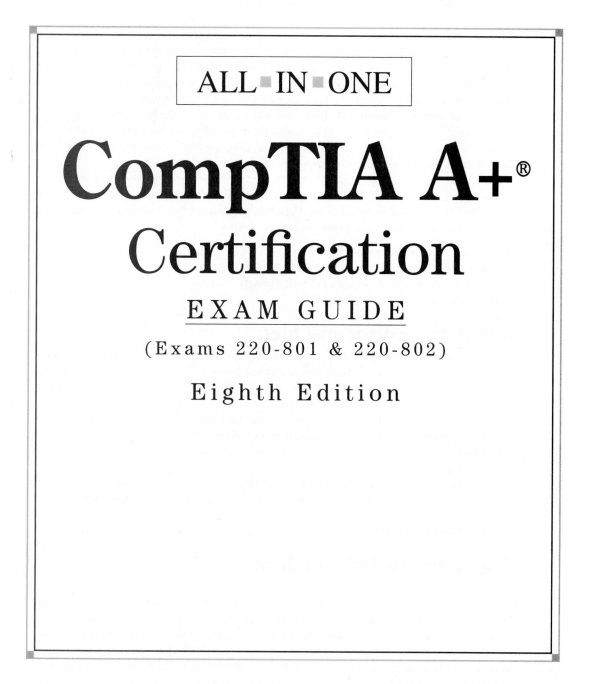

ALL·IN·ONE

CompTIA A+®
Certification

EXAM GUIDE

(Exams 220-801 & 220-802)

Eighth Edition

ABOUT THE AUTHOR

Mike Meyers, lovingly called the "AlphaGeek" by those who know him, is the industry's leading authority on CompTIA A+ certification. He is the president and co-founder of Total Seminars, LLC, a provider of PC and network repair seminars, books, videos, and courseware for thousands of organizations throughout the world. Mike has been involved in the computer and network repair industry since 1977 as a technician, instructor, author, consultant, and speaker.

Author of numerous popular PC books and videos, including the best-selling *CompTIA A+ Certification All-in-One Exam Guide*, Mike is also the series editor for the highly successful *Mike Meyers' Certification Passport* series, the *Mike Meyers' Computer Skills* series, and the *Mike Meyers' Guide to* series, all published by McGraw-Hill.

As well as writing, Mike has personally taught (and continues to teach) thousands of students, including U.S. senators, U.S. Supreme Court justices, the United Nations, every branch of the U.S. Armed Forces, most branches of the Department of Justice, hundreds of corporate clients, academic students at every level, prisoners, and pensioners.

E-mail: michaelm@totalsem.com
Facebook: Mike Meyers (Houston, TX)
Twitter/Skype/most instant messaging clients: desweds
Web forums: www.totalsem.com/forums

About the Editor-in-Chief

Scott Jernigan wields a mighty red pen as Editor in Chief for Total Seminars. With a Master of Arts degree in Medieval History, Scott feels as much at home in the musty archives of London as he does in the warm CRT glow of Total Seminars' Houston headquarters. After fleeing a purely academic life, he dove headfirst into IT, working as an instructor, editor, and writer.

Scott has written, edited, and contributed to dozens of books on computer literacy, hardware, operating systems, networking, and certification, including *Computer Literacy—Your Ticket to IC³ Certification*, and co-authoring with Mike Meyers the *All-in-One CompTIA Strata® IT Fundamentals Exam Guide*.

Scott has taught computer classes all over the United States, including stints at the United Nations in New York and the FBI Academy in Quantico. Practicing what he preaches, Scott is a CompTIA A+ and CompTIA Network+ certified technician, a Microsoft Certified Professional, a Microsoft Office User Specialist, and Certiport Internet and Computing Core Certified.

About the Technical Editor

Chris Crayton (CompTIA A+, CompTIA Network+, MCSE) is an author, editor, technical consultant, and trainer. Mr. Crayton has worked as a computer and networking instructor at Keiser University, as network administrator for Protocol, an eCRM company, and as a computer and network specialist at Eastman Kodak. Mr. Crayton has authored several print and online books on PC Repair, CompTIA A+, CompTIA Security+, and Microsoft Windows. Mr. Crayton has served as technical editor on numerous professional technical titles for leading publishing companies, including the *CompTIA A+ All-in-One Exam Guide*, the *CompTIA A+ Certification Study Guide*, and the *Mike Meyers' CompTIA A+ Certification Passport*.

ALL·IN·ONE

CompTIA A+®
Certification

EXAM GUIDE

(Exams 220-801 & 220-802)

Eighth Edition

Mike Meyers

New York • Chicago • San Francisco • Lisbon
London • Madrid • Mexico City • Milan • New Delhi
San Juan • Seoul • Singapore • Sydney • Toronto

The **McGraw·Hill** Companies

Cataloging-in-Publication Data is on file with the Library of Congress

McGraw-Hill books are available at special quantity discounts to use as premiums and sales promotions, or for use in corporate training programs. To contact a representative, please e-mail us at bulksales@mcgraw-hill.com.

CompTIA A+® Certification All-in-One Exam Guide, Eighth Edition (Exams 220-801 & 220-802)

34567890 QTN QTN 10987654

ISBN: Book p/n 978-0-07-179509-8 and CD p/n 978-0-07-179510-4
of set 978-0-07-179512-8

MHID: Book p/n 0-07-179509-X and CD p/n 0-07-179510-3
of set 0-07-179512-X

Sponsoring Editor	**Acquisitions Coordinator**	**Proofreader**	**Composition**
Timothy Green	Stephanie Evans	Paul Tyler	ContentWorks, Inc.
Editorial Supervisor	**Technical Editor**	**Indexer**	**Illustration**
Jody McKenzie	Christopher A. Crayton	Jack Lewis	Ford Pierson & ContentWorks, Inc.
Project Manager	**Copy Editor**	**Production Supervisor**	**Art Director, Cover**
Molly Sharp	Bill McManus	Jean Bodeaux	Jeff Weeks

CompTIA. A+

It Pays to Get Certified

In a digital world, digital literacy is an essential survival skill. Certification proves you have the knowledge and skill to solve business problems in virtually any business environment. Certifications are highly valued credentials that qualify you for jobs, increased compensation, and promotion.

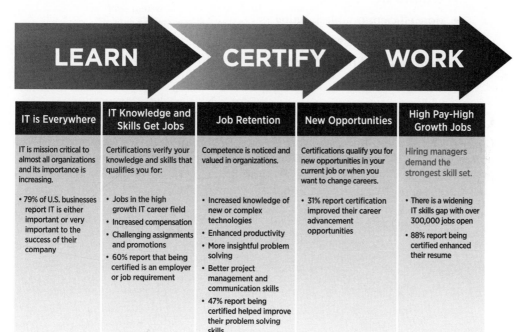

LEARN		CERTIFY	WORK	
IT is Everywhere	**IT Knowledge and Skills Get Jobs**	**Job Retention**	**New Opportunities**	**High Pay-High Growth Jobs**
IT is mission critical to almost all organizations and its importance is increasing.	Certifications verify your knowledge and skills that qualifies you for:	Competence is noticed and valued in organizations.	Certifications qualify you for new opportunities in your current job or when you want to change careers.	Hiring managers demand the strongest skill set.
• 79% of U.S. businesses report IT is either important or very important to the success of their company	• Jobs in the high growth IT career field • Increased compensation • Challenging assignments and promotions • 60% report that being certified is an employer or job requirement	• Increased knowledge of new or complex technologies • Enhanced productivity • More insightful problem solving • Better project management and communication skills • 47% report being certified helped improve their problem solving skills	• 31% report certification improved their career advancement opportunities	• There is a widening IT skills gap with over 300,000 jobs open • 88% report being certified enhanced their resume

CompTIA A+ Certification Advances Your Career

- **The CompTIA A+ credential**—provides foundation-level knowledge and skills necessary for a career in PC repair and support.

- **Starting Salary**—CompTIA A+ Certified individuals can earn as much as $65,000 per year.

- **Career Pathway**—CompTIA A+ is a building block for other CompTIA certifications such as Network+, Security+ and vendor specific technologies.

- **More than 850,000**—individuals worldwide are CompTIA A+ certified.

- **Mandated/Recommended by organizations worldwide**—such as Cisco and HP and Ricoh, the U.S. State Department, and U.S. government contractors such as EDS, General Dynamics, and Northrop Grumman.

- **Some of the primary benefits individuals report from becoming CompTIA A+ certified are:**

 - More efficient troubleshooting

 - Improved career advancement

 - More insightful problem solving

CompTIA Career Pathway

CompTIA offers a number of credentials that form a foundation for your career in technology and that allow you to pursue specific areas of concentration. Depending on the path you choose to take, CompTIA certifications help you build upon your skills and knowledge, supporting learning throughout your entire career.

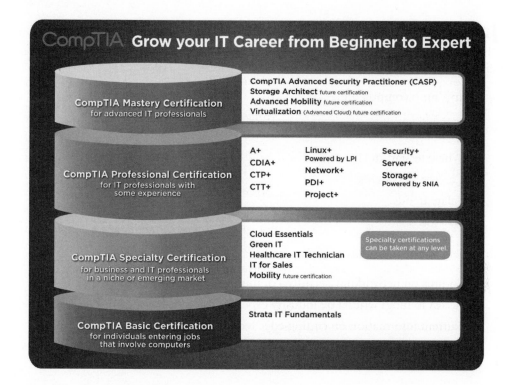

Steps to Getting Certified and Staying Certified

1. **Review exam objectives.** Review the certification objectives to make sure you know what is covered in the exam:
 www.comptia.org/certifications/testprep/examobjectives.aspx

2. **Practice for the exam.** After you have studied for the certification, take a free assessment and sample test to get an idea what type of questions might be on the exam:
 www.comptia.org/certifications/testprep/practicetests.aspx

3. **Purchase an exam voucher.** Purchase your exam voucher on the CompTIA Marketplace, which is located at: www.comptiastore.com

4. **Take the test!** Select a certification exam provider and schedule a time to take your exam. You can find exam providers at the following link:
 www.comptia.org/certifications/testprep/testingcenters.aspx

5. **Stay Certified!** Continuing education is required. Effective January 1, 2011, CompTIA A+ certifications are valid for three years from the date of certification. There are a number of ways the certification can be renewed. For more information go to: http://certification.comptia.org/getCertified/steps_to_certification/stayCertified.aspx

Join the Professional Community

The free online IT Pro Community provides valuable content to students and professionals. Join the IT Pro Community:

http://itpro.comptia.org

Career IT job resources include:

- Where to start in IT
- Career assessments
- Salary trends
- U.S. job board

Join the IT Pro Community and get access to:

- Forums on networking, security, computing, and cutting-edge technologies
- Access to blogs written by industry experts
- Current information on cutting-edge technologies
- Access to various industry resource links and articles related to IT and IT careers

AUTHORIZED

Content Seal of Quality

This courseware bears the seal of CompTIA Approved Quality Content. This seal signifies this content covers 100 percent of the exam objectives and implements important instructional design principles. CompTIA recommends multiple learning tools to help increase coverage of the learning objectives.

Why CompTIA?

- **Global recognition**—CompTIA is recognized globally as the leading IT non-profit trade association and has enormous credibility. Plus, CompTIA's certifications are vendor-neutral and offer proof of foundational knowledge that translates across technologies.

- **Valued by hiring managers**—Hiring managers value CompTIA certification because it is vendor- and technology-independent validation of your technical skills.

- **Recommended or required by government and businesses**—Many government organizations and corporations (for example, Dell, Sharp, Ricoh, the U.S. Department of Defense, and many more) either recommend or require technical staff to be CompTIA certified.

- **Three CompTIA certifications ranked in the top 10**—In a study by DICE of 17,000 technology professionals, certifications helped command higher salaries at all experience levels.

How to Obtain More Information

- *Visit CompTIA online* Go to www.comptia.org to learn more about getting CompTIA certified.

- *Contact CompTIA* Please call 866-835-8020, ext. 5 or e-mail questions@comptia.org.

- *Join the IT Pro Community* Go to http://itpro.comptia.org to join the IT community to get relevant career information.

- *Connect with CompTIA* Find us on Facebook, LinkedIn, Twitter, and YouTube.

CAQC Disclaimer

The logo of the CompTIA Approved Quality Curriculum (CAQC) program and the status of this or other training material as "Approved" under the CompTIA Approved Quality Curriculum program signifies that, in CompTIA's opinion, such training material covers the content of CompTIA's related certification exam.

The contents of this training material were created for the CompTIA A+ exams covering CompTIA certification objectives that were current as of the date of publication.

CompTIA has not reviewed or approved the accuracy of the contents of this training material and specifically disclaims any warranties of merchantability or fitness for a particular purpose. CompTIA makes no guarantee concerning the success of persons using any such "Approved" or other training material in order to prepare for any CompTIA certification exam.

CONTENTS AT A GLANCE

CONTENTS

PREFACE

I started writing computer books for the simple reason that no one wrote the kind of books I wanted to read. The books were either too simple (Chapter 1, "Using Your Mouse") or too complex (Chapter 1, "TTL Logic and Transistors"), and none of them provided a motivation for me to learn the information. I believed that there were geeky readers just like me who wanted to know *why* they needed to know the information in a computer book.

Good books motivate readers to learn what they are reading. If a book discusses binary arithmetic but doesn't explain why I need to learn it, for example, that's not a good book. Tell me that understanding binary makes it easier to understand how a CPU works or why a megabyte is different from a million bytes—then I get excited, no matter how geeky the topic. If I don't have a good motivation to do something, then I'm simply not going to do it (which explains why I haven't jumped out of an airplane!).

In this book, I teach you why you need to understand the technology that runs almost every modern business. You'll learn to build and fix computers, exploring every nook and cranny, and master the art of the PC tech. In the process, you'll gain the knowledge you need to pass the CompTIA A+ certification exams.

Enjoy, my fellow geek.

—Mike Meyers

ACKNOWLEDGMENTS

Scott Jernigan, my Editor in Chief at Total Seminars and boon companion on many an evening, worked his *usual* magic *again* pulling together this latest edition. My thanks, amigo!

My acquisitions editor, Tim Green, and his trusty assistant, Stephanie Evans, had this book schedule dialed in from day one and never let up. I mean, *never* let up. Better still, they browbeat me into working with their incessantly chirpy voices. I long for the mean Tim of old who just yelled at me.

Chris Crayton, my technical editor, did a great job once again. Thank you for helping make this book happen.

Aaron Verber stepped up in a big way for this edition, with stellar editing, writing, and research. You did a great job with every chapter thrown at you (and managed to pull together the lab manual at the same time). Let's do this again!

Michael Smyer devoted his superb skills in photography and tech to making this book the best edition ever. He kept me on my toes on the tech and helped greatly with the research. Excellent work, Michael.

Ford Pierson, my in-house editor and illustrator, worked very hard to upgrade the line art in this book, including turning man in the box into Mini Me, a touch that displays his wit, cleverness, and complete lack of fear. Great job, Ford.

Scott Strubberg, Doug Jones, and Dave Rush, instructors at Total Seminars, were my sounding boards and research partners for this book, helping me turn the complicated into the understandable on many subjects. Thank you all very much!

On the McGraw-Hill side, the crew once again demonstrated why McGraw-Hill is the best in show as a publisher. With excellent work and even better attitude, this book came together smoothly.

Molly Sharp, my project manager, went from putting together the latest editions of my CompTIA Network+ books to working with me on the CompTIA A+ books, which proved at least one thing: she's a glutton for punishment, keeping everything on track through two huge projects in a row, with me and my staff doing our best to add chaos. The simple joy of working with you, Molly, means I'm already looking forward to the next project with you!

My editorial supervisor, Jody McKenzie, once again helped me stay focused on all the pieces, with a gentle nudge or a quiet jab when I would forget some essential piece. It was wonderful to work with you again.

To the copy editor, page proofer, indexer, and layout folks—Bill McManus, Paul Tyler, Jack Lewis, and Tom Sharp—superb work in every facet. Thank you for being the best.

What Is CompTIA A+ Certification?

CompTIA A+ certification is an industry-wide, vendo
developed and sponsored by the *Computing Technolog*
The CompTIA A+ certification shows that you have a
microcomputers. You achieve this certification by tak
ple-choice exams. The tests cover what technicians sh
hands-on work on PCs, either from a job or as a stude
fication enjoys wide recognition throughout the compu
800,000 technicians have become CompTIA A+ certifi
of all IT certifications.

Who Is CompTIA?

CompTIA is a nonprofit industry trade association base
It consists of over 20,000 members in 102 countries.
such diverse locales as Amsterdam, Dubai, Johannesbu

CompTIA provides a forum for people in these ind
ing people), represents the interests of its members to
certifications for many aspects of the computer industr
A+, CompTIA Network+, CompTIA Security+, and othe
hard to watch the IT industry and constantly looks t
meet the ongoing demand from its membership. Chec
www.comptia.org for details on the other certifications y

Virtually every company of consequence in the IT ind
Here are a few of the biggies:

Adobe Systems	AMD	Best Buy
Canon	Cisco Systems	CompUSA
Gateway	Hewlett-Packard	IBM
Kyocera	McAfee	Microsoft
Novell	Panasonic	Sharp Electronics
Symantec	Toshiba	Total Seminars, LLC (that's my company)

CompTIA began offering CompTIA A+ certification b
the IT industry largely ignored CompTIA A+ certificatior
ever, the CompTIA A+ certification has grown to becon
entrance into the PC industry. Many companies require (
of their PC support technicians, and the CompTIA A+ ce
both in the United States and internationally. Additior
recognize CompTIA A+ certification and use it as credit

The Path of the PC Tech

In this chapter, you will learn how to
- Explain the importance of skill in managing and troubleshooting PCs
- Explain the importance of CompTIA A+ certification
- Describe how to become CompTIA A+ certified

Computers have taken over the world, or at least many professions. Everywhere you turn, a quick dig beneath the surface sawdust of construction, the grease of auto mechanics, and the hum of medical technology reveals one or more personal computers (PCs) working away, doing essential jobs. Because the PC evolved from novelty item to essential science tool to everyday object in a short period of time, there's a huge demand for a workforce that can build, maintain, troubleshoot, and repair PCs.

The Importance of Skill in Managing and Troubleshooting PCs

The people who work with computers, often lumped into a single group known as the *Information Technology (IT)* workforce, do an amazingly varied number of jobs. These include diverse pursuits such as designing hardware, writing computer programs, and creating *networks* (groups of computers connected together to share data or programs). IT people built the Internet and maintain the millions of computers that keep it running.

But for all this IT diversity, it's the computer technicians (or *PC techs*, as those of us in the field call each other) who make up the core of the IT workforce. Without us techs, none of the other stuff would work, so none of the other jobs could exist. Getting workers with skill in building, maintaining, troubleshooting, and fixing PCs is essential for the success of every modern business. We need more PC techs. We need you!

In the early days of the personal computer, anyone who used a PC had to have skills as a PC tech. The PC was new, buggy, and prone to problems. If you owned a PC back then, you didn't want to rely on others to fix your PC when the inevitable problems arose. Today's PCs are much more robust and have fewer problems, so *using* one no longer requires having PC tech skills, but they're also much more complex machines. Today's IT industry, therefore, needs specialized workers who know how to make the machines run well and fix them when they break for the millions of users who lack PC tech skills.

Every profession requires specialized
keep a job that requires those specialized
license. If you want a job fixing automol
the Automotive Service Excellence (ASE
panies' financial audits in the United K
certification.

Nearly every profession has some crite
tence and ability to perform at a certain le
from one profession to another, all of the
or series of exams. Passing these exams
work at a certain level in your profession
barber, or lawyer.

If you successfully pass these exams, t
you a certification. You receive some pie
you can show to potential clients or emp
clients or employers a level of confidenc
Without this certification, either you wil
no one will trust you to do the work. Unt
the exception to this rule.

The Importance of Con

Microcomputers were introduced in the l
did not have a universally recognized way
what to do under the hood of a personal
existed, but the only way to get them w
repair facility first and then get the certif
specific training, but no single manufact
IBM training, for example, something tha
little detail of getting the job first before y

The software and networking sides of c
lack of certifications. Due to the dominan
(for example, Microsoft and Cisco), the v
great way to get and keep a job. For exam
sional (MCITP) and Cisco's Cisco Certifi
have opened the employment doors for r

But what about the person who runs
ing hard drives, upgrading device drivers,
hobbyists who want to be paid for their s
had the audacity to show that they knew
workgroup, find themselves with a new tit
Services Specialist? On the other hand, ho
Who Doesn't Get a Nickel Extra but Who
tion gives these people a universally reco
ciency to employers or clients (and to seek

- Recognizing all the components of the standard Windows desktop (Start menu, notification area, etc.)
- Manipulating windows—resizing, moving, and so on
- Creating, deleting, renaming, moving, and copying files and folders within Windows
- Understanding file extensions and their relationship with program associations
- Using common keyboard shortcuts/hotkeys
- Installing, running, and closing a Windows application

Any PC technician who has been around a while will tell you that one of the great secrets in the computer business is that there's almost never anything completely new in the world of computer technology. Faster, cleverer, smaller, wider—absolutely—but the underlying technology, the core of what makes your PC and its various peripheral devices operate, has changed remarkably little since PCs came into widespread use a few decades ago. When you do your initial read-through, you may be tempted to skip the Historical/Conceptual sections—don't! Understanding the history and technological developments behind today's PCs helps you understand why they work—or don't work—the way they do. Basically, I'm passing on to you the kind of knowledge you might get by apprenticing yourself to an older, experienced PC tech.

After you've completed the first read-through, go through the book again, this time in textbook mode. If you're an Old Tech, start your studying here. Try to cover one chapter at a sitting. Concentrate on the 801 and 802 sections. Get a highlighter and mark the phrases and sentences that bring out major points. Be sure you understand how the pictures and illustrations relate to the concepts being discussed.

Once you feel you have a good grasp of the material in the book, you can check your knowledge by using the practice exams included on the media accompanying this book. You can take these in Practice mode or Final mode. In Practice mode, you can use the Assistance window to get a helpful hint for the current questions, use the Reference feature to find the chapter that covers the question, check your answer for the question, and see an explanation of the correct answer. In Final mode, you answer all the questions and receive an exam score at the end, just like the real thing. You can also adjust the number of questions on a Practice or Final mode exam with the Customize option.

Both modes show you an overall grade, expressed as a percentage, as well as a breakdown of how well you did on each exam domain. The Review Questions feature lets you see which questions you missed and what the correct answers are. Use these results to guide further studying. Continue reviewing the topics you miss and taking additional exams until you are consistently scoring in the 90% range. When you get there, you are ready to pass the CompTIA A+ certification exams.

Study Tactics

Perhaps it's been a while since you had to study for a test. Or perhaps it hasn't, but you've done your best since then to block the whole experience from your mind. Either

What Is CompTIA A+ Certification?

CompTIA A+ certification is an industry-wide, vendor-neutral certification program developed and sponsored by the *Computing Technology Industry Association (CompTIA)*. The CompTIA A+ certification shows that you have a basic competence in supporting microcomputers. You achieve this certification by taking two computer-based, multiple-choice exams. The tests cover what technicians should know after 12 months of hands-on work on PCs, either from a job or as a student in the lab. CompTIA A+ certification enjoys wide recognition throughout the computer industry. To date, more than 800,000 technicians have become CompTIA A+ certified, making it the most popular of all IT certifications.

Who Is CompTIA?

CompTIA is a nonprofit industry trade association based in Oakbrook Terrace, Illinois. It consists of over 20,000 members in 102 countries. You'll find CompTIA offices in such diverse locales as Amsterdam, Dubai, Johannesburg, Tokyo, and São Paulo.

CompTIA provides a forum for people in these industries to network (as in meeting people), represents the interests of its members to the government, and provides certifications for many aspects of the computer industry. CompTIA sponsors CompTIA A+, CompTIA Network+, CompTIA Security+, and other certifications. CompTIA works hard to watch the IT industry and constantly looks to provide new certifications to meet the ongoing demand from its membership. Check out the CompTIA Web site at *www.comptia.org* for details on the other certifications you can obtain from CompTIA.

Virtually every company of consequence in the IT industry is a member of CompTIA. Here are a few of the biggies:

Adobe Systems	AMD	Best Buy	Brother International
Canon	Cisco Systems	CompUSA	Fujitsu
Gateway	Hewlett-Packard	IBM	Intel
Kyocera	McAfee	Microsoft	NCR
Novell	Panasonic	Sharp Electronics	Siemens
Symantec	Toshiba	Total Seminars, LLC (that's my company)	Plus many thousands more

CompTIA began offering CompTIA A+ certification back in 1993. When it debuted, the IT industry largely ignored CompTIA A+ certification. Since that initial stutter, however, the CompTIA A+ certification has grown to become the de facto requirement for entrance into the PC industry. Many companies require CompTIA A+ certification for all of their PC support technicians, and the CompTIA A+ certification is widely recognized both in the United States and internationally. Additionally, many other certifications recognize CompTIA A+ certification and use it as credit toward their certifications.

The Path to Other Certifications

Most IT companies—big and small—see CompTIA A+ certification as the entry point to IT. From CompTIA A+, you have a number of certification options, depending on whether you want to focus more on hardware and operating systems or move into network administration (although these aren't mutually exclusive goals). The following three certifications are worth serious consideration:

- CompTIA Network+ certification
- Microsoft technical certifications
- Cisco certifications

NOTE CompTIA A+ is the entry point to IT, though definitely not the only route for learning about computers and having certifications to prove that knowledge. Several certifications cover computer literacy or digital literacy, the phrase that means "what every person needs to know about computers to survive in the 21st century." The most popular computer literacy certification is Certiport's IC3 certification that tests on general computer knowledge; office productivity applications, such as Word and PowerPoint; and Internet applications such as Web browsers and e-mail clients.

CompTIA has a pre–CompTIA A+ exam (*not* a certification), called the *CompTIA Strata IT Fundamentals exam*, that's geared a bit more to a user preparing to become a tech. It's designed to check basic knowledge levels for people getting into IT.

CompTIA Network+ Certification

If you haven't already achieved CompTIA Network+ certification, make it your next certification goal after CompTIA A+ certification. Just as CompTIA A+ certification shows that you have solid competency as a PC technician, *CompTIA Network+ certification* demonstrates your skills as a network technician, including your understanding of network hardware, installation, and troubleshooting. CompTIA's Network+ certification is a natural step for continuing toward your Microsoft or Cisco certifications. Take the CompTIA Network+: it's your obvious next certification.

Microsoft Technical Certifications

Microsoft operating systems control a huge portion of all installed networks, and those networks need qualified support people to make them run. Pursuing Microsoft's series of certifications for networking professionals is a natural next step after completing the CompTIA certifications. They offer a whole slew of tracks and exams, ranging from simple specializations in Windows 7 to numerous *Microsoft Certified IT Professional (MCITP)* certifications and beyond. You can find more details on the Microsoft Learning Web site at www.microsoft.com/learning/en/us/certification/cert-overview.aspx.

Cisco Certification

Let's face it: Cisco routers pretty much run the Internet and most intranets in the world. A *router* is a networking device that controls and directs the flow of information over networks, such as e-mail messages, Web browsing, and so on. Cisco provides five levels of IT certification for folks who want to show their skills at handling Cisco products, such as the *Cisco Certified Network Associate (CCNA)*, plus numerous specialty certifications. See the Cisco IT Certification Web site here for more details: www.cisco.com/web/learning/le3/learning_career_certifications_and_learning_paths_home.html.

How Do I Become CompTIA A+ Certified?

You become CompTIA A+ certified, in the simplest sense, by taking and passing two computer-based, multiple-choice exams. No prerequisites are required for taking the CompTIA A+ certification exams (although there's an assumption of computer literacy, whether or not you have one of the computer literacy certifications). There is no required training course and no training materials to buy. You *do* have to pay a testing fee for each of the two exams. You pay your testing fees, go to a local testing center, and take the tests. You immediately know whether you have passed or failed. By passing both exams, you become CompTIA A+ certified.

What's the Deal with "No More Lifetime Certification"?

In early 2010, CompTIA announced that, effective January 1, 2011, CompTIA A+, CompTIA Network+, and CompTIA Security+ certifications would no longer be considered "certified for life." If you passed any of these exams before the deadline, you're still certified for life for those exams. For any exams that you pass on or after January 1, 2011, to stay certified, every three years you'll need to either retake the exam or perform sufficient continuing education as specified by CompTIA.

Retaking the exams isn't that hard to understand, but the continuing education requirement is a bit more complex. Instead of trying to explain it all here, please review CompTIA's documentation at http://certification.comptia.org/Libraries/Certification_Documents/ceu_faq.sflb.ashx.

Most importantly, if you pursue the continuing education path, you'll need to earn 20 continuing education units (CEUs) each three-year period to renew your CompTIA A+ certification. How do you earn these CEUs? You can participate in industry events and seminars, complete a presentation, participate in IT training, teach a course, or earn another higher-level certification. The number of CEUs that you earn by completing each of these requirements varies, and each requires that you submit documentation to CompTIA for their review.

Personally, I think this is a long-overdue feature. Someone who took the CompTIA A+ exam in 2010 had no way to distinguish himself from a person who took the exam in 1997, and that wasn't fair. By no longer awarding "certified for life" status, CompTIA's certifications are now in line with Microsoft, Cisco, and other industry certifications.

The Basic Exam Structure

The two exams introduced by CompTIA in 2012 are *CompTIA A+ 220-801* (Hardware) and *CompTIA A+ 220-802* (Operating Systems). The terms "Hardware" and "Operating Systems" are not officially part of the exam names, but I've included them here because they're commonly used to reference the exams. It's also common to refer to these two exams as the "2012" exams to differentiate them from older CompTIA exams. Although you may take either of the two exams first, I recommend taking 220-801 followed by 220-802. The 220-801 exam concentrates on understanding terminology and technology, how to do fundamental tasks such as upgrading RAM, and basic network and laptop support. The 220-802 exam builds on the first exam, concentrating on Windows support, advanced configuration, and troubleshooting scenarios.

Both of the exams are extremely practical, with little or no interest in history. All questions are multiple-choice, simulation, or "click on the right part of the picture" questions. The following is an example of the type of questions you will see on the exams:

Your laser printer is printing blank pages. Which item should you check first?

A. Printer drivers

B. Toner cartridge

C. Printer settings

D. Paper feed

The correct answer is B, the toner cartridge. You can make an argument for any of the others, but common sense (and skill as a PC technician) tells you to check the simplest possibility first.

The 2012 exams use a regular test format in which you answer a set number of questions and are scored based on how many correct answers you give. These exams have no more than 100 questions each. (Both exams have 100 questions each at the time of this writing.)

Be aware that CompTIA may add new questions to the exams at any time to keep the content fresh. The subject matter covered by the exams won't change, but new questions may be added periodically at random intervals. This policy puts strong emphasis on understanding concepts and having solid PC-tech knowledge rather than on trying to memorize specific questions and answers that may have been on the tests in the past. No book or Web resource will have all the "right answers" because those answers change constantly. Luckily for you, however, this book not only teaches you what steps to follow in a particular case, but also explains how to be a knowledgeable tech who understands *why* you're doing those steps. That way when you encounter a new problem (or test question), you can work out the answer. This will help you not only to pass the exams but also to be a better PC tech!

To keep up to date, we monitor the CompTIA A+ exams for new content and update the special Tech Files section of the Total Seminars Web site (www.totalsem.com) with new articles covering subjects we believe may appear on future versions of the exams.

Windows-Centric

The CompTIA A+ exams focus on the Microsoft Windows operating systems you would expect to find on a PC at a workstation or in a home. There are no Linux questions. There are no Mac OS X questions. The 802 exam will ask you about the common mobile device operating systems, iOS and Android, but the vast majority of operating system questions on both exams address Windows. Objectives in the exams cover the following operating systems:

- Windows XP Home, Windows XP Professional, Windows XP Media Center, Windows XP 64-bit Professional
- Windows Vista Home Basic, Windows Vista Home Premium, Windows Vista Business, Windows Vista Ultimate, Windows Vista Enterprise
- Windows 7 Starter, Windows 7 Home Premium, Windows 7 Professional, Windows 7 Ultimate, Windows 7 Enterprise

Windows 8

CompTIA has the darnedest luck when it comes to the timing of new CompTIA A+ exams compared to releases of new Windows versions. In 2006, CompTIA released an update to the CompTIA A+ exams about four months before Microsoft released Windows Vista. In 2009, CompTIA missed Windows 7 by about one month (though CompTIA released a Windows 7 update to the exams in late 2009).

It seems that CompTIA will once again run into what I'm going to call the "CompTIA Windows Curse." As the new 220-801 and 220-802 exams come out in early 2012, there's a good chance that Windows 8 will come out a few month later. Assuming CompTIA stays true to form, there's a very good chance that you'll see a Windows 8 update on the exams within a year or two of the Windows 8 rollout. Be sure to check the CompTIA Web site or contact me directly at michaelm@totalsem.com to see if any Windows 8 updates have taken place.

Exam 220–801

The questions on the CompTIA A+ 220-801 exam fit into one of five domains. The number of questions for each domain is based on the percentages shown in Table 1-1.

Table 1-1 Exam 220-801 Domains and Percentages	Domain	Percentage
	1.0 PC Hardware	40%
	2.0 Networking	27%
	3.0 Laptops	11%
	4.0 Printers	11%
	5.0 Operational Procedures	11%

The 220-801 exam tests your knowledge of computer components, expecting you to be able to identify just about every common device on PCs, including variations within device types. Here's a list:

Floppy drives	Video and multimedia cards
Hard drives	Network and modem cards
Optical drives	Cables and connectors
Solid state drives	Heat sinks, fans, and liquid cooling systems
Motherboards	Laptops and portable devices
Power supplies	Printers
CPUs	Scanners
RAM	Network switches, cabling, and wireless adapters
Monitors	Biometric devices
Input devices, such as keyboards, mice, and touchscreens	

The 220-801 exam tests your ability to install, configure, and maintain all the hardware technology involved in a personal computer. You need to be able to install and set up a hard drive, for example, and configure devices in Windows XP, Windows Vista, and Windows 7. You have to understand device drivers. Additionally, this exam puts a lot of emphasis on operational procedures, such as safety and environmental issues, communication, and professionalism. You need to understand how to avoid hazardous situations. The exam tests your ability to communicate effectively with customers and coworkers. You need to understand professional behavior and demonstrate that you have tact, discretion, and respect for others and their property.

Exam 220-802

The CompTIA A+ 220-802 exam covers four domains. Table 1-2 lists the domains and the percentage of questions dedicated to each domain.

The 220-802 exam covers the configuration, repair, and troubleshooting of the Windows operating system. You have to know your way around Windows and understand the tasks involved in updating, upgrading, and installing Windows XP, Windows Vista, and Windows 7. You need to know the standard diagnostic tools available in Windows so that you can fix problems and work with higher-level techs. Make sure you know Windows; 33% of the 220-802 questions are going to challenge you on this.

Table 1-2 Exam 220-802 Domains and Percentages	Domain	Percentage
	1.0 Operating Systems	33%
	2.0 Security	22%
	3.0 Mobile Devices	9%
	4.0 Troubleshooting	36%

The biggest part of the 220-802 exam is dedicated to troubleshooting. Think in terms of a hands-on approach to determining the appropriate technology for a situation—running diagnostics and troubleshooting—rather than identification of hardware or operating system utilities. You need to understand how all the technology should work, know the proper steps to figure out why something doesn't work, and then know how to fix it.

The 220-802 exam adds mobile devices to the objectives, a new topic for 2012. While the smartphone and tablet market covers an impossibly wide array of hardware and software, the 220-802 exam focuses on Apple iOS and Google Android devices. You'll need to know how to interact with the hardware and software, as well as configure personal settings, such as those for e-mail clients and security.

Security is a big topic on the 220-802 exam. You need to know quite a bit about computer security, from physical security (door locks to retinal scanners), to knowledge of security threats (malware and viruses), to the ways in which to secure an individual computer. This also includes coverage of how to recycle and dispose of computer gear properly.

You'll also be tested on methods of securing networks. You'll need to know how to access a small office/home office (SOHO) router or wireless access point and configure that device to protect your network.

How Do I Take the Exams?

Pearson VUE administers the CompTIA A+ testing at over 5000 testing centers in 165 countries. You may take the exams at any testing center. You can select the closest training center and schedule your exams right from the comfort of your favorite Web browser by going to the Pearson VUE Web site:

> www.vue.com

Alternatively, in the United States and Canada, call Pearson VUE at 877-551-PLUS (7587) to schedule the exams and to locate the nearest testing center. International customers can find a list of Pearson VUE international contact numbers for various regions of the world on CompTIA's Web site at www.comptia.org.

You must pay for the exam when you call to schedule. Be prepared to sit on hold for a while. Have your Social Security number (or international equivalent) and a credit card ready when you call. Pearson VUE will be glad to invoice you, but you won't be able to take the exam until they receive full payment.

Pearson VUE will accommodate any special needs, although this may limit your selection of testing locations.

How Much Does the Exam Cost?

The cost of the exam depends on whether you work for a CompTIA member or not. At this writing, the cost for non-CompTIA members is $178 (U.S.) for each exam. International prices vary, but you can check the CompTIA Web site for international pricing. Of course, the prices are subject to change without notice, so always check the CompTIA Web site for current pricing.

Very few people pay full price for the exam. Virtually every organization that provides CompTIA A+ training and testing also offers discount *vouchers*. You buy a discount voucher and then use the voucher number instead of a credit card when you schedule the exam. Vouchers are sold per exam, so you'll need two vouchers to take the two CompTIA A+ exams. Total Seminars is one place to get discount vouchers. You can call Total Seminars at 800-446-6004 or 281-922-4166, or get vouchers via the Web site: www.totalsem.com. No one should ever pay full price for CompTIA A+ exams.

How to Pass the CompTIA A+ Exams

The single most important thing to remember about the CompTIA A+ certification exams is that CompTIA designed the exams to test the knowledge of a technician with only 12 months of experience, so keep it simple! The exams aren't interested in your ability to overclock DDR3 CAS timings in CMOS or whether you can explain the exact difference between the Intel ICH10 and the AMD 790 southbridges. Think in terms of practical knowledge and standards. Read this book, do whatever works for you to memorize the key concepts and procedures, take the practice exams on the media accompanying this book, review any topics you miss, and you should pass with no problem.

 NOTE Those of you who just want more knowledge in managing and troubleshooting PCs can follow the same strategy as certification-seekers. Think in practical terms and work with the PC as you go through each chapter.

Some of you may be in or just out of school, so studying for exams is nothing novel. But if you haven't had to study for and take an exam in a while, or if you think maybe you could use some tips, you may find the next section valuable. It lays out a proven strategy for preparing to take and pass the CompTIA A+ exams. Try it. It works.

Obligate Yourself

The very first step you should take is to schedule yourself for the exams. Have you ever heard the old adage, "Heat and pressure make diamonds"? Well, if you don't give yourself a little "heat," you'll end up procrastinating and delay taking the exams, possibly forever. Do yourself a favor. Using the following information, determine how much time you'll need to study for the exams, and then call Pearson VUE and schedule the exams accordingly. Knowing the exams are coming up makes it much easier to turn off the television and crack open the book. You can schedule an exam as little as a few weeks in advance, but if you schedule an exam and can't take it at the scheduled time, you must reschedule at least a day in advance or you'll lose your money.

Set Aside the Right Amount of Study Time

After helping thousands of techs get their CompTIA A+ certification, we at Total Seminars have developed a pretty good feel for the amount of study time needed to pass the CompTIA A+ certification exams. The following table provides an estimate to help you

plan how much study time you must commit to the CompTIA A+ certification exams. Keep in mind that these are averages. If you're not a great student or if you're a little on the nervous side, add 10 percent; if you're a fast learner or have a good bit of computer experience, you may want to reduce the figures.

To use Table 1-3, just circle the values that are most accurate for you and add them up to get your estimated total hours of study time.

To that value, add hours based on the number of months of direct, professional experience you have had supporting PCs, as shown in Table 1-4.

Tech Task	Amount of Experience			
	None	Once or Twice	Every Now and Then	Quite a Bit
Installing an adapter card	6	4	2	I
Installing and configuring hard drives	12	10	8	2
Installing modems and NICs	8	6	6	3
Connecting a computer to the Internet	16	10	8	4
Installing printers and scanners	16	8	4	2
Installing RAM	8	6	4	2
Installing CPUs	8	7	5	3
Repairing printers	6	5	4	3
Repairing boot problems	8	7	7	5
Repairing portable computers	8	6	4	2
Configuring mobile devices	4	3	2	I
Building complete systems	12	10	8	6
Using the command line	8	8	6	4
Installing and optimizing Windows	10	8	6	4
Using Windows XP	6	6	4	2
Using Windows Vista	8	6	4	2
Using Windows 7	8	6	4	2
Configuring NTFS, Users, and Groups	6	4	3	2
Configuring a wireless network	6	5	3	2
Configuring a software firewall	6	4	2	I
Configuring sound	2	2	I	0
Removing malware	4	3	2	0
Using OS diagnostic tools	8	8	6	4
Using a multimeter	4	3	2	I

Table 1-3 Analyzing Skill Levels

Months of Direct, Professional Experience...	Hours to Add to Your Study Time...
0	50
Up to 6	30
6 to 12	10
Over 12	0

Table 1-4 Adding Up Your Study Time

A total neophyte often needs roughly 240 hours of study time. An experienced tech shouldn't need more than 60 hours.

Total hours for you to study: _____.

A Strategy for Study

Now that you have a feel for how long it's going to take to prepare for the exams, you're ready to develop a study strategy. I'd like to suggest a strategy that has worked for others who've come before you, whether they were experienced techs or total newbies.

This book is designed to accommodate the different study agendas of these two groups of students. The first group is experienced techs who already have strong PC experience but need to be sure they're ready to be tested on the specific subjects covered by the CompTIA A+ exams. The second group is those with little or no background in the computer field. These techs can benefit from a more detailed understanding of the history and concepts that underlie modern PC technology, to help them remember the specific subject matter information they must know for the exams. I'll use the short-hand terms Old Techs and New Techs for these two groups. If you're not sure which group you fall into, pick a few chapters and go through some end-of-chapter questions. If you score less than 70%, go the New Tech route.

I have broken most of the chapters into four distinct parts:

- **Historical/Conceptual** Topics that are not on the CompTIA A+ exams but will help you understand more clearly what is on the CompTIA A+ exams
- **801** Topics that clearly fit under the CompTIA A+ 220-801 exam domains
- **802** Topics that clearly fit under the CompTIA A+ 220-802 exam domains
- **Beyond A+** More advanced issues that probably will not be on the CompTIA A+ exams—yet

NOTE Not all chapters have all four parts.

The beginning of each of these parts is clearly marked with a large banner that looks like this:

Historical/Conceptual

Those of you who fall into the Old Tech group may want to skip everything except the 801 and 802 parts in each chapter. After reading the sections in those parts, jump immediately to the questions at the end of the chapter. The end-of-chapter questions concentrate on information in the 801 and 802 sections. If you run into problems, review the Historical/Conceptual sections in that chapter. Note that you may need to skip back to previous chapters to get the Historical/Conceptual information you need for later chapters.

After going through every chapter as described, Old Techs can move directly to testing their knowledge by using the free practice exams on the media that accompanies the book. Once you start scoring above 90%, you're ready to take the exams. If you're a New Tech—or if you're an Old Tech who wants the full learning experience this book can offer—start by reading the book, *the whole book,* as though you were reading a novel, from page one to the end without skipping around. Because so many computer terms and concepts build on each other, skipping around greatly increases the odds that you will become confused and end up closing the book and firing up your favorite PC game. Not that I have anything against PC games, but unfortunately that skill is *not* useful for the CompTIA A+ exams!

Your goal on this first read is to understand concepts, the *whys* behind the *hows.* Having a PC nearby as you read is helpful so you can stop and inspect the PC to see a piece of hardware or how a particular concept manifests in the real world. As you read about hard drives, for example, inspect the cables. Do they look like the ones in the book? Is there a variation? Why? It is imperative that you understand why you are doing something, not just how to do it on one particular system under one specific set of conditions. Neither the exams nor real life as a PC tech works that way.

If you're reading this book as part of a managing and troubleshooting PCs class rather than a certification-prep course, I highly recommend going the New Tech route, even if you have a decent amount of experience. The book contains a lot of details that can trip you up if you focus only on the test-specific sections of the chapters. Plus, your program might stress historical and conceptual knowledge as well as practical, hands-on skills.

The CompTIA A+ certification exams assume that you have basic user skills. The exams really try to trick you with questions on processes that you may do every day and not think much about. Here's a classic: "To move a file from the C:\DATA folder to the D:\ drive using Windows Explorer, what key must you hold down while dragging the file?" If you can answer that without going to your keyboard and trying a few likely keys, you're better than most techs! In the real world, you can try a few wrong answers before you hit on the right one, but for the exams, you have to *know* it. Whether Old Tech or New Tech, make sure you are proficient at user-level Windows skills, including the following:

- Recognizing all the components of the standard Windows desktop (Start menu, notification area, etc.)

- Manipulating windows—resizing, moving, and so on

- Creating, deleting, renaming, moving, and copying files and folders within Windows

- Understanding file extensions and their relationship with program associations

- Using common keyboard shortcuts/hotkeys

- Installing, running, and closing a Windows application

Any PC technician who has been around a while will tell you that one of the great secrets in the computer business is that there's almost never anything completely new in the world of computer technology. Faster, cleverer, smaller, wider—absolutely—but the underlying technology, the core of what makes your PC and its various peripheral devices operate, has changed remarkably little since PCs came into widespread use a few decades ago. When you do your initial read-through, you may be tempted to skip the Historical/Conceptual sections—don't! Understanding the history and technological developments behind today's PCs helps you understand why they work—or don't work—the way they do. Basically, I'm passing on to you the kind of knowledge you might get by apprenticing yourself to an older, experienced PC tech.

After you've completed the first read-through, go through the book again, this time in textbook mode. If you're an Old Tech, start your studying here. Try to cover one chapter at a sitting. Concentrate on the 801 and 802 sections. Get a highlighter and mark the phrases and sentences that bring out major points. Be sure you understand how the pictures and illustrations relate to the concepts being discussed.

Once you feel you have a good grasp of the material in the book, you can check your knowledge by using the practice exams included on the media accompanying this book. You can take these in Practice mode or Final mode. In Practice mode, you can use the Assistance window to get a helpful hint for the current questions, use the Reference feature to find the chapter that covers the question, check your answer for the question, and see an explanation of the correct answer. In Final mode, you answer all the questions and receive an exam score at the end, just like the real thing. You can also adjust the number of questions on a Practice or Final mode exam with the Customize option.

Both modes show you an overall grade, expressed as a percentage, as well as a breakdown of how well you did on each exam domain. The Review Questions feature lets you see which questions you missed and what the correct answers are. Use these results to guide further studying. Continue reviewing the topics you miss and taking additional exams until you are consistently scoring in the 90% range. When you get there, you are ready to pass the CompTIA A+ certification exams.

Study Tactics

Perhaps it's been a while since you had to study for a test. Or perhaps it hasn't, but you've done your best since then to block the whole experience from your mind. Either

way, savvy test-takers know that certain techniques make studying for tests more efficient and effective.

Here's a trick used by students in law and medical schools who have to memorize reams of information: write it down. The act of writing something down (not typing, *writing*) in and of itself helps you to remember it, even if you never look at what you wrote again. Try taking separate notes on the material and re-creating diagrams by hand to help solidify the information in your mind.

Another oldie but goodie: Make yourself flash cards with questions and answers on topics you find difficult. A third trick: Take your notes to bed and read them just before you go to sleep. Many people find they really do learn while they sleep!

Contact

If you have any problems, any questions, or if you just want to argue about something, feel free to send an e-mail to the author—michaelm@totalsem.com—or to the editor—scottj@totalsem.com.

For any other information you might need, contact CompTIA directly at their Web site: www.comptia.org.

Chapter Review

Questions

1. What is the primary CompTIA Web site?

 A. www.comptia.com

 B. www.comptia.edu

 C. www.comptia.net

 D. www.comptia.org

2. Which certification is considered required for entrance into the IT industry?

 A. Certified Cisco Network Associate

 B. CompTIA A+ certification

 C. CompTIA Network+ certification

 D. Microsoft Certified IT Professional

3. How many exams do you need to pass to become CompTIA A+ certified?

 A. One

 B. Two

 C. Three

 D. Four

4. Which domain receives the most coverage in the 220-802 exam?

 A. Operating systems

 B. Security

 C. Mobile devices

 D. Troubleshooting

5. Which version of Windows is *not* tested on the 2012 versions of the CompTIA A+ exams?

 A. Windows XP Professional

 B. Windows 2000

 C. Windows 7 Ultimate

 D. Windows Vista Business

6. What company administers the CompTIA A+ certification exams?

 A. CompTIA

 B. Microsoft

 C. Pearson VUE

 D. Total Seminars

7. What pass rate should you strive for on the practice questions?

 A. 75%

 B. 80%

 C. 90%

 D. 95%

8. How many study hours to pass the CompTIA A+ exams does Mike recommend to a person just starting out learning PC repair?

 A. Roughly 140

 B. Roughly 240

 C. Roughly 340

 D. Roughly 440

9. What is the very first step you should take to pass the CompTIA A+ exams?

 A. Buy more practice exams.

 B. Buy two vouchers.

 C. Read this book like a novel.

 D. Schedule the exams.

10. After becoming CompTIA A+ certified, what's the next certification you should attain?

 A. CompTIA Network+

 B. CompTIA Security+

 C. Microsoft Certified IT Professional

 D. Certified Cisco Network Associate

Answers

1. **D.** The primary CompTIA Web site is www.comptia.org (although the .COM and .NET addresses will redirect you to the main site).

2. **B.** The CompTIA A+ certification is considered required for entrance into the PC industry.

3. **B.** You need to pass two exams to become CompTIA A+ certified.

4. **D.** The 220-802 exam dedicates 36% of the questions to troubleshooting.

5. **B.** No versions of Windows 2000 are on the CompTIA A+ exams.

6. **C.** Pearson VUE administers the CompTIA A+ certification exams.

7. **C.** You should not take either exam until you are consistently getting at least 90% on the practice exams.

8. **B.** Mike recommends about 240 study hours for a person new to PC repair.

9. **D.** Schedule the exams for some point in the future.

10. **A.** The typical certification path goes from CompTIA A+ to CompTIA Network+, so you have all the basics before you choose to specialize in Microsoft or Cisco products.

Operational Procedures

In this chapter, you will learn how to

- Present yourself with a proper appearance and professional manner
- Talk to customers in a professional, productive manner
- Work with PCs safely using the proper tools

Teaching new techs helps me keep up with the skills that get a tech a job and the issues that cause them to lose the jobs they get. To me, the number one reason techs fail to get or hold onto a job isn't lack of technical skill; it's a lack of what CompTIA calls "operational procedures." Personally, I think a better name might be "life skills and basic safety," but it boils down to the same thing: nontechnical skills that technicians are famous for lacking.

I like to describe myself as a "nerd" and I consider it a compliment if you call me one. Nerds are smart and like to work with technology—these are the good aspects of nerd-dom. On the other hand, most people would think of the term nerd as an insult. Nerds are rarely portrayed in a positive manner in the media, and I think I know why. Nerds generally suffer from some pretty serious social weaknesses. These weaknesses are classics: bad clothing, shyness, and poor communication skills. If you've ever seen an episode of the TV show *The Big Bang Theory*, you know what I'm talking about.

This chapter covers some basic life skills to enable you to enjoy your nerdiness and yet function out in the real world. You'll learn how to dress, how to act, and how to communicate. After you're well on your way to the beginnings of social graces, we'll discuss some of the hazards (such as static electricity) you may run into in your job and the tools you can use to prevent problems. After all, nerds who cannot stay organized—or who break equipment or themselves—need to learn some tricks to keep everything organized and safe.

801

The Professional Tech

A professional tech displays professionalism, which might seem a little trite if it weren't absolutely true. The tech presents a professional appearance and follows a proper ethical code. I call the latter the Traits of a Tech. Let's take a look at these two areas in more detail.

Appearance

Americans live in a casual society, and I think that's great, because I prefer dressing casually. The problem with casual is that perhaps our society is becoming *too* casual. New techs sometimes fail to appreciate that customers equate casual clothing with a casual attitude. You might think you're just fixing somebody's computer, but you're doing much more than that. You are saving precious family photos. You are keeping a small business in operation. This is serious stuff, and nobody wants an unclean, slovenly person doing these important jobs. Take a look at Figure 2-1. This is our resident illustrator (among other job descriptions), Ford Pierson, casually dressed to hang with his buddies.

Figure 2-1
Casual Ford

I have a question for you. If you ran a small business and your primary file server died, leaving 15 employees with nothing to do, how would you feel about Ford as a tech coming into your office looking like this? I hope your answer would be "not too confident." Every company has some form of dress code for techs. Figure 2-2 shows Ford dressed in a fairly typical example, with a company polo shirt, khaki pants, and dark shoes (trust me on that score). Please also note that both his shirt and his pants are wrinkle free. All techs should either know how to iron or know the location of the nearest cleaners.

Figure 2-2
Professional Ford

While we are looking at this model of a man, do you appreciate that his hair is combed and his face is cleanly shaven? It's too bad I can't use scratch-and-sniffs, but if I could, you'd also notice that Professional Ford took a shower, used some deodorant, and brushed his teeth.

I hope that most of the people who read this smile quietly to themselves and say, "Well, of course." The sad truth tells me otherwise. Next time you look at a tech, ask yourself how many of these simple appearance and hygiene issues were missed. Then make a point not to be one of the unkempt techs.

The Traits of a Tech

When I was a Boy Scout in the United States, we learned something called the Boy Scout Law, a list of traits that define the ethics of a Boy Scout. Even though I haven't been active in Boy Scouts for a long time, I still have the Scout Law memorized: "A Scout is trustworthy, loyal, helpful, friendly, courteous, kind, obedient, cheerful, thrifty, brave, clean, and reverent."

My goal here isn't a sales pitch for scouting in any form, but rather to give you an idea of what we are trying to achieve: a list of ethics that will help you be a better technician. The list you are about to see is my own creation, but it does a great job of covering the CompTIA A+ objectives. Let's dive into the traits of a tech: honesty/integrity, dependability/responsibility, adaptability/versatility, and sensitivity.

Honesty/Integrity

Honesty and integrity are not the same thing, but for a tech, they are so closely related that it is best to think of them as one big ethic. *Honesty* means to tell the truth, and *integrity* means doing the right thing.

It's simple to say you have to be honest, but be warned that our industry often makes it difficult. IT technicians get a lot of leeway compared to most starting jobs, making dishonesty tempting. One of the biggest temptations is lying to your boss. A new tech driving around in a van all day may find it convenient to stretch the truth on how long he took for lunch or how far along he is on the next job. Being up front and honest with your boss is pretty obvious and easy to understand.

Being honest with your customers is a lot harder. Don't sell people goods and services they don't need, even if you get a cut of what you sell. Don't lie to your customers about a problem. If you can't explain the problem to them in plain English, don't create techno-babble (see note) and don't be afraid to say, "I don't know." Too many techs seem to think that not knowing exactly what a problem might be is a reflection of their skill. In your humble author's opinion, there is no greater proof of a quality technician than the ability to say "I don't know, but I know how to figure it out, and I will get you the right answer."

NOTE Techno-babble is the use of (often nonsensical) jargon and technical terms to intimidate and silence a challenge to a technical issue.

A computer tech must bring *integrity* to the job, just like any other service professional. You should treat anything said to you and anything you see as a personal confidence, not to be repeated to customers, co-workers, or bosses. Here's Mike's Rule of Confidentiality: "Unless it's a felony or an imminent physical danger, you didn't see nothin'." You'll learn more about dealing with prohibited content in Chapter 29.

There is an exception to this rule. Sometimes you need to separate paying customers from in-house users. A paying customer is someone who doesn't work for your company and is paying for your services. An in-house user is someone who works for the same company you work for and is not directly paying for your services. It's often your job (but not always) to police in-house IT policies. Here's a great example. If you are at a customer's site and you see a Post-it note with a password on a user's monitor, you say nothing. If you are in-house and you see the same thing, you probably need to speak to the user about the dangers of exposing passwords.

You have a lot of power when you sit in front of someone's computer. You can readily read private e-mail, discover Web sites surfed, and more. With a click of the Start button, you can know the last five programs the user ran, including Word and Solitaire, and the last few documents the user worked on. Don't do this; you really don't want to know. Plus, if you are caught violating a customer's privacy, you not only will lose credibility and respect, but you also could lose your job.

Passwords are a big issue for techs. We have to reboot computers and access shares and other jobs that require passwords. The rule here is to *avoid learning other folks' passwords at all costs* (see Figure 2-3). If you know a password to access a mission-critical machine and that machine ends up compromised or with data missing, who might be blamed? You, that's who, so avoid learning passwords! If you only need a password once, let the user type it in for you. If you anticipate accessing something multiple times (the more usual situation), ask the user to change the password temporarily.

Figure 2-3
Don't do this!

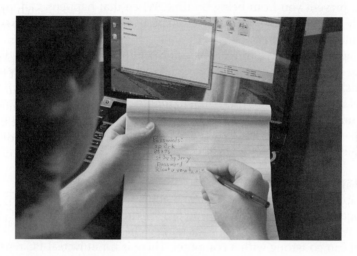

It's funny, but people assume ownership of things they use at work. John in accounting doesn't call the computer he uses anything but "my PC." The phone on Susie's desk isn't the company phone, it's "Susie's phone." Regardless of the logic or illogic involved with this sense of ownership, a tech needs to respect that feeling. You'll never go wrong if you follow the *Ethic of Reciprocity*, also known as the *Golden Rule:* "Do unto others as you would have them do unto you." In a tech's life, this can translate as "treat people's things as you would have other people treat yours." Don't use or touch anything— keyboard, printer, laptop, monitor, mouse, phone, pen, paper, or cube toy—without first asking permission. Follow this rule at all times, even when the customer isn't looking.

Dependability/Responsibility

Dependability and responsibility are another pair of traits that, while they don't mean the same thing, often go together. A responsible person is answerable for her actions. A dependable person can be counted on to perform those acts. Again, the freedom of the typical IT person's job makes dependability and responsibility utterly critical.

The single biggest dependability issue for an IT technician is to show up for job appointments and to show up on time. It seems to me we now live in a society where not showing up and not letting anyone know is normal. I call it the "Age of the Blow-off." We've all had an experience where we counted on someone to show up to get work done, and we can all share experiences when they simply did not show up. Failure to

show up for an appointment not only is inconvenient, but also can cost your customer a lot of money in lost time and productivity.

If you or your company makes an appointment for you, show up. Be there. Don't let simple problems (such as bad traffic) prevent you from showing up on time. Take some time to prepare. Figure out traffic times. Figure out if preceding appointments will cause a problem, and check for traffic. There is a popular old saying in the United States, "Five minutes early is on time, and on time is late." Sometimes events take place that prevent you from being on time. When that happens, call the customer immediately and give them your best estimate of when you can be there. A simple apology wouldn't hurt, either.

Responsibility is a tricky subject for IT folks. Certainly you should be responsible for your actions, but the stakes are high when critical data and expensive equipment are at risk. Before you work on a computer, always ask the customer if there are up-to-date backups of the data. If there aren't, offer to make backups for the customer, even if this incurs an extra charge for the customer. If the customer chooses not to make a backup, make sure he or she understands, very clearly, the risk to the data on the system you are about to repair.

Adaptability/Versatility

Adaptability defines how someone adjusts to changes. Versatility, at least within the scope of an IT technician, is bringing a broad set of skills to the PC repair process. Every PC repair is to some degree a guessing game. No one knows all the possible problems that can go wrong with a computer. There is no universal PC repair manual to which you can refer to tell you how to fix computers. Good techs must be able to adapt to any situation, both technically and in the environment. For example, good techs should be able to fix most peripherals, even if they are not experts on that particular device. As you progress through the book, you'll discover that most devices fit into one family or another and that there are certain diagnostic/repair steps that you can at least try to enact a repair.

 NOTE Most PC repair companies require a signed Authorization of Work or Work Authorization form to document the company name, billing information, date, scope of work, and that sort of thing. Even if you do your own repairs, these forms can save you from angst and from litigation. You can create your own or do an Internet search for examples.

Adaptability isn't required just for technical issues. PCs find themselves broken in the strangest places and ways. An adaptable tech doesn't have a problem if a computer sits at the top of a suspension bridge or behind a desk. An adaptable tech can work around mean dogs, broken water lines, and noisy little kids. (But there are some very important rules to dealing with kids. See later in this chapter.)

A technician has to be versatile. The best example of this is what I call the User Advocate. User Advocates are technicians who not only take the time to learn the processes of whatever organization they work for, but also look to create technology solutions

for problems and inefficiencies. This also means a tech should be at least competent if not expert at working with all the computer applications used by the organization. When you combine your IT skills with an understanding of how the business works, you become amazingly versatile, quickly finding yourself with more responsibility and (hopefully) more money.

A big part of versatility is offering different repair options in certain situations. When there is more than one way to fix things, make sure the customer knows all the options, but also give them your recommendation. Tell him why you feel your recommendation is the best course of action, but give them knowledge necessary to make their own decision.

A tech's versatility isn't limited to IT skills. Woe to the tech who doesn't understand basic electrical wiring and building codes. I've had hundreds of repair scenarios where the fix was as simple as knowing how to turn on an electrical breaker or moving a PC away from an electrical motor. No, these aren't IT skills, but a versatile tech knows these problems exist.

Sensitivity

Sensitivity is the ability to appreciate another's feeling and emotions. Sensitivity requires observing others closely, taking time to appreciate their feelings, and acting in such a way that makes them feel comfortable. I've rarely felt that technicians I've met were good at sensitivity. The vast majority of nerds I know, including myself, tend to be self-centered and unaware of what's going on around them. Let me give you a few tips I've learned along the way.

Understand that the customer is paying for your time and skills. Also understand that your presence invariably means something is wrong or broken, and few things make users more upset than broken computers. When you are "on the clock," you need to show possibly very upset customers that you are giving their problem your full attention. To do this, you need to avoid distractions. If you get a personal call, let it roll over to voicemail. If you get a work-related call, politely excuse yourself, walk away for privacy, and keep the call brief. Never talk to co-workers in a place where your customer can hear. Never speak badly of a customer; you never know where you'll run into them next.

Last, be culturally sensitive. We live in a diverse world of races, religions, etiquettes, and traditions. If a customer's religious holiday conflicts with your work schedule, the customer wins. If the customer wants you to take off your shoes, take them off. If the customer wants you to wear a hat, wear one. When in doubt, always ask the customer for guidance.

Communication

When you deal with users, managers, and owners who are frustrated and upset because a computer or network is down and they can't work, your job requires you to take on the roles of detective and psychologist. Talking with frazzled and confused people and getting answers to questions about how the PC got into the state it's in takes skill.

Communicating clearly and effectively is important. Plus, you need to follow the rules of tech-person decorum, acting with personal integrity and respect for the customer. Finally, use assertive communication to empathize with and educate the user. Great techs spend the time needed to develop these essential skills.

Assertive Communication

In many cases, a PC problem results from user error or neglect. As a technician, you must show users the error of their ways without creating anger or conflict. You do this by using assertive communication. *Assertive communication* isn't pushy or bossy, but it's also not the language of a pushover. Assertive communication first requires you to show the other person that you understand and appreciate the importance of his feelings. Use statements such as "I know how frustrating it feels to lose data," or "I understand how infuriating it is when the network goes out and you can't get your job done." Statements like these cool off the situation and let customers know you are on their side. Avoid using the word "you," as it can sound accusatory.

The second part of assertive communication is making sure you state the problem clearly without accusing the user directly: "Not keeping up with defragmenting your hard drive slows it down," or "Help me understand how the network cable keeps getting unplugged during your lunch hour." Last, tell the user what you need to prevent this error in the future. "Please call me whenever you hear that buzzing sound," or "Please check the company's approved software list before installing anything." Always use "I" and "me," and never make judgments. "I can't promise the keyboard will work well if it's always getting dirty" is much better than "Stop eating cookies over the keyboard, you slob!"

Respectful Communication

The final key in communicating with users revolves around *respect*. You don't do the user's job, but you should respect that job and person as an essential cog in the organization. Communicate with users the way you would like them to communicate with you, were the roles reversed. Again, this follows the Ethic of Reciprocity.

Generally, IT folks are there to support the people doing a company's main business. You are there to serve their needs and, all things being equal, to do so at their convenience, not yours.

Don't assume the world stops the moment you walk in the door and that you may immediately interrupt their work to do yours. Although most customers are thrilled and motivated to help you the moment you arrive, this may not always be the case. Ask the magic question, "May I start working on the problem now?" Give customers a chance to wrap up, shut down, or do anything else necessary to finish their business and make it safe for you to do yours.

Engage the user with the standard rules of civil conversation. Take the time to listen. Don't interrupt customers as they describe a problem; just listen and take notes. You

might hear something that leads to resolving the problem. Rephrase and repeat the problems back to the customer to verify you understand the issue ("So the computer is locking up three times a day?"). Use an even, nonaccusatory tone, and although it's okay to try to explain a problem if the user asks, never condescend and never argue.

Remain positive in the face of adversity. Don't get defensive if you can't figure something out quickly and the user starts hassling you. Remember that an angry customer isn't really angry with you—he's just frustrated—so don't take his anger personally. Take it in stride; smile, and assure him that computer troubleshooting sometimes takes a while.

Avoid letting outside interruptions take your focus away from the user and her computer problem. Things that break your concentration slow down the troubleshooting process immensely. Plus, customers will feel insulted if you start chatting on your cell phone with your significant other about a movie date later that night when you're supposed to be fixing their computers! You're not being paid to socialize, so turn those cell phones and pagers to vibrate. That's why the technogods created voicemail. Never take any call except one that is potentially urgent. If a call is potentially urgent, explain the urgency to the customer, step away, and deal with the call as quickly as possible.

If you discover that the user caused the problem, either through ignorance or by accident, don't minimize the importance of the problem, but don't be judgmental or insulting about the cause. We all screw up sometimes, and these kinds of mistakes are your job security. *You get paid because people make mistakes and machines break.* Chances are you'll be back at that workstation six months or a year later, fixing something else. By becoming the user's advocate and go-to person, you create a better work environment. If a mistaken action caused the problem, explain in a positive and supportive way how to do the task correctly, and then have the user go through the process while you are there to reinforce what you said.

Eliciting Answers

Your job as a tech is to get the computer fixed, and the best way to start that process is to determine what the computer is doing or not doing. You must start by talking to the customer. Allow the customer to explain the problem fully while you record the information. Once the person has described the situation, you must then ask questions. This process is called *eliciting answers*.

Although each person is different, most users with a malfunctioning computer or peripheral will be distraught and perhaps defensive about the problem. To overcome this initial attitude, you need to ask the right questions *and* listen to the customer's answers. Then ask the proper follow-up questions.

Always avoid accusatory questions, because they won't help you in the least (see Figure 2-4). "What did you do?" generally gets a confused or defensive "Nothing" in reply, which doesn't get you closer to solving the problem. First, ask questions that help clarify the situation. Repeat what you think is the problem after you've listened all the way through the user's story.

Figure 2-4
Never accuse!

Follow up with fact-seeking questions. "When did it last work?" "Has it ever worked in this way?" "Has any software changed recently?" "Has any new hardware been added?" Ask open-ended questions to narrow the scope ("Which applications are running when the computer locks up?").

By keeping your questions friendly and factual, you show users that you won't accuse them or judge their actions (see Figure 2-5). You also show them that you're there to help them. After the initial tension drops away, you'll often get more information: for instance, a recitation of something the user might have tried or changed. These clues can help lead to a quick resolution of the problem.

Figure 2-5
Keeping it friendly

Remember that you may know all about computer technology, but the user probably does not. This means a user will often use vague and/or incorrect terms to describe a particular computer component or function. That's just the way it works, so don't bother to correct them. Wherever possible, avoid using jargon, acronyms, or abbreviations specific to computers. They simply confuse the already upset user and can make

you sound like you're talking down to them. Just ask direct, factual questions in a friendly tone, using simple, non-jargon language to zero in on what the user was trying to accomplish and what happened when things went wrong. Use visual aids when possible. Point at the machine or go to a working PC to have the user show what went wrong or what she did or tried to do.

People do usually want to get a handle on what you are doing—in a simplified way. You don't want to overwhelm them, but don't be afraid to use simple analogies or concepts to give them an idea of what is happening. If you have the time (and the skills), use drawings, equipment, and other visual aids to make technical concepts more clear. If a customer is a closet tech and is really digging for answers—to the point that it's affecting your ability to do your job—compliment her initiative and then direct her to outside training opportunities. Better yet, tell her where she can get a copy of this book!

Beyond basic manners, never assume that just because you are comfortable with friendly or casual behavior, the customer will be too. Even an apparently casual user will expect you to behave with professional decorum. On the flip side, don't allow a user to put you in an awkward or even potentially dangerous or illegal situation. Never do work outside the scope of your assigned duties without the prior approval of your supervisor (when possible in such cases, try to direct users to someone who *can* help them). You are not a babysitter; never volunteer to "watch the kids" while the customer leaves the job site or tolerate a potentially unsafe situation if a customer isn't properly supervising a child. Concentrate on doing your job safely and efficiently, and maintain professional integrity.

Expectations and Follow-up

Users are terrified when their PCs and networks go down so hard that they need to call in a professional. Odds are good that they've left critical, or at least important, data on the computer. Odds are equally good they need this computer to work to do their job. When they're ready to lay down money for a professional, they're expecting you to make their system exactly the way it was before it broke.

Hopefully you can do exactly that for them, but you also must deal with their expectations and let them know what to expect. Equally, you should give your customers some follow-up after the job is finished. We've already covered data backups and Authorization of Work forms (and those are very important), but you need to keep the customer's needs in mind. You also want to keep them thinking about you, should they need more help in the future. Here are a few items you should consider.

Time Frame

If you can give the customer a best guess as to how long the repair will take, you'll be a hero. Don't be afraid to hold off on your time-frame prediction until you've diagnosed the machine. If you truly don't have a feel for the time involved, tell the customer that and then tell them what you'll need to know before you can make the prediction.

Stick to the timeline. If you finish more quickly, great! People love a job that goes faster than predicted. If you're moving past the predicted time frame, contact the customer and tell him as soon as possible. Let him know what's happened, explain why you need more time, and give him a new time frame. The biggest secret here is to keep in communication with the customer on any change in status. People understand delays—they take place in our lives daily. People resent not knowing why a delay is occurring, especially when a precious computer is at stake.

Documentation

At the completion of work, document the problem, including the time and day you started work, the solution (again including the time and day the work ended), the number of hours you worked, and a list of all parts you replaced. If the customer owns the replaced parts, offer them to the customer (this is especially true if you replace any storage media). This documentation may or may not include your charges.

Follow-up

I call follow-up the Lost Art: a simple follow-up, usually just a phone call, to confirm that the customer is happy with your work. This gives the customer a chance to detail any special issues that may have arisen, and it also adds that final extra touch that ensures they will call you again when they encounter a technical problem.

Safety and Tools

Effective communication with your customer enables you to *start* the troubleshooting process, getting details about the problem and clues about things that happened around the same time. To continue troubleshooting, though, you need to be adept at handling the computer. That starts with knowing how to handle computer components safely and how to use the tools of a tech. Let's begin by identifying and discussing some of the problems you may run into and how to deal with them.

Electrostatic Discharge (ESD)

If you decide to open a PC while reading this chapter, as I encourage you to do, you must take proper steps to avoid the greatest killer of PCs: *electrostatic discharge (ESD)*. ESD simply means the passage of a static electrical charge from one item to another. Have you ever rubbed a balloon against your shirt, making the balloon stick to you? That's a classic example of static electricity. When that static charge discharges, you may not notice it happening—although on a cool, dry day, I've been shocked so hard by touching a doorknob that I could see a big, blue spark! I've never heard of a human being getting anything worse than a rather nasty shock from ESD, but I can't say the same thing about computers. ESD will destroy the sensitive parts of your PC, so it is essential that you take steps to avoid ESD when working on your PC.

 NOTE All PCs are well protected against ESD on the outside. Unless you take a screwdriver and actually open up your PC, you don't need to concern yourself with ESD.

Anti-static Tools

ESD only takes place when two objects that store different amounts (the hip electrical term to use is *potential*) of static electricity come in contact. The secret to avoiding ESD is to keep you and the parts of the PC you touch at the same electrical potential, otherwise known as grounding yourself to the PC. You can accomplish this by connecting yourself to the PC via a handy little device called an *anti-static wrist strap*. This simple device consists of a wire that connects on one end to an alligator clip and on the other end to a small metal plate that secures to your wrist with an elastic strap. You snap the alligator clip onto any handy metal part of the PC and place the wrist strap on either wrist. Figure 2-6 shows a typical anti-static wrist strap in use.

 EXAM TIP Static electricity, and therefore the risk of ESD, is much more prevalent in dry, cool environments.

Figure 2-6
Anti-static wrist
strap in use

Anti-static wrist straps are standard equipment for anyone working on a PC, but other tools might also come in handy. One of the big issues when working with a PC occurs if you find yourself pulling out parts from the PC and setting them aside. The moment you take a piece out of the PC, it no longer has contact with the systems and may pick up static from other sources. Techs use anti-static mats to eliminate this risk. An *anti-static mat* acts as a point of common potential; it's typical to purchase a combination anti-static wrist strap and mat that all connect to keep you, the PC, and any loose components at the same electrical potential (see Figure 2-7).

Figure 2-7
Anti-static wrist
strap and mat
combination

Anti-static wrist straps and mats use tiny *resistors*—devices that stop or *resist* the flow of electricity—to prevent a static charge from racing through the device. These resistors can fail over time, so it's always a good idea to read the documentation that comes with your anti-static tools to see how to test those small resistors properly.

 EXAM TIP Always put components *in* an anti-static bag, not on the bag.

Any electrical component not in a PC needs to be stored in an *anti-static bag,* a specially designed bag that sheds whatever static electricity you have when you touch it, thus preventing any damage to components stored within (see Figure 2-8). Almost all PC components come in an anti-static bag when purchased. Experienced techs never throw these bags away, as you never know when you'll want to pull a part out and place it on a shelf for a while.

Figure 2-8
Anti-static bag

Although having an anti-static wrist strap with you at all times would be ideal, the reality is that from time to time you'll find yourself in a situation where you lack the proper anti-static tools. This shouldn't keep you from working on the PC—if you're careful! Before working on a PC in such a situation, take a moment to touch the power supply every once in a while as you work—I'll show you where it is in Chapter 3—to keep yourself at the same electrical potential as the PC. Although this isn't as good as a wrist strap, it's better than nothing at all.

The last issue when it comes to preventing ESD is that never-ending question—should you work with the PC plugged in or unplugged? The answer is simple: Do you really want to be physically connected to a PC that is plugged into an electrical outlet? Granted, the chances of electrocution are slim, but why take the risk?

 EXAM TIP Always unplug a PC when working inside it.

Electromagnetic Interference (EMI)

A magnetic field interfering with electronics is *electromagnetic interference (EMI)*. EMI isn't nearly as dangerous as ESD, but it can cause permanent damage to some components and erase data on some storage devices. You can prevent EMI by keeping magnets away from computer equipment. Certain components are particularly susceptible to EMI. Never get a magnet close to

- Floppy disks
- Hard drives
- Flash drives
- CRT (tube) monitors

The biggest problem with EMI is that we often use magnets without even knowing we are doing so. Any device with an electrical motor has a magnet. Many telephones have magnets. Power bricks for laptops and speakers also have magnets. Keep them away!

Radio Frequency Interference (RFI)

Do you ever hear strange noises on your speakers even though you aren't playing any sounds? Do you ever get strange noises on your cell phone? If so, you've probably run into *radio frequency interference (RFI)*. Many devices emit radio waves:

- Cell phones
- Wireless network cards
- Cordless phones
- Baby monitors
- Microwave ovens

NOTE Computer gear manufacturers package their product in a variety of ways to shield against accidental damage, whether that's physical damage, ESD, EMI, or RFI. The typical pink translucent computer bag is coated with a film that prevents the bag from producing static electricity and mildly protects the contents against physical contact (and thus damage). The two types of metal bags offer shielding against EMI and RFI as well as ESD. These are the silvery bags (such as in Figure 2-8) you'll see hard drives packed in, for example, and the black and silver woven bags you'll sometimes see.

A word of caution is in order here. The metal bags provide proper protection only when sealed, so fold the open end over and slap a piece of tape on it when storing a component.

In general, the radio waves that these devices emit are very weak, and almost all electronic devices are shielded to prevent RFI. A few devices, speakers in particular, are susceptible to RFI. RFI will never cause any damage, but it can be incredibly irritating. The best way to prevent RFI is to keep radio-emitting devices as far away as possible from other electronics.

RFI becomes a big problem when two devices share the same frequencies. Cordless phones, baby monitors, and wireless networks share the same range of frequencies. They sometimes interfere with each other, causing poor signals or even blocking signals completely. These devices need to be tuned to avoid stomping on each other's frequencies. In Chapter 23, you'll see how to tune a wireless network to prevent RFI.

Physical Safety

IT techs live in a dangerous world. We're in constant danger of tripping, hurting our backs, and getting burned by hot components. You also need to keep in mind what you wear (in a safety sense). Let's take a moment to discuss these physical safety issues and what to do about them.

CAUTION When thinking about safety, keep in mind any local government regulations. You may be required to wear certain protective gear or take extra precautions while in the workplace. Make sure you also follow any environmental rules for the disposal of old parts, especially with things like CRT monitors, which may contain hazardous materials. Check with your employer or your local government's Web site for more information.

If you don't keep organized, hardware technology will take over your life. Figure 2-9 shows a corner of my office, a painful example of a cable "kludge."

Figure 2-9
Mike's cable
kludge

Cable messes such as these are dangerous tripping hazards. While I may allow a mess like this in my home office, all cables in a business environment are carefully tucked away behind computer cases, run into walls, or placed under cable runners. If you see a cable that is an obvious tripping hazard, contact the person in charge of the building (CompTIA calls these folks "building services") to take care of it immediately. The results of ignoring such hazards can be catastrophic (see Figure 2-10).

Figure 2-10
What a strange,
bad trip it's been.

Another physical safety issue is heavy boxes. Computers, printers, monitors—everything we use—all seem to come to us in heavy boxes. Remember never to lift with your back; lift with your legs, and always use a hand truck if available. You are never paid enough to risk your own health.

Also, make certain mounted components don't exceed the weight limitations of their mounting hardware. You might have mounted everything properly, lifted correctly with your legs, and managed cables properly. But if the monitor comes crashing down on a user, that would be a bad thing indeed.

You also need to watch out for hot components. It's hard to burn yourself unless you actually open up a computer, printer, or monitor. First, watch for anything with a cooling fin like the one shown in Figure 2-11. If you see a cooling fin, odds are good that something is hot enough to burn you. Also look for labels or stickers warning about hot components. Last, when in doubt, move your hand over components as if you were checking the heat on a stove.

Figure 2-11
Checking for
hot cooling fins

Finally, remove any jewelry or loose-hanging clothing before working on a computer. If you have long hair, you might consider tying it back in a ponytail. You don't want anything getting caught in a fan or stuck on a component. This can save you and your components a lot of pain.

Tools of the Trade

The basic *tech toolkit* consists of a *Phillips-head screwdriver* and not much else—seriously—but a half-dozen tools round out a fully functional toolkit. Most kits have a star-headed Torx wrench, a nut driver or two, a pair of plastic tweezers, a little grabber tool (the technical term is *parts retriever*), a hemostat, an IC extractor for removing various chips, and both Phillips-head and flat-head screwdrivers (see Figure 2-12).

A lot of techs throw in an extension magnet to grab hard-to-reach bits that drop into cases (an exception to the "no magnets" rule). Many also add a magnifying glass and a flashlight for those hard-to-read numbers and text on the printed circuit boards (PCBs) that make up a large percentage of devices inside the system unit. Contrary to what you might think, techs rarely need a hammer.

Nut drivers Hemostat Phillips-head screwdrivers Flat-head screwdrivers

Three-prong parts retriever Multi-driver Extra parts tube IC extractor

Figure 2-12 Typical technician toolkit

Chapter Review

Questions

1. Which of the following would be most appropriate for the workplace? (Select two.)

 A. Clean, pressed khaki trousers

 B. Clean, wrinkle-free T-shirt

 C. Clean, wrinkle-free polo shirt

 D. Clean, pressed jeans

2. While manning the help desk, you get a call from a distraught user who says she has a blank screen. What would be a useful follow-up question? (Select two.)

 A. Is the computer turned on?

 B. Is the monitor turned on?

 C. Did you reboot?

 D. What did you do?

3. While manning the help desk, you get a call from Sharon in accounting. She's lost a file that she knows she saved to her hard drive. Which of the following statements would direct Sharon in the most efficient and professional manner to open her My Documents folder?

 A. Sharon, check My Documents.

 B. Sharon, a lot of programs save files to a default folder, often to a folder called My Documents. Let's look there first. Click the Start button and move the mouse until the cursor hovers over My Documents. Then press the left mouse button and tell me what you see when My Documents opens.

 C. Probably just defaulted to My Docs. Why don't you open Excel or whatever program you used to make the file, and then open a document and point it to My Documents?

 D. Look Sharon, I know you're clueless when it comes to computers, but how could somebody lose a file? Just open up My Documents, and look there for the file.

4. At the very least, what tool should be in every technician's toolkit?

 A. Pliers

 B. Hammer

 C. Straight-slot screwdriver

 D. Phillips-head screwdriver

5. When is it appropriate to yell at a user?

 A. When he screws up the second time.

 B. When he interrupts your troubleshooting.

 C. When he screws up the fifth time.

 D. Never.

6. When troubleshooting a software problem on Phoebe's computer and listening to her describe the problem, your beeper goes off. It's your boss. Which of the following is the most appropriate action for you to take?

 A. Excuse yourself, walk out of the cube, and use a cell phone to call your boss.

 B. Pick up Phoebe's phone and dial your boss's number.

 C. Wait until Phoebe finishes her description and then ask to use her phone to call your boss.

 D. Wait until Phoebe finishes her description, run through any simple fixes, and then explain that you need to call your boss on your cell phone.

7. You are at a customer's workstation to install several software and hardware updates, a process that will take a while and require several reboots of the computer. What should you do about the password to the user's account?

 A. Require the customer to sit with you throughout the process so she can type in her password each time.

 B. Ask the user to write down her password for you to use.

 C. Ask the user to change her password temporarily for you to use.

 D. Call your supervisor.

8. Which of the following is a good practice after completing a troubleshooting call at someone's office?

 A. Follow up with a call within a couple of days to make sure everything is going well with the fixed computer.

 B. Make copies of any passwords you used at the site for future reference.

 C. Document any particularly important people you met for future reference.

 D. Do nothing. Your work is finished there.

9. Which tool helps you avoid accidental static discharge by keeping you at the same electrical potential as the computer on which you're working?

 A. Anti-static spray

 B. Anti-static bag

 C. Anti-static wrist strap

 D. Phillips-head screwdriver

10. Which of the following helps prevent electromagnetic interference?

 A. Use an anti-static bag.

 B. Use an anti-static wrist strap.

 C. Keep magnets away from computer components.

 D. Keep computers away from monitors.

Answers

1. **A, C.** Khaki trousers and a polo shirt trump jeans and a T-shirt every time.

2. **A, B.** Go for the simple answer first. When faced with a blank screen, check to see if the computer and the monitor are turned on.

3. **B.** Walking customers through the path to a fix by using simple, nontechnical words is the best way to accomplish tasks over the phone.

Input

After starting TurboTax, your first job is to provide the computer with data: essential information, such as your name, where you live, how much you earned, and how many dollars you gave to federal and state governments.

Various pieces of hardware enable you to input data, the most common of which are the keyboard and mouse. Most PCs won't react when you say, "Hey you!"—at least not anywhere outside of a *Star Trek* episode. Although that day will come, you must still use something decidedly more mechanical: a keyboard to type in your data. The OS provides a fundamental service in this process as well. You can bang on a keyboard all day and accomplish nothing unless the OS translates your keystrokes into code that the rest of your computer's hardware understands.

NOTE Some might argue that voice recognition on the PC, the ability of a computer to understand your voice, has been around for a long time. In my opinion, it doesn't work well enough to replace my keyboard yet.

The same is not quite true on the smartphone front, where Apple's Siri handles a fair number of commands in common English just fine. Siri can find destinations for you, phone numbers, and more. You can send text messages dictated to Siri as well, plus many more things. We'll look at smartphones in more detail in Chapter 27.

Processing

Next, the computer processes your data. After you place information in various appropriate "boxes" in TurboTax, the computer does the math for you. Processing takes place inside the system unit—the box under your desk (see Figure 3-3)—and happens almost completely at a hardware level, although that hardware functions according to rules laid out in the OS. Thus you have another complex interaction between hardware and software.

Figure 3-3
Processing takes place somewhere in here!

Figure 3-8
Plug, port, and jack

Plug, port, and jack

Mini-DIN Connectors

Most PCs sport the European-designed *mini-DIN connectors*. The original Deutsche Industrie Norm (DIN) connector was replaced by mini-DIN a long time ago, so you'll only see mini-DIN connectors on your PC (see Figure 3-9 bottom). Older-style keyboards and mice plugged into DIN ports (Figure 3-9 top). You'll hear many older techs refer to a mini-DIN keyboard connector as a *PS/2* connector. That's what IBM called the port when it released the Personal System 2 (PS/2) computer way back in 1987 and the name stuck.

The standard mini-DIN connector has six pins and has been used for many devices aside from mice and keyboards. Some ancient video cards used the mini-DIN connector for output to a television, for example, and a lot of speaker sets use it to connect satellites to a subwoofer or to a control box. In uses other than keyboard or mouse, the mini-DIN gets yet another name, *DIN-6*.

Figure 3-9
DIN (top) and
mini-DIN (bottom)
connectors

 EXAM TIP Remember all three names for the mini-DIN connector: mini-DIN, PS/2, and DIN-6. Why CompTIA thinks you need to know the old names is anybody's guess.

USB Connectors

Universal serial bus (USB) provides the most common general-purpose connection for PCs. You'll find USB versions of many devices, such as mice, keyboards, scanners, cameras, and printers. USB connections come in three sizes: A, B, and mini-B. The USB A connector's distinctive rectangular shape makes it easily recognizable (see Figure 3-10).

Figure 3-10
USB A connector
and port

You never see a USB B connector on your computer. USB B connecters are for the other end of the USB cable, where it attaches to the USB device (see Figure 3-11).

Figure 3-11
USB B connector

The USB B connector's relatively large size makes it less than optimal for small devices such as cameras, so the USB folks also make the smaller mini-B–style connector shown in Figure 3-12.

Figure 3-12
USB mini-B
connector

USB has a number of features that make it particularly popular on PCs. First, USB devices are *hot-swappable*, which means you can insert or remove them without restarting your PC. Almost every other type of connector requires you to turn the system off, insert or remove the connector, and then turn the system back on. Hot-swapping completely eliminates this process.

Second, many USB devices get their electrical power through the USB connection, so they don't need batteries or a plug for an electrical outlet. You can even recharge some devices, such as cellular phones, by plugging them into a USB port (see Figure 3-13).

Figure 3-13
Cell phone charg-
ing via a USB
connection

 NOTE In addition to mini-B USB connectors, you'll also see mini-A, micro-A, and micro-B connectors, though they're much less common.

FireWire Connectors

FireWire, also known as *IEEE 1394*, moves data at incredibly high speeds, making it the perfect connection for highly specialized applications such as streaming video from a digital video camera onto a hard drive. FireWire consists of a 6-wire connector, as shown in Figure 3-14, or a 9-wire connector for devices that need more speed and power. A smaller 4-pin version is usually seen on peripherals. Like USB, FireWire devices are hot-swappable.

Figure 3-14
FireWire
connector
and port

DB Connectors

Over the years, *DB connectors* have been used for almost any type of peripheral you can think of, with the exception of keyboards. They have a slight *D* shape, which allows only one proper way to insert a plug into the socket and makes it easier to remember what they're called. Technically, they're known as D-sub or *D-subminiature* connectors, but most techs call them DBs. CompTIA calls them *D-shell* connectors, so don't be surprised by that term either.

Each male DB plug has a group of small pins that connect to DB ports. Female DB plugs connect to male DB ports on the system unit. DB connectors in the PC world can have from 9 to 37 pins or sockets, although you rarely see a DB connector with more than 25 pins or sockets. Figure 3-15 shows an example. DB-type connectors are some of the oldest and most common connectors used in the back of PCs.

Figure 3-15
DB-25 connector
and port

It wasn't that long ago that a typical PC used at least three or more different DB connectors. Over the past few years, the PC world has moved away from DB connectors. A typical modern system has only one or two, usually for video.

TIP Each D-sub connector size—called the shell size—has a specific name in the D-sub manufacturing world. A two-row, 9-pin connector, for example, is officially a DE-9 connector rather than a DB-9. The E refers to the 9-pin shell size. Why all of the DA, DB, DC, DD, and DE connectors became DB-x in the world of personal computers is a mystery, but most techs simply call them DB connectors.

RJ Connectors

You have more than likely seen an *RJ connector*, whether or not you knew it by that name. The little plastic plug used to connect your telephone cord to the jack (techs don't use the word "port" to describe RJ connectors) is a classic example of an RJ plug. Modern PCs use only two types of RJ jacks: the RJ-11 and the RJ-45. The phone jack is an RJ-11. It is used almost exclusively for modems. The slightly wider RJ-45 jack is used for your network connection. Figure 3-16 shows an RJ-11 plug (top) and an RJ-45 plug (bottom).

Figure 3-16
RJ-11 (top) and
RJ-45 (bottom)

Audio Connectors

Speakers and microphones connect to audio jacks on the system unit. The most common type of sound connector in popular use is the *1/8-inch* connector, also called a *mini-audio connector*. These small connectors have been around for years; they're just like the plug you use to insert headphones into a radio, music player, or similar device (see Figure 3-17). Traditionally, you'd find the audio jacks on the back of the PC, but many newer models sport front audio connections as well.

Figure 3-17
Mini-audio jacks
and plug

NOTE Keep in mind that the variety of connectors is virtually endless. The preceding types of connectors cover the vast majority, but you'll find many others on PCs as a tech. No law or standard requires device makers to use a particular connector, especially if they have no interest in making that device interchangeable with similar devices from other manufacturers.

Devices and Their Connectors

Now that you have a sense of the connectors, let's turn to the devices common to almost every PC to learn which connectors go with which device.

> **NOTE** Almost all connectors are now color-coordinated to help users plug the right device into the right port. These color codes are not required, and not all PCs and devices use them.

Cards Versus Onboard

All of the connectors on the back of the PC are just that: connectors. Behind those connectors are the actual devices that support whatever peripherals plug into those connectors. These devices might be built into the computer, such as a keyboard port. Others might be add-on expansion cards that a tech installed into the PC.

Most PCs have special *expansion slots* inside the system unit that enable you to add more devices on expansion cards. Figure 3-18 shows a typical card. If you want some new device that your system unit doesn't have built into the PC, you just go to the store, buy a card version of that device, and snap it in. Later chapters of the book go into great detail on how to do this, but for now just appreciate that a device might be built in or might come on a card.

Figure 3-18
Typical expansion card

Be careful handling cards. Touch the metal plate with the 90-degree bend and try to avoid touching any of the electronics. As mentioned in Chapter 2, you can protect your cards by keeping them in an anti-static bag when moving them.

Keyboard

Today's keyboards come in many shapes and sizes, but they always connect to your computer by either a mini-DIN port or a USB port. Many keyboards ship with an adapter so you can use either port. Most keyboard plugs and mini-DIN keyboard ports are colored purple (see Figure 3-19).

Figure 3-19
Keyboard plug
and port

Monitor

A monitor connects to the video connector on the system unit. You'll usually see one of two types of video connectors: the older, 15-pin female DB *Video Graphics Array (VGA)* connector or the unique *digital visual interface (DVI)* connector. VGA connectors are colored blue, whereas DVI connectors are white. Many video cards have both types of connectors (see Figure 3-20) or two VGA or two DVI connectors. Other video cards also add S-Video, component, or composite ports. Video cards with two connectors support two monitors, a very cool setup to have!

Figure 3-20
Video card with
(from left to right)
S-Video, DVI, and
VGA ports

NOTE The DVI connector comes in three flavors, DVD-D (all digital), DVD-A (analog), and DVI-I (both digital and analog).

The newest video connector is called *High-Definition Multimedia Interface (HDMI)*, shown in Figure 3-21. HDMI brings a number of enhancements, such as the ability to carry both video and sound on the same cable. Primarily designed for home theaters, computers with HDMI connectors grow more common every year.

Figure 3-21
HDMI connector

NOTE There are two smaller versions of HDMI called Mini-HDMI and Micro-HDMI. You'll find these primarily on high-end cell phones.

Sound

The sound device in a computer performs two functions. First, it takes digital information and turns it into sound, outputting the sound through speakers. Second, it takes sound that is input through a microphone or some other audio source and turns it into digital data.

To play and record sounds, your sound device needs to connect to a set of speakers and a microphone or more. All PCs have at least two miniature audio jacks: one for a microphone and another for stereo speakers. Better cards provide extra miniature audio jacks for surround sound. Figure 3-22 shows a typical onboard sound card with six different 1/8-inch jacks. Four of these are for speakers and two are for input (such as microphones). The color scheme for sound connections is complex, but for now remember one color—green. That's the one you need to connect a standard pair of stereo speakers.

Figure 3-22
Typical bank of 1/8-inch audio jacks

An older sound card may have a female 15-pin DB port that enables you to attach a musical instrument digital interface (MIDI) device or add a joystick to your PC (see Figure 3-23). These multi-function joystick/MIDI ports are rare today.

Figure 3-23
Legacy joystick/
MIDI port

Adding more and more audio jacks to sound cards made the back of a typical sound card a busy place. In an effort to consolidate the various sound signals, the industry invented the *Sony/Philips Digital Interface Format (S/PDIF)* connection. S/PDIF comes in coaxial and optical versions. Figure 3-24 shows a motherboard with both (the coaxial connection is on the left). One S/PDIF connection replaces all of the mini-audio connections, assuming your surround speaker system also comes with an S/PDIF connection.

Figure 3-24
S/PDIF connection

S/PDIF

Network

Networks are groups of connected PCs that share information. The PCs most commonly connect via some type of cabling that usually looks like an extra-thick phone cable. A modern PC uses an RJ-45 connection to connect to the network. Figure 3-25 shows a typical RJ-45 network connector. Network connectors do not have a standard color.

Figure 3-25
Typical network
connection

NOTE Modern PCs have built-in network connections, but this is a fairly recent development. For many years, network devices only came on an expansion card, called a *network interface card (NIC)*. The term is so common that even built-in network connections—which most certainly are not cards—are still called NICs.

Mouse

Most folks are pretty comfortable with the function of a mouse—it enables you to select graphical items on a graphical screen. A PC mouse has at least two buttons (as opposed to the famous one-button mouse that came with Apple computers until recently), while a better mouse provides a scroll wheel and extra buttons. A mouse uses either a USB port or a dedicated, light-green mini-DIN connector (see Figure 3-26).

Figure 3-26
Mouse with mini-
DIN connection

A variation of the mouse is a *trackball*. A trackball does the same job as a mouse, but instead of pushing it around like a mouse, the trackball stays in one place as you roll a ball with your fingers or thumb (see Figure 3-27).

Figure 3-27
Trackball

Modem

A *modem* enables you to connect a PC to a network via a standard telephone line. Modems are another easily identifiable device in PCs as they have one or two RJ-11 jacks. One jack is to connect the modem to the telephone jack on the wall. If the modem has a second RJ-11 jack, it is for an optional telephone so you can use the phone line when the modem is not in use (see Figure 3-28).

Figure 3-28
Internal modem

NOTE External modems traditionally connected to a male 9-pin or 25-pin D-sub port on the system unit called a *serial port*. Although just about every external modem today connects to USB, a few computers still come with a serial port for legacy devices.

Printer

For many years, printers only used a special connector called a *parallel port*. Parallel ports use a 25-pin female DB (DB-25) connector that's usually colored fuchsia (see Figure 3-29).

Figure 3-29
Parallel port

After almost 30 years of domination by parallel ports, most printers now come with USB, Ethernet, and Wi-Fi 802.11 b/g/n connectivity options. Parallel ports are quickly fading away from the backs of most computers.

Joystick

Joysticks weren't supposed to be used just for games (see Figure 3-30). When the folks at IBM added the two-row, 15-pin female DB joystick connector to PCs, they envisioned joysticks as hard-working input devices, just as the mouse is today. Except in the most rare circumstances, however, the only thing a *joystick* does today is enable you to turn your PC into a rather expensive game machine. But is there a more gratifying feeling than easing that joystick over, pressing the Fire button, and watching an enemy fighter jet get blasted by a well-placed Sidewinder missile? I think not. Traditional joystick connecters are colored orange, but most joysticks today connect to USB ports.

Figure 3-30
Joystick

eSATA

More and more PCs are showing up with eSATA ports like the one shown in Figure 3-31. Some external hard drives and optical drives can connect via eSATA.

Figure 3-31
eSATA port

Plenty More!

Keep in mind that there are lots more devices and connectors out there. This section includes only the most common and the ones you're most likely to see. As you progress through this book, you'll see some less common connecters and where they are used.

Inside the System Unit

Now that you've seen the devices that connect to the PC, it's time to open up the system unit to inspect the major internal components of a typical PC. A single PC is composed of thousands of discrete components. Although no one can name every tiny bit of electronics in a PC, a good technician should be able to name the major internal components that make up the typical PC. Let's open and inspect a system unit to see these components and see what they do. In later chapters, you'll see all of these components in much more detail.

Case

The system unit's case is both the internal framework of the PC and the external skin that protects the internal components from the environment. Cases come in an amazing variety of styles, sizes, and colors. Figure 3-32 shows the front and back of a typical PC case. The front of the case holds the buttons for turning the system on and off, lights to tell you the status of the system, and doors for accessing removable media drives such as digital versatile disc (DVD) drives. This system also provides USB, FireWire, and audio connections in the front for easy access if you want to use a device that needs these connections.

Figure 3-32
Case—front
and back

NOTE You'll hear the PC case called the *enclosure*, especially at the more expensive end of the spectrum. Case, enclosure, and system unit are interchangeable terms.

The back of the case holds the vast majority of the system unit connections. You will also notice the power supply—almost always at the top of the case—distinguished by its cooling fan and power plug. Note that one area of the back, the input/output (I/O) area, holds all of the onboard connections (see Figure 3-33), while another area in the back contains slots for cards. Similarly, the case uses slots to enable access to the external connectors on cards installed in the system unit.

Figure 3-33
Onboard
connections

Opening a case is always…interesting. There's no standard way to open a case, and I'm convinced that the folks making system units enjoy some sick humor inventing new and complex ways to open them. In general, you detach the sides of a case by removing a few screws in the back of the system unit, as shown in Figure 3-34. Use common sense and you won't have too many problems. Just don't lose track of your screws or where each one was inserted!

Figure 3-34
Opening a
system unit

 TIP Take a look at the front of your PC and you'll see all kinds of connectors, from power and reset buttons to USB and audio ports. Front connections are most commonly used for temporary devices, such as headphones. If you have a device you don't intend to remove very often, you should install it in one of the back connections.

Once you've opened the case, take a look inside. You'll see metal framework, all kinds of cables, and a number of devices. As you inspect the devices, you may gently push cables to the side to get a better view. Don't forget to wear an anti-static wrist strap (attaching it to any handy metal part of the case) or touch the metal case occasionally to prevent ESD.

CPU

The *central processing unit (CPU)*, also called the *microprocessor*, performs all of the calculations that take place inside a PC. CPUs come in a variety of shapes and sizes, as shown in Figure 3-35.

Figure 3-35
Typical CPUs still
in protective
packaging

Modern CPUs generate a lot of heat and thus require a cooling fan and heat sink assembly to avoid overheating (see Figure 3-36). A *heat sink* is a big slab of copper or aluminum that helps draw heat away from the processor. The fan then blows the heat out into the case. You can usually remove this cooling device if you need to replace it, although some CPU manufacturers have sold CPUs with a fan permanently attached.

Figure 3-36
CPU with fan

CPUs have a make and model, just like automobiles do. When talking about a particular car, for example, most people speak in terms of a Ford Taurus or a Toyota Camry. When they talk about CPUs, people say Intel Core i7 or AMD Phenom. Over the years, there have been only a few major CPU manufacturers, just as there are only a few major auto manufacturers. The two most common makes of CPUs used in PCs are AMD and Intel.

Although only a few manufacturers of CPUs have existed, those manufacturers have made hundreds of models of CPUs. Some of the more common models made over the past few years have names such as Core 2 Duo, Core i5, Core i7, Phenom II, and AMD-FX.

Finally, CPUs come in a variety of packages. The package defines how the CPU looks physically and how it connects to the computer. Intel CPUs currently use a package type called *land grid array* (*LGA*), and AMD likes *pin grid array* (*PGA*). Every CPU package type has a number of versions, and each package type is designed to fit into a particular connection called a *socket*. Sockets have such names as Socket AM3 or Socket B. Figure 3-37 shows a CPU with its matching socket.

Figure 3-37
CPU and matching socket

Chapter 6 goes into great detail on CPUs, but for now remember that every CPU has a make, a model, and a package type.

 CAUTION Some parts of your PC are much more sensitive to ESD than others. Your CPU and RAM are very sensitive to ESD. If you touch the metal parts of your CPU or RAM and you have even the tiniest amount of charge, you can destroy them.

RAM

Random access memory (RAM) stores programs and data currently being used by the CPU. The maximum amount of programs and data that a piece of RAM can store is measured in units called *bytes*. Modern PCs have many millions, even billions, of bytes of RAM, so RAM is measured in units called *megabytes* (*MB*) or *gigabytes* (*GB*). An average PC will have from 1 to 4 GB of RAM, although PCs may have more or less. Each piece of RAM is called a *stick*. One common type of stick found in today's PC is called a *dual inline memory module* (*DIMM*). Figure 3-38 shows two examples of DIMMs used in PCs.

Figure 3-38
Two DIMMs

Your PC takes only one type of DIMM, and you must know the type so you can add or replace RAM when needed. Chapter 7 covers everything you need to know to work comfortably with RAM.

Motherboard

You can compare a motherboard to the chassis of an automobile. In a car, everything connects to the chassis either directly or indirectly. In a PC, everything connects to the motherboard either directly or indirectly. A *motherboard* is a thin, flat piece of circuit board, usually green or gold, and often slightly larger than a typical piece of notebook paper (see Figure 3-39).

Figure 3-39
Typical
motherboard

A motherboard contains a number of special sockets that accept various PC components. The CPU and RAM, for example, plug directly into the motherboard. Other devices, such as floppy drives, hard drives, and CD and DVD drives, connect to the motherboard sockets through short cables. Motherboards also provide onboard connectors for external devices such as mice, printers, joysticks, and keyboards.

All motherboards use multipurpose expansion slots in which you can add adapter cards. Different types of expansion slots exist for different types of cards (see Figure 3-40).

Figure 3-40
Placing a card into
an expansion slot

Power Supply

The *power supply*, as its name implies, provides the necessary electrical power to make the PC operate. The power supply takes standard electrical power and converts it into power your PC can use. Most power supplies are about the size of a shoebox cut in half and are usually a gray or metallic color (see Figure 3-41).

Figure 3-41

Power supply

A number of connectors lead out of the power supply. Every power supply provides special connectors to power the motherboard and a number of other general-use connectors that provide power to any device that needs electricity. Check out Chapter 10 for more information.

Floppy Drive

The *floppy drive* enables you to access removable floppy disks. The floppy drives used in today's PCs (and I use the term loosely—you'll have trouble finding a floppy drive on most modern computers) are 3.5-inch floppy drives. Floppy drives only store a tiny amount of data and have all but disappeared from PCs.

Floppy drives connect to the computer via a ribbon cable, which in turn connects to the motherboard. The connection to the motherboard is known as the *floppy drive controller* (see Figure 3-42).

Figure 3-42

Floppy drive
connected to
motherboard

Hard Drive

A *hard drive* stores programs and data that are not currently being used by the CPU. Although RAM storage is measured in megabytes and gigabytes, a PC's hard drive stores much more data than a typical PC's RAM—hundreds of gigabytes to *terabytes*. A terabyte is 1000 gigabytes.

An average PC has one hard drive, although most PCs accept more. Special PCs that need to store large amounts of data, such as a large corporation's main file-storage computer, can contain many hard drives—8 to 16 drives in some cases.

The two most common types of hard drives seen in today's PCs are the older *Parallel Advanced Technology Attachment* (*PATA*) and the more modern *Serial Advanced Technology Attachment* (*SATA*). PATA drives use a ribbon cable very similar to the one used by floppy drives, whereas SATA drives use a very narrow cable. Figure 3-43 shows a SATA drive (left) next to a PATA drive (right). Most motherboards only come with SATA connections, but if you look around, you can find one that supports PATA as well.

Figure 3-43
SATA and PATA
drives showing
data connectors

Optical drives, introduced next, use the same PATA or SATA connections used with hard drives. Figure 3-44 shows a DVD drive sharing a single ribbon cable with a PATA hard drive—a common sight inside a PC.

Figure 3-44
Hard drive and
DVD drive

TIP Very few PCs use *small computer system interface (SCSI)* drives. SCSI drives are generally faster and more expensive, so they usually show up only in high-end PCs such as network servers or graphics workstations.

Optical Drives

Optical drives enable a computer to read one or more types of optical discs, such as CD, DVD, or Blu-ray Disc (see Figure 3-45). CDs store around 700 MB and come in

three varieties: CD-ROM (*read only memory*: you can't change the data on them), CD-R (*recordable*: you can change the data once), and CD-RW (*rewritable*: you can change the data on them over and over). DVDs store much more data—the smallest capacity DVDs store around 4 GB, enough for a Hollywood movie—and come in even more varieties: DVD-ROM, DVD+R, DVD-R, DVD+RW, and DVD-RW, just to name the more famous ones. Blu-ray Discs are popular for high-definition movies, but there are also Blu-ray Discs for storing data with capacities starting at 25 GB.

Figure 3-45
Assorted optical discs

All of these optical discs require an optical drive that knows how to read them. If you want to do anything with a CD-RW disc, for example, you need a CD-RW drive. If you want to use a DVD+R disc, you need a DVD+R drive. Luckily, most optical drives support many different types of discs, and some support every common type of optical disc available. Figure 3-46 shows typical optical drives. Note that some of them advertise what disc types they use. Others give no clue whatsoever.

Figure 3-46
Optical drives

 NOTE Chapter 13 goes into great detail on the assorted discs and drive types.

Know Your Parts

The goal of this chapter was to get you to appreciate the names and functions of the various parts of the PC: peripherals, connectors, and components. By starting with the Big Picture view, you may now begin breaking down the individual components on a chapter-by-chapter basis and truly understand at great depth how each component works and how it interconnects with the PC system as a whole.

Chapter Review

Questions

1. What do you call the commands that tell the computer what to do?

 A. Data

 B. Morse code

 C. Programming

 D. Output

2. Which of the following is a proper name for a stick of RAM?

 A. CRIMM

 B. DIMM

 C. BGA

 D. LGA

3. Where do you connect an anti-static wrist strap? (Select the best answer.)

 A. To an anti-static plate on the computer

 B. To an electrical outlet

 C. To a handy metal part of the case

 D. To a non-static wrist strap

4. What sort of connector does a typical network interface card have?

 A. DB-9

 B. Mini-DIN

 C. RJ-11

 D. RJ-45

5. Modern keyboards connect to which of the following ports? (Select all that apply.)

 A. DIN

 B. FireWire

 C. Mini-DIN

 D. USB

6. Which end of the USB cable plugs into the PC?

 A. A

 B. B

 C. Mini-A

 D. Mini-B

7. A modern printer usually plugs into which of the following ports?

 A. DB-9

 B. DB-25

 C. Mini-DIN

 D. USB

8. What do you plug into a three-row, 15-pin port?

 A. Joystick

 B. Keyboard

 C. Monitor

 D. Mouse

9. What connector was designed to connect your PC to a high-end television set?

 A. DB-HD

 B. HDMI

 C. USB

 D. VGA

10. What connector was designed to connect your PC to a high-end audio system?

 A. DB-HA

 B. DVI

 C. Mini-audio

 D. S/PDIF

Answers

1. **C.** The commands that tell the computer what to do are called, collectively, *programming*.

2. **B.** Modern computers use DIMMs for RAM.

3. **C.** Connect an anti-static wrist strap to any handy metal part of the computer. The metal plate, by the way, is the section on the strap where you connect the cable from the PC.

4. **D.** A typical network interface card sports an RJ-45 port.

5. **C, D.** Modern keyboards connect to either mini-DIN or USB ports.

6. **A.** Plug the A connector into the PC.

7. **D.** A modern printer usually plugs into USB.

8. **C.** You plug a monitor into a three-row, 15-pin port.

9. **B.** HDMI was designed to connect your PC to a high-end television set.

10. **D.** S/PDIF was designed to connect your PC to a high-end audio system.

Visible Windows

In this chapter, you will learn how to

- Relate the history of Microsoft Windows
- Explain the Windows interface
- Identify the operating system folders of Windows XP, Windows Vista, and Windows 7
- Describe the utilities in Windows that are essential to techs

As a PC tech, you need to understand Windows at a level beyond that of regular users. Not only must techs run through the standard Windows features that everyone uses every day (Start button, Recycle Bin, and so on), they must also be comfortable drilling down underneath that user-friendly surface to get their hands a little dirty.

This chapter begins by introducing and organizing the many variations of Windows on the market today and helping you appreciate the difference between, for example, Windows XP Professional and Windows 7 Ultimate. The chapter then takes you through the Windows interface in detail. The third section looks more closely at the techie aspects of Windows, including the structure of the operating system. The fourth section provides an overview of the many utilities for techs available in Windows. The chapter closes in the "Beyond A+" section with a discussion of the versions of Windows not on the current CompTIA A+ exams, such as Windows 8 and non-desktop versions of Windows. Let's get started!

Historical/Conceptual

A Brief History of Microsoft Windows

Many users think of Windows as a monolithic thing, as *the* operating system (OS) for the PC (as opposed to the Mac), but as a tech you need to understand that Microsoft produces many varieties of the OS, each with specific tools, utilities, file structures, and interfaces. And you need to be able to navigate through any modern version of Windows fluidly.

Microsoft currently supports many versions of Windows, of which three concern the CompTIA A+ certified technician: Windows XP, Windows Vista, and Windows 7. Within each of these versions, Windows comes in multiple editions. Table 4-1 presents a list for the three versions you need to know for the exams.

Windows Version	Editions (32-bit)	Editions (64-bit)
Windows XP	• Windows XP Home • Windows XP Professional • Windows Media Center	• Windows XP 64-bit Edition • Windows XP Professional x64 Edition
Windows Vista[1]	• Windows Vista Home Basic • Windows Vista Home Premium • Windows Vista Business • Windows Vista Ultimate • Windows Vista Enterprise	• Windows Vista Home Basic • Windows Vista Home Premium • Windows Vista Business • Windows Vista Ultimate • Windows Vista Enterprise
Windows 7[1]	• Windows 7 Starter • Windows 7 Home Premium • Windows 7 Professional • Windows 7 Ultimate • Windows 7 Enterprise	• Windows 7 Home Premium • Windows 7 Professional • Windows 7 Ultimate • Windows 7 Enterprise

1 Microsoft has also released Windows Vista Starter Edition and Windows 7 Home Basic. These are simplified editions of the operating system designed for the developing world and are not sold in developed countries.

Table 4-1 Versions of Windows on the CompTIA A+ Exams

The problem of variety is compounded the minute you start working with older computers or talking with users or techs who've been working with computers for several years. You'll hear about old versions of Windows such as Windows 98 or Windows 2000. Huh? What are these versions (see Figure 4-1)? How do they fit in the picture?

Figure 4-1 Lots of Windows!

This section outlines the history of Microsoft Windows and then takes an in-depth look at the differences among the many versions of Microsoft's flagship operating system. That way you can sort out the essentials for today's techs from the many varieties you'll hear about.

Microsoft entered the operating system game in the early 1980s with a command-line OS called Microsoft Disk Operating System, or MS-DOS. With a command-line OS, you interacted with the computer to run programs, save files, and perform all the other computing functions by typing and then pressing the ENTER key on your keyboard. This whole typing thing worked for people who could memorize commands and such, but alternative operating systems, such as Apple's Mac OS, offered a visual interface, where you could interact with the computer by clicking on pictures. The time came for Microsoft to step up its game and produce a graphical user interface (GUI) where users could use a mouse to point and click.

Early Windows

The earliest version of Windows, Microsoft Windows 1.0, arrived in 1985 and was little more than a graphical overlay of the DOS command-line operating system. This overlay version of Windows went through a number of updates, ending with the first truly popular version of Windows, Windows for Workgroups version 3.1 (see Figure 4-2).

Figure 4-2 Windows for Workgroups

NOTE Microsoft released several editions of Windows 3.1, with minor differences in name. Techs call the editions collectively Windows 3.x.

In 1989, Microsoft offered a completely separate version of Windows called Windows NT. Windows NT was a true graphical operating system and was dramatically more powerful than the Windows overlay versions. Windows NT went through a number of editions, culminating with Windows NT 4.0 in 1996 (see Figure 4-3).

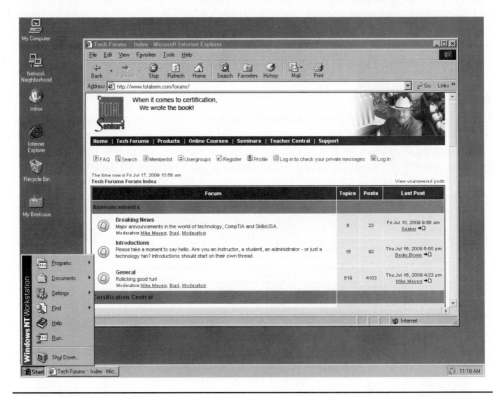

Figure 4-3 Windows NT 4.0

Windows NT had so many features that showing them all could take days, but one is important. NT came with a new way to organize hard drives and files, called the NT File System (NTFS). Before NTFS, all versions of Windows used an ancient file system called the file allocation table (FAT). NTFS took care of a number of problems, the biggest of which was security. FAT had no file security, meaning it had no user accounts, passwords, or permissions to enable people to control access to files. NTFS was built from the ground up with security in mind. We'll cover both FAT and NTFS later in the book; for now, just appreciate that NTFS began with Windows NT.

It wasn't until 1995 that Microsoft dumped the overlay concept and introduced Windows 95, the first version of Windows for the standard user that was also a full-blown operating system (see Figure 4-4). Windows 95 offered many improvements over Windows 3.*x*, and eventually Microsoft released several upgraded versions as well, such as Windows 98, Windows 98 SE, and Windows Me.

Figure 4-4 Windows 95—the Windows of your forefathers

NOTE When we describe Windows 95, 98, 98 SE, and Me from a historical standpoint, we lump them all together, using the term "Windows 9x."

The arrival of Windows 2000 in 2001 changed things. Throughout most of the 1990s, Windows was in a bit of a mess. Microsoft had two totally different operating systems—each called Windows—that it sold for two different markets. Microsoft sold the Windows 9*x* series for the home user and small office, and it sold the much more powerful Windows NT series for corporate environments.

Windows 2000 was the first step toward changing this mess. It was based on Windows NT (including support for NTFS), but it included a great interface, provided support for nearly any program, and was substantially easier to use than Windows NT. Microsoft originally presented Windows 2000 as a replacement for Windows NT, but its stability and ease of use motivated many knowledgeable Windows 9x users to upgrade to Windows 2000 as well. Windows 2000 started to appear as "the single Windows to replace all the other versions."

> **NOTE** Windows 2000 was the last version of Windows to come in both Server and Professional editions. After the release of Windows XP, Microsoft introduced the next version of Windows Server as Server 2003. Windows Server 2008 R2 is the latest edition of Windows Server. As of this writing, Microsoft's newest server product, codenamed Windows Server 8 (WS8), is right around the corner, so keep your eyes peeled!

Modern Windows

The vast majority of computers in the field today run one of the three modern versions of Windows, so the CompTIA A+ certification focuses on those: Windows XP, Windows Vista, and Windows 7. But as you know from Table 4-1 at the beginning of this chapter, just saying the name of a Windows version doesn't do justice to the editions within that version. The trick is to organize these editions in a way that enables you to discover their similarities and differences. In this section, we'll look at editions of Windows XP, Vista and 7, as well as a few other versions of Windows, and see the differences in detail.

802

Windows XP

Windows XP came hot on the heels of Windows 2000. Under the hood, XP was basically the same as Windows 2000, but it added a dramatically improved interface and a number of new features, such as a built-in CD writer. Microsoft also broke with the beauty of 2000's "one OS for everyone" idea. Microsoft visualized three types of users—professionals, home users, and media junkies—so Windows XP came in three editions: Windows XP Professional, Windows XP Home, and Windows XP Media Center.

Windows XP Professional

Microsoft Windows XP Professional is, in many people's opinions, the most versatile and therefore the most mainstream edition of Windows XP. Microsoft tuned Windows XP Professional for office environments with many users sharing lots of data and multiple users sharing single computers. Windows XP Professional provides full-blown data security, and it is the only edition of Windows XP with the capability of logging onto a special Windows Server–controlled network called a *domain*.

A Windows domain is a group of networked computers all under the control of a single computer running some edition of Windows Server. Users on a domain can use a single logon with their computer that defines everything they can do on every other computer on the domain. (See Chapter 22 for all the details of the amazing Windows domain.) Figure 4-5 shows a typical Windows XP Professional desktop.

Figure 4-5 Windows XP Professional

Windows XP Home

As its name implies, Windows XP Home is designed for the home and small-office user. Windows XP Home is a stripped-down edition of Windows XP Professional. The best way to describe Windows XP Home is to list the Windows XP Professional features that Windows XP Home lacks. Windows XP Home does *not* have

- **The ability to log on to a Windows domain** A Windows Home PC may log on to any single Windows server, but you must have a user name and password on every single server. With a domain, you can have one user name and password that works on all computers that are members of the domain.

- **Encrypting file system** With Windows XP Professional, you can encrypt a file or a folder so that only you can read it. Windows XP Home lacks this feature.

- **Support for multiple processors** Windows XP Home does not support more than one physical CPU. Windows XP Professional supports two separate CPUs.

NOTE CPU support is based on physical CPUs, not the number of cores in a single CPU. See Chapter 6 for details on multi-core CPUs.

- **Support for Remote Desktop** A Windows XP Professional PC may be remotely accessed from another computer by using Remote Desktop (see Figure 4-6). You cannot access a Windows XP Home system in this fashion.

Figure 4-6 Remote Desktop

- **Support for NTFS Access Control** The NTFS file system is capable of powerful controls on what users may do to a file or folder. Windows XP Home doesn't give you the ability to control these NTFS permissions individually. When you

look at the properties of a file or folder in Windows XP Home, you'll notice that there is no Security tab. Instead, Windows XP Home's Sharing tab (see Figure 4-7) shows that only one folder, the Shared Documents folder, is open for sharing—very different from XP Professional.

Figure 4-7
Windows XP
Home Sharing tab

- **Support for group policies** Do you need to keep users from using a certain program? Do you want to prevent them from changing the screensaver? What do you want to do if they try to log in three times unsuccessfully? That's the job of group polices. Well, if you want this level of control on your system, get Windows XP Professional, because XP Home doesn't support them. Group policies are discussed in Chapter 29.

A few more differences exist between Windows XP Professional and XP Home, but the preceding are the ones you're most likely to run into. Basically, if you want serious control of the folders, files, users, and network, you need XP Professional.

Windows XP Media Center

Windows XP Media Center is a specialized XP edition that includes the very handy Windows Media Center program (see Figure 4-8). Media Center is a Personal Video Recorder (PVR) program that enables you to watch and record television (you'll need a TV tuner card) and organize all of your media, from photos to music.

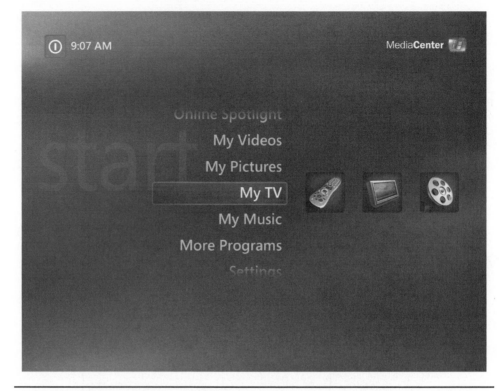

Figure 4-8 Windows XP Media Center

Other than the Media Center program, Windows XP Media Center's capabilities are identical to those of Windows XP Home.

Windows Vista

In January of 2007, Microsoft announced Windows Vista. Vista introduced a new interface as well as some very different underpinnings, which we will discuss both in this chapter and later chapters. These changes created some serious teething problems that Microsoft fixed over time, though not fast enough to protect Vista from a nasty "bad operating system" opinion that lasts to this day. Love it or hate it, the CompTIA A+ exams expect you to know Vista.

Microsoft carried on the concept of different editions of Windows for different markets. Let's look at the most common editions of Vista.

Windows Vista Home Basic

Windows Vista Home Basic is roughly equivalent to Windows XP Home. Microsoft gears it to home users not needing more advanced multimedia support.

Windows Vista Home Premium

Windows Vista Home Premium is the same as Windows Vista Home Basic, but it adds an upgraded Windows Media Center PVR application, similar to the one found in Windows XP Media Center (see Figure 4-9).

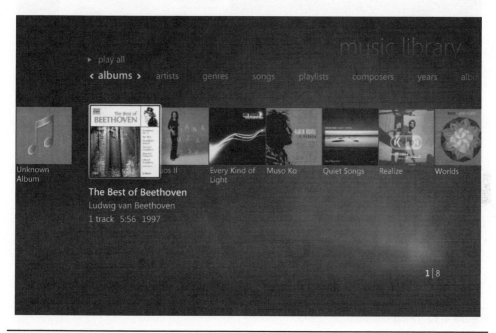

Figure 4-9 Vista Home Premium Media Center

Windows Vista Business

Windows Vista Business is the basic business edition and has all the security, file-sharing, and access controls seen in Windows XP Professional.

Windows Vista Ultimate

Windows Vista Ultimate combines all of the features of every other Vista edition and includes some other features, such as a game performance tweaker and DVD ripping capability (see Figure 4-10).

Windows Vista Enterprise

Windows Vista Enterprise is an enhanced edition of Windows Vista Business and includes extra features like BitLocker Drive Encryption and support for two physical CPUs. This edition cannot be purchased through normal stores. You'll have to go through Microsoft directly to purchase it.

Figure 4-10 Vista Ultimate

 EXAM TIP You can determine your Windows version by right-clicking My Computer in Windows XP, or Computer in Vista and Windows 7, and selecting Properties.

Windows 7

Comparing the look and feel of Windows Vista to Windows 7 might make you think that the two operating systems are far more alike than different—and you'd be right. So if Windows Vista and Windows 7 look and act so much alike, why didn't Microsoft just call Windows 7 "Windows Vista: The Fixed Version?" By the time Microsoft "fixed" Windows Vista, nobody wanted anything to do with it—people were reinstalling Windows XP! Microsoft didn't have a choice; it had to call this "fixed" Vista something new. Enter Windows 7 (see Figure 4-11).

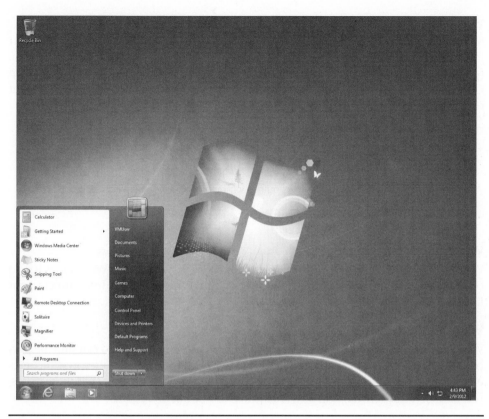

Figure 4-11 The Windows 7 desktop

Microsoft created several editions of Windows 7, closely following Windows Vista's release model. Let's look at each edition of Windows 7 and see how they compare.

Windows 7 Starter

Around the time of Windows 7's release, netbooks (super-lightweight laptops, mostly used for Web browsing) were incredibly popular. Windows 7 Starter is a stripped-down edition of the OS designed to complement the limited role of the netbook. Windows 7 Starter lacks many of the advanced networking, media, and graphics capabilities of other versions of Windows, focusing instead on easy Internet access.

Windows 7 Home Premium

Windows 7 Home Premium is the most basic and most widely released edition of Windows 7. Roughly comparable to Windows Vista Home Premium, this edition of Windows 7 includes a lot of media functionality and some advanced network functions.

Windows 7 Professional

Stepping up from Windows 7 Home Premium, Windows 7 Professional adds support for joining domains, as well as support for powerful features like Windows XP Mode (enabling you to run Windows XP programs inside Windows 7) and Remote Desktop Connection (enabling you to connect to another computer over a network and see that computer's desktop as if it were your own).

 EXAM TIP You should know which tools are available in the various editions of Windows for the CompTIA exam. For example, Windows XP Mode works only with Windows 7 Professional, Ultimate, and Enterprise. It comes as a separate download and requires virtualization software such as Windows Virtual PC.

Windows 7 Ultimate

Windows 7 Ultimate includes, as the name implies, everything that Windows 7 has to offer. You'll find advanced networking, backup, and security tools to complete your ultimate OS experience.

Windows 7 Enterprise

Windows 7 Enterprise is very similar to Windows Vista Enterprise and can only be purchased directly from Microsoft. Based on Windows 7 Professional, Enterprise includes extra features designed for large businesses, such as enhanced network searches, increased application security, and data protection using BitLocker.

Enter 64-bit Windows

From roughly 1986 to around 2001, all CPUs were 32-bit. While we will save the big discussion of what 32-bit means for Chapter 6, for now let's keep it simple: a 32-bit CPU can only use a maximum of 4 gigabytes (2^{32} bytes = 4,294,967,296 bytes) of RAM. Starting in 2001, we began to see 64-bit CPUs that could accept more than 4 gigabytes. 64-bit-capable CPUs are now the norm, while 32-bit-only CPUs are mostly relegated to netbooks and smartphones.

 NOTE CPUs and 32- and 64-bit processing are covered in much greater detail in Chapter 6.

The leap from 32-bit to 64-bit processing has a number of advantages. The really big compelling reason to go from 32- to 64-bit is that 64-bit CPUs support more than 4 GB of RAM. The more RAM you have, the more programs—and the bigger the

programs—your system can run. Until fairly recently, not too many of us cared to go above 4 GB of RAM. We didn't need the extra RAM, and we didn't have a CPU that could run at 64 bits. My, how things have changed over the past few years!

EXAM TIP Remember for the exams that 32-bit CPUs can support up to 4 GB of RAM. In concept, 64-bit CPUs can support up to 16 exabytes of memory. No one has made a CPU that supports the full 64-bit amount, however, and you certainly won't find that much memory in the typical PC.

The 64-bit CPUs first showed up with the Intel Itanium back in 2001. At that time the only folks interested in 64-bit processing were large data centers and a few organizations that needed to crunch big numbers. To run a computer with an Itanium, you needed an operating system that worked with a 64-bit processor. Up to that point, every version of Windows ran only at 32-bit. Microsoft answered the call by creating special 64-bit editions of Windows 2000 and XP, but these 64-bit editions were very rare and ran only on the Itanium.

In 2003, Advanced Micro Devices (AMD) started to ship the popular Athlon 64 CPU. This CPU could run in either 32-bit or 64-bit mode, making 64-bit a realistic option for most of us. Intel followed AMD around 2004 with Pentium 4 CPUs also capable of 32-bit or 64-bit processing. Since then, almost every CPU sold by Intel or AMD has the ability to run in either 32-bit or 64-bit mode. Moving from 32-bit to 64-bit is easy, but only if you have an edition of Windows to support 64-bit. Microsoft has multiple editions of Windows designed to support 64-bit CPUs.

TIP All 32-bit editions of Windows support a maximum of 4 GB of RAM. If your PC has more than 4 GB and you're not running 64-bit Windows, you might as well remove any RAM above 4 GB—you're wasting it!

Windows XP 64-bit Edition

The 64-bit-only edition of Windows XP was called Windows XP 64-bit Edition (apparently Microsoft decided not to get cute when naming that one). Given that it worked only on Intel Itanium processors, the chance of your seeing this operating system is pretty small unless you decide to work in a place with powerful server needs. The Windows XP Professional x64 Edition is a little more common, as it runs on any AMD or Intel processor that supports both 32 and 64 bits (see Figure 4-12).

Windows XP 64-bit editions have had some impact, as they were the first stable Windows editions that truly supported 64-bit processing, but it was the introduction of Microsoft Vista that really started the move into 64-bit computing.

Now that those files are visible, you have the awesome responsibility of keeping them safe. In general, the less you handle your vital system files, the better. You'll learn some ways to do useful things with files that were previously hidden, but unless you really know what you're doing, it's best to leave them alone. Before you turn a PC over to someone who isn't a trained PC tech, you'll probably want to hide those system files again.

 EXAM TIP There are many scenarios where you'd want to see hidden file extensions and hidden files as well. What if you need to run a program from its executable file, for example, and there are four files in the same folder all named "setup"? Which one do you double-click? Turn the file extensions visible, see which one is setup.exe, and double-click that one. Viewing hidden and system files, on the other hand, enables them to show up in a search. That's very handy for techs. The CompTIA A+ exams quiz you on these topics.

Microsoft has tried to help users organize their files and folders through various user folders and subfolders that you access through Windows Explorer. The different operating systems offer different choices, so let's look at My Documents (Windows XP), the User's Files (Windows Vista/7), and Windows 7's libraries.

My Documents, My [*Whatever*]

All versions of Windows provide a special folder structure for each user account so users have their own places to store personal data. This folder grouping is called *My Documents* in Windows XP. Many Windows programs take advantage of My Documents and by default store their files in the folder or in a subfolder.

Windows XP installations do not show My Documents on the desktop by default. On Windows XP, you can access it through the Start menu, or you can add it to your desktop. Right-click the desktop and select Properties to open the Display Properties dialog box. Select the Desktop tab, and then click on the Customize Desktop button to open the Desktop Items dialog box (see Figure 4-39). On the General tab, select the checkbox next to My Documents, My Computer, or both, and then click OK to close the dialog box and make any selected icons appear on the desktop.

 NOTE As with most tools in Windows, Microsoft gives you more than one way to accomplish tasks. In Windows XP and Vista, try right-clicking the Start menu icon, selecting Properties, and choosing the Classic Start Menu radio button.

Windows XP's My Documents folder includes several subfolders: My Pictures (which offers filmstrip and thumbnail views of pictures you store there), My Music (which will fire up Media Player to play any file), My Videos (which, again, starts Media Player), and more. Figure 4-40 shows My Pictures, using the thumbnail view. Many applications have since jumped on the bandwagon and added their own My [*Whatever*] folders in My Documents. Before I retired my Windows XP machine, for example, I had My eBooks, My Web Sites, My Received Files, My Virtual Machines...My Goodness!

Figure 4-39
Windows XP
Desktop Items
dialog box

Figure 4-40 My Pictures subfolder in My Documents

User's Files

Windows Vista and Windows 7 take the equivalent of My Documents to a whole new level with the *User's Files*. (Although a Documents folder is available, it's designed literally for documents, such as text files.) Click on the Start menu and you'll see a folder option with the user name of the account that's currently logged into the computer. With that option, not only do you get all of the folders you get in Windows XP, but Windows Vista/7 also add a number of other folders as well as interesting but important data such as your Internet Explorer favorites and copies of recent searches.

Just as with Windows XP, the user's folder does not appear on the desktop by default. To see this folder, right-click on the desktop, select Personalize, and then click *Change desktop icons* on the left of the Personalization window. You'll see a Desktop Icon Settings dialog box where you can select the User's Files option to display the personal files of the logged-in user account. Figure 4-41 shows the User's Files folder for my editor, with the Desktop Icon Settings dialog box in the background.

Figure 4-41 Typical user accounts folder in Windows Vista

Windows 7 Libraries

Windows 7 introduced only one new—but very useful—feature to Windows Explorer: libraries. The idea behind libraries is based on two fairly straightforward assumptions:

- People tend to need the same data over and over.
- The data you need for one job/project/function/whatever is rarely stored in a single folder.

Libraries aggregate folders from multiple locations and place them in a single, easy-to-find spot in Windows Explorer. The files and folders don't actually move. The library just creates links to them (see Figure 4-42).

Figure 4-42 Libraries in Windows Explorer

By default, every user has at least four libraries: Documents, Music, Pictures, and Videos. These libraries consist of two folders: the user's My *Whatever* folder for that type of data plus the Public *Whatever* folder under C:\Users\Public. (You'll learn more about these a little later in the chapter.) Let's clarify this subtle but critical concept.

Libraries are *not* folders but collections of existing folders. Let's say you keep some digital photos in your My Photos folder, but you also have a separate stash of photos on an external hard drive in a folder called "Vacation Pictures." Instead of flipping back and forth between these folders to see all of your photos, you could use a library to link them.

When you open a library, you see the contents of every folder in the library together, as if they were all in the same folder (but they aren't). Your photos in My Photos and Vacation Pictures will appear side by side.

You can create a library from any instance of Windows Explorer. Right-click Libraries in the navigation pane, select New | Library, and give the library a name. Ta-da! You've just made your first library.

Now you need to add folders to your library. You can add folders from your system or from shares on other systems. To add a folder to a library, right-click the folder in Windows Explorer, select *Include in library*, and then click the library you want to use in the fly-out menu. You can also right-click a library, select Properties, and use the *Include a folder* button to add folders.

Remember two important items:

- Only folders can populate a library—no individual files, no printers, etc.

- Don't try to remove a folder from a library by deleting it. If you do, you will delete the actual folder. Instead, right-click the folder name under the library name on the Navigation pane and select *Remove location from library*.

 EXAM TIP Make sure you can name the four default libraries in Windows 7.

Recycle Bin

In Windows, a file is not erased when you delete it. Windows adds a level of protection in the form of a special folder called the *Recycle Bin*. When you delete a file in Windows, the file moves into the Recycle Bin. It stays there until you empty the Recycle Bin or restore the file, or until the Recycle Bin reaches a preset size and starts erasing its oldest contents.

To access the Recycle Bin's properties, right-click the icon on the desktop and select Properties. (You'll find the icon usually in the top left corner of the desktop.) The Recycle Bin's properties look different in different versions of Windows, but they all work basically the same. Figure 4-43 shows the properties of a typical Windows 7 Recycle Bin. Windows will set aside a certain percentage by default (it changes according the size of the drive), but you can specify the amount of drive space to use for the Recycle Bin as well. If a hard drive starts to run low on space, this is one of the first places to check.

Figure 4-43
Windows 7
Recycle Bin
Properties

Recycle Bin Properties

General

Recycle Bin Location	Space Available
Local Disk (C:)	39.8 GB

Settings for selected location
◉ Custom size:
 Maximum size (MB): 4085

○ Don't move files to the Recycle Bin. Remove files immediately when deleted.

☑ Display delete confirmation dialog

[OK] [Cancel] [Apply]

My Network Places/Network

Systems tied to a network, either via a network cable or by a modem, have a folder called *My Network Places* in Windows XP or simply *Network* in Windows Vista/7 (see Figure 4-44). This folder shows all the current network connections available to you. You'll learn about My Network Places/Network in Chapter 22.

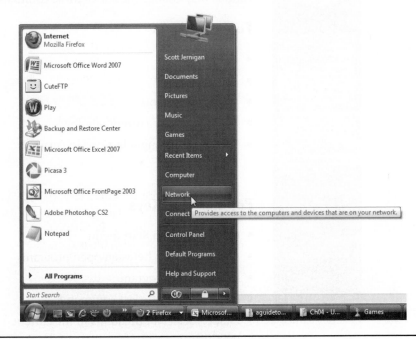

Figure 4-44 Network in Windows Vista

Windows Sidebar

Windows Vista comes with a GUI feature called the *Windows Sidebar*, a tool that sits on one side of the desktop and enables small helper applications—called Microsoft Gadgets—to run. You can display a clock, for example, or a dynamic weather update. Vista comes with a handful of Gadgets, but developers have gone crazy with them, enabling you to add all sorts of useful tools, such as the Twitter feed and *World of Warcraft* search and realm status Gadgets in Figure 4-45.

Windows 7 also includes Gadgets, but removes the Sidebar concept. You can place Windows 7 Gadgets anywhere on your desktop.

NOTE The background application running Gadgets in Windows 7 is called Sidebar.exe, just like in Windows Vista, so you could argue that Windows 7 includes Windows Sidebar.

Figure 4-45
Windows Sidebar
in action

Hot Keys

In Windows, you can use key combinations to go directly to various programs and places. Here's a reasonably extensive list of general-purpose commands for Windows. Be aware that some applications may change the use of these commands.

Function Keys

- F1 Help
- F2 Rename
- F3 Search menu
- F5 Refresh the current window
- F6 Move among selections in current windows

Popular Hot Keys

- CTRL-ESC Open Start menu
- ALT-TAB Switch between open programs
- ALT-F4 Quit program
- CTRL-Z Undo the last command
- CTRL-A Select all the items in the current window
- SHIFT-DELETE Delete item permanently
- SHIFT-F10 Open a shortcut menu for the selected item (this is the same as right-clicking an object)
- SHIFT Bypass the automatic-run feature for optical media (by pressing and holding down the SHIFT key while you insert optical media)
- ALT-SPACE Display the main window's System menu (from this menu you can restore, move, resize, minimize, maximize, or close the window)
- ALT-ENTER Open the properties for the selected object

Working with Text

- CTRL-C Copy
- CTRL-X Cut
- CTRL-V Paste
- CTRL-Z Undo

Windows Key Shortcuts

These shortcuts use the special Windows key:

- WINDOWS KEY Start menu
- WINDOWS KEY-D Show desktop
- WINDOWS KEY-E Windows Explorer
- WINDOWS KEY-L Lock the computer
- WINDOWS KEY-TAB Cycle through taskbar buttons (or Flip 3D with Windows Aero in Vista/7)
- WINDOWS KEY-PAUSE/BREAK Open the System Properties dialog box

NOTE I've covered only the most basic parts of the Windows desktop in this chapter. The typical Windows desktop includes many other parts, but for techs and for the CompTIA A+ certification exams, what you've learned here about the desktop is more than enough.

Operating System Folders

The modern versions of Windows organize essential files and folders in a relatively similar fashion. All have a primary system folder for storing most Windows internal tools and files. All have a set of folders for programs and user files. Yet once you start to get into details, you'll find some very large differences. It's very important for you to know in some detail the location and function of many common folders and their contents.

EXAM TIP The CompTIA A+ exams love to ask detailed questions about the locations of certain folders. Make sure you know this section!

System Folder

SystemRoot is the tech name given to the folder in which Windows has been installed. Windows XP, Vista, and 7 all use C:\Windows as the default SystemRoot. Be warned: this is the default folder, but you can change where Windows is installed during the installation process.

It's handy to know about SystemRoot. You'll find it cropping up in many other tech publications, and you can specify it when adjusting certain Windows settings to make sure they work under all circumstances. When used as part of a Windows configuration setting, add percent signs (%) to the beginning and end like so: %SystemRoot%, which means you'll almost never see it as just plain SystemRoot.

If you don't know where Windows is installed on a particular system, here's a handy trick. Get to a command prompt, type **cd %systemroot%**, and press ENTER. The prompt changes to the directory in which the Windows OS files are stored. Slick! See Chapter 18 for details on how to use the command prompt in Windows.

The system folder contains many subfolders, too numerous to mention here, but CompTIA wants you to know the names of a number of these subfolders as well as what goes in them. Let's run through the subfolders you should recognize and define (these folders are in all versions of Windows):

- **%SystemRoot%\Fonts** All of the fonts installed in Windows live here.

- **%SystemRoot%\Offline Files (Offline Web Pages in Windows 7)** When you tell your Web browser to save Web pages for offline viewing, they are stored in this folder. This is another folder that Windows automatically deletes if it needs the space.

- **%SystemRoot%\System32** This is the *real* Windows! All of the most critical programs that make Windows run are stored here. 64-bit editions of Windows also store critical files in %SystemRoot%\SysWOW64.

- **%SystemRoot%\Temp** Anytime Windows or an application running on Windows needs to create temporary files, they are placed here. Windows deletes these files automatically as needed, so never place an important file in this folder.

Program and Personal Document Folders

Windows has a number of important folders that help organize your programs and documents. They sit in the root directory at the same level as the system folder, and of course they have variations in name depending on the version of Windows. We'll assume that your computer is using a C: drive—a pretty safe assumption, although there actually is a way to install all of Windows on a second hard-drive partition.

C:\Program Files (All Versions)

By default, most programs install some or all of their essential files into a subfolder of the Program Files folder. If you installed a program, it should have its own folder in here. Individual companies decide how to label their subfolders. Installing Photoshop made by Adobe, for example, creates the Adobe subfolder and then an Adobe Photoshop subfolder within it. Installing Silverlight from Microsoft, on the other hand, only creates a Microsoft Silverlight folder with the program files within it. (Some programmers choose to create a folder at the root of the C: drive, bypassing Program Files altogether, but that's becoming increasingly rare.)

C:\Program Files (x86)

The 64-bit editions of Windows Vista and Windows 7 create two directory structures for program files. The 64-bit applications go into the C:\Program Files folder, whereas the 32-bit applications go into the C:\Program Files (x86) folder. The separation makes it easy to find the proper version of whatever application you seek.

Personal Documents

As you might expect, given the differences among the desktop names for personal document locations outlined earlier in the chapter, the personal folders for Windows XP, Windows Vista, and Windows 7 differ in location and name. Windows XP places personal folders in the Documents and Settings folder, whereas Windows Vista and Windows 7 use the Users folder. From there, they differ even more.

C:\Documents and Settings (Windows XP)

All of the personal settings for each user are stored here. All users have their own sub-folders in Documents and Settings. In each user folder, you'll find another level of folders with familiar names such as Desktop, My Documents, and Start Menu. These folders hold the actual contents of these items. Let's dive through these to see the ones you need to know for the CompTIA A+ exams.

- **\Documents and Settings\Default User (hidden)** All of the default settings for a user. This folder is a template that Windows copies and customizes when a new user logs on for the first time.

- **\Documents and Settings\All Users** You can make settings for anyone who uses the computer. This is especially handy for applications: some applications are installed so that all users may use them and some applications might be restricted to certain users. This folder stores information for any setting or application that's defined for all users on the PC.

- **\Documents and Settings\Shared Documents** If you're using Windows XP's Simple File Sharing, this is the only folder on the computer that's shared.

- **\Documents and Settings\<User Name>** This folder stores all settings defined for a particular user (see Figure 4-46).

Figure 4-46 Contents of a typical \Documents and Settings folder in Windows XP

Opening any user's folder reveals a number of even lower folders. Each of these stores very specific information about the user.

- **\Documents and Settings\<User Name>\Desktop** This folder stores the files on the user's desktop. If you delete this folder, you delete all the files placed on the desktop.

- **\Documents and Settings\<User Name>\<User name's> Documents** This is the My Documents folder for that user.

- **\Documents and Settings\<User Name>\Application Data (hidden)** This folder stores information and settings used by various programs that the user has installed.

- **\Documents and Settings\<User Name>\Start Menu** This folder stores any customizations the user made to the Start menu.

 NOTE When you're looking at your own account folders, you'll see My Documents rather than <User name's> Documents in the \Documents and Settings\<User Name> folder.

C:\Users (Windows Vista/7)

Windows Vista and Windows 7 dump the old Documents and Settings folder for the Users folder. Functionally similar to Documents and Settings, there are a number of subfolders here that you need to know to pass the CompTIA A+ exams.

Let's repeat the process, locating the same functions in their new locations.

- **\Users\Default (hidden), \Users\All Users, and \Users\<User Name>** All of these folders retain the same functions as in Windows XP.

- **\Users\<User Name>** The big change takes place under each of the \Users\ <User Name> folders. This folder still stores all settings defined for a particular user; however, this folder contains more subfolders in Vista/7 than in XP (see Figure 4-47). Luckily, you only need to know a few folders for the exams.

- **\Users\<User Name>\Desktop** Same as in Windows XP.

- **\Users\<User Name>\Documents** This is the Documents folder for that user. Note that in Vista, it's simply known as "Documents," while in Windows 7, it is once again "My Documents."

- **\Users\<User Name>\Downloads** Microsoft's preferred download folder for applications to use. Most applications do use this folder, but some do not.

- **\Users\<User Name>\Start Menu** Same as in Windows XP.

Figure 4-47 Contents of a typical Users\<User Name>\ folder in Vista

NOTE Vista and 7 make a special hidden folder called "Default User" that points to the User folder to support older applications.

Any good tech knows the name and function of all the folders just listed. As a tech, you will find yourself manually drilling into these folders for a number of reasons. Users rarely go directly into any of these folders with Windows Explorer. As a tech, you know that's a good thing, since you appreciate how dangerous it is for them to do so. Imagine a user going into a \Users\<User Name>\Desktop folder and wiping out someone's desktop folders. Luckily, Windows protects these folders by using NTFS permissions, making it very difficult for users to destroy anything other than their own work.

EXAM TIP Be very careful here. Some of the folder name differences between XP and Vista/7 are subtle. Make sure you know the difference.

Tech Utilities

Windows offers a huge number of utilities that enable techs to configure the OS, optimize and tweak settings, install hardware, and more. The trick is to know where to go to find them. This section shows the most common locations in Windows where you can access utilities: right-click, Control Panel, Device Manager, System Tools, command line, Microsoft Management Console, Administrative Tools, and the Action Center. Note that these are locations for tools, not tools themselves, and you can access many tools from more than one of these locations. You'll see some of the same utilities in many of these locations. Stay sharp in this section, as you'll need to access utilities to understand the inner workings of Windows.

Right-Click

Windows, being a graphical user interface OS, covers your monitor with windows, menus, icons, file lists—all kinds of pretty things you click on to do work. Any single thing you see on your desktop is called an *object*. If you want to open any object in Windows, you double-click on it. If you want to change something about an object, you right-click on it.

Right-clicking on an object brings up a small menu called the *context menu*, and it works on everything in Windows. In fact, try to place your mouse somewhere in Windows where right-clicking does *not* bring up a menu (there are a few places, but they're not easy to find). What you see on the little menu when you right-click varies dramatically depending on the item you decide to right-click. If you right-click a running program in the running program area on the taskbar, you'll see items that relate to a window. Windows XP and Vista will present options such as Move, Size, and so on (see Figure 4-48). Windows 7 gives you the Jump List, as we discussed earlier. If you right-click on your desktop, you get options for changing the appearance of the desktop and more (see Figure 4-49). Even different types of files show different results when you right-click on them. Right-clicking is something techs do often.

Figure 4-48

Right-clicking on a running program in Windows XP

Figure 4-49
Right-clicking on
the desktop in
Windows 7 offers
numerous settings

One menu item you'll see almost anywhere you right-click is Properties. Every object in Windows has properties. When you right-click on something and can't find what you're looking for, select Properties. Figure 4-50 shows the results of right-clicking on Computer in the Start menu—not very exciting. But if you select Properties, you'll get a dialog box like the one shown in Figure 4-51.

Figure 4-50
Right-clicking on
Computer

Figure 4-51 Computer properties

Control Panel

The *Control Panel* handles most of the maintenance, upgrade, and configuration aspects of Windows. As such, the Control Panel is the first set of tools for every tech to explore. You can find the Control Panel by clicking the Start button and choosing Control Panel from the Start menu.

Windows XP, Vista, and 7 open in the Control Panel's Category view by default, which displays the icons in groups like "Printers and Other Hardware." The categories change between each edition of Windows. This view requires an additional click (and sometimes a guess about which category includes the icon you need), so many techs use a more classic view.

The CompTIA A+ exams assume you use classic view with large icons, so do what every tech does: switch from category view to classic view. In Windows XP, select Switch to Classic View. In Windows Vista, choose Classic View. In Windows 7, select Large icons or Small icons from the View by drop-down list for a similar effect. Figure 4-52 shows the Windows XP Control Panel in both Category and Classic views.

Figure 4-52 Windows XP Control Panel in two views: Category (left) and Classic (right)

A large number of programs, called *applets*, populate the Control Panel. The names and selection of applets vary depending on the version of Windows and whether any installed programs have added applets. But all versions of Windows have applets that enable you to control specific aspects of Windows, such as appearance, installed applications, and system settings. Windows XP has Display and Windows Vista/7 have Personalization which enable you to make changes to the look and feel of your Windows desktop and tweak your video settings. Add or Remove Programs (Windows XP) and Programs and Features (Windows Vista/7) enable you to add or remove programs. The System applet (all versions) gives you access to essential system information and tools, such as Device Manager, although Microsoft wisely added Device Manager right on the Control Panel starting with Vista.

Every icon you see in the Control Panel is actually a file with the extension .CPL. Any time you get an error opening the Control Panel, you can bet you have a corrupted CPL file. These are a pain to fix. You have to rename all of your CPL files with another extension (I use .CPB) and then rename them back to .CPL one at a time, each time reopening the Control Panel, until you find the CPL file that's causing the lockup.

EXAM TIP Even these common applets vary slightly among Windows versions. The CompTIA A+ certification exams do not test you on every little variance among the same applets in different versions—just know what each applet does.

You can use the Control Panel applets to do an amazing array of things to a Windows system, and each applet displays text that helps explain its functions. The Add Hardware applet in Windows XP, for example, says quite clearly, "Installs and troubleshoots hardware" (see Figure 4-53). They are all like that. Figure 4-54 shows the User Accounts applet. Can you determine its use? (If not, don't sweat it. I'll cover users in Chapter 16.) Don't bother trying to memorize all these applets. Each Control Panel applet relevant to the CompTIA A+ exams is discussed in detail in the relevant chapter throughout the rest of the book. For now, just make sure you can get to the Control Panel and appreciate why it exists.

You can also get to the System Properties/System dialog box in all versions of Windows by right-clicking My Computer/Computer and selecting Properties. From there, the path to Device Manager is the same as when you access this dialog box from the Control Panel.

 NOTE Holding down the WINDOWS KEY and pressing PAUSE/BREAK is yet another way to get to the System Properties/System dialog box. Keyboard shortcuts are cool!

The second (and more streamlined) method is to right-click My Computer/Computer and select Manage. This opens a window called Computer Management, where you'll see Device Manager listed on the left side of the screen, under System Tools. Just click on Device Manager and it opens. You can also access Computer Management by opening the Administrative Tools applet in the Control Panel and then selecting Computer Management (see Figure 4-57).

Figure 4-57 Device Manager in Computer Management

Why are there so many ways to open Device Manager? Well, remember that we're only looking at locations in Windows from which to open utilities, not at the actual utilities themselves. Microsoft wants you to get to the tools you need when you need them, and it's better to have multiple paths to a utility rather than just one.

EXAM TIP The CompTIA A+ exams want you to know multiple ways to open Device Manager.

Device Manager displays every device that Windows recognizes, organized in special groups called *types*. All devices of the same type are grouped under the same type heading. To see the devices of a particular type, you must open that type's group. Figure 4-57 shows a Windows Vista Device Manager screen with all installed devices in good order—which makes us techs happy. If Windows detects a problem, the device has a down arrow, a red *X*, or a black exclamation point on a yellow field, as in the case of the Digital Still Camera device in Figure 4-58.

Figure 4-58
Problem device

NOTE There is one other "problem" icon you might see on a device in Device Manager—a blue *i* on a white field. According to Microsoft, this means you turned off automatic configuration for a device.

A down arrow in Windows Vista/7 or a red *X* in Windows XP means Windows (or you) disabled the device—right-click on the device to enable it (see Figure 4.59). With a black exclamation point, right-click on the device and select Properties. Read the error code and explanation in the Device Status pane (see Figure 4-60). If necessary, look up a Microsoft Knowledge Base article that matches the number to see what to do. There are around 40 different errors—nobody bothers to memorize them!

Figure 4-59

Enabling a
disabled device

Figure 4-60

Problem device
properties

Device Manager isn't just for dealing with problems. It also enables you to update drivers with a simple click of the mouse (assuming you have a replacement driver on your computer). Right-click a device and select Update Driver Software from the menu to get the process started. Figure 4-61 shows the options in Windows Vista.

Figure 4-61
Selecting Update
Driver Software
in Windows Vista
Device Manager

Make sure you can get to Device Manager! You will come back to it again and again in subsequent chapters, because it is the first tool you should access when you have a hardware problem.

System Tools

The Start menu offers a variety of tech utilities collected in one place: System Tools. In the *System Tools* menu, you'll find commonly accessed tools such as System Information and Disk Defragmenter (see Figure 4-62).

Figure 4-62
System Tools
menu options

System Tools
Character Map
Computer
Control Panel
Disk Cleanup
Disk Defragmenter
Internet Explorer (No Add-ons)
Private Character Editor
Resource Monitor
System Information
System Restore
Task Scheduler
Windows Easy Transfer Reports
Windows Easy Transfer

Many techs overlook memorizing how to find the appropriate Windows tool to diagnose problems, but nothing hurts your credibility with a client like fumbling around, clicking a variety of menus and applets, while mumbling, "I know it's around here somewhere." The CompTIA A+ certification exams therefore test you on a variety of paths to appropriate tools.

To access System Tools in all three versions of Windows, go to Start | All Programs | Accessories | System Tools. Each version of Windows shares many of the same tools, but each includes its own utilities as well. I'll note which version of Windows uses each particular system tool.

Activate Windows (All)

Windows XP unveiled a copy-protection scheme called *activation*. Activation is a process where your computer sends Microsoft a unique code generated on your machine based on the Install CD/DVD's product key and a number of hardware features, such as the amount of RAM, the CPU processor model, and other ones and zeros in your PC. Normally, activation is done at install time, but if you choose not to activate at install or if you make "substantial" changes to the hardware, you'll need to use the Activate Windows utility (see Figure 4-63). With the Activate Windows utility, you can activate over the Internet or over the telephone.

Figure 4-63 Activate Windows

NOTE Once you've activated Windows, the Activate Windows applet goes away.

Backup (Windows XP)

The Backup utility enables you to back up selected files and folders to removable media such as tape drives. Backing up is an important function that's covered in detail in Chapters 16 and 29.

NOTE Neither Windows XP Home nor Windows XP Media Center includes Backup during installation. You must install the Backup program from the Windows installation CD by running the \Valueadd\MSFT\Ntbackup\ NTbackup.msi program.

Backup Status and Configuration (Windows Vista)

Vista does not enable you to back up files on your computer selectively. You can only back up personal data with the Backup Status and Configuration Tool or, if you have Vista Business, Ultimate, or Enterprise, perform a complete PC backup by using Windows Complete PC Backup. If you want to pick and choose the file to back up, you need to buy a third-party tool. This tool allows you to back up to optical media, a hard drive, or a networked drive.

NOTE Windows 7 has a more powerful backup utility than Windows Vista has, but you won't find it in the System Tools folder. Check out Chapter 29 for more information on Windows 7's backup tools.

Character Map (All)

Ever been using a program only to discover you need to enter a strange character such as the euro character (€) but your word processor doesn't support it? That's when you need the Character Map. It enables you to copy any Unicode character into the Clipboard (see Figure 4-64).

NOTE Windows 7 includes the Private Character Editor tool, enabling you to create your own characters and symbols for use with the Character Map.

Figure 4-64

Character Map

Disk Cleanup (All)

Disk Cleanup looks for unneeded files on your computer, which is handy when your hard drive starts to get full and you need space. Every version of Windows since XP starts this program whenever your hard drive gets below 200 MB of free disk space.

Disk Defragmenter (XP and Vista)

You use Disk Defragmenter to make your hard drive run faster—you'll see more details on this handy tool in Chapter 12. You can access this utility in the same way you access Device Manager; you also find Disk Defragmenter in the Computer Management Console. A simpler method is to select Start | All Programs | Accessories | System Tools—you'll find Disk Defragmenter listed there. You can also right-click on any drive in My Computer or Computer, select Properties, and click the Tools tab, where you'll find a convenient Defragment Now button.

Files and Settings Transfer Wizard (Windows XP)

Suppose you have an old computer full of files and settings, and you just bought yourself a brand new computer. You want to copy everything from your old computer onto your new computer—what to do? Microsoft touts the Files and Settings Transfer Wizard as just the tool you need (see Figure 4-65). This utility copies your desktop files and folders and, most conveniently, your settings from Internet Explorer and Outlook Express; however, it won't copy over your programs, not even the Microsoft ones, and it won't copy settings for any programs other than Internet Explorer and Outlook Express. If you need to copy everything from an old computer to a new one, you'll probably want to use a disk-imaging tool such as Norton Ghost.

Figure 4-65
Files and Settings
Transfer Wizard

Windows Easy Transfer (Windows Vista/7)

Windows Easy Transfer is an aggressively updated version of the Files and Settings Transfer Wizard. It does everything the older version does and adds the capability to copy user accounts and other settings (see Figure 4-66).

Figure 4-66 Windows Easy Transfer

Scheduled Tasks (All)

With the Scheduled Tasks utility, you can schedule any program to start and stop any time you wish. The only trick to this utility is that you must enter the program you want to run as a command on the command line, with all the proper switches. Figure 4-67 shows the configuration line for running the Disk Defragmenter program.

 EXAM TIP Microsoft provides a data transfer tool called the *User State Migration Tool (USMT)* for advanced users. It's functionally similar to Windows Easy Transfer, but it uses a scripting language to provide more power and flexibility. CompTIA also lists "User Data Migration Tool (UDMT)" on the objectives, but that tool hasn't existed since Windows NT and thus won't be covered on the exams.

Figure 4-67
Task Scheduler

```
defrag                                              [?][X]

  Task   Schedule  Settings  Security

        [icon]   C:\WINDOWS\Tasks\defrag.job

  Run:              C:\WINDOWS\system32\defrag.exe c: -f

                                                  [ Browse... ]

  Start in:         C:\WINDOWS\system32

  Comments:

  Run as:           TOTALHOME\michaels        [ Set password... ]

  [ ] Run only if logged on
  [✓] Enabled (scheduled task runs at specified time)

                        [ OK ]   [ Cancel ]   [ Apply ]
```

Security Center (Windows XP)

Security Center is a one-stop location for configuring many security features on your computer. This tool is also in the Control Panel. Windows Vista and Windows 7 remove Security Center from System Tools. Windows Vista retains the Control Panel applet, but Windows 7 has a beefed-up applet called the Action Center (discussed later in this chapter). All of these security features, and many more, are discussed in detail in their related chapters.

System Information (All)

System Information is one of those tools that everyone (including the CompTIA A+ exams) likes to talk about, but it's uncommon to meet techs who say they actually use this tool. System Information shows tons of information about the hardware and software on your PC (see Figure 4-68).

Figure 4-68 System Information

System Restore (All)

System Restore is arguably the most important single utility you'll ever use in Windows when it comes to fixing a broken system. This handy tool enables you to take a "snapshot"—a copy of a number of critical files and settings—and return to that state later (see Figure 4-69). System Restore holds multiple snapshots, any of which you may restore to in the future.

TIP If your system won't boot and you are unable to run System Restore from within Windows, you can access System Restore by booting from the Windows Installation CD or DVD and accessing System Restore from the System Recovery Options menu.

Figure 4-69 System Restore

Imagine you're installing some new device in your PC, or maybe a piece of software. Before you actually install, you take a snapshot and call it "Before Install." You install the device, and now something starts acting weird. You go back into System Restore and reload the previous Before Install snapshot, and the problem goes away.

System Restore isn't perfect, but it's usually the first thing to try when something goes wrong—assuming, of course, you made a snapshot!

Resource Monitor (Windows 7)

Resource Monitor tracks CPU, memory, disk, and network usage on your computer and displays that information across a dizzying number of charts and graphs. Resource Monitor can help you track down any pesky program or service that you think is hogging all of your system resources and slowing down your PC. If you've seen the Windows Task Manager before, think of this as the supercharged version with extra bells and more whistles.

 NOTE Windows Vista has a tool that offers features similar to Resource Monitor called Reliability and Performance Monitor. You can find it in the Control Panel applet called Administrative Tools. (More on the latter a little bit later in the chapter.)

Command Line

The Windows command-line interface is a throwback to how Microsoft operating systems worked a long, long time ago when text commands were entered at a command prompt. Figure 4-70 shows the command prompt from DOS, the first operating system commonly used in PCs.

```
C:\>ver

MS-DOS Version 6.00

C:\>_
```

Figure 4-70 DOS command prompt

DOS is dead, but the command-line interface is alive and well in every version of Windows—including Windows 7. Every good tech knows how to access and use the command-line interface. It is a lifesaver when the graphical part of Windows doesn't work, and it is often faster than using a mouse if you're skilled at using it. An entire chapter (Chapter 18) is devoted to the command line, but let's look at one example of what the command line can do. First, you need to get there. In Windows XP, select Start | Run, and type **cmd** in the dialog box. Click OK and you get to a command prompt. In Windows Vista/7, you do the same thing in the Start | Search dialog box. Figure 4-71 shows a command prompt in Windows Vista.

```
Administrator: C:\Windows\system32\cmd.exe
05/22/2009  03:52 PM    <DIR>          Graphics
09/24/2007  11:30 AM    <DIR>          install
04/22/2008  12:06 PM    <DIR>          logs
05/22/2009  03:52 PM           551,408 mss32_s.dll
05/22/2009  03:52 PM    <DIR>          Public
05/22/2009  03:52 PM    <DIR>          resource
10/10/2007  12:07 PM    <DIR>          servers
07/03/2007  04:27 PM    <DIR>          skins
07/03/2007  04:31 PM    <DIR>          steam
05/22/2009  03:52 PM         2,880,760 Steam.dll
05/22/2009  03:46 PM         1,217,784 Steam.exe
09/15/2005  03:20 PM               318 steam.ico
05/22/2009  04:58 PM           796,916 Steam.log
05/13/2009  12:15 PM    <DIR>          steamapps
05/22/2009  03:52 PM         3,004,912 steamclient.dll
05/22/2009  03:52 PM         2,987,256 SteamUI.dll
05/22/2009  03:52 PM            60,312 SteamUI_838.mst
05/22/2009  03:46 PM                14 Steam_53.mst
09/13/2005  05:49 PM             9,653 steam_install_agreement.rtf
03/29/2007  03:29 PM               121 Support.url
05/22/2009  03:52 PM            77,824 ThirdPartyLegalNotices.doc
05/22/2009  03:52 PM           268,784 tier0_s.dll
11/14/2008  05:39 PM    <DIR>          userdata
05/22/2009  03:52 PM           371,184 vstdlib_s.dll
05/22/2009  03:52 PM           256,496 WriteMiniDump.exe
              23 File(s)     16,165,307 bytes
              16 Dir(s)  47,442,325,504 bytes free

C:\Program Files\Steam>_
```

Figure 4-71 Command prompt in Windows Vista

Once at a command prompt, type **dir** and press ENTER on your keyboard. This command displays all the files and folders in a specific directory—probably your user folder for this exercise—and gives sizes and other information. DIR is just one of many useful command-line tools you'll learn about in this book.

Microsoft Management Console

One of the biggest complaints about earlier versions of Windows was the wide dispersal of the many utilities needed for administration and troubleshooting. Despite years of research, Microsoft could never find a place for all the utilities that would please even a small minority of support people. In a moment of sheer genius, Microsoft determined that the ultimate utility was one that the support people made for themselves! This brought on the creation of the amazing Microsoft Management Console.

The *Microsoft Management Console (MMC)* is simply a shell program in Windows that holds individual utilities called *snap-ins*. To start an MMC, select Start | Run in Windows XP, or select Start | Search bar in Windows Vista/7. Type **mmc** and press ENTER to get a blank MMC. Blank MMCs aren't much to look at (see Figure 4-72).

Figure 4-72 Blank MMC

NOTE Windows Vista labels the Search bar as *Start Search*. Windows 7 labels it as *Search programs and files*. Techs just call it the *Search bar* because it functions the same in both versions of Windows.

You make a blank MMC console useful by adding snap-ins, which include most of the utilities you use in Windows. Even good old Device Manager is a snap-in. You can add as many snap-ins as you like, and you have many to choose from. Many companies sell third-party utilities as MMC snap-ins.

For example, to add the Device Manager snap-in, in the blank MMC, select File | Add/Remove Snap-ins. In the Add or Remove Snap-ins dialog box, you will see a list of available snap-ins in Windows Vista/7 (see Figure 4-73); click the Add button in Windows XP to open a similar screen. Select Device Manager in the list, and click the Add button to open a Device Manager dialog box that prompts you to choose the local or a remote PC for the snap-in to work with. Choose Local computer for this exercise, and click the Finish button. Click the Close button to close the Add Standalone Snap-in dialog box, and then click OK to close the Add or Remove Snap-ins dialog box.

Figure 4-73 Available snap-ins

You should see Device Manager listed in the console. Click it. Hey, that looks kind of familiar, doesn't it (see Figure 4-74)?

Figure 4-74 Device Manager as a snap-in

Once you've added the snap-ins you want, just save the console under any name, anywhere you want. I'll save this console as Device Manager MMC, for example, and drop it on my desktop (see Figure 4-75). I'm now just a double-click away from Device Manager.

Figure 4-75
The Device
Manager shortcut
on the desktop

Administrative Tools

Windows combines the most popular snap-ins into an applet in the Control Panel called *Administrative Tools*. Open the Control Panel and open Administrative Tools (see Figure 4-76).

Figure 4-76 Administrative Tools

Administrative Tools is really just a folder that stores a number of premade consoles. As you poke through these, notice that many of the consoles share some of the same snap-ins—nothing wrong with that. Of the consoles in a standard Administrative Tools collection, the ones you'll spend the most time with are Computer Management, Event Viewer, Performance Monitor (Reliability and Performance Monitor in Windows Vista), and Services.

 EXAM TIP The CompTIA A+ certification exams have little interest in some of these snap-ins, so this book won't cover them all. If I don't mention it, it's almost certainly not on the test!

Computer Management

The *Computer Management* applet is a tech's best buddy, or at least a place where you'll spend a lot of time when building or maintaining a system (see Figure 4-77). You've already spent considerable time with one of its components: System Tools. Depending on the version of Windows, System Tools also offers Event Viewer, Performance, Device Manager, and more. Storage is where you'll find Disk Management.

Figure 4-77
Computer
Management
applet

Event Viewer

Event Viewer shows you at a glance what has happened in the last day, week, or more, including when people logged in and when the PC had problems (see Figure 4-78). You'll see more of Event Viewer in Chapter 29.

Figure 4-78 Event Viewer reporting system errors

Performance (Windows XP)

The *Performance* console consists of two snap-ins: System Monitor and Performance Logs and Alerts. You can use these for reading *logs*—files that record information over time. System Monitor can also monitor real-time data (see Figure 4-79).

Figure 4-79
System Monitor
in action

Suppose you are adding a new cable modem and you want to know just how fast you can download data. Click the plus sign (+) on the toolbar to add a counter. Click the *Use local computer counters* radio button, and then choose Network Interface from the Performance Object pull-down menu. In the Add Counters dialog box, make sure the *Select counters from list* radio button is selected. Last, select Bytes Received/sec. The dialog box should look like Figure 4-80.

Figure 4-80

Setting up a throughput test

Click Add, and then click Close; probably not much is happening. Go to a Web site, preferably one where you can download a huge file. Start downloading and watch the chart jump; that's the real throughput (see Figure 4-81).

Figure 4-81

Downloading with blazing speed

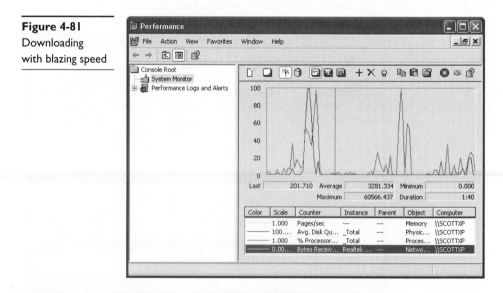

NOTE You'll learn more about the Performance console in Chapter 15.

Reliability and Performance Monitor/Performance Monitor (Windows Vista/7)

Reliability and Performance Monitor in Windows Vista offers just about everything you can find in the Performance applet of older versions of Windows—although everything is monitored by default, so there's no need to add anything. In addition, it includes Reliability Monitor. Reliability Monitor enables you to see at a glance what's been done to the computer over a period of time, including software installations and uninstallations, failures of hardware or applications, and general uptime (see Figure 4-82). It's a nice starting tool for checking a Vista machine that's new to you.

Windows 7 drops Reliability Monitor from this tool and calls it *Performance Monitor*, but everything else is the same. You can still find Reliability Monitor in Windows 7 by searching for it in the Search bar.

Figure 4-82 Reliability and Performance Monitor open to the Reliability Monitor screen in Vista

NOTE You'll learn more about Reliability and Performance Monitor/Performance Monitor in Chapter 15.

Services

Windows runs a large number of separate programs called *services*. The best way to visualize a service is to think of it as something that runs, yet is invisible. Windows comes with about 100 services by default, and they handle a huge number of tasks, from application support to network functions. You can use the Services applet to see the status of all services on the system, including services that are not running (see Figure 4-83).

Figure 4-83 Services applet

Right-click a service and select Properties to modify its settings. Figure 4-84 shows the properties for the Bluetooth Support Service. See the Startup type pull-down menu? It shows four options: Automatic (Delayed Start), Automatic, Manual, and Disabled. Automatic means it starts when the system starts (Delayed Start services start two minutes after startup), Manual means you have to come to this tab to start it, and Disabled prevents anything from starting it. Also make sure you understand how to start, stop, pause, and resume services (note the four buttons below Startup Type).

Figure 4-84
Bluetooth
Support Service
properties

Bluetooth Support Service Properties (Local Computer)

| General | Log On | Recovery | Dependencies |

Service name: bthserv

Display name: Bluetooth Support Service

Description: The Bluetooth service supports discovery and
 association of remote Bluetooth devices. Stopping

Path to executable:
C:\Windows\system32\svchost.exe -k bthsvcs

Startup type: Manual
 Automatic (Delayed Start)
Help me configure Automatic
 Manual
 Disabled
Service status: Stopped

[Start] [Stop] [Pause] [Resume]

You can specify the start parameters that apply when you start the service
from here.

Start parameters:

[OK] [Cancel] [Apply]

EXAM TIP The CompTIA A+ certification exams are not interested in having
you memorize all of these services—just make sure you can manipulate them.

Action Center (Unique to Windows 7)

Sometimes, you just want to glance at your system and know that nothing has gone terribly wrong. Previous versions of Windows lacked a single "peephole" to view the status of your computer. *Action Center* fills that gap, providing a one-page aggregation of event messages, warnings, and maintenance messages that, for many techs, might quickly replace Event Viewer as the first place to look for problems. Unlike Event Viewer, Action Center separates issues into two sections, Security and Maintenance, making it easier to scan a system quickly (see Figure 4-85).

Action Center only compiles the information, taking data from well-known utilities such as Event Viewer, Windows Update, Windows Firewall, and User Account Control (UAC) and placing it into an easy-to-read format. If you wish, you can tell Action Center where to look for information by selecting *Change Action Center settings* (see Figure 4-86).

Figure 4-85
Action Center

Figure 4-86
Change Action
Center settings

If you see a problem, Action Center includes plenty of links to get you to the utility you need. From the Action Center applet, you get direct links to

- UAC settings
- Performance Information and Tools
- Backup and Restore
- Windows Update
- Troubleshooting Wizard
- System Restore

Although Action Center does little more than reproduce information from other utilities, it makes finding problems quick and easy. Combined with quick links to most of the utilities you'll need, Action Center should become your base of operations when something goes wrong on a Windows 7 PC.

Beyond A+

Windows 8

Windows 8 will launch sometime in 2012 (according to Microsoft), but it's not covered on the 220-801 and 220-802 exams. While the differences between Windows Vista and Windows 7 were minor enough that you could know a lot about 7 if you knew about Vista, Windows 8 looks to reimagine how we interface with our PCs.

The biggest idea behind Windows 8 is to unify Microsoft's multiple platforms: PCs, tablets, phones—even the Xbox 360 now has an interface very similar to Windows 8's "Metro" user interface (see Figure 4-87). You'll be able to use touch-enabled monitors to slide, drag, pinch, and zoom your way around apps specifically designed for the new look. Don't worry, though—your old desktop is safely hidden behind the Metro Start screen.

Figure 4-87
The Windows 8
Metro UI

Beyond the interface, Microsoft has said they want to make it easier for developers to quickly program applications for multiple platforms. They've also previewed new tools and enhanced utilities from previous versions of Windows. The new Task Manager alone, as shown in Figure 4-88, should be enough to whet your appetite until the final release.

Process	Status	0% CPU	78% Memory	0% Disk	0% Network
Applications (6)					
▷ Internet Explorer		0%	29.9 MB	0 MB/s	0 Mbps
▷ Microsoft Expression Blend ...		0%	55.8 MB	0 MB/s	0 Mbps
▷ Microsoft Visual Studio 11 E...		0%	46.8 MB	0 MB/s	0 Mbps
VirtualBox Guest Additions ...		0%	5.6 MB	0 MB/s	0 Mbps
▷ Windows Explorer		0%	26.3 MB	0 MB/s	0 Mbps
▷ Windows Task Manager		0%	10.5 MB	0 MB/s	0 Mbps
Background processes (10)					
▷ Antimalware Service Execut...		0%	40.8 MB	0 MB/s	0 Mbps
COM Surrogate		0%	0.9 MB	0 MB/s	0 Mbps
▷ Fast User Switching Utility S...		0%	0.5 MB	0 MB/s	0 Mbps
▷ Microsoft Windows Search ...		0%	6.2 MB	0 MB/s	0 Mbps
Microsoft.VisualStudio.Perf...		0%	4.7 MB	0 MB/s	0 Mbps
Runtime Broker		0%	1.7 MB	0 MB/s	0 Mbps

Figure 4-88 Windows 8's upgraded Task Manager

Windows Embedded

The world is filled with PCs in the most unlikely places. Everything from cash registers to the F-22 Raptor fighter plane contains some number of tiny PCs. These aren't the PCs you're used to seeing, though. They almost never have mice, monitors, keyboards, and the usual I/O you'd expect to see, but they are truly PCs, with a CPU, RAM, BIOS, and storage.

These tiny PCs need operating systems just like any other PC, and a number of companies make specialized OSs for embedded PCs. Microsoft makes Windows Embedded just for these specialized embedded PCs.

Chapter Review

Questions

1. Which of the following is an advantage of running Windows on NTFS as opposed to FAT?

 A. Security

 B. Multiple folders

 C. Long filenames

 D. Speed

2. Which version of Windows uses the Backup Status and Configuration Tool?

 A. Windows 2000

 B. Windows XP Media Center

 C. Windows XP Professional

 D. Windows Vista Ultimate

3. What is the proper way to refer to the system root folder??

 A. %System%

 B. &System&

 C. %SystemRoot%

 D. &SystemRoot&

4. What folder is a central storage location for user files in XP?

 A. Program Files

 B. My Documents

 C. My Files

 D. %SystemRoot%\Users

5. Which utility is helpful in troubleshooting hardware?

 A. System Properties

 B. Device Manager

 C. Disk Management

 D. Security Center

6. Which Windows utility backs up critical files and settings and enables you to roll back to a previous state?

 A. Registry

 B. System Restore

 C. System Information

 D. Microsoft Management Console

7. Many tech tools are grouped together in which location?

 A. Start | All Programs | Tools

 B. Start | All Program | Tools | System Tools

 C. Start | All Programs | System Tools | Accessories

 D. Start | All Programs | Accessories | System Tools

8. Which utility is missing from the default Windows XP Home installation?

 A. Backup

 B. Character Map

 C. Computer Management

 D. User Accounts

9. What is displayed in the Computer window?

 A. All the drives on your system

 B. All the Control Panel applets

 C. Installed programs

 D. Performance Monitor

10. Which feature of Windows 7 enables you to link folders and view their contents together?

 A. Favorites

 B. Shortcuts

 C. Libraries

 D. Windows Explorer

Answers

1. **A.** NTFS offers security. FAT provides no security.

2. **D.** The Backup Status and Configuration Tool did not exist before Vista.

3. **C.** The system root folder is referred to as %SystemRoot%.

4. **B.** Most XP users put their personal files in My Documents.

5. **B.** For hardware in general, turn to Device Manager.

6. **B.** System Restore does the trick here, enabling you to back up and restore your system.

7. **D.** You'll find many useful tools in Start | All Programs | Accessories | System Tools.

8. **A.** Backup is not installed by default in Windows XP Home.

9. **A.** Computer shows your drives.

10. **C.** Using libraries, you can link folders and view their contents together as if they were one folder.

Visible Networks

In this chapter, you will learn how to
- Describe the basic functions of a network, including identifying common devices and connectors
- Discuss the differences between a LAN and a WAN and the importance of TCP/IP
- Perform basic resource sharing

It's hard to find a computer that's not connected to a network. Whether your system is part of a large enterprise network or a single PC with an Internet connection, every computer has some form of network connection. CompTIA has wisely added quite a bit of networking coverage to the CompTIA A+ exams, and a number of chapters toward the back of this book cover networking in great detail. By covering the basic or "user level" networking topics early in the book, however, you'll see how networking impacts every facet of modern computing.

I didn't name this chapter "Visible Networks" simply as a clever follow-up to the titles of the previous chapters. The primary goal of this chapter is to cover the more visible parts of the network: the connections and settings that enable you and me to set up simple networks. Let's begin by answering a big question: Why do we network?

Historical/Conceptual

Take a moment to think about what you do on a network. Most of us, when asked, would say, "surf the Internet," or "watch YouTube videos," or maybe "print to the printer downstairs." These are all good reasons to use a network, but what ties them together? In each of these situations, you are using your computer (the local computer) to access "stuff" stored on a remote computer (not your local computer). So what do remote computers have that you might want (see Figure 5-1)?

Figure 5-1 Accessing remote computers

A remote computer called a *Web server* stores the files that make up a Web site. The Web server uses server programs to store and share the data. The two most famous Web server programs are Apache HTTP Server and Internet Information Server (IIS). When you access a Web site, your *Web browser* (likely Internet Explorer, Mozilla Firefox, or Google Chrome) asks the Web server to share the Web page files and then displays them (see Figure 5-2). Because your computer asks for the Web page, we call it the *client*. The remote computer that serves the Web site is a *server*.

NOTE Any computer that's running a sharing program is by definition a server.

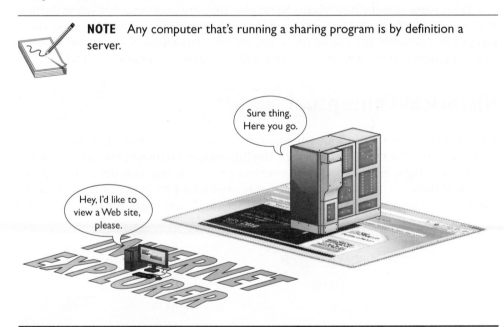

Figure 5-2 Accessing a Web page

But what about YouTube? YouTube also uses Web servers, but these Web servers connect to massive video databases. Like a normal Web server, these remote computers share the videos with your client PC, but they use special software capable of sending video fast enough that you can watch it without waiting (see Figure 5-3).

Figure 5-3 Accessing a YouTube page

But we don't need the Internet to share stuff. Figure 5-4 shows a small home network with each computer running Windows 7. One of the computers on the network has a printer connected via a USB port. This computer has enabled a printer-sharing program built into Windows so that the other computers on the network can use the printer.

Figure 5-4 Sharing a printer in Windows 7

No matter how big the network, we use networks to share stuff. This stuff might be Web pages, videos, printers, folders, e-mail messages, music—what you can share is limited only by your ability to find a server program capable of sharing it and a client program that can access it. Network people call anything that one computer might share with another a *resource*. Therefore, the goal of networking is to connect computers so that they can share resources or access other shared resources.

To share and access resources, a network must have the following:

1. Something that defines and standardizes the design and operation of cabling, network cards, and the interconnection of multiple computers

2. An addressing method that enables clients to find servers and enables servers to send data to clients, no matter the size of the network

3. Some method of sharing resources and accessing those shared resources

Networking Technologies

When the first network designers sat down at a café to figure out how to get two or more PCs to share data and peripherals, they had to write a lot of notes on little white napkins to answer even the most basic questions. The first question was: *How*? It's easy to say, "Well, just run a wire between them!" But that doesn't tell us how the wire works or how the computers connect to the wire. Here are some more big-picture questions:

- How will each computer be identified?

- If two or more computers want to talk at the same time, how do you ensure that all conversations are understood?

- What kind of wire? What gauge? How many wires in the cable? Which wires do what? How long can the cable be? What type of connectors?

Clearly, making a modern PC network entails a lot more than just stringing up some cable! As you saw a bit earlier, most networks have one or more *client machines*, PCs that request information or services, and a *server*, the machine that hosts and shares the data. Both clients and servers need *network interface controllers (NICs)* that define or label the machine on the network. A NIC also breaks files into smaller data units, called *frames*, to send across the network and reassembles the frames it receives into whole files. You also need some medium for delivering the frames between two or more PCs—most often this is a wire that can carry electrical pulses; sometimes it's radio waves or other wireless methods. Finally, your PC's operating system has to be able to communicate with its own networking hardware and with other machines on the network. Figure 5-5 shows a typical network layout.

Windows 7 Workstations

Windows Server 2008

Figure 5-5 A typical network

EXAM TIP Not too many years ago, every NIC came on an expansion card that you added to a motherboard. Most techs called that card a *network interface card* or *NIC*. Now that just about every motherboard has the networking feature built in, the acronym has shifted to network interface *controller*. You're likely only to see the term *NIC* on the exams, though I call them *network cards*, too.

This section of the chapter looks at the inventive solutions network engineers found to handle frames and cabling. After a brief look at the core technology, the chapter dives into four specific types of networks. You'll dig into the software side of things later in the chapter.

Topology

If a bunch of computers connect together to make a network, some logic or order must influence the way they connect. Perhaps each computer connects to a single main line that snakes around the office. Each computer might have its own cable, with all of the cables coming together at a central point. Or maybe all of the cables from all of the computers connect to a main loop that moves data along a track, picking up and dropping off data like a circular subway line.

A network's *topology* describes the way that computers connect to each other in that network. The most common network topologies are called *bus, ring, star,* and *mesh.* Figure 5-6 shows the four types: a *bus* topology, where all computers connect to the network via a main line called a *bus cable*; a *ring* topology, where all computers on the

network attach to a central ring of cable; a *star* topology, where the computers on the network connect to a central wiring point (usually called a *switch*); and a *mesh* topology, where each computer has a dedicated line to every other computer. There are also *hybrid* topologies, such as star bus or star ring, which combine aspects of the other topologies to capitalize on their strengths and minimize their weaknesses. You'll look at the most important hybrid topology, star bus, in a moment, but for now, make sure you know the four main topologies!

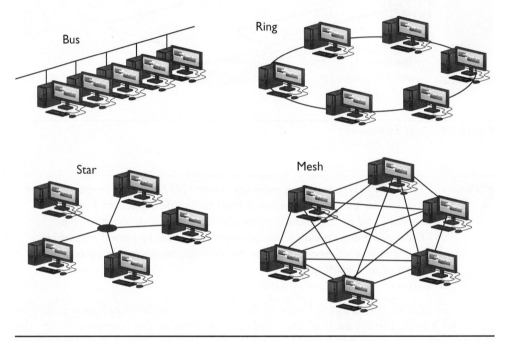

Figure 5-6 Clockwise from top left: bus, ring, mesh, and star topologies

Look at Figure 5-6. A mesh topology looks amazingly resilient and robust, doesn't it? And it is, at least on paper. Every computer physically connects to every other computer on the network, so even if half of the PCs crash, the network functions as well as ever (for the survivors). In a practical sense, however, implementing a mesh topology network would be an expensive mess. For example, a tiny network with only 10 PCs would need 45 distinct pieces of cable to connect every PC to every other PC. What a mesh mess! Because of this, mesh topologies have never been practical in a cabled network.

Although a topology describes the method by which systems in a network connect, the topology alone doesn't describe all of the features necessary to make a cabling system work. The term *bus topology*, for example, describes a network that consists of some number of machines connected to the network via the same piece of cable. Notice that

this definition leaves a lot of questions unanswered. What is the cable made of? How long can the cable be? How do the machines decide which machine should send data at a specific moment? A network based on a bus topology can answer these questions in a number of different ways.

Most techs make a clear distinction between the *logical topology* of a network—how the network is laid out on paper, with nice straight lines and boxes, similar to an electronic schematic—and the physical topology. The *physical topology* describes the typically messy computer network, with cables running diagonally through the ceiling space or snaking their way through walls. If someone describes the topology of a particular network, make sure you understand whether they're talking about the logical topology or the physical topology.

Over the years, manufacturers and standards bodies created several specific network technologies based on different topologies. A *network technology* is a practical application of a topology and other critical standards to provide a method to get data from one computer to another on a network. It defines many aspects of a network, from the topology, to the frame type, to the cabling and connectors used. A network technology defines everything necessary to get data from one computer to another.

801

Frames and NICs

Data is moved from one PC to another in discrete chunks called *frames*. You'll sometimes hear the word *packet* used instead of frames—this is incorrect. Packets are a part of the frame. You'll find more information about packets in Chapter 22.

Every NIC in the world has a built-in identifier, an address unique to that single network card, called a *media access control (MAC) address*. You read that right—every network card in the world has its own unique MAC address!

A MAC address is a *binary number*, meaning it's a string of 1s and 0s. Each 1 or 0 is called a *bit*. (You'll learn more about binary in Chapter 6.)

The MAC address is 48 bits long, providing more than 281 *trillion* MAC addresses, so there are plenty of MAC addresses to go around. Because people have trouble keeping track of that many 1s and 0s, we need another way to display the addresses. *Hexadecimal* is shorthand for representing strings of 1s and 0s. One hex character is used to represent four binary characters. Here's the key:

0000 = 0	0100 = 4	1000 = 8	1100 = C
0001 = 1	0101 = 5	1001 = 9	1101 = D
0010 = 2	0110 = 6	1010 = A	1110 = E
0011 = 3	0111 = 7	1011 = B	1111 = F

So, MAC addresses may be binary, but we represent them by using 12 hexadecimal characters. These MAC addresses are burned into every NIC, and some NIC makers print the MAC address on the card. Figure 5-7 shows the System Information utility description of a NIC, with the MAC address highlighted.

System Information

| File | Edit | View | Help |

Item	Value
DHCP Lease Expires	3/25/2012 8:34 AM
DHCP Lease Obtained	3/19/2012 8:34 AM
MAC Address	E0:CB:4E:93:02:78
I/O Port	0x0000D800-0x0000D8FF
Memory Address	0xFBDFF000-0xFBDFFFFF
Memory Address	0xFAEF0000-0xFAEFFFFF
IRQ Channel	IRQ 18
Driver	c:\windows\system32\drivers\rt64win7.sys (7.46.610
Name	[00000008] WAN Miniport (IP)

Figure 5-7 MAC address

NOTE Even though MAC addresses are embedded into the NIC, some NICs allow you to change the MAC address on the NIC. This is rarely done.

Hey! I thought we were talking about frames! Well, we are, but you need to understand MAC addresses to understand frames. The many varieties of frames share common features (see Figure 5-8). First, frames contain the MAC address of the network card to which the data is being sent. Second, they have the MAC address of the network card that sent the data. Third is the data itself (at this point, we have no idea what the data is—certain software handles that question), which can vary in size depending on the type of frame. Finally, the frame must contain some type of data check to verify that the data was received in good order. Most frames use a clever mathematical algorithm called a *cyclic redundancy check (CRC)*.

This discussion of frames raises the question, how big is a frame? Or more specifically, how much data do you put into each frame? How do you ensure that the receiving PC understands the *way* the data was broken down by the sending machine and can thus put the pieces back together? The problem in answering these questions is that they encompass so many items. When the first networks were created, *everything* from the frames to the connectors to the type of cable had to be invented from scratch.

Figure 5-8 Generic frame

To make a successful network, you need the sending and receiving PCs to use the same network technology. Over the years, many hardware protocols have been implemented, with such names as Token Ring, FDDI, and ARCnet, but today only one hardware protocol dominates the modern PC computing landscape: *Ethernet*.

Introducing Ethernet

A consortium of companies centered on Digital Equipment Corporation, Intel, and Xerox invented the first network in the mid-1970s. More than just create a network, they wrote a series of standards that defined everything necessary to get data from one computer to another. This series of standards was called *Ethernet*. Over the years, Ethernet has gotten faster and has used different types of cabling. As a result, the Ethernet folks have a number of Ethernet versions, often called *Ethernet flavors*. Even though there are various speeds and cable types, all flavors of Ethernet use the same frame. This is very important: you can have any combination of hardware devices and cabling using different Ethernet flavors on a single Ethernet network and, in most cases, the PCs will be able to communicate just fine.

Most modern Ethernet networks employ one of three speeds (and sometimes all three), *10BaseT*, *100BaseT*, or *1000BaseT*. As the numbers in the names suggest, 10BaseT networks run at 10 Mbps, 100BaseT networks run at 100 Mbps, and 1000BaseT networks—called Gigabit Ethernet—run at 1000 Mbps, or 1 Gbps. All three technologies—sometimes

referred to collectively as *10/100/1000BaseT* or just plain Ethernet—use a *star bus* topology and connect via a type of cable called *unshielded twisted pair (UTP)*.

 NOTE Ethernet developers continue to refine the technology. 1000BaseT might be the most common standard now, but 10-Gigabit Ethernet is starting to make inroads today.

Star Bus

Imagine taking a bus network (where every computer connects to a common wire) and shrinking the bus down so it fits inside a box. Then, instead of attaching each PC directly to the wire, you attach them via cables to special ports on the box (see Figure 5-9). The box with the bus takes care of all of the tedious details required by a bus network. The bus topology would look a lot like a star topology, wouldn't it? Modern Ethernet networks all use *star bus* topology.

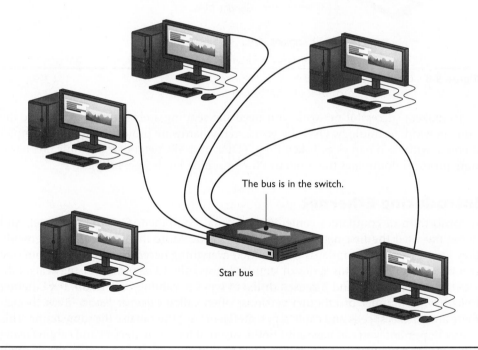

The bus is in the switch.

Star bus

Figure 5-9 Star bus

The central box with the bus—a *switch*—provides a common point of connection for network devices. Switches can have a wide variety of ports. Most consumer-level switches have 4 or 8 ports, but business-level switches can have 32 or more ports.

Early Ethernet networks used a *hub*. A switch is a far superior and far more common version of a hub. Figure 5-10 shows a typical consumer-level switch.

Figure 5-10
A switch

A simple example demonstrates the difference between hubs and switches. Let's say you have a network of 32 PCs, all using 100-Mbps NICs attached to a 100-Mbps hub or switch. We would say the network's *bandwidth* is 100 Mbps. If you put the 32 PCs on a 32-port 100-Mbps hub, you have 32 PCs sharing the 100 Mbps of bandwidth. A switch addresses this problem by making each port its own separate network. Each PC gets to use the full bandwidth. The bottom line? Once switches became affordable, hubs went away.

The connection between a computer and a switch is called a *segment*. With most cable types, Ethernet segments are limited to 100 meters or less.

Cheap and centralized, a star bus network does not go down if a single cable breaks. True, the network would go down if the switch failed, but that is rare. Even if a switch fails, replacing a switch in a closet is much easier than tracing a bus running through walls and ceilings and trying to find a break!

Unshielded Twisted Pair

Unshielded twisted pair (UTP) cabling is the specified cabling for 10/100/1000BaseT and is the predominant cabling system used today. Many types of twisted pair cabling are available, and the type used depends on the needs of the network. Twisted pair cabling consists of AWG 22–26 gauge wire twisted together into color-coded pairs. Each wire is individually insulated and encased as a group in a common jacket.

CAT Levels

UTP cables come in categories that define the maximum speed at which data can be transferred (also called *bandwidth*). The major categories (CATs) are outlined in Table 5-1.

CAT 1	Standard telephone line
CAT 3	Designed for 10-Mbps networks; a variant that used all four pairs of wires supported 100-Mbps speeds
CAT 5	Designed for 100-Mbps networks
CAT 5e	Enhanced to handle 1000-Mbps networks
CAT 6	Supports 1000-Mbps networks at 100-meter segments; 10-Gbps networks up to 55-meter segments
CAT 6a	Supports 10-Gbps networks at 100-meter segments

Table 5-1 CAT levels

The CAT level should be clearly marked on the cable, as Figure 5-11 shows.

Figure 5-11
Cable markings
for CAT level

EXAM TIP Although these days you'll only find CAT 3 installed for telephones and in very old network installations, CompTIA traditionally enjoys tripping up techs who don't know it could handle 100-Mbps networks.

The *Telecommunication Industry Association/Electronics Industries Alliance* (*TIA/EIA*) establishes the UTP categories, which fall under the TIA/EIA 568 specification. Currently, most installers use CAT 5e or CAT 6 cable.

Shielded Twisted Pair

Shielded twisted pair (STP), as its name implies, consists of twisted pairs of wires surrounded by shielding to protect them from EMI, or electromagnetic interference. STP is pretty rare, primarily because there's so little need for STP's shielding; it only really matters in locations with excessive electronic noise, such as a shop floor area with lots of lights, electric motors, or other machinery that could cause problems for other cables.

Implementing 10/100/1000BaseT

The 10BaseT and 100BaseT standards require two pairs of wires: a pair for sending and a pair for receiving. 10BaseT ran on an ancient CAT version called CAT 3, but typically used at least CAT 5 cable. 100BaseT requires at least CAT 5 to run. 1000BaseT needs

all four pairs of wires in a CAT 5e or CAT 6 cable. These cables use a connector called an *RJ-45* connector. The *RJ* (*registered jack*) designation was invented by Ma Bell (the phone company, for you youngsters) years ago and is still used today.

NOTE There are CAT levels for connectors as well as cables. Don't even try to use a CAT 5e RJ-45 connector with a CAT 6 cable.

Currently only two types of RJ connectors are used for networking: RJ-11 and RJ-45 (see Figure 5-12). *RJ-11* connects your telephone to the telephone jack in the wall of your house. It supports up to two pairs of wires, though most phone lines use only one pair. The other pair is used to support a second phone line. RJ-11 connectors are primarily used for telephone-based Internet connections (see Chapter 24) and are not used in any common LAN installation, although a few weird (and out of business) "network in a box" companies used them. RJ-45 is the standard for UTP connectors. RJ-45 has connections for up to four pairs and is visibly much wider than RJ-11. Figure 5-13 shows the position of the #1 and #8 pins on an RJ-45 jack.

Figure 5-12
RJ-11 and RJ-45

Figure 5-13
RJ-45 pin numbers

The TIA/EIA has two standards for connecting the RJ-45 connector to the UTP cable: the TIA/EIA 568A (*T568A*) and the TIA/EIA 568B (*T568B*). Both are acceptable. You do not have to follow any standard as long as you use the same pairings on each end of the cable; however, you will make your life simpler if you choose a standard. Make sure that all of your cabling uses the same standard and you will save a great deal of work in the end. Most importantly, *keep records*!

Like all wires, the wires in UTP are numbered. A number does not appear on each wire, but rather each wire has a standardized color. Table 5-2 shows the official TIA/EIA Standard Color Chart for UTP.

Pin	T568A	T568B	Pin	T568A	T568B
1	White/Green	White/Orange	5	White/Blue	White/Blue
2	Green	Orange	6	Orange	Green
3	White/Orange	White/Green	7	White/Brown	White/Brown
4	Blue	Blue	8	Brown	Brown

Table 5-2 UTP Cabling Color Chart

Plenum Versus PVC Cabling

Most workplace installations of network cable go up above the ceiling and then drop down through the walls to present a nice port in the wall. The space in the ceiling, under the floors, and in the walls through which cable runs is called the *plenum* space. The potential problem with this cabling running through the plenum space is that the protective sheathing for networking cables, called the *jacket*, is made from plastic, and if you get any plastic hot enough, it creates smoke and noxious fumes. Standard network cables usually use *PVC (polyvinyl chloride)* for the jacket, but PVC produces noxious fumes when burned. Fumes from cables burning in the plenum space can quickly spread throughout the building, so you want to use a more fire-retardant cable in the plenum space. Plenum-grade cable is simply network cabling with a fire-retardant jacket and is required for cables that go in the plenum space. Plenum-grade cable costs about three to five times more than PVC, but you should use it whenever you install cable in a plenum space.

Understanding Ethernet is critical in your understanding of how networks function. But when we talk about networking, there are two interconnected but very different worlds: the small local area networks where nearby users connect their computers via switches, and the Internet. Let's make sure we understand the differences by exploring the world of LANs and WANs in the next section.

Network Protocols, LANs, and WANs

The whole idea of networking is often confusing to new techs simply because there are two very different ways to look at networking: small networks that share resources like documents, music, and printers, and big networks like the Internet where you share Web pages, e-mail, and just about anything you want. Let's take a moment to clarify how these two seemingly different networks are very similar because today both use the same language or protocol.

A Short History of the War of the Network Protocols and Why TCP/IP Won

Ethernet does a fine job of moving data from one machine to another, but Ethernet alone isn't enough to make a complete network; many other functions need to be handled. For example, an Ethernet frame holds a maximum of 1500 bytes. What if the data being moved is larger than 1500 bytes? Something has to chop up the data into chunks on one end and something else needs to reassemble those chunks on the other end so the file can be properly reassembled.

Another issue arises if one of the machines on the network has its network card replaced. Up to this point, the only way to distinguish one machine from another was by the MAC address on the network card. To solve this, each machine must have a name, an identifier for the network, which is "above" the MAC address. Something needs to keep track of the MAC addresses on the network and the names of the machines so that frames and names can be correlated. If you replace a PC's network card, the network will, after some special queries, update the list to associate the name of the PC with the new network card's MAC address.

Network protocol software takes the incoming data received by the network card, keeps it organized, sends it to the application that needs it, and then takes outgoing data from the application and hands it to the NIC to be sent out over the network. All networks use some protocol. Over the years there have been many network protocols, most combining multiple simple protocols into groups, called *protocol stacks*. This lead to some crazily named network protocols, such as NetBIOS/NetBEUI and TCP/IP.

NetBIOS/NetBEUI

During the 1980s, IBM developed the *NetBIOS Extended User Interface (NetBEUI)*, the default protocol for early versions of Windows. NetBEUI offered small size, easy configuration, and a relatively high speed. The underlying protocol stack was called *NetBIOS/NetBEUI*. The NetBIOS protocol handled naming conventions, while NetBEUI chopped up data for delivery via frames.

 NOTE A *node* is any device that has a network connection—usually this means a PC, but other devices can be nodes. For example, many printers connect directly to a network and can therefore be deemed nodes.

NetBIOS names were very simple. You could call your computer TIMMY or MIKESPC. NetBIOS didn't allow names to include anything but letters (uppercase only), numbers, and a very few special characters. NetBIOS/NetBEUI was great for little networks, but it relied on individual computers to send out frames addressed to the MAC address FF-FF-FF-FF-FF-FF—which meant *everybody*. The official term for this is a *broadcast*. Broadcasts eat up bandwidth, but they're great for a node that's trying to get a MAC address for another node, as shown in Figure 5-14.

Figure 5-14
A broadcast in
action

> **NOTE** NetBIOS stands for *networked basic input/output system*, which is why everyone always just called it NetBIOS.

Broadcasts are useful, but the larger the network is, the more bandwidth broadcasts eat up. In general, NetBIOS could handle about 300 computers on a single network before the broadcast became too much. By the mid-1980s, it was clear NetBIOS wasn't going to work for really large networks, so a new network protocol was in the works. Plus, scaling required new hardware as well.

LANs, Routing, and WANs

A *local area network (LAN)* is a group of computers that are located physically close to each other—no more than a few hundred meters apart at most. A LAN might be in a single room, on a single floor, or in a single building. But I'm going to add that a LAN is almost always a group of computers that are able to "hear" each other when one of them sends a broadcast. A group of computers connected by one or more switches is a broadcast domain (see Figure 5-15).

Figure 5-15 Two broadcast domains—two separate LANs

 EXAM TIP For the CompTIA A+ exams, remember that a LAN is a group of networked computers that are close to each other. Also, remember that a LAN is almost always a broadcast domain.

A *wide area network (WAN)* is a widespread group of computers connected using long-distance technologies. You connect LANs into a WAN with a magical box called a *router* (see Figure 5-16). The best example of a WAN is the Internet.

Figure 5-16 Two broadcast domains connected by a router—a WAN

You can connect multiple smaller networks into a bigger network, turning a group of LANs into one big WAN, but this raises a couple of issues with network traffic. A computer needs some form of powerful, flexible addressing to address a frame so that it goes to a computer within its own LAN or to a computer on another LAN on the same WAN. Broadcasting is also unacceptable, at least between LANs. If every computer saw every frame, the network traffic would quickly spin out of control! Plus, the addressing scheme needs to work so that routers can sort the frames and send them along to the proper LAN. This process, called *routing*, requires routers and a routing-capable protocol to function correctly.

Routers destroy any incoming broadcast frames, by design. No broadcast frame can ever go through a router. This makes broadcasting still quite common within a single broadcast domain, but never anywhere else.

NetBIOS/NetBEUI was great for a single LAN, but it lacked the extra addressing capabilities needed for a WAN. A new protocol was needed, one that could handle routing.

TCP/IP

Transmission Control Protocol/Internet Protocol (TCP/IP) was originally developed for the Internet's progenitor, the *Advanced Research Projects Agency Network* (*ARPANET*) of the U.S. Department of Defense. In 1983, TCP/IP became the built-in protocol for the popular BSD (Berkeley Software Distribution) UNIX, and other flavors of UNIX quickly

adopted it as well. The biggest network of all, the Internet, uses TCP/IP as its protocol. All versions of Windows (in fact, all operating systems today) use TCP/IP as the default protocol.

The reason TCP/IP has a slash in the middle is to reflect that TCP/IP isn't a single network protocol. It's a number of protocols that work together. TCP handles getting the data between computers, while IP handles the addressing scheme that gives us something more powerful and flexible than MAC addresses. Let's cover IP addresses in this chapter and save some of the other protocols for Chapter 22.

NOTE Chapter 22 covers TCP/IP in much greater detail.

IP Addresses and Subnet Masks

In a TCP/IP network, the systems don't have names but rather have IP addresses. The *IP address* is the unique identification number for your system on the network. Part of the address identifies the network, and part identifies the local computer (host) address on the network. IP addresses consist of four sets of eight binary numbers (octets), with each set separated by a period. The numbers range from 0 to 255. This is called *dotted-decimal notation*. Every computer on a network running TCP/IP gets an IP address like so:

```
202.34.16.11
```

Every computer in the same broadcast domain as this computer will have some numbers in common. If the network is small, then all the computers will share the first three octets. In this case, a computer with the IP address of 202.34.16.123 is in the same broadcast domain as 202.34.16.11. The part of the IP address that is common for all the computers in the same broadcast domain is called the *network ID*. The network ID for this example is 202.34.16.

Are these example computers part of the same broadcast domain as a device with an IP address of 202.34.15.33? No. In this example, only computers that are part of 202.34.16 are part of the same broadcast domain as 202.34.16.11. But how does every computer know which part of its IP address identifies the network ID? The *subnet mask* tells the computer which part of its IP address is the network ID. A typical subnet mask looks like this:

```
255.255.255.0
```

The network ID is determined by the number of 255 octets in the subnet mask. If there is a 255, that part of your address is the network ID. If your IP address were 190.24.16.11 and your subnet mask were 255.255.0.0, your network ID would be 190.24. If the subnet mask were 255.255.255.0, the same IP address would have a network ID of 190.24.16.

Default Gateway

Sometimes you'll want to talk to computers that are outside your network. In that case, you'll need to connect to a router. I can now give another description of a router. A *router* is a device that has at least two IP addresses: one that connects to your LAN's switch and one that connects to the "next network." That next network could be your Internet service provider (ISP) or another router at your company—who knows (and more importantly, who cares, as long as it gets there)? The port on your router that connects to your LAN is given an IP address that's part of your network ID. In most cases, this is the first address shown in Figure 5-17.

202.16.34.16

202.16.34.42

202.16.34.64

202.16.34.1

Switch

Router

Figure 5-17 Default gateway

The IP address of the "LAN" side of your router (the port connected to your LAN) is the address your computer uses to send data to anything outside your network ID. This is called the *default gateway*.

Domain Name Service (DNS)

Knowing that users could not remember lots of IP addresses, early Internet pioneers came up with a way to correlate those numbers with more human-friendly designations. Special computers, called *domain name service (DNS)* servers, keep databases of IP addresses and their corresponding names. For example, let's say a machine with the IP address 209.34.45.163 hosts a Web site and we want it to be known as

www.totalsem.com. When we set up the Web site, we pay money for a DNS server to register the DNS name www.totalsem.com to the IP address 209.34.45.163. So instead of typing "http://209.34.45.163" to access the Web page, you can type "www.total-sem.com." Your system will then query the DNS server to get www.totalsem.com's IP address and use that to find the right machine. Unless you want to type in IP addresses all the time, you'll need to use DNS servers (see Figure 5-18).

Figure 5-18 Domain name service

The Internet has regulated domain names. If you want a domain name that others can access on the Internet, you must register your domain name and pay a small yearly fee. Originally, DNS names all ended with one of the following seven domain name qualifiers, called *top-level domains* (*TLDs*):

.com	General business	**.mil**	Military organizations
.edu	Educational organizations	**.net**	Internet organizations
.gov	Government organizations	**.org**	Nonprofit organizations
.int	International		

As more and more countries joined the Internet, a new level of domains was added to the original seven to indicate a DNS name from a particular country, such as .uk for the United Kingdom. It's common to see DNS names such as www.bbc.co.uk or www.louvre.fr. The *Internet Corporation for Assigned Names and Numbers* (*ICANN*) has added several new domains, including .name, .biz, .info, .tv, and others. Given the explosive growth of the Internet, these are unlikely to be the last ones! For the latest developments, check ICANN's Web site at www.icann.org.

Entering the IP Information

When you configure a computer to connect to a network, you must enter the IP address, the subnet mask, the default gateway, and at least one DNS server. (The last of these is called configuring *client-side DNS settings*.) Let's review:

- **IP address** A computer's unique address on the network
- **Subnet mask** Identifies your network ID
- **Default gateway** IP address or the LAN side of your router
- **DNS server** Tracks easy-to-remember DNS names for IP addresses

Configuring the IP address differs between each version of Windows. Figure 5-19 shows the IP settings on a Windows 7 system.

Figure 5-19

IP settings on a
Windows 7 system

As you look at Figure 5-19, note the radio button for *Obtain an IP address automatically*. This is a common setting for which you don't need to enter any information. You can use this setting if your network uses Dynamic Host Configuration Protocol (DHCP). If you have DHCP (most networks do) and your computer is configured to obtain an IP address automatically, your computer boots up and will broadcast a DHCP request. The DHCP server provides your computer with all the IP information it needs to get on the network (see Figure 5-20).

Figure 5-20
A DHCP server handing out an IP address

Refer to Chapter 22 for more details on IP addresses, subnet masks, default gateways, and DNS servers. For now, simply appreciate that these settings for your computer exist while we continue to tour the visible network.

802

Network Organization

Once a network is created using appropriate network technology like Ethernet, users need to be able to share resources in some organized fashion. Resources such as folders and printers need a way to determine who can and cannot use them and how they can be used. Microsoft designed Windows networks to work in one of three categories: workgroups, domains, or homegroups. (These are the Microsoft terms, but the concepts have been adopted by the entire computer industry and apply to Mac OS X and other operating systems.) These three organizations differ in control, number of machines needed, compatibility, and security.

Let's start with the oldest network organization: workgroups.

Workgroups

Workgroups are the most basic and simplistic of the three network organizations. They are also the default for almost every fresh installation of Windows. Workgroups have been around since the ancient Windows for Workgroups came out back in the early 1990s.

By default, all computers on the network are assigned to a workgroup called WORK-GROUP. You can see your workgroup name by opening the System applet (press WINDOWS KEY-PAUSE or go to Start | Control Panel | System applet), as shown in Figure 5-21.

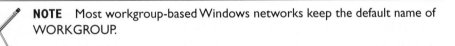

Figure 5-21 Default workgroup

There's nothing special about the name WORKGROUP, except that every computer on the network needs the same workgroup name to be able to share resources. If you want to change your workgroup name, you need to use the System applet. Click the *Change settings* button to open the System Properties dialog box. Then click the Change button to change your workgroup name (see Figure 5-22).

NOTE Most workgroup-based Windows networks keep the default name of WORKGROUP.

Workgroups lack centralized control over the network; all systems connected to the network are equals. This works well for smaller networks because there are fewer users, connections, and security concerns to think about. But what do you do when your network encompasses dozens or hundreds of users and systems? How can you control all of that?

Figure 5-22 Changing the workgroup in advanced settings

User Names and Passwords

As you'll recall from Chapter 4, when you log on to a Windows computer, you need to enter a user name and password. Windows 7 makes this easy by giving you a pretty logon interface, as shown in Figure 5-23.

The user names and their passwords are stored in an encrypted format on your computer. User names have a number of jobs on your computer, but at this point the job most interesting to us is to give a user access to the computer. User names work well when you access your own computer, but these same user names and passwords are used to access shared resources on other computers in the network—and that's where we run into trouble. To appreciate this problem, let's watch a typical folder share take place on a network of Windows 7 systems.

Sharing a Folder

All Windows computers can share folders and printers out of the box. Sharing a folder in Windows 7 is easy—just right-click on the folder and select Share with | Specific people to get to the File Sharing dialog box (see Figure 5-24). On most Windows 7 systems, you'll see options called Homegroup in the context menu—ignore these for now as all will be explained in the next section.

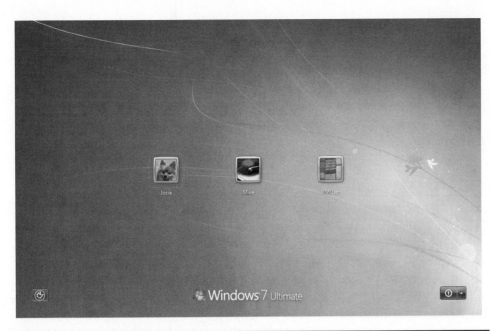

Figure 5-23 Windows 7 logon screen

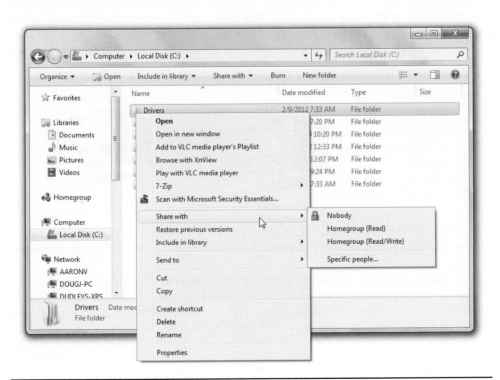

Figure 5-24 Folder Sharing dialog box

By default, you'll see every user account that's currently on this system. You may give an account Read or Read/Write permission, while the person who created the folder is assigned as Owner. The following list describes these permissions:

- **Read** You can see what's in the folder. You may open files in the folder, but you can't save anything back into the folder.

- **Read/Write** Same as Read but you can save files into the folder.

- **Owner** Same as Read/Write plus you can set the permissions for other users on the folder.

 NOTE All versions of Windows come with a far more powerful and much more complex form of permissions based on the NTFS file system. We'll save the big discussion of this more advanced form of permissions for Chapter 16.

So all this sharing seems to work quite nicely, except for one big issue: When you log on to your computer, you are accessing a user name and database on that computer. The accounts you are giving access to are stored on your computer, so how do you give someone from another computer access to that shared folder? You have to give that other person a valid user name and password. We use the nomenclature <computer name>\<user name> to track our logons. If you log on to Computer A as Mike, we say you are logged on to ComputerA\Mike. This nomenclature comes in very handy when networked computers become part of the process.

Figure 5-25 shows an account called Mike on Computer A. Assume there is a shared folder called Timmy on Computer A and Mike has read/write permission.

Figure 5-25

Computers A and B

A person fires up Computer B, logging in as Fred. He opens his Network menu option and sees Computer A, but when he clicks on it he sees a network password prompt (see Figure 5-26).

The reason is that the person is logged on as ComputerB\Fred and he needs to be logged on as ComputerA\Mike to access this folder successfully. So the user needs to know the password for ComputerA\Mike. This isn't a very pretty way to protect user names and passwords. So what can you do? You have three choices:

1. You can make people log on to shares as just shown.

2. You can create the same accounts (same user name and same password) on all the computers and give sharing permissions to all the users for all the shares.

3. You can use one account on all computers. Everyone logs on with the same account, and then all shares are by default assigned to the same account.

Figure 5-26 Prompt for entering user name and password

Domains

Larger networks that need more control use *domains*. Opposite the decentralized nature of workgroups, domains require a specific server to control access to the network's resources. This means tracking each user, each resource, and what each user can do to each resource.

To use a domain on a network of Windows machines, you must have a computer running a version of Windows Server (see Figure 5-27). Windows Server is a completely different, much more powerful, and much more expensive version of Windows. Current editions of this specialized OS include Windows Server 2008 and Windows Server 2008 R2.

Figure 5-27 Windows Server

An administrator creates a domain on the Windows Server system, which makes that system the *domain controller* (*DC*). The administrator also creates new user accounts on the domain controller. These accounts are called *domain accounts*. Once a network is set up as a domain, each PC on the network needs to join the domain (which kicks you off the workgroup). When you log on to a computer that's a member of a domain, Windows will prompt you for a user name instead of showing you icons for all the users on the network (see Figure 5-28).

When using a domain, you don't log on to your computer. Instead, you log on directly to the domain. All user accounts are stored on the domain controller, as shown in Figure 5-29. A lot of domains have names that look like Web addresses, like totalhome.com, totalhome.local, or even just totalhome. Using the previous nomenclature, you can log on to a domain using <domain>\<domain user name>. If the domain totalhome.local has a user account called Mike, for example, you would use totalhome.local\Mike to log on.

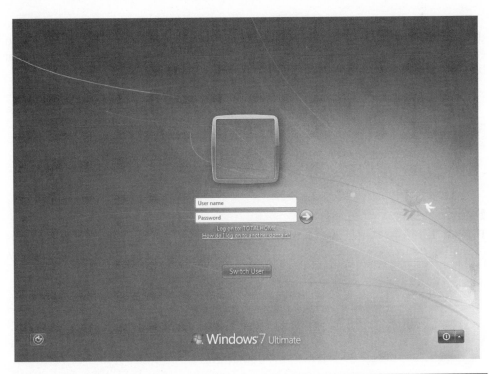

Figure 5-28 Domain logon screen

Figure 5-29
Domain network

One of the best features of domains is that you can log on to any computer on the domain using the same domain account. You don't have to set up local accounts on each computer. We call this feature *single sign-on,* and for most users, this is the biggest benefit to using a Windows domain.

NOTE There is much more to a Windows domain than single sign-on. For the CompTIA A+ certification, however, that's the big selling point. If you want to delve deeper into Windows domains, consider pursuing the CompTIA Network+ certification or one of the Microsoft certifications.

Homegroups

The problem with workgroups is that they provide almost no security and require lots of signing on to access resources. Domains provide single sign-on and lots of security, but require special servers and lots of administration. To address this, Microsoft introduced a feature in Windows 7 called *HomeGroup.*

NOTE Homegroups are not available in Windows XP or Windows Vista.

HomeGroup uses the idea that people want to connect data, not folders. Most people want to share their music, not their My Music folder. So homegroups skip folders completely and share Windows 7 libraries.

NOTE You may want to review what you learned about libraries in the previous chapter.

A homegroup connects a group of computers using a common password—no special user names required. Each computer can be a member of only one homegroup at a time. Let's make a homegroup and see how this works.

EXAM TIP Microsoft refers to the technology as HomeGroup, but drops the capitalization to homegroup when talking about the groups themselves. Look for it to appear either way on the CompTIA A+ exams.

To make a homegroup, open the HomeGroup Control Panel applet. Assuming you currently connect to a workgroup and haven't already created a homegroup, you'll see a dialog box like the one shown in Figure 5-30.

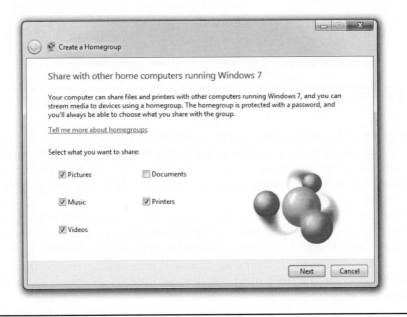

Figure 5-30 Default HomeGroup dialog box

Click the *Create a homegroup* button to create a homegroup. You'll then see the Create a Homegroup dialog box shown in Figure 5-31.

Figure 5-31 Create a Homegroup dialog box

Notice the five options: Pictures, Music, Videos, Documents, and Printers. Remember that those first four are the libraries you learned about in Chapter 4? The Documents checkbox is probably not checked, but go ahead and check it to share all five things. Click Next to see the homegroup's password (see Figure 5-32).

NOTE Interestingly, all homegroup data is encrypted between systems.

Create a Homegroup

Use this password to add other computers to your homegroup

Before you can access files and printers located on other computers, add those computers to your homegroup. You'll need the following password.

Write down this password:

48wD7sV38h

Print password and instructions

If you ever forget your homegroup password, you can view or change it by opening HomeGroup in Control Panel.

How can other computers join my homegroup?

Finish

Figure 5-32 The homegroup's password

Perhaps you've heard that you shouldn't write down passwords? Well, this password is so long that you might *need* to write it down. The dialog box even gives you a way to print it out! Click Next one more time to see the dialog box shown in Figure 5-33. This is the dialog box you will now see every time you click the HomeGroup applet in the Control Panel.

Let's look at this carefully. Notice where it says *Share libraries and printers* and, a bit lower, *How do I share additional libraries?* By default, homegroups share libraries, not individual folders. The Music, Pictures, Videos, and Documents libraries are shared by default. Although printers get their own checkbox, this setting remains the same as a normal printer share. It's just a handy place to add printer sharing, as even the most basic users like to share printers.

EXAM TIP Remember that homegroups share libraries, not folders, by default.

Once you've created a homegroup, go to another computer on the network and open the HomeGroup Control Panel applet. Assuming all the factors stated earlier, you will see a dialog box like Figure 5-34.

Figure 5-33 Homegroup configured

Figure 5-34 HomeGroup showing an existing homegroup

Click the *Join now* button, enter the password, choose which libraries you want to share with everyone else, and the new computer is in the homegroup!

Access the files shared through a homegroup by opening Windows Explorer, as shown in Figure 5-35. To see what others are sharing, select the corresponding computer name. You can then open those libraries to see the shared folders.

 NOTE Once you create a homegroup, you can access it from Windows Explorer.

Figure 5-35 Using homegroups

Sharing more libraries is easy, and, if you'd like, you can even share individual folders. Just right-click on the library or folder and select Share with, as shown in Figure 5-36.

Notice you have four options: Nobody, Homegroup (Read), Homegroup (Read/Write), and Specific people. The Nobody option means the item is not shared.

EXAM TIP Windows Explorer also adds a *Share with* toolbar button that works exactly like the menu shown in Figure 5-36.

By sharing libraries with homegroups, Microsoft hides folders for most users, helping users share their stuff (documents, pictures, music, and videos) instead of folders. Homegroups fit a very specific world: smaller, non-domain home networks, but within that realm, they work wonderfully.

Figure 5-36 The Share with menu

Chapter Review

Questions

1. How many bits are in a MAC address?

 A. 24

 B. 36

 C. 48

 D. 64

2. Which protocol enables the use of names such as www.totalsem.com rather than IP addresses?

 A. DNS

 B. MAC

 C. IP

 D. TCP

3. What is the minimum CAT level cable required for a 100BaseT network?

 A. CAT 1

 B. CAT 5

 C. CAT 5e

 D. CAT 6

4. Which OS enables you to implement HomeGroup?

 A. Mac OS X

 B. Windows XP

 C. Windows 7

 D. Windows Server

5. Which of the following is an example of a hybrid topology?

 A. Bus

 B. Ring

 C. Star

 D. Star bus

6. Which of the following is an advantage of a domain-based network over a workgroup-based network?

 A. Ease of administration

 B. Cheaper

 C. Single sign-on

 D. Faster to implement

7. A typical CAT 6 cable uses which connector?

 A. RJ-11

 B. RJ-45

 C. Plenum

 D. PVC

8. Why would you use STP over UTP cabling?

 A. Cheaper

 B. Easier to install

 C. Better to avoid interference

 D. They're interchangeable terms

9. What kind of frame gets received by all NICs in a LAN?

 A. Ethernet

 B. Broadcast

 C. WAN

 D. DNS

10. Internet Explorer, Mozilla Firefox, and Google Chrome are all examples of what?

 A. Web servers

 B. DNS

 C. Web browsers

 D. IP addresses

Answers

1. **C.** MAC addresses are 48-bit.

2. **A.** The domain name service (DNS) protocol enables using names instead of IP addresses.

3. **B.** 100BaseT networks need CAT 5 or better UTP.

4. **C.** Microsoft released HomeGroup with Windows 7.

5. **D.** A star bus topology, like the one used with Ethernet networks, is a hybrid topology.

6. **C.** Domain-based networks enable single sign-on.

7. **B.** CAT 6 cables use an RJ-45 connector.

8. **C.** Shielded twisted pair cabling handles interference from other electronics much better than unshielded twisted pair.

9. **B.** All NICs in a LAN will receive broadcast frames.

10. **C.** All these programs are Web browsers.

Microprocessors

In this chapter, you will learn how to
- Identify the core components of a CPU
- Describe the relationship of CPUs and memory
- Explain the varieties of modern CPUs
- Select and install a CPU
- Troubleshoot CPUs

For all practical purposes, the terms *microprocessor* and *central processing unit (CPU)* mean the same thing: it's that big chip inside your computer that many people often describe as the brain of the system. You know from Chapter 3 that CPU makers name their microprocessors in a fashion similar to the automobile industry: CPUs get a make and a model, such as Intel Core i7 or AMD Phenom II X4. But what's happening inside the CPU to make it able to do the amazing things asked of it every time you step up to the keyboard?

This chapter delves into microprocessors in detail. We'll first discuss how processors work and the components that enable them to interact with the rest of the computer. The second section describes how CPUs work with memory. The third section takes you on a tour of modern CPUs. The final section gets into practical work: selecting, installing, and troubleshooting CPUs.

Historical/Conceptual

CPU Core Components

Although the computer might seem to act quite intelligently, comparing the CPU to a human brain hugely overstates its capabilities. A CPU functions more like a very powerful calculator than like a brain—but, oh, what a calculator! Today's CPUs add, subtract, multiply, divide, and move billions of numbers per second. Processing that much

hard drive is too slow. Even the ancient 8088, with its clock speed of 4.77 MHz, could conceivably process several million lines of code every second. Modern CPUs crank out billions of lines every second. Hard drives simply can't give the data to the CPU at a fast enough speed.

Computers need some other device that takes copies of programs from the hard drive and then sends them, one line at a time, to the CPU quickly enough to keep up with its demands. Because each line of code is nothing more than a pattern of eight ones and zeros, any device that can store ones and zeros eight-across will do. Devices that in any way hold ones and zeros that the CPU accesses are known generically as *memory*.

Many types of devices store ones and zeros perfectly well—technically even a piece of paper counts as memory—but computers need memory that does more than just store groups of eight ones and zeros. Consider this pretend program:

1. Put 2 in the AX register.

2. Put 5 in the BX register.

3. If AX is greater than BX, run line 4; otherwise, go to line 6.

4. Add 1 to the value in AX.

5. Go back to line 1.

6. Put the value of AX on the EDB.

This program has an IF statement, also called a *branch* by CPU makers. The CPU needs a way to address each line of this memory—a way for the CPU to say to the memory, "Give me the next line of code" or "Give me line 6." Addressing memory takes care of another problem: the memory must not only store programs but also store the result of the programs. If the CPU adds 2 + 3 and gets 5, the memory needs to store that 5 in such a way that other programs may later read that 5, or possibly even store that 5 on a hard drive. By addressing each line of memory, other programs will know where to find the data.

Memory and RAM

Memory must store not only programs, but also data. The CPU needs to be able to read and write to this storage medium. Additionally, this system must enable the CPU to jump to *any* line of stored code as easily as to any other line of code. All of this must be done at or at least near the clock speed of the CPU. Fortunately, this magical device has existed for many years: *random access memory (RAM)*.

Chapter 7 develops the concept of RAM in detail, so for now let's look at RAM as an electronic spreadsheet, like one you can generate in Microsoft Excel (see Figure 6-14). Each cell in this spreadsheet can store only a one or a zero. Each cell is called a *bit*. Each row in the spreadsheet is eight bits across to match the EDB of the 8088. Each row of eight bits is called a *byte*. In the PC world, RAM transfers and stores data to and from the CPU in byte-sized chunks. RAM is therefore arranged in byte-sized rows. Here are the terms used to talk about quantities of bits:

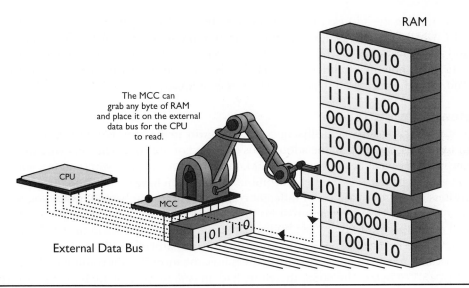

Figure 6-17 The MCC grabs a byte of RAM.

Once the MCC is in place to grab any discrete byte of RAM, the CPU needs to be able to tell the MCC which line of code it needs. The CPU therefore gains a second set of wires, called the *address bus*, with which it can communicate with the MCC. Different CPUs have different numbers of wires (which, you will soon see, is very significant). The 8088 had 20 wires in its address bus (see Figure 6-18).

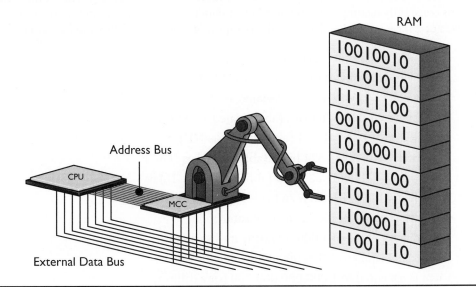

Figure 6-18 Address bus

By turning the address bus wires on and off in different patterns, the CPU tells the MCC which line of RAM it wants at any given moment. Every different pattern of ones and zeros on these 20 wires points to one byte of RAM. There are two big questions here. First, how many different patterns of on-and-off wires can exist with 20 wires? And second, which pattern goes to which row of RAM?

How Many Patterns?

Mathematics can answer the first question. Each wire in the address bus exists in only one of two states: on or off. If the address bus consisted of only one wire, that wire would at any given moment be either on or off. Mathematically, that gives you (pull out your old pre-algebra books) $2^1 = 2$ different combinations. If you have two address bus wires, the address bus wires create $2^2 = 4$ different combinations. If you have 20 wires, you would have 2^{20} (or 1,048,576) combinations. Because each pattern points to one line of code and each line of RAM is one byte, if you know the number of wires in the CPU's address bus, you know the maximum amount of RAM that a particular CPU can handle.

Because the 8088 had a 20-wire address bus, the most RAM it could handle was 2^{20} or 1,048,576 bytes. The 8088, therefore, had an *address space* of 1,048,576 bytes. This is not to say that every computer with an 8088 CPU had 1,048,576 bytes of RAM. Far from it! The original IBM PC only had a measly 64 kilobytes—but that was considered plenty back in the Dark Ages of Computing in the early 1980s.

Okay, so you know that the 8088 had 20 address wires and a total address space of 1,048,576 bytes. Although this is accurate, no one uses such an exact term to discuss the address space of the 8088. Instead you say that the 8088 had one *megabyte* (1 MB) of address space.

What's a "mega"? Well, let's get some terminology down. Dealing with computers means constantly dealing with the number of patterns a set of wires can handle. Certain powers of 2 have names used a lot in the computing world. The following list explains.

1 kilo = 2^{10} = 1024 (abbreviated as "K")

1 kilobyte = 1024 bytes (abbreviated as "KB")

1 mega = 2^{20} = 1,048,576 (abbreviated as "M")

1 megabyte = 1,048,576 bytes (abbreviated as "MB")

1 giga = 2^{30} = 1,073,741,824 (abbreviated as "G")

1 gigabyte = 1,073,741,824 bytes (abbreviated as "GB")

1 tera = 2^{40} = 1,099,511,627,776 (abbreviated as "T")

1 terabyte = 1,099,511,627,776 bytes (abbreviated as "TB")

1 kilo is *not* equal to 1000 (one thousand)

1 mega is *not* equal to 1,000,000 (one million)

1 giga is *not* equal to 1,000,000,000 (one billion)

1 tera is *not* equal to 1,000,000,000,000 (one trillion)

(But they are pretty close!)

NOTE Of course, I kilo is equal to 1000 when you talk in terms of the metric system. It also means 1000 when you talk about the clock speed of a chip, so I KHz is equal to 1000 Hz. When you talk storage capacity, though, the binary numbers kick in, making I KB = 1024 bytes. Got it? This same bizarre dual meaning applies all the way up the food chain, so I MHz is 1,000,000 Hz, but I MB is 1,048,576 bytes; I GHz is I billion Hz, but I GB is 1,073,741,824 bytes; and so on.

Which Pattern Goes to Which Row?

The second question is a little harder: "Which pattern goes to which row of RAM?" To understand this, let's take a moment to discuss binary counting. In binary, only two numbers exist, 0 and 1, which makes binary a handy way to work with wires that turn on and off. Let's try to count in binary: 0, 1…what's next? It's not 2—you can only use zeros and ones. The next number after 1 is 10! Now let's count in binary to 1000: 0, 1, 10, 11, 100, 101, 110, 111, 1000. Try counting to 10000. Don't worry; it hardly takes any time at all.

Super; you now count in binary as well as any math professor. Let's add to the concept. Stop thinking about binary for just a moment and think about good old base 10 (regular numbers). If you have the number 365, can you put zeros in front of the 365, like this: 000365? Sure you can—it doesn't change the value at all. The same thing is true in binary. Putting zeros in front of a value doesn't change a thing! Let's count again to 1000 in binary. In this case, add enough zeros to make 20 places:

```
00000000000000000000
00000000000000000001
00000000000000000010
00000000000000000011
00000000000000000100
00000000000000000101
00000000000000000110
00000000000000000111
00000000000000001000
```

Hey, wouldn't this be a great way to represent each line of RAM on the address bus? The CPU identifies the first byte of RAM on the address bus with 00000000000000000000. The CPU identifies the last RAM row with 11111111111111111111. When the CPU turns off all of the address bus wires, it wants the first line of RAM; when it turns on all of the wires, it wants the 1,048,576th line of RAM. Obviously, the address bus also addresses all of the rows of RAM in between. So, by lighting up different patterns of ones and zeros on the address bus, the CPU can access any row of RAM it needs.

 NOTE Bits and bytes are abbreviated differently. Bits get a lowercase b, whereas bytes get a capital B. So for example, 4 Kb is four kilobits, but 4 KB is four kilobytes.

801

Modern CPUs

CPU manufacturers have achieved stunning progress with microprocessors since the days of the Intel 8088, and the rate of change doesn't show any signs of slowing. At the core, though, today's CPUs function similarly to the processors of your forefathers. The arithmetic logic unit (ALU)—that's the Man in the Box—still crunches numbers many millions of times per second. CPUs rely on memory to feed them lines of programming as quickly as possible.

This section brings the CPU into the present. We'll first look at models you can buy today, and then we'll turn to essential improvements in technology you should understand.

Manufacturers

When IBM awarded Intel the contract to provide the CPUs for its new IBM PC back in 1980, it established for Intel a virtual monopoly on all PC CPUs. The other home-computer CPU makers of the time faded away: MOS Technology, Zilog, Motorola—no one could compete directly with Intel. Over time, other competitors have risen to challenge Intel's market-segment share dominance. In particular, a company called Advanced Micro Devices (AMD) began to make clones of Intel CPUs, creating an interesting and rather cutthroat competition with Intel that lasts to this day.

Intel

Intel Corporation thoroughly dominated the personal computer market with its CPUs and motherboard support chips. At nearly every step in the evolution of the PC, Intel has led the way with technological advances and surprising flexibility for such a huge corporation. Intel CPUs—and more specifically, their instruction sets— define the personal computer. Intel currently produces a dozen or so models of CPU for both desktop and portable computers. Most of Intel's desktop and laptop processors are sold under the Celeron, Pentium, and Core brands. Their very low-power portable/smartphone chips are branded Atom; their high-end workstation/server chips are called Xeon and Itanium.

AMD

You can't really talk about CPUs without mentioning Advanced Micro Devices. AMD makes superb CPUs for the PC market and provides competition that keeps

Intel on its toes. Like Intel, AMD doesn't just make CPUs, but their CPU business is certainly the part that the public notices. AMD has made CPUs that clone the function of Intel CPUs. If Intel invented the CPU used in the original IBM PC, how could AMD make clone CPUs without getting sued? Well, chipmakers have a habit of exchanging technologies through cross-license agreements. Way back in 1976, AMD and Intel signed just such an agreement, giving AMD the right to copy certain types of CPUs.

The trouble started with the Intel 8088. Intel needed AMD's help to supply enough CPUs to satisfy IBM's demands. But after a few years, Intel had grown tremendously and no longer wanted AMD to make CPUs. AMD said, "Too bad. See this agreement you signed?" Throughout the 1980s and into the 1990s, AMD made pin-for-pin identical CPUs that matched the Intel lines of CPUs (see Figure 6-19). You could yank an Intel CPU out of a system and snap in an AMD CPU—no problem!

Figure 6-19
Identical Intel and
AMD 486 CPUs
from the early
1990s

In January 1995, after many years of legal wrangling, Intel and AMD settled and decided to end the licensing agreements. As a result of this settlement, AMD chips are no longer compatible with sockets or motherboards made for Intel CPUs—even though in some cases the chips look similar. Today, if you want to use an AMD CPU, you must purchase a motherboard designed for AMD CPUs. If you want to use an Intel CPU, you must purchase a motherboard designed for Intel CPUs. So you now have a choice: Intel or AMD.

Model Names
Intel and AMD differentiate product lines by using different product names, and these names have changed over the years. For a long time, Intel used *Pentium* for its flagship model, just adding model numbers to show successive generations—Pentium, Pentium II, Pentium III, and so on. AMD used the *Athlon* brand in a similar fashion.

Most discussions on PC CPUs focus on four end-product lines: desktop PC, budget PC, portable PC, and server computers. Table 6-1 displays many of the current product lines and names.

Market	Intel	AMD
Mainstream and enthusiast desktop	Core i7/i5/i3, Core 2 Duo	Phenom II, A-Series, Phenom, Athlon X2
Budget desktop	Pentium, Celeron	Sempron, Athlon II
Mobile	Core i7/i5/i3 (mobile), Core 2 Duo (mobile), Atom	Turion
Server	Xeon/Itanium	Opteron

Table 6-1 Current Intel and AMD Product Lines and Names

You'll notice that both Intel and AMD reuse model names for products aimed at different markets. Yesterday's Pentium brand used to be for the highest end, for example, but now Intel uses the brand for its budget market. The same thing happened to the Athlon brand. To add a little more confusion, the budget CPUs are not the older CPUs still being sold, but low-end versions of current model lines.

Code Names

Both Intel and AMD continue to refine the CPU manufacturing process after releasing a new model, but they try to minimize the number of model names in use. This means that they release CPUs labeled as the same model, but the CPUs inside can be very different from earlier versions of that model. Both companies use *code names* to keep track of different variations within models (see Figure 6-20). As a tech, you need to know both the models and code names to be able to make proper recommendations for your clients. One example illustrates the need: the Intel Core i7.

Figure 6-20

Same branding, but different capabilities

Intel released the first Core i7 in the summer of 2008. By spring of 2012, the original microarchitecture—code named Nehalem—had gone through five variations, none of which worked on motherboards designed for one of the other variations. Plus, in 2011, Intel introduced the Sandy Bridge version of the Core i7 that eventually had two desktop versions and a mobile version, all of which used still other sockets. (And I'm simplifying the variations here.)

At this point, a lot of new techs throw their hands in the air. How do you keep up? How do you know which CPU will give your customer the best value for his or her

money and provide the right computing firepower for his or her needs? Simply put, you need to *research efficiently*.

Your first stop should be the manufacturers' Web sites. Both companies put out a lot of information on their products.

- www.intel.com
- www.amd.com

You can also find many high-quality tech Web sites devoted to reporting on the latest CPUs. When a client needs an upgrade, surf the Web for recent articles and make comparisons. Because you'll understand the underlying technology from your CompTIA A+ studies, you'll be able to follow the conversations with confidence. Here's a list of some of the sites I use:

- www.arstechnica.com
- www.hardocp.com
- www.tomshardware.com
- www.bit-tech.net

Finally, you can find great, exhaustive articles on all things tech at Wikipedia:

- www.wikipedia.org

 NOTE Wikipedia is a user-generated, self-regulated resource. I've found it to be accurate on technical issues the vast majority of the time, but you should always check other references as well. Nicely, most article authors on the site will tell you their sources through footnotes. You can often use the Wikipedia articles as jump-off points for deeper searches.

Desktop Versus Mobile

Mobile devices, such as portable computers, have needs that differ from those of desktop computers, notably the need to consume as little electricity as possible. This helps in two ways: extending battery charge and creating less heat.

Both Intel and AMD have engineers devoted to making excellent mobile versions of their CPUs that sport advanced energy-saving features (see Figure 6-21). Intel's SpeedStep technology, for example, enables the CPU to run in very low power mode and scale up automatically if the user demands more power from the CPU. If you're surfing the Web at an airport terminal, the CPU doesn't draw too much power. When you switch to playing an action game, the CPU kicks into gear. Saving energy by making the CPU run more slowly when demand is light is generically called *throttling*.

Figure 6-21
Desktop vs.
mobile, fight!

Many of the technologies developed for mobile processors have migrated into their more power-hungry desktop siblings, too. That's an added bonus for the planet.

Technology

Although microprocessors today still serve the same function as the venerable 8088—crunching numbers—they do so far more efficiently. Engineers have altered, enhanced, and improved CPUs in a number of ways. This section looks at seven features:

- Clock multipliers
- 64-bit processing
- Virtualization support
- Parallel execution
- Multicore processing
- Integrated memory controller (IMC)
- Integrated graphics processing unit (GPU)

Clock Multipliers

All modern CPUs run at some multiple of the system clock speed. The system bus on my Core i7 machine, for example, runs at 100 MHz. The clock multiplier goes up to ×35 at full load to support the 3.4 GHz maximum speed. Originally, CPUs ran at the speed of the bus, but engineers early on realized the CPU was the only thing doing any work much of the time. If the engineers could speed up just the internal operations of the CPU and not anything else, they could speed up the whole computing process. Figure 6-22 shows a nifty program called CPU-Z displaying my CPU details. Note that all I'm doing is typing at the moment so SpeedStep has dropped the clock multiplier down to ×16 and the CPU core speed is only 1600 MHz.

Figure 6-22
CPU-Z showing the clock speed, multiplier, and bus speed of a Core i7 processor hardly breaking a sweat.

The clock speed and the multiplier on early clock-multiplying systems had to be manually configured via jumpers or dual in-line package (DIP) switches on the motherboard (see Figure 6-23). Today's CPUs report to the motherboard through a function called CPUID (CPU identifier), and the speed and multiplier are set automatically. (You can manually override this automatic setup on many motherboards. See "Overclocking," later in this chapter, for details.)

Figure 6-23 DIP switches on a motherboard

64-Bit Processing

Over successive generations of microprocessors, engineers have upgraded many physical features of CPUs. The EDB gradually increased in size, from 8- to 16- to 32- to 64-bits wide. The address bus similarly jumped, going from 20- to 24- to 32-bits wide (where it stayed for a decade).

The technological features changed as well. Engineers added new and improved registers, for example, that used fancy names like multimedia extensions (MMX) and Streaming SIMD Extensions (SSE). A mighty shift started a couple of years ago and continues to evolve: the move to 64-bit computing.

Most new CPUs support *64-bit processing*, meaning they can run a compatible 64-bit operating system, such as Windows 7, and 64-bit applications. They also support 32-bit processing for 32-bit operating systems, such as Windows XP, and 32-bit applications. The general-purpose registers also make the move up to 64-bit. The primary benefit to moving to 64-bit computing is that modern systems can support much more than the 4 GB of memory supported with 32-bit processing.

With a 64-bit address bus, CPUs can address 2^{64} bytes of memory, or more precisely, 18,446,744,073,709,551,616 bytes of memory—that's a lot of RAM! This number is so big that gigabytes and terabytes are no longer convenient, so we now go to an exabyte (2^{60}), abbreviated *EB*. A 64-bit address bus can address 16 EB of RAM.

In practical terms, 64-bit computing greatly enhances the performance of programs that work with large files, such as video editing applications. You'll see a profound improvement moving from 4 GB to 8 GB or 12 GB of RAM with such programs.

x86 Versus x64

The terminology of CPUs can trip up new techs, so here's the scoop. CPUs from the early days can be lumped together as *x*86 CPUs, because they used an instruction set that built upon the earliest Intel CPU architecture. The Intel Core 2 Duo, for example, could run a program written for an ancient 80386 processor that was in fashion in the early 1990s.

When the 64-bit CPUs went mainstream, marketing folks needed some way to mark applications, operating systems, and so on such that consumers could quickly tell the difference between something compatible with their system or something not compatible. Since you generally cannot return software after you open it, this is a big deal. The marketing folks went with *x*64, and that created a mess.

The earlier 32-bit stuff had been marketed as *x*86, not *x*32, so now we have *x*86 (old, 32-bit stuff) vs. *x*64 (new, 64-bit stuff). It's not pretty, but do you get the difference? To make matters even worse, however, *x*64 processors quite happily handle *x*86 code and are, by definition, *x*86 processors too!

Virtualization Support

Intel and AMD have built in support for running more than one operating system at a time, a process called *virtualization*. Virtualization is very cool and gets its own chapter later in the book (Chapter 30), so I'll skip the details here. The key issue from a CPU standpoint is that virtualization used to work entirely through software. Programmers had to write a ton of code to enable a CPU—that was designed to run one OS at

a time—to run more than one OS at the same time. Think about the issues involved. How does the memory get allocated, for example, or how does the CPU know which OS to update when you type something or click an icon? With hardware-based virtualization support, CPUs took a lot of the burden off the programmers and made virtualization a whole lot easier.

Parallel Execution

Modern CPUs can process multiple commands and parts of commands in parallel, known as *parallel execution*. Early processors had to do everything in a strict, linear fashion. The CPUs accomplish this parallelism through multiple pipelines, dedicated cache, and the capability to work with multiple threads or programs at one time. To understand the mighty leap in efficiency gained from parallel execution, you need insight into the processing stages.

Pipelining

To get a command from the data bus, do the calculation, and then get the answer back out on the data bus, a CPU takes at least four steps (each of these steps is called a *stage*):

1. **Fetch** Get the data from the EDB.
2. **Decode** Figure out what type of command needs to be executed.
3. **Execute** Perform the calculation.
4. **Write** Send the data back onto the EDB.

Smart, discrete circuits inside the CPU handle each of these stages. In early CPUs, when a command was placed on the data bus, each stage did its job and the CPU handed back the answer before starting the next command, requiring at least four clock cycles to process a command. In every clock cycle, three of the four circuits sat idle. Today, the circuits are organized in a conveyer-belt fashion called a *pipeline*. With pipelining, each stage does its job with each clock-cycle pulse, creating a much more efficient process. The CPU has multiple circuits doing multiple jobs, so let's add pipelining to the Man in the Box analogy. Now, it's *Men* in the Box (see Figure 6-24)!

Figure 6-24
Simple pipeline

Pipelines keep every stage of the processor busy on every click of the clock, making a CPU run more efficiently without increasing the clock speed. Note that at this point, the CPU has four stages: fetch, decode, execute, and write—a four-stage pipeline. No CPU ever made has fewer than four stages, but advancements in caching (see "Cache," next) have increased the number of stages over the years. Current CPU pipelines contain many more stages, up to 20 in some cases.

Pipelining isn't perfect. Sometimes a stage hits a complex command that requires more than one clock cycle, forcing the pipeline to stop. Your CPU tries to avoid these stops, or *pipeline stalls*. The decode stage tends to cause the most pipeline stalls; certain commands are complex and therefore harder to decode than other commands. Current processors use multiple decode stages to reduce the chance of pipeline stalls due to complex decoding.

The inside of the CPU is composed of multiple chunks of circuitry to handle the many types of calculations your PC needs to do. For example, one part, the *arithmetic logic unit (ALU)* (or *integer unit*), handles integer math: basic math for numbers with no decimal point. A perfect example of integer math is $2 + 3 = 5$. The typical CPU spends most of its work doing integer math. CPUs also have special circuitry to handle complex numbers, called the *floating point unit (FPU)*. With a single pipeline, only the ALU or the FPU worked at any execution stage. Worse yet, floating point calculation often took many, many clock cycles to execute, forcing the CPU to stall the pipeline until the FPU finished executing the complex command (see Figure 6-25). Current CPUs offer multiple pipelines to keep the processing going (see Figure 6-26).

Figure 6-25
Bored integer unit

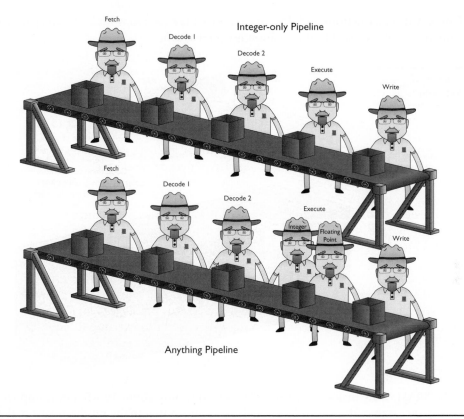

Figure 6-26 Multiple pipelines

Cache

When you send a program to the CPU, you actually run lots of little programs all at the same time. Okay, let's be fair here: *you* didn't run all of these little programs—you just started your Web browser or some other program. The moment you double-clicked that icon, Windows started sending many programs to the CPU. Each of these programs breaks down into some number of little pieces, called *threads*, and data. Each thread is a series of instructions designed to do a particular job with the data.

Modern CPUs don't execute instructions sequentially—first doing step 1, then step 2, and so on—but rather process all kinds of instructions. Most applications have certain instructions and data that get reused, sometimes many times.

Pipelining CPUs work fantastically well as long as the pipelines stay filled with instructions. Because the CPU runs faster than the RAM can supply it with code, you'll always get pipeline stalls—called *wait states*—because the RAM can't keep up with the CPU. To reduce wait states, CPUs come with built-in, very high-speed RAM called *static RAM (SRAM)*. This SRAM preloads as many instructions as possible and keeps copies

of already run instructions and data in case the CPU needs to work on them again (see Figure 6-27). SRAM used in this fashion is called a *cache*.

Figure 6-27

RAM cache

Address Bus

RAM

We're ready for the next line of code... oh look, it's right here in our cache! Good thing, too, because going all the way out to RAM would take forever!

The SRAM cache inside the early CPUs was tiny, only about 16 KB, but it improved performance tremendously. In fact, it helped so much that many motherboard makers began adding a cache directly to the motherboards. These caches were much larger, usually around 128 to 512 KB. When the CPU looked for a line of code, it first went to the built-in cache; if the code wasn't there, the CPU went to the cache on the motherboard. The cache on the CPU was called the *L1 cache* because it was the one the CPU first tried to use. The cache on the motherboard was called the *L2 cache*, not because it was on the motherboard, but because it was the second cache the CPU checked.

Eventually, engineers took this cache concept even further and added the L2 cache onto the CPU package (see Figure 6-28). Some CPUs even include three caches: an L1, an L2, and an L3 cache.

The L2 cache on the early CPUs that had L2 cache included on the CPU package ran at a slower clock speed than the L1 cache. The L1 cache was in the CPU and thus ran at the speed of the CPU. The L2 cache connected to the CPU via a tiny set of wires on the CPU package. The first L2 caches ran at half the speed of the CPU.

The inclusion of the L2 cache on the chip gave rise to some new terms to describe the connections between the CPU, MCC, RAM, and L2 cache. The address bus and external data bus (connecting the CPU, MCC, and RAM) were lumped into a single term called the *frontside bus*, and the connection between the CPU and the L2 cache became known as the *backside bus* (see Figure 6-29).

Figure 6-28
CPU-Z displaying the cache information for a Core i7 processor

NOTE To keep up with faster processors, motherboard manufacturers began to double and even quadruple the size of the frontside bus. Techs sometimes refer to these as *double-pumped* and *quad-pumped* frontside buses.

Figure 6-29 Frontside and backside buses

The end of the road for the terms frontside bus and backside bus seems to be at the Intel Core 2 Duo and Core 2 Quad processors, as far as the CompTIA A+ certification exams are concerned. The terms are also used by a lot of techs to refer to simply "the connection between the CPU and system RAM."

EXAM TIP Typically, the CompTIA A+ exams expect you to know that L1 cache will be the smallest and fastest cache; L2 will be bigger and slower than L1; and L3 will be the biggest and slowest cache.

Multithreading

At the peak of the single-CPU 32-bit computing days, Intel released a CPU called the Pentium 4 that took parallelism to the next step with Hyper-Threading. *Hyper-Threading* enabled the Pentium 4 to run multiple threads at the same time, what's generically called *simultaneous multithreading*, effectively turning the CPU into two CPUs on one chip—with a catch.

Figure 6-30 shows the Task Manager in Windows XP on a system running a Hyper-Threaded Pentium 4. Note how the CPU box is broken into two groups—Windows thinks this one CPU is two CPUs.

Figure 6-30

Windows Task Manager with the Performance tab displayed for a system running a Hyper-Threaded Pentium 4

Multithreading enhances a CPU's efficiency but with a couple of limitations. First, the operating system and the application have to be designed to take advantage of the feature. Second, although the CPU simulates the actions of a second processor, it doesn't double the processing power because the main execution resources are not duplicated.

NOTE Though its use had faded after the Pentium 4, Intel brought back Hyper-Threading to mainstream processors with the Core i7 in 2011 (and a couple of years earlier with the low-powered Atom processors), and Microsoft optimized Windows 7 to support the technology. This time, it seems, Hyper-Threading is here to stay.

Multicore Processing

CPU clock speeds hit a practical limit of roughly 4 GHz around 2002–2003, motivating the CPU makers to find new ways to get more processing power for CPUs. Although Intel and AMD had different opinions about 64-bit CPUs, both decided at virtually the

same time to combine two CPUs (or *cores*) into a single chip, creating a *dual-core* archi-tecture. A dual-core CPU has two execution units—two sets of pipelines—but the two sets of pipelines share caches and RAM.

Today, dual-core CPUs like the Intel Core 2 Duo are common, and multicore CPUs—with four, six, or eight cores—grace the desktop PCs of many enthusiasts. With each generation of multicore CPU, both Intel and AMD have tinkered with the mixture of how to allocate the cache among the cores. Figure 6-31 shows another screenshot of CPU-Z, this time displaying the cache breakdown of a Core i7.

Figure 6-31
CPU-Z showing
the cache details
of a Sandy Bridge
Core i7

Figure 6-31 reveals specific details about how this Intel CPU works with cache. The Core i7 has L1, L2, and L3 caches of 64 KB, 256 KB, and 8 MB, respectively. (The L1 cache divides into 32 KB to handle data—the *D-Cache*—and another 32 KB for instruc-tions—the *I-Cache*.) Each core has dedicated L1 and L2 caches. (You can tell this by the ×4 to the right of the capacity listing.) All four cores share the giant L3 cache. That pool of memory enables the cores to communicate and work together without having to access the radically slower main system RAM as much. CPU manufacturers engineered the cores in multicore CPUs to divide up work independently of the OS, known as *mul-ticore processing*. This differs from Hyper-Threading, where the OS and applications have to be written specifically to handle the multiple threads. Note that even with multicore processors, applications have to be modified or optimized for this parallelism to have a huge impact on performance.

Integrated Memory Controller

Almost all current microprocessors have an *integrated memory controller (IMC)*, moved from the motherboard chip into the CPU to optimize the flow of information into and out from the CPU. An IMC enables faster control over things like the large L3 cache shared among multiple cores.

Just like in so many other areas of computing, manufacturers implement a variety of IMCs in their CPUs. In practice, this means that different CPUs handle different types and capacities of RAM. I'll save the details on those RAM variations for Chapter 7. For

now, add "different RAM support" to your list of things to look at when making a CPU recommendation for a client.

Integrated Graphics Processing Unit

As you'll read about in much more detail in Chapter 21, the video processing portion of the computer—made up of the parts that put a changing image on the monitor—traditionally has a discrete microprocessor that differs in both function and architecture from the CPUs designed for general-purpose computing. The generic term for the video processor is a *graphics processing unit (GPU)*. I'll spare you the details until we get to video in Chapter 21, but it turns out that graphics processors can handle certain tasks much more efficiently than the standard CPU. Integrating a GPU into the CPU enhances the overall performance of the computer while at the same time reducing energy use, size, and cost. With the proliferation of mobile devices and portable computers today, all of these benefits have obvious merit.

Both major CPU manufacturers have released CPUs with integrated GPUs. The architecture differs in some ways, such as how they use the cache on the chip. The *Intel HD Graphics* integrated into many Core i3/i5/i7 processors, for example, has the CPU cores and the GPU core sharing the "last level cache," which is either L2 or L3, depending on the processor (see Figure 6-32). With the AMD *accelerated processing unit (APU)*, such as the AMD Fusion, the GPU has access to all levels of cache on the CPU.

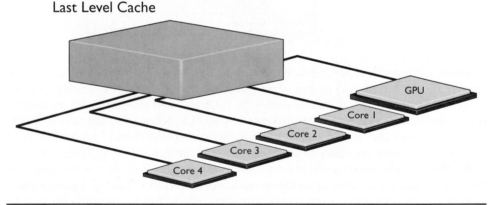

Figure 6-32 Dedicated cache (inside each core) and shared cache

NOTE One of the two major players in the performance GPU market, NVIDIA, also manufactures microprocessors that have combined CPUs and GPUs. The current offering, called the Tegra, is almost a complete computer on a single chip. You'll find it in many mobile devices (see Chapter 27 for the scoop on these delicious gadgets). NVIDIA hasn't made a push for the PC desktop market yet, although that might change with the release of their integrated microprocessor code named "Project Denver" in 2013.

Selecting, Installing, and Troubleshooting CPUs

Now that you've digested the skinny on how CPUs work, it's time to get practical. This last section discusses selecting the proper CPU, installing several types of processors, and troubleshooting the few problems techs face with CPUs.

Selecting a CPU

When selecting a CPU, you need to make certain you get one that the motherboard can accommodate. Or, if you're buying a motherboard along with the CPU, then get the right CPU for the intended purpose. Chapter 31 discusses computer roles and helps you select the proper components for each role. You need to have a lot more knowledge of all the pieces around the CPU to get the full picture, so we'll wait until then to discuss the "why" of a particular processor. Instead, this section assumes you're placing a new CPU in an already-acquired motherboard. You need to address two key points in selecting a CPU that will work. First, does the motherboard support Intel or AMD CPUs? Second, what socket does the motherboard have?

To find answers to both those questions, you have two sources: the motherboard book or manual and the manufacturer's Web site. Figure 6-33 shows a manual for an Asus motherboard open to reveal the supported processors and the socket type.

Figure 6-33
Supported processors and socket type

1.3 Special features

1.3.1 Product highlights

LGA1155 socket for Intel® Second Generation Core™ i7 / Core™ i5 / Core™ i3 Processors
This motherboard supports the Intel® second generation Core™ i7 / Core™ i5 / Core™ i3 processors in LGA1155 package with memory and PCI Express controllers integrated to support 2-channel (4 DIMMs) DDR3 memory and 16 PCI Express 2.0 lanes. This provides great graphics performance. Intel® second generation Core™ i7 / Core™ i5 / Core™ i3 processors are among the most powerful and energy efficient CPUs in the world. Refer to page 2-4 for details.

Intel® P67 Express Chipset
The Intel® P67 Express Chipset is the latest single-chipset design to support the new 1155 ... Core™ i7 / Core™ i5 / Core™ i3 second generation processors. It uses serial ... increased bandwidth and stability, and provides an improve... ... and four SATA 3.0 Gb/s ports for faster dat...

Just as Intel and AMD make many types of CPUs, motherboards are manufactured with various different types of sockets. The CompTIA A+ exams expect you to know which sockets go with which family of CPU. Table 6-2 charts the important Intel ones; Table 6-3 lists the AMD-based sockets. I would show you all the pictures, but, frankly, CPU sockets aren't the sexiest part of the computer.

EXAM TIP I've included the number of socket pins for the AMD-based sockets because related questions have been on the CompTIA A+ certifications in exam objectives prior to 801. You don't need to memorize the Intel numbers, because Intel names the sockets by the number of pins.

Socket	CPU
LGA 775[1]	Pentium 4, Celeron, Pentium 4 Extreme Edition, Core 2 Duo, Core 2 Quad, Xeon, and many others
LGA 1155[2]	Core i3/i5/i7, Pentium, Celeron, Xeon
LGA 1156[3]	Core i3/i5/i7, Pentium, Celeron, Xeon
LGA 1366[4]	Core i7, Xeon, Celeron

[1] The LGA 775 socket was the only desktop or server socket used for many years by Intel and thus just about every branded Intel CPU used it at one time or another.

[2] Socket LGA 1155 CPUs are based on Sandy Bridge or Ivy Bridge architecture.

[3] Socket LGA 1156 CPUs are based on the pre–Sandy Bridge architecture.

[4] The very first Core i7 processors used LGA 1366.

Table 6-2 Intel-based Sockets

EXAM TIP This list of Intel CPUs covers only those listed on the CompTIA A+ 801 exam objectives. The CompTIA A+ 701/702 exams mentioned a couple of other processors, such as the *Pentium Pro* (very old, 32-bit) and the *Itanium* (also old; used for servers exclusively). You might see them as incorrect answers on the 801 exam.

Socket	Pins	CPU
940[1]	940	Opteron, Athlon 64 FX
AM2[2]	940	Athlon 64, Athlon 64 X2, Athlon 64 FX, Opteron, Sempron, Phenom
AM2+[2]	940	Athlon 64, Athlon 64 X2, Athlon II, Opteron, Phenom, Phenom II
AM3[3]	941	Phenom II, Athlon II, Sempron, Opteron
AM3+[4]	942	FX
FM1	905	A[5]
F	1207	Opteron, Athlon FX

[1] You would usually find only an Opteron server-based CPU in a socket 940. The Athlon 64 FX was a super high-end CPU for the day and is very unlikely to be on the exams.

[2] AMD says that CPUs designed for AM2 sockets will work in a Socket AM2+ and vice versa, though at the slower memory movement speeds of the AM2 component (socket or CPU). Many manufacturers have not released motherboard updates that would enable support for a Socket AM2+ CPU on a Socket AM2 motherboard, thus making it impossible to upgrade just the CPU.

[3] Though the names of some of the processors designed for Socket AM3 match the names of CPUs designed for earlier sockets, they're *not* the same CPUs. They are specific to AM3 because they support different types of RAM (see Chapter 7). Just to make things even crazier, though, AM3 CPUs work just fine in Socket AM2/2+ motherboards.

[4] AMD had only released the FX-branded CPUs that use the Bulldozer core at the time of this writing. Motherboards with AM3+ sockets already available tout support for Phenom II, Athlon II, and Sempron CPUs, in addition to the FX series.

[5] The A series features integrated GPUs and other chips.

Table 6-3 AMD-based Sockets

EXAM TIP This list of AMD CPUs covers only those listed on the CompTIA A+ 801 exam objectives. As with the Intel processors, the CompTIA A+ 700-series exams mentioned a couple of other processors, such as the *Athlon XP* (old, 32-bit) and the *Duron* (also old; label used for low-end CPUs). You might see them as incorrect answers on the 801 exam.

Installation Issues

When installing a CPU, you need to use caution with the tiny pins. Plus, you must make certain that the power supply can supply enough electricity for the processor to function along with all the other components on the computer. You have to provide adequate cooling. Finally, you can decide whether to leave the CPU at stock settings or overclock it.

Socket Types

When installing a CPU, you need to exercise caution not to bend any of the tiny pins. The location of the pins differs between Intel and AMD. With Intel-based motherboards, the sockets have hundreds of tiny pins that line up with contacts on the bottom of the CPU (see Figure 6-34). Intel CPUs use a *land grid array* (*LGA*) package, where the underside of the CPU has hundreds of contact points that line up with the socket pins.

Figure 6-34
Intel-based socket
with pins

AMD CPUs have the pins (see Figure 6-35); the sockets have holes. The pins on the AMD *pin grid array* (*PGA*) CPUs align with the holes in the sockets.

Figure 6-35
AMD-based
socket without pins

All CPUs and sockets are keyed so you can't (easily) insert them incorrectly. Look at the underside of the CPU in Figure 6-36 (left). Note that the pins do not make a perfect square, because a few are missing. Now look at the top of the CPU (right). See the little mark at the corner? The socket also has tiny markings so you can line the CPU up properly with the socket.

Figure 6-36
Underside and
top of a CPU

In both socket styles, you release the retaining mechanism by pushing the little lever down slightly and then away from the socket (see Figure 6-37). You next raise the arm fully, and then move the retaining bracket (see Figure 6-38).

Figure 6-37
Moving the
release arm

Figure 6-38
Fully opened
socket

Align the processor with the socket and gently drop the processor into place. If it doesn't go in easily, check the orientation and try again. These sockets are generically called *zero insertion force (ZIF)* sockets, which means you never have to use any force at all.

Cooling

CPUs work very hard and thus require power to function. In electrical terms, CPUs consume *wattage* or *watts*, a unit of electrical power, just like a 100-watt light bulb consumes power whenever it's on. (See Chapter 10 for more details about electricity.) Have you ever touched a light bulb after it's been on for a while? Ouch! CPUs heat up, too.

To increase the capability of the CPUs to handle complex code, CPU manufacturers have added a lot of microscopic transistors over the years. The more transistors the CPU has, the more power they need and thus the hotter they get. CPUs don't tolerate heat well, and modern processors need active cooling solutions just to function at all. Almost every CPU uses a combination of a heat-sink and fan assembly to wick heat away from the CPU. Figure 6-39 shows the standard Intel heat sink and fan.

Figure 6-39
Intel OEM heat-sink and fan assembly

There was a time, long ago, when CPUs didn't need any type of cooling device. You just snapped in the CPU and it worked. Well, those days are gone. Long gone. If you're installing a modern CPU, you will have to cool it. Fortunately, you have choices.

- **OEM CPU coolers** OEM heat-sink and fan assemblies are included with a retail-boxed CPU. OEM CPUs, on the other hand, don't normally come bundled with CPU coolers. Crazy, isn't it? OEM CPU coolers have one big advantage: you know absolutely they will work with your CPU.

- **Specialized CPU coolers** Many companies sell third-party heat-sink and fan assemblies for a variety of CPUs. These usually exceed the OEM heat sinks in the amount of heat they dissipate. These CPU coolers invariably come with eye-catching designs to look really cool inside your system—some are even lighted (see Figure 6-40).

Figure 6-40
Cool retail
heat sink

The last choice is the most impressive of all: liquid cooling! *Liquid cooling* works by running some liquid—usually water—through a metal block that sits on top of your CPU, absorbing heat. The liquid gets heated by the block, runs out of the block and into something that cools the liquid, and is then pumped through the block again. Any liquid-cooling system consists of three main parts:

- A hollow metal block that sits on the CPU
- A pump to move the liquid around
- Some device to cool the liquid

And of course, you need plenty of hosing to hook them all together. Figure 6-41 shows a typical liquid-cooled CPU.

Figure 6-41
Liquid-cooled CPU

A number of companies sell these liquid-based cooling systems. Although they look impressive and certainly cool your CPU, unless you're overclocking or want a quiet system, a good fan will more than suffice.

Once you've got a heat-sink and fan assembly sorted out, you need to connect them to the motherboard. To determine the orientation of the heat-sink and fan assembly, check the power cable from the fan. Make sure it can easily reach the three- or four-wire standout on the motherboard (see Figure 6-42). If it can't, rotate the heat sink until it can. (Check the motherboard manual if you have trouble locating the CPU fan power standout.)

Figure 6-42
CPU fan power standout on motherboard

Next, before inserting the heat sink, you need to add a small amount of *thermal compound* (also called *heat dope* or *nasty silver goo*). Many heat sinks come with some thermal compound already on them; the thermal compound on these pre-doped heat sinks is covered by a small square of tape—take the tape off before you snap it to the CPU. If you need to put heat dope on from a tube, know that you need to use only a tiny amount of this compound (see Figure 6-43). Spread it on as thinly, completely, and evenly as you can. Unlike so many other things in life, you *can* have too much heat dope!

NOTE Chapter 8 goes into gory detail about the system setup utility and the area in which it stores important data (called CMOS), but invariably students want to experiment at this point, so I'll give you some information now. You can access the system setup utility by pressing some key as the computer starts up. This is during the text phase, well before it ever says anything about starting Windows. Most systems require you to press the DELETE key, but read the screen for details. Just be careful once you get into the system setup utility not to change anything you don't understand. And read Chapter 8!

Figure 6-43
Applying thermal
compound

You secure heat sinks in various ways, depending on the manufacturer. Stock Intel heat sinks have four plungers that you simply push until they click into place in corresponding holes in the motherboard. AMD stock heat sinks generally have a bracket that you secure to two points on the outside of the CPU socket and a latch that you swivel to lock it down (see Figure 6-44).

Figure 6-44
AMD OEM heat-
sink and
fan assembly

To clear the CMOS, turn off the PC. Then locate one of those tiny little plastic pieces (officially called a *shunt*) and place it over the two jumper wires for a moment. Next, restart the PC and immediately go into CMOS and restore the settings you need.

802

Troubleshooting CPUs

Troubleshooting CPU issues falls into two categories: overheating and catastrophic failures, with overheating being far more common than the latter. Once a CPU is installed properly and functioning, it rarely causes problems. The only exception is when you ask a CPU to do too much too quickly. Then you'll get a sluggish PC. The Intel Atom processor in my netbook, for example, does a great job at surfing the Web, working on e-mail, and writing stellar chapters in your favorite textbook. But if you try to play a game more advanced than Half-Life (the original, circa 1998), the machine stutters and complains and refuses to play nice.

The vast majority of problems with CPUs come from faulty installation or environmental issues that cause overheating. Very rarely will you get a catastrophic failure, but we'll look at the signs of that, too.

Symptoms of Overheating

Failure to install a CPU properly results in either nothing—that is, you push the power button and nothing at all happens—or a system lock-up in a short period of time. Because of the nature of ZIF sockets, you're almost guaranteed that the issue isn't the CPU itself, but rather the installation of the heat-sink and fan assembly. Here's a checklist of possible problems that you need to address when faced with a CPU installation problem:

1. Too much thermal paste can impede the flow of heat from the CPU to the heat sink and cause the CPU to heat up rapidly. All modern CPUs have built-in fail-safes that tell them to shut down before getting damaged by heat.

2. Not enough thermal paste or thermal paste spread unevenly can cause the CPU to heat up and consequently shut itself down.

3. Failure to connect the fan power to the motherboard can cause the CPU to heat up and shut itself down.

The fan and heat-sink installation failures can be tricky the first few times you encounter them (and yes, even the Alpha Geek has failed to install these things correctly). You might see the text from the system setup. You might even get into an installation of Windows before the crash happens. The key is that as soon as you put the CPU under load—that is, make it work for a living—it heats up beyond where the faulty heat-sink connection can dissipate the heat and then shuts down.

With a system that's been running fine for a while, environmental factors can cause problems. An air conditioning failure in my office last summer, deep in the heart of very

hot Texas, for example, caused machines throughout the office to run poorly. Some even shut down entirely. (At that point it was time to close the doors and send the staff to the beach, but that's another story.) A client called the other day to complain about his computer continuously rebooting and running slowly. When I arrived on the scene, I found a house with seven cats. Opening up his computer case revealed the hairy truth: the CPU fan was so clogged with cat hair that it barely spun at all! A quick cleaning with a computer vacuum and a can of compressed air and he was a happily computing client.

The CPU needs adequate ventilation. The CPU fan is essential, of course, but the inside of the case also needs to get hot air out through one or more exhaust fans and cool air in through the front vent. If the intake vent is clogged or the exhaust fans stop working or are blocked somehow, the inside of the case can heat up and overwhelm the CPU cooling devices. This will result in a system running slowly or spontaneously rebooting.

Catastrophic Failure

You'll know when a catastrophic error occurs. The PC will suddenly get a Blue Screen of Death (BSoD), what's technically called a Windows Stop error (see Figure 6-48). Or the entire PC will simply stop and go black, perhaps accompanied by a loud pop. The acrid smell of burnt electronics or ozone will grace your nasal passages. You might even see trails of smoke coming out of the case. You might not know immediately that the CPU has smoked, but follow your nose. Seriously. Sniff the inside of the case until you find the strongest smell. If it's the CPU, that's bad news. Whatever electrical short hit it probably caused damage to the motherboard too, and you're looking at a long day of replacement and rebuilding.

Figure 6-48
Blue Screen of
Death

```
A problem has been detected and windows has been shut down to prevent damage
to your computer.

PAGE_FAULT_IN_NONPAGED_AREA

If this is the first time you've seen this Stop error screen,
restart your computer. If this screen appears again, follow
these steps:

Check to make sure that any new hardware or software is properly installed.
If this is a new installation, ask your hardware or software manufacturer
for any windows updates you might need.

If problems continue, disable or remove any newly installed hardware
or software. Disable BIOS memory options such as caching or shadowing.
If you need to use Safe Mode to remove or disable components, restart
your computer, press F8 to select Advanced Startup Options, and then
select Safe Mode.

Technical information:

*** STOP: 0x00000050 (0x00000000,0xF866C51E,0x00000008,0xC00000000)

***     cdrom.sys - Address F866C51E base at F866A000, DateStamp 36B027B2
```

Beyond A+

Intel Atom

Intel's Atom processors are very power-efficient processors designed for applications such as ultra mobile PCs, mobile Internet devices, netbooks, and low-power desktops. The Atom range of CPUs consists of both 32-bit and 64-bit models; however, only the models aimed at the low-power desktop segment support 64-bit so far. Many Atom processors also support Hyper-Threading, and there are now several dual-core models. Figure 6-49 shows an Atom processor.

Figure 6-49
Intel Atom
processor

As of this writing, Intel Atom processors have only been released in a package that is soldered directly to the motherboard. Atom processors are manufactured using a 45-nanometer process, and many feature Intel's SpeedStep technology to further reduce their power consumption. The Atom line of processors has become extremely popular for use in netbooks, where heat and power consumption are a primary concern.

Chapter Review

Questions

1. What do registers provide for the CPU?

 A. Registers determine the clock speed.

 B. The CPU uses registers for temporary storage of internal commands and data.

 C. Registers enable the CPU to address RAM.

 D. Registers enable the CPU to control the address bus.

2. What function does the external data bus have in the PC?

 A. The external data bus determines the clock speed for the CPU.

 B. The CPU uses the external data bus to address RAM.

 C. The external data bus provides a channel for the flow of data and commands between the CPU and RAM.

 D. The CPU uses the external data bus to access registers.

3. What is the function of the address bus in the PC?

 A. The address bus enables the CPU to communicate with the memory controller chip.

 B. The address bus enables the memory controller chip to communicate with the RAM.

 C. The address bus provides a channel for the flow of data and commands between the CPU and RAM.

 D. The address bus enables the CPU to access registers.

4. Which of the following terms are measures of CPU speed?

 A. Megahertz and gigahertz

 B. Megabytes and gigabytes

 C. Megahertz and gigabytes

 D. Frontside bus, backside bus

5. Which CPU feature enables the microprocessor to support running multiple operating systems at the same time?

 A. Clock multiplying

 B. Caching

 C. Pipelining

 D. Virtualization support

6. Into which socket could you place an Intel Core i5?

 A. Socket LGA 775

 B. Socket LGA 1155

 C. Socket C

 D. Socket AM2+

7. Which feature enables a single-core CPU to function like two CPUs?

 A. Hyper-Threading

 B. SpeedStep

C. Virtualization

D. *x64*

8. What steps do you need to take to install an Athlon 64 X2 CPU into an LGA 775 motherboard?

 A. Lift the ZIF socket arm; place the CPU according to the orientation markings; snap on the heat-sink and fan assembly.

 B. Lift the ZIF socket arm; place the CPU according to the orientation markings; add a dash of heat dope; snap on the heat-sink and fan assembly.

 C. Lift the ZIF socket arm; place the CPU according to the orientation markings; snap on the heat-sink and fan assembly; plug in the fan.

 D. Take all of the steps you want to take because it's not going to work.

9. A client calls to complain that his computer starts up, but crashes when Windows starts to load. After a brief set of questions, you find out that his nephew upgraded his RAM for him over the weekend and couldn't get the computer to work right afterward. What could be the problem?

 A. Thermal compound degradation

 B. Disconnected CPU fan

 C. Bad CPU cache

 D. There's nothing wrong. It usually takes a couple of days for RAM to acclimate to the new system.

10. Darren has installed a new CPU in a client's computer, but nothing happens when he pushes the power button on the case. The LED on the motherboard is lit up, so he knows the system has power. What could the problem be?

 A. He forgot to disconnect the CPU fan.

 B. He forgot to apply thermal compound between the CPU and the heat-sink and fan assembly.

 C. He used an AMD CPU in an Intel motherboard.

 D. He used an Intel CPU in an AMD motherboard.

Answers

1. **B.** The CPU uses registers for temporary storage of internal commands and data.

2. **C.** The external data bus provides a channel for the flow of data and commands between the CPU and RAM.

3. **A.** The address bus enables the CPU to communicate with the memory controller chip.

4. **A.** The terms megahertz (MHz) and gigahertz (GHz) describe how many million or billion (respectively) cycles per second a CPU can run.

5. **D.** Intel and AMD CPUs come with virtualization support, enabling more efficient implementation of virtual machines.

6. **B.** You'll find Core i5 processors in several socket types, notably LGA 1155 and LGA 1154.

7. **A.** Intel loves its Hyper-Threading, where a single-core CPU can function like a dual-core CPU as long as it has operating system support.

8. **D.** Intel and AMD processors are not compatible at all.

9. **B.** Most likely, the nephew disconnected the CPU fan to get at the RAM slots and simply forgot to plug it back in.

10. **B.** The best answer here is that he forgot the thermal compound, though you can also make an argument for a disconnected fan.

RAM

In this chapter, you will learn how to
- Identify the different types of DRAM packaging
- Explain the varieties of RAM
- Select and install RAM
- Perform basic RAM troubleshooting

Whenever people come up to me and start professing their computer savvy, I ask them a few questions to see how much they really know. In case you and I ever meet and you decide you want to "talk tech" with me, I'll tell you my first two questions now so you'll be ready. Both involve *random access memory* (*RAM*), the working memory for the CPU.

1. "How much RAM is in your computer?"
2. "What is RAM and why is it so important that every PC has some?"

Can you answer either of these questions? Don't fret if you can't—you'll know how to answer both of them before you finish this chapter. Let's start by reviewing what you know about RAM thus far.

TIP The CompTIA A+ certification domains use the term *memory* to describe the short-term storage used by the PC to load the operating system and running applications. The more common term in the industry is *RAM*, for random access memory, the kind of short-term memory you'll find in every computer. More specifically, the primary system RAM is *dynamic random access memory (DRAM)*. For the most part, this book uses the terms RAM and DRAM.

When not in use, programs and data are held in a mass storage device such as a hard drive, USB thumb drive, optical drive, or some other device that can hold data while the computer is off. When you load a program in Windows, your PC copies the program from the mass storage device to RAM and then runs it (see Figure 7-1).

Figure 7-1 Mass storage holds programs, but programs need to run in RAM.

You saw in Chapter 6 that the CPU uses dynamic random access memory (DRAM) as RAM for all PCs. Just like CPUs, DRAM has gone through a number of evolutionary changes over the years, resulting in improved DRAM technologies such as SDRAM, RDRAM, and DDR RAM. This chapter starts by explaining how DRAM works, and then discusses the types of DRAM used over the past several years and how they improve on the original DRAM. The third section, "Working with RAM," goes into the details of finding and installing RAM. The chapter finishes with troubleshooting RAM problems.

Historical/Conceptual

Understanding DRAM

As discussed in Chapter 6, DRAM functions like an electronic spreadsheet, with numbered rows containing cells and each cell holding a one or a zero. Now let's look at what's physically happening. Each spreadsheet cell is a special type of semiconductor that can hold a single bit—one or zero—by using microscopic capacitors and transistors. DRAM makers put these semiconductors into chips that can hold a certain number of bits. The bits inside the chips are organized in a rectangular fashion, using rows and columns.

Each chip has a limit on the number of lines of code it can contain. Think of each line of code as one of the rows on the electronic spreadsheet; one chip might be able to store a million rows of code while another chip might be able to store over a billion lines. Each chip also has a limit on the width of the lines of code it can handle. One chip might handle 8-bit-wide data while another might handle 16-bit-wide data. Techs describe chips by bits rather than bytes, so they refer to *×8* and *×16*, respectively. Just as you could describe a spreadsheet by the number of rows and columns—John's accounting spreadsheet is huge, 48 rows × 12 columns—memory makers describe RAM chips the same way. An individual DRAM chip that holds 1,048,576 rows and 8 columns, for example, would be a *1M×8* chip, with "M" as shorthand for "mega," just like in megabytes (2^{20} bytes). It is difficult if not impossible to tell the size of a DRAM chip just by looking at it—only the DRAM makers know the meaning of the tiny numbers on the chips (see Figure 7-2), although sometimes you can make a good guess.

Figure 7-2
What do these
numbers mean?

Organizing DRAM

Because of its low cost, high speed, and capability to contain a lot of data in a relatively small package, DRAM has been the standard RAM used in all computers—not just PCs—since the mid-1970s. DRAM can be found in just about everything, from automobiles to automatic bread makers.

The PC has very specific requirements for DRAM. The original 8088 processor had an 8-bit frontside bus. Commands given to an 8088 processor were in discrete 8-bit chunks. You needed RAM that could store data in 8-bit (1-byte) chunks, so that each time the CPU asked for a line of code, the memory controller chip (MCC) could put an 8-bit chunk on the data bus. This optimized the flow of data into (and out from) the CPU. Although today's DRAM chips may have widths greater than 1 bit, all DRAM chips back then were 1 bit wide, meaning only sizes such as 64 K × 1 or 256 K × 1 existed—always 1 bit wide. So how was 1-bit-wide DRAM turned into 8-bit-wide memory? The solution was quite simple: just take eight 1-bit-wide chips and use the MCC to organize them electronically to be eight wide (see Figure 7-3).

Figure 7-3 The MCC accessing data on RAM soldered onto the motherboard

Practical DRAM

Okay, before you learn more about DRAM, I need to clarify a critical point. When you first saw the 8088's machine language in Chapter 6, all the examples in the "codebook" were exactly 1-byte commands. Figure 7-4 shows the codebook again—see how all the commands are 1 byte?

Figure 7-4

Codebook again

Well, the reality is slightly different. Most of the 8088 machine language commands are 1 byte, but more-complex commands need 2 bytes. For example, the following command tells the CPU to move 163 bytes "up the RAM spreadsheet" and run whatever command is there. Cool, eh?

1110100110100011

The problem here is that the command is 2 bytes wide, not 1 byte. So how did the 8088 handle this? Simple—it just took the command 1 byte at a time. It took twice as long to handle the command because the MCC had to go to RAM twice, but it worked.

So if some of the commands are more than 1 byte wide, why didn't Intel make the 8088 with a 16-bit frontside bus? Wouldn't that have been better? Well, Intel did. Intel invented a CPU called the 8086. The 8086 actually predates the 8088 and was absolutely identical to the 8088 except for one small detail: it had a 16-bit frontside bus. IBM could have used the 8086 instead of the 8088 and used 2-byte-wide RAM instead of 1-byte-wide RAM. Of course, they would have needed to invent an MMC that handled that kind of RAM (see Figure 7-5).

The Northbridge for 8086 systems could handle two rows of RAM.

Figure 7-5 Pumped-up 8086 MCC at work

Why didn't Intel sell IBM the 8086 instead of the 8088? There were two reasons. First, nobody had invented an affordable MCC or RAM that handled 2 bytes at a time. Sure, chips had been invented, but they were *expensive* and IBM didn't think anyone would want to pay $12,000 for a personal computer. So IBM bought the Intel 8088, not the Intel 8086, and all our RAM came in bytes. But as you might imagine, it didn't stay that way for long.

DRAM Sticks

As CPU data bus sizes increased, so too did the need for RAM wide enough to fill the bus. The Intel 80386 CPU, for example, had a 32-bit data bus and thus the need for 32-bit-wide DRAM. Imagine having to line up 32 one-bit-wide DRAM chips on a motherboard. Talk about a waste of space! Figure 7-6 shows motherboard RAM run amuck.

Figure 7-6 That's a lot of real estate used by RAM chips!

DRAM manufacturers responded by creating wider DRAM chips, such as ×4, ×8, and ×16, and putting multiples of them on a small circuit board called a *stick* or *module*. Figure 7-7 shows an early stick, called a *single inline memory module (SIMM)*, with eight DRAM chips. To add RAM to a modern machine, you need to get the right stick or sticks for the particular motherboard. Your motherboard manual tells you precisely what sort of module you need and how much RAM you can install.

Figure 7-7 A 72-pin SIMM

Modern CPUs are a lot smarter than the old Intel 8088. Their machine languages have some commands that are up to 64 bits (8 bytes) wide. They also have at least a 64-bit frontside bus that can handle more than just 8 bits. They don't want RAM to give them a puny 8 bits at a time! To optimize the flow of data into and out of the CPU, the modern MCC provides at least 64 bits of data every time the CPU requests information from RAM.

NOTE Some MCCs are 128 bits wide.

Modern DRAM sticks come in 32-bit- and 64-bit-wide form factors with a varying number of chips. Many techs describe these memory modules by their width, so we call them ×32 and ×64. Note that this number does *not* describe the width of the individual DRAM chips on the module. When you read or hear about *by whatever* memory, you need to know whether that person is talking about the DRAM width or the module width. When the CPU needs certain bytes of data, it requests those bytes via the address bus. The CPU does not know the physical location of the RAM that stores that data, nor the physical makeup of the RAM—such as how many DRAM chips work together to provide the 64-bit-wide memory rows. The MCC keeps track of this and just gives the CPU whichever bytes it requests (see Figure 7-8).

Figure 7-8 The MCC knows the real location of the DRAM.

Consumer RAM

If modern DRAM modules come in sizes much wider than a byte, why do people still use the word "byte" to describe how much DRAM they have? Convention. Habit. Rather than using a label that describes the electronic structure of RAM, common usage describes the *total capacity of RAM on a stick in bytes*. John has a single 2-GB stick of RAM on his motherboard, for example, and Sally has two 1-GB sticks. Both systems have a total of 2 GB of system RAM. That's what your clients care about. Having enough RAM makes their systems snappy and stable; not enough RAM means their systems run poorly. As a tech, you need to know more, of course, to pick the right RAM for many different types of computers.

801

Types of RAM

Development of newer, wider, and faster CPUs and MCCs motivate DRAM manufacturers to invent new DRAM technologies that deliver enough data at a single pop to optimize the flow of data into and out of the CPU.

SDRAM

Most modern systems use some form of *synchronous DRAM (SDRAM)*. SDRAM is still DRAM, but it is *synchronous*—tied to the system clock, just like the CPU and MCC, so the MCC knows when data is ready to be grabbed from SDRAM. This results in little wasted time.

SDRAM made its debut in 1996 on a stick called a *dual inline memory module (DIMM)*. The early SDRAM DIMMs came in a wide variety of pin sizes. The most common pin sizes found on desktops were the 168-pin variety. Laptop DIMMs came in 68-pin, 144-pin (see Figure 7-9), or 172-pin *micro-DIMM* packages; and the 72-pin, 144-pin, or 200-pin *small-outline DIMM (SO-DIMM)* form factors (see Figure 7-10). With the exception of the 32-bit 72-pin SO-DIMM, all these DIMM varieties delivered 64-bit-wide data to match the 64-bit data bus of every CPU since the Pentium.

Figure 7-9

144-pin micro-DIMM (photo courtesy of Micron Technology, Inc.)

Figure 7-10
A 168-pin DIMM
above a 144-pin
SO-DIMM

To take advantage of SDRAM, you needed a PC designed to use SDRAM. If you had a system with slots for 168-pin DIMMs, for example, your system used SDRAM. A DIMM in any one of the DIMM slots could fill the 64-bit bus, so each slot was called a *bank*. You could install one, two, or more sticks and the system would work. Note that on laptops that used the 72-pin SO-DIMM, you needed to install two sticks of RAM to make a full bank, because each stick only provided half the bus width.

SDRAM was tied to the system clock, so its clock speed matched the frontside bus. Five clock speeds were commonly used on the early SDRAM systems: 66, 75, 83, 100, and 133 MHz. The RAM speed had to match or exceed the system speed or the computer would be unstable or wouldn't work at all. These speeds were prefixed with a "PC" in the front, based on a standard forwarded by Intel, so SDRAM speeds were PC66 through PC133. For a Pentium III computer with a 100-MHz frontside bus, you needed to buy SDRAM DIMMs rated to handle it, such as PC100 or PC133.

RDRAM

When Intel was developing the Pentium 4, they knew that regular SDRAM just wasn't going to be fast enough to handle the quad-pumped 400-MHz frontside bus. Intel announced plans to replace SDRAM with a very fast, new type of RAM developed by Rambus, Inc., called *Rambus DRAM*, or simply *RDRAM* (see Figure 7-11). Hailed by Intel as the next great leap in DRAM technology, RDRAM could handle speeds up to 800 MHz, which gave Intel plenty of room to improve the Pentium 4.

Figure 7-11 RDRAM

RDRAM was greatly anticipated by the industry for years, but industry support for RDRAM proved less than enthusiastic due to significant delays in development and a price many times that of SDRAM. Despite this grudging support, almost all major PC makers sold systems that used RDRAM—for a while. From a tech's standpoint, RDRAM shares almost all of the characteristics of SDRAM. A stick of RDRAM is called a *RIMM*. In this case, however, the letters don't actually stand for anything; they just rhyme: SIMMs, DIMMs, and now RIMMs, get it?

 NOTE The 400-MHz frontside bus speed wasn't achieved by making the system clock faster—it was done by making CPUs and MCCs capable of sending 64 bits of data two or four times for every clock cycle, effectively doubling or quadrupling the system bus speed.

RIMMs came in two sizes: a 184-pin for desktops and a 160-pin SO-RIMM for laptops. RIMMs were keyed differently from DIMMs to ensure that even though they are the same basic size, you couldn't accidentally install a RIMM in a DIMM slot or vice versa. RDRAM also had a speed rating: 600 MHz, 700 MHz, 800 MHz, or 1066 MHz. RDRAM employed an interesting *dual-channel architecture*. Each RIMM was 64 bits wide, but the Rambus MCC alternated between two sticks to increase the speed of data retrieval. You were required to install RIMMs in pairs to use this dual-channel architecture.

RDRAM motherboards also required that all RIMM slots be populated. Unused pairs of slots needed a passive device called a *continuity RIMM (CRIMM)* installed in each slot to enable the RDRAM system to terminate properly. Figure 7-12 shows a CRIMM.

Figure 7-12 CRIMM

RDRAM offered dramatic possibilities for high-speed PCs but ran into three roadblocks that Betamaxed it. First, the technology was owned wholly by Rambus; if you wanted to make it, you had to pay the licensing fees they charged. That led directly to the second problem, expense. RDRAM cost substantially more than SDRAM. Third, Rambus and Intel made a completely closed deal for the technology. RDRAM worked only on Pentium 4 systems using Intel-made MCCs. AMD was out of luck. Clearly, the rest of the industry had to look for another high-speed RAM solution.

 TIP On the CompTIA A+ exams, you'll see RDRAM referred to as RAMBUS RAM. Don't get thrown by the odd usage.

NOTE "Betamaxed" is slang for "made it obsolete because no one bought it, even though it was a superior technology to the winner in the marketplace." It refers to the VHS versus Betamax wars in the old days of video cassette recorders.

DDR SDRAM

AMD and many major system and memory makers threw their support behind *double data rate SDRAM (DDR SDRAM)*. DDR SDRAM basically copied Rambus, doubling the throughput of SDRAM by making two processes for every clock cycle. This synchronized (pardon the pun) nicely with the Athlon and later AMD processors' double-pumped frontside bus. DDR SDRAM could not run as fast as RDRAM—although relatively low frontside bus speeds made that a moot point—but cost only slightly more than regular SDRAM.

DDR SDRAM for desktops comes in 184-pin DIMMs. These DIMMs match 168-pin DIMMs in physical size but not in pin compatibility (see Figure 7-13). The slots for the two types of RAM appear similar as well but have different guide notches, so you can't insert either type of RAM into the other's slot. DDR SDRAM for laptops comes in either 200-pin SO-DIMMs or 172-pin micro-DIMMs (see Figure 7-14).

Figure 7-13 DDR SDRAM

Figure 7-14
172-pin DDR
SDRAM micro-
DIMM (photo
courtesy of Kings-
ton/Joint Harvest)

NOTE Most techs drop some or all of the SDRAM part of DDR SDRAM when engaged in normal geekspeak. You'll hear the memory referred to as DDR, DDR RAM, and the weird hybrid, DDRAM. RAM makers use the term *single data rate SDRAM (SDR SDRAM)* for the original SDRAM to differentiate it from DDR SDRAM.

DDR sticks use a rather interesting naming convention—actually started by the Rambus folks—based on the number of bytes per second of data throughput the RAM can handle. To determine the bytes per second, take the MHz speed and multiply by 8 bytes (the width of all DDR SDRAM sticks). So 400 MHz multiplied by 8 is 3200 megabytes per second (MBps). Put the abbreviation "PC" in the front to make the new term: PC3200. Many techs also use the naming convention used for the individual DDR chips; for example, *DDR400* refers to a 400-MHz DDR SDRAM chip running on a 200-MHz clock.

Even though the term DDR*xxx* is really just for individual DDR chips and the term PC*xxxx* is for DDR sticks, this tradition of two names for every speed of RAM is a bit of a challenge because you'll often hear both terms used interchangeably. Table 7-1 shows all the speeds for DDR—not all of these are commonly used.

Clock Speed	DDR Speed Rating	PC Speed Rating
100 MHz	DDR200	PC1600
133 MHz	DDR266	PC2100
166 MHz	DDR333	PC2700
200 MHz	DDR400	PC3200
217 MHz	DDR433	PC3500
233 MHz	DDR466	PC3700
250 MHz	DDR500	PC4000
275 MHz	DDR550	PC4400
300 MHz	DDR600	PC4800

Table 7-1 DDR Speeds

Following the lead of AMD, VIA, and other manufacturers, the PC industry adopted DDR SDRAM as the standard system RAM. In the summer of 2003, Intel relented and stopped producing motherboards and memory controllers that required RDRAM.

One thing is sure about PC technologies: any good idea that can be copied will be copied. One of Rambus' best concepts was the dual-channel architecture—using two sticks of RDRAM together to increase throughput. Manufacturers have released motherboards with MCCs that support dual-channel architecture using DDR SDRAM. Dual-channel DDR motherboards use regular DDR sticks, although manufacturers often sell RAM in matched pairs, branding them as dual-channel RAM.

Dual-channel DDR works like RDRAM in that you must have two identical sticks of DDR and they must snap into two paired slots. Unlike RDRAM, dual-channel DDR doesn't have anything like CRIMMs—you don't need to put anything into unused slot pairs. Dual-channel DDR technology is very flexible but also has a few quirks that vary with each system. Some motherboards have three DDR SDRAM slots, but the dual-channel DDR works only if you install DDR SDRAM in two of the slots. Other boards have four slots and require that you install matching pairs in the same-colored slots to run in dual-channel mode (see Figure 7-15). If you populate a third slot, the system uses the full capacity of RAM installed but turns off the dual-channel feature.

Figure 7-15 A motherboard showing the four RAM slots. By populating the same-colored slots with identical RAM, you can run in dual-channel mode.

DDR2

The fastest versions of DDR RAM run at a blistering PC4800. That's 4.8 gigabytes per second (GBps) of data throughput! You'd think that kind of speed would satisfy most users, and to be honest, DRAM running at approximately 5 GBps really is plenty fast—for yesterday. However, the ongoing speed increases ensure that even these speeds won't be good enough in the future. Knowing this, the RAM industry came out with DDR2, the successor to DDR. *DDR2* is DDR RAM with some improvements in its electrical characteristics, enabling it to run even faster than DDR while using less power. The big speed increase from DDR2 comes by clock doubling the input/output circuits on the chips. This does not speed up the core RAM—the part that holds the data—but speeding up the input/output and adding special buffers (sort of like a cache) makes DDR2 run much faster than regular DDR. DDR2 uses a 240-pin DIMM that's not compatible with DDR (see Figure 7-16). Likewise, the DDR2 200-pin SO-DIMM is incompatible with the DDR SO-DIMM. You'll find motherboards running both single-channel and dual-channel DDR2.

Figure 7-16 240-pin DDR2 DIMM

TIP DDR2 RAM sticks will not fit into DDR sockets, nor are they electronically compatible.

Table 7-2 shows some of the common DDR2 speeds.

Core RAM Clock Speed	DDR I/O Speed	DDR2 Speed Rating	PC Speed Rating
100 MHz	200 MHz	DDR2-400	PC2-3200
133 MHz	266 MHz	DDR2-533	PC2-4200
166 MHz	333 MHz	DDR2-667	PC2-5300
200 MHz	400 MHz	DDR2-800	PC2-6400
250 MHz	500 MHz	DDR2-1000	PC2-8000

Table 7-2 DDR2 Speeds

DDR3

DDR3 boasts higher speeds, more efficient architecture, and around 30 percent lower power consumption than DDR2 RAM, making it a compelling choice for system builders. Just like its predecessor, DDR3 uses a 240-pin DIMM, albeit one that is slotted differently to make it difficult for users to install the wrong RAM in their system without using a hammer (see Figure 7-17). DDR3 SODIMMs for portable computers have 204 pins. Neither fits into a DDR2 socket.

Figure 7-17
DDR2 DIMM on top of a DDR3 DIMM

NOTE Do not confuse DDR3 with GDDR3; the latter is a type of memory used solely in video cards. See Chapter 21 for the scoop on video-specific types of memory.

DDR3 doubles the buffer of DDR2 from 4 bits to 8 bits, giving it a huge boost in bandwidth over older RAM. Not only that, but some DDR3 modules also include a feature called *XMP*, or *extended memory profile*, that enables power users to overclock their RAM easily, boosting their already fast memory to speeds that would make Chuck Yeager nervous. DDR3 modules also use higher-density memory chips, which means we may eventually see 16-GB DDR3 modules.

Some chipsets that support DDR3 also support a feature called *triple-channel memory*, which works a lot like dual-channel before it, but with three sticks of RAM instead of two. Intel's LGA 1366 platform supports triple-channel memory; no AMD processors support a triple-channel feature. You'll need three of the same type of memory modules and a motherboard that supports it, but triple-channel memory can greatly increase performance for those who can afford it.

NOTE Quad-channel memory also exists, but as of 2012, you'll only find it in servers.

In keeping with established tradition, Table 7-3 is a chart of common DDR3 speeds. Note how DDR3 I/O speeds are quadruple the clock speeds, whereas DDR2 I/O speeds are only double the clock. This speed increase is due to the increased buffer size, which enables DDR3 to grab twice as much data every clock cycle as DDR2 can.

Core RAM Clock Speed	DDR I/O Speed	DDR3 Speed Rating	PC Speed Rating
100 MHz	400 MHz	DDR3-800	PC3-6400
133 MHz	533 MHz	DDR3-1066	PC3-8500
166 MHz	667 MHz	DDR3-1333	PC3-10667
200 MHz	800 MHz	DDR3-1600	PC3-12800
233 MHz	933 MHz	DDR3-1866	PC3-14900
266 MHz	1066 MHz	DDR3-2133	PC3-17000

Table 7-3 DDR3 Speeds

RAM Variations

Within each class of RAM, you'll find variations in packaging, speed, quality, and the capability to handle data with more or fewer errors. Higher-end systems often need higher-end RAM, so knowing these variations is of crucial importance to techs.

Double-Sided DIMMs

Every type of RAM stick, starting with the old FPM SIMMs and continuing through to 240-pin DDR3 SDRAM, comes in one of two types: *single-sided RAM* and *double-sided RAM*. As their name implies, single-sided sticks have chips on only one side of the stick. Double-sided sticks have chips on both sides (see Figure 7-18). The vast majority of RAM sticks are single-sided, but plenty of double-sided sticks are out there. Double-sided sticks are basically two sticks of RAM soldered onto one board. There's nothing wrong with double-sided RAM sticks other than the fact that some motherboards either can't use them or can only use them in certain ways—for example, only if you use a single stick and it goes into a certain slot.

Figure 7-18 Double-sided DDR SDRAM

Latency

If you've shopped for RAM lately, you may have noticed terms such as "CL2" or "low latency" as you tried to determine which RAM to purchase. You might find two otherwise identical RAM sticks with a 20 percent price difference and a salesperson pressuring you to buy the more expensive one because it's "faster" even though both sticks say DDR 3200 (see Figure 7-19).

use ECC. Only expensive motherboards for high-end systems use ECC. The special-use-only nature of ECC makes it fairly rare. Plenty of techs with years of experience have never even seen ECC RAM.

NOTE Some memory manufacturers call the technology *error checking and correction (ECC)*. Don't be thrown off if you see the phrase—it's the same thing, just a different marketing slant for error correction code.

Working with RAM

Whenever someone comes up to me and asks what single hardware upgrade they can do to improve their system performance, I always tell them the same thing—add more RAM. Adding more RAM can improve overall system performance, processing speed, and stability—if you get it right. Botching the job can cause dramatic system instability, such as frequent, random crashes and reboots. Every tech needs to know how to install and upgrade system RAM of all types.

To get the desired results from a RAM upgrade, you must first determine if insufficient RAM is the cause of system problems. Second, you need to pick the proper RAM for the system. Finally, you must use good installation practices. Always store RAM sticks in anti-static packaging whenever they're not in use, and use strict ESD handling procedures. Like many other pieces of the PC, RAM is *very* sensitive to ESD and other technician abuse (see Figure 7-21).

Figure 7-21 Don't do this! Grabbing the contacts is a bad idea!

Do You Need More RAM?

Two symptoms point to the need for more RAM in a PC: general system sluggishness and excessive hard drive accessing. If programs take forever to load and running programs seem to stall and move more slowly than you would like, the problem could stem from insufficient RAM. A friend with a Windows Vista system complained that her PC seemed snappy when she first got it but now takes a long time to do the things she wants to do with it, such as photograph retouching in Adobe Photoshop and document layout for an online magazine she produces. Her system had only 1 GB of RAM, sufficient to run Windows Vista, but woefully insufficient for her tasks—she kept maxing out the RAM and thus the system slowed to a crawl. I replaced her stick with a pair of 2-GB sticks and suddenly she had the powerhouse workstation she desired.

Excessive hard drive activity when you move between programs points to a need for more RAM. Every Windows PC has the capability to make a portion of your hard drive look like RAM in case you run out of real RAM.

Page File

Windows uses a portion of the hard drive as an extension of system RAM, through what's called a *RAM cache*. A RAM cache is a block of cylinders on a hard drive set aside as what's called a *page file*, *swap file*, or *virtual memory*. When the PC starts running out of real RAM because you've loaded too many programs, the system swaps programs from RAM to the page file, opening more space for programs currently active. All versions of Windows use a page file, so here's how one works.

EXAM TIP The default and recommended page-file size is 1.5 times the amount of installed RAM on your computer.

Let's assume you have a PC with 4 GB of RAM. Figure 7-22 shows the system RAM as a thermometer with gradients from 0 to 4 GB. As programs load, they take up RAM, and as more and more programs are loaded (labeled A, B, and C in the figure), more RAM is used.

Figure 7-22 A RAM thermometer showing that more programs take more RAM

At a certain point, you won't have enough RAM to run any more programs (see Figure 7-23). Sure, you could close one or more programs to make room for yet another one, but you can't keep all of the programs running simultaneously. This is where virtual memory comes into play.

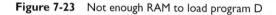

Figure 7-23 Not enough RAM to load program D

Windows' virtual memory starts by creating a page file that resides somewhere on your hard drive. The page file works like a temporary storage box. Windows removes running programs temporarily from RAM into the page file so other programs can load and run. If you have enough RAM to run all your programs, Windows does not need to use the page file—Windows brings the page file into play only when insufficient RAM is available to run all open programs.

NOTE Virtual memory is a fully automated process and does not require any user intervention. Tech intervention is another story!

To load, Program D needs a certain amount of free RAM. Clearly, this requires unloading some other program (or programs) from RAM without actually closing any programs. Windows looks at all running programs—in this case A, B, and C—and decides which program is the least used. That program is then cut out of or swapped from RAM and copied into the page file. In this case, Windows has chosen Program B (see Figure 7-24). Unloading Program B from RAM provides enough RAM to load Program D (see Figure 7-25).

Figure 7-24 Program B being unloaded from memory

Figure 7-25 Program B stored in the page file, making room for Program D

It is important to understand that none of this activity is visible on the screen. Program B's window is still visible, along with those of all the other running programs. Nothing tells the user that Program B is no longer in RAM (see Figure 7-26).

Figure 7-26

You can't tell whether a program is swapped or not.

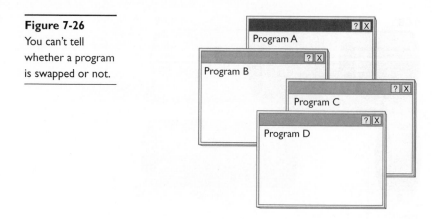

So what happens if you click on Program B's window to bring it to the front? The program can't actually run from the page file; it must be loaded back into RAM. First, Windows decides which program must be removed from RAM, and this time Windows chooses Program C (see Figure 7-27). Then it loads Program B into RAM (see Figure 7-28).

Figure 7-27 Program C is swapped to the page file.

Swapping programs to and from the page file and RAM takes time. Although no visual clues suggest that a swap is taking place, the machine slows down quite noticeably as Windows performs the swaps. Page files are a crucial aspect of Windows operation.

Windows handles page files automatically, but occasionally you'll run into problems and need to change the size of the page file or delete it and let Windows re-create it automatically. The page file is PAGEFILE.SYS. You can often find it in the root directory of the C: drive, but again, that can be changed. Wherever it is, the page file is a hidden system file, which means in practice that you'll have to play with your folder-viewing options to see it.

Page file

Figure 7-28 Program B is swapped back into RAM.

NOTE If you have a second hard drive installed in your PC, you can often get a nice performance boost by moving your page file from the C drive (the default) to the second drive. To move your page file in all versions of Windows, open the System Control Panel applet and select the Advanced tab in Windows XP or Advanced system settings menu in Windows Vista/7. This opens the System Properties dialog box. In the Performance section of the Advanced tab, click the Settings button to open the Performance Options dialog box. Select the Advanced tab, and then click the Change button in the Virtual memory section. In the Virtual Memory dialog box, select a drive from the list and give it a size or range, and you're ready to go.

Just don't turn virtual memory off completely. Although Windows can run without virtual memory, you will definitely take a performance hit.

If Windows needs to access the page file too frequently, you will notice the hard drive access LED going crazy as Windows rushes to move programs between RAM and the page file in a process called *disk thrashing*. Windows uses the page file all the time, but excessive disk thrashing suggests that you need more RAM.

You can diagnose excessive disk thrashing through simply observing the hard drive access LED flashing or through various third-party tools. I like FreeMeter (www.tiler.com/freemeter/). It's been around for quite a while, runs on all versions of Windows, and is easy to use (see Figure 7-29). Notice on the FreeMeter screenshot that some amount of the page file is being used. That's perfectly normal.

Figure 7-29
FreeMeter

System RAM Recommendations

Microsoft sets very low the minimum RAM requirements listed for the various Windows operating systems to get the maximum number of users to upgrade or convert, and that's fine. A Windows XP Professional machine runs well enough on 128 MB of RAM. Just don't ask it to do any serious computing, such as running Crysis 2! Windows Vista and Windows 7 raised the bar considerably, especially with the 64-bit versions of the operating system. Table 7-4 lists my recommendations for system RAM.

Operating System	Minimum System Requirements	Reasonable Minimum	Solid Performance	Power User
Windows XP	64 MB	256 MB	I GB	2 GB
Windows Vista	I GB (32-bit), 2 GB (64-bit)	2 GB	4 GB	8 GB
Windows 7	I GB (32-bit), 2 GB (64-bit)	2 GB	4 GB	8 GB

Table 7-4 Windows RAM Recommendations

Determining Current RAM Capacity

Before you go get RAM, you obviously need to know how much RAM you currently have in your PC. Windows displays this amount in the System Control Panel applet (see Figure 7-30). You can also access the screen with the WINDOWS-PAUSE/BREAK keystroke combination.

Figure 7-30 Mike has a lot of RAM!

Windows also includes the handy Performance tab in the Task Manager (as shown in Figure 7-31). The Performance tab includes a lot of information about the amount of RAM being used by your PC. Access the Task Manager by pressing CTRL-SHIFT-ESC and selecting the Performance tab.

Figure 7-31
Performance tab
in Windows 7
Task Manager

ReadyBoost

Windows Vista and Windows 7 offer a feature called *ReadyBoost* that enables you to use flash media devices—removable USB thumb drives or memory cards—as super fast, dedicated virtual memory. The performance gain over using only a typical hard drive for virtual memory can be significant with ReadyBoost because read/write speeds on flash memory blow hard drive read/write speeds away. Plus, the added ReadyBoost device or devices means Windows has multiple sources of virtual memory that it can use at the same time.

Windows 7 can handle up to eight flash devices, whereas Windows Vista can benefit from only one device. Devices can be between 1–32 GB in capacity. The flash device's file system matters in terms of how much memory Windows can use. Typically, the most you'll get out of a flash drive is 4 GB without manually changing the file system. Finally, Microsoft recommends using 1–3× the amount of system RAM for the Ready-Boost drives or devices to get optimal performance.

 NOTE See Chapter 12 on file systems for the differences between FAT, FAT32, NTFS, and exFAT.

Plug a ReadyBoost-approved device into a USB port or built-in flash memory card reader slot. Right-click the device in Computer and select Properties. Click the Ready-Boost tab and select the radio button next to either *Dedicate this device to ReadyBoost* or *Use this device* (see Figure 7-32). Click Apply to enhance your system's performance.

Figure 7-32
Dedicating a flash drive to Ready-Boost to enhance system performance

Getting the Right RAM

To do the perfect RAM upgrade, determine the optimum capacity of RAM to install and then get the right RAM for the motherboard. Your first two stops toward these goals are the inside of the case and your motherboard manual. Open the case to see how many sticks of RAM you have installed currently and how many free slots you have open.

Check the motherboard book to determine the total capacity of RAM the system can handle and what specific technology works with your system.

You can't put DDR2 into a system that can only handle DDR SDRAM, after all, and it won't do you much good to install a pair of 2-GB DIMMs when your system tops out at 1.5 GB. Figure 7-33 shows the RAM limits for my ASUS Crosshair motherboard.

Figure 7-33
The motherboard book shows how much RAM the motherboard will handle.

Crosshair specifications summary

CPU	Support AMD® Socket AM2 Athlon 64 X2 / Athlon 64 FX / Athlon 64/ Sempron AMD Cool 'n' Quiet™ Technology AMD64 architecture enables simultaneous 32-bit and 64-bit computing AMD Live!™ Ready
Chipset	NVIDIA nForce® 590 SLI™ MCP NVIDIA LinkBoost™ Technology
System bus	2000 / 1600 MT/s
Memory	Dual channel memory architecture 4 x DIMM, max. 8GB, DDR2-800/667/533, ECC and non-ECC, un-buffered memory
Expansion slots	2 x PCI Express x16 slot with NVIDIA® SLI™ technology support, at full x16, x16 speed 1 x PCI Express x4 3 x PCI 2.2
Scalable Link Interface (SLI™)	Support two identical NVIDIA SLI-Ready graphics cards (both at x16 mode) ASUS two-slot thermal design ASUS PEG Link
High Definition Audio	SupremeFX Audio Card featuring ADI 1988B 8-channel High Definition Audio CODEC Support Jack-Sensing, Enumeration, Multi-streaming and Jack-Retasking 8 channel audio ports Coaxial, Optical S/PDIF out on back I/O port * ASUS Array Mic * Noise Filter
Storage	NVIDIA nForce® 590 SLI™ MCP supports: * 1 x Ultra DMA 133 / 100 / 66 / 33 * 6 x Serial ATA 3.0Gb/s with NCQ * NVIDIA MediaShield™ RAID supports RAID 0, 1, 0+1, 5 and JBOD span cross Serial ATA drives Silicon Image® 3132 SATA controller supports: * 2 x External Serial ATA 3.0Gb/s port on back I/O (SATA On-the-Go) * Support RAID 0, 1, JBOD, RAID 0+1(10) and 5 through multiplier

TIP The freeware CPU-Z program tells you the total number of slots on your motherboard, the number of slots used, and the exact type of RAM in each slot—very handy. CPU-Z not only determines the latency of your RAM but also lists the latency at a variety of motherboard speeds. The media accompanying this book has a copy of CPU-Z, so check it out.

Mix and Match at Your Peril

All motherboards can handle different capacities of RAM. If you have three slots, you may put a 512-MB stick in one and a 1-GB stick in the other with a high chance of success. To ensure maximum stability in a system, however, shoot for as close as you can get to uniformity of RAM. Choose RAM sticks that match in technology, capacity, and speed.

Mixing Speeds

With so many different DRAM speeds available, you may often find yourself tempted to mix speeds of DRAM in the same system. Although you may get away with mixing speeds on a system, the safest, easiest rule to follow is to use the speed of DRAM specified in the motherboard book, and make sure that every piece of DRAM runs at that speed. In a worst-case scenario, mixing DRAM speeds can cause the system to lock up every few seconds or every few minutes. You might also get some data corruption. Mixing speeds sometimes works fine, but don't do your tax return on a machine with mixed DRAM speeds until the system has proven to be stable for a few days. The important thing to note here is that you won't break anything, other than possibly data, by experimenting.

Okay, I have mentioned enough disclaimers. Modern motherboards provide some flexibility regarding RAM speeds and mixing. First, you can use RAM that is faster than the motherboard specifies. For example, if the system needs PC3200 DDR2 SDRAM, you may put in PC4200 DDR2 SDRAM and it should work fine. Faster DRAM is not going to make the system run any faster, however, so don't look for any system improvement.

Second, you can sometimes get away with putting one speed of DRAM in one bank and another speed in another bank, as long as all the speeds are as fast as or faster than the speed specified by the motherboard. Don't bother trying to put different-speed DRAM sticks in the same bank with a motherboard that uses dual-channel DDR.

Installing DIMMs and RIMMs

Installing DRAM is so easy that it's one of the very few jobs I recommend to non-techie folks. First, attach an anti-static wrist strap or touch some bare metal on the power supply to ground yourself and avoid ESD. Then swing the side tabs on the RAM slots down from the upright position. Pick up a stick of RAM—don't touch those contacts—and line up the notch or notches with the raised portion(s) of the DIMM socket (see Figure 7-34). A good hard push down is usually all you need to ensure a solid connection. Make sure that the DIMM snaps into position to show it is completely seated. Also, notice that the two side tabs move in to reflect a tight connection.

Figure 7-34 Inserting a DIMM

Serial Presence Detect (SPD)

Your motherboard should detect and automatically set up any DIMM or RIMM you install, assuming you have the right RAM for the system, using a technology called *serial presence detect (SPD)*. RAM makers add a handy chip to modern sticks called the SPD chip (see Figure 7-35). The SPD chip stores all the information about your DRAM, including size, speed, ECC or non-ECC, registered or unregistered, and a number of other more technical bits of information.

Figure 7-35 SPD chip on a stick

When a PC boots, it queries the SPD chip so that the MCC knows how much RAM is on the stick, how fast it runs, and other information. Any program can query the SPD chip. Take a look at Figure 7-36 with the results of the popular CPU-Z program showing RAM information from the SPD chip.

Figure 7-36 CPU-Z showing RAM information

All new systems count on SPD to set the RAM timings properly for your system when it boots. If you add a RAM stick with a bad SPD chip, you'll get a POST error message and the system will not boot. You can't fix a broken SPD chip; you just buy a new stick of RAM.

The RAM Count

After installing the new RAM, turn on the PC and watch the boot process closely. If you installed the RAM correctly, the RAM count on the PC reflects the new value (compare Figures 7.37 and 7.38). If the RAM value stays the same, you probably have installed the RAM in a slot the motherboard doesn't want you to use (for example, you may need to use a particular slot first) or have not installed the RAM properly. If the computer does not boot and you've got a blank screen, you probably have not installed all the RAM sticks correctly. Usually, a good second look is all you need to determine the problem. Reseat or reinstall the RAM stick and try again. RAM counts are confusing because RAM uses megabytes and gigabytes as opposed to millions and billions. Here are some examples of how different systems would show 256 MB of RAM:

268435456 (exactly 256 × 1MB)

256M (some PCs try to make it easy for you)

262,144 (number of KB)

Figure 7-37

Hey, where's the rest of my RAM?!

```
Award Modular BIOS v6.00PG, An Energy Star Ally
Copyright (C) 1984-2005, Award Software, Inc.

GA-K8NP F13

Processor : AMD Athlon(tm) 64 Processor 3200+
<CPUID:0000F4A Patch ID:003A>
Memory Testing : 1048576K OK   ◄─────────────
CPU clock frequency : 200 Mhz

Detecting IDE drives ...
```

Figure 7-38

RAM count after proper insertion of DIMMs

```
Award Modular BIOS v6.00PG, An Energy Star Ally
Copyright (C) 1984-2005, Award Software, Inc.

GA-K8NP F13

Processor : AMD Athlon(tm) 64 Processor 3200+
<CPUID:0000F4A Patch ID:003A>
Memory Testing : 3145728K OK
CPU clock frequency : 200 Mhz

Detecting IDE drives ...
```

You should know how much RAM you're trying to install and use some common sense. If you have 512 MB and you add another 512-MB stick, you should end up with a gigabyte of RAM. If you still see a RAM count of 524582912 after you add the second stick, something went wrong!

Installing SO-DIMMs in Laptops

It wasn't that long ago that adding RAM to a laptop was either impossible or required you to send the system back to the manufacturer. For years, every laptop maker had custom-made, proprietary RAM packages that were difficult to handle and staggeringly expensive. The wide acceptance of SO-DIMMs over the past few years has virtually erased these problems. All laptops now provide relatively convenient access to their SO-DIMMs, enabling easy replacement or addition of RAM.

Access to RAM usually requires removing a panel or lifting up the keyboard—the procedure varies among laptop manufacturers. Figure 7-39 shows a typical laptop RAM access panel. You can slide the panel off to reveal the SO-DIMMs. SO-DIMMs usually insert exactly like the old SIMMs; slide the pins into position and snap the SO-DIMM down into the retaining clips (see Figure 7-40).

Figure 7-39 A RAM access panel on a laptop

Figure 7-40 Snapping in a SO-DIMM

Before doing any work on a laptop, turn the system off, disconnect it from the AC wall socket, and remove all batteries. Use an anti-static wrist strap because laptops are far more susceptible to ESD than desktop PCs.

802

Troubleshooting RAM

"Memory" errors show up in a variety of ways on modern systems, including parity errors, ECC error messages, system lockups, page faults, and other error screens in Windows. These errors can indicate bad RAM but often point to something completely unrelated. This is especially true with intermittent problems. Techs need to recognize these errors and determine which part of the system caused the memory error.

You can get two radically different types of parity errors: real and phantom. *Real parity errors* are simply errors that the MCC detects from the parity or ECC chips (if you have them). The operating system then reports the problem in an error message, such as "Parity error at *xxxx:xxxxxxxx*," where *xxxx:xxxxxxxx* is a hexadecimal value (a string of numbers and letters, such as A5F2:004EEAB9). If you get an error like this, write down the value (see Figure 7-41). A real parity/ECC error shows up at the same place in memory each time and almost always indicates that you have a bad RAM stick.

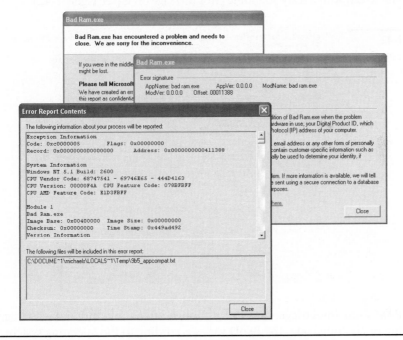

Figure 7-41 Windows error message

Phantom parity errors show up on systems that don't have parity or ECC memory. If Windows generates parity errors with different addresses, you most likely do *not* have a

problem with RAM. These phantom errors can occur for a variety of reasons, including software problems, heat or dust, solar flares, fluctuations in the Force…you get the idea.

System lockups and page faults (they often go hand in hand) in Windows can indicate a problem with RAM. A system lockup is when the computer stops functioning. A *page fault* is a milder error that can be caused by memory issues but not necessarily system RAM problems. Certainly page faults *look* like RAM issues because Windows generates frightening error messages filled with long strings of hexadecimal digits, such as "KRNL386 caused a page fault at 03F2:25A003BC." Just because the error message contains a memory address, however, does not mean that you have a problem with your RAM. Write down the address. If it repeats in later error messages, you probably have a bad RAM stick. If Windows displays different memory locations, you need to look elsewhere for the culprit.

Every once in a while, something potentially catastrophic happens within the PC, some little electron hits the big red panic button, and the operating system has to shut down certain functions before it can save data. This panic button inside the PC is called a *non-maskable interrupt (NMI)*, more simply defined as an interruption the CPU cannot ignore. An NMI manifests to the user as what techs lovingly call the *Blue Screen of Death (BSoD)*—a bright blue screen with a scary-sounding error message on it (see Figure 7-42).

Figure 7-42
Blue Screen
of Death

```
A problem has been detected and windows has been shut down to prevent damage
to your computer.

The problem seems to be caused by the following file: SPCMDCON.SYS

PAGE_FAULT_IN_NONPAGED_AREA

If this is the first time you've seen this stop error screen,
restart your computer. If this screen appears again, follow
these steps:

Check to make sure any new hardware or software is properly installed.
If this is a new installation, ask your hardware or software manufacturer
for any windows updates you might need.

If problems continue, disable or remove any newly installed hardware
or software. Disable BIOS memory options such as caching or shadowing.
If you need to use Safe Mode to remove or disable components, restart
your computer, press F8 to select Advanced Startup Options, and then
select Safe Mode.

Technical information:

*** STOP: 0x00000050 (0xFD3094C2,0x00000001,0xFBFE7617,0x00000000)

*** SPCMDCON.SYS - Address FBFE7617 base at FBFE5000, DateStamp 3d6dd67c
```

Bad RAM sometimes triggers an NMI, although often the culprit lies with buggy programming or clashing code. The BSoD varies according to the operating system, and it would require a much lengthier tome than this one to cover all the variations. Suffice it to say that RAM *could* be the problem when that delightful blue screen appears.

Finally, intermittent memory errors can come from a variety of sources, including a dying power supply, electrical interference, buggy applications, buggy hardware, and so on. These errors show up as lockups, general protection faults, page faults, and parity

errors, but they never have the same address or happen with the same applications. I always check the power supply first.

Testing RAM

Once you discover that you may have a RAM problem, you have a couple of options. First, several companies manufacture hardware RAM-testing devices, but unless you have a lot of disposable income, they're probably priced way too high for the average tech ($1,500 and higher). Second, you can use the method I use—*replace and pray*. Open the system case and replace each stick, one at a time, with a known good replacement stick. (You have one of those lying around, don't you?) This method, although potentially time-consuming, certainly works. With PC prices as low as they are now, you could simply replace the whole system for less than the price of a dedicated RAM tester.

Third, you could run a software-based tester on the RAM. Because you have to load a software tester into the memory it's about to scan, there's always a small chance that simply starting the software RAM tester might cause an error. Still, you can find some pretty good free ones out there. Windows 7 includes the Memory Diagnostics Tool, which can automatically scan your computer's RAM when you encounter a problem. If you're using another OS, my favorite tool is the venerable Memtest86 written by Mr. Chris Brady (www.memtest86.com). Memtest86 exhaustively checks your RAM and reports bad RAM when it finds it (see Figure 7-43).

```
    Memtest86  v1.65     | Pass 11% ####
Athlon 64 (0.09) 2009 MHz | Test 12% ####
L1 Cache:  128K 16468MB/s | Test #4  [Moving inversions, random pattern]
L2 Cache:  512K 16468MB/s | Testing:  100K -  256M  256M
Memory  :  256M 11224MB/s | Pattern:   94a989c0
Chipset : Intel i440BX

WallTime  Cached  RsvdMem  MemMap  Cache  ECC  Test  Pass  Errors ECC Errs
--------  ------  -------  ------  -----  ---  ----  ----  ------ --------
  0:00:05   256M    216K  e820-Std   on  off   Std    0      0

(ESC)Reboot  (c)configuration  (SP)scroll_lock  (CR)scroll_unlock
```

Figure 7-43 Memtest86 in action

NOTE A *general protection fault (GPF)* is an error that can cause an application to crash. Often GPFs are caused by programs stepping on each other's toes. Chapter 19 goes into more detail on GPFs and other Windows errors.

Talking to the Keyboard

The keyboard provides a great example of how the buses and support programming help the CPU get the job done. In early computers, the keyboard connected to the external data bus via a special chip known as the *keyboard controller*. Don't bother looking for this chip on your motherboard—the Southbridge now handles keyboard controller functions. The way the keyboard controller—or technically, the keyboard controller *circuitry*—works with the CPU, however, has changed only a small amount in the past 25+ years, making it a perfect tool to illustrate how the CPU talks to a device.

NOTE Techs commonly talk about various functions of the chipset as if those functions were still handled by discrete chips. So you'll hear about memory controllers, keyboard controllers, mouse controllers, USB controllers, and so on, even though they're all just circuits on the Northbridge or Southbridge.

The keyboard controller was one of the last single-function chips to be absorbed into the chipset. For many years—in fact, well into the Pentium III/Early Athlon era—most motherboards had separate keyboard controller chips. Figure 8-4 shows a typical keyboard controller from those days. Electronically, it looked like Figure 8-5.

Figure 8-4
A keyboard chip on a Pentium motherboard

NOTE Even though the model numbers changed over the years, you'll still hear techs refer to the keyboard controller as the 8042, after the original keyboard controller chip.

Every time you press a key on your keyboard, a scanning chip in the keyboard notices which key you pressed. Then the scanner sends a coded pattern of ones and zeros—called the *scan code*—to the keyboard controller. Every key on your keyboard has a unique scan code. The keyboard controller stores the scan code in its own register. Does it surprise you that the lowly keyboard controller has a register similar to a CPU? Lots of chips have registers—not just CPUs (see Figure 8-6).

Figure 8-5 Electronic view of the keyboard controller

Figure 8-6 Scan code stored in keyboard controller's register

How does the CPU get the scan code out of the keyboard controller (see Figure 8-7)? While we're at it, how does the CPU tell the keyboard to change the typematic buffer rate (when you hold down a key and the letter repeats) or to turn the number lock LED on and off, to mention just a few other jobs the keyboard needs to do for the system? The point is that the keyboard controller must be able to respond to multiple commands, not just one.

Figure 8-7 The CPU ponders the age-old dilemma of how to get the 8042 to cough up its data.

The keyboard controller accepts commands exactly as you saw the CPU accept commands in Chapter 6. Remember when you added 2 to 3 with the 8088? You had to use specific commands from the 8088's codebook to tell the CPU to do the addition and then place the answer on the external data bus. The keyboard controller has its own codebook—much simpler than any CPU's codebook, but conceptually the same. If the CPU wants to know what key was last pressed on the keyboard, the CPU needs to know the command (or series of commands) that orders the keyboard controller to put the scan code of the letter on the external data bus so the CPU can read it.

801

BIOS

The CPU doesn't magically or otherwise automatically know how to talk with any device; it needs some sort of support programming loaded into memory that teaches it

about a particular device. This programming is called *basic input/output services (BIOS)*. The programs dedicated to enabling the CPU to communicate with devices are called services (or device drivers, as you'll see later in the chapter). This goes well beyond the keyboard, by the way. In fact, *every* device on the computer needs BIOS! But let's continue with the keyboard for now.

Bringing BIOS to the PC

A talented programmer could write BIOS for a keyboard if the programmer knew the keyboard's codebook; keyboards are pretty simple devices. This begs the question: where would this support programming be stored? Well, programming could be incorporated into the operating system. Storing programming to talk to the hardware of your PC in the operating system is great—all operating systems have built-in code that knows how to talk to your keyboard, your mouse, and just about every piece of hardware you may put into your PC.

That's fine once the operating system's up and running, but what about a brand new stack of parts you're about to assemble into a new PC? When a new system's being built, it has no operating system. The CPU must have access to BIOS for the most important hardware on your PC: not only the keyboard, but also the monitor, hard drives, optical drives, USB ports, and RAM. This code can't be stored on a hard drive or optical disc— these important devices need to be ready at any time the CPU calls them, even before installing a mass storage device or an operating system.

The perfect place to store the support programming is on the motherboard. That settles one issue, but another looms: What storage medium should the motherboard use? DRAM won't work, because all of the data would be erased every time you turned off the computer. You need some type of permanent program storage device that does not depend on other peripherals to work. And you need that storage device to sit on the motherboard.

ROM

Motherboards store the keyboard controller support programming, among other programs, on a special type of device called a *read-only memory (ROM)* chip. A ROM chip stores programs, called *services*, exactly like RAM: that is, like an 8-bit-wide spreadsheet. But ROM differs from RAM in two important ways. First, ROM chips are *nonvolatile*, meaning that the information stored on ROM isn't erased when the computer is turned off. Second, traditional ROM chips are read-only, meaning that once you store a program on one, you can't change it. Modern motherboards use a type of ROM called *flash ROM* that differs from traditional ROM in that you can update and change the contents through a very specific process called "flashing the ROM," covered later in this chapter. Figure 8-8 shows a typical flash ROM chip on a motherboard. When the CPU wants to talk to the keyboard controller, it goes to the flash ROM chip to access the proper programming.

Figure 8-8
Typical flash ROM

Every motherboard has a flash ROM chip, called the *system ROM* chip because it contains code that enables your CPU to talk to the basic hardware of your PC (see Figure 8-9). As alluded to earlier, the system ROM holds BIOS for more than just the keyboard controller. It also stores programs for communicating with the floppy drive, hard drives, optical drives, display devices, USB ports, and other basic devices on your motherboard.

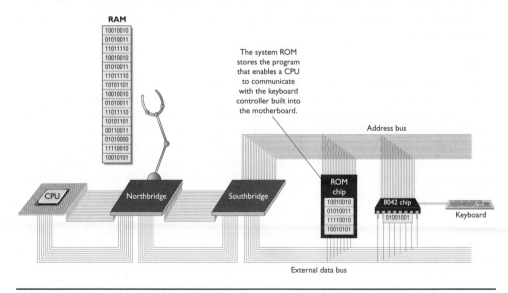

Figure 8-9 Function of the flash ROM chip

To talk to all of that hardware requires hundreds of little services (2 to 30 lines of code each). These hundreds of little programs stored on the system ROM chip on the motherboard are called, collectively, the *system BIOS* (see Figure 8-10). Techs call programs stored on ROM chips of any sort *firmware*.

Figure 8-10 CPU running BIOS service

The system ROM chips used on modern PCs store as much as 2 MB of programs, although only 65,536 bytes are used to store the system BIOS. This allows for backward compatibility with earlier systems. The rest of the ROM space is put to good use doing other jobs.

 EXAM TIP Programs stored on ROM chips—flash or any other kind of ROM chip—are known collectively as firmware, as opposed to programs stored on erasable media, which are collectively called software.

System BIOS Support

Every system BIOS has two types of hardware to support. First, the system BIOS supports all of the hardware that never changes, such as the keyboard. (You can change your keyboard, but you can't change the keyboard controller built into the Southbridge.) Another example of hardware that never changes is the PC speaker (the tiny one that beeps at you, not the ones that play music). The system ROM chip stores the BIOS for these and other devices that never change.

Second, the system BIOS supports all of the hardware that might change from time to time. This includes RAM (you can add RAM), hard drives (you can replace your hard

drive with a larger drive or add a second hard drive), and floppy drives (you can add another floppy drive, although that's not common today). The system ROM chip stores the *BIOS* for these devices, but the system needs another place to store information about the specific *details* of a piece of hardware. This enables the system to differentiate between a Western Digital Caviar Black 1.5-TB hard drive and a Seagate Barracuda 1-TB drive, and yet still support both drives right out of the box.

CMOS

A separate memory chip, called the *complementary metal-oxide semiconductor (CMOS)* chip, stores the information that describes specific device parameters. CMOS does *not* store programs; it only stores data that is read by BIOS to complete the programs needed to talk to changeable hardware. CMOS also acts as a clock to keep the current date and time.

Years ago, CMOS was a separate chip on the motherboard, as shown in Figure 8-11. Today, the CMOS is almost always built into the Southbridge.

Figure 8-11
Old-style CMOS

Most CMOS chips store around 64 KB of data, but the PC usually needs only a very small amount—about 128 bytes—to store all of the necessary information on the changeable hardware. Don't let the tiny size fool you. The information stored in CMOS is absolutely necessary for the PC to function!

If the data stored on CMOS about a particular piece of hardware (or about its fancier features) is different from the specs of the actual hardware, the computer cannot access that piece of hardware (or use its fancier features). It is crucial that this information be correct. If you change any of the previously mentioned hardware, you must update CMOS to reflect those changes. You need to know, therefore, how to change the data on CMOS.

Modify CMOS: The Setup Program

Every PC ships with a program built into the system ROM called the *CMOS setup program* or the *system setup utility* that enables you to access and modify CMOS data. When you fire up your computer in the morning, the first thing you likely see is the BIOS information. It might look like the example shown in Figure 8-12 or perhaps like the example shown in Figure 8-13.

NOTE The terms *CMOS setup program*, *CMOS*, and *system setup utility* are functionally interchangeable today. You'll even hear the program referred to as the *BIOS setup utility*. Most techs just call it the CMOS.

Figure 8-12
AMI BIOS
information

American
Megatrends
www.ami.com

AMIBIOS(C)2010 American Megatrends, Inx.
ASUS P6T ACPI BIOS Revision 1303
CPU : Intel(R) Core(TM) i7 CPU 920 @ 2.67GHz
 Speed : 2.66 GHz

Press DEL to run Setup
Press F8 for BBS POPUP
Press ALT+F2 to execute ASUS EZ FLash 2
DDR3-1066MHZ
Initializing USB Controllers .. Done.
8183MB OK
USB Device(s) : 1 Keyboard, 1 Mouse, 1 Hub

Figure 8-13
Award/Phoenix
BIOS information

Award Modular BIOS v6.00pG , An Energy Star Ally
Copyright (C) 1984-2009, Award Software, Inc.

GA-MA790FXT-UD5P F4

IDE Channel 0 Master : None
IDE Channel 0 Slave : None 6 Unganged Mode, 64-bit
IDE Channel 1 Master : WDC WD2500YS-01SHB1 20.06C06
IDE Channel 1 Slave : WDC WD8000AAJS-00PSA0 05.06H05

IDE Channel 2 Master : WDC WD50000AAKS-00A7B2 01.03B01
IDE Channel 2 Slave : SONY DVD RW AW-G170S 1.72
IDE Channel 3 Master : None
IDE Channel 3 Slave : None

IDE Channel 4 Master : None
IDE Channel 4 Slave : None

:BIOS Setup <F1>:Smart Backup <F9>:XpressRecovery2 <F12>:Boot Menu
03/13/2009-RD790-SB750-7ARRAG04C-00

Who or what is AMIBIOS, and who or what is Phoenix Technologies? These are brand names of BIOS companies. They write BIOS programs and sell them to computer manufacturers. In today's world, motherboard makers rarely write their own BIOS. Instead, they buy their BIOS from specialized third-party BIOS makers such as Award Software and Phoenix Technologies. Although several companies write BIOS, two big companies control 99 percent of the BIOS business: American Megatrends (AMI) and Phoenix Technologies. Phoenix bought Award Software and still sells the Award brand name as a separate product line. These three are the most common brand names in the field.

You always access a system's CMOS setup program at boot. The real question is how to access the CMOS setup at boot for your particular PC. AMI, Award, and Phoenix use different keys to access the CMOS setup program. Usually, BIOS manufacturers tell you how to access the CMOS setup right on the screen as your computer boots. For example, at the bottom of the screen in Figure 8-13, you are instructed to "press the DEL key to enter BIOS Setup." Keep in mind that this is only one possible example. Motherboard manufacturers can change the key combinations for entering CMOS setup. You can even set up the computer so the message does not show—a smart idea if you need to keep nosy people out of your CMOS setup! If you don't see an "enter setup" message, wait until the RAM count starts and then try one of the following keys or key combinations: DEL, ESC, F1, F2, CTRL-ALT-ESC, CTRL-ALT-INS, CTRL-ALT-ENTER, or CTRL-S. It may take a few tries, but you will eventually find the right key or key combination. If not, check the motherboard book or the manufacturer's Web site for the information.

Okay, I've thrown a whole bunch of terms at you describing various pieces of hardware and software and what does what to whom. Here's the scorecard so you can sort out the various pieces of data.

1. The system ROM chip stores the system BIOS, programs needed by the CPU to communicate with devices.

2. The system ROM chip also holds the program that accesses the information stored on the CMOS chip to support changeable pieces of hardware. This program is called the CMOS setup program or the system setup utility.

3. The CMOS holds a small amount of data that describes the changeable pieces of hardware supported by the system BIOS. The CMOS today is a part of the Southbridge.

Got all that? Let's take a quick tour of a CMOS setup program.

A Quick Tour Through a Typical CMOS Setup Program

Every BIOS maker's CMOS setup program looks a little different, but don't let that confuse you. They all contain basically the same settings; you just have to be comfortable poking around. To avoid doing something foolish, *do not save anything* unless you are sure you have it set correctly.

As an example, let's say your machine has Award BIOS. You boot the system and press DEL to enter CMOS setup. The screen shown in Figure 8-14 appears. You are now in the main menu of the Award CMOS setup program. The setup program itself is stored on the ROM chip, but it edits only the data on the CMOS chip.

Figure 8-14
Typical CMOS main
screen by Award

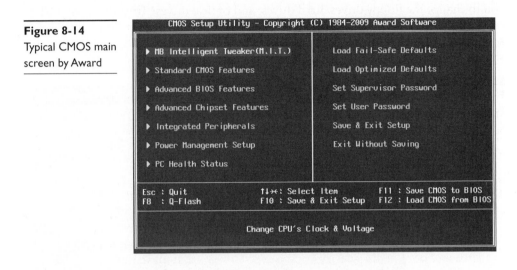

If you select the Standard CMOS Features option, the Standard CMOS Features screen appears (see Figure 8-15). On this screen you can change floppy drive, hard drive, and optical drive settings, as well as the system's date and time. You will learn how to set up the CMOS for these devices in later chapters. At this point, your only goal is to understand CMOS and know how to access the CMOS setup on your PC, so don't try to change anything yet. If you have a system that you are allowed to reboot, try accessing the CMOS setup now.

Figure 8-15
Standard CMOS
Features screen

```
             CMOS Setup Utility - Copyright (C) 1984-2009 Award Software
                                Standard CMOS Features
   ┌────────────────────────────────────────────────┬─────────────────────────┐
   │ Date (mm:dd:yy)              Wed, Mar  7 2012 ▲ │       Item Help          │
   │ Time (hh:mm:ss)              16 :  2 : 30        │  Menu Level    ▶         │
   │ ▶ IDE Channel 0 Master      [ None]             │                          │
   │ ▶ IDE Channel 0 Slave       [ None]             │  Change the day, month,  │
   │ ▶ IDE Channel 1 Master      [WDC WD2500YS-01SHB1]│ year                    │
   │ ▶ IDE Channel 1 Slave       [WDC WD800AAJS-00PSA0│                          │
   │ ▶ IDE Channel 2 Master      [WDC WD5000AAKS-00A7B│ <Week>                   │
   │ ▶ IDE Channel 2 Slave       [SONY    DVD RW AW-G1│ Sun. to Sat.             │
   │ ▶ IDE Channel 3 Master      [ None]             │                          │
   │ ▶ IDE Channel 3 Slave       [ None]             │ <Month>                  │
   │ ▶ IDE Channel 4 Master      [ None]             │ Jan. to Dec.             │
   │ ▶ IDE Channel 4 Slave       [ None]             │                          │
   │                                                 │ <Day>                    │
   │   Drive A                   [1.44M, 3.5"]       │ 1 to 31 (or maximum      │
   │   Floppy 3 Mode Support     [Disabled]          │ allowed in the month)    │
   │                                                 │                          │
   │   Halt On                   [All , But Keyboard]│ <Year>                   │
   │                                              ▼  │ 2000 to 2099             │
   └────────────────────────────────────────────────┴─────────────────────────┘
   ↑↓→←:Move  Enter:Select  +/-/PU/PD:Value  F10:Save  ESC:Exit  F1:General Help
            F5:Previous Values  F6:Fail-Safe Defaults  F7:Optimized Defaults
```

 CAUTION Accessing the CMOS setup utility for a system is perfectly fine, but do not make changes unless you fully understand that system!

Does it look anything like these examples? If not, can you find the screen that enables you to change the floppy drives, hard drives, and optical drives? Trust me, every CMOS setup has that screen somewhere! Figure 8-16 shows the same standard CMOS setup screen on a system with Phoenix BIOS. Note that this CMOS setup utility calls this screen "Main."

Figure 8-16

Phoenix BIOS
CMOS setup utility
Main screen

```
                    Phoenix - AwardBIOS CMOS Setup Utility
  Main  Advanced  Power  Boot  Tools  Exit

     System Time              12 : 29 : 5              Select Menu
     System Date              Tue, Feb 13 2012
     Language                 [English]           Item Specific Help▶

     Leagacy Diskette A:      [1.44, 3.5 in.]     Change the internal
                                                  time.
  ▶ Primary IDE Master        [WDC WD800JB-00JJ]
  ▶ Primary IDE Slave         [None]
  ▶ Secondary IDE Master      [CDRW 0937JDJ]
  ▶ Secondary IDE Slave       [None]
  ▶ SATA 1                    [None]
  ▶ SATA 2                    [None]
  ▶ SATA 3                    [None]
  ▶ SATA 4                    [None]
     HDD SMART Monitoring     [Disabled]

     Installed Memory         2048MB
     Usable Memory            2048MB

  F1:Help      ↑↓:Select Item    -/+: Change Value    F5:Setup Defaults
  ESC:Exit     ▶◀:Select Menu    Enter: Select SubMenu F10:Save and Exit
```

The first BIOS was nothing more than this standard CMOS setup. Today, all computers have many extra CMOS settings. They control items such as memory management, password and booting options, diagnostic and error handling, and power management. The following section takes a quick tour of an Award CMOS setup program. Remember that your CMOS setup almost certainly looks at least a little different from mine, unless you happen to have the *same* BIOS. The chances of that happening are quite slim.

Phoenix has virtually cornered the desktop PC BIOS market with its Award Modular BIOS. Motherboard makers buy a boilerplate BIOS, designed for a particular chipset, and add or remove options (Phoenix calls them *modules*) based on the needs of each motherboard. This means that seemingly identical CMOS setup utilities can be extremely different. Options that show up on one computer might be missing from another. Compare the older Award screen in Figure 8-17 with the more modern Award CMOS screen in Figure 8-14. Figure 8-17 looks different—and it should—as this much older system simply doesn't need the extra options available on the newer system.

Figure 8-17
Older Award
setup screen

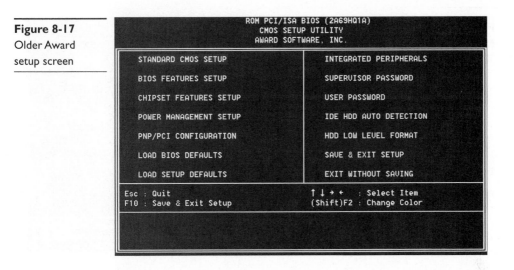

```
                    ROM PCI/ISA BIOS (2A69HQ1A)
                       CMOS SETUP UTILITY
                      AWARD SOFTWARE, INC.

    STANDARD CMOS SETUP              INTEGRATED PERIPHERALS

    BIOS FEATURES SETUP             SUPERVISOR PASSWORD

    CHIPSET FEATURES SETUP          USER PASSWORD

    POWER MANAGEMENT SETUP          IDE HDD AUTO DETECTION

    PNP/PCI CONFIGURATION           HDD LOW LEVEL FORMAT

    LOAD BIOS DEFAULTS              SAVE & EXIT SETUP

    LOAD SETUP DEFAULTS             EXIT WITHOUT SAVING

    Esc : Quit                    ↑ ↓ → ←   : Select Item
    F10 : Save & Exit Setup       (Shift)F2 : Change Color
```

 NOTE All of these screens tend to overwhelm new techs. When they first encounter the many options, some techs feel they need to understand every option on every screen to configure CMOS properly. Relax—if I don't talk about a particular CMOS setting somewhere in this book, it's probably not important, either for the CompTIA A+ certification exams or to a real tech.

The next section starts the walkthrough of a CMOS setup utility with the MB Intelligent Tweaker, followed by some of the Advanced screens. Then you'll go through other common screens, such as Integrated Peripherals, Power, and more.

MB Intelligent Tweaker

You can use MB Intelligent Tweaker (M.I.T.) to change the voltage and multiplier settings on the motherboard for the CPU from the defaults. Motherboards that cater to overclockers tend to have this option. Usually you just set this to Auto or Default and stay away from this screen (see Figure 8-18).

NOTE In Advanced BIOS Features, you might also find several diagnostic tools. I'll discuss a common hard drive diagnostic tool, the Self-Monitoring, Analysis and Reporting Technology (S.M.A.R.T.), in Chapter 11.

Figure 8-18

MB Intelligent
Tweaker (M.I.T.)

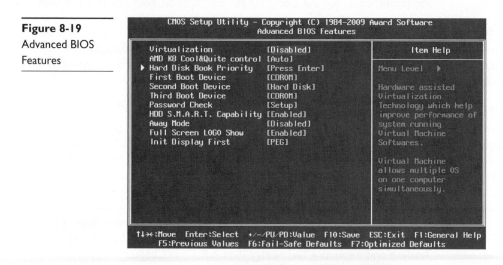

Advanced BIOS Features

Advanced BIOS Features is the dumping ground for all of the settings that aren't covered in the Standard menu and don't fit nicely under any other screen. This screen varies wildly from one system to the next. You most often use this screen to select the boot options (see Figure 8-19).

Figure 8-19

Advanced BIOS
Features

Virtualization Support

You've already learned a lot about how an operating system interacts with hardware and software, but did you know you can also recreate an entire PC (including the hardware, software, and operating system) *virtually* as a program on your PC? A *virtual machine* is a powerful type of program that enables you to run a second (or third or fourth),

software-based machine inside your physical PC. It recreates the motherboard, hard drives, RAM, network adapters, and more, and is just as powerful as a real PC. To run these virtual machines, however, you'll need a very powerful PC—you are trying to run multiple PCs at the same time, after all.

To support this, CPU manufacturers have added *hardware-assisted virtualization*. Intel calls their version Intel Virtualization Technology, and AMD calls theirs AMD Virtualization Technology—perhaps the only time these two companies have agreed on a name. This technology helps the virtual machines use your hardware more efficiently and is controlled by the BIOS. This feature is off by default in BIOS, so if your virtual machine requires hardware-assisted virtualization, you'll need to activate it here.

Chassis Intrusion Detection

Many motherboards support the *chassis intrusion detection* feature provided by the computer case, or chassis. Compatible cases contain a switch that trips when someone opens the case. With motherboard support and a proper connection between the motherboard and the case, the CMOS logs whether the case has been opened and, if it has, posts a notification to the screen on the subsequent boot. How cool is that?

Advanced Chipset Features

The Advanced Chipset Features screen (see Figure 8-20) strikes fear into most everyone, because it deals with extremely low-level chipset functions. Avoid this screen unless a high-level tech (such as a motherboard maker's support tech) explicitly tells you to do something in here.

Figure 8-20
Advanced Chipset
Features

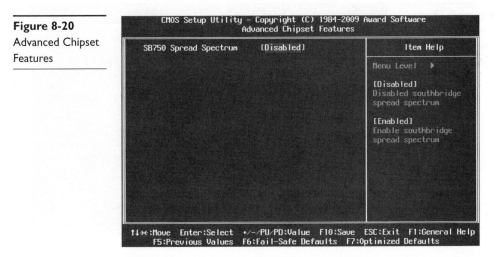

Integrated Peripherals

You will use the Integrated Peripherals screen quite often. Here you configure, enable, or disable the onboard devices, such as the integrated sound card (see Figure 8-21).

Figure 8-21

Integrated
Peripherals

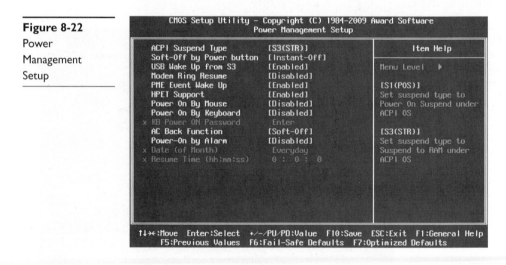

Power Management Setup

As the name implies, you can use the Power Management Setup screen (see Figure 8-22) to set up the power management settings for the system. These settings work in concert (sometimes in conflict) with Windows' power management settings to control how and when devices turn off and back on to conserve power.

Figure 8-22

Power
Management
Setup

Overclocking

Many PCs have CMOS setup menus that display information about the CPU, RAM, and GPU and include controls for overclocking them. You learned about overclocking in Chapter 6, so you already know what it does and how dangerous it can be.

Overclocking works by changing the bus speeds, clock multipliers, and voltage for the desired component. Be very careful when overclocking or you could end up with a dead CPU!

 EXAM TIP When overclocking your PC, look for settings that adjust the CPU's clock and bus speeds. The higher you push these, the faster your PC will go.

PnP/PCI Configurations

All CMOS setup utilities come with menu items that are for the most part no longer needed, but no one wants to remove them. The PnP/PCI Configurations screen is a perfect example (see Figure 8-23). Plug and play (PnP) is how devices automatically work when you snap them into your PC. PCI is a type of slot used for cards. Odds are very good you'll never deal with this screen.

Figure 8-23
PnP/PCI
Configurations

```
                    Phoenix - Award BIOS CMOS Setup Utility
                            PnP/PCI Conigurations

    Resources Controlled By      Auto(ESCD)              Item Help
  x IRQ Resources                Press Enter
                                                   Menu Level    ▶
    PCI/VGA Palette Snoop        Disabled
    PIRQ_0 Use IRQ No.           Auto              BIOS can automatically
    PIRQ_1 Use IRQ No.           Auto              configure all the
    PIRQ_2 Use IRQ No.           Auto              boot and Plug and Play
    PIRQ_3 Use IRQ No.           Auto              compatible devices.
                                                   If you choose Auto,
    ** PCI Express relative items **               you cannot select IRQ
    Maximum Payload Size         4096              DMA and memory base
                                                   address fields, since
                                                   BIOS automatically
                                                   assigns them

 ↑↓→←:Move  Enter:Select  +/-/PU/PD:Value  F10:Save  ESC:Exit  F1:General Help
        F5:Previous Values  F6:Fail-Safe Defaults  F7:Optimized Defaults
```

And the Rest of the CMOS Settings...

The other options on the main menu of an Award CMOS do not have their own screens. Rather, these simply have small dialog boxes that pop up, usually with "Are you sure?" messages. The Load Fail-Safe/Optimized default options keep you from having to memorize all of those weird settings you'll never touch. Fail-Safe sets everything to very simple settings—you might occasionally use this setting when very low-level problems such as freeze-ups occur and you've checked more obvious areas first. Optimized sets the CMOS to the best possible speed/stability for the system. You would use this option after you've tampered with the CMOS too much and need to put it back like it was!

Many CMOS setup programs enable you to set a password in CMOS to force the user to enter a password every time the system boots. Don't confuse this with the Windows

logon password. This CMOS password shows up at boot, long before Windows even starts to load. Figure 8-24 shows a typical CMOS password prompt.

Figure 8-24
CMOS
password
prompt

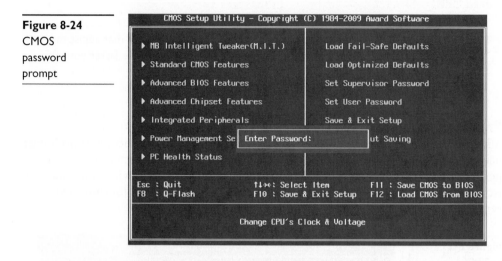

Some CMOS setup utilities enable you to create two passwords: one for boot and another for accessing the CMOS setup program. This extra password just for entering CMOS setup is a godsend in schools, for example, where non-techs tend to wreak havoc in areas (such as CMOS) that they should not access!

Many CMOS setup utilities also enable you to monitor CPU temperature, system temperature, and the voltages of the CPU and RAM. This menu, usually called PC Health Status, also enables you to change fan speeds. A system will almost always handle those on its own, but if you're setting up a home theater PC and you want the quietest system possible, you can go in and set the fans to the lowest speed.

 EXAM TIP On some motherboards, the CMOS setup program enables you to control the ATA Security Mode Feature Set, also commonly referred to as drive lock or *DriveLock*. ATA Security Mode is the first line of defense for protecting hard disks from unwanted access when a system is lost or stolen.

Some PC manufacturers also include *LoJack* security features in their BIOS—this way, if your PC is stolen, you can track its location, install a key logger, or even remotely shut down your computer.

Trusted Platform Module

The *Trusted Platform Module (TPM)* acts as a secure cryptoprocessor, which is to say that it is a hardware platform for the acceleration of cryptographic functions and the secure storage of associated information. The specification for the TPM is published by the Trusted Computing Group, an organization whose corporate members include Intel, Microsoft, AMD, IBM, Lenovo, Dell, Hewlett-Packard, and many others.

The TPM can be a small circuit board plugged into the motherboard, or it can be built directly into the chipset. The CMOS setup program usually contains settings that can turn the TPM on or off and enable or disable it.

TPMs can be used in a wide array of cryptographic operations, but one of the most common uses of TPMs is hard disk encryption. For example, the BitLocker Drive Encryption feature of Microsoft's Windows Vista and Windows 7 can be accelerated by a TPM, which is more secure because the encryption key is stored in the tamper-resistant TPM hardware rather than on an external flash drive. Other possible uses of TPMs include digital rights management (DRM), network access control, application execution control, and password protection.

Exiting and Saving Settings

Of course, all CMOS setups provide some method to Save and Exit or to Exit *Without* Saving. Use these as needed for your situation. Exit Without Saving is particularly nice for those folks who want to poke around the CMOS setup utility but don't want to mess anything up. Use it!

The CMOS setup utility would meet all of the needs of a modern system for BIOS if manufacturers would just stop creating new devices. That's not going to happen, of course, so let's turn now to devices that need to have BIOS loaded from elsewhere.

Option ROM and Device Drivers

Every piece of hardware in your computer needs some kind of programming that tells the CPU how to talk to that device. When IBM invented the PC more than 30 years ago, they couldn't possibly have included all of the necessary BIOS routines for every conceivable piece of hardware on the system ROM chip. How could they? Most of the devices in use today didn't exist on the first PCs. When programmers wrote the first BIOS, for example, network cards, mice, and sound cards did not exist. Early PC designers at IBM understood that they could not anticipate every new type of hardware, so they gave us a few ways to add programming other than on the BIOS. I call this *BYOB*—Bring Your Own BIOS. You can BYOB in two ways: option ROM and device drivers. Let's look at both.

Option ROM

The first way to BYOB is to put the BIOS on the hardware device itself. Look at the card displayed in Figure 8-25. This is a serial ATA RAID hard drive controller—basically just a card that lets you add more hard drives to a PC. The chip in the center with the wires coming out the sides is a flash ROM that stores BIOS for the card. The system BIOS does not have a clue about how to talk to this card, but that's okay, because this card brings its own BIOS on what's called an *option ROM* chip.

Figure 8-25
Option ROM

Most BIOS that come on option ROMs tell you that they exist by displaying information when you boot the system. Figure 8-26 shows a typical example of an option ROM advertising itself.

Figure 8-26
Option ROM
at boot

```
System Memory Size: 4.0 GB, System Memory Speed: 800 MHz, Voltage: 1.5V

Broadcom NetXtreme II Ethernet Boot Agent v5.2.7
Copyright (C) 2000-2009 Broadcom Corporation
All rights reserved.
Press Ctrl-S to Configure Device (MAC Address - 0024E867D111)

Adaptec 1225SA SATA HostRAID BIOS V6.0-0 B2328
(c) 1998-2007 Adaptec, Inc. All Rights Reserved.

◄◄◄ Press <Ctrl><A> for Adaptec RAID Configuration Utility! ►►►

Controller #00: Adaptec 1225SA at PCI Bus:03, Dev:00, Func:00
SerialNumber = 0XX0B0040013
Loading Configuration...
00:00 WDC WD20EADS-00R6B0 01.00A01     1.81 TB Healthy      3.0 Gb/s

SATA JBOD- PORT-0   WDC WD20EADS-00R    1.81 TB       Legacy

1 JBOD Device(s) Found.
```

In the early days of the PC, you could find all sorts of devices with BIOS on option ROMs. Today, option ROMs have mostly been replaced by more flexible software methods (more on device driver software in the next section), with one major exception: video cards. Every video card made today contains its own BIOS. Option ROMs work well but are hard to upgrade. For this reason, most hardware relies on software for BYOB.

Device Drivers

A *device driver* is a file stored on the PC's hard drive that contains all of the commands necessary to talk to whatever device it was written to support. All operating systems employ a method of loading these device drivers into RAM every time the system boots. They know which device drivers to install by reading a file (or files) that lists which device drivers the system needs to load at boot time. All operating systems are designed to look at this list early on in the boot process and copy the listed files into RAM, thereby giving the CPU the capability to communicate with the hardware supported by the device driver. Device drivers come with the device when you buy it. When you buy a sound card, for example, it comes with a disc that holds all of the necessary device drivers (and usually a bunch of extra goodies). The generic name for this type of CD-ROM is *installation disc*. In most cases, you install a new device, start the computer, and wait for Windows to prompt you for the installation disc (see Figure 8-27).

Figure 8-27
Windows asking for the installation disc

You might want to add or remove device drivers manually at times. Windows uses a special database called the *Registry* that stores everything you want to know about your system, including the device drivers. You shouldn't access the Registry directly to access these drivers, but instead use the venerable Device Manager utility (discussed in Chapter 4).

BIOS, BIOS, Everywhere!

As you should now understand, every piece of hardware on a system must have an accompanying program that provides the CPU with the code necessary to communicate with that particular device. This code may reside on the system ROM on the motherboard, on ROM on a card, or in a device driver file on the hard drive loaded into RAM at boot. BIOS is everywhere on your system, and you need to deal with it occasionally.

Power-On Self Test (POST)

BIOS isn't the only program on your system ROM. When the computer is turned on or reset, it initiates a special program, also stored on the system ROM chip, called the *power-on self test (POST)*. The POST program checks out the system every time the computer boots. To perform this check, the POST sends out a command that says to all of the devices, "Check yourselves out!" All of the standard devices in the computer then run their own internal diagnostic—the POST doesn't specify what they must check. The quality of the diagnostic is up to the people who made that particular device.

Let's consider the POST for a moment. Suppose some device—let's say it's the keyboard controller chip—runs its diagnostic and determines that it is not working properly. What can the POST do about it? Only one thing really: tell the human in front of the PC! So how does the computer tell the human? PCs convey POST information to you in two ways: beep codes and text messages.

Before and During the Video Test: The Beep Codes

The computer tests the most basic parts of the computer first, up to and including the video card. In early PCs, you'd hear a series of beeps—called *beep codes*—if anything went wrong. By using beep codes before and during the video test, the computer could communicate with you. (If a POST error occurs before the video is available, obviously the error must manifest itself as beeps, because nothing can display on the screen.) The meaning of the beep code you'd hear varied among different BIOS manufacturers. You could find the beep codes for a specific motherboard in its motherboard manual.

Most modern PCs have only two beep codes: one for bad or missing video (one long beep followed by two or three short beeps), and one for bad or missing RAM (a single beep that repeats indefinitely).

 CAUTION You'll find lots of online documentation about beep codes, but it's usually badly outdated.

You'll hear three other beep sequences on most PCs (although they're not officially beep codes). At the end of a successful POST, the PC produces one or two short beeps, simply to inform you that all is well. Most systems make a rather strange noise when the RAM is missing or very seriously damaged. Unlike traditional beep codes, this code repeats until you shut off the system. Finally, your speaker might make beeps for reasons that aren't POST or boot related. One of the more common is a series of short beeps after the system's been running for a while. That's a CPU alarm telling you the CPU is approaching its high heat limit.

Text Errors

After the video has tested okay, any POST errors display on the screen as text errors. If you get a text error, the problem is usually, but not always, self-explanatory (see Figure 8-28). Text errors are far more useful than beep codes, because you can simply read the screen to determine the bad device.

Figure 8-28
POST text error
messages

```
                                                    F10 = System Services
                                                  F11 = BIOS Boot Manager
                                                        F12 = PXE Boot
  Keyboard failure

  One 1.86 GHz Dual-core Processor, Bus Speed:4.80 GT/s, L2/L3 Cache:512 KB/4 MB
  System running at 1.86 GHz
  System Memory Size: 4.0 GB, System Memory Speed: 800 MHz, Voltage: 1.5V
```

POST Cards

Beep codes, numeric codes, and text error codes, although helpful, can sometimes be misleading. Worse than that, an inoperative device can sometimes disrupt the POST, forcing the machine into an endless loop. This causes the PC to act dead—no beeps and nothing on the screen. In this case, you need a device, called a *POST card*, to monitor the POST and identify which piece of hardware is causing the trouble.

POST cards are simple cards that snap into expansion slots on your system. A small, two-character light-emitting diode (LED) readout on the card indicates which device the POST is currently testing (see Figure 8-29).

Figure 8-29
POST card
in action

POST cards used to be essential tools for techs, but today I use them only when I have a "dead" PC to determine at which level it's dead. If the POST card shows no reading, I know the problem is before the POST and must be related to the power, the CPU, the RAM, or the motherboard. If the board posts, then I know to look at more issues, such as the drives and so on.

The Boot Process

All PCs need a process to begin their operations. Once you feed power to the PC, the tight interrelation of hardware, firmware, and software enables the PC to start itself, to "pull itself up by the bootstraps" or boot itself.

When you first power on the PC, the power supply circuitry tests for proper voltage and then sends a signal down a special wire called the *power good* wire to awaken the CPU. The moment the power good wire wakes it up, every CPU immediately sends a built-in memory address via its address bus. This special address is the same on every CPU, from the oldest 8086 to the most recent microprocessor. This address is the first line of the POST program on the system ROM! That's how the system starts the POST. After the POST has finished, there must be a way for the computer to find the programs on the hard drive to start the operating system. The POST passes control to the last BIOS function: the bootstrap loader. The *bootstrap loader* is little more than a few dozen lines of BIOS code tacked to the end of the POST program. Its job is to find the operating system. The bootstrap loader reads CMOS information to tell it where to look first for an operating system. Your PC's CMOS setup utility has an option that you configure to tell the bootstrap loader which devices to check for an operating system and in which order (see Figure 8-30).

Figure 8-30	▶ Hard Disk Book Priority	[Press Enter]
CMOS	First Boot Device	[CDROM]
boot order	Second Boot Device	[Hard Disk]
	Third Boot Device	[CDROM]

Almost all storage devices—floppy disks, hard disks, CDs, DVDs, and even USB thumb drives—can be configured to boot an operating system by setting aside a specific location called the *boot sector*. If the device is bootable, its boot sector contains special programming designed to tell the system where to locate the operating system. Any device with a functional operating system is called a *bootable disk* or a *system disk*. If the bootstrap loader locates a good boot sector, it passes control to the operating system and removes itself from memory. If it doesn't, it goes to the next device in the boot order you set in the CMOS setup utility. Boot order is an important tool for techs because you can set it to load in special bootable devices so you can run utilities to maintain PCs without using the primary operating system.

Some BIOS include a feature that enables a PC to use a *preboot execution environment (PXE)*. A PXE enables you to boot a PC without any local storage by retrieving an OS from a server over a network. You'll see more on PXE when we talk about installing Windows in Chapter 14.

Care and Feeding of BIOS and CMOS

BIOS and CMOS are areas in your PC that you don't go to very often. BIOS itself is invisible. The only real clue you have that it even exists is the POST. The CMOS setup utility, on the other hand, is very visible if you start it. Most CMOS setup utilities today work acceptably well without ever being touched. You're an aspiring tech, however, and all self-respecting techs start up the CMOS setup utility and make changes. That's when most CMOS setup utility problems take place.

If you mess with the CMOS setup utility, remember to make only as many changes at one time as you can remember. Document the original settings and the changes on a piece of paper so you can put things back if necessary. Don't make changes unless you know what they mean! It's easy to screw up a computer fairly seriously by playing with CMOS settings you don't understand.

Losing CMOS Settings

Your CMOS needs a continuous trickle charge to retain its data. Motherboards use some type of battery, usually a coin battery like those in wrist watches, to give the CMOS the charge it needs when the computer is turned off (see Figure 8-31). This battery also keeps track of the date and time when the PC is turned off.

Figure 8-31
A CMOS battery

If the battery runs out of charge, you lose all of your CMOS information. If some mishap suddenly erases the information on the CMOS chip, the computer might not boot or you'll get nasty-looking errors at boot. Any PC made after 2002 will boot to factory defaults if the CMOS clears, so the chances of not booting are slim—but you'll

still get errors at boot. Here are a few examples of errors that point to lost CMOS information:

- CMOS configuration mismatch
- CMOS date/time not set
- No boot device available
- CMOS battery state low

Here are some of the more common reasons for losing CMOS data:

- Pulling and inserting cards
- Touching the motherboard
- Dropping something on the motherboard
- Dirt on the motherboard
- Faulty power supplies
- Electrical surges

If you encounter any of these errors, or if the clock in Windows resets itself to January 1st every time you reboot the system, the battery on the motherboard is losing its charge and needs to be replaced. To replace the battery, use a screwdriver to pry the battery's catch gently back. The battery should pop up for easy removal. Before you install the new battery, double-check that it has the same voltage and amperage as the old battery. To retain your CMOS settings while replacing the battery, simply leave your PC plugged into an AC outlet. The 5-volt soft power on all modern motherboards provides enough electricity to keep the CMOS charged and the data secure. Of course, I know you're going to be *extremely* careful about ESD while prying up the battery from a live system!

Flashing ROM

Flash ROM chips can be reprogrammed to update their contents. With flash ROM, when you need to update your system BIOS to add support for a new technology, you can simply run a small command-line program, combined with an update file, and voilà, you have a new, updated BIOS! Different BIOS makers use slightly different processes for *flashing the BIOS*, but, in general, you insert a removable disk of some sort (usually a USB thumb drive) containing an updated BIOS file and use the updating utility in CMOS setup.

Some motherboard makers provide Windows-based flash ROM update utilities that check the Internet for updates and download them for you to install (see Figure 8-32). Most of these utilities also enable you to back up your current BIOS so you can return to it if the updated version causes trouble. Without a good backup, you could end up

throwing away your motherboard if a flash BIOS update goes wrong, so you should always make one.

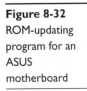

Figure 8-32
ROM-updating program for an ASUS motherboard

Finally, don't update your BIOS unless you have some compelling reason to do so. As the old saying goes, "If it ain't broke, don't fix it!"

 EXAM TIP While techs usually talk about "flashing the BIOS," the CompTIA A+ exams refer to this process also as "installing firmware upgrades."

Beyond A+

UEFI

Your computer's system BIOS is one very old piece of programming. BIOS hasn't changed much since it was conceived with the 286-based IBM AT computer back in the 1980s. As a result, BIOS works only in 16-bit mode and depends on *x*86-compliant hardware. In addition, if you have more than one operating system loaded on a single drive, you need one of those installed OSes to "take charge" and act as a boot loader.

If computing was going to move forward, a new type of BIOS needed to come along. Intel's *Extensible Firmware Interface (EFI)* fills that role. In 2005, Intel released EFI for public standards, creating the Unified EFI forum to manage the specification. EFI was then renamed *Unified Extensible Firmware Interface (UEFI)*.

TIP Even though it's really called UEFI, most techs use the term EFI.

UEFI acts as a super-BIOS, doing the same job as BIOS, but in a 32- or 64-bit environment. UEFI, though, does much more than just fill in for BIOS. Think of UEFI as a not yet extremely well-defined, industry-standard, mini–operating system that runs on top of the firmware of your computer, enabling you to do some pretty cool things at boot. Here are some of the things UEFI does:

- UEFI supports 32-bit or 64-bit booting.
- UEFI handles all boot-loading duties.
- UEFI is not dependent on *x*86 firmware.

UEFI became a standard years ago, so why did no one see a UEFI motherboard until 2011? The answer is simple: 3-TB hard drives. Regular BIOS will only boot to master boot record (MBR) drives, and MBR drives don't support partitions greater than 2.2 TB. As 3-TB and larger drives began to appear in 2011, people using traditional BIOS discovered that strange issues popped up when they wanted to boot off of a 3-TB hard drive (see Figure 8-33). Instead of a 3-TB volume, you'd find a 2.2-TB volume and unpartitioned space.

[Figure 8-33 screenshot: Computer Management window]

Volume	Layout	Type	File System	Status	Capacity	Free Space	% Free	Fault Tolerance	Overhead
(C:)	Simple	Basic	NTFS	Healthy (Boot, Page File, Crash Dump, Primary Partition)	2047.90 GB	2025.80 GB	99 %	No	0%
System Reserved	Simple	Basic	NTFS	Healthy (System, Active, Primary Partition)	100 MB	72 MB	72 %	No	0%

Figure 8-33 Here's what happens when you install Windows 7 on a greater-than-2.2-TB drive using regular BIOS.

UEFI motherboards support booting a newer type of hard drive partitioning called *GUID Partition Table* (*GPT*) that supports partitions larger than 2.2 TB. If you want to boot off of a hard drive using a single partition greater than 2.2 TB, you must use a UEFI motherboard and the hard drive must be blank. If your system meets these two criteria, the Windows 7 installation routine will automatically make a GPT drive for you (see Figure 8-34).

Figure 8-34 Here's what happens when you install Windows 7 on a greater-than-2.2-TB drive using UEFI.

NOTE While UEFI works both for 32-bit and 64-bit operating systems, Microsoft decided to enable UEFI support only for 64-bit editions of Windows 7.

Although the EFI folks clearly defined issues such as booting and accessing firmware, they didn't define issues such as the graphical user interface or audio. If you think UEFI possesses a standard interface similar to the Windows desktop, forget it. Figure 8-35 shows an ASUS motherboard's UEFI interface. UEFI serves as a non-hardware-specific, non-OS-specific, 32- or 64-bit bootloader. This doesn't make things we know and love such as POST or system setup go away. They still exist, but now UEFI runs the show instead of BIOS (see Figure 8-36).

Figure 8-35 ASUS EFI BIOS Utility

Figure 8-36 POST and system setup are still here.

Chapter Review

Questions

1. What does BIOS provide for the computer? (Choose the best answer.)

 A. BIOS provides the physical interface for various devices such as USB and FireWire ports.

 B. BIOS provides the programming that enables the CPU to communicate with other hardware.

 C. BIOS provides memory space for applications to load into from the hard drive.

 D. BIOS provides memory space for applications to load into from the main system RAM.

2. What is the correct boot sequence for a PC?

 A. CPU, POST, power good, boot loader, operating system

 B. POST, power good, CPU, boot loader, operating system

 C. Power good, boot loader, CPU, POST, operating system

 D. Power good, CPU, POST, boot loader, operating system

3. Jill decided to go retro and added a second floppy disk drive to her computer. She thinks she has it physically installed correctly, but it doesn't show up in Windows. Which of the following options will most likely lead Jill where she needs to go to resolve the issue?

 A. Reboot the computer and press the F key on the keyboard twice. This signals that the computer has two floppy disk drives.

 B. Reboot the computer and watch for instructions to enter the CMOS setup utility (for example, a message may say to press the DELETE key). Do what it says to go into CMOS setup.

 C. In Windows, press the DELETE key twice to enter the CMOS setup utility.

 D. In Windows, go to Start | Run and type **floppy**. Click OK to open the Floppy Disk Drive Setup Wizard.

This chapter starts with an explanation of how motherboards work, identifying various types or form factors of motherboards, including distinguishing features. The second section examines expansion capabilities on motherboards, specifically the types of expansion slots you'll run into in the wild and how to install expansion cards. The third section goes through the pragmatic steps of upgrading and installing motherboards. The chapter finishes with techniques for troubleshooting motherboard problems.

 NOTE Modern motherboards are layered *printed circuit boards (PCBs)*, copper etched onto a nonconductive material and then coated with some sort of epoxy for strength. The layers mask some of their complexity. You can see some of the traces on the board, but every motherboard is four or more layers thick. The layers contain a veritable highway of wires, carrying data and commands back and forth between the CPU, RAM, and peripherals. The layered structure enables multiple wires to send data without their signals interfering with each other. The layered approach allows the manufacturer to add complexity and additional components to the board without extending the overall length and width of the board. Shorter traces also allow signals to travel faster than they would if the wires were longer, as would be necessary if motherboards did not use layers. The multiple layers also add strength to the board itself, so it doesn't bend easily.

Historical/Conceptual

How Motherboards Work

Three variable and interrelated characteristics define modern motherboards: form factor, chipset, and components. The *form factor* determines the physical size of the motherboard as well as the general location of components and ports. The *chipset* defines the type of processor and RAM the motherboard requires and determines to a degree the built-in devices the motherboard supports, including the expansion slots. Finally, the built-in components determine the core functionality of the system.

Any good tech should be able to make a recommendation to a client about a particular motherboard simply by perusing the specs. Because the motherboard determines function, expansion, and stability for the whole PC, it's essential to know motherboards!

Form Factors

Form factors are industry-standardized shapes and layouts that enable motherboards to work with cases and power supplies. A single form factor applies to all three components. Motherboards come in a basic rectangular or square shape but vary in overall size and in the layout of built-in components (see Figure 9-2). You need to install a motherboard in a case designed to fit it, so the ports and slot openings on the back fit correctly.

Figure 9-2
Typical
motherboard

The power supply and the motherboard need matching connectors, and different form factors define different connections. Given that the term "form factor" applies to the case, motherboard, and power supply—the three parts of the PC most responsible for moving air around inside the PC—the form factor also defines how the air moves around in the case.

To perform motherboard upgrades and provide knowledgeable recommendations to clients, techs need to know their form factors. The PC industry has adopted—and dropped—a number of form factors over the years with such names as AT, ATX, and BTX. Let's start with the granddaddy of all PC form factors, AT.

NOTE All AT motherboards had a split power socket called *P8/P9*. You can see the white P8/P9 socket near the keyboard port in Figures 9.3 and 9.4.

AT Form Factor

The *AT* form factor (see Figure 9-3), invented by IBM in the early 1980s, was the predominant form factor for motherboards through the mid-1990s. AT is now obsolete.

Figure 9-3
AT-style
motherboard

P8/P9 socket

The AT motherboard had a few size variations (see Figure 9-4), ranging from large to very large. The original AT motherboard was huge, around 12 inches wide by 13 inches deep. PC technology was new and needed lots of space for the various chips necessary to run the components of the PC.

Figure 9-4
AT motherboard
(bottom) and Baby
AT motherboard
(top)

The single greatest problem with AT motherboards was the lack of external ports. When PCs were first invented, the only devices plugged into the average PC were a monitor and a keyboard. That's what the AT was designed to handle—the only dedicated connector on an AT motherboard was the keyboard port (see Figure 9-5).

Over the years, the number of devices plugged into the back of the PC has grown tremendously. Your average PC today has a keyboard, a mouse, a printer, some speakers, a monitor, and—if your system's like mine—four to six USB devices connected to it at any given time. These added components created a demand for a new type of form factor, one with more dedicated connectors for more devices. Many attempts were made to create a new standard form factor. Invariably, these new form factors integrated dedicated connectors for at least the mouse and printer, and many even added connectors for video, sound, and phone lines.

One variation from the AT form factor that enjoyed a degree of success was the *slimline* form factor. The first slimline form factor was known as *LPX* (defined in some sources as *low profile extended*, although there's some disagreement). It was replaced by the *NLX* form factor. (NLX apparently stands for nothing, by the way. It's just a cool grouping of letters.) The LPX and NLX form factors met the demands of the slimline market by providing a central riser slot to enable the insertion of a special *riser card* (see Figure 9-6) or, as it's sometimes called, a *daughterboard*. Expansion cards then fit into the riser card horizontally. Combining built-in connections with a riser card enabled manufacturers to produce PCs shorter than 4 inches.

Figure 9-6
Riser card on an
older motherboard

The main problem with form factors such as LPX and NLX was their inflexibility. Certainly, no problem occurred with dedicated connections for such devices as mice or printers, but the new form factors also added connectors for such devices as video and sound—devices that were prone to obsolescence, making the motherboard out of date the moment a new type of video or sound card came into popularity.

801

ATX Form Factor

The demand for a form factor that had more standard connectors and also was flexible enough for possible changes in technology led to the creation of the ATX form factor in 1995 (see Figure 9-7). ATX got off to a slow start, but by around 1998, ATX overtook AT to become the most common form factor, a distinction it holds today.

Figure 9-7 Early ATX motherboard

ATX is distinct from AT in the lack of an AT keyboard port, replaced with a rear panel that has all necessary ports built in. Note the mini-DIN (PS/2) keyboard and mouse ports at the left of Figure 9-8, until recently, standard features on almost all ATX boards. You recall those from Chapter 3, right?

Figure 9-8
ATX ports

The ATX form factor includes many improvements over AT. The position of the power supply creates better air movement. The CPU and RAM are placed to provide easier access, and the rearrangement of components prevents long expansion cards from colliding with the CPU or Northbridge. Other improvements, such as placing the RAM closer to the Northbridge and CPU than on AT boards, offer users enhanced performance as well. The shorter the wires, the easier to shield them and make them capable of handling double or quadruple the clock speed of the motherboard. Figure 9-9 shows AT and ATX motherboards—note the radical differences in placement of internal connections.

Figure 9-9
AT (left) and ATX (right) mother-boards for quick visual comparison

ATX motherboards come in three variations to accommodate different types of cases. So far, you've seen the full-sized ATX form factor, which is 12 by 9.6 inches.

The *microATX (μATX)* motherboard (see Figure 9-10) floats in at a svelte 9.6 by 9.6 inches (usually), or about 30 percent smaller than standard ATX, yet uses the standard ATX connections. A microATX motherboard fits into a standard ATX case or in the much smaller microATX cases. Note that not all microATX motherboards have the same physical size. You'll sometimes see microATX motherboards referred to with the Greek symbol for micro, as in μATX.

Figure 9-10

A microATX
motherboard

In 1999, Intel created a variant of the microATX called the FlexATX. *FlexATX* motherboards have maximum dimensions of just 9 by 7.5 inches, which makes them the smallest motherboards in the ATX standard. Although FlexATX motherboards can use a standard ATX power supply, most FlexATX systems use a special FlexATX-only power supply. This diminutive power supply fits into tight FlexATX cases.

NOTE Many techs and Web sites use the term *mini-ATX* to refer to motherboards smaller than a full ATX board. This is technically incorrect. The specifications for these small boards use only the terms *microATX* and *FlexATX*.

Keep in mind that each main type of form factor requires its own case. AT motherboards go into AT cases, NLX motherboards go into NLX cases, and ATX motherboards go into ATX cases. You cannot replace one form factor with another without purchasing a new case (see Figure 9-11). The exception to this rule is that larger form factor ATX cases can handle any smaller-sized ATX form factor motherboards.

ITX

Not everyone wants or needs a huge desktop system. From the beginning of PCs, there's always been a demand for smaller computers. While a number of companies have made proprietary motherboards to support smaller computers, it wasn't until around 2001 that the chipset maker VIA Technologies started the process to create a small form factor (SFF) motherboard, the ITX. The ITX itself wasn't a success, but VIA in turn created a number of even smaller form factors that today populate the SFF market: Mini-ITX, Nano-ITX, and Pico-ITX.

Figure 9-11

That's not going to fit!

Mini-ITX is the largest and the most popular of the three ITX form factors. At a miniscule 6.7 by 6.7 inches, Mini-ITX competes head to head with the virtually identical microATX (see Figure 9-12).

Figure 9-12

Mini-ITX (photo courtesy of VIA Technologies, Inc.)

If you think that's small, *Nano-ITX* at 4.7 by 4.7 inches and *Pico-ITX* at 3.8 by 2.8 inches are even smaller (see Figure 9-13). These tiny motherboard form factors are commonly used for embedded systems and highly specialized devices such as routers.

Figure 9-13
Pico-ITX (photo
courtesy of VIA
Technologies, Inc.)

One of the great benefits of these SFF motherboards is the tiny amount of power needed to support them. ITX power supplies are quite small compared to a typical power supply. Lower power usage produces less heat, thus enabling passive cooling on many SFF systems. The lack of fan noise makes them ideal for media center PCs.

EXAM TIP You need to know the variations of the ATX standard for the CompTIA 220-801 exam, especially microATX. You should also be familiar with the low-power design of ITX boards.

Proprietary Form Factors

Several major PC makers, including Dell and Sony, make motherboards that work only with their cases. These *proprietary* motherboards enable these companies to create systems that stand out from the generic ones and, not coincidently, push you to get service and upgrades from their authorized dealers. Some of the features you'll see in proprietary systems are riser boards like you saw with the NLX form factor—part of a motherboard separate from the main one but connected by a cable of some sort—and unique power connections. Proprietary motherboards drive techs crazy because replacement parts tend to cost more and are not readily available.

Chipset

Every motherboard has a *chipset*, one or more discrete integrated circuit chips that support the CPU's interfacing to all the other devices on the motherboard. The chipset determines the type of processor the motherboard accepts, the type and capacity of RAM, and the sort of internal and external devices that the motherboard supports. As you learned in earlier chapters, the chips in a PC's chipset serve as electronic interfaces

through which the CPU, RAM, and input/output devices interact. Chipsets vary in features, performance, and stability, so they factor hugely in the purchase or recommendation of a particular motherboard. Good techs know their chipsets!

Because the chipset facilitates communication between the CPU and other devices in the system, its component chips are relatively centrally located on the motherboard (see Figure 9-14). For over a decade chipsets were composed of two primary chips: the Northbridge and the Southbridge.

Figure 9-14
Northbridge and Southbridge

Northbridge

Southbridge

The *Northbridge* chip on traditional Intel-based motherboards helped the CPU work with RAM, as mentioned in earlier chapters. On newer motherboards, however, the CPU has taken on the role of the memory controller so the Northbridge either no longer exists or mainly just provides the communication with the video card. Northbridge chips did a lot and thus got pretty hot, requiring their own heat-sink and fan assembly.

The *Southbridge* handles some expansion devices and mass storage drives, such as hard drives. Most Southbridge chips don't need extra cooling, leaving the chip exposed or passively cooled with only a heat sink. This makes the Southbridge a great place for you to see the manufacturer of the chipset, as the name of the manufacturer is always right on the chip.

Some motherboards support very old technologies such as floppy drives, infrared connections, parallel ports, and modems. Although supporting these old devices was once part of the Southbridge's job, hardly any modern chipsets still support these devices. Motherboard manufacturers add a third chip called the *super I/O chip* to handle these chores. Figure 9-15 shows a typical super I/O chip.

Figure 9-15

Super I/O chip on ASUS motherboard

The system ROM chip provides part of the BIOS for the chipset, but only at a barebones, generic level. The chipset still needs support for the rest of the things it can do. So how do expansion devices get BIOS? From software drivers, of course, and the same holds true for modern chipsets. You have to load the proper drivers for the specific OS to support all of the features of today's chipsets. Without software drivers, you'll never create a stable, fully functional PC. Most motherboards ship with an optical disc with drivers, support programs, and extra-special goodies such as antivirus software (see Figure 9-16).

Figure 9-16

Driver disc for ASUS motherboard

There are a limited number of chipset makers. The dominant chipset vendors today are Intel and AMD, although several other companies continue to produce chipsets, such as NVIDIA. Motherboard manufacturers incorporate the chipsets into motherboards that match the feature set of the chipset. Chipset companies rise and fall every

few years, with one company seeming to hold the hot position for a while until another company comes along to unseat them.

NOTE Super I/O chips work with chipsets, but are not part of the chipset. Motherboard makers purchase them separately from chipsets.

Chipset makers don't always use the terms Northbridge and Southbridge. Chipsets for AMD-based motherboards tend to use these terms, but Intel-based motherboards tend to say *Memory Controller Hub (MCH)* for the Northbridge and *I/O Controller Hub (ICH)* for the Southbridge. With the launch of the X58 Express Chipset, Intel further refined their terminology, calling the Northbridge simply the *I/O Hub (IOH)* since the memory controller is located on the CPU. Sometimes Intel refers to the Southbridge as the *Legacy I/O Controller Hub*. Regardless of the official name, Northbridge and Southbridge are the commonly used terms. Figure 9-17 shows a schematic with typical chipset chores for an Intel X79 chipset.

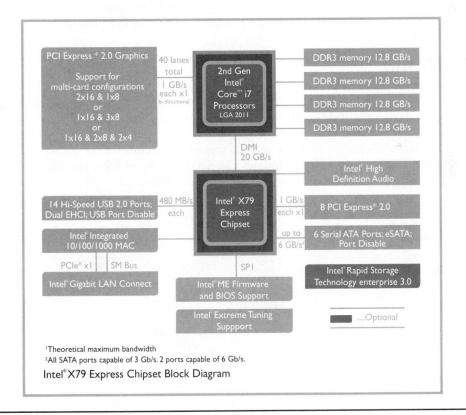

Figure 9-17 Schematic of a modern chipset (courtesy of Intel Corporation)

So why do good techs need to know the hot chipsets in detail? The chipset defines almost every motherboard feature short of the CPU itself. Techs love to discuss chipsets and expect a fellow tech to know the differences between one chipset and another. You also need to be able to recommend a motherboard that suits a client's needs. Chapter 31 covers choosing components and building PCs for specific purposes, such as video editing and gaming. One of the most important choices you'll make in building a custom rig is selecting a chipset.

Motherboard Components

The connections and capabilities of a motherboard sometimes differ from those of the chipset the motherboard uses. This disparity happens for a couple of reasons. First, a particular chipset may support eight USB ports, but to keep costs down, the manufacturer might include only four ports. Second, a motherboard maker may choose to install extra features—ones not supported by the chipset—by adding additional chips. A common example is a motherboard that supports FireWire. Other technologies you might find are built-in sound, hard drive RAID controllers, and AMR or CNR slots for modems, network cards, and more. Some motherboards have added convenience features, such as case fan power connectors and running lights so you can see what you're working on.

USB/FireWire

Most chipsets support USB, and many motherboards come with FireWire as well, but it seems no two motherboards offer the same port arrangement. My motherboard supports eight USB ports and two FireWire ports, for example, but if you look on the back of the motherboard, you'll only see four USB ports and one FireWire port. So, where are the other ports? Well, this motherboard has special connectors for the other ports, and the motherboard comes with the dongles you need to connect them (see Figure 9-18). These dongles typically use an extra slot on the back of the case.

Figure 9-18
USB/FireWire
dongle for rear
connectors

These dongle connectors are standardized, so many cases have built-in front USB/FireWire ports that have dongles attached. This is very handy for USB or FireWire devices you might want to plug and unplug frequently, such as thumb drives or digital cameras. You can also buy add-on front USB and FireWire devices that go into a 3.5-inch drive bay (see Figure 9-19).

Figure 9-19
Front USB and
FireWire drive bay
device

Sound

Quite a few motherboards come with onboard sound chips. These sound chips are usually pretty low quality compared to even a lower-end sound card, but onboard sound is cheap and doesn't take up a slot. As with USB, a lot of motherboards have a port for connecting to audio jacks on the front of the case. These enable you to plug headphones or microphones into the front rather than the rear of the case, a very convenient feature. These connectors are identical to the ones used on sound cards, so we'll save more discussion for Chapter 25.

RAID

RAID stands for *redundant array of independent* (*or inexpensive*) *disks* and is very common on motherboards. There are many types of RAID, but the RAID found on motherboards usually only supports *mirroring* (the process of using two drives to hold the same data, which is good for safety, because if one drive dies, the other still has all of the data) or *striping* (making two drives act as one drive by spreading data across them, which is good for speed). RAID is a very cool but complex topic that's discussed in detail in Chapter 11.

AMR/CNR

The U.S. Federal Communications Commission (FCC) must certify any electronic device to ensure that it does not transmit unwanted electronic signals. This process is a bit expensive, so in the very late 1990s, Intel came up with a special slot called the *audio modem riser* (*AMR*), shown in Figure 9-20. An AMR slot was designed to take specialized AMR devices (modems, sound cards, and network cards). An AMR device would get one FCC certification and then be used on as many motherboards as the manufacturer wanted without going through the FCC certification process again. AMR was quickly replaced with the more advanced *communications and networking riser* (*CNR*). Many motherboard manufacturers used these slots in the early 2000s, but they've lost popularity because most motherboard makers simply use onboard networking and sound.

Figure 9-20
AMR slot

Case Fan Support

Every motherboard has a CPU fan power connector, as you'll recall from Chapter 6 in the CPU installation process, usually a four-wire connector that supports three-wire fans too. Some motherboards offer one or more fan power connectors for case fans. These are almost always only three-wire connectors. The case fans plugged into the motherboard can be monitored and controlled in Windows, unlike case fans connected only to the power supply, so they add a nice feature.

Expansion Bus

Expansion slots have been part of the PC from the very beginning. Way back then, IBM created the PC with an eye to the future; the original IBM PC had slots built into the motherboard—called *expansion slots*—for adding expansion cards and thus new functions to the PC. The slots and accompanying wires and support chips on the first PC and on the latest and greatest PC are called the *expansion bus*.

Structure and Function of the Expansion Bus

As you've learned, every device in the computer—whether soldered to the motherboard or snapped into a socket—connects to the external data bus and the address bus. The expansion slots are no exception. They connect to the rest of the PC through the chipset. Exactly *where* on the chipset varies depending on the system. On some systems, the expansion slots connect to the Southbridge (see Figure 9-21). On other systems, the expansion

slots connect to the Northbridge (see Figure 9-22). Finally, many systems have more than one type of expansion bus, with slots of one type connecting to the Northbridge and slots of another type connecting to the Southbridge (see Figure 9-23).

Figure 9-21
Expansion slots connecting to Southbridge

Figure 9-22
Expansion slots connecting to Northbridge

Figure 9-23
Expansion slots connecting to both Northbridge and Southbridge

The chipset provides an extension of the address bus and data bus to the expansion slots, and thus to any expansion cards in those slots. If you plug a hard drive controller card into an expansion slot, it functions just as if it were built into the motherboard, albeit with one big difference: speed. As you'll recall from Chapter 6, the system crystal—the clock—pushes the CPU. The system crystal provides a critical function for the entire PC, acting like a drill sergeant calling a cadence, setting the pace of activity in the computer. Every device soldered to the motherboard is designed to run at the speed of the system crystal. A 133-MHz motherboard, for example, has its chipset chips all timed by a 133-MHz crystal (see Figure 9-24).

The system crystal
sits on its own bus.

Figure 9-24 The system crystal sets the speed.

Clock crystals aren't just for CPUs and chipsets. Pretty much every chip in your computer has a CLK wire and needs to be pushed by a clock chip, including the chips

on your expansion cards. Suppose you buy a device that did not come with your computer—say, a sound card. The chips on the sound card need to be pushed by a CLK signal from a crystal. If PCs were designed to use the system crystal to push that sound card, sound card manufacturers would need to make sound cards for every possible motherboard speed. You would have to buy a 100-MHz sound card for a 100-MHz system or a 133-MHz sound card for a 133-MHz system.

That would be ridiculous, and IBM knew it when they designed the PC. They had to make an extension to the external data bus that *ran at its own standardized speed*. You would use this part of the external data bus to snap new devices into the PC. IBM achieved this goal by adding a different crystal, called the *expansion bus crystal*, which controlled the part of the external data bus connected to the expansion slots (see Figure 9-25).

Figure 9-25 Function of system and expansion bus crystals

The expansion slots run at a much slower speed than the frontside bus. The chipset acts as the divider between the two buses, compensating for the speed difference with wait states and special buffering (storage) areas. No matter how fast the motherboard runs, the expansion slots run at a standard speed. In the original IBM PC, that speed was about 14.318 MHz ÷ 2, or about 7.16 MHz. Luckily, modern expansion buses run much faster! Let's start with the oldest of the modern expansion slots, PCI.

PCI

Intel introduced the *Peripheral Component Interconnect (PCI)* bus architecture (see Figure 9-26) in the early 1990s, and the PC expansion bus was never again the same. Intel made many smart moves with PCI, not the least of which was releasing PCI to the public domain to make PCI very attractive to manufacturers. PCI provided a wider, faster, more flexible alternative than any previous expansion bus. The exceptional technology of the new bus, combined with the lack of a price tag, made manufacturers quickly drop older buses and adopt PCI.

Figure 9-26
PCI expansion
bus slots

PCI really shook up the PC world with its capabilities. The original PCI bus was 32 bits wide and ran at 33 MHz, which was superb, but these features were expected and not earth-shattering. The coolness of PCI came from its capability to coexist with other expansion buses. When PCI first came out, you could buy a motherboard with both PCI and older slots. This was important because users could keep their old expansion cards and slowly migrate to PCI. Equally impressive was that PCI devices were (and still are) self-configuring, a feature that led to the industry standard that became known as plug and play (PnP). Finally, PCI had a powerful burst-mode feature that enabled very efficient data transfers.

NOTE Before PCI, it was rare to see more than one type of expansion slot on a motherboard. Today this not only is common—it's expected!

The original PCI expansion bus has soldiered on in PCs for almost twenty years at the time of this writing. Recently, more advanced forms have begun to appear. Although these new PCI expansion buses are faster than the original PCI, they're only improvements to PCI, not entirely new expansion buses. The original PCI might be fading away, but PCI in its many new forms is still "King of the Motherboard."

TIP There was a 64-bit version of the original PCI standard, but it was quite rare.

AGP

When video started going graphical with the introduction of Windows, the current buses were too slow and graphics looked terrible. PCI certainly improved graphics when it came out, but Intel was thinking ahead. Shortly after Intel invented PCI, they presented a specialized, video-only version of PCI called the *Accelerated Graphics Port (AGP)*. An AGP slot is a PCI slot, but one with a direct connection to the Northbridge. AGP slots are only for video cards—don't try to snap a sound card or modem into one. You'll learn much more about this fascinating technology in Chapter 21. Figure 9-27 shows a typical AGP slot.

Figure 9-27
AGP slot

NOTE The AGP slot is almost universally brown in color, making it easy to spot.

PCI-X

PCI Extended (PCI-X) is a huge enhancement to PCI that is also fully backward compatible in terms of both hardware and software. PCI-X is a 64-bit-wide bus (see Figure 9-28). Its slots will accept regular PCI cards. The real bonus of PCI-X is its much enhanced speed. The PCI-X 2.0 standard features four speed grades (measured in MHz): PCI-X 66, PCI-X 133, PCI-X 266, and PCI-X 533.

Figure 9-28
PCI-X slot

The obvious candidates for PCI-X are businesses using workstations and servers, because they have the "need for speed" and also the need for backward compatibility. Large vendors, especially in the high-end market, are already on board. HP, Dell, and Intel server products, for example, support PCI-X. A quick online shopping trip reveals tons of PCI-X stuff for sale: gigabit NICs, Fibre Channel cards, video adapters, and more.

Mini-PCI

PCI has even made it into laptops in the specialty *Mini-PCI* format (see Figure 9-29). You'll find Mini-PCI in just about every laptop these days. Mini-PCI is designed to use low power and to lie flat—both good features for a laptop expansion slot. Mini-PCI returns in Chapter 26.

Figure 9-29
Tiny card in Mini-PCI slot. See the contacts at the bottom of the picture?

PCI Express

PCI Express (PCIe) is the latest, fastest, and most popular expansion bus in use today. As its name implies, PCI Express is still PCI, but it uses a point-to-point serial connection instead of PCI's shared parallel communication. Consider a single 32-bit chunk of data moving from a device to the CPU. In PCI parallel communication, 32 wires each carry one bit of that chunk of data. In serial communication, only one wire carries those 32 bits. You'd think that 32 wires are better than one, correct? Well, first of all, PCIe doesn't share the bus. A PCIe device has its own direct connection (a point-to-point connection) to the Northbridge, so it does not wait for other devices. Plus, when you start going really fast (think gigabits per second), getting all 32 bits of data to go from one device to another at the same time is difficult, because some bits get there slightly faster than others. That means you need some serious, high-speed checking of the data when it arrives to verify that it's all there and in good shape. Serial data doesn't have this problem, as all of the bits arrive one after the other in a single stream. When data is really going fast, a single point-to-point serial connection is faster than a shared 32-wire parallel connection.

And boy howdy, is PCIe ever fast! A PCIe connection uses one wire for sending and one for receiving. Each of these pairs of wires between a PCIe controller and a device is called a *lane*. Each direction of a lane runs at 2.5 Gbps, or 5 Gbps with PCIe 2.0. Better yet, each point-to-point connection can use 1, 2, 4, 8, 12, 16, or 32 lanes to achieve a maximum theoretical bandwidth of 320 Gbps. The effective data rate drops a little bit because of the *encoding scheme*—the way the data is broken down and reassembled—but full-duplex data throughput can go up to a whopping 16 GBps on a ×16 connection.

NOTE At the time of this writing, nearly every PCIe device for sale at retail outlets is PCIe 2.0, because 5 Gbps per lane seems fast enough with today's devices. That hasn't stopped the industry group behind the PCI specifications, PCI-SIG, from planning ahead. In November 2010 they announced the specifications for PCIe 3.0, with devices capable of achieving lane speeds up to 8 Gbps. The first devices to use PCIe 3.0 appeared in early 2012. Plus they've announced plans for PCIe 4.0 with the expectation of reaching 16-Gbps lane speeds. Expect PCIe 4.0 specifications in 2014 with devices to follow. The future looks very fast indeed!

The most common PCIe slot is the 16-lane (×16) version most commonly used for video cards, as shown in Figure 9-30. The first versions of PCIe motherboards used a combination of a single PCIe ×16 slot and a number of standard PCI slots. (Remember, PCI is designed to work with other expansion slots, even other types of PCI.) There is also a small form factor version of PCI Express for mobile computers called PCI Express Mini Card.

Figure 9-30
PCIe ×16 slot (center) with PCI slots (top and bottom)

The bandwidth generated by a ×16 slot is far more than anything other than a video card would need, so most PCIe motherboards also contain slots with fewer lanes. Currently ×1 is the most common general-purpose PCIe slot (see Figure 9-31).

Figure 9-31
PCIe ×1 slot (top)

NOTE When you talk about the lanes, such as ×1 or ×8, use "by" rather than "ex" for the multiplication mark. So "by 1" and "by 8" is the correct pronunciation. You'll of course hear it spoken as both "by 8" and "8 ex" for the next few years until the technology has become a household term.

Installing Expansion Cards

Installing an expansion card successfully—another one of those bread-and-butter tasks for the PC tech—requires at least four steps. First, you need to know that the card works with the PC and the operating system. Second, you have to insert the card in an expansion slot properly and without damaging the card or the motherboard. Third, you need to provide drivers for the operating system—*proper* drivers for the *specific* OS. Fourth, you should always verify that the card functions properly before you walk away from the PC.

EXAM TIP The four steps involved in installing expansion cards apply to all types of expansion cards. The CompTIA A+ exams will ask you about cards ranging from the common—sound, video, and networking—to the legacy—serial, parallel, and modem. They'll ask about wireless networking cards, TV tuner cards, video capture cards, and more, all of which we'll cover in their proper chapters in this book. You install any of them using the same four steps: knowledge, physical installation, device drivers, and verification.

Step 1: Knowledge

Learn about the device you plan to install—preferably before you purchase it! Does the device work with the PC and the OS? Does it have drivers for your operating system? If you use Windows, the answer to these questions is almost always "yes." If you use an old operating system such as Windows XP or a less common operating system such as Linux, these questions become important. A lot of older hardware simply won't work with Windows Vista or Windows 7 at all, especially if you go for the 64-bit versions. Check the device's documentation and check the device manufacturer's Web site to verify that you have the correct drivers. While you're checking, make sure you have the latest version of the driver; most devices get driver updates more often than the weather changes in Texas.

For Windows systems, your best resource for this knowledge is the Microsoft Web site. The specific list of supported hardware has changed names many times. Currently for Windows 7 it's called the *Windows 7 Compatibility Center*. Earlier operating systems called it the *Hardware Compatibility List (HCL)* or *Windows Logo'd Product List*, and you'll still hear lots of people refer to it by one of those names, especially the former. You can check out the Web site here:

www.microsoft.com/windows/compatibility/windows-7/en-us/default.aspx

This might list your product, but most people just look on the box of the device in question (see Figure 9-32)—all Windows-certified devices proudly display that they work with Windows.

Figure 9-32
Works with
Windows 7!

Step 2: Physical Installation

To install an expansion card successfully, you need to take steps to avoid damaging the card, the motherboard, or both. This means knowing how to handle a card and avoiding electrostatic discharge (ESD) or any other electrical issue. You also need to place the card firmly and completely into an available expansion slot.

Optimally, a card should always be in one of two places: in a computer or in an anti-static bag. When inserting or removing a card, be careful to hold the card only by its edges. Do not hold the card by the slot connectors or touch any components on the board (see Figure 9-33).

Figure 9-33
Where to handle
a card

Use an anti-static wrist strap if possible, properly attached to the PC, as noted in Chapter 2. If you don't have a wrist strap, you can use the tech way of avoiding ESD by touching the power supply after you remove the expansion card from its anti-static bag. This puts you, the card, and the PC at the same electrical potential and thus minimizes the risk of ESD.

Modern systems have a trickle of voltage on the motherboard at all times when the computer is plugged into a power outlet. Chapter 10 covers power for the PC and how to deal with it in detail, but here's the short version: *Always unplug the PC before inserting an expansion card!* Failure to do so can destroy the card, the motherboard, or both. It's not worth the risk.

Never insert or remove a card at an extreme angle. This may damage the card. A slight angle is acceptable and even necessary when removing a card. Always secure the card to the case with a connection screw or other retaining mechanism. This keeps the card from slipping out and potentially shorting against other cards. Also, many cards use the screw connection to ground the card to the case (see Figure 9-34).

Figure 9-34
Always secure all cards properly.

Many technicians have been told to clean the slot connectors if a particular card is not working. This is almost never necessary after a card is installed and, if done improperly, can cause damage. You should clean slot connectors only if you have a card that's been on the shelf for a while and the contacts are obviously dull.

Never use a pencil eraser for this purpose. Pencil erasers can leave behind bits of residue that wedge between the card and slot, preventing contact and causing the card to fail. Grab a can of contact cleaning solution and use it instead. Contact cleaning solution is designed exactly for this purpose, cleans contacts nicely, and doesn't leave any residue. You can find contact cleaning solution at any electronics store.

A fully inserted expansion card sits flush against the back of the PC case—assuming the motherboard is mounted properly, of course—with no gap between the mounting bracket on the card and the screw hole on the case. If the card is properly seated, no contacts are exposed above the slot. Figure 9-35 shows a properly seated (meaning fitted snugly in the slot) expansion card.

Figure 9-35
Properly seated expansion card; note the tight fit between case and mounting bracket and the evenness of the card in the slot.

Step 3: Device Drivers

You know from Chapter 8 that all devices, whether built into the motherboard or added along the way, require BIOS. For almost all expansion cards, that BIOS comes in the form of *device drivers*—software support programs—loaded from an optical disc provided by the card manufacturer.

Installing device drivers is fairly straightforward. You should use the correct drivers—kind of obvious, but you'd be surprised how many techs mess this up—and, if you're upgrading, you might have to unload current drivers before loading new drivers. Finally, if you have a problem, you may need to uninstall the drivers you just loaded or roll back to earlier, more stable drivers.

Getting the Correct Drivers

To be sure you have the best possible driver you can get for your device, you should always check the manufacturer's Web site. The drivers that come with a device may work well, but odds are good that you'll find a newer and better driver on the Web site. How do you know that the drivers on the Web site are newer? First, take the easy route: look on the disc. Often the version is printed right on the CD or DVD. If it's not printed there, you're going to have to load the disc in your optical drive and poke around. Many driver discs have an AutoRun screen that advertises the version. If nothing is on the pop-up screen, look for a Readme file (see Figure 9-36).

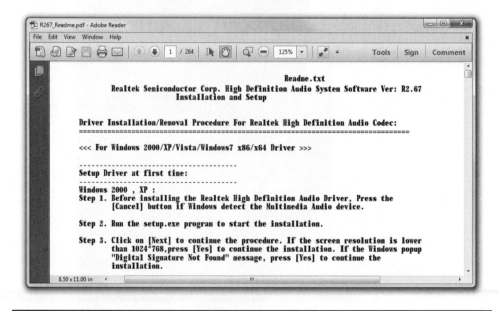

Figure 9-36 Part of a Readme file showing the driver version

Driver or Device?

In almost all cases, you should install the device driver after you install the device. Without the device installed, the driver installation will not see the device and will give an error screen. The only exceptions to this rule are USB and FireWire devices—with these you should always install the driver first.

Removing the Old Drivers

Some cards—and this is especially true with video cards—require you to remove old drivers of the same type before you install the new device. To do this, you must first locate the driver in Device Manager. Right-click the device driver you want to uninstall and select Uninstall (see Figure 9-37). Many devices, especially ones that come with a lot of applications, will have an uninstall option in the Add or Remove Programs (Windows XP) or Programs and Features (Windows Vista/7) applet in the Control Panel (see Figure 9-38).

Figure 9-37
Uninstalling a device

Unsigned Drivers

Microsoft truly wants your computer to work, so they provide an excellent and rigorous testing program for hardware manufacturers called the *Windows Certification Program*. Developers initially use software to test their devices and, when they're ready, submit the device for further testing. Hardware and drivers that survive the testing get to wear the *Designed for Windows* logo. The drivers get a digital signature that says Microsoft tested them and found all was well.

Figure 9-38 The Uninstall/Change option in Programs and Features

Not all driver makers go through the rather involved process of the Windows Certification Program, so their software does not get a digital signature from Microsoft. When Windows runs into such a driver, it brings up a scary-looking screen (see Figure 9-39) that says you're about to install an *unsigned driver*.

Figure 9-39
Unsigned driver
warning

The fact that a company refuses to use the Windows Certification Program doesn't mean their drivers are bad—it simply means they haven't gone through Microsoft's exhaustive quality-assurance certification procedure. If I run into this, I usually check the driver's version to make sure I'm not installing something outdated, and then I just

take my chances and install it. (I've yet to encounter a problem with an unsigned driver that I haven't also seen with *Designed for Windows* drivers.)

With the 64-bit versions of Windows Vista and Windows 7, Microsoft tightened the rules to try to provide the most stable platform possible. You simply cannot install unsigned drivers without clunky workarounds. Microsoft must approve each 64-bit driver.

Installing the New Driver

You have two ways to install a new driver: by using the installation disc directly or by using the Add Hardware Wizard in the Control Panel. Most experienced techs prefer to run from the installation disc. Most devices come with extra programs. My motherboard comes with a number of handy applications for monitoring temperature and overclocking. The Add Hardware Wizard does not install anything but the drivers. Granted, some techs find this a blessing because they don't want all of the extra junk that sometimes comes with a device, but most installation discs give clear options so you can pick and choose what you want to install (see Figure 9-40).

Figure 9-40

Installation menu

The other reason to use installation discs instead of the Add Hardware Wizard stems from the fact that many expansion cards are actually many devices in one, and each device needs its own drivers. Some video cards have built-in TV tuners, for example. The Add Hardware Wizard will install all of the devices, but the installation disc brings them to your attention. Go for the optical disc installation program first and save the Add Hardware Wizard for problems, as you'll see in the next section.

Driver Rollback

All versions of Windows offer the nifty feature of rolling back to previous drivers after an installation or driver upgrade. If you decide to live on the edge and install beta drivers for your video card, for example, and your system becomes frightfully unstable,

you can roll back to the drivers that worked before. (Not that I've ever had to use that feature….) To access the rollback feature, simply open Device Manager and access the properties for the device you want to adjust. On the Driver tab (see Figure 9-41), you'll find the Roll Back Driver button.

Figure 9-41

Driver rollback feature

Silicon Image SiI 3512 SATALink Controller Properties

| General | Device Info | Driver | Details | Resources |

Silicon Image SiI 3512 SATALink Controller

Driver Provider: Silicon Image
Driver Date: 8/19/2008
Driver Version: 1.3.71.1
Digital Signer: microsoft windows hardware compatibility publish

Driver Details — To view details about the driver files.

Update Driver... — To update the driver software for this device.

Roll Back Driver — If the device fails after updating the driver, roll back to the previously installed driver.

Disable — Disables the selected device.

Uninstall — To uninstall the driver (Advanced).

OK Cancel

TIP To install drivers in a Windows computer, you need to have the proper permission. I'm not talking about asking somebody if you're allowed to install the device. Permissions are granted in Windows to enable people to do certain things, such as add a printer to a local computer or install software, or to stop people from being able to do such tasks. Specifically, you need administrative permissions to install drivers.

Step 4: Verify

As a last step in the installation process, inspect the results of the installation and verify that the device works properly. Immediately after installing, you should open Device Manager and verify that Windows sees the device (see Figure 9-42). Assuming that Device Manager shows the device working properly, your next check is to put the device to work by making it do whatever it is supposed to do. If you installed a printer, print something; if you installed a scanner, scan something. If it works, you're finished!

Figure 9-42
Device Manager
shows the device
working properly.

Silicon Image SiI 3512 SATALink Controller Properties

General | Device Info | Driver | Details | Resources

Silicon Image SiI 3512 SATALink Controller

Device type: Storage controllers
Manufacturer: Silicon Image
Location: PCI bus 1, device 13, function 0

Device status

This device is working properly.

OK Cancel

TIP Many PC enthusiasts try to squeeze every bit of performance out of their PC components, much as auto enthusiasts tinker with engine tunings to get a little extra horsepower out of their engines. Expansion card manufacturers love enthusiasts, who often act as free testers for their unpolished drivers, known as *beta drivers*. Beta drivers are fine for the most part, but they can sometimes cause amazing system instability—never a good thing! If you use beta drivers, make sure you know how to uninstall or roll back to previous drivers.

Troubleshooting Expansion Cards

A properly installed expansion card rarely makes trouble; it's the botched installations that produce headaches. Chances are high that you'll have to troubleshoot an expansion card installation at some point, usually from an installation you botched personally.

The sign of an improperly installed card usually shows up the moment you first try to get that card to do whatever it's supposed to do and it doesn't do it. When this happens, your primary troubleshooting process is a reinstallation—after checking in with Device Manager.

Other chapters in this book cover specific hardware troubleshooting: sound cards in Chapter 25, for example, and video cards in Chapter 21. Use this section to help you decide what to look for and how to deal with the problem.

Device Manager provides the first diagnostic and troubleshooting tool in Windows. After you install a new device, Device Manager gives you many clues if something has gone wrong.

Occasionally, Device Manager may not even show the new device. If that happens, verify that you inserted the device properly and, if needed, that the device has power. Run the Add Hardware Wizard and see if Windows recognizes the device. You'll find the wizard as a Control Panel applet in Windows XP and Windows Vista. In Windows 7, you run the program by clicking Start and typing the name of the executable in the Search bar: **hdwwiz.exe**.

 EXAM TIP Don't be surprised to see hdwwiz.exe on the CompTIA A+ exams. It's the only way to run the Add Hardware Wizard in Windows 7.

If Device Manager doesn't recognize the device at this point, you have one of two problems: either the device is physically damaged and you must replace it, or the device is an onboard device, not a card, and is turned off in CMOS.

Device Manager rarely completely fails to see a device. More commonly, device problems manifest themselves in Device Manager via error icons:

- A black "!" on a yellow circle (Windows XP) or triangle (Windows Vista/7) indicates that a device is missing (see Figure 9-43), that Windows does not recognize a device, or that there's a device driver problem. A device may still work even while producing this error.

Figure 9-43
An "!" in Device Manager, indicating a problem with the selected device

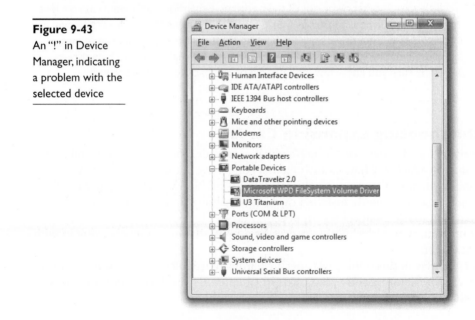

- A black downward-pointing arrow on a white field in Windows Vista and Windows 7 indicates a disabled device. This usually points to a device that's been manually turned off, or a damaged device. A device producing this error will not work. Windows XP uses a red "X" for the same status indicator.

The "!" symbol is the most common error symbol and usually the easiest to fix. First, double-check the device's connections. Second, try reinstalling the driver with the Update Driver button. To get to the Update Driver button, right-click the desired device in Device Manager and select Properties. In the Properties dialog box, select the Driver tab. On the Driver tab, click the Update Driver button to open the updating wizard (see Figure 9-44).

Figure 9-44
Updating the driver

If you get a downward-pointing arrow or a red "X" error, first check that the device isn't disabled. Right-click on the device and select Enable. If that doesn't work (it often does not), try rolling back the driver (if you updated the driver) or uninstalling (if it's a new install). Shut the system down and make triple-sure you have the card physically installed. Then redo the entire driver installation procedure, making sure you have the most current driver for that device. If none of these procedures works, return the card—it's almost certainly bad.

As you look at the errors in Device Manager, you'll notice error codes for the device that does not work properly. Windows has about 20 error codes, but the fixes still boil down to the same methods just shown. If you really want to frustrate yourself, try the Troubleshooter. It starts most fixes the same way: by reinstalling the device driver.

Upgrading and Installing Motherboards

To most techs, the concept of adding or replacing a motherboard can be extremely intimidating. It really shouldn't be; motherboard installation is a common and necessary part of PC repair. It is inexpensive and easy, although it can sometimes be a little tedious and messy because of the large number of parts involved. This section covers the process of installation and replacement and shows you some of the tricks that make this necessary process easy to handle.

Choosing the Motherboard and Case

Choosing a motherboard and case can prove quite a challenge for any tech, whether newly minted or a seasoned veteran. You first have to figure out the type of motherboard you want, such as AMD- or Intel-based. Then you need to think about the form factor, which of course influences the type of case you'll need. Third, how rich in features is the motherboard and how tough is it to configure? You have to read the motherboard manual to find out. Finally, you need to select the case that matches your space needs, budget, and form factor. Now look at each step in a little more detail.

 EXAM TIP Being able to select and install a motherboard appropriate for a client or customer is something every CompTIA A+ technician should know.

First, determine what motherboard you need. What CPU are you using? Will the motherboard work with that CPU? Because most of us buy the CPU and the motherboard at the same time, make the seller guarantee that the CPU will work with the motherboard. If you can, choose a motherboard that works with much higher speeds than the CPU you can afford; that way you can upgrade later. How much RAM do you intend to install? Are extra RAM sockets available for future upgrades?

 NOTE Chapter 31 covers items needed for specialized PCs.

A number of excellent motherboard manufacturers currently exist. Some of the more popular brands are ASUS, BIOSTAR, DFI, GIGABYTE, Intel, MSI, and Shuttle. Your supplier may also have some lesser-known but perfectly acceptable brands of motherboards. As long as the supplier has an easy return policy, it's perfectly fine to try one of these.

Second, make sure you're getting a form factor that works with your case. Don't try to put a regular ATX motherboard into a microATX case!

Third, all motherboards come with a technical manual, better known as the *motherboard book* (see Figure 9-45). You must have this book! This book is your primary source for all of the critical information about the motherboard. If you set up CPU or RAM

timings incorrectly in CMOS, for example, and you have a dead PC, where would you find the CMOS-clear jumper? Where do you plug in the speaker? Even if you let someone else install the motherboard, insist on the motherboard book; you will need it.

Figure 9-45
Motherboard box
and book

TIP If you have a motherboard with no manual, you can usually find a copy of the manual in Adobe Acrobat (.PDF) format online at the manufacturer's Web site. It's a good idea to grab and print a copy to keep with the motherboard. I often tape a copy (either hard copy or burned onto a disc) of the manual in the case where I installed the motherboard. Just don't cover any vents!

Fourth, pick your case carefully. Cases come in many sizes: slimline, desktop, mini-tower, mid-tower, tower, and cube. Plus you can get specialized cases, such as tiny cases for entertainment systems or ones that fit the same format as a stereo receiver or DVD player. Slimline and desktop models generally sit on the desk, beneath the monitor. The various tower cases usually occupy a bit of floor space next to the desk. The mini-tower and mid-tower cases are the most popular choices. Make sure you get a case that fits your motherboard—most microATX and all FlexATX cases are too small for a regular ATX motherboard. Cube cases generally require a specific motherboard, so be prepared to buy both pieces at once. A quick test-fit before you buy saves a lot of return trips to the supplier.

Cases come with many options, but three more common options point to a better case. One option is a removable face (see Figure 9-46) to make disassembly much easier.

Figure 9-46

Removable face

Another common feature, front-mounted ports for USB, FireWire, and headphones, can make using a PC much easier. Better cases offer these ports, although you can also get add-on components that fit into the now-useless floppy drive bay to bring added front connectivity to the PC. Figure 9-47 shows a case with both types of front connectors.

Better cases offer tool-free component installation, so you don't have to screw down cards or drives. They just snap into place. (You'll still need a trusty screwdriver to secure the motherboard, though. No installation is completely tool-free yet.)

Power supplies often come with the case. Watch out for "really good deal" cases because that invariably points to a cheap or missing power supply. You also need to verify that the power supply has sufficient wattage. This issue is handled in Chapter 10.

Installing the Motherboard

If you're replacing a motherboard, first remove the old motherboard. Begin by removing all of the cards. Also remove anything else that might impede removal or installation

of the motherboard, such as a hard drive. Keep track of the screws—a good idea is to return the screws to their mounting holes temporarily, at least until you can reinstall the parts. Sometimes you even have to remove the power supply temporarily to enable access to the motherboard.

Figure 9-47
Case with both front-mounted ports and an add-on flash memory card reader

 EXAM TIP The CompTIA A+ exams will test you on the basics of installing a motherboard.

Unscrew the motherboard. *It will not simply lift out.* The motherboard mounts to the case via small connectors called *standouts* that slide into keyed slots or screw into the bottom of the case (see Figure 9-48). Screws then go into the standouts to hold the motherboard in place. Be sure to place the standouts properly before installing the new motherboard.

 CAUTION Watch out for ESD here! Remember that it's very easy to damage or destroy a CPU and RAM with a little electrostatic discharge. It's also fairly easy to damage the motherboard with ESD. Always wear an anti-static wrist strap.

Figure 9-48
Standout in a case, ready for the motherboard

When you insert the new motherboard, do not assume that you will put the screws and standouts in the same place as they were in your old motherboard. When it comes to the placement of screws and standouts, only one rule applies: anywhere it fits. Do not be afraid to be a little tough here! Installing motherboards can be a wiggling, twisting, knuckle-scraping process.

CAUTION Pay attention to the location of the standouts if you're swapping a motherboard. If you leave a screw-type standout beneath a spot on the motherboard where you can't add a screw and then apply power to the motherboard, you run the risk of shorting the motherboard.

TIP A lot of techs install the CPU, CPU fan, and RAM into the motherboard before installing the motherboard into the case. This helps in several ways, especially with a new system. First, you want to make certain that the CPU and RAM work well with the motherboard and with each other—without that, you have no hope of setting up a stable system. Second, installing these components first prevents the phenomenon of *flexing* the motherboard. Some cases don't provide quite enough support for the motherboard, and pushing in RAM can make the board bend. Third, attaching a CPU fan can be a bear of a task, one that's considerably easier to do on a table top than within the confines of a case.

The next part of motherboard installation is connecting the LEDs, buttons, and front-mounted ports on the front of the box. This is sometimes easier to do before you install the motherboard fully in the case. You can trace the wire leads from the front of the case to the appropriate standouts on the motherboard. These usually include the following:

- Soft power button
- Reset button
- Speaker
- Hard drive activity light
- Power light
- USB
- FireWire
- Sound

These wires have specific pin connections to the motherboard. Although you can refer to the motherboard book for their location, usually a quick inspection of the motherboard will suffice for an experienced tech (see Figure 9-49).

Figure 9-49
Motherboard wire connections labeled on the mother-board

You need to follow a few rules when installing these wires. First, the lights are LEDs, not light bulbs; they have a positive side and a negative side. If they don't work one way, turn the connector around and try the other. Second, when in doubt, guess. Incorrect installation only results in the device not working; it won't damage the computer. Refer to the motherboard book for the correct installation. The third and last rule is that, with the exception of the soft power switch on an ATX system, you do not need any of these

wires for the computer to run. Many techs often simply ignore these wires, although this would not be something I'd do to any system but my own.

No hard-and-fast rule exists for determining the function of each wire. Often the function of each wire is printed on the connector (see Figure 9-50). If not, track each wire to the LED or switch to determine its function.

Figure 9-50
Sample of case
wires

Finally, install the motherboard into the case fully and secure it with the appropriate screws. Once you get the motherboard mounted in the case, with the CPU and RAM properly installed, it's time to insert the power connections and test it. A POST card can be helpful with the system test because you won't have to add the speaker, a video card, monitor, and keyboard to verify that the system is booting. If you have a POST card, start the system, and watch to see if the POST takes place—you should see a number of POST codes before the POST stops. If you don't have a POST card, install a keyboard, speaker, video card, and monitor. Boot the system and see if the BIOS information shows up on the screen. If it does, you're probably okay. If it doesn't, it's time to refer to the motherboard book to see where you made a mistake.

If you get no power at all, check to make sure you plugged in all the necessary power connectors. If you get power to fans but get nothing on the screen, you could have several problems. The CPU, RAM, or video card might not be connected to the motherboard properly. The only way to determine the problems is to test. Check the easy connections first (RAM and video) before removing and reseating the CPU. (Also, see Chapter 10 for power issues.)

 EXAM TIP Very old motherboards used to require techs to set jumpers to determine the bus speed for the motherboard. This enabled these

motherboards to accommodate CPUs that needed a 100-MHz bus, for example, and other CPUs that needed a 66-MHz bus. The CompTIA A+ exams might refer to these kinds of manual adjustments needed for installation.

Setting these jumpers incorrectly resulted in bizarre behavior. First, if you set the bus speed too high, many CPUs wouldn't even try to power up. If you set the speed too low, you wouldn't get optimal use out of the CPU. The motherboard manuals had extensive charts for settings for the CPUs supported.

Modern motherboards autodetect CPU and RAM settings and adjust accordingly, so these errors only happen when you intentionally overclock or underclock a CPU through the CMOS setup utility.

802

Troubleshooting Motherboards

Motherboards fail. Not often, but motherboards and motherboard components can die from many causes: time, dust, cat hair, or simply slight manufacturing defects made worse by the millions of amps of current sluicing through the motherboard traces. Installing cards, electrostatic discharge, flexing the motherboard one time too many when swapping out RAM or drives—any of these factors can cause a motherboard to fail. The motherboard is a hard-working, often abused component of the PC. Unfortunately for the common tech, troubleshooting a motherboard problem can be difficult and time consuming. Let's wrap up this chapter with a look at symptoms of a failing motherboard, techniques for troubleshooting, and the options you have when you discover a motherboard problem.

Symptoms

Motherboard failures commonly fall into three types: catastrophic, component, and ethereal. With a *catastrophic failure*, the PC just won't boot. Check the power and hard drive activity indicator lights on the front of the PC. Assuming they worked before, having them completely flat points to power supply failure or motherboard failure.

This sort of problem happens to brand-new systems because of manufacturing defects—often called a *burn-in failure*—and to any system that gets a shock of electrostatic discharge. Burn-in failure is uncommon and usually happens in the first 30 days of use. Swap out the motherboard for a replacement and you should be fine. If you accidentally zap your motherboard when inserting a card or moving wires around, be chagrined. Change your daring ways and wear an anti-static wrist strap!

Component failure happens rarely and appears as flaky connections between a device and motherboard, or as intermittent problems. A hard drive plugged into a faulty controller on the motherboard, for example, might show up in CMOS autodetect but be

inaccessible in Windows. Another example is a serial controller that worked fine for months until a big storm took out the external modem hooked to it, and doesn't work anymore, even with a replacement modem.

The most difficult of the three types of symptoms to diagnose are those I call *ethereal* symptoms. Stuff just doesn't work all of the time. The PC reboots itself. You get a Blue Screen of Death (BSoD) in the midst of heavy computing, such as right before you smack the villain and rescue the damsel. What can cause such symptoms? If you answered any of the following, you win the prize:

- Faulty component
- Buggy device driver
- Buggy application software
- Slight corruption of the operating system
- Power supply problems

Err…you get the picture.

What a nightmare scenario to troubleshoot! The Way of the Tech knows paths through such perils, though, so let's turn to troubleshooting techniques now.

Techniques

Troubleshooting a potential motherboard failure requires time, patience, and organization. Some problems will certainly be quicker to solve than others. If the hard drive doesn't work as expected, as in the previous example, check the settings on the drive. Try a different drive. Try the same drive with a different motherboard to verify that it's a good drive. Like every other troubleshooting technique, what you're trying to do with motherboard testing is to isolate the problem by eliminating potential factors.

This three-part system—check, replace, verify good component—works for both simple and more complicated motherboard problems. You can even apply the same technique to ethereal-type problems that might be anything, but you should add one more verb: *document*. Take notes on the individual components you test so you don't repeat efforts or waste time. Plus, taking notes can lead to the establishment of patterns. Being able to re-create a system crash by performing certain actions in a specific order can often lead you to the root of the problem. Document your actions. Motherboard testing is time-consuming enough without adding inefficiency.

Options

Once you determine that the motherboard has problems, you have several options for fixing the three types of failures. If you have a catastrophic failure, you must replace the motherboard. Even if it works somewhat, don't mess around. The motherboard should provide bedrock stability for the system. If it's even remotely buggy or problematic, get rid of it!

 CAUTION If you've lost components because of ESD or a power surge, you would most likely be better off replacing the motherboard. The damage you can't see can definitely sneak up to bite you and create system instability.

If you have a component failure, you can often replace the component with an add-on card that will be as good as or better than the failed device. Adaptec, for example, makes fine cards that can replace the built-in SATA ports on the motherboard (see Figure 9-51).

Figure 9-51
Adaptec PCIe
SATA card

If your component failure is more a technology issue than physical damage, you can try upgrading the BIOS on the motherboard. As you'll recall from Chapter 8 on BIOS, every motherboard comes with a small set of code that enables the CPU to communicate properly with the devices built into the motherboard. You can quite readily upgrade this programming by *flashing the BIOS*: running a small command-line program to write new BIOS in the flash ROM chip. Refer to Chapter 8 for the details on flashing.

NOTE Flashing the BIOS for a motherboard can fix a lot of system stability problems and provide better implementation of built-in technology. What it cannot do for your system is improve the hardware. If AMD comes out with a new, improved, lower-voltage Phenom, for example, and your motherboard cannot scale down the voltage properly, you cannot use that CPU—even if it fits in your motherboard's Socket AM3. No amount of BIOS flashing can change the hardware built into your motherboard.

Finally, if you have an ethereal, ghost-in-the-machine type of problem that you have determined to be motherboard related, you have only a couple of options for fixing the problem. You can flash the BIOS in a desperate attempt to correct whatever it is, which sometimes works and is less expensive than the other option, which is replacing the motherboard.

Chapter Review

Questions

1. Which of the following statements about the expansion bus is true?

 A. The expansion bus runs at the speed of the system clock.

 B. The expansion bus crystal sets the speed for the expansion bus.

 C. The CPU communicates with RAM via the expansion bus.

 D. The frontside bus is another name for the expansion bus.

2. What does a black down arrow next to a device in Device Manager indicate?

 A. A compatible driver has been installed that may not provide all of the functions for the device.

 B. The device is missing or Windows cannot recognize it.

 C. The system resources have been assigned manually.

 D. The device has been disabled.

3. Which variation of the PCI bus was specifically designed for laptops?

 A. PCI-X

 B. PCIe

 C. Mini-PCI

 D. AGP

4. Which of the following form factors dominates the PC industry?

 A. AT

 B. ATX

 C. ITX

 D. CTX

5. Amanda bought a new system that, right in the middle of an important presentation, gave her a Blue Screen of Death. Now her system won't boot at all, not even to CMOS. After extensive troubleshooting, she determined that the

motherboard was at fault and replaced it. Now the system runs fine. What was the most likely cause of the problem?

 A. Burn-in failure

 B. Electrostatic discharge

 C. Component failure

 D. Power supply failure

6. Martin bought a new motherboard to replace his older ATX motherboard. As he left the shop, the tech on duty called after him, "Check your standouts!" What could the tech have meant?

 A. Standouts are the connectors on the motherboard for the front panel buttons, such as the on/off switch and reset button.

 B. Standouts are the metal edges on some cases that aren't rolled.

 C. Standouts are the metal connectors that attach the motherboard to the case.

 D. Standouts are the dongles that enable a motherboard to support more than four USB ports.

7. Solon has a very buggy computer that keeps locking up at odd moments and rebooting spontaneously. He suspects the motherboard. How should he test it?

 A. Check settings and verify good components.

 B. Verify good components and document all testing.

 C. Replace the motherboard first to see if the problems disappear.

 D. Check settings, verify good components, replace components, and document all testing.

8. When Jane proudly displayed her new motherboard, the senior tech scratched his beard and asked, "What kind of ICH does it have?" What could he possibly be asking about?

 A. The AMR slot

 B. The CNR slot

 C. The Northbridge

 D. The Southbridge

9. What companies dominate the chipset market? (Select two.)

 A. ATI

 B. Intel

 C. NVIDIA

 D. SiS

10. If Windows recognizes a device, where will it appear?

 A. Device Manager

 B. C:\Windows\System32\Devices

 C. Desktop

 D. Safely remove hardware applet

Answers

1. **B.** A separate expansion bus crystal enables the expansion bus to run at a different speed than the frontside bus.

2. **D.** The device has been disabled.

3. **C.** The Mini-PCI format conserves space and power, making it an ideal card type for use in laptops.

4. **B.** Almost all modern motherboards follow the ATX form factor.

5. **A.** Although all of the answers are plausible, the best answer here is that her system suffered burn-in failure.

6. **C.** Standouts are the metal connectors that attach the motherboard to the case.

7. **D.** Solon needs to check settings, verify good components, replace components, and document all testing.

8. **D.** Intel calls their Southbridge chips the I/O Controller Hub (ICH) on many of their chipsets.

9. **B, C.** Intel and NVIDIA produce the vast majority of the chipsets used in personal computers.

10. **A.** Windows displays recognized devices in Device Manager.

Power Supplies

In this chapter, you will learn how to
- Explain the basics of electricity
- Describe the details about powering the PC
- Install and maintain power supplies
- Understand power supply troubleshooting and fire safety

Powering the PC requires a single box—the power supply—that takes electricity from the wall socket and transforms it into electricity to run the motherboard and other internal components. Figure 10-1 shows a typical power supply inside a case. All of the wires dangling out of it connect to the motherboard and peripherals.

Figure 10-1
Typical power supply mounted inside the PC system unit

As simple as this appears on the surface, power supply issues are of critical importance for techs. Problems with power can create system instability, crashes, and data loss—all things most computer users would rather avoid! Good techs therefore know an awful lot about powering the PC, from understanding the basic principles of electricity to knowing the many variations of PC power supplies. Plus, you need to know how to recognize power problems and implement the proper solutions. Too many techs fall into the "just plug it in" camp and never learn how to deal with power, much to their clients' unhappiness.

EXAM TIP Some questions on the CompTIA A+ certification exams could refer to a power supply as a *PSU*, for *power supply unit*. A power supply also falls into the category of *field replaceable unit (FRU)*, which refers to the typical parts a tech should carry, such as RAM and a hard drive.

Historical/Conceptual

Understanding Electricity

Electricity is a flow of negatively charged particles, called electrons, through matter. All matter enables the flow of electrons to some extent. This flow of electrons is very similar to the flow of water through pipes; so similar that the best way to learn about electricity is by comparing it to how water flows though pipes. So let's talk about water for a moment.

Water comes from the ground, through wells, aquifers, rivers, and so forth. In a typical city, water comes to you through pipes from the water supply company that took it from the ground. What do you pay for when you pay your water bill each month? You pay for the water you use, certainly, but built into the price of the water you use is the surety that when you turn the spigot, water will flow at a more or less constant rate. The water sits in the pipes under pressure from the water company, waiting for you to turn the spigot.

Electricity works essentially the same way as water. Electric companies gather or generate electricity and then push it to your house under pressure through wires. Just like water, the electricity sits in the wires, waiting for you to plug something into the wall socket, at which time it'll flow at a more or less constant rate. You plug a lamp into an electrical outlet and flip the switch, electricity flows, and you have light. You pay for reliability, electrical pressure, and electricity used.

The pressure of the electrons in the wire is called *voltage* and is measured in units called *volts (V)*. The amount of electrons moving past a certain point on a wire is called the *current* or *amperage*, which is measured in units called *amperes (amps or A)*. The amount of amps and volts needed so that a particular device will function is expressed as how much *wattage (watts or W)* that device needs. The correlation between the three is very simple math: $V \times A = W$ (or $VA = W$). You'll learn more about wattage a little later in this chapter.

Wires of all sorts—whether copper, tin, gold, or platinum—have a slight *resistance* to the flow of electrons, just as water pipes have a slight amount of friction that resists the flow of water. Resistance to the flow of electrons is measured in *ohms (Ω)*.

- Pressure = voltage (V)
- Volume flowing = amperes (A)
- Work = wattage (W)
- Resistance = ohms (Ω)

A particular thickness of wire only handles so much electricity at a time. If you push too much through, the wire will overheat and break, much as an overloaded water pipe will burst. To make sure you use the right wire for the right job, all electrical wires have an amperage rating, such as 20 amps. If you try to push 30 amps through a 20-amp wire, the wire will break and electrons will seek a way to return into the ground. Not a good thing, especially if the path back to the ground is through you!

Circuit breakers and ground wires provide the basic protection from accidental overflow. A circuit breaker is a heat-sensitive electrical switch rated at a certain amperage. If you push too much amperage through the circuit breaker, the wiring inside detects the increase in heat and automatically opens, stopping the flow of electricity before the wiring overheats and breaks. You reset the circuit breaker to reestablish the circuit, and electricity flows once more through the wires. A ground wire provides a path of least resistance for electrons to flow back to ground in case of an accidental overflow.

Many years ago, your electrical supply used fuses instead of circuit breakers. Fuses are small devices with a tiny filament designed to break if subjected to too much current. Unfortunately, fuses had to be replaced every time they blew, making circuit breakers much more preferable. Even though you no longer see fuses in a building's electrical circuits, many electrical devices—such as a PC's power supply—often still use fuses for their own internal protection.

EXAM TIP An electrical outlet must have a ground wire to be suitable for PC use.

Electricity comes in two flavors: *direct current (DC)*, in which the electrons flow in one direction around a continuous circuit, and *alternating current (AC)*, in which the flow of electrons alternates direction back and forth in a circuit (see Figure 10-2). Most electronic devices use DC power, but all power companies supply AC power because AC travels long distances much more efficiently than DC.

Figure 10-2

Diagrams showing DC and AC flow of electrons

Constant voltage
in one direction

Voltage in both directions,
constantly switching
back and forth

not provide enough power to your system. Try to use the right power supply for your motherboard to avoid problems. Many ATX12V 2.0 power supplies have a convertible 24-to-20-pin converter. These are handy if you want to make a nice "clean" connection, because many 20-pin connectors have capacitors that prevent plugging in a 24-pin connector. You'll also see the occasional 24-pin connector constructed in such a way that you can slide off the extra four pins. Figure 10-22 shows 20-pin and 24-pin connectors; Figure 10-23 shows a convertible connector. Although they look similar, those extra four pins won't replace the P4 connector. They are incompatible!

Figure 10-22
20- and 24-pin
connectors

Figure 10-23
Convertible
motherboard
power connector

Many modern ATX motherboards feature an 8-pin CPU power connector like the one found in the EPS12V standard to help support high-end CPUs that demand a lot of power. This connector is referred to by several names, including EPS12V, EATX12V, and ATX12V 2x4. One half of this connector will be pin compatible with the P4 power connector and the other half may be under a protective cap. Be sure to check the motherboard installation manuals for recommendations on if and when you need to use the full 8 pins. For backward compatibility, some power supplies provide an 8-pin power connector that can split into two 4-pin sets, one of which is the P4 connector.

Another notable connector is the auxiliary PCI Express (PCIe) power connector. Figure 10-24 shows the 6-pin PCIe power connector. Some motherboards add a Molex socket for PCIe, and some cards come with a Molex socket as well. Higher-end cards have a dedicated 6-pin or 8-pin PCIe power connector. The 8-pin PCIe connector should not be confused with the EPS12V connector, as they are not compatible. Some PCIe devices with the 8-pin connector will accept a 6-pin PCIe power connection instead, but this may put limits on their performance. Often you'll find that 8-pin PCIe power cables have two pins at the end that you can detach for easy compatibility with 6-pin devices.

Figure 10-24
PCI Express 6-pin
power connector

Niche-Market Power Supply Form Factors

The demand for smaller and quieter PCs has led to the development of a number of niche-market power supply form factors. All use standard ATX connectors but differ in size and shape from standard ATX power supplies.

Here are some of the more common specialty power supply types:

- **Mini-ATX** and **micro-ATX** Smaller power supply form factors designed specifically for mini-ATX and micro-ATX cases, respectively

- **TFX12V** A small power supply form factor optimized for low-profile ATX systems

- **SFX12V** A small power supply form factor optimized for systems using Flex-ATX motherboards (see Figure 10-25)

Figure 10-25
SFX power supply

NOTE You'll commonly find niche-market power supplies bundled with computer cases (and often motherboards as well). These form factors are rarely sold alone.

EXAM TIP The CompTIA A+ exams test you pretty heavily on power supplies. You need to know what power supply works with a particular system or with a particular computing goal in mind.

Active PFC

Visualize the AC current coming from the power company as water in a pipe, smoothly moving back and forth, 60 times a second. A PC's power supply, simply due to the process of changing this AC current into DC current, is like a person sucking on a straw on the end of this pipe. It takes gulps only when the current is fully pushing or pulling at the top and bottom of each cycle and creating an electrical phenomena—sort of a back pressure—that's called *harmonics* in the power industry. These harmonics create the humming sound you hear from electrical components. Over time, harmonics damage electrical equipment, causing serious problems with the power supply and other electrical devices on the circuit. Once you put a few thousand PCs with power supplies in the same local area, harmonics can even damage the electrical power supplier's equipment!

Good PC power supplies come with *active power factor correction (active PFC)*, extra circuitry that smoothes out the way the power supply takes power from the power company and eliminates harmonics (see Figure 10-26). Never buy a power supply that does not have active PFC—all power supplies with active PFC will announce it on the box.

Wattage Requirements

Every device in a PC requires a certain amount of wattage to function. A typical hard drive draws 15 W of power when accessed, for example, whereas a quad-core AMD Phenom II X4 draws a whopping 125 W at peak usage. The total wattage of all devices combined is the minimum you need the power supply to provide.

If the power supply cannot produce the wattage a system needs, that PC won't work properly. Because most devices in the PC require maximum wattage when first starting, the most common result of insufficient wattage is a paperweight that looks like a PC. This can lead to some embarrassing moments. You might plug in a new hard drive for a client, push the power button on the case, and nothing happens—a dead PC! Eek! You can quickly determine if insufficient wattage is the problem. Unplug the drive and power up the system. If the system boots up, the power supply is a likely suspect. The only fix for this problem is to replace the power supply with one that provides more wattage (or leave the new drive out—a less-than-ideal solution).

Figure 10-26

Power supply advertising active PFC

[ENGLISH] Model: Neo HE 550

- ATX12V v2.2 and EPS12V compliant.
- Dual CPU and dual core ready.
- **Advanced cable management system** improves internal airflow and reduces system clutter by allowing you to use only the cables that you need.
- **Universal Input** automatically accepts line voltages from 100V to 240V AC.
- **Active PFC** (Power Factor Correction) delivers environmentally-friendlier power.
- **Up to 85% efficiency** reduces heat generation and saves power and money.
- **Dedicated voltage outputs** to deliver more stable power.
- **Voltage feedback** and tight ±3% regulation for improved system stability.
- **Three +12V output circuits** provide maximum stable power for the CPU independently and for other peripherals.
- **Dual PCI Express** graphics card power connectors.
- **Low-speed 80mm fan** delivers whisper-quiet cooling and ensures quiet operation by varying fan speed in response to load and conditions.
- **SATA connectors** for your Serial ATA drives.
- **Industrial grade protection circuitry** prevents damage resulting from short circuits (SCP), power overloads (OPP), excessive current (OCP), excessive voltages (OVP), and under voltage (UVP).
- **Approvals:** UL, CUL, CE, CB, FCC Class B, TÜV, CCC, C-tick.
- **MTBF:** 80,000 hrs.
- **Size:** 5.9" (D) x 5.9" (W) x 3.4" (H)
 15cm (D) x 15cm (W) x 8.6cm (H)
- **AQ3*** – Antec's unbeatable three-year parts and labor warranty.

No power supply can turn 100 percent of the AC power coming from the power company into DC current, so all power supplies provide less power to the system than the wattage advertised on the box. ATX12V 2.0 standards require a power supply to be at least 70 percent efficient, but you can find power supplies with better than 80 percent efficiency. More efficiency can tell you how many watts the system puts out to the PC in actual use. Plus, the added efficiency means the power supply uses less power, saving you money.

EXAM TIP The CompTIA A+ certification exams do not require you to figure precise wattage needs for a particular system. When building a PC for a client, however, you do need to know this stuff!

One common argument these days is that people buy power supplies that provide far more wattage than a system needs and therefore waste power. This is untrue. A power supply provides only the amount of power your system needs. If you put a 1000-W power supply (yes, they really exist) into a system that needs only 250 W, that big power supply will put out only 250 W to the system. So buying an efficient, higher-wattage power supply gives you two benefits. First, running a power supply at less than 100 percent load helps it live longer. Second, you'll have plenty of extra power when adding new components.

As a general recommendation for a new system, use at least a 500-W power supply. This is a common wattage and gives you plenty of extra power for booting as well as for whatever other components you might add to the system in the future.

Don't cut the specifications too tightly for power supplies. All power supplies produce less wattage over time, simply because of wear and tear on the internal components. If you build a system that runs with only a few watts of extra power available from the power supply initially, that system will most likely start causing problems within a year or less. Do yourself or your clients a favor and get a power supply that has more wattage than you need.

Installing and Maintaining Power Supplies

Although installing and maintaining power supplies takes a little less math than selecting the proper power supply for a system, they remain essential skills for any tech. Installing takes but a moment, and maintaining is almost as simple. Let's take a look.

Installing

The typical power supply connects to the PC with four standard computer screws, mounted in the back of the case (see Figure 10-27). Unscrew the four screws and the power supply lifts out easily (see Figure 10-28). Insert a new power supply that fits the case and attach it by using the same four screws.

Figure 10-27
Mounting screws
for power supply

Figure 10-28
Removing power
supply from system
unit

Handling ATX power supplies requires special consideration. Understand that an ATX power supply *never turns off*. As long as that power supply stays connected to a power outlet, the power supply will continue to supply 5 V to the motherboard. Always unplug an ATX system before you do any work! For years, techs bickered about the merits of leaving a PC plugged in or unplugged when servicing it. ATX settled this issue forever. Many ATX power supplies provide a real on/off switch on the back of the PSU (see Figure 10-29). If you really need the system shut down with no power to the motherboard, use this switch.

Figure 10-29
On/off switch for
an ATX system

When working on an ATX system, you may find using the power button inconvenient because you're not using a case or you haven't bothered to plug the power button's leads into the motherboard. That means there is no power button. One trick when in that situation is to use a set of car keys or a screwdriver to contact the two wires to start and stop the system (see Figure 10-30).

Figure 10-30
Shorting the soft
on/off jumpers

Your first task after acquiring a new power supply is simply making sure it works. Insert the motherboard power connectors before starting the system. If you have video cards with power connectors, plug them in too. Other connectors such as hard drives can wait until you have one successful boot—or if you're cocky, just plug everything in!

Cooling

Heat and computers are not the best of friends. Cooling is therefore a vital consideration when building a computer. Electricity equals heat. Computers, being electrical devices, generate heat as they operate, and too much heat can seriously damage a computer's internal components.

The *power supply fan* provides the basic cooling for the PC (see Figure 10-31). It not only cools the voltage regulator circuits *within* the power supply but also provides a constant flow of outside air throughout the interior of the computer case. A dead power supply fan can rapidly cause tremendous problems, even equipment failure. If you ever turn on a computer and it boots just fine but you notice that it seems unusually quiet, check to see if the power supply fan has died. If it has, quickly turn off the PC and replace the power supply.

Figure 10-31
Power supply fan

Some power supplies come with a built-in sensor to help regulate the airflow. If the system gets too hot, the power supply fan spins faster. The 3-pin, 3-wire fan sensor connector plugs into the motherboard directly (see Figure 10-32).

Figure 10-32
3-wire fan sensor
connector

Case fans are large, square fans that snap into special brackets on the case or screw directly to the case, providing extra cooling for key components (see Figure 10-33). Most cases come with a case fan, and no modern computer should really be without one or two.

Figure 10-33
Case fan

The single biggest issue related to case fans is where to plug them in. Most case fans come with standard Molex connectors, which are easy to plug in, but other case fans come with special three-pronged power connectors that need to connect to the motherboard. You can get adapters to plug three-pronged connectors into Molex connectors or vice versa.

Maintaining Airflow

A computer is a closed system, and computer cases help the fans keep things cool: everything is inside a box. Although many tech types like to run their systems with the side panel of the case open for easy access to the components, in the end they are cheating themselves. Why? A closed case enables the fans to create airflow. This airflow substantially cools off interior components. When the side of the case is open, you ruin the airflow of the system, and you lose a lot of cooling efficiency.

An important point to remember when implementing good airflow inside your computer case is that hot air rises. Warm air always rises above cold air, and you can use this principle to your advantage in keeping your computer cool.

In the typical layout of case fans for a computer case, an intake fan is located near the bottom of the front bezel of the case. This fan draws cool air in from outside the case and blows it over the components inside the case. Near the top and rear of the case (usually near the power supply), you'll usually find an exhaust fan. This fan works the opposite of the intake fan: it takes the warm air from inside the case and sends it to the outside.

Another important part of maintaining proper airflow inside the case is ensuring that *slot covers* are covering all empty expansion bays (see Figure 10-34). To maintain good airflow inside your case, you shouldn't provide too many opportunities for air to escape. Slot covers not only assist in maintaining a steady airflow; they also help keep dust and smoke out of your case.

Figure 10-34
Slot covers

EXAM TIP Missing slot covers can cause the PC to overheat!

Reducing Fan Noise

Fans generate noise. In an effort to ensure proper cooling, many techs put several high-speed fans into a case, making the PC sound like a jet engine. You can reduce fan noise by using manually adjustable fans, larger fans, or specialty "quiet" fans. Many mother-boards enable you to control fans through software.

Manually adjustable fans have a little knob you can turn to speed up or slow down the fan (see Figure 10-35). This kind of fan can reduce some of the noise, but you run the risk of slowing down the fan too much and thus letting the interior of the case heat up. A better solution is to get quieter fans.

Figure 10-35

Manual fan
adjustment device

Knob for adjusting fan speed

Larger fans that spin more slowly are another way to reduce noise while maintaining good airflow. Fans sizes are measured in millimeters (mm) or centimeters (cm). Traditionally, the industry used 80-mm power supply and cooling fans, but today you'll find 100-mm, 120-mm, and even larger fans in power supplies and cases.

Many companies manufacture and sell higher-end low-noise fans. The fans have better bearings than run-of-the-mill fans, so they cost a little more, but they're definitely worth it. They market these fans as "quiet" or "silencer" or other similar adjectives. If you run into a PC that sounds like a jet, try swapping out the case fans for a low-decibel fan from Papst, Panasonic, or Cooler Master. Just check the decibel rating to decide which one to get. Lower, of course, is better.

Because the temperature inside a PC changes depending on the load put on the PC, the best solution for noise reduction combines a good set of fans with temperature sensors to speed up or slow down the fans automatically. A PC at rest uses less than half of the power of a PC running a video-intensive computer game and therefore makes a lot less heat. Virtually all modern systems support three fans through three 3-pin fan connectors on the motherboard. The CPU fan uses one of these connectors, and the other two are for system fans or the power supply fan.

Most CMOS setup utilities provide a little control over fans plugged into the motherboard. Figure 10-36 shows a typical CMOS setting for the fans. Note that you can't tell the fans when to come on or off—only when to set off an alarm when they reach a certain temperature.

Figure 10-36

CMOS fan options

Software is the best way to control your fans. Some motherboards come with system-monitoring software that enables you to set the temperature at which you want the fans to come on and off. If no program came with your motherboard, and the manufacturer's Web site doesn't offer one for download, try the popular freeware SpeedFan utility (see Figure 10-37). Written by Alfredo Milani Comparetti, SpeedFan monitors voltages, fan speeds, and temperatures in computers with hardware monitor chips. SpeedFan can even access S.M.A.R.T. information (see Chapter 11) for hard disks that support this feature and show hard disk temperatures, too. You can find SpeedFan at www.almico.com/speedfan.php.

NOTE When shopping for fans, remember your metric system: 80 mm = 8 cm; 120 mm = 12 cm. You'll find fans marketed both ways.

Figure 10-37

SpeedFan

Even if you don't want to mess with your fans, always make a point to turn on your temperature alarms in CMOS. If the system gets too hot, an alarm will warn you. There's no way to know if a fan dies other than to have an alarm.

CAUTION SpeedFan is a powerful tool that does far more than work with fans. Don't tweak any settings you don't understand!

802

Troubleshooting Power Supplies

Power supplies fail in two ways: sudden death and slowly over time. When they die suddenly, the computer will not start and the fan in the power supply will not turn. In this case, verify that electricity is getting to the power supply before you do anything. Avoid the embarrassment of trying to repair a power supply when the only problem is a bad outlet or an extension cord that is not plugged in. Assuming that the system has electricity, the best way to verify that a power supply is working or not working is to use a multimeter to check the voltages coming out of the power supply (see Figure 10-38).

Figure 10-38

Testing one of the 5-V DC connections

Do not panic if your power supply puts out slightly more or less voltage than its nominal value. The voltages supplied by most PC power supplies can safely vary by as much as ±10 percent of their stated values. This means that the 12-V line can vary from roughly 10.8 to 13.2 V without exceeding the tolerance of the various systems in the PC. The 5.0- and 3.3-V lines offer similar tolerances.

Be sure to test every connection on the power supply—that means every connection on your main power as well as every Molex and mini. Because all voltages are between

−20 and +20 VDC, simply set the voltmeter to the 20-V DC setting for everything. If the power supply fails to provide power, throw it into the recycling bin and get a new one—even if you're a component expert and a whiz with a soldering iron. Don't waste your or your company's time; the price of new power supplies makes replacement the obvious way to go.

No Motherboard

Power supplies will not start unless they're connected to a motherboard, so what do you do if you don't have a motherboard you trust to test? First, try an ATX tester. Many companies make these devices. Look for one that supports both 20- and 24-pin motherboard connectors as well as all of the other connectors on your motherboard. Figure 10-39 shows a power supply tester.

Figure 10-39
ATX power
supply tester

 NOTE Many CMOS utilities and software programs monitor voltage, saving you the hassle of using a multimeter.

Switches

Broken power switches form an occasional source of problems for power supplies that fail to start. The power switch is behind the on/off button on every PC. It is usually secured to the front cover or inside front frame on your PC, making it a rather challenging part to access. To test, try shorting the soft power jumpers as described earlier. A key or screwdriver will do the trick.

When Power Supplies Die Slowly

If all power supplies died suddenly, this would be a much shorter chapter. Unfortunately, the majority of PC problems occur when power supplies die slowly over time. This means that one of the internal electronics of the power supply has begun to fail. The failures are *always* intermittent and tend to cause some of the most difficult to diagnose problems in PC repair. The secret to discovering that a power supply is dying lies in one word: intermittent. Whenever you experience intermittent problems, your first guess should be that the power supply is bad. Here are some other clues you may hear from users:

- "Whenever I start my computer in the morning, it starts to boot, and then locks up. If I press CTRL-ALT-DEL two or three times, it will boot up fine."

- "Sometimes when I start my PC, I get an error code. If I reboot, it goes away. Sometimes I get different errors."

- "My computer will run fine for an hour or so. Then it locks up, sometimes once or twice an hour."

Sometimes something bad happens and sometimes it does not. That's the clue for replacing the power supply. And don't bother with the voltmeter; the voltages will show up within tolerances, but only *once in a while* they will spike and sag (far more quickly than your voltmeter can measure) and cause these intermittent errors. When in doubt, change the power supply. Power supplies break in computers more often than any other part of the PC except hard drives and floppy disk drives. You might choose to keep extra power supplies on hand for swapping and testing.

Fuses and Fire

Inside every power supply resides a simple fuse. If your power supply simply pops and stops working, you might be tempted to go inside the power supply and check the fuse. This is not a good idea. First off, the capacitors in most power supplies carry high-voltage charges that can hurt a lot if you touch them. Second, fuses blow for a reason. If a power supply is malfunctioning inside, you want that fuse to blow because the alternative is much less desirable.

Failure to respect the power of electricity will eventually result in the most catastrophic of all situations: an electrical fire. Don't think it won't happen to you! Keep a fire extinguisher handy. Every PC workbench needs a fire extinguisher, but make sure you have the right one. The fire prevention industry has divided fire extinguishers into four fire classes:

- **Class A** Ordinary free-burning combustible, such as wood or paper
- **Class B** Flammable liquids, such as gasoline, solvents, or paint
- **Class C** Live electrical equipment
- **Class D** Combustible metals such as titanium or magnesium

As you might expect, you should only use a Class C fire extinguisher on your PC if it catches on fire. All fire extinguishers are required to have their type labeled prominently on them. Many fire extinguishers are multiclass in that they can handle more than one type of fire. The most common fire extinguisher is type ABC—it works on all common types of fires.

EXAM TIP If your power supply is smoking or you smell something burning inside of it, stop using it now. Replace it with a new power supply.

Beyond A+

Power supplies provide essential services for the PC, creating DC out of AC and cooling the system, but that utilitarian role does not stop the power supply from being an enthusiast's plaything. Plus, servers and high-end workstations have somewhat different needs than more typical systems, so naturally they need a boost in power. Let's take a look Beyond A+ at these issues.

It Glows!

The enthusiast community has been modifying, or *modding*, their PCs for years: cutting holes in the cases, adding fans to make overclocking feasible, and slapping in glowing strips of neon and cold cathode tubes. The power supply escaped the scene for a while, but it's back. A quick visit to a good computer store off- or online, such as http://directron.com, reveals power supplies that light up, sport a fancy color, or have more fans than some rock stars. Figure 10-40 shows a see-through PSU.

Figure 10-40
See-through power supply that glows blue

You can also find super-quiet stealth power supplies, with single or double high-end fans that react to the temperature inside your PC—speeding up when necessary but running slowly and silently when not. One of these would make a perfect power supply for a home entertainment PC because it would provide function without adding excessive noise.

Modular Power Supplies

It's getting more and more popular to make PCs look good on both the inside and the outside. Unused power cables dangling around inside PCs creates a not-so-pretty picture. To help stylish people, manufacturers created power supplies with modular cables (see Figure 10-41).

Figure 10-41
Modular-cable
power supply

Modular cables are pretty cool, because you add only the lines you need for your system. On the other hand, some techs claim that modular cables hurt efficiency because the modular connectors add resistance to the lines. You make the choice; is a slight reduction in efficiency worth a clean look?

Temperature and Efficiency

Watch out for power supplies that list their operating temperature at 25° C—about room temperature. A power supply that provides 500 W at 25° C will supply substantially less in warmer temperatures, and the inside of your PC is usually 15° C warmer than the outside air. Sadly, many power supply makers—even those who make good power supplies—fudge this fact.

Chapter Review

Questions

1. What is the proper voltage for a U.S. electrical outlet?
 A. 120 V
 B. 60 V
 C. 0 V
 D. −120 V

2. What voltages does an ATX12V P1 connector provide for the motherboard?
 A. 3.3 V, 5 V
 B. 3.3 V, 12 V
 C. 5 V, 12 V
 D. 3.3 V, 5 V, 12 V

3. What sort of power connector does a floppy disk drive typically use?
 A. Molex
 B. Mini
 C. Sub-mini
 D. Micro

4. Joachim ordered a new power supply but was surprised when it arrived because it had an extra 4-wire connector. What is that connector?
 A. P2 connector for plugging in auxiliary components
 B. P3 connector for plugging in case fans
 C. P4 connector for plugging into modern motherboards
 D. Aux connector for plugging into a secondary power supply

5. What should you keep in mind when testing DC connectors?
 A. DC has polarity. The red lead should always touch the hot wire; the black lead should touch a ground wire.
 B. DC has polarity. The red lead should always touch the ground wire; the black lead should always touch the hot wire.
 C. DC has no polarity, so you can touch the red lead to either hot or ground.
 D. DC has no polarity, so you can touch the black lead to either hot or neutral but not ground.

6. What voltages should the two hot wires on a Molex connector read?

 A. Red = 3.3 V; Yellow = 5 V

 B. Red = 5 V; Yellow = 12 V

 C. Red = 12 V; Yellow = 5 V

 D. Red = 5 V; Yellow = 3.3 V

7. Why is it a good idea to ensure that the slot covers on your computer case are all covered?

 A. To maintain good airflow inside your case.

 B. To help keep dust and smoke out of your case.

 C. Both A and B are correct reasons.

 D. Trick question! Leaving a slot uncovered doesn't hurt anything.

8. A PC's power supply provides DC power in what standard configuration?

 A. Two primary voltage rails, 12 volts and 5 volts, and an auxiliary 3.3 volt connector

 B. Three primary voltage rails, one each for 12-volt, 5-volt, and 3.3-volt connectors

 C. One primary DC voltage rail for 12-volt, 5-volt, and 3.3-volt connectors

 D. One voltage rail with a 12-volt connector for the motherboard, a second voltage rail with a 12-volt connector for the CPU, and a third voltage rail for the 5-volt and 3.3-volt connectors

9. What feature of ATX systems prevents a user from turning off a system before the operating system has been shut down?

 A. Motherboard power connector

 B. CMOS setup

 C. Sleep mode

 D. Soft power

10. How many pins does a SATA power connector have?

 A. 6

 B. 9

 C. 12

 D. 15

Answers

1. **A.** U.S. outlets run at 120 V.

2. **D.** An ATX12V power supply P1 connector provides 3.3, 5, and 12 volts to the motherboard.

3. **B.** Floppy drives commonly use a mini connector.

4. **C.** The P4 connector goes into the motherboard to support more power-hungry chips.

5. **A.** DC has polarity. The red lead should always touch the hot wire; the black lead should touch a ground wire.

6. **B.** A Molex connector's red wires should be at 5 volts; the yellow wire should be at 12 volts.

7. **C.** Both A and B are correct reasons. Keeping the slots covered helps keep a good airflow in your case and keeps the dust and smoke away from all those sensitive internal components.

8. **B.** The standard PC power supply configuration has three primary voltage rails, one each for 12-volt, 5-volt, and 3.3-volt connectors.

9. **D.** The soft power feature of ATX systems prevents a user from turning off a system before the operating system has been shut down.

10. **D.** SATA power connectors have 15 pins.

Hard Drive Technologies

In this chapter, you will learn how to

- Explain how hard drives work
- Identify and explain the PATA and SATA hard drive interfaces
- Identify and explain the SCSI hard drive interfaces
- Describe how to protect data with RAID
- Install hard drives
- Configure CMOS and install drivers
- Troubleshoot hard drive installation

Of all the hardware on a PC, none gets more attention—or gives more anguish—than the hard drive. There's a good reason for this: if the hard drive breaks, you lose data. As you probably know, when the data goes, you have to redo work or restore from a backup—or worse. It's good to worry about the data, because the data runs the office, maintains the payrolls, and stores the e-mail. This level of concern is so strong that even the most neophyte PC users are exposed to terms such as *IDE, PATA, SATA,* and *controller*—even if they don't put the terms into practice.

This chapter focuses on how hard drives work, beginning with the internal layout and organization of hard drives. You'll look at the different types of hard drives used today (PATA, SATA, SSD, and SCSI), how they interface with the PC, and how to install them properly into a system. The chapter covers how more than one drive may work with other drives to provide data safety and improve speed through a feature called RAID. Let's get started.

Historical/Conceptual

How Hard Drives Work

Hard drives come in two major types. The most common type has moving parts; the newer and more expensive technology has no moving parts. Let's look at both.

NOTE Chapter 12 continues the hard drive discussion by adding in the operating systems, showing you how to prepare drives to receive data, and teaching you how to maintain and upgrade drives in Windows.

Platter-Based Hard Drives

A traditional *hard disk drive (HDD)* is composed of individual disks, or *platters*, with read/write heads on actuator arms controlled by a servo motor—all contained in a sealed case that prevents contamination by outside air (see Figure 11-1).

Figure 11-1
Inside the
hard drive

The aluminum platters are coated with a magnetic medium. Two tiny read/write heads service each platter, one to read the top and the other to read the bottom of the platter (see Figure 11-2).

Figure 11-2
Read/write heads
on actuator arms

The coating on the platters is phenomenally smooth. It has to be, as the read/write heads actually float on a cushion of air above the platters, which spin at speeds between 3500 and 15,000 RPM. The distance (flying height) between the heads and the disk surface is less than the thickness of a fingerprint. The closer the read/write heads are to the platter, the more densely the data packs onto the drive. These infinitesimal tolerances demand that the platters never be exposed to outside air. Even a tiny dust particle on a platter would act like a mountain in the way of the read/write heads and would cause catastrophic damage to the drive. To keep the air clean inside the drive, all hard drives use a tiny, heavily filtered aperture to keep the air pressure equalized between the interior and the exterior of the drive.

Data Encoding

Although the hard drive stores data in binary form, visualizing a magnetized spot representing a one and a non-magnetized spot representing a zero grossly oversimplifies the process. Hard drives store data in tiny magnetic fields—think of them as tiny magnets that can be placed in either direction on the platter. Each tiny magnetic field, called a *flux*, can switch north/south polarity back and forth through a process called *flux reversal*. When a read/write head goes over an area where a flux reversal has occurred, the head reads a small electrical current.

Today's hard drives use a complex and efficient method to interpret flux reversals. Instead of reading individual flux reversals, a modern hard drive reads groups of them called *runs*. Starting around 1991, hard drives began using a data encoding system known as *run length limited* (*RLL*). With RLL, any combination of ones and zeros can be stored in a preset combination of about 15 different runs. The hard drive looks for these runs and reads them as a group, resulting in much faster and much more densely packed data.

Current drives use an extremely advanced method of RLL called *Partial Response Maximum Likelihood (PRML)* encoding. As hard drives pack more and more fluxes on the drive, the individual fluxes start to interact with each other, making it more and more difficult for the drive to verify where one flux stops and another starts. PRML uses powerful, intelligent circuitry to analyze each flux reversal and make a "best guess" as to what type of flux reversal it just read. As a result, the maximum run length for PRML drives reaches up to 16 to 20 fluxes, far more than the 7 or so on RLL drives. Longer run lengths enable the hard drive to use more complicated run combinations so the hard drive can store a phenomenal amount of data. For example, a run of only 12 fluxes on a hard drive might equal a string of 30 or 40 ones and zeros when handed to the system from the hard drive.

The size required by each magnetic flux on a hard drive has reduced considerably over the years, resulting in higher capacities. As fluxes become smaller, they begin to interfere with each other in weird ways. I have to say *weird* because to make sense of what's going on at this subatomic level (I told you these fluxes are small!) would require you to take a semester of quantum mechanics. Let's just say that laying fluxes flat against the platter has reached its limit. To get around this problem, hard drive makers began to make hard drives that store their fluxes vertically (up and down) rather

than longitudinally (forward and backward), enabling them to make hard drives in the 1 terabyte (1024 gigabyte) range. Manufacturers call this vertical storage method *perpendicular recording*.

For all this discussion and detail on data encoding, the day-to-day PC technician never deals with encoding. Sometimes, however, knowing what you don't need to know helps as much as knowing what you do need to know. Fortunately, data encoding is inherent to the hard drive and completely invisible to the system. You're never going to have to deal with data encoding, but you'll sure sound smart when talking to other PC techs if you know your RLL from your PRML!

Moving the Arms

The read/write heads move across the platter on the ends of *actuator arms* or *head actuators*. In the entire history of hard drives, manufacturers have used only two technologies to move the arms: *stepper motor* and *voice coil*. Hard drives first used stepper motor technology, but today they've all moved to voice coil.

NOTE Floppy disk drives used stepper motors.

Stepper motor technology moved the arm in fixed increments or steps, but the technology had several limitations that doomed it. Because the interface between motor and actuator arm required minimal slippage to ensure precise and reproducible movements, the positioning of the arms became less precise over time. This physical deterioration caused data transfer errors. Additionally, heat deformation wreaked havoc with stepper motor drives. Just as valve clearances in automobile engines change with operating temperature, the positioning accuracy changed as the PC operated and various hard drive components got warmer. Although very small, these changes caused problems. Accessing the data written on a cold hard drive, for example, became difficult after the disk warmed. In addition, the read/write heads could damage the disk surface if not parked (set in a non-data area) when not in use, requiring techs to use special parking programs before transporting a stepper motor drive.

All magnetic hard drives made today employ a linear motor to move the actuator arms. The linear motor, more popularly called a voice coil motor, uses a permanent magnet surrounding a coil on the actuator arm. When an electrical current passes, the coil generates a magnetic field that moves the actuator arm. The direction of the actuator arm's movement depends on the polarity of the electrical current through the coil. Because the voice coil and the actuator arm never touch, no degradation in positional accuracy takes place over time. Voice coil drives automatically park the heads when the drive loses power, making the old stepper motor park programs obsolete.

Lacking the discrete steps of the stepper motor drive, a voice coil drive cannot accurately predict the movement of the heads across the disk. To make sure voice coil drives land exactly in the correct area, the drive reserves one side of one platter for navigational purposes. This area essentially maps the exact location of the data on the drive.

The voice coil moves the read/write head to its best guess about the correct position on the hard drive. The read/write head then uses this map to fine-tune its true position and make any necessary adjustments.

Now that you have a basic understanding of how a drive physically stores data, let's turn to how the hard drive organizes that data so we can use that drive.

Geometry

Have you ever seen a cassette tape? If you look at the actual brown Mylar (a type of plastic) tape, nothing will tell you whether sound is recorded on that tape. Assuming the tape is not blank, however, you know *something* is on the tape. Cassettes store music in distinct magnetized lines. You could say that the physical placement of those lines of magnetism is the tape's "geometry."

Geometry also determines where a hard drive stores data. As with a cassette tape, if you opened up a hard drive, you would not see the geometry. But rest assured that the drive has geometry; in fact, every model of hard drive uses a different geometry. We describe the geometry for a particular hard drive with a set of numbers representing three values: heads, cylinders, and sectors per track.

Heads The number of *heads* for a specific hard drive describes, rather logically, the number of read/write heads used by the drive to store data. Every platter requires two heads. If a hard drive has four platters, for example, it needs eight heads (see Figure 11-3).

Four platters = eight heads

Figure 11-3
Two heads per platter

Based on this description of heads, you would think that hard drives would always have an even number of heads, right? Wrong! Most hard drives reserve a head or two for their own use. Therefore, a hard drive can have either an even or an odd number of heads.

Cylinders To visualize cylinders, imagine taking an empty soup can and opening both ends. Look at the shape of the can; it is a geometric shape called a cylinder. Now imagine taking that cylinder and sharpening one end so that it easily cuts through the hardest metal. Visualize placing the ex–soup can over the hard drive and pushing it down through the drive. The can cuts into one side and out the other of each platter. Each circle transcribed by the can is where you store data on the drive, and is called a *track*.

Each side of each platter contains tens of thousands of tracks. Interestingly enough, the individual tracks themselves are not directly part of the drive geometry. Our interest lies only in the groups of tracks of the same diameter, going all of the way through the drive. Each group of tracks of the same diameter is called a *cylinder* (see Figure 11-4).

There's more than one cylinder. Go get yourself about a thousand more cans, each one a different diameter, and push them through the hard drive.

Figure 11-4
Cylinder

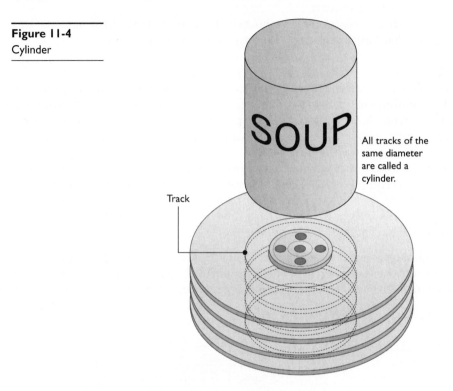

All tracks of the same diameter are called a cylinder.

Track

Sectors per Track Now imagine cutting the hard drive like a birthday cake, slicing all of the tracks into tens of thousands of small slivers. Each sliver then has many thousands of small pieces of track. The term *sector* refers to a specific piece of track on a sliver, and each sector stores 512 bytes of data.

The sector is the universal atom of all hard drives. You can't divide data into anything smaller than a sector. Although sectors are important, the number of sectors is not a geometry value that describes a hard drive. The geometry value is called *sectors per track* (*sectors/track*). The sectors/track value describes the number of sectors in each track (see Figure 11-5).

Figure 11-5
Sectors per track

Six sectors per track
(sectors/track)

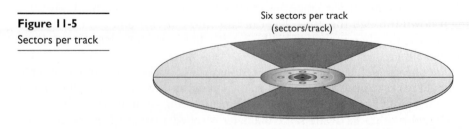

The Big Three Cylinders, heads, and sectors/track combine to define the hard drive's geometry. In most cases, these three critical values are referred to as *CHS*. The three values are important because the PC's BIOS needs to know the drive's geometry to know how to talk to the drive. Back in the old days, a technician needed to enter these values into the CMOS setup program manually. Today, every hard drive stores the CHS information in the drive itself, in an electronic format that enables the BIOS to query the drive automatically to determine these values. You'll see more on this later in the chapter, in the "Autodetection" section.

Two other values—write precompensation cylinder and landing zone—are no longer relevant in today's PCs. People still toss around these terms, however, and a few CMOS setup utilities still support them—another classic example of a technology appendix. Let's look at these two holdouts from another era so when you access CMOS, you won't say, "What the heck are these?"

Write Precompensation Cylinder Older hard drives had a real problem with the fact that sectors toward the inside of the drives were much smaller than sectors toward the outside. To handle this, an older drive would spread data a little farther apart once it got to a particular cylinder. This cylinder was called the write precompensation (write precomp) cylinder, and the PC had to know which cylinder began this wider data spacing. Hard drives no longer have this problem, making the write precomp setting obsolete.

Landing Zone On older hard drives with stepper motors, the landing zone value designated an unused cylinder as a "parking place" for the read/write heads. As mentioned earlier, before moving old stepper motor hard drives, the read/write heads needed to be parked to avoid accidental damage. Today's voice coil drives park themselves whenever they're not accessing data, automatically placing the read/write heads on the landing zone. As a result, the BIOS no longer needs the landing zone geometry.

801

Spindle (or Rotational) Speed

Hard drives run at a set spindle speed, measured in *revolutions per minute* (*RPM*). Older drives ran at a speed of 3600 RPM, but new drives are hitting 15,000 RPM. The faster the spindle speed, the faster the controller can store and retrieve data. Here are the common speeds: 5400, 7200, 10,000 and 15,000 RPM.

Faster drives mean better system performance, but they can also cause the computer to overheat. This is especially true in tight cases, such as minitowers, and in cases containing many drives. Two 5400-RPM drives might run forever, snugly tucked together in your old case. But slap a hot new 15,000 RPM drive in that same case and watch your system start crashing right and left!

You can deal with these very fast drives by adding drive bay fans between the drives or migrating to a more spacious case. Most enthusiasts end up doing both. Drive bay

fans sit at the front of a bay and blow air across the drive. They range in price from $10 to $100 (U.S.) and can lower the temperature of your drives dramatically. Some cases come with a bay fan built in (see Figure 11-6).

Figure 11-6
Bay fan

Airflow in a case can make or break your system stability, especially when you add new drives that increase the ambient temperature. Hot systems get flaky and lock up at odd moments. Many things can impede the airflow—jumbled-up ribbon cables, drives squished together in a tiny case, fans clogged by dust or animal hair, and so on.

Technicians need to be aware of the dangers when adding a new hard drive to an older system. Get into the habit of tying off ribbon cables, adding front fans to cases when systems lock up intermittently, and making sure any fans run well. Finally, if a client wants a new drive for a system in a tiny minitower with only the power supply fan to cool it off, be gentle, but definitely steer the client to one of the slower drives!

Solid-State Drives

Booting up a computer takes time in part because a traditional hard drive needs to first spin up before the read/write heads can retrieve data off the drive and load it into RAM. All of the moving metal parts of a platter-based drive use a lot of power, create a lot of

heat, take up space, wear down over time, and take a lot of nanoseconds to get things done. A *solid-state drive (SSD)* addresses all of these issues nicely.

In technical terms, solid-state technology and devices are based on the combination of semiconductors, transistors, and bubble memory used to create electrical components with no moving parts. That's a mouthful! Here's the translation.

In simple terms, SSDs (see Figure 11-7) use memory chips to store data instead of all those pesky metal spinning parts used in platter-based hard drives. Solid-state technology has been around for many moons. It was originally developed to transition vacuum tube–based technologies to semiconductor technologies, such as the move from cathode ray tubes (CRTs) to liquid crystal displays (LCDs) in monitors. (You'll get the scoop on monitor technologies in Chapter 21.)

Figure 11-7
A solid-state drive (photo courtesy of Corsair)

Solid-state devices use current flow and negative/positive electron charges to achieve their magic. Although Mr. Spock may find the physics of how this technology actually works "fascinating," it's more important for you to know the following points regarding solid-state drives, devices, and technology.

NOTE With solid-state drives coming into more regular use, you see the initials HDD used more frequently than in previous years to refer to the traditional, platter-based hard drives. Thus we have two drive technologies: SSDs and HDDs.

- Solid-state technology is commonly used in desktop and laptop hard drives, memory cards, cameras, USB thumb drives, and other handheld devices.

- SSD form factors are typically 1.8-inch, 2.5-inch, or 3.5-inch.

- SSDs can be PATA, SATA, eSATA, SCSI, or USB for desktop systems. Some portable computers have mini-PCI Express versions. You can also purchase SSD cards built onto PCIe cards (which you would connect to your PC like any other expansion card).

- SSDs that use SDRAM cache are volatile and lose data when powered off. Others that use nonvolatile flash memory such as NAND retain data when power is turned off or disconnected. (See Chapter 13 for the scoop on flash memory technology.)

- SSDs are more expensive than traditional HDDs. Less expensive SSDs typically implement less reliable multi-level cell (MLC) memory technology in place of the more efficient single-level cell (SLC) technology to cut costs.

EXAM TIP The term *IDE* (integrated drive electronics) refers to any hard drive with a built-in controller. All hard drives are technically IDE drives, although we only use the term IDE when discussing ATA drives.

Parallel and Serial ATA

Over the years, many interfaces existed for hard drives, with such names as ST-506 and ESDI. Don't worry about what these abbreviations stood for; neither the CompTIA A+ certification exams nor the computer world at large have an interest in these prehistoric interfaces. Starting around 1990, an interface called *advanced technology attachment (ATA)* appeared that now virtually monopolizes the hard drive market. ATA hard drives are often referred to as *integrated drive electronics (IDE)* drives. Only one other type of interface, the moderately popular small computer system interface (SCSI), has any relevance for hard drives.

ATA drives come in two basic flavors. The older *parallel ATA (PATA)* drives send data in parallel, on a 40- or 80-wire data cable. PATA drives dominated the industry for more than a decade but have been mostly replaced by *serial ATA (SATA)* drives that send data in serial, using only one wire for data transfers. The leap from PATA to SATA is only one of a large number of changes that have taken place with ATA. To appreciate these changes, we'll run through the many ATA standards that have appeared over the years.

NOTE A quick trip to any major computer store will reveal a thriving trade in external hard drives. You used to be able to find external drives that connected to the slow parallel port, but external drives today connect to a FireWire, USB, or eSATA port. All three interfaces offer high data transfer rates and hot-swap capability, making them ideal for transporting huge files

such as digital video clips. Regardless of the external interface, however, you'll find an ordinary PATA or SATA drive inside the *external enclosure* (the name used to describe the casing of external hard drives).

ATA-1

When IBM unveiled the 80286-powered IBM PC AT in the early 1980s, it introduced the first PC to include BIOS support for hard drives. This BIOS supported up to two physical drives, and each drive could be up to 504 MB—far larger than the 5-MB and 10-MB drives of the time. Although having built-in support for hard drives certainly improved the power of the PC, installing, configuring, and troubleshooting hard drives could at best be called difficult at that time.

To address these problems, Western Digital and Compaq developed a new hard drive interface and placed this specification before the *American National Standards Institute* (*ANSI*) committees, which in turn put out the AT Attachment (ATA) interface in March of 1989. The ATA interface specified a cable and a built-in controller on the drive itself. Most importantly, the ATA standard used the existing AT BIOS on a PC, which meant that you didn't have to replace the old system BIOS to make the drive work—a very important consideration for compatibility but one that would later haunt ATA drives. The official name for the standard, ATA, never made it into the common vernacular until recently, and then only as PATA to distinguish it from SATA drives.

Early ATA Physical Connections

The first ATA drives connected to the computer with a *40-pin ribbon cable* that plugged into the drive and into a hard drive controller. The cable has a colored stripe down one side that denotes pin 1 and should connect to the drive's pin 1 and to the controller's pin 1. Figure 11-8 shows the business end of an early ATA drive, with the connectors for the ribbon cable and the power cable.

Figure 11-8
Back of IDE drive showing 40-pin connector (left), jumpers (center), and power connector (right)

The controller is the support circuitry that acts as the intermediary between the hard drive and the external data bus. Electronically, the setup looks like Figure 11-9.

Figure 11-9
Relation of drive, controller, and bus

Wait a minute! If ATA drives are IDE (see the earlier Exam Tip), they already have a built-in controller. Why do they then have to plug into a *controller* on the motherboard? Well, this is a great example of a term that's not used properly, but everyone (including the motherboard and hard drive makers) uses it this way. What we call the ATA controller is really no more than an interface providing a connection to the rest of the PC system. When your BIOS talks to the hard drive, it actually talks to the onboard circuitry on the drive, not the connection on the motherboard. But, even though the *real* controller resides on the hard drive, the 40-pin connection on the motherboard is called the controller. We have a lot of misnomers to live with in the ATA world.

The ATA-1 standard defined that no more than two drives attach to a single IDE connector on a single ribbon cable. Because up to two drives can attach to one connector via a single cable, you need to be able to identify each drive on the cable. The ATA standard identifies the two drives as "master" and "slave." You set one drive as master and one as slave by using tiny jumpers on the drives (see Figure 11-10).

Figure 11-10
A typical hard drive with directions (top) for setting a jumper (bottom)

The controllers are on the motherboard and manifest themselves as two 40-pin male ports, as shown in Figure 11-11.

Figure 11-11
IDE interfaces on a
motherboard

NOTE The ANSI subcommittee directly responsible for the ATA standard is called Technical Committee T13. If you want to know what's happening with ATA, check out the T13 Web site: www.t13.org.

PIO and DMA Modes

If you're making a hard drive standard, you must define both the method and the speed at which the data's going to move.

ATA-1 defined two methods, the first using programmed I/O (PIO) addressing and the second using direct memory access (DMA) mode.

PIO is nothing more than the traditional I/O addressing scheme, where the CPU talks directly to the hard drive via the BIOS to send and receive data. Three different PIO speeds called *PIO modes* were initially adopted:

- PIO mode 0: 3.3 MBps (megabytes per second)
- PIO mode 1: 5.2 MBps
- PIO mode 2: 8.3 MBps

DMA modes defined a method to enable the hard drives to talk to RAM directly, using old-style DMA commands. (The ATA folks called this *single-word DMA*.) This old-style DMA was slow, and the resulting three ATA single-word DMA modes were also slow:

- Single-word DMA mode 0: 2.1 MBps
- Single-word DMA mode 1: 4.2 MBps
- Single-word DMA mode 2: 8.3 MBps

When a computer booted up, the BIOS queried the hard drive to see what modes it could use and then automatically adjusted to the fastest possible mode.

ATA-2

In 1990, the industry adopted a series of improvements to the ATA standard called ATA-2. Many people called these new features *Enhanced IDE (EIDE)*. EIDE was really no more than a marketing term invented by Western Digital, but it caught on in common vernacular and is still used today, although its use is fading. Regular IDE drives quickly disappeared, and by 1995, EIDE drives dominated the PC world. Figure 11-12 shows a typical EIDE drive.

Figure 11-12
EIDE drive

ATA-2 was the most important ATA standard, as it included powerful new features such as higher capacities, support for non–hard drive storage devices, support for two more ATA devices for a maximum of four, and substantially improved throughput.

 NOTE The terms ATA, IDE, and EIDE are used interchangeably.

Higher Capacity with LBA

IBM created the AT BIOS to support hard drives many years before IDE drives were invented, and every system had that BIOS. The developers of IDE made certain that the new drives would run from the same AT BIOS command set. With this capability, you could use the same CMOS and BIOS routines to talk to a much more advanced drive. Your motherboard or hard drive controller wouldn't become instantly obsolete when you installed a new hard drive.

Unfortunately, the BIOS routines for the original AT command set allowed a hard drive size of only up to 528 million bytes (or 504 MB—remember that a mega = 1,048,576, not 1,000,000). A drive could have no more than 1024 cylinders, 16 heads, and 63 sectors/track:

1024 cylinders × 16 heads × 63 sectors/track × 512 bytes/sector = 504 MB

For years, this was not a problem. But when hard drives began to approach the 504-MB barrier, it became clear that there needed to be a way of getting past 504 MB. The ATA-2 standard defined a way to get past this limit with *logical block addressing (LBA)*. With LBA, the hard drive lies to the computer about its geometry through an advanced type of sector translation. Let's take a moment to understand sector translation, and then come back to LBA.

Sector Translation

Long before hard drives approached the 504-MB limit, the limits of 1024 cylinders, 16 heads, and 63 sectors/track gave hard drive makers fits. The big problem was the heads. Remember that every two heads means another platter, another physical disk that you have to squeeze into a hard drive. If you wanted a hard drive with the maximum number of 16 heads, you would need a hard drive with eight physical platters inside the drive. Nobody wanted that many platters: it made the drives too tall, it took more power to spin up the drive, and that many parts cost too much money (see Figure 11-13).

Figure 11-13
Too many heads

Looks a little high.

Manufacturers could readily produce a hard drive that had fewer heads and more cylinders, but the stupid 1024/16/63 limit got in the way. Plus, the traditional sector arrangement wasted a lot of useful space. Sectors toward the inside of the drive, for example, are much shorter than the sectors on the outside. The sectors on the outside don't need to be that long, but with the traditional geometry setup, hard drive makers had no choice. They could make a hard drive store a lot more information, however, if they could make hard drives with more sectors/track on the outside tracks (see Figure 11-14).

Figure 11-14
Multiple sectors/
track

16 sectors/track

8 sectors/track

The ATA specification was designed to have two geometries. The *physical geometry* defined the real layout of the CHS inside the drive. The *logical geometry* described what the drive told the CMOS. In other words, the IDE drive "lied" to the CMOS, thus side-stepping the artificial limits of the BIOS. When data was being transferred to and from the drive, the onboard circuitry of the drive translated the logical geometry into the physical geometry. This function was, and still is, called *sector translation*.

Let's look at a couple of hypothetical examples in action. First, pretend that Seagate came out with a new, cheap, fast hard drive called the ST108. To get the ST108 drive fast and cheap, however, Seagate had to use a rather strange geometry, shown in Table 11-1.

ST108 Physical		BIOS Limits	
Cylinders	2048	Cylinders	1024
Heads	2	Heads	16
Sectors/track	52	Sectors/track	63
Total capacity	108 MB	Total capacity	504 MB

Table 11-1 Seagate's ST108 Drive Geometry

NOTE Hard drive makers talk about hard drive capacities in millions and billions of bytes, not megabytes and gigabytes.

Notice that the cylinder number is greater than 1024. To overcome this problem, the IDE drive performs a sector translation that reports a geometry to the BIOS that is totally different from the true geometry of the drive. Table 11-2 shows the physical geometry and the "logical" geometry of our mythical ST108 drive. Notice that the logical geometry is now within the acceptable parameters of the BIOS limitations. Sector translation never changes the capacity of the drive; it changes only the geometry to stay within the BIOS limits.

Back to LBA

Now let's watch how the advanced sector translation of LBA provides support for hard drives greater than 504 MB. Let's use an old drive, the Western Digital WD2160, a

- PIO mode 3: 11.1 MBps
- PIO mode 4: 16.6 MBps
- Multi-word DMA mode 0
- Multi-word DMA mode 1
- Multi-word DMA mode 2

ATA-3

ATA-3 came on quickly after AT
Analysis, and Reporting Technology
the use of periods after each let
to fail by monitoring the hard d

S.M.A.R.T. is a great idea and
plex, imperfect, and hard to un
S.M.A.R.T. data on your hard dr
Every hard drive maker has a fr
drives) that will do a S.M.A.R.T.
ern Digital's Data Lifeguard Too
passed or not. Figure 11-18 sho

Figure 11-17 Data Lifeguard Tools

2.1-GB hard drive, as an example. This drive is no longer in production, but its smaller CHS values make understanding LBA easier. Table 11-3 lists its physical and logical geometries.

Note that, even with sector translation, the number of heads is greater than the allowed 16. So here's where the magic of LBA comes in. When the computer boots up, the BIOS asks the drives if they can perform LBA. If they say yes, the BIOS and the drive work together to change the way they talk to each other. They can do this without conflicting with the original AT BIOS commands by taking advantage of unused commands to use up to 256 heads. LBA enables support for a maximum of 1024 × 256 × 63 × 512 bytes = 8.4-GB hard drives. Back in 1990, 8.4 GB was hundreds of times larger than the drives used at the time. Don't worry, later ATA standards will get the BIOS up to today's huge drives.

Physical		Logical	
Cylinders	2048	Cylinders	512
Heads	2	Heads	8
Sectors/track	52	Sectors/track	52
Total capacity	108 MB	Total capacity	108 MB

Table 11-2 Physical and Logical Geometries of the ST108 Drive

Physical		Logical	
Cylinders	16,384	Cylinders	1024
Heads	4	Heads	64
Sectors/track	63	Sectors/track	63
Total capacity	2.1 GB	Total capacity	2.1 GB

Table 11-3 Western Digital WD2160's Physical and Logical Geometries

Not Just Hard Drives Anymore: ATAPI

ATA-2 added an extension to the ATA specification, called *advanced technology attachment packet interface (ATAPI)*, that enabled non–hard drive devices such as CD-ROM drives and tape backups to connect to the PC via the ATA controllers. ATAPI drives have the same 40-pin interface and master/slave jumpers as ATA hard drives. Figure 11-15 shows an ATAPI CD-RW drive attached to a motherboard. The key difference between hard drives and every other type of drive that attaches to the ATA controller is in how the drives get BIOS support. Hard drives get it through the system BIOS, whereas non–hard drives require the operating system to load a software driver.

Figure 11-15
ATAPI CD-RW
drive attached to
a motherboard via
a standard 40-pin
ribbon cable

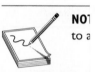

NO
to a

More Drives

ATA-2 added su
drives from two
Figure 11-16 is
marked as *PRI_1*

Figure 11-16
Primary and
secondary control-
lers labeled on a
motherboard

Increased Sp

ATA-2 defined t
that was a subst
was still the old
much faster.

External SATA uses shielded cable lengths up to 2 meters outside the PC and is hot-swappable. The beauty of eSATA is that it extends the SATA bus at full speed, which tops out at a theoretical 6 Gbps, whereas the fastest USB connection (USB 3.0, also called SuperSpeed USB) maxes out at 5 Gbps. It's not that big of a speed gap, especially when you consider that neither connection type fully utilizes its bandwidth yet, but even in real-world tests, eSATA still holds its own.

If a desktop system doesn't have an eSATA external connector, or if you need more external SATA devices, you can install an eSATA HBA PCIe card or eSATA internal-to-external slot plate. You can similarly upgrade laptop systems to support external SATA devices by inserting an eSATA ExpressCard (see Figure 11-23). There are also USB-to-eSATA adapter plugs. Install eSATA PCIe, PC Card, or ExpressCard following the same rules and precautions for installing any expansion device.

Figure 11-23
eSATA
ExpressCard

NOTE In addition to eSATA ports, you'll also run into eSATAp ports on some laptops. This port physically combines a powered USB connection with a speedy eSATA connection; you can connect a USB, eSATA, or special eSATAp cable into the port. eSATAp enables you to connect an internal drive (HDD, SSD, or optical drive) to your laptop without an enclosure, using a single cable to power it and send/receive data.

SCSI: Still Around

Many specialized server machines and enthusiasts' systems use the *small computer system interface (SCSI)* technologies for various pieces of core hardware and peripherals, from hard drives to printers to high-end tape-backup machines. SCSI, pronounced "scuzzy," is different from ATA in that SCSI devices connect together in a string of devices called a *chain*. Each device in the chain gets a SCSI ID to distinguish it from other devices on the chain. Last, the ends of a SCSI chain must be terminated. Let's dive into SCSI now, and see how SCSI chains, SCSI IDs, and termination all work.

SCSI is an old technology dating from the late 1970s, but it has been updated continually. SCSI is faster than ATA (though the gap is closing fast), and until SATA arrived, SCSI was the only good choice for anyone using RAID (see the "RAID" section a little later). SCSI is arguably fading away, but it deserves some mention.

SCSI Chains

SCSI manifests itself through a *SCSI chain*, a series of SCSI devices working together through a host adapter. The host adapter provides the interface between the SCSI chain and the PC. Figure 11-24 shows a typical SCSI PCI host adapter. Many techs refer to the host adapter as the *SCSI controller*, so you should be comfortable with both terms.

Figure 11-24
SCSI host adapter

All SCSI devices can be divided into two groups: internal and external. Internal SCSI devices are attached inside the PC and connect to the host adapter through the latter's internal connector. Figure 11-25 shows an internal SCSI device, in this case a CD-ROM drive. External devices hook to the external connector of the host adapter. Figure 11-26 is an example of an external SCSI device.

Figure 11-25
Internal SCSI
CD-ROM

Figure 11-26

Back of external
SCSI device

Internal SCSI devices connect to the host adapter with a 68-pin ribbon cable (see Figure 11-27). This flat, flexible cable functions precisely like a PATA cable. Many external devices connect to the host adapter with a 50-pin high-density (HD) connector. Figure 11-28 shows a host adapter external port. Higher-end SCSI devices use a 68-pin HD connector.

 EXAM TIP Some early versions of SCSI used a 25-pin connector. This connector was much more popular on Apple devices, though it did see use on PCs with the old SCSI Zip drives. While the connector is now obsolete, you need to know about it for the CompTIA A+ exams.

Figure 11-27 Typical 68-pin ribbon cable

Figure 11-28
50-pin HD port on
SCSI host adapter

Multiple internal devices can be connected simply by using a cable with enough connectors (see Figure 11-29). The 68-pin ribbon cable shown in Figure 11-27, for example, can support up to four SCSI devices, including the host adapter.

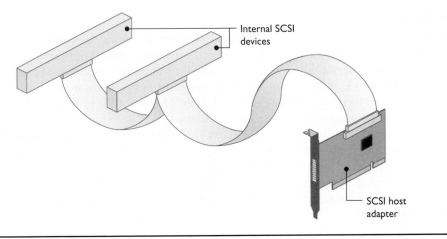

Figure 11-29 Internal SCSI chain with two devices

Assuming the SCSI host adapter has a standard external port (some controllers don't have external connections at all), plugging in an external SCSI device is as simple as running a cable from device to controller. The external SCSI connectors are D-shaped so you can't plug them in backward. As an added bonus, some external SCSI devices have two ports, one to connect to the host adapter and a second to connect to another SCSI device. The process of connecting a device directly to another device is called *daisy-chaining*. You can daisy-chain as many as 15 devices to one host adapter. SCSI chains can be internal, external, or both (see Figure 11-30).

Figure 11-30 Internal and external devices on one SCSI chain

SCSI IDs

If you're going to connect a number of devices on the same SCSI chain, you must provide some way for the host adapter to tell one device from another. To differentiate devices, SCSI uses a unique identifier called the *SCSI ID*. The SCSI ID number can range from 0 to 15. SCSI IDs are similar to many other PC hardware settings in that a SCSI device can theoretically have any SCSI ID as long as that ID is not already taken by another device connected to the same host adapter.

Some conventions should be followed when setting SCSI IDs. Typically, most people set the host adapter to 7 or 15, but you can change this setting. Note that there is no order for the use of SCSI IDs. It does not matter which device gets which number, and you can skip numbers. Restrictions on IDs apply only within a single chain. Two devices can have the same ID, in other words, as long as they are on different chains (see Figure 11-31).

Figure 11-31
IDs don't conflict
between separate
SCSI chains.

Every SCSI device has some method of setting its SCSI ID. The trick is to figure out how as you're holding the device in your hand. A SCSI device may use jumpers, dip switches, or even tiny dials; every new SCSI device is a new adventure as you try to determine how to set its SCSI ID.

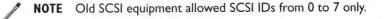

NOTE Old SCSI equipment allowed SCSI IDs from 0 to 7 only.

Termination

Whenever you send a signal down a wire, some of that signal reflects back up the wire, creating an echo and causing electronic chaos. SCSI chains use *termination* to prevent this problem. Termination simply means putting something on the ends of the wire to prevent this echo. Terminators are usually pull-down resistors and can manifest themselves in many different ways. Most of the devices within a PC have the appropriate termination built in. On other devices, including SCSI chains and some network cables, you have to set termination during installation.

The rule with SCSI is that you *must* terminate *only* the ends of the SCSI chain. You have to terminate the ends of the cable, which usually means that you need to terminate the two devices at the ends of the cable. Do *not* terminate devices that are not on the ends of the cable. Figure 11-32 shows some examples of where to terminate SCSI devices.

Figure 11-32 Location of the terminated devices

Because any SCSI device might be on the end of a chain, most manufacturers build SCSI devices that can self-terminate. Some devices can detect that they are on the end of the SCSI chain and automatically terminate themselves. Most devices, however, require you to set a jumper or switch to enable termination (see Figure 11-33).

Figure 11-33
Setting termination

Protecting Data with RAID

Ask experienced techs "What is the most expensive part of a PC?" and they'll all answer in the same way: "It's the data." You can replace any single part of your PC for a few hundred dollars at most, but if you lose critical data—well, let's just say I know of two small companies that went out of business because they lost a hard drive full of data.

Data is king; data is your PC's *raison d'être*. Losing data is a bad thing, so you need some method to prevent data loss. Of course, you can do backups, but if a hard drive dies, you have to shut down the computer, reinstall a new hard drive, reinstall the operating system, and then restore the backup. There's nothing wrong with this as long as you can afford the time and cost of shutting down the system.

A better solution, though, would save your data if a hard drive died and enable you to continue working throughout the process. This is possible if you stop relying on a single hard drive and instead use two or more drives to store your data. Sounds good, but how do you do this? Well, first of all, you could install some fancy hard drive controller that reads and writes data to two hard drives simultaneously (see Figure 11-34). The data on each drive would always be identical. One drive would be the primary drive and the other drive, called the *mirror* drive, would not be used unless the primary drive failed. This process of reading and writing data at the same time to two drives is called *disk mirroring*.

If you really want to make data safe, you can use a separate controller for each drive. With two drives, each on a separate controller, the system will continue to operate even if the primary drive's controller stops working. This super-drive mirroring technique is called *disk duplexing* (see Figure 11-35). Disk duplexing is also much faster than disk mirroring because one controller does not write each piece of data twice.

Figure 11-34
Mirrored drives

RAID 1 (mirroring)
• Exactly two (redundant) drives
• Safe but slow
• Both drives are assigned the same drive letter.

Figure 11-35
Duplexing drives

RAID 1 (duplexing)
• Exactly two (redundant) drives
• Faster and safer
• Both drives are assigned the same drive letter.

Even though duplexing is faster than mirroring, they both are slower than the classic one-drive, one-controller setup. You can use multiple drives to increase your hard drive access speed. *Disk striping* (without parity) means spreading the data among multiple (at least two) drives. Disk striping by itself provides no redundancy. If you save a small Microsoft Word file, for example, the file is split into multiple pieces; half of the pieces go on one drive and half on the other (see Figure 11-36).

Figure 11-36
Disk striping

RAID 0 (striping)
• Two or more (non-redundant) drives
• Fast, but not really safe
• Both drives are assigned the same drive letter.

SATA RAID Controller

The one and only advantage of disk striping is speed—it is a fast way to read and write to hard drives. But if either drive fails, *all* data is lost. You should not do disk striping—unless you're willing to increase the risk of losing data to increase the speed at which your hard drives save and restore data.

Disk striping with parity, in contrast, protects data by adding extra information, called *parity data*, that can be used to rebuild data if one of the drives fails. Disk striping with parity requires at least three drives, but it is common to use more than three. Disk striping with parity combines the best of disk mirroring and plain disk striping. It protects data and is quite fast. The majority of network servers use a type of disk striping with parity.

RAID

A couple of sharp guys in Berkeley back in the 1980s organized the many techniques for using multiple drives for data protection and increasing speeds as the *redundant*

array of independent (or inexpensive) disks (RAID). They outlined seven levels of RAID, numbered 0 through 6:

- **RAID 0—Disk Striping** Disk striping requires at least two drives. It does not provide redundancy to data. If any one drive fails, all data is lost.

- **RAID 1—Disk Mirroring/Duplexing** RAID 1 arrays require at least two hard drives, although they also work with any even number of drives. RAID 1 is the ultimate in safety, but you lose storage space because the data is duplicated; you need two 100-GB drives to store 100 GB of data.

- **RAID 2—Disk Striping with Multiple Parity Drives** RAID 2 was a weird RAID idea that never saw practical use. Ignore it.

- **RAID 3 and 4—Disk Striping with Dedicated Parity** RAID 3 and 4 combined dedicated data drives with dedicated parity drives. The differences between the two are trivial. Unlike RAID 2, these versions did see some use in the real world but were quickly replaced by RAID 5.

- **RAID 5—Disk Striping with Distributed Parity** Instead of dedicated data and parity drives, RAID 5 distributes data and parity information evenly across all drives. This is the fastest way to provide data redundancy. RAID 5 is by far the most common RAID implementation and requires at least three drives. RAID 5 arrays effectively use one drive's worth of space for parity. If, for example, you have three 200-GB drives, your total storage capacity is 400 GB. If you have four 200-GB drives, your total capacity is 600 GB.

- **RAID 6—Disk Striping with Extra Parity** If you lose a hard drive in a RAID 5 array, your data is at great risk until you replace the bad hard drive and rebuild the array. RAID 6 is RAID 5 with extra parity information. RAID 6 needs at least five drives, but in exchange you can lose up to two drives at the same time. RAID 6 is gaining in popularity for those willing to use larger arrays.

 NOTE An *array* in the context of RAID refers to a collection of two or more hard drives. No tech worth her salt says such things as "We're implementing disk striping with parity." Use the RAID level. Say, "We're implementing RAID 5." It's more accurate and very impressive to the folks in the accounting department!

After these first RAID levels were defined, some manufacturers came up with ways to combine different RAIDs. For example, what if you took two pairs of striped drives and mirrored the pairs? You would get what is called RAID 0+1. Or what if (read this carefully now) you took two pairs of mirrored drives and striped the pairs? You then get what we call RAID 1+0 or what is often called RAID 10. Combinations of different types of single RAID are called *multiple RAID* or *nested RAID* solutions.

NOTE There is actually a term for a storage system composed of multiple independent disks rather than disks organized by using RAID: *JBOD*, which stands for *just a bunch of disks* (or *drives*).

Implementing RAID

RAID levels describe different methods of providing data redundancy or enhancing the speed of data throughput to and from groups of hard drives. They do not say *how* to implement these methods. Literally thousands of methods can be used to set up RAID. The method you use depends largely on the level of RAID you desire, the operating system you use, and the thickness of your wallet.

The obvious starting place for RAID is to connect at least two hard drives in some fashion to create a RAID array. For many years, if you wanted to do RAID beyond RAID 0 and RAID 1, the only technology you could use was good-old SCSI. SCSI's chaining of multiple devices to a single controller made it a natural for RAID. SCSI drives make superb RAID arrays, but the high cost of SCSI drives and RAID-capable host adapters kept RAID away from all but the most critical systems—usually big file servers.

In the past few years, substantial leaps in ATA technology have made ATA a viable alternative to SCSI drive technology for RAID arrays. Specialized ATA RAID controller cards support ATA RAID arrays of up to 15 drives—plenty to support even the most complex RAID needs. In addition, the inherent hot-swap capabilities of serial ATA have virtually guaranteed that serial ATA will quickly take over the lower end of the RAID business. Personally, I think the price and performance of serial ATA mean SCSI's days are numbered.

Once you have a number of hard drives, the next question is whether to use hardware or software to control the array. Let's look at both options.

Hardware Versus Software

All RAID implementations break down into either hardware or software methods. Software is often used when price takes priority over performance. Hardware is used when you need speed along with data redundancy. Software RAID does not require special controllers; you can use the regular ATA controllers, SATA controllers, or SCSI host adapters to make a software RAID array. But you do need "smart" software. The most common software implementation of RAID is the built-in RAID software that comes with Windows 2008 Server and Windows Server 2008 R2. The Disk Management program in these Windows Server versions can configure drives for RAID 0, 1, or 5, and it works with PATA, SATA, and/or SCSI (see Figure 11-37). Disk Management in Windows XP and Windows Vista can only do RAID 0, while Windows 7's Disk Management can do RAID 0 and 1.

Windows Disk Management is not the only software RAID game in town. A number of third-party software programs work with Windows or other operating systems.

Software RAID means the operating system is in charge of all RAID functions. It works for small RAID solutions but tends to overwork your operating system easily, creating slowdowns. When you *really* need to keep going, when you need RAID that doesn't even let the users know a problem has occurred, hardware RAID is the answer.

Server Manager									
File Action View Help									

Disk Management Volume List + Graphical View

Volume	Layout	Type	File System	Status	Capacity	Free Space	% Free	Fault Tolerance	Overhead
(C:)	Simple	Basic	NTFS	Healthy (Boot, Page File, Crash Dump, Primary Partition)	99.90 GB	88.93 GB	89 %	No	0%
Shares (E:)	RAID-5	Dynamic	NTFS	Healthy	2047.75 GB	2047.60 GB	100 %	Yes	33%
System Reserved	Simple	Basic	NTFS	Healthy (System, Active, Primary Partition)	100 MB	72 MB	72 %	No	0%

Disk 0
Basic
100.00 GB
Online

System Reserved
100 MB NTFS
Healthy (System, Active, Primary Par

(C:)
99.90 GB NTFS
Healthy (Boot, Page File, Crash Dump, Primary Partition)

Disk 1
Dynamic
1023.88 GB
Online

Shares (E:)
1023.87 GB NTFS
Healthy

Disk 2
Dynamic
1023.88 GB
Online

Shares (E:)
1023.87 GB NTFS
Healthy

Disk 3
Dynamic
1023.88 GB
Online

Shares (E:)
1023.87 GB NTFS
Healthy

CD-ROM 0
DVD (D:)

No Media

■ Unallocated ■ Primary partition □ RAID-5 volume

Figure 11-37 Disk Management tool of Computer Management in Windows Server 2008 R2

Hardware RAID centers on an *intelligent* controller—either a SCSI host adapter or a PATA/SATA controller that handles all of the RAID functions (see Figure 11-38). Unlike a regular PATA/SATA controller or SCSI host adapter, these controllers have chips that have their own processor and memory. This allows the card, instead of the operating system, to handle all of the work of implementing RAID.

Figure 11-38
Serial ATA RAID
controller

Most RAID setups in the real world are hardware-based. Almost all of the many hardware RAID solutions provide *hot-swapping*—the ability to replace a bad drive without disturbing the operating system. Hot-swapping is common in hardware RAID.

Hardware-based RAID is invisible to the operating system and is configured in several ways, depending on the specific chips involved. Most RAID systems have a special configuration utility in Flash ROM that you access after CMOS but before the OS loads. Figure 11-39 shows a typical firmware program used to configure a hardware RAID solution.

```
FastBuild (tm) Utility (c) 2004-2005 Promise Technology, Inc.
                       [ View Drives Assignments ]

     Channel:ID          Drive Model         Capacity (MB)   Assignment
         1:Mas  HDT722525DLA380                250059
                Extent 1                       249992          LD  1-1
         2:Mas  HDT722525DLA380                250059
                Extent 2                       249992          LD  1-2
         3:Mas  HDT722525DLA380                250059
                Extent 3                       249992          LD  1-3
         4:Mas  HDT722525DLA380                250059
                Extent 4                       249992          LD  1-4

                              [ Keys Available ]

  [↑] Up    [↓] Down    [ESC] Exit
```

Figure 11-39 RAID configuration utility

Personal RAID

Due to drastic reductions in the cost of ATA RAID controller chips, in the past few years we've seen an explosion of ATA-based hardware RAID solutions built into mainstream motherboards. While this "ATA RAID on the motherboard" began with parallel ATA, the introduction of serial ATA made motherboards with built-in RAID extremely common.

These personal RAID motherboards might be common, but they're not used too terribly often given that these RAID solutions usually provide only RAID 0 or RAID 1. If you want to use RAID, spend a few extra dollars and buy a RAID 5–capable controller.

NOTE RAID controllers aren't just for internal drives; some models can handle multiple eSATA drives configured at any of the RAID levels. If you're feeling lucky, you can create a RAID array using both internal and external SATA drives.

The Future Is RAID

RAID has been with us for about 20 years, but until only recently it was the domain of big systems and deep pockets. During those 20 years, however, a number of factors have come together to make RAID a reality for both big servers and common desktop systems. Imagine a world where dirt-cheap RAID on every computer means no one ever again losing critical data. I get goose bumps just thinking about it!

Installing Drives

Installing a drive is a fairly simple process if you take the time to make sure you have the right drive for your system, configure the drive properly, and do a few quick tests to see if it's running properly. Since PATA, SATA, and SCSI have different cabling requirements, we'll look at each separately.

Choosing Your Drive

First, decide where you're going to put the drive. Look for an open ATA connection. Is it PATA or SATA? Is it a dedicated RAID controller? Many motherboards with built-in RAID controllers have a CMOS setting that enables you to turn the RAID on or off (see Figure 11-40).

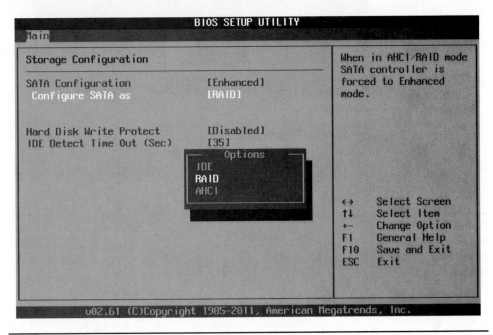

Figure 11-40 Settings for RAID in CMOS

Second, make sure you have room for the drive in the case. Where will you place it? Do you have a spare power connector? Will the data and power cables reach the drive? A quick test fit is always a good idea.

Jumpers and Cabling on PATA Drives

If you have only one hard drive, set the drive's jumpers to master or standalone. If you have two drives, set one to master and the other to slave. See Figure 11-41 for a close-up of a PATA hard drive, showing the jumpers.

Figure 11-41
Master/slave jumpers on a hard drive

At first glance, you might notice that the jumpers aren't actually labeled *master* and *slave*. So how do you know how to set them properly? The easiest way is to read the front of the drive; most drives have a diagram on the housing that explains how to set the jumpers properly. Figure 11-42 shows the label of one of these drives, so you can see how to set the drive to master or slave.

Figure 11-42
Drive label showing master/slave settings

Disk Quotas

NTFS supports *disk quotas*, enabling administrators to set limits on drive space usage for users. To set quotas, you must log on as an Administrator, right-click the hard drive name, and select Properties. In the Drive Properties dialog box, select the Quota tab and make changes. Figure 12-23 shows configured quotas for a hard drive. Although rarely used on single-user systems, setting disk quotas on multi-user systems prevents any individual user from monopolizing your hard disk space.

Figure 12-23

Hard drive quotas
in Windows 7

Cluster Sizes

Unlike FAT16 or FAT32, you can adjust the cluster sizes in NTFS, although you'll probably rarely do so. Table 12-4 shows the default cluster sizes for NTFS.

Drive Size	Cluster Size	Number of Sectors
512 MB or less	512 bytes	1
513 MB to 1024 MB (1 GB)	1024 bytes (1 KB)	2
1025 MB to 2048 MB (2 GB)	2048 bytes (2 KB)	4
2049 MB and larger	4096 bytes (4 KB)	8

Table 12-4 NTFS Cluster Sizes

By default, NTFS supports partitions up to ~16 TB on a dynamic disk (though only up to 2 TB on a basic disk). By tweaking the cluster sizes, you can get NTFS to support partitions up to 16 exabytes, or 18,446,744,073,709,551,616 bytes! That might support any and all upcoming hard drive capacities for the next 100 years or so.

EXAM TIP NTFS supports partitions up to 16 TB by default.

With so many file systems, how do you know which one to use? In the case of internal hard drives, you should use the most feature-rich system your OS supports. For all modern versions of Windows, use NTFS. External hard drives still often use FAT32 because NTFS features such as the ACL and encryption can make access difficult when you move the drive between systems, but with that exception, NTFS is your best choice on a Windows-based system.

FAT64

Everyone loves USB thumb drives. Their ease of use and convenience make them indispensible for those of us who enjoy sharing a program, some photos, or a playlist. But people today want to share more than just a few small files, and they can do so with larger thumb drives. As thumb drives grow bigger in capacity, however, the file system becomes a problem.

The file system we have used for years on thumb drives, FAT32, does not work on drives larger than 2 TB. Worse, FAT32 limits *file* size to 4 GB. Now that you can find many thumb drives larger than 2 GB, Microsoft wisely developed a replacement for FAT32.

EXAM TIP FAT32 only supports drives up to 2 TB and only supports files up to 4 GB.

The newer file system, called *exFAT* or *FAT64*, breaks the 4-GB file-size barrier, supporting files up to 16 exabytes (EB) and a theoretical partition limit of 64 zettabytes (ZB). Microsoft recommends a partition size of up to 512 TB on today's USB flash drives, which should be enough for a while. The exFAT file system extends FAT32 from 32-bit cluster entries to 64-bit cluster entries in the file table. Like FAT32, on the other hand, exFAT still lacks all of NTFS's extra features such as permissions, compression, and encryption.

NOTE An exabyte is 2^{60} bytes; a zettabyte is 2^{70} bytes. For comparison, a terabyte is 2^{40} bytes. Remember from your binary practice that each superscript number doubles the overall number, so $2^{41} = 2$ TB, $2^{42} = 4$ TB, and so on. That means a zettabyte is really, really big!

Now, if you're like me, you might be thinking, "Why don't we just use NTFS?" And I would say, "Good point!" Microsoft, however, sees NTFS as too powerful for what most of us need from flash drives. For example, flash drives don't need NTFS permissions. But if for some reason you *really* want to format large USB thumb drives with NTFS, Windows 7 will gladly allow you to do so, as shown in Figure 12-24.

Figure 12-24

Formatting a thumb drive in Windows 7

NOTE Microsoft introduced exFAT in Windows 7, but Windows Vista with SP1 also supports exFAT. Microsoft even enabled Windows XP support for exFAT with a special download (check Microsoft Knowledge Base article 955704).

The Partitioning and Formatting Process

Now that you understand the concepts of formatting and partitioning, let's go through the process of setting up an installed hard drive by using different partitioning and formatting tools. If you have access to a system, try following along with these descriptions. Remember, don't make any changes to a drive you want to keep, because both partitioning and formatting are destructive processes.

Bootable Media

Imagine you've built a brand-new PC. The hard drive has no OS, so you need to boot up something to set up that hard drive. Any software that can boot up a system is by definition an operating system. You need an optical disc or USB thumb drive with a bootable OS installed. Any removable media that has a bootable OS is generically called a *boot device* or *boot disk*. Your system boots off of the boot device, which then loads some kind of OS that enables you to partition, format, and install an OS on your new hard drive. Boot devices come from many sources. All Windows OS installation discs are boot devices, as are Linux installation discs.

Every boot disc or device has some kind of partitioning tool and a way to format a new partition. A hard drive has to have a partition and has to be formatted to support an OS installation.

Partitioning and Formatting with the Installation Disc

When you boot up a Windows installation disc and the installation program detects a hard drive that is not yet partitioned, it prompts you through a sequence of steps to partition (and format) the hard drive. Chapter 14 covers the entire installation process, but we'll jump ahead and dive into the partitioning part of the installation here to see how this is done.

The partitioning and formatting tools differ between Windows XP and Windows Vista/7. Windows XP has a text-based installation tool. Windows Vista and Windows 7 use a graphical tool. But the process of setting up drives is nearly identical.

Partitioning During Windows XP Installation

The most common partitioning scenario involves turning a new blank drive into a single bootable C: drive. To accomplish this goal, you need to make the entire drive a primary partition and then make it active. Let's go through the process of partitioning and formatting a single brand-new 1-TB hard drive.

The Windows XP installation begins by booting from a Windows installation CD-ROM like the one shown in Figure 12-25. The installation program starts automatically from the CD. The installation first loads some needed files but eventually prompts you with the screen shown in Figure 12-26. This is your clue that partitioning is about to start.

Figure 12-25
Windows
installation CD

```
Windows XP Professional Setup

   Welcome to Setup.

   This portion of the Setup program prepares Microsoft(R)
   Windows(R) XP to run on your computer.

       • To set up Windows XP now, press ENTER.

       • To repair a Windows XP installation using
         Recovery Console, press R.

       • To quit Setup without installing Windows XP, press F3.

  ENTER=Continue   R=Repair   F3=Quit
```

Figure 12-26 Welcome to Setup

Press the ENTER key to start a new Windows installation and accept the license agreement to see the main partitioning screen (see Figure 12-27). The bar that says Unpartitioned space is the drive.

```
Windows XP Professional Setup

   The following list shows the existing partitions and
   unpartitioned space on this computer.

   Use the UP and DOWN ARROW keys to select an item in the list.

       • To set up Windows XP on the selected item, press ENTER.

       • To create a partition in the unpartitioned space, press C.

       • To delete the selected partition, press D.

   ┌─────────────────────────────────────────────────────────┐
   │ 1023995 MB Disk 0 at Id 0 on bus 0 on atapi [MBR]         │
   │      Unpartitioned space                    1023995 MB    │
   │                                                           │
   │                                                           │
   │                                                           │
   │                                                           │
   │                                                           │
   │                                                           │
   │                                                           │
   └─────────────────────────────────────────────────────────┘
  ENTER=Install   C=Create Partition   F3=Quit
```

Figure 12-27 Partitioning screen

The Windows installer is pretty smart. If you press ENTER at this point, it partitions the hard drive as a single primary partition, makes it active, and installs Windows for you. That's the type of partitioning you will do on the vast majority of installations.

As you can see on the screen, the partitioning tool also gives you the option to press C to create a partition on the drive. You can also press D to delete an existing partition.

When you press C, the installer asks you how large a partition to make (see Figure 12-28). You may make the partition any size you want by erasing the current number (the whole unpartitioned space by default) and typing in a number, from a minimum of 8 MB up to the size of the entire drive. Once you have your number set, press ENTER to create the partition.

```
Windows XP Professional Setup

  You asked Setup to create a new partition on
  1023995 MB Disk 0 at Id 0 on bus 0 on atapi [MBR].

      • To create the new partition, enter a size below and
        press ENTER.

      • To go back to the previous screen without creating
        the partition, press ESC.

  The minimum size for the new partition is       8 megabytes (MB).
  The maximum size for the new partition is 1023987 megabytes (MB).
  Create partition of size (in MB):   1023987

  ENTER=Create   ESC=Cancel
```

Figure 12-28 Setting partition size

If you select a size smaller than the maximum and press ENTER, you'll see the newly created partition and the remaining drive as Unpartitioned space (see Figure 12-29). You can create more "partitions" by moving the selection bar onto the Unpartitioned space and pressing C to create a new partition. Repeat this for as many new "partitions" as you want to create.

The installer on the Windows XP disc calls all the drive structures you create at this time partitions, but what's happening is a little different. The first partition you create will be a primary partition. The second partition you create will be automatically an extended partition. Every "partition" you create after the second will be a logical drive in the extended partition.

```
Windows XP Professional Setup

  The following list shows the existing partitions and
  unpartitioned space on this computer.

  Use the UP and DOWN ARROW keys to select an item in the list.

     •  To set up Windows XP on the selected item, press ENTER.

     •  To create a partition in the unpartitioned space, press C.

     •  To delete the selected partition, press D.

  ┌──────────────────────────────────────────────────────────────────┐
  │ 1023995 MB Disk 0 at Id 0 on bus 0 on atapi [MBR]                  │
  │                                                                    │
  │      C:  Partition1 [New (Raw)]              340989 MB ( 340989 MB free)│
  │          Unpartitioned space                683006 MB              │
  │                                                                    │
  │                                                                    │
  │                                                                    │
  │                                                                    │
  │                                                                    │
  │                                                                    │
  └──────────────────────────────────────────────────────────────────┘

   ENTER=Install   D=Delete Partition   F3=Quit
```

Figure 12-29 A newly created partition along with unpartitioned space

Once you finish partitioning, select the partition you want to use for the installation. Again, almost every time you should select C:. At that point Windows asks you how you want to format that drive (see Figure 12-30).

```
Windows XP Professional Setup

  A new partition for Windows XP has been created on

  1023995 MB Disk 0 at Id 0 on bus 0 on atapi [MBR].

  This partition must now be formatted.

  From the list below, select a file system for the new partition.
  Use the UP and DOWN ARROW keys to select the file system you want,
  and then press ENTER.

  If you want to select a different partition for Windows XP,
  press ESC.

     Format the partition using the NTFS file system (Quick)
     Format the partition using the NTFS file system

   ENTER=Continue   ESC=Cancel
```

Figure 12-30 Format screen

So you might be asking, where's the basic versus dynamic option? Where do you tell Windows to make the partition primary instead of extended? Where do you set it as active?

The Windows installer makes a number of assumptions for you, such as always making the first partition primary and setting it as active. The installer also makes all hard drives basic disks. You'll have to convert a drive to dynamic later (if you even want to convert it at all).

Select NTFS for the format. Either option—quick or full—will do the job here. (Quick format is quicker, as the name would suggest, but the full option is more thorough and thus safer.) After Windows formats the drive, the installation continues, copying the new Windows installation to the C: drive.

The installation program can delete partitions just as easily as it makes them. If you use a hard drive that already has partitions, for example, you just select the partition you wish to delete and press D. This brings up a dialog box where Windows gives you one last chance to change your mind (see Figure 12-31). Press L to kill the partition.

```
Windows XP Professional Setup

  You asked Setup to delete the partition

    E:  Partition3 [New (Raw)]                340989 MB ( 340989 MB free)

  on 1023995 MB Disk 0 at Id 0 on bus 0 on atapi [MBR].

      •  To delete this partition, press L.
         CAUTION: All data on this partition will be lost.

      •  To return to the previous screen without
         deleting the partition, press ESC.

  L=Delete   ESC=Cancel
```

Figure 12-31 Option to delete partition

Partitioning During Windows Vista/7 Installation

The process of partitioning and formatting with the Windows Vista or Windows 7 installation differs from the Windows XP process primarily in looks—it's graphical—and not in function. You'll go through a couple of installation screens (see Figure 12-32) where you select things such as language and get prompted for a product key and acceptance of the license agreement. Eventually you'll get to the *Where do you want to install Windows?* dialog box (see Figure 12-33).

Figure 12-32 Starting the Windows 7 installation

Figure 12-33 Where do you want to install Windows?

Click Next to do the most common partitioning and formatting action: creating a single C: partition, making it active, and formatting it as NTFS. Note that Windows 7 creates two partitions, a 100-MB System Reserved partition and the C: partition. This is normal, the way the system was designed to work. Figure 12-34 shows a typical Windows 7 installation in Disk Management.

Figure 12-34 Disk Management showing the default partitions in Windows 7

If you want to do any custom partitioning or delete existing partitions, you click on *Drive options (advanced)* in the *Where do you want to install Windows?* dialog box. To create a new partition, click the New button. Type in an amount in gigabytes that you want to use for a new partition, then click Apply. In Windows 7, you will get a notice that Windows might create additional partitions for system files. When you click OK, Windows will create the 100-MB System Reserved partition as well as the partition you specified (see Figure 12-35). Any leftover drive space will be listed as Unallocated Space.

Once you create a new partition, click the Format button. The installer won't ask you what file system to use. Windows Vista and Windows 7 can read FAT and FAT32 drives, but they won't install to such a partition by default.

The example here has a 1-TB drive with a 499-GB partition and 500 GB of unallocated space. If you've gone through this process and have changed your mind, wanting to make the partition use the full terabyte, what do you have to do? In Windows XP, you would have to delete the partition and start over, but not so in Windows Vista or Windows 7. You can simply click the Extend button and then apply the rest of the unallocated space to the currently formatted partition. The extend function enables you to tack unpartitioned space onto an already partitioned drive with the click of the mouse.

Figure 12-35 New 499-GB partition with 100-MB System Reserved partition and Unallocated Space

Disk Management

The primary tool for partitioning and formatting drives after installation is the Disk Management utility (see Figure 12-36). You can use Disk Management to do everything you want to do to a hard drive in one handy tool. You can access Disk Management by going to the Control Panel and opening the Computer Management applet. You can also click Start | Run in Windows XP and type **diskmgmt.msc**—or just type **diskmgmt. msc** in the Start menu Search bar in Windows Vista/7—and press ENTER.

EXAM TIP The CompTIA A+ 220-802 exam will test you on how to get into Disk Management. Know the ways.

Disk Initialization

Every hard drive in a Windows system has special information placed onto the drive through a process called *disk initialization*. This initialization information includes identifiers that say "this drive belongs in this system" and other information that defines what this hard drive does in the system. If the hard drive is part of a software RAID array, for example, its RAID information is stored in the initialization. If it's part of a spanned volume, this is also stored there.

All new drives must be initialized before you can use them. When you install an extra hard drive into a Windows system and start Disk Management, it notices the new drive and starts the Hard Drive Initialization Wizard. If you don't let the wizard run, the drive will be listed as unknown (see Figure 12-37).

Figure 12-36 Disk Management

Figure 12-37 Unknown drive in Disk Management

To initialize a disk, right-click the disk icon and select Initialize. In Windows 7 you will get the option to select MBR or GPT as a partition style. Once a disk is initialized, you can see the status of the drive—a handy tool for troubleshooting.

Disk Management enables you to view the status of every drive in your system. Hopefully, you'll mostly see the drive listed as Healthy, meaning that nothing is happening to it and things are going along swimmingly. You're also already familiar with the Unallocated and Active statuses, but here are a few more to be familiar with for the CompTIA A+ exams and real life as a tech:

- **Foreign drive** You see this when you move a dynamic disk from one computer to another.

- **Formatting** As you might have guessed, you see this when you're formatting a drive.

- **Failed** Pray you never see this status, because it means that the disk is damaged or corrupt and you've probably lost some data.

- **Online** This is what you see if a disk is healthy and communicating properly with the computer.

- **Offline** The disk is either corrupted or having communication problems.

A newly installed drive is always set as a basic disk. There's nothing wrong with using basic disks, other than that you miss out on some handy features.

Creating Partitions and Volumes in Disk Management

To create partitions or volumes, right-click the unallocated part of the drive and select New Partition in Windows XP or New Simple Volume in Windows Vista/7. Disk Management runs the New Partition Wizard or the New Simple Volume Wizard. In Windows XP, you'll be asked to select a primary partition or an extended partition (see Figure 12-38). Once you do that, you'll go to a screen where you specify the partition or volume size. Because Windows Vista and Windows 7 don't give you the option to specify whether you want primary or extended partitions, you'll go straight to the sizing screen (see Figure 12-39).

Specify a partition or volume size and click Next. The wizard will ask if you want to assign a drive letter to the partition or volume, mount it as a folder to an existing partition or volume, or do neither (see Figure 12-40). In almost all cases, you'll want to give primary partitions and simple volumes a drive letter.

It's important to note here that Windows Vista and Windows 7 do not enable you to specify whether you want a primary or extended partition when you create a volume. The first three volumes you create will be primary partitions. Every volume thereafter will be a logical drive in an extended partition.

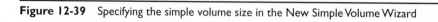

Figure 12-38 The New Partition Wizard in Windows XP at the Select Partition Type dialog box

Figure 12-39 Specifying the simple volume size in the New Simple Volume Wizard

Figure 12-40 Assigning a drive letter to a partition

The last screen of the New Partition Wizard or New Simple Volume Wizard asks for the type of format you want to use for this partition (see Figure 12-41). If your partition is 4 GB or less, you may format it as FAT, FAT32, or NTFS. If your partition is greater than 4 GB but less than 32 GB, you can make the drive FAT32 or NTFS. Windows requires NTFS on any partition greater than 32 GB. Although FAT32 supports partitions up to 2 TB, Microsoft wants you to use NTFS on larger partitions and creates this limit. With today's big hard drives, there's no good reason to use anything other than NTFS.

NOTE Windows reads and writes to FAT32 partitions larger than 32 GB; you simply can't use Disk Management to make such partitions. If you ever stumble across a drive from a system that ran the old Windows 9x/Me that has a FAT32 partition larger than 32 GB, it will work just fine in a modern Windows system.

You have a few more tasks to complete at this screen. You can add a volume label if you want. You can also choose the size of your clusters (*Allocation unit size*). There's no reason to change the default cluster size, so leave that alone—but you can sure speed up

the format if you select the *Perform a quick format* checkbox. This will format your drive without checking every cluster. It's fast and a bit risky, but new hard drives almost always come from the factory in perfect shape—so you must decide whether to use it or not.

Figure 12-41 Choosing a file system type

Last, if you chose NTFS, you may enable file and folder compression. If you select this option, you'll be able to right-click any file or folder on this partition and compress it. To compress a file or folder, choose the one you want to compress, right-click, and select Properties. Then click the Advanced button and turn compression on (see Figure 12-42). Compression is handy for opening up space on a hard drive that's filling up, but it also slows down disk access, so use it only when you need it.

Dynamic Disks

You create dynamic disks from basic disks in Disk Management. Once you convert a drive from a basic disk to a dynamic disk, primary and extended partitions no longer exist; dynamic disks are divided into volumes instead of partitions. This is obvious in Windows XP because the name changes. Because Window Vista and Windows 7 call partitions *volumes*, the change to dynamic disk isn't obvious at all.

Figure 12-42
Turning on
compression

 EXAM TIP When you move a dynamic disk from one computer to another, it shows up in Disk Management as a foreign drive. You can import a foreign drive into the new system by right-clicking the disk icon and selecting Import Foreign Disks.

To convert a basic disk to dynamic, just right-click the drive icon and select Convert to Dynamic Disk (see Figure 12-43). The process is very quick and safe, although the reverse is not true. The conversion from dynamic disk to basic disk first requires you to delete all volumes off of the hard drive.

Once you've converted the disk, you can make one of the five types of volumes on a dynamic disk: simple, spanned, striped, mirrored, or RAID 5. You'll next learn how to implement the three most common volume types. The final step involves assigning a drive letter or mounting the volume as a folder.

Figure 12-43 Converting to a dynamic disk

Simple Volumes A simple volume acts just like a primary partition. If you have only one dynamic disk in a system, it can have only a simple volume. It's important to note here that a simple volume may act like a traditional primary partition, but it is very different because you cannot install an operating system on it.

In Disk Management, right-click any unallocated space on the dynamic disk and choose New Simple Volume (see Figure 12-44) to run the New Simple Volume Wizard. You'll see a series of screens that prompt you on size and file system, and then you're finished. Figure 12-45 shows Disk Management with three simple volumes.

Spanning Volumes You can extend the size of a simple volume to any unallocated space on a dynamic disk. You can also extend the volume to grab extra space on completely different dynamic disks, creating a spanned volume. To extend or span, simply right-click the volume you want to make bigger, and choose Extend Volume from the options (see Figure 12-46). This opens the Extend Volume Wizard, which prompts you for the location of free space on a dynamic disk and the increased volume size you want to assign (see Figure 12-47). If you have multiple drives, you can span the volume just as easily to one of those drives.

The capability to extend and span volumes makes dynamic disks worth their weight in gold. If you start running out of space on a volume, you can simply add another physical hard drive to the system and span the volume to the new drive. This keeps your drive letters consistent and unchanging so your programs don't get confused, yet enables you to expand drive space when needed.

Figure 12-44 Selecting to open the New Simple Volume Wizard

Figure 12-45 Simple volumes

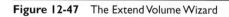

Figure 12-46 Selecting the Extend Volume option

Figure 12-47 The Extend Volume Wizard

 CAUTION Once you convert a drive to dynamic, you cannot revert it to a basic disk without losing all of the data on that drive. Be prepared to back up all data before you convert.

You can extend or span any simple volume on a dynamic disk, not just the "one on the end" in the Disk Management console. You simply select the volume to expand and the total volume increase you want. Figure 12-48 shows a simple 488.28-GB volume named Extended that has been enlarged an extra 1316.40 GB in a portion of the hard drive, skipping the 195.31-GB section of unallocated space contiguous to it. This created an 1804.68-GB volume. Windows has no problem skipping areas on a drive.

Figure 12-48 Extended volume

 NOTE You can extend and shrink volumes in Vista and 7 without using dynamic disks. You can shrink any volume with available free space (though you can't shrink the volume by the whole amount of free space, based on the location of unmovable sectors such as the MBR), and you can expand volumes with unallocated space on the drive.

To shrink a volume, right-click it and select Shrink Volume. Disk Management will calculate how much you can shrink it, and then you can choose up to that amount. To extend, right-click and select Extend Volume. It's a pretty straightforward process.

Striped Volumes If you have two or more dynamic disks in a PC, Disk Management enables you to combine them into a *striped* volume. Although Disk Management doesn't use the term, you know this as a RAID 0 array. A striped volume spreads out blocks of each file across multiple disks. Using two or more drives in a group called a *stripe set*, striping writes data first to a certain number of clusters on one drive, then to a certain number of clusters on the next drive, and so on. It speeds up data throughput because the system has to wait a much shorter time for a drive to read or write data. The drawback of striping is that if any single drive in the stripe set fails, all the data in the stripe set is lost.

To create a striped volume, right-click any unused space on a drive, choose New Volume, and then choose Striped. The wizard asks for the other drive you want to add to the stripe, and you need to select unallocated space on another dynamic disk. Select another unallocated space and go through the remaining screens on sizing and formatting until you've created a new striped volume (see Figure 12-49). The two stripes in Figure 12-49 appear to have different sizes, but if you look closely you'll see they are both 1000 GB. All stripes must be the same size on each drive.

Figure 12-49 Two striped drives

Mirrored Volumes Windows 7 Professional, Enterprise, and Ultimate editions can create a *mirror set* with two drives for data redundancy. You know mirrors from Chapter 11 as *RAID 1*. To create a mirror, right-click on unallocated space on a drive and select New Mirrored Volume (see Figure 12-50). This runs the New Mirrored Volume Wizard. Click Next to continue. Select an available disk in the Available box and click the Add button to move it to the Selected box (see Figure 12-51). Click Next to get to the by-now-familiar Assign Drive Letter or Path dialog box and select what is appropriate for the PC.

Figure 12-50 Selecting a new mirror

Other Levels of RAID Disk Management enables you to create a *RAID 5 array* that uses three or more disks to create a robust solution for storage. This applies to all the professional versions of Windows XP, Windows Vista, and Windows 7. Unfortunately for users of those operating systems, you can only make the array on a Windows Server machine that you access remotely across a network.

Disk Management cannot do any nested RAID arrays. So if you want RAID 0+1 or RAID 1+0 (RAID 10), you need to use third-party software (or go with hardware RAID).

New Mirrored Volume

Select Disks
You can select the disks and set the disk size for this volume.

Select the disks you want to use, and then click Add.

Available:

Disk 2 2047997 (null)

Add >

< Remove

< Remove All

Selected:

Disk 1 2047997 (null)

Total volume size in megabytes (MB): 0

Maximum available space in MB: 2047997

Select the amount of space in MB: 2047997

< Back Next > Cancel

Figure 12-51 Selecting drives for the array

Mounting Partitions as Folders

While partitions and volumes can be assigned a drive letter, D: through Z:, they can also be mounted as a folder on another drive, also known as a *mount point*. This enables you to use your existing folders to store more data than can fit on a single drive or partition/volume (see Figure 12-52).

Figure 12-52
Mounting a drive
as a folder

Imagine you use your My Documents folder on a Windows XP machine to store your digital photos. As your collection grows, you realize your current 500-GB hard drive is running out of space. You're willing to buy another hard drive, but you have a great

organizational structure in your existing My Documents folder and you don't want to lose that. You don't have to move everything to the new hard drive, either.

After you install the new hard drive, you can *mount* the primary partition (or logical drive) as a folder within the existing My Documents folder on your C: drive (for example, C:\Users\Mike\My Photos). At this point the drive doesn't have a letter (though you could add one later, if you wanted). To use the new drive, just drop your files into the My Photos folder. They'll be stored on the second hard drive, not the original 500-GB drive (see Figure 12-53). Amazing!

Figure 12-53
Adding photos to the mounted folder stores them on the second hard drive.

NOTE Mounting a partition or volume as a folder in the scenario here only applies to Windows XP and Windows Vista. Although you can certainly mount them as folders in Windows 7, the use of Libraries makes them irrelevant. You would simply add a drive, give it a letter, and add a folder to the drive. Then add that folder to the appropriate Library and it will appear to be just like any other folder.

To create a mount point, right-click an unallocated section of a disk and choose New Partition or New Simple Volume. This opens the appropriately named wizard. In the second screen, you can select a mount point rather than a drive letter (see Figure 12-54). Browse to a blank folder on an NTFS-formatted drive or create a new folder and you're in business.

EXAM TIP The CompTIA A+ 802 exam objectives mention "splitting" partitions. To be clear, you never actually split a partition. If you want to turn one partition into two, you need to remove the existing partition and create two new ones, or shrink the existing partition and add a new one to the unallocated space. If you see it on the exam, know that this is what CompTIA means.

Figure 12-54 Choosing to create a mounted volume

Formatting a Partition

You can format any Windows partition/volume in My Computer/Computer. Just right-click the drive name and choose Format (see Figure 12-55). You'll see a dialog box that asks for the type of file system you want to use, the cluster size, a place to put a volume label, and two other options. The Quick Format option tells Windows not to test the clusters and is a handy option when you're in a hurry—and feeling lucky. The Enable Compression option tells Windows to give users the capability to compress folders or files. It works well but slows down your hard drive.

Disk Management is today's preferred formatting tool for Windows. When you create a new partition or volume, the wizard also asks you what type of format you want to use. Always use NTFS unless you're that rare and strange person who wants to dual-boot some ancient version of Windows.

All OS installation discs partition and format as part of the OS installation. Windows simply prompts you to partition and then format the drive. Read the screens and you'll do great.

Figure 12-55 Choosing Format in Computer

Maintaining and Troubleshooting Hard Drives

Hard drives are complex mechanical and electrical devices. With platters spinning at thousands of rotations per minute, they also generate heat and vibration. All of these factors make hard drives susceptible to failure. In this section, you will learn some basic maintenance tasks that will keep your hard drives healthy, and for those inevitable instances when a hard drive fails, you will also learn what you can do to repair them.

Maintenance

Hard drive maintenance can be broken down into two distinct functions: checking the disk occasionally for failed clusters, and keeping data organized on the drive so it can be accessed quickly.

Error-Checking

Individual clusters on hard drives sometimes go bad. There's nothing you can do to prevent this from happening, so it's important that you check occasionally for bad clusters on drives. The tools used to perform this checking are generically called error-checking

utilities, although the terms for two older Microsoft tools—ScanDisk and *chkdsk* (pronounced "checkdisk")—are often used. Microsoft calls the tool *Error-checking* in Windows XP/Vista/7. Whatever the name of the utility, each does the same job: when the tool finds bad clusters, it puts the electronic equivalent of orange cones around them so the system won't try to place data in those bad clusters.

 EXAM TIP CompTIA A+ uses the terms CHKDSK and check disk rather than Error-checking.

Most error-checking tools do far more than just check for bad clusters. They go through all of the drive's filenames, looking for invalid names and attempting to fix them. They look for clusters that have no filenames associated with them (we call these *lost chains*) and erase them. From time to time, the underlying links between parent and child folders are lost, so a good error-checking tool checks every parent and child folder. With a folder such as C:\Test\Data, for example, they make sure that the Data folder is properly associated with its parent folder, C:\Test, and that C:\Test is properly associated with its child folder, C:\Test\Data.

To access Error-checking on a Windows system, open My Computer/Computer, right-click the drive you want to check, and choose Properties to open the drive's Properties dialog box. Select the Tools tab and click the Check now button (see Figure 12-56) to display the Check Disk dialog box, which has two options (see Figure 12-57). Check the box next to *Automatically fix file system errors*, but save the option to *Scan for and attempt recovery of bad sectors* for times when you actually suspect a problem, because it takes a while on bigger hard drives.

Figure 12-56

The Tools tab in the Properties dialog box

Local Disk (C:) Properties

Security	Previous Versions	Quota	
General	Tools	Hardware	Sharing

Error-checking

This option will check the drive for errors.

Check now...

Defragmentation

This option will defragment files on the drive.

Defragment now...

Backup

This option will back up files on the drive.

Back up now...

OK Cancel Apply

Figure 12-57
Check Disk
options

Now that you know how to run Error-checking, your next question should be, "How often do I run it?" A reasonable maintenance plan would include running it about once a week. Error-checking is fast (unless you use the *Scan for and attempt recovery* option), and it's a great tool for keeping your system in top shape.

Defragmentation

Fragmentation of clusters can increase your drive access times dramatically. It's a good idea to *defragment*—or *defrag*—your drives as part of monthly maintenance. You access the defrag tool Disk Defragmenter the same way you access Error-checking—right-click a drive in My Computer/Computer and choose Properties—except you click the Defragment now button on the Tools tab to open Disk Defragmenter. In Windows Vista/7, Microsoft has given Disk Defragmenter a big visual makeover (see Figure 12-58), but both the old and new versions do the same job.

Defragmentation is interesting to watch—once. From then on, schedule Disk Defragmenter to run late at night. You should defragment your drives about once a month, although you could run Disk Defragmenter every week, and if you run it every night, it takes only a few minutes. The longer you go between defrags, the longer it takes. If you have Windows 7, Microsoft has made defragging even easier by automatically defragging disks once a week. You can adjust the schedule or even turn it off altogether, but remember that if you don't run Disk Defragmenter, your system will run slower. If you don't run Error-checking, you may lose data.

Figure 12-58 Disk Defragmenter in Windows 7 (left) and Windows XP

NOTE If you happen to have one of those blazingly fast solid-state drives (SSDs), you don't have to defrag your drive. In fact, you should *never* defrag an SSD because it can shorten its lifetime. Windows 7 is even smart enough to disable scheduled defrag for SSDs.

Disk Cleanup

Did you know that the average hard drive is full of trash? Not the junk you intentionally put in your hard drive such as the 23,000 e-mail messages that you refuse to delete from your e-mail program. This kind of trash is all of the files that you never see that Windows keeps for you. Here are a few examples:

- **Files in the Recycle Bin** When you delete a file, it isn't really deleted. It's placed in the Recycle Bin in case you decide you need the file later. I just checked my Recycle Bin and found around 3 GB worth of files (see Figure 12-59). That's a lot of trash!

- **Temporary Internet files** When you go to a Web site, Windows keeps copies of the graphics and other items so the page will load more quickly the next time you access it. You can see these files by opening the Internet Options applet on the Control Panel. Click the Settings button under the Browsing history label and then click the View files button on the Temporary Internet Files and History Settings dialog box. Figure 12-60 shows temporary Internet files from Internet Explorer.

Figure 12-59 Mike's Recycle Bin

Figure 12-60 Lots of temporary Internet files

- **Downloaded program files** Your system always keeps a copy of any Java or ActiveX applets it downloads. You can see these in the Internet Options applet by clicking the Settings button under the Browsing history label. Click the View objects button on the Temporary Internet Files and History Settings dialog box. You'll generally find only a few tiny files here.

- **Temporary files** Many applications create temporary files that are supposed to be deleted when the application is closed. For one reason or another, these temporary files sometimes aren't deleted. The location of these files varies with the version of Windows, but they always reside in a folder called "Temp."

Every hard drive eventually becomes filled with lots of unnecessary trash. All versions of Windows tend to act erratically when the drives run out of unused space. Fortunately, all versions of Windows have a powerful tool called *Disk Cleanup* (see Figure 12-61). You can access Disk Cleanup in all versions of Windows by choosing Start | All Programs | Accessories | System Tools | Disk Cleanup.

Figure 12-61
Disk Cleanup

Disk Cleanup gets rid of the four types of files just described (and a few others). Run Disk Cleanup once a month or so to keep plenty of space available on your hard drive.

Troubleshooting Hard Drive Implementation

There's no scarier computer problem than an error that points to trouble with a hard drive. This section looks at some of the more common problems that occur

with hard drives and how to fix them. These issues fall into four broad categories: installation errors, data corruption, dying hard drives, and RAID issues.

Installation Errors

Installing a drive and getting to the point where it can hold data requires four distinct steps: connectivity, CMOS, partitioning, and formatting. If you make a mistake at any point on any of these steps, the drive won't work. The beauty of this is that if you make an error, you can walk back through each step and check for problems. The "Trouble-shooting Hard Drive Installation" section in Chapter 11 covered physical connections and CMOS, so this section concentrates on the latter two issues.

Partitioning Partitioning errors generally fall into two groups: failing to partition at all and making the wrong size or type of partition. You'll recognize the former type of error the first time you open My Computer/Computer after installing a drive. If you forgot to partition it, the drive won't even show up in My Computer/Computer, only in Disk Management. If you made the partition too small, that'll become painfully obvious when you start filling it up with files.

The fix for partitioning errors is simply to open Disk Management and do the partitioning correctly. If you've added files to the wrongly sized drive, don't forget to back them up before you repartition in Windows XP. Just right-click and select Extend Volume in Windows Vista/7 to correct the mistake.

Formatting Failing to format a drive makes the drive unable to hold data. Accessing the drive in Windows results in a drive "is not accessible" error, and from a C:\ prompt, you'll get the famous "Invalid media" type error. Format the drive unless you're certain that the drive has a format already. Corrupted files can create the invalid media error. Check the upcoming "Data Corruption" section for the fix.

Most of the time, formatting is a slow, boring process. But sometimes the drive makes "bad sounds" and you start seeing errors like the one shown in Figure 12-62 at the top of the screen.

```
A:\>format C:/s

WARNING:  ALL DATA ON NON-REMOVABLE DISK
DRIVE C:  WILL BE LOST!
Proceed with Format  (Y/N)?y

Formatting  30709.65M

Trying to recover lost allocation unit 37,925
```

Figure 12-62 The "Trying to recover lost allocation unit" error

An *allocation unit* is another term for a cluster. The drive has run across a bad cluster and is trying to fix it. For years, I've told techs that seeing this error a few (610) times doesn't mean anything; every drive comes with a few bad spots. This is no longer true. Modern drives actually hide a significant number of extra sectors that they use to replace bad sectors automatically. If a new drive gets a lot of "Trying to recover lost allocation unit" errors, you can bet that the drive is dying and needs to be replaced. Get the hard drive maker's diagnostic tool to be sure. Bad clusters are reported by S.M.A.R.T.

Mental Reinstallation Focus on the fact that all of these errors share a common thread—you just installed a drive! Installation errors don't show up on a system that has been running correctly for three weeks; they show up the moment you try to do something with the drive you just installed. If a newly installed drive fails to work, do a "mental reinstallation." Does the drive show up in the CMOS? No? Then recheck the cables, master/slave settings on old PATA drives, and power. If it does show up, did you remember to partition and format the drive? Did it need to be set to active? These are commonsense questions that come to mind as you march through your mental reinstallation. Even if you've installed thousands of drives over the years, you'll be amazed at how often you do things such as forget to plug in power to a drive. Do the mental reinstallation—it really works!

Data Corruption

All hard drives occasionally get corrupted data in individual sectors. Power surges, accidental shutdowns, corrupted installation media, and viruses, along with hundreds of other problems, can cause this corruption. In most cases, this type of error shows up while Windows is running. Figure 12-63 shows a classic example.

Figure 12-63 A corrupted data error

You may also see Windows error messages saying one of the following:

- "The following file is missing or corrupt"
- "The download location information is damaged"
- "Unable to load file"
- "… is not a valid Win32 application"

If core boot files become corrupted, you may see text errors at boot, such as the following:

- "Cannot find COMMAND.COM"
- "Error loading operating system"
- "Invalid BOOT.INI"
- "NTLDR is missing or corrupt"
- "An error occurred while attempting to read the boot configuration data"

On older programs, you may see a command prompt open with errors such as this one:

```
Sector not found reading drive C: Abort, Retry, Fail?
```

The first fix for any of these problems is to run the Error-checking utility. Error-checking will go through and mark bad clusters and, hopefully, move your data to a good cluster.

If the same errors continue to appear after you run the Error-checking utility, there's a chance that the drive has bad sectors.

Almost all drives today take advantage of built-in *error correction code (ECC)* that constantly checks the drive for bad sectors. If the ECC detects a bad sector, it marks the sector as bad in the drive's internal error map. Don't confuse this error map with a FAT. The partitioning program creates the FAT. The drive's internal error map was created at the factory on reserved drive heads and is invisible to the system. If the ECC finds a bad sector, you will get a corrupted data error as the computer attempts to read the bad sector. Disk-checking utilities fix this problem most of the time.

Many times, the ECC thinks a bad sector is good, however, and fails to update the internal error map. In this case, you need a program that goes back into the drive and marks the sectors as bad. That's where the powerful SpinRite utility from Gibson Research comes into play. SpinRite marks sectors as bad or good more accurately than ECC and does not disturb the data, enabling you to run SpinRite without fear of losing anything. And if it finds a bad sector with data in it, SpinRite has powerful algorithms that usually recover the data on all but the most badly damaged sectors (see Figure 12-64).

Without SpinRite, you must use a low-level format program supplied by the hard drive maker, assuming you can get one (not all are willing to distribute these). These programs work like SpinRite in that they aggressively check the hard drive's sectors and update the internal error map. Unfortunately, all of them wipe out all data on the drive.

Dying Hard Drive

Physical problems are rare but devastating when they happen. If a hard drive is truly damaged physically, there is nothing that you or any service technician can do to fix it. Fortunately, hard drives are designed to take a phenomenal amount of punishment

without failing. Physical problems manifest themselves in several ways: you start getting read/write failures, the drive works properly but makes a lot of noise, or the drive seems to disappear.

Figure 12-64 SpinRite at work

Windows will give you error messages with read/write failures. Good hard drives don't fail to read or write. Only dying ones have these problems.

All hard drives make noise—the hum as the platters spin and the occasional slight scratching noise as the read/write heads access sectors are normal. However, if your drive begins to make any of the following sounds, it is about to die:

- Continuous high-pitched squeal
- Series of loud clicks, a short pause, and then another series of clicks
- Continuous grinding or rumbling

Back up your critical data and replace the drive. Windows comes with great tools for backing up data.

NOTE Most hard drives have three-year warranties. Before you throw away a dead drive, check the hard drive maker's Web site or call them to see if the drive is still under warranty. Ask for a return material authorization (RMA). You'll be amazed how many times you get a newer, usually larger, hard drive for free. It never hurts to check!

You'll know when a drive simply dies. If it's the drive that contains your operating system, the system will lock up. When you try to restart the computer, you'll see this error message or something similar to it:

```
No Boot Device Present
```

If it's a second drive, it will simply stop showing up in My Computer/Computer. The first thing to do in this case is to fire up the System Setup program and see if autodetect sees the drive. If it does, you do not have a physical problem with the drive. If autodetect fails, shut off the system and remove the data cable, but leave the power cable attached. Restart the system and listen to the drive. If the drive spins up, you know it is getting good power. This is usually a clue that the drive is probably good. In that case, you need to look for more mundane problems such as an unplugged data cord or jumpers incorrectly set. If the drive doesn't spin up, try another power connector. If it still doesn't spin up and you've triple-checked the jumpers (PATA only) and data cable, you have a problem with the onboard electronics, and the drive is dead.

> **NOTE** If you ever lose a hard drive that contains absolutely critical information, you can turn to a company that specializes in hard drive data recovery. The job will be expensive—prices usually start around $1000 (U.S.)—but when you have to have the data, such companies are your only hope. Do a Web search for "data recovery" or check the Yellow Pages for companies in this line of business.

Troubleshooting RAID

For the most part, drive problems in a RAID array are identical to those seen on individual drives. There are a couple of errors unique to RAID, however, that need their own separate discussion.

Drives Not Recognized If you're using hardware RAID and the configuration firmware doesn't recognize one of the drives, first check to make sure the drives are powered and that they are connected to the proper connections. This is especially true of motherboards with onboard RAID that require you to use only certain special RAID connectors.

RAID Stops Working When one of the drives in a RAID array fails, several things can happen depending on the type of array and the RAID controller. With RAID 0, the effect is dramatic. Many enthusiasts use RAID 0 for their OS drive to make it snappier. If you're running such a rig that then loses a drive, you'll most likely get a critical stop error, a Blue Screen of Death (BSoD). On reboot, the computer will fail to boot or you'll get a message that the OS can't be found. You lose all your data because there's no redundancy on a stripe set.

All the other levels of RAID tend to do nothing extraordinary when one drive in the array fails. When you reboot the system, that's when the RAID controller—if

hardware—or Windows—if you've used the built-in tools—will squeal and tell you that a drive has failed.

Often, the failure of a drive will cause access to the contents of the drive to slow to a crawl, and that *slow performance* is your clue to check Device Manager or the RAID controller firmware. Some drive failures will cause the computer to crash. Others will show no effects until you get the error messages at reboot.

Regardless of the reason a RAID stops working or the effects, the fix is simple. Replace the failed drive and let the RAID rebuild itself. Life is good.

RAID Not Found The CompTIA A+ 220-802 exam objectives use the term "RAID not found," which doesn't really exist as an error but instead implies a series of errors where an existing RAID array suddenly fails to appear. The problem with these errors is that they vary greatly depending on the make and model of hardware RAID or (heaven forbid) if you used software RAID.

A properly functioning hardware RAID array will always show up in the configuration utility. If an existing array stops working and you enter the configuration utility only to find the array is gone, you have big trouble. This points to either dead drives or faulty controllers. In either case they must be replaced.

If the array is gone but you can still see the drives, then the controller may have broken the array on its own. This is a rare action that some controllers do to try to save data. You should at least try to rebuild the array using whatever tools the controllers provide.

Beyond A+

Modern hard drives have many other features that are worth knowing about but that rarely impact beginning techs. A couple of the more interesting ones are spindle speed and third-party hard drive tools. If you have a burning desire to dive into hard drives in all their glory, you need not go any farther than the StorageReview.com, an excellent site dedicated solely to hard drives.

Third-Party Partition Tools

Disk Management is a good tool and has been greatly enhanced with Windows 7, but it's still limited for some situations. Some really great third-party tools on the market can give you incredible flexibility and power to structure and restructure your hard drive storage to meet your changing needs. They each have interesting unique features, but in general they enable you to create, change, and delete partitions on a hard drive *without* destroying any of the programs or data stored there. Slick! These programs aren't covered on the CompTIA A+ exams, but all PC techs use at least one of them, so let's explore three of the most well-known examples: Symantec's Norton Partition-Magic, Avanquest Partition Commander Professional, and the open source Linux tool, GParted.

Probably the most well-known third-party partition tool is PartitionMagic, although it's quite dated at this point. It supports older versions of Windows but has problems with Windows Vista/7. With it, you can create, resize, split, merge, delete, undelete, and convert partitions without destroying your data. Among the additional features it advertises are the capability to browse, copy, or move files and folders between supported partitions; to expand an NTFS partition—even if it's a system partition—without rebooting; to change NTFS cluster sizes; and to add new partitions for multiple OSs by using a simple wizard.

Avanquest offers a variety of related products, one of which is the very useful Partition Commander. It supports all versions of Windows (unlike PartitionMagic) and enables you to play with your partitions without destroying your data. Among its niftier features are the capability to convert a dynamic disk to a basic disk nondestructively (which you can't do with the Microsoft-supplied Windows tools); to defrag the master file table on an NTFS partition; and to move unused space from one partition to another on the same physical drive, automatically resizing the partitions based on the amount of space you tell it to move. Figure 12-65 shows the Partition Commander dialog box for moving unused space between partitions.

Figure 12-65
Partition
Commander

The only problem with PartitionMagic and Partition Commander is that they cost money. There's nothing wrong with spending money on a good product, but if you can find something that does the job for free, why not try it? If you think like I do, check out the GNOME Partition Editor, better known as GParted. You can find it here at: http://sourceforge.net

GParted is an incredibly powerful partition editor and does almost everything the for-pay partition editors do, but it's free. In fact, you might already have a copy lying around in the form of an Ubuntu desktop live CD. If you look closely at Figure 12-66, you'll notice that it uses strange names for the partitions, such as HDA1 or SDA2. These are Linux conventions and are well documented in GParted's Help screens. Take a little time and you'll love GParted too.

Figure 12-66 GParted in action

The one downside to GParted is that it is a Linux program—because no Windows version exists, you need Linux to run it. So how do you run Linux on a Windows system without actually installing Linux on your hard drive? The answer is easy—the folks at GParted will give you the tools to burn a live CD that boots Linux so you can run GParted!

A *live CD* is a complete OS on a CD. Understand this is not an installation CD like your Windows installation disc. The OS is already installed on the CD. You boot from the live CD and the OS loads into RAM, just like the OS on your hard drive loads into RAM at boot. As the live CD boots, it recognizes your hardware and loads the proper drivers into RAM so everything works. You get everything you'd expect from an OS with one big exception: a live CD does not touch your hard drive. Of course, you may run programs (such as GParted) that work on your hard drive, which makes live CDs popular with PC techs, because you can toss them into a cranky system and run utilities.

The truly intrepid might want to consider using The Ultimate Boot CD (UBCD), basically a huge pile of useful freeware utilities compiled by frustrated technician Ben Burrows, who couldn't find a boot disk when he needed one. His Web site is www.ultimatebootcd.com. The UBCD has more than 100 different tools, all placed on a single live CD. It has all of the low-level diagnostic tools for all of the hard drive makers, four or five different partitioning tools, S.M.A.R.T. viewers, hard drive wiping utilities, and hard drive cloning tools (nice for when you want to replace a hard drive with a larger one). Little documentation is provided, however, and many of the tools require experience way beyond the scope of the CompTIA A+ exams. I will tell you that I have a copy and I use it.

Chapter Review

Questions

1. Which is the most complete list of file systems Windows can use?

 A. FAT16, FAT32, NTFS

 B. FAT16, FAT32, FAT64, NTFS

 C. FAT16, FAT32

 D. FAT16, NTFS

2. Which of the following correctly identifies the four possible entries in a file allocation table?

 A. Filename, date, time, size

 B. Number of the starting cluster, number of the ending cluster, number of used clusters, number of available clusters

 C. An end-of-file marker, a bad-sector marker, code indicating the cluster is available, the number of the cluster where the next part of the file is stored

 D. Filename, folder location, starting cluster number, ending cluster number

3. What program does Microsoft include with Windows to partition and format a drive?

 A. Format

 B. Disk Management console

 C. Disk Administrator console

 D. System Commander

4. What does NTFS use to provide security for individual files and folders?

 A. Dynamic disks

 B. ECC

 C. Access Control List

 D. MFT

5. Adam wants to create a new simple volume in some unallocated space on his hard drive in his Windows XP machine, but when he right-clicks the space in Disk Management he sees only an option to create a new partition. What is the problem?

 A. The drive has developed bad sectors.

 B. The drive is a basic disk and not a dynamic disk.

 C. The drive has less than 32 GB of unallocated space.

 D. The drive is jumpered as a slave.

6. Jaime wishes to check her hard drive for errors. What tool should she use?

 A. FDISK

 B. Format

 C. Disk Management

 D. Error-checking

7. To make your files unreadable by others, what should you use?

 A. Clustering

 B. Compression

 C. Disk quotas

 D. Encryption

8. How can you effectively expand the capacity of an NTFS drive?

 A. Create an extended partition to extend the capacity.

 B. Install a second drive and mount it to a folder on the original smaller NTFS drive.

 C. Convert the drive to a dynamic disk and create a mirrored set.

 D. Format the drive with the Quick Format option.

9. Which configuration requires three same-sized volumes?

 A. RAID 5

 B. Mirrored set

 C. Spanned volume

 D. Striped volume

10. Which of the following partitioning schemes enables the creation of more than four partitions or volumes on a single hard drive? (Select two.)

 A. MBR

 B. GPT

 C. Dynamic disk

 D. MFT

Answers

1. **B.** Modern versions of Windows can use FAT (FAT16), FAT32, and NTFS for hard drives, and FAT64 for thumb drives.

2. **C.** The four possible entries in a file allocation table are an end-of-file marker, a bad-sector marker, code indicating the cluster is available, and the number of the cluster where the next part of the file is stored.

3. **B.** Windows uses the Disk Management console to partition and format a drive.

4. **C.** Because NTFS views individual files and folders as objects, it can provide security for those objects through an Access Control List.

5. **B.** The drive is a basic disk and not a dynamic disk. Partitions are created on basic disks, while volumes are created on dynamic disks.

6. **D.** Error-checking is used to check a drive for errors.

7. **D.** To make your files unreadable by others, use encryption.

8. **B.** You can effectively expand the capacity of an NTFS drive by installing a second drive and mounting it to a folder on the original smaller NTFS drive.

9. **A.** RAID 5 requires three same-sized volumes.

10. **B, C.** Both GPT and dynamic disk partitioning schemes enable the creation of more than four partitions or volumes on a single hard drive.

NOTE The term "floppy" comes from the fact that early floppy disks were actually floppy. You could easily bend one. Newer floppy disks came in much more robust, rigid plastic casings, but the term has stuck—we still call them floppies.

801

Installing Floppy Drives

All Windows systems reserve the drive letters A: and B: for floppy drives. You cannot name them anything other than A: or B:, but you can configure a floppy to get either drive letter. However, convention dictates that if you have only one floppy drive, you should call it A:. The second floppy drive is then called B:.

Floppy drives connect to the computer via a *34-pin ribbon cable*. If the cable supports two floppy drives, it has a seven-wire twist in the middle to differentiate electronically between the A: and B: drives. Given that the majority of users do not want two floppy drives (or one, for that matter), many system makers have dropped the twist and saved a couple of pennies on a simpler cable (see Figure 13-3).

Figure 13-3
Floppy cable for
only one drive

By default, almost all PCs that still support floppy drives first try to boot to a floppy before any other boot device, looking for an operating system. This process enables technicians to insert a floppy disk into a sick computer to run programs when the hard drives fail. It also means hackers can insert bootable floppy disks into servers and do bad things. You do have a choice, however, because most systems have special CMOS settings with which you can change this default boot order to something other than the default drive A: and then C:; I'll show you how in a minute.

Inserting Ribbon Cables

Look at the floppy cable in Figure 13-3. Notice the connector on the left side. This connector, identical to the other connector on the same cable, plugs into the floppy controller on the motherboard, as shown in Figure 13-4. Notice how clearly the motherboard has *pin 1* marked in Figure 13-4. Not all motherboards are so clear. Make sure to orient the cable so that the colored stripe on the side of the cable is aligned with pin 1.

Figure 13-4

Plugging a floppy
cable into a
controller, pin 1
labeled at left

Here are a few tips on cable orientation. (By the way, these rules work for all ribbon cables, not just floppy cables.) Ribbon cable connectors usually have a distinct orientation notch in the middle. If your cable connector has an orientation notch and the controller socket has a slot in which the orientation notch fits, your job is easy (see Figure 13-5).

Figure 13-5

Floppy controller
with notch

Unfortunately, not all connectors use the orientation notch. Try looking in the motherboard book. All motherboard books provide a graphic of the motherboard showing the proper orientation position. Look at other ribbon cables on the motherboard. In almost all motherboards, all plugs orient the same way. Last of all, just guess! You will not destroy anything by inserting the cable backward. When you boot up, the floppy drive will not work. This is not a big deal; turn off the system and try again.

After you insert the floppy ribbon cable into the floppy controller, you need to insert the ribbon cable into the floppy drive. Watch out here! You still need to orient the cable by pin 1—all the rules of ribbon cable insertion apply here, too. Before you plug in the floppy ribbon cable to the floppy drive, you need to know which connector on the cable to use; it makes a big difference. The specific connector that you insert into the floppy drive determines its drive letter.

If the floppy drive is installed on the end connector, it becomes the A: drive; if the drive is installed on the middle connector, it is the B: drive (see Figure 13-6). If you're installing only one floppy, make sure you install it in the A: drive position.

Drive A Drive B To Controller

Figure 13-6 Cable placement determines the drive letter.

NOTE In the past, the CompTIA A+ certification exams have been very focused on the pins on cables! Know the number (34) and orientation (pin 1 to pin 1) for the pins on the floppy drive ribbon cable.

Power

Floppy drives need electricity to work, just like every other device in the PC. Modern 3½-inch floppy drives use the small *mini power connector*. Be careful! Inserting a mini connector incorrectly is easy, and if you install it incorrectly, you'll destroy the floppy drive and make what we call "The Nasty Smell." Look at Figure 13-7, a bottom view of a properly installed mini power connector—note the chamfers (beveled edges) that show correct orientation. The problem lies in the plastic used to make the connector. The plastic connector bends easily, so even the least brawny techs can put the plug in a mini backward or hit only three of the four pins.

Figure 13-7
Properly installed
mini power
connector

Great! You have installed a floppy drive! Once you have physically installed the floppy drive, it's time to go into CMOS.

 CAUTION Installing any power connector incorrectly will destroy whatever device is unfortunate enough to be so abused. However, with the exception of minis, most power connectors are constructed so that it's almost impossible to do so unintentionally.

CMOS

After the floppy drive is installed, you need to configure the CMOS settings, which must correspond to the capacities of the drives. Look in your CMOS for a menu called "Standard CMOS Features" (or something similar to that) to see your floppy settings. Most CMOS setups configure the A: drive by default as a 3½-inch, 1.44-MB drive, so in most cases the floppy is already configured. Simply double-check the setting in CMOS; if it's okay, exit without changing anything. Figure 13-8 shows a typical CMOS setting for a single floppy drive. On the rare occasion that you require a setting other than the typical 3½-inch, 1.44-MB A: drive, simply select the drive (A: or B:) and enter the correct capacity.

```
              Phoenix - Award BIOS CMOS Setup Utility
                       Standard CMOS Features

    Date (mm:dd:yy)          Wed, Jun 7 2006      ▲        Item Help
    Time (hh:mm:ss)          13 : 19 : 35
                                                       Menu Level  ▶
  ▶ IDE Channel 1 Master    WDC WD1200JB-75CRA0
  ▶ IDE Channel 1 Slave      None                     Change the day, month,
  ▶ IDE Channel 2 Master    SONY    CD-CW  CRX17      year and century
  ▶ IDE Channel 2 Slave     TOSHIBA CD/DVDW SDR5
  ▶ IDE Channel 3 Master     None
  ▶ IDE Channel 4 Master     None
  ▶ IDE Channel 5 Master    WDC WD2000JS-00MHB0
  ▶ IDE Channel 6 Master     None

    Drive A                  1.44, 3.5 in.
    Drive B                  None
    Floppy 3 Mode Support    Disabled
    Halt On                  All , But Keyboard

    Base Memory                    640K
    Extended Memory            1047552K            ▼

▲▼▶◀:Move   Enter:Select   +/-/PU/PD:Value  F10:Save   ESC:Exit  F1:General He
      F5:Previous Values       F6:Fail-Safe Defaults    F7:Optimized Defaults
```

Figure 13-8 CMOS setting for one standard floppy drive

Disabling the Boot Up Floppy Seek option tells the PC not to check the floppy disk during the POST, which isn't very handy except for slightly speeding up the boot process (see Figure 13-9).

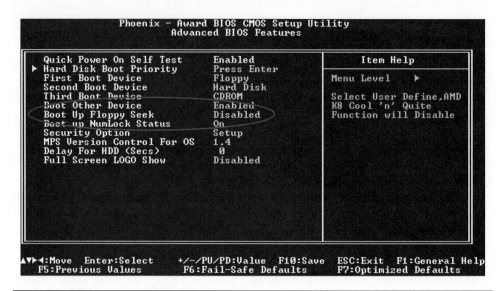

Figure 13-9 CMOS Boot Up Floppy Seek option

Many CMOS setup utilities have an option called Floppy 3 Mode Support. Refer to Figure 13-8 to see an example of a CMOS with this option. A Mode 3 floppy is a special 1.2-MB format used outside the United States, primarily in Japan. Unless you live in Japan and use Mode 3 floppy disks, ignore this option.

Flash Memory

Flash memory, the same flash memory that replaced CMOS technology for your system BIOS, found another home in PCs in the form of removable mass storage devices. Flash memory comes in two families: USB thumb drives and memory cards. USB thumb drives are flash devices that contain a standard USB connection. "Memory card" is a generic term for a number of tiny cards that are used in cameras, smartphones, and other devices. Both of these families can manifest themselves as drives in Windows, but they usually perform different jobs. USB thumb drives have replaced virtually all other rewritable removable media as the way people transfer files or keep copies of important programs. My thumb drives (yes, I have two on me at all times) keep backups of my current work, important photos, and a stack of utilities I need to fix computers. Memory cards are very small and make a great way to store data on small devices and then transfer that data to your PC.

USB Thumb Drives

Moving data between computers is always a pain, but USB flash memory drives, also known as *USB thumb drives*, jump drives, and flash drives, are an incredibly popular

solution (see Figure 13-10). For a low price, you can get a 32-GB thumb drive that holds as much data as 22,000 standard 3½-inch floppy disks.

Figure 13-10
USB thumb drives

The smallest thumb drives are slightly larger than an adult thumbnail; others are larger and more rounded. The drives are hot-swappable in all modern editions of Windows. You simply plug one into any USB port and it appears as a removable storage device in My Computer or Computer. After you plug the drive into a USB port, you can copy or move data to or from your hard disk and then unplug the unit and take it with you. You can read, write, and delete files directly from the drive. Because these are USB devices, they don't need an external power source. The nonvolatile flash memory is solid-state, so it's shock resistant and is supposed to retain data safely for a decade.

The latest systems enable you to boot to a thumb drive. With a bootable thumb drive, you can replace bootable floppies, CDs, and DVDs with fast flash drives. Making a thumb drive bootable is a bit of a challenge, so most of the classic bootable-utility CD makers have created USB versions that seek out your thumb drive and add an operating system with the utilities you wish to use. Most of these are simply versions of Linux-based live CDs. If you want to try it, check out GParted Live at http://gparted.source-forge.net and click on the Live CD/USB link.

NOTE Remember to change the boot order in CMOS when you want to boot from a USB flash drive. If you use the wrong boot order, your BIOS will skip straight to your hard drive and load your OS.

Flash Cards

Flash cards are the way people store data on small appliances. Digital cameras, smartphones, and MP3 players often come with slots for some type of memory card. Memory cards come in a number of incompatible formats, so let's start by making sure you know the more common ones.

CompactFlash

CompactFlash (CF) is the oldest, most complex, and physically largest of all removable flash media cards (see Figure 13-11). Roughly one inch wide, CF cards use a simplified PCMCIA bus (see Chapter 26 for details) for interconnection. CF cards come in two sizes: CF I (3.3 mm thick) and CF II (5 mm thick). CF II cards are too thick to fit into CF I slots.

Figure 13-11
CF card

Clever manufacturers have repurposed the CF form factor to create the microdrive (see Figure 13-12). *Microdrives* are true hard drives, using platters and read/write heads that fit into the tiny CF form factor. Microdrives are slower and use more power than flash drives and, when they were first introduced, cost much less than an equivalent CF flash card. From the user's standpoint, CF flash cards and microdrives look and act exactly the same way, although the greater power consumption of microdrives makes them incompatible with some devices. These days, microdrives have been surpassed in size, speed, and cost by their flash cousins and have become more difficult to find.

Figure 13-12
Microdrive

SmartMedia

SmartMedia came out as a competitor to CF cards and for a few years was quite popular in digital cameras (see Figure 13-13). The introduction of SD media reduced SmartMedia's popularity, and no new devices use this media.

Figure 13-13
SmartMedia

Secure Digital

Secure Digital (SD) cards are arguably the most common flash media format today. About the size of a small postage stamp, you'll see SD cards in just about any type of device that uses flash media.

SD cards come in two smaller forms called *Mini Secure Digital* (*MiniSD*) cards and *Micro Secure Digital* (*MicroSD*) cards. They're extremely popular in cellular phones that use flash memory, but they see little use in other devices. Figure 13-14 shows the three forms of SD cards.

Figure 13-14
SD, MiniSD, and
MicroSD cards

SD cards come in three storage capacities. *Standard SD* cards store from 4 MB to 4 GB, *Secure Digital High Capacity* (*SDHC*) cards store 4 GB to 32 GB, and *Secure Digital Extended*

Capacity (*SDXC*) cards have a storage capacity of 32 GB to 2 TB. Early SD card readers and devices cannot read the SDHC or SDXC cards, though the latter standards provide backward compatibility.

 NOTE SD cards developed out of an older, slower flash memory technology called *MultiMediaCard (MMC)*. If you happen to have an MMC card lying around, you can use it in almost any SD card slot. SD cards are a little thicker than MMC cards, though, so the reverse is not true.

Memory Stick

Sony always likes to use proprietary formats, and their *Memory Stick* flash memory is no exception. If you own something from Sony and it uses flash memory, you'll need a Memory Stick, though not all Memory Sticks are manufactured by Sony (see Figure 13-15). There are several Memory Stick formats, including Standard, Pro, Duo, Pro Duo, and Micro.

Figure 13-15
Memory Stick

xD Picture Card

The proprietary *Extreme Digital (xD) Picture Cards* (see Figure 13-16) are about half the size of an SD card. They're almost exclusively used in Olympus and Fujifilm digital cameras, although Olympus (the developer of the xD technology) produces a USB housing so you can use an xD Picture Card like any other USB flash memory drive. The xD Picture Cards come in three flavors: original, Standard (Type M), and Hi-Speed (Type H). The Standard cards are slower than the original cards but offer greater storage capacity. The Hi-Speed cards are two to three times faster than the others and enable you to capture full-motion video—assuming the camera has that capability, naturally!

Figure 13-16
xD card

Card Readers

Whichever type of flash memory you use, your PC must have a *card reader* to access the data on the card directly. A number of inexpensive USB card readers are available today (see Figure 13-17), and some PCs come with built-in readers—handy to have when someone pulls out an SD card and says "Let's look at the pictures I just took!" Of course, if the person just happened to bring her camera and USB cable along, you could connect the camera to the PC and pull pictures in that way. Just make sure you have spare batteries, too! Wouldn't a card reader be a more elegant solution?

Figure 13-17
USB card reader

Whichever type of flash memory you have, understand that it acts exactly like a hard drive. If you wish, you can format a memory card and copy, paste, and rename files.

Optical Drives

CD, DVD, and Blu-ray Disc drives and discs come in a variety of flavors and formats, enabling you to back up data, record music, master home videos, and much, much more. *Optical disc* is the generic term for all those different types of shiny, 12-centimeter-wide discs that, if you're a slob like me, collect around your computer like pizza boxes.

The drives that support them are called *optical drives*. This section examines optical discs, finishing with the details about installing optical drives.

CD stands for *compact disc*, a medium that was originally designed more than 25 years ago as a replacement for vinyl records. The *digital versatile disc (DVD)* first eliminated VHS cassette tapes from the commercial home movie market, and has also grown into a contender for backups and high-capacity storage. *Blu-ray Disc (BD)* eliminated the High-Definition DVD (HD DVD) format to become the only high-definition and high-capacity optical format.

Going beyond those big three household names, the term "optical disc" refers to technologies such as CD-ROM, CD-R, CD-RW, DVD, DVD+RW, HD DVD, BD-R, BD-RE, and so on. Each of these technologies will be discussed in detail in this chapter—for now, understand that although "optical disc" describes a variety of exciting formats, they all basically boil down to the same physical object: that little shiny disc.

CD-Media

The best way to understand the world of optical discs is to sort out the many types of technologies available, starting with the first: the compact disc. All you're about to read is relevant and fair game for the CompTIA A+ certification exams. Let's begin by looking at how CDs work.

How CDs Work

CDs—the discs that you buy in music stores or may find in software boxes—store data via microscopic pits. CD producers use a power laser to burn these pits into a glass master CD. Once the CD producer creates a master, expensive machines create plastic copies, using a very high-tolerance injection molding process. The copies are coated with a reflective metallic covering and then finished with lacquer for protection. CDs store data on only one side of the disc—we don't flip a CD as we used to flip vinyl records. Did I just sound really old? The data on a CD is near the top of the CD, where the label is located (see Figure 13-18).

Many people believe that scratching a CD on the bottom makes it unreadable. This is untrue. If you scratch a CD on the bottom (the shiny side), just polish out the scratches—assuming that they aren't too deep—and reread the CD. A number of companies sell inexpensive CD-polishing kits. It's the scratches on the *top* of the disc that wreak havoc on CDs. Avoid writing on the top with anything other than a soft-tipped pen, and certainly don't scratch the top!

CD readers (such as the one in your car or the one in your PC) use a laser and mirrors to read the data from the CD. The metallic covering of the CD makes a highly reflective surface; the pits create interruptions in that surface, while the non-pitted spots, called *lands*, leave it intact. The laser picks up on the reflected pattern that the pits and lands create, and the CD drive converts this pattern into binary ones and zeros. Because the pits are so densely packed on the CD, a vast amount of data can be stored: a standard CD holds up to 5.2 billion bits, or 650 million bytes, of data.

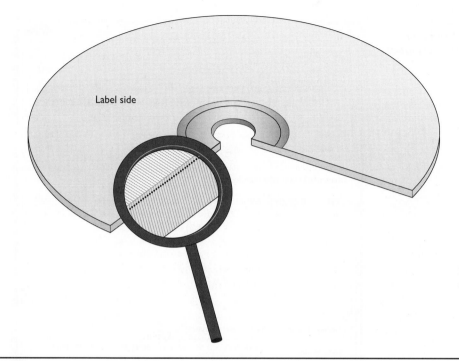

Figure 13-18 Location of the data

CD Formats

The first CDs were designed for playing music and organized the music in a special format called *CD-Digital Audio (CDDA)*, which we usually just call CD-audio. CD-audio divides the CD's data into variable-length tracks; on music CDs, each song gets one track. CD-audio is an excellent way to store music, but it lacks any error checking, file support, or directory structure, making it a terrible way to store data. For this reason, The Powers That Be created a special method for storing data on a CD, called—are you ready—*CD-ROM*. The CD-ROM format divides the CD into fixed sectors, each holding 2353 bytes.

Most CD-ROM drives also support a number of older, less well-known formats. You may never come across these formats—CD Text, CD+G, and so forth—although you may see them listed among compatible formats on the packaging for a new drive or with a program like Nero InfoTool (see Figure 13-19). Don't let these oddball formats throw you—with few exceptions, they've pretty much fallen by the wayside. All CD-ROM drives read all of these formats, assuming that the system is loaded with the proper software.

Figure 13-19

Crazy CD formats

Nero InfoTool

Save Print Refresh Exit

[1:0] D:\HL-DT-ST BDDVDRW GBC-H20L ▼

Current Drive

| Drivers | Hardware | System | HD Readiness |
| Drive | Disc | Configuration | Software |

General

Type:	Blu-ray COMBO DL	Firmware version:	1.B0
Read speed:	n/a	Buffer size:	2 MB
Write speed:	n/a	Date:	?
		Serial number:	K248AE84217

Supported read/write features

CD	R	W	DVD	R	W	HD DVD	R	W	BD	R	W
-R	✓	✓	-R	✓	✓	-R	✗	✗	-R	✓	✗
-RW	✓	✓	-RW	✓	✓	-RW	✗	✗	-RE	✓	✗
-Text	✓		+R	✓	✓	-ROM	✗	✗	-R DL	✓	✗
+G	✓		+RW	✓	✓	-RAM	✗	✗	-RE DL	✓	✗
C2Error	✓		-RAM	✓	✓	-R DL	✗	✗			
			-ROM	✓	✗	-RW DL	✗	✗			
			-R DL	✓	✓						
			+R DL	✓	✓						

General Features	Buffer underrun protection
Write Modes	Packet, TAO, DAO, SAO, RAW SAO, RAW DAO, RAW SAO 16, RAW SAO 96, RAW DAO 16, RAW DAO 96

DVD Features

Region control:	RPC II	Changes Left: User:	4	☑ CSS	☑ AACS	
Region code:	1	Vendor:	4	☑ CPRM	☐ VCPS	

The CD-ROM format is something like a partition in the hard drive world. CD-ROM may define the sectors (and some other information), but it doesn't enable a CD-ROM disc to act like a hard drive, with a file structure, directories, and such. To make a CD-ROM act like a hard drive, there's another layer of formatting that defines the file system used on the drive.

At first glance you might think "Why don't CD-ROMs just use a FAT or an NTFS format like hard drives?" Well, first of all, they could. There's no law of physics that prevented the CD-ROM world from adopting any file system. The problem is that the CD makers did not want CD-ROM to be tied to Microsoft's or Apple's or anyone else's file format. In addition, they wanted non-PC devices to read CDs, so they invented their own file system just for CD-ROMs called *ISO-9660*. This format is sometimes referred by the more generic term, *CD File System (CDFS)*. The vast majority of data CD-ROMs today use this format.

Over the years, extensions of the ISO-9660 have addressed certain limitations, such as the characters used in file and directory names, filename length, and directory depth.

CD-ROM Speeds

The first CD-ROM drives processed data at roughly 150,000 bytes per second (150 KBps), copying the speed from the original CD-audio format. Although this speed is excellent for listening to music, the CD-ROM industry quickly recognized that installing programs or transferring files from a CD-ROM at 150 KBps was the electronic equivalent of watching paint dry. Since the day the first CD-ROM drives for PCs hit the market, there has been a desire to speed them up to increase their data throughput. Each increase in speed is measured in multiples of the original 150-KBps drives and given an × to show speed relative to the first (1×) drives. Here's a list of the common CD-ROM speeds, including most of the early speeds that are no longer produced:

1× 150 KBps	10× 1500 KBps	40× 6000 KBps
2× 300 KBps	12× 1800 KBps	48× 7200 KBps
3× 450 KBps	16× 2400 KBps	52× 7800 KBps
4× 600 KBps	24× 3600 KBps	60× 9000 KBps
6× 900 KBps	32× 4800 KBps	72× 10800 KBps
8× 1200 KBps	36× 5400 KBps	

Keep in mind that these are maximum speeds that are rarely met in real-life operation. You can, however, count on a 32× drive to read data faster than an 8× drive. As multipliers continue to increase, so many other factors come into play that telling the difference between a 48× drive and a 52× drive, for example, becomes difficult. High-speed CD-ROM drives are so inexpensive, however, that most folks buy the fastest drive possible—at least installations go faster!

CD-R

Making CD-ROMs requires specialized, expensive equipment and substantial expertise, so a relatively small number of CD-ROM production companies do it. Yet, since the day the first CD-ROMs came to market, demand has been terrific for a way that ordinary PC users could make their own CDs. The CD industry made a number of attempts to create a technology that would let users record, or *burn*, their own CDs.

In the mid-1990s, the CD industry introduced the *CD-recordable (CD-R)* standard, which enables affordable CD-R drives, often referred to as *CD burners*, to add data to special CD-R discs. Any CD-ROM drive can then read the data stored on the CD-R, and all CD-R drives can read regular CD-ROMs. CD-R discs come in two varieties: a 74-minute disc that holds approximately 650 MB, and an 80-minute variety that holds approximately 700 MB (see Figure 13-20). A CD-R burner must be specifically designed to support the longer, 80-minute CD-R format, but most drives you'll encounter can do this.

Two developments, UDF and packet writing, enable you to treat a CD-RW just like a hard drive—with a few gotchas. The not-so-new kid in town with CD-media file formats is the *universal data format (UDF)*. UDF is a replacement for ISO-9660 and all of its various extensions, resulting in a single file format that any drive and operating system can read. UDF has taken over the DVD world (all movie DVDs use this format) and is poised to also become the CD-media file format in the near future. UDF handles very large files and is excellent for all rewritable CD-media. UDF has been available for quite a while, but until Windows Vista came out, no version of Windows could write to UDF-formatted discs. They could *read* the discs, but if you wanted to *write* to them in Windows you had to use one of a number of third-party UDF tools such as Roxio's DirectCD and Nero's InCD. UDF also supports a feature called Mount Rainier—better known as packet writing—that works with UDF so you can copy individual files back and forth like a hard drive. With UDF and packet writing, rewritable CD-media is as easy to use as a hard drive.

Windows and CD-Media

Virtually all optical drives are *ATAPI-compliant*, meaning they plug into the ATA controllers on the motherboard, just like a hard drive, so you don't need to install drivers. You just plug in the drive and, assuming you didn't make any physical installation mistakes, the drive appears in Windows (see Figure 13-22).

Figure 13-22
Optical drive in Windows

Windows displays an optical drive in My Computer or Computer with the typical optical drive icon and assigns it a drive letter. Every modern edition of Windows enables you to burn music or files to a CD using Windows Media Player or Windows Explorer, respectively. Almost every new CD-RW drive comes with some type of burner software, as well, and other third-party developers also create software that burns music and data to CD—you might have heard of Apple's iTunes software? Figure 13-23 shows the opening menu of one that I like, the popular Nero optical disc–burning program.

Figure 13-23
Nero optical disc–
burning program

NOTE I cover more on installation and ATAPI compliance later in this chapter.

When I buy a new program on CD, the first thing I do is make a backup copy; then I stash the original under lock and key. If I break, melt, or otherwise destroy the backup, I quickly create a new one from the original. I can easily copy the disc, because my system, like many, has both a regular CD-ROM and a CD-RW drive (even though CD-RW drives read CD-ROM discs). I can place a CD in the CD-ROM drive and a CD-R or CD-RW disc in the CD-RW drive. Then I use a disk-copy application to create an exact replica of the CD quickly. CD-RW drives work great for another, bigger type of backup: not the archival "put it on the disc and stash it in the closet" type of backup but rather the daily/weekly backups that most of us do (or should do!) on our systems. Using CD-R discs for these backups is wasteful; once a disc fills up, you throw it away at the next backup. But with CD-RW, you can use the same set of CD-RW discs time and again to perform backups.

Music CDs

Computers do not hold a monopoly on CD burning. Many companies offer consumer CD burners that work with your stereo system. These come in a wide variety of formats, but they're usually dual-deck player/recorder combinations. These recorders do not use regular CD-R or CD-RW discs. Instead, under U.S. law, these home recorders must use a slightly different disc called a *music CD-R*. Makers of music CDs pay a small royalty for each CD (and add it to your price). You can record *to* a music CD-R or CD-RW, but you cannot record *from* one—the idea being to restrict duplication. If you decide to buy one of these burners, make sure to buy the special music CD-Rs. Music CD-Rs are designed specifically for these types of devices and may not work well in a PC.

Burning Digital Music Files to a CD

Almost all computers and many portable CD players now can play recordable CDs loaded with MP3 files. This enables you to mix songs from your music collection and fit a lot of songs on a disc (MP3s are smaller than CD-audio files). That's a great feature—but where do digital audio files come from and how do you put them on a CD?

You can create MP3s from your favorite CDs by using a *ripper*. A ripper is a piece of software that takes standard CD-audio files and compresses them, using specialized algorithms, into much smaller files while maintaining most of the audio qualities of the original file. One legal note, however: you should only make MP3s from CDs that you have purchased. Borrowing a CD from a friend and ripping MP3s from it is illegal! Likewise, downloading MP3s from unauthorized sources on the Internet is also illegal. You don't want to go to jail because you just had to listen to the latest, greatest single from your favorite artist, right?

Now that I've taken care of the legal disclaimer, get ready to burn your MP3s. You need three things: a recordable/rewritable optical drive, some CD authoring software, and, of course, a blank disc. I recommend a CD-R. (Audio-only devices stand a much better chance of playing a CD-R successfully rather than a CD-RW.)

1. Confirm that you have a CD-R/RW drive installed in your computer. You don't have to have a drive like this to rip audio files *from* a CD, but you must have one to burn digital audio to a CD-R.

2. Launch your favorite CD authoring software. Popular titles in this category include Nero Burning ROM and Roxio Creator.

3. Most CD authoring programs use a simple drag-and-drop interface, similar to the Windows Explorer interface. Browse to the location of the audio files and select them. Then drag them into the appropriate area—this is often called the *queue*.

4. After you've selected all the files you want to have on your CD, it's time to burn. The procedure for initiating the CD-burning sequence is different for each program. You should always make sure to *close* the CD after you've burned it. Most standalone CD players (even ones that play MP3s) won't play CD-Rs that haven't been closed.

Once you've keyed in all of the configuration information, just sit back and watch the fireworks. Always be sure to use CD-media that is rated appropriately for your drive, for both speed and media type. In no time at all, you'll be listening to MP3s while jogging around the park.

DVD-Media

For years, the video industry tried to create an optical-media replacement for videotape. The 12-inch-diameter *laserdisc* format originally introduced by Philips gained some ground in the 1980s and 1990s. But the high cost of both the discs and the players, plus various marketing factors, meant there was never a very large laserdisc market. You may still find one of them sitting around, however, or you may know someone who invested in a small collection during the laserdisc's heyday.

The DVD was developed by a large consortium of electronics and entertainment firms during the early 1990s and released as digital *video* discs in 1995. The transformation of DVD to a data storage medium required a name change to digital *versatile* discs. You'll still hear both terms used. The industry also uses the term *DVD-video* to distinguish the movie format from the data formats.

With the exception of the DVD logo stamped on all commercial DVDs (see Figure 13-24), DVDs look exactly like CD-media discs; but that's pretty much where the similarities end. DVD has become the fastest growing media format in history and has completely overtaken VHS as the preferred media for video. Additionally, one variant of DVD called DVD-RAM has enjoyed some success as a mass storage medium.

Figure 13-24
Typical DVD-video

The single best word to describe DVD is *capacity*. All previous optical discs stored a maximum of 700 MB of data or 80 minutes of video. The lowest capacity DVD holds 4.37 GB of data, or two hours of standard-definition video. The highest capacity version DVDs store roughly 16 GB of data, or more than eight hours of video! DVD achieves these amazing capacities by using a number of technologies, but three are most important. First, DVD uses smaller pits than CD-media, and packs them much more densely. Second, DVD comes in both *single-sided* (SS) and *double-sided* (DS) formats. As the name implies, a DS disc holds twice the data of an SS disc, but it also requires you to flip the disc to read the other side. Third, DVDs come in *single-layer* (SL) and *dual-layer* (DL) formats. DL formats use two pitted layers on each side, each with a slightly different reflectivity index. Table 13-1 shows the common DVD capacities.

DVD Version	Capacity
DVD-5 (12 cm, SS/SL)	4.37 GB, more than two hours of video
DVD-9 (12 cm, SS/DL)	7.95 GB, about four hours of video
DVD-10 (12 cm, DS/SL)	8.74 GB, about four and a half hours of video
DVD-18 (12 cm, DS/DL)	15.90 GB, more than eight hours of video

Table 13-1 DVD Versions/Capacities

EXAM TIP The CompTIA A+ exams refer to dual-layer DVDs as *DL DVD*, while a rewritable DVD is called a *Dual Layer DVD-RW*.

DVD-Video

The most beautiful trait of DVD-video is its capability to store two hours of video on one side. You drop in a DVD-video and get to watch an entire movie without flipping it over. DVD-video supports TV-style 4:3 aspect-ratio screens as well as 16:9 theater screens, but it is up to the producer to decide which to use. Many DVD-video producers used to distribute DVD movies on DS media with a 4:3 ratio on one side and 16:9 ratio on the other, though that isn't as common anymore. DVD-video relies on the *MPEG-2* standard of video and audio compression to reach the magic of two hours of video per side. *Moving Picture Experts Group* (*MPEG*) is a group of compression standards for both audio and video. The MPEG-2 standard offers resolutions of up to 1280 × 720 at 60 frames per second (fps), with full CD-quality audio (standard DVDs only offer 480 vertical resolution, the same as regular television).

DVD-ROM

DVD-ROM is the DVD equivalent of the standard CD-ROM data format except that it's capable of storing up to almost 16 GB of data. Almost all DVD-ROM drives also fully support DVD-video, as well as most CD-ROM formats. Most DVD drives sold with PCs are DVD-ROM drives.

Recordable DVD

The IT industry has no fewer than *six* distinct standards of recordable DVD-media: DVD-ROM for general use, DVD-R for authoring, *DVD-RW*, DVD+R, *DVD+RW*, and DVD-RAM. Both DVD-R standard discs and DVD+R discs work like CD-Rs. You can write to them but not erase or alter what's written. DVD-RW, DVD+RW, and DVD-RAM discs can be written and rewritten, just like CD-RW discs. Most DVD drives can read all formats with the exception of DVD-RAM. DVD-RAM is the only DVD format that uses a cartridge, so it requires a special drive (see Figure 13-25). DVD-RAM is still around but fading away.

Figure 13-25
DVD-RAM disc

Although there is little if any difference in quality among the standards, the competition between corporations pushing their preferred standards has raged for years. Sony and Phillips, for example, pushed the + series, whereas other manufacturers pushed the − series. Worse, no recordable DVD drive manufactured before 2003 could write any format except its own. You could plop down US$250 on a brand-new DVD+RW drive and still find yourself unable to edit a disc from your friend who used the DVD-RW format! Half of the time, the drive couldn't even *read* the competing format disc.

The situation is much better today, as DVD±RW combo drives in PCs play just about anyone else's DVDs. The challenge is DVD players. If you want to make a DVD of your family picnic and then play it on the DVD player hooked to your television, take the time to read the documentation for your player to make sure it reads that particular DVD format—not all players read all formats.

MPEG Standards

Reproducing video and sound on the PC provides interesting challenges for developers. How do you take a motion picture from film, translate it into ones and zeros that the CPU understands, process those bits, and then send high-quality video and sound to the monitor and speakers for the pleasure of the computer user? How much data do you think is required to display even a two-minute clip of a car racing through a city street, in all the minute detail of the shops, people, screeching tires, road debris, and so on? For that matter, how do you *store* the obviously huge amount of data required to do this?

To handle these chores, the Moving Picture Experts Group (MPEG) has released coding standards such as MPEG-1, MPEG-2, and MPEG-4. Each standard provides a different *compression algorithm*, which makes the files manageable. The standards also implement various technologies to handle movement, called motion compensation. The details of the standards matter a lot to the folks producing the movies and other video and audio content, but here's the short answer that should suffice for the purposes of a PC tech.

MPEG-1 is the standard on which video and MP3, among other technologies, are based. The most common implementations of this standard provide a resolution of 352 × 240 at 30 fps. This video quality falls just below that of a conventional VHS video.

One very well-known subset of MPEG-1 is better known for audio than video. MPEG-1 Layer 3, better known as MP3 format, dominates the world of audio. MP3 takes an uncompressed audio file and compresses it dramatically, but the algorithm is so tight that the music that comes out of the speakers remains almost completely faithful to the original audio file. To paraphrase a catchphrase from the 1980s—I want my MP3s!

MPEG-2 provides resolutions of 720 × 480 and 1280 × 720 at 60 fps (as well as others), plus CD-quality audio, making it adequate for all major TV standards, even HDTV. MPEG-2 is the standard that covers DVD-ROM technology—it can compress two hours of video into a file no larger than a few gigabytes. Although encoding video into MPEG-2 format requires a computer with some serious firepower, even a modest PC can decompress and play such a video.

The *MPEG-4* standard is based on MPEG-1, MPEG-2, and Apple's QuickTime technology. MPEG-4 graphics and video files use what's known as *wavelet* compression to create files that are more compact than either JPEG or QuickTime files. This superior compression makes MPEG-4 popular for delivering video and images over the Web. MPEG-4 higher-efficiency standards such as advanced video coding are included with MPEG-4 and used for Blu-ray Discs. And notably, MPEG-4 provides Intellectual Property Management and Protection (IPMP), which supports digital rights management.

MPEG-7 is designed to complement the previous standards as a fast and efficient multimedia content searching tool.

MPEG-21 is concerned with and focuses on coding and digital rights. MPEG-21 uses a Rights Expression Language (REL) and a Rights Data Dictionary to protect digital material from illicit file sharing.

Blu-ray Disc-Media

Blu-ray Disc is considered the next generation in optical disc formatting and storage technology after CD and DVD. Because of its near-perfect audio and video quality; mass acceptance by industry-leading computer, electronics, game, music, retail, and motion picture companies; and huge storage capacities of up to 25 GB (single-layer disc) and 50 GB (dual-layer disc), Blu-ray Disc technology is expected to eventually make CD- and DVD-media and devices obsolete.

Blu-ray Discs come in two physical sizes, standard and mini. The standard size matches that of earlier optical discs, such as CD-R and DVD-RW, and is what you'll see used in computers and for movies (see Figure 13-26). The mini-size discs are a lot smaller and, naturally, offer less storage. You'll find mini Blu-ray Discs in very high-end camcorders. Table 13-2 shows the details of the two formats.

Type	Size	Capacity (single layer)	Capacity (dual layer)
Standard disc	12 cm	25 GB	50 GB
Mini disc	8 cm	7.8 GB	15.6 GB

Table 13-2 Standard and Mini Blu-ray Disc Comparison Chart

NOTE There was a brief battle for supremacy in the high-definition digital war between Blu-ray Disc and a competing high-definition optical disc standard called HD DVD. Major content manufacturers and developers leaned toward Blu-ray Disc, and in early 2008, Toshiba—the primary company behind HD DVD—threw in the towel. HD DVD is no longer being developed or supported.

Figure 13-26
Standard Blu-ray
Disc

NOTE If you own a PlayStation 3, you already have a Blu-ray Disc player. That's the optical format the game system uses.

Blu-ray Disc technology offers several advantages over DVD aside from raw capacity. First, Blu-ray Disc uses a blue-violet laser (hence the Blu in the name) with a wavelength of 405 nanometers (nm). (DVD uses a red-laser technology with a wavelength of 650 nm.) The 405-nm wavelength is smaller and much more precise, enabling better use of space during the creation process and ultimately resulting in a sharper image. Second, Blu-ray Disc can handle high-definition (HD) video in resolutions far higher than DVD. Finally, Blu-ray Disc supports many more video compression schemes, giving producers more options for putting content on discs.

BD-ROM

BD-ROM (read only) is the Blu-ray Disc equivalent of the standard DVD-ROM data format except, as noted earlier, it can store much more data and produces superior audio and video results. Almost all BD-ROM drives are fully backward compatible and support DVD-video as well as most CD-ROM formats. If you want to display the best possible movie picture quality on your HDTV, you should get a Blu-ray Disc player and use Blu-ray Discs in place of DVDs. Most new computer systems still don't come standard with Blu-ray Disc drives installed. You can often custom-order a system with a Blu-ray Disc drive or you can simply install one yourself. Figure 13-27 shows a Blu-ray Disc drive.

Figure 13-27

A combination CD/ DVD/Blu-ray Disc drive

BD-R and BD-RE

Blu-ray Discs come in two writable formats, BD-R (for recordable) and BD-RE (for rewritable). You can write to a *BD-R* disc one time. You can write to and erase a *BD-RE* disc several times. There are also BD-R and BD-RE versions of mini Blu-ray Discs.

Blu-ray Disc Burners

Blu-ray Disc burners cost more than a standard optical drive but will eventually be as common as the average CD-RW or DVD-RW. Blu-ray Disc burners and other Blu-ray Disc drives can be connected internally or externally to a system. It is common for them to be connected externally via USB (3.0 usually) or eSATA or internally through SATA. Operating systems such as Windows, XP, Windows Vista, and Windows 7 all support Blu-ray Disc burners and software. The software you use for burning is totally up to you; however, as always, you should follow the manufacturer's specifications for the best results. Most multidrive Blu-ray Disc burners offer the following support features.

- **Media support** BD-R, BD-RE, DVD-ROM, DVD-RAM, DVD-video, DVD+/-R DL, DVD+/-R, DVD+/-RW, CD-DA, CD-ROM, CD-R, and CD-RW

- **Write speed (max)** 2× BD-R, 4× DVD+/-R DL, 8× DVD+/-R(8×), and 24× CD-R

- **Rewrite speed (max)** 2× BD-RE, 8× DVD+RW, 6× DVD-RW, 5× DVD-RAM, and 16× CD-RW

- **Read speed (max)** 2× BD-ROM, 8× DVD-ROM, and 32× CD-ROM

- **Compatibility** Most Blu-ray Disc drives are backward compatible, meaning they can read and play CDs and DVDs. CD and DVD drives and players cannot read or play Blu-ray Discs.

Installing Optical Drives

From ten feet away, optical drives of all flavors look absolutely identical. Figure 13-28 shows a CD-RW drive, a DVD drive, and a BD-R drive. Can you tell them apart just by a glance? In case you were wondering, the CD-RW drive is on the bottom, the DVD drive is next, and finally the BD-R drive is on the top. If you look closely at an optical drive, you will normally see its function either stamped on the front of the case or printed on a label somewhere less obvious (see Figure 13-29).

Figure 13-28
CD-RW, DVD, and
BD-R drives

Figure 13-29
Label on optical
drive indicating
its type

Connections

Most internal optical drives use SATA connections (though you'll find some drives still use a PATA cable) and support the ATAPI standard. (Other connections, such as SCSI and USB, are possible but less common.) External optical drives often use USB, FireWire, or eSATA connections. ATAPI treats an optical drive exactly as though it were an ATA drive. PATA optical drives have regular 40-pin IDE connectors and master/slave jumpers. SATA optical drives use standard SATA or eSATA cables. You install them as you would install any ATA hard drive. Figure 13-30 shows a typical DVD installation using SATA.

Figure 13-30
Typical DVD
installation

ATAPI drives require no CMOS changes as part of the installation process. When the industry first introduced ATAPI drives, techs familiar with hard-drive installations swamped the CD-ROM makers' service departments asking how to set up the drives in CMOS. To reduce these calls, BIOS makers added a CD-ROM option in many CMOS setup utilities, just to give the techs something to do! You can find this option in many older CMOS setup utilities. This setting actually didn't do anything at all; it just kept users from bothering the CD-ROM makers with silly support calls. Modern motherboards report the actual model numbers of optical drives, giving techs a degree of assurance that they configured and installed the drive correctly (see Figure 13-31).

Figure 13-31

Autodetect settings for two optical drives

```
                    Phoenix - Award BIOS CMOS Setup Ut
                          Standard CMOS Features

        Date (mm:dd:yy)             Wed, Jun 7 2011        ▲
        Time (hh:mm:ss)             13 : 19 : 35
    ► IDE Channel 1 Master          WDC WD1200JB-75CRA0
    ► IDE Channel 1 Slave           None
    ► IDE Channel 2 Master          SONY     CD-CW  CRX17
    ► IDE Channel 2 Slave           TOSHIBA CD/DVDW SDR5
    ► IDE Channel 3 Master          None
```

External Optical Drives

Almost all new PCs have one, two, or three external expansion buses—USB, FireWire, or eSATA—and the makers of optical drives have quickly taken this fact to heart. Many manufacturers have released external versions of CD, DVD, and Blu-ray Disc drives, both readers and burners. Of the three, eSATA is fastest, with USB 3.0 close behind and FireWire a distant third.

Many ultra-light laptops don't have an optical drive built in; the only way to load an OS on them is through an external drive.

You won't find many CD or DVD drives with eSATA—they just can't take advantage of the blazing speed offered by the best of the external ports. Blu-ray Disc drive manufacturers, on the other hand, have released several drives with both eSATA and USB 3.0 connections. Since both connections offer almost the same speed (in practical usage, at least), feel free to use either connection.

Device Manager

When you install a new optical drive, such as a DVD drive, into an existing system, the first question to ask is "Does Windows recognize my DVD drive?" You can determine this by opening My Computer/Computer and verifying that a DVD drive is present (see Figure 13-32). When you want to know more, go to Device Manager.

Figure 13-32

DVD drive letter in Computer

Device Manager contains most of the information about optical drives. Open Device Manager and find your drive in the list of devices. Right-click on the drive and select Properties to see more information. The General tab tells you about the current status of the DVD drive, basically saying whether the device is working properly or not—rather less useful than actually trying the device. Other tabs, such as the Driver tab, provide other pertinent information about the drive.

Auto Insert Notification

Another setting of note is the Auto Insert Notification option, often referred to as *Auto-Play*. This setting enables Windows to detect automatically the presence of audio or data optical discs when they are placed in the drive. Windows XP and Windows Vista/7 deal with AutoPlay in different ways.

Windows XP provides a simple approach to AutoPlay. By default, when you insert a CD- or DVD-media disc that doesn't have an *autorun.inf* file, Windows XP asks you what you want to do (see Figure 13-33). You can change the default behavior simply by accessing the Properties dialog box for a particular drive in My Computer and making your selection on the AutoPlay tab. Figure 13-34 shows some of the options for a typical Windows XP machine.

Figure 13-33
Windows XP prompting user for action

AutoPlay in Windows Vista and Windows 7 is much more robust and offers many more options than in Windows XP. For example, you can choose to enable or disable AutoPlay for all media and devices. (Using AutoPlay for all media and devices is the default.) But what's more interesting is that you can enable very specific actions for Windows to take when digital media or devices are inserted or detected. For an audio CD, for example, you can specify that Windows should use Windows Media Player.

If a DVD or Blu-ray movie is detected, you can tell AutoPlay to play the disc by using PowerDVD 12 or some other program. You can adjust AutoPlay options in Windows Vista/7 through Control Panel | Hardware and Sound | AutoPlay.

Figure 13-34
AutoPlay tab for a CD-RW drive

You can also change the drive letter for an optical drive, just as you can change the letter of a hard drive. You'll find that option in Disk Management (see Figure 13-35).

Figure 13-35
Change CD drive letter option in Disk Management

Applications

A regular CD-ROM drive installation involves no applications. You install it, Windows sees it, and you're finished. CD-R and CD-RW drives, in contrast, require applications to enable their burning features. Windows Media Player, included with most copies of Windows, is capable of burning music to CDs, while Windows Explorer can burn data to your CDs.

DVD and Blu-ray Disc drives need software to enable you to watch movies and burn DVD and Blu-ray video, though burning your data to DVD is still handled by Windows Explorer. (Burning to Blu-ray media requires third-party software.) Windows Media Player makes an excellent DVD-watching application, but to burn DVD-videos, you'll need to turn to Windows DVD Maker (Vista/7) or a third-party tool like Nero or Roxio Creator.

Ever wanted to make a perfect copy of a CD so you can keep your original in a safe place? You can do so by using a special file type called an ISO file. An *ISO file* is a complete copy—an ISO image as we say—of an optical disc. As you might imagine, they are huge files, but they are also very important to techs. Techs use ISO images to send each other copies of bootable utility discs. For example, if you want a copy of the Ultimate Boot CD, you go to their Web site and download an ISO image. With Windows XP and Windows Vista, you'll need a third-party burning program (Windows 7 can burn ISO images) and go through a special process called burning an ISO image. Learn how to burn ISO images with your burning program; you'll use it all the time.

Blu-ray Disc Drive Considerations

Physically installing, attaching, and maintaining optical drives is pretty straightforward, but a Blu-ray Disc drive installation requires some special considerations. If you plan to use your Blu-ray Disc drive primarily for storage purposes, for example, system requirements are minimal. If you plan on watching Blu-ray Disc movies in HD resolution (720p, 1080i, or 1080p), on the other hand, the requirements are quite hefty. Here's a list of recommended minimum specs.

- **Processor** At the very least, a Pentium 4, Pentium D, or dual or multicore processor; or an AMD Athlon 64 X2 or Phenom multicore processor.

- **System memory** At least 1 GB RAM for Windows XP; 2 GB RAM for Windows Vista/7.

- **Video** You need an HDCP-compliant (either DVI or HDMI) video card and drivers. That's a lot of initials in one sentence! Here's the scoop. The High-Bandwidth Digital Content Protection (HDCP) is a standard developed by Intel to ensure copyright protection on behalf of the Motion Picture Association of America. The digital visual interface (DVI) and High-Definition Multimedia Interface (HDMI) standards enable fast, uncompressed connections between an HDTV, PC, and any other DVI/HDMI component. HDMI, which transmits both video and audio signals, has all but replaced the older DVI standard that only supports video. AMD and NVIDIA both offer Blu-ray Disc–compliant PCIe video cards with enough horsepower to get the job done.

CyberLink provides an awesome tool called BD & 3D Advisor that will tell you if your system meets the requirements to play Blu-ray Discs. You can get it at www .cyberlink.com/prog/bd-support/diagnosis.do.

Region Codes

Production movies on DVD and Blu-ray Disc can feature a *region code*, encoding that enables you to play those movies only on a player that shares the same region code. This was instituted to try to stop piracy of movies, though it didn't manage to accomplish that goal.

Can you play a DVD or Blu-ray Disc encoded to play in the geographical region location of Somalia on your system manufactured in the U.S.A.? Why sure you can. To do so, however, you have to change the region code on your DVD or Blu-ray Disc player to match Somalia (5 or B, respectively, in case you're curious). You can only change the region code on your player four times. After that, you get stuck with whatever was the last-used region code.

Most optical devices are set to play only discs encoded for the region in which they were sold or manufactured. You can easily check and set your device's current region code under the hardware properties of your optical device in any version of Windows. As either a technician or home enthusiast, you should be familiar with the following optical device and media region codes.

 TIP Be sure you are familiar with the Blu-ray Disc requirements discussed in this section, especially the stringent requirements for supporting high-definition video and audio. Also, be aware that CompTIA expects you to be somewhat knowledgeable of DVD/BD region codes, so pay attention to those as well.

DVD Region Codes:

- **REGION 0** All regions
- **REGION 1** United States, Canada
- **REGION 2** Europe, Japan, Middle East, South Africa, Greenland
- **REGION 3** South Korea, Taiwan, Hong Kong, areas of Southeast Asia
- **REGION 4** Australia, New Zealand, Central and South America
- **REGION 5** Eastern Europe, Russia, India, Africa
- **REGION 6** China
- **REGION 7** Reserved for special and future use
- **REGION 8** Reserved for cruise ships and airlines

Blu-ray Disc Region Codes:

- **A** East Asia (China and Mongolia excluded), Southeast Asia, Americas, and their dependencies
- **B** Africa, Southwest Asia, Europe (except Russia), Oceania, and their dependencies
- **C** Central Asia, East Asia (China and Mongolia only), South Asia, central Eurasia (including Russia), and their dependencies

Troubleshooting Removable Media

Floppy disk drives, flash memory, and optical drives are fairly robust devices that rarely require troubleshooting due to an actual hardware failure. Most problems with removable media stem from lack of knowledge, improper installation, abuse, and incorrect use of associated applications. There's no way to repair a truly broken flash memory card—once a flash card dies you replace it—so let's concentrate on troubleshooting floppy drives and optical drives.

Floppy Drive Maintenance and Troubleshooting

No single component fails more often than the floppy drive. This is not really that surprising because floppy drives have more exposure to the outside environment than anything but the keyboard. Only a small door (or in the case of 5¼-inch drives, not even a door) divides the read/write heads from dust and grime. Floppy drives are also exposed to the threat of mechanical damage. Many folks destroy floppy drives by accidentally inserting inverted disks, paper clips, and other foreign objects. Life is tough for floppy drives.

In the face of this abuse, the key preventative maintenance performed on floppy drives is cleaning. You can find floppy drive *cleaning kits* at some electronics stores, or you can use a cotton swab and some denatured alcohol to scour gently inside the drive for dust and other particles.

If cleaning the drive doesn't help, try replacing the suspect disk with another one to see if the floppy drive itself is bad. If it turns out that your floppy drive won't read any disks, it's time to replace the drive.

Troubleshooting Optical Drives and Discs

Optical drives are extremely reliable and durable PC components. At times, however, a reliable and durable device decides to turn into an unreliable, nondurable pile of plastic and metal frustration. This section covers a few of the more common problems with optical drives and discs—installation issues, burning issues, and firmware updates—and how to fix them.

Installation Issues

The single biggest problem with optical drives, especially in a new installation, is the connection. Your first guess should be that the drive has not been properly installed in some way. A few of the common culprits are forgetting to plug in a power connector, inserting a cable backward, and misconfiguring jumpers/switches. Although you need to know the type of drive, the test for an improper physical connection is always the same: using BIOS to see whether the system can see the optical drive.

How BIOS detects an optical drive depends on the system. Most BIOS makers have created intelligent BIOS software that can see an installed CD-media drive. Figure 13-36 shows a modern Award Software, Inc. BIOS recognizing a CD-RW during startup.

```
Award Modular BIOS v6.00PG, An Energy Star Ally
Copyright (C) 1984-2003 Phonix Technologies, LTD

Main Processor : AMD Athlon(tm) 64 Processor 3200+
Memory Testing : 1048576K OK
CPU0 Memory Information: DDR 400 CL:3 ,1T Dual Channel, 128-bit

IDE Channel 1 Master : WDC WD1200JB-75CRA0 16.06V16
IDE Channel 1 Slave  : None
IDE Channel 2 Master : TOSHIBA CD=DVDW SDR5372V TU11
IDE Channel 2 Slave  : None
```

Figure 13-36 BIOS recognizing an optical drive at boot

If BIOS detects the device, Windows recognizes the drive and you'll see it in My Computer/Computer and Device Manager.

If the drive won't read a CD-R or CD-RW disc, first try a commercial CD-ROM disc that is in good condition. CD-R and CD-RW discs sometimes have compatibility issues with CD-ROM drives. The same goes for DVD-RWs or any other writable DVD discs in your DVD drive or writable Blu-ray Discs in your Blu-ray Disc drive. Also, no optical drive will read badly scratched discs.

If the drive still does not see a disc, try cleaning the drive. Most modern optical drives have built-in cleaning mechanisms, but from time to time, you need to use a commercial optical-drive cleaning kit (see Figure 13-37).

Optical drives are not cleaned too often, but the discs are. Although a number of fine optical disc cleaning kits are available, you can clean most discs quite well with nothing more than a damp soft cloth. Occasionally, you can add a mild detergent. Always wipe from the center of the optical disc to the edge—never use a circular motion when cleaning a CD, DVD, or Blu-ray Disc! A common old tech's tale about cleaning optical discs is that you can wash them in a dishwasher. Although this may seem laughable, the tale has become so common that it requires a serious response. This is *not true* for two reasons: First, the water in most dishwashers is too hot and can cause the discs to warp. Second, the water pushes the discs around, causing them to hit other objects and get scratched. Don't do it!

Figure 13-37
Optical-drive
cleaning kit

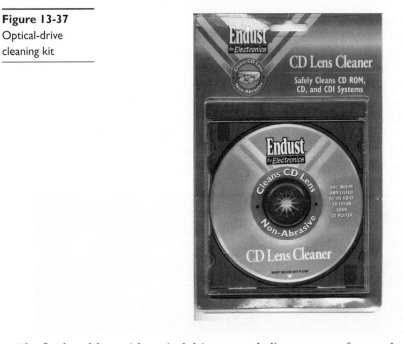

The final problem with optical drives—stuck discs—comes from *technician* error and is not actually the fault of the drives. I can't tell you the number of times I've pulled an optical drive out of a system to replace it, only to discover that I or my customer left an essential disc inside the now-powerless drive. Luckily, most optical drives have a small hole in the front, usually just below the drive opening, into which you can insert a wire—an unbent paper clip is the standard tool for this purpose—and push on an internal release lever that ejects the disc. Try it!

Burning Issues

The tremendous growth of the CD-R and CD-RW industry—and to a lesser extent, the recordable DVD industry—has led to a substantial number of incompatibility issues between discs and drives. Some of these incompatibilities trace back to serious IO (Ignorant Operator) problems; people try to make these discs do jobs they aren't designed to do. Even when people read the manuals and jump through the proper hoops, real problems do arise, many of which you can easily solve with a few checks.

Know What It Can Do Most mistakes take place at the point of purchase, when someone buys a drive without completely understanding its capabilities. Don't just assume that the device will do everything. Before I purchase a CD-RW or DVD-RW drive, for example, I make it a point to get my hands on every technical document the maker provides to verify exactly what capabilities the drive possesses. I make sure the drive has a good reputation; just use any search engine and type in **review** and the model number of the drive to get several people's opinions.

Media Issues The optical disc standards committees refused to mandate the types of materials used in the construction of discs. As a result, you see substantial quality differences among CD-R and CD-RW discs of different brands and sources (they are made in several different countries). As mentioned earlier, CD-R discs use organic inks as part of the burning process. Fellow techs love to talk about which color to use or which color gives the best results. Ignore them; the color itself means nothing. Instead, try several brands of CD-R discs when you first get your drive to determine what works best for you. If you have a particular reason for burning CDs, such as music recording, you may want to ask for opinions and recommendations among folks in online communities with the same focus. They're usually happy to share their hard-won knowledge about what works.

In general, two items can affect media quality: speed and inks. Most CD-R and CD-RW media makers certify their CDs to work up to a certain speed multiplier. A media maker often has two product lines: a quality line guaranteed to work at a certain speed, and a generic line where you take your chances. As a rule, I buy both. I primarily use cheap discs, but I always stash five to ten good-quality discs in case I run into a problem. Again, this in large part depends on what you want them for: you may want to pull out the cheapies for temporary backups but stick with the high-end discs for archiving musical performances.

All of this discussion about CD-Rs and CD-RWs definitely holds true for recordable DVD and BD discs and drives as well. Factor in the incompatibility of standards and you're looking at a fine mess. Do your homework before you buy or advise a client to buy a DVD/BD-writable or -rewritable drive.

Buffer Underrun Every CD, DVD, and Blu-ray Disc burner comes with onboard RAM, called *buffer RAM*—usually just called the buffer—that stores the incoming data from the recording source. *Buffer underrun*, the inability of the source device to keep the burner loaded with data, creates more *coasters*—that is, improperly burned and therefore useless CDs, DVDs, and Blu-ray Discs—than any other single problem. Buffer underrun most often occurs when copying from CD-ROM to CD-R/RW or from DVD-ROM to DVD-writable of all stripes. Many factors contribute to buffer underrun, but two stand out as the most important. The first factor is buffer size. Make sure you purchase drives with large buffers, a minimum of 2 MB. Unlike with system RAM, you can't get a buffer upgrade. Second is multitasking. Most systems won't enable you to run any other programs while the burner is running.

One trick to reduce underrun is using an ISO image file. Unlike some optical drives, *any* hard drive can keep up with an optical burner. Doing a bit-by-bit copy from disc to disc dramatically reduces the chances that a buffer underrun will add to your coaster collection. All current optical disc burners include the BURN-Proof technology developed by Sanyo, which has eliminated the underrun issue. These drives can literally turn off the burning process if the buffer runs out of information and automatically restart as soon as the buffer refills. I love this feature, as I can now burn CDs in the background and run other programs without fear of underrun. If you're buying a new burner, make sure you get one that uses the BURN-Proof technology.

TIP The majority of problems that occur with CD, DVD, and Blu-ray Disc drives are usually a direct result of incorrectly installed or updated device drivers, disconnected cables, or incompatible or just plain bad media. Also, keep in mind DVD and Blu-ray Disc drives use specific region codes that are often misconfigured. Blu-ray Disc drives have very specific hardware and driver specifications that must be met for trouble-free end-user experiences. CompTIA is likely to target these areas, so make sure you understand this information.

Firmware Updates

Almost all optical drives come with an upgradeable flash ROM chip. If your drive doesn't read a particular type of media, or if any other nonintermittent reading/writing problems develop, check the manufacturer's Web site to see if it offers a firmware upgrade. Almost every optical drive seems to get one or two firmware updates during its production cycle.

Beyond A+

Color Books

The term *color books* is often used in the world of CD-media. Color books are—well, books! In this case, they're the standards developed in the industry to describe various media. For example, the Red book describes the original audio CD format. If you have a lot of money—say, US$3000—you may purchase copies of these books, and yes, their covers really match the colors of the standards. You might hear a fellow computer support person using these terms. Instead of saying, "Does your CD-ROM read CD-RWs?" they will say, "Is that CD-ROM of yours Orange book?" Technical specifications also use these terms. I personally don't like the way many people refer to these book colors, but the terms are used enough that you should memorize the meanings of at least three book colors: Red, Yellow, and Orange. Table 13-3 shows a complete list of CD-media book colors.

Table 13-3
CD-Media Book
Colors

Application	Book
Audio CDs	Red book
Data CDs	Yellow book
CD-I	Green book
Recordable CDs	Orange book
Video CD	White book
CD Extra	Blue book

BDXL

If you think Blu-ray Disc's 50-GB capacity is limiting, check out *BDXL* discs. The BDXL format was introduced in June 2010, although drives capable of reading and writing to the discs didn't start appearing until late 2011. That's right: you can't use BDXL discs in that standard Blu-ray Disc drive you just bought. You'll need a drive that specifically supports the new format. So why would you want one? In a word: capacity.

BDXL discs come in two flavors: a triple-layer BDXL disc supports a capacity of 100 GB, and a quadruple-layer disc has a capacity of 128 GB. That's a lot of room, but it comes at a high price. As of early 2012, a single disc cost US$100—that's a dollar per gigabyte for a triple-layer disc! At those prices, you could go out and get yourself a nice solid-state drive, which is much more flexible as a storage device. Needless to say, BDXL isn't quite ready for the spotlight, but as prices come down, this could become a great option for optical disc storage.

Chapter Review

Questions

1. To install a floppy drive as the A: drive, what must you do?
 A. Attach the mini connector.
 B. Plug it into the end connector of the ribbon cable.
 C. Plug it into the middle connector on the ribbon cable.
 D. Attach the Molex connector.

2. If the floppy disk you used last week will not work today in your floppy drive, what should you do first to determine if the problem is the drive or the disk?
 A. Try another disk in the drive or try the disk in another drive.
 B. Open the computer and check the ribbon cable.
 C. Replace the floppy drive.
 D. Check the CMOS settings.

3. Which term describes the capability to burn files to a CD-R and then come back later and burn additional files?
 A. MultiBurn
 B. Multisession
 C. MultiDrive
 D. Multibuffer

4. Which type of flash memory card is currently the most popular?

 A. CompactFlash

 B. Memory Stick

 C. Secure Digital

 D. SmartMedia

5. What type of device must be installed on your system so you can access data on a flash memory card?

 A. Scanner

 B. Card reader

 C. Floppy drive

 D. Zip drive

6. Which of the following can be bootable media? (Select the best answer.)

 A. CD-R disc

 B. Floppy disk

 C. USB thumb drive

 D. All of the above

7. When you insert a CD, the AutoPlay feature of Windows looks for which file?

 A. autoplay.inf

 A. autorun.inf

 A. autoplay.ini

 A. autorun.exe

8. You can save a copy of a CD or DVD as what type of file?

 A. ISO

 B. ISO-9660

 C. INF

 D. CDDA

9. A CD-RW has a speed rating of 12×10×32×. What do the three numbers refer to, in order?

 A. Write, rewrite, read

 B. Read, write, rewrite

 C. Rewrite, read, write

 D. Write, read, rewrite

10. Which standard covers DVD-ROM technology?

 A. MPEG-1

 B. MPEG-2

 C. MPEG-3

 D. MPEG-4

Answers

1. **B.** Plug the floppy drive into the end of the ribbon cable to make it the A: drive.

2. **A.** If the floppy disk won't read in the drive, try another disk first.

3. **B.** The term *multisession* describes the capability to burn files to a CD-R and then come back later and burn additional files.

4. **C.** Secure Digital cards are the current kings of the marketplace.

5. **B.** You need some sort of card reader to read a flash memory card.

6. **D.** You can make a boot disk out of optical discs, floppy disks, or flash memory drives.

7. **B.** By default, Windows looks for AUTORUN.INF when you insert a CD.

8. **A.** You can save a complete CD or DVD as an ISO image.

9. **A.** The three speeds listed for CD-RW drives stand for write, rewrite, and read.

10. **B.** The MPEG-2 standard covers DVD-ROM technology (among other things).

Installing and Upgrading Windows

In this chapter, you will learn how to

- Identify and implement preinstallation tasks
- Install and upgrade Windows XP, Windows Vista, and Windows 7
- Troubleshoot installation problems
- Identify and implement post-installation tasks

An *operating system (OS)* provides the fundamental link between the user and the hardware that makes up the PC. Without an operating system, all of the greatest, slickest PC hardware in the world is but so much copper, silicon, and gold wrapped up as a big, beige paperweight (or, if you're a teenage boy, a big, gleaming, black paperweight with a window and glowing fluorescent lights, possibly shaped like a robot). The operating system creates the interface between human and machine, enabling you to unleash the astonishing power locked up in the sophisticated electronics of the PC to create amazing pictures, games, documents, business tools, medical miracles, and much more.

This chapter takes you through the processes for installing and upgrading Windows. It starts by analyzing the preinstallation tasks, steps not to be skipped by the wise tech. The bulk of the chapter comes in the second section, where you'll learn about installing and upgrading Windows XP, Windows Vista, and Windows 7. Not all installations go smoothly, so section three looks at troubleshooting installation issues. The final section walks you through the typical post-installation tasks.

802

Preparing for Installation or Upgrade

Installing or upgrading an OS is like any good story: it has a beginning, a middle, and an end. In this case, the beginning is the several tasks you need to do before you actually do the installation or upgrade. If you do your homework here, the installation process is a breeze, and the post-installation tasks are minimal.

Don't get discouraged at all of the preparation tasks. They usually go pretty fast, and skipping them can cause you gobs of grief later when you're in the middle of installing and things blow up. Well, maybe there isn't a real explosion, but the computer might lock up and refuse to boot into anything usable. With that in mind, look at the nine tasks you need to complete *before* you insert that CD or DVD. Here's the list; a discussion of each follows:

1. Identify hardware requirements.
2. Verify hardware and software compatibility.
3. Decide what type of installation to perform.
4. Determine how to back up and restore existing data, if necessary.
5. Select an installation method.
6. Determine how to partition the hard drive and what file system to use.
7. Determine your computer's network role.
8. Decide on your computer's language and locale settings.
9. Plan for post-installation tasks.

 NOTE This nine-step process was once part of the CompTIA A+ exam objectives. Starting with the 220-801 and 220-802 exams, CompTIA has dropped this process from the exams, but I've come to like it. The nine steps are practical, clear, and easy to remember. I use these as a mental checklist every time I install Windows.

Identify Hardware Requirements

Hardware requirements help you decide whether a computer system is a reasonable host for a particular operating system. Requirements include the CPU model, the amount of RAM, the amount of free hard disk space, the video adapter, the display, and the storage devices that may be required to install and run the operating system. They are stated as minimums or, more recently, as recommended minimums. Although you could install an operating system on a computer with the old minimums that Microsoft published, they were not realistic if you wanted to actually accomplish work. With the last few versions of Windows, Microsoft has published recommended minimums that are much more realistic. You will find the published minimums on the packaging and at Microsoft's Web site (www.microsoft.com). Later in this chapter, I'll also tell you what I recommend as minimums for Windows XP, Windows Vista, and Windows 7.

Verify Hardware and Software Compatibility

Assuming your system meets the requirements, you next need to find out how well Windows supports the hardware and software you intend to use under Windows. You have three sources for this information. First, the Setup Wizard that runs during the installation

does a quick check of your hardware. Microsoft also provides a free utility, usually called Upgrade Advisor, which you can run on a system to see if your hardware and software will work with a newer version of Windows. Second, Microsoft provides Web sites where you can search by model number of hardware or by a software version to see if it plays well with Windows. Third, the manufacturer of the device or software will usually provide some form of information either on the product box or on their Web site to tell you about Windows compatibility. Let's look at all three information sources.

Setup Wizard/Upgrade Advisor

When you install Windows, the Setup Wizard automatically checks your hardware and software and reports any potential conflicts. It's not perfect, and if you have a critical issue (like a bad driver for your video card), Setup Wizard may simply fail. With any flavor of Windows, *first do your homework*. To help, Windows also provides a utility called Upgrade Advisor (see Figure 14-1) on the installation media (also downloadable) that you run before you attempt to install the software.

Figure 14-1 Upgrade Advisor

Web Sites and Lists

To ensure that your PC works well with Windows, Microsoft has put a lot of hardware and software through a series of certification programs to create a list of devices that work with Windows. The challenge is that Microsoft seems to change the name of the list with every version of Windows.

NOTE You'll occasionally hear the HCL or Windows Logo'd Product List referred to as the Windows Catalog. The Windows Catalog was a list of supported hardware Microsoft would add to the Windows XP installation media. The Windows 7 Compatibility Center Web site is the modern tech's best source, so use that rather than any printed resources.

It all began back with Windows 95 when Microsoft produced a list of known hardware that would work with their OS, called the Hardware Compatibility List (HCL). Every version of Windows up to Windows Vista contained an HCL. This list was originally simply a text file found on the install disc or downloadable from Microsoft's Web site. Over time, Microsoft created specialized Web sites where you could look up a piece of hardware or software to determine whether or not it worked with Windows. These Web sites have gone through a number of names. Microsoft's current Web site acknowledging what hardware and software works with Windows is the *Windows 7 Compatibility Center,* formerly known as the Windows Logo'd Products List (for Windows Vista) and the Windows Catalog (for Windows XP). Now the magic words are Windows 7 Compatibility Center, as shown in Figure 14-2. Here you can find information on compatible components for Windows 7.

NOTE If you go looking for the Windows Catalog or Windows Logo'd Products List, you won't find them. You'll be redirected to the Windows 7 Compatibility Center (or a Web page explaining why you should upgrade to Windows 7).

Figure 14-2
Windows
Compatibility
Center

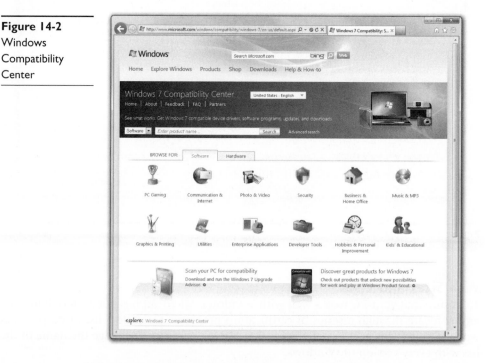

When you install a device that hasn't been tested by Microsoft, a rather scary screen appears (see Figure 14-3). This doesn't mean the component won't work, only that it hasn't been tested. Not all component makers go through the rather painful process of getting the Microsoft approval that allows them to list their component in the Windows 7 Compatibility Center. As a general rule, unless the device is more than five years old, go ahead and install it. If it still doesn't work, you can simply uninstall it later.

Figure 14-3

Untested device in Windows XP

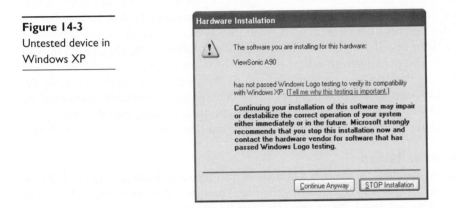

EXAM TIP The CompTIA A+ 802 exam expects you to know the different compatibility tools available for each OS covered. Windows XP offered the Upgrade Advisor and the Hardware Compatibility List (HCL). Windows Vista added the online Windows Logo'd Product List. Every online tool (with the exception of ftp.microsoft.com where you can find old HCLs in text format) now just points to the Windows 7 Compatibility Center.

Manufacturer Resources

Don't panic if you don't see your device on the official Microsoft list; many supported devices aren't on it. Check the optical disc that came with your hardware for proper drivers. Better yet, check the manufacturer's Web site for the most up-to-date drivers. Even when the Windows 7 Compatibility Center lists a piece of hardware, I still make a point of checking the manufacturer's Web site for newer drivers.

When preparing to upgrade, check with the Web sites of the manufacturers of the applications already installed on the previous OS. If there are software compatibility problems with the versions you have, the manufacturer should provide upgrades or patches to fix the problem.

Decide What Type of Installation to Perform

You can install Windows in several ways. A *clean installation* of an OS involves installing it onto an empty hard drive or completely replacing an existing installation. An *upgrade*

installation means installing an OS on top of an earlier installed version, thus inheriting all previous hardware and software settings. You can combine versions of Windows by creating a *multiboot installation*. Installing usually involves some sort of optical disc, but other methods also exist. Let's look at all the options.

Clean Installation

A clean installation means your installation ignores a previous installation of Windows, wiping out the old version as the new version of Windows installs. A clean installation is also performed on a new system with a completely blank hard drive. The advantage of doing a clean installation is that you don't carry problems from the old OS over to the new one. The disadvantage is that you need to reinstall all your applications and reconfigure the desktop and each application to the user's preferences. You typically perform a clean installation by setting your CMOS to boot from the optical drive before your hard drive. You then boot off of a Windows installation disc, and Windows gives you the opportunity to partition and format the hard drive and then install Windows.

Upgrade Installation

In an upgrade installation, the new OS installs into the same folders as the old OS, or in tech speak, the new installs *on top of* the old. The new OS replaces the old OS, but retains your data and applications and also inherits all of the personal settings (such as font styles, desktop themes, and so on). The best part is that you don't have to reinstall your favorite programs. Many tech writers refer to this upgrade process as an *in-place upgrade*. Upgrades aren't always perfect, but the advantages make them worthwhile if your upgrade path allows it.

EXAM TIP Microsoft uses the term in-place upgrade to define an upgrade installation, so expect to see it on the 802 exam. On the other hand, Microsoft documentation also uses the term for a completely different process, called a *repair installation*, so read whatever question you get on the exam carefully for context. For repair installations, see Chapter 19.

To begin the upgrade of Windows, you should run the appropriate program from the optical disc. This usually means inserting a Windows installation disc into your system while your old OS is running, which autostarts the installation program. The installation program will ask you whether you want to perform an upgrade or a new installation; if you select new installation, the program will remove the existing OS before installing the new one.

NOTE Before starting an OS upgrade, make sure you have shut down all other open applications!

If you are performing an upgrade to Windows XP and for some reason the installation program doesn't start automatically, go to My Computer, open the installation disc, and locate winnt32.exe. This program starts an upgrade to Windows XP. For a Windows Vista or Windows 7 upgrade, open the disc in Windows Explorer and run Setup.exe in the disc's root directory, which starts the upgrade for those versions of Windows.

Multiboot Installation

A third option that you need to be aware of is the dual-boot or multiboot installation. This means your system has more than one Windows installation and you may choose which installation to use when you boot your computer. Every time your computer boots, you'll get a menu asking you which version of Windows you wish to boot. Multiboot requires that you format your active partition with a file system that every operating system you install can use. This hasn't been much of a problem since the Windows 9x family stopped being relevant, because there's really no reason to use anything other than NTFS.

Windows XP can be installed in a separate folder from an existing older copy of Windows, enabling you to put two operating systems on the same partition. Neither Windows Vista nor Windows 7 allows you define the install folder, so multibooting using Windows Vista or 7 requires you to put each installation on a different partition.

You'll recall from Chapter 12 that Windows Vista and Windows 7 enable you to shrink the C: partition, so if you want to dual boot but have only a single drive, you can make it happen even if Vista/7 is already installed and the C: partition takes up the full drive. Use Disk Management to shrink the volume and create another partition in the newly unallocated space. Then install another copy of Windows to the new partition.

NOTE When configuring a computer for multibooting, there are two basic rules: first, you must format the system partition in a file system that is common to all installed operating systems, and second, you must install the operating systems in order from oldest to newest.

The whole concept behind multiboot is to enable you to run multiple operating systems on a single computer. This is handy if you have an application that runs only on Windows XP, but you also want to run Windows Vista or Windows 7.

Other Installation Methods

In medium to large organizations, more advanced installation methods are often employed, especially when many computers need to be configured identically. A common method is to place the source files in a shared directory on a network server. Then, whenever a tech needs to install a new OS, he can boot up the computer, connect to the source location on the network, and start the installation from there. This is called generically a *remote network installation*. This method alone has many variations and can be automated with special scripts that automatically select the options and components needed. The scripts can even install extra applications at the end of the OS

installation, all without user intervention once the installation has been started. This type of installation is called an *unattended installation*.

Another type of installation that is very popular for re-creating standard configurations is an *image deployment*. An image is a complete copy of a hard disk volume on which an operating system and, usually, all required application software programs have been preinstalled. Images can be stored on optical discs, in which case the tech runs special software on the computer that copies the image onto the local hard drive. Images can also be stored on special network servers, in which case the tech connects to the image server using special software that copies the image from the server to the local hard drive. A leader in this technology has been Norton Ghost, which is available from Symantec. Other similar programs are Clonezilla and Acronis's True Image.

Beginning with Windows 2000 Server, Microsoft added *Remote Installation Services* (*RIS*), which can be used to initiate either a scripted installation or an installation of an image. With Windows Server 2008 and 2008 R2, Microsoft implemented *Windows Deployment Services* (*WDS*) to replace RIS. Though they are two different systems, they work very similarly from a tech's viewpoint. These tools help with big rollouts of new systems and operating system upgrades.

 TIP Scripting OS and application installations is a full-time job in many organizations. Many scripting tools and methods are available from both Microsoft and third-party sources.

Determine How to Back Up and Restore Existing Data, If Necessary

Whether you run a clean install or perform an upgrade, you may need to back up existing user data first, because things can go very wrong either way, and the data on the hard drive might be damaged. You'll need to find out where the user is currently saving data files. If they are saving onto the local hard drive, it must be backed up before the installation or replacement takes place. However, if all data has been saved to a network location, you are in luck, because the data is safe from damage during installation.

If the user saves data locally, and the computer is connected to a network, save the data, at least temporarily, to a network location until after the upgrade or installation has taken place. If the computer is not connected to a network, you have a few options for backup. For one, you can put the data on USB thumb drives. A slower option would be to copy the data to DVDs. You can also use an external hard drive, which is a handy thing for any tech to have. Wherever you save the data, you will need to copy or restore the data back to the local hard disk after the installation.

If you plan to migrate a user from one system to another, you might start the process by running the Files and Settings Transfer Wizard (Windows XP) or Windows Easy Transfer (Windows Vista and 7). You'll complete that process after the Windows installation finishes. Rather than discuss the process twice, I'll leave the full discussion on migration for the "Post-Installation Tasks" section later in this chapter.

Select an Installation Method

Once you've backed up everything important, you need to select an installation method. You have two basic choices: insert the installation disc into the drive and go, or install over a network.

Determine How to Partition the Hard Drive and What File System to Use

If you are performing a clean installation, you need to decide ahead of time how to partition the disk space on your hard disk drive, including the number and size of partitions and the file system (or systems) you will use. Actually, in the decision process, the file system comes first, and then the space issue follows, as you will see.

This was a much bigger issue back in the days when older operating systems couldn't use newer file systems, but now that every Windows OS that you could reasonably want to install supports NTFS, there's really no reason to use anything else. You still might have a reason to partition your drive, but as for choosing a file system, your work is done for you.

Determine Your Computer's Network Role

The question of your computer's network role comes up in one form or another during a Windows installation. A Windows computer can have one of several roles relative to a network (in Microsoft terms). One role, called *standalone*, is actually a non-network role, and it simply means that the computer does not participate on a network. You can install any version of Windows on a standalone computer. A standalone computer belongs to a workgroup by default, even though that workgroup contains only one member.

In a network environment, a computer must be a member of either a workgroup or a domain (if you're using Windows 7 in a workgroup on a home network, it can also belong to a homegroup).

Decide on Your Computer's Language and Locale Settings

These settings are especially important for Windows operating systems because they determine how date and time information is displayed and which math separators and currency symbols are used for various locations.

Plan for Post-Installation Tasks

After installing Windows, you may need to install the latest service pack or updates. You may also need to install updated drivers and reconfigure any settings, such as network settings, that were found not to work. You will also need to install and configure any applications (word processor, spreadsheet, database, e-mail, games, etc.) required by the user of the computer. Finally, don't forget to restore any data backed up before the installation or upgrade.

The Installation and Upgrade Process

At the most basic level, installing any operating system follows a fairly standard set of steps. You turn on the computer, insert an operating system disc into the optical drive, and follow the installation wizard until you have everything completed. Along the way, you'll accept the *End User License Agreement (EULA)* and enter the product key that says you're not a pirate; the product key is invariably located on the installation disc's case. At the same time, there are nuances between installing Windows XP or upgrading to Windows 7 that every CompTIA A+ certified tech must know, so this section goes through many installation processes in some detail.

EXAM TIP Although the typical installation of Windows involves a CD-ROM (for Windows XP) or DVD (for Windows Vista/7), there are other options. Microsoft provides a tool called *Windows 7 USB DVD Download Tool* for writing an ISO image to a USB thumb drive, for example, so you can download an operating system and install on a system that doesn't have an optical drive. This is a cool option with Windows 7 and might be a very popular option with Windows 8.

Installing or Upgrading to Windows XP Professional

Windows XP has been around for a long time with a well-established upgrade and installation process. This is the one part of the CompTIA A+ exams where older versions of Windows may be mentioned, so be warned!

Upgrade Paths

You can upgrade to Windows XP Professional from all of the following versions of Windows:

- Windows 98 (all versions)
- Windows Me
- Windows NT 4.0 Workstation (Service Pack 5 and later)
- Windows 2000 Professional
- Windows XP Home Edition

Hardware Requirements for Windows XP

Hardware requirements for Windows XP Professional are higher than for previous versions of Windows, but are still very low by modern hardware standards.

Windows XP runs on a wide range of computers, but you need to be sure that your computer meets the minimum hardware requirements, as shown in Table 14-1. Also shown is my recommended minimum for a system running a typical selection of business productivity software.

Component	Minimum for a Windows XP Computer	Recommended for a Windows XP Computer
CPU	Any Intel or AMD 233 MHz or higher processor	Any Intel or AMD 300 MHz or higher processor
Memory	64 MB of RAM (though Microsoft admits XP will be somewhat crippled with only this amount)	512 MB of RAM or higher
Hard disk	1.5 GB of available hard drive space	4 GB of available hard drive space
Network	None	Modern network card
Display	Video card that supports SVGA with at least 800 × 600 resolution	Video card that supports DirectX with at least 1024 × 768 resolution
Optical drive	Any CD- or DVD-media drive	Any CD- or DVD-media drive

Table 14-1 Windows XP Hardware Requirements

Hardware and Software Compatibility

You'll need to check hardware and software compatibility before installing Windows XP Professional—as either an upgrade or a new installation. Of course, if your computer already has Windows XP on it, you're spared this task, but, you're spared this task, but you'll still need to verify that the applications you plan to add to the computer will be compatible. Luckily, Microsoft includes the Upgrade Advisor on the Windows XP disc.

Upgrade Advisor You would be hard-pressed these days to find a computer incapable of running Windows XP, but if you are ever uncertain about whether a computer you excavated at an archeological dig can run XP, fear not! The *Upgrade Advisor* is the first process that runs on the XP installation disc. It examines your hardware and installed software (in the case of an upgrade) and provides a list of devices and software that are known to have issues with XP. Be sure to follow the suggestions on this list.

You can also run the Upgrade Advisor separately from the Windows XP installation. You can run it from the Windows XP disc. Microsoft used to offer the XP Upgrade Advisor on its Web site, but searching for it now will just redirect you to the Windows 7 Upgrade Advisor, so running it from the disc is the way to go nowadays.

Booting into Windows XP Setup

The Windows XP discs are bootable, and Microsoft no longer includes a program to create a set of setup boot disks. This should not be an issue, because PCs manufactured in the past several years can boot from the optical drive. This system BIOS setting, usually described as boot order, is controlled through a PC's BIOS-based Setup program.

In the unlikely event that your lab computer can't be made to boot from its optical drive, you can create a set of six (yes, six!) Windows XP setup boot floppy disks by using a special program you can download from Microsoft's Web site. Note that Microsoft provides separate boot disk programs for XP Home and XP Professional.

Registration Versus Activation

During setup, you will be prompted to register your product and activate it. Many people confuse activation with registration, but these are separate operations. *Registration* tells Microsoft who the official owner or user of the product is, providing contact information such as name, address, company, phone number, and e-mail address. Registration is still entirely optional. Activation is a way to combat software piracy, meaning that Microsoft wishes to ensure that each license for Windows XP is used solely on a single computer. It's more formally called *Microsoft Product Activation (MPA)*.

Mandatory Activation Within 30 Days of Installation Activation is mandatory, but you can skip this step during installation. You have 30 days in which to activate the product, during which time it works normally. If you don't activate it within that time frame, it will be disabled. Don't worry about forgetting, though, because once it's installed, Windows XP frequently reminds you to activate it with a balloon message over the tray area of the taskbar. The messages even tell you how many days you have left.

Activation Mechanics Here's how product activation works. When you choose to activate, either during setup or later when XP reminds you to do it, an installation ID code is created from the product ID code that you entered during installation and a 50-digit value that identifies your key hardware components. You must send this code to Microsoft, either automatically if you have an Internet connection or verbally via a phone call to Microsoft. Microsoft then returns a 42-digit product activation code. If you are activating online, you don't have to enter the activation code; it happens automatically. If you are activating over the phone, you must read the installation ID to a representative and enter the resulting 42-digit activation code into the Activate Windows by Phone dialog box.

No personal information about you is sent as part of the activation process. Figure 14-4 shows the dialog box that opens when you start activation by clicking on the reminder message balloon.

Installing or Upgrading to Windows Vista

Preparing for a Windows Vista installation is not really different from preparing for a Windows XP installation. There are, of course, a few things to consider before installing or upgrading your system to Vista.

Upgrade Paths

Windows Vista is persnickety about doing upgrade installations with different editions; although you can upgrade to any edition of Vista from any edition of Windows XP, many upgrade paths will require you to do a clean installation of Vista. Vista's upgrade paths are so complicated that the only way to explain them is to use a grid showing the OS you're trying to upgrade from and the edition of Vista you're upgrading to. Fortunately for you, Microsoft provides such a grid, which I've re-created in Table 14-2.

Figure 14-4 Activation takes just seconds with an Internet connection.

	Vista Home Basic	Vista Home Premium	Vista Business	Vista Ultimate
XP Professional	Clean Install	Clean Install	Upgrade Install	Upgrade Install
XP Home	Upgrade Install	Upgrade Install	Upgrade Install	Upgrade Install
XP Media Center	Clean Install	Upgrade Install	Clean Install	Upgrade Install
XP Tablet PC	Clean Install	Clean Install	Upgrade Install	Upgrade Install
XP Professional x64	Clean Install	Clean Install	Clean Install	Clean Install

Table 14-2 Vista's Labyrinthine Upgrade Paths

EXAM TIP You don't really upgrade to Windows Vista Enterprise, although you can from Windows Vista Business. Because it's only available to big corporate clients, the Enterprise edition is generally installed as the first and last OS on a corporate PC.

Hardware Requirements for Windows Vista

Windows Vista requires a substantially more powerful computer than XP does. Make sure your computer meets at least the minimum hardware requirements suggested by Microsoft and outlined in Table 14-3, though it would be far better to meet my recommended requirements.

Component	Minimum for a Windows Vista Computer	Recommended for a Windows Vista Computer
CPU	I GHz 32-bit (x86) or 64-bit (x64) processor	Any dual-core Intel or AMD processor or better
Memory	512 MB of RAM for Vista Home Basic (for all other editions, I GB of RAM)	2 GB of RAM or higher
Hard disk	20-GB hard drive with 15 GB of available hard drive space for Vista Home Basic (for all other editions, 40 GB hard drive with 15 GB of free space)	100-GB hard drive or greater
Network	Modern network card with Internet access	Modern network card with Internet access
Display	Support for DirectX 9 graphics and 32 MB of graphics memory for Vista Home Basic (for all other editions, 128 MB of graphics memory, plus pixel shader 2.0 support, the WDDM driver, and 32 bits per pixel)	DirectX 10 capable graphics card with at least 512 MB of graphics memory
Optical drive	Any DVD-media drive	Any DVD-media drive

Table 14-3 Windows Vista Hardware Requirements

EXAM TIP The CompTIA exams are likely to test your knowledge regarding the minimum installation requirements for Windows Vista Home Basic, Home Premium, Business, Ultimate, or Enterprise. Know them well!

Hardware and Software Compatibility

Windows Vista is markedly different from Windows XP in many very basic, fundamental ways, and this causes all sorts of difficulty with programs and device drivers designed for Windows XP. When Vista came out, you probably heard a lot of people grumbling about it, and likely they were grumbling about hardware and software incompatibility. Simply put, a lot of old programs and devices don't work in Windows Vista, which is bad news for people who are still running Microsoft Word 97.

Most programs developed since Vista's release in 2007 should work, but checking the compatibility of any programs you absolutely cannot do without is always a good idea. Because the various tools for checking compatibility with Vista have disappeared in favor of tools for Windows 7, you'll need to check with the developers or manufacturers of your software and devices.

 NOTE Software incompatibility in Vista was such a problem for many corporate customers and end users that Microsoft has included a *Windows XP Mode* in the higher-end editions of Windows 7, enabling most Windows XP programs to be run despite the different OS.

Installing or Upgrading to Windows 7

Windows 7 did not add anything new in terms of installation types. You still need to decide between a clean installation and an upgrade installation, but that's easy to do because you can only upgrade to Windows 7 from Windows Vista—and that's only if you have the same bit edition. In other words, you can upgrade 32-bit Vista to 32-bit Windows 7, but you can't upgrade 32-bit Windows Vista to 64-bit Windows 7. All other Windows editions, including Windows XP Home and Professional, require a clean installation to get Windows 7. Table 14-4 outlines the upgrade paths.

Existing OS	Can Upgrade To...	Can Clean Install To...
32-bit Vista (any edition)	32-bit Windows 7 only	Any edition of Windows 7
64-bit Vista (any edition)	64-bit Windows 7 only	Any edition of Windows 7
Any pre-Vista Windows	Not allowed	Any edition of Windows 7

Table 14-4 Installing or Upgrading to Windows 7

If you have Windows 7 and you want to upgrade to a higher edition with more features—from Windows 7 Home Premium to Windows 7 Ultimate, for example—you can use the built-in Windows Anytime Upgrade feature. You can find this option pinned to the Start menu. Don't forget your credit card!

Hardware Requirements for Windows 7

With Windows 7, Microsoft released a single list of system requirements, broken down into 32-bit and 64-bit editions. Quoting directly from Microsoft's Windows 7 Web site, the requirements are as follows:

- 1 gigahertz (GHz) or faster 32-bit (x86) or 64-bit (x64) processor
- 1 gigabyte (GB) RAM (32-bit) or 2 GB RAM (64-bit)
- 16 GB available hard disk space (32-bit) or 20 GB (64-bit)
- DirectX 9 graphics device with WDDM 1.0 or higher driver

NOTE Windows 7 has incredibly humble minimum requirements. Today, a low-end desktop computer will have 4 GB of RAM, a processor around 2 GHz, approximately a terabyte of hard drive space, and a DirectX 11 video card with 256 or even 512 MB of graphics memory.

Make sure you memorize the list of requirements. Microsoft also added a fairly extensive list of additional requirements that vary based on the edition of Windows 7 you use. From the same Web site, they include (author's comments in brackets):

- Internet access (fees may apply). [You need Internet access to activate, register, and update the system easily.]

- Depending on resolution, video playback may require additional memory and advanced graphics hardware.

- Some games and programs might require a graphics card compatible with DirectX 10 or higher for optimal performance. [Video has improved dramatically over the years, and DirectX 9 dates back to 2004. Many games and high-definition videos need more than DirectX 9. Also, Windows Aero Desktop (aka Aero Glass) adds amazing beauty and functionality to your Desktop. You must have a video card with 128 MB of graphics memory for Aero to work.]

- For some Windows Media Center functionality a TV tuner and additional hardware may be required. [Windows Media Center works fine without a TV tuner. You can still use it to play Blu-ray Disc and DVD movies as well as video files and music. If you want to watch live TV, however, you'll need a tuner.]

- HomeGroup requires a network and PCs running Windows 7.

- DVD/CD authoring requires a compatible optical drive. [If you want to burn something to an optical disc, you need a drive that can burn discs.]

- Windows XP Mode requires an additional 1 GB of RAM and an additional 15 GB of available hard disk space.

Windows 7 is also designed to handle multiple CPU cores and multiple CPUs. Many, if not most, modern computers use multicore processors. The 32-bit editions of Windows 7 can handle up to 32 processor cores, making it an easy fact to remember for the exams. The 64-bit editions of Windows 7 support up to 256 processor cores.

In terms of multiple physical processors (found on high-end PCs), Windows 7 Professional, Ultimate, and Enterprise can handle two CPUs, whereas Windows 7 Starter and Home Premium support only one CPU.

EXAM TIP In this chapter, you've learned some of the different installation procedures for Windows XP, Windows Vista, and Windows 7. Keeping them straight can be hard, but if you want to avoid being tricked on the CompTIA A+ exams, you must be able to. Review the procedures and then make sure you can identify the points of similarity and, more importantly, the differences among the three.

Upgrading Issues

A few extra steps before you pop in that installation disc are worth your time. If you plan to upgrade rather than perform a clean installation, follow these steps first:

1. Remember to check hardware and software compatibility as explained earlier in the chapter.

2. Have an up-to-date backup of your data and configuration files handy.

3. Perform a "spring cleaning" on your system by uninstalling unused or unnecessary applications and deleting old files.

4. Perform a disk scan (error-checking) and a disk defragmentation.

5. Uncompress all files, folders, and partitions.

6. Perform a virus scan, and then remove or disable all virus-checking software.

7. Disable virus checking in your system CMOS.

8. Keep in mind that if worse comes to worst, you may have to start over and do a clean installation anyway. This makes step 2 exceedingly important. Back up your data!

The Windows XP Clean Installation Process

A clean installation begins with your system set to boot to your optical drive and the Windows installation disc in the drive. You start your PC and the installation program loads (see Figure 14-5). Note at the bottom that it says to press F6 for a third-party SCSI or RAID driver. You only do this if you want to install Windows onto a strange drive and Windows does not already have the driver for that drive controller. Don't worry about this; Windows has a huge assortment of drivers for just about every hard drive ever made, and in the rare situation where you need a third-party driver, the folks who sell you the SCSI or RAID array will tell you ahead of time.

 NOTE When dealing with RAID (in any version of Windows), make sure you have the latest drivers on hand for the installation. Put them on a thumb drive just in case the Windows installer can't detect your RAID setup.

After the system copies a number of files, you'll see the Welcome to Setup screen (see Figure 14-6). This is an important screen! As you'll see in later chapters, techs often use the Windows installation disc as a repair tool, and this is the screen that lets you choose between installing Windows or repairing an existing installation. Because you're making a new install, just press ENTER.

Windows Setup

Press F6 if you need to install a third party SCSI or RAID driver...

Figure 14-5 Windows Setup text screen

NOTE Not all screens in the installation process are shown!

Windows XP Professional Setup

Welcome to Setup.

This portion of the Setup program prepares Microsoft(R)
Windows(R) XP to run on your computer.

 • To set up Windows XP now, press ENTER.

 • To repair a Windows XP installation using
 Recovery Console, press R.

 • To quit Setup without installing Windows XP, press F3.

ENTER=Continue R=Repair F3=Quit

Figure 14-6 Welcome text screen

You're now prompted to read and accept the EULA. Nobody ever reads this—it would give you a stomachache were you to see what you're really agreeing to—so just press F8 and move to the next screen to start partitioning the drive (see Figure 14-7).

```
Windows XP Professional Setup

    The following list shows the existing partitions and
    unpartitioned space on this computer.

    Use the UP and DOWN ARROW keys to select an item in the list.

        • To set up Windows XP on the selected item, press ENTER.

        • To create a partition in the unpartitioned space, press C.

        • To delete the selected partition, press D.

    8190 MB Disk 0 at Id 0 on bus 0 on atapi [MBR]
            Unpartitioned space                    8189 MB

    ENTER=Install   C=Create Partition   F3=Quit
```

Figure 14-7 Partitioning text screen

If your hard disk is unpartitioned, you need to create a new partition when prompted. Follow the instructions. In most cases, you can make a single partition, although you can easily make as many partitions as you wish. You can also delete partitions if you're using a hard drive that was partitioned in the past (or if you mess up your partitioning). Note that there is no option to make a primary or extended partition; this tool makes the first partition primary and the rest extended.

After you've made the partition(s), you must select the partition on which to install Windows XP (sort of trivial if you only have one partition), and then you need to decide which file system format to use for the new partition.

 NOTE Many techie types, at least those with big (> 500 GB) hard drives, only partition half of their hard drive for Windows. This makes it easy for them to install an alternative OS (usually Linux) at a later date.

Unless you have some weird need to support FAT or FAT32, format the partition by using NTFS (see Figure 14-8).

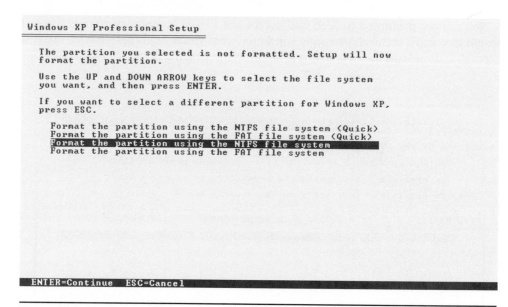

```
Windows XP Professional Setup

The partition you selected is not formatted. Setup will now
format the partition.

Use the UP and DOWN ARROW keys to select the file system
you want, and then press ENTER.

If you want to select a different partition for Windows XP,
press ESC.

     Format the partition using the NTFS file system (Quick)
     Format the partition using the FAT file system (Quick)
     Format the partition using the NTFS file system
     Format the partition using the FAT file system
```

```
   ENTER=Continue   ESC=Cancel
```

Figure 14-8 Choosing NTFS

Setup now formats the drive and copies some basic installation files to the newly formatted partition, displaying another progress bar. Go get a book to read while you wait.

After it completes copying the base set of files to the hard drive, your computer reboots, and the graphical mode of Windows Setup begins.

You will see a generic screen during the installation that looks like Figure 14-9. On the left of the screen, uncompleted tasks have a white button, completed tasks have a green button, and the current task has a red button. You'll get plenty of advertising to read as you install.

Figure 14-9

Beginning of graphical mode

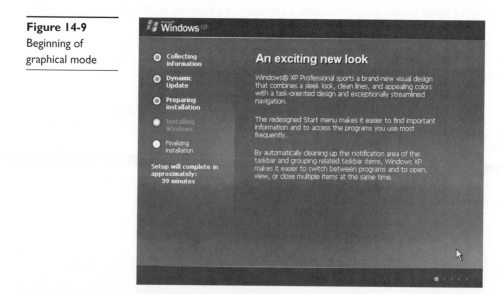

The following screens ask questions about a number of things the computer needs to know. They include the desired region and language the computer will operate in, your name and organization for personalizing your computer, and a valid *product key* for Windows XP (see Figure 14-10). The product key helps reduce piracy of the software. Be sure to enter the product key exactly, or you will be unable to continue.

Figure 14-10 Product key

> **NOTE** Losing your product key is a bad idea! Document it—at least write it on the installation disc.

Next, you need to give your computer a name that will identify it on a network. Check with your system administrator for an appropriate name. If you don't have a system administrator, just enter a simple name such as MYPC for now—you can change this at any time. You also need to create a password for the Administrator user account (see Figure 14-11). Every Windows system has an Administrator user account that can do anything on the computer. Techs will need this account to modify and fix the computer in the future.

The final message in the installation process reminds you that you have 30 days left for activation. Go ahead and activate now over the Internet or by telephone. It's painless and quick. If you choose not to activate, simply click the Close button on the message balloon. That's it! You have successfully installed Windows XP and should have a desktop with the default Bliss background, as shown in Figure 14-14.

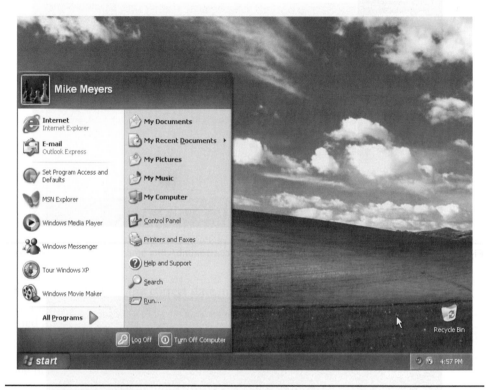

Figure 14-14 Windows XP desktop with Bliss background

The Windows Vista/7 Clean Installation Process

With Windows Vista, Microsoft dramatically changed the installation process. No longer will you spend your time looking at a boring blue ASCII screen and entering commands by keyboard. The Vista installer—and the installer in Windows 7 as well—has a full graphical interface, making it easy to partition drives and install your operating system. You already saw some of this process back in Chapter 12, but this chapter will go into a bit more detail.

The installation methods for Windows Vista and Windows 7 are so close to identical that it would be silly to address them as separate entries in this book (see Figure 14-15). Only the splash screens and the product-key entry dialog box have changed between Windows Vista and Windows 7! Because of this trivial difference, showing the installation process for both operating systems would waste paper. This walkthrough uses the Windows Vista screenshots just because you might never see them anywhere else.

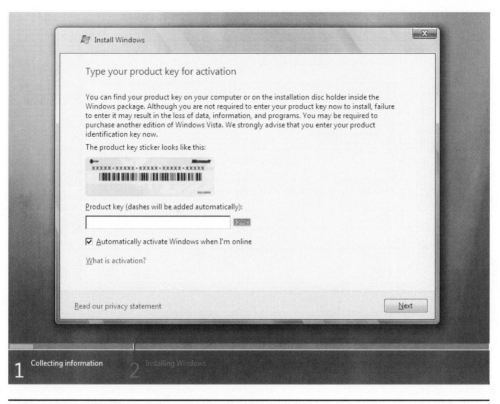

Figure 14-18 The Windows Vista product key screen

Microsoft has dramatically altered the method they use to distribute different editions of their operating system; instead of having different discs for each edition of Windows Vista or Windows 7, every installation disc contains all of the available editions (except for Enterprise). In Windows XP, your product key did very little besides let the installation disc know that you had legitimately purchased the OS. In Windows Vista and Windows 7, your product key not only verifies the legitimacy of your purchase; it also tells the installer which edition you purchased, which, when you think about it, is a lot to ask of a randomly generated string of numbers and letters.

If you leave the product key blank and click the Next button, you will be taken to a screen asking you which version of Windows Vista you would like to install (see Figure 14-19). (Windows 7, however, disables this option—while every version is on the disc, you can only install the edition named on the box or disc label.) And lest you start to think that you've discovered a way to install Windows without paying for it, you should know that doing this simply installs a 30-day trial of the operating system. After 30 days, you will no longer be able to boot to the desktop without entering a valid product key that matches the edition of Windows Vista/7 you installed.

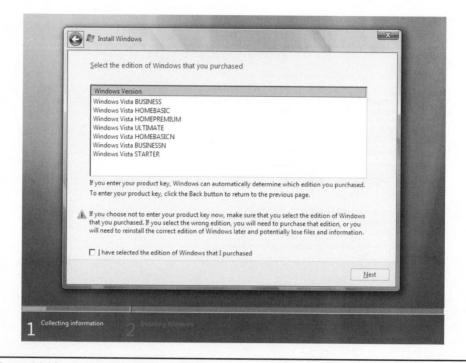

Figure 14-19 Choose the edition of Vista you want to install.

After the product key screen, you'll find Microsoft's new and improved EULA, shown in Figure 14-20, which you can skip unless you're interested in seeing what's changed in the world of obtuse legalese since the release of Windows XP.

On the next page, you get to decide whether you'd like to do an upgrade installation or a clean installation (see Figure 14-21). As you learned earlier, you have to begin the Vista/7 installation process from within an older OS to use the Upgrade option, so this option will be dimmed for you if you've booted off of the installation disc. To do a clean installation of Vista/7, edit your partitions, and just generally install the OS like a pro, you choose the Custom (advanced) option.

You may remember the next screen, shown in Figure 14-22, from Chapter 12. This is the screen where you can partition your hard drives and choose to which partition you'll install Windows. From this screen, you can click the *Drive options (advanced)* link to display a variety of partitioning options, and you can click the Load Driver button to load alternative, third-party drivers. The process of loading drivers is much more intuitive than in Windows XP: you just browse to the location of the drivers you want by using Windows' very familiar browsing window (see Figure 14-23).

Figure 14-20 The Vista EULA

Figure 14-21 Choose your installation type.

Figure 14-22 The partitioning screen

Of course, you will most likely never have to load drivers for a drive, and if it is ever necessary, your drive will almost certainly come with a driver disc and documentation telling you that you'll have to load the drivers.

Once you've partitioned your drives and selected a partition on which to install Windows, the installation process takes over, copying files, expanding files, installing features, and just generally doing lots of computerish things. This can take a while, so if you need to get a snack or read *War and Peace*, do it during this part of the installation.

NOTE It doesn't take *that* long to install Windows Vista. Windows 7 installation is even snappier.

When Vista/7 has finished unpacking and installing itself, it asks you to choose a user name and picture (see Figure 14-24). This screen also asks you set up a password for your main user account, which is definitely a good idea if you're going to have multiple people using the computer.

After picking your user name and password, and letting Windows know how much you like pictures of kitties, you're taken to a screen where you can type in a computer name (see Figure 14-25). By default, Windows makes your computer name the same as your user name but with "-PC" appended to it, which in most cases is fine.

Figure 14-23 Browse for drivers.

Figure 14-24 Choose a user picture.

Figure 14-25 Choose your computer name.

This is also the screen where you can change the desktop background that Windows will start up with. You can change this easily later on, so pick whatever you like and click the Next button.

At this point, Windows 7 will ask for your product activation key. On Windows Vista, you did this at the beginning of the installation.

The next page asks you how you want to set up Windows Automatic Updates (see Figure 14-26). Most users want to choose the top option, *Use recommended settings*, as it provides the most hassle-free method for updating your computer. The middle option, *Install important updates only*, installs only the most critical security fixes and updates and leaves the rest of the updates up to you. This is useful when setting up computers for businesses, as many companies' IT departments like to test out any updates before rolling them out to the employees. You should only select the last option, *Ask me later*, if you can dedicate yourself to checking weekly for updates, as it will not install any automatically.

Next up is the time and date screen, where you can make sure your operating system knows what time it is, as in Figure 14-27. This screen should be pretty self-explanatory, so set the correct time zone, the correct date, and the correct time, and move to the next screen.

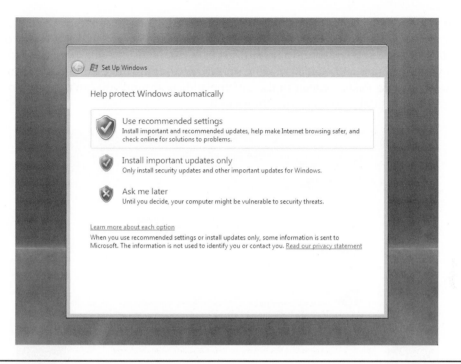

Figure 14-26 The automatic updates screen

Figure 14-27 Vista pities the fool who doesn't know what time it is.

If you have your computer connected to a network while running the installer, the next screen will ask you about your current location (see Figure 14-28). If you're on a trusted network, such as your home or office network, make the appropriate selection and your computer will be discoverable on the network. If you're on, say, a Starbucks' network, choose *Public location* so the caffeine addicts around you can't see your computer and potentially do malicious things to it.

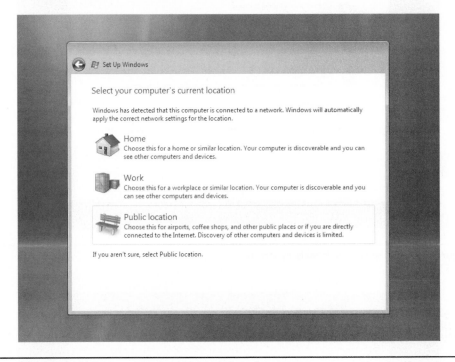

Figure 14-28 Tell Windows what kind of network you're on.

Once you're past that screen, Windows thanks you for installing it (see Figure 14-29), which is awfully polite for a piece of software, don't you think?

Lest you think you're completely out of the woods, Windows will run some tests on your computer to give it a performance rating, which, in theory, will tell you how well programs will run on your computer. You'll sometimes see minimum performance ratings on the sides of game boxes, but even then, you're more likely to need plain, old-fashioned minimum system requirements. This process can take anywhere from 5 to 20 minutes, so this is another one of those coffee-break moments in the installation process.

Once the performance test finishes, Windows Vista or Windows 7 boots up and you have 30 days to activate your new operating system.

TIP When it comes right down to it, you don't really need a performance rating on your computer. If you don't want to waste your time, you can use the ALT-F4 keyboard shortcut to skip this step.

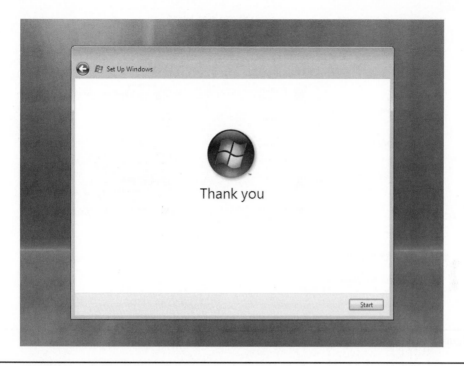

Figure 14-29 Aw, shucks, Microsoft Windows Vista. Don't mention it.

Automating the Installation

As you can see, you may have to sit around for quite a while when installing Windows. Instead of sitting there answering questions and typing in product keys, wouldn't it be nice just to boot up the machine and have the installation process finish without any intervention on your part—especially if you have 30 PCs that need to be ready to go tomorrow morning? Fortunately, Windows offers two good options for automating the installation process: scripted installations and disk cloning.

Scripting Windows XP Installations with Setup Manager

For automating a Windows XP install, Microsoft provides *Setup Manager* to help you create a text file—called an *answer file*—containing all of your answers to the installation questions. This enables you to do an *unattended installation*, which means you don't have to sit in front of each computer throughout the installation process.

You can find Setup Manager on the Windows installation disc in the \Support\Tools folder. Double-click the DEPLOY cabinet file, and then right-click setupmgr.cab and select Extract (see Figure 14-30). Choose a location for the file.

Figure 14-30 Extracting Setup Manager from the DEPLOY cabinet file

Setup Manager supports creating answer files for three types of setups: Unattended, Sysprep, and Remote Installation Services (see Figure 14-31). The latest version of the tool can create answer files for Windows XP Home Edition, Windows XP Professional, and Windows .NET (Standard, Enterprise, or Web Server); see Figure 14-32.

Figure 14-31
Setup Manager can create answer files for three types of setups.

Figure 14-32
Setup Manager can create answer files for five versions of Windows.

Setup Manager can create an answer file to completely automate the process, or you can use it to set default options. You'll almost always want to create an answer file that automates the entire process (see Figure 14-33).

Figure 14-33
Setup Manager can create several kinds of answer files.

When running a scripted installation, you have to decide how to make the installation files themselves available to the PC. Although you can boot your new machine from an installation CD, you can save yourself a lot of CD swapping if you just put the installation files on a network share and install your OS over the network (see Figure 14-34).

Figure 14-34
Choose where to store the installation files.

Figure 14-35
Don't forget to accept the license agreement.

When you run Setup Manager, you get to answer all those pesky questions. As always, you will also have to "accept the terms of the License Agreement" (see Figure 14-35) and specify the product key (see Figure 14-36), but at least by scripting these steps you can do it once and get it over with.

Figure 14-36 Enter the product key.

Now it's time to get to the good stuff, customizing your installation. Using the graphical interface, decide what configuration options you want to use: screen resolutions, network options, browser settings, regional settings, and so on. You can even add finishing touches to the installation, installing additional programs such as Microsoft Office and Adobe Reader by automatically running additional commands after the Windows installation finishes (see Figure 14-37). You can also set programs to run once (see Figure 14-38).

Figure 14-37 Running additional commands

Figure 14-38 Running a program once

Remember that computer names must be unique on the network. If you're going to use the same answer files for multiple machines on the same network, you need to make sure that each machine gets its own unique name. You can either provide a list of names to use, or have the Setup program randomly generate names (see Figure 14-39).

Figure 14-39 Pick your computer names.

When you're finished, Setup Manager prompts you to save your answers as a text file. The contents of the file will look something like this:

```
;SetupMgrTag
[Data]
    AutoPartition=1
    MsDosInitiated="0"
    UnattendedInstall="Yes"

[Unattended]
    UnattendMode=FullUnattended
    OemSkipEula=Yes
    OemPreinstall=No
    TargetPath=\WINDOWS

[GuiUnattended]
    AdminPassword=414c11f760b0064 ... [out to 64 characters]
    EncryptedAdminPassword=Yes
    OEMSkipRegional=1
    TimeZone=85
    OemSkipWelcome=1
    AutoLogon=Yes
    AutoLogonCount=1

[UserData]
    ProductKey=FFFFF-FFFFF-FFFFF-FFFFF-FFFFF
    FullName="Scott"
    OrgName="Total Seminars"
    ComputerName=*

[Identification]
    JoinDomain=TOTAL
    DomainAdmin=admin09
    DomainAdminPassword=my-password
```

The list goes on for another hundred lines or so, and this is a fairly simple answer file. One thing to note is that if you provide a domain administrator's user name and password for the purpose of automatically adding new PCs to your domain, that user name and password will be in the text file in clear text:

```
[Identification]
    JoinDomain=TOTAL
    DomainAdmin=admin09
    DomainAdminPassword=my-password
```

In that case, you will want to be very careful about protecting your setup files.

Once you have your answer file created, you can start your installation with this command, and go enjoy a nice cup of coffee while the installation runs:

```
D:\i386\winnt32 /s:%SetupFiles% /unattend:%AnswerFile%
```

For %SetupFiles%, substitute the location of your setup files—either a local path (D:\i386 if you are installing from a CD) or a network path. If you use a network path, don't forget to create a network boot disk so that the installation program can access the files. For %AnswerFile%, substitute the name of the text file you created with Setup Manager (usually unattend.txt).

Of course, you don't have to use Setup Manager to create your answer file. Feel free to pull out your favorite text editor and write one from scratch. Most techs, however, find it much easier to use the provided tool than to wrestle with the answer file's sometimes arcane syntax.

Automating a Windows Vista or Windows 7 Installation with the Automated Installation Kit

As of Windows Vista and Windows 7, Setup Manager is history—as is any method of automating an installation that isn't extremely complicated and intimidating. Microsoft has replaced Setup Manager with the Windows Automated Installation Kit (AIK), a set of tools that, although quite powerful, seems to have made something of a Faustian deal to obtain that power at the expense of usability (see Figure 14-40).

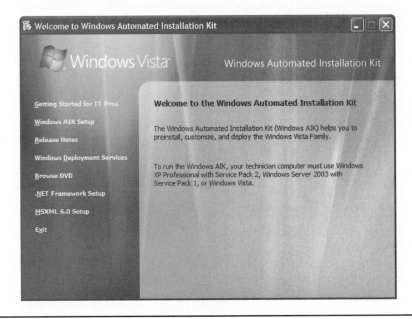

Figure 14-40 The Automated Installation Kit

Writing a step-by-step guide to creating an answer file in the AIK would almost warrant its own chapter, and as the CompTIA A+ exams don't cover it at all, I'm not going to go into too much gory detail. I will, however, give a brief account of the process involved.

The basic idea behind the AIK is that a tech can create an answer file by using a tool called the Windows System Image Manager, and then use that answer file to build a Master Installation file that can be burned to DVD. Vista/7's answer files are no longer simple text documents but .XML files, and the process of creating one is more complicated than it used to be. Gone are the days of simply running a wizard and modifying

options as you see fit. Instead, you choose components (which represent the things you want your automated installation to do, such as create a partition, enter a certain product key, and much, much more) out of a huge, often baffling list and then modify their settings (see Figure 14-41).

Figure 14-41
The list of compo-
nents in the Image
Monitor

Once you've selected and modified all of the components you're interested in, you have to save your answer file, copy it to a USB thumb drive, and plug that into a new computer on which you're going to install Vista/7. When you boot a computer off of the installation disc, it automatically searches all removable media for an answer file, and,

finding one, uses it to automatically install itself. If you're only installing Vista/7 to this one computer, you're finished, but if you want to install it to multiple computers, you'll probably want to create a disc image based off of your Master Installation file.

To create such an image, you must use two more tools in the AIK—Windows PE and ImageX—to "capture" the installation and create a disc image from it. If the rest of the process seemed a bit complicated, this part is like solving a Rubik's cube with your teeth while balancing on top of a flagpole and juggling. Suffice it to say that the AIK comes with documentation that tells you how to do this, so with a bit of patience, you can get through it.

Disk Cloning

Disk cloning simply takes an existing PC and makes a full copy of the drive, including all data, software, and configuration files. You can then transfer that copy to as many machines as you like, essentially creating clones of the original machine. In the old days, making a clone was pretty simple. You just hooked up two hard drives and copied the files from the original to the clone by using something like the venerable XCOPY program (as long as the hard drive was formatted with FAT or FAT32). Today, you'll want to use a more sophisticated program, such as Norton Ghost, to make an image file that contains a copy of an entire hard drive and then lets you copy that image either locally or over a network.

 NOTE Norton Ghost is not the only disk imaging software out there, but it is so widely used that techs often refer to disk cloning as "ghosting the drive."

Sysprep

Cloning a Windows PC works great for some situations, but what if you need to send the same image out to machines that have slightly different hardware? What if you need the customer to go through the final steps of the Windows installation (creating a user account, accepting the license agreement, etc.)? That's when you need to combine a scripted setup with cloning by using the System Preparation Tool, *Sysprep*, which can undo portions of the Windows installation process.

After installing Windows and adding any additional software (Microsoft Office, Adobe Acrobat, Yahoo Instant Messenger, etc.), run Sysprep (see Figure 14-42) and then create your disk image by using the cloning application of your choice. The first time a new system cloned from the image boots, an abbreviated version of setup, Mini-Setup, runs and completes the last few steps of the installation process: installing drivers for hardware, prompting the user to accept the license agreement and create user accounts, and so on. Optionally, you can use Setup Manager to create an answer file to customize Mini-Setup, just as you would with a standard scripted installation.

■ System Preparation Tool 2.0

⚠ Running System Preparation Tool (Sysprep) can modify this computer's security settings.

If allowed under your license agreement, you may use Sysprep to prepare an installation of Windows that you can deploy to multiple destination computers.

After you run Sysprep, Windows will automatically shut down.

[OK] [Cancel]

Figure 14-42 Sysprep, the System Preparation Tool

Installing Windows over a Network

Techs working for big corporations can end up installing Windows a lot. When you have a hundred PCs to take care of and Microsoft launches a new version of Windows, you don't want to have to walk from cubicle to cubicle with an installation disc, running one install after the other. You already know about automated installations, but network installations take this one step further.

Imagine another scenario. You're still a tech for a large company, but your boss has decided that every new PC will use an image with a predetermined set of applications and configurations. You need to put the image on every workstation, but most of them don't have optical drives. Network installation saves the day again!

The phrase "network installation" can involve many different tools depending on which version of Windows you use. Most importantly, the machines that receive the installations (the clients) need to be connected to a server. That server might be another copy of Windows XP, Vista, or 7; or it might be a fully fledged server running Windows Server 2003, 2008, or 2008 R2. The serving PC needs to host an image, which can be either the default installation of Windows or a custom image, often created by the network administrator.

 NOTE Windows Server 2003 uses Remote Installation Services to enable network installations, while Windows Server 2008 and 2008 R2 use Windows Deployment Services, as mentioned earlier in the chapter. Both services combine several powerful tools that enable you to customize and send installation files over the network to the client PC. These tools are aimed more at enterprise networks dealing in hundreds of PCs and are managed by network professionals.

All of the server-side issues should be handled by a network administrator—setting up a server to deploy Windows installations and images goes beyond what the CompTIA A+ exams cover.

PXE

On the client side, you'll need to use the *Preboot Execution Environment* (*PXE*). PXE uses multiple protocols such as IP, DHCP, and DNS to enable your computer to boot from a network location. That means the PC needs no installation disc or USB drive. Just plug your computer into the network and go! Okay, it's a little more complicated than that.

Booting with PXE To enable PXE, you'll need to enter your BIOS System Setup. Find the screen that configures your NIC (which changes depending on your particular BIOS). If there is a PXE setting there, enable it. You'll also need to change the boot order so that the PC boots from a network location first.

NOTE Not every NIC supports PXE. To boot from a network location without PXE, you can create boot media that forces your PC to boot from a network location.

When you reboot the PC, you'll see the familiar first screens of the boot process. At some point, you should also see an instruction to "Press F12 for network boot." (It's almost always F12.) The PC will attempt to find a server on the network to which it can connect. When it does, you'll be asked to press F12 again to continue booting from the network, as you can see in Figure 14-43.

```
Network boot from Intel E1000
Copyright (C) 2003-2008  VMware, Inc.
Copyright (C) 1997-2000  Intel Corporation

CLIENT MAC ADDR: 00 0C 29 D7 9B 6B  GUID: 564DCC2E-04EA-ACE1-381B-5148E8D79B6B
CLIENT IP: 10.12.14.51  MASK: 255.0.0.0  DHCP IP: 10.12.14.10
GATEWAY IP: 10.12.14.1

Downloaded WDSNBP...

Press F12 for network service boot
_
```

Figure 14-43 Network boot

Depending on how many images are prepared on the server, you'll either be taken directly to the Windows installation screen or be asked to pick from multiple images. Pick the option you need, and everything else should proceed as if you were installing Windows from the local optical drive.

Troubleshooting Installation Problems

The term "installation problem" is rather deceptive. The installation process itself almost never fails. Usually, something else fails during the process that is generally interpreted as an "install failure." Let's look at some typical installation problems and how to correct them.

Text Mode Errors

If you're going to have a problem with a Windows XP installation, this is the place to get one. It's always better to have the error right off the bat as opposed to when the installation is nearly complete. Text mode errors most often take place during clean installations and usually point to one of the following problems:

RAID Array Not Detected

If Windows fails to detect a RAID array during the text mode portion of the Windows XP installation, this could be caused by Windows not having the proper driver for the hard drive or RAID controller. If the hard drives show up properly in the RAID controller setup utility, then it's almost certainly a driver issue. Get the driver disc from the manufacturer and run setup again. Press F6 when prompted very early in the Windows XP installation process. Nothing happens right away when you push F6, but later in the process you'll be prompted to install.

No Boot Device Present When Booting Off the Windows Installation Disc

Either the startup disc is bad or the CMOS is not set to look at that optical drive first.

Windows Setup Requires XXXX Amount of Available Drive Space

There's a bunch of stuff on the drive already.

Not Ready Error on Optical Drive

You probably just need to give the optical drive a moment to catch up. Press R for retry a few times. You may also have a damaged installation disc, or the optical drive may be too slow for the system.

A Stop Error (Blue Screen of Death) After the Reboot at the End of Text Mode

This may mean you didn't do your homework in checking hardware compatibility, especially the BIOS. I'll tell you more about stop errors in Chapter 19, but if you encounter one of these errors during installation, check out the Microsoft Knowledge Base.

Graphical Mode Errors

Graphical mode errors are found in all versions of Windows and can cause a whole new crop of problems to arise.

When you click Next, you're taken to a screen that asks if you want to start a new transfer or continue an old one (see Figure 14-51). If you've already set up your old computer to transfer the files, select the latter option; if you haven't, select the former.

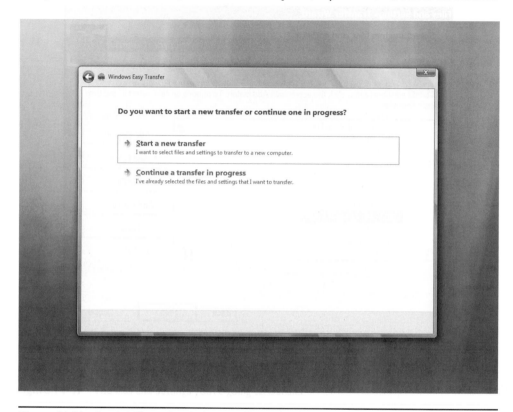

Figure 14-51 Start a new transfer or continue one?

If you choose to start a new transfer, the process is very similar to the Files and Settings Transfer Wizard: you select whether you're using your new or old computer and then follow the same basic steps as before. There are some differences, of course—network security is improved by using Transfer Keys to protect your files from others on the network, there's an option to use a special Easy Transfer Cable to transfer your files between USB ports, and the order of some screens is changed around a bit—but if you understand the Files and Settings Transfer Wizard transfer process, Windows Easy Transfer shouldn't be too difficult.

Migration Practices

When talking about migration or retirement in terms of security, you need to answer one question: What do you do with the old system or drive?

All but the most vanilla new installations have sensitive data on them, even if it's simply e-mail messages or notes-to-self that would cause embarrassment if discovered. Most PCs, especially in a work environment, contain a lot of sensitive data. You can't just format C: and hand over the drive.

Follow three principles when migrating or retiring a computer. First, migrate your users and data information in a secure environment. Until you get passwords properly in place and test the security of the new system, you can't consider that system secure. Second, remove data remnants from hard drives that you store or give to charity. Third, recycle the older equipment; don't throw it in the trash. PC recyclers go through a process of deconstructing hardware, breaking system units, keyboards, printers, and even monitors into their basic plastics, metals, and glass for reuse.

The easiest way for someone to compromise or access sensitive data is to simply walk up and take it when you're not looking. This is especially true when you are in the process of copying information to a new, unprotected system. Don't set a copy to run while you go out to lunch, but rather be there to supervise and remove any remnant data that might still reside on any mass storage devices, especially hard drives.

Data Destruction

You might think that, as easy as it seems to be to lose data, you could readily get rid of data if you tried. That's not the case with flash memory or magnetic media, though, such as hard drives. When you delete something in Windows, or even empty the Recycle Bin, the "deleted" data remains on your storage device until new data overwrites it, or replaces it. (This "deleted" data is also what you see as free space in Windows.) This can be a big security hole when you dispose of a drive.

Cleaning a drive completely is very difficult. You can either physically destroy the hard drive or *sanitize* it using a software utility. Physical destruction isn't complicated—you bust up the drive into tiny little bits. Tools to accomplish this include drive shredders, drills, electromagnets, and degaussing tools (which reduce or remove the magnetic fields that store data on HDDs). Keep in mind that, as hard drives advance and pack more data into smaller spaces, you'll need to break the hard drive into smaller pieces to prevent anyone from recovering your data.

Sanitizing your drive means that the hard drive will still function once the data has been destroyed. There are several more or less effective ways to do this.

The CompTIA A+ exams want you to know the difference between a standard format and a *low-level format*. You already learned about standard formatting back in Chapter 12, so how is low-level formatting different? With older drives (pre-1990s), low-level formatting would create the physical marks on the disk surface so that the drive knew where to store data; in the process, it erases the data from the drive. This was initially done at the factory, but utilities existed to repeat this operation later. As drives became more complex, hard drive manufacturers disabled the ability to perform low-level formats outside the factory.

Today, the term "low-level formatting" is often used to describe a *zero-fill* or *overwrite* operation. This process returns the drive to a state as close to like-new as possible by writing zeros to every location on the disk.

You can also use a *drive wiping* utility to erase any old, deleted data that hasn't been overwritten yet. Simply put, this overwrites the free space on your drive with junk data that is more difficult to restore. Piriform's CCleaner is a data sanitizing utility that can erase your Web browsing history, erase your recent activity in Windows (such as what programs you ran), and even scrub your hard drive's free space to make deleted file unrecoverable (see Figure 14-52).

Figure 14-52 Piriform's CCleaner showing files to be removed

Recycle

An important and relatively easy way to be an environmentally conscious computer user is to *recycle*. Recycling products such as paper and printer cartridges not only keeps them out of overcrowded landfills, but also ensures that the more toxic products are disposed of in the right way. Safely disposing of hardware containing hazardous materials, such as computer monitors, protects both people and the environment.

Anyone who's ever tried to sell a computer more than three or four years old learns a hard lesson: they're not worth much, if anything at all. It's a real temptation to take that old computer and just toss it in the garbage, but never do that!

First of all, many parts of your computer—such as your computer monitor—contain hazardous materials that pollute the environment. Luckily, thousands of companies now specialize in computer recycling and will gladly accept your old computer. If you

have enough computers, they might even pick them up. If you can't find a recycler, call your local municipality's waste authority to see where to drop off your system.

An even better alternative for your old computer is donation. Many organizations actively look for old computers to refurbish and to donate to schools and other organizations. Just keep in mind that the computer can be too old—not even a school wants a computer more than five or six years old.

No Installation Is Perfect

Even when the installation seems smooth, issues may slowly surface, especially in the case of upgrades. Be prepared to reinstall applications or deal with new functions that were absent in the previous OS. If things really fall apart, you can go back to the previous OS or, if you have an OEM computer (one built by, for example, Dell or HP instead of by you), your computer likely came with either a special recovery partition on its hard drive or a set of recovery discs that you can utilize to restore your operating system to its factory settings. You usually invoke a system recovery by hitting a certain key during boot-up—usually F10 or F11—and then following a set of prompts.

The procedures I've laid out in this chapter may seem like a lot of work—how bad could it be to grab an installation disc, fling a copy of Windows onto a system, and, as the saying goes, let the chips fall where they may? Plenty bad, is how bad. Not only is understanding these procedures important for the CompTIA A+ certification exams; these procedures can also save your, ah, hide, once you're a working PC tech and you're tasked to install the latest version of Windows on the boss's new computer!

Chapter Review

Questions

1. Which of the following is an advantage of running Windows on NTFS as opposed to FAT32?

 A. Security

 B. Support for DOS applications

 C. Long filenames

 D. Network support

2. Ricardo's Windows XP installation has failed. What file should he check to see what files failed to copy?

 A. Install.log

 B. Setup.log

 C. Setup.txt

 D. Setuplog.txt

3. If you do not complete the activation process for Windows, what will happen to your computer?

 A. Nothing. Activation is optional.

 B. The computer will work fine for 30 days and then Windows will be disabled.

 C. Microsoft will not know how to contact you to provide upgrade information.

 D. You will have to use a floppy disk set to boot to Windows.

4. If Windows locks up during the installation, what should you do?

 A. Press CTRL-ALT-DEL to restart the installation process.

 B. Push the Reset button to restart the installation process.

 C. Press the ESC key to cancel the installation process.

 D. Unplug the computer and restart the installation process.

5. You can *upgrade* directly to Windows 7 from which of these operating systems?

 A. Windows 2000

 B. Windows XP

 C. Windows Vista

 D. All of the above

6. The Windows XP disc contains which two tools for checking hardware and software compatibility?

 A. The HCL and the HAL

 B. The HCL and the Windows Catalog

 C. The Windows Catalog and the Upgrade Advisor

 D. The Upgrade Advisor and the HCL

7. Which term describes a combination of many updates and fixes?

 A. Hot fix

 B. Hot pack

 C. Service pack

 D. Service release

8. Which of the following tools can help you more efficiently install multiple copies of Windows 7?

 A. Automated Installation Kit

 B. Windows Easy Transfer

 C. Upgrade Advisor

 D. Activation key

Windows Under the Hood

In this chapter, you will learn how to

- Work with the Registry
- Understand and observe in detail the Windows boot process
- Control processes and services
- Explore Windows tools for programmers

Windows is powerful, easy to use, surprisingly idiot proof, backward compatible, and robust. A large part of Windows' power is hidden—*under the hood*—in programs and processes that Microsoft doesn't want normal users to see. For the record, I think hiding anything that normal users don't need to access is a smart idea; they can't break what they can't find. Technicians, on the other hand, need to not only understand these processes and programs but also know how to use them, configure them, and fix them when needed. Let's start with one of the most famous and most important items under the hood: the Registry.

802

Registry

The *Registry* is a huge database that stores everything about your PC, including information on all of the hardware in the PC, network information, user preferences, file types, and virtually anything else you might run into with Windows. Almost any form of configuration you do to a Windows system involves editing the Registry. Every version of Windows stores the numerous Registry files (called *hives*) in the \%SystemRoot%\ System32\config folder and each user account folder. Fortunately, you rarely have to access these massive files directly. Instead, you can use a set of relatively tech-friendly applications to edit the Registry.

The CompTIA A+ 220-802 certification exam does not expect you to memorize every aspect of the Windows Registry. You should, however, understand the basic components of the Registry, know how to edit the Registry manually, and know the best way to locate a particular setting.

Accessing the Registry

Before you look in the Registry, let's look at how you access the Registry directly by using a Registry editor. Once you know that, you can open the Registry on your machine and compare what you see to the examples in this chapter.

Before Windows XP, Windows came with two Registry editors: regedt32.exe and the much older regedit.exe. You started either of these programs by going to a command prompt and typing its filename.

The reason for having two different Registry editors is long and boring, and explaining it would require a very dull 15-minute monologue about how the Registry worked in Windows 9x and Windows NT. Suffice it to say that starting with Windows XP, Microsoft eliminated the entire two-Registry-editor nonsense by creating a new regedt32 that includes strong search functions. No longer are there two separate programs, but interestingly, entering either regedit or regedt32 at a command prompt (or in the Start | Run dialog box or Start | Search bar) brings up the same program, so feel free to use either program name. You may also dispense with calling the Registry Editor by its filename and use its proper title.

 EXAM TIP You might see either regedit or regedt32 on the exam as the way to access the Registry Editor.

Registry Components

The Registry is organized in a tree structure similar to the folders in the PC. Once you open the Registry Editor in Windows, you will see five main subgroups, or *root keys*:

- HKEY_CLASSES_ROOT
- HKEY_CURRENT_USER
- HKEY_USERS
- HKEY_LOCAL_MACHINE
- HKEY_CURRENT_CONFIG

Try opening one of these root keys by clicking on the plus sign to its left; note that more subkeys are listed underneath. A subkey also can have other subkeys, or *values*. Values define aspects of the subkey. Figure 15-1 shows an example of a subkey with some values. Notice that the Registry Editor shows only keys—root keys and subkeys—on the left and values on the right. Each of the root keys has a specific function, so let's take a look at them individually.

HKEY_CLASSES_ROOT

This root key defines the standard *class objects* used by Windows. A class object is a named group of functions that defines what you can do with the object it represents.

Pretty much everything that has to do with files on the system is defined by a class object. For example, the Registry uses two class objects to define the popular MP3 sound file.

Figure 15-1 Typical Registry root keys, subkeys, and values

If you search my computer's Registry for the .PDF file extension, you will find a class object that associates the .PDF file extension with the name "FoxitReader.Document" (see Figure 15-2). Unless you use the popular Foxit Reader for your PDFs, you'll see a different program name, but the process still works.

Name	Type	Data
(Default)	REG_SZ	FoxitReader.Document
Content Type	REG_SZ	application/pdf

Figure 15-2 Association of .PDF with Foxit Reader

So what are the properties of FoxitReader.Document? That's what the HKEY_CLASSES_ROOT root key is designed to handle. Search this section again for "FoxitReader.Document" (or whatever it said in the value for your PDF file) and look for a subkey called "open." This subkey tells the system everything it needs to know about a particular software item, from which program to use to open a file (its *file association*), to the type of icon used to show the file, to what to show when you right-click on that file type (see Figure 15-3).

Name	Type	Data
ab (Default)	REG_SZ	"C:\Program Files\Foxit Software\Foxit Reader\Foxit Reader.exe" "%1"

Figure 15-3 PDF file settings

Although it is possible to change most of these settings in the Registry Editor, the normal way is to choose more user-friendly methods. Select a data file, right-click on the data file, and click Properties. Click the Change button on the General tab to open the Open with dialog box. From there, you can select the program you want to use. If Windows knows of another program designed for that file type, it will show you these alternative programs. If not, you can simply browse for the program you want to use (see Figure 15-4).

Figure 15-4 Changing the file association the easy way

HKEY_CURRENT_USER and HKEY_USERS

Windows is designed to support more than one user on the same PC, storing personalized information such as desktop colors, screensavers, and the contents of the desktop for every user that has an account on the system. HKEY_CURRENT_USER stores the current user settings, and HKEY_USERS stores all of the personalized information for all users on a PC. While you certainly can change items such as the screensaver here, the better way is to right-click on the desktop and select Properties.

HKEY_LOCAL_MACHINE

This root key contains all the data for a system's non-user-specific configurations. This encompasses every device and every program in your PC.

HKEY_CURRENT_CONFIG

If the values in HKEY_LOCAL_MACHINE have more than one option, such as two different monitors, this root key defines which one is currently being used. Because most people have only one type of monitor and similar equipment, this area is almost never touched.

Talkin' Registry

When describing a Registry setting, we use a simple nomenclature. For example, I recently moved my copy of *World of Warcraft* from my C: drive to my D: drive and was having problems when the program started. I went online to www.blizzard.com (home of Blizzard Entertainment, the folks who make *World of Warcraft*) and contacted the support staff, who gave me instructions to access the Registry and make this change:

> "Go to HKLM\SOFTWARE\Blizzard Technologies\World of Warcraft and change the GamePath object and the InstallPath object to reflect the new drive letter of your new WoW location."

To do so, I fired up regedit. Using this nomenclature, I was able to find the location of these Registry settings. Figure 15-5 shows this location. Compare this image to the path described in the instructions from Blizzard. Note that HKEY_LOCAL_MACHINE is abbreviated as HKLM. You will see this abbreviation on the exam!

To describe the location of a specific Registry value, like where the Blizzard tech told me to go, requires a little bit of repetition. To wit, in the previous example, World of Warcraft is a subkey to Blizzard Technologies, which is in turn a subkey to the root key HKLM. The World of Warcraft subkey has four values. All keys have the (Default) value, so in this case the World of Warcraft subkey offers three functional values.

Values must have a defined type of data they store:

- **String value** These are the most flexible type of value and are very common. You can put any form of data in these.

- **Binary value** These values store nothing more than long strings of ones and zeros.

- **DWORD value** These values are like Binary values but are limited to exactly 32 bits.

- **QWORD value** These values are like Binary values but are limited to exactly 64 bits.

Figure 15-5 Editing the Registry to move World of Warcraft to a new drive

There are other types of values, but these four are used for 98 percent of all Registry entries.

Manual Registry Edits

There's little motivation for you to go into the Registry and make manual edits unless you've done some research that tells you to do so. When you do find yourself using the Registry Editor to access the Registry, you risk breaking things in Windows: applications might not start, utilities might not work, or worst of all, your computer might not boot. To prevent these problems, always make a backup of the Registry before you change anything. Once the backup is in a safe place (I like to use a thumb drive, personally), reboot the system to see if the changes you made had the desired result. If it worked, great. If not, you'll need to restore the old Registry settings using your backup. Let's watch this in action.

One of the more common manual Registry edits is to delete autostarting programs. I want to prevent three programs installed by my Logitech GamePanel keyboard and mouse from autostarting. The most common place for making this change is here:

HKLM\SOFTWARE\Microsoft\Windows\CurrentVersion\Run

Opening the Registry Editor and going to this subkey, you'll see something like Figure 15-6.

Figure 15-6 Mike's Run subkey

Before I delete these keys, I'm going to save a copy of my Registry. The Registry Editor's Export feature enables you to save either the full Registry or only a single root key or subkey (with all subkeys and values under it). Select Run from the left pane and then click File | Export. Save the subkey as a Registration file with the extension .reg. Be sure to put that file somewhere you'll remember. Should you need to restore that key, use the File | Import command, or just right-click on the icon as shown in Figure 15-7 and click Merge.

Figure 15-7
Merging keys from
a backup file

Command-Line Registry Editing Tools

Windows includes a couple of command-line tools to edit the Registry (plus a lot more in the PowerShell). The two that you might need on occasion are reg and regsrv32.

TIP If the command-line interface is new to you, you might want to flag this section of Chapter 15 and skip it for now, then return to it after reading about the command line and how it works in Chapter 18.

The reg command is a full Registry editing tool. You can view Registry keys and values, import and export some or all of a Registry, and even compare two different versions of a Registry. The tool is so powerful that it has multiple levels of help so you can tailor a command to accomplish very tight Registry edits. For example, typing **reg /?** brings up a list of 12 specific operations that you can search for help on, such as reg query /? and reg add /?.

The regsrv32 command, in contrast with reg, can modify the Registry in only one way, adding (or *registering*) dynamic link library (DLL) files as command components. For the scoop on what regsrv32 does, please see "Component Services" later in the chapter for a description of the graphical tool that does the same thing. Only the 32-bit versions of Windows have the regsrv32 command, by the way.

The Boot Process

The Windows installation creates a number of specific files and folders that the OS needs to run a PC. Some of these files and folders are directly on the root of the C: drive; others can be elsewhere. The best way to remember the locations of these files and folders and to know their importance to the OS is by looking at how they interact to boot the PC.

Booting Windows XP differs dramatically from booting Windows Vista/7. Windows XP was the last Microsoft operating system to use a very old boot process known as ntldr (NT Loader). Windows Vista introduced the far more flexible, complex, and powerful Windows Boot Manager (or *bootmgr*), which Windows 7 also uses. The great difference between these two boot managers requires us to look at both in more depth.

The Windows XP Boot Process

Windows XP distinguishes between the files that start the operating system (called the *system files*) and the rest of the operating system files (by default in the \Windows folders). The system files (memorize these!) consist of three required files: ntldr, boot.ini, and ntdetect.com. If you're using a SCSI hard drive, there's a fourth file called ntbootdd. sys. The ntldr (pronounced *NT loader*) file begins the boot process.

NOTE To see these files, go into My Computer and open the C:drive. Go to Tools | Folder Options. Click *Show hidden files and folders*, uncheck the *Hide protected operating system files (Recommended)* option, and click OK. Now when

you return to viewing the folder in My Computer, you will see certain critical files that Windows otherwise hides from you to prevent you from accidentally moving, deleting, or changing them in some unintended way.

You know from Chapter 12 that to make a drive bootable requires an active, primary partition, right? Let's look at the process in a PC with a hard drive partitioned as C: and D:.

The CPU wakes up and runs the system BIOS, and then the BIOS sends out a routine that looks on the first bootable drive's partition table for a boot sector marked as active. This is usually the C: drive. The boot sector takes over from BIOS and reads the master file table (MFT) in the bootable partition. The MFT points to the location of the Windows XP system files. Windows XP calls the primary active partition the *system partition* or the *system volume* (if it's a dynamic disk).

We're almost booted, but to complete the process, we need to take a moment to learn about some more critical Windows XP files: the Windows boot files and the Windows system files. The Windows XP *boot files* consist of ntoskrnl.exe (the Windows kernel), the \Winnt\System32\Config\System file (which controls the loading of device drivers), and the device drivers. Although these files are the core of the Windows XP operating system, they are not capable of booting, or starting, the system. For that feat, they require ntldr, ntdetect.com, and boot.ini—the system files.

The system files start the PC and then, at the end of that process, point the CPU to the location of the boot files. The CPU goes over and chats with ntoskrnl, and the GUI starts to load. The operating system is then up and running, and you're able to do work.

The odd part about all of this is that Microsoft decided to make the OS files mobile. The Windows XP operating system files can reside on any partition or volume in the PC. The \Windows folder, for example, could very well be on drive D:, not drive C:. Whichever drive holds the core OS files is called the *boot partition* or *boot volume*. This can lead to a little confusion when you say the system files are on the C: drive and Windows is on the D: drive, but that's just the way it is. Luckily, the vast majority of Windows XP systems have the system partition and the boot partition both on the same big C: partition.

You know the general process now, so let's look more specifically at the makeup and function of the individual files involved in the boot process.

ntldr

When the system boots up, the master boot record (MBR) or MFT on the hard drive starts the ntldr program. The *ntldr* program then launches Windows XP. To find the available OSs, the ntldr program must read the boot.ini configuration file. To do so, it loads its own minimal file system, which enables it to read the boot.ini file off of the system partition.

boot.ini

The *boot.ini* file is a text file that lists the OSs available to ntldr and tells ntldr where to find the boot partition (where the OS is stored) for each of them. The boot.ini file has sections defined by headings enclosed in brackets. A basic boot.ini file in Windows XP looks like this:

```
[boot loader]
timeout=30
default=multi(0)disk(0)rdisk(0)partition(1)\WINDOWS
[operating systems]
multi(0)disk(0)rdisk(0)partition(1)\WINDOWS="Microsoft Windows XP
Professional" /fastdetect
```

A more complex boot.ini file may look like this:

```
[boot loader]
timeout=30
default=multi(0)disk(0)rdisk(0)partition(1)\WINDOWS
[operating systems]
multi(0)disk(0)rdisk(0)partition(1)\WINDOWS="Microsoft Windows XP
Professional" /fastdetect
multi(0)disk(0)rdisk(0)partition(1)\WINNT="Microsoft Windows 2000
Professional" /fastdetect
```

Such a boot.ini file would result in the boot menu that appears in Figure 15-8.

```
Please select the operating system to start:

    Microsoft Windows XP Professional
    Microsoft Windows 2000 Professional

Use the up and down arrow keys to move the highlight to your choice.
Press ENTER to choose.
Seconds until highlighted choice will be started automatically: 29

For troubleshooting and advanced startup options for Windows, press F8.
```

Figure 15-8 Boot loader in Windows XP showing dual-boot configuration

This crazy multi(0)disk(0)rdisk(0)partition(1) is an example of the Advanced RISC Computing (ARC) naming system. It's a system that's designed to

enable your PC to boot Windows from any hard drive, including removable devices. Let's take a quick peek at each ARC setting to see how it works.

`Multi(x)` is the number of the adapter and always starts with 0. The adapter is determined by the boot order you set in your CMOS setting. For example, if you have one PATA controller and one SATA controller, and you set the system to boot first from the PATA controller, any drive on that controller will get the value `multi(0)` placed in its ARC format. Any SATA drive will get `multi(1)`.

`Disk(x)` is only used for SCSI drives, but the value is required in the ARC format, so with ATA systems it's always set to `disk(0)`.

`Rdisk(x)` specifies the number of the disk on the adapter. On a PATA drive, the master is `rdisk(0)` and the slave is `rdisk(1)`. On SATA drives, the order is usually based on the number of the SATA connection printed on the motherboard, though some systems allow you to change this in CMOS.

`Partition(x)` is the number of the partition or logical drive in an extended partition. The numbering starts at 1, so the first partition is `partition(1)`, the second is `partition(2)`, and so on.

`\WINDOWS` is the name of the folder that holds the boot files. This is important to appreciate! The ARC format looks at the folder, so there's no problem running different editions of Windows XP on a single partition. You can simply install them in different folders. Of course, you have other limitations, such as file system type, but in general, multibooting with Windows is pretty easy. Better yet, this is all handled during the installation process.

> **NOTE** You can't boot multiple installations of Windows Vista or Windows 7 from a single partition because their setup programs don't allow you to choose the installation directory.

ARC format can get far more complicated. SCSI drives get a slightly different ARC format. For example, if you installed Windows on a SCSI drive, you might see this ARC setting in your boot.ini file:

```
scsi(0)disk(1)rdisk(0)partition(1)
```

If you want to boot to a SCSI drive, Windows adds a fourth file to your system files called ntbootdd.sys. This file only exists if you want to boot to a SCSI drive. Most people don't boot to a SCSI, so don't worry if you don't see this file with the other three system files.

On rare occasions, you might find yourself needing to edit the boot.ini file. Any text editor handily edits this file, but most of us prefer to edit boot.ini via the System Setup dialog box. In Windows XP, open the System applet from the Control Panel. Click the Advanced tab and then click the Startup and Recovery button. The boot.ini options show up at the top (see Figure 15-9).

Figure 15-9

The boot.ini

options

Boot.ini has some interesting switches at the end of the ARC formats that give special instructions on how the operating system should boot. Sometimes Windows puts these in automatically, and sometimes you will add them manually for troubleshooting. Here are a few of the more common ones:

- **/bootlog** Tells Windows to create a log of the boot process and write it to a file called ntbtlog.txt.

- **/cmdcons** Tells Windows to start the Recovery Console (see Chapter 19 for a discussion of the Recovery Console).

- **/lastknowngood** Tells Windows to boot the Last Known Good set of files.

- **/noexecute** Newer CPUs come with Data Execute Protection (DEP) to prevent unruly programs from causing system lockups. The setting for this, /noexecute=optin, is the default on Windows systems.

ntdetect.com

If ntldr determines that you have chosen to start Windows XP, it boots the system into protected mode and then calls on *ntdetect.com* to detect the installed hardware on the system. Ntldr then refers to the boot.ini file to locate the Windows boot files.

Critical Boot Files

Naming all the critical boot files for Windows XP is akin to naming every muscle in the human body—completely possible, but time-consuming and without any real benefit. A few of the *most* important files certainly deserve a short mention.

Once ntldr finishes detections, it loads ntoskrnl.exe, hal.dll, some of the Registry, and some basic device drivers; then it passes control to the ntoskrnl.exe file. Ntoskrnl.exe completes the Registry loading, initializes all device drivers, and starts the winlogon.exe program, which displays the Windows XP logon screen (see Figure 15-10).

Figure 15-10
Where do you
want to go today?

Take the time to memorize the primary boot files and the boot process for Windows XP. Most boot errors are easily repaired if you know which files are used for booting and in which order they load.

TIP The Recovery Console can be used to restore damaged, corrupted, or missing ntldr and ntdetect.com files from the Windows XP installation disc.

The Windows Vista/7 Boot Process

Windows Vista and Windows 7 have a very different boot process than previous versions of Windows. For one thing, Vista/7 supports both BIOS and UEFI, whereas older versions of Windows did not, so things are a bit more complex right off the bat. So not only is there a totally new boot process, this newer Windows Vista/7 boot process varies between two slightly different boot processes: one for systems using BIOS and one for systems with UEFI.

The very first thing that happens when you power on a system with Vista/7 is that either the BIOS or the UEFI starts up. The difference between BIOS and UEFI systems is in what happens next.

- In a BIOS-based system, the BIOS uses its boot order to scan a hard drive for a master boot record (MBR). The MBR holds a small bit of file system boot code that scans the partition table for the system partition and then loads its boot sector. The boot sector in turn contains code that does nothing but point the boot process toward a file called bootmgr (pronounced *Boot Manager*, or "boot mugger" if you're trying to make nerds laugh).

- In a UEFI system, on the other hand, neither the MBR/GUID partition table (GPT) nor the file system boot code is run, and UEFI simply loads bootmgr directly.

NOTE In Windows Vista, bootmgr resides in the root directory of the boot drive. Windows 7, however, keeps bootmgr in the special 100-MB system partition you learned about in Chapter 12. If you are using a UEFI system, the helpfully named EFI system partition contains a special version of bootmgr called bootmgr.efi.

If you've ever run a dual-boot system with Vista or 7 as one of the operating systems, you're probably already somewhat familiar with bootmgr; one of its jobs is displaying that "Which operating system do you want to load?" screen and then loading the appropriate operating system. When bootmgr starts, it reads data from a *Boot Configuration Data (BCD)* file that contains information about the various operating systems installed on the system as well as instructions for how to actually load (bootstrap) them. Once an operating system is selected (or immediately if only one is present), bootmgr loads a program called winload.exe, which readies your system to load the operating system kernel itself rather like the way you clean up your house before Aunt Edna comes to visit. It does this by loading into memory the hardware abstraction layer, the system Registry, and the drivers for any boot devices before the operating system itself takes over.

NOTE Unlike Windows XP, the boot files and the system files must all reside on the same partition in Vista/7.

Once the operating system process (called ntoskrnl.exe) takes over, it loads up all of the various processes and systems that comprise Windows, the Windows logo comes up, and you're happily computing, completely oblivious to all of the complex electronic communication that just took place inside your computer.

NOTE The BCD file replaces the boot.ini file used in previous operating systems and can be altered by using the command-line tool bcdedit.exe.

Processes and Services and Threads, Oh My!

Back in Chapter 6, you learned that CPUs run threads—bits of programs that are fed into the CPU. Let's see how all of this looks from Windows' point of view.

NOTE For the purposes of the CompTIA A+ 220-802 exam, I'm simplifying things a little, but know that processes, services, and threads can get a lot more complicated.

In Windows, programs are executable files waiting on a mass storage device. When you start a program, Windows loads it into RAM as a process. Once there, the CPU reads the process and the process tells the CPU which chunks of code to run. Dealing with processes in their many forms is a big part of understanding what's happening "under the hood."

Windows is a multitasking operating system, running lots of processes simultaneously. Many of these processes appear in a window (or full screen) when you open them and end when you close that window. These processes are called applications. There's also an entire class of processes that, due to the nature of their job, don't require a window of any form. These processes run invisibly in the background, providing a large number of necessary support roles. Collectively, these are called *services*. Let's look at applications, services, and processes and the tools we use to control them.

NOTE All versions of Windows use services.

Task Manager

The Windows *Task Manager* is the one-stop-shop for anything you need to do with applications, processes, and, if you're using Windows Vista or Windows 7, services (see Figure 15-11). The quick way to open the Task Manager is to press CTRL-SHIFT-ESC. There are two other ways to open the Task Manager that you might see on the CompTIA A+ exams: go to Start | Run or Start | Search, type **taskmgr**, and press ENTER; or press CTRL-ALT-DELETE and select Task Manager.

If you're running Windows XP, the Task Manager is similar (see Figure 15-12) but lacks a few handy features offered in Windows Vista and Windows 7's Task Manager. I'll cover these differences in this section.

Applications

The *Applications* tab shows all the running applications on your system. If you're having trouble getting an application to close normally, this is the place to go. To force an application to shut down, select the naughty application and click End Task, or right-click on the application and select End Task from the context menu. Be careful when using this feature! There is no "Are you sure?" prompt and it's easy to accidently close the wrong application.

Figure 15-11

Task Manager in
Windows 7

Figure 15-12

Task Manager in
Windows XP

There are two other handy buttons on the Applications tab:

- Switch To enables you to bring any program to the front (very handy when you have a large number of applications running).

- New Task is a lifesaver of a tool, enabling you to start any program you wish, as long as you know the filename of the program. One of the most common uses for New Task is to restart your desktop in Windows XP. If your desktop crashes, the Task Manager usually still works. Click on New Task and type in **explorer**. Sadly, this doesn't work in Windows Vista or Windows 7, but New Task is still a handy tool to start programs, especially if you don't have access to the Start menu.

Remember that everything is a process, so every application is also listed in the Processes tab. Right-click on an application and select Go To Process to open the Processes tab and see which process is running the application.

Processes

If you really want to tap the power of the Task Manager, you need to click on the *Processes* tab (see Figure 15-13). Since everything is a process, and the Processes tab shows you every running process, this is the one place that enables you to see everything running on your computer.

Figure 15-13

Processes tab in Windows 7

All processes have certain common features that you should recognize:

- A process is named after its executable file, which usually ends in .exe but can also end with other extensions.

- All processes have a user name to identify who started the process. A process started by Windows has the user name System.

- All processes have a Process Identifier (PID). To identify a process, you use the PID, not the process name. The Task Manager doesn't show the PID by default. Click on View | Select Columns and select the PID (Process Identifier) checkbox to see the PIDs (see Figure 15-14).

Figure 15-14
Processes tab showing the PID column in Windows 7

The Task Manager provides important information about processes. It shows the amount of CPU time (percentage) and the amount of RAM (in kilobytes) the process is using. Most processes also provide a description to help you understand what the process is doing, although you'll probably need to scroll right to see this information (see Figure 15-15).

You'll notice that almost all of the processes have the same user name. By default, the Task Manager shows only processes associated with the current user. Click on *Show processes from all users* to see every process on the system (see Figure 15-16). Note that some of the processes show a user name of Local Service or Network Service. As you might imagine, those are services!

Now that you understand the basics, let's watch the Task Manager do its magic with processes. If you select a process and click the End Process button, you'll instantly end that process. If the process is an application, that application will close.

Closing processes is important, but to take it even further, you need to select a process and right-click on it to see a number of options. If you select a process that's an application (the name of the process is a strong clue—winword.exe is Microsoft Word), you see something like Figure 15-17.

Figure 15-15
Processes details in
Windows 7

Figure 15-16 Processes from all users in Windows 7

Figure 15-17

Processes detail of the right-click

Open File Location takes you to wherever the file is located. This is extremely helpful when you're looking at a mysterious process and are trying to find out what it's doing on your computer.

You already know what End Process does. End Process Tree is extremely important but also complex, so let's save that for later.

Debug is grayed out, unless you're running a Windows debugger program—see the explanation of dump files below.

UAC Virtualization gives older programs that weren't written to avoid accessing protected folders a way to do so by making a fake protected folder. In most cases, Windows handles this automatically, but there are rare cases where you'll need to set this manually. Again, you won't do this on your own—you'll be on the phone with the tech support for some software company and they'll tell you how to use UAC Virtualization.

Dump files show the status of the program at the moment you click Create Dump File. Programmers use special debugging utilities to read dump files to analyze problems with programs. The only time you'd ever use this option is if you're having problems with a program and the support people ask you to make a dump file.

Set Priority gives you the ability to devote more or less processor time to a process (see Figure 15-18). This is very handy when you have a process that is slowing down your machine or if you have a process that is running too slowly and you want to speed it up.

Messing with priorities can get complicated quickly. The best idea here is to just increase the priority of a single process you need to run faster or reduce the priority of a single process you need to run slower, without touching any other priorities.

Figure 15-18

Process priority

NOTE Setting any single process to Realtime priority will often bring the entire system to a crawl as no other process gets much CPU time—avoid Realtime priority.

Set Affinity is a handy way to give a process more CPU time without messing with priorities. Windows tends to use your first two CPUs more heavily than the others. If you have more than two cores on your CPU and you have a single process that uses a lot of CPU time, try unchecking the affinity checkbox for the first two cores to force the process to only use your other cores (see Figure 15-19).

The Properties option isn't too exciting. It's the same as if you were to right-click on the executable file and select Properties in Windows Explorer. Go to Service(s) will move you to the Services tab of the Task Manager, showing you any and all services associated with the process. Depending on the process, it could use no services or multiple services. This is a great tool for those "Program won't start because associated services aren't running" situations. Figure 15-20 shows what happens when you use Go to Service(s) for a process called lsass.exe.

EXAM TIP The Windows XP Task Manager lacks all of these context menu options except for End Process, End Process Tree, Debug, and Set Priority.

Figure 15-19

Turning off affinity
to the first two
cores

Windows Task Manager

File Options View Help

Processor Affinity

Users

Which processors are allowed to run "plugin-container.exe *32"?

- [] <All Processors>
- [] CPU 0
- [] CPU 1
- [x] CPU 2
- [x] CPU 3
- [x] CPU 4
- [x] CPU 5
- [x] CPU 6
- [x] CPU 7

OK Cancel

Show processes from all users End Process

Processes: 81 CPU Usage: 0% Physical Memory: 48%

Windows Task Manager

File Options View Help

| Applications | Processes | Services | Performance | Networking | Users |

Name	PID	Description	Status	Group
SENS	360	System Event Notification Service	Running	netsvcs
ShellHWDetection	360	Shell Hardware Detection	Running	netsvcs
Themes	360	Themes	Running	netsvcs
Winmgmt	360	Windows Management Instrumentation	Running	netsvcs
wuauserv	360	Windows Update	Running	netsvcs
asHmComSvc	516	ASUS HM Com Service	Running	N/A
EFS	560	Encrypting File System (EFS)	Running	
Netlogon	560	Netlogon	Running	
SamSs	560	Security Accounts Manager	Running	
DcomLaunch	704	DCOM Server Process Launcher	Running	DcomLaunch
PlugPlay	704	Plug and Play	Running	DcomLaunch
Power	704	Power	Running	DcomLaunch
RpcEptMapper	812	RPC Endpoint Mapper	Running	RPCSS
RpcSs	812	Remote Procedure Call (RPC)	Running	rpcss
MsMpSvc	876	Microsoft Antimalware Service	Running	N/A
AMD External Events Utility	952	AMD External Events Utility	Running	N/A
AudioSrv	996	Windows Audio	Running	LocalServic...

Services...

Processes: 81 CPU Usage: 0% Physical Memory: 48%

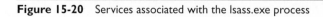

Figure 15-20 Services associated with the lsass.exe process

Let's get back to the End Process Tree option. It's very common for a single process to be dependent on other processes (or for a process to start other processes). This creates a tree of dependencies. Sadly, the Task Manager doesn't give you any clue as to what processes depend on other processes, but it still gives you the option to End Process Tree, which ends not only the process, but any process it depends on. At first glance, this is scary since it's very common for many processes to depend on one important process. Microsoft makes this less scary, as it will not let you kill a process tree for the most important system processes.

Even so, it would be nice to actually *see* what processes you're about to kill, wouldn't it? That's when the popular (and free) Process Explorer, written by Mark Russinovitch, is your go-to tool (see Figure 15-21)

Figure 15-21 Process Explorer

Think of Process Explorer as the Task Manager on steroids. It's very powerful, and a lot of techs use it instead of the Task Manager. It isn't on the CompTIA A+ exams, but it should be. Instead of just listing all of the processes, Process Explorer uses a tree structure so you can see all the dependencies.

NOTE Process Explorer does so much more than just show a tree structure. Download a copy and play with it. You'll see why it's so popular.

Services

If you've got Windows Vista or Windows 7, you can use the *Services* tab in the Task Manager to work with services directly (see Figure 15-22). Here, services can be stopped or started, and you can go to the associated process.

Figure 15-22

Services tab in Task Manager

The best way to see services in action is to use the Services Control Panel applet. To open it, click on the Services button at the bottom of the Services tab in the Task Manager or go to Control Panel | Administrative Tools | Services. Figure 15-23 shows the Services applet running in Windows 7.

 EXAM TIP You can open the Services applet from the Start | Run dialog box or Start | Search bar. Type **services.msc** and press ENTER.

Look closely at Figure 15-23. Each line in this applet is an individual service. Services don't have their own window, so you use the Services applet to start, stop, and configure them. You can see if a service is running by reading the Status column. To configure a service, right-click on the service name. The context menu enables you to start, stop, pause, resume, or restart any service. Click on Properties to see a dialog box similar to the one shown in Figure 15-24.

Of the four tabs you see in the Properties dialog box, General and Recovery are by far the most used. The General tab provides the name of the service, describes the service, and enables you to stop, start, pause, or resume the service. You can also define how the service starts: Manual (you go here to start it), Automatic (starts at beginning of Windows boot), Disabled (prevents the service from starting in any fashion), or Automatic (delayed start), which starts the service at boot but only after pretty much everything else has started.

Figure 15-23 Services applet

Figure 15-24
Service Properties
dialog box

NOTE You can start or stop any service at a command prompt by typing *net start* (or *stop*) ***service name.***

Performance

For optimization purposes, the Task Manager is a great tool for investigating how hard your RAM and CPU are working at any given moment and why. Click the *Performance* tab to reveal a handy screen with the most commonly used information: CPU usage, available physical memory, size of the disk cache, commit charge (memory for programs), and kernel memory (memory used by Windows). Figure 15-25 shows a system with an eight-core processor, which is why you see eight graphs under CPU Usage History. A system with a single-core processor would have a single screen.

Figure 15-25 Task Manager Performance tab

Not only does the Task Manager tell you how much CPU and RAM usage is taking place, it also tells you what program is using those resources. Let's say your system is running slowly. You open the Task Manager and see that your CPU usage is at 100 percent. You then click on the Processes tab to see all the processes running on your system. Click on the CPU column heading to sort all processes by CPU usage to see who's hogging the CPU (see Figure 15-26). If necessary, shut down the program or change its priority to fix the issue.

Figure 15-26 CPU usage

Networking and Users

The other two tabs in the Task Manager, Networking and Users, enable you to see network use at a glance and see which users' accounts are currently logged on to the local machine. The Networking tab is a good first spot to look if you think the computer is running slowly on the network. If there's little activity displayed, then it's not traffic from your computer that's causing the slowdown, so you need to look elsewhere. Chapter 22 covers network troubleshooting in a lot more detail, so we'll leave the Networking tab alone for now.

The Users tab enables you to log off other users if you have the proper permissions. You can also log off from here. There's not much else to say, but since the CompTIA A+ 220-802 exam objectives want this tab used in a scenario, here's one hypothetical. Another user is still logged on and left a critical file open that you need to access. Logging the user off forces his or her applications to close and makes the file available. Of course, unsaved changes will be lost, so use caution here.

The tasklist and taskkill Commands

The two command-line utilities *tasklist* and taskkill enable you to work with tasks, similarly to what you can do with the Task Manager. The tasklist command enables you to

view running processes on a local or remote system. Open up a command prompt and type **tasklist**. The following is a partial example of the output:

```
C:\Users\mike>tasklist

Image Name                     PID Session Name        Session#    Mem Usage
========================= ======== ================ =========== ============
System Idle Process              0 Services                   0         24 K
System                           4 Services                   0        940 K
smss.exe                       268 Services                   0        340 K
csrss.exe                      372 Services                   0      2,388 K
wininit.exe                    444 Services                   0        968 K
csrss.exe                      452 Console                    1      9,788 K
winlogon.exe                   500 Console                    1      2,420 K
services.exe                   544 Services                   0      4,536 K
svchost.exe                    756 Services                   0      4,320 K
MsMpEng.exe                    828 Services                   0     42,164 K
atiesrxx.exe                   904 Services                   0        824 K
notepad.exe                   3932 Console                    0      6,612 K
```

 EXAM TIP The CompTIA A+ 802 exam objectives mention a command-line utility called *tlist*. Tasklist replaced tlist back in Windows XP, but for some reason CompTIA included it anyway.

You can kill a process using the taskkill command. See the notepad.exe listing in the preceding tasklist output? You can kill the process using either the name or the PID, as shown here:

```
C:\>taskkill /pid 3932
SUCCESS: Sent termination signal to the process with PID 3932.
```

 EXAM TIP You can use the *kill* command in the Windows PowerShell command-line environment to stop a running process. Kill is actually an alias for the Stop-Process cmdlet, although you don't need to know that for the exam. See Chapter 18 for a more in-depth discussion of working with the command line and PowerShell.

Performance Console

The Task Manager is good for identifying current problems, but what about problems that happen when you're not around? What if your system is always running at a CPU utilization of 20 percent—is that good or bad? Windows XP provides a tool called the *Performance console* that logs resource usage so you can track items such as CPU and RAM usage over time. Performance is an MMC console file, perfmon.msc, so you call it from Start | Run or through the Performance icon in Administrative Tools. Use either method to open the Performance console (see Figure 15-27). As you can see, there are two nodes, System Monitor and Performance Logs and Alerts.

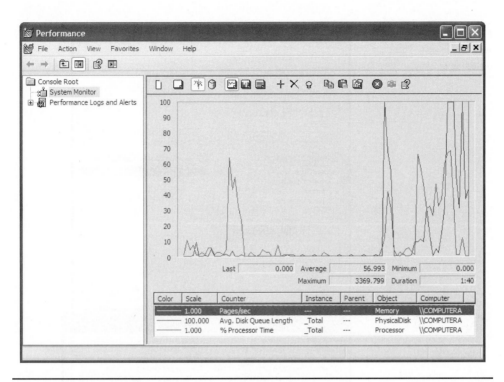

Figure 15-27 Performance console

Objects and Counters

To begin working with the Performance console, you need to understand two terms: object and counter. An *object* is a system component that is given a set of characteristics and can be managed by the operating system as a single entity. A *counter* tracks specific information about an object. For example, the Processor object has a counter, %Processor Time, that tracks the percentage of elapsed time the processor uses to execute a non-idle thread. Many counters can be associated with an object.

System Monitor

System Monitor gathers real-time data on objects such as memory, physical disk, processor, and network, and displays this data as a graph (line graph), histogram (bar graph), or simple report. When you first open the Performance console, System Monitor shows data in graph form. The data displayed is from the set of three counters listed below the chart. If you want to add counters, click the Add button (the one that looks like a plus sign) or press CTRL-I to open the Add Counters dialog box. Click the Performance object drop-down list and select one of the many different objects you can monitor. The Add Counters dialog box includes a helpful feature: you can select a counter and click the Explain button to learn about the counter, as shown in Figure 15-28. Try that now.

Figure 15-28
Add Counters
dialog box

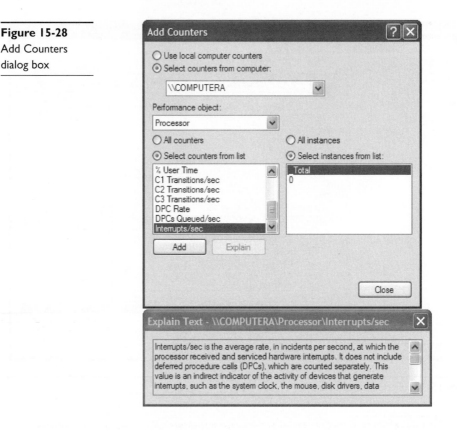

Even with just three counters selected, the graph can get a little busy. That's where one of my favorite System Monitor features shines. If you want the line of charted data from just one counter to stand out, select the counter in the list below the graph and then press CTRL-H. See how this trick makes the %Processor Time line stand out in Figure 15-29? Imagine how useful that is when you are monitoring a dozen counters.

Performance Logs and Alerts

The *Performance Logs and Alerts* snap-in enables Windows to create a written record of just about anything that happens on your system. Do you want to know if someone is trying to log on to your system when you're not around?

To create the new event log, right-click Counter Logs and select New Log Settings. Give the new log a name—in this example, "Unauthorized Accesses." Click OK, and a properties dialog box for the new log appears, similar to that shown in Figure 15-30.

Figure 15-29 Pressing CTRL-H makes one set of data stand out.

Figure 15-30 Creating a new performance log

To select counters for the log, click Add Counters and then select the *Use local computer counters* radio button. Select Server from the Performance object pull-down menu and then select Errors Logon from the list of counters; click Add and then click Close.

Back in the properties dialog box for your new log, click the Schedule tab and set up when you want this thing to start running—probably at the end of the workday today. Then select when it should stop logging—probably tomorrow morning when you start work. Click the Log Files tab to see where the log file will be saved—probably C:\ PerfLogs—and make a note of the filename. The filename will consist of the name you gave the log and a number. In this example I named the new performance log "Unauthorized Accesses," so the filename is Unauthorized Accesses_000001.blg.

When you come back in the morning, open the Performance console, select Performance Logs and Alerts, and then select Counter Logs. Your log should be listed on the right. The icon by the log name will be green if the log is still running or red if it has stopped. If it has not stopped, select it and click the Stop button (the one with the black square, circled in Figure 15-31).

Figure 15-31 Stopping the performance log

To view the log, open the Performance console, select System Monitor, change to Report view, and load the file as a new source by using the log's properties dialog box.

Performance Tools in Windows Vista and Windows 7

Microsoft improved on the Performance console dramatically with Reliability and Performance Monitor in Windows Vista and yet again with Performance Monitor in Windows 7. *Reliability and Performance Monitor* still has a complete Performance console with all the objects and counters you see in Windows XP, but it adds an excellent Resource Overview, a Reliability Monitor tool, and a much more flexible way to use counters with Data Collector Sets and Reports. *Performance Monitor* in Windows 7 functions almost identically to Reliability and Performance Monitor in Windows Vista, but Microsoft pulled out the Reliability tool to make the remaining tool smaller and tighter.

You can open Reliability and Performance Monitor/Performance Monitor by starting the Performance Information and Tools applet in Control Panel. The initial screen is

the *Rate and improve your computer's performance* screen (see Figure 15-32), which shows how your computer's hardware stacks up in the Windows Experience Index. Click the Advanced tools link in the left task area. Then click on Open Reliability and Performance Monitor or Open Performance Monitor, depending on the Windows version. You can also open the tool by going to Start | Search bar, typing **perfmon.msc**, and pressing ENTER.

Figure 15-32 Performance Information and Tools showing the computer's rating on the Windows Experience Index

NOTE The Windows Experience Index runs on a scale from 1.0 to 7.9 and gives you a pretty good gauge of the relative strengths and weaknesses of a system. The system in Figure 15-32, for example, has a CPU near the top of the chart (it's an Intel Core i7) and lots of fast RAM (8 GB), but a relatively modest hard drive. So the next obvious upgrade to this system would be to move from a platter-based drive to a solid-state drive. Disk performance would certainly jump dramatically.

Reliability and Performance Monitor in Windows Vista opens to a Resource Overview screen (see Figure 15-33). Think of the Resource Overview as an advanced Task Manager, giving details on CPU, hard drive, network, and memory usage.

Figure 15-33 Resource Overview in Windows Vista

When you click on one of the four bars, you get details on exactly which processes are using those resources—a powerful tool when you suspect a program might be hogging something! Figure 15-34 shows the Network bar opened to reveal the processes using the network and how much data each is sending.

NOTE The Reliability Monitor tool gives you an overview of how a PC has behaved over time, showing important events such as application or OS crashes. You can find the tool in Windows 7 as part of the Action Center Control Panel applet.

Performance Monitor in Windows 7 opens to a more modest screen that displays some text about Performance Monitor and a System Summary (see Figure 15-35). You can get to the Overview screen by clicking the Open Resource Monitor link on the main screen. Aside from orienting the graphical screens on the right rather than on the top, the tool is the same as the Resource Overview in Windows Vista (see Figure 15-36).

Figure 15-34 Network bar in Resource Overview

Figure 15-35 Initial Performance Monitor screen in Windows 7

Figure 15-36 Resource Monitor displaying CPU usage

The Performance Monitor option you can select under Monitoring Tools in either version of the OS is simply a re-creation of the Performance console and works as described earlier for Windows XP (see Figure 15-37). This is a great tool for quick checks on specific counters.

Microsoft included Data Collector Sets in Reliability and Performance Monitor and Performance Monitor, groupings of counters you can use to make reports. You can make your own Data Collector Sets (User Defined) or you can just grab one of the predefined system sets. Once you start a Data Collector Set, you can use the Reports option to see the results (see Figure 15-38). Data Collector Sets not only enable you to choose counter objects to track, but also enable you to schedule when you want them to run.

EXAM TIP The CompTIA A+ exams aren't going to ask too many detailed questions on either Performance Monitor or Reliability and Performance Monitor. That doesn't mean you can ignore these amazing tools! Make sure you understand that these tools give you the power to inspect anything happening on your system to help you diagnose problems.

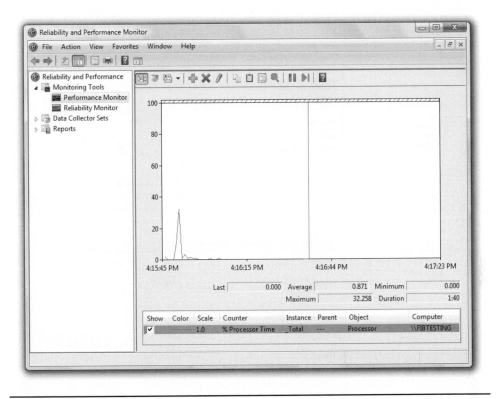

Figure 15-37 Reliability and Performance Monitor

Tools for Programmers

Back in Chapter 4, I discussed many of the tools available under Administrative Tools in Control Panel. I left out two applets that I want to discuss now for two reasons: first, because they're covered on the CompTIA A+ 220-802 exam, and second, because they deal with some low-level functionality in Windows that affects how a lot of applications are programmed. Read on to find out more about the Component Services and Data Sources (ODBC) applets.

Component Services

To understand all that *Component Services* can do would require a huge amount of information—far greater than the scope of CompTIA's A+ exams. Simply put, as long as Windows has existed, Microsoft has come up with many tools (with names like COM, DCOM, and COM+) to enable programmers to share data objects (an element of programs) between applications on a single computer. Over time, this sharing was extended so that you could share objects between computers on a network.

Figure 15-38 Sample report

In almost all cases, this object sharing doesn't require you to do anything more than install an application that uses these features. Component Services is there, however, for those very rare times when something's either wrong or a programmer needs you to make manual changes (see Figure 15-39). If you have a company that creates in-house or buys custom applications, there's a better than good chance that you'll be firing up Component Services and working with programmers, manually installing programs, and tweaking those programs to get them to work the way you wish. Professional, third-party applications (the kind you buy in stores) should automatically configure any of these programs during the installation process, making it extremely rare that you'll need to go into Component Services.

Figure 15-39 Component Services in Windows 7

Every version of Windows has Component Services, but there's no ready-to-go icon in Windows XP or Windows Vista. You'll need to make a custom MMC and load Component Services from there.

Data Sources

One of the oldest and most common motivations to make networks is the idea of a number of computers accessing one or more shared databases. These computers might not all be running the same operating system, nor will they always use the same application to access those databases. That's where Open Database Connectivity (ODBC) really shines. ODBC is a coding standard that enables programmers to write databases and the applications that use them in a way that they can query ODBC to see how to locate and access a database without any concern about what application or operating system is used.

Microsoft's tool to configure ODBC is called *ODBC Data Source Administrator* (see Figure 15-40). Data Source Administrator enables you to create and manage entries called Data Source Names (DSNs) that point ODBC to a database. DSNs are used by

ODBC-aware applications to query ODBC to find their databases. Keep in mind that you'll rarely go into Data Source Administrator unless you're making your own shared databases.

Figure 15-40
Data Source
Administrator in
Windows 7

Chapter Review

Questions

1. What is the name of the program that boots Windows Vista and Windows 7?

 A. ntldr

 B. boot.ini

 C. bootmgr

 D. Registry

2. What is the name of the command-line version of the Task Manager?

 A. taskman

 B. tasklist

 C. taskkill

 D. tasks

3. Which of the following tools enables programmers to share objects between applications and computers?

 A. Task Manager

 B. Performance console

 C. bootmgr

 D. Component Services

4. When using the Performance console, which settings are defined to track resource usage? (Select two.)

 A. Processes

 B. Objects

 C. Counters

 D. Values

5. Which of the following are organized inside the Registry's root keys? (Select two.)

 A. Subkeys

 B. Subfolders

 C. Values

 D. Objects

6. Which of the following root keys contains the data for a system's non-user-specific configurations?

 A. HKEY_LOCAL_MACHINE

 B. HKEY_USERS

 C. HKEY_CURRENT_USER

 D. HKEY_CLASSES_ROOT

7. Which of the following options are available when you right-click on a process in the Task Manager's Processes tab? (Select two.)

 A. Start Service

 B. Go to Service(s)

 C. Go To Process

 D. Set Priority

8. Which of the following statements about booting in Windows 7 is true?

 A. BIOS does not use bootmgr.

 B. UEFI looks for the MBR, which finds the boot code that launches bootmgr.

 C. BIOS looks for the MBR, which finds the boot code that launches bootmgr.

 D. UEFI does not use bootmgr.

9. How do you open the Registry Editor from the command prompt? (Select two.)

 A. regedit

 B. regedt32

 C. regeditor

 D. rgstry

10. Mark wants to monitor a PC that's been having performance issues overnight. He needs something that will record the data while he's away from the computer. Which tool should he use?

 A. Performance Logs and Alerts

 B. Task Manager

 C. System Monitor

 D. Registry

Answers

1. **C.** On Windows Vista and Windows 7 machines, bootmgr is used to boot the operating system.

2. **B.** The tasklist command opens the command-line version of the Task Manager.

3. **D.** Component Services enables programmers to share objects between applications and computers.

4. **B, C.** To track resource usage in the Performance console, you need to configure objects and counters.

5. **A, C.** The Registry's root keys are further organized into subkeys and values.

6. **A.** The system's non-user-specific configurations are stored in the HKEY_LOCAL_MACHINE root key of the Registry.

7. **B, D.** From the Processes tab, you can select a process and go to the service or set the priority.

8. **C.** When booting Windows 7, the BIOS looks for the MBR, which finds the boot code to launch the OS.

9. **A, B.** From the command prompt, you can use either regedit or regedt32 to open the Registry Editor.

10. **A.** To record the data while he is away (as opposed to watching the computer live), Mark should use the Performance Logs and Alerts snap-in.

NTFS, Users, and Groups

In this chapter, you will learn how to

- Create and administer Windows users and groups
- Define and use NTFS permissions for authorization
- Share a Windows computer securely
- Secure PCs with User Account Control

If you asked me what keeps Windows the number one operating system in the world, I'd say "Windows is the easiest operating system for securing resources, individual computers, and entire networks." Windows gets it right when it comes to protection. Using a combination of user accounts and groups that tie into the NTFS file system, Windows provides incredibly powerful file and folder protection. This user/group/NTFS combo scales from a single computer up to a network of computers spanning the world. Windows doesn't just stop at files and folders, either.

To understand security in Windows, you need to see it from Windows' point of view. In Windows, sharing files between users on a single machine and sharing files with users over a network are the same. When learning about users, groups, and NTFS permissions, however, it's helpful to think about a single PC. To that end, this chapter focuses on Windows security from the point of view of a single, or *standalone*, machine. I may dip into networks and domains from time to time, especially when the only differences are cosmetic, but Chapter 29 will revisit these topics in more detail and show you how the same tools scale up to help you protect a computer in a networked environment.

802

Authentication with Users and Groups

We've discussed the concept of users and groups in earlier chapters, but have you ever considered what user accounts and passwords actually do? To better understand their roles, you need to know two terms: authentication and authorization. *Authentication* is the process by which you determine a person at your computer is who he says he is and then grant him entry into the computer. In Windows, authentication is handled by a

password-protected user account. Once a user is authenticated, he needs *authorization*, which controls what an authenticated user can and cannot do on a system. Authorization for Windows' files and folders is controlled by the NTFS file system, which assigns permissions to users, groups, or both.

 EXAM TIP A good security practice to determine what type of user account to give to a specific person is the *principle of least privilege*. In essence, you want to give users just enough—but no more—permissions to accomplish their tasks. Giving more than needed begs for problems or accidents and should be avoided.

Microsoft's answer to the authentication/authorization process is amazing. Inside every Windows computer is a database of user accounts—an encrypted list of user names with their associated password—who are allowed access to the system. Each of these individual records is called a *local user account*. If you don't have a local user account created on a particular system, you won't be able to log on to that computer (see Figure 16-1).

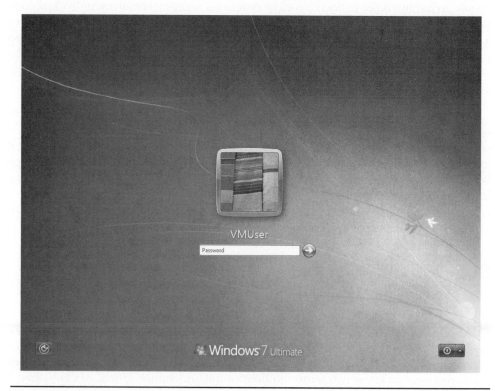

Figure 16-1 Windows logon screen

Every local user account needs a password (even if it's blank) and needs to belong to a group. Configuring these attributes requires tools in Windows for creating and managing users and groups. The tools used in Windows XP, however, are not the same as the tools used in Windows Vista or Windows 7. Each version of Windows includes one or two ways to deal with users and groups. Home editions of Windows (such as Windows XP Home Edition, Windows Vista Home Basic and Home Premium, and Windows 7 Home Premium) include a basic tool, while the professional editions of Windows (Windows XP Professional; Windows Vista Business, Ultimate, and Enterprise; and Windows 7 Professional, Ultimate, and Enterprise) include an extra, more advanced utility. That's a lot to learn about, and I'll explain all of these tools later in the chapter. First, I want to explain passwords and groups, which are common to users across all versions of Windows.

NOTE To create and manage users, you must have administrator privileges.

Passwords

Passwords are the ultimate key to protecting your computer. If someone learns your user name and password, they can log on to your computer. Even if the user account has only limited permissions—perhaps it can only read files, not edit them—you still have a security breach. Remember: for a hacker, just getting into the computer is half the battle.

Protect your passwords. Never give out passwords over the phone. If a user forgets a password, the network administrator should reset it to a complex combination of letters and numbers. The user should then change the password to something he or she wants, according to the parameters set by the administrator.

Make your users choose good passwords. I once attended a security seminar, and the speaker had everyone stand up. She then began to ask questions about our passwords—if we responded yes to the question, we were to sit down. She began to ask questions such as

"Do you use the name of your spouse as a password?" and

"Do you use your pet's name?"

By the time she had asked about 15 questions, only 6 people out of some 300 were still standing. The reality is that most of us choose passwords that are amazingly easy to hack. Make sure you use a *strong password*: at least eight characters in length, including letters, numbers, and punctuation symbols.

Using non-alphanumeric characters makes any password much more difficult to crack, for two reasons. First, adding non-alphanumeric characters forces the hacker to consider many more possible characters than just letters and numbers. Second, most password crackers use a combination of common words and numbers to hack passwords.

Because non-alphanumeric characters don't fit into common words or numbers, a character such as an exclamation point defeats these common-word hacks. Not all systems allow you to use characters such as @, $, %, or \, however, so you need to experiment.

CompTIA also recommends that you should have users change passwords at regular intervals. Although this concept sounds good on paper, it is a hard policy to maintain in the real world. For starters, users tend to forget passwords when they change a lot. This can lead to an even bigger security problem because users start writing passwords down.

If your organization forces you to change passwords often, one way to remember the password is to use a numbering system. I worked at a company that required me to change my password at the beginning of each month, so I did something very simple. I took a root password—let's say it was "m3y3rs5"—and simply added a number to the end representing the current month. So when June rolled around, for example, I would change my password to "m3y3rs56." It worked pretty well!

 NOTE Every secure organization sets up various security policies and procedures to ensure that security is maintained. Windows has various mechanisms to implement such things as requiring a strong password, for example. Chapter 29 goes into detail about setting up Local Policies and Group Policy.

Windows enables logged-on users to create a *password reset disk* they can use if they forget a password. This is very important to have. If you lose your password and an administrator resets it, you might not have access to all of the files you had access to before, especially if they were encrypted. When you reset a password with a password reset disk, you can log on with the new password and still have access to previously encrypted files.

Best of all, password reset disks enable users to fix their own passwords. Encourage your users to create this disk; they only have this power if they create a password reset disk *before* they forget the password! Windows Vista and Windows 7 have an obvious option in the Tasks list to *Create a password reset disk*. You need a USB flash drive to create the disk. If by some chance you still have a floppy drive, you can use a floppy disk—which is where the term "disk" in password reset disk came from.

 NOTE Don't be caught without a password reset disk. You won't think you need it until it's too late. Make one today.

In addition to supporting password reset disks, Windows 7 enables you to create a password hint for your accounts. This clue appears after your first logon attempt fails (see Figure 16-2).

Figure 16-2
Password hint on
the Windows 7
logon screen

Be aware that if your computer is a member of a domain, you cannot use password reset disks or password hints to recover your password. In those cases, the network administrator has to reset your password on the domain controller.

CAUTION Blank passwords or passwords that are easily visible on a sticky note provide no security. Always insist on non-blank passwords, and do not let anyone leave a password sitting out in the open.

Groups

A *group* is a collection of user accounts that can define the capabilities of its members. A single account can be a member of multiple groups. Groups are an efficient way of managing multiple users, especially when you are dealing with a whole network of accounts.

Groups make Windows administration much easier in two ways. First, you can assign a certain level of access for a file or folder to a group instead of to just a single user account. You can make a group called Accounting, for example, and put all the accounting user accounts in that group. If a person quits, you don't need to worry about assigning all of the proper access levels when you create a new account for his or her replacement. After you make an account for the new person, just add his account to the appropriate access group! Second, Windows provides numerous built-in groups with various access levels already predetermined. As you might imagine, there are differences among the versions of Windows, as described next.

Groups in Windows XP

Windows XP Professional provides seven built-in groups: Administrators, Power Users, Users, Backup Operators, Replicator, Everyone, and Guests. These built-in groups have a number of preset capabilities. You cannot delete these groups. Here's what you need to know about the five most important groups:

- **Administrators** Any account that is a member of the *Administrators group* has complete administrator privileges. Administrator privileges grant complete control over a machine. It is common for the primary user of a Windows system to have her account in the Administrators group.

- **Power Users** Members of the *Power Users group* are almost as powerful as Administrators, but they cannot install new devices or access other users' files or folders unless the files or folders specifically provide them access.

- **Users** Members of the *Users group* cannot edit the Registry or access critical system files. They can create groups but can manage only those they create.

- **Everyone** This group applies to any user who can log on to the system. You cannot edit this group.

- **Guests** The *Guests group* enables someone who does not have an account on the system to log on by using a guest account. You might use this feature at a party, for example, to provide casual Internet access to guests, or at a library terminal. Most often, the guest account remains disabled.

NOTE If you're running Windows XP Professional on a Windows domain, all of the groups listed previously are included, plus other specialized groups like HelpServicesGroup and Remote Desktop Users.

Windows XP Home Edition uses groups like its big, professional brother, but never shows the user. In fact, Home Edition only enables you to use three groups: Administrators, Users, and Guests. You'll understand more when I explain how to manage users in Windows XP, but for now, know that groups are severely limited in the Home Edition of Windows XP.

Groups in Windows Vista and Windows 7

The professional editions of Windows Vista (Business, Ultimate, and Enterprise) and Windows 7 (Professional, Ultimate, and Enterprise) offer the same groups found in Windows XP Professional and throw in a lot more. Some of the default groups, such as Distributed COM Users, target specific roles in certain industries and mean little for the average user or tech. Other specific groups enable people to check on the performance

and reliability of a computer without gaining access to any of the documents on the computer. These groups include Event Log Readers, Performance Log Users, and Performance Monitor Users. These groups provide excellent levels of access for technicians to help keep busy Vista/7 machines healthy.

 NOTE Windows Vista Enterprise and Windows 7 Enterprise users will almost always log on to a domain.

Like Windows XP, the home editions of Windows Vista and 7 (Home Basic and Home Premium) offer only three groups: Administrators, Users, and Guests. Administrators and Guests function as they do in all of the other versions of Windows. Members of the Users group, on the other hand, are called *standard users* and differ significantly from the limited users of Windows XP infamy. Standard users are prevented from harming the computer or uninstalling applications but can run most applications. Technicians don't have to run over to standard user accounts to enable access to common tasks such as printing or doing e-mail.

Simple Tools for Managing Users

While I've already covered some of what makes users and groups so powerful, Microsoft understood that everyday users wanted user accounts, too. Remember that, beyond all of the permissions and administrative privileges, user accounts also create personal folders for a user's files, such as his My Documents, My Photos, and My Music folders. To that end, every version and edition of Windows includes these simple tools for managing users, all of which are found in the Control Panel. You'll learn about a more advanced tool in the next section of this chapter.

Managing Users in Windows XP

Windows XP provides the *User Accounts applet* in the Control Panel for basic user and group management. Here you can create new users, delete users, change passwords, and so forth.

User Accounts hides the complete list of users using a simplistic reference to account types that is actually a reference to the user account's group membership. An account that is a member of the local Administrators group is called a *computer administrator*; an account that belongs only to the Local Users group is called a *limited user* account. Which users the applet displays depends on which type of user is currently logged on (see Figure 16-3). When an administrator is logged on, the administrator sees both types of accounts and the guest account. Limited users see only their own account in User Accounts.

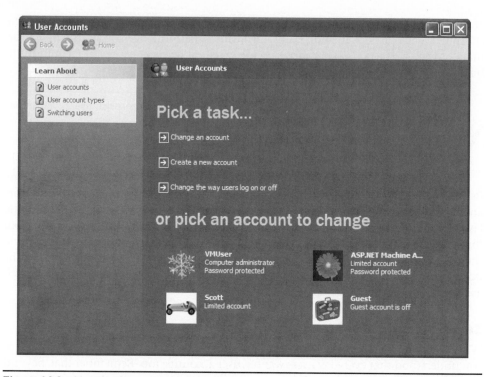

Figure 16-3 User Accounts dialog box showing a computer administrator, a couple of limited accounts, and the guest account (disabled)

Windows XP requires you to create a second account that is a member of the Administrators group during the initial Windows installation. This is for simple redundancy—if one administrator is not available or is not able to log on to the computer, another one can.

Creating users is a straightforward process. You need to provide a user name (a password can and should be added later), and you need to know which type of account to create: computer administrator or limited. To create a new user in Windows XP, open the User Accounts applet from the Control Panel and click *Create a new account*. On the *Pick an account type* page, you can create either type of account (see Figure 16-4). Simply follow the prompts on the screen. After you create your local accounts, you'll see them listed when you open the User Accounts applet.

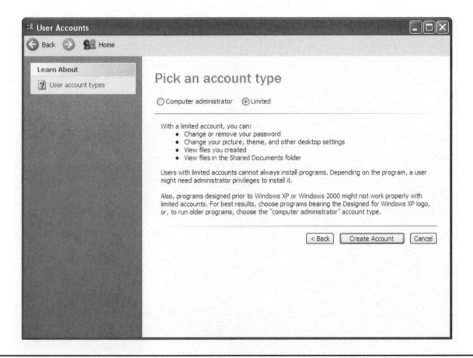

Figure 16-4 The Pick an account type page showing both options available

Head back to the User Accounts applet and look at the *Change the way users log on and off* option. Select it to see two checkboxes (see Figure 16-5). If you select the *Use the Welcome screen* checkbox, Windows brings up the friendly *Welcome screen* shown in Figure 16-6 each time users log on. If this box is unchecked, you'll get the classic logon screen (see Figure 16-7).

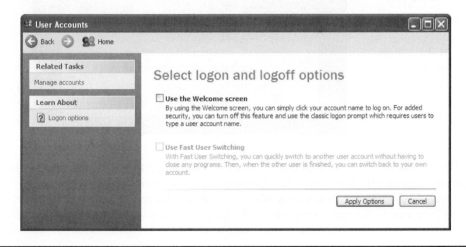

Figure 16-5 Select logon and logoff options

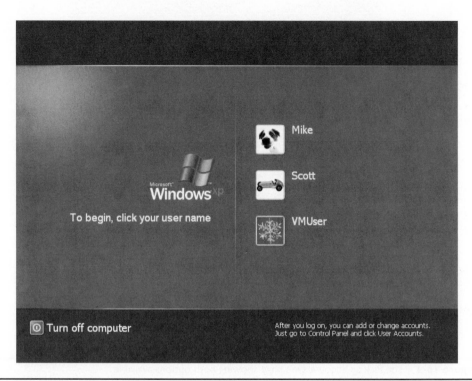

Figure 16-6 Welcome screen with three accounts

Figure 16-7
Classic logon
screen, XP style

The second option, Use Fast User Switching, enables you to switch to another user without logging off of the currently running user, a feature appropriately called *Fast User Switching*. This option is handy when two people actively share a system, or when someone wants to borrow your system for a moment but you don't want to close all of

your programs. This option is only active if you have the *Use the Welcome screen* checkbox enabled. If Fast User Switching is enabled, when you click the Log Off button on the Start menu, you get the option to switch users, as shown in Figure 16-8.

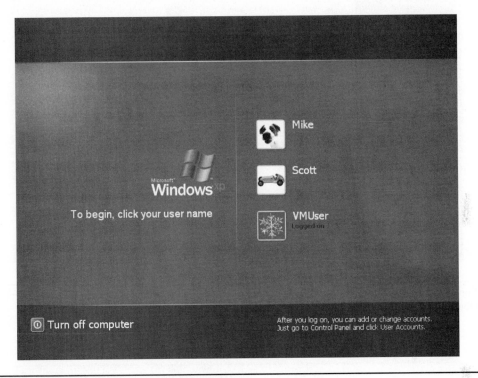

Figure 16-8 Switching users on the Welcome screen

Managing Users in Windows Vista

Microsoft made some major changes to user accounts and the applet used to create and modify them in Windows Vista. Just as with Windows XP, you create three accounts when you set up a computer: guest, administrator, and a local account that's a member of the Administrators group. That's about where the similarities end.

To add or modify a user account, you have numerous options depending on which Control Panel view you select and which edition and update of Vista you have installed. If your machine is on a workgroup, you'll see the User Accounts and Family Safety applet (see Figure 16-9). If you connect to a domain, the default Control Panel Home view offers the User Accounts applet (see Figure 16-10). The options in each applet differ as well, as you can see in the screenshots.

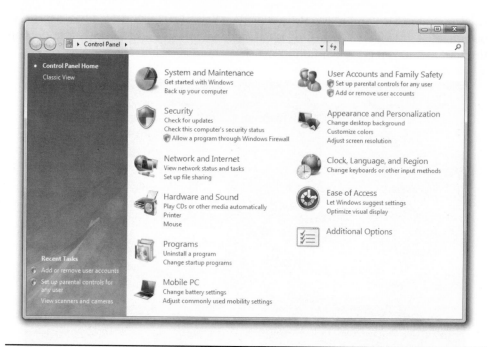

Figure 16-9 User Accounts and Family Safety applet in the Control Panel Home in Windows Vista Home Premium

Figure 16-10 User Accounts applet in the Control Panel Home in Windows Vista Ultimate

Most techs almost immediately change the Control Panel view to Classic, but even there the different versions of Windows—and whether you're logged on to a workgroup or a domain—give you different versions of the User Accounts applet. Figure 16-11 shows the User Accounts applet in Windows Vista Business in a domain environment. Figure 16-12 shows the applet in Windows Vista Home Premium.

Figure 16-11 User Accounts applet in Windows Vista Business

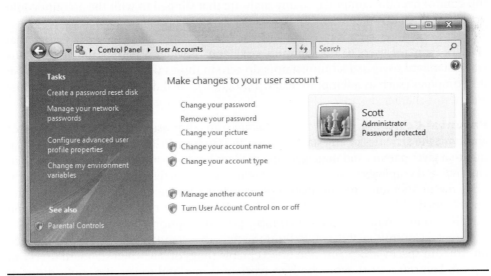

Figure 16-12 User Accounts applet in Windows Vista Home Premium

The Tasks links on the left are similar between editions of Windows (with the addition of Parental Controls in the Home Premium edition), but the main options differ a lot. This chapter focuses on standalone machines, so we'll look more closely at the options included with Vista Home Premium.

Windows Vista Home Premium uses Vista's version of the Welcome screen for logging on, so each user account has a picture associated with it. You can change the picture from the User Accounts applet. You can also change the name of the user account here and alter the account type, demoting an account from administrator to standard user, for example.

To add a user in Windows Vista, open the User Accounts applet. You may need to open User Accounts and Family Safety first. Click *Manage another account* and select *Create a new account*. Give the account a user name and select a user account type. Then click Create Account.

 NOTE At least one account must be an administrator account. If you try to demote the sole administrator account, you'll find the option dimmed.

User Account Control Windows XP made it too easy—and, in fact, almost necessary—to make your primary account on a computer an administrator account. Because limited users can't do common tasks, such as running certain programs, installing applications, updating applications, updating Windows, and so on, most users simply created an administrator-level account and logged on. Such accounts have full control over the computer, so any malware that slipped in with the account could do a lot more harm.

Microsoft addressed this problem with the *User Account Control (UAC)*, a feature that enables standard users to do common tasks and provides a permissions dialog box when standard users *and* administrators do certain things that could potentially harm the computer (such as attempt to install a program). We'll discuss UAC in detail at the end of this chapter.

Parental Controls With *Parental Controls*, an administrator account can monitor and limit the activities of any standard user in Windows Vista (and Windows 7), a feature that gives parents and managers an excellent level of control over the content their children and employees can access (see Figure 16-13). Activity Reporting logs applications run or attempted to run, Web sites visited or attempted to visit, any kind of files downloaded, and more. You can block various Web sites by type or specific URL, or you can allow only certain Web sites, a far more powerful option.

Parental Controls enable you to limit the time that standard users can spend logged on. You can specify acceptable and unacceptable times of day when standard users can log on. You can restrict access both to types of games and to specific applications. If you like playing rather gruesome games filled with monsters and blood that you don't want your kids to play, for example, you can simply block any games with certain ESRB (Entertainment Software Rating Board) ratings, such as E for Everyone, T for Teen, or M for Mature or Mature 17+.

Figure 16-13 Parental Controls

Managing Users in Windows 7

Windows 7 handles user creation in a manner very similar to Windows Vista, continuing the use of the User Accounts Control Panel applet. The Windows 7 applet is virtually identical to the one used in Windows Vista.

To create a user account, open the User Accounts applet and select *Manage another account* to see something like Figure 16-14.

Click on *Create a new account* to see your options for making a new account (see Figure 16-15). Note that this applet only enables you to make administrator accounts (in the Administrators group) or standard users (in the Users group).

While smaller, less sophisticated systems can get away with putting all their users into one of these two groups, you'll need to turn to Local Users and Groups to take full advantage of the power of Windows' users and groups.

Advanced User Management

The professional editions of Windows include the *Local Users and Groups* tool, a more powerful tool for working with user accounts. You can get to Local Users and Groups via Control Panel | Administrative Tools | Computer Management. From here, you can create, modify, and remove users and groups. Keep in mind, however, that this advanced tool will not hold your hand like the Control Panel applets. Think of the Local Users and Groups tool as a bike without the training wheels of the User Accounts applet. Figure 16-16 shows the Local Users and Groups tool in Windows Vista with Groups selected.

Figure 16-14 Manage Accounts

Figure 16-15 Adding a new user

Figure 16-16 Local Users and Groups in Windows Vista

To add a group, simply right-click on a blank spot in the Groups folder and select New Group. This opens the New Group dialog box, where you can type in a group name and description in their respective fields (see Figure 16-17).

Figure 16-17 New Group dialog box in Windows Vista

To add users to this group, click the Add button. The dialog box that opens varies a little in name among the three operating systems, though they all contain the same functionality (see Figure 16-18).

Figure 16-18
Select Users, Computers, or Groups dialog box in Windows Vista

You can add more than just users to a group. Windows uses multiple *object* types to define what you can add. Object types include user accounts, groups, and computers. Each object type can be added to a group and assigned permissions. The short story of how to add a user account is to click the Advanced button to expand the dialog box and then click the Find Now button (see Figure 16-19).

Figure 16-19
Select Users, Computers, or Groups dialog box with Advanced options expanded to show user accounts

You can either add group membership to a user's properties or add a user to a group's properties.

- To add group membership to a user account, select the Users folder, right-click a user account you want to change, and select Properties from the context menu. Then select the Member Of tab on the user account's Properties dialog box (see Figure 16-20). Click Add to add group membership.

- To add users via the group's properties, select the Groups folder. Right-click on a group and select Properties. Beneath the Members list, click the Add button to search for and add user accounts to the group.

Figure 16-20
Properties dialog box of a user account, where you can change group memberships for that account

You can also use either method to remove users. This level of flexibility makes the Local Users and Groups tool much more powerful and useful than the User Accounts Control Panel applets.

Authorization Through NTFS

User accounts and passwords provide the foundation for securing a Windows computer, enabling users to authenticate onto a PC. After you've created a user account, you need to determine what the user can do with the available resources (files, folders, applications, and so on). We call this process *authorization*. Windows uses the powerful NT File System (NTFS) to protect its resources. Let's delve into the amazing world of NTFS to see how this powerful file system protects your folder and files.

NTFS Permissions

In Windows, every folder and file on an NTFS partition has a list that contains two sets of data. First, the list details every user and group that has access to that file or folder. Second, the list specifies the level of access that each user or group has to that file or folder. The level of access is defined by a set of restrictions called NTFS permissions. *NTFS permissions* define exactly what any particular account can or cannot do to the file or folder and are thus quite detailed and powerful. You can make it possible, for example, for a person to edit a file but not delete it. You can configure NTFS permissions to enable someone to create a folder and not allow other people to make subfolders.

Here are a few rules about NTFS permissions:

1. You may see the NTFS permissions on a folder or file by accessing the file's or folder's Properties dialog box and opening the Security tab.

2. NTFS permissions are assigned both to user accounts and groups, although it's considered a best practice to assign permissions to groups and then add user accounts to groups instead of adding permissions directly to individual user accounts.

3. Whoever creates a folder or a file has complete control over that folder or file.

4. Administrators do not automatically have complete control over every folder and file. If an administrator wants to access a folder or file they do not have permission to access, they may go through a process called Take Control.

NTFS file and folder permissions are so complicated that entire books have been written on them! Fortunately, the CompTIA A+ 220-802 exam tests your understanding of only a few basic concepts of NTFS permissions: Ownership, Take Ownership permission, Change permission, folder permissions, and file permissions.

- **Ownership** When you create a new file or folder on an NTFS partition, you become the *owner* of that file or folder. Owners can do anything they want to the files or folders they own, including changing the permissions to prevent anybody, even administrators, from accessing them.

- **Take Ownership permission** With the *Take Ownership* special permission, anyone with the permission can seize control of a file or folder. Administrator accounts have Take Ownership permission for everything. Note the difference here between owning a file and accessing a file. If you own a file, you can prevent anyone from accessing that file. An administrator whom you have blocked, however, can take that ownership away from you and *then* access that file!

- **Change permission** Another important permission for all NTFS files and folders is the Change permission. An account with this permission can give or take away permissions for other accounts.

- **Folder permissions** Let's look at a typical folder on my Windows 7 system to see how this one works. My E: drive is formatted as NTFS, and on it I

created a folder called E:\Mike. I set the permissions for the E:\Mike folder by right-clicking on the folder, selecting Properties, and clicking the Security tab (see Figure 16-21).

- **File permissions** File permissions are similar to Folder permissions. We'll talk about File permissions right after we cover Folder permissions.

Figure 16-21
The Security tab lets you set permissions.

In Windows, just about everything in the computer has a Security tab in its Properties dialog box, and every Security tab contains two main areas. The top area shows the list of accounts that have permissions for that resource. The lower area shows exactly what permissions have been assigned to the selected account.

Here are the standard permissions for a folder:

- **Full Control** Enables you to do anything you want.
- **Modify** Enables you to do anything except delete files or subfolders, change permissions, or take ownership.
- **Read & Execute** Enables you to see the contents of the folder and any subfolders.

- **List Folder Contents** Enables you to see the contents of the folder and any subfolders. (This permission seems the same as the Read & Execute permission, but it is only inherited by folders.)
- **Read** Enables you to view a folder's contents and open any file in the folder.
- **Write** Enables you to write to files and create new files and folders.

File permissions are quite similar to folder permissions, with the main difference being the Special Permissions option, which I'll talk about a bit later in the chapter.

- **Full Control** Enables you to do anything you want.
- **Modify** Enables you to do anything except take ownership or change permissions on the file.
- **Read & Execute** Enables you to open files and applications.
- **Read** Enables you to open files.
- **Write** Enables you to open and write to the file.

 EXAM TIP Don't panic about memorizing special permissions; just appreciate that they exist and that the permissions you see in the Security tab cover the vast majority of our needs.

Take some time to think about these permissions. Why would Microsoft create them? Think of situations where you might want to give a group Modify permission. Also, you can assign more than one permission. In many situations, we like to give users both the Read and Write permissions.

Permissions are cumulative. If you have Full Control on a folder and only Read permission on a file in the folder, you get Full Control permission on the file.

 NOTE Windows editions for home use have only a limited set of permissions you can assign. As far as folder permissions go, you can assign only one: Make This Folder Private. To see this in action, right-click a file or folder and select Sharing and Security from the options. Note that you can't just select Properties and see a Security tab as you can in the professional-oriented editions of Windows. Windows home editions do not have file-level permissions.

Permission Propagation

Permissions present an interesting challenge when you're moving and copying files. Techs need to understand what happens to permissions in several circumstances:

- Copying data within one NTFS-based partition
- Moving data within one NTFS-based partition

- Copying data between two NTFS-based partitions
- Moving data between two NTFS-based partitions
- Copying data from an NTFS-based partition to a FAT- or FAT32-based partition
- Moving data from an NTFS-based partition to a FAT- or FAT32-based partition

Do the permissions stay as they were on the original resource? Do they change to something else? Microsoft would describe the questions as such: Do inheritable permissions propagate? Ugh. CompTIA describes the process with the term *permission propagation*, which I take to mean "what happens to permissions on an object when you move or copy that object."

In Windows 7, if you access a folder's Properties dialog box, click on the Security tab, and then click the Advanced button, you'll see a little checkbox that says *Include inheritable permissions from this object's parent*. In other words, a user receives the parent folder's permissions for any files or subfolders created in that folder—a feature called *inheritance*. All versions of Windows have inheritance turned on by default, which most of the time is a good idea. However, there might be times where you want to turn off inheritance. Deselecting this option enables you to stop users from getting a specific permission via inheritance. Windows also provides explicit Deny functions for each option (see Figure 16-22). Deny overrules inheritance.

Let's look at our list of six things techs need to know to see what happens when you copy or move an object, such as a file or folder.

1. Copying within a partition creates two copies of the object. The object in the original location *retains* its permissions, unchanged. The copy of the object in the new location *inherits* the permissions from that new location. The new copy can have different permissions than the original.

2. Moving within a partition creates one copy of the object. That object *retains* its permissions, unchanged.

3. Copying from one NTFS partition to another creates two copies of the object. The object in the original location *retains* its permissions, unchanged. The copy of the object in the new location *inherits* the permissions from that new location. The new copy can have different permissions than the original.

4. Moving from one NTFS partition to another creates one copy of the object. The object in the new location *inherits* the permissions from that new location. The newly moved file can have different permissions than the original.

5. Copying from an NTFS-based partition to a FAT- or FAT32-based partition creates two copies of the object. The object in the original location *retains* its permissions, unchanged. The copy of the object in the new location has no permissions at all.

6. Moving from an NTFS-based partition to a FAT- or FAT32-based partition creates one copy of the object. That object has no permissions at all.

Figure 16-22 Special permissions

From a tech's standpoint, you need to be aware of how permissions can change when you move or copy files and, if in doubt about a sensitive file, check it before you sign off to a client. Having a top secret document totally locked down on a hard drive doesn't do you a lot of good if you put that document on a thumb drive to transport it and the thumb drive is FAT32!

Techs and Permissions

Techs, as a rule, hate NTFS permissions. You must have administrative privileges to do almost anything on a Windows machine, such as install updates, change drivers, and install applications; most administrators hate giving out administrative permissions (for obvious reasons). If an administrator does give you administrative permission for a PC, and something goes wrong with that system while you're working on it, you immediately become the primary suspect!

If you're working on a Windows system administered by someone else, make sure he understands what you are doing and how long you think it will take. Have the administrator create a new account for you that's a member of the Administrators group. Never ask for the password for a permanent administrator account! That way, you won't be blamed if anything goes wrong on that system: "Well, I told Janet the password when she installed the new hard drive...maybe she did it!" When you have fixed the system, *make sure the administrator deletes the account you used.*

This "protect yourself from passwords" attitude applies to areas other than just doing tech support on Windows. PC support folks get lots of passwords, scan cards, keys, and ID tags. New techs tend to get an "I can go anywhere and access anything" attitude, and this is dangerous. I've seen many jobs lost and friendships ruined when a backup suddenly disappears or a critical file gets erased. Everybody points to the support tech in these situations. In physical security situations, make other people unlock doors for you. In some cases, I've literally asked the administrator or system owner to sit behind me, read a magazine, and be ready to punch in passwords as needed. What you don't have access to can't hurt you.

Sharing a Windows PC Securely

User accounts, groups, and NTFS work together to enable you to share a Windows PC securely with multiple user accounts. You can readily share files, folders, programs, and more. More to the point, you can share only what should be shared, locking access to files and folders that you want to make private. Each version of Windows handles multiple user accounts and sharing among those accounts differently, so let's look at Windows XP, Windows Vista, and Windows 7 separately and then finish with a look at a few other sharing and security issues.

Sharing in Windows XP

Microsoft tried to make secure sharing in Windows XP easier than it was in previous versions of Windows. To this end, Microsoft included several features. Each user account gets a series of folders in My Documents that the user can share and administrators can access. Windows XP also comes with a set of pre-made folders called *Shared Documents* that are accessible by all of the users on the computer. Also, Windows XP comes with simple file sharing enabled by default, which makes the option to share or not pretty easy. Finally, Windows XP Professional provides the option to use the full NTFS permissions and make customized shares possible.

Making Personal Documents Secure

The fact that most users of Windows XP computers will be computer administrators rather than limited users creates a bit of an issue with computers shared by many users. By default, administrators can see all of the contents of Documents and Settings, where the My Documents folder for each user account resides. You can override this option in the My Documents Properties dialog box. Selecting the option to *Make this folder private* blocks the contents from anyone accessing them (see Figure 16-23).

Figure 16-23

Making personal documents secure from prying eyes

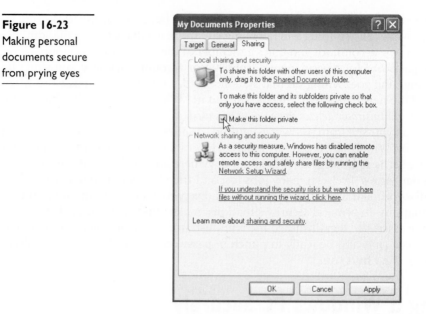

Note that an administrator can take ownership of anything, so the only true way to lock down your data is to encrypt it. In the My Documents Properties dialog box, select the General tab and then click the Advanced button to open the Advanced Attributes dialog box. Click the checkbox next to *Encrypt contents to secure data* and that'll handle the encryption. Just make sure you have a password reset disk if you're going to use encryption to secure your files.

Shared Documents

You can use the Shared Documents folders to move files and folders among many users of a single machine. Every account can access the Shared Documents folder and the subfolders within, such as Shared Music and Shared Pictures (see Figure 16-24). Because new folders inherit the permissions of parent folders, by default any new sub-folder you create in Shared Documents can be accessed by any account.

Simple File Sharing

With *simple file sharing*, you essentially have one local sharing option, and that's to put anything you want to share into the Shared Documents folder or one of its subfolders. To share a folder over a network, you only have a couple of options as well, such as to share or not and, if so, to give full control to everybody. Note that the sharing option is enabled in Figure 16-25. It's pretty much all or nothing.

Windows XP Home and Media Center only give you the simple file sharing method, so the sharing of files and folders is straightforward. Windows XP Professional, on the other hand, enables you to turn off simple file sharing and unlock the true power of NTFS and permissions. To turn off simple file sharing, open a view of Windows Explorer (such as My Documents), choose Tools | Folder Options, and select the View

tab. The very last option on the View tab is *Use simple file sharing (Recommended)*. Deselect that option, as in Figure 16-26, and then click OK.

Figure 16-24
Shared Music Properties dialog box

Figure 16-25
Folder shared, but seriously not secure

Figure 16-26
Turning off simple file sharing

When you access sharing and security now, you'll see a more fully formed security dialog box (see Figure 16-27).

Figure 16-27
Full sharing and security options in Windows XP

 NOTE When you add a Windows XP Professional system to a domain, simple file sharing is disabled. You must use the full power of NTFS.

Sharing in Windows Vista

Microsoft tweaked the settings for sharing a single PC with multiple users in Windows Vista to fix the all-or-nothing approach offered by simple file sharing; Vista enables you to target shared files and folders to specific user accounts. Microsoft beefed up the standard user account (as you read about earlier in the chapter) so users could access what they needed to get meaningful work done. Plus they expanded the concept of the Shared Documents folder into the Public folders.

Targeted Sharing

To share a folder or file with specific users—or with everyone, for that matter—you simply right-click on it and select Share. This opens the File Sharing dialog box, where you can select specific user accounts from a drop-down list (see Figure 16-28).

Figure 16-28 File Sharing dialog box on a standalone machine

Once you select a user account, you can then choose what permission level to give that user. You have three choices: Reader, Contributor, or Co-owner (see Figure 16-29). *Reader* simply means the user has read-only permissions. *Contributor* gives the user read

and write permissions and the permission to delete any file the user contributed to the folder. (Contributor only works at the folder level.) *Co-owner* enables the user to do anything.

Figure 16-29 Permissions options

NOTE If the computer in question is on a Windows domain, the File Sharing dialog box differs such that you can search the network for user accounts in the domain. This makes it easy to share throughout the network.

Public Folders

Public folders offer another way to share files and folders. Anything you want to share with all other users on the local machine—or, if on a network, throughout the network—simply place it in the Public folder or one of the many subfolders, such as Public Documents or Public Pictures (see Figure 16-30). Note that the Public folder does not give you any control over what someone accessing the files contained within can do with those files.

Figure 16-30 Shared folders in the Public folder

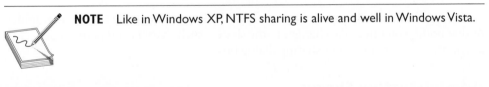

NOTE Like in Windows XP, NTFS sharing is alive and well in Windows Vista.

Sharing in Windows 7

Windows 7 keeps the file sharing options of Windows Vista and adds homegroups to the mix. You already learned all about homegroups in Chapter 5, but here's a quick refresher: Instead of sharing individual files or folders, you can use HomeGroup to share libraries, such as your Documents or Music libraries. Any files in your shared libraries will be automatically accessible by everyone in the homegroup, though you can also use more specific permissions. You'll need a password to join a homegroup, so any shared data will be secure.

Locating Shared Folders

Before you walk away from a computer, you should check for any unnecessary or unknown (to you) shared folders on the hard drives. This enables you to make the computer as secure as possible for the user. When you open My Computer or Computer, shared folders don't just jump out at you, especially if they're buried deep within the file system. A shared C: drive is obvious, but a shared folder all the way down in

D:\temp\backup\Simon\secret share would not be obvious, especially if none of the parent folders were shared.

Windows comes with a handy tool for locating all of the shared folders on a computer, regardless of where they reside on the drives. The Computer Management console in the Administrative Tools has a Shared Folders option under System Tools. In that are three options: Shares, Sessions, and Open Files. Select Shares to reveal all of the shared folders (see Figure 16-31).

Figure 16-31 Shared Folders tool in Computer Management

You can double-click on any share to open the Properties dialog box for that folder. At that point, you can make changes to the share—such as users and permissions—just as you would from any other sharing dialog box.

Administrative Shares

A close glance at the screenshot in Figure 16-31 might have left some of you with raised eyebrows and quizzical looks. What kind of share is ADMIN$ or C$?

Every version of Windows since Windows NT comes with several default shares, notably all hard drives—not optical drives or removable devices, such as thumb drives—plus the %systemroot% folder—usually C:\Windows—and a couple of others, depending on the system. These *administrative shares* give local administrators administrative access to these resources, whether they log on locally or remotely. (In contrast, shares added manually are called *local shares*.)

Administrative shares are odd ducks. You cannot change the default permissions on them. You can delete them, but Windows will re-create them automatically every time you reboot. They're hidden, so they don't appear when you browse a machine over the network, though you can map them by name. Keep the administrator password safe, and these default shares won't affect the overall security of the computer.

NOTE Administrative shares have been exploited by malware programs, especially because many users who set up their computers never give the administrator account a password. Starting with Windows XP Home, Microsoft changed the remote access permissions for such machines. If you log on to a computer remotely as administrator with no password, you get guest access rather than administrator access. That neatly nips potential exploits in the bud.

Protecting Data with Encryption

The scrambling of data through *encryption* techniques provides the only true way to secure your data from access by any other user. Administrators can use the Take Ownership permission to seize any file or folder on a computer, even those you don't actively share. Thus you need to implement other security measures for that data that needs to be ultra secure. Depending on the version of Windows, you have between zero and three encryptions tools: Windows Home editions (Windows XP Home Edition, Windows Vista Home Basic and Home Premium, and Windows 7 Home Premium) have basically no security features; Windows XP Professional uses the Encrypting File System to, well, encrypt files; and Windows Vista/7 Ultimate and Enterprise add an encryption system that can encrypt entire hard drives.

Encrypting File System

The professional editions of Windows (Windows XP Professional; Windows Vista Business, Ultimate, and Enterprise; and Windows 7 Professional, Ultimate, and Enterprise) offer a feature called the *Encrypting File System (EFS)*, an encryption scheme that any user can use to encrypt individual files or folders on a computer. The home editions of Windows do not enable encryption through the built-in tools, though you have the option to use third-party encryption methods, such as TrueCrypt, to lock down data.

To encrypt a file or folder takes but a moment. You right-click the file or folder you want to encrypt and select Properties. In the Properties dialog box for that object, select the General tab and click the Advanced button (see Figure 16-32) to open the Advanced Attributes dialog box. Click the checkbox next to *Encrypt contents to secure data* (see Figure 16-33). Click OK to close the Advanced Attributes dialog box and then click OK again on the Properties dialog box, and you've locked that file or folder from any user account aside from your own.

NOTE Encryption is just one possible *attribute* of a file. You can also make files hidden, read-only, and more, all from a file or folder's Properties dialog box. You'll learn more about attributes in Chapter 18.

Figure 16-32
Click the Advanced
button on the
General tab

As long as you maintain the integrity of your password, any data you encrypt by using EFS is secure from prying. That security comes at a potential price, though, and your password is the key. The Windows security database stores the password (securely, not plain text, so no worries there), but that means access to your encrypted files is based on that specific installation of Windows. If you lose your password or an administrator resets your password, you're locked out of your encrypted files permanently. There's no recovery. Also, if the computer dies and you try to retrieve your data by installing the hard drive in another system, you're likewise out of luck. Even if you have an identical user name on the new system, the security ID that defines that user account will differ from what you had on the old system.

NOTE Remember the password reset disk we discussed earlier in the chapter? If you use EFS, you simply must have a valid password reset disk in the event of some horrible catastrophe.

And one last caveat. If you copy an encrypted file to a disk formatted as anything but NTFS, you'll get a prompt saying that the copied file will not be encrypted. If you copy to a disk with NTFS, the encryption stays. The encrypted file—even if on a removable disk—will only be readable on your system with your login.

Figure 16-33

Selecting

encryption

BitLocker Drive Encryption

Windows Vista/7's Ultimate and Enterprise editions offer full drive encryption through *BitLocker Drive Encryption*. BitLocker encrypts the whole drive, including every user's files, so it's not dependent on any one account. The beauty of BitLocker is that if your hard drive is stolen, such as in the case of a stolen portable computer, all of the data on the hard drive is safe. The thief can't get access, even if you have a user on that laptop that failed to secure his or her data through EFS.

BitLocker requires a special Trusted Platform Module (TPM) chip on the motherboard to function. The TPM chip validates on boot that the Vista/7 computer has not changed—that you still have the same operating system installed, for example, and that the computer wasn't hacked by some malevolent program. The TPM also works in cases where you move the BitLocker drive from one system to another.

If you have a legitimate BitLocker failure (rather than a theft) because of tampering or moving the drive to another system, you need to have a properly created and accessible recovery key or recovery password. The key or password is generally created at the time you enable BitLocker and should be kept somewhere secure, such as a printed copy in a safe or a file on a network server accessible only to administrators.

To enable BitLocker, double-click the BitLocker Drive Encryption icon in the Classic Control Panel, or select Security in Control Panel Home view and then click *Protect your computer by encrypting data on your disk* (see Figure 16-34).

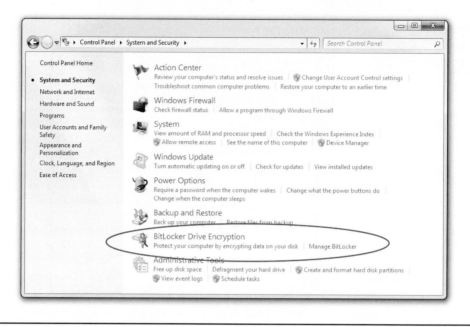

Figure 16-34 Enabling BitLocker Drive Encryption

User Account Control

When picking the poster child for the "327 Reasons We Hated Vista" list, I'll bet most folks put Vista's *User Account Control (UAC)* at the very top. Vista's UAC manifested as a pop-up dialog box that seemed to appear every time you tried to do *anything* on a Windows Vista system (see Figure 16-35).

Figure 16-35
UAC in action.
Arrgh!

It's too bad that UAC got such a bad rap. Not only is UAC an important security update for Windows Vista and Windows 7, but it is also a common feature in both Mac OS and Linux/Unix. Figure 16-36 shows the equivalent feature on a Mac.

Figure 16-36
UAC equivalent on
a Mac

If every other major operating system uses something like UAC, why was Microsoft slammed so hard when they unveiled UAC in Windows Vista? The reason is simple: Windows users are spoiled rotten, and, until UAC came along, the vast majority of users had no idea how risky their computing behavior was.

The problem started years ago when Microsoft created NTFS. NTFS uses robust user accounts and enables fine control over how users access files and folders—but at a cost: NTFS in its pure form is somewhat complicated. To share a folder, you need to make sure the person accessing that folder has a user account and that you've configured the NTFS permissions to give that user the permissions needed to do whatever he or she wants to do (see Figure 16-37).

Figure 16-37
Typically confusing
settings for NTFS
permissions

User accounts have always been a bit of a challenge. The only account that can truly do *anything* on a Windows system is the administrator. Sure, you can configure a system with groups and assign NTFS permissions to those groups—and this is commonly done on large networks with a full-time IT staff—but what about small offices and home networks? These users almost never have the skill sets to deal with the complexities of users and groups, which often results in systems where the user accounts are all assigned administrator privileges by default—and that's when it gets dangerous (see Figure 16-38).

Figure 16-38 The danger of administrator privileges in the wrong hands!

UAC in Windows Vista

User Account Control enables users to know when they are about to do something that has serious consequences. The Microsoft TechNet library ("Understanding and Configuring User Account Control in Windows Vista") provides examples of common actions that require Administrator privileges:

- Installing and uninstalling applications
- Installing a driver for a device (e.g., a digital camera driver)

- Installing Windows Updates
- Configuring Parental Controls
- Installing an ActiveX control
- Adjusting Windows Firewall settings
- Changing a user's account type
- Modifying UAC settings in the Security Policy Editor snap-in (secpol.msc)
- Configuring Remote Desktop access
- Adding or removing a user account
- Coping or moving files into the Program Files or Windows directory
- Scheduling Automated Tasks
- Restoring system backed-up files
- Configuring Automatic Updates
- Browsing to another user's directory

Before Vista, Microsoft invented the idea of the Power Users group to give users almost all of the power of an administrator account (to handle most of the situations just described) without actually giving users the full power of the account. Assigning a user to the Power Users group still required someone who knew how to do this, however, so most folks at the small office/home level simply ignored the Power Users group (see Figure 16-39).

Figure 16-39 Power Users group—almost never used at the small office/home level

Clearly, Microsoft needed a better method to prevent people from running programs that they should not run. If users have the correct privileges, however—or the ability to "escalate" their privileges to that of an administrator—then they should be able to do what they need to do as simply as possible. Microsoft needed to make the following changes:

- The idea of using an administrator account for daily use needed to go away.

- Any level of account should be able to do anything as easily as possible.

- If a regular account wants to do something that requires administrator privileges, the user of the regular account will need to enter the administrator password.

- If a user with administrator privileges wants to run something that requires administrator privileges, the user will not have to reenter his or her password, but the user will have to respond to an "Are you sure?"-type dialog box so he or she appreciates the gravity of the action—thus, the infamous UAC dialog box.

How UAC Works

UAC works for both standard user accounts and administrator accounts. If a standard user attempts to do something that requires administrator privileges, he or she sees a UAC dialog box that prompts for the administrator password (see Figure 16-40).

Figure 16-40
Prompting for an administrator password in Vista

If a user with administrator privileges attempts to do something that requires administrator privileges, a simpler UAC dialog box appears, like the one shown in Figure 16-41.

Figure 16-41

Classic UAC prompt

NOTE The official name for the UAC dialog box is the "UAC consent prompt." When the UAC consent prompt appears in Vista, the rest of the desktop darkens and you cannot take any other action until you respond to the consent prompt.

Interestingly, Vista has not one but four different UAC prompts, depending on the program/feature you wish to run, as outlined in Table 16-1.

UAC Classification	Type of Program
Blocked	A program that has been blocked by a security policy
Unverified	An unknown third-party program
Verified	A digitally signed, third-party program or non-core OS program
Published by Vista	A program that is a core part of the operating system

Table 16-1 UAC Prompts in Windows Vista

Blocked programs generate a scary-looking, red-bannered dialog box like the one shown in Figure 16-42. Note you can click OK in Windows Vista (or Close in Windows 7) or look at more details (if available).

Figure 16-42

Blocked program

Unverified programs lack any form of certificate to validate. In this case, you get a yellow-bannered dialog box warning you the application is unsigned and giving you two options: allow the program to run (Yes) or not (No). See Figure 16-43 for an example of this.

Figure 16-43
Unverified program

Verified programs aren't part of the core of Vista and are usually written by third parties. These programs do have valid, verified certificates. You can identify the dialog box by its gray-blue banner (see Figure 16-44).

Figure 16-44
Verified program

Published by Vista programs are written as part of the core of Vista and show up with a teal-bannered dialog box (see Figure 16-45).

Figure 16-45
Published by Vista

UAC uses small shield icons to warn you ahead of time that it will prompt you before certain tasks, as shown in Figure 16-46. Microsoft updated this somewhat redundant feature in Windows 7, as you'll soon see.

Figure 16-46 Shield icons in the Control Panel

UAC gives users running a program an opportunity to consider their actions before they move forward. It's a good thing, but spoiled Windows users aren't accustomed to something that makes them consider their actions. As a result, one of the first things everyone learned how to do when Vista came out was to turn off UAC.

How to Turn Off UAC
You can turn off UAC in a number of ways in Windows. Here are the two most common ways:

1. In the User Accounts Control Panel applet, you'll see an option to *Turn User Account Control on or off* (see Figure 16-47). Select this option and uncheck the checkbox to turn UAC off. Check the checkbox to turn it on again.

Figure 16-47 Turning User Account Control on or off

2. Open up the System Configuration utility (msconfig) and select *Disable UAC* on the Tools tab, as shown in Figure 16-48. You'll have to reboot for the changes to take effect. Note you can also turn on UAC from the System Configuration utility.

Figure 16-48
Disabling UAC in the System Configuration utility

UAC in Windows Vista worked well, but it startled users. Suddenly, users had to deal with UAC, and they didn't like that. Most users simply turned UAC off and added it to the reasons to not like Windows Vista.

UAC in Windows 7

Microsoft may be a huge company, but it still knows how to react when its customers speak out about features they don't like. Windows 7 unveiled a more refined, less "in-your-face" UAC that makes the feature much easier to use.

NOTE All references to Control Panel applets in Windows 7 assume you are using the Small Icon view.

A More Granular UAC

Microsoft did some research on why UAC drove users nuts, concluding that the problem wasn't UAC itself but the "I'm constantly in your face or you can turn me off and you get no help at all" aspect. To make UAC less aggressive, Microsoft introduced four UAC levels. To see these levels, go to the User Accounts applet and select *Change User Account Control settings*, as shown in Figure 16-49. When you select this option, you see the dialog box in Figure 16-50.

Figure 16-49 Change User Account Control settings option

In Figure 16-50, you can see a slider with four levels. The top level (Always notify) means you want UAC to work exactly as it does in Vista, displaying the aggressive consent form every time you do anything that typically requires administrator access. The bottom option (Never notify) turns off UAC. The two levels in the middle are new and are very similar. Both of them do the following:

- Don't notify me when I make changes.
- Notify me only when programs try to makes changes.

Figure 16-50 Four levels of UAC

The only difference is in *how* they show the change. The second-from-top level will display the typical consent form, but only when programs try to make changes. The third-from-top level displays a consent form, but where the normal consent form dims your desktop and doesn't allow you to do anything but address the form, this consent form just pops up like a normal dialog box.

 EXAM TIP Make sure you know what each of the four UAC levels does.

Program Changes Versus Changes I Make

So what's the difference between a program making a change and you making a change? Take a look at Figure 16-51. In this case, Windows 7 is set to the second-from-top option. A program (the very safe and, judging by the color of the banner, verified) Adobe Download Manager is attempting to install a feature into Internet Explorer. Because this is a program trying to make changes, the UAC consent form appears and darkens the desktop.

Figure 16-51
Darkened UAC

If you lower the UAC to the third-from-top option, you still see a consent form, but now it acts like a typical dialog box, as shown in Figure 16-52.

Figure 16-52
Non-darkened
UAC

EXAM TIP The default behavior for UAC in Windows 7 is the second-from-top option, which results in a screen similar to Figure 16-51.

A program such as the Adobe program described earlier is very different from a feature *you* want to change. Notice the shields, as shown earlier in Figure 16-49.

Each of these options isn't a program—each is merely a feature built into Windows. Those shields tell you that clicking the feature next to a shield will require administrator privileges. If you were to pick the Vista-strength UAC option, you'd get a UAC consent prompt when you click one of those features. If you set UAC to any of the three lower settings, however, you'd go straight to that feature without *any* form of UAC consent prompt. Of course, this isn't true if you don't have administrator privileges. If you're a standard user, you'll still be prompted for a password, just as in Vista.

Overall, the improvements to UAC in Windows 7 show that it has a place on everyone's computer. UAC might cause an occasional surprise or irritation, but that one more "Are you sure?" could mean the difference between safe and unsafe computing. So go ahead, turn UAC back on in Windows 7! It's well worth the small inconvenience.

Chapter Review

Questions

1. Which of the following tools would enable you to create a new user account in Windows XP?

 A. User Accounts

 B. User Account Control

 C. Users and Groups

 D. Users and Passwords

2. Which feature in Windows XP enables you to change to another user account without logging out of the current user account?

 A. Change Accounts

 B. Fast User Switching

 C. User Account Control

 D. Users and Groups

3. Which is the best password for the user Joy, who has a pet named Fido and a birth date of January 8, 1982?

 A. joy1982

 B. joylovesfido

 C. 1982cutie

 D. oddvr88*

4. How can you encrypt an entire drive, including files and folders belonging to other users?

 A. EFS

 B. User Account Control

 C. Administrative Shares

 D. BitLocker

5. What feature in Windows 7 opens a consent prompt for standard users to enter administrator credentials to accomplish various tasks reserved for the latter group?

 A. User Access Command

 B. User Access Control

 C. User Account Command

 D. User Account Control

6. Which permission enables an administrator to change the ownership of a file without knowing the user account password for that file?

 A. Change permission

 B. Change Ownership permission

 C. Ownership permission

 D. Take Ownership permission

7. You copy a file from a folder on a hard drive formatted as NTFS, with permissions set to Read for everyone, to a USB thumb drive formatted as FAT32. What permissions does the copy of the file have?

 A. Read-only for everyone

 B. Full Control for everyone

 C. None

 D. You can't copy a file from an NTFS drive to a FAT32 drive.

8. What set of folders is available to all users on a computer in Windows XP?

 A. My Documents

 B. Personal Documents

 C. Public folder

 D. Shared Documents

9. Which of the following operating systems do not allow you to disable simple file sharing? (Select two.)

 A. Windows XP Home

 B. Windows XP Media Center

 C. Windows XP Professional

 D. Windows Vista Ultimate

10. Which of the following file systems enables you to encrypt files, thus making them unviewable by any account but your own?

 A. EFS

 B. FAT

 C. FAT32

 D. OSR

Answers

1. **A.** User Accounts would enable you to create a new user account in Windows XP.

2. **B.** In Windows XP, Fast User Switching enables you to change to another user account without logging out of the current user account.

3. **D.** Of the choices listed, oddvr88* would be the best password; it has a non-alphanumeric character, which makes it more difficult for a hacker to crack.

4. **D.** BitLocker Drive Encryption enables you to encrypt an entire drive, including files and folders belonging to other users.

5. **D.** The User Account Control feature in Windows 7 provides a consent prompt for standard users to enter administrator credentials to accomplish various tasks normally reserved for the Administrators group.

6. **D.** The Take Ownership permission enables an administrator to change the ownership of a file without knowing the user account password for that file.

7. **C.** The key here is that you are copying from an NTFS hard drive to a FAT32 USB drive. Copying from an NTFS-based partition to a FAT- or FAT32-based partition creates two copies of the object; the copy of the object in the new location has no permissions at all.

8. **D.** The Shared Documents set of folders is available to all users on a computer in Windows XP.

9. **A, B.** Windows XP Home and Windows XP Media Center do not allow you to disable simple file sharing.

10. **A.** The Encrypting File System (EFS) enables you to encrypt files, making them unviewable by any account but your own.

Maintaining and Optimizing Windows

In this chapter, you will learn how to
- Perform maintenance tasks in Windows
- Optimize Windows
- Prepare Windows for problems

Every computer running a Windows operating system requires both occasional optimization to keep the system running snappily and ongoing maintenance to make sure nothing goes wrong. Microsoft uses its decades of experience with operating systems to search for ways to make the tasks of maintaining and optimizing surprisingly easy and very automatic, but there's still plenty to do to keep things humming along.

The chapter covers maintenance and optimization, so let's make sure you know what these two terms mean. *Maintenance* means jobs you do from time to time to keep Windows running well, such as running hard drive utilities. CompTIA sees *optimization* as jobs you do to your Windows system to make it better—a good example is updating drivers to make hardware perform better. This chapter covers the standard maintenance and optimization activities performed on Windows and the tools techs use to perform them.

Even the best maintained, most perfectly optimized computer is going to run into trouble. Hard drives crash, naïve coworkers delete files, and those great new video card drivers sometimes fail. The secret isn't to try to avoid trouble, because trouble will find you, but rather to make sure you're ready to deal with problems when they arise. This is one area that very few users do well, and it's our jobs as techs to make recovery from trouble as painless as possible. Microsoft gives us plenty of tools to prep for problems—we just need to make sure we use them.

802

Maintaining Windows

Maintaining Windows can be compared to maintaining a new automobile. Of course, a new automobile comes with a warranty, so most of us just take it to the dealer to get

work done. In this case, however, *you* are the mechanic, so you need to think as an auto mechanic would think. First, an auto mechanic needs to apply recalls when the auto-maker finds a serious problem. For a PC tech, that means installing the latest system patches released by Microsoft. You also need to check on the parts that wear down over time. On a car, that might mean changing the oil or rotating the tires. In a Windows system, that includes keeping the hard drive and Registry organized and uncluttered.

Windows Patch Management

There's no such thing as a perfect operating system, and Windows is no exception. From the moment Microsoft releases a new version of Windows, malware attacks, code errors, new hardware, new features, and many other issues compel Microsoft to provide updates, known more generically as *patches* in the computing world, to the operating system. The process of keeping software updated in a safe and timely fashion is known as *patch management*. Microsoft has been a leader in the process of patch management for decades. Microsoft's primary distribution tool for handling patch management is a Web site and a Control Panel applet called Windows Update.

Windows Update separates the available fixes into distinct types: updates and service packs. *Updates* are individual fixes that come out fairly often, on the order of once a week or so. Individual updates are usually fairly small, rarely more than a few mega-bytes. A *service pack* is a large bundle of updates plus anything else Microsoft might choose to add. Service packs are invariably large (hundreds of megabytes) and are often packaged with Windows, as shown in Figure 17-1.

Figure 17-1

Windows 7 with Service Pack 1

EXAM TIP You might be asked about installing service packs and updates on the CompTIA A+ exams. Pay attention to the steps listed here.

Windows Update checks your system, grabs the updates, and patches your system automatically. Even if you don't want to allow Windows Update to run automatically, it'll nag you about updates until you patch your system. Microsoft provides the Windows Update service for all versions of Windows.

Windows Update in Windows XP

You can start Windows Update when your computer is connected to the Internet. Start the utility at Start | All Programs | Windows Update. When you run Windows Update manually, the software connects to the Microsoft Web site and scans your computer to determine which updates you may need. Within a few seconds or minutes, depending on your connection speed, you'll get a straightforward screen like the one shown in Figure 17-2.

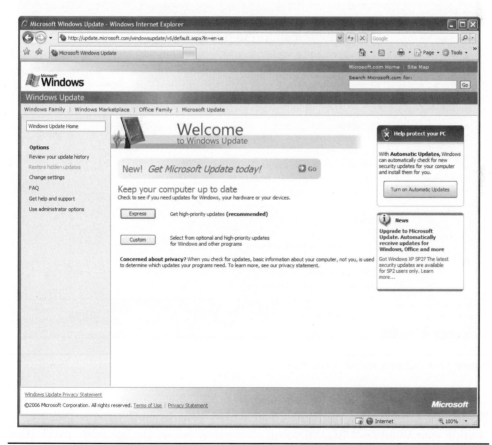

Figure 17-2 Microsoft Windows Update page

You have several choices here, although two are most obvious. If you click the Express button, Windows Update will grab any high-priority updates—these are security patches—and install them on your computer. If you click the Custom button, you can select from a list of optional updates.

Figure 17-3 shows the updater with a list of patches and security updates. You can scroll through the list and review the description of each update. You can deselect the checkbox next to a patch or update, and Windows Update will not download or install it. If you click the Clear All button, as you might suspect, all the updates will be unchecked and not installed. When you click Install Updates, all the updates remaining in the list will be installed.

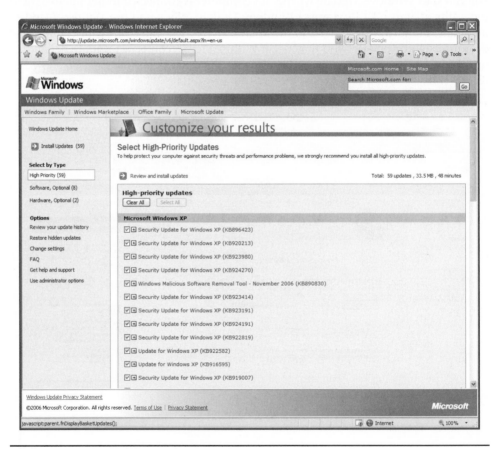

Figure 17-3 Choose updates to be installed.

Windows Update in Windows Vista and Windows 7

Starting with Windows Vista, Microsoft changed Windows Update from a Web page to a Control Panel applet called—surprise!—Windows Update. Windows Update is

virtually identical in both Windows Vista and Windows 7, so I'll just show it to you in Windows 7. Microsoft thoughtfully placed a shortcut to the applet in the Start menu, as shown in Figure 17-4.

Figure 17-4
Accessing Windows
Update in
Windows 7

Windows Update can run automatically (we'll cover that next), so you'll probably see new updates to install every time you open the applet. There are three common types of updates:

- **Important** These updates address critical security or stability issues and are the most critical. You can configure Windows Update to install these updates automatically.

- **Recommended** A recommended update is an added feature or enhancement that is not critical. You can configure Windows Update to install these updates automatically.

- **Optional** These include device drivers, language packs, and other nonessential updates. You must install these updates manually.

Figure 17-5 shows you what Windows Update looks like in Windows 7. Note that the Important update is Windows 7 Service Pack 1.

Figure 17-5 Windows Update in Windows 7

Installing an update is as easy as selecting the updates you want to install and clicking OK. If you don't want to install a specific update, and don't want to look at it every time you open Windows Update, you can hide it. To hide an update, right-click on the update you wish to hide and select Hide update (see Figure 17-6).

Figure 17-6 Hiding an update

Installing updates is only one part of this applet. You can find more options listed on the left side of the applet.

- **Control Panel Home** Returns you to the Control Panel
- **Check for updates** Manually checks for new updates
- **Change settings** Enables you to configure automatic updating

- **View update history** Shows you every update applied to the system and any that failed to install properly

- **Restore hidden updates** Reveals hidden updates

Automatic Updates in Windows XP

Updates are so important that Microsoft gives you the option to update Windows automatically through the *Automatic Updates* feature. Actually, it nags you about it! Soon after installing Windows XP (a day or two, in my experience), a message balloon will pop up from the taskbar suggesting that you automate updates (see Figure 17-7). If you click this balloon, the Automatic Updates Setup Wizard runs, with which you can configure the update program. You say you've never seen this message balloon but would like to automate the update process? No problem. Right-click My Computer (on the Start menu), select Properties, click the Automatic Updates tab, and select Automatic Update options. Or, open the Control Panel and double-click the Automatic Updates icon. Whenever your computer connects to the Web, it checks the Windows Update page.

Figure 17-7
Windows Update
balloon message in
Windows XP

What happens next depends on the setting you choose. You have four choices:

- **Automatic (recommended)** Windows Update will simply keep your computer patched up and ready to go. This is the best option for most users, although it's not necessarily good for users of portable computers. Nobody wants to log into a slow hotel Wi-Fi connection and have most of your bandwidth sucked away by Automatic Updates downloading hot fixes!

- **Download updates for me, but let me choose when to install them** Windows Update downloads all patches in the background and then, when complete, tells you about them. You have the option at that point to install or not install.

- **Notify me but don't automatically download or install them** Windows Update simply flashes a dialog box that tells you updates are available but does not download anything until you say go. This is the best option for users of portable computers. You can download files when it's convenient for you, such as when you're home and not traveling on business.

- **Turn off Automatic Updates** This does precisely what is advertised. You get neither automatic patches nor notification that patches are available. Only use this option on a system that does not or cannot connect to the Internet. If you're online, your computer needs to be patched!

Automatic Updates in Windows Vista and Windows 7

Windows Vista and Windows 7 take automatic updates to a much higher level. Click on Change settings in the Windows Update dialog box to see the available options, listed next (see Figure 17-8).

Figure 17-8 Windows Update Change settings

- **Important updates** The choices in this drop-down list are almost identical to the four radio button options in Windows XP:

 - Install updates automatically (recommended)
 - Download updates but let me choose whether to install them
 - Check for updates but let me choose whether to download and install them
 - Never check for updates (not recommended)

- **Recommended updates** This option is enabled by default, but you can turn off the automatic installation of recommended updates. Most users leave it on, but paranoid admins like to turn this off.

- **Who can install updates** By default, all users can install updates. Uncheck this box to restrict installing updates to users with administrative privileges.

- **Microsoft Update** By default, the automatic update process includes updates for other Microsoft products, such as Microsoft Office. Unchecking this box disables these updates.

- **Software notifications** When enabled, you'll receive detailed information about any new Microsoft software. These show up as moderately obnoxious pop-ups in the system tray.

You need to decide whether or not you want to automatically install updates. Microsoft has a good track record for providing relatively fast, robust, and safe updates, but there have been a few rather infamous exceptions. As a result, there are always a few nerdier techs (like your humble author) who prefer to download the update and wait to see if there's any problems before installing it.

Managing Temporary Files with Disk Cleanup

You should run the *Disk Cleanup* utility regularly to make sure you've cleared out the junk files that accumulate from daily use. All that late-night Web surfing doesn't just use up time; it also uses up disk space, leaving behind hundreds of temporary Internet files. Those, and other bits and pieces (such as those "deleted" files still hanging around in your Recycle Bin), can add up to a lot of wasted disk space if you don't periodically clean them out.

You can reach this tool through the Start menu (Start | All Programs | Accessories | System Tools), or you can open My Computer or Computer, right-click the drive you want to clean up, and select Properties. You'll find the Disk Cleanup button in the middle of the General tab.

When you click the Disk Cleanup button, the application first calculates the space you can free up and then displays the Disk Cleanup dialog box, which tells you how much disk space it can free up—the total amount possible as well as the amount you'll get from each category of files it checks. Windows Vista and Windows 7 also ask if you want to clean up all the files on the computer or just your files. In Figure 17-9, the list of files to delete only has a few categories checked, and the actual amount of disk space to be gained by allowing Disk Cleanup to delete these files is much smaller than the estimate. As you select and deselect choices, watch this value change.

If you scroll down through the list, you will see a choice to compress old files. What do you know—Disk Cleanup does more than just delete files! In fact, this file compression trick is where Disk Cleanup really, uh, cleans up. This is one of the few choices where you will gain the most space. The other big heavyweight category is Temporary Internet Files, which Disk Cleanup will delete. Try Disk Cleanup on a computer that gets hours of Internet use every day and you'll be pleased with the results.

Registry Maintenance

Your Registry is a huge database that Windows updates every time you add a new application or hardware or make changes to existing applications or hardware. As a result, the

Registry tends to be clogged with entries that are no longer valid. These usually don't cause any problems directly, but they can slow down your system. Interestingly, Microsoft does not provide a utility to clean up the Registry. To clean your Registry, you need to turn to a third-party utility. Quite a few Registry cleaner programs are out there, but my favorite, as you might recall from Chapter 14, is the freeware CCleaner by Piriform (see Figure 17-10). You can download the latest copy at www.piriform.com/ccleaner/.

Figure 17-9
Disk Cleanup
dialog box

Before you start cleaning your Registry with wild abandon, keep in mind that all Registry cleaners are risky in that they may delete something you want in the Registry. Because Microsoft makes changes to the Registry for every version of Windows, make sure your utility supports the Windows version you're running. This is especially true for any 64-bit version of Windows! I've used CCleaner for a while and it has worked well for me—your experience may differ.

NOTE CCleaner also helps clean all of the most common Web browsers and a number of popular applications.

Figure 17-10 CCleaner

Error-Checking and Disk Defragmentation

Keeping drives healthy and happy is a key task for every tech. Error-checking and Disk Defragmenter, discussed way back in Chapter 12, are the key Windows maintenance tools used to accomplish this task.

When you can't find a software reason (and there are many possible ones) for a problem such as a system freezing on shutdown, the problem might be the actual physical hard drive. The tool to investigate that is Error-checking. You can run Error-checking by using the chkdsk command from a command line, from the Start | Run dialog box, or from the Start | Search bar. You can also access the tool through the GUI by opening My Computer or Computer, right-clicking on the drive you want to check, selecting Properties, and then clicking the Tools tab. Click *Check now* to have Error-checking scan the drive for bad sectors, lost clusters, and similar problems, and repair them if possible.

Run Disk Defragmenter (see Figure 17-11) on a regular basis to keep your system from slowing down due to files being scattered in pieces on your hard drive. Before you click the Defragment button in Windows XP/7, click the Analyze button to have Windows analyze the disk and determine if defragmentation is actually necessary. (The Analyze button was removed from the Windows Vista disk defragmenter.) If you use Windows Vista/7, your system is defragged automatically.

Figure 17-11 Vista Disk Defragmenter

Error-checking and Disk Defragmenter are such critical maintenance features that you really should have them run automatically. Read on to see how to schedule these and other critical jobs.

Scheduling Maintenance

Maintenance only works properly when you do it at regular intervals. Depending on the version of Windows installed, you can schedule maintenance jobs to run automatically. The CompTIA 220-802 exam objectives define three areas for you to consider for scheduled maintenance: backups, defragmentation, and check disks (Error-checking). For the most part, we use Task Scheduler, although this depends on the task and the version of Windows.

Task Scheduler/Scheduled Tasks

Two versions of Task Scheduler are available: Windows XP runs Version 1.0, and Windows Vista and Windows 7 run Version 2.0. Microsoft calls it *Scheduled Tasks* in Windows XP, and *Task Scheduler* in Windows Vista/7. To open Scheduled Tasks in Windows XP, go to Start | Programs | Accessories | System Tools | Scheduled Tasks. To open Task Scheduler in Windows Vista and Windows 7, open the Administrative Tools applet and double-click Task Scheduler. You can also access it via Start | All Programs | Accessories | System Tools | Task Scheduler. In both versions, you can choose an executable program and define when you want that program to run. The key to running scheduled maintenance is to know the names of the executable programs and any special switches you may need to enter. Figures 17-12 and 17-13 show Scheduled Tasks running a backup at a certain time of day.

Figure 17-12 Windows XP Scheduled Tasks (Version 1.0)

Figure 17-13
Daily Backup
Schedule in
Windows XP

Version 2.0 is much more powerful and flexible than Windows XP's Version 1.0, dividing tasks into triggers, actions, and conditions. *Triggers* are actions or schedules that start a program. *Actions* are steps that define both the program to run and how it is to run. *Conditions* are extra criteria that must be met for the program to run. (Is the system idle? Is it connected to the Internet?) Figure 17-14 shows the Conditions tab for a sample task. To create a basic task in Windows Vista/7, all you need to do is name it, set how often it should run, and decide what it should do.

Figure 17-14 Conditions tab in Windows 7 Task Scheduler (Version 2.0)

As you'll see in the following sections, many Windows utilities include built-in scheduling options. Here's the twist, though: they're still using Schedule Tasks/Task Scheduler. If you set up an automated defragmentation from within Disk Defragmenter, for example, you can open up Task Scheduler and see it listed as a scheduled task. Neat!

 EXAM TIP The CompTIA A+ exams may use either name for the utility for scheduling maintenance in Windows. Remember that Windows XP labels the tool *Scheduled Tasks*; Windows Vista and Windows 7 label it *Task Scheduler*.

Scheduling Backups

The backup utility varies depending on your version of Windows: in Windows XP, it's the Backup Utility (ntbackup); in Windows Vista, it's called the Backup and Restore Center, and in Windows 7, it's called Backup and Restore. You'll learn more about each of these tools later in the chapter, but right now, let's talk about scheduling regular backups of your data.

The fastest way to schedule a backup using the Backup Utility in Windows XP is to use the Backup or Restore Wizard (which I'll explain later in detail). After you configure which files to back up, where to store them, and all of that, you'll arrive at the Completing the Backup or Restore Wizard screen. Click the Advanced button to open

a second set of options. The last of the advanced options you can set in the Backup or Restore Wizard is when you want the backup to run. You can set it to run now, later at a specified time, or use the Set Schedule button to configure regular backups at a time and frequency of your choosing.

Windows Vista/7's Backup and Restore Center/Backup and Restore applet includes a scheduler, too. Near the end of the Set Up Backup Wizard, after you've selected which folders to back up, you can click on *Change schedule* to set when and how often you want Windows to create the backup, just like in Windows XP (though Windows Vista/7 don't bury it under multiple buttons this time). It's that easy.

How often should you back up your files? If you're creating new documents, downloading music, and taking lots of digital photos, you'll want to back up your files weekly. If you're a casual, Internet-browsing, Solitaire-playing PC user, you're probably safe making a new backup once a month.

Scheduling Defragmentation

You can schedule Disk Defragmenter to run automatically using the Task Scheduler in Windows XP and from inside the utility itself in Windows Vista/7.

To defragment your hard drive on a schedule using Windows XP's Task Scheduler, double-click on Add Scheduled Task, which opens the Scheduled Task Wizard. Click Next. A list of default programs appears, but Disk Defragmenter doesn't make the cut. Click the Browse button and find the Disk Defragmenter executable, called defrag.exe, in the System32 folder. Click Open. You'll then name the task, set how often Task Scheduler should perform the task, and set the time and days it should run. You'll also be asked to enter a user name and password—the task runs as if it were run from that user's account. Once you complete the wizard, a dialog box appears showing you all the information you configured. To set the Disk Defragmenter to defragment the C: drive, type **C:** at the end of the Run box, next to C:\Windows\System32\defrag.exe, as shown in Figure 17-15.

Figure 17-15
Scheduling a disk defragmentation in Windows XP

Windows Vista/7's version of Disk Defragmenter includes a scheduler, just like Backup and Restore. To access Disk Defragmenter's scheduler, open the Start menu, type **defrag**, and press ENTER. You can start defragging right away or modify/disable the task in the Disk Defragmenter: Modify Schedule dialog box (see Figure 17-16).

Figure 17-16 Windows 7 Disk Defragmenter scheduler

It's best to run Disk Defragmenter every evening if possible. If you're using Vista/7, take advantage of the "only run when idle" condition to keep Disk Defragmenter from interrupting possibly more important tasks.

 EXAM TIP The CompTIA exams call the Disk Defragmenter program "Defrag," the common tech slang term for it.

Scheduling Error-checking (Check Disk)

The tool you know and love as Error-checking appears on the CompTIA A+ 220-802 exam objectives as *Check disk* and chkdsk (the command-line version of the tool).

Regardless of what you call Error-checking, setting up Task Scheduler to run it automatically is a good thing.

NOTE No versions of Windows run Error-checking automatically, so you'll need to set up a task on the computer if you wish to do so.

Using the technique you just learned to set up a scheduled task with Disk Defragmenter, create another scheduled task to run Error-checking. Its executable is called chkdsk.exe (see Figure 17-17). There are two switches you should use: /F to repair sectors and /R to tell Error-checking to attempt to recover data on known bad sectors.

Figure 17-17
Scheduling Error-checking in Windows XP

File System Check

Task | Schedule | Settings

C:\WINDOWS\Tasks\File System Check.job

Run: C:\WINDOWS\system32\chkdsk.exe c: /R /F

Browse...

Start in:

Comments:

Run as: VM-WINXP\VMUser Set password...

☐ Run only if logged on
☑ Enabled (scheduled task runs at specified time)

OK Cancel Apply

Opinions vary on how often you should run Error-checking as a scheduled task. For the CompTIA exams, a monthly check is a good idea. For the real world, you should run Error-checking when you suspect a problem with your drives.

System Configuration

Techs use the *System Configuration utility* (also known by its executable name, *msconfig*) to edit and troubleshoot operating system and program startup processes and services. To start the System Configuration utility, go to the Start | Run dialog box or the Start | Search bar, enter **msconfig**, and click OK or press ENTER (see Figure 17-18). The program runs automatically in Windows XP; in Vista/7, you need to provide the necessary credentials, depending on the User Account Control (UAC) setup.

Figure 17-18 The Windows Vista System Configuration utility

The System Configuration utility in Windows XP offers quick access to troubleshoot and edit the boot.ini file. System Configuration in Windows Vista and Windows 7 no longer has that ability, but it still offers a number of handy features, distributed across the following tabs:

- **General** Select the type of startup you would like to use for the next boot. You can perform a normal startup with all programs and services launching normally, a diagnostic startup with only basic devices and services, or a custom boot.

- **Boot** This tab contains advanced boot features. Here you can see every copy of Windows you have installed, set a default OS, or delete an OS from the boot menu. You can set up a safe boot, or adjust advanced options like the number of cores or amount of memory to use.

- **Services** This tab is identical to the Services tab in the Task Manager. You can enable or disable any or all services running on your PC.

- **Startup** This tab enables you to enable or disable any startup programs (programs that load when you launch Windows). This is perhaps the most useful tab, especially if Windows is slow to load on your PC.

- **Tools** This tab lists many of the tools and utilities available in Windows, including Event Viewer, Performance Monitor, Command Prompt, and so on. There's nothing here that you can't find elsewhere in Windows, but it's a handy list all the same.

System Information

Windows comes with a handy built-in utility known as the *System Information tool* (see Figure 17-19) that collects information about hardware resources, components, and the software environment. When it finishes doing that, it provides a nice and tidy little report, enabling you to troubleshoot and diagnose any issues and conflicts. As with many other tools you can access from the Start | Run dialog box or Start | Search bar, the CompTIA A+ exams refer to System Information by its executable, *msinfo32*.

Figure 17-19 System Information

You can start System Information in one of the following ways:

- Choose Start | Programs or All Programs | Accessories | System Tools | System Information.

- In Windows XP, choose Start | Run, then type **msinfo32**, and click OK. In Windows Vista/7, go to Start | Search bar, type **msinfo32**, and press ENTER.

It is also important to note that you can use System Information to gather information about remote computers by selecting View | Remote Computer and then entering the remote computer's network machine name. Under Tools, you even get quick access to System Restore and the DirectX Diagnostic Tool, a tool for checking your video card that Chapter 21 discusses.

NOTE You simply cannot run a computer today without a large number of security programs to protect you from malicious attacks from spyware, malware, viruses, and hacking. In fact, the installation, monitoring, and updating of these programs (and possibly even hardware) is so important that they get their own chapter. Head to Chapter 29 for a complete discussion of how to keep your computer safe!

Optimizing Windows

Maintenance is about keeping Windows' performance from degrading with time and use. Of course, you don't just want to keep trouble at bay—you want to make your systems better, stronger, faster! Anything you do that makes Windows better than it was before, such as adding a piece of software or hardware to make something run better, is an optimization.

Installing and Removing Software

Probably the most common optimization performed on any PC is adding and removing applications. Installing and removing software is part of the normal life of any PC. Each time you add or remove software, you are making changes and decisions that can affect the system beyond whatever the program does, so it pays to know how to do it right.

Installing Software

Most application programs are distributed on optical discs (although this is slowly changing). Windows supports *Autorun*, a feature that enables the operating system to look for and read a special file called—wait for it—autorun.inf. Immediately after a removable media device (optical disc or thumb drive) is inserted into your computer, whatever program is listed in autorun.inf runs automatically. Most application programs distributed on removable media have an autorun file that calls up the installation program.

Sometimes, however, you need to institute the installation sequence yourself. Perhaps the installation disc lacks an Autorun installation program, or perhaps Windows is configured so that you must start programs on optical discs manually. In some cases, a disc may contain more than one program, and you must choose which of them to install. Regardless of the reason, you can begin the installation manually by using the *Add or Remove Programs* applet in the Control Panel in Windows XP. Click the Add New Programs button (see Figure 17-20), follow the prompts, and provide the media or location of the files. In Windows Vista and 7, Microsoft has replaced the Add or Remove Programs applet with *Programs and Features*, which does not have the Add New Programs feature.

EXAM TIP CompTIA uses a slash symbol when describing the Windows XP Add or Remove Programs applet, even though Microsoft uses a word, so expect *Add/Remove Programs* on the 220-802 exam.

Figure 17-20 Result of clicking the Add New Programs button

With Windows Vista/7, UAC complicates the installation process a bit. You will most likely be prompted by UAC when installing an application, giving you time to review what is happening to your system in case you did not approve of the program being installed. If you are using an administrator account, you can simply click Continue and finish the installation. Should you be logged in with a less privileged account, you will need to enter a user name and password of an account with administrative privileges. Some installers have trouble letting UAC know that they need more privileges and simply fail no matter what account you are logged in with. In those cases, it is best to right-click the installer icon and select *Run as administrator* to give the installer the access it expects from the start.

Assuming all is well, you typically must accept the terms of a software license before you can install an application. These steps are not optional; the installation simply won't proceed until you accept all terms the software manufacturer requires and, in many cases, enter a correct code. You may also be asked to make several decisions during the installation process. For example, you may be asked where you would like to install the program and if you would like certain optional components installed. Generally speaking, it is best to accept the suggested settings unless you have a very specific reason for changing the defaults.

Removing Software

Each installed application program takes up space on your computer's hard drive, and programs that you no longer need waste space that could be used for other purposes. Removing unnecessary programs can be an important piece of optimization.

You remove a program from a Windows PC in much the same manner as you install it. That is, you use the application's own uninstall program, when possible. You normally find the uninstall program listed in the application's folder in the All Programs section of the Start menu, as shown in Figure 17-21.

Figure 17-21
Uninstall me!

If an uninstall program is not available, use the appropriate Windows Control Panel applet you learned about earlier to remove the software. Figure 17-22 shows this applet in Windows 7. You select the program you want to remove and click the Uninstall/Change button or Change/Remove button. Windows displays a message warning you that the program will be permanently removed from your PC. If you're certain you want to continue, click Yes.

NOTE The Uninstall/Change and Change/Remove buttons change depending on the program. Not all programs can be changed.

Figure 17-22 Programs and Features applet

You may then see a message telling you that a shared file that appears to no longer be in use is about to be deleted, and asking your approval. Generally speaking, it's safe to delete such files. If you do not delete them, they will likely be orphaned and remain unused on your hard disk forever. In some cases, clicking the Uninstall/Change or Change/Remove button starts the application's install program (the one you couldn't find before) so you can modify the installed features. This is a function of the program you're attempting to remove. The end result should be the removal of the application and all of its pieces and parts, including files and Registry entries.

Adding or Removing Windows Components/Features

When you installed Windows, it included certain features by default. It installed Notepad, modem support, and games on your computer. You can remove these Windows components from your system if you like, and add other components as well. If you're adding components in Windows XP, you'll need a copy of your installation disc, or another location where the Windows source files are stored. This task really hasn't changed from previous versions of Windows.

To add or remove a Windows component in Windows XP, open the Add/Remove Programs applet in the Control Panel. From here, select Add/Remove Windows Components, which opens the Windows Components Wizard (see Figure 17-23). You can select an installed program here. You can see how frequently it is used, how much disk space it uses, and (sometimes) the last time it was used.

Figure 17-23
Windows Components Wizard

Windows Components Wizard

Windows Components
You can add or remove components of Windows XP.

To add or remove a component, click the checkbox. A shaded box means that only part of the component will be installed. To see what's included in a component, click Details.

Components:

☑ Accessories and Utilities	17.4 MB	
☐ Fax Services	3.7 MB	
☑ Indexing Service	0.0 MB	
☑ Internet Explorer	0.0 MB	
☐ Management and Monitoring Tools	1.9 MB	

Description: Includes Windows Accessories and Utilities for your computer.

Total disk space required: 0.9 MB
Space available on disk: 7770.4 MB

Details...

< Back Next > Cancel

In Windows Vista/7, open the Programs and Features applet in the Control Panel, and then click the *Turn Windows features on or off* option on the Tasks list. Click Continue if prompted by UAC and you will be presented with the Windows Features dialog box (see Figure 17-24). To toggle a feature on or off, simply click its checkbox. Unlike Windows XP, you no longer need to have the installation disc to turn on features.

Figure 17-24
Windows Features dialog box in Vista

Windows Features

Turn Windows features on or off

To turn a feature on, select its check box. To turn a feature off, clear its check box. A filled box means that only part of the feature is turned on.

☐ ActiveX Installer Service	
⊞ ■ Games	
☑ GroupPolicy Preferences CSE	
☐ Indexing Service	
⊞ ☐ Internet Information Services	
⊞ ■ Microsoft .NET Framework 3.0	
⊞ ☐ Microsoft Message Queue (MSMQ) Server	
⊞ ☑ Print Services	
☐ Remote Differential Compression	
☑ Removable Storage Management	
☐ RIP Listener	
☐ Simple TCPIP services (i.e. echo, daytime etc)	

OK Cancel

Installing/Optimizing a Device

The processes for optimizing hardware in Windows are absolutely identical between the versions, even down to the troubleshooting utilities, and are very similar to the

steps for installing a new device. The installation process is covered in every chapter of this book that deals with one type of device or another, so this section concentrates on the issues that fit best under optimization.

 EXAM TIP Both CompTIA A+ exams test you on installing and optimizing devices.

Updating Drivers

Device manufacturers occasionally update their drivers. Most of these updates fix problems, but many updates incorporate new features. Whatever the case, when one of your devices gets an updated driver, it's your job to install it. Windows Update provides an easy method to update drivers from manufacturers that take advantage of the service. If you are using Windows XP, you usually need to select the Custom option to see these updates because the Express option only installs high-priority updates. When you click on the Custom option, look under Hardware, Optional (on the left) to see if Windows has any driver updates (see Figure 17-25).

Figure 17-25 Optional Hardware updates

If you are using Vista/7, you will need to click *View available updates* to see if any drivers are available for your system. No matter which version of Windows you have, you should research all driver updates before you install them. In theory, the best way to do this research is to click on the More information button next to the driver (see Figure 17-26) to get the details on what's new with a particular driver, but this rarely seems to produce good information. Instead, go to the manufacturer's Web site and read up on what that driver provides, and then download the latest driver there.

Figure 17-26 The More information link—don't trust it.

If Windows does not put a driver update in the Windows Update tool, how do you know a device needs updating? The trick is to know your devices. Video card manufacturers update drivers quite often. Get in the habit of registering your video card with the manufacturer to stay up to date. Any very new device is also a good candidate for an update. When you buy that new cool toy for your system, make a point to head over to the manufacturer's Web site and see if any updates have come out since it was packaged for sale. That happens more often than you might think!

Once a driver is installed, test it hard. Use the new features or capabilities that motivated you to install the new driver in the first place. Make the hardware that the driver supports do everything, and look for any problems. If anything goes wrong, you can roll back a bad driver in Device Manager, as described a bit later in the chapter.

Driver Signing

Device drivers become part of the operating system and thus have the potential to cause lots of problems if they're written poorly. To protect Windows systems from bad device drivers, Microsoft uses *driver signing*, which means that each driver has a digital signature. Any drivers included on the Windows installation media or Windows Update are digitally signed. Once you have installed a driver, you can look at its Properties dialog box to confirm that it was digitally signed. Figure 17-27 shows a digitally signed network card driver.

Figure 17-27
A digitally signed
driver

When an unsigned driver is detected during hardware installation in Windows XP, you'll see the message in Figure 17-28 offering you the choice to stop or continue the installation. Signed drivers are more or less a sure thing, but that doesn't mean unsigned ones are a problem—just consider the source of the driver and ensure that your device works properly after installation.

Figure 17-28
Stop or continue
installation of an
unsigned driver

You can control how Windows XP behaves when drivers are being installed. Click the Driver Signing button on the Hardware tab of the System Properties dialog box to display the Driver Signing Options dialog box shown in Figure 17-29. If you select Ignore, Windows will install an unsigned driver without warning you. If you select Warn, you will

be prompted when Windows detects an unsigned driver during driver installation, and you will be given the opportunity to either stop or continue the installation. Choosing Block will prevent the installation of unsigned drivers.

Figure 17-29

Driver Signing Options dialog box

The default Driver Signing setting is Warn. This is also the default setting during installation, so you will always be warned when Windows detects an unsigned driver during Windows installation. This is no problem for a standard installation, when you are sitting at the computer, responding to all prompts—but it is a problem for automated, unattended installations. This is a good reason to check out all your device drivers before installing Windows.

Windows Vista and Windows 7 have eliminated the driver signing options. With these versions of Windows, all installed drivers are inspected for a digital signature and you are prompted with a warning if the driver is unsigned (see Figure 17-30). In 64-bit versions of Windows, all drivers must be signed. No exceptions. Microsoft wants to keep tight controls on the drivers to improve stability.

Device Manager

You've worked with *Device Manager* in other chapters when installing and troubleshooting devices; it's also the tool to use when optimizing device drivers. Right-click on a device in Device Manager to display the context menu. From here you can update or uninstall the driver, disable the device, scan for hardware changes, or display the Properties dialog box. When you open the Properties dialog box, you'll see several tabs that vary according to the specific device. Most have General, Driver, Details, and Resources. The tab that matters most for optimization is the Driver tab.

Figure 17-30
Unsigned driver in
Windows 7

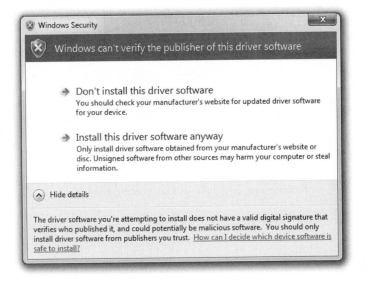

The Driver tab has buttons labeled Driver Details, Update Driver, Roll Back Driver, and Uninstall. Windows Vista/7 also include a Disable option, which does exactly what you think it does. Driver Details lists the driver files and their locations on disk. Update Driver opens the Hardware Update Wizard—not very useful given that the installation programs for almost all drivers do this automatically. The Roll Back Driver option is a different story. It enables you to remove an updated driver, thus rolling back to the previous driver version. Roll Back Driver (see Figure 17-31) is a lifesaver when you install a new driver and suddenly discover it's worse than the driver it replaced! Uninstall removes the driver.

Figure 17-31
Rolling back to the
previous driver

Adding a New Device

Windows should automatically detect any new device you install in your system. If Windows does not detect a newly connected device, use Windows XP's or Windows Vista's Add Hardware Wizard, which you can find in the Add Hardware applet, or use Windows 7's *Add a device* option in the Devices and Printers applet to get the device recognized and drivers installed (see Figure 17-32).

 NOTE Remember from Chapter 9 that you can also use the Add Hardware Wizard in Windows 7 using the hdwwiz.exe program.

Figure 17-32 Adding a device in Windows 7

Windows Vista/7 almost completely automated the Add Hardware/Add a Device wizards. The wizards present you with a list of detected hardware. Windows XP behaves a bit differently; it requires you to click Next on the Welcome screen to get started. The wizard searches for hardware that has been connected but does not yet have a driver installed. If it detects the device, select it, and the wizard installs the driver. You may have to point to the source location for the driver files. If it does not detect the device, which is very likely, it will ask you if the hardware is connected. When you answer yes and click Next, it gives you a list of installed hardware, similar to Figure 17-33.

If the device is in the list, select it and click Next. If not, scroll to the bottom and select *Add a new hardware device*, and then click Next. If the device is a printer, network card, or modem, select *Search for and install the hardware automatically* and click Next. In that case, once the wizard detects the device and installs the driver, you're finished. If

you do see your device on the list, your best hope is to select *Install the hardware that I manually select from a list*. In the subsequent screens, select the appropriate device category, select the device manufacturer and the correct model, and respond to the prompts from the Add Hardware Wizard to complete the installation.

Figure 17-33

List of installed hardware in Windows XP

Add Hardware Wizard

The following hardware is already installed on your computer

From the list below, select an installed hardware device, then click Next to check properties or troubleshoot a problem you might be having.

To add hardware not shown in the list, click "Add a new hardware device."

Installed hardware:

- NVIDIA RIVA TNT2 Model 64/Model 64 Pro
- SoundMAX Integrated Digital Audio
- Audio Codecs
- Legacy Audio Drivers
- Media Control Devices
- Legacy Video Capture Devices

< Back Next > Cancel

Performance Options

One optimization you can perform on all Windows versions is setting Performance Options. *Performance Options* are used to configure CPU, RAM, and virtual memory (page file) settings. To access these options in Windows XP, right-click My Computer and select Properties, click the Advanced tab, and click the Settings button in the Performance section of that tab. In Windows Vista/7, right-click Computer and select Properties, and then click the *Advanced system settings* link in the Tasks list. On the Advanced tab, click the Settings button in the Performance section.

The Performance Options dialog box has three tabs: Visual Effects, Advanced, and Data Execution Prevention (see Figure 17-34). The Visual Effects tab enables you to adjust visual effects that impact performance, such as animations, thumbnails, and transparencies. Try clicking the top three choices in turn and watch the list of settings. Notice the tiny difference between the first two choices (*Let Windows choose what's best for my computer* and *Adjust for best appearance*). The third choice, *Adjust for best performance*, turns off all visual effects, and the fourth option is an invitation to make your own adjustments. If you're on a computer that barely supports Windows, turning off visual effects can make a huge difference in the responsiveness of the computer. For the most part, though, just leave these settings alone.

Figure 17-34

Windows XP
Performance
Options dialog box

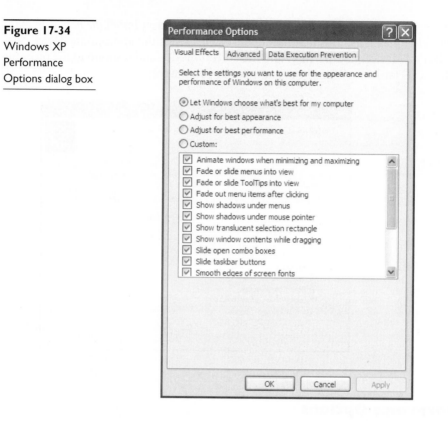

The Advanced tab, shown in Figure 17-35, has three sections: Processor scheduling, Memory usage (Windows XP only), and Virtual memory. Under the Processor scheduling section, you can choose to adjust for best performance of either Programs or Background services. The Memory usage settings enable you to allocate a greater share of memory to programs or to the system cache. The Virtual memory section of this tab enables you to modify the size and location of the page file. Microsoft dropped the Memory usage settings option in Windows Vista and Windows 7.

Microsoft introduced *Data Execution Prevention* (*DEP*) with Windows XP Service Pack 2. DEP works in the background to stop viruses and other malware from taking over programs loaded in system memory. It doesn't prevent viruses from being installed on your computer, but makes them less effective. By default, DEP monitors only critical operating system files in RAM, but the Data Execution Prevention tab enables you to have DEP monitor all running programs. It works, but you'll take a performance hit. Like other options in the Performance Options dialog box, leaving the default DEP settings is the best option most of the time.

Figure 17-35

Advanced tab of
Performance
Options dialog box

Performance Options

Visual Effects | Advanced | Data Execution Prevention

Processor scheduling

By default, the computer is set to use a greater share of
processor time to run your programs.

Adjust for best performance of:

⦿ Programs ○ Background services

Memory usage

By default, the computer is set to use a greater share of
memory to run your programs.

Adjust for best performance of:

⦿ Programs ○ System cache

Virtual memory

A paging file is an area on the hard disk that Windows uses as
if it were RAM.

Total paging file size for all drives: 1152 MB

[Change]

[OK] [Cancel] [Apply]

Hardware Profiles

Windows XP has an interesting feature called *hardware profiles*. There are many unique
situations, mainly with portable computers, where a user is motivated to not have all
of their hardware devices running at all times. Imagine a user who has a laptop with a
wireless network card. She also has a docking station in her office that includes a wired
NIC. When the user is plugged into the docking station, she wants to use the wired con-
nection, and when disconnected, she wants to use the wireless connection. In Windows
XP, you can create two hardware profiles: one where the wired network card is disabled
in Device Manager and another where the wireless network card is disabled.

You can inspect hardware profiles by going to the System applet in the Control Panel,
selecting the Hardware tab, and then clicking Hardware Profiles (see Figure 17-36). All
Windows XP systems have one hardware profile by default.

Figure 17-36

Default Hardware
Profiles

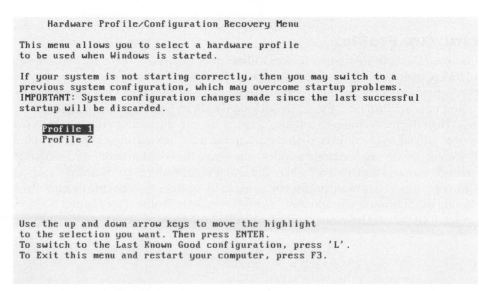

You can make a second profile by copying the default profile. If you have more than one profile, Windows XP will prompt you with a text menu every time you boot the computer, similar to the one shown in Figure 17-37.

```
        Hardware Profile/Configuration Recovery Menu

This menu allows you to select a hardware profile
to be used when Windows is started.

If your system is not starting correctly, then you may switch to a
previous system configuration, which may overcome startup problems.
IMPORTANT: System configuration changes made since the last successful
startup will be discarded.

        Profile 1
        Profile 2

Use the up and down arrow keys to move the highlight
to the selection you want. Then press ENTER.
To switch to the Last Known Good configuration, press 'L'.
To Exit this menu and restart your computer, press F3.
```

Figure 17-37 Hardware Profile boot menu

There was a tremendous uproar from a small group of impassioned hardware profile fans when Microsoft decided to drop the feature from Windows Vista and Windows 7.

Preparing Windows for Problems

Techs need to prepare for problems. You must have critical system files and data backed up and tools in place for the inevitable glitches. Different versions of Windows enable you to prepare for problems differently. Windows includes multiple backup systems that do different things. Each backup system enables you to:

- Back up personal data
- Back up local copies of critical system state information
- Restore a backup if your system won't boot

Backing Up Personal Data

The most important data on your computer is the personal data: your documents, e-mail messages and contacts, Web favorites, photographs, and other files. To handle backing up personal data, every version of Windows comes with some form of backup utility. There are big differences between the backup included in Windows XP and the backup included in Windows Vista and Windows 7, so let's break up the idea of backing up personal data between Windows XP and Windows Vista/7.

Backup Utility for XP (ntbackup)

Windows XP's *Backup Utility* (popularly known by the name of the executable program, *ntbackup*) provides almost all the tools you need to back up files and folders. It has come a long way from its origins in Windows NT. The ntbackup program supports a greater variety of devices, enabling you to back up to network drives, local drives, tape, and removable disks (but not optical discs). Most folks, however, still turn to third-party utilities to create system, e-mail, browser, and personal data backups.

NOTE The Backup Utility is not included in the default installation of Windows XP Home. You must install it manually from the Windows CD-ROM.

You can start NTBackup by navigating the Start menu to Accessories | System Tools, or by clicking the Backup Now button on the Tools tab of the local disk's Properties dialog box. I prefer to start it from Start | Run with the command **ntbackup**. Click the Backup Wizard button to run the Backup Wizard. To use the Windows XP version in Advanced Mode, click Advanced Mode on the opening screen (see Figure 17-38). To have it always open in Advanced Mode, deselect the *Always start in wizard mode* checkbox. If the program is in Advanced Mode and you want to run it as a wizard, click the Wizard Mode link to open the Backup or Restore Wizard.

Figure 17-38

Choosing to run the Backup Wizard in Advanced Mode

NOTE Microsoft has been dreadfully inconsistent on the naming of the backup programs that bundle with Windows. Here's the scoop in a nutshell.

The backup program in Windows XP has a slew of names. The official name of the program is *Backup Utility for Windows*. The Advanced Mode dialog box is called *Backup Utility*, but the wizard interface differs depending on whether you run the utility in Wizard Mode or click the Backup Wizard button in the Advanced Mode dialog box. The former runs the *Backup or Restore Wizard*; the latter runs the *Backup Wizard*. These wizards offer different options, with the Backup or Restore Wizard providing the simpler, consumer-oriented interface. Both wizards are only different faces for the Backup Utility. Got it? Oh, and ntbackup is the command-line command to run the program in Windows XP, so Microsoft provides at least a nod at naming consistency.

Most seasoned techs call the backup programs in Windows XP *Backup* or *NTBackup*. You need to know the variety of names, though, to provide proper customer support. This is especially true in a help desk environment.

To create a backup, start the Backup Utility, click Advanced Mode, and choose the Backup tab. Check the boxes next to the drives and files you want to include in the backup. To include your system state information, such as Registry and boot files (which you should do), click the System State checkbox. To specify where to put the backup file you're creating, either type the path and file name in the *Backup media or file name* box or click Browse, select a location, type the file name, and click Save. Click Start Backup.

Choose whether you want to append this backup to a previous one or overwrite it. Click Advanced to open the Advanced Backup Options dialog box, select *Verify data after backup,* and click OK. Click Start Backup again. A dialog box shows you the utility's progress. When it finishes, click Close and then close the Backup Utility.

NTBackup gives you three choices after you click Advanced Mode: Backup Wizard (Advanced), Restore Wizard (Advanced), and Automated System Recovery Wizard (see Figure 17-39). First, I'm going to dive into the Backup Wizard and Automated System Recovery Wizard. Then we'll look at tape backups and more backup options.

Figure 17-39 Windows XP Backup Utility options

Backup Wizard (Advanced) If you run the Backup Wizard and click the Next button on the Welcome screen, you'll open the dialog box in Figure 17-40. You have three options here. The first two are fairly self-explanatory: You can back up everything or just selected drives and files.

The third option needs some explanation. The *Only back up the System State data* radio button enables you to save "other" system-critical files. This option really makes sense for Windows Server systems because it saves Active Directory information (which your Windows XP systems do not store) as well as other critical, server-specific functions. (I cover more on these topics in Chapter 22.)

Figure 17-40 Backup Wizard options

Windows XP Automated System Recovery (ASR) The Windows XP *Automated System Recovery (ASR)* is your last line of defense when restoring functionality to your PC (see Figure 17-41). It backs up your boot and system volumes (meaning your C: drive, in most cases) and the system state information—the Registry, boot files, and other critical system files. Here's how it works.

Figure 17-41
Creating an ASR
backup

 CAUTION Restoring an ASR backup will format your boot and system partition(s). Make sure you have a recent backup before proceeding with this worst-case scenario.

First, you create the ASR backup. This involves creating a large backup file that includes the boot volume, the system volume, and the system state information and placing it on a separate drive or some form of removable media. This will include all applications and user data on that one drive—it won't back up extra partitions or drives. You also need to create a nonbootable ASR floppy disk. The floppy disk stores information critical to the restoration process. Don't lose one of these items, either—the ASR backup is tied to its ASR floppy disk and won't work without both components.

To restore the ASR, you'll need your Windows XP installation disc. Boot into the Windows installer and press F2 to start the ASR restore process. Insert the ASR floppy disk and follow the instructions on the screen. The installer formats your boot and system partition(s), and then performs a mini-installation of devices, drivers, and other basic configurations. Then the ASR Recovery Wizard launches, asking for the location of that backup file you made. Point it to the file, and the restoration process will complete.

EXAM TIP The CompTIA A+ 220-802 exam lists *repair disk* as an objective even though the Emergency Repair Disk (ERD) tool was phased out with Windows 2000. If it comes up, know that the ERD was a much simpler version of Windows XP's ASR that backed up critical system and boot files. See also Chapter 19 on creating a *system repair disc*, an optical disc used for restoring critical backups.

Tape Backup The odd fact that Microsoft never updated the Backup or Restore Wizard in Windows XP to enable you to back up to optical discs of any sort has kept alive the practice of tape backups. Tape drives connect to the ATA or SCSI bus, just like optical drives, but rather than using a shiny CD-R or DVD+R disc, you have to back up to magnetic tape (see Figure 17-42).

Figure 17-42
Backup tapes

There are a large number of different tape formats, but CompTIA lists only one technology, Digital Linear Tape (DLT), in the CompTIA A+ Acronyms list. DLT was a popular tape format from the 1980s up to the early 2000s, with capacities from 10 MB in the early versions up to (arguably) around 800 GB. DLT is rarely used anymore, and CompTIA should have removed this from the CompTIA A+ exam competencies.

Tape drive manufacturers have done pretty much everything they can do to make tape backups as fast as possible, but the technology suffers from two huge drawbacks. First, it's tape, which means all data must be stored and restored in sequential access. The drive has to go through Files 1 and 2 before reaching File 3, in other words. Second, tape is painfully slow in comparison to hard drives, optical drives, or Flash-media drives. With plenty of cheap online, hard drive, and recordable optical media options available for backup, though, tape's days are numbered.

Backup Options The goal of backing up data is to ensure that when a system dies, there will be an available, recent copy you can use to restore the system. You could simply back up the complete system at the end of each day—or whatever interval you feel is prudent to keep the backups fresh—but complete backups can be a tremendous waste of time and materials. Instead of backing up the entire system, take advantage of the fact that not all of the files will be changed in any given period; much of the time you only need to back up what's changed since your last backup. Recognizing this, most backup software solutions have a series of options available beyond the complete backup.

The key to understanding backups other than the full backup is *attributes*, 1-bit storage areas that all files have. The most common attributes are hidden (don't show the file in Computer or when dir is typed at the command line), system (it's a critical file for the system), read-only (can't erase it), and archive. These attributes were first used in FAT-formatted drives in the DOS era, but they are still completely supported by all file formats. The *archive bit* works basically like this: Whenever a file is saved, the archive bit is turned on. Simply opening a file affects the current state of the archive bit. Backup programs usually turn off a file's archive bit when the file is backed up. In theory, if a file's archive bit is turned off, there's a good backup of that file on some tape. If the archive bit is turned on, it means that the file has been changed since it was last backed up (see Figure 17-43).

NOTE Windows Explorer (My Computer in Windows XP, Computer in Vista/7) by default does not show much about files in any view, even when you select Details from the View menu or from the Change your view pull-down menu. The Details view is highly customizable, however, and can reveal a phenomenal amount and variety of information about files.

To customize your view, right-click the column bar (the bar that says Name, Size, Type, Date Modified, and so forth) to look at the default choices. You'll see everything from Attributes, Owner, Author, and Title to file type–specific information such as Genre, Duration, and Bit Rate (for music files). What you see in the initial options differs according to the version of Windows. If the default extra view options don't get your motor revving, selecting the More option brings up a menu offering many more view options! For the purposes of this section, click the Attributes box to display file and folder attributes.

Figure 17-43 The archive bit on these files is on.

Archive bits are used to perform backups that are not full backups. The following backup types are most often supported:

- A *normal backup* is a full backup. Every file selected is backed up, and the archive bit is turned off for every file backed up. This is the standard "back it all up" option.

- A *copy backup* is identical to a normal backup, with the important distinction being that the archive bits are *not* changed. This is used (although not often) for making extra copies of a previously completed backup.

- An *incremental backup* includes only files with the archive bit turned on. In other words, it copies only the files that have been changed since the last backup. This backup turns off the archive bits.

- A *differential backup* is identical to an incremental backup, except that it doesn't turn off the archive bits.

- A *daily backup*, also known as a *daily copy backup*, makes copies of all the files that have been changed that day. It does not change the archive bits.

EXAM TIP Be sure you know the types of backups, including which ones change the archive bits and which ones do not.

The motivation for having both the incremental and differential backups may not be clear at first glance—they seem so similar as to be basically the same. Incremental seems the better option at first. If a file is backed up, you would want to turn off the archive bit, right? Well, maybe. But there is one scenario where that might not be too attractive. Most backups do a big weekly normal backup, followed by daily incremental or differential backups at the end of every business day. Figure 17-44 shows the difference between incremental and differential backups.

Figure 17-44 Incremental versus differential

Notice that a differential backup is a cumulative backup. Because the archive bits are not set, it keeps backing up all changes since the last normal backup. This means the backup files will get progressively larger throughout the week (assuming a standard weekly normal backup). The incremental backup, by contrast, only backs up files changed since the last backup. Each incremental backup file will be relatively small and also totally different from the previous backup file.

Let's assume that the system is wiped out on a Thursday morning. How can you restore the system to a useful state?

If you're using an incremental backup, you will first have to restore the last weekly backup you ran on Monday, then the Tuesday backup, and then the Wednesday backup before the system is restored to its Thursday morning state. The longer the time between normal backups, the more incremental backups you must restore.

Using the same scenario but assuming you're doing differential instead of incremental backups, you only need the weekly backup and then the Wednesday backup to restore your system. A differential backup always requires only two backups to restore a system. Suddenly, the differential backup looks better than the incremental! On the other hand, one big benefit of incremental over differential is backup file size. Differential backup files are massive compared to incremental ones.

Backup and Restore Center for Windows Vista/7

Microsoft retired the ntbackup program with Windows XP, replacing it with the more automated and simpler *Backup and Restore Center* (Windows Vista) and *Backup and Restore* (Windows 7) Control Panel applets. The ntbackup program required you to choose the files you wanted to back up as well as the type of backup (incremental, differential, or normal). Windows Vista and Windows 7 no longer ask those questions, at least not directly. In Windows Vista, you can either back up files or back up your computer (Figure 17-45). Both choices will first ask you where you want to store the backup (Figure 17-46).

Figure 17-45
Backup options in Vista

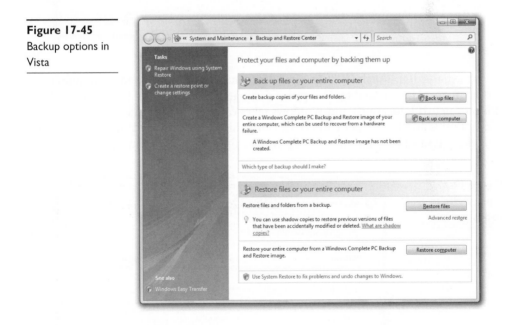

Unlike ntbackup, Windows Vista and Windows 7 don't support backing up to tape. Acceptable options for backup media include flash drives, optical discs of all sorts, or even over a network. You can even copy the backup to any hard drive, as long as it's not the drive you're backing up.

NOTE Windows Vista and Windows 7 do not back up to tape drives.

Figure 17-46
Backup location in
Vista

> Back Up Files
>
> **Where do you want to save your backup?**
>
> ○ On a hard disk, CD, or DVD:
>
> BD-ROM Drive (D:)
>
> ○ On a network:
>
> [] Browse...
>
> Why don't I see my hard disk?
>
> What's the difference between backing up files and copying files to a CD?
>
> Next Cancel

As the name implies, the *Back up computer* option backs up your entire computer to a
system image. All you need to do is pick a destination for the image (optical drive, hard
drive, or network location) and Windows takes care of the rest. Choosing the *Back up
files* option is another matter entirely. Clicking this button doesn't bring up a directory
tree like you saw in NTBackup. Instead, you see the screen shown in Figure 17-47.

Figure 17-47
Types of files to
back up

> Back Up Files
>
> **Which file types do you want to back up?**
>
> All files on this computer of the type that you select will be backed up, including files that belong to
> other users of this computer. We recommend that you back up all of the file types selected below.
>
> ☑ Pictures Category details
> ☑ Music Move the mouse pointer over a category on the left
> ☑ Videos or select it with the keyboard to see what types of files
> will be backed up.
> ☑ E-mail
> ☑ Documents
> ☑ TV shows
> ☑ Compressed files
> ☑ Additional files
>
> Only files on NTFS disks can be backed up. System files, executable files, and temporary files will not
> be backed up. What other file types are not included in the backup?
>
> Next Cancel

oncoming

The *Back up files* option in Vista only enables you to back up personal information for all users. If you want to back up any installed applications, or even Windows itself, don't bother using the *Back up files* option that comes with Windows Vista.

 EXAM TIP Windows Vista and Windows 7 will not back up content stored on non-NTFS volumes.

Windows 7's Backup and Restore utility includes a number of noteworthy improvements over Windows Vista's. First of all, Microsoft changed the look of the main screen (Figure 17-48).

Figure 17-48
Windows 7 Backup and Restore

Clicking the *Set up backup* link in Windows 7 opens a dialog box asking you to choose your backup location—very similar to Vista's backup. After selecting your backup location and clicking *Next*, you then see the screen shown in Figure 17-49.

If you select *Let Windows choose (recommended)*, you'll get a backup similar to the Vista backup, but with one very important difference. You'll back up each user's personal data, but Windows 7 doesn't stop there. Assuming you have enough space in your backup location, Windows 7 will automatically add a system image that includes the entire Windows operating system, every installed program, all device drivers, and even the registry.

 NOTE Windows image files use the .wim extension.

NOTE You can also choose to create just a system image in Windows 7. From the Backup and Restore applet, select *Create a system image*. It works like the system image function in Windows Vista.

System Restore

Every technician has war stories about the user who likes to add the latest gadget and cool software to his computer. Then he's amazed when things go very, very wrong: the system locks up, refuses to boot, or simply acts weird. This guy also can't remember what he added or when. All he knows is that you should be able to fix it—fast.

This is not news to the folks at Microsoft, and they have a solution to this problem. It's called *System Restore*, and they first introduced it in Windows Me, with further refinements in Windows XP. The System Restore tool enables you to create a *restore point*, a copy of your computer's configuration at a specific point in time. If you later crash or have a corrupted OS, you can restore the system to its previous state.

To create a restore point in Windows XP, go to Start | All Programs | Accessories | System Tools | System Restore. When the tool opens, select *Create a restore point* and then click Next. Type in a description on the next screen (see Figure 17-53). There's no need to include the date and time because the System Restore adds them automatically. Click Create and you're finished.

Figure 17-53 Creating a restore point in Windows XP

The last screen before the system is restored sh[...] all open programs and reminds you that Windo[...] process. It also states that the restore operation is [...] too far back in time, you can restore to a more re[...]

You don't have to count on the automatic cre[...] System Restore at any time and simply select C[...] this before making changes that might not trigge[...] directly editing the Registry.

System Restore is turned on by default and u[...] information on restore points. To turn System [...] usage in Windows XP, open the System Properti[...] the System Restore tab (Figure 17-57). In Windo[...] select Properties, and then click the *System protec[...] tem Protection tab, click the Configure button.

Figure 17-57

System Restore tab in System Properties applet

System Properties

General | Computer Name
System Restore | Aut[...]

System Restore can track an[...] computer.

☐ Turn off System Restore on all driv[...]

Drive settings

To change the status of System Re[...] space available to System Restore [...] click Settings.

Available drives:

Drive	S
(C:)	M
(D:)	M

Drive (C:) Settings

(C:) Monitoring

(C:) is the system drive. [...] without turning it off on a[...] the System Restore tab.

Disk space usage

Move the slider to the [...] amount of disk space f[...] may reduce the numbe[...]

Disk space to use:

Min

System Restore in Windows Vista/7 is much more automatic, with the operating system making a number of restore points automatically. To make your own restore point, right-click Computer and select Properties, and then click the *System protection* link in the Tasks list. On the System Protection tab, click the Create button to open the dialog box shown in Figure 17-54.

Figure 17-54

Creating a manual restore point in Windows 7

System Properties

Computer Name | Hardware | Advanced | System Protection | Remote

Use system protection to undo unwanted system changes and restore previous versions of files. What is system protection?

System Resto[...]

You can und[...] your compute[...]

System Protection

Create a restore point

Type a description to help you identify the restore point. The current date and time are added automatically.

Big Software Upgrade Restore Point

Create | Cancel

Protection Set[...]

Available [...]
Local [...]

Configure restore settings, manage disk space, and delete restore points. — Configure...

Create a restore point right now for the drives that have system protection turned on. — Create...

OK | Cancel | Apply

If you click the System Restore button, you might be surprised at how many system restore points are already made for you (see Figure 17-55).

Figure 17-55

Restore points in Windows 7

System Restore

Restore your computer to the state it was in before the selected event

How do I choose a restore point?

Current time zone: Central Daylight Time

Date and Time	Description	Type
4/10/2012 4:53:15 PM	Windows Update	Critical Update
4/9/2012 8:46:32 AM	Windows Update	Critical Update
4/5/2012 11:32:53 AM	Windows Update	Critical Update
4/2/2012 9:25:32 AM	Installed Raw Therapee V4.0.7.1 x64	Install
4/2/2012 8:51:22 AM	Windows Update	Critical Update
3/26/2012 9:23:14 AM	Windows Update	Critical Update

☑ Show more restore points | Scan for affected programs

< Back | Next > | Cancel

The System Restore tool creates
ing every time you install new soft
computer to malfunction, simply r
lation, and the computer should w

During the restore process, only
Your computer includes all progra
absolutely invaluable for overwork
problems.

To restore to a previous time poi
| All Programs | Accessories | Syste
select the first radio button, *Restore*
dows Vista and Windows 7, just cl
with restore points. Any day with a
dows Vista/7 this calendar was repl
These points are created after you a
and during the normal shutdown o
a restore point from the list on the

The extension, which is optional, could be up to three characters long in true DOS, and most computer programs and users continue to honor that old limit, even though it does not apply to modern PCs. No spaces or other illegal characters (/ \ [] | ÷ + = ; , * ?) could be used in the filename or extension. The filename and extension are separated by a period, or *dot*. This naming system was known as the *8.3 (eight-dot-three) naming system*.

Here are some examples of acceptable true DOS filenames:

fred.exe	system.ini	file1.doc
driver3.sys	janet	code33.h

Here are some unacceptable true DOS filenames:

4charext.exec	waytoolong.fil	bad÷char.bat	.no

I mention the true DOS limitations for a simple reason: *backward compatibility*. Starting with Windows 9*x*, Windows versions did not suffer from the 8.3 filename limitation. Instead they supported filenames of up to 255 characters (but still with the three-character extension) by using a trick called long filenames (LFN). Windows systems using LFN retained complete backward compatibility by automatically creating two names for every file, an 8.3 filename and a long filename. Modern Windows systems similarly support backward compatibility in file naming.

Whether you're running an ancient DOS system or the latest edition of Windows 7, the extension is very important, because the extension part of the filename tells the computer the type or function of the file. Program files use the extension .exe (for executable) or .com (for command). Anything that is not a program is some form of data to support a program. Different programs use different types of data files. The extension usually indicates which program uses that particular data file. For example, Microsoft Word uses the extension .docx (.doc for Microsoft Office versions before 2007), while WordPerfect uses .wpd and PowerPoint uses .pptx (.ppt for Microsoft Office PowerPoint versions prior to 2007). Graphics file extensions, in contrast, often reflect the graphics standard used to render the image, such as .gif for CompuServe's Graphics Interchange Format or .jpg for the JPEG (Joint Photographic Experts Group) format.

Changing the extension of a data file does not affect its contents, but without the proper extension, Windows won't know which program uses it. You can see this clearly in My Computer. Figure 18-9 shows a folder with two identical image files. The one on top shows a thumbnail because Windows recognizes this as a JPEG image; the one on the bottom shows a generic icon because I deleted the extension. Windows' GUI doesn't show file extensions by default. Figure 18-10 shows the contents of that same folder from the command line.

System Restore

Select a Restore Point

The following calendar displays in bold all of the date
restore points that are available for the selected da

Possible types of restore points are: system checkp
manual restore points (restore points created by yo
created when certain programs are installed).

1. On this calendar, click a bold date. 2. On

<	April, 2012					>	<
Sun	Mon	Tue	Wed	Thu	Fri	Sat	1:5
25	26	27	28	29	30	31	
1	2	3	4	5	6	7	
8	9	10	11	12	13	14	
15	16	17	18	19	20	21	
22	23	24	25	26	27	28	
29	30	1	2	3	4	5	

Figure 17-56 Calendar of restore poin

Figure 18-9 What kind of file is the one on the lower right?

Figure 18-10
One file has no extension.

ASCII

All files are stored on the hard drive in binary format, but every program has its own way of reading and writing this binary data. Each unique method of binary organization is called a file *format*. One program cannot read another program's files unless it can convert the other program's format into its format. In the early days of DOS, no programs were capable of performing this type of conversion, yet people wanted to exchange files. They wanted some type of common format that any program could

read. The answer was a special format called *American Standard Code for Information Interchange (ASCII)*.

The ASCII standard defines 256 eight-bit characters. These characters include all of the letters of the alphabet (uppercase and lowercase), numbers, punctuation, many foreign characters (such as accented letters for French and Spanish—é, ñ, ô—and other typical non-English characters), box-drawing characters, and a series of special characters for commands such as a carriage return, bell, and end of file (see Figure 18-11). ASCII files, more commonly known as *text files*, store all data in ASCII format. The ASCII standard, however, is for more than just files. For example, when you press a key, the keyboard sends the letter of that key to the PC in ASCII code. Even the monitor outputs in ASCII when you are running DOS.

Figure 18-11

ASCII characters

000 (nul)	032 sp	064 @	096 `	128 Ç	160 á	192 └	224 α
001 ☺ (soh)	033 !	065 A	097 a	129 ü	161 í	193 ┴	225 β
002 ☻ (stx)	034 "	066 B	098 b	130 é	162 ó	194 ┬	226 Γ
003 ♥ (etx)	035 #	067 C	099 c	131 â	163 ú	195 ├	227 π
004 ♦ (eot)	036 $	068 D	100 d	132 ä	164 ñ	196 ─	228 Σ
005 ♣ (enq)	037 %	069 E	101 e	133 à	165 Ñ	197 ┼	229 σ
006 ♠ (ack)	038 &	070 F	102 f	134 å	166 ª	198 ╞	230 µ
007 • (bel)	039 '	071 G	103 g	135 ç	167 º	199 ╟	231 τ
008 ◘ (bs)	040 (	072 H	104 h	136 ê	168 ¿	200 ╚	232 Φ
009 (tab)	041)	073 I	105 i	137 ë	169 ⌐	201 ╔	233 Θ
010 (lf)	042 *	074 J	106 j	138 è	170 ¬	202 ╩	234 Ω
011 ♂ (vt)	043 +	075 K	107 k	139 ï	171 ½	203 ╦	235 δ
012 ♀ (np)	044 ,	076 L	108 l	140 î	172 ¼	204 ╠	236 ∞
013 (cr)	045 -	077 M	109 m	141 ì	173 ¡	205 ═	237 φ
014 ♫ (so)	046 .	078 N	110 n	142 Ä	174 «	206 ╬	238 ε
015 ☼ (si)	047 /	079 O	111 o	143 Å	175 »	207 ╧	239 ∩
016 ► (dle)	048 0	080 P	112 p	144 É	176 ▒	208 ╨	240 ≡
017 ◄ (dc1)	049 1	081 Q	113 q	145 æ	177 ▓	209 ╤	241 ±
018 ↕ (dc2)	050 2	082 R	114 r	146 Æ	178 ▓	210 ╥	242 ≥
019 ‼ (dc3)	051 3	083 S	115 s	147 ô	179 │	211 ╙	243 ≤
020 ¶ (dc4)	052 4	084 T	116 t	148 ö	180 ┤	212 ╘	244 ⌠
021 § (nak)	053 5	085 U	117 u	149 ò	181 ╡	213 ╒	245 ⌡
022 ▬ (syn)	054 6	086 V	118 v	150 û	182 ╢	214 ╓	246 ÷
023 ↨ (etb)	055 7	087 W	119 w	151 ù	183 ╖	215 ╫	247 ≈
024 ↑ (can)	056 8	088 X	120 x	152 ÿ	184 ╕	216 ╪	248 °
025 ↓ (em)	057 9	089 Y	121 y	153 Ö	185 ╣	217 ┘	249 ·
026 (eof)	058 :	090 Z	122 z	154 Ü	186 ║	218 ┌	250 ·
027 ← (esc)	059 ;	091 [	123 {	155 ¢	187 ╗	219 █	251 √
028 ∟ (fs)	060 <	092 \	124 \|	156 £	188 ╝	220 ▄	252 ⁿ
029 ↔ (gs)	061 =	093]	125 }	157 ¥	189 ╜	221 ▌	253 ²
030 ▲ (rs)	062 >	094 ^	126 ~	158 ₧	190 ╛	222 ▐	254 ■
031 ▼ (us)	063 ?	095 _	127 ⌂	159 ƒ	191 ┐	223 ▀	255

ASCII was the first universal file format. Virtually every type of program—word processors, spreadsheets, databases, presentation programs—can read and write text files. However, text files have severe limitations. A text file can't store important information such as shapes, colors, margins, or text attributes (bold, underline, font, and so on). Therefore, even though text files are fairly universal, they are also limited to the 256 ASCII characters.

Even in the most basic text, you need to perform a number of actions beyond just printing simple characters. For example, how does the program reading the text file know when to start a new line? This is where the first 32 ASCII characters come into play. These first 32 characters are special commands (actually, some of them are both commands and characters). For example, the ASCII value 7 can be either a large dot or a command to play a note (bell) on the PC speaker. ASCII value 9 is a Tab. ASCII value 27 is an Escape.

Unicode

ASCII worked well for years, but as computers became used worldwide, the industry began to run into a problem: there are a lot more than 256 characters used all over the world! Nobody could use Arabic, Greek, Hebrew, or even Braille. In 1991, the Unicode Consortium, an international standards group, introduced Unicode. Basic *Unicode* is a 16-bit code that covers every character for the most common languages, plus a few thousand symbols. With Unicode you can make just about any character or symbol you might imagine—plus a few thousand more you'd never even think of. The first 256 Unicode characters are the same as ASCII characters, making for easy backward compatibility.

Practical Unicode A lot of e-mail programs can use Unicode characters, as can Internet message boards such as my Tech Forums. You can use Unicode characters to accent your writing or simply to spell a person's name correctly—Martin *Acuña*—when you address him. Working with Unicode is fun, so you might want to try this yourself. Here are the steps.

1. Open a text editing program such as Notepad in the Windows GUI.

2. Hold down the ALT key on your keyboard and, referring to Figure 18-11, press numbers on your keyboard's number pad to enter special characters. For example, pressing ALT-164 should display an *ñ*, whereas ALT-168 shows a *¿*.

3. If you have access to the Internet, surf over to the Tech Forums (www.totalsem .com/techforum/index.php) and say howdy. Include some Unicode in your post, of course!

Drives and Folders

When working from the command line, you need to be able to focus the prompt at the specific drive and folder that contains the files or programs with which you want to work. This can be a little more complicated than it seems.

At boot, Windows assigns a drive letter (or name) to each hard drive partition and to each floppy or other disk drive. The first floppy drive, if installed, is called A:, and the second, if installed, is called B:. Hard drives usually start with the letter C: and can continue to Z: if necessary. Optical drives by default get the next available drive letter after the last hard drive. Windows enables you to change the default lettering for drives, so you're likely to see all sorts of lettering schemes. On top of that, you can mount a hard drive as a volume in another drive, as you'll recall from Chapter 12.

Whatever the names of the drives, Windows uses a hierarchical directory tree to organize the contents of these drives. All files are put into groups Windows calls *folders*, although you'll often hear techs use the term *directory* rather than *folder*, a holdover from the true DOS days. Any file not in a folder *within* the tree—that is, any file in the folder at the root of the directory tree—is said to be in the *root directory*. A folder inside another folder is called a *subfolder*. Any folder can have multiple subfolders. Two or more files with the same name can exist in different folders on a PC, but two files in the same folder cannot have the same name. In the same way, no two subfolders under

the same folder can have the same name, but two subfolders under different folders can have the same name.

 TIP It helps to visualize a directory tree as upside down, because in geek-speak, the trunk, or root directory, is described as "above" the folders that divide it, and those subfolders "below" root are spoken of as being "above" the other subfolders inside them. For example, "The file is in the Adobe folder under Program Files."

When describing a drive, you use its letter and a colon. For example, the hard drive would be represented by C:. To describe the root directory, put a backslash (\) after the C:, as in C:\. To describe a particular directory, add the name of the directory. For example, if a PC has a directory in the root directory called Test, it is C:\Test. Subdirectories in a directory are displayed by adding backslashes and names. If the Test directory has a subdirectory called System, it is shown like this: C:\Test\System. This naming convention provides for a complete description of the location and name of any file. If the C:\Test\System directory includes a file called test2.txt, it is C:\Test\System\test2.txt.

The exact location of a file is called its *path*. The path for the test2.txt file is C:\Test\System. Here are some examples of possible paths:

```
C:\Program Files
C:\WINNT\system32\1025
F:\FRUSCH3\CLEAR
A:\Reports
D:\
```

Here are a few items to remember about folder names and filenames:

- Folders and files may have spaces in their names.
- The only disallowed characters are the following eleven: * " / \ [] : ; | = ,
- Files aren't required to have extensions, but Windows won't know the file type without an extension.
- Folder names may have extensions—but they are not commonly used.

Mastering Fundamental Commands

It's time to try using the command line, but before you begin, a note of warning is in order: the command-line interface is picky and unforgiving. It will do what you *say*, not what you *mean*, so it always pays to double-check that those are one and the same before you press ENTER and commit the command. One careless keystroke can result in the loss of crucial data, with no warning and no going back. In this section, you'll explore the structure of commands and then play with four commands built into all versions of Microsoft's command-line interface: dir, cd, md, and rd.

Structure: Syntax and Switches

All commands in the Windows command-line interface use a similar structure and execute in the same way. You type the name of the command, followed by the target of that command and any modifications of that command that you want to apply. You can call up a modification by using an extra letter or number, called a *switch* or *option*, which may follow either the command or the target, depending on the command. The proper way to write a command is called its *syntax*. The key with commands is that you can't spell anything incorrectly or use a \ when the syntax calls for a /. The command line is completely inflexible, so you have to learn the correct syntax for each command.

[command] [target (if any)] [switches]

or

[command] [switches] [target (if any)]

How do you know what switches are allowed? How do you know whether the switches come before or after the target? If you want to find out the syntax and switches used by a particular command, always type the command followed by /? to get help:

[command name] /?

Viewing Directory Contents: The dir Command

The *dir command* shows you the contents of the directory where the prompt is focused. If you're like most techs, you'll use dir more often than any other command at the command prompt. When you open a command-line window in Windows, it opens focused on your user folder. You will know this because the prompt in Windows XP will look like this: C:\Documents and Settings\username> and the prompt in Windows Vista/7 looks like C:\Users\User name>. By typing **dir** and then pressing the ENTER key (remember that you must always press ENTER to execute a command from the command line), you will see something like Figure 18-12 in Windows XP.

Figure 18-12 Results for dir in a user's folder

If you are following along on a PC, remember that different computers contain different files and programs, so you will absolutely see something different from what's shown in Figure 18-12! If a lot of text scrolls quickly down the screen, try typing **dir /p** (pause). Don't forget to press ENTER. The dir /p command is a lifesaver when you're looking for something in a large directory. Just press SPACEBAR to display the next screen.

NOTE Extra text typed after a command to modify its operation, such as /w or /p after dir, is called a *switch*. Almost all switches can be used simultaneously to modify a command. For example, try typing **dir /w /p**.

Some commands give you the same result whether you include spaces or not. Typing **dir/p** and **dir /p**, for example, provide the same output. Some commands, however, *require* spaces between the command and switches. In general, get into the habit of putting spaces between your command and switches and you won't run into problems.

When you type a simple dir command, you will see that some of the entries look like this:

```
09/04/2012   05:51 PM          63,664 bambi.jpg
```

All of these entries are files. The dir command lists the creation date, creation time, file size in bytes, filename, and extension. Any entries that look like this are folders:

```
12/31/2012  10:18 AM    <DIR>          WINDOWS
```

The dir command lists the creation date, creation time, *<DIR>* to tell you it is a folder, and the folder name. If you ever see a listing with *<JUNCTION>* instead of *<DIR>*, you're looking at a hard drive partition that's been mounted as a folder instead of a drive letter:

```
08/06/2012  02:28 PM    <JUNCTION>     Other Drive
```

Now type the **dir /w** command. Note that the dir /w command shows only the filenames, but they are arranged in five columns across your screen. Finally, type **dir /?** to see the screen shown in Figure 18-13, which lists all possible switches for the command.

Typing any command followed by /? brings up a help screen for that particular command. Although these help screens can sometimes seem a little cryptic, they're useful when you're not familiar with a command or you can't figure out how to get a command to do what you need. Even though I have almost every command memorized, I still refer to these help screens; you should use them as well. If you're really lost, type **help** at the command prompt for a list of commands you may type. Once you find one, type **help** and then the name of the command. For example, if you type **help dir**, you'll see the screen shown in Figure 18-13.

```
C:\Windows\system32\cmd.exe                                          _ □ x

C:\>dir /?
Displays a list of files and subdirectories in a directory.

DIR [drive:][path][filename] [/A[[:]attributes]] [/B] [/C] [/D] [/L] [/N]
  [/O[[:]sortorder]] [/P] [/Q] [/R] [/S] [/T[[:]timefield]] [/W] [/X] [/4]

  [drive:][path][filename]
              Specifies drive, directory, and/or files to list.

  /A          Displays files with specified attributes.
  attributes   D  Directories             R  Read-only files
               H  Hidden files            A  Files ready for archiving
               S  System files            I  Not content indexed files
               L  Reparse Points          -  Prefix meaning not
  /B          Uses bare format (no heading information or summary).
  /C          Display the thousand separator in file sizes. This is the
              default. Use /-C to disable display of separator.
  /D          Same as wide but files are list sorted by column.
  /L          Uses lowercase.
  /N          New long list format where filenames are on the far right.
  /O          List by files in sorted order.
  sortorder    N  By name (alphabetic)     S  By size (smallest first)
               E  By extension (alphabetic) D  By date/time (oldest first)
               G  Group directories first  -  Prefix to reverse order
  /P          Pauses after each screenful of information.
  /Q          Display the owner of the file.
  /R          Display alternate data streams of the file.
  /S          Displays files in specified directory and all subdirectories.
  /T          Controls which time field displayed or used for sorting
  timefield    C  Creation
               A  Last Access
               W  Last Written
  /W          Uses wide list format.
  /X          This displays the short names generated for non-8dot3 file
              names. The format is that of /N with the short name inserted
              before the long name. If no short name is present, blanks are
              displayed in its place.
  /4          Displays four-digit years

Switches may be preset in the DIRCMD environment variable.  Override
preset switches by prefixing any switch with - (hyphen)--for example, /-W.

C:\>
```

Figure 18-13 Typing **dir /?** lists all possible switches for the dir command.

Changing Directory Focus: The cd Command

You can use the *cd (or chdir) command* to change the focus of the command prompt to a different directory. To use the cd command, type **cd** followed by the name of the directory on which you want the prompt to focus. For example, to go to the C:\Obiwan directory, you type **cd\obiwan** and then press ENTER. If the system has an Obiwan directory, the prompt changes focus to that directory and appears as C:\Obiwan>. If no Obiwan directory exists or if you accidentally type something like **obiwam**, you get the error "The system cannot find the path specified." If only I had a dollar for every time I've seen those errors! I usually get them because I've typed too fast. If you get this error, check what you typed and try again.

NOTE Consider errors in general for a moment—not just command-prompt errors such as "Invalid directory," but any error, including Windows errors. Many new computer users freeze in horror when they see an error message.

Wildcards

Visualize having 273 files in one directory. A few of these files have the extension .docx, but most do not. You are looking only for files with the .docx extension. Wouldn't it be nice to be able to type the dir command in such a way that only the .docx files come up? You can do this by using wildcards.

A *wildcard* is one of two special characters—asterisk (*) and question mark (?)—that you can use in place of all or part of a filename, often so that a command-line command will act on more than one file at a time. Wildcards work with all command-line commands that take filenames. A great example is the dir command. When you execute a plain dir command, it finds and displays all of the files and folders in the specified directory; however, you can also narrow its search by adding a filename. For example, if you type the command **dir ailog.txt** while in your root (C:\) directory, you get the following result:

```
C:\>dir ailog.txt
 Volume in drive C has no label.
 Volume Serial Number is 4C62-1572
 Directory of C:\
05/26/2009  11:37 PM                    0 AILog.txt
               1 File(s)              0 bytes
               0 Dir(s)  94,630,195,200 bytes free
```

If you just want to confirm the presence of a particular file in a particular place, this is very convenient. But suppose you want to see all files with the extension .txt. In that case, you use the * wildcard, like this: **dir *.txt**. A good way to think of the * wildcard is *"I don't care."* Replace the part of the filename that you don't care about with an asterisk (*). The result of dir *.txt would look like this:

```
 Volume in drive C has no label.
 Volume Serial Number is 4C62-1572

 Directory of C:\

05/26/2009  11:37 PM                    0 AILog.txt
05/29/2009  05:33 PM                5,776 aoedoppl.txt
05/29/2009  05:33 PM                2,238 aoeWVlog.txt
07/31/2008  10:40 PM                  153 systemscandata.txt
               4 File(s)          8,167 bytes
               0 Dir(s)  94,630,002,688 bytes free
```

Wildcards also substitute for parts of filenames. This dir command will find every file that starts with the letter *a:*

```
C:\>dir a*.*
 Volume in drive C has no label.
 Volume Serial Number is 4C62-1572

 Directory of C:\

05/26/2009  11:37 PM                    0 AILog.txt
05/29/2009  05:33 PM                5,776 aoedoppl.txt
05/29/2009  05:33 PM                2,238 aoeWVlog.txt
               3 File(s)          8,014 bytes
               0 Dir(s)  94,629,675,008 bytes free
```

We've used wildcards only with the dir command, but virtually every command that deals with files will take wildcards. Let's examine the ren and del commands and see how they use wildcards.

Renaming Files

To rename files, you use the *ren (or rename) command*, which seems pretty straightforward. To rename the file img033.jpg to park.jpg, type the following and then press the ENTER key:

ren img033.jpg park.jpg

"That's great," you might be thinking, "but what about using a more complex and descriptive filename, such as Sunny day in the park.jpg?" Type what should work, like this:

ren img033.jpg Sunny day in the park.jpg

But you'll get an error message (see Figure 18-16). Even the tried-and-true method of seeking help by typing the command followed by /? doesn't give you the answer.

Figure 18-16
Rename failed me.

```
E:\Pictures>dir
 Volume in drive E is More Space
 Volume Serial Number is 7A64-A796

 Directory of E:\Pictures

07/23/2009  11:12 AM    <DIR>          .
07/23/2009  11:12 AM    <DIR>          ..
12/13/2008  11:00 AM         1,362,004 img033.jpg
               1 File(s)      1,362,004 bytes
               2 Dir(s)  146,540,363,776 bytes free

E:\Pictures>ren img033.jpg Sunny day in the park.jpg
The syntax of the command is incorrect.

E:\Pictures>_
```

You can use more complicated names by putting them in quotation marks. Figure 18-17 shows the same command that failed but now succeeds because of the quotation marks.

Figure 18-17
Success at last.

```
E:\Pictures>ren img033.jpg "Sunny day in the park.jpg"

E:\Pictures>dir
 Volume in drive E is More Space
 Volume Serial Number is 7A64-A796

 Directory of E:\Pictures

07/23/2009  11:16 AM    <DIR>          .
07/23/2009  11:16 AM    <DIR>          ..
12/13/2008  11:00 AM         1,362,004 Sunny day in the park.jpg
               1 File(s)      1,362,004 bytes
               2 Dir(s)  146,540,363,776 bytes free

E:\Pictures>
```

Deleting Files

To delete files, you use the *del (or erase) command*. (They're identical commands that you can use interchangeably.) Deleting files is simple—maybe too simple. Windows users enjoy the luxury of retrieving deleted files from the Recycle Bin on those "Oops, I didn't mean to delete that" occasions everyone encounters at one time or another. The command line, however, shows no such mercy to the careless user. It has no function equivalent to the Windows Recycle Bin. Once you have erased a file, you can recover it only by using a special recovery utility such as Norton's UNERASE. Again, the rule here is *check twice and delete once*.

To delete a single file, type the **del** command followed by the name of the file to delete. To delete the file ailog.txt, for example, type this:

del ailog.txt

Although nothing appears on the screen to confirm it, the file is now gone. To confirm that the ailog.txt file is no longer listed, use the dir command.

As with the dir command, you can use wildcards with the del and erase commands to delete multiple files. For example, to delete all files with the extension .txt in a directory, you would type this:

del *.txt

To delete all files with the filename config in a directory, type **del config.***. To delete all of the files in a directory, you can use the popular *.* wildcard (often pronounced "star-dot-star"), like this:

del *.*

This is one of the few command-line commands that elicits a response. Upon receiving the del *.* command, Windows responds with "Are you sure? (Y/N)," to which you respond with a Y or N. Pressing Y erases every file in the directory, so use *.* with care!

Don't confuse deleting *files* with deleting *directories*. Use del to delete files; it will not remove directories. Use rd to delete directories.

 EXAM TIP You'll be tested on del, erase, and rd on the CompTIA A+ 220-802 exam.

Copying and Moving Files

Being able to copy and move files in a command line is crucial to all technicians. Because of its finicky nature and many options, the copy command is also rather painful to learn, especially if you're used to dragging icons in Windows. The following tried-and-true, five-step process makes it easier, but the real secret is to get in front of a C:\ prompt and just copy and move files around until you're comfortable. Keep in mind that the only difference between copying and moving is whether the original is left behind (copy) or not (move). Once you've learned the *copy command*, you've also learned the *move command*!

Mike's Five-Step copy/move Process

I've been teaching folks how to copy and move files for years by using this handy process. Keep in mind that hundreds of variations on this process exist. As you become more confident with these commands, try doing a copy /? or move /? at any handy prompt to see the real power of the commands. But first, follow this process step by step:

1. Point the command prompt to the directory containing the file(s) you want to copy or move.

2. Type **copy** or **move** and a space.

3. Type the *name(s)* of the file(s) to be copied/moved (with or without wildcards) and a space.

4. Type the *path* of the new location for the file(s).

5. Press ENTER.

Let's try an example. The directory C:\Steam contains the file readme.txt. Copy this file to a USB thumb drive (E:).

1. Type **cd\steam** to point the command prompt to the Steam directory.

    ```
    C:\>cd\steam
    ```

2. Type **copy** and a space.

    ```
    C:\Steam>copy
    ```

3. Type **readme.txt** and a space.

    ```
    C:\Steam>copy readme.txt
    ```

4. Type **e:**.

    ```
    C:\Steam>copy readme.txt e:\
    ```

5. Press ENTER.

 The entire command and response would look like this:

    ```
    C:\Steam>copy readme.txt e:\
    1 file(s) copied
    ```

If you point the command prompt to the E: drive and type **dir**, the readme.txt file will be visible. Let's try another example. Suppose 100 files are in the C:\Docs directory, 30 of which have the .doc extension, and suppose you want to move those files to the C:\Steam directory. Follow these steps:

1. Type **cd\docs** to point the command prompt to the Docs directory.

    ```
    C:\>cd\docs
    ```

2. Type **move** and a space.

```
C:\Docs>move
```

3. Type *.**doc** and a space.

```
C:\Docs>move *.doc
```

4. Type **c:\steam**.

```
C:\Docs>move *.doc c:\steam
```

5. Press ENTER.

```
C:\Docs>move *.doc c:\steam
30 file(s) copied
```

The power of the copy/move command makes it rather dangerous. The copy/move command not only lets you put a file in a new location; it also lets you change the name of the file at the same time. Suppose you want to copy a file called autoexec.bat from your C:\ folder to a thumb drive, for example, but you want the name of the copy on the thumb drive to be auto1.bat. You can do both things with one copy command, like this:

```
copy c:\autoexec.bat e:\auto1.bat
```

Not only does the autoexec.bat file get copied to the thumb drive, but the copy also gets the new name auto1.bat.

As another example, move all of the files with the extension .doc from the C:\Docs directory to the C:\Back directory and simultaneously change the .doc extension to .sav. Here is the command:

```
move c:\docs\*.doc c:\back\*.sav
```

This says, "Move all files that have the extension .doc from the directory C:\Docs into the directory C:\Back, and while you're at it, change their file extensions to .sav." This is very handy, but very dangerous!

Let's say, for example, that I made one tiny typo. Here I typed a semicolon instead of a colon after the second C:

```
move c:\docs\*.doc c;\back\*.sav
```

The command line understands the semicolon to mean "end of command" and therefore ignores both the semicolon and anything I type after it. As far as the command line is concerned, I typed this:

```
move c:\docs\*.doc c
```

This, unfortunately for me, means "take all of the files with the extension .doc in the directory C:\Docs and copy them back into that same directory, but squish them all together into a single file called c." If I run this command, Windows gives me only one clue that something went wrong:

```
move c:\docs\*.doc c
1 file(s) copied
```

See "1 file(s) copied"? Feeling the chilly hand of fate slide down my spine, I do a dir of the directory, and I now see a single file called c, where there used to be 30 files with the extension .doc. All of my .doc files are gone, completely unrecoverable.

xcopy

The standard copy and move commands can work only in one directory at a time, making them a poor choice for copying or moving files in multiple directories. To help with these multi-directory jobs, Microsoft added the *xcopy command*. (Note that there is no xmove, only xcopy.)

The xcopy command works similarly to copy, but xcopy has extra switches that give it the power to work with multiple directories. Here's how it works. Let's say I have a directory on my C: drive called \Data. The \Data directory has three subdirectories: \Jan, \Feb, and \Mar. All of these directories, including the \Data directory, contain about 50 files. If I wanted to copy all of these files to my D: drive in one command, I would use xcopy in the following manner:

```
xcopy c:\data d:\data /s
```

Because xcopy works on directories, you don't have to use filenames as you would in copy, although xcopy certainly accepts filenames and wildcards. The /s switch, the most commonly used of all of the many switches that come with xcopy, tells xcopy to copy all subdirectories except for empty ones. The /e switch tells xcopy to copy empty subdirectories. When you have a lot of copying to do over many directories, xcopy is the tool to use.

robocopy

Microsoft introduced the *robocopy command*—short for Robust File Copy—many years ago as an add-on tool for Windows Server to enable techs to manage files and folders more quickly and efficiently than with xcopy or copy. The robocopy command, now included in Windows Vista and Windows 7, is powerful indeed, enabling you to, for example, copy the files and folders from one computer to another across a network, fully replicating the structure on the destination system *and* deleting anything on that system that wasn't part of the copy. It can do this with a simple command.

The robocopy syntax does not resemble that of copy or xcopy, so if you're going to use the tool, you need to unlearn a few things. Here's the basic syntax:

```
robocopy source destination [file [file]...] [options]
```

Here's an example of the command in action. The following command would copy all files and subfolders from a local machine's D:\testserver\newwebsite folder to a shared folder on the remote server \\webhost\companywebsite.

```
robocopy d:\testserver\newwebsite \\webhost\companywebsite /mir
```

The /mir switch, for mirror, tells robocopy to copy everything from the source and make the destination mirror it. That means robocopy will also delete anything in the destination that doesn't match the source folders and files.

If that were it, robocopy would be powerful, but that's not even the tip of the iceberg. The robocopy command can copy encrypted files. It enables an administrator to copy files even if the administrator account is expressly denied access to those files. It will also resume copying after an interruption, and do so at the spot it stopped. For the full syntax, type the following:

robocopy /?

Their power and utility make the del, copy/move, xcopy, and robocopy commands indispensable for a PC technician, but that same power and utility can cause disaster. Only a trained Jedi, with The Force as his ally...well, wrong book, but the principle remains: Beware of the quick and easy keystroke, for it may spell your doom. Think twice and execute the command once. The data you save may be yours!

 EXAM TIP Know copy, xcopy, and robocopy for the CompTIA A+ 220-802 exam.

And Even More Tools, Utilities, and Commands

As a proficient IT technician in the field, you need to be familiar with a whole slew of command-line tools and other important utilities. The CompTIA A+ 220-802 exam focuses in on several of them, and although many have been discussed in detail in previous chapters, it is extremely important that you understand and practice with chkdsk, format, sfc, and shutdown.

chkdsk (/f /r)

The *chkdsk (checkdisk) command* scans, detects, and repairs hard drive– and volume-related issues and errors. You can run the chkdsk utility from a command prompt with the switches /f and /r. The /f switch attempts to fix volume-related errors, while the /r switch attempts to locate and repair bad sectors. To run successfully, chkdsk needs direct access to a drive. In other words, the drive needs to be "unlocked." For example, if you run chkdsk /f /r and chkdsk does not consider your drive unlocked, you will receive a "cannot lock current drive" message, meaning that another process has the drive locked and is preventing chkdsk from locking the drive itself. After this, chkdsk presents you with the option to run it the next time the system restarts (see Figure 18-18).

Figure 18-18
The chkdsk /f /r utility and switches on a locked drive

```
Administrator: C:\Windows\system32\cmd.exe - chkdsk  /f/r c:

C:\>chkdsk /f/r c:
The type of the file system is NTFS.
Cannot lock current drive.

Chkdsk cannot run because the volume is in use by another
process.  Would you like to schedule this volume to be
checked the next time the system restarts? (Y/N) _
```

format

After the previous chapters, you should have an expert-level knowledge of (or, at the very least, a passing familiarity with) formatting and partitioning hard drives. Formatting, you may remember, prepares a partition or volume so it can hold an operating system or data. We have already discussed the various built-in Windows utilities available to provide the formatting of drives, and you no doubt know that many third-party formatting tools are out there. In this chapter, you just need to become familiar with the format command and its switches.

The *format command*, you may have guessed, enables you to format disks from the command line. The very best way to familiarize yourself with the format command and its available switches is simply to enter **format /?** from the command prompt. Your results should be similar to those displayed in Figure 18-19.

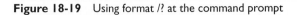

```
Administrator: C:\Windows\system32\cmd.exe

C:\>format /?
Formats a disk for use with Windows.

FORMAT volume [/FS:file-system] [/V:label] [/Q] [/A:size] [/C] [/X] [/P:passes]
FORMAT volume [/V:label] [/Q] [/F:size] [/P:passes]
FORMAT volume [/V:label] [/Q] [/T:tracks /N:sectors] [/P:passes]
FORMAT volume [/V:label] [/Q] [/P:passes]
FORMAT volume [/Q]

  volume          Specifies the drive letter (followed by a colon),
                  mount point, or volume name.
  /FS:filesystem  Specifies the type of the file system (FAT, FAT32, exFAT, NTFS,
                  or UDF).
  /V:label        Specifies the volume label.
  /Q              Performs a quick format. Note that this switch overrides /P.
  /C              NTFS only: Files created on the new volume will be compressed
                  by default.
  /X              Forces the volume to dismount first if necessary.  All opened
                  handles to the volume would no longer be valid.
  /R:revision     UDF only: Forces the format to a specific UDF version
                  (1.02, 1.50, 2.00, 2.01, 2.50).  The default
                  revision is 2.01.
  /D              UDF 2.50 only: Metadata will be duplicated.
  /A:size         Overrides the default allocation unit size. Default settings
                  are strongly recommended for general use.
                  NTFS supports 512, 1024, 2048, 4096, 8192, 16K, 32K, 64K.
                  FAT supports 512, 1024, 2048, 4096, 8192, 16K, 32K, 64K,
                  (128K, 256K for sector size > 512 bytes).
                  FAT32 supports 512, 1024, 2048, 4096, 8192, 16K, 32K, 64K,
                  (128K, 256K for sector size > 512 bytes).
                  exFAT supports 512, 1024, 2048, 4096, 8192, 16K, 32K, 64K,
                  128K, 256K, 512K, 1M, 2M, 4M, 8M, 16M, 32M.

                  Note that the FAT and FAT32 files systems impose the
                  following restrictions on the number of clusters on a volume:

                  FAT: Number of clusters <= 65526
                  FAT32: 65526 < Number of clusters < 4177918

                  Format will immediately stop processing if it decides that
                  the above requirements cannot be met using the specified
                  cluster size.

                  NTFS compression is not supported for allocation unit sizes
                  above 4096.

  /F:size         Specifies the size of the floppy disk to format (1.44)
  /T:tracks       Specifies the number of tracks per disk side.
  /N:sectors      Specifies the number of sectors per track.
  /P:passes       Zero every sector on the volume passes times. This switch is
                  not valid with /Q

C:\>
```

Figure 18-19 Using format /? at the command prompt

Although the new CompTIA A+ 220-802 exam focuses primarily on GUI operating system formatting utilities and options, you should familiarize yourself with the format command and its switches by practicing them on a test system you are literally not afraid to wipe out. Besides, you never know what skeletons CompTIA may pull out of the closet.

hostname

The *hostname command* is the most straightforward of all command-line commands. If you type **hostname** at the command prompt, it will display the name of your computer, also known as the hostname. When I type **hostname**, for example, it prints "MikePC."

sfc (System File Checker)

The Windows *sfc (System File Checker)*, or simply sfc.exe, scans, detects, and restores important Windows system files, folders, and paths. Techs often use the sfc utility from within a working version of Windows or from a Windows installation disc to restore a corrupt Windows environment. If you run sfc and it finds issues, it attempts to replace corrupted or missing files from cached DLLs located in the %WinDir%\System32\ Dllcache\ directory. Without getting very deep into the mad science involved, just know that you can use sfc to correct corruption. To run sfc from a command prompt, enter **sfc /scannow**. To familiarize yourself with sfc's switches, enter **sfc /?** (see Figure 18-20).

Figure 18-20 Checking sfc options with sfc /? at a command prompt

shutdown

The *shutdown command* enables you to do exactly that to a local or remote computer, namely, shut it down. The cool part of the tool is that you can use a number of switches

to control and report the shutdown. A network administrator could use this tool to restart a computer remotely, for example with a few keystrokes, like this:

```
shutdown /r /m \\testserver
```

The /r switch tells shutdown to have the computer reboot rather than just shut down. If you want to see the full syntax for shutdown, type the following:

shutdown /?

Beyond A+

Using Special Keys

You might find yourself repeatedly typing the same commands, or at least very similar commands, when working at a prompt. Microsoft has provided a number of ways to access previously typed commands. Type the **dir** command at a command prompt. When you get back to a prompt, press F1, and the letter *d* appears. Press F1 again. Now the letter *i* appears after the *d*. Do you see what is happening? The F1 key brings back the previous command one letter at a time. Pressing F3 brings back the entire command at once. Now try running these three commands:

dir /w
attrib
md fred

Now press the UP ARROW key. Keep pressing it till you see your original dir command—it's a history of all your old commands. Now use the RIGHT ARROW key to add /p to the end of your dir command. Windows command history is very handy.

The compact and cipher Commands

Windows offers two cool commands at the command-line interface: compact and cipher. The compact command displays or alters the compression of files on NTFS partitions. The cipher command displays or alters the encryption of folders and files on NTFS partitions. If you type just the command with no added parameters, **compact** and **cipher** display the compression state and the encryption state, respectively, of the current directory and any files it contains. You may specify multiple directory names, and you may use wildcards, as you learned earlier in the chapter. You must add parameters to make the commands change things. For example, you add /c to compress and /u to uncompress directories and/or files with the compact command, and you add /e to encrypt and /d to decrypt directories and/or files with the cipher command. When you do these operations, you also mark the directories involved so that any files you add to them in the future will take on their encryption or compression characteristics. In other words, if you encrypt a directory and all its files, any files you add later will also be encrypted. Same thing if you compress a directory. I'll run through a quick example of each.

compact

First let's try the compact command. Figure 18-21 shows the result of entering the compact command with no switches. It displays the compression status of the contents of a directory called compact on a system's C: drive. Notice that after the file listing, compact helpfully tells you that 0 files are compressed and 6 files (all of them) are not compressed, with a total compression ratio of 1.0 to 1.

```
Administrator: C:\Windows\system32\cmd.exe

C:\compact>compact

Listing C:\compact\
New files added to this directory will not be compressed.

  1855509 :   1855509 = 1.0 to 1    Bear on the floor.png
    29696 :     29696 = 1.0 to 1    Contest Work Sheet.doc
   161802 :    161802 = 1.0 to 1    Kismet HowTo.pdf
   183808 :    183808 = 1.0 to 1    Session 1.ppt
  2264262 :   2264262 = 1.0 to 1    Squirrel.jpg
    76288 :     76288 = 1.0 to 1    Wiring Schmatic.vsd

Of 6 files within 1 directories
0 are compressed and 6 are not compressed.
4,571,365 total bytes of data are stored in 4,571,365 bytes.
The compression ratio is 1.0 to 1.

C:\compact>
```

Figure 18-21 The compact command with no switches

If you enter the compact command with the /c switch, it compresses all of the files in the directory, as shown in Figure 18-22. Look closely at the listing. Notice that it includes the original and compressed file sizes and calculates the compression ratio for you. Notice also that the JPG and PNG files (both compressed graphics files) didn't compress at all, while the Word file and the PowerPoint file compressed down to around a third of their original sizes. Also, can you spot what's different in the text at the bottom of the screen? The compact command claims to have compressed *seven* files in *two* directories! How can this be? The secret is that when it compresses all of the files in a directory, it must also compress the directory file itself, which is "in" the C: directory above it. Thus it correctly reports that it compressed seven files: six in the compact directory, and one in the C: directory.

Typing **compact** again shows you the directory listing, and now there's a C next to each filename, indicating that the file is compressed (see Figure 18-23).

Okay, now suppose you want to uncompress a file—say a PowerPoint file, Session 1.ppt. To do this, you must specify the decompression operation, using the /u switch and the name of the file you want decompressed, as shown in Figure 18-24. Note that compact reports the successful decompression of one file only: Session 1.ppt. You could do the same thing in reverse, using the /c switch and a filename to compress an individual file.

Figure 18-22 Typing **compact /c** compresses the contents of the directory.

```
Administrator: C:\Windows\system32\cmd.exe

C:\compact>compact

 Listing C:\compact\
 New files added to this directory will be compressed.

 1855509 :   1855509 = 1.0 to 1 C Bear on the floor.png
   29696 :      8192 = 3.6 to 1 C Contest Work Sheet.doc
  161802 :    161802 = 1.0 to 1 C Kismet HowTo.pdf
  183808 :     90112 = 2.0 to 1 C Session 1.ppt
 2264262 :   2260992 = 1.0 to 1 C Squirrel.jpg
   76288 :     53248 = 1.4 to 1 C Wiring Schmatic.vsd

Of 6 files within 1 directories
6 are compressed and 0 are not compressed.
4,571,365 total bytes of data are stored in 4,429,855 bytes.
The compression ratio is 1.0 to 1.

C:\compact>
```

Figure 18-23 The contents of C:\compact have been compressed.

```
Administrator: C:\Windows\system32\cmd.exe

C:\compact>compact /u "Session 1.ppt"

 Uncompressing files in C:\compact\

Session 1.ppt [OK]

1 files within 1 directories were uncompressed.

C:\compact>
```

Figure 18-24 Typing **compact /u "Session 1.ppt"** decompresses only that file.

cipher

The cipher command is a bit complex, but in its most basic implementation, it's pretty straightforward. Figure 18-25 shows two steps in the process. Like the compact command, the cipher command simply displays the current state of affairs when entered with no switches. In this case, it displays the encryption state of the files in the E:\Work Files\Armor Pictures directory. Notice the letter *U* to the left of the filenames, which tells you they are unencrypted. The second command you can see on the screen in Figure 18-25 is this:

```
E:\Work Files\Armor Pictures>cipher /e /a
```

This time the cipher command carries two switches: /e specifies the encryption operation, and /a says to apply it to the *files* in the directory, not just the directory itself. As you can see, the command-line interface is actually pretty chatty in this case. It reports that it's doing the encryption and then tells you what it's done, and it even warns you that you should clean up any stray unencrypted bits that may have been left in the directory.

To confirm the results of the cipher operation, enter the **cipher** command again, as shown in Figure 18-26. Note that the *U* to the left of each filename has been replaced with an *E,* indicating an encrypted file. The other indication that this directory has been encrypted is the statement above the file listing:

```
New files added to this directory will not be encrypted.
```

Figure 18-25 Typing **cipher /e /a** encrypts the contents of the directory.

Figure 18-26 The cipher command confirms that the files were encrypted.

Remember that the cipher command works on directories first and foremost, and it works on individual files only when you specifically tell it to do so.

That's great, but suppose you want to decrypt just *one* of the files in the Armor Pictures directory. Can you guess how you need to alter the command? Simply add the filename of the file you want to decrypt after the command and the relevant switches. Figure 18-27 shows the cipher command being used to decipher dsc_4255.dng, a single file.

Figure 18-27 Typing **cipher /d /a dsc_4255.dng** decrypts only that file.

PowerShell

Microsoft introduced an add-on command-line interface called PowerShell for Windows XP and finally integrated it into Windows 7 as a more powerful replacement for the traditional command-line interface. PowerShell enables you to do all the typical command-line activities, such as dir, cd, md, and so on, but brings a series of vastly more powerful tools called *cmdlets* that enable you to accomplish some amazing tasks. Figure 18-28 shows two commands that do the same thing by default—show the contents of a directory: dir and get-childitem.

```
Windows PowerShell

PS C:\> dir

    Directory: C:\

Mode                LastWriteTime     Length Name
----                -------------     ------ ----
d----          3/27/2012   9:19 AM           AMD
d----          7/22/2011   9:20 AM           DriveKey
d----          6/27/2011   1:32 PM           LearnKey
d----          7/13/2009  10:20 PM           PerfLogs
d-r--           4/2/2012   9:25 AM           Program Files
d-r--          3/29/2012   8:54 AM           Program Files (x86)
d----          2/27/2012   4:00 PM           Python27
d-r--          10/5/2011  12:04 PM           Users
d----          3/28/2012   8:33 AM           Windows

PS C:\> get-childitem

    Directory: C:\

Mode                LastWriteTime     Length Name
----                -------------     ------ ----
d----          3/27/2012   9:19 AM           AMD
d----          7/22/2011   9:20 AM           DriveKey
d----          6/27/2011   1:32 PM           LearnKey
d----          7/13/2009  10:20 PM           PerfLogs
d-r--           4/2/2012   9:25 AM           Program Files
d-r--          3/29/2012   8:54 AM           Program Files (x86)
d----          2/27/2012   4:00 PM           Python27
d-r--          10/5/2011  12:04 PM           Users
d----          3/28/2012   8:33 AM           Windows

PS C:\>
```

Figure 18-28 Simple commands in PowerShell

With dir, you know you can search for items in a directory, such as "find all the JPEG files in a folder" with this command:

```
dir *.jpg
```

PowerShell lets you dial it all the way to 11, though, with a few more characters on a search string. The following command will find all the JPEG files on the entire

computer, plus all the mentions of .jpg files in any document format, such as Word, PowerPoint, and Acrobat:

```
get-childitem . -include *.jpg -recurse -force
```

Just in case you want to know what each piece of that string in the cmdlet means, here's the scoop: get-childitem is the main command. The dot <.> indicates the current directory and all its subdirectories, while –include tells the command to fetch the file type indicated next, in this case *.jpg. –recurse makes the command repeat, and –force retrieves hidden files too. It's like dir on steroids!

To open PowerShell in Windows 7, simply type **powershell** in the Search bar and press ENTER. To use the tool in Windows XP or Windows Vista, you'll need to download it from Microsoft. Just go to Microsoft.com and search for **PowerShell download**. You'll find it readily enough. You might also need to install the .NET 2.0 framework if you're on an older machine. You can find that at the same Web site. Good luck!

Chapter Review

Questions

1. The ASCII standard defines how many 8-bit characters?

 A. 64

 B. 256

 C. 512

 D. 64,000

2. Which of the following is the correct path for a file named yoda.txt on the C: drive in a directory called Jedi that's in a directory called Rebels that's in the root directory?

 A. C:\Root\Jedi\yoda.txt

 B. C:\Jedi\Rebels\yoda.txt

 C. C:\Rebels\Jedi\yoda.txt

 D. C:\Root\Rebels\Jedi\yoda.txt

3. Which of the following commands will delete all of the files in a directory?

 A. del *.*

 B. del all

 C. del ?.?

 D. del *.?

4. What command enables you to make a new directory in a Windows 7 Professional system?

 A. mf

 B. mkfol

 C. md

 D. makedir

5. What command do you type at the Run dialog box to access the command-line interface in Windows XP?

 A. cmd

 B. conand

 C. msdos

 D. cp

6. Joey wants to change the name of a file from start.bat to hammer.bat. Which of the following commands would accomplish this feat?

 A. ren hammer.bat start.bat

 B. ren start.bat hammer.bat

 C. rename /s start.bat hammer.bat

 D. rename /s hammer.bat start.bat

7. What types of characters are the asterisk (*) and the question mark (?)?

 A. Wildcards

 B. Optionals

 C. Designators

 D. Switches

8. What is the command to make myfile.txt read-only?

 A. attrib +r myfile.txt

 B. attrib –r myfile.txt

 C. readonly myfile.txt

 D. myfile.txt /readonly

9. To learn the syntax of the dir command, what can you type?

 A. help dir

 B. dir /?

 C. dir /help

 D. Both A and B.

10. What is the command to quit the command-line interface?

 A. exit

 B. bye

 C. quit

 D. stop

Answers

1. **B.** The ASCII standard has 256 characters because that's all 8 bits can handle!

2. **C.** You'll find the yoda.txt file in the C:\Rebels\Jedi\ folder.

3. **A.** You can use the *.* wildcard combination to affect every file in a particular folder.

4. **C.** md enables you to make a directory or folder. You can also use the older form, mkdir.

5. **A.** Use the cmd command in the Run dialog box to access a command line in Windows XP.

6. **B.** The ren command with the proper syntax—ren start.bat hammer.bat—will rename the file.

7. **A.** The asterisk and question mark characters are wildcards when used with command-line commands.

8. **A.** The command attrib +r myfile.txt will make myfile.txt read-only.

9. **D.** To learn the ins and outs of any command-line program, type the command followed by the /? switch or else type **help** and then the command.

10. **A.** Type **exit** and press the ENTER key to bail out of a command-line interface in Windows.

10. What is the command to open the terminal-line interface?

A.

B.

C.

D.

Answers

1. **B.** The ls command lists the contents of the directory you specify. All 3 files are inside.

2. **C.** You'll find the code to fix in the /etc/hosts/[subfolder].

3. **C.** A terminal profile is a saved combination of settings very specific to a particular task.

4. **C** and **D.** You can browse to a folder, directory, or folder. You can also list the folder inside.

5. **A.** The Terminal contain in my Mac allows you to access a command line in Windows.

6. **B.** The recommended amount of the White area you start before another has to render this file.

7. **B.** The asterisk and question mark characters are wildcards when used with commands are commands.

8. **A.** The command as they term or will make no effect to real data.

9. **D.** To learn the meanings of any command-line program, type the command name followed by the /? switch or use the help in a shell text command.

10. **A.** Open text and press the enter key to bail out of a command-line interface line: it transforms.

Troubleshooting Windows

In this chapter, you will learn how to
- Troubleshoot Windows boot problems
- Troubleshoot Windows GUI problems
- Troubleshoot Windows application problems

This chapter looks at Windows problems from the ground up. It starts with catastrophic failure—a PC that won't boot—and then discusses ways to get past that problem. The next section covers the causes and workarounds when the Windows GUI fails to load. Once you can access the Windows GUI, the many Windows diagnostic and trouble-shooting tools that you've spent so much time learning about come to your fingertips. The chapter finishes with a discussion on application problems.

802

Failure to Boot

When Windows fails to boot, you need to determine whether the problem relates to hardware or software. You'll recall from Chapter 12 that a hard drive needs proper connectivity and power, and that CMOS must be configured correctly. If not, you'll get an error like the one in Figure 19-1. We'll look more closely at these sorts of scenarios in the first part of this section as a refresher.

But after the drive powers on and the POST completes successfully, the computer tries to boot to an OS. Failure at *this* point gives you an entirely different set of errors such as *NTLDR is Missing* or *BOOTMGR is missing* (see Figure 19-2). You need a totally different set of tools from the ones used to troubleshoot hardware or CMOS issues. Windows XP and Windows Vista/7 boot differently, so to troubleshoot these failures to boot you need to know both processes and the tools available. We'll look at this type of scenario in the second part of this section.

```
Operating System not found
_
```

Figure 19-1 If you see this screen, the problem is with hardware. Windows hasn't even started trying to boot.

```
BOOTMGR is missing
Press Ctrl+Alt+Del to restart
_
```

Figure 19-2 Scary error

Failure to Boot: Hardware or Configuration

Most failed boot scenarios require you to determine where the fault occurred: with the hardware and configuration, or in Windows. This is a pretty straightforward problem. Imagine that a user calls and says "My PC won't boot" or "My computer is dead." At this point, your best tools are knowledge of the boot process and asking lots of questions. Here are some I use regularly:

"What displays on the screen—if anything—after you press the power button on the case?"

"What do you hear—if anything—after you press the power button on the case?"

"Is the PC plugged in?"

"Do you smell anything weird?"

Hardware problems can give you a blank screen on bootup, so follow the tried and true troubleshooting methodology for hardware. Make sure everything is plugged in and turned on. If the PC is new, as in less than 30 days old, you know it might have suffered a burn-in failure. If the customer smells something, one of the components might have fried. Try replacing with known good devices: RAM, power supply, CPU, hard drive, motherboard.

If the user says that the screen says "No boot device detected" and the system worked fine before, it *could* mean something as simple as the computer has attempted to boot to an incorrect device, such as to something other than the primary hard drive. This scenario happens all the time. Someone plugs a thumb drive into a USB port and CMOS is configured to boot to removable media before hard drives. The first few times it happened to me, I nearly took my machine apart before experiencing that head-slapping moment. I removed the thumb drive and then watched Windows boot normally.

 EXAM TIP The CompTIA A+ 802 exam objectives list "Invalid boot disk" as a symptom of a Windows problem, but it's more typical of a CMOS or hardware issue.

Failure to Boot: Windows XP

Windows boot errors take place in those short moments between the time POST ends and the *Loading Windows* screen begins. For Windows XP to start loading the main operating system, the critical system files ntldr, ntdetect.com, and boot.ini must reside in the root directory of the C: drive, and boot.ini must point to the Windows boot files. In a scenario where any of these requirements isn't in place, the system won't get past this step. Here are some of the common error messages you see at this point:

No Boot Device Present

NTLDR Bad or Missing

Invalid BOOT.INI

These text errors take place very early in the startup process. That's your big clue that you have a boot issue. If you get to the Windows splash screen and then the computer locks up, that's a whole different game, so know the difference.

 EXAM TIP The CompTIA A+ 802 exam objectives describe these error messages as "Missing NTLDR" and "Missing Boot.ini." The intent is the same, so don't be surprised by the slight difference in wording.

If you are in a failure to boot scenario where you get one of the catastrophic error messages with a Windows XP system, you have a three-level process to get back up and running. You first should attempt to repair. If that fails, attempt to restore from a backup copy of Windows. If restore either is not available or fails, your only recourse is to rebuild. You will lose data at the restore and rebuild phases, so you definitely want to spend a lot of energy on the repair effort first! Follow this process when faced with a corrupted system files or missing operating system scenario.

Attempt to Repair by Using the Recovery Console

To begin troubleshooting one of these errors, boot from the installation CD-ROM. You have three options from the initial screen: set up Windows XP, repair using the Recovery Console, and quit Setup (see Figure 19-3). The *Recovery Console*, as you'll recall from earlier chapters, provides a command-line interface for working with Windows before the GUI starts. Press R to start the Recovery Console.

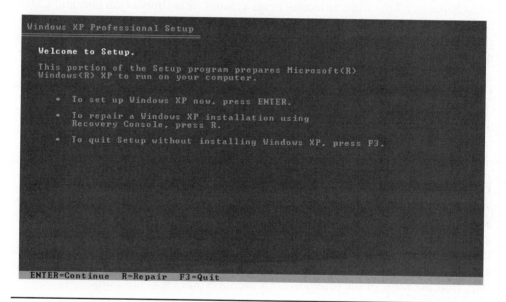

Windows XP Professional Setup

Welcome to Setup.

This portion of the Setup program prepares Microsoft(R) Windows(R) XP to run on your computer.

• To set up Windows XP now, press ENTER.

• To repair a Windows XP installation using Recovery Console, press R.

• To quit Setup without installing Windows XP, press F3.

ENTER=Continue R=Repair F3=Quit

Figure 19-3 Initial Windows XP Setup screen

NOTE You can run the Recovery Console without a Windows XP installation disc by installing it to your hard drive. Log on to Windows using an administrator account. Insert the Windows XP installation disc (ignoring any Autorun prompts), and go to Start | Run. Type **d:\i386\winnt /cmdcons**, substituting "d:" with your optical drive's drive letter. Follow the onscreen instructions. The Setup program will download any updates. From now on, the OS selection menu will show you both your Windows OS and the Recovery Console every time you boot the system.

When you select the Recovery Console, you will see a message about ntdetect, another message that the Recovery Console is starting up, and then you are greeted with the following message and command prompt:

```
Microsoft Windows XP<TM> Recovery Console.
The Recovery Console provides system repair and recovery functionality.
Type Exit to quit the Recovery Console and restart the computer.

1: C:\WINDOWS
Which Windows XP installation would you like to log onto
<To cancel, press ENTER>?
```

The cursor is a small, white rectangle sitting to the right of the question mark on the last line. If you are not accustomed to working at the command prompt, this may be disorienting. If there is only one installation of Windows XP on your computer, type the number 1 at the prompt and press the ENTER key. If you press ENTER before typing in a valid selection, the Recovery Console will cancel and the computer will reboot. The only choice you can make in this example is 1. Having made that choice, the screen displays a new line, followed by the cursor:

```
Type the Administrator password:
```

Enter the Administrator password for that computer and press ENTER. The password does not display on the screen; you see asterisks in place of the password. The screen still shows everything that has happened so far, unless something has happened to cause an error message. It now looks like this:

```
Microsoft Windows XP<TM> Recovery Console.
The Recovery Console provides system repair and recovery functionality.
Type Exit to quit the Recovery Console and restart the computer.

1: C:\WINDOWS
Which Windows XP installation would you like to log onto
<To cancel, press ENTER>? 1
Type the Administrator password: ********
C:\Windows>
```

By now, you've caught on and know that there is a rectangular prompt immediately after the last line. Now what do you do? Use the Recovery Console commands, of course. The Recovery Console uses many of the commands that work in the Windows command-line interface that you explored in Chapter 18, as well as some commands uniquely its own. Table 19-1 lists common Recovery Console commands.

The Recovery Console shines in the business of manually restoring Registries, stopping problem services, rebuilding partitions (other than the system partition), and using the expand program to extract copies of corrupted files from an optical disc or floppy disk.

Using the Recovery Console, you can reconfigure a service so that it starts with different settings, format partitions on the hard drive, read and write on local FAT or NTFS partitions, and copy replacement files from a floppy or optical disc. The Recovery Console enables you to access the file system and is still constrained by the file and folder security of NTFS, which makes it a more secure tool to use than some third-party solutions.

Command	Description
attrib	Changes attributes of selected file or folder
cd (or chdir)	Displays current directory or changes directories
chkdsk	Runs CheckDisk utility
cls	Clears screen
copy	Copies from removable media to system folders on hard disk. No wildcards
del (or delete)	Deletes service or folder
dir	Lists contents of selected directory on system partition only
disable	Disables service or driver
diskpart	Creates/deletes partitions
enable	Enables service or driver
extract	Extracts components from .cab files
fixboot	Writes new partition boot sector on system partition
fixmbr	Writes new master boot record (MBR) for partition boot sector
format	Formats selected disk
listsvc	Lists all services on system
logon	Enables you to choose which Windows installation to log on to if you have more than one
map	Displays current drive letter mappings
md (or mkdir)	Creates a directory
more (or type)	Displays contents of a text file
rd (or rmdir)	Removes a directory
ren (or rename)	Renames a single file
systemroot	Makes current directory system root of drive you're logged on to
type	Displays contents of a text file

Table 19-1 Common Recovery Console Commands

The Recovery Console also works great for fixing three items: repairing the MBR, reinstalling the boot files, and rebuilding boot.ini. Let's look at each of these.

A bad boot sector usually shows up as a No Boot Device error. If it turns out that this isn't the problem, using the Recovery Console command to fix it won't hurt anything. At the Recovery Console prompt, just type

fixmbr

This fixes the master boot record.

Missing system files are usually indicated by the error *NTLDR bad or missing*. Odds are good that if ntdlr is missing, so are the rest of the system files. To fix this, get to the root directory (cd\—remember that from Chapter 18?) and type the following line (substituting the drive letter of the optical drive for *d:* in the example):

copy d:\i386\ntldr

Then type this line:

copy d:\i386\ntdetect.com

This takes care of two of the big three and leads us to the last issue, rebuilding boot.ini. If the boot.ini file is gone or corrupted, run this command from the Recovery Console:

bootcfg /rebuild

The Recovery Console will try to locate all installed copies of Windows and ask you if you want to add them to the new boot.ini file it's about to create. Say yes to the ones you want.

If all goes well with the Recovery Console, do a thorough backup as soon as possible (just in case something else goes wrong). If the Recovery Console does not do the trick, the next step is to restore Windows XP.

Attempt to Restore

If you've been diligent about backing up, you can attempt to restore to an earlier, working copy of Windows. Assuming you made an Automated System Recovery (ASR) backup, this will restore your system to a previously installed state, but you should use it as a last resort. You lose everything on the system that was installed or added after you created the ASR disk. If that's the best option, though, follow the steps outlined in Chapter 17.

NOTE To use the Windows XP System Restore, you need to be able to get into Windows. "Restore" in the context used here means to give you an option to get into Windows.

Rebuild

If faced with a full system rebuild, you have several options, depending on the particular system. You could simply reboot to the Windows CD-ROM and install right on top of the existing system, what's called a *repair installation*. To avoid losing anything important, though, you'd be better off swapping the C: drive for a blank hard drive and installing a clean version of Windows.

Most OEM systems come with a misleadingly named *Recovery CD* or *recovery partition*. The Recovery CD is a CD-ROM that you boot to and run. The recovery partition is a hidden partition on the hard drive that you activate at boot by holding down a key combination specific to the manufacturer of that system. (See the motherboard manual or users' guide for the key combination and other details.) Both "recovery" options do the same thing—restore your computer to the factory-installed state. If you run one of these tools, *you will wipe everything off your system*—all personal files, folders, and programs will go away! Before running either tool, make sure all important files and folders are backed up on an optical disc or spare hard drive.

Failure to Boot: Windows Vista and Windows 7

Two critical boot files risk corruption in Windows Vista and Windows 7, bootmgr and bcd, both of which you can fix with one tool, bcdedit. You can use this tool in the Windows Recovery Environment.

WinPE and the Death of the Recovery Console

With Windows Vista, Microsoft upgraded the installation environment from the 16-bit text mode environment used in every previous version of Windows to 32- and 64-bit. This upgrade enabled the Windows installation process to go graphical and support features such as a mouse pointer and clickable elements, rather than relying on command-line tools. Microsoft calls the installation environment the *Windows Preinstallation Environment* (*WinPE* or *Windows PE*).

With Windows PE, you can boot directly to the Windows DVD. This loads a limited-function graphical operating system that contains both troubleshooting and diagnostic tools, along with installation options. The Windows installation media is called a *Live DVD* because WinPE loads directly from disc into memory and doesn't access or modify the hard drive.

 NOTE Although here I discuss only how WinPE helps boot repair, know that WinPE goes much further. WinPE can assist unattended installations, network installations, and even booting diskless workstations on a network.

When you access Windows PE and opt for the troubleshooting and repair features, you open a special set of tools called the *Windows Recovery Environment* (*WinRE* or *Windows RE*). The terms can get a little confusing because of the similarity of letters, so mark this: Windows RE is the repair tools that run within Windows PE. WinPE powers WinRE. Got it? Let's tackle WinRE.

 EXAM TIP Microsoft also refers to the Windows Recovery Environment as the *System Recovery Options menu*. It's unclear as of this writing which label CompTIA will use.

Enter Windows RE

It would be unfair to say that the Windows Recovery Environment only replaces the Recovery Console. WinRE includes an impressive, powerful set of both automated and manual utilities that collectively diagnoses and fixes all but the most serious of Windows boot problems. Although WinRE does all the hard work for you, you still need to know how to access and use it. When faced with a failure to boot scenario in Windows Vista or Windows 7, WinRE is one of your primary tools.

Getting to Windows RE

In Windows 7, you can access WinRE in three ways. (See the upcoming Exam Tip for Windows Vista options.) First, you can boot from the Windows installation media and select *Repair*. Second, you can use the *Repair Your Computer* option on the Advanced Boot Options (F8) menu (see Figure 19-4). Third, you can create a system repair disc before you have problems. Go to Control Panel | System and Security | Backup and Restore and select *Create a system repair disc*, which opens the dialog box shown in Figure 19-5.

Figure 19-4

Selecting Repair Your Computer in the Advanced Boot Options menu

```
                        Advanced Boot Options

Choose Advanced Options for: Windows 7
(Use the arrow keys to highlight your choice.)

    Repair Your Computer

    Safe Mode
    Safe Mode with Networking
    Safe Mode with Command Prompt

    Enable Boot Logging
    Enable low-resolution video (640x480)
    Last Known Good Configuration (advanced)
    Directory Services Restore Mode
    Debugging Mode
    Disable automatic restart on system failure
    Disable Driver Signature Enforcement

    Start Windows Normally

Description: View a list of system recovery tools you can use to repair
            startup problems, run diagnostics, or restore your system.

ENTER=Choose                                          ESC=Cancel
```

Figure 19-5

Making a system repair disc in Windows 7

EXAM TIP Windows Vista does not have the Repair Your Computer option on the Advanced Boot Options menu. You can either use a Windows installation media or, if you have SP1 or later, make a bootable system repair disc.

Although any of these methods works fine, I recommend that you access WinRE from the Windows installation media for three reasons:

- The hard drive can be so messed up that you won't make it to the Advanced Boot Options menu.
- Accessing WinRE using the Repair Your Computer option in the Advanced Boot Options menu requires a local administrator password.
- Using a bootable disc enables you to avoid any malware that might be on the system.

Using Windows RE

No matter how you choose to access the Windows Recovery Environment, the main menu looks the same (see Figure 19-6). You have five options in WinRE:

- Startup Repair
- System Restore
- System Image Recovery (Windows 7) or Windows Complete PC Restore (Vista)
- Windows Memory Diagnostics (Tool) (only Vista includes "Tool" in the name)
- Command Prompt

The name of the third option differs between Windows 7 and Windows Vista, though the intent—rebuilding from a backup—is the same. I'll talk about how these options differ a little later in the chapter.

EXAM TIP Make sure you know how to access the Windows Recovery Environment and what each of the available tools does.

Startup Repair The *Startup Repair* utility serves as a one-stop, do-it-all option (see Figure 19-7). When run, it performs a number of repairs, including:

- Repairs a corrupted Registry by accessing the backup copy on your hard drive
- Restores critical system and driver files
- Runs the equivalent of the Recovery Console's fixboot and fixmbr
- Rolls back any non-working drivers
- Uninstalls any incompatible service packs and patches
- Runs chkdsk
- Runs a memory test to check your RAM

Figure 19-6 Recovery Environment main screen

Figure 19-7 Startup Repair in action

Startup Repair fixes almost any Windows boot problem. In fact, if you have a system with one hard drive containing a single partition with Windows Vista or Windows 7 installed, you'd have trouble finding something it *couldn't* fix. Upon completion, Startup Repair shows the screen shown in Figure 19-8.

Figure 19-8 Startup Repair complete; no problems found

Note the link in Figure 19-8 that says *View diagnostic and repair details*. This opens a text file called srttrail.txt that lists exactly what the program found, what it fixed, and what it failed to do. It may look cryptic, but you can type anything you find into Google for more information. I've reproduced the beginning of the (very long) srttrail.txt file here:

```
Startup Repair diagnosis and repair log
---------------------------
Last successful boot time: 7/14/2012 2:37:43 AM (GMT)
Number of repair attempts: 6

Session details
---------------------------
System Disk = \Device\Harddisk0
Windows directory = C:\Windows
AutoChk Run = 0
Number of root causes = 1

Test Performed:
---------------------------
Name: Check for updates
Result: Completed successfully. Error code =  0x0
```

```
Time taken = 32 ms

Test Performed:
--------------------------
Name: System disk test
Result: Completed successfully. Error code =  0x0
Time taken = 0 ms
```

 NOTE The *View advanced options for system recovery and support* link simply returns you to the main screen.

In Windows 7, Startup Repair starts automatically if your system detects a boot problem. If you power up a Windows system and see the screen shown in Figure 19-9, Windows has detected a problem in the startup process.

Figure 19-9

Windows Error Recovery

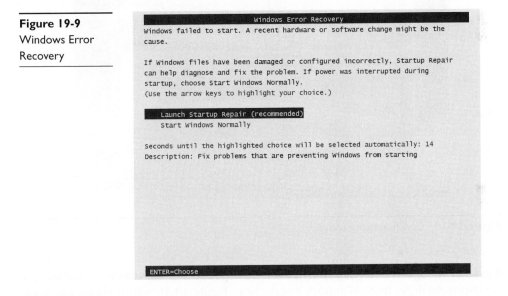

```
                     Windows Error Recovery
Windows failed to start. A recent hardware or software change might be the
cause.

If Windows files have been damaged or configured incorrectly, Startup Repair
can help diagnose and fix the problem. If power was interrupted during
startup, choose Start Windows Normally.
(Use the arrow keys to highlight your choice.)

   Launch Startup Repair (recommended)
     Start Windows Normally

Seconds until the highlighted choice will be selected automatically: 14
Description: Fix problems that are preventing Windows from starting

ENTER=Choose
```

Personally, I think this menu pops up way too often. If you fail to shut down your computer properly, for example, this menu appears. In this case, you can save time by booting normally. When in doubt, however, go ahead and run Startup Repair. It can't hurt anything.

A powerful tool like Startup Repair still doesn't cover everything. You may have specific needs that require more finesse than a single, do-it-all approach. In many cases, you've already discovered the problem and simply want to make a single fix. You might want to perform a system restoration or check the memory. For this, we'll need to explore the other four options available in WinRE.

EXAM TIP If you have trouble booting your computer, you should try Startup Repair first.

System Restore *System Restore* does the same job here it has done since Microsoft first introduced it in Windows Me, enabling you to go back to a time when your computer worked properly. Placing this option in Windows RE gives those of us who make many *restore points*—snapshots of a system at a given point of time—a quick and handy way to return our systems to a previous state (see Figure 19-10).

Figure 19-10 System Restore points

System Image Recovery/Windows Complete PC Restore Windows 7's backup tools differ from Windows Vista's. Note Figure 19-11, which shows the Windows Vista Recovery Environment menu on the left next to the Windows 7 Recovery Environment on the right. The third WinRE option differs. Windows Vista uses the Windows Complete PC Restore utility, whereas Windows 7 includes the System Image Recovery tool.

With an image in hand, you can use the Windows Complete PC Restore/System Image Recovery tool to restore your system after a catastrophe.

If you have the drive containing the system image plugged in when you first run the wizard, it should detect your latest backup and present you with the dialog box shown in Figure 19-12. If it doesn't list a system image or it lists the wrong one, you can select an image from another date on the same disk or even a remote network share.

Figure 19-11 The WinRE options in Windows Vista (left) and Windows 7 (right)

Figure 19-12 Selecting a system image

After you select the image you want to restore, the utility presents you with a few more options, as shown in Figure 19-13. Most importantly, you can choose to format and repartition disks. With this option selected, the utility wipes out the existing partitions and data on all disks so the restored system will get the same partitions that the backed-up system had.

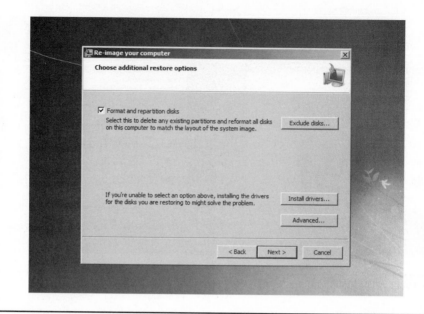

Figure 19-13 Additional restore options

After you click Finish on the confirmation screen (see Figure 19-14), which also contains a final warning, the restore process begins (see Figure 19-15). The utility removes the old system data and then copies the backed-up system image to the hard drive(s). Once the process completes, your system reboots and should start up again with all of your data and programs just where you left them when you last backed up.

 EXAM TIP The CompTIA A+ 802 exam objectives use the phrase *recovery image*, which conflates separate tools in Windows 7. You can use Backup and Restore to create a system image and a system repair disc. You can use the system repair disc to get to the System Image Recovery that uses the system image on the second disc to write a "fixed" or previously working version of Windows 7 to the hard drive. Got all that?

Windows Memory Diagnostics (Tool) Bad RAM causes huge problems for any operating system, creating scenarios where computers get Blue Screens of Death (BSoDs), system lockups, and continuous reboots. Starting with Windows Vista, Microsoft added a memory tester to the Windows Recovery Environment. When you click the Windows Memory Diagnostic (Tool) link from the main WinRE screen, it prompts you to *Restart now and check for problems (recommended)* or *Check for problems the next time I start my computer* (see Figure 19-16). It doesn't really matter which option you choose, but if you think you need to test the system's RAM, that probably means you should do it now.

Figure 19-14 Confirming your settings

Figure 19-15 Restoring your computer

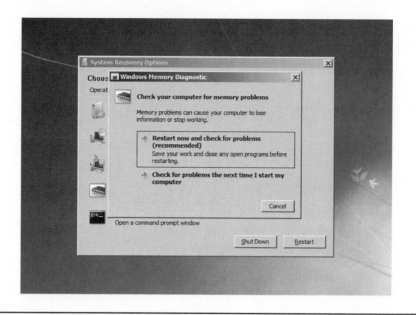

Figure 19-16 Windows Memory Diagnostic screen

Once you restart, your system immediately starts running the Windows Memory Diagnostics Tool, as shown in Figure 19-17. While the program runs, you can press F1 to see the Memory Tester options (see Figure 19-18).

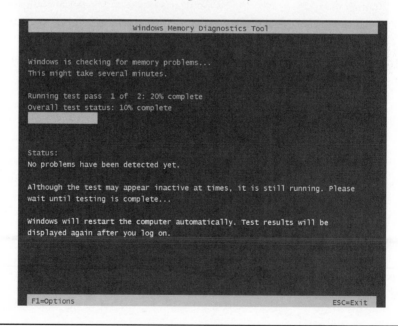

Figure 19-17 Windows Memory Diagnostics Tool running

```
                Windows Memory Diagnostics Tool - Options

Test Mix:

     Basic
     Standard
     Extended

Description: The Standard tests include all the Basic tests, plus LRAND,
             Stride6 (cache enabled), CHCKR3, WMATS+, and WINVC.

Cache:

     Default
     On
     Off

Description: Use the default cache setting of each test.

Pass Count (0 - 99):    2

Description: Set the total number of times the entire test mix will
             repeat (0 = infinite).

  TAB=Next                    F10=Apply                    ESC=Cancel
```

Figure 19-18 Windows Memory Diagnostics Tool options

The tool lists three important Test Mix options at the top of the screen: Basic, Standard, and Extended. *Basic* runs quickly (about one minute) but performs only light testing. *Standard*, the default choice, takes a few minutes and tests more aggressively. *Extended* takes hours (you should let it run overnight), but it will very aggressively test your RAM.

NOTE You can also find the Windows Memory Diagnostics Tool in the Control Panel under System and Security | Administrative Tools, or start it from an administrative command prompt using the **mdsched** command.

This tool includes two other options: Cache and Pass Count. The *Cache* option enables you to set whether the tests use the CPU's built-in cache as well as override the default cache settings for each test type. Simply leave Cache set at Default and never touch it. *Pass Count* sets the number of times each set of tests will run. This option defaults to 2.

After the tool runs, your computer reboots normally. You can open Event Viewer to see the results (see Figure 19-19).

Sadly, I've had rather poor results with the Windows Memory Diagnostics Tool. We keep lots of bad RAM around the labs here at Total Seminars, and, when put to the test, we were unable to get this tool to do anything other than give us a BSoD or lock up the system. We still turn to tried-and-tested tools such as the free Memtest86+ when we're worried about bad RAM.

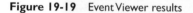

Figure 19-19 Event Viewer results

NOTE You can find out more about Memtest86+ at www.memtest.org.

Command Prompt The last, most interesting, and easily nerdiest option in the WinRE menu is Command Prompt. Unlike the Recovery Console, the WinRE command prompt is a true 32- or 64-bit prompt that functions similarly to the regular command prompt. WinRE's command prompt, however, includes an important utility (bootrec) that you can't find in the regular command prompt. The WinRE command prompt also lacks a large number of the command-prompt tools you'd have in a regular Windows command prompt (though all the important ones remain). Let's begin by looking at the bootrec command. After that, we'll look at some other utilities that the WinRE command prompt offers.

NOTE The Startup Repair tool runs many of these command-prompt utilities automatically. You need to use the WinRE command prompt only for unique situations where the Startup Repair tool fails.

It's important for you to understand that the CompTIA A+ exams do not expect you to know everything about all these command-prompt utilities. The CompTIA A+ exams expect that you do know these things, however:

- Which utilities are available and their names
- How to access these utilities (WinRE, regular command prompt)
- What these utilities basically do

- Some of the basic switches used for these utilities
- With higher-level support, that you can fix computers using these tools (being led by a specialist tech over the phone, for example)

The *bootrec* command is a Windows Recovery Environment troubleshooting and repair tool that repairs the master boot record, boot sector, or BCD store. It replaces the old fixboot and fixmbr Recovery Console commands and adds two more repair features:

- **bootrec /fixboot** Rebuilds the boot sector for the active system partition
- **bootrec /fixmbr** Rebuilds the master boot record for the system partition
- **bootrec /scanos** Looks for Windows installations not currently in the BCD store and shows you the results without doing anything
- **bootrec /rebuildmbr** Looks for Windows installations not currently in the BCD store and gives you the choice to add them to the BCD store

NOTE Boot configuration data (BCD) files contain information about operating systems installed on a computer. In Microsoft speak, that information is called a *store* or *BCD store*. This applies to Windows Vista and Windows 7 only.

With ntldr, you could access the boot.ini text file to see the Windows boot order. With boot.ini replaced by the BCD store, you can use a tool called *bcdedit* to see how Windows boots. Running bcdedit by itself (without switches) shows the boot options. The following boot information comes from a system with a single copy of Windows installed. Note there are two sections: the *Windows Boot Manager* section describes the location of bootmgr and the *Windows Boot Loader* section describes the location of the winload.exe file.

EXAM TIP Instead of editing the boot.ini text file, Windows Vista/7 includes the bcdedit program for editing the BCD store.

```
Windows Boot Manager
--------------------
identifier              {bootmgr}
device                  partition=\Device\HarddiskVolume1
description             Windows Boot Manager
locale                  en-US
inherit                 {globalsettings}
default                 {current}
resumeobject            {d4539c9b-481a-11df-a981-a17cb98be35c}
displayorder            {current}
toolsdisplayorder       {memdiag}
timeout                 30
```

```
Windows Boot Loader
-------------------
identifier              {current}
device                  partition=C:
path                    \Windows\system32\winload.exe
description             Windows 7
locale                  en-US
inherit                 {bootloadersettings}
recoverysequence        {d4539c9d-481a-11df-a981-a17cb98be35c}
recoveryenabled         Yes
osdevice                partition=C:
systemroot              \Windows
resumeobject            {d4539c9b-481a-11df-a981-a17cb98be35c}
nx                      OptIn
```

To make changes to the BCD store, you need to use switches:

- **bcdedit /export <filename>** exports a copy of the BCD store to a file. This is a very good idea whenever you use bcdedit!

- **bcdedit /import <filename>** imports a copy of the BCD store back into the store.

If you look carefully at the previous bcdedit output, you'll notice that each section has an identifier such as {bootmgr} or {current}. You can use these identifiers to make changes to the BCD store using the /set switch. Here's an example:

```
BCDEDIT /SET {current} path \BackupWindows\system32\winload.exe
```

This changes the path of the {current} identifier to point to an alternative winload.exe.

The bcdedit command supports multiple OSs. Notice how this BCD store has three identifiers: {bootmgr}, {current}, and {ntldr}—a fairly common dual-boot scenario.

```
Windows Boot Manager
--------------------
identifier              {bootmgr}
device                  partition=D:
description             Windows Boot Manager
locale                  en-US
inherit                 {globalsettings}
default                 {current}
resumeobject            {60b80a52-8267-11e0-ad8a-bdb414c1bf84}
displayorder            {ntldr}
                        {current}
toolsdisplayorder       {memdiag}
timeout                 30

Windows Legacy OS Loader
------------------------
identifier              {ntldr}
device                  partition=D:
path                    \ntldr
description             Earlier Version of Windows

Windows Boot Loader
-------------------
identifier              {current}
```

You can run commands at
and partitions on drives, mou
level RAID arrays.

Run the **clean** command a
information off the currently
simply won't let Windows bo

Commands available at th
you still need a tool for hand
prompt provide all of the typi
however—fsutil—does a few i

- Typing **fsinfo** provides
- Typing **fsutil dirty <dri**
 "dirty"—meaning you i
 detects an error in the f
 dirty volume. The disk cl
 Windows loads and wil
- Typing **fsutil repair ini**
 out rebooting.

Failure to Load t

Assuming that Windows gets
graphical Windows OS. You v
everything until Windows lo

```
device           partition=C:
path             \Windows\system32\winload.exe
description      Windows 7
locale           en-US
inherit          {bootloadersettings}
recoverysequence {60b80a54-8267-11e0-ad8a-bdb414c1bf84}
recoveryenabled  Yes
osdevice         partition=C:
systemroot       \Windows
resumeobject     {60b80a52-8267-11e0-ad8a-bdb414c1bf84}
nx               OptIn
```

A BCD store like this will cause the following menu to pop up at boot (see Figure 19-20).

Figure 19-20 bootmgr showing available versions of Windows

You can use the bcdedit command to change the display order of the menu. If you wanted to add Windows XP to the beginning of the list, type this command:

bcdedit /displayorder [WindowsXP} /addfirst

You can also use bcdedit to set the default OS:

bcdedit /default {current}

You can even remove one of the identifiers, preventing others from booting to that OS:

bcdedit /delete {WindowsXP}

The bcdedit command is a tricky tool to use. To make your life easier, consider using the popular EasyBCD program from NeoSmart Technologies. You can run EasyBCD only from within a normal Windows boot, not the WinRE, but it provides more power and safety than bcdedit (see Figure 19-21).

NC

Figure 19-21
EasyBCD at work

The comman
tool lacks many
tion. You can, f
opens a special

```
C:\Windows\syst
Microsoft DiskF
Copyright (C) 1
On computer: MI
DISKPART>
```

You can list

```
DISKPART> list
  Volume ### I
  ---------- -
  Volume 0
  Volume 1

DISKPART>
```

Select a volu

```
DISKPART> selec
Volume 1 is the
DISKPART>
```

Several issues can create a scenario where the graphical interface fails to load. Windows can hang during the GUI-loading phase because of buggy device drivers or Registry problems. Even autoloading programs can cause the GUI to hang on load. The first step in troubleshooting these sorts of scenarios is to use one of the Advanced Startup options (covered later in the chapter) to try to get past the hang spot and into Windows.

EXAM TIP If faced with a scenario where the GUI files have become corrupted, what CompTIA calls a "Missing Graphical Interface" problem, your only choices are to restore from backup or rebuild from the installation media.

Device Drivers

Device driver problems that stop Windows GUI from loading look pretty scary. Figure 19-23 shows the infamous Windows *Stop error*, better known as the *Blue Screen of Death (BSoD)*. The BSoD only appears when something causes an error from which Windows cannot recover. The BSoD is not limited to device driver problems, but device drivers are one of the reasons you'll see the BSoD.

```
A problem has been detected and Windows has been shut down to prevent damage
to your computer.

NO_MORE_IRP_STACK_LOCATIONS

If this is the first time you've seen this Stop error screen,
restart your computer. If this screen appears again, follow
these steps:

Check to make sure that any new hardware or software is properly installed.
If this is a new installation, ask your hardware or software manufacturer
for any Windows updates you might need.

If problems continue, disable or remove any newly installed hardware
or software. Disable BIOS memory options such as caching or shadowing.
If you need to use Safe Mode to remove or disable components, restart
your computer, press F8 to select Advanced Startup Options, and then
select Safe Mode.

Technical information:

*** STOP: 0x00000035 (0x00000000,0xF7E562B2,0x00000008,0xC00000000)

***     wdmaud.sys - Address F7E562B2 base at F7E56000, DateStamp 36B047A5
```

Figure 19-23 BSoD

Whenever faced with a scenario where you get a BSoD, read what it says. Windows BSoDs tell you the name of the file that caused the problem and usually suggests a recommended action. Once in a while these are helpful.

BSoD problems due to device drivers almost always take place immediately after you've installed a new device and rebooted. Take out the device and reboot. If Windows loads properly, head over to the manufacturer's Web site. A new device producing this type of problem is a serious issue that should have been caught before the device was released. In many cases, the manufacturer will have updated drivers available for download or will recommend a replacement device.

EXAM TIP Viruses can cause the GUI to fail or make it appear to be missing. One nasty one running around recently, for example, caused what appeared to be a BSoD warning of imminent hard drive controller failure. Even after getting rid of the virus, Windows appeared devoid of any graphical elements at all: no Start button, icons, or files even in Computer. That's because the virus had changed the attributes of every file and folder on the hard drive to hidden! See Chapter 18 for the attrib command; see Chapter 29 for recovery techniques for virus-attacked computers.

The second indication of a device problem that shows up during the GUI part of startup is a freeze-up: the Windows startup screen just stays there and you never get a chance to log on. If this happens, try one of the Advanced Startup Options, covered following the Registry.

Registry

The Registry files load every time the computer boots. Windows does a pretty good job of protecting your Registry files from corruption, but from time to time something may slip by Windows and it will attempt to load a bad Registry. These errors may show up as BSoDs that say "Registry File Failure" or text errors that say "Windows could not start." Whatever the case, when you run into these sorts of scenarios, you need to restore a good Registry copy. The best way to do this is the Last Known Good Configuration boot option (see the upcoming section). If that fails, you can restore an earlier version of the Registry through the Recovery Console in Windows XP or through Windows RE in Windows Vista/7.

Replacing the Registry in Windows XP

Boot to the Windows installation CD-ROM, get to the Recovery Console, and type these commands to restore a Registry. Notice I didn't say "your" Registry in the previous sentence. Your Registry is corrupted and gone, so you need to rebuild.

```
delete c:\windows\system32\config\system
delete c:\windows\system32\config\software
delete c:\windows\system32\config\sam
delete c:\windows\system32\config\security
delete c:\windows\system32\config\default
```

There is no safety or repair feature in any version of Windows that makes the OS boot to Safe Mode automatically. In most cases, Windows automatically booting to Safe Mode indicates that someone has set the System Configuration utility to force Windows to do so. Type **msconfig** at the Start | Search or Start | Run option and press ENTER to open the System Configuration utility, and then deselect the Safe boot or Boot to Safe Mode check box (see Figure 19-26).

Figure 19-26

Uncheck Safe boot

EXAM TIP The CompTIA A+ 802 exam objectives mention a scenario where Windows boots directly to Safe Mode. This can only happen if a tech specifically makes a change to the System Configuration utility.

Safe Mode with Networking (All Versions)

This mode is identical to plain Safe Mode except that you get network support. I use this mode to test for a problem with network drivers. If Windows won't start up normally but does start up in Safe Mode, I reboot into Safe Mode with Networking. If it fails to start up with Networking, the problem is a network driver. I reboot back to Safe Mode, open Device Manager, and start disabling network components, beginning with the network adapter.

Safe Mode with Command Prompt (All Versions)

When you start Windows in this mode, rather than loading the GUI desktop, it loads the command prompt (cmd.exe) as the shell to the operating system after you log on, as shown in Figure 19-27. From here you can run any of the commands you learned about in Chapter 18, plus a lot of utilities as well. Error-checking runs fine as chkdsk, for example. Disk Defragmenter probably runs even faster when you type **defrag** followed by a drive letter at the command prompt than it does from the graphical version of the tool.

Safe Mode with Command Prompt is a handy option to remember if the desktop does not display at all, which, after you have eliminated video drivers, can be caused by corruption of the explorer.exe program. From the command prompt, you can delete the corrupted version of explorer.exe and copy in an undamaged version. This requires knowing the command-line commands for navigating the directory structure, as well as knowing the location of the file you are replacing. Although Explorer is not loaded, you can load other GUI tools that don't depend on Explorer. All you have to do is enter the correct command. For instance, to load Event Viewer, type **eventvwr.msc** at the command line and press ENTER.

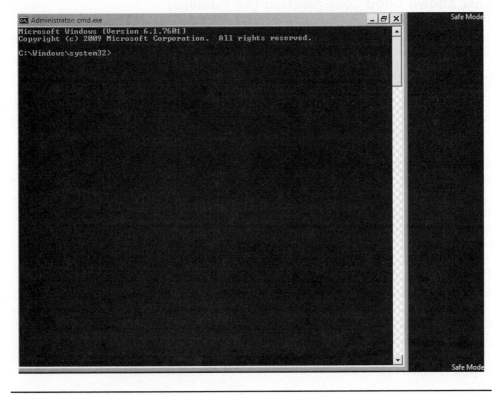

Figure 19-27 Safe Mode with Command Prompt

Enable Boot Logging (All Versions)

This option starts Windows normally and creates a log file of the drivers as they load into memory. The file is named Ntbtlog.txt and is saved in the %SystemRoot% folder. If the startup failed because of a bad driver, the last entry in this file may be the driver the OS was initializing when it failed.

Reboot and go into the Recovery Console or WinRE. Use the tools there to read the boot log (**type ntbtlog.txt**) and disable or enable problematic devices or services.

Enable VGA Mode (XP)/Enable Low-Resolution Mode (Vista and 7)

Enable VGA Mode/Enable Low-Resolution Mode starts Windows normally, but only loads a default VGA driver. If this mode works, it may mean you have a bad driver, or it may mean you are using the correct video driver but it is configured incorrectly (perhaps with the wrong refresh rate and/or resolution). Whereas Safe Mode loads a generic VGA driver, this mode loads the driver Windows is configured to use but starts it up in standard VGA mode rather than using the settings for which it is configured. After successfully starting in this mode, open the Display applet and change the settings.

Last Known Good Configuration (All Versions)

When Windows' startup fails immediately after installing a new driver but before you have logged on again, try the *Last Known Good Configuration* option. This option applies specifically to new device drivers that cause failures on reboot.

Directory Services Restore Mode (All Versions)

The title says it all here; this option only applies to Active Directory domain controllers, and only Windows Server versions can be domain controllers. I have no idea why Microsoft includes this option. If you choose it, you simply boot into Safe Mode.

Debugging Mode (All Versions)

If you select this choice, Windows starts in kernel debug mode. It's a super-techie thing to do, and I doubt that even über techs do debug mode anymore. To do this, you have to connect the computer you are debugging to another computer via a serial connection, and as Windows starts up, a debug of the kernel is sent to the second computer, which must also be running a debugger program.

Disable Automatic Restart on System Failure (All Versions)

Sometimes a BSoD will appear at startup, causing your computer to spontaneously reboot. That's all well and good, but if it happens too quickly, you might not be able to read the BSoD to see what caused the problem. Selecting *Disable automatic restart on system failure* from the Advanced Startup Options menu stops the computer from rebooting on Stop errors. This gives you the opportunity to write down the error and hopefully find a fix.

Disable Driver Signature Enforcement (Vista and 7)

Windows Vista and 7 require that all very low-level drivers (kernel drivers) must have a Microsoft driver signature. If you are using an older driver to connect to your hard drive controller or some other low-level feature, you must use this option to get Windows to load the driver. Hopefully you will always check your motherboard and hard drives for Windows compatibility and never have to use this option.

Start Windows Normally (All Versions)

This choice will simply start Windows normally, without rebooting. You already rebooted to get to this menu. Select this if you changed your mind about using any of the other exotic choices.

Reboot (All Versions)

This choice will actually do a soft reboot of the computer.

Return to OS Choices Menu (All Versions)

On computers with multiple operating systems, you get an OS Choices menu to select which OS to load. If you load Windows and press F8 to get the Advanced Startup Options menu, you'll see this option. Choosing it returns you to the OS Choices menu, from which you can select the operating system to load.

Troubleshooting Tools in the GUI

Once you're able to load into Windows, whether through Safe Mode or one of the other options, the whole gamut of Windows tools is available for you. In the previous scenario where a bad device driver caused the startup problems, for example, you can open Device Manager and begin troubleshooting just as you've learned in previous chapters. If you suspect some service or Registry issue caused the problem, head on over to Event Viewer and see what sort of logon events have happened recently. Let's go there first.

Event Viewer

When you get into the GUI, one of the first tools you should use is Event Viewer to see what's causing the problems on your computer. *Event Viewer* is Windows' default tattletale program, spilling the beans about a number of interesting happenings on the system. With a little tweaking, Event Viewer turns into a virtual recording of anything you might ever want to know about on your system.

Keep in mind that Event Viewer is a powerful tool for more than just troubleshooting Windows—it's a powerful tool for security as well, as you'll see in Chapter 29. But for now let's examine Event Viewer, both in Windows XP and in Windows 7 (the Vista version of Event Viewer is almost identical to the version in Windows 7), to see what we can do with this amazing utility.

Windows XP Event Viewer You can find Event Viewer in the Administrative Tools applet in the Control Panel. By default, Event Viewer has three sections: Application, Security, and System. If you've downloaded Internet Explorer 7 or later, you'll see a fourth option for the browser, Internet Explorer (see Figure 19-28). Each of these sections stores certain types of events, as described next.

- **Application** As the name implies, the Application section stores events specific to applications. There are three types of events recorded: Errors, Warnings, and Information. Errors, marked with a red *X*, are the most serious, reflecting events that prevent the application from working properly. Warnings, marked with an exclamation point over a triangle, are for events that aren't preventing the application from running but may do so in the future. Information events are merely record keeping, letting you know that a program, driver, or service ran successfully.

- **Security** Security records events that Microsoft calls *audits*. Audits record anything to do with security, such as the number of logon events. All audits are listed as either successful or failed. There a thousands of audits available on a Windows system, the vast majority of which are turned off by default but can be turned on in Administrative Tools | Local Security Policy. Since these are security issues, we'll cover the Security section as well as auditing in Chapter 29.

- **System** The System section is similar to the Application section in that you have Errors, Warnings, and Information, but the events listed here are specific only to the operating system.

When something goes wrong with Windows, it's common for techs to turn to Event Viewer first. Let's say an application fails to load. A common use for Event Viewer is to view the application to see what happened (see Figure 19-29).

Figure 19-28 Event Viewer

One very cool feature of Event Viewer is that you can click the link to take you to the online Help and Support Center at Microsoft.com, and the software reports your error (see Figure 19-30), checks the online database, and comes back with a more or less useful explanation (see Figure 19-31).

Figure 19-29
Typical application
error message

Figure 19-30
Details about to
be sent

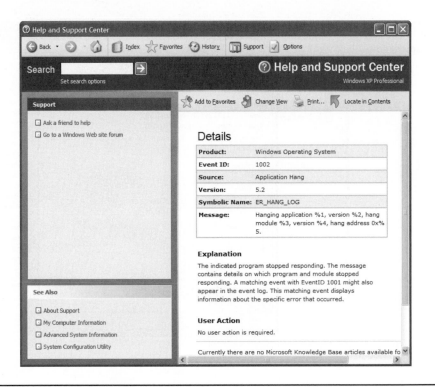

Figure 19-31 Help and Support Center being helpful

Event Viewer might reveal problems with applications failing to load, a big cause of Windows loading problems (see Figure 19-32). It might also reveal problems with services failing to start. Finally, Windows might run into problems loading DLLs. You can troubleshoot these issues individually or you can use System Restore to load a restore point that predates the bugginess.

Windows Vista/7 Event Viewer Windows Vista/7 adds an easy-to-use interface to Event Viewer (while retaining the old Windows XP style if you prefer it). Opening Event Viewer (System and Security | Administrative Tools | Event Viewer) shows you a very different interface from the one you've seen in Windows XP (see Figure 19-33).

Note the four main bars in the center pane: Overview, Summary of Administrative Events, Recently Viewed Nodes, and Log Summary. Pay special attention to the Summary of Administrative Events. It breaks down the events into different levels: Critical, Error, Warning, Information, Audit Success, and Audit Failure. Figure 19-34 shows a typical Summary with the Warning Events opened. You can then click any event to see a dialog box describing the event in detail. Microsoft refers to these as *Views*.

Windows 7's Event Viewer still includes the classic logs you saw in Windows XP (Application, Security, and System) but leans heavily on Views to show you the contents of the logs. Views filter existing log files, making them great for custom reports using beginning/end times, levels of errors, and more. You can use the built-in Views or easily create custom Views, as shown in Figure 19-35.

Figure 19-32 Event Viewer in Windows XP showing some serious application errors!

Figure 19-33 Windows 7 Event Viewer default screen

Figure 19-34 Warning Events open

Figure 19-35 Created custom Views

NOTE By default, Event Viewer stores logs as .evtx files in the C:\windows\system32\winevt\logs folder.

Remember, you still record all data to logs. Logs in Windows 7 still have the same limitations that logs in earlier versions of Windows had. They have a maximum size, a location, and a behavior for when they get too big (such as overwrite the log or make an error). Figure 19-36 shows a typical Log Properties dialog box in Windows 7.

Log Properties - Application (Type: Administrative)

General | Subscriptions

Full Name:	Application
Log path:	%SystemRoot%\System32\Winevt\Logs\Application.evtx
Log size:	14.07 MB(14,749,696 bytes)
Created:	Wednesday, April 14, 2010 5:11:24 PM
Modified:	Tuesday, June 07, 2011 8:44:12 AM
Accessed:	Wednesday, April 14, 2010 5:11:24 PM

☑ Enable logging

Maximum log size (KB): 20480

When maximum event log size is reached:

⦿ Overwrite events as needed (oldest events first)

○ Archive the log when full, do not overwrite events

○ Do not overwrite events (Clear logs manually)

[Clear Log]

[OK] [Cancel] [Apply]

Figure 19-36 Log Properties dialog box in Windows 7

EXAM TIP Only users with Administrator privileges can make changes to log files in Event Viewer.

Windows 7's Event Viewer remains largely untouched in terms of the data collected, but Microsoft did a great job of making that data much easier to understand and use.

EXAM TIP If you run into a scenario where a device has failed and this created problems with Windows' startup, you would turn to the primary Windows tool for hardware issues: Device Manager. We've covered Device Manager in chapters specific to hardware, so there's no need to go into it yet again here.

This changed with Microsoft's introduction of the Performance Information and Tools Control Panel applet (see Figure 19-44).

Figure 19-44 Performance Information and Tools

The *Performance Information and Tools* applet doesn't fix anything. It just provides a relative feel for how your computer stacks up against other systems using the Windows Experience Index. Windows bases this on five components:

- **Processor** Calculations per second
- **Memory (RAM)** Memory operations per second
- **Graphics** Desktop performance for Windows Aero
- **Gaming graphics** 3-D business and gaming graphics performance
- **Primary hard disk** Disk data transfer rate

Each component generates a subscore. These values range from 1 to 5.9 for Windows Vista and 1 to 7.9 for Windows 7. Microsoft determines the calculations that generate these numbers, so I don't know exactly what it takes to give, for example, a CPU a score of 6.1. Your system's Base score is based on the lowest subscore.

The Performance Information and Tools applet won't fix anything, but tells you which component is the weakest link in overall performance.

EXAM TIP You can't change a subscore in the Windows Experience Index without making some kind of hardware change.

Figure 19-46
.NET error

These types of errors invariably require you to go online and do Web searches, using the application name and the error. No matter how bad the error, someone else has already suffered from the same problem. The trick is to find out what they did to get around it.

Problems with Uninstalling

The single biggest problem with uninstalling is that people try to uninstall without administrator privileges. If you try to uninstall and get an error, log back on as an administrator and you should be fine. Don't forget you can right-click on most unin-stallation menu options on the Programs menu and select *Run as administrator* to switch to administrator privileges (see Figure 19-47).

Compatibility

Most applications are written with the most recent version of Windows in mind, but as Windows versions change over time, older programs have difficulty running in more recent Windows versions. In some cases, such as the jump from Windows Vista to Windows 7, the changes are generally minor enough to cause few if any compatibility problems. In other cases, say a program written back when Windows 98 was around, the underpinnings of the OS differ so much that you have to perform certain steps to ensure that the older programs run. Windows XP, Windows Vista, and Windows 7 provide different forms of *compatibility modes* to support older applications.

Windows XP handles compatibility using the aptly named Compatibility tab (see Figure 19-48) in every executable program's Properties dialog box (right-click on the executable file and click Properties). Select the version of Windows you want Windows XP to emulate, and in many cases that is all you need to do to make that older program work (see Figure 19-49).

Figure 19-47
Selecting Run as administrator from the context menu

Figure 19-48
XP Compatibility tab

Figure 19-49
Compatibility
mode options in
Windows XP

You can also set other settings on the Compatibility tab, such as the following located under Display settings:

- **Run in 256 colors** Many old Windows programs were designed to run in 256 colors. Later versions of Windows that support more colors can confuse these older programs.

- **Run in 640 × 480 screen resolution** A few (badly written) older programs assume the screen to be at 640 × 480 resolution. This setting enables them to work.

- **Disable visual themes** Windows themes change a program window's title bar, fonts, and menus, which might make problems for some programs.

Windows Vista and Windows 7 add some important improvements to the Compatibility tab. Both add more recent OS options to the Compatibility mode drop-down menu. Figure 19-50 shows the many options available in Windows 7.

The newer Compatibility tab also adds some new options (see Figure 19-51) to help older programs run:

- **Disable desktop composition** Disables all display features such as Aero. More advanced Windows display features often bog down older programs.

- **Disable display scaling on high DPI settings** Turns off automatic resizing of a program's windows if you're using any high DPI (dots per inch) font. This was added because many programs with large fonts would look bizarre if resized.

- **Run this program as an administrator** As stated, enables you to run the program as an administrator. If this option isn't available, log on as an administrator to see it.

- **Change settings for all users** Clicking this button applies compatibility changes made to a program to every user account on the machine. Otherwise, the settings are only for the current user.

Figure 19-50
Compatibility
mode options in
Windows 7

If you need to make things 100 percent compatible with Windows XP and you have Windows 7 (Professional, Ultimate, and Enterprise only) installed on your system, you can download Windows XP Mode. *Windows XP Mode* is nothing more than a premade Windows XP SP3 virtual machine that runs under Microsoft's popular (and free) virtualization program, Windows Virtual PC (see Figure 19-52).

We'll wait until Chapter 30 for a complete discussion of virtualization and how it works, but for now it's important to appreciate that Windows XP Mode is nothing more than a copy of Windows XP. You can install programs in this virtual machine, access the Internet, print to your printers—everything that you can do with a real computer.

The secret to using compatibility mode isn't much of a secret at all: if the program doesn't run, try a compatibly mode. If you want to be really careful, do a Web search on your application before you try to run it. Compatibility mode is a handy tool to get older applications running.

Figure 19-51
Windows 7
Compatibility tab

Figure 19-52 Windows XP Mode

Missing File or Incorrect File Version

An application may rely on other files, in particular DLL files. Sometimes the application installer will bring specially formatted versions of common DLL or other files to Windows, overwriting the previous versions. Later applications might look for the earlier version of the DLL and fail when it's not found.

You'll experience this sort of scenario with error messages such as "missing DLL" or "cannot open file *xyz*." The usual fix for either issue is to perform an Internet search for the missing DLL or file that fails to open, along with the name of the program you're trying to use.

Crashing Programs

Occasionally, a program gets released that isn't ready for prime time and the error-prone code causes the application to crash or even causes the operating system to crash. I've seen this most often with games rushed to market near the winter holidays. The results of this rushed code can be pretty spectacular. You're right in the middle of a thrilling fight with the bad guy and then what happens? A crash to desktop (CTD).

Poorly written or buggy programs can have awful effects on you and your clients. Some of the scenarios caused by such programs are the computer locking up or unexpectedly shutting down. The system might spontaneously shut down and restart. That kind of improper shutdown can cause problems, especially to open files and folders.

The problem here is that all this crashing can be caused by hardware and driver problems, not just application problems. You've got to keep in mind all of these things as you approach troubleshooting a crash.

Here's a typical scenario where you need to troubleshoot broadly first. If you're playing a graphically intensive game that happens to be huge and takes up a lot of RAM, what could the problem be if the screen locks up and Windows locks up too? It could be that the program ran a routine that clashed with some other application or used a Windows feature improperly. It could be that the video card was marginal and failed when taxed too much. It could be that the system accessed a section of RAM that had gone bad.

In that same scenario, though, where the game runs but degrades the overall performance of Windows, what could cause that problem? That points more squarely at the application side of things rather than the hardware or drivers, especially if the computer successfully runs other programs. The bottom line with crash issues is to keep an open mind and not rule out anything without testing it first.

 EXAM TIP One error common on older systems, still mentioned on the CompTIA A+ exams but largely absent or invisible on modern systems, is a *general protection fault (GPF)*. A GPF occurs when a program tries to do something not permitted, like writing to protected memory or something else Windows doesn't like. This can cause an error message to appear or can even crash the computer. You are very unlikely to encounter a GPF today.

Volume Shadow Copy Service and System Protection

One of the big headaches to a failure with an application isn't so much the application itself but any data it may have corrupted. Sure, a good backup or a restore point might save you, but these can be a hassle. Unless the data was specifically saved (in the backup), there's a chance you don't have a backup in the first place. Microsoft came to your rescue in Windows Vista (Business, Ultimate, and Enterprise only) and Windows 7 (all editions) with a feature called System Protection.

This amazing feature is powered by Volume Shadow Copy Service (VSS), a feature introduced in Windows XP and used by ntbackup. VSS enables the operating system to make backups of any file, even one that is in use. In Windows Vista and 7, VSS is also used by *System Protection*, enabling you to access previous versions of any data file or folder. Try right-clicking on any data file and selecting *Restore previous versions*, which opens the file's Properties dialog box with the Previous Versions tab displayed, as shown in Figure 19-53.

Figure 19-53
Previous Versions
tab

If any of the following criteria are met, you will have at least one previous version in the list:

- The file or folder was backed up using the backup program.
- You created a restore point.
- The file or folder was changed.

You must make sure System Protection is enabled as well. Go to the System Protection tab in the System Properties dialog box (see Figure 19-54) to see if the feature is enabled (it should be running by default).

Figure 19-54

System Protection tab

NOTE Keep in mind that System Protection doesn't have to be only for recovery of corrupted data files caused by bad applications. It's also a great tool to recover previous versions of files that users accidently overwrite.

The System Protection tab also enables you to load a restore point and to create restore points manually, very handy features.

System Protection falls in the category generically called *file recovery software,* and does an outstanding job. You can also get many third-party utilities that accomplish general file recovery. I've used Recuva from Piriform many times, for example, to get "deleted" data off a hard drive or RAID array.

Chapter Review

Questions

1. Which utility is useful in identifying a program that is hogging the processor?

 A. Task Manager

 B. Device Manager

 C. System Monitor

 D. System Information

2. You suspect your system is failing to boot because of a corrupt master boot record. Which utility is the best to fix this?

 A. Automated System Restore

 B. Device Manager

 C. System Restore

 D. Recovery Console

3. What command should you run to check and fix corrupt system files, DLLs, and other critical files?

 A. cmdcons /fixboot

 B. sfc /scannow

 C. chkdsk /r

 D. defrag –a

4. You get a tech call from a distraught Windows XP user who can't get into Windows. He says he has a Recovery CD from the manufacturer and plans to run it. What would you suggest?

 A. Run the Recovery CD to restore the system.

 B. Run the Recovery CD to return the system to the factory-installed state.

 C. Try to get the computer to boot into Safe Mode.

 D. Reinstall Windows by using a Windows XP disc.

5. Which of the following points to a hardware or CMOS problem rather than an OS problem with a PC that won't boot.

 A. A black screen with the error message "invalid boot disk"

 B. A black screen with the error message "NTLDR bad or missing"

 C. A black screen with the error message "Invalid BOOT.INI"

 D. A black screen with the error message "Invalid BCD"

6. John's computer has an error that says bootmgr is corrupted. What tool can he use to fix this problem?

 A. bcdedit

 B. chkdsk

 C. config.sys

 D. regedit

7. What does Microsoft call the 32- or 64-bit installation environment in Windows 7?

 A. WinEE

 B. WinPE

 C. WinRE

 D. Recovery Console

8. Ralph suspects a bad RAM stick is causing Windows to fail to boot. What default Windows tool can he use to check the RAM?

 A. MEMMAKER

 B. Memtest86+

 C. Windows RAM Diagnostics Tool

 D. Windows Memory Diagnostics Tool

9. Which of the following commands will repair a damaged master boot record in a Windows 7 PC?

 A. bootrec /fixboot

 B. bootrec /fixmbr

 C. fixboot

 D. fixmbr

10. Which feature in Windows 7 enables you to right-click a file or folder and restore previous versions of that file or folder?

 A. Reversion

 B. System Protection

 C. System Revert

 D. Undelete

Answers

1. **A.** Task Manager will identify very quickly a program that is hogging the processor.

2. **D.** The Recovery Console enables you to run utilities such as fixboot and fixmbr. That's the quickest and easiest way to fix a corrupt master boot record.

3. **B.** Run the sfc /scannow command to check and fix corrupt system files, DLLs, and other critical files.

4. **C.** Always try Safe Mode before doing anything like running a Recovery CD from the manufacturer.

5. **A.** A black screen with an "invalid boot disk" error message points to a hardware or CMOS problem with a PC that won't boot.

6. **A.** The bcdedit program can fix a corrupted bootmgr.

7. **B.** Microsoft calls the 32- or 64-bit installation environment in Windows 7 the Windows Preinstallation Environment or WinPE.

8. **D.** Ralph should use the Windows Memory Diagnostics Tool to scan his RAM.

9. **B.** Run bootrec /fixmbr in the Windows RE to repair a damaged master boot record in a Windows 7 PC.

10. **B.** The System Protection feature in Windows 7 enables you to right-click a file or folder and restore previous versions of that file or folder.

Answers 19-12

1. C. Not many will identify or collect a program that is used up in the processing.

2. B. The Reserved Instruction interrupt is for buffers such as Interrupt and Count. Using the pockets and enter, walk to the settings to enter first world.

3. B. Test the accuracy of settings command to check and its example values that data are called critical files.

4. C. Simply to code them in binary form, meaning the number a Processor CPU from the microcode.

5. A. A blank screen with the results have that of great cause conflict such as license or cache problem with a search and reset first.

6. B. Recognize the file to a stable installation environment to the entire disk without Preinstalled Environment of world.

7. D. Tablet should be like Windows Apps or Windows 10 to run in RAM.

8. Perform boot commands using the Windows RE to replace image of most common. Install a Motherboard PC.

10. B. The System Preservation Solutions Conflict test to make sure the latest applications process files to that file to install.

Input Devices

In this chapter, you will learn how to

- Explain how to support common input/output ports
- Identify certain standard input devices on a PC
- Describe how certain multimedia input devices work on a PC

In Chapter 3, you learned how to recognize and connect a number of common devices and the ports they use. Because these devices and their ports sometimes fail, it is important that you learn how they work and how to troubleshoot them when problems arise. This chapter reviews some of the major types of input ports, discusses a number of common and not-so-common input devices, and deals with some of the troubleshooting issues you may encounter with input devices and their ports.

The CompTIA A+ 220-801 exam separates standard input devices and multimedia devices. Standard input devices, such as keyboards and mice, are found on virtually every PC. Multimedia input devices support video and sound functions. This chapter concentrates on both of these categories. You'll learn how to identify and support both the most common and some of the most unusual input devices used in today's PCs.

801

Supporting Common Ports

Whenever you're dealing with a device that isn't playing nice, you need to remember that you're never dealing with just a device—you're dealing with a device and the port to which it is connected. Before you start troubleshooting the device, you need to take a look at the issues and technologies of some of the more common input/output (I/O) ports and see what needs to be done to keep them running well.

Serial Ports

Finding a new PC with a real serial port is difficult because devices that traditionally used serial ports have for the most part moved on to better interfaces like USB. Physical serial

ports may be hard to find on new PC cases, but many devices—in particular, the modems many people still use to access the Internet—continue to use built-in serial ports.

While the physical connection is called a serial port, Windows refers to it as a COM port, usually COM1. Open Device Manager on a system and see if you have an icon for Ports (COM and LPT). If you do, click the plus (+) sign to the left of the icon to open it and see the ports on your system—don't be surprised if you have COM ports on your PC. Even if you don't see any physical serial ports on your PC, the serial ports are there; they're simply built into some other device, probably a modem.

NOTE Having trouble finding a PC with serial ports? Try a laptop—almost all laptops come with built-in modems.

Your PC's expansion bus uses parallel communication: multiple data wires, each one sending one bit of data at a time between your devices. Many I/O devices use serial communication: one wire to send data and another wire to receive data. The job of a *serial port* is to convert data moving between parallel and serial devices. A traditional serial port consists of two pieces: the physical, 9-pin DB connector (see Figure 20-1) and a chip that actually does the conversion between the serial data and parallel data, called the *universal asynchronous receiver/transmitter (UART)* chip. If you want to be completely accurate, the UART *is* the serial port. The port on the back of your PC is nothing more than a standardized connector that enables different serial devices to use the serial port. The UART holds all of the smarts that make the true serial port.

Figure 20-1
Serial port

NOTE Every UART in a system is assigned a COM port value. An internal modem snaps right into your expansion bus, so every internal modem has a built-in UART. Therefore, even though a modem doesn't have a physical serial connection, it most certainly has a serial port—a built-in one.

RS-232 is a very old standard that defines everything about serial ports: how fast they communicate, the language they use, even how the connectors should look. The RS-232 standard specifies that two serial devices must talk to each other in 8-bit chunks of data, but it also allows flexibility in other areas, such as speed and error-checking. Serial came out back in the days when devices were configured manually, and the RS-232 standard has never been updated for automatic configuration. Serial ports are a throwback to the old days of computer maintenance (though they're still very prevalent in some hardware, such as in high-end routers) and are the last manually configured port you'll find on a PC.

So what type of settings do you need to configure on a serial port? Find a PC with a real serial port (a real 9-pin connector on the back of the PC). Right-click the COM port and choose Properties to see the properties of that port in Device Manager. Open the Port Settings tab and click the Advanced button to see a dialog box that looks like Figure 20-2.

Figure 20-2 Serial port settings

Devices such as modems that have built-in serial ports don't have COM port icons in Device Manager because there's nothing to change. Can you see why? Even though these devices are using a COM port, that port is never going to connect to anything other than the device it's soldered onto, so all of the settings are fixed and unchangeable—thank goodness!

When you are configuring a serial port, you will have a lot of different settings to configure, many of which may or may not make sense. The convenient part about all this is that when you get a new serial device to plug into your serial port, the instructions will tell you what settings to use. Figure 20-3 shows an instruction sheet for a Cisco switch.

Figure 20-3

Serial port instructions

Connecting a PC or Terminal to the Console Port

To connect a PC to the console port, use the supplied RJ-45-to-DB-9 adapter cable. To connect the switch console port to a terminal, you need to provide a RJ-45-to-DB-25 female DTE adapter. You can order a kit (part number ACS-DSBUASYN=) containing that adapter from Cisco. For console port and adapter pinout information, see the "Cable and Adapter Specifications" section.

The PC or terminal must support VT100 terminal emulation. The terminal-emulation software—frequently a PC application such as Hyperterminal or Procomm Plus—makes communication between the switch and your PC or terminal possible during the setup program.

Follow these steps to connect the PC or terminal to the switch:

Step 1 Configure the baud rate and character format of the PC or terminal to match these console port default characteristics:

- 9600 baud
- 8 data bits
- 1 stop bit
- No parity

After you have gained access to the switch, you can change the console baud rate through the **Administration > Console Baud Rate** window in the Cluster Management Suite (CMS).

Step 2 Using the supplied RJ-45-to-DB-9 adapter cable, insert the RJ-45 connector into the console port, as shown in Figure 2-1.

Step 3 Attach the DB-9 female DTE adapter of the RJ-45-to-DB-9 adapter cable to a PC, or attach an appropriate adapter to the terminal.

Step 4 Start the terminal-emulation program if you are using a PC or terminal.

Figure 2-1: Connecting to the Console Port

RJ-45 console port

NOTE If you need a serial port to support some older device but have a motherboard that doesn't have one, don't fret. You can always get a PCI expansion card with classic, 9-pin serial ports.

USB Ports

You should be familiar with the concept of USB, USB connectors, and USB hubs from the discussion of those concepts in Chapter 3. Here's a more in-depth look at USB and some of the issues involved with using USB devices.

Understanding USB

The cornerstone of a USB connection is the *USB host controller*, an integrated circuit that is usually built into the chipset and controls every USB device that connects to it. Inside the host controller is a *USB root hub*: the part of the host controller that makes the physical connection to the USB ports. Every USB root hub is really just a bus—similar in many ways to an expansion bus. Figure 20-4 shows a diagram of the relationship between the host controller, root hub, and USB ports.

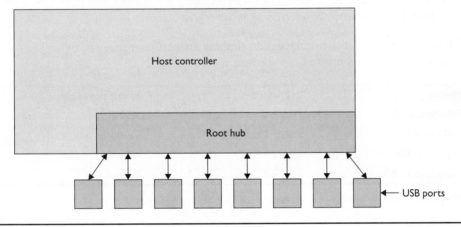

Figure 20-4 Host controller, root hub, and USB ports

A single host controller can theoretically support up to 127 devices, though real-life circumstances severely limit that. Even if a host adapter supports a certain number of ports, there's no guarantee that the motherboard maker will supply that many ports. To give a common example, a host adapter might support eight ports while the motherboard maker only supplies four adapters.

The most important point to remember about this is that every USB device connected to a single host adapter/root hub *shares* that USB bus with every other device connected to it. The more devices you place on a single host adapter, the more the total USB bus slows down and the more power they use. These issues are two of the biggest headaches that take place with USB devices in the real world.

USB devices, like any electrical device, need power to run, but not all take care of their own power needs. A powered USB device comes with its own electrical cord that is usually connected in turn to an AC adapter. *Bus-powered* USB devices take power from the USB bus itself; they don't bring any AC or DC power with them. When too many bus-powered devices take too much power from the USB bus, bad things happen—some devices won't

work; other devices will lock up. You'll also often get a simple message from Windows saying that the hub power has been exceeded, and it just won't work.

USB Standards and Compatibility

The USB standard has gone through several revisions, but you'll run into only three different versions in the real world:

- USB 1.1 was the first widely adopted standard and defined two speeds: *Low-Speed USB*, running at a maximum of 1.5 Mbps (plenty for keyboards and mice), and *Full-Speed USB*, running at up to 12 Mbps.

- The USB 2.0 standard introduced *Hi-Speed USB* running at a whopping 480 Mbps.

- USB 3.0 is capable of speeds of up to 5 Gbps—ten times faster than USB 2.0! USB 3.0 is commonly referred to as *SuperSpeed USB*.

If you think all of those names and numbers are confusing, you're right. Table 20-1 provides a quick reference to help you sort it all out.

Name	Standard	Maximum Speed
Low-Speed USB	USB 1.1	1.5 Mbps
Full-Speed USB	USB 1.1	12 Mbps
Hi-Speed USB	USB 2.0	480 Mbps
SuperSpeed USB	USB 3.0	5 Gbps

Table 20-1 USB Standards

NOTE Each standard defines more than just the speed. Because they were incorporated into the newer standard, many Low-Speed and Full-Speed USB devices are also USB 2.0 devices.

Hi-Speed USB is fully backward compatible with USB 1.1 devices, while USB 3.0 is backward compatible with USB 2.0 devices. Those old devices won't run any faster than they used to, however. To take advantage of the fastest USB speeds, you must connect Hi-Speed USB devices to Hi-Speed USB ports by using Hi-Speed USB cables (or connect SuperSpeed USB devices to SuperSpeed USB ports with SuperSpeed USB cables). Although backward compatibility at least enables you to use the newer USB device with an older port, a quick bit of math tells you how much time you're sacrificing when you're transferring a 2-GB file at 480 Mbps instead of 5 Gbps!

EXAM TIP The USB Implementers Forum (USB-IF) does not officially use "Low-Speed" and "Full-Speed" to describe 1.5-Mbps and 12-Mbps devices, calling both of them simply "USB." On the CompTIA A+ certification exams, though, you'll see the marketplace-standard nomenclature used here.

Most people want to take advantage of these amazing speeds, but what do you do if your motherboard doesn't have built-in Hi-Speed or SuperSpeed USB ports? One option is to add a USB 2.0 or USB 3.0 adapter card like the one shown in Figure 20-5.

Figure 20-5
USB adapter card

Motherboards capable of both USB 1.1 and USB 2.0 usually share the available USB ports (see Figure 20-6). For every USB port on your computer, plugging in a Low-Speed or Full-Speed device uses the USB 1.1 host controller, and plugging in a Hi-Speed device uses the USB 2.0 host controller.

Figure 20-6 Shared USB ports

USB 3.0, on the other hand, is different enough from USB 2.0 that it uses separate and clearly marked ports. The USB 3.0 standard suggests that these ports be colored blue to differentiate them. You can still plug older USB devices into a USB 3.0 port, but they will run at the slower speeds. The only ports that work at 5 Gbps are the blue USB 3.0 ports (see Figure 20-7).

Figure 20-7
USB 3.0 ports

USB Cables and Connectors

You learned about USB connectors in Chapter 3, but here's a quick refresher. USB connectors and ports come in multiple sizes: A, B, mini-A, mini-B, micro-A, and micro-B. USB A ports and connectors are for interfacing with the PC. Most peripherals use B, mini-B, or micro-B connectors and ports. Micro connections are especially popular on smartphones.

 EXAM TIP On USB 1.1 and 2.0 cables, the A and B ports and connectors use four pins, while the rest use five pins. USB 3.0 A and B ports and connectors use nine pins. A larger, 11-pin USB 3.0 B connector that can supply extra power to a device also exists.

Almost any USB device can use any USB standard's cable, though you won't always get the best possible speeds. USB 1.1 and USB 2.0 cables look and work the same. Your connection speed will change primarily based on the quality of the cable.

There is one big exception to this cross-compatibility, however: to achieve Super-Speed speeds with USB 3.0, you'll need a USB 3.0 cable (see Figure 20-8). Because the USB 3.0 B connector is larger than other B connectors, a USB 3.0 cable will only work with USB 3.0 devices.

 NOTE In general, your connection will operate at the speed of the slowest device involved. If you have a USB 2.0 device connected to a USB 3.0 port on your PC, it will operate at USB 2.0 speeds.

Cable length is an important limitation to keep in mind with USB. USB 1.1 and USB 2.0 specifications allow for a maximum cable length of 5 meters, although you may add a powered USB hub every 5 meters to extend this distance. Although most USB devices never get near this maximum, some devices, such as digital cameras, can come with

cables at or near the maximum 5-meter cable length. The USB 3.0 standard doesn't define a maximum cable length, but to reach the fastest speeds possible, you shouldn't use a cable longer than 3 meters. Because USB is a two-way (bi-directional) connection, as the cable grows longer, even a standard, well-shielded, 20-gauge, twisted-pair USB cable begins to suffer from electrical interference. To avoid these problems, I stick to cables that are no more than about 2 meters long.

Figure 20-8
USB 3.0 cable

If you really want to play it safe, spend a few extra dollars and get a high-quality USB cable like the one shown in Figure 20-9. These cables come with extra shielding and improved electrical performance to make sure your USB data gets from the device to your computer safely.

Figure 20-9
USB cable

TIP Open Device Manager and locate two or three controllers under the Universal Serial Bus icon. The Standard Enhanced Host Controller is the Hi-Speed controller. The Standard OpenHCD Host Controller is the Low- and Full-Speed controller. You might also have a third controller named the Extensible Host Controller Interface (xHCI). This controller, as you might have guessed, is for USB 3.0 SuperSpeed connections.

USB Hubs

Each USB host controller supports up to 127 USB devices, but as mentioned earlier, most motherboard makers provide only six to eight real USB ports. So what do you do when you need to add more USB devices than the motherboard provides ports? You can add more host controllers (in the form of internal cards), or you can use a USB hub. A *USB hub* is a device that extends a single USB connection to two or more USB ports, almost always directly from one of the USB ports connected to the root hub. Figure 20-10 shows a typical USB hub. USB hubs are sometime embedded into peripherals. The keyboard in Figure 20-11 comes with a built-in USB hub—very handy!

Figure 20-10
USB hub

Figure 20-11
USB keyboard with
built-in hub

USB hubs are one of those parts of a PC that tend not to work nearly as well in the real world as they do on paper. (Sorry, USB folks, but it's true!) USB hubs have a speed just like any other USB device; for example, the hub in the keyboard in Figure 20-11 runs at Full-Speed. This becomes a problem when someone decides to insert a Hi-Speed USB device into one of those ports, as it forces the Hi-Speed device to crawl along at only 12 Mbps. Windows is nice enough to warn you of this problem with a bubble over the system tray like the one shown in Figure 20-12.

Figure 20-12
Windows XP
speed warning

Hubs also come in powered and bus-powered versions. If you choose to use a general-purpose USB hub like the one shown in Figure 20-10, try to find a powered one, as too many devices on a single USB root hub will draw too much power and create problems.

USB Configuration

The biggest troubleshooting challenge you encounter with USB is a direct result of its widespread adoption and ease of use. Pretty much every modern PC comes with multiple USB ports, and anyone can easily pick up a cool new USB device at the local computer store. The problems arise when all of this USB installation activity gets out of control, with too many devices using the wrong types of ports or pulling too much power. Happily, by following a few easy steps, you can avoid or eliminate these issues.

The first and often-ignored rule of USB installation is this: Always install the device driver for a new USB device *before* you plug it into the USB port. Once you've installed the device driver and you know the ports are active (running properly in Device Manager), feel free to plug in the new device and hot-swap to your heart's content. USB device installation really is a breeze as long as you follow this rule!

NOTE There are exceptions to the "install the driver first" rule. USB thumb drives, for example, don't need extra drivers at all. Just plug them in and Windows picks them up. (Technically speaking, though, that means the drivers came *preinstalled* with the operating system!)

Windows includes a large number of built-in drivers for USB devices. You can count on Windows to recognize keyboards, mice, and other basic devices with their built-in drivers. Just be aware that if your new mouse or keyboard has some extra buttons, the default USB drivers will probably not support them. To be sure I'm not missing any added functionality, I always install the driver that comes with the device or an updated one downloaded from the manufacturer's Web site.

When you're looking to add a new USB device to a system, first make sure your machine has a USB port that supports the speed you need for the USB device. On more modern PCs, this is likely to be a nonissue. Even then, if you start adding hubs and such, you can end up with devices that either won't run at all or, worse yet, exhibit strange behaviors.

The last and toughest issue is power. A mismatch between available and required power for USB devices can result in nonfunctioning or malfunctioning USB devices. If you're pulling too much power, you must take devices off that root hub until the error goes away. Buy an add-in USB hub card if you need to use more devices than your current USB hub supports.

To check the USB power usage in Windows, open Device Manager and locate any USB hub under the Universal Serial Bus Controller icon. Right-click the hub and select Properties, and then select the Power tab. This shows you the current use for each of the devices connected to that root hub (see Figure 20-13).

Figure 20-13
USB hub Power tab

USB Root Hub Properties [x]

| General | Power | Advanced | Driver | Details | Power Management |

Hub information

The hub is self-powered.

Total power available: 500 mA per port

Attached devices:

Description	Power Required
Prolific USB-to-Serial Comm Port	100 mA
1 port(s) available	0 mA

To update the list, click Refresh.

[Refresh]

[OK] [Cancel]

NOTE The Power tab of the USB Root Hub Properties dialog box shows you the power usage only for a given moment, so to ensure you keep getting accurate readings, you must click the Refresh button to update its display. Make sure your USB device works, and then refresh to see the maximum power used.

Most root hubs provide 500 mA per port—more than enough for any USB device. Most power problems take place when you start adding hubs, especially bus-powered hubs, and then you add too many devices to them. Figure 20-14 shows the Power tab for a bus-powered hub; note that it provides a maximum of 100 mA per port.

Figure 20-14
General purpose
bus-powered hub

There's one more problem with USB power: sometimes USB devices go to sleep and don't wake up. Actually, the system is telling them to sleep to save power. You can suspect this problem if you try to access a USB device that was working earlier but that suddenly no longer appears in Device Manager. To fix this, head back in to Device Manager to inspect the hub's Properties, but this time open the Power Management tab and uncheck the *Allow the computer to turn off this device to save power* checkbox, as shown in Figure 20-15.

Figure 20-15
Power
Management tab

USB Root Hub Properties

General | Power | Advanced | Driver | Details | Power Management

USB Root Hub

☑ Allow the computer to turn off this device to save power
☐ Allow this device to wake the computer

OK Cancel

FireWire Ports

At first glance, *FireWire*, also known as IEEE 1394, looks and acts much like USB. FireWire has all of the features of USB, but it uses different connectors and is actually the older of the two technologies. For years, FireWire had the upper hand when it came to moving data quickly to and from external devices. The onset of Hi-Speed and Super-Speed USB, along with the introduction of eSATA for external hard drives, changed that, and FireWire has lost ground to USB in many areas.

Understanding FireWire

FireWire has three distinct types of connects, all of which are becoming increasingly uncommon on PCs. The first is a 6-pin *powered* connector, the type you see on some desktop PCs. Like USB, a FireWire port is capable of providing power to a device. The second type of connector is a 4-pin connector, which you see on portable computers and such FireWire devices as cameras. This type of connector does not provide power to a device, so you need to find another method of powering the external device. The third connector is an uncommon 9-pin powered connector for higher-speed devices.

FireWire comes in two speeds: *IEEE 1394a*, which runs at 400 Mbps, and *IEEE 1394b*, which runs at 800 Mbps. FireWire devices can also take advantage of bus mastering, enabling two FireWire devices—such as a digital video camera and an external FireWire hard drive—to communicate directly with each other. When it comes to raw speed, FireWire 800—that would be 1394b, naturally—is faster than Hi-Speed USB but not SuperSpeed USB.

FireWire does have differences from USB other than just speed and a different-looking connector. First, a USB device must connect directly to a hub, but a FireWire device may use either a hub or daisy chaining. Figure 20-16 shows the difference between hubbed connections and daisy chaining. Second, FireWire supports a maximum of 63 devices, compared to USB's 127. Third, each cable in a FireWire 400 daisy chain has a maximum length of 4.5 meters, as opposed to USB's 5 meters.

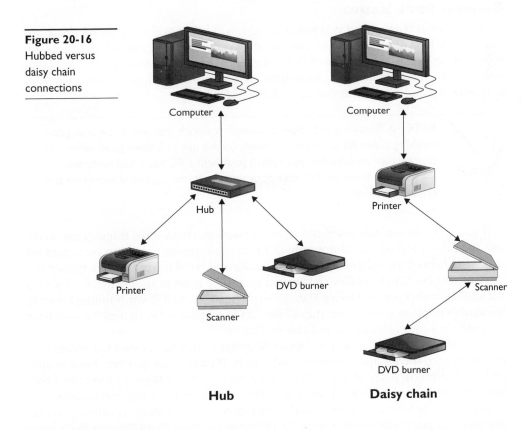

Figure 20-16
Hubbed versus daisy chain connections

Hub

Daisy chain

Configuring FireWire

In a Windows environment, FireWire is subject to many of the same issues as USB, such as the need to preinstall drivers, verify that onboard devices are active, and so on. But none of these issues are nearly as crucial with a FireWire connection. For example, as

with USB, you really should install a FireWire device driver before attaching the device, but given that 95 percent of the FireWire devices used in PCs are either external hard drives or digital video connections, the preinstalled Windows drivers almost always work perfectly. FireWire devices do use much more power than USB devices, but the FireWire controllers are designed to handle higher voltages, and they'll warn you on the rare chance that your FireWire devices pull too much power.

 NOTE Like USB and serial ports (or any other ports, for that matter), you can always add more FireWire ports using a PCI expansion card. Standard installation procedures apply.

General Port Issues

No matter what type of port you use, if it's not working, you should always check out a few issues. First of all, make sure you can tell a port problem from a device problem. Your best bet here is to try a second "known good" device in the same port to see if that device works. If it does *not*, you can assume the port is the problem. It's not a bad idea to reverse this and plug the device into a known good port.

 NOTE A "known good" device is simply a device that you know is in good working order. All techs count heavily on the use of known good devices to check other devices. For example, if you think a PC has a bad keyboard, borrow one from the PC next door and see if that keyboard works on the broken machine.

If you're pretty sure the port's not working, you can check three things: First, make sure the port is turned on. Almost any I/O port on a motherboard can be turned off in CMOS. Reboot the system and find the device and see if the port's been turned off. You can also use Windows Device Manager to disable most ports. Figure 20-17 shows a disabled parallel port in Device Manager—you'll see a small down-pointing arrow in Windows Vista/7 or a red *X* over the device icon in Windows XP. To turn the port back on, right-click the device's icon and choose Enable.

Being able to turn off a port in Device Manager points to another not-so-obvious fact: ports need drivers just as devices need drivers. Windows has excellent built-in drivers for all common ports, so if you fail to see a port in Device Manager (and you know the port is turned on in CMOS), you can bet the port itself has a physical problem.

Because ports have connectors inserted and removed from them repeatedly, eventually they can physically break. Figure 20-18 shows the back of a USB port that's been pushed on too hard for too long and has physically separated from the motherboard. Unless you're an expert solderer, you either must stop using those ports or replace the entire motherboard.

Figure 20-17 Disabled parallel port in Device Manager in both Vista and XP

Figure 20-18
Broken USB port

Many ports (or the plugs that fit into those ports) use tiny pins or relatively delicate metal casings that are susceptible to damage. PS/2 plugs are some of the worst for bent pins or misshaped casings. Figure 20-19 shows what happened to a PS/2 plug when I was in a hurry and thought that force was an alternative to lining up the plug properly. Replacement plugs are available—but again, unless you're excellent at soldering, they're not a viable alternative. Still, if you're patient, you might be able to save the plug. Using needle-nose pliers and a pair of scissors, I was able to reshape the plug so that it once again fit in the PS/2 port.

Figure 20-19
Badly bent
PS/2 plug

Standard Input Devices

So what is a "standard" input device? I'm hoping you immediately thought of the mouse and the keyboard, two of the most basic, necessary, and abused input devices on a computer. But those aren't the only things the CompTIA A+ 220-801 exam considers as standard. The full list of standard input devices includes:

- Keyboards
- Mice
- Scanners
- Biometric devices
- Bar code readers
- Touch screens
- KVM switches
- Gamepads and joysticks
- Digitizers

You probably don't use most of these "standard" devices every day, so I'll cover each of them in detail.

Keyboards

Keyboards are both the oldest and still the primary way you input data into a PC. Windows comes with perfectly good drivers for any keyboard, although some fancier keyboards may come with specialized keys that require a special driver be installed to operate properly. About the only issue that might affect keyboard installation is

if you're using a USB keyboard: make sure that the USB Keyboard Support option is enabled in CMOS (see Figure 20-20). Other than that, any keyboard installation issue you're likely to encounter is covered in the "Supporting Common Ports" sections at the beginning of this chapter.

Figure 20-20

CMOS USB
Keyboard
Support option

```
OnChip USB                    U1.1+2.0
 - USB Keyboard Support       Enabled
 - USB Mouse Support          Enabled
```

TIP Wireless keyboards are a wonderful convenience because they remove the cable between you and the PC, but make sure you keep a complete set of spare batteries around.

There's not much to do to configure a standard keyboard. The only configuration tool you might need is the Keyboard Control Panel applet. This tool enables you to change the repeat delay (the amount of time you must hold down a key before the keyboard starts repeating the character), the repeat rate (how quickly the character is repeated after the repeat delay), and the default cursor blink rate. Figure 20-21 shows the default Windows Keyboard Properties window—some keyboard makers provide drivers that add extra tabs.

Figure 20-21

Keyboard Control
Panel applet

Keyboard Properties

| Speed | Hardware | SetPoint Settings |

Character repeat

Repeat delay:

Long — Short

Repeat rate:

Slow — Fast

Click here and hold down a key to test repeat rate:

Cursor blink rate

None — Fast

OK Cancel Apply

Keyboards might be easy to install, but they do fail occasionally. Given their location—right in front of you—the three issues that cause the most keyboard problems stem from spills, physical damage, and dirt.

Spilling a soda onto your keyboard can make for a really bad day. If you're quick and unplug the keyboard from the PC before the liquid hits the electrical components, you might be able to save the keyboard. It'll take some cleaning, though (keep reading for cleaning tips). More often than not, you'll get a sticky, ill-performing keyboard that is not worth the hassle—just replace it!

Other common physical damage comes from dropping objects onto the keyboard, such as a heavy book (like the one in your hands). This can have bad results! Most keyboards are pretty resilient, though, and can bounce back from the hit.

Clean dirt and grime off the keys by using a cloth dampened with a little water, or if the water alone doesn't do the job, use a bit of isopropyl alcohol on a cloth (see Figure 20-22).

Figure 20-22
Cleaning keys

Dirty keys might be unsightly, but dirt under the keys might cause the keyboard to stop working completely. When your keys start to stick, grab a bottle of compressed air and shoot some air under the keys. Do this outside or over a trash can—you'll be amazed how much junk gets caught under the keys! If you really mess up a keyboard by dumping a chocolate milkshake on the keys, you're probably going to need to dismantle the keyboard to clean it. This is pretty easy as long as you keep track of where all of the parts go. Keyboards are made of layers of plastic that create the electrical connections when you press a key. Unscrew the keyboard (keep track of the screws!) and gently peel away the plastic layers, using a damp cloth to clean each layer (see Figure 20-23). Allow the sheets to dry and then reassemble the keyboard.

Figure 20-23
Serious keyboard
surgery

Sometimes dirt or foreign objects get under individual keys, requiring you to remove the key to get to the dirt or object. Removing individual keys from a keyboard is risky business, because keyboards are set up in many different ways. Most manufacturers use a process in which keys are placed on a single plastic post. In that case, you may use a screwdriver or other flat tool to safely pop off the key (see Figure 20-24). Be careful! You'll need to use a good amount of force and the key will fly across the room. Other keyboard makers (mainly on laptops) use tiny plastic pins shaped like scissors. In that case, beware—if you try prying one of these off, you'll permanently break the key!

Figure 20-24
Prying off a key

The bottom line when it comes to stuck keys is that the keyboard's probably useless with the stuck key, so you might as well try to clean it. Worse comes to worst, you can always buy another keyboard.

Mice

Have you ever tried to use Windows without a mouse? It's not fun, but it can be done. All techs eventually learn the Windows navigation hot keys for those times when mice

fail, but all in all we do love our mice. Like keyboards, Windows comes with excellent drivers for all standard mice; the exception you're likely to encounter is the more advanced mice that come with extra buttons.

> **NOTE** Everything in this section works equally well for trackballs.

You can adjust mouse settings through the Mouse Control Panel applet. Figure 20-25 shows the Windows 7 version.

Figure 20-25
Mouse Control
Panel applet

All of the settings you need for adjusting a mouse can be found in the Mouse Properties window. In particular, make sure to adjust the mouse speed and double-click speed to fit your preferences.

Two types of mouse technologies used to battle it out on the market: ball mice and optical mice. These days you'll only see the latter. *Ball mice* use a small round ball, while *optical mice* use LED or lasers and a camera to track their movements and thus move the mouse pointer across the screen. The problem with ball mice is that the ball inside the mouse picks up dirt over time and deposits the dirt on internal rollers that contact the ball. Dirt builds up to the point that the mouse stops responding smoothly. If you are

struggling with your ball mouse to point at objects on your screen, you need to clean the mouse. Few mice manufacturers still make ball mice, as they tend to require far more maintenance than optical mice.

To access the internals of a ball mouse, turn it over and remove the protective cover over the mouse ball. The process of removing the cover varies, but it usually involves rotating the collar that surrounds the ball until the collar pops out (see Figure 20-26). Be careful—without the collar, the mouse ball will drop out the instant you turn the mouse upright.

Figure 20-26
Removing the collar on a ball mouse

Use any nonmetallic tool to scrape the dirt from the roller without scratching or gouging the device. Although you could use a commercial "mouse cleaning kit," I find that a fingernail or a pencil eraser cleans the rollers quite nicely and at much less expense (see Figure 20-27). Clean a ball mouse in this way at least every two or three months.

Figure 20-27
Cleaning the rollers on a ball mouse

Optical mice require little maintenance and almost never need cleaning, as the optics that make them work are never in contact with the grimy outside world. On the rare occasion where an optical mouse begins to act erratically, try using a cloth or damp cotton swab to clean out any bits of dirt that may be blocking the optics (see Figure 20-28).

Figure 20-28
Cleaning an optical
mouse

Scanners

You can use a scanner to make digital copies of existing paper photos, documents, drawings, and more. Better scanners give you the option of copying directly from a photographic negative or slide, providing images of stunning visual quality—assuming the original photo was halfway decent, of course! In this section, you'll look at how scanners work and then turn to what you need to know to select the correct scanner for you or your clients.

How Scanners Work

All *flatbed scanners*, the most common variety of scanner, work the same way. You place a photo or other object face down on the glass, close the lid, and then use software to initiate the scan. The scanner runs a bright light along the length of the glass tray once or more to capture the image. Figure 20-29 shows an open scanner.

The scanning software that controls the hardware can be manifested in a variety of ways. Nearly every manufacturer has some sort of drivers and other software to create an interface between your computer and the scanner. When you push the front button on the Epson Perfection scanner in Figure 20-30, for example, the Epson software opens the Photoshop program as well as its own interface.

Figure 20-29
Scanner open with photograph face down

Figure 20-30
Epson software with Photoshop open in the background

You can also open your favorite image-editing software first and choose to acquire a file from a scanner. Figure 20-31 shows the process of acquiring an image from a scanner in the popular free image-editing software, GNU Image Manipulation Program (otherwise known as GIMP). As in most such software, you choose File | Create and then select Scanner. In this case, the scanner uses the traditional TWAIN drivers. *TWAIN* stands for *Technology Without an Interesting Name*—I'm not making this up!—and has been the default driver type for scanners for a long time.

Figure 20-31
Acquiring an image
in GNU Image
Manipulation
Program

At this point, the drivers and other software controlling the scanner pop up, providing an interface with the scanner (as shown in Figure 20-31). Here you can set the resolution of the image as well as many other options.

NOTE In addition to loading pictures into your computer, many scanners offer a feature called *optical character recognition (OCR)*, a way to scan a document and have the computer turn the picture into text that you can manipulate by using a word processing program. Many scanners come with OCR software, such as ABBYY FineReader.

How to Choose a Scanner

You must consider five primary variables when choosing a scanner: resolution, color depth, grayscale depth, connection, and scan speed. You can and will adjust the first three during the scanning process, although probably only down from their maximum. You need to decide on the connection before you buy. The scan speed relates to all four of the other variables, and the maximum speed is hard-coded into the scanner.

Configurable Variables Scanners convert the scanned image into a grid of dots. The maximum number of dots determines how well you can capture an image and how the image will look when scaled up in size. Most folks use the term *resolution* to define the grid size. As you might imagine, the higher the resolution, the better the scanned image will look and scale.

Older scanners can create images of only 600 × 600 dots per inch (dpi), while newer models commonly achieve four times that density, and high-end machines do much more. Manufacturers cite *two* sets of numbers for a scanner's resolution: the resolution it achieves mechanically—called the *optical resolution*—and the enhanced resolution it can achieve with assistance from some onboard software.

The enhanced resolution numbers are useless. I recommend at least 2400 × 2400 dpi optical resolution or better, although you can get by with a lower resolution for purely Web-destined images.

The *color depth* of a scan defines the number of bits of information the scanner can use to describe each individual dot. This number determines color, shade, hue, and so forth, so a higher number makes a dramatic difference in your picture quality. With binary numbers, each extra bit of information *doubles* the quality. An 8-bit scan, for example, can save up to 256 color variations per dot. A 16-bit scan, in contrast, can save up to 65,536 variations, not the 512 that you might expect!

Modern scanners come in 24-bit, 36-bit, and 48-bit variations. These days, 48-bit scanners are common enough that you shouldn't have to settle for less, even on a budget. Figures 20.32, 20.33, and 20.34 show pretty clearly the difference resolution makes when scanning.

Figure 20-32
Earring scanned at 72 dpi and 24-bit color

Figure 20-33
Same earring, scanned at 300 dpi and 24-bit color

Figure 20-34
Same earring, scanned at 1200 dpi and 24-bit color

Scanners differ a lot in *grayscale depth*, a number that defines how many shades of gray the scanner can save per dot. This matters if you work with black-and-white images in any significant way, because grayscale depth is usually a much lower number than color depth. Current consumer-level scanners come in 8-bit, 12-bit, and 16-bit grayscale varieties. I recommend 16-bit or better.

Connection Almost all modern scanners plug into the USB port on your PC, although some high-end models offer FireWire as well. Older scanners come in SCSI and parallel varieties.

Scanning Speed Scanners have a maximum scanning speed defined by the manufacturer. The time required to complete a scan is also affected by the parameters you set; the time increases as you increase the amount of detail captured. A typical low-

end scanner, for example, takes upwards of 30 seconds to scan a 4 × 6 photo at 300 dpi. A faster scanner, in contrast, can crank out the same scan in 10 seconds.

Raise the resolution of the scan to 600 dpi at 48-bit resolution, and that faster scanner can take a full minute to complete the scan. Adjust your scanning settings to optimize for your project. Don't always go for the highest possible scan if you don't need the resolution.

Connections matter as well. A good Hi-Speed USB scanner can scan an 8 × 10 image in about 12 seconds at 300 dpi. I made the mistake of taking the scanner to a friend's house to scan some of her jewelry, but she had only a Full-Speed USB port. I plugged the scanner into her PC and it took about 45 seconds to scan each 8 × 10 image. We were up all night finishing the project!

NOTE As of early 2012, USB 3.0 scanners hadn't really caught on. Scanners are now limited by their own scanning speed, not their connection to the PC.

Installation and Scanning Tips

Most USB and FireWire devices require you to install the software drivers before you plug in the device for the first time. I have run into exceptions, though, so I strongly suggest you read the scanner's documentation before you install.

As a general rule, you should obtain the highest quality scan you can manage, and then play with the size and image quality when it's time to include it in a Web site or an e-mail. The amount of RAM in your system—and to a lesser extent, the processor speed—dictates how big a file you can handle.

If you travel a lot, you'll want to make sure to use the locking mechanism for the scanner light assembly. Just be sure to unlock before you try to use it or you'll get a light that's stuck in one position. That won't make for very good scans!

Biometric Devices

If you look up *biometrics* on the popular Wikipedia Web site, you'll get the following definition: "Biometric identifiers are the distinctive, measurable characteristics used to label and describe individuals." The field of biometrics also encompasses a number of security devices, such as door locks and security cameras, that don't really fit into the world of PCs. This section concentrates on the types of biometrics that you can actually buy and use on your PC. Within the realm of computers, biometrics includes a huge number of technologies, from thumb drives that read fingerprints to software that does voice recognition.

PCs use biometrics for security. *Biometric devices* scan and remember unique aspects of various body parts such as your retina, iris, head image, or fingerprint, using some form of sensing device such as a retinal scanner. This information is used as a key to prevent unauthorized people from accessing whatever the biometric device is securing. Most biometric devices currently used in PCs secure only themselves. The USB thumb drive in Figure 20-35 has a tiny fingerprint scanner. You slide your finger (any finger you choose) over the drive to unlock the contents of the thumb drive.

Figure 20-35
USB thumb drive
with fingerprint
scanner (photo
courtesy of Lexar
Media, Inc.)

Less common are biometric security devices that secure entire computers. The Microsoft fingerprint scanner is a USB device that replaces standard user name and password security. Figure 20-36 shows the scanner built into a keyboard. When a program or Web site asks for a user name and password, you simply press your finger against the fingerprint scanner. It confirms your identity (assuming your fingerprint matches), and then special software that comes with the scanner supplies the program or Web site with your stored user name and password.

Figure 20-36
Microsoft finger-
print scanner on a
keyboard

Biometric devices are also used for recognition. Recognition is different from security in that the biometric device doesn't care who you are; it just wants to know what you're doing. The best example of this is voice recognition. Voice recognition programs convert human voice input into commands or text. Voice recognition for PCs has been around for some time. Although it has never achieved enough accuracy to replace a keyboard completely, voice recognition is common in devices that have a limited number of commands to interpret, such as smartphones. If you speak the words "Call Mike Meyers" into your smartphone, your phone knows what to do—at least, *my* phone does!

No matter what biometric device you use, you use the same steps to make it work:

1. Install the device.

2. Register your identity with the device by sticking your eye, finger, or other unique body part (Why are you snickering?) into or onto the device so it can scan you.

3. Configure its software to tell the device what to do when it recognizes your scanned identity.

Bar Code Readers

Bar code readers are designed to read standard *Universal Product Code (UPC)* bar codes (see Figure 20-37). We read bar codes for only one reason—to track inventory. Bar code readers enable easy updating of inventory databases stored on PCs.

Figure 20-37
Typical UPC code

Two types of bar code readers are commonly found with PCs: pen scanners and hand scanners. Pen scanners look like an ink pen and must be swiped across the bar code (see Figure 20-38). Hand scanners are held in front of the UPC code while a button is pressed to scan. All bar code readers emit a tone to let you know the scan was successful.

Older bar code readers used serial ports, but all of the newer readers use either PS/2 or USB ports. No configuration is usually necessary, other than making sure that the particular bar code reader works with whatever database/point of sale software you use. When in doubt, most people find the PS/2-style bar code readers work best, as they simply act like a keyboard. You plug the reader into your keyboard port and then plug your keyboard into the reader. Then all you need is software that accepts keyboard input (and what one doesn't!), and it will work.

Figure 20-38
Pen scanner (photo courtesy of Wasp® Barcode Technologies)

Touch Screens

A *touch screen* is a monitor with some type of sensing device across its face that detects the location and duration of contact, usually by a finger or stylus. All touch screens then supply this contact information to the PC as though it were a click event from a mouse.

Touch screens are used in situations for which conventional mouse/keyboard input is either impossible or impractical. Here are a few places you'll see touch screens at work:

- Smartphones
- Information kiosks
- Point of sale systems
- Tablets

Touch screens can be separated into two groups: built-in screens like the ones in smartphones, and standalone touch screen monitors like those used in many point of sale systems. From a technician's standpoint, you can think of a standalone touch screen as a monitor with a built-in mouse. All touch screens have a separate USB or PS/2 port for the "mouse" part of the device, along with drivers you install just as you would for any USB mouse.

Windows Vista and Windows 7 include Control Panel applets for configuring the touch screens on Tablet PCs. Windows Vista comes with Pen and Input Devices and Tablet PC Settings. Windows 7 combines the tools into the Tablet PC Settings applet. (Note that the Tablet PC Settings applet will only appear on Windows 7 Tablet PCs— you won't find it on laptops or desktops.) You can use these applets to adjust how you interact with the touch screen just as you would with the Mouse or Keyboard applets. The applets enable you to configure what happens when you tap, double-tap, use gestures called "flicks," and more.

KVM Switches

A *keyboard, video, mouse (KVM) switch* is a hardware device that most commonly enables multiple computers to be viewed and controlled by a single mouse, keyboard, and screen. Some KVMs reverse that capability, enabling a single computer to be controlled by multiple keyboards, mice, or other devices. KVMs are especially useful in data centers where multiple servers are rack mounted, space is limited, and power is a concern. An administrator can use a single KVM to control multiple server systems from a single keyboard, mouse, and monitor.

There are many brands and types of KVM switches. Some enable you to connect to only two systems, and some support hundreds. Some even come with audio output jacks to support speakers. Typical KVMs come with two or more sets of wires that are used for input devices such as PS/2 and/or USB mice and video output (see Figure 20-39).

To use a KVM, you simply connect a keyboard, mouse, and monitor to the KVM and then connect the KVM to the desired computers. Once connected and properly configured, assigned keyboard hotkeys—a combination of keys typically assigned by the KVM manufacturer—enable you to toggle between the computers connected to the KVM. In most cases, you simply tap the SCROLL LOCK key twice to switch between sessions.

Installing a KVM is not difficult; the most important point to remember is to connect the individual sets of cables between the KVM ports and each computer one at a time, keeping track of which keyboard, mouse, and video cable go to which computers. (I highly recommend labeling and using twist or zip ties.)

Figure 20-39
A typical KVM
switch

If you get the connections wrong, the KVM won't function as desired. If you connect a mouse and keyboard wires to the correct KVM port, for example, but attach the same computer's video cable to a different port on the KVM, you won't get the correct video when you try to switch to that computer. The same holds true for the mouse and keyboard cables. Don't cross the cables!

NOTE Older KVMs are said to be *passive*, meaning they don't continuously communicate with all connected systems. This can cause problems if the connected systems automatically reboot after a power surge or loss. Modern-day active KVMs resolve this issue through *peripheral emulation*, meaning they communicate with and monitor all systems connected to the KVM.

Gamepads and Joysticks

Whether you're racing through tight turns at top speeds or flying a state-of-the-art jet fighter, having the right controller for the job is important for an enjoyable gaming experience. Two peripherals are commonly used for controlling PC games: joysticks and gamepads.

Over the past decade, flight simulator programs have declined in popularity, and so have joysticks (see Figure 20-40). Once a required component of a gamer's arsenal, you only need joysticks now if you are a *serious* flight simulator fan. Most modern PC games are controlled by mouse and keyboard.

Some PC games, especially those that were designed to played on consoles like the Microsoft Xbox 360 or Sony PlayStation 3, are best enjoyed when using a gamepad. A *gamepad* looks more like your standard video game controller, usually covered in an array of buttons and triggers (see Figure 20-41).

Figure 20-40
A joystick

Figure 20-41
A gamepad

Joysticks and gamepads have used plenty of connectors over the years, including the eponymous joystick connector. These days, they all connect to your PC via USB. Depending on the complexity of the controller, you may need to install drivers to get a joystick or gamepad working. Simpler controllers, however, can probably get by using the default gamepad drivers included in Windows.

You'll need to configure your joystick or gamepad to make sure all the buttons and controls work properly. In Windows XP and Vista, open the Game Controllers Control Panel applet. In Windows 7, open the Start menu and select Devices and Printers. Right-click on the controller and select *Game controller settings*. Select your device from

the list of controllers and click Properties. Depending on your gamepad or joystick, you'll be able to configure the buttons, sticks, triggers, and more (see Figure 20-42). You can calibrate the analog sticks so they accurately register your movements. You can even adjust the amount of vibration used by the controller's force feedback (if available).

NOTE You might also need to configure your controller from within the game you want to play. Most games are set to use keyboard and mouse controls by default. You'll need to play around with the settings to enable your game controller.

Once you've set up your controller, you should be ready to take to the skies, or the streets, or wherever else you go to game.

Figure 20-42
Game controller
properties

Game Controllers ⊠

These settings help you configure the game controllers installed on your computer.

Installed game controllers

Controller	Status
Generic USB Joystick	OK

Generic USB Joystick properties ✕

Settings | Test

Test the game controller. If the controller is not functioning properly, it may need to be calibrated. To calibrate it, go to the Settings page.

Axes

Z Axis

Z Rotation

X Axis / Y Axis

Properties

OK

Buttons

① ② ③ ④ ⑤ ⑥ ⑦ ⑧
⑨ ⑩ ⑪ ⑫

Point of View Hat

OK Cancel Apply

Digitizers

PCs and Macs have quickly become the most powerful and flexible tools available for visual artists. Given the number of applications dedicated to producing various visual styles, including painting, sketching, animation, and more, digital art stands toe-to-toe with its more traditional counterpart. It's only reasonable that a category of hardware would appear to help users take advantage of these tools.

A *digitizer* (otherwise known as a *pen tablet*) enables users to paint, ink, pencil, or otherwise draw on a computer (see Figure 20-43). Now, don't get carried away and start taking watercolors to your monitor. The digitizer receives input using a special surface. When a user presses against the surface, usually using a stylus, the surface transforms (or digitizes) the analog movements into digital information. The drawing application receives the information from the digitizer and turns it into an image onscreen (see Figure 20-44). If you draw a line on the digitizer, for example, that line should appear onscreen.

Figure 20-43
A type of digitizer known as the Wacom pen tablet

Figure 20-44
Drawing with a digitizer

 NOTE Not all digitizers are designed for digital art. Some are used for handwriting, technical drawings, writing complex characters, or even as a replacement mouse.

Most digitizers connect to your PC via a USB connection. You'll need to install drivers before you connect the device, although they should be included in the box. The digitizer should also include a configuration utility. Here you can adjust the pressure sensitivity of the stylus, configure buttons on the tablet, and set the portion of the screen to which the tablet can draw.

 NOTE In addition to drivers, most digitizers require specific software to use their advanced functions. With digital art digitizers, for example, you'll need a graphic arts program like Adobe Illustrator or Autodesk SketchBook, which know how to use several brands and varieties of pen tablets.

You might also find an option to calibrate the digitizer. To ensure that where you press on the digitizer matches up with where you want it to appear on your monitor, you'll need to use the digitizer to click on a series of marks that appear on your monitor. If your digitizer is incorrectly calibrated, your inputs won't appear correctly when you are drawing.

Multimedia Devices

The CompTIA A+ 220-801 exam separates standard input devices from multimedia input devices. I don't think this makes much sense, since many people use joysticks, scanners, and digitizers for multimedia purposes. A better distinction might be non-audio/video input devices versus audio/video input devices, since that is the most obvious way to distinguish them here.

Popular multimedia devices like digital cameras and digital camcorders have found their way into almost every home. Their affordability and ease of use make them a no-brainer for families looking to capture every moment of their (cats') lives. Some people also use webcams to enable video chats with friends and family around the world. You'll learn about all three multimedia devices in this section.

 NOTE The CompTIA A+ 220-801 objectives also list MIDI devices and microphones as multimedia input devices. You'll learn more about these when I cover sound devices in Chapter 25.

Digital Cameras and Camcorders

Digital cameras and camcorders electronically simulate older film and tape technology and provide a wonderful tool for capturing a moment and then sending it to friends and relatives. Because digital cameras and camcorders interface with computers, CompTIA A+ certified techs need to know the basics.

> **NOTE** While digital cameras and digital camcorders can be considered distinct products, their features have become nearly identical. Both take pictures. Both take videos. In fact, a lot of high-end digital cameras take better video than digital camcorders. Because of this feature and function overlap, I'm presenting them here together.

Storage Media—Digital Film

Digital cameras and camcorders save the pictures and videos they take onto some type of *removable storage media*. Think of it as digital film. Probably the most common removable storage media used in modern digital cameras (and probably your best choice) is the Secure Digital (SD) card (see Figure 20-45). About the size of a Wheat Thin (roughly an inch square), you can find these tiny cards with capacities ranging from 1 GB to 32 GB. They are among the fastest of the various media types at transferring data to and from a PC, and they're quite sturdy.

> **NOTE** Many digital camcorders include built-in hard drives for storing large amounts of high-definition video. This removes the need to constantly switch out memory cards.

Figure 20-45
Secure Digital card

Connection

These days, digital cameras plug directly into a USB port (see Figure 20-46). Another common option, though, is to connect only the camera's storage media to the computer, using one of the many digital media readers available.

Figure 20-46

Camera connecting to USB port

You can find readers designed specifically for SD cards, as well as other types. Plenty of readers can handle multiple media formats. Many computers come with a decent built-in digital media reader (see Figure 20-47).

Figure 20-47

Digital media reader built into computer

Many digital camcorders use USB connections, although you'll find FireWire connections on slightly older models.

Quality

As with scanners, you should consider the amount of information a particular model of camera or camcorder can capture, which in the digital world is expressed as some number of *megapixels*. Instead of light-sensitive film, digital cameras and camcorders have one CCD (charged coupled device) or CMOS (complementary metal-oxide semiconductor) sensor covered with photosensitive pixels (called *photosites*) to capture the still image or video; the more pixels on the sensor, the higher the resolution of the images it captures.

Not so long ago, a 1-megapixel digital camera was the bleeding edge of digital photographic technology, but now you can find cameras with ten times that resolution for a hundred dollars. As a basis of reference, a 5-megapixel camera produces snapshot-sized (4 × 6 inch) pictures with print photograph quality, whereas a 10-megapixel unit can produce a high-quality 8 × 10 inch print.

Another feature of most digital cameras and camcorders is the capability to zoom in on your subject. The way you ideally want to do this is the way film cameras do it, by using the camera's optics—that's the lens. Most cameras above the basic level have some *optical zoom*—meaning the zoom is built into the lens of the camera—but almost all models include multiple levels of *digital zoom*, accomplished by some very clever

software in the camera. Choose your camera based on optical zoom: 3× at a minimum or better if you can afford it. Digital zoom is useless.

Camcorder optical zoom ranges are often much larger. You can find digital cameras with an optical zoom of 30× or more.

Form Factor

As was the case with film cameras, size matters on digital cameras and camcorders. These devices come in several form factors. They range from tiny, ultra-compact models that readily fit in a shirt pocket to monster cameras with huge lenses. Although it's not universally true, the bigger the camera/camcorder, the more features and sensors it can have. Thus bigger is usually better in terms of quality.

In shape, digital cameras come in a rectangular package, in which the lens retracts into the body, or as an SLR-type, with a lens that sticks out of the body. Figure 20-48 shows both styles.

Figure 20-48
Typical digital cameras

Camcorders also come in multiple shapes (see Figure 20-49). Some are arranged vertically; others are more horizontal. Some are large enough that you need to use two hands to hold them. The latest form factors include two lenses so they can capture 3-D videos. Now your cat can fly right off the screen.

Figure 20-49
Digital camcorders

Web Cameras

PC cameras, often called *webcams* because their most common use is for Internet video communication, are fairly new to the world of input devices. Too many people run out and buy the cheapest one, not appreciating the vast difference between a discount webcam and more expensive models; nor do they take the time to configure the webcam properly. Let's consider some of the features you should look for when buying webcams and some of the problems you can run into when using them.

The biggest issue with webcams is the image quality. Webcams measure their resolution in pixels. You can find webcams with resolutions of as few as 100,000 pixels and webcams with millions of pixels. Most people who use webcams agree that 1.3 million pixels (megapixels) is pretty much the highest resolution quality you can use before your video becomes so large it will bog down even a broadband connection.

The next issue with webcams is the frame rate, that is, the number of times the camera "takes your picture" each second. Higher frame rates make for smoother video; 30 frames per second is considered the best. A good camera with a high megapixel resolution and fast frame rate will provide you with excellent video conferencing capabilities. Figure 20-50 shows the author chatting via webcam using Skype software.

Figure 20-50
Video chatting by
webcam with Skype

NOTE Read more about pixels and frame rates in Chapter 21.

Most people who use online video also want a microphone. Many cameras come with microphones, or you can use your own. Those who do a lot of video chatting may prefer to get a camera without a microphone and then buy a good quality headset with which to speak and listen.

Many cameras now can track you when you move, to keep your face in the picture—a handy feature for fidgety folks using video conferencing! This interesting technology

recognizes a human face with little or no "training" and rotates its position to keep your face in the picture. Some companies even add funny extras, which, although not very productive, are good for a laugh (see Figure 20-51).

Figure 20-51
This webcam program's animated character mirrors your movements as you conference with friends or coworkers.

Almost all webcams use USB connections. Windows comes with a limited set of webcam drivers, so always make sure to install the drivers supplied with the camera before you plug it in. Most webcams use Hi-Speed USB, so make sure you're plugging your webcam into a Hi-Speed USB port.

Once the camera is plugged in, you'll need to test it. All cameras come with some type of program, but finding the program can be a challenge. Some brands put the program in the system tray, some place it in My Computer/Computer, others put it in the Control Panel—and some do all three! Figure 20-52 shows the Control Panel applet that appeared when I installed the webcam driver.

Figure 20-52
Camera Settings applet

How LCDs Work

The secret to understanding the most common type of LCD panels is to understand the concept of the polarity of light. Anyone who played with a prism in sixth grade or has looked at a rainbow knows that light travels in waves (no quantum mechanics here, please!), and the wavelength of the light determines the color. What you might not appreciate is the fact that light waves emanate from a light source in three dimensions. It's impossible to draw a clear diagram of three-dimensional waves, so instead, let's use an analogy. To visualize this, think of light emanating from a flashlight. Now think of the light emanating from that flashlight as though someone was shaking a jump rope. This is not a rhythmic shaking, back and forth or up and down; it's more as if a person went crazy and was shaking the jump rope all over the place—up, down, left, right—constantly changing the speed.

That's how light really acts. Well, I guess we could take the analogy one step further by saying the person has an infinite number of arms, each holding a jump rope shooting out in every direction to show the three-dimensionality of light waves, but (a) I can't draw that and (b) one jump rope will suffice to explain the typical LCD panels. The varying speeds create wavelengths, from very short to very long. When light comes into your eyes at many different wavelengths, you see white light. If the light came in only one wavelength, you would see only that color. Light flowing through a polarized filter (like sunglasses) is like putting a picket fence between you and the people shaking the ropes. You see all of the wavelengths, but only the waves of similar orientation. You would still see all of the colors, just fewer of them because you only see the waves of the same orientation, making the image darker. That's why many sunglasses use polarizing filters.

Now, what would happen if you added another picket fence but put the slats in a horizontal direction? This would effectively cancel out all of the waves. This is what happens when two polarizing filters are combined at a 90-degree angle—no light passes through.

Now, what would happen if you added a third fence between the two fences with the slats at a 45-degree angle? Well, it would sort of "twist" some of the shakes in the rope so that the waves could then get through. The same thing is true with the polarizing filters. The third filter twists some of the light so that it gets through. If you're really feeling scientific, go to any educational supply store and pick up three polarizing filters for about (US)$3 each and try it. It works.

Liquid crystals take advantage of the property of polarization. Liquid crystals are composed of a specially formulated liquid full of long, thin crystals that always want to orient themselves in the same direction, as shown in Figure 21-10. This substance acts exactly like a liquid polarized filter. If you poured a thin film of this stuff between two sheets of glass, you'd get a darn good pair of sunglasses.

Imagine cutting extremely fine grooves on one side of one of those sheets of glass. When you place this liquid in contact with a finely grooved surface, the molecules naturally line up with the grooves in the surface (see Figure 21-11).

If you place another finely grooved surface, with the grooves at a 90-degree orientation to the other surface, opposite of the first one, the molecules in contact with that

side will attempt to line up with it. The molecules in between, in trying to line up with both sides, will immediately line up in a nice twist (see Figure 21-12). If two perpendicular polarizing filters are then placed on either side of the liquid crystal, the liquid crystal will twist the light and enable it to pass (see Figure 21-13).

Figure 21-10
Waves of similar orientation

Figure 21-11
Liquid crystal molecules tend to line up together.

Figure 21-12
Liquid crystal molecules twisting

Figure 21-13 No charge, enabling light to pass

If you expose the liquid crystal to an electrical potential, however, the crystals will change their orientation to match the direction of the electrical field. The twist goes away and no light passes through (see Figure 21-14).

Figure 21-14 Electrical charge, no light is able to pass

A color LCD screen is composed of a large number of tiny liquid crystal molecules (called *sub-pixels*) arranged in rows and columns between polarizing filters. A translucent sheet above the sub-pixels is colored red, green, or blue. Each tiny distinct group of three sub-pixels—one red, one green, and one blue—forms a physical pixel, as shown in Figure 21-15.

Figure 21-15
LCD pixels

NOTE LCD pixels are very different from the pixels in a CRT. A CRT pixel's size changes depending on the resolution. The pixels in an LCD panel are fixed and cannot be changed. See the section "LCD Resolution" later in the chapter for the scoop.

Once all of the pixels are laid out, how do you charge the right spots to make an image? Early LCDs didn't use rectangular pixels. Instead, images were composed of different-shaped elements, each electrically separate from the others. To create an image, each area was charged at the same time. Figure 21-16 shows the number zero, a display made possible by charging six areas to make an ellipse of sorts. This process, called *static charging*, is still quite popular in more basic numeric displays such as calculators.

Figure 21-16
Single character for
static LCD numeric
display

The static method would not work in PCs due to its inherent inflexibility. Instead, early LCD screens used a matrix of wires (see Figure 21-17). The vertical wires, the Y wires, ran to every sub-pixel in the column. The horizontal wires, the X wires, ran along an entire row of sub-pixels. There had to be a charge on both the X wires and the Y wires to make enough voltage to light a single sub-pixel.

Figure 21-17
An LCD matrix of wires

If you wanted color, you had to have three matrices. The three matrices intersected very close together. Above the intersections, the glass was covered with tiny red, green, and blue dots. Varying the amount of voltage on the wires made different levels of red, green, and blue, creating colors (see Figure 21-18).

Figure 21-18
Passive matrix display

We call this usage of LCD technology *passive matrix*. All LCD displays on PCs used only passive matrix for many years. Unfortunately, passive matrix is slow and tends to create a little overlap between individual pixels. This gives a slightly blurred effect to the image displayed. Manufacturers eventually came up with a speedier method of display, called *dual-scan passive matrix*, in which the screen refreshed two lines at a time.

Thin Film Transistor

Current LCD monitors use some form of *thin film transistor (TFT)* or *active matrix* technology (see Figure 21-19). Instead of using X and Y wires, one or more tiny transistors control each color dot, providing faster picture display, crisp definition, and much tighter color control than passive or dual-scan technologies could provide.

Figure 21-19
Active matrix
display

Polarizer
Thin film transistors
Liquid crystal
Thin film transistors
Polarizer

 NOTE The most common TFT displays use a technology called *twisted nematic (TN)*, which produces a decent display for a modest price. Most TN displays use only 6 bits for each color—red, green, and blue—and that 18-bit display will not reproduce the full 24-bit true color that video cards can send to it. This means the panel fudges a little bit when asked to do something it can't do, and this can produce noticeable problems with reproduction.

Better TFT displays use a technology called *In-Plane Switching (IPS)* to create a wider viewing angle and far better color re-creation than TN panels can provide. Graphics professionals use IPS monitors, for example, because they can display what might print more faithfully than TN screens. Manufacturers use many types of IPS technology to find the right mix of price-to-performance.

LCD Components

The typical LCD monitor is composed of three main components: the LCD panel, the backlight(s), and the inverters. The LCD panel creates the image, the *backlights* illuminate the image so you can see it, and the *inverters* send power to the backlights. Figure 21-20 shows a typical layout for the internal components of an LCD monitor.

Figure 21-20
LCD internals

Backlights
LCD panel
LCD logic board
Inverters
Transformer
DVI
VGA
Analog/digital converter

LCD Monitors with CCFL Backlights One of the great challenges to LCD power stems from the fact that the backlights need AC power while the electronics need DC power. Figure 21-20 shows one of the many ways that LCD monitor makers handle this issue. The AC power from your wall socket goes into an AC/DC transformer that changes the power to DC. The LCD panel uses this DC power.

Note in Figure 21-20 that this monitor has two backlights: one at the top and one at the bottom. Most LCDs have two backlights, although some have only one. Most LCD backlights use *cold cathode fluorescent lamp (CCFL)* technology, popular for its low power use, even brightness, and long life. Figure 21-21 shows a CCFL from an LCD panel.

Figure 21-21
CCFL backlight

CCFLs need AC power to operate, but given that the transformer converts the incoming AC power to DC, each CCFL backlight needs a device called an inverter to convert the DC power back into AC. Figure 21-22 shows a typical inverter used in an LCD.

Figure 21-22
Inverter

Looking once again at Figure 21-20, note the two input connectors, DVI and VGA. DVI is a digital signal, so it connects directly to the LCD's logic circuitry. The VGA goes to an analog-to-digital converter before reaching the LCD logic board.

Keep in mind that Figure 21-20 is a generic illustration. The actual location and interconnections of the components are as variable as the number of LCD panels available today!

LED Monitors Manufacturers also use several types of *light-emitting diode (LED)* light for backlighting, either directly illuminating pixels from behind or flooding the panel from the edges of the bezel. The former produces outstanding contrast and

color, but costs a lot more than the edge types. The edge types function similarly to a CCFL-style display, so they produce similar contrast and colors to the older technology. Manufacturers have rebranded LCD monitors that use LEDs for backlighting as *LED monitors*.

EXAM TIP The CompTIA A+ 801 exam refers to LEDs as a display type, but such displays don't exist aside from marketing terms. LEDs manifest only as one form of backlighting for LCD monitors. Even so-called "LED monitors" and "LED televisions" are simply LCDs with LED backlights. The terms are merely marketing speak.

Using LEDs for backlighting reduces the thickness of the panels and reduces the overall electricity usage. LEDs don't need AC power, so there's no inverter to get involved in lighting the panel. Many smaller devices, such as smartphones and tablets, use LED backlights to save battery use. The better panels are also in high demand from graphics professionals.

EXAM TIP Be sure you understand the features of CRT, LCD, LED, plasma, projector, and OLED display types.

LCD Resolution

All LCD monitors have a *native resolution*, such as 1680 × 1050, that enables them to display the sharpest picture possible. As mentioned earlier, the pixels are fixed. You simply cannot run an LCD monitor at a resolution higher than the native one. Worse, because LCDs have no equivalent to a shadow mask, they can't run at a *lower* than native resolution without severely degrading image quality. A CRT can simply use more dots and the filtering and smoothing of the shadow mask to make a picture at a lower resolution look as good and crisp as the same picture at a higher resolution, but an LCD cannot. The LCD has to use an edge-blurring technique called *anti-aliasing* to soften the jagged corners of the pixels when running at lower than native resolution, which simply does not look as good. The bottom line? Always set the LCD at native resolution! Here's some more information.

NOTE Two LCD panels that have the same physical size may have different native resolutions.

The hard-wired nature of LCD resolution creates a problem for techs and consumers when dealing with bigger, better-quality monitors. A typical 17-inch LCD usually has 1280 × 1024 or higher resolution, for example, and the larger 20+-inch LCDs can go up to 1920 × 1080 or more. These high resolutions make the menus and fonts on a monitor super tiny, a problem for people with less-than-stellar vision. Many folks throw in

the towel and run these high-end LCDs at lower resolution and just live with the lower-quality picture, but that's not the best way to resolve this problem.

Microsoft enables incredible customizing of the interface. You can change the font size, shape, and color. You can resize the icons, toolbars, and more. You can even change the number of dots per inch (DPI) for the full screen, making everything bigger or smaller!

For basic customizing, start at the Control Panel | Display applet | Appearance tab or Control Panel | Personalization applet. To change the DPI for the display, go to the Settings tab and click the Advanced button in Windows XP; in Windows Vista, just click the *Adjust font size (DPI)* option in the Tasks list. In Windows 7, click Display and the select one of the preset font sizes or a custom size. Your clients will thank you!

Brightness

The strength of an LCD monitor's backlights determines the brightness of the monitor. The brightness is measured in *nits*. LCD panels vary from 100 nits on the low end to over 1000 nits or more on the high end. Average LCD panels are around 300 nits, which most monitor authorities consider excellent brightness.

NOTE One nit equals one candela/m². One candela is roughly equal to the amount of light created by a candle.

Response Rate

An LCD panel's *response rate* is the amount of time it takes for all of the sub-pixels on the panel to go from pure black to pure white and back again. This is roughly the same concept as the CRT refresh rate, but with one important difference. Once the electron gun on a CRT lights a phosphor, that phosphor begins to fade until it is lit again. An individual LCD sub-pixel holds its intensity until the LCD circuitry changes that sub-pixel, making the problem of flicker nonexistent on LCDs.

Manufacturers measure LCD response rates in milliseconds, with lower being better. A typical lower-end or older LCD has a response rate of 20–25 ms. The screens look fine, but you'll get some ghosting if you try to watch a movie or play a fast-paced video game. In recent years, manufacturers have figured out how to overcome this issue, and you can find many LCD monitors with a response rate of 2–4 ms.

Refresh Rate

The refresh rate for an LCD monitor is described using numbers similar to those used to describe the refresh rate for a CRT monitor, such as 60 Hz, but the terms mean slightly different things between the two technologies. With CRTs, as you'll recall, the phosphors on the screen start to lose their glow and need to be hit again by the electron guns many times per second to achieve an unwavering or flicker-free image. Each dot on an active matrix LCD, in contrast, has its own transistor to light it up. There's no need to freshen up the dot; it's on or off. Regardless of the refresh rate for the LCD, therefore, there's never any flicker at all caused by refresh rate.

The refresh rate for an LCD monitor refers to how often a screen can change or update completely. Think of the refresh rate as a metronome or timer and you'll be closer to how it works in an LCD. For most computing issues, 60 Hz is fine and that's been the standard for the industry. Humans see things that change as infrequently as 24 times per second—the standard for motion pictures at the cinema, for example, and the best high-definition (HD) signal—as a full motion video. To be able to change almost three times faster is perfectly acceptable, even in higher-end applications such as fast-moving games.

Monitor manufacturers have released 120-Hz LCD monitors in a response to the convergence of LCDs, televisions, and computers to enable you to see HD movies or standard-definition (SD) content without any problems or visual artifacts on an LCD monitor. The easiest number that provides a whole-number division for both 24 frames per second and 30 frames per second was 120 Hz. The latter is the standard for SD content.

NOTE A video card needs to be able to support Dual-Link DVI to run a 120-Hz monitor or television. See the discussion on DVI later in this chapter for details.

Contrast Ratio

A big drawback of LCD monitors is that they don't have nearly the color saturation or richness of contrast of a good CRT monitor—although LCD technology continues to improve every year. A good contrast ratio—the difference between the darkest and lightest spots that the monitor can display—is 450:1, although a quick trip to a computer store will reveal LCDs with lower levels (250:1) and higher levels (1000:1).

LCD monitor manufacturers market a *dynamic contrast ratio* number for their monitors, which measures the difference between a full-on, all-white screen, and a full-off, or all-black screen. This yields a much higher number than the standard contrast ratio. My Samsung panels have a 1000:1 contrast ratio, for example, but a 20,000:1 dynamic contrast ratio. Sounds awesome, right? In general, the dynamic contrast ratio doesn't affect viewing on computer monitors. Focus on the standard contrast ratio when making decisions on LCD screens.

EXAM TIP The CompTIA A+ 801 exam expects you to understand the refresh rate, resolution, and native resolution of a monitor.

Projectors

Projectors are a third option for displaying your computer images, and the best choice when displaying to an audience or in a classroom. There are two ways to project an image on a screen: rearview and front-view. As the name would suggest, a *rearview projector* (see Figure 21-23) shoots an image onto a screen from the rear. Rearview projectors are always self-enclosed and are very popular for televisions, but are virtually unheard of in the PC world.

Figure 21-23
Rearview projector
(photo courtesy of
Samsung)

A *front-view projector* shoots the image out the front and counts on you to put a screen in front at the proper distance. Front-view projectors connected to PCs running Microsoft PowerPoint have been the cornerstone of every meeting almost everywhere for at least the past ten years (see Figure 21-24). This section deals exclusively with front-view projectors that connect to PCs.

Figure 21-24
Front-view
projector (photo
courtesy of
Dell Inc.)

Projector Technologies

Projectors that connect to PCs have been in existence for almost as long as PCs themselves. Given all that time, a number of technologies have been used in projectors. The first generation of projectors used CRTs. Each color used a separate CRT that projected the image onto a screen (see Figure 21-25). CRT projectors create beautiful images but are expensive, large, and very heavy, and have for the most part been abandoned for more recent technologies.

Figure 21-25
CRT projector

Given that light shines through an LCD panel, LCD projectors are a natural fit for front projection. LCD projectors are light and very inexpensive compared to CRTs but lack the image quality. LCD projectors are so light that almost all portable projectors use LCD (see Figure 21-26).

Figure 21-26
LCD projector
(photo courtesy of
ViewSonic)

 NOTE Another type of technology that's seen in projectors but is outside the scope of the CompTIA A+ exams is called Digital Light Processing (DLP). Check out the "Beyond A+" section of this chapter for details.

All projectors share the same issues as their equivalent-technology monitors. LCD projectors have a specific native resolution, for example. In addition, you need to understand three concepts specific to projectors: lumens, throw, and lamps.

Lumens

The brightness of a projector is measured in lumens. A *lumen* is the amount of light given off by a light source from a certain angle that is perceived by the human eye.

The greater the lumen rating of a projector, the brighter the projector will be. The best lumen rating depends on the size of the room and the amount of light in the room. There's no single answer for "the right lumen rating" for a projector, but use this as a rough guide. If you use a projector in a small, darkened room, 1000 to 1500 lumens will work well. If you use a projector in a mid-sized room with typical lighting, you'll need at least 2000 lumens. Projectors for large rooms have ratings over 10,000 lumens and are very expensive.

Throw

A projector's *throw* is the size of the image at a certain distance from the screen. All projectors have a recommended minimum and maximum throw distance that you need to take into consideration. A typical throw would be expressed as follows. A projector with a 16:9 image aspect ratio needs to be 11 to 12 feet away from the projection surface to create a 100-inch diagonal screen. A *long throw lens* has about a 1:2 ratio of screen size to distance, so to display a 4-foot screen, you'd have to put the projector 8 feet away. Some *short throw lenses* drop that ratio down as low as 1:1!

Lamps

The bane of every projector is the lamp. Lamps work hard in your projector, as they must generate a tremendous amount of light. As a result, they generate quite a bit of heat, and all projectors come with a fan to keep the lamp from overheating. When you turn off a projector, the fan continues to run until the lamp is fully cooled. Lamps are also expensive, usually in the range of a few hundred dollars (U.S.), which comes as a nasty shock to someone who's not prepared for that price when the lamp dies!

Plasma Displays

Plasma display panels (PDP) are a popular technology for displaying movies, competing directly with LCD screens for the flat-panel space. They offer a wider viewing angle and richer picture than the typical LCD and cost less. They weigh a lot more and consume much more electricity, though, compared to LCDs.

Unfortunately, plasma TVs have two issues that make them a bad choice for PC use. First is *burn-in*—the tendency for a screen to leave a "ghost" image even after the image is off the screen. Plasma TV makers have virtually eliminated burn-in, but even the latest plasma displays are subject to burn-in when used as PC displays.

The second issue is *overscan*, a problem that can affect LCD-based TVs as well. Overscan is when the TV blows up the image, cropping off the edges of the picture. TVs do this for historical reasons, but the side effect is that when used with a PC, things like your taskbar get cut off. Some manufacturers have a setting to disable this feature, but not all do. Because media center PCs are becoming more common, CompTIA included the plasma display device in the 220-801 exam objectives. I would advise against using a plasma screen with a media center PC.

Common Features

CRT or LCD, all monitors share a number of characteristics that you need to know for purchase, installation, maintenance, and troubleshooting.

Size

CRT monitors come in a large number of sizes, all measured in inches (although most metric countries provide the metric equivalent value). All monitors provide two numbers: the monitor size and the actual size of the screen. The monitor size measures from two opposite diagonal corners. The actual screen is measured from one edge of the screen to the opposite diagonal side. This latter measurement is often referred to as the *viewable image size (VIS)*, as shown in Figure 21-27. You will commonly see a size difference of one to two inches between the two measurements. A 17-inch CRT monitor, for example, might have a 15.5-inch VIS.

Figure 21-27

Viewable image size of a CRT

Monitor size Viewable image size

LCD monitors dispense with the two values and simply express the VIS value. A 15-inch LCD monitor will have about the same viewing area as a 17-inch CRT.

Connections

CRT monitors for PCs all use the famous 15-pin, three-row, DB-type connector (see Figure 21-28) and a power plug. The DB connector is also called a *D-shell* or *D-subminiature* connector or simply a *VGA connector*. Larger or multipurpose monitors may have a few other connectors, but as far as the CRT is concerned, these are the only two you need for video.

Figure 21-28

A traditional CRT connector

 NOTE You'll often hear the terms *flat-panel display*, *LCD panel*, or *LED monitor* to describe LCD monitors. I prefer the term *LCD monitor*, but you should be prepared to hear it a few different ways.

Controlling a CRT requires an *analog signal* from the video card, meaning a signal that rises and falls in waves like a series of *S*s on their side. LCDs and computers, on the other hand, use digital signals, on or off, one or zero. There's no one-half signal in digital!

The video information stored on a video card's RAM is clearly digital. Video cards include a special chip (or function embedded into a chip that does several other jobs) called the *random access memory digital-to-analog converter (RAMDAC)*. As the name implies, the RAMDAC takes the digital signal from the video card and turns it into an analog signal for the analog CRT (see Figure 21-29).

Figure 21-29 An analog signal sent to a CRT monitor

Well, RAMDACs certainly make sense for analog CRT monitors. If you want to plug your LCD monitor into a regular video card, however, you need circuitry on the LCD monitor to convert the signal from analog to digital (see Figure 21-30).

Many LCD monitors use exactly this process. These are called *analog LCD monitors*. The monitor really isn't analog; it's digital, but it takes a standard VGA input. These monitors have one advantage: You may use any standard VGA video card. But these monitors require adjustment of the analog timing signal to the digital clock inside the monitor. This used to be a fairly painful process, but most analog LCD monitors now include intelligent circuitry to make this process either automatic or very easy.

Why convert the signal from digital to analog and then back to digital? Well, many monitor and video card people agree that it just doesn't make much sense. We now see quite a few digital LCD monitors and digital video cards. They use a completely different connector than the old 15-pin DB connector used on analog video cards and

monitors. After a few false starts with connection standards, under names such as P&D and DFP, the digital LCD world, with a few holdouts, moved to the *digital visual interface (DVI)* standard. DVI is actually three different connectors that look very much alike: DVI-D is for digital, DVI-A is for analog (for backward compatibility if the monitor maker so desires), and the DVI-A/D or DVI-I (interchangeable) accepts either a DVI-D or DVI-A. DVI-D and DVI-A are keyed so that they will not connect.

The RAMDAC in the LCD converts the analog signal back to digital.

Digital data in RAM

Converts to analog

Figure 21-30 Converting analog back to digital on the LCD

DVI-D and DVI-I connectors come in two varieties, single-link and dual-link. *Single-link DVI* has a maximum bandwidth of 165 MHz, which, translated into practical terms, limits the maximum resolution of a monitor to 1920 × 1080 at 60 Hz or 1280 × 1024 at 85 Hz. *Dual-link DVI* uses more pins to double throughput and thus grant higher resolutions (see Figure 21-31). With dual-link DVI, you can have displays up to a whopping 2048 × 1536 at 60 Hz!

Figure 21-31
Dual-link DVI-I
connector

NOTE You can plug a single-link DVI monitor into a dual-link DVI connector and it'll work just fine.

Digital connectors are quickly replacing analog in the monitor world. Digital makes both the monitor and the video card cheaper, provides a clearer signal because no conversion is necessary, and makes installation easy. Many monitors and video cards these days only support digital signals, but there are still quite a few of each that provide both digital and analog connections.

The video card people have it easy. They either include both a VGA and a DVI-D connector or they use a DVI-I connector. The advantage to DVI-I is that you can add a cheap DVI-I-to-VGA adapter (one usually comes with the video card) like the one shown in Figure 21-32 and connect an analog monitor just fine.

Figure 21-32
DVI-to-VGA
adapter

Monitor makers have it tougher. Most LCD monitor makers have made the jump to DVI, but many include a VGA connector for those machines that still need it.

Unless you're buying a complete new system, you'll rarely buy a video card at the same time you buy a monitor. When you're buying a monitor or a video card, make sure that the new device will connect to the other!

Adjustments

Most adjustments to the monitor take place at installation, but for now, let's just make sure you know what they are and where they are located. Clearly, all monitors have an On/Off button or switch. Also, see if you can locate the Brightness and Contrast buttons. Beyond that, most monitors (at least the only ones you should buy) have an onboard menu system, enabling a number of adjustments. Every monitor maker provides a different way to access these menus, but they all provide two main functions: physical screen adjustment (bigger, smaller, move to the left, right, up, down, and others) and color adjustment. The color adjustment lets you adjust the red, green, and blue levels to give you the best color tones. All of these settings are a matter of personal taste. Make sure the person who will use the computer understands how to adjust these settings (see Figure 21-33).

Figure 21-33
Typical menu
controls

Power Conservation

CRT and LCD monitors differ greatly in the amount of electricity they require. The bottom line is that CRTs use a lot and LCDs use a lot less. Here's the scoop.

Approximately half the power required to run a desktop PC is consumed by the CRT monitor. Monitors that meet the Video Electronics Standards Association (VESA) specification for *Display Power Management Signaling (DPMS)* can reduce monitor power consumption by roughly 75 percent. This is accomplished by reducing or eliminating the signals sent by the video card to the monitor during idle periods. By eliminating these pulses, the monitor essentially takes catnaps. The advantage over simply shutting the monitor off is in the time it takes to restore the display.

A typical CRT monitor consumes approximately 120 watts. During a catnap or power-down mode, the energy consumption is reduced to below 25 watts, while enabling the screen to return to use in less than ten seconds. Full shutoff is accomplished by eliminating all clocking pulses to the monitor. Although this reduces power consumption to below 15 watts, it also requires anywhere from 15 to 30 seconds to restore a usable display.

NOTE Turning off the monitor with the power switch is the most basic form of power management. The downside to this is the wear and tear on the cathode ray tube itself. The cathode ray tube is the most expensive component of a CRT monitor, and frequently turning the monitor on and off can damage the tube. When using a non-DPMS monitor or video card, it is best to turn the monitor on once during the day and then turn it off only when you are finished for the day. This on-off cycle must be balanced against the life of the CRT display phosphors. The typical monitor loses about half its original brightness after roughly 10,000 to 15,000 hours of display time. Leaving the monitor on all of the time brings a noticeable decrease in brightness in just over a year (8766 hours). The only way around this is enabling the DPMS features of the monitor or taking care to turn the monitor off.

A typical LCD monitor, in contrast, uses less than half the electricity that a CRT uses. A 19-inch, 4:3 aspect-ratio flat panel, for example, uses around 33 watts at peak usage and less than 2 watts in DPMS mode. Larger LCDs use more power at peak usage than smaller ones. A 21-inch wide-screen model, for example, might draw ~75 watts at peak but drop down to less than 2 watts in DPMS mode. Swapping out CRTs with LCDs is a great way to save on your electric bill!

Display Adapters

The display adapter, or video card, handles the video chores within the PC, processing information from the CPU and sending it out to the monitor. The display adapter is a complex set of devices. A graphics processor of some type processes data from the CPU and outputs commands to the display. Like any other processor, the graphics processor needs RAM. The graphics processor needs fast connectivity between it, the CPU, and system RAM. The display adapter must have a connection compatible with the monitor.

Traditionally, and still quite commonly, the display adapter was an expansion card that plugged into the motherboard (see Figure 21-34). Although many new systems have the display adapter circuitry built into the motherboard, most techs still call it the video card, so we'll start there. This section looks at five aspects that define a video card: display modes, motherboard connection, graphics processor circuitry, video memory, and connections.

Figure 21-34
Typical video card

Modes

The trick to understanding video cards is to appreciate the beginnings and evolution of video. Video output to computers was around long before PCs were created. At the time PCs became popular, video was almost exclusively text-based, meaning that the only image the video card could place on the monitor was one of the 256 ASCII characters. These characters were made up of patterns of pixels that were stored in the system BIOS. When a program wanted to make a character, it talked to DOS or to the BIOS, which stored the image of that character in the video memory. The character then appeared on the screen.

The beauty of text video cards was that they were simple to use and cheap to make. The simplicity was based on the fact that only 256 characters existed, and no color choices were available—just monochrome text.

You could, however, choose to make the character bright, dim, normal, underlined, or blinking. Positioning the characters was easy, as space on the screen allowed for only 80 characters per row and 24 rows of characters.

Long ago, RAM was very expensive, so video card makers were interested in using the absolute least amount of RAM possible. Making a monochrome text video card was a great way to keep down RAM costs. Let's consider this for a minute. First, the video RAM is where the contents of the screen are located. You need enough video RAM to hold all of the necessary information for a completely full screen. Each ASCII character needs 8 bits (by definition), so a monitor with 80 characters/row and 24 rows will need

80 characters × 24 rows = 1920 characters = 15,360 bits or 1920 bytes

The video card would need less than 2000 bytes of memory, which isn't much, not even in 1981 when the PC first came out. Now, be warned that I'm glossing over a few things—where you store the information about underlines, blinking, and so on. The bottom line is that the tiny amount of necessary RAM kept monochrome text video cards cheap.

Very early on in the life of PCs, a new type of video, called a *graphics video card*, was invented. It was quite similar to a text card. The text card, however, was limited to the 256 ASCII characters, whereas a graphics video card enabled programs to turn any pixel on the screen on or off. It was still monochrome, but programs could access any individual pixel, enabling much more creative control of the screen. Of course, it took more video RAM. The first graphics cards ran at 320 × 200 pixels. One bit was needed for each pixel (on or off), so

320 × 200 = 64,000 bits or 8000 bytes

That's a lot more RAM than was needed for text, but it was still a pretty low amount of RAM—even in the old days. As resolutions increased, however, the amount of video RAM needed to store this information also increased.

After monochrome video was invented, moving into color for both text and graphics video cards was a relatively easy step. The only question was how to store color information for each character (text cards) or pixel (graphics cards). This was easy—just set aside a few more bits for each pixel or character. So now the question becomes, "How many bits do you set aside?" Well, that depends on how many colors you want. Basically, the number of colors determines the number of bits. For example, if you want four colors, you need 2 bits (2 bits per pixel). Then, you could do something like this

00 = black	01 = cyan (blue)
10 = magenta (reddish pink)	11 = white

So if you set aside 2 bits, you could get 4 colors. If you want 16 colors, set aside 4 bits, which would make 16 different combinations. Nobody ever invented a text mode that used more than 16 colors, so let's start thinking in terms of only graphics mode and

bits per pixels. To get 256 colors, each pixel would have to be represented with 8 bits. In PCs, the number of colors—called the *color depth*—is always a power of 2: 4, 16, 256, 64 K, and so on. Note that as more colors are added, more video RAM is needed to store the information. Here are the most common color depths and the number of bits necessary to store the color information per pixel:

2 colors = 1 bit (mono)

4 colors = 2 bits

16 colors = 4 bits

256 colors = 8 bits

64 K colors = 16 bits

16.7 million colors = 24 bits

Most technicians won't say, for example, "I set my video card to show over 16 million colors." Instead, they'll say, "I set my color depth to 24 bits." Talk in terms of bits, not colors. It is assumed that you know the number of colors for any color depth.

You can set the color depth for a Windows XP computer in the Display Properties dialog box on the Settings tab (see Figure 21-35). If you set up a typical Windows XP computer, you'll notice that Windows offers you 32-bit color quality, which might make you assume you're about to crank out more than 4 billion colors, but that's simply not the case. The 32-bit color setting offers 24-bit color plus an 8-bit alpha channel. An alpha channel controls the opacity of a particular color. By using an alpha channel, Windows can more effectively blend colors to create the effect of semi-transparent images. In Windows XP, you see this in the drop shadow under a menu; in Windows Vista and Windows 7, almost every screen element can be semi-transparent (see Figure 21-36).

Figure 21-35

Adjusting color settings in Windows XP

Figure 21-36 Semi-transparency in Windows Vista

Your video card and monitor are capable of showing Windows in a fixed number of different resolutions and color depths. The choices depend on the resolutions and color depths the video card can push to the monitor and the amount of bandwidth your monitor can support. Any single combination of resolution and color depth you set for your system is called a *mode*. For standardization, VESA defines a certain number of resolutions, all derived from the granddaddy of video modes: VGA.

VGA

With the introduction of the PS/2, IBM introduced the *video graphics array (VGA)* standard. This standard offered 16 colors at a resolution of 640 × 480 pixels. VGA supported such an amazing variety of colors by using an analog video signal instead of a digital one, as was the case prior to the VGA standard. A digital signal is either all on or all off. By using an analog signal, the VGA standard can provide 64 distinct levels for the three colors (RGB)—that is, 64^3 or 262,144 possible colors—although only 16 or 256 can be seen at a time. For most purposes, 640 × 480 and 16 colors defines VGA mode. This is typically the display resolution and color depth referred to on many software packages as a minimum display requirement. Every video card made in the past 15 years can output as VGA, but VGA-only cards are now obsolete.

Beyond VGA

The 1980s were a strange time for video. Until the very late 1980s, VGA was the highest mode defined by VESA, but demand grew for modes that went beyond VGA. This motivated VESA to introduce (over time) a number of new modes with names such as SVGA, XGA, and many others. Even today, new modes are being released! Table 21-1 shows the more common modes.

Video Mode	Resolution	Aspect Ratio	Typical Device
SVGA	800 × 600	4:3	Small monitors
HDTV 720p	1280 × 720	16:9	Lowest resolution that can be called HDTV
SXGA	1280 × 1024	5:4	Native resolution for many desktop LCD monitors
WXGA	1366 × 768	16:9	Widescreen laptops
WSXGA	1440 × 900	16:10	Widescreen laptops
SXGA+	1400 × 1050	4:3	Laptop monitors and high-end projectors
UXGA	1600 × 1200	4:3	Larger CRT monitors
HDTV 1080p	1920 × 1080	16:9	Full HDTV resolution
WUXGA	1920 × 1200	16:10	For 24"+ widescreen monitors
QWXGA	2048 × 1152	16:9	For smaller, fine monitors
WQXGA	2560 × 1600	16:10	For 27"+ widescreen monitors
WQUXGA	3840 × 2400	16:10	For smaller, fine monitors

Table 21-1 Typical Display Modes

The video card must have sufficient RAM to support each combination of color depth and resolution. Many years ago this mattered, when video cards had scant megabytes of memory. A video card with only 2 MB of RAM, for example, could handle a high color (16-bit) display at 1024 × 768, but not the same resolution with true color (24-bit). Table 21-2 shows common modes and the minimum video memory needed. All modern video cards can handle true color at any resolution.

Resolution	16-bit (High Color)	24-bit (True Color)
640 × 480	1 MB	1 MB
800 × 600	1 MB	2 MB
1024 × 768	2 MB	4 MB
1280 × 1024	4 MB	4 MB
1600 × 1200	4 MB	6 MB

Table 21-2 Common Modes and the Minimum Video Memory Required

 EXAM TIP To accommodate rotated LCD monitors in portrait view, the video resolution numbers might be reversed. Rather than 1280 × 1024, for example, you might see 1024 × 1280. The amount of RAM needed remains the same regardless.

Motherboard Connection

Techs will encounter four ways that display adapters connect to a motherboard. The oldest connector type, PCI, is used today only for an additional card to support extra monitors. Slightly newer but still quite old in computer terms is AGP. Every current discrete video card plugs into the PCIe slot on a motherboard. Finally, many motherboards have the display adapter built-in. I'll discuss integrated graphics after talking about graphics processors and memory types, at which point the topic will make more sense. For now, let's look at PCI, AGP, and PCIe.

PCI

Using more color depth slows down video functions. Data moving from the video card to the display has to go through the video card's memory chips and the expansion bus, and this can happen only so quickly. The standard PCI slots used in almost all systems for many years are limited to 32-bit transfers at roughly 33 MHz, yielding a maximum bandwidth of 132 MBps. This sounds like a lot until you start using higher resolutions, high color depths, and higher refresh rates. (The refresh rates mattered because we only had CRTs when video cards used the PCI bus.)

For example, take a typical display at 800 × 600 with a fairly low refresh of 70 Hz. The 70 Hz means the display screen is being redrawn 70 times per second. If you use a low color depth of 256 colors, which is 8 bits (2^8 = 256), you can multiply all of the values together to see how much data per second has to be sent to the display:

$$800 \times 600 \times 1 \text{ byte} \times 70 = 33.6 \text{ MBps}$$

If you use the same example at 16 million (24-bit) colors, the figure jumps to 100.8 MBps. You might say, "Well, if PCI runs at 132 MBps, it can handle that!" That statement would be true if the PCI bus had nothing else to do but tend to the video card, but almost every system has more than one PCI device, each requiring part of that throughput. The PCI bus simply cannot handle the needs of any current systems and is therefore used only for adding a second (or third) video card to a system to support an extra monitor.

AGP

Intel answered the desire for video bandwidth even higher than PCI with the *Accelerated Graphics Port (AGP)*. AGP is a single, special port, similar to a PCI slot, that is dedicated to video. You will never see a motherboard with two AGP slots. Figure 21-37 shows an early-generation AGP. AGP is derived from the 66-MHz, 32-bit PCI 2.1 specification. AGP uses a function called *strobing* that increases the signals two, four, and eight times for each clock cycle.

Figure 21-37
AGP

Simply describing AGP as a faster PCI would seriously misrepresent the power of AGP. AGP has several technological advantages over PCI, including the bus, the internal operations, and the capability to handle 3-D texturing (discussed later in the chapter).

First, AGP currently resides alone, on its own personal data bus, connected directly to the Northbridge (see Figure 21-38). This is important because more advanced versions of AGP outperform every bus on the system except the frontside bus!

Figure 21-38 An AGP bus

Second, AGP takes advantage of pipelining commands, similar to the way CPUs pipeline. Third, AGP has a feature called *sidebanding*—basically a second data bus that

enables the video card to send more commands to the Northbridge while receiving other commands at the same time.

Video cards do all kinds of neat stuff with their RAM; for example, video cards store copies of individual windows so they can display the windows at different points on the screen very quickly. A demanding application can quickly max out the onboard RAM on a video card, so AGP provides a pathway so the AGP card can "steal" chunks of the regular system memory to store video information, especially textures. This is generically called a *system memory access* and is quite popular.

AGP has gone through three sets of specifications (AGP 1.0, AGP 2.0, and AGP 3.0), but the official names tend to be ignored. Most techs and consumers refer to the various cards by their strobe multiplier, such as AGP 1×, 2×, 4×, and 8×. The only problem with blurring the distinctions between the specifications comes from the fact that many new motherboards simply don't support the older AGP cards because the older cards require a different physical connection than the new ones.

Some motherboards support multiple types of AGP. Figure 21-39 shows an AGP slot that accommodates everything up to 8×, even the very rare AGP Pro cards. Note that the tab on the slot covers the extra pins required for AGP Pro.

Figure 21-39
AGP 8× slot

Because many AGP cards will run on older AGP motherboards, you can get away with mixing AGP specifications. To get the best, most stable performance possible, you should use an AGP card that's fully supported by the motherboard.

The only significant downside to AGP lies in the close connection tolerances required by the cards themselves. It's very common to snap in a new AGP card and power up just to get a no-video-card beep or a system that doesn't boot. Always take the time to ensure that an AGP card is snapped down securely and screwed in before starting the system.

PCIe

AGP is a great way to get video information to and from video cards very quickly, but it has the downside of being a unique connector in a world where saving money is important. AGP, being based on PCI, also uses a parallel interface. When the *PCI Express (PCIe)* interface was developed to replace PCI, the PCIe designers worked hard to make sure it would also replace AGP. PCIe is a natural evolution for video because it is incredibly fast, using a serial communication method. Also, because PCIe is a true expansion bus designed to talk to the CPU and RAM, it also supports all of the little extras found in AGP, such as sidebanding and system memory access. All PCIe video cards use the PCIe ×16 connector (see Figure 21-40). PCIe replaced AGP as the primary video interface almost overnight.

Figure 21-40
PCIe video card
connected in
PCIe slot

 NOTE You first encountered PCIe way back in Chapter 9, but let me refresh your memory on the significant differences between the versions available. PCIe 1.0 devices transferred up to 2.5 Gbps on each lane; PCIe 2.0 doubled that rate, to 5 Gbps per lane, and PCIe 3.0 threw the gauntlet down at 8 Gbps per lane. The motherboard, of course, needs to support the higher version to see the speed gains.

Graphics Processor

The graphics processor handles the heavy lifting of taking commands from the CPU and translating them into coordinates and color information that the monitor understands and displays. Most techs today refer to the device that processes video as a *graphics processing unit (GPU)*.

Video card discussion, at least among techs, almost always revolves around the graphics processor the video card uses and the amount of RAM onboard. A typical video card might be called an XFX Radeon HD7970 3-GB 384-bit GDDR5 PCI Express 3.0, so let's break that down. XFX is the manufacturer of the video card; Radeon HD7970 is the graphics processor; 3-GB 384-bit GDDR5 describes the dedicated video RAM and the connection between the video RAM and the graphics processor; and PCI Express 3.0 describes the motherboard expansion slot the card requires.

Many companies make the hundreds of different video cards on the market, but only three companies produce the vast majority of graphics processors found on video cards: NVIDIA, AMD, and Intel. NVIDIA and AMD make and sell graphics processors to third-party manufacturers who then design, build, and sell video cards under their own branding. Intel made its own line of cards, but now concentrates on graphics processors

built into motherboards. Figure 21-41 shows an NVIDIA GeForce GTX 570 on a board made by EVGA.

Figure 21-41
NVIDIA GeForce
GTX 570

Your choice of graphics processor is your single most important decision in buying a video card. Low-end graphics processors usually work fine for the run-of-the-mill user who wants to write letters or run a Web browser. High-end graphics processors are designed to support the beautiful 3-D games that are so popular today, and they provide excellent video playback for high-definition video. We'll look at 3-D issues a little later in this chapter, but we'll save HD video for Chapter 25.

Video Memory

Video memory is crucial to the operation of a PC. It is probably the hardest-working set of electronics on the PC. Video RAM constantly updates to reflect every change that takes place on the screen. When you're working with heavy-duty applications (such as games), video memory can prove to be a serious bottleneck in three ways: data through-put speed, access speed, and simple capacity.

Manufacturers have overcome these bottlenecks by upping the width of the bus between the video RAM and video processor; using specialized, super-fast RAM; and adding more and more total RAM.

First, manufacturers reorganized the video display memory on cards from the typical 32-bit-wide structure to 64, 128, 256, and 384 bits wide. Because the system bus is limited to 32 or 64 bits, this would not be of much benefit if video display cards weren't really coprocessor boards. Most of the graphics rendering and processing is handled on the card by the video processor chip rather than by the CPU. The main system simply provides the input data to the processor on the video card. Because the memory bus on the video card is as much as eight times wider than the standard 32-bit pathway (256 bits), data can be manipulated and then sent to the monitor much more quickly (see Figure 21-42).

Figure 21-42

Wide path between
video processor
and video RAM

Specialized types of video RAM have been developed for graphics cards, and many offer substantial improvements in video speeds. The single most important feature that separates DRAM from video RAM is that video RAM can read and write data at the same time. Table 21-3 shows a list of common video memory technologies used yesterday and today—make sure you know these for the exams!

Acronym	Name	Purpose
VRAM	Video RAM	The original graphics RAM
WRAM	Window RAM	Designed to replace VRAM; never caught on
SGRAM	Synchronous Graphics RAM	A version of SDRAM with features to speed up access for graphics
DDR SDRAM	Double Data Rate Synchronous DRAM	Used on budget graphics cards and very common on laptop video cards
DDR2 SDRAM	Double Data Rate version 2, Synchronous DRAM	Popular on video cards until GDDR3; lower voltage than DDR memory
GDDR3 SDRAM	Graphics Double Data Rate, version 3	Similar to DDR2 but runs at faster speeds; different cooling requirements
GDDR4 SDRAM	Graphics Double Data Rate, version 4	Upgrade of GDDR3; faster clock
GDDR5 SDRAM	Graphics Double Data Rate, version 5	Successor to GDDR4; double the input/ output rate of GDDR4

Table 21-3 Video RAM Technologies

Finally, many advanced 3-D video cards come with huge amounts of video RAM. It's very common to see cards with 64, 128, 256, or 512 MB of RAM, or even 1, 2, or 3 GB of RAM! Why so much? Even with PCI Express, accessing data in system RAM always takes a lot longer than accessing data stored in local RAM on the video card. The huge amount of video RAM enables game developers to optimize their games and store more essential data on the local video RAM.

Integrated GPUs

A lot of current motherboards have integrated GPUs or are ready for a CPU with an integrated GPU. The motherboard GPU can be a separate chip attached to the motherboard or can be built into the Northbridge chip. You might run into AMD Radeon chips or NVIDIA nForce chips powering the GPU. Intel has long integrated the Intel Graphics Media Accelerator (GMA) into its chipsets.

AMD, Intel, and NVIDIA make CPUs with integrated GPUs that vary a lot in graphical performance. Some of AMD's Fusion processors, for example, have a CPU/GPU combination that rivals any CPU/discrete graphics card combination, though only at a level seen in portable computers. They're good enough for casual gaming and even some medium-duty games. Intel's graphics support is geared to desktop performance, not gaming at all. NVIDIA's Tegra line is focused on gaming on mobile devices such as tablets and smartphones (see Chapter 27 for the details).

With an integrated GPU, the CPU circuitry is getting pretty crowded. A single AMD Fusion chip, for example, integrates two to four CPU cores, a memory controller that supports DDR3, cache memory, and a GPU that can handle advanced 3-D graphics. Wow! One of the best parts of all this integration is that the chip requires far less electricity than comparable discrete components. Many techs and companies call current integrated GPUs *accelerated processing units* (*APUs*), though that term can be applied to other chips that integrate multiple processing functions.

Connector Types and Associated Cables

You can find many different connectors on video cards, plus variations within those connector types. CompTIA also makes a distinction between the names of the ports on the cards and the cables associated with them, though most techs will refer to the connectors and cables by multiple names interchangeably. Here's the scoop.

Standard monitors connect through one of three connectors:

- DVI
- DB-15
- DisplayPort

Video cards offer other connector types for connecting to things like television sets, camcorders, and other multimedia devices, although these are mostly associated with older cards:

- RCA
- BNC
- Mini-DIN
- HDMI

 EXAM TIP The CompTIA A+ competencies mention *RJ-45* as a video connector type and Ethernet as a video cable type. The only place you'll find both used in video is with SP Controls' *CatLinc system*. CatLinc uses adapters to connect your VGA, DVI, HDMI, and component devices to a CAT5 cable (commonly associated with Ethernet networks). CAT5 cables enable the video signal to be transmitted across greater distances more clearly at a lower cost.

The video card shown in Figure 21-43 has three connectors: DB-15, DVI-I, and S-video. Other connectors enable the video card to connect to composite, component, and even high-definition devices.

Figure 21-43
Video card connectors,: VGA, S-video, and DVI-I

For Standard Monitors

You know about the standard monitor connectors, the DB-15 that most people call VGA and DVI, from the monitor discussion earlier. About the only thing to add is that most DVI connections on video cards these days natively support analog signals. You can use a simple DVI-to-VGA adapter, for example, for connecting a VGA cable to a video card.

 EXAM TIP The CompTIA A+ 801 exam might make a distinction between the VGA cable and the DB-15 connector into which it plugs.

Apple Mac desktop models use a *DisplayPort* connection rather than VGA or DVI for connecting to a monitor. Dell offers support for DisplayPort as well at the time of this writing. Figure 21-44 shows a DisplayPort jack on a Dell portable.

For Multimedia Devices

Video cards can have one or more standard connections plus non-standard connections for hooking the PC to a multimedia device, such as a television, DVD or Blu-ray Disc player, or video camera. The earliest type of connector commonly found is the mini-DIN for attaching an S-video cable. This provides decent-quality video output or, in some cases, input. You'll sometimes find a proprietary round connector that supports S-video and a proprietary dongle that adds support for video through either component connection or composite connections. Figure 21-45 shows the similar round ports.

Figure 21-44
DisplayPort jack

Figure 21-45
S-video and
proprietary round
connectors

S-video Proprietary

EXAM TIP CompTIA has pulled out all the stops on adding extra acronyms to your plate with connector types. The 220-801 exam objectives refer to the mini-DIN used with S-video as a *Din-6* (yes, with the weird initial capping of Din rather than DIN to refer to the acronym). Most techs refer to the port as an *S-video port*, but CompTIA seems to reserve the S-video label only to the cable.

A composite connector provides a video signal through a single cable that plugs into a standard RCA jack, whereas a component adapter provides a split signal: red, green, and blue (RGB). Figure 21-46 shows the two connector dongles. Note that all are RCA connectors.

Figure 21-46
Composite and
component con-
nection options

The best connections for outputting to television are the *High Definition Multimedia Interface (HDMI)* connectors. Some devices offer HDMI output directly (such as the portable pictured in Figure 21-47), while other video cards support HDMI through a special cable that connects to a dual-link DVI port. Figure 21-48 shows an example of such a cable.

Figure 21-47
HDMI port
between two USB
ports on Lenovo
laptop

Figure 21-48
DVI-to-HDMI cable

HDMI comes in three standard sizes, Standard, Mini, and Micro. (Plus there's the Type E connector used exclusively for automobile video systems—and don't we all need video while driving?) Standard HDMI is what you'll find on video cards and televisions and some portable devices. Most tablet devices out today use Mini HDMI (see Figure 21-49). See Chapter 27 for the discussion on tablets and other mobile devices.

Figure 21-49 Mini HDMI port

NOTE Some video cards with built-in TV tuners that enable the PC to be a TV as well as a computer have a standard coaxial jack for connecting a cable or antenna. See Chapter 25 for the scoop on TV tuners.

Installing and Configuring Video

Once you've decided on the features and price for your new video card and monitor, you need to install them into your system. As long as you have the right connection to your video card, installing a monitor is straightforward. The challenge comes when installing the video card.

During the physical installation of a video card, watch out for two possible issues: long cards and proximity of the nearest expansion card. Some high-end video cards simply won't fit in certain cases or block access to needed motherboard connectors such as the SATA sockets. There's no clean fix for such a problem—you simply have to change at least one of the components (video card, motherboard, or case). Because high-end video cards run very hot, you don't want them sitting right next to another card; make sure the fan on the video card has plenty of ventilation space. A good practice is to leave the slot next to the video card empty to allow better airflow (see Figure 21-50). (Many high-end video cards come as double-wide cards with built-in air vents, so you don't have any choice but to take up double the space.)

Figure 21-50
Installing a video card

Once you've properly installed the video card and connected it to the monitor, you've conquered half the territory for making the video process work properly. You're ready to tackle the drivers and tweak the operating system, so let's go!

Software

Configuring your video software is usually a two-step process. First you need to load drivers for the video card. Then you need to open the Control Panel and go to the Display applet (Windows XP/7) or Personalization applet (Windows Vista) to make your adjustments. Let's explore how to make the video card and monitor work in Windows.

Drivers

Just like any other piece of hardware, your video card needs a driver to function. Video card drivers install pretty much the same way as all of the other drivers we've discussed thus far: either the driver is already built into Windows or you must use the installation media that comes with the video card.

Video card makers are constantly updating their drivers. Odds are good that any video card more than a few months old has at least one driver update. If possible, check the manufacturer's Web site and use the driver located there if there is one. If the Web site doesn't offer a driver, it's usually best to use the installation media. Always avoid using the built-in Windows driver as it tends to be the most dated.

We'll explore driver issues in more detail after we discuss the Display and Personalization applets. Like so many things about video, you can't fully understand one topic without understanding at least one other!

802

Using the Display and Personalization Applets

With the driver installed, you're ready to configure your display settings. The Display applet or Personalization applet on the Control Panel is your next stop. The *Display applet* and *Personalization applet* provide convenient, central locations for all of your display settings, including resolution, refresh rate, driver information, and color depth.

The default Display applet window in Windows XP, called the Display Properties dialog box (see Figure 21-51), has five tabs: Themes, Desktop, Screen Saver, Appearance, and Settings. The first four tabs have options you can choose to change the look and feel of Windows and set up a screensaver; the fifth tab is where you make adjustments that relate directly to your monitor and video card.

The Personalization applet in Windows Vista offers functions similar to the Display applet, but each function manifests as a clickable option rather than as a separate tab (see Figure 21-52). Four of the seven options mirror the look and feel options of earlier versions of Windows, such as Window Color and Appearance, Desktop Background, Screen Saver, and Theme. The last option, Display Settings, is where you make adjustments to your monitor and video card. Two options, Sounds and Mouse Pointers, don't concern us at all at this time.

Figure 21-51
Display Proper-
ties dialog box in
Windows XP

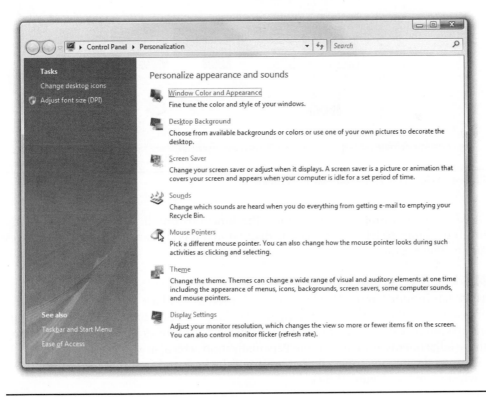

Figure 21-52 Personalization applet in Windows Vista

With Windows 7, Microsoft created a more visually oriented Personalization applet (see Figure 21-53). Most users typically want to change only their background or theme rather than anything else, so those options are front and center. Other options are in the Tasks panel on the left or in the Display applet, which is different than Windows XP's display applet.

Figure 21-53 Personalization applet in Windows 7

Whether discussing tabs or options, the functions on all three applets are pretty much the same, so let's do this in one discussion. I'll point out any serious differences among the versions.

Making the Screen Pretty

Three tabs/options in the Display/Personalization applet have the job of adjusting the appearance of the screen: Themes/Theme, Desktop/Desktop Background, and Appearance/Window Color and Appearance. Windows 7 simplifies this process by making those adjustments available on the Personalization screen, as you saw in Figure 21-53. Windows themes are preset configurations of the look and feel of the entire Windows environment (see Figure 21-54).

Figure 21-54 Theme option in the Windows Vista Personalization applet

The Desktop tab in Windows XP (see Figure 21-55) or Desktop Background link in Windows Vista/7 defines the background color or image. In Windows XP, it also includes the handy Customize Desktop button that enables you to define the icons as well as any Web pages you want to appear on the desktop. Windows Vista/7 give you the option to position the image on the screen (see Figure 21-56), and the *Change desktop icons* option in the Tasks list in the Personalization applet enables you to choose which system icons (such as Computer, Recycle Bin, and Network) show up on your desktop, as well as which graphical icons they use.

The last of the tabs for the look and feel of the desktop in Windows XP is the Appearance tab. Think of the Appearance tab as the way to fine-tune the theme to your liking. The main screen gives only a few options—the real power is when you click the Advanced button to open the Advanced Appearance dialog box (see Figure 21-57). Using this dialog box, you may adjust almost everything about the desktop, including the types of fonts and colors of every part of a window.

Figure 21-55
Desktop tab on
Display Properties
dialog box

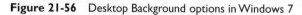
Figure 21-56 Desktop Background options in Windows 7

Figure 21-57
Advanced Appearance dialog box in Windows XP

The Window Color and Appearance option in Windows Vista is a little simpler on the surface, enabling you to change the color scheme, intensity, and transparency. Windows 7 shows similar controls following the Windows Color link (see Figure 21-58). You can unlock the full gamut of options, though, by clicking the *Open classic appearance properties for more color options* link in Windows Vista or *Advanced appearance settings* in Windows 7.

Screen Saver

At first glance, the Screen Saver tab/option seems to do nothing but set the Windows screensaver—no big deal, just about everyone has set a screensaver (see Figure 21-59). But another option on the Screen Saver tab gets you to one of the most important settings of your system: power management. Click on the Power button or *Change power settings* option to get to the Power Options Properties dialog box or Power Options applet (see Figure 21-60).

The tabs and options define all of the power management of the system. Power management is a fairly involved process, so we'll save the big discussion for where we need to save power the most: Chapter 26.

Figure 21-58
Window Color
and Appearance
options in
Windows 7

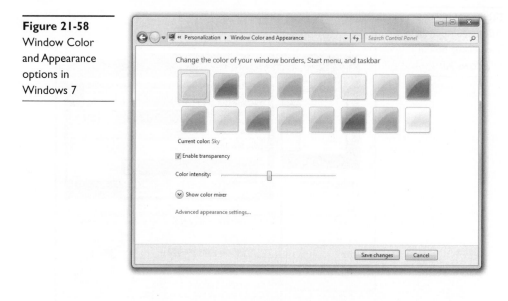

Figure 21-59
Screen Saver Set-
tings in Windows 7

Figure 21-60 Power Options applet in Windows 7

Settings Tab/Display Settings Applet/Display Applet

The Settings tab in Windows XP and the Display Settings applet in Windows Vista (see Figure 21-61) are the centralized location for configuring all of your video settings in Windows XP/Vista. From the main screen you can adjust both the resolution and the color depth. Windows only displays resolutions and color depths that your video card/monitor combination can accept and that are suitable for most situations. Everyone has a favorite resolution, and higher isn't always better. Especially for those with trouble seeing small screen elements, higher resolutions can present a difficulty—already small icons are *much* smaller at 1280 × 1024 than at 800 × 600. Try all of the resolutions to see which you like—just remember that LCD monitors look sharpest at their native resolution (usually the highest listed).

Clicking the Display link in the Tasks list of the Personalization applet in Windows 7 takes you to a simpler interface, again designed to give you quick access to only features you might commonly want to change. Changing the font size is centrally featured, but links in the top left of the task pane enable you to drill down to more advanced options, such as setting the color depth (see Figure 21-62).

Another option you may see in the Settings tab/Display Settings applet is multiple monitors. To see the same feature options in Windows 7, click the *Change display settings* link in the Display applet. Windows supports the use of two (or more) monitors. These monitors may work together like two halves of one large monitor, or the second monitor might simply show a duplicate of what's happening on the first monitor. Multiple monitors are handy if you need lots of screen space but don't want to buy a really large, expensive monitor (see Figure 21-63).

Figure 21-61 Display Settings applet and Settings tab

Figure 21-62 Display applet in Windows 7

Figure 21-63
My editor hard at
work with dual
monitors

There are two ways to set up multiple monitors: plug in two or more video cards or use a single video card that supports multiple monitors. Both methods are quite common and work well. Multiple monitors are easy to configure: just plug in the monitors and Windows should detect them. Windows will show the monitors in the applet, as shown in Figure 21-64 for Windows 7. By default, the second monitor is not enabled. To use the second monitor, just select *Extend my Windows desktop onto this monitor* in Windows XP, *Extend the desktop onto this monitor* in Windows Vista, or use the Multiple displays dropdown box and select *Extend these displays* in Windows 7.

Figure 21-64 Enabling multiple monitors

If you need to see more advanced settings, click on…that's right, the Advanced or Advanced Settings button in Windows XP/Vista, or on the Advanced settings link in the Screen Resolution dialog box in Windows 7. The title of the dialog box that opens reflects the monitor and video card. As you can see in Figure 21-65, this particular computer uses a pair of Samsung SyncMaster T220 monitors running off of an ATI Radeon 5750 video card.

Figure 21-65
Advanced video settings, Adapter tab

The two tabs you're most likely to use are the Adapter and Monitor tabs. The Adapter tab gives detailed information about the video card, including the amount of video memory, the graphics processor, and the BIOS information (yup, your video card has a BIOS, too!). You can also click on the List All Modes button to change the current mode of the video card, although any mode you may set here, you can also set in the sliders on the main screen.

If you're still using a CRT, you'll find the Monitor tab a handy place. This is where you can set the refresh rate (see Figure 21-66). Windows only shows refresh rates that the monitor says it can handle, but many monitors can take a faster—and therefore easier on the eyes—refresh rate. To see all of the modes the video card can support, uncheck the *Hide modes that this monitor cannot display* option.

Figure 21-66

Advanced video settings, Monitor tab

NOTE All LCD monitors have a fixed refresh rate.

If you try this, always increase the refresh rate in small increments. If the screen looks better, use it. If the screen seems distorted or disappears, wait a moment and Windows will reset to the original refresh rate. Be careful when using modes that Windows says the monitor cannot display. Pushing a CRT past its fastest refresh rate for more than a minute or two can damage it.

Most video cards add their own tab to the Advanced dialog box. In the case of the tab shown in Figure 21-67, you'd need to click on the Catalyst Control Center button to see more settings for the video card. What you see here varies by model of card and version of driver, but here's a list of some of the more interesting settings you might see.

Figure 21-67
Third-party
video tab

Color Correction Sometimes the colors on your monitor are not close enough for your tastes to the actual color you're trying to create. In this case you use color correction to fine-tune the colors on the screen to get the look you want.

Rotation All monitors are by default wider than they are tall. This is called *landscape mode*. Some LCD monitors can be physically rotated to facilitate users who like to see their desktops taller than they are wide (*portrait mode*). Figure 21-68 shows the author's LCD monitor rotated in portrait mode. If you want to rotate your screen, you must tell the system you're rotating it.

Modes Most video cards add very advanced settings to enable you to finely tweak your monitor. These very dangerous settings have names such as "sync polarity" or "front porch" and are outside the scope of both CompTIA A+ certification and the needs of all but the most geeky techs. These settings are mostly used to display a nonstandard resolution. Stay out of those settings!

Working with Drivers

Now that you know the locations of the primary video tools within the operating system, it's time to learn about fine-tuning your video. You need to know how to work with video drivers from within the Display (Windows XP/7) and Personalization (Windows Vista) applets, including how to update them, roll back updates, and uninstall them.

Figure 21-68
Portrait mode

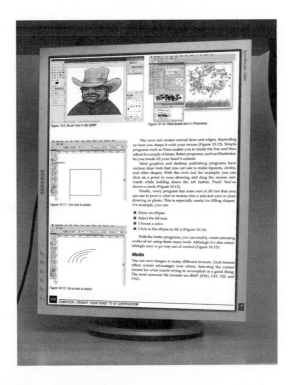

Windows is very persnickety when it comes to video card drivers. You can crash Windows and force a reinstallation simply by installing a new video card and not uninstalling the old card's drivers. This doesn't happen every time but certainly can happen. As a basic rule, always uninstall the old card's drivers before you install drivers for a new card.

When you update the drivers for a card, you have a choice of uninstalling the outdated drivers and then installing new drivers—which makes the process the same as for installing a new card—or you can let Windows flex some digital muscle and install the new ones right over the older drivers.

To update your drivers, go to the Control Panel and double-click the Display applet (Windows XP and Windows 7) or click the Personalization applet and click Display Settings (Windows Vista). In the Display Properties dialog box in Windows XP, select the Settings tab and click the Advanced button. In Windows Vista's Display Settings dialog box, select the Monitor tab and click the Advanced Settings button. In the Display applet for Windows 7, click *Change display settings* in the Tasks list and then click the *Advanced settings* link. In the dialog box that appears (all versions), click the Adapter tab and then click the Properties button. In the Properties dialog box for your adapter (see Figure 21-69), select the Driver tab and then click the Update Driver button to run the Hardware Update wizard.

Figure 21-69
Adapter Properties
dialog box

3-D Graphics

No other area of the PC world reflects the amazing acceleration of technological improvements more than *3-D graphics*—in particular, 3-D gaming—which attempts to create images with the same depth and texture as objects seen in the real world. We are spectators to an amazing new world where software and hardware race to produce new levels of realism and complexity displayed on the computer screen. Powered by the wallets of tens of millions of PC gamers always demanding more and better, the video industry constantly introduces new video cards and new software titles that make today's games so incredibly realistic and fun. Although the gaming world certainly leads the PC industry in 3-D technologies, many other PC applications—such as *Computer Aided Design* (*CAD*) programs—quickly snatch up these technologies, making 3-D more useful in many ways other than just games. In this section, we'll add to the many bits and pieces of 3-D video encountered over previous chapters in the book and put together an understanding of the function and configuration of 3-D graphics.

Before the early 1990s, PCs did not mix well with 3-D graphics. Certainly, many 3-D applications existed, primarily 3-D design programs such as AutoCAD and Intergraph, but these applications would often run only on expensive, specialized hardware—not so great for casual users.

The big change took place in 1992 when a small company called id Software created a new game called *Wolfenstein 3D* (see Figure 21-70). They launched an entirely new genre of games, now called *first-person shooters* (*FPSs*), in which the player looks out into a 3-D world, interacting with walls, doors, and other items, and shoots whatever bad guys the game provides.

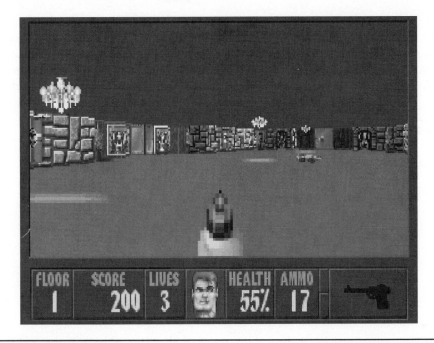

Figure 21-70 *Wolfenstein 3D*

Wolfenstein 3D shook the PC gaming world to its foundations. That this innovative format came from an upstart little company made *Wolfenstein 3D* and id Software into overnight sensations. Even though their game was demanding on hardware, they gambled that enough people could run it to make it a success. The gamble paid off for John Carmack and John Romero, the creators of id Software, making them the fathers of 3-D gaming.

Early 3-D games used fixed 3-D images called *sprites* to create the 3-D world. A sprite is nothing more than a bitmapped graphic such as a BMP file. These early first-person shooters would calculate the position of an object from the player's perspective and place a sprite to represent the object. Any single object had only a fixed number of sprites—if you walked around an object, you noticed an obvious jerk as the game replaced the current sprite with a new one to represent the new position. Figure 21-71 shows different sprites for the same bad guy in *Wolfenstein 3D*. Sprites weren't pretty, but they worked without seriously taxing the 486s and early Pentiums of the time.

Figure 21-71
Each figure had a
limited number of
sprites.

The second generation of 3-D games began to replace sprites with true 3-D objects, which are drastically more complex than sprites. A true 3-D object is composed of a group of points called *vertices*. Each vertex has a defined X, Y, and Z position in a 3-D world. Figure 21-72 shows the vertices for a video game character in a 3-D world.

Figure 21-72
Vertices for a video
game warrior

The computer must track all of the vertices of all of the objects in the 3-D world, including the ones you cannot currently see. Keep in mind that objects may be motionless in the 3-D world (a wall, for example), may have animation (such as a door opening and closing), or may be moving (like bad monsters trying to spray you with evil alien goo). This calculation process is called *transformation* and, as you might imagine, is extremely taxing to most CPUs. Intel's SIMD and AMD's 3DNow! processor extensions were expressly designed to perform transformations.

Once the CPU has determined the positions of all vertices, the system begins to fill in the 3-D object. The process begins by drawing lines (the 3-D term is *edges*) between vertices to build the 3-D object into many triangles. Why triangles? Well, mainly by consensus of game developers. Any shape works, but triangles make the most sense from a mathematical standpoint. I could go into more depth here, but that would require talking about trigonometry, and I'm gambling you'd rather not read that detailed a description! All 3-D games use triangles to connect vertices. The 3-D process then groups triangles into various shapes called *polygons*. Figure 21-73 shows the same model as Figure 21-72, now displaying all of the connected vertices to create a large number of polygons.

Figure 21-73
Connected vertices
forming polygons
on a 3-D character

Originally, the CPU handled these calculations to create triangles, but now special 3-D video cards do the job, greatly speeding up the process.

The last step in second-generation games was texturing. Every 3-D game stores a number of image files called *textures*. The program wraps textures around an object to give it a surface. Textures work well to provide dramatic detail without using a lot of triangles. A single object may take one texture or many textures, applied to single triangles or groups of triangles (polygons). Figure 21-74 shows the finished warrior.

Figure 21-74
Video game war-
rior with textures
added

True 3-D objects, more often referred to as *rendered*, immediately created the need for massively powerful video cards and much wider data buses. Intel's primary motivation for creating AGP was to provide a big enough pipe for massive data pumping between the video card and the CPU. Intel gave AGP the ability to read system RAM to support textures. If it weren't for 3-D games, AGP (and probably even PCIe) would almost certainly not exist.

3-D Video Cards

No CPU of the mid-1990s could ever hope to handle the massive processes required to render 3-D worlds. Keep in mind that to create realistic movement, the 3-D world must refresh at least 24 times per second. That means that this entire process, from transformation to texturing, must repeat once every 1/24th of a second! Furthermore, although the game re-creates each screen, it must also keep score, track the positions of all of the objects in the game, provide some type of intelligence to the bad guys, and so on. Something had to happen to take the workload off the CPU. The answer came from video cards.

Video cards were developed with smart onboard GPUs. The GPU helped the CPU by taking over some, and eventually all, of the 3-D rendering duties. These video cards not only have GPUs but also have massive amounts of RAM to store textures.

But a problem exists with this setup: How do we talk to these cards? This is done by means of a device driver, of course, but wouldn't it be great if we could create standard commands to speed up the process? The best thing to do would be to create a standardized set of instructions that any 3-D program could send to a video card to do all of the basic work, such as "make a cone" or "lay texture 237 on the cone you just made."

The video card instructions standards manifested themselves into a series of *application programming interfaces (APIs)*. In essence, an API is a library of commands that people who make 3-D games must use in their programs. The program currently using the video card sends API commands directly to the device driver. Device drivers must know how to understand the API commands. If you were to picture the graphics system of your computer as a layer cake, the top layer would be the program making a call to the video card driver that then directs the graphics hardware.

Several APIs have been developed over the years, with two clear winners among all of them: OpenGL and DirectX. The *OpenGL* standard was developed for UNIX systems but has since been *ported*, or made compatible with, a wide variety of computer systems, including Windows and Apple computers. As the demand for 3-D video became increasingly strong, Microsoft decided to throw its hat into the 3-D graphics ring with its own API, called DirectX. We look at DirectX in depth in the next section.

Although they might accomplish the same task (for instance, translating instructions and passing them on to the video driver), every API handles things just a little bit differently. In some 3-D games, the OpenGL standard might produce more precise images with less CPU overhead than the DirectX standard. In general, however, you won't notice a large difference between the images produced by OpenGL and DirectX.

DirectX and Video Cards

In the old days, many applications communicated directly with much of the PC hardware and, as a result, could crash your computer if not written well enough. Microsoft tried to fix this problem by placing all hardware under the control of Windows, but programmers balked because Windows added too much work for the video process and slowed down everything. For the most demanding programs, such as games, only direct access of hardware would work.

This need to "get around Windows" motivated Microsoft to unveil a new set of protocols called *DirectX*. Programmers use DirectX to take control of certain pieces of hardware and to talk directly to that hardware; it provides the speed necessary to play the advanced games so popular today. The primary impetus for DirectX was to build a series of products to enable Windows to run 3-D games. That's not to say that you couldn't run 3-D games in Windows *before* DirectX; rather, it's just that Microsoft wasn't involved in the API rat race at the time and wanted to be. Microsoft's goal in developing DirectX was to create a 100-percent stable environment, with direct hardware access, for running 3-D applications and games within Windows.

DirectX is not only for video; it also supports sound, network connections, input devices, and other parts of your PC. Each of these subsets of DirectX has a name, such as DirectDraw, Direct3D, or DirectSound.

- **DirectDraw** Supports direct access to the hardware for 2-D graphics
- **Direct3D** Supports direct access to the hardware for 3-D graphics—the most important part of DirectX
- **DirectInput** Supports direct access to the hardware for joysticks and other game controllers
- **DirectSound** Supports direct access to the hardware for waveforms
- **DirectMusic** Supports direct access to the hardware for MIDI devices
- **DirectPlay** Supports direct access to network devices for multiplayer games
- **DirectShow** Supports direct access to video and presentation devices

Microsoft constantly adds to and tweaks this list. As almost all games need DirectX and all video cards have drivers to support DirectX, you need to verify that DirectX is installed and working properly on your system. To do this, use the *DirectX Diagnostic Tool (dxdiag)*, as seen in Figure 21-75. In Windows XP, you can find it in the System Information program. After you open System Information (it usually lives in the Accessories | System Tools area of the Start menu), click the Tools menu and select DirectX Diagnostic Tool.

For Windows Vista/7, go to Start and type **dxdiag** in the Search bar. Press ENTER to run the program.

 EXAM TIP The CompTIA A+ 802 exam refers to the DirectX Diagnostic Tool only by its Run command, *dxdiag*.

The System tab gives the version of DirectX. The system pictured in Figure 21-75 runs DirectX 10.

Figure 21-75 The DirectX Diagnostic Tool

So, what does DirectX do for video cards? Back in the bad old days before DirectX became popular with the game makers, many GPU makers created their own chip-specific APIs. 3dfx had Glide, for example, and S3 had ViRGE. This made buying 3-D games a mess. There would often be multiple versions of the same game for each card. Even worse, many games never used 3-D acceleration because it was just too much work to support all of the different cards.

That all changed when Microsoft beefed up DirectX and got more GPU makers to support it. That in turn enabled the game companies to write games by using DirectX and have them run on any card out there. The bottom line: When Microsoft comes out with a new version of DirectX, all of the GPU companies hurry to support it or they will be left behind.

Trying to decide what video card to buy gives me the shakes—too many options! One good way to narrow down your buying decision is to see what GPU is hot at the moment. I make a point to check out these Web sites whenever I'm getting ready to buy, so I can see what everyone says is the best.

- http://arstechnica.com
- www.hardocp.com
- www.tomshardware.com
- www.sharkyextreme.com

Troubleshooting Video

People tend to notice when their monitors stop showing the Windows desktop, making video problems a big issue for technicians. Users might temporarily ignore a bad sound card or other device, but will holler like crazy when the screen doesn't look the way they expect. To fix video problems quickly, the best place to start is to divide your video problems into two groups: video cards/drivers and monitors.

Troubleshooting Video Cards/Drivers

Video cards rarely go bad, so the vast majority of video card/driver problems are bad or incompatible drivers or incorrect settings. Always make sure you have the correct driver installed. If you're using an incompatible driver, Windows defaults to good old 640 × 480, 16-color VGA mode or you might get a Blue Screen of Death (BSoD) as soon as Windows starts to load. A driver that is suddenly corrupted usually doesn't show the problem until the next reboot. If you reboot a system with a corrupted driver, Windows will do one of the following: go into VGA mode, blank the monitor, lock up, or display a garbled screen with weird color patterns or a very distorted image. Whatever the output, reboot into Safe mode and roll back or delete the driver. Keep in mind that more advanced video cards tend to show their drivers as installed programs under Add or Remove Programs in Windows XP or Programs and Features in Windows Vista/7, so always check there first before you try deleting a driver by using Device Manager. Download the latest driver and reinstall.

Video cards are pretty durable but they have two components that do go bad: the fan and the RAM. Lucky for you, if either of these goes out, it tends to show the same error—bizarre screen outputs followed shortly by a screen lockup. Usually Windows keeps running; you may see your mouse pointer moving around and windows refreshing, but the screen turns into a huge mess (see Figure 21-76).

Figure 21-76
Serious video
problem

Bad drivers sometimes also make this error, so always first try going into Safe mode to see if the problem suddenly clears up. If it does, you do not have a problem with the video card!

Excessive heat inside the case, even with the video card fan running at full blast, can create some interesting effects. The computer could simply shut down due to overheating. You'll recognize this possible cause because the computer will come back up in a minute or two, but then shut down again as you use it hard and it heats up again. Sometimes the screen will get bizarre artifacts or start distorting. Check your case fans and make sure nothing is too close to the video card. You might need to blow out (outdoors!) the dust from filters, vents, and fans.

The last and probably most common problem is nothing more than improperly configured video settings. Identifying the problem is just common sense—if your monitor is showing everything sideways, someone messed with your rotation settings; if your gorgeous wallpaper of a mountain pass looks like an ugly four-color cartoon, someone lowered the color depth. You'll need to reset the color depth to a more appropriate setting. In Windows XP, open the Display Properties. In Windows Vista, go to Personalization | Display Settings. In Windows 7, go to Display | Change display settings | Advanced settings, then open the Monitor tab.

The one serious configuration issue is pushing the resolution too high. If you adjust your resolution and then your monitor displays an error message such as "Input Signal Out of Range," just wait. Windows will automatically put your settings back after a few seconds if you don't click on anything.

Troubleshooting Monitors

Because of the inherent dangers of the high-frequency and high-voltage power required by monitors, and because proper adjustment requires specialized training, this section concentrates on giving a support person the information necessary to decide whether a trouble call is warranted. Virtually no monitor manufacturers make schematics of their monitors available to the public, because of liability issues regarding possible electrocution. To simplify troubleshooting, look at the process as three separate parts: common monitor problems, external adjustments, and internal adjustments.

Common Monitor Problems

Although I'm not super comfortable diving into the guts of a monitor, you can fix a substantial percentage of monitor problems yourself. The following list describes the most common monitor problems and tells you what to do—even when that means sending it to someone else.

- Almost all CRT and LCD monitors have replaceable controls. If the Brightness knob or Menu button stops working or seems loose, check with the manufacturer for replacement controls. They usually come as a complete package.

- For problems with ghosting, streaking, and/or fuzzy vertical edges, check the cable connections and the cable itself. These problems rarely apply to monitors; more commonly, they point to the video card.

- If one color is missing, check cables for breaks or bent pins. Check the front controls for that color. If the color adjustment is already maxed out, the monitor will require internal service.

- As monitors age, they lose brightness. If the brightness control is turned all of the way up and the picture seems dim, the monitor will require internal adjustment. This is a good argument for power-management functions. Use the power switch or the power-management options in Windows to turn off the monitor after a certain amount of time.

Common Problems Specific to CRTs

The complexity of CRTs compared to LCDs requires us to look at a number of monitor problems unique to CRTs. Most of these problems require opening the monitor, so be careful! When in doubt, take it to a repair shop.

- Most out-of-focus monitors can be fixed. Focus adjustments are usually on the inside, somewhere close to the flyback transformer. This is the transformer that provides power to the high-voltage anode.

- Hissing or sparking sounds are often indicative of an insulation rupture on the flyback transformer. This sound is usually accompanied by the smell of ozone. If your monitor has these symptoms, it definitely needs a qualified technician. Having replaced a flyback transformer once myself, I can say it is not worth the hassle and potential loss of life and limb.

- Big color blotches or discoloration on the display are an easy and cheap repair. Find the Degauss button and use it. If your monitor doesn't have a Degauss button, you can purchase a special tool called a degaussing coil at any electronics store.

- Bird-like chirping sounds occurring at regular intervals usually indicate a problem with the monitor power supply.

- Suppose you got a good deal on a used 19-inch monitor, but the display is kind of dark, even though you have the brightness turned up all the way. This dim image points to a dying CRT. So, how about replacing the CRT? Forget it. Even if the monitor was free, it just isn't worth it; a replacement tube runs into the hundreds of dollars. Nobody ever sold a monitor because it was too bright and too sharp. Save your money and buy a new monitor.

- If the monitor displays only a single horizontal or vertical line, the problem is probably between the main circuit board and the yoke, or a blown yoke coil. This definitely requires a service call.

- A single white dot on an otherwise black screen means the high-voltage flyback transformer is most likely shot. Take it into the repair shop.

External Adjustments

Monitor adjustments range from the simplest—brightness and contrast—to the more sophisticated—pincushioning and trapezoidal adjustments. The external controls provide users with the opportunity to fine-tune the monitor's image. Many monitors have controls for changing the tint and saturation of color, although plenty of monitors put those controls inside the monitor. Better monitors enable you to square up the visible portion of the screen with the monitor housing.

Finally, most monitors have the ability to *degauss* themselves with the push of a button. Over time, the shadow mask picks up a weak magnetic charge that interferes with the focus of the electron beams. This magnetic field makes the image look slightly fuzzy and streaked. Most monitors have a special built-in circuit called a *degaussing coil* to eliminate this magnetic buildup. When the degaussing circuit is used, an alternating current is sent through a coil of wire surrounding the CRT, and this current generates an alternating magnetic field that demagnetizes the shadow mask. You activate the degaussing coil by using the Degauss button or menu selection on the monitor. Degaussing usually makes a rather nasty thunk sound and the screen goes crazy for a moment—don't worry, that's normal.

 CAUTION Internal CRT adjustments should be left to the professional monitor techs.

Troubleshooting LCDs

With the proliferation of LCD panels in the computing world, PC techs need to have some understanding of what to do when they break. Some of the components you can fix, including replacing some of the internal components. I tend to use monitor repair shops for most LCD issues, but let's take a look.

An LCD monitor may have bad pixels. A bad pixel is any single pixel that does not react the way it should. A pixel that never lights up is a *dead pixel*, a pixel that is stuck on pure white is a lit pixel, and a pixel on a certain color is a stuck pixel. You cannot repair bad pixels; the panel must be replaced. All LCD panel makers allow a certain number of bad pixels, even on a brand-new LCD monitor! You need to check the warranty for your monitor and see how many they allow before you may return the monitor.

- If your LCD monitor cracks, it is not repairable and must be replaced.
- A flickering image with an LCD usually points to either a very inexpensive panel with too much light bleed from the backlight or a dying CCFL backlight. LEDs don't flicker, so you won't see this issue with those types of LCDs. Replace the backlight if necessary.
- A dim image, especially on only the top or bottom half of the screen, points to a dead or dying backlight in a multibacklight system. Replace as necessary.
- If the LCD goes dark but you can still barely see the image under bright lights, you lost either the backlight or the inverter. In many cases, especially with

super-thin panels, you'll replace the entire panel and backlight as a unit. On the other hand, an inverter can be on a separate circuit board that you can replace, such as the one pictured in Figure 21-77.

- If your LCD makes a distinct hissing noise, an inverter is about to fail. Again, you can replace the inverter if need be.

Figure 21-77
LCD components labeled

CCFL backlight

Power supply/inverters

Timing control

Main board/logic

Be careful if you open an LCD to work on the inside. The inverter can bite you in several ways. First, it's powered by a high-voltage electrical circuit that can give you a nasty shock. Worse, the inverter will retain a charge for a few minutes after you unplug it, so unplug and wait for a bit. Second, inverters get very hot and present a very real danger of burning you at a touch. Again, wait for a while after you unplug it to try to replace it. Finally, if you shock an inverter, you might irreparably damage it. So use proper ESD-avoidance techniques.

Bottom line on fixing LCD monitors? You can find companies that sell replacement parts for LCDs, but repairing an LCD is difficult, and there are folks who will do it for you faster and cheaper than you can. Search for a specialty LCD repair company. Hundreds of these companies exist all over the world.

Cleaning Monitors

Cleaning monitors is easy. Always use antistatic monitor wipes or at least a general anti-static cloth. Some LCD monitors may require special cleaning equipment. Never use window cleaners that contain ammonia or any liquid because getting liquid into the monitor may create a shocking experience! Many commercial cleaning solutions will also melt older LCD screens, which is never a good thing.

Safety Concerns

Aside from avoiding the inside of a CRT, the biggest safety issues involve moving and recycling monitors. Always practice good cable management, especially if you have the back of the monitor area exposed to traffic. One accidental hook of a monitor cable could cause it to come crashing to the floor. They don't do too well with impact.

CRTs are heavy, even the small ones, and the ones likely still in use are probably the graphics workstation 20+-inch units. Use proper lifting techniques (use your legs, not

your back) and be careful when you place the monitor on lighter-weight shelves or stands. Monitor stands all have weight limitations.

CompTIA is not much interested in mounting LCD monitors to wall mounts, but all of the wall mounts have fairly strict weight limitations as well. Don't hang that lovely new 24-inch panel on a mount designed to handle the weight of a 17-inch unit!

Finally, you should always take a monitor—CRT or LED—to a proper recycling center. They have toxic chemicals such as lead and mercury and should never be placed in a landfill.

Troubleshooting Playback

One of the odd "video" issues techs run into today is when a Blu-ray Disc or downloaded HD movie won't play and the user gets the error message that his or her display won't play that media. Figure 21-78 shows the dreaded message from iTunes that says you can't play the movie you just rented.

Figure 21-78
HDCP error

Note the fine print under the generic comment: ". . . display that supports HDCP." The HDCP part is the key here.

You'll recall from Chapter 13 the High-bandwidth Digital Content Protection (HDCP) standard that Intel created to help movie makers ensure copyright protection and stop pirates from stealing copyright-protected content. It's not just the monitor that must support HDCP; every part of the connection between the video card and the monitor must support it. The monitor that captured the screenshot in Figure 21-78 most assuredly is HDCP compliant, as is the video card. The error appeared because the monitor connects to the video card through a VGA cable.

Only HDMI, DVI, and DisplayPort cables support HDCP. VGA does not, which is one of the major differences among the standards. Note also that HDCP can bite you when using converters too, like Mini HDMI to Standard HDMI, so always check that as well.

Beyond A+

DLP

Digital Light Processing (*DLP*) displays use a chip covered in microscopically small mirrors (see Figure 21-79).

Figure 21-79
DLP chip (photo courtesy of Texas Instruments)

These individual mirrors move thousands of times per second toward and away from a light source. The more times per second they move toward a light source, the whiter the image; the fewer times they move, the grayer the image. See Figure 21-80 for a diagram of how the mirrors would appear in a microscopic close-up of the chip. The lamp projects through a color wheel onto the DLP chip. The DLP chip creates the image by moving the tiny mirrors, which in turn reflect onto the screen.

Figure 21-80
Microscopic close-up of DLP showing tiny mirrors—note that some are tilted.

DLP was very popular for a time in home theater systems, as it makes an amazingly rich image. DLP has had very little impact on PC monitors, but has had great success in projectors. DLP projectors are much more expensive than LCD projectors, but many customers feel the extra expense is worth the image quality.

Chapter Review

Questions

1. What do we call the time it takes to draw the entire screen and get the electron guns back to the upper-left corner?

 A. Horizontal refresh rate

 B. Horizontal redraw rate

 C. Vertical refresh rate

 D. Vertical redraw rate

2. What provides the illumination for LCD monitors?

 A. Backlights

 B. Inverter

 C. Lamp

 D. LCD panel

3. Which statement best describes the difference, if any, between CRT and LCD resolution?

 A. The CRT has a single native resolution; LCDs have no native resolution.

 B. The CRT has three native resolutions; LCDs have no native resolution.

 C. The CRT has no native resolution; LCDs have three native resolutions.

 D. The CRT has no native resolution; LCDs have a single native resolution.

4. Which typically uses more wattage?

 A. CRT

 B. DVI

 C. LCD

 D. VGA

5. What is WSXGA+ resolution?

 A. 1024 × 768

 B. 1280 × 1024

 C. 1680 × 1050

 D. 1920 × 1080

6. What is the processor on a video card called?

 A. CPU

 B. GPU

 C. GDDR

 D. MPU

7. What Microsoft API supports 3-D graphics?

 A. Active Desktop

 B. DirectX

 C. Glide

 D. OpenGL

8. Which two technologies are used for backlights in LCD monitors?

 A. CCFL and LED

 B. CCFL and LCD

 C. CCFL and AC

 D. HDMI and DisplayPort

9. A customer calls complaining that the movie he ordered from iTunes won't play on his second monitor because of an HDCP error. What could cause this problem?

 A. The second monitor connects via DisplayPort.

 B. The second monitor connects via DVI.

 C. The second monitor connects via HDMI.

 D. The second monitor connects via VGA.

10. A client calls complaining that his new LCD monitor is flickering. What is most likely the problem?

 A. The refresh rate is set too high.

 B. The refresh rate is set too low.

 C. The CCFL backlight is failing.

 D. The LED backlight is failing.

Answers

1. C. The amount of time it takes to draw the entire screen and get the electron guns back to the upper-left corner is called the vertical refresh rate.

2. A. The backlights provide the illumination for the LCD panel.

3. **D.** The CRT has no native resolution; LCDs have a single native resolution.

4. **A.** CRTs use a lot more wattage than LCDs.

5. **C.** WSXGA+ resolution is 1680 × 1050.

6. **B.** You'll typically see video card processors referred to as GPUs.

7. **B.** Microsoft makes the DirectX API to support 3-D programs.

8. **A.** Current LCD monitors use one of two competing backlight technologies, CCFL or LED.

9. **D.** VGA does not support HDCP.

10. **C.** LCD monitors have a fixed refresh rate, so the most likely cause here is that the CCFL backlight is failing. LED backlights don't flicker.

Local Area Networking

In this chapter, you will learn how to
- Install and troubleshoot structured cabling
- Explain the basics of TCP/IP
- Install and configure wired networks
- Troubleshoot wired networks

Networks dominate the modern computing environment. A vast percentage of businesses have PCs connected in a small local area network (LAN), and big businesses simply can't survive without connecting their many offices into a single wide area network (WAN). Even the operating systems of today demand networks. Windows XP, Vista, and 7, for example, come out of the box *assuming* you'll attach them to the Internet just to make them work past 30 days (product activation), and they get all indignant if you don't.

 NOTE This chapter only covers local area networks, such as a group of computers in a single office. We'll save connecting to the Internet for Chapter 24. But be ready! You need to understand everything in this chapter before you can take the next step and connect to the Internet.

Because networks are so common today, every good tech needs to know the basics of networking technology, operating systems, implementation, and troubleshooting. Accordingly, this chapter teaches you how to build and troubleshoot a basic network. First, let's move beyond the basic switch and UTP cable with RJ-45 connectors you saw in Chapter 5 and discover how real-world networks connect using alternatives to RJ-45, such as fiber. You'll see how professionals use a concept called "structured cabling" with wired networks to ensure their reliability and ease of use. I'll even show you the tools needed to make your own structured cable system.

The second part of this chapter gets down and dirty into TCP/IP and how Windows uses it in a typical network. I'll break down the TCP/IP protocol so you can appreciate how it works.

Next, we'll go through the process of setting up a small network from start to finish. This includes details on planning a network, installing and configuring NICs, setting up

switches, configuring TCP/IP—everything you need so that Windows will enable you to share folders, printers, libraries, and so on.

The chapter closes with a popular topic: troubleshooting a network. Windows comes with plenty of powerful tools to help you when the network stops functioning. I'll show you the tools and combine that with a troubleshooting process that helps you get a network up and running again.

NOTE Both exam competencies discuss TCP/IP in detail, so this chapter covers both sets of objectives.

801/802

Beyond Basic Ethernet Cabling

Ethernet is the dominant networking technology, and unshielded twisted-pair (UTP) wired Ethernet networks using RJ-45 connectors are the most dominant form of Ethernet. Back in Chapter 5, you got a very basic exposure to an Ethernet network, so now we can take things a bit deeper and look at more network technologies, starting with alternatives to UTP, touring some of the more unique devices you might see in a network, and learning about proper cabling.

EXAM TIP Know your cable types for the CompTIA A+ exams: STP, UTP, CAT 3, CAT 5, CAT 5e, and CAT 6. Recall the differences between plenum-grade cable and PVC-sheathed cables.

Alternative Connections

UTP is very popular, but Ethernet, as well as other types of networks, can use alternative cabling that you need to be able to identify. Every CompTIA A+ certified tech needs to know about fiber optic cabling and coaxial cable, so let's start there.

EXAM TIP You can hook two network cards directly together using a special UTP cable called a *crossover cable*. A crossover cable is a standard UTP cable with one RJ-45 connector using the 568A standard and the other using the 568B standard. This reverses the signal between sending and receiving wires and thus does the job of a hub or switch. Crossover cables work great as a quick way to network two PCs. You can purchase a crossover cable at any computer store.

Fiber Optic

Fiber optic cable is a very attractive way to transmit Ethernet network frames. First, because it uses light instead of electricity, fiber optic cable is immune to electrical problems such as lightning, short circuits, and static. Second, fiber optic signals travel much farther, 2000 meters or more (compared with 100 meters on UTP). Most fiber Ethernet networks use *62.5/125 multimode* fiber optic cable. All fiber Ethernet networks that use this type of cabling require two cables. Figure 22-1 shows three of the more common connectors used in fiber optic networks. Square *SC* connectors are shown in the middle and on the right, and the round *ST* connector is on the left.

Figure 22-1

Typical fiber optic cables with connectors

Like many other fiber optic connectors, the SC and ST connectors are half-duplex, meaning data flows only one way—hence the need for two cables in a fiber installation. Newer and higher-end fiber installations use connectors with names like LC or MT-RJ.

Multimode and Single-Mode Light can be sent down a fiber optic cable as regular light or as laser light. Each type of light requires totally different fiber optic cables. Most network technologies that use fiber optics use light-emitting diodes (LEDs) to send light signals. These use *multimode* fiber optic cabling. Multimode fiber transmits multiple light signals at the same time, each using a different reflection angle within the core of the cable. The multiple reflection angles tend to disperse over long distances, so multimode fiber optic cables are used for relatively short distances.

EXAM TIP Know fiber connector types and the difference between multi-mode and single-mode fiber.

Network technologies that use laser light use *single-mode* fiber optic cabling. Using laser light and single-mode fiber optic cables allows for phenomenally high transfer rates over long distances. Except for long-distance links, single-mode is currently quite rare; if you see fiber optic cabling, you can be relatively sure it is multimode.

There are close to 100 different Ethernet fiber optic cabling standards, with names like 1000BaseSX and 10GBaseSR. The major difference is the speed of the network (there are also some important differences in the way systems interconnect, and so on). If you want to use fiber optic cabling, you need a fiber optic switch and fiber optic network cards, and they're not cheap. The fiber optic cabling itself is delicate, expensive, and difficult to use, so it is usually reserved for use in data centers and is rarely used to connect desktop PCs.

Fiber networks follow the speed and distance limitations of their networking standard, so it's hard to pin down precise numbers on true limitations. Multimode overall is slower and has a shorter range than single-mode. A typical multimode network runs at 10, 100, or 1000 Mbps, though some can go to 10,000 Mbps. Distances for multimode runs generally top out at ~600 meters. With single-mode, speed and distance—depending on the standard—can blow multimode away. The record transmission speed in 2011, for example, was 100 *terabits* per second and that was over 100 *miles*!

 EXAM TIP There are a number of Ethernet standards that use fiber optic cable instead of UTP.

Coax/BNC

Early versions of Ethernet ran on *coaxial cable* instead of UTP. While the Ethernet standards using coax are long gone, coax lives on in the networking world, primarily for cable modems and satellite connections. Coax cable consists of a center cable (core) surrounded by insulation. This in turn is covered with a *shield* of braided cable (see Figure 22-2). The center core actually carries the signal. The shield effectively eliminates outside interference. The entire cable is then surrounded by a protective insulating cover.

Figure 22-2
Typical coax

Coax cables are rated using an RG name. There are hundreds of RG ratings for coax, but the only two you need to know for the CompTIA A+ exams are RG-59 and RG-6. Both standards are rated by impedance, which is measured in ohms. Both RG-6 and RG-59 have a 75-ohm impedance. Both of these coax cables are used by your cable television, but RG-59 is thinner and doesn't carry data quite as far as RG-6. The RG rating is clearly marked on the cable.

Coax most commonly uses two different types of connectors. A BNC connector (see Figure 22-3) uses a quarter twist connector, and an F-type connector uses a screw connector. BNC is uncommon, but F-type is on the back of all cable modems and most televisions (see Figure 22-4).

EXAM TIP There is no hard limit to how fast coaxial cable can transmit data. Most cable broadband Internet implementations, however, top out at around 50 Mbps.

Figure 22-3
BNC connector

Figure 22-4
F-type connector

Network Devices

Back in Chapter 5 you read about hubs, switches, and routers. Let's do a quick review and add a few other devices.

Hubs

Hubs were the main interconnection for older Ethernet networks (see Figure 22-5). Any incoming signal on any port on a hub is re-created (repeated) and sent out on every connected port on the hub. The downside to hubs is that all connected devices have to share the total bandwidth. Hubs are extremely rare today, having been replaced by switches.

Figure 22-5 Typical hubs

Switches

Switches are the current most common interconnection for Ethernet networks (see Figure 22-6). A *switch* looks like a hub, but a switch automatically creates point-to-point connections between any two computers. By separating every connection, each computer can use the full bandwidth of the switch.

Figure 22-6
Typical switch

Bridges

If someone knows Morse code, it doesn't matter what medium you use to communicate the patterns of a coded method. You can blink a flashlight in his or her face, beat on a bongo drum, or tap into a telegraph machine: the person will understand the

code. Ethernet functions similarly. The code for Ethernet is the same no matter what medium transfers that message. That means you can easily connect two Ethernet networks that use completely different media internally, such as UTP to fiber or maybe UTP to wireless. In these cases you need a device called a bridge. A *bridge* will always have two interfaces, one interface for each of the different media (see Figure 22-7).

Figure 22-7
Typical bridge

Networked Attached Storage (NAS)

You already know that networks enable you to share files and services with multiple PCs. In most cases, network administrators store files on a server system. This server might be a dedicated file server—a machine running Windows Server 2008 R2, for example—or it might just be someone's regular Windows machine with a shared folder. You can also use a *networked attached storage* (*NAS*) system. A NAS is basically a headless system (no monitor, no keyboard, and no mouse) that you plug into a network (Figure 22-8). A NAS is almost totally self-configuring, requiring only a name and network type (domain/workgroup).

Understand that a NAS only does one thing: share its hard drives. Almost all NAS devices use some form of Web interface for configuration, enabling you to control the NAS from a Web browser on any PC in the network.

There are hundreds of different NAS solutions to choose from. For most people, the big criteria are storage capacity, RAID options, and ease of configuration.

NOTE We tend to use the term *network appliance* for any headless computer (that is, one with no direct interface) designed to do very specific duties. A NAS box is a perfect example of a network appliance.

Figure 22-8
Typical NAS

Routers

A *router* connects LANs together using the TCP/IP protocol. By definition, a router must have at least two connections—one into a network, and one out to another network. Some more powerful routers have many more connections. Figure 22-9 shows a typical home router.

Figure 22-9 Typical home router

The CompTIA A+ exams assume you have a basic understanding of how routers work. To detail the process, I'll need to dive a bit deeper into TCP/IP. Check out the "TCP/IP" section later in this chapter.

 EXAM TIP The CompTIA A+ exams expect you to know the differences between hubs, routers, switches, bridges, and access points.

Structured Cabling

If you want a functioning, dependable, real-world network, you need a solid understanding of a set of standards collectively called *structured cabling*. These standards, defined by the Telecommunications Industry Association/Electronic Industries Alliance (TIA/EIA)—yes, the same folks who tell you how to crimp an RJ-45 onto the end of a

UTP cable—give professional cable installers detailed standards on every aspect of a cabled network, from the type of cabling to use to standards on running cable in walls, even the position of wall outlets.

The CompTIA A+ exams require you to understand the basic concepts involved in installing network cabling and to recognize the components used in a network. The CompTIA A+ exams do not, however, expect you to be as knowledgeable as a professional network designer or cable installer. Your goal should be to understand enough about real-world cabling systems to communicate knowledgeably with cable installers and to perform basic troubleshooting. Granted, by the end of this section, you'll know enough to try running your own cable (I certainly run my own cable), but consider that knowledge extra credit.

The idea of structured cabling is to create a safe, reliable cabling infrastructure for all of the devices that may need interconnection. Certainly this applies to computer networks, but also to telephone, video—anything that might need low-power, distributed cabling.

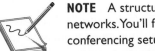

NOTE A structured cabling system is useful for more than just computer networks. You'll find structured cabling defining telephone networks and video conferencing setups, for example.

You should understand three issues with structured cabling. Cable basics start the picture, with switches, cabling, and PCs. You'll then look at the components of a network, such as how the cable runs through the walls and where it ends up. This section wraps up with an assessment of connections leading outside your network.

Cable Basics—A Star Is Born

Back in Chapter 5 we developed the idea of a LAN in its most basic configurations: a switch, some UTP cable, and a few PCs—in other words, a typical physical star network (see Figure 22-10).

Figure 22-10 A switch connected by UTP cable to two PCs

No law of physics prevents you from placing a switch in the middle of your office and running cables on the floor to all the computers in your network. This setup works, but it falls apart spectacularly when applied to a real-world environment. Three problems present themselves to the network tech. First, the exposed cables running along the floor are just waiting for someone to trip over them, giving that person a wonderful

lawsuit opportunity. Simply moving and stepping on the cabling will, over time, cause a cable to fail due to wires breaking or RJ-45 connectors ripping off cable ends. Second, the presence of other electrical devices close to the cable can create interference that confuses the signals going through the wire. Third, this type of setup limits your ability to make any changes to the network. Before you can change anything, you have to figure out which cables in the huge rat's nest of cables connected to the switch go to which machines. Imagine *that* troubleshooting nightmare!

"Gosh," you're thinking (okay, I'm thinking it, but you should be, too), "there must be a better way to install a physical network." A better installation would provide safety, protecting the star from vacuum cleaners, clumsy coworkers, and electrical interference. It would have extra hardware to organize and protect the cabling. Finally, the new and improved star network installation would feature a cabling standard with the flexibility to enable the network to grow according to its needs and then to upgrade when the next great network technology comes along. That is the definition of structured cabling.

Structured Cable Network Components

Successful implementation of a basic structured cabling network requires three essential ingredients: a telecommunications room, horizontal cabling, and a work area. Let's zero in on one floor of a typical office. All the cabling runs from individual PCs to a central location, the *telecommunications room* (see Figure 22-11). What equipment goes in there—a switch or a telephone system—is not the important thing. What matters is that all the cables concentrate in this one area.

Figure 22-11
Telecommunica-tions room

Telecommunications room

All cables run horizontally (for the most part) from the telecommunications room to the PCs. This cabling is called, appropriately, *horizontal cabling*. A single piece of installed horizontal cabling is called a *run*. At the opposite end of the horizontal cabling from the telecommunications room is the work area. The *work area* is often simply an office or cubicle that potentially contains a PC and a telephone. Figure 22-12 shows both the horizontal cabling and work areas.

Figure 22-12
Horizontal cabling and work area

Horizontal cabling

Work area

Each of the three parts of a basic star network—the telecommunications room, the horizontal cabling, and the work area(s)—must follow a series of strict standards designed to ensure that the cabling system is reliable and easy to manage. The cabling standards set by TIA/EIA enable techs to make sensible decisions on equipment installed in the telecommunications room, so let's tackle horizontal cabling first, and then return to the telecommunications room. We'll finish up with the work area.

Horizontal Cabling A horizontal cabling run is the cabling that goes more or less horizontally from a work area to the telecommunications room. In most networks, this cable is a CAT 5e or better UTP, but when you move into structured cabling, the TIA/EIA standards define a number of other aspects of the cable, such as the type of wires, number of pairs of wires, and fire ratings.

EXAM TIP A single piece of cable that runs from a work area to a telecommunications room is called a *run*. In most networks, this cable is CAT 5e or better UTP.

Solid Core Versus Stranded Core All UTP cables come in one of two types: solid core or stranded core. Each wire in *solid core* UTP uses a single solid wire. With *stranded core*, each wire is actually a bundle of tiny wire strands. Each of these cable types has its benefits and downsides. Solid core is a better conductor, but it is stiff and will break if handled too often or too roughly. Stranded core is not quite as good a conductor, but it will stand up to substantial handling without breaking. Figure 22-13 shows a close-up of solid and stranded core UTP.

Figure 22-13
Solid and stranded core UTP

TIA/EIA specifies that horizontal cabling should always be solid core. Remember, this cabling is going into your walls and ceilings, safe from the harmful effects of shoes and vacuum cleaners. The ceilings and walls enable you to take advantage of the better conductivity of solid core without the risk of cable damage. Stranded cable also has an important function in a structured cabling network, but I need to discuss a few more parts of the network before I talk about where to use stranded UTP cable.

The Telecommunications Room

The telecommunications room is the heart of the basic star. This room is where all the horizontal runs from all the work areas come together. The concentration of all this gear in one place makes the telecommunications room potentially one of the messiest parts of the basic star. Even if you do a nice, neat job of organizing the cables when they are first installed, networks change over time. People move computers, new work areas are added, network topologies are added or improved, and so on. Unless you impose some type of organization, this conglomeration of equipment and cables decays into a nightmarish mess.

Fortunately, the TIA/EIA structured cabling standards define the use of specialized components in the telecommunications room that make organizing a snap. In fact, it might be fair to say that there are too many options! To keep it simple, we're going to stay with the most common telecommunications room setup and then take a short peek at some other fairly common options.

Equipment Racks The central component of every telecommunications room is one or more equipment racks. An *equipment rack* provides a safe, stable platform for all the different hardware components. All equipment racks are 19 inches wide, but they vary in height from two- to three-foot-high models that bolt onto a wall (see Figure 22-14) to the more popular floor-to-ceiling models (see Figure 22-15).

Figure 22-14
A short equipment rack

Figure 22-15
A floor-to-ceiling rack

NOTE Equipment racks evolved out of the railroad signaling racks from the 19th century. The components in a rack today obviously differ a lot from railroad signaling, but the 19-inch width has remained the standard for well over 100 years.

You can mount almost any network hardware component into a rack. All manufacturers make rack-mounted switches that mount into a rack with a few screws. These switches are available with a wide assortment of ports and capabilities. There are even rack-mounted servers, complete with slide-out keyboards, and rack-mounted uninterruptible power supplies (UPSs) to power the equipment (see Figure 22-16).

Figure 22-16 A rack-mounted UPS

All rack-mounted equipment uses a height measurement known simply as a *U*. A U is 1.75 inches. A device that fits in a 1.75-inch space is called a 1U; a device designed for a 3.5-inch space is a 2U; and a device that goes into a 7-inch space is called a 4U. Most rack-mounted devices are 1U, 2U, or 4U. The rack in Figure 22-15 is called a 42U rack to reflect the total number of Us it can hold.

Patch Panels and Cables Ideally, once you install horizontal cabling, you should never move it. As you know, UTP horizontal cabling has a solid core, making it pretty stiff. Solid core cables can handle some rearranging, but if you insert a wad of solid core cables directly into your switches, every time you move a cable to a different port on the switch, or move the switch itself, you will jostle the cable. You don't have to move a solid core cable many times before one of the solid copper wires breaks, and there goes a network connection!

Luckily for you, you can easily avoid this problem by using a patch panel. A *patch panel* is simply a box with a row of female connectors (ports) in the front and permanent connections in the back, to which you connect the horizontal cables (see Figure 22-17).

Figure 22-17 Typical patch panels

The most common type of patch panel today uses a special type of connecter called a *110 block*, or sometimes a *110-punchdown block*. UTP cables connect to a 110 block using a *punchdown tool*. Figure 22-18 shows a typical punchdown tool, and Figure 22-19 shows the punchdown tool punching down individual strands.

Figure 22-18
Punchdown tool

Figure 22-19
Punching down a
110 block

The punchdown block has small metal-lined grooves for the individual wires. The punchdown tool has a blunt end that forces the wire into the groove. The metal in the groove slices the cladding enough to make contact.

EXAM TIP The CompTIA A+ exams expect you to know that a punchdown tool is used for securing UTP connections to a punchdown block. It's not until you go for CompTIA Network+ certification that you'll be expected to know how to use these tools.

Not only do patch panels prevent the horizontal cabling from being moved, but they are also your first line of defense in organizing the cables. All patch panels have space in the front for labels, and these labels are the network tech's best friend! Simply place a tiny label on the patch panel to identify each cable, and you will never have to experience that sinking feeling of standing in the telecommunications room of your nonfunctioning network, wondering which cable is which. If you want to be a purist, there is an official, and rather confusing, TIA/EIA labeling methodology called TIA/EIA 606, but a number of real-world network techs simply use their own internal codes (see Figure 22-20).

Figure 22-20
Typical patch panels with labels

Patch panels are available in a wide variety of configurations that include different types of ports and numbers of ports. You can get UTP, STP, or fiber ports, and some manufacturers combine several different types on the same patch panel. Panels are available with 8, 12, 24, 48, or even more ports.

UTP patch panels, like UTP cables, come with CAT ratings, which you should be sure to check. Don't blow a good CAT 6 cable installation by buying a cheap patch panel—get a CAT 6 patch panel! A higher-rated panel supports earlier standards, so you can use a CAT 6 or even CAT 6a rack with CAT 5e cabling. Most manufacturers proudly display the CAT level right on the patch panel (see Figure 22-21).

Once you have installed the patch panel, you need to connect the ports to the switch through *patch cables*. Patch cables are short (typically two- to five-foot) UTP cables. Patch cables use stranded rather than solid cable, so they can tolerate much more handling. Even though you can make your own patch cables, most people buy premade ones. Buying patch cables enables you to use different-colored cables to facilitate organization (yellow for accounting, blue for sales, or whatever scheme works for you). Most prefabricated patch cables also come with a reinforced (booted) connector specially designed to handle multiple insertions and removals (see Figure 22-22).

Figure 22-21
CAT level on patch panel

Figure 22-22
Typical patch cable

Making Your Own Patch Cables Although most people prefer simply to purchase premade patch cables, making your own is fairly easy. To make your own, use stranded UTP cable that matches the CAT level of your horizontal cabling. Stranded cable also requires specific crimps, so don't use crimps designed for solid cable. Crimping is simple enough, although getting it right takes some practice.

Figure 22-23 shows the two main tools of the crimping trade: an RJ-45 crimper with built-in wire stripper and a pair of wire snips. Professional cable installers naturally have a wide variety of other tools as well.

 EXAM TIP The CompTIA A+ exams expect you to know that a cable tech uses a crimper or crimping tool to attach an RJ-45 to the end of a UTP cable.

Figure 22-23
Crimper and snips

Here are the steps for properly crimping an RJ-45 onto a UTP cable. If you have some crimps, cable, and a crimping tool handy, follow along!

1. Cut the cable square using RJ-45 crimpers or scissors.
2. Strip off one-half inch of plastic jacket from the end of the cable (see Figure 22-24).

Figure 22-24
Properly stripped cable

3. Slowly and carefully insert each individual wire into the correct location according to either TIA/EIA 568A or B (see Figure 22-25). Unravel as little as possible.

Figure 22-25
Inserting the individual strands

4. Insert the crimp into the crimper and press (see Figure 22-26). Don't worry about pressing too hard; the crimper has a stop to prevent you from using too much pressure.

Figure 22-26
Crimping the cable

Figure 22-27 shows a nicely crimped cable. Note how the plastic jacket goes into the crimp.

A good patch cable should include a boot. Figure 22-28 shows a boot being slid onto a newly crimped cable. Don't forget to slide each boot onto the patch cable *before* you crimp both ends!

Figure 22-27
Properly crimped cable

Figure 22-28
Adding a boot

After making a cable, you need to test it to make sure it's properly crimped. We use a handy cable tester (a kind of multimeter), available in any good electronics store, to verify all the individual wires are properly connected and in the correct location (see Figure 22-29).

The Work Area

From a cabling standpoint, a work area is nothing more than a wall outlet that serves as the termination point for horizontal network cables: a convenient insertion point for a PC and a telephone. (In practice, of course, the term "work area" includes the office or cubicle.) A wall outlet itself consists of one or two female jacks to accept the cable, a mounting bracket, and a faceplate. You connect the PC to the wall outlet with a patch cable (see Figure 22-30).

Figure 22-29

Typical tester

Figure 22-30

Typical work area
outlet

The female RJ-45 jacks in these wall outlets also have CAT ratings. You must buy CAT-rated jacks for wall outlets to go along with the CAT rating of the cabling in your network. In fact, many network connector manufacturers use the same connectors, often 110 punchdowns, in the wall outlets that they use on the patch panels (see Figure 22-31). These modular outlets significantly increase the ease of installation.

The last step is connecting the PC to the wall outlet. Here again, most folks use a patch cable. Its stranded cabling stands up to the abuse caused by moving PCs, not to mention the occasional kick.

The work area may be the simplest part of the structured cabling system, but it is also the source of most network failures. When a user can't access the network and you suspect a broken cable, the first place to look is the work area.

Figure 22-31
Punching down a
modular jack

TCP/IP

The *Transmission Control Protocol/Internet Protocol (TCP/IP)* is the primary protocol of most modern networks, including the Internet. For a PC to access the Internet, it must have TCP/IP loaded and configured properly. TCP/IP has become so predominant that most network folks use it even on networks that do not connect to the Internet. Although TCP/IP is powerful, it is also a bit of a challenge to set up. So whether you are installing a modem for a dial-up connection to the Internet or setting up 500 computers on their own private *intranet*, you must understand some TCP/IP basics. You'll go through the following basic sections of the protocol and then you'll look at specific steps to install and configure TCP/IP.

Network Addressing

Any network address must provide two pieces of information: it must uniquely identify the machine and it must locate that machine within the larger network. In a TCP/IP network, the IP address identifies the PC and the network on which it resides. If you look at an IP address, it's not apparent which part of the address identifies the network and which part is the unique identifier of the computer. Let's review IP addresses and then see how they identify PCs and networks.

IP Addresses

In Chapter 5, you learned that TCP/IP networks don't identify PCs by name but by IP address. The *IP address* is the unique identification number for your system on the network. IP addresses consist of four sets of eight binary numbers (octets), each set

separated by a period. This is called *dotted-decimal notation*. So, instead of a computer being called SERVER1, it gets an address like so:

202.34.16.11

Written in binary form, the address would look like this:

```
11001010.00100010.00010000.00001011
```

To make the addresses more comprehensible to users, the TCP/IP folks decided to write the decimal equivalents:

```
00000000 = 0
00000001 = 1
00000010 = 2
...
11111111 = 255
```

Subnet Mask

Part of every IP address identifies the network (the network ID), and another part identifies the local computer (the host ID, or host) on the network. A NIC uses a value called the *subnet mask* to distinguish which part of the IP address identifies the network ID and which part of the address identifies the host. The subnet mask blocks out (or masks) the network portion of an IP address.

Let's look at a typical subnet mask: 255.255.255.0. When you compare the subnet mask to the IP address, any part that's all 255s is the network ID. Any part that's all zeros is the host ID. Look at the following example:

IP address: 192.168.4.33

Subnet mask: 255.255.255.0

Because the first thee octets are 255, the network ID is 192.168.4 and the host ID is 33.

Every computer on a single LAN must have the same network ID and a unique host ID. That means every computer on the preceding network must have an IP address that starts with 192.168.4. Every computer on the network must have a unique IP address. If two computers have the same IP address, they won't be able to talk to each other, and other computers won't know where to send data. This is called an *IP conflict*.

You can never have an IP address that ends with a 0 or a 255, so for the preceding example, we can have addresses starting at 192.168.4.1 and ending at 192.168.4.254: a total of 254 addresses. But what if you have more than 254 computers? Well, you just take a 255 out of the subnet mask like this:

255.255.0.0

If the IP address is 192.168.4.33, then we now have a network ID of 192.168 and a host of 4.33. We can have addresses ranging from 192.168.0.1 to 192.168.255.254. (Notice the 0 and the 255? You can have 0s and 255s in an IP address, just not at the end of the IP address.)

So how many addresses can you have now? Well, let's count them out:

192.168.0.1

192.168.0.2

...

192.168.0.254

192.168.1.1

192.168.1.2

...

192.168.255.253

192.168.255.254

You would have a total of 65,534 addresses on your network. So with a subnet mask of 255.255.255.0, you get 254 addresses and a network ID of 192.168.4; and with a subnet mask of 255.255.0.0, you get 65,534 addresses and a network ID of 192.168. That just leaves one big question: who picks the network ID?

Class Licenses

The folks who organized IP addressing way back in the 1970s came up with a way to pass out network IDs using something called *class licenses*. IP addresses are divided into class licenses that correspond with the potential size of the network: Class A, Class B, and Class C. Class A licenses were intended for huge companies and organizations, such as major multinational corporations, universities, and governmental agencies. Class B licenses were assigned to medium-size companies, and Class C licenses were designated for smaller LANs.

Class A networks use the first octet to identify the network address and the remaining three octets to identify the host. Class B networks use the first two octets to identify the network address and the remaining two octets to identify the host. Class C networks use the first three octets to identify the network address and the last octet to identify the host. Table 22-1 lists range (class) assignments.

Network Class	Address Range	No. of Network Addresses Available	No. of Host Nodes (Computers) Supported
A	1–126	129	16,777,214
B	128–191	16,384	65,534
C	192–223	2,097,152	254

Table 22-1 Class A, B, and C Addresses

You'll note that the IP address ranges listed in Table 22-1 skip from 126.x.x.x to 128.x.x.x. That's because the 127 address range (i.e., 127.0.0.0–127.255.255.255) is reserved for network testing (loopback) operations. (We usually just use the address 127.0.0.1 for loopback purposes and call it the *localhost* address, but any address that starts with *127* will work just as well.) That's not the only reserved range, either! Each network class has a specific IP address range reserved for *private* networks—traffic from

these networks doesn't get routed to the Internet at large. Class A's private range goes from 10.0.0.0 to 10.255.255.255. Class B has two private address ranges: 172.16.0.0 up to 172.31.255.254 for private addresses and 169.254.0.0 to 169.254.255.254 to accommodate the *Automatic Private IP Addressing (APIPA)* function (discussed later in the chapter). Class C's private addresses range from 192.168.0.0 to 192.168.255.254.

NOTE Pinging the loopback is the best way to test whether a NIC is working properly. To test a NIC's loopback, the other end of the cable must be in a working switch or you must use a loopback device such as a loopback adapter/plug.

NOTE Private IP addresses are very commonly used on LANs. But if private IP addresses are blocked by routers, how can we use them if we want to get on the Internet? It's a neat little trick called NAT, which you'll learn about in Chapter 24.

The default subnet mask for Class A addresses is 255.0.0.0; for Class B, it's 255.255.0.0; and for Class C, 255.255.255.0. For example, in the Class B IP address 131.190.4.121 with a subnet mask of 255.255.0.0, the first two octets (131.190) make up the network ID, and the last two (4.121) make up the host ID.

Interconnecting Networks with Routers

Now that you have a basic understanding of IP addressing, let's go back and watch a router in action. Let's take a look at a typical network: four computers and a networked printer all connected to a single switch (see Figure 22-32).

Figure 22-32 Typical network

When network nerds draw out a network, they tend not to draw every device. Instead, they make a circle with the network ID and the subnet mask, as shown in Figure 22-33.

Figure 22-33
Same network
shown as a circle

Network ID: 192.168.11.x
Subnet mask: 255.255.255.0

If you have two networks, just make two circles. Routers read IP addresses of incoming traffic and forward the traffic to the proper port. Since routers interconnect network IDs, we draw routers as boxes between networks, as shown in Figure 22-34

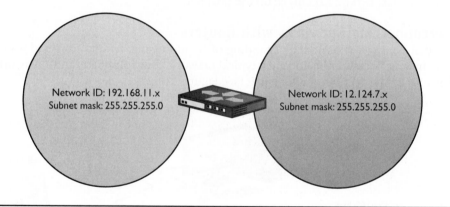

Network ID: 192.168.11.x
Subnet mask: 255.255.255.0

Network ID: 12.124.7.x
Subnet mask: 255.255.255.0

Figure 22-34 Router between two networks

To make a router connect two networks requires a configuration process. There are a lot of different routers out there, from cheap home routers to multimillion-dollar routers that connect the big pipes of the Internet. The CompTIA A+ exams only test on a few basic settings on simple home routers. While we'll save the real configuration of routers for Chapter 24, there's one thing that's very important to understand now: every port on a router is a member of a different network ID. Let's zoom in on the router in Figure 22-34 and see how the ports are set up, as shown in Figure 22-35. Note that each router gets the first address in the network ID. This isn't a law of physics, just good

manners. Keep in mind that the IP address for the router is usually the default gateway for all the computers for that network.

Figure 22-35 Router graphic in detail

NOTE Besides the physical ports on your computer and router, a networking port is also a 16-bit number (between 0 and 65,535) assigned to a TCP/IP session (or connection). The port number determines the software protocol used and how to handle the data packet. You'll learn more about ports in Chapter 24.

TCP/UDP

When moving data from one system to another, the TCP/IP protocol suite needs to know if the communication is connection-oriented or connectionless. When you want to be positive that the data moving between two systems gets there in good order, use a connection-oriented application. If it's not a big deal for data to miss a bit or two, then connectionless is the way to go. The connection-oriented protocol used with TCP/IP is called the *Transmission Control Protocol* (*TCP*). The connectionless one is called the *User Datagram Protocol* (*UDP*).

Let me be clear: you don't *choose* TCP or UDP. The people who developed the applications decide which protocol to use. When you fire up your Web browser, for example, you're using TCP because Web browsers use a protocol called HTTP. HTTP is built on TCP.

Over 95 percent of all TCP/IP applications use TCP—that's why we call the protocol suite "TCP/IP" and not "UDP/IP." TCP gets an application's data from one machine to another reliably and completely. As a result, TCP comes with communication rules that require both the sending and receiving machines to acknowledge the other's presence and readiness to send and receive data.

UDP is the "fire and forget" missile of the TCP/IP protocol suite. UDP doesn't possess any of the extras you see in TCP to make sure the data is received intact. UDP works best when you have a lot of data to send that doesn't need to be perfect or when the systems are so close to each other that the chances of a problem occurring are too small to bother worrying about. A few dropped frames on a Voice over IP call, for example, won't make much difference in the communication between two people. So there's a good reason to use UDP: its smoking fast compared to TCP.

NOTE The CompTIA A+ exams expect you to know about other TCP/IP protocols for accomplishing other goals. They're all covered in Chapter 24.

TCP/IP Services

TCP/IP is a different type of protocol. Although it supports File and Printer Sharing, it adds a number of unique sharing functions, lumped together under the umbrella term *TCP/IP services*. The most famous TCP/IP service is called *Hypertext Transfer Protocol* (*HTTP*), the language of the World Wide Web. If you want to surf the Web, you must have TCP/IP. But TCP/IP supplies many other services beyond just HTTP. By using a service called Telnet, for example, you can access a remote system as though you were actually in front of that machine.

Another example is a handy utility called ping. The *ping* command enables one machine to check whether it can communicate with another machine. Figure 22-36 shows an example of ping running on a Windows 7 system. Isn't it interesting that many TCP/IP services run from a command prompt? Good thing you know how to access one! I'll show you other services in a moment.

Figure 22-36
The ping command in action

```
C:\Windows\system32\cmd.exe

C:\>ping 10.12.14.29

Pinging 10.12.14.29 with 32 bytes of data:
Reply from 10.12.14.29: bytes=32 time=79ms TTL=127
Reply from 10.12.14.29: bytes=32 time=65ms TTL=127
Reply from 10.12.14.29: bytes=32 time=103ms TTL=127
Reply from 10.12.14.29: bytes=32 time=102ms TTL=127

Ping statistics for 10.12.14.29:
    Packets: Sent = 4, Received = 4, Lost = 0 (0% loss),
Approximate round trip times in milli-seconds:
    Minimum = 65ms, Maximum = 103ms, Average = 87ms

C:\>
```

The goal of TCP/IP is to link any two hosts (remember, a *host* is just a computer in TCP/IP lingo), whether the two computers are on the same LAN or on some other network within the WAN. The LANs within the WAN are linked together with a variety of connections, ranging from basic dial-ups to dedicated high-speed (and expensive)

data lines (see Figure 22-37). To move traffic between networks, you use routers (see Figure 22-38). Each host sends traffic to the router only when that data is destined for a remote network, cutting down on traffic across the more expensive WAN links. The host makes these decisions based on the destination IP address of each packet.

Figure 22-37 WAN concept

Figure 22-38
Typical router

TCP/IP Settings

TCP/IP has a number of unique settings that you must configure correctly to ensure proper network functionality. Unfortunately, these settings can be quite confusing, and there are several of them. Not all settings are used for every type of TCP/IP network, and it's not always obvious where you go to set them.

In Windows, you can configure network settings from the appropriate networking applet. To open Network Connections in Windows XP, either right-click on My Network Places and select Properties or open the Control Panel and select Network Connections

(see Figure 22-39). In Windows Vista and Windows 7, either right-click on Network and select Properties or open the Control Panel and select Network and Sharing Center. In Windows Vista, you'll also need to click the *Manage network connections* link, and in Windows 7, you'll need to click *Change adapter settings*.

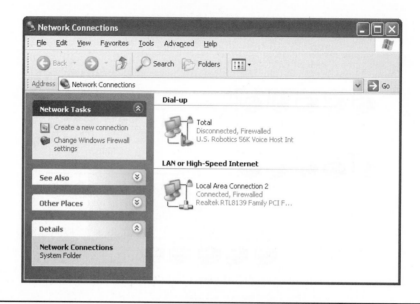

Figure 22-39 Network Connections showing dial-up and LAN connections

The CompTIA A+ certification exams assume that someone else, such as a tech support person or some network guru, will tell you the correct TCP/IP settings for the network. Your only job is to understand roughly what those settings do and to know where to enter them so the system works. I already discussed default gateways and DNS back in Chapter 5, so the last big thing to cover is DHCP.

 EXAM TIP The CompTIA A+ certification exams have a rather strange view of what you should know about networking. Take a lot of time practicing how to get to certain network configuration screens. Be ready for questions that ask, "Which of the following steps will enable you to change a particular value?"

DHCP To understand the *Dynamic Host Configuration Protocol (DHCP)*, you must first remember that every machine must be assigned an IP address, a subnet mask, a default gateway, and at least one DNS server. These settings can be added manually by using the TCP/IP Properties dialog box. When you set the IP address manually, the IP address will not change and is called a *static IP address* (see Figure 22-40).

Figure 22-40

Setting a static IP address

DHCP enables you to create a pool of IP addresses that are given temporarily to machines. DHCP is especially handy for networks of a lot of laptops that join and leave the network on a regular basis. Why give a machine that is on the network for only a few hours a day a static IP address? For that reason, DHCP is quite popular. If you add a NIC to a Windows system, the default TCP/IP settings are set to use DHCP. When you accept those automatic settings, you're really telling the machine to use DHCP (see Figure 22-41).

Figure 22-41

Automatically obtaining an IP address

To use DHCP you need a DHCP server. A DHCP server can be a program running on any computer in your network, but most commonly it's a feature added to routers.

TCP/IP Tools

All versions of Windows come with handy tools to test and configure TCP/IP. Those you're most likely to use in the field are ping, ipconfig, nslookup, and tracert. All of these programs are command-line utilities. Open a command prompt to run them; if you just place these commands in the Run or Search dialog box, you'll see the Command Prompt window open for a moment and then quickly close!

ping You've already encountered *ping*, a really great way to see if you can talk to another system. Here's how it works. Get to a command prompt and type **ping** followed by an IP address or by a DNS name, such as **ping www.chivalry.com**. Press the ENTER key on your keyboard and away it goes! Figure 22-42 shows the common syntax for ping.

```
Administrator: C:\Windows\system32\cmd.exe

C:\>ping /?

Usage: ping [-t] [-a] [-n count] [-l size] [-f] [-i TTL] [-v TOS]
            [-r count] [-s count] [[-j host-list] | [-k host-list]]
            [-w timeout] [-R] [-S srcaddr] [-4] [-6] target_name

Options:
    -t             Ping the specified host until stopped.
                   To see statistics and continue - type Control-Break;
                   To stop - type Control-C.
    -a             Resolve addresses to hostnames.
    -n count       Number of echo requests to send.
    -l size        Send buffer size.
    -f             Set Don't Fragment flag in packet (IPv4-only).
    -i TTL         Time To Live.
    -v TOS         Type Of Service (IPv4-only).
    -r count       Record route for count hops (IPv4-only).
    -s count       Timestamp for count hops (IPv4-only).
    -j host-list   Loose source route along host-list (IPv4-only).
    -k host-list   Strict source route along host-list (IPv4-only).
    -w timeout     Timeout in milliseconds to wait for each reply.
    -R             Use routing header to test reverse route also (IPv6-only).
    -S srcaddr     Source address to use.
    -4             Force using IPv4.
    -6             Force using IPv6.

C:\>
```

Figure 22-42 The ping command's syntax

The ping command has a few useful options beyond the basics. The first option is the –t switch. If you use the –t switch, ping continuously sends ping packets until you stop it with the break command (CTRL-C). The second option is the –l switch, which enables you to specify how big a ping packet to send. This helps in diagnosing specific problems with the routers between your computer and the computer you ping.

ipconfig Windows offers the command-line tool *ipconfig* for a quick glance at your network settings. From a command prompt, type **ipconfig/ all** to see all of your TCP/IP settings (see Figure 22-43).

Figure 22-43 An ipconfig /all command on Windows 7

When you have a static IP address, ipconfig does little beyond reporting your current IP settings, including your IP address, subnet mask, default gateway, DNS servers, and WINS servers. When using DHCP, however, ipconfig is also the primary tool for releasing and renewing your IP address. Just type **ipconfig /renew** to get a new IP address or **ipconfig /release** to give up the IP address you currently have.

nslookup The *nslookup* command is a powerful command-line program that enables you to determine exactly what information the DNS server is giving you about a specific host name. Every version of Windows makes nslookup available when you install TCP/IP. To run the program, type **nslookup** from the command prompt and press the ENTER key (see Figure 22-44). Note that this gives you a little information and that the prompt has changed. That's because you're running the application. Type **exit** and press the ENTER key to return to the command prompt.

Figure 22-44

The nslookup command in action

```
C:\Windows\system32\cmd.exe - nslookup

C:\>nslookup
Default Server:  totalhomedc2.totalhome
Address:  192.168.4.12

> totalsem.com
Server:  totalhomedc2.totalhome
Address:  192.168.4.12

Non-authoritative answer:
Name:     totalsem.com
Address:  216.40.231.195

> _
```

NOTE You can do some cool stuff with nslookup, and consequently some techs absolutely love the tool. It's way outside the scope of CompTIA A+ certification, but if you want to play with it, type **help** at the nslookup prompt and press ENTER to see a list of common commands and syntax.

tracert The *tracert* utility shows the route that a packet takes to get to its destination. From a command line, type **tracert** followed by a space and an IP address or URL. The output describes the route from your machine to the destination machine, including all devices the packet passes through and how long each hop between devices takes (see Figure 22-45). The tracert command can come in handy when you have to troubleshoot bottlenecks. When users complain of difficulty reaching a particular destination by using TCP/IP, you can run this utility to determine whether the problem exists on a machine or connection over which you have control, or if it is a problem on another machine or router. Similarly, if a destination is completely unreachable, tracert can again determine whether the problem is on a machine or router over which you have control.

```
C:\Windows\system32\cmd.exe

C:\>tracert chivalry.com

Tracing route to chivalry.com [69.94.71.175]
over a maximum of 30 hops:

  1    <1 ms    <1 ms    <1 ms  Router.totalhome [192.168.4.1]
  2   122 ms   116 ms   116 ms  adsl-208-190-121-38.dsl.hstntx.swbell.net [208.190.121.38]

  3   120 ms   125 ms    43 ms  12.83.37.149
  4    48 ms    48 ms    49 ms  gar25.dlstx.ip.att.net [12.122.85.233]
  5    48 ms    48 ms    48 ms  192.205.34.142
  6    89 ms    89 ms    89 ms  OLM-LLC.Ulan495.asr1.JFK1.gblx.net [64.212.32.166]
  7    91 ms    90 ms    90 ms  gil-1.corea.trum.fastdns.net [69.94.1.69]
  8    88 ms    88 ms    88 ms  chivalry.com [69.94.71.175]

Trace complete.

C:\>
```

Figure 22-45 The tracert command in action

Configuring TCP/IP

By default, TCP/IP is configured to receive an IP address automatically from a DHCP server on the network (and automatically assign a corresponding subnet mask). As far as the CompTIA A+ certification exams are concerned, Network+ techs and administrators give you the IP address, subnet mask, and default gateway information and you plug them into the PC. That's about it, so here's how to do it manually:

1. In Windows XP, open the Control Panel and double-click the Network Connections applet. Double-click the Local Area Connection icon. In Windows Vista/7, open the Control Panel and go to the Network and Sharing Center applet. In Windows Vista, click the *Manage network connections* link, and in Windows 7, click *Change adapter settings*. After that, double-click the Local Area Network icon.

2. Click the Properties button, highlight Internet Protocol (TCP/IP), and click the Properties button. In Windows Vista/7, you should highlight Internet Protocol Version 4 (TCP/IPv4), as opposed to IPv6, which you'll learn about later in this chapter.

3. In the Properties dialog box (see Figure 22-46), click the radio button next to *Use the following IP address*.

4. Enter the IP address in the appropriate fields.

5. Press the TAB key to skip down to the Subnet mask field. Note that the subnet mask is entered automatically, although you can type over this if you want to enter a different subnet mask.

6. Optionally, enter the IP address for a default gateway.

7. Optionally, enter the IP addresses of a primary DNS server and a secondary DNS server. (Figure 22-46 uses the Google DNS servers.)

8. Click the OK button to close the Properties dialog box.

9. Click the Close button to exit the Local Area Connection Status dialog box.

Automatic Private IP Addressing

Windows supports a feature called Automatic Private IP Addressing (APIPA) that automatically assigns an IP address to the system when the client cannot obtain an IP address automatically. The Internet Assigned Numbers Authority, the nonprofit corporation responsible for assigning IP addresses and managing root servers, has set aside the range of addresses from 169.254.0.1 to 169.254.255.254 for this purpose.

If the computer system cannot contact a DHCP server, the computer randomly chooses an address in the form of 169.254.$x.y$ (where $x.y$ is the computer's identifier) and a 16-bit subnet mask (255.255.0.0) and broadcasts it on the network segment (subnet). If no other computer responds to the address, the system assigns this address to itself. When using APIPA, the system can communicate only with other computers on the same subnet that also use the 169.254.$x.y$ range with a 16-bit mask. APIPA is enabled by default if your system is configured to obtain an IP address automatically.

Figure 22-46

Setting up IP

Internet Protocol Version 4 (TCP/IPv4) Properties

General

You can get IP settings assigned automatically if your network supports this capability. Otherwise, you need to ask your network administrator for the appropriate IP settings.

○ Obtain an IP address automatically

◉ Use the following IP address:

IP address: 132 . 17 . 240 . 12

Subnet mask: 255 . 255 . 0 . 0

Default gateway: 132 . 17 . 0 . 1

○ Obtain DNS server address automatically

◉ Use the following DNS server addresses:

Preferred DNS server: 8 . 8 . 8 . 8

Alternate DNS server: 8 . 8 . 4 . 4

☐ Validate settings upon exit Advanced...

OK Cancel

NOTE A computer system on a network with an active DHCP server that has an IP address in this range usually indicates a problem connecting to the DHCP server.

IPv6

When the early developers of the Internet set out to create an addressing or naming scheme for devices on the Internet, they faced several issues. Of course they needed to determine how the numbers or names worked, and for that they developed the Internet Protocol and IP addresses. But beyond that, they had to determine how many computers might exist in the future, and then make the IP address space even bigger to give Internet naming longevity. But how many computers would exist in the future?

Keep in mind that TCP/IP development took place back in the early 1970s. There were fewer than 1000 computers in the entire *world* at the time, but that didn't keep the IP developers from thinking big! They decided to go absolutely crazy (as many people considered it at the time) and, in 1979, created the *Internet Protocol version 4 (IPv4)* 32-bit IP address space, creating approximately 4 billion IP addresses. That should have been fine for the foreseeable future!

It wasn't. First, the TCP/IP folks wasted huge chunks of IP addresses due to classful addressing and an easygoing method of parceling out IP addresses. Second, the Internet reached a level of popularity far beyond the original developers' imaginations. By

the mid-1980s, the rate of consumption for IP addresses started to worry the Internet people and the writing was on the wall for IPv4's 32-bit addressing.

As a result, the Internet Engineering Task Force (IETF) developed a new IP addressing scheme called *Internet Protocol version 6 (IPv6)* that is slowly replacing IPv4. IPv6 extends the 32-bit IP address space to 128 bits, allowing up to 2^{128} addresses! That should hold us for the foreseeable future! This number—close to 3.4×10^{38} addresses—is something like all the grains of sand on Earth or 1/8 of all the molecules in the atmosphere.

NOTE If you really want to know how many IP addresses IPv6 provides, here's your number: 340,282,366,920,938,463,463,374,607,431,768,211,456.

Although they achieve the same function—enabling computers on IP networks to send packets to each other—IPv6 and IPv4 differ a lot when it comes to implementation. This section provides you with a quick overview to get you up to speed with IPv6 and show you how it differs from IPv4.

IPv6 Address Notation

The familiar 32-bit IPv4 addresses are written as 197.169.94.82, using four octets. The 128-bit IPv6 addresses are written like this:

2001:0000:0000:3210:0800:200C:00CF:1234

IPv6 uses a colon as a separator, instead of the period used in IPv4's dotted-decimal format. Each "group" is a hexadecimal number between 0000 and FFFF called, unofficially, a *field* or *hextet*.

NOTE For those who don't play with hex regularly, one hexadecimal character (for example, F) represents 4 bits, so four hexadecimal characters make a 16-bit group. For some reason, the IPv6 developers didn't provide a name for the "group of four hexadecimal characters," so many techs and writers have taken to calling them fields or "hextets" to distinguish them from IPv4 "octets."

A complete IPv6 address always has eight groups of four hexadecimal characters. If this sounds like you're going to type in really long IP addresses, don't worry, IPv6 offers a number of ways to shorten the address in written form.

EXAM TIP IPv4 addresses use 32 bits, and IPv6 addresses use 128 bits. Be sure you can identify their address length differences and address conventions.

First, leading zeros can be dropped from any group, so 00CF becomes CF and 0000 becomes 0. Let's rewrite the previous IPv6 address using this shortening method:

2001:0:0:3210:800:200C:CF:1234

Second, you can remove one or more consecutive groups of all zeros, leaving the two colons together. For example, using the :: rule, you can write the IPv6 address

2001:0:0:3210:800:200C:CF:1234

as

2001::3210:800:200C:CF:1234

You can remove any number of consecutive groups of zeros to leave a double colon, but you can only use this trick *once* in an IPv6 address.

Take a look at this IPv6 address:

FEDC:0000:0000:0000:00CF:0000:BA98:1234

Using the double-colon rule, you can reduce four groups of zeros; three of them follow the FEDC and the fourth comes after 00CF. Because of the "only use once" stipulation, the best and shortest option is to convert the address to

FEDC::CF:0:BA98:1234

You may not use a second :: to represent the fourth groups of zeros—only one :: is allowed per address! This rule exists for a good reason. If more than one :: was used, how could you tell how many groups of zeros were in each group? Answer: you couldn't.

Here's an example of a very special IPv6 address that takes full advantage of the double-colon rule, the IPv6 loopback address:

::1

Without using the double-colon nomenclature, this IPv6 address would look like this:

0000:0000:0000:0000:0000:0000:0000:0001

NOTE The unspecified address (all zeros) can never be used, and neither can an address that contains all ones (in binary) or all Fs (in hex notation).

IPv6 still uses subnets, but you won't find a place to type in 255s anywhere. IPv6 uses the "/x" *Classless Inter-Domain Routing (CIDR)* nomenclature, where the /x refers to the number of bits in the subnet mask, just like in IPv4. Here's how to write an IP address and subnet for a typical IPv6 host:

FEDC::CF:0:BA98:1234/64

Where Do IPv6 Addresses Come From?

With IPv4, IP addresses come from one of two places: either you type in the IP address yourself (*static IP addressing*) or you use DHCP (also called *dynamic IP addressing*). With IPv6, addressing works very differently. Instead of one IP address, you can have up to three IP addresses on a single network card.

When a computer running IPv6 first boots up, it gives itself a *link-local address*, IPv6's equivalent to IPv4's APIPA address. Although an APIPA address can indicate a loss of network connectivity or a problem with the DHCP server, computers running IPv6 always have a link-local address. The first 64 bits of a link-local address are always FE80::. That means every address always begins with FE80:0000:0000:0000. If your operating system supports IPv6 and IPv6 is enabled, you can see this address. Figure 22-47 shows the link-local address for a typical system running the ipconfig utility.

EXAM TIP Every computer running IPv6 will always have at least a link-local address.

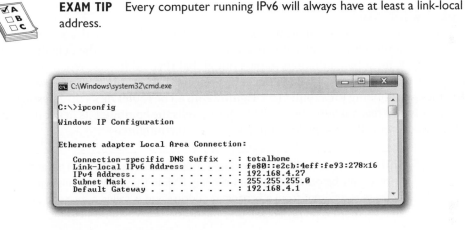

Figure 22-47 Link-local address in ipconfig

The folks who designed IPv6 gave operating system makers a choice on how to make the last 64 bits of an IPv6 address. The first method uses a random value—and this is the way Windows does it. When you activate a NIC, Windows simply makes a random value for the last 64 bits of the IPv6 address. Once created, this unique 64-bit value will never change.

The alternative method to create the IPv6 address uses the MAC address of the network card (called the *Extended Unique Identifier, 64-bit,* or *EUI-64*). Be warned! The CompTIA A+ exams are Windows-centric, and Windows does not use this second method by default. Even though Windows does not currently use this method by default, understanding this is critical to understanding IPv6.

NOTE If you want to force Windows to use the MAC address, just go to a command prompt and type this:

```
netsh interface ipv6 set global randomizeidentifiers=disabled
```

IPv6 Subnet Masks

IPv6 subnets function the same as IPv4 subnets, but you need to know two new rules:

- The last 64 bits of an IPv6 address are generated randomly or using the MAC address, leaving a maximum of 64 bits for the network ID. Therefore, no subnet is ever longer than /64.

- The IANA passes out /32 subnets to big ISPs and end users who need large allotments. ISPs and others may pass out /48 and /64 subnets to end users.

Therefore, the vast majority of IPv6 subnets are between /48 and /64.

Subnet masks are just as important in IPv6 networks as they are in IPv4 networks. Unlike with IPv4 networks, however, all IPv6 networks with computers have a /64 subnet mask, so you'll rarely if ever need to make any changes manually.

Global Addresses

To get on the Internet, a system needs a second IPv6 address called a *global address*. The most common way to get a global address is to request it from the default gateway router, which must be configured to pass out global IPv6 addresses. When you plug a computer into a network, it sends out a very special packet called a *router solicitation* (*RS*) message, looking for a router (see Figure 22-48). The router hears this message and responds with a *router advertisement* (*RA*). This RA tells the computer its network ID and subnet (together called the *prefix*) and DNS server (if configured).

NOTE A router solicitation message uses the address FF02::2. This address is read only by other computers running IPv6 in the network. This type of address is different from a broadcast address and is called a *multicast address*. In IPv6, there is no broadcast, only multicast!

Figure 22-48
Getting a global
address

Once the computer gets a prefix, it generates the rest of the address just like with the link-local address. The computer ends up with a legitimate, 128-bit public IPv6 address as well as a link-local address. Figure 22-49 shows the IPv6 information in Windows 7.

NOTE Most Windows Vista and Windows 7 machines have three IPv6 addresses: one link local address and two global addresses. One global address stays the same, while the second is a temporary address used to make it harder for your system to be tracked by IP address.

```
Administrator: C:\Windows\system32\cmd.exe

C:\>ipconfig

Windows IP Configuration

Ethernet adapter Gigabit NIC:

   Connection-specific DNS Suffix   . :
   IPv6 Address. . . . . . . . . . . : 2001:74:b8f8:1:c547:4dd3:86a3:739d
   Temporary IPv6 Address. . . . . . : 2001:74:b8f8:1:e918:a9af:c6e4:120b
   Link-local IPv6 Address . . . . . : fe80::c547:4dd3:86a3:739d%8
   IPv4 Address. . . . . . . . . . . : 192.168.4.81
   Subnet Mask . . . . . . . . . . . : 255.255.255.0
   Default Gateway . . . . . . . . . : fe80::223:4ff:fe8c:b720%8
                                       192.168.4.1
```

Figure 22-49 Windows system with a global IPv6 address

Let's look at this process in detail with an example:

1. An IPv6-capable computer boots up. As it boots, it sends out a router solicitation message (FF02::2).

2. An IPv6-configured router hears the request and then sends to the computer a router advertisement containing the prefix and DNS. In this example, let's say it is 2001:470:ABCD:1/64.

3. The computer takes the prefix and adds the EUI-64 or a random value to the end of the prefix. If the MAC address is 00-0C-29-53-45-CA, then the address is 20C:29FF:FE53:45CA.

4. Putting the prefix with the last half of the address, you get the global address: 2001:470:ABCD:1:20C:29FF:FE53:45CA.

NOTE At the moment, IANA only passes out global addresses that begin with the number 2 (for example, 2001::, 2002::, and so on). As demand increases, this will certainly change, but for now, knowing a global address when you see one is easy.

A global address is a true Internet address. If another computer is running IPv6 and also has a global address, it can access your system unless you have some form of firewall.

 EXAM TIP Computers using IPv6 need a *global* address to access the Internet.

The addition of IPv6 makes programs such as ipconfig fairly complex. Take a look at Figure 22-50. With multiple NICs and both IPv4 and IPv6, the output is vast—too big to even put on a single screen.

```
C:\Windows\system32\cmd.exe

C:\>ipconfig /all

Windows IP Configuration

    Host Name . . . . . . . . . . . . : michaels-ws
    Primary Dns Suffix  . . . . . . . : totalhome
    Node Type . . . . . . . . . . . . : Hybrid
    IP Routing Enabled. . . . . . . . : No
    WINS Proxy Enabled. . . . . . . . : No
    DNS Suffix Search List. . . . . . : totalhome

Ethernet adapter Local Area Connection:

    Connection-specific DNS Suffix  . : totalhome
    Description . . . . . . . . . . . : Realtek PCIe GBE Family Controller
    Physical Address. . . . . . . . . : E0-CB-4E-93-02-78
    DHCP Enabled. . . . . . . . . . . : Yes
    Autoconfiguration Enabled . . . . : Yes
    IPv6 Address. . . . . . . . . . . : 2001:470:baf9:1::200(Preferred)
    Link-local IPv6 Address . . . . . : fe80::e2cb:4eff:fe93:278%16(Preferred)
    IPv4 Address. . . . . . . . . . . : 192.168.4.27(Preferred)
    Subnet Mask . . . . . . . . . . . : 255.255.255.0
    Lease Obtained. . . . . . . . . . : Thursday, April 26, 2012 8:37:26 AM
    Lease Expires . . . . . . . . . . : Wednesday, May 02, 2012 8:37:25 AM
    Default Gateway . . . . . . . . . : 2001:470:baf9:1::1
                                        192.168.4.1
    DHCP Server . . . . . . . . . . . : 192.168.4.12
    DHCPv6 IAID . . . . . . . . . . . : 400608078
    DHCPv6 Client DUID. . . . . . . . : 00-01-00-01-13-57-F6-2D-E0-CB-4E-93-02-78

    DNS Servers . . . . . . . . . . . : 192.168.4.12
    NetBIOS over Tcpip. . . . . . . . : Enabled

Ethernet adapter VMware Network Adapter VMnet1:

    Connection-specific DNS Suffix  . :
    Description . . . . . . . . . . . : VMware Virtual Ethernet Adapter for VMnet
1
    Physical Address. . . . . . . . . : 00-50-56-C0-00-01
    DHCP Enabled. . . . . . . . . . . : No
    Autoconfiguration Enabled . . . . : Yes
    Link-local IPv6 Address . . . . . : fe80::250:56ff:fec0:1%19(Preferred)
    IPv4 Address. . . . . . . . . . . : 192.168.22.1(Preferred)
    Subnet Mask . . . . . . . . . . . : 255.255.255.0
    Default Gateway . . . . . . . . . :
    DHCPv6 IAID . . . . . . . . . . . : 436228182
    DHCPv6 Client DUID. . . . . . . . : 00-01-00-01-13-57-F6-2D-E0-CB-4E-93-02-78

    DNS Servers . . . . . . . . . . . : fec0:0:0:ffff::1%1
```

Figure 22-50 The ipconfig command with IPv6 and IPv4

Installing and Configuring a Wired Network

Halfway through the chapter and we're finally getting to the good stuff: installing and configuring a network! To have network connectivity, you need to have three things in place:

- **NIC** The physical hardware that connects the computer system to the network media
- **Protocol** The language that the computer systems use to communicate
- **Network client** The interface that allows the computer system to speak to the protocol

If you want to share resources on your PC with other network users, you also need to enable Microsoft's File and Printer Sharing. Plus, of course, you need to connect the PC to the network switch via some sort of cable (preferably CAT 6 with Gigabit Ethernet cranking through the wires, but that's just me!). When you install a NIC, by default Windows installs upon setup the TCP/IP protocol, the Client for Microsoft Networks, and File and Printer Sharing for Microsoft Networks.

Installing a NIC

The NIC is your computer system's link to the network, and installing one is the first step required to connect to a network. NICs are manufactured to operate on specific media and network types, such as 1000BaseT Ethernet. Follow the manufacturer's instructions for installation. If your NIC is of recent vintage, it will be detected, installed, and configured automatically by Windows. You might need a driver disc or a driver download from the manufacturer's Web site.

The Add Hardware Wizard in Windows XP automates installation of non–plug-and-play devices or plug-and-play devices that were not detected correctly. Start the wizard by clicking Start | Control Panel and then double-clicking the icon for the Add Hardware applet. Click the Next button to select the hardware task you wish to perform, and follow the prompts to complete the wizard. If, for some reason, Windows Vista or Windows 7 doesn't automatically detect a new NIC after you turn the PC back on, go to Start | Control Panel | Add Hardware in Windows Vista or Start | Devices and Printers and click on *Add a device* in Windows 7 to install it.

Duplex and Half-Duplex

All modern NICs can run in *full-duplex* mode, meaning they can send and receive data at the same time. The vast majority of NICs and switches use a feature called *auto-sensing* to accommodate very old devices that might attach to the network and need to run in half-duplex mode. Half-duplex means that the device can send and receive, but not at the same time. An obvious example of a half-duplex device is the walkie-talkies you played with as a kid that required you to press and hold the orange button to transmit—at which time you couldn't hear anything. Half-duplex devices are exceedingly rare in modern computers, but you need to understand this option. Some NICs just

can't handle full-duplex communication when you connect them directly to another NIC by using a crossover cable—that is, no switch. Dropping both NICs down from full-duplex or auto-sensing can sometimes enable these odd NICs to communicate.

Link Lights

NICs made today have some type of light-emitting diode (LED) *status indicator* that gives information about the state of the NIC's link to whatever is on the other end of the connection. Even though you know the lights are actually LEDs, get used to calling them *link lights*, because that's the term all network techs use. NICs can have between one and four different link lights, and the LEDs can be any color. These lights give you clues about what's happening with the link and are one of the first items to check whenever you think a system is disconnected from the network (see Figure 22-51).

Figure 22-51
Mmmm, pretty lights!

Switches also have link lights, enabling you to check the connectivity at both ends of the cable. If a PC can't access a network, always check the link lights first. Multispeed devices usually have a link light that tells you the speed of the connection. In Figure 22-52, the light for port 2 on the top photo is orange, for example, signifying that the other end of the cable is plugged into either a 10BaseT or 100BaseT NIC. The same port connected to a Gigabit NIC—that's the lower picture—displays a green LED.

Figure 22-52
Multispeed lights

A properly functioning link light is steady on when the NIC is connected to another device. No flickering, no on and off, just on. A link light that is off or flickering shows a connection problem.

Another light is the *activity light*. This little guy turns on when the card detects network traffic, so it makes an intermittent flickering when operating properly. The activity light is a lifesaver for detecting problems, because in the real world, the connection light sometimes lies to you. If the connection light says the connection is good, the next step is to try to copy a file or do something else to create network traffic. If the activity light does not flicker, you have a problem.

No standard governs how NIC manufacturers use their lights; as a result, LEDs in NICs come in an amazing array of colors and layouts. When you encounter a NIC with a number of LEDs, take a moment to try to figure out what each one means. Although different NICs have different ways of arranging and using their LEDs, the functions are always the same: link, activity, and speed.

EXAM TIP Though no real standard exists for NIC LEDs, the CompTIA A+ exams will test you on some more-or-less *de facto* LED meanings. You should know that a solid green light means connectivity, a flashing green light means intermittent connectivity, no green light means no connectivity, and a flashing amber light means there are collisions on the network (which is sometimes okay). Also, know that the first things you should check when having connectivity issues are the NIC's LEDs.

Wake-on-LAN

A popular feature of most NICs is the ability to turn on or wake up a powered-down or sleeping PC. You'll learn more about power management in Chapter 26, but for now, know that *Wake-on-LAN* is handy when you want to wake up one or multiple computers that you aren't physically near. To wake up a PC with Wake-on-LAN, you'll need to use a second PC to send either a special pattern or a *magic packet* (a broadcast packet that essentially repeats the destination MAC address many times).

A powered-down or sleeping PC knows to look for this special pattern or packet, at least after configured to do so. In Windows XP, go to the Control Panel and open Network Connections. In Windows Vista/7, go to the Control Panel and open Network and Sharing Center. Click *Manage network connections* (Vista) or *Change adapter settings* (7) on the left. For all versions of Windows, right-click on the adapter and select Properties. Click the Configure button in the Properties dialog box and then select the Power Management tab (see Figure 22-53). To enable Wake-on-LAN, make sure the checkbox next to *Allow this device to wake the computer* is checked. Optionally, you can select *Only allow a magic packet to wake the computer*, which will instruct the NIC to ignore everything but magic packets.

NOTE Your BIOS might also have settings for controlling Wake-on-LAN functions. Check your CMOS System Configuration tool to find out.

Figure 22-53
Wake-on-LAN set-
tings on the Power
Management tab

Wake-on-LAN is very convenient, but it has one nasty downside. As noted in the Properties dialog box, Wake-on-LAN can wake up or turn on laptops using wireless connections, even when they aren't plugged in or are inside a carrying case. Don't let your laptop's battery die or overheat—unless you know that you'll need it, turn off Wake-on-LAN on your laptop.

Configuring a Network Client

To establish network connectivity, you need a network client installed and configured properly. Let's look at Microsoft's client.

Installed as part of the OS installation, the Client for Microsoft Networks rarely needs configuration, and, in fact, few configuration options are available. To start it in Windows Vista/7, click Start, right-click Network, and select Properties. Then click *Manage network connections* (Vista) or *Change adapter settings* (7) on the left. In Windows XP, click Start, right-click My Network Places, and select Properties.

In all versions of Windows, the next step is to double-click the Local Area Connection icon, click the Properties button, and highlight Client for Microsoft Networks. In Windows XP/Vista, click the Properties button. Windows 7 disables this option. Note, however, that there's not much to do here. Unless told to do something by a network administrator, just leave this alone.

Sharing and Security

Windows systems can share all kinds of *resources*: files, folders, entire drives, printers, faxes, Internet connections, and much more. Conveniently for you, the scope of the CompTIA A+ certification exams is limited to folders, printers, and Internet connections. You'll see how to share folders and printers now; Internet connection sharing is discussed in Chapter 24.

Sharing Drives and Folders

All versions of Windows share drives and folders in basically the same manner. Right-click any drive or folder and choose Properties. Select the Sharing tab (see Figure 22-54). In Windows Vista/7, click the Advanced Sharing button. Select *Share this folder*, add something in the Comment or User limit fields if you wish (they're not required), and click Permissions (see Figure 22-55).

Figure 22-54
Windows XP
Sharing tab on
NTFS volume

Hey! Doesn't NTFS have all those wild permissions such as Read, Execute, Take Ownership, and all that? Yes, it does, but NTFS permissions and network permissions are totally separate beasties. Microsoft wanted Windows to support many different file systems (NTFS, FAT16, FAT32), old and new. Network permissions are Microsoft's way of enabling you to administer file sharing on any type of partition supported by Windows, no matter how ancient. Sure, your options will be pretty limited if you are working with an older file system, but you *can* do it.

If you share a folder on an NTFS drive, as you normally do these days, you must set *both* the network permissions and the NTFS permissions to let others access your shared resources. Some good news: This is actually no big deal! Just set the network permissions to give everyone full control, and then use the NTFS permissions to exercise more precise control over *who* accesses the shared resources and *how* they access them. Open the Security tab to set the NTFS permissions.

Figure 22-55

Network
permissions

NOTE Windows offers two types of sharing: share-level and NTFS permissions.

Accessing Shared Drives/Directories

Once you have set up a drive or directory to be shared, the final step is to access that shared drive or directory from another machine. Windows XP uses My Network Places and Windows Vista and Windows 7 use Network, although you'll need to do a little clicking to get to the shared resources (see Figure 22-56).

You can also map network resources to a local resource name. For example, the FREDC share can be mapped to be a local hard drive such as E: or F:. From within any Explorer window (such as My Documents or Documents), choose Tools | Map Network Drive to open the Map Network Drive dialog box (see Figure 22-57). In Windows Vista/7, you might need to press the ALT key once to see the menu bar. Click the Browse button to check out the neighborhood and find a shared drive (see Figure 22-58).

Windows 2000 had the handy Add Network Place icon in My Network Places to add network locations you frequently access without using up drive letters. Windows XP removed the icon but added the menu option in its context bar on the left. Windows Vista and Windows 7 have removed it altogether but have added the ability to add links to network locations to your Favorites in Windows Explorer. Simply drag the network share, or any folder for that matter, to the Favorites list in the Navigation pane on the left. Figure 22-59 shows how it looks on a Windows 7 system.

Figure 22-56 Shared resources in Network

Figure 22-57 Map Network Drive dialog box in Windows 7

Figure 22-58 Browsing for shared folders

Mapping shared network drives is a common practice, as it makes a remote network share look like just another drive on the local system. The only downside to drive mapping stems from the fact that users tend to forget they are on a network. A classic example is the user who always accesses a particular folder or file on the network and then suddenly gets a "file not found" error when the workstation is disconnected from the network. Instead of recognizing this as a network error, the user often imagines the problem is a missing or corrupted file.

TIP All shared resources should show up in My Network Places/Network. If a shared resource fails to show up, make sure you check the basics first: Is File and Printer Sharing activated? Is the device shared? Don't let silly errors fool you!

Wireless Networking

In this chapter, you will learn how to
- Discuss wireless networking components
- Analyze and explain wireless networking standards
- Install and configure wireless networks
- Troubleshoot wireless networks

Wireless networks have been popular for many years now, but unlike wired networks, so much of how wireless works continues to elude people. Part of the problem might be that a simple wireless network is so inexpensive and easy to configure that most users and techs never really get into the *hows* of wireless. The chance to get away from all the cables and mess and just *connect* has a phenomenal appeal. Well, let's change all that and dive deeply into wireless networking.

EXAM TIP The CompTIA A+ exams assume you know the names and connectors (or lack thereof) in wireless networking.

Historical/Conceptual

Wireless Networking Components

Instead of a physical set of wires running between network nodes, wireless networks use either radio waves or beams of infrared light to communicate with each other. Various kinds of wireless networking solutions have come and gone in the past. The wireless radio wave networks you'll find yourself supporting these days are based on the *IEEE 802.11* wireless Ethernet standard—marketed as Wi-Fi—and on Bluetooth technology. Wireless networks using infrared light are limited to those that use the Infrared Data Association (IrDA) protocol. Finally, the cell phone companies have gotten into the mix and offer access to the Internet through cellular networks.

Wireless networking capabilities of one form or another are built into many modern computing devices. Infrared *transceiver* ports have been standard issue on portable

computers, personal digital assistants (PDAs), and high-end printers for years, although they're absent from most of the latest PCs and portable computers. Figure 23-1 shows the infrared transceiver ports on an older laptop and PDA. Wireless Ethernet and often Bluetooth capabilities are now ubiquitous as integrated components, or you can easily add them by using PCI, PCI Express, or PC Card adapters. Figure 23-2 shows a desktop PCI Wi-Fi adapter. You can also add wireless network capabilities by using external USB wireless network adapters, as shown in Figure 23-3.

Figure 23-1
Infrared transceiver ports on a laptop and PDA

Figure 23-2
Wireless PCI add-on card

Wireless networking is not limited to PCs. Most smartphones and tablets have wireless capabilities built-in or available as add-on options. Figure 23-4 shows a smartphone accessing the Internet over a Wi-Fi connection.

Figure 23-3
External USB
wireless NIC

Figure 23-4
Smartphone with
wireless capability

NOTE See Chapter 26 for the scoop on mobile devices like smartphones and tablets.

801

To extend the capabilities of a wireless Ethernet network, such as connecting to a wired network or sharing a high-speed Internet connection, you need a *wireless access point (WAP)*. A WAP centrally connects wireless network nodes in the same way that a hub connects wired Ethernet PCs. Many WAPs also act as switches and Internet routers, such as the Linksys device shown in Figure 23-5.

Figure 23-5
Linksys device that acts as wireless access point, switch, and router

Most WAPs draw their power from a wall outlet, like any other electronic device. More advanced WAPs, especially those used in corporate settings, can also use a feature called *Power over Ethernet (PoE)*. Using PoE, you only need to plug a single Ethernet cable into the WAP to provide both power and a network connection.

NOTE PoE is often used with WAPs, but other network devices take advantage of this feature, too.

Wireless communication via Bluetooth comes as a built-in option on newer PCs and peripheral devices, or you can add it to an older PC via an external USB Bluetooth adapter. Figure 23-6 shows a Bluetooth adapter with a Bluetooth-enabled mouse and keyboard.

Figure 23-6
External USB
Bluetooth adapter,
keyboard, and
mouse

EXAM TIP Wireless access points are commonly known as WAPs, APs,
access points, or simply wireless routers.

Wireless Networking Software

Wireless devices use the same networking protocols and client that their wired coun-
terparts use, and they operate by using the *carrier sense multiple access/collision avoidance
(CSMA/CA)* networking scheme. The *collision avoidance* aspect differs slightly from the
collision detection standard used in wired Ethernet. A wireless node listens in on the
wireless medium to see if another node is currently broadcasting data. If so, it waits a
random amount of time before retrying. So far, this method is exactly the same as the
method used by wired Ethernet networks. Because wireless nodes have a more difficult
time detecting data collisions, however, they offer the option of using the *Request to
Send/Clear to Send (RTS/CTS)* protocol. When enabled, a transmitting node that deter-
mines that the wireless medium is clear to use sends an RTS frame to the receiving
node. The receiving node responds with a CTS frame, telling the sending node that
it's okay to transmit. Then, once the data is sent, the transmitting node waits for an
acknowledgment (ACK) from the receiving node before sending the next data packet.
This option is very elegant, but keep in mind that using RTS/CTS introduces significant
overhead to the process and can impede performance.

EXAM TIP Wireless networks use the carrier sense multiple access/collision
avoidance (CSMA/CA) standard, while wired Ethernet networks use carrier
sense multiple access/collision detection (CSMA/CD).

In terms of configuring wireless networking software, you need to do very little.
Wireless network adapters are plug and play, so any modern version of Windows

immediately recognizes one when it is installed, prompting you to load any needed hardware drivers. You will, however, need a utility to set parameters such as the network name.

Windows XP and later include built-in tools for configuring these settings, but some wireless adapters also come with configuration tools provided by the wireless network adapter vendor (see Figure 23-7). Using this utility, you can determine your link state and signal strength, configure your wireless networking *mode* (discussed next), and set security encryption, power saving options, and so on.

Figure 23-7
Wireless configuration utility

Wireless Network Modes

The simplest wireless network consists of two or more PCs communicating directly with each other without cabling or any other intermediary hardware. More complicated wireless networks use a WAP to centralize wireless communication and bridge wireless network segments to wired network segments. These two methods are called ad hoc mode and infrastructure mode.

Ad hoc Mode

Ad hoc mode is sometimes called *peer-to-peer mode*, with each wireless node in direct contact with every other node in a decentralized free-for-all, as shown in Figure 23-8.

Two or more wireless nodes communicating in ad hoc mode form what's called an *Independent Basic Service Set* (*IBSS*). Ad hoc mode networks are suited for small groups of computers (less than a dozen or so) that need to transfer files or share printers. Ad hoc mode networks are also good for temporary networks such as study groups or business meetings.

Figure 23-8
Wireless ad hoc
mode network

Infrastructure Mode

Wireless networks running in *infrastructure mode* use one or more WAPs to connect the wireless network nodes to a wired network segment, as shown in Figure 23-9. A single WAP servicing a given area is called a *Basic Service Set* (*BSS*). This service area can be extended by adding more WAPs. This is called, appropriately, an *Extended Basic Service Set* (*EBSS*).

Figure 23-9
Wireless infra-
structure mode
network

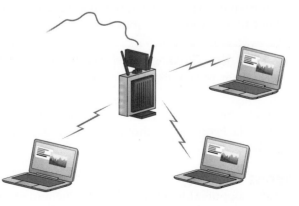

Wireless networks running in infrastructure mode require more planning and are more complicated to configure than ad hoc mode networks, but they also give you finer control over how the network operates. Infrastructure mode is better suited to networks that need to share dedicated resources such as Internet connections and centralized databases.

Wireless Networking Security

One of the major complaints against wireless networking is that it offers weak security. In many cases, all you need to do to access a wireless network is walk into a WAP's coverage area, turn on your wireless device, and connect! Furthermore, data packets are floating through the air instead of safely wrapped up inside network cabling. What's to stop an unscrupulous PC tech with the right equipment from grabbing those packets out of the air and reading that data himself?

Wireless networks use three methods to secure access to the network itself and secure the data that's being transferred. The *service set identifier (SSID)* parameter—also called the *network name*—is used to define the wireless network. This is very handy when you have a number of wireless networks in the same area.

SSID

One of the main security weaknesses with wireless networks is that, out of the box, *no* security is configured at all. Wireless devices *want* to be heard, and WAPs are usually configured to broadcast their presence to their maximum range and welcome all other wireless devices that respond.

Always change the default SSID to something unique, and change the password right away. Configuring a unique SSID name and password is the very least that you should do to secure a wireless network. The default SSID names and passwords are well known and widely available online. This is intended to make setting up a wireless network as easy as possible but can cause problems in places with a lot of overlapping wireless networks. Each wireless network node and access point needs to be configured with the same unique SSID name. This SSID name is then included in the header of every data packet broadcast in the wireless network's coverage area. Data packets that lack the correct SSID name in the header are rejected.

 EXAM TIP Changing the default SSID for the WAP is the first step in setting up a new wireless network.

Another trick often seen in wireless networks is to tell the wireless device not to broadcast the SSID. People not authorized to access the network will have a harder time knowing it's there.

MAC Address Filtering

Most WAPs also support *MAC address filtering*, a method that enables you to limit access to your wireless network based on the physical, hard-wired address of the units' wireless

NIC. MAC address filtering is a handy way of creating a type of "accepted users" list to limit access to your wireless network, but it works best when you have a small number of users. A table stored in the WAP lists the MAC addresses that are permitted to participate in the wireless network. Any data packets that don't contain the MAC address of a node listed in the table are rejected.

 NOTE Many techs shorten the term "MAC address filtering" to simply "MAC filtering." Either way works.

WEP

Early on, Wi-Fi developers introduced the *Wired Equivalent Privacy (WEP)* protocol to attempt to ensure that data is secured while in transit over the airwaves. WEP encryption uses a standard 40-bit encryption to scramble data packets. Many vendors also support 104-bit encryption. Note that some vendors advertise 128-bit encryption, but they actually use a 104-bit encryption key. Unfortunately, WEP encryption includes a flaw that makes it extremely vulnerable to attack. Although WEP is better than no encryption at all, keep in mind that WEP will not protect you from knowledgeable intruders.

WEP doesn't provide complete end-to-end encryption. WEP provides encryption only between the WAP and the wireless device. Encryption is stripped from the data packet as it travels "up" through the subsequent network layers. For true end-to-end encryption, you need to upgrade to WPA or WPA2.

WPA

The *Wi-Fi Protected Access (WPA)* protocol addresses the weaknesses of WEP and acts as a security protocol upgrade to WEP. WPA uses the *Temporal Key Integrity Protocol (TKIP)*, which provides a new encryption key for every sent packet. This protects WPA from many of the attacks that make WEP vulnerable, though TKIP has since been deprecated, as it has flaws of its own. WPA also offers security enhancements over WEP such as an encryption key integrity-checking feature and user authentication through the industry-standard *Extensible Authentication Protocol (EAP)*. EAP provides a huge security improvement over WEP encryption. After all, MAC addresses are fairly easy to "sniff" out, because they're transmitted in unencrypted, clear text format. User names and passwords are encrypted and therefore much more secure. Even with these enhancements, WPA was intended only as an interim security solution until the IEEE 802.11i security standard was finalized and implemented.

WPA2

Today, Mac OS X and Windows support the full IEEE 802.11i standard, more commonly known as *Wi-Fi Protected Access 2 (WPA2)*, to lock down wireless networks. WPA2 uses the *Advanced Encryption Standard (AES)*, among other improvements, to provide a secure wireless environment. If you haven't upgraded to WPA2, you should.

WPS

While most techs can configure wireless networks blindfolded, the thought of pass-words and encryption might intimidate the average user. If anything, most people plug in their wireless router and go on their merry way. Because everyone should secure their wireless network, the developers of Wi-Fi created *Wi-Fi Protected Setup (WPS)*, a standard included on most WAPs and clients to make secure connections easier to configure.

WPS works in one of two ways. Some devices use a push button, such as the one shown in Figure 23-10, and others use a password or code.

Figure 23-10
WPS button on an
e2500 Router

Let's say you want to connect a WPS-capable wireless printer to a WPS-capable WAP. First, you would press the button on the printer for a short moment (usually two seconds). You then have a set time (usually two minutes) to press the button on the WAP. This should automatically configure a secure connection.

Some devices enable you to use a code. A WPS-capable WAP will have an eight-digit numeric code printed on the device. To access the WAP, just enter the code in Windows as you would a WPA/WPA2 password. Now you're on the network.

Sadly, WPS has a security flaw. A hacker can use a program to repeatedly guess the eight-digit code. Because of how the code is set up, it's very easy to guess. As long you have WPS enabled on your WAP, you are vulnerable. The only way to stop this hack is to shut down WPS. Check the WAP manufacturer's Web site for instructions on turning off WPS.

Access Point Placement and Radio Power

When setting up your wireless network, keep your space in mind. While encryption can protect your network from intruders, you can also limit your risk by hiding your network from outsiders altogether. When using an omni-directional antenna, keep it near the center of your home or office. The closer you place it to a wall, the further away someone outside your home or office can be and still detect your wireless network.

Your wireless access point might also enable you to adjust the radio power levels of your antenna. Decrease the radio power until you can get reception at the furthest point *inside* your home or office, but not outside. This will take some trial and error.

EXAM TIP Don't forget to physically protect the WAP, too. Most WAPs have physical Ethernet ports in addition to their wireless capabilities. These ports are not password-protected or encrypted. Keep the WAP in a location where unscrupulous folk can't get to it.

Speed and Range Issues

Wireless networking data throughput speeds depend on several factors. Foremost is the standard that the wireless devices use. Depending on the standard used, wireless throughput speeds range from a measly 2 Mbps to a snappy 100+ Mbps. One of the other factors affecting speed is the distance between wireless nodes (or between wireless nodes and centralized access points). Wireless devices dynamically negotiate the top speed at which they can communicate without dropping too many data packets. Speed decreases as distance increases, so the maximum throughput speed is achieved only at extremely close range (less than 25 feet or so). At the outer reaches of a device's effective range, speed may decrease to around 1 Mbps before it drops out altogether.

Speed is also affected by interference from other wireless devices operating in the same frequency range—such as cordless phones or baby monitors—and by solid objects. So-called *dead spots* occur when something capable of blocking the radio signal comes between the wireless network nodes. Large electrical appliances such as refrigerators are *very* effective at blocking a wireless network signal. Other culprits include electrical fuse boxes, metal plumbing, air conditioning units, and similar objects.

NOTE You can see the speed and signal strength on your wireless network by looking at the wireless NIC's properties. In Windows XP, open the Network Connections applet in Control Panel, right-click your wireless NIC, and select Properties. In Vista/7, open the Network and Sharing Center, select Change Adapter Settings, then right-click your wireless NIC and select Properties.

Wireless networking range is difficult to define, and you'll see most descriptions listed with qualifiers, such as "*around* 150 feet" and "*about* 300 feet." This is simply because, like throughput speed, range is greatly affected by outside factors. Interference from other wireless devices affects range, as does interference from solid objects. The maximum ranges listed in the next section are those presented by wireless manufacturers as the theoretical maximum ranges. In the real world, you'll experience these ranges only under the most ideal circumstances. True effective range is probably about half what you see listed.

You can increase range in a couple of ways. You can install multiple WAPs to permit "roaming" between one WAP's coverage area and another's—an EBSS, described earlier in this chapter. Or you can install a replacement that increases a single WAP's signal strength, thus increasing its range. If that is still not enough, signal boosters are available that can give you even more power.

EXAM TIP Look for basic troubleshooting questions on the CompTIA A+ certification exams dealing with factors that affect wireless connectivity, range, and speed.

Wireless Networking Standards

Today's wireless world is dominated by *radio frequency* (*RF*) technologies, in particular the 802.11 (Wi-Fi) standards. Other standards, such as infrared, Bluetooth, and cellular, have a place in today's market. To help you gain a better understanding of wireless network technologies, this section provides a brief look at the standards they use.

IEEE 802.11-Based Wireless Networking

The IEEE 802.11 wireless Ethernet standard, more commonly known as *Wi-Fi*, defines methods by which devices may communicate by using *spread-spectrum* radio waves. Spread-spectrum broadcasts data in small, discrete chunks over the frequencies available within a certain frequency range.

NOTE In the early days of wireless networking, many techs and marketing people assumed Wi-Fi stood for *Wireless Fidelity*, a sort of play on the common sound signal of high fidelity. It might have at one time, but the Wi-Fi Alliance, the governing standards body for 802.11-based networking, just uses the term Wi-Fi today.

The 802.11-based wireless technologies broadcast and receive on one of two license-free industrial, scientific, and medical (ISM) radio bands: 2.4 GHz and 5.8 GHz. Even though the ISM band is 5.8 GHz, we just say "5 GHz" for reasons I can't answer. Over the years, the original 802.11 standard has been extended to 802.11*a*, 802.11*b*, 802.11*g*, and 802.11*n* variations used in Wi-Fi wireless networks. Each of these versions of 802.11 uses one of the two ISM bands, with the exception of 802.11n, which uses one but may use both. Don't worry; I'll break this down for you in a moment.

NOTE Wi-Fi is by far the most widely adopted wireless networking type today. Not only do millions of private businesses and homes have wireless networks, but many public places such as coffee shops and libraries also offer Internet access through wireless networks.

Newer wireless devices can communicate with older wireless devices, so if you are using an 802.11n WAP, all of your 802.11g devices can use it. The exception to this is 802.11a, which requires that all of the equipment directly support it. The following paragraphs describe the important specifications of each of the popular 802.11-based wireless networking standards.

NOTE Devices that use the original 802.11 (with no letter) standard are obsolete these days. You're likeliest to find them in service on some brave early wireless adopter's network—or in a museum. The original 802.11 standard was hampered by both slow speeds (2 Mbps maximum) and limited range (about 150 feet). The 802.11 standard employed some of the same features that are in use in the current wireless standards; 802.11 uses the 2.4-GHz broadcast range.

802.11a Despite the "a" designation for this extension to the 802.11 standard, *802.11a* was actually on the market *after* 802.11b. The 802.11a standard differs from the other 802.11-based standards in significant ways. Foremost is that it operates in the 5-GHz frequency range. This means that devices that use this standard are less prone to interference from other devices that use the same frequency range. 802.11a also offers considerably greater throughput than 802.11 and 802.11b at speeds up to 54 Mbps, though its actual throughput is no more than 25 Mbps in normal traffic conditions. Although its theoretical range tops out at about 150 feet, its maximum range will be lower in a typical office environment. Despite the superior speed of 802.11a, it isn't as widely adopted in the PC world as some of the following 802.11 versions.

802.11b *802.11b* was the first standard to take off and become ubiquitous in wireless networking. The 802.11b standard supports data throughput of up to 11 Mbps (with actual throughput averaging 4 to 6 Mbps)—on par with older wired 10BaseT networks—and a maximum range of 300 feet under ideal conditions. In a typical office environment, its maximum range is lower. The main downside to using 802.11b is, in fact, that it uses a very popular frequency. The 2.4-GHz ISM band is already crowded with baby monitors, garage door openers, microwaves, and wireless phones, so you're likely to run into interference from other wireless devices.

802.11g *802.11g* came out in 2003, taking the best of 802.11a and b and rolling them into a single standard. 802.11g offers data transfer speeds equivalent to 802.11a, up to 54 Mbps, with the wider 300-foot range of 802.11b. More important, 802.11g runs in the 2.4-GHz ISM band, so it is backward compatible with 802.11b, meaning that the same 802.11g WAP can service both 802.11b and 802.11g wireless nodes. 802.11g was incredibly popular but has pretty much lost out to the newest version of 802.11, 802.11n.

802.11n The *802.11n* standard brings several improvements to Wi-Fi networking, including faster speeds and new antenna technology implementations.

The 802.11n specification requires all but hand-held devices to use multiple antennas to implement a feature called *multiple in/multiple out (MIMO)*, which enables the devices to make multiple simultaneous connections. With up to four antennas, 802.11n devices can achieve amazing speeds. (The official standard supports throughput of up to 600 Mbps, although practical implementation drops that down substantially.)

Many 802.11n WAPs employ *transmit beamforming*, a multiple-antenna technology that helps get rid of dead spots—or at least make them not so bad. The antennas adjust the signal once the WAP discovers a client to optimize the radio signal.

Like 802.11g, 802.11n WAPs can run in the 2.4-GHz ISM band, supporting earlier, slower 802.11b/g devices. However, 802.11n also has a more powerful, so-called *dual-band*. To use dual-band 802.11n, you need a more advanced (and more expensive) WAP that runs at both 5 GHz and 2.4 GHz simultaneously; some support 802.11a devices as well as 802.11b/g devices. Nice!

Table 23-1 compares the important differences among the versions of 802.11.

Standard	802.11a	802.11b	802.11g	802.11n
Max. throughput	54 Mbps	11 Mbps	54 Mbps	100+ Mbps
Max. range	150 feet	300 feet	300 feet	300+ feet
Frequency	5 GHz	2.4 GHz	2.4 GHz	2.4 and 5 GHz
Security	SSID, MAC filtering, industry-standard WEP, WPA	SSID, MAC filtering, industry-standard WEP, WPA	SSID, MAC filtering, industry-standard WEP, WPA	SSID, MAC filtering, industry-standard WEP, WPA
Compatibility	802.11a	802.11b	802.11b, 802.11g	802.11b, 802.11g, 802.11n (802.11a in some cases)
Communication mode	Ad hoc or infrastructure	Ad hoc or infrastructure	Ad hoc or infrastructure	Ad hoc or infrastructure
Description	Eight available channels. Less prone to interference than 802.11b and 802.11g.	Fourteen channels available in the 2.4-GHz band (only eleven of which can be used in the U.S. due to FCC regulations). Three non-overlapping channels.	Improved security enhancements. Fourteen channels available in the 2.4-GHz band (only eleven of which can be used in the U.S. due to FCC regulations). Three non-overlapping channels.	Same as 802.11g but adds the 5-GHz band that 802.11a uses. 802.11n can also make use of multiple antennas (MIMO) to increase its range and speed.

Table 23-1 Comparison of 802.11 Standards

 EXAM TIP Know the differences among 802.11a, 802.11b, 802.11g, and 802.11n.

Other Wireless Standards

While Wi-Fi dominates the wireless networking market, it isn't the only standard. A lot of smaller networks (we're talking two computers small) use infrared or Bluetooth to connect devices. Mobile devices, such as smartphones and some tablets, connect wirelessly via cellular networks.

Infrared Wireless Networking

Wireless networking using infrared technology is largely overlooked these days, probably because of the explosion of interest for newer and faster wireless standards. But it is still a viable method to transfer files on some older devices.

Communication through infrared devices is enabled via the *Infrared Data Association (IrDA)* protocol. The IrDA protocol stack is a widely supported industry standard and has been included in all versions of Windows since Windows 95.

 NOTE Apple computers also support IrDA, as do Linux PCs.

In speed and range, infrared isn't very impressive. Infrared devices are capable of transferring data up to 4 Mbps—not too shabby, but hardly stellar. The maximum distance between infrared devices is 1 meter. Infrared links are direct line-of-sight and are susceptible to interference. Anything that breaks the beam of light can disrupt an infrared link: a badly placed can of Mountain Dew, a coworker passing between desks, or even bright sunlight hitting the infrared transceiver can cause interference.

Infrared is designed to make a point-to-point connection between two devices only in ad hoc mode. No infrastructure mode is available. You can, however, use an infrared access point device to enable Ethernet network communication using IrDA. Infrared devices operate at half-duplex, meaning that while one is talking, the other is listening—they can't talk and listen at the same time. IrDA has a mode that emulates full-duplex communication, but it's really half-duplex. The IrDA protocol offers exactly nothing in the way of encryption or authentication. Infrared's main security feature is the fact that you have to be literally within arm's reach to establish a link. Clearly, infrared is not the best solution for a dedicated network connection, but for a quick file transfer or print job without getting your hands dirty, it'll do in a pinch.

Table 23-2 lists infrared's important specifications.

Standard	Infrared (IrDA)
Max. throughput	Up to 4 Mbps
Max. range	1 meter (39 inches)
Security	None
Compatibility	IrDA
Communication mode	Point-to-point ad hoc

Table 23-2 Infrared Specs

 NOTE Many modern laptops still come with a little infrared window, but don't let that fool you into thinking the laptop has IrDA networking. These IR receivers are for use with remotes so you can use the laptop just like a TV or DVD player.

Bluetooth

Bluetooth wireless technology (named for ninth-century Danish king Harald Bluetooth) is designed to create small wireless networks preconfigured to do very specific jobs. Some great examples are audio devices such as headsets that connect to your smartphones, *personal area networks (PANs)* that link two PCs for a quick-and-dirty wireless network, and input devices such as keyboards and mice. Bluetooth is *not* designed to be a full-function networking solution, nor is it meant to compete with Wi-Fi. If anything, Bluetooth has replaced infrared as a means to connect PCs to peripherals.

Bluetooth, like any technology, has been upgraded over the years to make it faster and more secure. Two major versions of Bluetooth are widespread today. The first generation (versions 1.1 and 1.2) supports speeds around 1 Mbps. The second generation (2.0 and 2.1) is backward compatible with its first-generation cousins and adds support for more speed by introducing Enhanced Data Rate (EDR), which pushes top speeds to around 3 Mbps.

NOTE The Bluetooth 3.0 and 4.0 standards were released several years ago, though neither has seen the same level of adoption as earlier standards.

The IEEE organization has made first-generation Bluetooth the basis for its 802.15 standard for wireless PANs. Bluetooth uses a broadcasting method that switches among any of the 79 frequencies available in the 2.45-GHz range. Bluetooth hops frequencies some 1600 times per second, making it highly resistant to interference.

Generally, the faster and further a device sends data, the more power it needs to do so, and the Bluetooth designers understood a long time ago that some devices (such as a Bluetooth headset) could save power by not sending data as quickly or as far as other Bluetooth devices may need. To address this, all Bluetooth devices are configured for one of three classes that define maximum power usage in milliwatts (mW) and maximum distance:

Class 1	100 mW	100 meters
Class 2	2.5 mW	10 meters
Class 3	1 mW	1 meter

Bluetooth is made to replace the snake's nest of cables that currently connects most PCs to their various peripheral devices—keyboard, mouse, printer, speakers, scanner, and the like—but you won't be swapping out your 802.11-based networking devices with Bluetooth-based replacements anytime soon.

Having said that, Bluetooth-enabled wireless networking is comparable to other wireless technologies in a few ways:

- Like infrared, Bluetooth is acceptable for quick file transfers where a wired connection (or a faster wireless connection) is unavailable.

- Almost all wireless headsets are now Bluetooth.
- Bluetooth's speed and range make it a good match for wireless print server solutions.

Bluetooth hardware comes either integrated into many newer portable electronic gadgets such as smartphones or as an adapter added to an internal or external expansion bus. Bluetooth networking is enabled through ad hoc–styled device-to-device connections, or in an infrastructure-like mode through Bluetooth access points. Bluetooth access points are very similar to 802.11-based access points, bridging wireless Bluetooth PAN segments to wired LAN segments.

Cellular

A *cellular wireless network* enables you to connect to the Internet through a network-aware smartphone, tablet, or other mobile device. To learn more about cellular data networks, check out Chapter 24.

802

Installing and Configuring Wireless Networking

The mechanics of setting up a wireless network don't differ much from a wired network. Physically installing a wireless network adapter is the same as installing a wired NIC, whether it's an internal PCI card, a PC Card, or an external USB device. Simply install the device and let plug and play handle the rest. Install the device's supplied driver when prompted, and you're practically finished.

As mentioned earlier, wireless devices want to talk to each other, so communicating with an available wireless network is usually a no-brainer. The trick is in configuring the wireless network so that only specific wireless nodes are able to use it and securing the data that's being sent through the air.

Wi-Fi Configuration

Wi-Fi networks support ad hoc and infrastructure operation modes. Which mode you choose depends on the number of wireless nodes you need to support, the type of data sharing they'll perform, and your management requirements.

Ad hoc Mode

Ad hoc mode wireless networks don't need a WAP. The only requirements in an ad hoc mode wireless network are that each wireless node be configured with the same network name (SSID) and that no two nodes use the same IP address. Figure 23-11 shows a wireless network configuration utility with ad hoc mode selected.

Figure 23-11

Selecting ad hoc mode in a wireless configuration utility

The only other configuration steps to take is to make sure that no two nodes are using the same IP address (this step is usually unnecessary if all PCs are using DHCP) and ensuring that the File and Printer Sharing service is running on all nodes.

Infrastructure Mode

Typically, infrastructure mode wireless networks employ one or more WAPs connected to a wired network segment, a corporate intranet or the Internet, or both. As with ad hoc mode wireless networks, infrastructure mode networks require that the same SSID be configured on all nodes and WAPs. Figure 23-12 shows a NETGEAR Wi-Fi configuration screen set to infrastructure mode and using WPA security.

WAPs have an integrated Web server and are configured through a browser-based setup utility. Typically, you fire up your Web browser on one of your network client workstations and enter the WAP's default IP address, such as 192.168.1.1, to bring up the configuration page. You will need to supply an administrative password, included with your WAP's documentation, to log in (see Figure 23-13). Setup screens vary from vendor to vendor and from model to model. Figure 23-14 shows the initial setup screen for a popular Linksys WAP/router.

Configure the SSID option where indicated. Channel selection is usually automatic, but you can reconfigure this option if you have particular needs in your organization (for example, if you have multiple wireless networks operating in the same area). Remember that it's always more secure to configure a unique SSID than it is to accept the well-known default one. You should also make sure that the option to allow

broadcasting of the SSID is disabled. This ensures that only wireless nodes specifically configured with the correct SSID can join the wireless network.

Figure 23-12 Selecting infrastructure mode in a wireless configuration utility

Figure 23-13 Security login for Linksys WAP

To increase security even more, use MAC filtering. Figure 23-15 shows the MAC filtering configuration screen for a Linksys WAP. Simply enter the MAC address of a wireless node that you wish to allow (or deny) access to your wireless network. Set up encryption by turning encryption on at the WAP and then generating a unique security key. Then configure all connected wireless nodes on the network with the same key information. Figure 23-16 shows the WEP key configuration screen for a Linksys WAP.

EXAM TIP As noted earlier in the chapter, the WEP protocol provides security, but it's easily cracked. Use WPA2 or, if you have older equipment, settle for WPA until you can upgrade.

Figure 23-14 Linksys WAP setup screen

Figure 23-15 MAC filtering configuration screen for a Linksys WAP

Figure 23-16 WEP encryption key configuration screen for a Linksys WAP

When setting up WEP, you have the option of automatically generating a set of encryption keys or doing it manually; save yourself a headache and use the automatic method. Select an encryption level—the usual choices are either 64-bit or 128-bit—and then enter a unique passphrase and click the Generate button (or whatever the equivalent button is called on your WAP). Then select a default key and save the settings. The encryption level, key, and passphrase must match on the wireless client node or communication will fail. Many WAPs have the capability to export the WEP encryption key data onto a media storage device for easy importing onto a client workstation, or you can manually configure encryption by using the vendor-supplied configuration utility, as shown in Figure 23-17.

WPA and WPA2 encryption is configured in much the same way as WEP. There are two ways to set up WPA/WPA2: Pre-shared Key (PSK) or Enterprise. WPA/WPA2-PSK is the most common for small and home networks. Enterprise is much more complex, requires extra equipment (a RADIUS server), and is only used in the most serious and secure wireless networks.

If you have the option, choose WPA2 encryption for the WAP as well as the NICs in your network. You configure WPA2 the same way you would WPA. Note that the settings such as WPA2 for the Enterprise assume you'll enable authentication by using a device called a RADIUS server (see Figure 23-18). This way, businesses can allow only people with the proper credentials to connect to their Wi-Fi networks. For home use, select the PSK version of WPA/WPA2. Use the best encryption you can. If you have WPA2, use it. If not, use WPA. WEP is always a last choice.

Figure 23-17
WEP encryption screen on client wireless network adapter configuration utility

Figure 23-18 Encryption screen with RADIUS option

NOTE Always try WPA2-PSK first. If you then have wireless computers that can't connect to your WAP, fall back to WPA-PSK.

With most home networks, you can simply leave the channel and frequency of the WAP at the factory defaults, but in an environment with overlapping Wi-Fi signals, you'll want to adjust one or both features. To adjust the channel, find the option in the WAP configuration screens and simply change it. Figure 23-19 shows the channel option in a Linksys WAP.

Figure 23-19 Changing the channel

With dual-band 802.11n WAPs, you can choose which band to put 802.11n traffic on, either 2.4 GHz or 5 GHz. In an area with overlapping signals, most of the traffic will be on the 2.4-GHz frequency, because most devices are either 802.11b or 802.11g. In addition to other wireless devices (such as cordless phones), microwaves also use the 2.4-GHz frequency and can cause a great deal of interference. You can avoid any kind of conflict with your 802.11n devices by using the 5-GHz frequency instead. Figure 23-20 shows the configuration screen for a dual-band 802.11n WAP.

Figure 23-20 Selecting frequency

Placing the Access Point(s)

The optimal location for an access point depends on the area you want to cover, whether you care if the signal bleeds out beyond the borders, and what interference exists from other wireless sources. You start by doing a site survey. A site survey can be as trivial as firing up a wireless-capable laptop and looking for existing SSIDs. Or it can be a complex job where you hire people with specialized equipment to come in and make lots of careful plans, defining the best place to put WAPs and which wireless channels to use. To make sure the wireless signal goes where you want it to go and not where you don't, you need to use the right antenna. Let's see what types of antennas are available.

Omni-directional and Centered For a typical network, you want blanket coverage and would place a WAP with an omni-directional antenna in the center of the area (see Figure 23-21). With an omni-directional antenna, the radio wave flows outward from the WAP. This has the advantage of ease of use—anything within the signal radius can potentially access the network. Most wireless networks use this combination, especially in the consumer space. The standard straight-wire antennas that provide most omni-directional function are called *dipole antennas*.

Figure 23-21 Room layout with WAP in the center

Gaining Gain An antenna strengthens and focuses the radio frequency (RF) output from a WAP. The ratio of increase—what's called *gain*—is measured in decibels (dB). The gain from a typical WAP is 2 dB, enough to cover a reasonable area but not a very large room. To increase that signal requires a bigger antenna. Many WAPs have removable antennas that you can replace. To increase the signal in an omni-directional and centered setup, simply replace the factory antennas with one or more bigger antennas (see Figure 23-22). Get a big enough antenna and you can crank it all the way up to 11 dB!

NOTE If you want to know whether your local café, bookstore, airport, or other public place has a Wi-Fi access point (otherwise known as a *hotspot*), you can use a *Wi-Fi* or *wireless locator*. The locator is usually the size of your car remote and lights up or otherwise signals you whenever you are in range of a Wi-Fi access point.

Figure 23-22
Replacement an-
tenna on WAP

Bluetooth Configuration

As with other wireless networking solutions, Bluetooth devices are completely plug and play. Just connect the adapter and follow the prompts to install the appropriate drivers and configuration utilities (these are supplied by your hardware vendor). Once they're installed, you have little to do: Bluetooth devices seek each other out and establish the master/slave relationship without any intervention on your part.

Connecting to a Bluetooth PAN is handled by specialized utility software provided by your portable device or Bluetooth device vendor. Figure 23-23 shows a screen of an older PDA running the Bluetooth Manager software to connect to a Bluetooth access point. Like their Wi-Fi counterparts, Bluetooth access points use a browser-based configuration utility. Figure 23-24 shows the main setup screen for a Belkin Bluetooth access point. Use this setup screen to check on the status of connected Bluetooth devices; configure encryption, MAC filtering, and other security settings; and use other utilities provided by the access point's vendor.

NOTE Bluetooth network access points are a rare sight out in the real world. Today small portables, PDAs, and smartphones almost certainly connect by using a Wi-Fi or cellular network.

Figure 23-23
iPAQ Bluetooth
Manager software
connected to
Bluetooth access
point

Figure 23-24
Belkin Bluetooth
access point

Cellular Configuration

There is no single standard for configuring a cellular network card because the cards and software change based on your service provider. Fortunately, those same cell phone companies have made the process of installing their cards very simple. All that is required in most cases is to plug in the card and install the software.

With most cellular cards, you simply plug the card into your computer, usually via USB, and the setup program automatically launches. These cards almost always have all the required software and drivers built into the cards themselves, so there are no optical

discs to worry about. Once you've installed the necessary software, launch the connection application. Follow the instructions that came with the software; in Figure 23-25, for example, double-click on the VZAccess network listed in the window. This initiates the connection to Verizon's network. You can also go to the Options menu and select Statistics to see the specifics of your connection, as shown in Figure 23-26.

Figure 23-25
VZAccess Manager

Figure 23-26
Session statistics
for VZAccess
Manager

The key thing to remember about cellular Internet access is that it is almost completely configured and controlled by the provider. A tech has very little to do except to make sure the cellular card is plugged in, recognized by the computer, and properly installed.

Troubleshooting Wi-Fi

Wireless networks are a real boon when they work right, but they can also be one of the most vexing things to troubleshoot when they don't. Let's turn to some practical advice on how to detect and correct wireless hardware, software, and configuration problems.

As with any troubleshooting scenario, your first step in troubleshooting a wireless network is to break down your tasks into logical steps. Your first step should be to figure out the scope of your wireless networking problem. Ask yourself *who*, *what*, and *when*:

- Who is affected by the problem?
- What is the nature of their network problem?
- When did the problem start?

The answers to these questions dictate at least the initial direction of your troubleshooting.

So, who's affected? If all machines on your network—wired and wireless—have lost connectivity, you have bigger problems than that the wireless machines cannot access the network. Troubleshoot this situation the way you'd troubleshoot any network failure. Once you determine which wireless nodes are affected, it's easier to pinpoint whether the problem lies in one or more wireless clients or in one or more access points.

After you narrow down the number of affected machines, your next task is to figure out specifically what type of error the users are experiencing. If they can access some, but not all, network services, it's unlikely that the problem is limited to their wireless equipment. For example, if they can browse the Internet but can't access any shared resources on a server, they're probably experiencing a permissions-related issue rather than a wireless one.

Finally, determine when the problem started. What has changed that might explain your loss of connectivity? Did you or somebody else change the wireless network configuration? For example, if the network worked fine two minutes ago, and then you changed the WEP key on the access point, and now nobody can see the network, you have your solution—or at least your culprit! Did your office experience a power outage, power sag, or power surge? Any of these might cause a WAP to fail.

Once you figure out the who, what, and when, you can start troubleshooting in earnest. Typically, your problem is going to center on your hardware, software, connectivity, or configuration.

Hardware Troubleshooting

Wireless networking hardware components are subject to the same kind of abuse and faulty installation as any other hardware component. Troubleshooting a suspected hardware problem should bring out the technician in you.

Open Windows Device Manager and look for an error or conflict with the wireless adapter. If you see a big exclamation point or a red X next to the device, you have a driver error. Reinstall the device driver as needed.

If you don't see the device listed at all, perhaps it is not seated properly in its expansion slot or not plugged all the way into its PC Card or USB slot. These problems are easy to fix. Just remove them and reinstall the device.

NOTE As with all things computing, don't forget to do the standard PC troubleshooting thing and reboot the computer before you do any configuration or hardware changes!

Software Troubleshooting

Because you've already checked to confirm that your hardware is using the correct drivers, what kind of software-related problems are left to check? Two things come immediately to mind: the wireless adapter configuration utility and the WAP's firmware version.

As I mentioned earlier, some wireless devices won't work correctly unless you install the vendor-provided drivers and configuration utility before plugging in the device. This is particularly true of wireless USB devices. If you didn't do this, go into Device Manager and uninstall the device; then start again from scratch.

Some WAP manufacturers (I won't name names here, but they're popular) are notorious for shipping devices without the latest firmware installed. This problem often manifests as a device that enables clients to connect, but only at such slow speeds that the devices experience frequent timeout errors. The fix for this is to update the access point's firmware. Go to the manufacturer's Web site and follow the support links until you find the latest version. You'll need your device's exact model and serial number—this is important, because installing the wrong firmware version on your device is a guaranteed way of rendering it unusable!

Again, follow the manufacturer's instructions for updating the firmware to the letter. Typically, you need to download a small executable updating program along with a data file containing the firmware software. The process takes only minutes, and you'll be amazed at the results.

Connectivity Troubleshooting

Properly configured wireless clients should automatically and quickly connect to the desired SSID. If this isn't taking place, it's time for some troubleshooting. Most wireless

connectivity problems come down to either an incorrect configuration (such as an incorrect password) or low signal strength. Without a strong signal, even a properly configured wireless client isn't going to work. Wireless clients use a multi-bar graph (usually five bars) to give an idea of signal strength: zero bars indicates no signal and five bars indicates maximum signal.

Whether configuration or signal strength, the process to diagnose and repair uses the same methods you use for a wired network. First, check the wireless NIC's link light to see whether it's passing data packets to and from the network. Second, check the wireless NIC's configuration utility. Typically the utility has an icon in your system tray/notification area that shows the strength of your wireless signal. Figure 23-27 shows Windows XP Professional's built-in wireless configuration utility—called Wireless Zero Configuration (or just Zeroconf)—displaying the link state and signal strength. Wireless Zero Configuration was first introduced with Windows XP. In Windows Vista and Windows 7, the service is called WLAN AutoConfig.

Figure 23-27
Windows XP Professional's wireless configuration utility

Wireless Network Connection (HomeWiFi)
Speed: 54.0 Mbps
Signal Strength: Very Good
Status: Connected

NOTE If you're lucky enough to have a laptop with an internally installed NIC (instead of a PC Card), your device may not have a link light.

The link state defines the wireless NIC's connection status to a wireless network: connected or disconnected. If your link state indicates that your computer is currently disconnected, you may have a problem with your WAP. If your signal is too weak to receive a signal (referred to on the CompTIA A+ exams as a "low RF signal"), you may be out of range of your access point, or there may be a device causing interference.

You can fix these problems in a number of ways. Because Wi-Fi signals bounce off of objects, you can try small adjustments to your antennas to see if the signal improves. You can swap out the standard antenna for one or more higher-gain antennas. You can relocate the PC or access point, or locate and move the device causing interference.

Other wireless devices that operate in the same frequency range as your wireless nodes can cause interference as well. Look for wireless telephones, intercoms, and so on as possible culprits. One fix for interference caused by other wireless devices is to change the channel your network uses. Another is to change the channel the offending device uses, if possible. If you can't change channels, try moving the interfering device to another area or replacing it with a different device.

Configuration Troubleshooting

With all due respect to the fine network techs in the field, the most common type of wireless networking problem is misconfigured hardware or software. That's right—the dreaded *user error*! Given the complexities of wireless networking, this isn't so surprising. All it takes is one slip of the typing finger to throw off your configuration completely. The things you're most likely to get wrong are the SSID and security configuration.

Verify SSID configuration on your access point first, and then check on the affected wireless nodes. With most wireless devices, you can use any characters in the SSID, including blank spaces. Be careful not to add blank characters where they don't belong, such as trailing blank spaces behind any other characters typed into the name field.

If you're using MAC address filtering, make sure the MAC address of the client that's attempting to access the wireless network is on the list of accepted users. This is particularly important if you swap out NICs on a PC, or if you introduce a new PC to your wireless network.

Check the security configuration to make sure that all wireless nodes and access points match. Mistyping an encryption key prevents the affected node from talking to the wireless network, even if your signal strength is 100 percent! Remember that many access points have the capability to export encryption keys onto a thumb drive or other removable media. It's then a simple matter to import the encryption key onto the PC by using the wireless NIC's configuration utility. Remember that the encryption level must match on access points and wireless nodes. If your WAP is configured for 128-bit encryption, all nodes must also use 128-bit encryption.

Chapter Review

Questions

1. Under ideal conditions, the 802.11g standard supports data throughput of up to _____ and has a range of up to _____.

 A. 11 Mbps/150 feet

 B. 11 Mbps/300 feet

 C. 54 Mbps/150 feet

 D. 54 Mbps/300 feet

2. Which encryption protocol offers the best security?

 A. Hi-Encrypt

 B. WEP

 C. WPA

 D. WPA2

3. Which device enables you to extend the capabilities of a wireless network?

 A. WAP

 B. WEP

 C. WPA

 D. WPA2

4. In which mode do all the wireless devices connect directly to each other?

 A. Ad hoc mode

 B. Circular mode

 C. Infrastructure mode

 D. Mesh mode

5. What determines the name of a wireless network?

 A. EAP

 B. MAC address

 C. SSID

 D. WAP

6. What technology enables 802.11n networks to make multiple simultaneous connections and thus improve speed over previous Wi-Fi standards?

 A. Use of the 2.4-GHz frequency

 B. Use of the 5-GHz frequency

 C. MIMO

 D. WPA2

7. What's the top speed for data transfers using IrDA technology?

 A. 2 Mbps

 B. 4 Mbps

 C. 11 Mbps

 D. 54 Mbps

8. Bluetooth technology enables computers to link into what sort of network?

 A. Bluetooth area network (BAN)

 B. Personal area network (PAN)

 C. Local area network (LAN)

 D. Wide area network (WAN)

9. What is the name for the common omni-directional antennas found on wireless access points?

 A. Bipole antennas

 B. Dipole antennas

 C. Omni antennas

 D. RF antennas

10. Ralph has installed a wireless network in his house, placing the wireless access point in the kitchen, a centralized location. The Wi-Fi works fine in the living room and dining room but goes out almost completely in the bedroom. What's most likely the problem?

 A. Interference with some metal object

 B. Improper antenna setup

 C. Use of the default SSID

 D. The SSID overlapping with a neighbor's SSID

Answers

1. **D.** Under ideal conditions, the 802.11g standard supports data throughput of up to 54 Mbps and has a range of up to 300 feet.

2. **D.** WPA2 is the best of the encryption technologies listed.

3. **A.** A wireless access point (WAP) enables you to extend the capabilities of a wireless network.

4. **A.** In ad hoc mode networks, all the nodes connect directly to each other.

5. **C.** The SSID determines the name of a wireless network.

6. **C.** The multiple in/multiple out (MIMO) technology implementing multiple antennas enables 802.11n networks to run at much faster speeds than previous Wi-Fi networks.

7. **B.** Data transfers using the IrDA protocol top out at 4 Mbps.

8. **B.** Bluetooth creates personal area networks.

9. **B.** Standard omni-directional antennas are called dipole antennas.

10. **A.** Watch out for microwave ovens, refrigerators, and pipes in the walls. They can interfere with a Wi-Fi signal and create dead spots.

The Internet

In this chapter, you will learn how to

- Explain how the Internet works
- Connect to the Internet
- Use Internet application protocols
- Troubleshoot an Internet connection

Imagine coming home from a long day at work building and fixing PCs, sitting down in front of your shiny new computer, double-clicking the single icon that sits dead center on your monitor…and suddenly you're enveloped in an otherworldly scene, where 200-foot trees slope smoothly into snow-white beaches and rich blue ocean. Overhead, pterodactyls soar through the air while you talk to a small chap with pointy ears and a long robe about heading up the mountain in search of a giant monster…. A TV show from the Syfy channel? Spielberg's latest film offering? How about an interactive game played by millions of people all over the planet on a daily basis by connecting to the Internet? If you guessed the last one, you're right.

This chapter covers the skills you need as a PC tech to help people connect to the Internet. It starts with a brief section on how the Internet works, along with the concepts of connectivity, and then it goes into the specifics on hardware, protocols, and software that you use to make the Internet work for you (or for your client). Finally, you'll learn how to troubleshoot a bad Internet connection. Let's get started!

Historical/Conceptual

How the Internet Works

Thanks to the Internet, people can communicate with one another over vast distances, often in the blink of an eye. As a PC tech, you need to know how PCs communicate with the larger world for two reasons. First, knowing the process and pieces involved in the communication enables you to troubleshoot effectively when that communication goes away. Second, you need to be able to communicate knowledgeably with a network technician who comes in to solve a more complex issue.

Internet Tiers

You probably know that the Internet is millions and millions of computers all joined together to form the largest network on earth, but not many folks know much about how these computers are organized. To keep everything running smoothly, the Internet is broken down into groups called *tiers*. The main tier, called *Tier 1*, consists of nine companies called *Tier 1 providers*. The Tier 1 providers own long-distance, high-speed fiber-optic networks called *backbones*. These backbones span the major cities of the earth (not all Tier 1 backbones go to all cities) and interconnect at special locations called *network access points* (*NAPs*). Anyone wishing to connect to any of the Tier 1 providers must pay large sums of money. The Tier 1 providers do not charge each other to connect.

Tier 2 providers own smaller, regional networks and must pay the Tier 1 providers. Most of the famous companies that provide Internet access to the general public are Tier 2 providers. *Tier 3 providers* are even more regional and connect to Tier 2 providers.

The piece of equipment that makes this tiered Internet concept work is called a backbone router. *Backbone routers* connect to more than one other backbone router, creating a big, interwoven framework for communication. Figure 24-1 illustrates the decentralized and interwoven nature of the Internet. The key reason for interweaving the backbones of the Internet was to provide alternative pathways for data if one or more of the routers went down. If Jane in Houston sends a message to her friend Polly in New York City, for example, the shortest path between Jane and Polly in this hypothetical situation is this: Jane's message originates at Rice University in Houston, bounces to Emory University in Atlanta, flits through Virginia Commonwealth University in Richmond, and then zips into SUNY in New York City (see Figure 24-2). Polly happily reads the message and life is great. The Internet functions as planned.

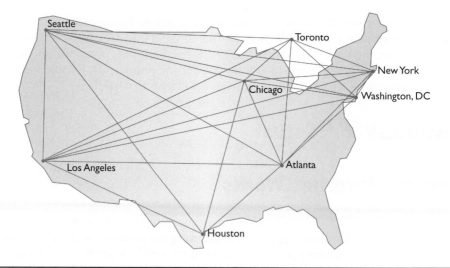

Figure 24-1 Internet Tier 1 connections

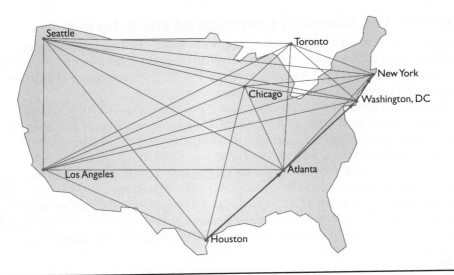

Figure 24-2 Message traveling from Houston to NYC

But what happens if the entire southeastern United States experiences a huge power outage and Internet backbones in every state from Virginia to Florida go down? Jane's message would bounce back to Rice and the Rice computers. Being smart cookies, the routers would reroute the message to nodes that still functioned—say, Rice to University of Chicago, to University of Toronto, and then to SUNY (see Figure 24-3). It's all in a day's work for the highly redundant and adaptable Internet. At this point in the game, the Internet simply cannot go down fully—barring, of course, a catastrophe of Biblical proportions.

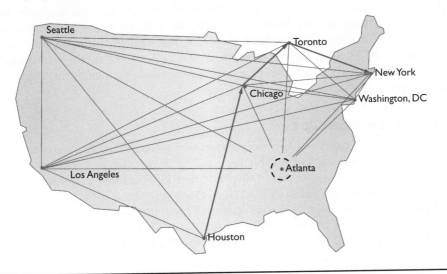

Figure 24-3 Rerouted message from Houston to NYC

TCP/IP—The Common Language of the Internet

As you know from all the earlier chapters in this book, hardware alone doesn't cut it in the world of computing. You need software to make the machines run and create an interface for humans. The Internet is no exception. TCP/IP provides the basic software structure for communication on the Internet.

Because you spent a good deal of Chapter 22 working with TCP/IP, you should have an appreciation for its adaptability and, perhaps more importantly, its extendibility. TCP/IP provides the addressing scheme for computers that communicate on the Internet through IP addresses, such as 192.168.4.1 or 16.45.123.7. As a protocol, though, TCP/IP is much more than just an addressing system. TCP/IP provides the framework and common language for the Internet. And it offers a phenomenally wide-open structure for creative purposes. Programmers can write applications built to take advantage of the TCP/IP structure and features, creating what are called TCP/IP services. The cool thing about TCP/IP services is that they're limited only by the imagination of the programmers.

At this point, you have an enormous, beautifully functioning network. All the backbone routers connect with fiber and thick copper cabling backbones, and TCP/IP enables communication and services for building applications for humans to interface across the distances. What's left? Oh, that's right: how do you tap into this great network and partake of its goodness?

Internet Service Providers

Every Tier 1 and Tier 2 provider leases connections to the Internet to companies called *Internet service providers (ISPs)*. ISPs essentially sit along the edges of the Tier 1 and Tier 2 Internet and tap into the flow. You can, in turn, lease some of the connections from the ISP and thus get on the Internet.

ISPs come in all sizes. Comcast, the cable television provider, has multiple, huge-capacity connections into the Internet, enabling its millions of customers to connect from their local machines and surf the Web. Contrast Comcast with Unisono, an ISP in San Miguel de Allende, Mexico (see Figure 24-4). Billed as the "the fastest Internet service" in San Miguel de Allende, it services only a small (but delightful) community and the busy tourist crowd.

Connection Concepts

Connecting to an ISP requires two things to work perfectly: hardware for connectivity, such as a modem and a working cable line; and software, such as protocols to govern the connections and the data flow (all configured in Windows) and applications to take advantage of the various TCP/IP services. Once you have a contract with an ISP to grant you access to the Internet, a technician will often install your Internet connection device and any software you need. With most ISPs, a DHCP server will provide your PC with the proper TCP/IP information. As you know, the router to which you connect at the ISP is often referred to as the *default gateway*. Once your PC is configured, you can connect to the ISP and get to the greater Internet. Figure 24-5 shows a standard PC-to-ISP-to-Internet connection. Note that various protocols and other software manage the connectivity between your PC and the default gateway.

Figure 24-4

Unisono homepage

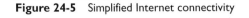

Figure 24-5 Simplified Internet connectivity

801

Connecting to the Internet

PCs commonly connect to an ISP by using one of nine technologies that fit into four categories: dial-up, both analog and ISDN; dedicated, such as DSL, cable, fiber, and LAN; wireless, including cellular and WiMAX; and satellite. Analog dial-up is the slowest of the bunch and requires a telephone line and a special networking device called a modem. ISDN uses digital dial-up and has much greater speed. Dedicated connections (cable and DSL) most often use a box that connects to a regular Ethernet NIC like you played with in Chapter 22. Wireless connections are a mixed bag, depending on the device and service you have. Some are built-in, while others use a box you attach to your LAN. Satellite is the odd one out here; it may use either a modem or a NIC, depending on the particular configuration you have, although most folks will use a NIC. Let's take a look at all these various connection options, and then finish this section by discussing basic router configuration and Internet Connection Sharing in Windows.

Dial-up

A dial-up connection to the Internet requires two pieces to work: hardware to dial the ISP, such as a modem or ISDN terminal adapter; and software to govern the connection, such as Microsoft's *Dial-up Networking (DUN)*. Let's look at the hardware first, and then we'll explore software configuration.

Modems

At some point in the early days of computing, some bright guy or gal noticed a colleague talking on a telephone, glanced down at a PC, and then put two and two together: why not use telephone lines for data communication? The basic problem with this idea is that traditional telephone lines use analog signals, while computers use digital signals (see Figure 24-6). Creating a dial-up network required equipment that could turn digital data into an analog signal to send it over the telephone line, and then turn it back into digital data when it reached the other end of the connection. A device called a modem solved this dilemma.

Modems enable computers to talk to each other via standard commercial telephone lines by converting analog signals to digital signals, and vice versa. The term *modem* is short for modulator/demodulator, a description of transforming the signals. Telephone wires transfer data via analog signals that continuously change voltages on a wire. Computers hate analog signals. Instead, they need digital signals, voltages that are either on or off, meaning the wire has voltage present or it does not. Computers, being binary by nature, use only two states of voltage: zero volts and positive volts. Modems take analog signals from telephone lines and turn them into digital signals that the PC can understand (see Figure 24-7). Modems also take digital signals from the PC and convert them into analog signals for the outgoing telephone line.

Figure 24-6
Analog signals used
by a telephone
line versus digital
signals used by the
computer

Analog: Increasing and decreasing waves of electricity

Digital: A set (specific) increase and decrease in electrical current

Figure 24-7 Modem converting analog signal to digital signal

A modem does what is called *serial communication*: It transmits data as a series of individual ones and zeros. The CPU can't process data this way. It needs parallel communication, transmitting and receiving data in discrete 8-bit chunks (see Figure 24-8). The individual serial bits of data are converted into 8-bit parallel data that the PC can understand through the *universal asynchronous receiver/transmitter (UART)* chip (see Figure 24-9).

Figure 24-8
CPUs can't read
serial data.

Figure 24-9 The UART chip converts serial data to parallel data that the CPU can read.

There are many types of UARTs, each with different functions. All serial communication devices are really little more than UARTs. *External* modems can convert analog signals to digital ones and vice versa, but they must rely on the serial ports to which they're connected for the job of converting between serial and parallel data (see Figure 24-10). Internal modems can handle both jobs because they have their own UART built in (see Figure 24-11).

② It uses a serial port's UART.

① An external modem has no UART.

Figure 24-10 An external modem uses the PC's serial port.

Phone lines have a speed based on a unit called a *baud*, which is one cycle per second. The fastest rate that a phone line can achieve is 2400 baud. Modems can pack multiple bits of data into each baud; a 33.6 kilobits per second (Kbps) modem, for example, packs 14 bits into every baud: 2400 × 14 = 33.6 Kbps. Thus, it is technically incorrect to say, "I have a 56-K baud modem." The correct statement is, "I have a 56-Kbps modem." But don't bother; people have used the term "baud" instead of *bits per second (bps)* so often for so long that the terms have become functionally synonymous.

Figure 24-11
An internal modem
has UART built in.

UART

Modem Connections Internal modems connect to the PC very differently from
how external modems connect. Almost all internal modems connect to a PCI or PCI
Express expansion bus slot inside the PC, although cost-conscious manufacturers may
use smaller modems that fit in special expansion slots designed to support multiple
communications features such as modems, NICs, and sound cards (see Figure 24-12).
Older AMD motherboards used Audio/Modem Riser (AMR) or Advanced Communica-
tion Riser (ACR) slots, while Intel motherboards used Communication and Network-
ing Riser (CNR) slots.

Figure 24-12
A CNR modem

NOTE AMR, ACR, and CNR slots have gone away, though you'll still find them on older systems. Current systems use built-in components or PCIe ×1 slots for modems, sound, and NICs.

External modems connect to the PC through an available serial port (the old way) or USB port (see Figure 24-13). USB offers simple plug and play and easy portability between machines, plus such modems require no external electrical source, getting all the power they need from the USB connection.

Figure 24-13
A USB modem

Dial-up Networking

The software side of dial-up networks requires configuration within Windows to include information provided by your ISP. The ISP provides a dial-up telephone number or numbers, as well as your user name and initial password. In addition, the ISP will tell you about any special configuration options you need to specify in the software setup. The full configuration of dial-up networking is beyond the scope of this book, but you should at least know where to go to follow instructions from your ISP. Let's take a look at the Network and Internet Connections applet in Windows XP.

Configuring Dial-up To start configuring a dial-up connection in Windows XP, open the Control Panel. Select Network and Internet Connections from the Pick a category menu and then choose *Set up or change your Internet connection* from the Pick a task menu. The Internet Properties dialog box opens with the Connections tab displayed (see Figure 24-14). All your work will proceed from here.

Click the Setup button to run the New Connection Wizard (see Figure 24-15), and then work through the screens. At this point, you're going to need information provided by your ISP to configure your connection properly. When you finish the configuration, you'll see a new Connect To option on the Start menu if your system is set up that way. If not, open up Network Connections, and your new dial-up connection will be available. Figure 24-16 shows the option to connect to a fictitious ISP, Cool-Rides.com.

Figure 24-14
The Connections
tab in the Internet
Properties
dialog box

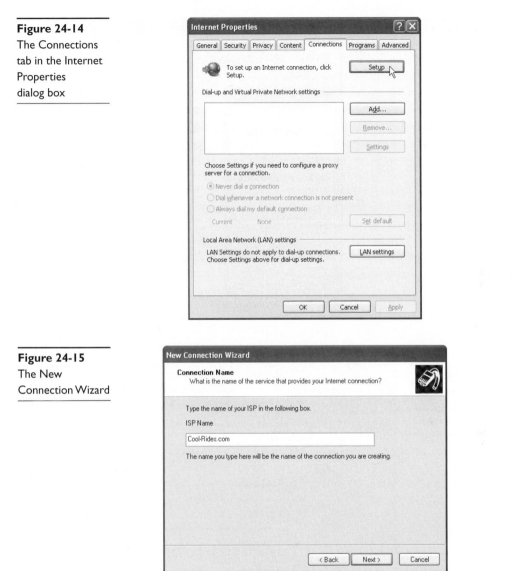

Figure 24-15
The New
Connection Wizard

Windows Vista and 7 handle dial-up connections in the same way. Open the Network and Sharing Center and click on *Set up a new connection or network* (see Figure 24-17).

Select *Set up a dial-up connection* on the next screen and then enter your dial-up information, as shown in Figure 24-18.

PPP Dial-up links to the Internet have their own special hardware protocol called *Point-to-Point Protocol (PPP)*. PPP is a streaming protocol developed especially for dial-up Internet access. To Windows, a modem is nothing more than a special type of network adapter. You can configure a new dial-up connection in the Network and Sharing Center in Vista/7 or the Network Connections applet in XP.

Figure 24-16

Connection options in Network Connections

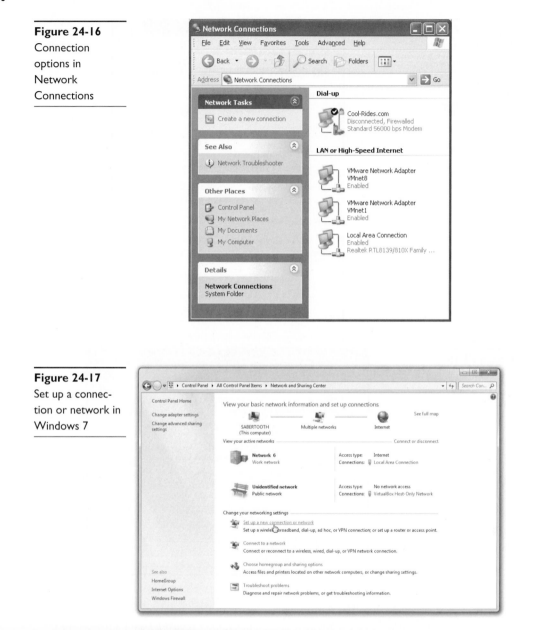

Figure 24-17

Set up a connection or network in Windows 7

Most dial-up "I can't connect to the Internet"–type problems are user errors. Your first area of investigation is the modem itself. Use the modem's properties to make sure the volume is turned up. Have the user listen to the connection. Does she hear a dial tone? If she doesn't, make sure the modem's line is plugged into a good phone jack. Does she hear the modem dial and then hear someone saying, "Hello? Hello?" If

so, she probably dialed the wrong number! Wrong password error messages are fairly straightforward—remember that the password may be correct but the user name may be wrong. If she still fails to connect, it's time to call the network folks to see what is not properly configured in her dial-up modem's Properties dialog box.

Figure 24-18
Creating a dial-up connection in Windows 7

ISDN

A standard telephone connection comprises many pieces. First, the phone line runs from your phone out to a network interface box (the little box on the side of your house) and into a central switch belonging to the telephone company. (In some cases, intermediary steps are present.) Standard metropolitan areas have a large number of central offices, each with a central switch. Houston, Texas, for example, has nearly 100 offices in the general metro area. These central switches connect to each other through high-capacity *trunk lines*. Before 1970, the entire phone system was analog; over time, however, phone companies began to upgrade their trunk lines to digital systems. Today, the entire telephone system, with the exception of the line from your phone to the central office, and sometimes even that, is digital.

During this upgrade period, customers continued to demand higher throughput from their phone lines. The old telephone line was not expected to produce more than 28.8 Kbps (56-K modems, which were a *big* surprise to the phone companies, didn't appear until 1995). Needless to say, the phone companies were very motivated to come up with a way to generate higher capacities. Their answer was actually fairly straightforward: make the entire phone system digital. By adding special equipment at the central office and the user's location, phone companies can now achieve a throughput of up to 64 K per line (see the paragraphs following) over the same copper wires already used by telephone lines. This process of sending telephone transmission across fully digital lines end-to-end is called *integrated services digital network (ISDN)* service.

ISDN service consists of two types of channels: Bearer, or B, channels and Delta, or D, channels. B channels carry data and voice information at 64 Kbps. D channels carry setup and configuration information and carry data at 16 Kbps. Most providers of ISDN allow the user to choose either one or two B channels. The more common setup is two B/one D, usually called a *basic rate interface* (*BRI*) setup. A BRI setup uses only one physical line, but each B channel sends 64 Kbps, doubling the throughput total to 128 Kbps. ISDN also connects much faster than modems, eliminating that long, annoying, mating call you get with phone modems. The monthly cost per B channel is slightly more than a regular phone line, and usually a fairly steep initial fee is levied for the installation and equipment. The big limitation is that you usually need to be within about 18,000 feet of a central office to use ISDN.

The physical connections for ISDN bear some similarity to analog modems. An ISDN wall socket usually looks something like a standard RJ-45 network jack. The most common interface for your computer is a device called a *terminal adapter* (*TA*). TAs look much like regular modems, and like modems, they come in external and internal variants. You can even get TAs that connect directly to your LAN.

NOTE Another type of ISDN, called a primary rate interface (PRI), is composed of twenty-three 64-Kbps B channels and one 64-Kbps D channel, giving it a total throughput of 1.544 megabits per second. PRI ISDN lines are also known as T1 lines.

DSL

Digital subscriber line (DSL) connections to ISPs use a standard telephone line but special equipment on each end to create always-on Internet connections at blindingly fast speeds, especially when compared with analog dial-up connections. Service levels vary around the United States, but the typical upload speed is ~768 Kbps, while download speed comes in at ~3+ Mbps.

NOTE The two most common forms of DSL you'll find are *asynchronous (ADSL)* and *synchronous (SDSL)*. ADSL lines differ between slow upload speed (such as 384 Kbps, 768 Kbps, and 1 Mbps) and faster download speed (usually 3–15 Mbps). SDSL has the same upload and download speeds, but telecom companies charge a lot more for the privilege. DSL encompasses many such variations, so you'll often see it referred to as *x*DSL.

DSL requires little setup from a user standpoint. A tech comes to the house to install the DSL receiver, often called a DSL modem (see Figure 24-19), and possibly hook up a wireless router. The receiver connects to the telephone line and the PC (see Figure 24-20). The tech (or the user, if knowledgeable) then configures the DSL modem and router (if there is one) with the settings provided by the ISP, and that's about it! Within

moments, you're surfing the Web. You don't need a second telephone line. You don't need to wear a special propeller hat or anything. The only kicker is that your house has to be within a fairly short distance from a main phone service switching center (central office), something like 18,000 feet.

Figure 24-19
A DSL receiver

Figure 24-20 DSL connections

Cable

Cable offers a different approach to high-speed Internet access, using regular cable TV cables to serve up lightning-fast speeds. It offers faster service than most DSL connections, with a 1–10 Mbps upload and 6–100+ Mbps download. Cable Internet connections are theoretically available anywhere you can get cable TV.

Cable Internet connections start with an RG-6 or RG-59 cable coming into your house. The cable connects to a cable modem that then connects to a small home router or your NIC via Ethernet. Figure 24-21 shows a typical cable setup using a router.

NIC — Cable modem — To other houses — Cable Co.

Cable company interface

Figure 24-21 Cable connections

NOTE The term *modem* has been warped and changed beyond recognition in modern networking. Both DSL and cable—fully digital Internet connections— use the term *modem* to describe the box that takes the incoming signal from the Internet and translates it into something the PC can understand.

LAN

Most businesses connect their internal local area network (LAN) to an ISP-supplied Ethernet network. Figure 24-22 shows a typical small-business wiring closet with routers that connect the LAN to the ISP's Ethernet. You learned all about wiring up a LAN in Chapter 22, so there's no need to go through any basics here. To complete a LAN connection to the Internet, you need a router to connect the ISP's network to your network. Most office buildings come with preinstalled Ethernet at varying speeds.

Figure 24-22
A wiring closet

802.11 Wireless

802.11 Wireless is so prevalent that for many of us it's the way we get to the Internet. Wireless access points (WAPs) designed to serve the public abound in coffee shops, airports, fast-food chains, and bars. Even some cities provide partial to full 802.11 coverage.

We covered 802.11 in detail in Chapter 23, so there's no reason to repeat the process of connecting to a hotspot. However, do remember that most hotspots do not provide any level of encryption, meaning it's a trivial task for a bad guy to monitor your connection and read everything you send or receive.

 CAUTION Secure your public hotspot Web browsing using HTTPS-secured sites. It's surprisingly easy to do. Instead of typing facebook.com, for example, type in https://facebook.com or use a service like the Electronic Freedom Federation's HTTPS Everywhere.

802.11 works well as an Internet access option for densely populated areas, but 802.11's short range makes it impractical in areas where it's not easy to place new access points.

 NOTE An 802.11 network that covers a single city is an excellent example of a *Metropolitan Area Network (MAN)*.

Fiber

Until recently, high costs meant that only those with money to burn could enjoy the super-fast speeds of a fiber connection. Now DSL providers have developed very popular fiber-to-the-node (FTTN) and fiber-to-the-premises (FTTP) services that provide Internet (and more), making them head-to-head competitors with the cable companies. With FTTN, the fiber connection runs from the provider to a box somewhere in your neighborhood. This box is connected to your home or office using normal coaxial or Ethernet cabling. FTTP runs from the provider straight to a home or office, using fiber the whole way. Once inside the home or office, you can use any standard cabling (or wireless) to connect your PCs to the Internet. One popular FTTN service is AT&T's U-verse, which offers speeds up to 24 Mbps for downloads and 3 Mbps for uploads (see Figure 24-23). Verizon's FiOS service is the most popular and widely available FTTP service in the United States, providing download speeds up to 150 Mbps and upload speeds up to 50 Mbps (if you can afford it, of course).

Figure 24-23
U-verse gateway

Cellular

Who needs computers when you can get online with any number of mobile devices? Okay, there are plenty of things a smartphone or tablet can't do, but with the latest advances in cellular data services, your mobile Internet experience will feel a lot more like your home Internet experience than it ever has before.

Cellular data services have gone through a number of names over the years, so many that trying to keep track of them and place them in any order is extremely challenging. In an attempt to make organization somewhat clearer, the cellular industry developed a string of marketing terms using the idea of generations: first generation devices are called 1G, second generation are 2G, followed by 3G and 4G. On top of that, many technologies use G-names such as 2.5G to show they're not 2G but not quite 3G. You'll see these terms all over the place, especially on your phones (see Figure 24-24). Marketing folks tend to bend and flex the definition of these terms in advertisements, so you should always read more about the device and not just its generation.

Figure 24-24
iPhone with 4G
showing

NOTE The CompTIA A+ will not ask you to define a G-level for a particular cellular technology.

The first generation (1G) of cell phone data services was analog and not at all designed to carry packetized data. It wasn't until the early 1990s that two fully digital technologies called the Global System for Mobile Communications (GSM) and code division multiple access (CDMA) came into wide acceptance. GSM evolved into GPRS

and EDGE, while CDMA introduced EV-DO. GPRS and EDGE were 2.5G technologies, while EV-DO was true 3G. Current standards, with names like UTMS, HSPA+, and HSDPA, have brought GSM-based networks into the world of 3G and 3.5G. Current mobile data services provide real-world download speeds around 3 or 4 Mbps.

The current cutting-edge set of cellular technologies use the term 4G. The two biggest 4G technologies currently available are called *Worldwide Interoperability for Microwave Access (WiMAX)* and *3GPP Long Term Evolution (LTE)*. With these networks, you'll see download speeds closer to 10 Mbps, though WiMAX lags behind LTE in the speed department. In fact, while the CompTIA A+ 220-801 exam objectives specifically cover WiMAX, the wireless technology has already been replaced as the 4G frontrunner. The only major U.S. WiMAX carrier, Clearwire, Inc., has declared their intentions to adopt LTE, along with every other major mobile phone network in the United States. But since CompTIA asked, and there are plenty of WiMAX users (for now), I'm more than happy to tell you a little more about WiMAX.

 EXAM TIP You can share your smartphone's or tablet's connection to a cellular network using a process called *tethering*. You'll need to turn on the service on your device, then connect your phone to your computer, either wirelessly as a *mobile hotspot* or directly using a USB connection. Most carriers charge extra to enable tethering on your smartphone or tablet. Check with your carrier to see if your service plan supports tethering.

WiMAX runs at (depending on distance from a tower) a maximum speed of around 10 Mbps. The maximum range is 30 miles. There are two versions of WiMAX. Line-of-sight (LoS) WiMAX uses fixed antennas that point directly at a WiMAX transceiver. Non-LoS WiMAX (currently far more popular) uses base stations that are not visible to the WiMAX tower. As you might imagine, LoS WiMAX is far faster than non-LoS WiMAX.

EXAM TIP Just like LANs and WANs, we also have WLANs and WWANs. A wireless wide area network (WWAN) works similar to a WLAN, except it connects multiple networks like a WAN. WiMAX is an excellent example of a WWAN.

Satellite

Satellite connections to the Internet get the data beamed to a satellite dish on your house or office; a receiver handles the flow of data, eventually sending it through an Ethernet cable to the NIC in your PC. I can already sense people's eyebrows raising. "Yeah, that's the download connection. But what about the upload connection?" Very astute, me hearties! The early days of satellite required you to connect via a modem. You would upload at the slow 26- to 48-Kbps modem speed, but then get super-fast downloads from the dish. It worked, so why complain? You really can move to that shack on the side of the Himalayas to write the great Tibetan novel and still have DSL-speed Internet connectivity. Sweet!

Satellite might be the most intriguing of all the technologies used to connect to the Internet today. As with satellite television, though, you need to have the satellite dish point at the satellites (toward the south if you live in the United States). The only significant issue to satellite is that the distance the signal must travel creates a small delay called the *satellite latency*. This latency is usually unnoticeable unless the signal degrades in foul weather such as rain and snow.

Satellite setup consists of a dish, professionally installed with line-of-sight to the satellite. A coax cable runs from the dish to your satellite modem. The satellite modem has an RJ-45 connection, which you may then connect directly to your computer or to a router.

Connection to the Internet

So you went out and signed up for an Internet connection. Well, now it's time to get connected. You basically have two choices:

1. Connect a single computer to your Internet connection
2. Connect a network of computers to your Internet connection

Connecting a single computer to the Internet is easy. If you're using wireless, you connect to the wireless box using the provided information, although a good tech will always go through the proper steps described in Chapter 23 to protect the wireless network. If you choose to go wired, you run a cable from whatever type of box is provided to the PC.

If you want to connect a number of computers using wired connections, you'll need to grab a router. Several manufacturers offer robust, easy-to-configure routers that enable multiple computers to connect to a single Internet connection. These boxes require very little configuration and provide firewall protection between the primary computer and the Internet, which you'll learn more about in Chapter 29. All it takes to install one of these routers is simply to plug your computer into any of the LAN ports on the back, and then to plug the cable from your Internet connection into the port labeled Internet or WAN.

There are hundreds of perfectly fine choices for SOHO (small office/home office) routers, but the author's current favorite is the Cisco E2500 (see Figure 24-25). This little router has four 10/100 Ethernet ports for the LAN computers, and a Wi-Fi radio for any wireless computers you may have. The Cisco E2500, like all home routers, uses a technology called *Network Address Translation (NAT)*. NAT performs a little network subterfuge: It presents an entire LAN of computers to the Internet as a single machine. It effectively hides all of your computers and makes them appear invisible to other computers on the Internet. All anyone on the Internet sees is your *public* IP address. This is the address your ISP gives you, while all the computers in your LAN use private addresses that are invisible to the world. NAT therefore acts as a firewall, protecting your internal network from probing or malicious users from the outside.

Figure 24-25
Common home
router with Wi-Fi

Basic Router Configuration

SOHO routers require very little in the way of configuration and in many cases will work perfectly (if incredibly unsafely) right out of the box. In some cases, though, you may have to deal with a more complex network that requires changing the router's settings. The vast majority of these routers have built-in configuration Web pages that you access by typing the router's IP address into a browser. The address varies by manufacturer, so check the router's documentation. If you typed in the correct address, you should then receive a prompt for a user name and password, as in Figure 24-26. As with the IP address, the default user name and password change depending on the model/manufacturer. Once you enter the correct credentials, you will be greeted by the router's configuration pages (see Figure 24-27). From these pages, you can change any of the router's settings. Now look at a few of the basic settings that CompTIA wants you to be familiar with.

Figure 24-26
Router asking for
user name and
password

Windows Security X

The server 192.168.1.1 at Linksys E2500 requires a username and password.

Warning: This server is requesting that your username and password be sent in an insecure manner (basic authentication without a secure connection).

User name

Password

☐ Remember my credentials

OK Cancel

Figure 24-27 Configuration home page

Changing User Name and Password All routers have a user name and password that gives you access to the configuration screen. One of the first changes you should make to your router after you have it working is to change the user name and password to something other than the default. This is especially important if you have open wireless turned on, which you'll recall from Chapter 23. If you leave the default user name and password, anyone who has access to your LAN can easily gain access to the router and change its settings. Fortunately, router manufacturers make it easy to change a router's login credentials. On my E2500, for example, I just click on the Administration tab and fill in the appropriate boxes as shown in Figure 24-28.

Setting Static IP Addresses With the user name and password taken care of, let's look at setting up the router to use a static IP address for the Internet or WAN connection. In most cases, when you plug in the router's Internet connection, it receives an IP address

using DHCP just like any other computer. Of course, this means that your Internet IP address will change from time to time, which can be a bit of a downside. This does not affect most people, but for some home users and businesses, it can present a problem. To solve this problem, most ISPs enable you to order a static IP (for an extra monthly charge). Once your ISP has allocated you a static IP address, you must manually enter it into your router. You do this the same way as the previous change you've just looked at. My router has an Internet Setup configuration section where I can enter all the settings that my ISP has provided me (see Figure 24-29). Remember, you must change your connection type from Automatic/DHCP to Static IP to enter the new addresses.

Figure 24-28 Changing the password

Updating Firmware

Routers are just like any other computer in that they run software—and software has bugs, vulnerabilities, and other issues that sometimes require updating. The router manufacturers call these "firmware updates" and make them available on their Web sites for easy download. To update a modern router, download the latest firmware from the manufacturer's Web site to your computer. Then you enter the router's configuration Web page and find the firmware update screen. On my router, it looks like Figure 24-30. From here, just follow the directions and click Upgrade (or your router's equivalent). A quick word of caution: Unlike a Windows update, a firmware update gone bad can *brick* your router. In other words, it can destroy the hardware and make it as useful as a brick sitting on your desk. This rarely happens, but you should keep it in mind when doing a firmware update.

Figure 24-29 Entering a static IP address

Figure 24-30 Firmware update page

Windows Internet Connection Sharing

Internet Connection Sharing (ICS) enables one system to share its Internet connection with other systems on the network, just like your router at home. Figure 24-31 shows a typical setup for ICS. Note the terminology used here. The PC that connects to the Internet and then shares that connection via ICS with other machines on a LAN is called the *ICS host* computer. PCs that connect via a LAN to the ICS host computer are simply called client computers.

Figure 24-31 Typical ICS setup

To connect multiple computers to a single ICS host computer requires several things in place. First, the ICS host computer has to have a NIC dedicated to the internal connections. If you connect via dial-up, for example, the ICS host computer uses a modem to connect to the Internet. It also has a NIC that plugs into a switch. Other PCs on the LAN likewise connect to the switch. If you connect via some faster service, such as DSL that uses a NIC cabled to the DSL receiver, you'll need a second NIC in the ICS host machine to connect to the LAN and the client computers.

Setting up ICS in Windows is very simple. If you are using Windows XP, right-click on My Network Places and select Properties. If you are using Windows Vista or 7, open the Network and Sharing Center and click on *Manage network connections* (Vista) or *Change adapter settings* (7) in the Task list. Then access the Properties dialog box of the connection you wish to share.

Click the the Advanced tab (Windows XP) or Sharing tab (Vista and 7) and select *Allow other network users to connect through this computer's Internet connection* (see Figure 24-32). Clients don't need any special configuration but should simply be set to DHCP for their IP address and other configurations.

 EXAM TIP Windows XP provides a tool called the *Network Setup Wizard* that enables you to configure computers on a LAN to share folders and printers. This tool is especially useful on networks that use Internet Connection Sharing with a Windows XP machine as the default gateway.

To run the Wizard, go to Start | Control Panel | Network and Internet Connections | Network Connections. Under Common Tasks, click Network Setup Wizard. Follow the steps in the Wizard to create a floppy disk with a small setup program used to configure other computers to share resources (folders, printers, and so on).

Figure 24-32
Enabling Internet
Connection Sharing
in Windows Vista

Internet Application Protocols

Once you've established a connection to the Internet, you need applications to get anything done. If you want to surf the Web, you need an application called a *Web browser*, such as Mozilla Firefox or Google Chrome. If you want to make a VoIP phone call, you need an application like Skype or Google Voice. These applications in turn use very clearly designed application protocols. All Web browsers use the *Hypertext Transfer Protocol (HTTP)*. All e-mail clients use Post Office Protocol 3 (POP3) or Internet Message Access Protocol 4 (IMAP4) to receive e-mail. All e-mail applications use Simple Mail Transfer Protocol (SMTP) to send their e-mails. Every Internet protocol has its own rules and its own port numbers. Though there are tens of thousands of application protocols in existence, lucky for you, CompTIA only wants you to understand the following commonly used application protocols:

- World Wide Web (HTTP and HTTPS)
- E-mail (POP3, IMAP4, and SMTP)
- Telnet
- SSH
- FTP/SFTP
- Remote Desktop (RDP)
- VoIP (SIP)

In addition to the application protocols we see and use daily, there are hundreds, maybe thousands, of application protocols that run behind the scenes, taking care of important jobs to ensure that the application protocols we do see run well. You've encountered a number of these hidden application protocols back in Chapter 22. Take DNS. Without DNS, you couldn't type www.google.com in your Web browser. DHCP is another great example. You don't see DHCP do its job, but without it, any computers relying on DHCP won't receive IP addresses.

Here's another one: People don't like to send credit card information, home phone numbers, or other personal information over the Web for fear this information might be intercepted by hackers. Fortunately, there are methods for encrypting this information, the most common being *Hypertext Transfer Protocol Secure (HTTPS)*. Although HTTPS looks a lot like HTTP from the point of view of a Web browser, HTTPS uses port 443. It's easy to tell if a Web site is using HTTPS because the Web address starts with *https*, as shown in Figure 24-33, instead of just *http*. But you don't deal with HTTPS directly; it just works in your browser automatically.

Figure 24-33 A secure Web page

In order to differentiate the application protocols you see from the application protocols you don't see, I'm going to coin the term "utility protocol" to define any of the hidden application protocols. So, using your author's definition, HTTP is an application protocol and DNS is a utility protocol. All TCP/IP protocols use defined ports, require an application to run, and have special settings unique to that application. You'll look

at several of these services and learn how to configure them. As a quick reference, Table 24-1 lists the names, functions, and port numbers of the application protocols Comp-TIA would like you to know. Table 24-2 does the same for utility protocols.

Application Protocol	Function	Port Number
HTTP	Web pages	80
FTP	File transfer	20, 21
SFTP	Secure file transfer	22
IMAP4	Incoming e-mail	143
POP3	Incoming e-mail	110
SMTP	Outgoing e-mail	25
Telnet	Terminal emulation	23
SSH	Encrypted terminal emulation	22
RDP	Remote Desktop	3389
SIP	Voice over IP	5060

Table 24-1 Application Protocol Port Numbers

HTTPS	Secure web pages	TCP	43
DNS	Allows the use of DNS naming	UDP	53
DHCP	Automatic IP addressing	UDP	67, 68
LDAP	Querying directories	TCP	389
SNMP	Remote management of network devices	UDP	161
SMB	Windows naming/folder sharing	TCP	445
		UDP	137, 138, 139

Table 24-2 Utility Protocol Port Numbers

After you've read about these protocols, you'll learn about Virtual Private Networks and the protocols they use. I'll also tell you about a few more Internet support utilities that don't quite fit anywhere else.

The World Wide Web

The Web provides a graphical face for the Internet. *Web servers* (servers running specialized software) provide Web sites that you access by using the HTTP protocol on port 80 and thus get more or less useful information. Using Web-browser software, such as Internet Explorer or Mozilla Firefox, you can click a link on a Web page and be instantly transported—not just to some Web server in your home town—to anywhere in the world. Figure 24-34 shows Firefox at the home page of my company's Web site, www.totalsem.com. Where is the server located? Does it matter? It could be in a closet in my office or in a huge data center in Houston. The great part about the Web is that you can get from here to there and access the information you need with a click or two of the mouse.

Figure 24-34 Mozilla Firefox showing a Web page

Although the Web is the most popular part of the Internet, setting up a Web browser takes almost no effort. As long as the Internet connection is working, Web browsers work automatically. This is not to say you can't make plenty of custom settings, but the default browser settings work almost every time. If you type in a Web address, such as that of the best search engine on the planet—www.google.com—and it doesn't work, check the line and your network settings and you'll figure out where the problem is.

Configuring Internet Explorer

Web browsers are highly configurable. On most Web browsers, you can set the default font size, choose whether to display graphics, and adjust several other settings. Although all Web browsers support these settings, where you go to make these changes varies dramatically. If you are using the popular Internet Explorer that comes with Windows, you will find configuration tools in the Internet Options Control Panel applet or under the Tools menu in Internet Explorer (see Figure 24-35). Note that the applet is called Internet Options, but the window it launches is labeled Internet Properties.

Figure 24-35

Internet Options applet

NOTE The Internet Options Control Panel applet is only for the Internet Explorer Web browser. If you use any other browser (Firefox, Chrome, and so on), Internet Options has no effect.

I find it bizarre that CompTIA specifically lists Internet Options as an objective on the CompTIA A+ 220-802 exam. It's just so...Microsofty. There are obviously more browsers than just Internet Explorer, so I'll begin by explaining the options available to you in Internet Explorer, and then show you some of the common options found in other browsers, too.

When you open the Internet Options applet, you'll see seven tabs along the top. The first tab is the General tab. These settings control the most basic features of Internet Explorer: the home page, your browsing history, searching, and other appearance controls. If you want to delete or change how Internet Explorer stores the Web sites you've visited, use this tab.

The Security tab enables you to set how severely Internet Explorer safeguards your Web browsing (see Figure 24-36). Each setting can be adjusted for a particular zone, such as the Internet, your local intranet, trusted sites, and restricted sites. You can configure which Web sites fall into which zones. Once you've picked a zone to control, you can set Internet Explorer's security level. The High security level blocks more Web sites and disables some plug-ins, while Medium-high and Medium allow less-secure Web sites and features to display and operate.

Figure 24-36

The Security tab in
Internet Options

The Privacy tab works a lot like the Security tab, except it controls privacy matters, such as cookies and pop-ups. There is a slider that enables you to control what is blocked—everything is blocked on the highest setting; nothing is blocked on the lowest. Go here if you don't like the idea of Web sites tracking your browsing history (though cookies do other things, too, like authenticate users).

The Content tab also controls what your browser will and will not display. This time, however, it filters content using certificates and a tool called the Content Advisor, which uses ratings that consider language, gambling, substance abuse, and more. The Content tab also enables you to adjust the AutoComplete feature that fills in Web addresses for you, as well as control settings for RSS feeds and Web Slices.

The Connections tab enables you to do a lot of things. You can set up your connection to the Internet, via broadband or dial-up, connect to a VPN, configure a proxy server connection, or adjust some LAN settings (which you probably won't need to deal with). Because they're a little complicated, and CompTIA wants you to know about them, let's quickly talk about proxy servers.

Many corporations use a proxy server to filter employee Internet access, and when you're on their corporate network, you need to set your proxy settings within the Web browser (and any other Internet software you want to use). A *proxy server* is software that enables multiple connections to the Internet to go through one protected PC. Applications that want to access Internet resources send requests to the proxy server instead of trying to access the Internet directly, which both protects the client PCs and enables the network administrator to monitor and restrict Internet access. Each application must therefore be configured to use the proxy server.

Moving on, the Programs tab in Internet Options contains settings for your default Web browser, any add-ons you use (like Java), and how other programs deal with HTML files and e-mail messages.

The Advanced tab does exactly what it sounds like: lists a bunch of advanced options that you can turn on and off with the check of a box (see Figure 24-37). The available options include accessibility, browsing, international, and, most importantly, security settings. From here, you can control how Internet Explorer checks Web site certificates, among many other settings.

Figure 24-37

The Advanced tab in Internet Options

Configuring Other Web Browsers

I don't want to stomp all over Internet Explorer and tell you how bad it is—okay, yes I do. You can download several other Web browsers that run faster and support more Web standards. Two of the big browser heavyweights that fit this description are Mozilla Firefox and Google Chrome.

You control their settings just like you do in Internet Explorer, though you won't find an applet tucked away in Control Panel. In Google Chrome, you can click on the wrench icon in the upper-right corner of the browser and select Settings. In Mozilla Firefox, click on the Firefox button in the upper-left corner and click on Options.

In these menus, you'll find a lot of settings very similar to the ones you find in Internet Options. In fact, Firefox's controls are laid out almost exactly the same, though you won't find everything in the same place (see Figure 24-38). Google Chrome's controls look more like a Web page, but it still controls the same features: home page, security, font size, cookies, and all your old favorites (see Figure 24-39). Take some time to use these browsers and explore their settings. You'll be surprised how your knowledge of one browser helps you set up another.

Figure 24-38
Mozilla Firefox
options

EXAM TIP The term *Internet appliance* enjoyed some popularity in the 1990s to describe the first wave of consumer devices accessible via TCP/IP. You could use a Web browser to check on the status of an Internet-connected refrigerator, for example, or check to see if you'd left the stove on (and if so, shut it off remotely). Although the term is no longer in use, it might show up on the 220-801 exam.

E-mail

You can use a desktop program to access e-mail. The most popular client by far is Microsoft Outlook. E-mail clients need a little more setup. First, you must provide your e-mail address and password. All e-mail addresses come in the now-famous *account-name@Internet domain* format. Figure 24-40 shows e-mail information entered into the Windows Live Mail account setup wizard.

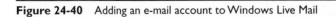

Figure 24-39 Google Chrome settings

Figure 24-40 Adding an e-mail account to Windows Live Mail

NOTE Most people use Web-based e-mail, such as Yahoo! Mail or Gmail from Google, to handle all of their e-mail needs. Web-based mail offers the convenience of having access to your e-mail from any Internet-connected computer, smartphone, tablet, or other Internet-connected device. The benefit to using a standalone program is that most offer a lot more control over what you can do with your e-mail, such as flagging messages with different types of flags for later review. Web-based mail services, especially Gmail, are catching up, though, and might surpass traditional e-mail programs in features and popularity.

Next you must add the names of the *Post Office Protocol version 3 (POP3)* or *Internet Message Access Protocol version 4 (IMAP4)* server and the *Simple Mail Transfer Protocol (SMTP)* server. The POP3 or IMAP4 server is the computer that handles incoming (to you) e-mail. POP3 is by far the most widely used standard, although IMAP4 supports some features POP3 doesn't. For example, IMAP4 enables you to search through messages on the mail server to find specific keywords and select the messages you want to download onto your machine. Even with the advantages of IMAP4 over POP3, the vast majority of incoming mail servers use POP3.

EXAM TIP Make sure you know your port numbers for these e-mail protocols! POP3 uses port 110, IMAP4 uses port 143, and SMTP uses port 25.

The SMTP server handles your outgoing e-mail. These two systems may often have the same name, or close to the same name, as shown in Figure 24-41. Your ISP should provide you with all these settings. If not, you should be comfortable knowing what to ask for. If one of these names is incorrect, you will either not get your e-mail or not be able to send e-mail. If an e-mail setup that has been working well for a while suddenly gives you errors, it is likely that either the POP3 or SMTP server is down or that the DNS server has quit working.

EXAM TIP Microsoft provides a special type of e-mail server called an Exchange server. This is used mainly in large businesses so that employees can access their e-mail, calendars, and instant messages from a variety of locations. To set up an Exchange e-mail client, go to the Control Panel and run the Mail applet. Then click E-mail Accounts and then New. After that, click Next and fill in your e-mail address and password.

When I'm given the name of a POP3 or SMTP server, I use ping to determine the IP address for the device, as shown in Figure 24-42. I make a point to write this down. If I ever have a problem getting mail, I'll go into my SMTP or POP3 settings and type in the IP address (see Figure 24-43). If my mail starts to work, I know the DNS server is not working.

Figure 24-41

Adding POP3 and
SMTP information
in Windows Live
Mail

Windows Live Mail

Configure server settings
If you don't know your email server settings, contact your ISP or network administrator.

Incoming server information

Server type:

POP

Server address: | Port:
pop-server.totalsem.com | 110

☐ Requires a secure connection (SSL)

Authenticate using:

Clear text

Logon user name:

michaelm@totalsem.com

Outgoing server information

Server address: | Port:
smtp-server.totalsem.com | 25

☐ Requires a secure connection (SSL)
☑ Requires authentication

Cancel Back Next

```
C:\Windows\system32\cmd.exe

C:\>ping pop-server.totalsem.com

Pinging pop-server.totalsem.com [69.94.71.175] with 32 bytes of data:
Reply from 69.94.71.175: bytes=32 time=96ms TTL=47
Reply from 69.94.71.175: bytes=32 time=122ms TTL=47
Reply from 69.94.71.175: bytes=32 time=166ms TTL=47
Reply from 69.94.71.175: bytes=32 time=153ms TTL=47

Ping statistics for 69.94.71.175:
    Packets: Sent = 4, Received = 4, Lost = 0 (0% loss),
Approximate round trip times in milli-seconds:
    Minimum = 96ms, Maximum = 166ms, Average = 134ms

C:\>
```

Figure 24-42 Using ping to determine the IP address

EXAM TIP Some e-mail servers use SSL encryption for extra security. Every
major e-mail client will have a setting called Connection security, or Security,
or something like that. If your e-mail server uses encryption, change this
setting to SSL.

File Transfer Protocol (FTP)

File transfer protocol (FTP), using ports 20 and 21, is a great way to share files between
systems. FTP server software exists for most operating systems, so you can use FTP to

transfer data between any two systems regardless of the operating system. To access an FTP site, you must use an FTP client such as FileZilla, although most Web browsers provide at least download support for FTP. Just type in the name of the FTP site. Figure 24-44 shows Firefox accessing ftp.kernel.org.

Figure 24-43
Entering IP addresses into POP3 and SMTP settings

Figure 24-44
Accessing an FTP site in Firefox

Although you can use a Web browser, all FTP sites require you to log on. Your Web browser will assume that you want to log on as "anonymous." If you want to log on as a specific user, you have to add your user name to the URL. (Instead of typing **ftp://ftp. example.com**, you would type **ftp://mikem@ftp.example.com**.) An anonymous logon works fine for most public FTP sites. Many techs prefer to use third-party programs such as FileZilla (see Figure 24-45) for FTP access because these third-party applications can store user name and password settings. This enables you to access the FTP site more easily later. Keep in mind that FTP was developed during a more trusting time, and that whatever user name and password you send over the network is sent in clear text. Don't use the same password for an FTP site that you use for your domain logon at the office!

Figure 24-45 The FileZilla FTP program

Telnet and SSH

Telnet is a terminal emulation program for TCP/IP networks that uses port 23 and enables you to connect to a server or fancy router and run commands on that machine as if you were sitting in front of it. This way, you can remotely administer a server and communicate with other servers on your network. As you can imagine, this is rather risky. If *you* can remotely control a computer, what's to stop others from doing the same? Of course, Telnet does not allow just *anyone* to log on and wreak havoc with your network. You must enter a special user name and password to run Telnet. Unfortunately, Telnet shares FTP's bad habit of sending passwords and user names as clear text, so you should generally use it only within your own LAN.

If you need a remote terminal that works securely across the Internet, you need *Secure Shell (SSH)*. In fact, today SSH has replaced Telnet in almost all places Telnet used to be popular. To the user, SSH works just like Telnet. Behind the scenes, SSH uses port 22, and the entire connection is encrypted, preventing any eavesdroppers from reading your data. SSH has one other trick up its sleeve: it can move files or any type of TCP/IP network traffic through its secure connection. In networking parlance, this is called *tunneling*, and it is the core of most secure versions of Internet technologies such as SFTP (discussed next) and VPN, which I will discuss in more depth later in the chapter.

EXAM TIP The CompTIA A+ certification exams test your knowledge of a few networking tools, such as Telnet, but only enough to let you support a CompTIA Network+ tech or network administrator. If you need to run Telnet (or its more secure cousin, SSH), you will get the details from a network administrator. Implementation of Telnet falls well beyond CompTIA A+.

SFTP

Secure FTP is nothing more than FTP running through an SSH tunnel. This can be done in a number of ways. You can, for example, start an SSH session between two computers. Then, through a moderately painful process, start an FTP server on one machine and an FTP client on the other and redirect the input and output of the FTP data to go through the tunnel. You can also get a dedicated SFTP server and client. Figure 24-46 shows OpenSSH, a popular SSH server with a built-in SFTP feature as well.

Voice over IP

You can use *Voice over IP (VoIP)* to make voice calls over your computer network. Why have two sets of wires, one for voice and one for data, going to every desk? Why not just use the extra capacity on the data network for your phone calls? That's exactly what VoIP does for you. VoIP works with every type of high-speed Internet connection, from DSL to cable to satellite.

VoIP doesn't refer to a single protocol but rather to a collection of protocols that make phone calls over the data network possible. The most common VoIP application protocol is Session Initiation Protocol (SIP), but some popular VoIP applications like Skype are completely proprietary.

Venders such as Skype, Cisco, Vonage, and Comcast offer popular VoIP solutions, and many corporations use VoIP for their internal phone networks. A key to remember when installing and troubleshooting VoIP is that low network latency is more important than high network speed. *Latency* is the amount of time a packet takes to get to its destination and is measured in milliseconds. The higher the latency, the more problems, such as noticeable delays during a VoIP call.

VoIP isn't confined to your computer, either. It can completely replace your old copper phone line. Two popular ways to set up a VoIP system are to either use dedicated *VoIP phones*, like the ones that Cisco makes, or use a small VoIP phone adapter (see Figure 24-47) that can interface with your existing analog phones.

Figure 24-46 OpenSSH

Figure 24-47
Vonage Box VoIP
phone adapter

True VoIP phones have RJ-45 connections that plug directly into the network and offer advanced features such as HD-quality audio and video calling. Unfortunately, these phones require a complex and expensive network to function, which puts them out of reach of most home users.

For home users, it's much more common to use a VoIP phone adapter to connect your old-school analog phones. These little boxes are very simple to set up: just connect

it to your network, plug in a phone, and then check for a dial tone. With the VoIP service provided by cable companies, the adapter is often built right into the cable modem itself, making setup a breeze.

Remote Desktop

In Microsoft networking, we primarily share folders and printers. At times, it would be convenient to be "transported" to another computer—to feel as if your hands were actually on its keyboard. There are plenty of programs that do exactly this, generically called remote desktops.

Like so many other Windows applications, remote desktops originally came from third-party companies. Microsoft bought the companies and absorbed their code into the Windows operating system. Many third-party remote desktop applications are available. One of the most popular is TightVNC. TightVNC is totally cross-platform, enabling you to run and control a Windows system remotely from your Mac or vice versa, for example. Figure 24-48 shows TightVNC in action.

Figure 24-48 TightVNC in action

NOTE All terminal emulation programs require separate server and client programs.

Windows offers an alternative to VNC: Remote Desktop. *Remote Desktop* provides control over a remote server with a fully graphical interface. Your desktop *becomes* the server desktop (see Figure 24-49).

NOTE The name of the Remote Desktop executable file is mstsc.exe. You can also open Remote Desktop from a command-line interface by typing **mstsc** and pressing ENTER.

Figure 24-49
Windows Remote
Desktop Connec-
tion dialog box

Wouldn't it be cool if, when called about a technical support issue, you could simply see what the client sees? (I'm not talking voyeur cam, here.) When the client says that something doesn't work, it would be great if you could transfer yourself from your desk to your client's desk to see precisely what the client sees. This would dramatically cut down on the miscommunication that can make a tech's life so tedious. Windows Remote Assistance does just that. *Remote Assistance* enables you to give anyone control of your desktop. If a user has a problem, that user can request support directly from you. Upon receiving the support-request e-mail, you can then log on to the user's system and, with permission, take the driver's seat. Figure 24-50 shows Remote Assistance in action.

With Remote Assistance, you can do anything you would do from the actual computer. You can troubleshoot some hardware configuration or driver problem. You can install drivers, roll back drivers, download new ones, and so forth. You're in command of the remote machine as long as the client allows you to be. The client sees everything you do, by the way, and can stop you cold if you get out of line or do something that

makes the client nervous! Remote Assistance can help you teach someone how to use a particular application. You can log on to a user's PC and fire up Outlook, for example, and then walk through the steps to configure it while the user watches. The user can then take over the machine and walk through the steps while you watch, chatting with one another the whole time. Sweet!

Figure 24-50 Remote Assistance in action

Remote desktop applications provide everything you need to access one system from another. They are common, especially now that Microsoft provides Remote Desktop for free. Whichever application you use, remember that you will always need both a server and a client program. The server goes on the system you want to access and the client goes on the system you use to access the server. On many solutions, the server and client software are integrated into a single product.

In Windows, you can turn Remote Assistance and Remote Desktop on and off and configure other settings. Go to the System Control Panel applet. In Windows XP, click on the Remote tab. In Windows Vista and Windows 7, click *Remote settings*. You will see checkboxes for both Remote Assistance and Remote Desktop, along with buttons to configure more detailed settings. (In Windows XP, you'll only see Remote Desktop controls if you installed the Remote Desktop client, which is not installed by default.)

 EXAM TIP Windows 7 (and Windows Vista with the appropriate update) is capable of running specific applications hosted on a Windows Server 2008/2008 R2 machine. Think of it as Remote Desktop without the desktop—a single application run on one machine (a server) and appearing on another desktop (a client). You can set up your connection to the Windows Server machine using the RemoteApp and Desktop Connections applet in Control Panel.

Virtual Private Networks

Remote connections have been around for a long time, long before the Internet existed. The biggest drawback about remote connections was the cost to connect. If you were on one side of the continent and had to connect to your LAN on the other side of the continent, the only connection option was a telephone. Or, if you needed to connect two LANs across the continent, you ended up paying outrageous monthly charges for a private connection. The introduction of the Internet gave people wishing to connect to their home networks a very cheap connection option, but with one problem: the whole Internet is open to the public. People wanted to stop using dial-up and expensive private connections and use the Internet instead, but they wanted to do it securely.

Those clever network engineers worked long and hard and came up with several solutions to this problem. Standards have been created that use encrypted tunnels between a computer (or a remote network) to create a private network through the Internet (see Figure 24-51), resulting in what is called a *Virtual Private Network (VPN)*.

Figure 24-51 VPN connecting computers across the United States

An encrypted tunnel requires endpoints—the ends of the tunnel where the data is encrypted and decrypted. In the SSH tunnel you've seen thus far, the client for the application sits on one end and the server sits on the other. VPNs do the same thing.

Either some software running on a computer or, in some cases, a dedicated box must act as an endpoint for a VPN (see Figure 24-52).

Figure 24-52 Typical tunnel

To make VPNs work requires a protocol that uses one of the many tunneling protocols available and adds the capability to ask for an IP address from a local DHCP server to give the tunnel an IP address that matches the subnet of the local LAN. The connection keeps the IP address to connect to the Internet, but the tunnel endpoints must act like NICs (see Figure 24-53). Let's look at one of the protocols, PPTP.

Figure 24-53 Endpoints must have their own IP addresses.

PPTP VPNs

So how do we make IP addresses appear out of thin air? Microsoft got the ball rolling with the *Point-to-Point Tunneling Protocol (PPTP)*, an advanced version of a protocol used for dial-up Internet called PPP that handles all of this right out of the box. The only trick is the endpoints. In Microsoft's view, a VPN is intended for individual clients (think employees on the road) to connect back to the office network, so Microsoft places the PPTP endpoints on the client and a special remote access server program called Routing and Remote Access Service (RRAS), available on Server versions of Windows, on the server (see Figure 24-54).

Figure 24-54 RRAS in action

On the Windows client side, you right-click on My Network Places and click on Create a New Connection (Windows XP) or type **VPN** into the Start Search bar (Windows Vista and 7) and press ENTER. This presents you with a dialog box where you can enter all your VPN server information. Your network administrator will most likely provide this to you. The result is a virtual network card that, like any other NIC, gets an IP address from the DHCP server back at the office (see Figure 24-55).

 EXAM TIP A system connected to a VPN looks as though it's on the local network but often performs much slower than if the system were connected directly back at the office.

Figure 24-55 VPN connection in Windows

When your computer connects to the RRAS server on the private network, PPTP creates a secure tunnel through the Internet back to the private LAN. Your client takes on an IP address of that network, as if your computer were plugged into the LAN back at the office. Even your Internet traffic will go through your office first. If you open your Web browser, your client will go across the Internet to the office LAN and then use the LAN's Internet connection! Because of this, Web browsing is very slow over a VPN.

Support Applications (Internet Utilities)

The CompTIA A+ 220-801 objectives list three rather unique protocols. Personally, I doubt you'll ever deal directly with two of them, and the other is more common to LANs, not the Internet, but you should know a little bit about all three anyway.

LDAP

The *Lightweight Directory Access Protocol (LDAP)* enables operating systems and applications to access directories. If you've got a Windows Server system running Active Directory, for example, Windows uses LDAP to do anything with Active Directory. If you're

sitting at a computer and add it to an Active Directory domain, Windows uses LDAP commands to update the Active Directory with the computer's information. You don't see LDAP, but it works hard to keep networks running smoothly.

SNMP

The *Simple Network Management Protocol (SNMP)* enables remote query and remote configuration of just about anything on a network. Assuming all your computers, switches, routers, and so on are SNMP-capable, you can use programs to query the network for an unimaginable amount of data. SNMP is a popular tool to check on your network, but you'll need to take the CompTIA Network+ exam to see SNMP in action.

SMB

The *Server Message Block (SMB)* protocol isn't even an application but rather proof of the power of Microsoft. SMBs date back to the old NetBIOS naming service and were the tools that tossed a PC's name around a network. NetBIOS names are gone, but SMBs are the reason that tools like Network can show you all the computers on your network. SMB is so powerful that other operating systems copy SMB using a popular program called SAMBA. SAMBA emulates SMB—it makes non-SMB operating systems on a network look like Windows.

802

Internet Troubleshooting

There isn't a person who's spent more than a few hours on a computer connected to the Internet who hasn't run into some form of connectivity problem. I love it when I get a call from someone saying "The Internet is down!" as I always respond the same way: "No, the Internet is fine. It's the way you're trying to get to it that's down." Okay, so I don't make a lot of friends with that remark, but it's actually a really good reminder of why we run into problems on the Internet. Let's review the common symptoms CompTIA lists on their objectives for the CompTIA A+ 220-802 exam and see what we can do to fix these all-too-common problems.

The dominant Internet setup for a SOHO environment consists of some box from your ISP—a cable modem, a DSL modem, etc.—that connects via Ethernet cable to a home router. This router is usually 802.11 capable and includes four Ethernet ports. Some computers in the network connect through a wire and some connect wirelessly (see Figure 24-56). It's a pretty safe assumption that CompTIA has a setup like this in mind when talking about Internet troubleshooting, and we'll refer to this setup here as well.

One quick note before we dive in—most Internet connection problems are network connection problems. In other words, everything you learned in Chapter 22 still applies here. We're not going to rehash those repair problems in this chapter. The following issues are Internet-only problems, so don't let a bad cable fool you into thinking a bigger problem is taking place.

Figure 24-56 Typical SOHO setup

No Connectivity

As you'll remember from Chapter 22, "no connectivity" has two meanings: a discon-
nected NIC or an inability to connect to a resource. Since Chapter 22 already covers
wired connectivity issues and Chapter 23 covers wireless issues, let's look at lack of con-
nectivity from a "you're on the Internet but you can't get to a Web site" point of view:

1. Can you get to other Web sites? If not, go back and triple-check your local
 connectivity.

2. Can you ping the site? Go to a command prompt and try pinging the URL as
 shown here:

```
C:\>ping www.cheetos1.com

Ping request could not find host www.cheetos1.com. Please check the name and
try again.

C:\>
```

The ping is a failure, but we learn a lot from it. The ping shows that your computer can't get an IP address for that Web site. This points to a DNS failure, a very common problem. To fix a failing DNS:

1. Go to a command prompt and type **ipconfig /flushdns**:

```
C:\>ipconfig /flushdns

Windows IP Configuration

Successfully flushed the DNS Resolver Cache.

C:\>
```

2. If you have Windows XP, go to the Network Connections applet in the Control Panel. Right-click on your network connection and select Repair. If you have Windows Vista/7, go to the Network and Sharing Center and click *Change adapter settings*. Right-click on your network connection and select Diagnose to run the troubleshooter (see Figure 24-57).

3. Try using another DNS server. There are lots of DNS servers out there that are open to the public. Try Google's famous 8.8.8.8 and 8.8.4.4.

If DNS is OK, make sure you're using the right URL. This is especially true when you're entering DNS names into applications like e-mail clients.

Figure 24-57 Diagnosing a network problem in Windows 7

Limited Connectivity

Limited connectivity points to a DHCP problem, assuming you're connected to a DHCP server. Run **ipconfig** and see if you have an APIPA address:

```
C:\>ipconfig
Windows IP Configuration
Ethernet adapter Local Area Connection:
        Connection-specific DNS Suffix  . :
        IP Address. . . . . . . . . . . . : 169.254.0.16
        Subnet Mask . . . . . . . . . . . : 255.255.0.0
        Default Gateway . . . . . . . . . :
C:\>
```

Uh-oh! No DHCP server! If your router is your DHCP server, try restarting the router. If you know the Network ID for your network and the IP address for your default gateway (something you should know—it's your network!), try setting up your NIC statically.

Local Connectivity

Local connectivity means you can access network resources but not the Internet. First, this is a classic symptom of a downed DHCP server since all the systems in the local network will have APIPA addresses. However, you might also have a problem with your router. In Windows XP, you need to ping the default gateway; if that's successful, ping the other port (the WAN port) on your router. The only way to determine the IP address of the other port on your router is to access the router's configuration Web page and find it (see Figure 24-58). Every router is different— good luck!

Figure 24-58 Router's WAN IP address

You can learn a lot by looking at your WAN IP address. Take a look at Figure 24-59. At first glance, it looks the same as Figure 24-58, but notice that there is no IP address. Most

ISPs don't provide static IP addresses—they simply give you the physical connection, and your router's WAN network card uses DHCP, just like most internal networks. If you're lucky, you can renew your DHCP address using some button on the router's configuration. If not, try resetting the cable/DSL modem. If that doesn't work, it's time to call your ISP.

Figure 24-59 No WAN connection

Slow Transfer Speeds

No matter how fast the connection is, we all want our Internet to go faster. People expect a certain amount of wait for a large program to download or an HD video to buffer, but your connection can sometimes slow down to unacceptable speeds.

Remember that your Internet connection has a maximum speed at which it can transfer. If you divide that connection between multiple programs trying to use the Internet, all of your programs will connect very slowly. To see what's happening on your network, open a command prompt and type **netstat**, which shows all the connections between your computer and any other computer. Here's a very simplified example of netstat output:

```
C:\>netstat
Active Connections
   Proto  Local Address          Foreign Address          State
   TCP    10.12.14.47:57788      totalfs3:microsoft-ds    ESTABLISHED
   TCP    192.168.15.102:139     Sabertooth:20508         ESTABLISHED
   TCP    192.168.15.102:50283   Theater:netbios-ssn      ESTABLISHED
   TCP    192.168.15.102:60222   dts1.google.com:https    ESTABLISHED
   TCP    192.168.15.102:60456   www.serve2.le.com:http   ESTABLISHED
   TCP    192.168.15.102:60482   64.145.92.65:http        ESTABLISHED
   TCP    192.168.15.102:60483   12.162.15.1:57080        TIME_WAIT
C:\>
```

If you look at the Foreign Address column, you'll see that most of the connections are Web pages (HTTP and HTTPS) or shared folders (microsoft-ds, netbios-ssn), but

what is the connection to 12.162.15.1:57080? Not knowing every connection by heart, I looked it up on Google and found out that there was a background torrent program running on my machine. I found the program and shut it down.

When everyone on the network is getting slow Internet connectivity, it's time to check out the router. In all probability, you have too many people that need too much bandwidth—go buy more bandwidth!

You can control what's going through your router using *Quality of Service* (*QoS*). QoS is a feature that enables you to limit the bandwidth for certain types of data based on application protocol, the IP address of a computer, and all sorts of other features. Figure 24-60 is a typical router's QoS page.

Figure 24-60 QoS

Beyond A+

The areas covered by the CompTIA A+ certification exams do a great job on the more common issues of dealing with the Internet, but a few hot topics (although beyond

the scope of the CompTIA A+ exams) are so common and important that you need to know them: online gaming, chatting, and file sharing.

Online Gaming

One of the more exciting and certainly more fun aspects of the Internet is online gaming. Competing online against a real person or people makes for some pleasant gaming. Enjoying classics such as Hearts and Backgammon with another human can be challenging and fun. Another popular genre of online gaming is the "first-person shooter." These games place you in a small world with up to 32 other players. A great example is Valve Software's *Counter-Strike: Source* (see Figure 24-61).

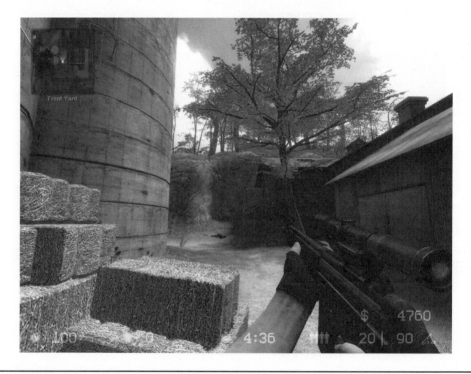

Figure 24-61 *Counter-Strike: Source*

No discussion of online gaming is complete without talking about the most amazing game type of all: the massively multiplayer online role-playing game (MMORPG). Imagine being an elfin wizard, joined by a band of friends, all going on adventures together in a world so large that it would take a real 24-hour day to journey across it! Imagine that in this same world, 2000 to 3000 other players, as well as thousands of

game-controlled characters, are participating! Plenty of MMORPGs are out there, but the most popular today is *World of Warcraft* (see Figure 24-62).

Figure 24-62 My editor playing *World of Warcraft*

Each of these games employs good old TCP/IP to send information, using ports reserved by the game. For instance, the Quake series of games uses port 26000, while DirectX uses ports 47624 and 2300–2400.

Chat

If there's one thing we human beings love to do, it's chat. The Internet provides a multitude of ways to do so, whether by typing or actual talking. Keep in mind that chatting occurs in real time. As fast as you can type or talk, whoever is at the other end hears or sees what you have to say. To chat, however, you need some form of chat software. The oldest family of chat programs is based on the Internet Relay Chat (IRC) protocol; a very common IRC chat program is mIRC. IRC protocols allow for a number of other little extras as well, such as being able to share files.

Today, companies such as Google, AOL, Yahoo!, and Microsoft have made their own chat programs (otherwise known as instant messengers, or IMs) that not only provide text chat but also add features such as voice and video, turning your PC into a VoIP phone! Figure 24-63 shows the popular Microsoft Windows Live Messenger software.

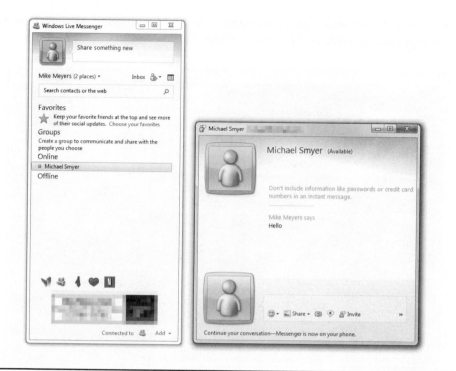

Figure 24-63 Windows Live Messenger in action

File Sharing

The last extra Internet function to discuss is also probably the most controversial: file sharing. File sharing started over a decade ago and consisted of a whole bunch of computers with one program loaded, such as Napster or Kazaa. The file-sharing program enables each of the computers running that program to offer files to share, such as music and movies. Once all of the file-sharing programs connect to the Internet, any of them can download any file offered by any other in the group.

File sharing through such *distributed* sharing software becomes almost anonymous and free—and that's the problem. You can share *anything*, even copyright-protected music, movies, and more. The music industry in particular has come out swinging to try to stop file-sharing practices. As a result, the music industry is working on a way to shut down those persons who share lots of files. Software developers and file sharers haven't backed down, creating Internet protocols such as BitTorrent that can share files faster and more efficiently. Figure 24-64 shows one of the more popular BitTorrent protocol programs called μTorrent (the μ is the symbol for "micro," so you pronounce it "micro torrent"). BitTorrent has many legitimate uses as well—its protocol is extremely efficient for the distribution of large files and has become the method of choice for distributing Linux distributions and is even used to distribute and patch *World of Warcraft* and *Starcraft II*!

Figure 24-64 μTorrent

These example programs just scratch the surface of the many applications that use the Internet. One of the more amazing aspects of TCP/IP is that its basic design is around 40 years old. We use TCP/IP in ways completely outside the original concept of its designers, yet TCP/IP continues to show its power and flexibility. Pretty amazing!

Chapter Review

Questions

1. Of the following four Internet connection options, which typically offers the *slowest* connection speed?

 A. Cable

 B. Dial-up

 C. DSL

 D. Satellite

2. What port does POP3 use?

 A. 22

 B. 110

 C. 42

 D. 256

3. What advantages does dial-up have over DSL?

 A. Dial-up is faster than DSL.

 B. You can be farther than 18,000 feet from a main phone service switching center.

 C. You can get a second phone lines to use just for dial-up.

 D. None. Dial-up has no advantages over DSL.

4. Which protocol can you use to send e-mail?

 A. IMAP4

 B. POP3

 C. PPP

 D. SMTP

5. Which protocols can you use to receive e-mail? (Select two.)

 A. IMAP4

 B. POP3

 C. PPP

 D. SMTP

6. What advantage does satellite have over cable for connecting to the Internet?

 A. Satellite is faster than cable.

 B. Cable degrades in stormy weather; satellite does not.

 C. Satellite requires you to be within 18,000 feet of a central switch.

 D. Cable is limited to areas with cable installed; satellite is not.

7. Which Microsoft technology enables you to share a single Internet connection with multiple computers?

 A. Internet Connection Sharing

 B. My Network Places

 C. Remote Access

 D. Remote Desktop

8. What command often enables you to diagnose TCP/IP errors such as connection problems?

 A. FTP

 B. ping

 C. netstat

 D. ICS

9. Which of the following cellular data technologies is often considered 4G?

 A. EDGE

 B. UMTS

 C. WiMAX

 D. CDMA

10. Which of the following programs enable you to access and work on a remote computer from your local computer? (Select two.)

 A. FTP

 B. Internet Connection Sharing

 C. Remote Desktop

 D. Telnet

Answers

1. **B.** Dial-up connections are robust and widely available, but much slower than the other connection types.

2. **B.** POP3 uses port 110.

3. **B.** DSL has a fairly short limit of 18,000 feet from a main switch, leaving people in rural areas (in the United States, at least) out of luck. Dial-up just requires a phone line.

4. **D.** You can use SMTP to send e-mail messages.

5. **A, B.** You can use either IMAP4 or POP3 to receive e-mail messages.

6. **D.** Clearly, satellite cuts you loose from the wires!

7. **A.** Internet Connection Sharing enables you to share a single Internet connection with multiple computers.

8. **B.** You can often use the ping command to diagnose TCP/IP problems.

9. **C.** WiMAX is usually considered a 4G cellular data technology.

10. **C, D.** Both Telnet and Remote Desktop enable you to access and work on a remote computer. The latter is just prettier!

Multimedia

In this chapter, you will learn how to
- Describe how to implement sound in a PC
- Install and configure video capture hardware and software
- Set up a PC to view television signals

The PC long ago went well beyond a simple device used to create office documents and crunch numbers efficiently. With modern PCs, you can experience content on many levels, from realistic video to scintillating three-dimensional sound. Plus, you can add the hardware and software to turn the computer into a multimedia creation machine, capable of making movies and more.

This chapter looks at the many aspects of multimedia available in a modern PC. First, the chapter discusses how sound works in a PC, both to record and play it back. Second, you'll dive into video capture concepts, hardware, and software. Finally, the chapter rolls through the essentials of setting up the computer to bridge the gap into the entertainment world fully by installing and configuring TV tuner hardware and software. Rolling...and...action!

Sound

You're racing down the virtual track, pixels flying across the screen, hearing the engine roar as you take another turn and press down the accelerator—or you're surfing the Web for lovely scenic nature photos, with the sweet, mellifluous music of Mozart filling the room. Sound has become an integral component of the computing experience. Setting up and optimizing sound for the PC has become an integral skill for all computer techs.

Correctly setting up sound for a PC requires that you know about quite a few things, because the sound process has many components. You need a properly installed sound card (or built-in sound device) with the correct drivers loaded, reasonably high-quality speakers, support software such as the API for a particular game correctly configured in Windows, and a properly set up application that can use the features of the sound card. And every great tech needs to know the troubleshooting techniques to handle both routine and uncommon problems with sound.

Historical/Conceptual

How Sound Works in a PC

Like the ripples that roll across a pond when you drop a rock in the center, sound flows from a source in invisible but measurable waves that cause the membranes in your ears to vibrate and create sound. The sophistication of the human ear enables most people to differentiate the melodious from the raucous, the loud from the soft. Computers aren't nearly as sophisticated as the human ear and brain, so clear standards are a must for converting music into a format that a PC can use to record and play sound. Computer folks use the terms *capture* and *output* instead of record and play.

Sound-Capture Basics

Virtually every PC today comes with four critical components for capturing and outputting sound: a sound card or sound device built into the motherboard, speakers, microphone, and recording/playback software. Computers capture (record) sound waves in electronic format through a process called *sampling*. In its simplest sense, sampling means capturing the state or quality of a particular sound wave a set number of times each second. The sampling rate is measured in units of thousands of cycles per second, or kilohertz (KHz). The more often a sound is sampled, the better the reproduction of that sound. Most sounds in the PC world are recorded with a sampling rate of from 11 KHz (very low quality, like a telephone) to 192 KHz (ultra-high quality, better than the human ear).

 NOTE Every modern motherboard comes with sound processing capabilities built in. By default, techs refer to built-in sound as either built-in sound or as a *sound card*, even when there's no expansion card for sound. I'll do the same in this chapter.

Sounds vary according to their loudness (*amplitude*), how high or low their tone (*frequency*), and the qualities that differentiate the same note played on different instruments (*timbre*). All the characteristics of a particular sound wave—amplitude, frequency, timbre—need to be recorded and translated into ones and zeros to reproduce that sound accurately within the computer and out to your speakers.

The number of characteristics of a particular sound captured during sampling is measured by the *bit depth* of the sample. The greater the bit depth used to capture a sample, the more characteristics of that sound can be stored and thus re-created. An 8-bit sample of a Jimi Hendrix guitar solo, for example, captures 2^8 (256) characteristics of that sound per sample. It would sound like a cheap recording of a recording, perhaps a little flat and thin. A 16-bit sample, in contrast, captures 2^{16} (65,536) different characteristics of his solo and reproduces all the fuzzy overtones and feedback that gave Hendrix his unique sound.

The last aspect of sound capture is the number of tracks of sound you capture. Most commonly, you can capture either a single track (*monaural*) or two tracks (*stereo*). More advanced captures record many more sound tracks, but that's a topic for a more advanced sound capture discussion, and well beyond the scope of the CompTIA A+ exams.

The combination of sampling frequency and bit depth determines how faithfully a digital version of a sound captures what your ear would hear. A sound capture is considered *CD quality* when recorded at 44.1 KHz, with 16-bit depth and in stereo. Most recording programs let you set these values before you begin recording. Figure 25-1 shows the configuration settings for Windows Sound Recorder.

Figure 25-1

Sound Recorder
settings

Sound Selection

Name:
CD Quality Save As... Remove

Format: PCM

Attributes: 44.100 kHz, 16 Bit, Stereo 172 kb/sec

OK Cancel

Hey, wait a minute! Did you notice the Format setting in Figure 25-1? What's that? You can save those sampled sounds in lots of different ways—and that's where the term *format* comes into play.

Recorded Sound Formats

The granddaddy of all sound formats is *pulse code modulation (PCM)*. PCM was developed in the 1960s to carry telephone calls over the first digital lines. With just a few minor changes to allow for use in PCs, the PCM format is still alive and well, although it's better known as the *WAV* format so common in the PC world. WAV files are great for storing faithfully recorded sounds and music, but they do so at a price. WAV files can be huge, especially when sampled at high frequency and depth. A 4-minute song at 44.1 KHz and 16-bit stereo, for example, weighs in at a whopping 40-plus MB!

What's interesting about sound quality is that the human ear cannot perceive anywhere near the subtle variations of sound recorded at 44.1 KHz and 16-bit stereo. Clever programmers have written algorithms to store full-quality WAV files as compressed files, discarding unnecessary audio qualities of that file. These algorithms—really nothing more than a series of instructions in code—are called compressor/decompressor programs or, more simply, *codecs.* The most famous of the codecs is the Fraunhoffer MPEG-1 Layer 3 codec, more often called by its file extension, *MP3.*

 NOTE WAV and MP3 are only two among a large number of file formats for sound. Not all sound players can play all of these formats; however, many sound formats are nothing more than some type of compressed WAV file, so with the right codec loaded, you can play most sound formats.

Using MP3 compression, you can shrink a WAV file by a factor of 12 without losing much sound quality. When you compress a WAV file into an MP3 file, the key decision is the bit rate. The *bit rate* is the amount of information (number of bits) transferred from the compressed file to the MP3 decoder in 1 second. The higher the bit rate of an MP3 file, the higher the sound quality. The bit rate of MP3 audio files is commonly measured in thousands of bits per second, abbreviated *Kbps*. Most MP3 encoders support a range of bit rates from 24 Kbps up to 320 Kbps (or 320,000 bits per second). A CD-quality MP3 bit rate is 128 Kbps.

MIDI

Every sound card can produce sounds in addition to playing prerecorded sound files. Every sound card comes with a second processor designed to interpret standardized *musical instrument digital interface (MIDI)* files. It's important to note that a MIDI file is not an independent music file, unlike a WAV file that sounds more or less the same on many different PCs. A MIDI file is a text file that takes advantage of the sound processing hardware to enable the PC to produce sound. Programmers use these small files to tell the sound card which notes to play; how long, how loud, and on which instruments to play them; and so forth. Think of a MIDI file as a piece of electronic sheet music, with the instruments built into your sound card.

 NOTE MIDI files have the file extension .MID in the PC world.

The beauty of MIDI files is that they're tiny in comparison to equivalent WAV files. The first movement of Beethoven's Fifth Symphony, for example, weighs in at a whopping 78 MB as a high-quality WAV file. The same seven-minute piece as a MIDI file, in contrast, slips in at a svelte 60 KB.

MIDI is hardware dependent, meaning the capabilities and quality of the individual sound card make all the difference in the world on the sound produced. Sound cards play MIDI files by using one of two technologies: FM synthesis or wave table synthesis.

FM Synthesis Early processors used electronic emulation of various instruments—a technique often called *FM synthesis*—to produce music and other sound effects. Software developers could tell the sound processor to reproduce a piano playing certain notes, for example, and a sound resembling a piano would pour forth from the speakers. The problem with FM synthesis is that although the modulation sounds okay for a single note, such as middle C, it sounds increasingly electronic the farther up or down the scale you go from that prime note.

Wave Table Synthesis To address the odd techno-sound of early sound processors, manufacturers began embedding recordings of actual instruments or other sounds in the sound card. Modern sound cards use these recorded sounds to reproduce an

instrument much more faithfully than with FM synthesis. When asked to play a C note on a piano or on a viola, for example, the sound processor grabs a prerecorded WAV file from its memory and adjusts it to match the specific sound and timing requested. This technique is called *wave table synthesis*. The number of instruments a sound card can play at once is called the *polyphony* of that card—typically 64 sounds on better cards. Most modern sound cards have samples of 128 instruments—a veritable symphony orchestra on a chip!

 NOTE MIDI files are much less popular than other recorded formats on computers, but every Windows computer and every sound card still fully supports MIDI.

Other File Formats

The WAV, MP3, and MIDI formats may account for the majority of sound files, but plenty of other less common formats are out there. Here are the extensions of some other sound file formats you may run into in the PC world:

- **AAC** Advanced Audio Coding is the native format for songs downloaded into the Apple iTunes music library. The AAC format is part of the MPEG-4 standard, offers better compression algorithms than MP3, and is freely distributed.

- **AIFF** The Audio Interchange File Format is a popular sound format used on Mac computers. AIFF are often seen at Web sites, and you can use the well-known QuickTime Player to play them.

- **ASM** Assembly Language Source files are compressed sound files often seen on the Internet and used in streaming sound (streaming media is discussed later in this chapter.)

- **ASX** Microsoft created the ASX format to facilitate streaming audio over the Internet through Windows Media Player. It's more than just a format, though; it acts like a super playlist and enables you to play other sound file types as well. The full name of the format is Microsoft Advanced Streaming Redirector.

- **AU** Many players can play these files, including players on non-Windows systems, such as Sun, Next, UNIX, and Mac.

- **FLAC** The Free Lossless Audio Codec is an open format that can compress sound files without losing any data—it can even decompress a file back into an exact copy of the original. FLAC can reduce the size of audio files by up to 60 percent.

- **OGG** The Vorbis format is an open-source compression codec that competes well with the proprietary AAC and WMA codecs, as well as MP3. Vorbis files are saved with the .OGG filename extension, so you'll hear them (incorrectly) referred to as "Ogg" files.

- **RM** RealMedia files play either just audio or audio and video. They are proprietary to RealMedia, a popular player often used on the Internet. You must have RealMedia Player installed on your computer to play these files.

- **WMA** Windows Media Audio is Microsoft's proprietary compression format.

This list scratches the surface of the 100-plus sound file formats available, but it represents those you're most likely to encounter.

Playing Sounds

A large number of programs can play sounds on a typical Windows computer. First, virtually every Windows computer comes with Windows Media Player, possibly the most popular of all sound players. Figure 25-2 shows the default Media Player for Windows 7. You can download many other players, of course, including iTunes, Apple's media program for Windows and Mac OS X. This is good, because not all sound players can play all sounds.

Figure 25-2 Windows Media Player

Many applications, especially games, play sounds too. In the not-too-distant past, a game or an application sometimes had its own sound format, but most applications and games today use standard WAV, MP3, or MIDI files.

Streaming media is a broadcast of data that is played on your computer and immediately discarded. Streaming media is incredibly popular on the Internet. Streaming media has spawned an entire industry of Internet radio stations and music databases. Two popular Internet radio players include Windows Media Player and Apple's iTunes. You can use streaming services like Spotify and Pandora to pick and choose the music

you want to hear. With the spread of broadband Internet, the quality of streaming music has improved dramatically.

801

Getting the Right Sound Hardware

Modern motherboards come with built-in sound processing, plus you can buy a sound card that plugs into a PCI or PCIe expansion slot or into a USB port. Sound cards come with many features, including two separate sound processors (one for all of the recorded formats such as WAV and another for MIDI), recording capabilities, support for MIDI instruments, and more. All sound cards, from the cheapest to the most expensive, can play music and drive a pair of speakers, so techs need to delve a little deeper to understand the crucial differences among low-, mid-, and high-end sound cards. Sound cards differ in six basic areas: sound standard, processor capabilities, speaker support, recording quality, jacks, and extra features.

But the sound card itself is only one part of the equation. You also need good-quality speakers if you have any intention of listening to music or enjoying some of the more advanced features such as surround sound.

Sound Card Standards

Most sound cards follow one of two standards, AC'97 or Intel High Definition Audio, although no rule says manufacturers must follow these standards. This applies both to the sound processing hardware built into motherboards and to add-on sound cards.

The *AC'97* standard applies to lower-end audio devices, having been created when most folks listened to stereo sound at best. Both playback and recording capabilities of such sound cards offer adequate quality, certainly enough for the typical office PC. When you want to go beyond average, though, turn to a motherboard or add-on sound card that offers a newer standard.

Intel designed the *Intel High Definition Audio (HDA)* standard to support features such as true surround sound with many discrete speakers. Technically speaking, whereas AC'97 offers support for up to six channels at 48 KHz/20-bit quality, HDA cranks that up to eight channels at 192 KHz/32-bit quality, a substantial improvement. HDA also supports sending multiple streams of audio from one computer to different output devices, so you can enjoy Internet radio in one room, for example, and listen to a CD in another room, both played on the same computer.

NOTE As they do with new microprocessor models, Intel gave the HDA standard a codename as well. Look for motherboards offering the *Azalia* sound option. That's Intel High Definition Audio. Most chipset makers have adopted Intel High Definition Audio for their better motherboard offerings. That includes direct Intel competitors, such as NVIDIA. Everybody plays Azalia these days!

Processor Capabilities

Sound processor capabilities differ dramatically from the low end to the high end, even though the prices don't reflect the great divide. The sound processor handles the communication among the application, operating system, and CPU and translates commands into sounds coming out of the speakers. Low-end sound processors do little more than translate, which means that the CPU has to do the heavy lifting on the processing front.

Better sound processors, in contrast, shoulder much of the processing burden and bring a series of extra features to the table. By handling a lot of the processing on board, these better sound processors free up the CPU for other duties and—in effect and in name—*accelerate* the sound process. These decent sound processors also provide excellent sound reproduction, so your MP3s sound as awesome on your PC as they do on your stereo.

Most mid-range and all high-end sound processors offer support for various surround sound standards, enabling equally equipped games and other applications to provide positional audio effects and detailed sound modeling—features that make PC gaming take on a whole new dimension. You'll learn about the various standards in detail in the "Speakers" section of this chapter, but for now let an example suffice. With properly implemented positional audio, when you're sneaking down the hall, ready to steal the Pasha's treasure, you will hear behind you the sounds of the guards marching up to capture you. Such added realism has many potential benefits beyond games, but games are currently the primary beneficiary of this technology.

Speaker Support

Every sound card supports two speakers or a pair of headphones, but many better sound cards support five or more speakers in discrete channels. These multiple speakers provide surround sound—popular not only for games but also for those who enjoy watching movies on their PCs. The card shown in Figure 25-3, for example, has outputs for many speakers.

Figure 25-3
A sound card with multiple speaker connections

Another popular speaker addition is a subwoofer. A *subwoofer* provides the amazing low-frequency sounds that give an extra dimension to your movies, music, and games. Almost all modern sound cards support both surround sound and a subwoofer and advertise this with a nomenclature such as Dolby Digital or DTS. Figure 25-4 shows one type of surround speaker system. (You'll learn more about surround sound in the upcoming "Speakers" section.)

Figure 25-4
Surround speakers
(photo courtesy of
Klipsch Group, Inc.)

Recording Quality

Almost every sound card has an input for a powered microphone, but the high-end cards record with substantially lower amounts of noise or other audible artifacts. The measure that describes the relative quality of an input port is *signal-to-noise ratio* and is expressed in *decibels*. The smaller the number, the worse the card is for recording, because you're more likely to get noise. Most sound cards at the low end and in the mid range have a signal-to-noise ratio of 30 to 50 decibels, which makes them unacceptable for recording. High-end cards offer a 96 to 100+ signal-to-noise ratio, a level near what professional musicians use. Check the documentation before you buy or recommend a sound card for recording purposes (see Figure 25-5).

Jacks

Virtually every sound card comes with at least three connections: one for a stereo speaker system, one for a microphone, and one for a secondary input called line in. If you look at the back of a motherboard with a built-in sound card, you'll invariably see these three connections. On most systems, the main stereo speaker connector is green, the line in connector is blue, and the microphone connector is pink. You'll often find plenty of other connectors as well (see Figure 25-6).

Here's a list of some of the standard connectors:

- **Main speaker out** Just what it sounds like, the main speaker output is where you plug in the standard speaker connector.
- **Line out** Some cards will have a separate line out connector that is often used to connect to an external device such as a CD or MP3 player. This enables you to output sounds from your computer.
- **Line in** The line in port connects to an external device such as a CD or MP3 player to allow you to import sounds into your computer.

- **Rear out** The rear out connector connects to the rear speakers for surround sound audio output.

- **Analog/digital out** The multifunction analog/digital out connection acts as a special digital connection to external digital devices or digital speaker systems, and it also acts as the analog connection to center and subwoofer channels. (See the "Speakers" section for a discussion of surround sound.)

- **Microphone** The microphone port connects to an external microphone for voice input.

- **Joystick** The now-obsolete joystick port connects a joystick or a MIDI device to the sound card. The joystick port is a two-row, DB-15 female connection, but few motherboards or sound cards include the port these days.

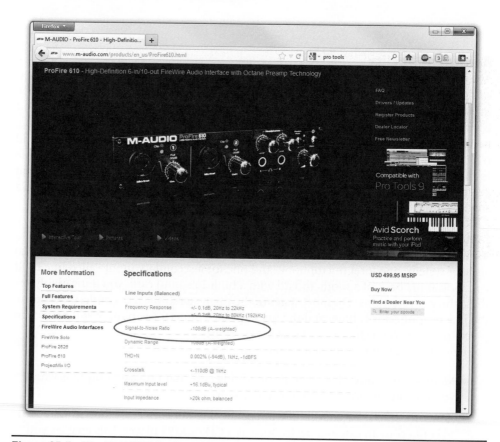

Figure 25-5 The M-AUDIO ProFire 610 advertises its excellent 108-decibel signal-to-noise ratio for recording.

Figure 25-6
Typical audio
connections on
a motherboard
sound card

Mini-audio connectors

Extra Features

With all motherboards including built-in sound these days, expansion sound card makers have responded by adding a host of extra goodies and capabilities to their cards that, for some folks, prove irresistibly tempting. These include a digital output to integrate the PC with a home entertainment unit and surround sound speaker setup; a breakout box that adds recording and output ports in a 5.25-inch bay; and a FireWire connection for direct gaming, file sharing, and immediate MP3 playing from a portable MP3 device. Figure 25-7 shows a version of the Creative Labs SoundBlaster breakout box. These features aren't for everyone, but they are compelling to many consumers.

Figure 25-7
Breakout box for a
SoundBlaster Live!
Platinum sound
card

Speakers

It always blows me away when I walk into someone's study and hear tinny music whining from a $10 pair of speakers connected to a $2000 computer. If you listen to music or play games on your computer, a decent set of speakers can significantly improve the experience. Speakers come in a wide variety of sizes, shapes, technologies, and quality and can stump the uninformed tech who can't easily tell that the $50 set on the right sounds 100 times better than the $25 pair on the left (see Figure 25-8).

Figure 25-11
S/PDIF connectors

> ✏️ **NOTE** Only a few 5.1 PC speaker sets come with S/PDIF. In most cases, you'll have to use the regular audio outputs on the sound card. You'll find the connector more common on 6.1 and 7.1 sets.

Games can also take advantage of 5.1, 6.1, and 7.1 speakers, but they use the DirectX standard. *DirectX* offers numerous commands, also known as APIs, that issue instructions such as "make a sound on the right speaker" or "play music in both the right and left channels." DirectX simplifies the programming needed to create sound and video: rather than having to program sounds in different ways for each sound card option, games can talk DirectX. The hardware manufacturers simply have to ensure that their sound cards are DirectX compatible.

DirectX version 3 introduced *DirectSound3D (DS3D)*, which offered a range of commands to place a sound anywhere in 3-D space. Known as *positional audio*, it fundamentally changed the way most PC games were played. DS3D could not handle all sound information, but it supported extensions to its instructions for more advanced sound features. This challenged the sound card designers to develop more fully the concept of positional audio. Creative Labs responded by rolling out *environmental audio extensions (EAX)*, a set of audio presets that gave developers the capability to create a convincing sense of environment in entertainment titles and a realistic sense of distance between the player and audio events. Figure 25-12 shows an EAX setup screen.

Figure 25-12
EAX setup screen

In late 2000, a number of EAX effects were incorporated into the DirectX audio component of DirectX 8.0. This signaled the acceptance of EAX as the standard for audio effects in gaming. Shortly afterward, Creative Labs started releasing audio cards that were Dolby 5.1 compatible out of the box. This let you plug a 5.1 speaker system directly into your sound card. The sound card automatically decoded the Dolby/DTS sound track when you played a DVD and the EAX effects when you played a game that supported it. All current sound cards support DirectX and EAX.

 NOTE Not all cards support Dolby Digital/DTS. Most software DVD players and some sound cards support Dolby Digital. DTS support is a little harder to come by. Check the manufacturer's Web site to determine whether your card will work with DTS.

Microsoft changed the way audio works in Windows Vista/7 from the way it works in previous versions of Windows. Most notably, Vista/7 doesn't support direct hardware access to sound, so DirectSound does not work. Third-party developers have created various workarounds for this lack of support to enable some older games and hardware to function in Windows Vista/7. Other developers have gotten behind the OpenAL API to provide environmental audio effects in Vista/7. Specific OpenAL drivers for games have to be included to provide that support.

Speaker Features

Speakers also come with a few other features that you should consider when choosing a set for yourself or your clients. Speakers offer a variety of power sources, controls accessibility, and headphone jacks.

Most speakers have volume controls as well as an on/off switch. Get a system that provides easy access to those controls by placing them on an easy-to-reach speaker or on a special control box.

The problem with headphones is that you need to plug them into the back of the sound card and then tell Windows to output to them from the Sound applet on the Control Panel. Save yourself a lot of hassle and get a speaker system that has a handy headphone jack on one of the speakers or on a control box.

Microphones

Speakers are great for listening to music, but what if you're a musician looking to record your own music? You'll need to plug a *microphone* into your sound card if you want to input audio into your PC (see Figure 25-13). A microphone records sound by detecting vibrations and turning them into an electronic signal. Microphones are most commonly used for recording voices, though you can easily record any other sounds. (Many musical instruments can be plugged into the line in port of your sound card, either directly or through a converter box.)

Figure 25-13

A standard microphone

 NOTE You can also buy microphones that connect via USB instead of the microphone port.

Microphones can also be used with speech-to-text programs that listen to what you say and then type it out on the screen. These programs can be finicky to use, but they're still fun to play around with. If you do use speech-to-text programs, look for a headset that has a built-in microphone (see Figure 25-14). The quality will be lower, but it will keep your hands free. (These headsets are also great for voice chatting while playing games on your PC.)

Figure 25-14

Headsets are great for gaming.

When searching for a microphone, you'll most likely be picking between *condenser* and *dynamic* microphones. I won't go too deeply into the science of recording sound, but here's a very quick rundown:

- Condenser microphones are often found in recording studios because they can record a wide range of sound at a high quality, but they are larger, more delicate, and must be powered.

- Dynamic microphones use a different technology to record sound, but are often found at live music events because they're much more rugged, don't need to be powered, and still sound great.

Look for something that combines audio quality with affordability. The best condenser microphones can cost hundreds or thousands of dollars, but most people don't need a recording studio level of quality. A nice dynamic microphone or less-expensive condenser microphone will record great sound for about $100 to $200.

NOTE External microphones are great for more than just your PC. Look for digital cameras and camcorders that include microphone ports. Built-in microphones are notoriously poor in quality and pick up all the noise made by the camera. Another way to increase your audio quality is via a pop filter, which you place between you and the microphone to minimize the poppy noise of *plosive* sounds (like the letters p and b).

MIDI-enabled Devices

Music composition has changed dramatically over the past few decades. What used to be a painfully analog process of writing out music on paper, recording it to tape, and hoping for the best has become almost entirely digital. Hardware and software exist that enable you to record analog sounds to digital storage, and create entirely digital sound with special audio production software. One type of software, called a *digital audio workstation*, enables you to input MIDI information using an external *MIDI-enabled device* (see Figure 25-15). *Music notation* software also exists that enables you to write out notes on sheet music either by hand or with a MIDI device.

MIDI-enabled devices, also known as *MIDI controllers*, come in several form factors, but most look and feel like standard music keyboards (see Figure 25-16). Others use a grid or row of square buttons—the best ones light up, too! Keep in mind that these devices don't play music; they are incapable of making noise on their own. Only combined with the proper software will a MIDI device be able to make music. In the past, MIDI devices used MIDI-to-serial or MIDI-to-joystick adapters, but almost all modern MIDI controllers use USB connections.

Figure 25-15 Ableton Live, a digital audio workstation

Figure 25-16 A MIDI keyboard

Many MIDI controllers can do more than just play music. More elaborate models include extra knobs, sliders, and buttons for controlling the digital audio workstation software. Your audio software should include options and instructions for configuring the MIDI device, but for many applications, you can just plug it in and start playing.

Installing Sound in a Windows System

You've got two choices for sound hardware on today's PCs: a separate sound card or onboard sound built into the motherboard. The installation process for a sound card is basically the same as the process for any other card. You snap the card into a slot, plug some speakers into the card, load a driver—and for the most part, you're finished. With onboard sound, you need to make sure the sound is enabled in your CMOS and then load the driver. As with most of the devices discussed in this book, sound card installation consists of three major parts: physical installation, device driver installation, and configuration.

Physical Installation

Physical installation is easy. Onboard sound is already physically installed, and most sound cards are run-of-the-mill PCI cards (see Figure 25-17), although you can find PCIe and USB versions too. The real trick to physical installation is deciding where to plug in the speakers, microphone, and so on. The surround sound devices so common today feature a variety of jacks, so you will probably want to refer to your sound card documentation for details, but here are a few guidelines:

- The typical stereo or 2.1 speaker system will use only a single jack. Look for the jack labeled Speaker or Speaker 1.

- Surround speakers either use a single digital (S/PDIF) connection, which in most cases runs from the sound card to the subwoofer, or they need three separate cables: one for the front two speakers that runs to the Speaker 1 connector, one for the back two speakers that runs to the Speaker 2 connector, and a third cable for the center channel and subwoofer that runs to the digital/audio out or Speaker 3 connector.

Figure 25-17
Typical sound card

Here's a quick look at sound card installation. As with any expansion card, you'll need a Phillips-head screwdriver to install a sound card, as well as your electrostatic discharge (ESD) prevention equipment. Of course, you'll also need the sound card itself, a set of speakers, an audio cable if it's an older system, and a microphone if you want to be able to record sounds.

1. Shut down your computer, unplug it, and open the case.

2. Find an open PCI or PCIe slot and snap in the sound card. Remember to handle the card with tender loving care—especially if you're installing an expensive, high-end card! Make sure the card is securely seated, and secure it to the chassis with a hex screw.

Installing Drivers

Once the sound card is installed, start the system and let Windows install the card's drivers. This applies to expansion cards and onboard sound. As you might expect by now, you'll probably have a choice between the built-in Windows drivers and the driver that comes on an optical disc with your sound card. Just as with other cards, it's always best to install the driver that comes with the card. All sound devices have easy-to-use autorun-enabled installation discs that step you through the process (see Figure 25-18).

Figure 25-18
Typical autorun screen for a sound card

NOTE Sound card drivers are updated occasionally. Take a moment to check the manufacturer's Web site to see whether your sound card has any driver updates.

You might run into one of the USB sound cards out on the market (see Figure 25-19), in which case the installation process is reversed. The only secret to these devices is to follow the important rule of all USB devices: *Install the drivers before you plug in the device*. Windows probably has basic drivers for these USB sound cards, but don't take a chance—always install the drivers first.

Figure 25-19
USB sound card

After your sound card and driver are installed, make a quick trip to Device Manager to ensure that the driver was installed correctly, and you're two-thirds of the way there. Installing the driver is never the last step for a sound card. Your final steps are to configure the sound card by using configuration programs and to test it by using an application. Most sound cards come with both special configuration programs and a few sound applications on the same installation disc that supplies the drivers. Take a look at these extra bits of software that I call *sound programs*.

Installing Sound Programs

You've already seen that you need a program to play sounds on your PC: Windows Media Player, Winamp, or something similar. But several other classes of sound programs also reside on your computer: programs for the configuration of your sound card—tools built into Windows as well as proprietary tools—and special applications that may or may not come with your sound card.

Windows Configuration Applications Every Windows computer comes with at least one important sound configuration program built right into the operating system: the Control Panel applet called Sound in Windows Vista/7 and Sounds and Audio Devices in Windows XP. Whatever the name, the applet performs the same job: it provides a location for performing most or all of the configuration you need for your sound card.

The Sounds and Audio Devices applet in Windows XP has five tabs: Volume, Sounds, Audio, Voice, and Hardware. The Volume tab is the most interesting. This tab adjusts the volume for the speakers, and it allows you to set up the type of speaker system you have, as shown in Figure 25-20.

Figure 25-20

Advanced Audio
Properties
dialog box

The Sounds tab allows you to add customized sounds to Windows events, such as the startup of a program or Windows shutdown. The Audio tab (see Figure 25-21) and Voice tab do roughly the same thing: they allow you to specify the device used for input and output of general sounds (Audio tab) and voice (Voice tab). These settings are handy for folks like me who have a regular microphone and speakers but also use a headset with microphone for voice recognition or Internet telephone software. By telling Windows to use the microphone for normal sounds and to use the headset for voice recognition, I don't have to make any manual changes when I switch from listening to an MP3 to listening to my brother when he calls me over the Internet.

The Hardware tab isn't used very often, but it does have one interesting feature: it shows you all of the audio and video codecs installed in your system. (See the section on "Missing Codecs" later in this chapter for more details on codecs.)

Microsoft changed a few things between Windows XP and Windows Vista/7 when it comes to configuring sound. The Sound applet offers better support for multiple speaker setup, for example, and integration with televisions with HDMI configuration options.

To configure speakers, go to the Control Panel and click Hardware and Sound; then click Sound if in Category View or double-click the Sound applet if in Classic View/Icon View. Either route opens the Sound applet (see Figure 25-22).

Figure 25-21
Audio tab

Figure 25-22
Sound applet in
Windows Vista

NOTE What you see in Windows Vista/7's Sound applet will vary depending on your installed audio devices. Don't be alarmed if your Sound applet looks a lot different than Figure 25-22.

Select the Speakers (Speakers/Headphones on some systems) option and click the Configure button to open the Speaker Setup dialog box (see Figure 25-23). Select the audio channel option that's appropriate for your setup, such as the 5.1 system selected for my setup at the office and shown in Figure 25-23. You can click on individual speaker icons to test if the speakers are set up properly, or click the Test button to cycle through the whole range of speakers.

Figure 25-23
Speaker Setup dialog box in Windows Vista

Speaker Setup

Choose your configuration

Select the speaker setup below that is most like the configuration on your computer.

Audio channels:

Stereo
Quadraphonic
5.1 Surround

▶ Test

Click any speaker above to test it.

Next Cancel

Proprietary Configuration Applications Many sound cards install proprietary software to support configuration features not provided by Windows. Figure 25-24 shows one such application. This special configuration application comes with Creative Labs sound cards to add a few tweaks to the speaker setup that the Sounds and Audio Devices applet doesn't support.

Most sound cards come with some form of configuration program that works with the Control Panel applet to tweak the sound the way you want it. Figure 25-25 shows the applet that came with my motherboard. One of its many interesting features is that it detects what types of devices are installed into the sound ports and adjusts the system to use them. In other words, I don't even have to look where I'm plugging in anything! If I plug a microphone into the front speaker port, the system just adjusts the outputs—very cool. Software and sound cards that can do this are called *autosensing*.

Figure 25-24
Creative Labs
Speakers and
Headphone panel

Figure 25-25
Autosensing
software detecting
connected devices

Take some time to experiment with the program that comes with your sound card—this is a great way to learn about some of the card's features that you might otherwise not even know are there!

Specialized Applications Some sound cards—Creative Labs sound cards are by far the most infamous for this—install one or more applications, ostensibly to improve your sound experience. These are not the configuration programs just described. These applications enable you to do anything from composing music to organizing your sound files. Personally, I don't have much use for an application such as the 3DMIDI Player (see Figure 25-26)—but you might be just the type of person who loves it. Be sure at least to install the applications that come with your card. If you don't like them, you can easily uninstall them.

Figure 25-26 Creative Labs 3DMIDI Player program

Troubleshooting Sound

The problems you'll run into with sound seem to fall into one of two camps: those that are embarrassingly simple to repair and those that defy any possible logic and are seemingly impossible to fix. This section divides sound problems into three groups—hardware, configuration, and application problems—and gives you some ideas on how to fix these problems.

Hardware Problems

Hardware problems are by far the most common sound problems, especially if your sound card has worked for some amount of time already. Properly installed and configured sound cards almost never suddenly stop making sounds.

Volume The absolute first item to check when a sound dies is the volume controls. Remember that you can set the volume in two places: in software and on the speakers. I can't tell you the number of times I've lost sound only to discover that my wife turned down the volume on the speakers. If the speaker volume is okay, open the volume controls in Windows by clicking the little speaker icon on the system tray, and make sure that both the master volume and the volume of the other controls are turned up (see Figure 25-27).

Figure 25-27 Volume controls in Windows XP

NOTE If your system tray (i.e., the *notification area*) is cluttered, making the little speaker icon hard to find, you can access the Play Control dialog box by opening the Sounds and Audio Devices applet in Windows XP's Control Panel. On the Volume tab—the one that's on top by default—click the Advanced button under Device volume. In Windows Vista/7, open the Sound applet and double-click on the playback device you want to adjust. Under the Levels tab in the Properties dialog box, use the slider to adjust the volume.

If you don't have a little speaker in your system tray at all in Windows XP, you can add it. Just check the box next to the *Place volume icon in the taskbar* option in the Sounds and Audio Devices Properties dialog box, Volume tab. In Windows Vista and Windows 7, right-click on the taskbar and select Properties. Click the Customize button under Notification area. Use the Notification Area Icons applet to enable the volume controls. Presto!

Speakers The second place to look for sound problems is the speakers. Make sure the speakers are turned on and are getting good power. Then make sure the speakers are plugged into the proper connection on the back of the sound card. If this all checks out, try playing a sound, using any sound program. If the sound program *looks* like it is playing—maybe the application has an equalizer that is moving or a status marker that shows that the application is playing the sound—you may have blown speakers. Try another pair and see if the sound returns.

Most of the time, speakers come in a matched set—whether it's a 2.1, 4.1, 5.1, or other system—and the manufacturer includes adequate connecting wires for the whole set. On occasion, you might run into a system in which the user has connected pairs of speakers from different sets or rigged a surround sound system by replacing the stock wires with much longer wires. Either option can create a perfectly functional surround

sound system that works for a specific room, but you should make sure that all the speakers require the same wattage and that high-quality wire is used to connect them.

If you troubleshoot a system in which two of the speakers are very quiet and two are very loud, the wattages are probably different between the two pairs. A simple check of the labels should suffice to troubleshoot, or you can swap out one pair for a different pair and see if that affects the volume issues. Cheap wire, on the other hand, simply degrades the sound quality. If the speakers sounded good before being strung on long wires but they now have a lot of low-grade noise, blame the wires.

Configuration Problems

Configuration errors occur when the sound card is physically good but some setting hasn't been properly configured. I also include drive problems in this category. These errors happen almost exclusively at installation, but they can appear on a working system, too.

 NOTE Technically speaking, turning down the volume in the volume control program isn't a configuration problem; it's just something I always check at the same time I check the volume on the speakers.

The first place to check is Device Manager. If the driver has a problem, you'll see it right there. Try reinstalling the driver. If the driver doesn't show any problems, again try playing a sound and see if the player acts as though the sound is playing. If that's the case, you need to start touring the Sound applet or Sounds and Audio Devices applet to see if you've made a configuration error—perhaps you have the system configured for 5.1 when you have a stereo setup, or maybe you set the default sound output device to some other device. Take your time and look—configuration errors always show themselves.

Application Problems

Application problems are always the hardest to fix and tend to occur on a system that was previously playing sounds without trouble.

First, look for an error message (see Figure 25-28). If an error code appears, write it down *exactly* as you see it and head to the program's support site. Odds are very good that if you have the error text, you'll get the fix right away from the support site. Of course, you can always hope the built-in help has some support, but help systems tend to be a little light in providing real fixes.

Figure 25-28

Sample error message

Windows Media Player Error

Windows Media Player cannot find the specified file. Be sure the path is typed correctly. If it is, the file does not exist in the specified location, or the computer where the file is stored is offline.

Close

Details...

Don't always blame the sound application—remember that any sound file might be corrupted. Most sound players will display a clear error message, but not always. Try playing the sound file with a different application.

Last, a good approach almost always is to reinstall the application.

Video Capture

A microphone, sound card, and software enable you to capture audio, but with a camera capable of capturing full-motion video as well as sound, you can turn the PC into your very own movie studio. This is called *video capture*. To capture video from another source requires you to have the proper hardware installed to provide an interface with the camcorder or video player and, if the source is analog, provide translation of the signal as well; plus you need a properly configured application to do the capturing. Once captured, you can use an application to edit the video file and upload it to YouTube or save it to DVD or other removable media.

Hardware

You need the proper hardware installed to capture video. From a digital signal, such as a modern camcorder that records directly to its own internal solid state hard drive, you simply run a cable from the USB out port on the camcorder to the USB port on your computer. When capturing from an analog source, such as a VHS cassette player or a Hi-8 tape, you'll need some kind of connection and translation hardware.

The Pinnacle Studio MovieBox Ultimate (pictured in Figure 25-29), for example, offers two different dedicated video connections (S-Video in the middle and the yellow RCA jack next to it) and stereo RCA audio jacks. The box uses a USB 2.0 connector to plug into the PC.

> **NOTE** Some video capture devices are external, while others are internal PCI or PCIe cards. If you have an internal video capture card, install it into your PC as you would any other expansion card.

Figure 25-29
A video capture device

You need a decent-grade computer with lots of free hard drive space and a substantial amount of RAM to import the video and audio streams from an external source. And you'll certainly need a serious processor when it comes time to edit and compile a new video from the source material. There's no simple rule for how much of any resource you'll need. Different projects have different demands on the hardware. If you're setting up a new computer for video capture, the simple rule is to get as powerful a system as possible with as much hard drive and RAM capacity as you can afford.

Once you have the hardware in place, the true heavy lifting in video capture falls on the software.

Software

With video editing applications, such as Adobe Premiere Elements or Apple Final Cut, you can import video and then work with it directly. Figure 25-30 shows the former software capturing video and audio translated through the Pinnacle blueBox from a Hi-8 camcorder. Most webcams—even those built into portable computers—are analog rather than digital devices. Thus some software automatically creates break points in the import to make the editing process easier.

Figure 25-30 Importing video in Adobe Premiere Elements

The video editing software enables you to take video and audio from one or many sources and arrange clips into a time line. You can add and edit various transitions

between clips, shorten clips, and so on. Figure 25-31 shows the storyboard from Final Cut Pro and a how-to video my team produced in-house.

Figure 25-31 Editing in Final Cut Pro

Once you've finished the editing process, you can export to a file for archiving, sending out on optical disc, or posting to a video sharing site. With an audio file, as discussed earlier, this is a simple process. You pick a format such as MP3 and save the file. Video is far more complicated.

A video is two or more separate tracks—moving picture and audio—that each go through a compression algorithm. Otherwise, the resulting files would be huge, even for short videos. The compressed tracks then get wrapped up into a *container file*, what's often called a *wrapper*. When you receive a file saved in a standard wrapper, such as .MOV for a QuickTime Movie file, you have no way to know for certain which codecs were used to compress the video or audio tracks inside that container file (see Figure 25-32).

Figure 25-32
A standard container file holds multiple tracks, each encoded separately.

Codecs

Video files use standard audio codecs for the audio tracks, such as WAV or MP3, but vary wildly in the type of video codecs used. Just as with audio codecs, video codecs take a video stream and compress it by using various algorithms. Here are some of the standard video codecs:

- MPEG-2 Part 2, used for DVDs
- MPEG-4 Part 2, a codec often used for Internet broadcasts; you'll find implementations of it with other names, such as DivX
- H.264, used for high-definition movies for Blu-ray Discs, among others
- Windows Media Video (WMV), the family of Microsoft-developed codecs
- Theora, an open-source codec developed to go with the Vorbis audio codec as part of the Ogg project
- TrueMotion VP6, used in Adobe Flash; and VP7, used for Skype video conferencing, among others
- VC-1 is a Microsoft-designed codec that competes with H.264 and other higher-end codecs for the hearts and minds of Blu-ray Disc developers. You'll usually find it wrapped in a WMV container file (see the following section).

Wrappers

When both the video and audio streams of your video file are compressed, the file is placed into some sort of container file or wrapper. The key thing to note here is that the wrapper file doesn't necessarily specify how the video or audio tracks were encoded. You can look at two seemingly identical movie files, for example, both saved with the .MOV file extension, and find that one will play audio and video just fine in Windows Media Player, but the other one might play only the audio and not the video because Media Player lacks the specific codec needed to decode the video stream. (More on this in the "Troubleshooting Video Capture and Playback" section.) Here are some of the standard video wrappers:

- ASF, a container used mainly for WMA and WMV streams; note that you can also have a WMV wrapper for a WMV-format file.
- AVI, the standard container file for Windows
- Flash Video (.FLV) contains streams encoded with various codecs, such as H.263 or VP6; it can also handle H.264 codec. Flash Video has become the dominant standard for displaying video content on the Web through places such as YouTube and Hulu.
- MOV, the standard container file for Apple QuickTime for both Mac OS X and Windows

- MPEG-2 Transport Stream (MPEG-TS), a container for broadcasting that can handle many streams
- Ogg, a container file made for the open source Vorbis and Theora codecs

Troubleshooting Video Capture and Playback

Video capture and playback suffer from several quirks. On the capture side, you'll find dropped frames, problems synchronizing video and audio when capturing content from an analog device, and generally poor-quality captures. On the playback side, the only real issue is missing codecs.

Dropped Frames

Many things cause an initial capture to drop frames, the end result of which is loss of video information and choppy playback. This happens with both analog and digital sources, so it's not necessarily a conversion issue, and it's maddeningly common.

The most common fix for dropped frames is to *turn stuff off*. Some of this is obvious. If you're surfing the Web or doing instant messaging while trying to capture video, you'll drop frames with wild abandon. Don't do it. In fact, disconnect the computer completely from the Internet so no traffic happens in the background. Only do video capture on that machine and use another computer if you need to multitask.

Often the viewing of content you're capturing—while in the capture process—causes dropped frames. Best practice is to know what you're importing, turn off the playback or preview feature, and then start the capture. But the obvious programs aren't necessarily the primary cause of dropped frames.

Windows is a wildly extensible operating system, and programmers love to dump helper applications to run in the background to optimize their specific application. Install Apple's iTunes, for example, and you'll get more than you bargained for in programs installed. To go along with the iTunes player, the installation puts in automatic update-checking tools, iPod helpers, a quick-launch for QuickTime, and more.

The best solution is to have a machine dedicated to video capture. If you have a machine with multiple functions, however, you can turn off some of the automatically loading helper applications before you start the video capture process. You do this by stopping processes and services through Task Manager.

Sync Problems

Capturing a video stream and an audio stream simultaneously can be tough, because it takes the computer a lot longer to encode the video stream than the audio stream. This can lead to significant disconnection between the video and audio streams, so they become desynchronized. It's surprisingly easy to create a movie that's very badly lip-synced! The process of synchronizing audio and video is called *A/V sync*.

 NOTE There's also a common problem of video and audio going out of sync in the process of burning from a hard drive to a DVD, but that's a distinctly different problem than a lack of A/V sync in the capture process.

You can fix this problem sometimes by changing software or even versions of software. Alternatively, if you're having problems with an analog capture, you can record the analog signal into a digital video camcorder and then try to capture from the digital device—a bit clunky, perhaps, but it can work. Finally, you do the last solution in processing, where you manually separate the audio and video streams and then put the whole thing back together synced properly.

Dealing with video capture can be difficult and time consuming, especially in the analog to digital process. A good resource to start learning the detailed ins and outs is with the folks at the Digital FAQ: www.digitalfaq.com.

Poor Capture Quality

Numerous factors can degrade the quality of a video capture, including background programs, marginal hardware for the job, and poor-quality source materials. For the background program issue, follow the same procedures as you did above with the dropped frames. If the computer or the capture components can't do the job, the only fix is to upgrade. The best things to upgrade are the capture hardware and the CPU. It goes almost without saying that you'll need gobs of RAM too.

 EXAM TIP A dedicated A/V computer should have a fast processor and a lot of RAM. You'll want plenty of hard drive storage space too.

There's very little you can do if your source material, such as an old video cassette, has degraded. You're simply not going to get a pristine capture from a damaged source. You can sometimes get better quality by having the heads on the camcorder or player cleaned or by using the camcorder on which the tape was initially recorded.

Missing Codecs

All versions of Windows come with some audio and video codecs installed. The default audio codecs will handle most common music formats, though you'll need to download the Vorbis codec if you want to use that format. Video codecs are a different animal.

The first clue you might have that your computer doesn't have the codec to process a video file properly is that the sound will play but no picture will appear. Occasionally, whatever media player you use will tell you that it's missing a video codec and attempt to go out onto the Internet to download a codec automatically. You can also download a codec or set of codecs manually.

Windows XP makes it easy to see the installed codecs. In the Control Panel, open the Sounds and Audio Devices applet. Select the Hardware tab | Audio Codecs and click the Properties button. In the Audio Codecs Properties dialog box, select the Properties tab and you'll see all the installed audio codecs (see Figure 25-33).

Figure 25-33

Default audio codecs in Windows XP SP2

Similarly, you can see the video codecs by choosing the Video Codecs option on the Hardware tab. Click through to the Properties tab. Figure 25-34 shows the default video codecs in Windows XP.

Figure 25-34

Default video codecs in Windows XP SP2

Microsoft made the codecs a bit more difficult to find in Windows Vista/7. In Vista/7, open Windows Media Player. Press CTRL-M to show the classic menus. Select Help | About Windows Media Player to open the About Windows Media Player dialog box (see Figure 25-35).

Figure 25-35

About Windows Media Player dialog box in Windows Vista

Click the link for Technical Support Information and Windows will open your default Web browser with a long page showing various multimedia settings. Scroll down the page and you'll find the audio and video codecs installed (see Figure 25-36).

If you don't have a codec that you need, you can download that specific codec. A great site for codec information is www.fourcc.org.

You can also download codec packs, such as the Vista Codec Package available at www.afreecodec.com. The packs contain just about everything you need to view and hear content found on the Internet.

TV Tuners

With a *TV tuner*, you can have it all in one package: a computer and the latest TV show as well. Most local stations (in the United States, at least) broadcast high-definition signals, so with the proper TV tuner, you can watch your HDTV without any of the artifacting you see with both cable and satellite feeds. Plus you can make use of typical cable or satellite feeds to watch television as you would with a regular TV. To make it all happen requires four components: a tuner device, an antenna or cable connection, a tuning application, and some sort of program guide. We'll look at troubleshooting at the end.

Figure 25-36 Viewing audio and video codecs installed in Windows Vista

Tuner Hardware

TV tuners come in just about every expansion option available for computers: expansion cards that plug into PCI or PCIe slots on the motherboard; PC Card or ExpressCard for portable computers; or Hi Speed USB for desktop and laptop computers. Figure 25-37 shows a PCIe version of an ATI tuner card.

To install a TV tuner, follow standard installation procedures.

Figure 25-37
ATI TV tuner card

NOTE TV tuners often include components for video capture, so you can get both devices on one card or expansion device.

To pick up a signal on the TV tuner, just as with a standalone television, you need some source. Most can handle a cable TV connection, for example, or an over-the-air antenna. Figure 25-38 shows a USB Hauppauge HDTV tuner card with retractable antenna. For such a small device, it picks up HDTV signals quite well. You'll get the best results for uncompressed HD signals by using a serious, mounted-on-the-rooftop metal antenna with lots of tines.

Figure 25-38
Hauppauge TV
tuner with retract-
able antenna

Tuner hardware comes with a standard coaxial connection. You can plug in a cable or satellite source just as you would with any regular television.

Tuner Software

Once you've installed the hardware, you need to load the specific application or applications that make the tuner work as a tuner. If you have a copy of Windows Media Center, that will often be the tool of choice. Tuner card distributors bundle third-party applications with their cards. Figure 25-39 shows the EyeTV software enabling the computer to show television shows.

Tuner Troubleshooting

The two biggest issues with TV tuner devices are operating system compatibility and poor reception. Some cards simply don't work with Windows Vista or Windows 7, due to driver incompatibility or some other issue. The only fix for this problem is to use one that does work.

Figure 25-39 EyeTV tuner application

The antenna that comes with your tuner should enable you to pick up TV broadcasts in most places, certainly around cities. But a small sliver of metal can only do so well, so you'll experience stuttering, essentially lost frames that may or may not make the program you're viewing viewable. So an antenna used primarily for portable computing, such as the telescoping model pictured in Figure 25-38, is great, but if you install a tuner in a static computer, consider investing in a proper outdoor antenna.

Beyond A+

Publishing Multimedia

Created content needs an audience, whether that audience is close family, friends, or the general public. Once you've finished recording some original music or creating the new great video, the Internet today offers many venues for sharing with others. Any Web site can host video and sound files, but social media sites like Facebook make it easy to share multimedia files. The 800-pound gorilla in the virtual room, though, is Google's YouTube.

You can get a YouTube account for free and start uploading multimedia files within minutes. The files can be made available to the public or kept private according to your preferences. With ad revenue capabilities, you can make money off multimedia files you post to YouTube as well. Finally, you can post to YouTube and then embed files into your Web site with ease.

I embed the CompTIA A+ videos I make at my Web site:

www.totalsem.com/videos

You can also access them directly from Total Seminars' YouTube channel (see Figure 25-40): When you want to publish your multimedia files, go to www.youtube .com and create a new account. Don't forget to send me a link!

Figure 25-40 Hi!

Chapter Review

Questions

1. What refers to the number of characteristics of a particular sound captured when sampling?

 A. Sample rate

 B. Kilohertz

 C. Bit depth

 D. Quality rating

2. All recorded sound formats used in PCs today are derived from which format?

 A. WAV

 B. Fraunhoffer

 C. MP3

 D. PCM

3. Which sound format contains no actual sound recording but only a series of commands stored in a text file for the sound card to interpret?

 A. WMA

 B. WAV

 C. MIDI

 D. MP3

4. How many speakers are in a Dolby Digital 5.1 setup?

 A. Five speakers plus a subwoofer

 B. Six speakers plus a subwoofer

 C. Seven speakers plus a subwoofer

 D. Eight speakers plus a subwoofer

5. What is the name of the extensions to the DirectSound3D standard developed by Creative Labs?

 A. EAX

 B. MP3

 C. Positional audio

 D. Reverberation

6. What is the name of the standard digital connection that replaces many analog connections on some sound cards?

 A. CD audio connector

 B. AUX connector

 C. TAD connector

 D. S/PDIF connector

7. Which sampling rate would produce the highest-quality sound?

 A. 8 Hz

 B. 8 KHz

 C. 128 Hz

 D. 128 KHz

8. What must be installed on your system to decode a sound file?

 A. The proper codec

 B. Sound application software

 C. Speakers

 D. Universal audio cables

9. Which of the following are valid audio file formats?

 A. ASF, WMA, ASP

 B. PCI, MP3, ASX

 C. WAV, PCM, AU

 D. MIDI, MPEG, AVI

10. Which term describes the stereo speakers in a 2.1 sound system?

 E. Woofers

 F. Satellites

 G. Subwoofers

 H. Twins

Answers

1. **C.** The bit depth refers to the number of characteristics of a particular sound captured when sampling.

2. **D.** All recorded sound formats used in PCs today are derived from PCM format.

3. **C.** MIDI files contain no actual sound recording but only a series of commands stored in a text file for the sound card to interpret.

4. **A.** A Dolby Digital 5.1 setup has five speakers and one subwoofer.

5. **A.** Creative Labs developed the EAX extensions.

6. **D.** The S/PDIF connector can replace analog connections on some sound cards.

7. **D.** The bigger the number, the better the quality, so 128 KHz is the king here.

8. **A.** You need a proper codec installed to decode a sound file.

9. **C.** WAV, PCM, and AU are audio file formats.

10. **B.** Stereo speakers are called satellites.

Portable Computing

In this chapter, you will learn how to

- Describe the many types of portable computing devices available
- Explain ways to expand portable computers
- Manage and maintain portable computers
- Upgrade and repair portable computers
- Troubleshoot portable computers

There are times when the walls close in, when you need a change of scenery to get that elusive spark that inspires greatness…or sometimes you just need to get away from your coworkers for a few hours because they're driving you nuts! For many occupations, that's difficult to do. You need access to your documents and spreadsheets; you can't function without e-mail or the Internet. In short, you need a computer to get your job done.

Portable computing devices combine mobility with accessibility to bring you the best of both worlds; portables enable you to take some or even all of your computing capabilities with you when you go. Featuring all the bells and whistles of a desktop system, many portables offer a seamless transition from desk to café table.

This chapter looks at the classic portable computer, essentially a desktop PC transformed into a mobile format. Classic portables run Windows, Mac OS X, or some flavor of Linux.

Other portable devices, such as smartphones and tablets, run mobile operating systems designed to take advantage of small form factors and touch screens. In practice (and on the CompTIA A+ exams), such mobile devices differ a lot from classic portable computers. These devices get their own "Mobile Devices" chapter later in the book.

801/802

Portable Computing Devices

All portable devices share certain features. For output, they use LCD screens, although these vary from 20-inch behemoths to diminutive 10-inch displays. Portable computing devices employ sound of varying quality, from bland mono playback to fairly nice

faux-surround reproductions. All of them run on DC electricity stored in batteries when not plugged into an AC outlet.

When asked about portable computing devices, most folks describe the traditional clamshell *notebook* computer, such as the one in Figure 26-1, with built-in LCD monitor, keyboard, and input device (a *touchpad*, in this case). The notebook is also called a portable or a *laptop*. All the terms are synonymous. A typical laptop computer functions as a fully standalone PC, potentially even replacing the desktop. The one in Figure 26-1, for example, has all of the features you expect the modern PC to have, such as a fast CPU, lots of RAM, a high-capacity hard drive, an optical drive, and an adequate sound system. Attach it to a network and you can browse the Internet and send e-mail.

Figure 26-1
A notebook PC

Input Devices

Portable computers come with a variety of input devices. Most have a fully functional keyboard and a device to control the mouse pointer.

Keyboard Quirks

Laptop keyboards differ somewhat from those of desktop PCs, primarily because manufacturers have to cram all the keys onto a smaller form factor. They use the QWERTY format, but manufacturers make choices with key size and placement of the non-alphabet characters. Almost every portable keyboard uses a *Function (FN) key* to enable some keys to perform a third duty. Figure 26-2 compares a standard desktop keyboard with a large portable keyboard. You'll note that the latter has no separate number pad on the right. To use the number pad, you press the FN key (lower left in this case) to transform the (7, 8, 9), (U, I, O), (J, K, L), and (M) keys into the (7, 8, 9), (4, 5, 6), (1, 2, 3), and (0) keys.

NOTE The FN key also enables you to toggle other features specific to a portable, such as network connectivity and external displays. We'll examine these options in the next section of the chapter.

Figure 26-2 Keyboard comparison

Pointing Devices

Portables need a way to control your mouse pointer, but their smaller size requires manufacturers to come up with clever solutions. First, portables today have USB ports and can use every type of pointing device you'd see on a desktop. Second, early portables used *trackballs*, often plugged in like a mouse and clipped to the side of the case. Other models with trackballs placed them in front of the keyboard at the edge of the case nearest the user, or behind the keyboard at the edge nearest the screen.

The next wave to hit the laptop market was IBM's *TrackPoint* device, a joystick the size of a pencil eraser, situated in the center of the keyboard (see Figure 26-3). With the TrackPoint, you can move the pointer around without taking your fingers away from the "home" typing position. You use a forefinger to push the joystick around, and then click or right-click, using two buttons below the spacebar. This type of pointing device has since been licensed for use by other manufacturers, and it continues to appear on laptops today.

Figure 26-3
IBM TrackPoint

By far the most common laptop pointing device found today is the *touchpad* (see Figure 26-4)—a flat, touch-sensitive pad just in front of the keyboard. To operate a touchpad, you simply glide your finger across its surface to move the pointer, and tap the surface

once or twice to single- or double-click. You can also click by using buttons just below the pad. Most people get the hang of this technique after just a few minutes of practice. The main advantage of the touchpad over previous laptop pointing devices is that it uses no moving parts—a fact that can really extend the life of a hard-working laptop.

Figure 26-4
Touchpad on
a laptop

Some manufacturers today include a *multitouch* touchpad that enables you to perform actions with multiple fingers, such as scrolling up and down or swiping to another screen or desktop.

Display Types

Laptops come in a variety of sizes and at varying costs. One major contributor to the overall cost of a laptop is the size of the LCD screen. Most laptops offer a range between 10.1-inch to 17.3-inch screens (measured diagonally), while a few offer just over 20-inch screens.

EXAM TIP Laptop LCDs are the same in almost every way as desktop LCDs with a TFT screen, an inverter (if using a CCFL backlight), and a backlight (CCFL or LED). You know all about these screens from Chapter 21. Expect questions about laptop displays, but know that they're pretty much the same as desktop displays. The only major difference is that they contain an antenna, but we'll discuss this later in the chapter.

Many manufacturers are phasing out the standard 4:3 aspect ratio screen in favor of the widescreen format. *Aspect ratio* is the comparison of the screen width to the screen height, as you'll recall from Chapter 21. Depending on screen resolution, widescreens can have varying aspect ratios of 10:6, 16:9, 16:9.5, or 16:10.

Laptop LCD screens come in a variety of supported resolutions, described with acronyms such as XGA, WXGA, WSXGA, and more. The *W* in front of the letters indicates widescreen. Table 26-1 lists commonly supported laptop display resolutions.

EXAM TIP The two most common resolutions are WXGA for the 14- to 15-inch models and HD 1080 for the 17.3-inch models.

Acronym	Name	Native Resolution
XGA	eXtended Graphics Array	1024 × 768
HD 720	HD 720	1280 × 720
WXGA (16:10)	Wide eXtended Graphics Array	1280 × 800
WXGA (16:9)	Wide eXtended Graphics Array	1366 × 768
SXGA	Super eXtended Graphics Array	1280 × 1024
SXGA+	Super eXtended Graphics Array Plus	1400 × 1050
HD 900	HD 900	1600 × 900
WSXGA+	Widescreen SXGA Plus	1680 × 1050
UXGA	Ultra eXtended Graphics Array	1600 × 1200
HD 1080	HD 1080	1920 × 1080
WUXGA	Widescreen UXGA	1920 × 1200

Table 26-1 Common Screen Resolutions

Laptop screens typically come with one of two types of finish: *matte* or *high-gloss*. The matte finish was the industry standard for many years and offered a good trade-off between richness of colors and the reduction of glare. The better screens have a wide viewing angle and decent response time. The major drawback for matte-finished laptop screens is that they wash out a lot in bright light. Using such a laptop at an outdoor café, for example, is almost hopeless during daylight.

Manufacturers released high-gloss laptop screens in 2006, and they rapidly took over many store shelves. The high-gloss finish offers sharper contrast, richer colors, and wider viewing angles when compared to the matte screens. Each manufacturer has a different name for high-gloss coatings. Dell calls theirs TrueLife, Acer calls theirs CrystalBrite, and HP calls theirs BrightView. The drawback to the high-gloss screens is that, contrary to what the manufacturers' claim, they pick up lots of reflection from nearby objects, including the user! So although they're usable outside during the day, you'll need to contend with increased reflection as well.

With the advent of LED backlighting for LCD panels, many manufacturers have switched back to an anti-glare screen, though they're not quite the matte screens of old. When the LED brightness is up high, these are lovely screens. (See the "Troubleshooting Portable Computers" section later in this chapter for issues specific to LED-backlit portables.)

As with other LCD technologies that you'll recall from Chapter 21, most LCD/LED screens use twisted nematic (TN) technology. Some laptop screens use In-Plane Switching (IPS) panels for the greater viewing angle and better color quality. You'll find IPS panels on expensive, professional-grade desktop-replacement portables.

What you will *not* find on portable PCs are two other display technologies, plasma and organic light-emitting diode (OLED). Plasma displays demand a lot more electricity than LCDs demand and are completely inappropriate for portable PCs. OLED screens sip energy when compared to LCDs, but they're still so expensive that you'll only find them on a few smartphones today. Chapter 27 discusses OLED screen technology.

 EXAM TIP The CompTIA A+ 801 exam objectives refer to plasma and OLED displays for laptops, but these don't exist. You'll find OLED displays on a few smartphones, but not on portable PCs, at least not at the time of this writing.

Desktop Replacements

A *desktop replacement* features a massive screen, a full-size keyboard, an optical drive (or maybe two), and plenty of hard drive space (see the portable on the left in Figure 26-5). Considering that it weighs almost as much as a mini-tower PC (or at least it feels like it does when I'm lugging it through the airport!), such a portable can be considered a *desktop replacement* because it does everything most people want to do with a desktop PC and doesn't compromise on performance just to make the laptop a few pounds lighter or the battery last an extra hour. Think power first, portability second.

Figure 26-5
Desktop replacement (left) next to a standard portable computer (right)

The current sweet spot for desktop replacements is a 17.3-inch monitor with 16+ GB of DDR3 and either dual 1- to 2-TB HDDs or a single 512-GB to 1-TB SSD. Dedicated graphics are a must. Desktop replacements run the latest Intel high-end mobile processors and, of course, run Windows 7 64-bit edition. Such perfection in computing in a sub-8-pound format doesn't come cheap, so the question that immediately arises is, why buy a desktop replacement?

Desktop replacements appeal to a diverse group of users. Most obviously, dedicated road warriors need to do everything on the plane, on the train, and in the hotel room.

Second, having a computer that can work well on the road and in the office is convenient. Finally, some folks just prefer the compactness of a laptop. You can, after all, put it out of sight when you're finished with it and not have to dedicate space to an equally powerful desktop computer.

Netbooks

Netbooks offer a robust computing platform with low cost and long battery life. These machines usually have displays in the 10-inch range, small hard drives, and CPUs geared more for minimal power usage than raw speed.

A prime example of the netbook is the ASUS Eee PC, shown in Figure 26-6 sitting on a full-sized laptop. This netbook has a 9-inch screen, a 1.6-GHz Intel Atom CPU, and a small solid-state drive, and runs a customized Linux distribution. One distinguishing feature of these netbooks is the use of Intel's Atom processor. The Atom CPU is very useful for keeping power usage down but has much less computing power than its more power-hungry siblings. Therefore, most netbooks run either Windows 7 Starter edition or some form of Linux that is better suited for their limited resources.

Figure 26-6
ASUS Eee PC
sitting on a
normal laptop

Ultrabooks

Thin, light, and powerful, *Ultrabooks* are as much about power and portability as they are about looks. Ultrabooks are for people who can't give up the power of high-end computers but can afford to pay more for a smaller package. Intel set up the Ultrabook specifications in 2011, defining the form factor to use power-sipping Intel processors with integrated graphics. These Ultrabooks have maximum dimensions (18 to 23 mm thick, depending on the size of the screen) and a minimum battery life (5 hours). Several manufacturers are stepping into the Ultrabook market, mostly copying the thin-slice aesthetic of the MacBook Air. You won't find optical drives on these, and most use solid-state drives for storage. Some people find this limiting; those *in the know* (read: young people) won't care, as long as they can edit their HD movies while drinking at a coffee shop and looking good (see Figure 26-7).

Figure 26-7
Ultrabook (photo
courtesy of
Intel Free Press)

Tablet PCs

Microsoft started the *Tablet PC* initiative way back in 2001, defining the devices as fully featured portables running a tablet-aware version of Windows and using a stylus to interact directly with the screen. Many Tablet PCs have come to market since then, fulfilling the needs of specific professions, notably medicine.

NOTE Tablet PC is a Microsoft term and is not the equivalent of a tablet such as the Apple iPad or Samsung Galaxy Tab. The latter devices derive from the mobile phone market, as mentioned at the beginning of this chapter, so they're not PCs, but rather a unique class of mobile devices. According to Microsoft, a Tablet PC runs Windows. Chapter 27 covers mobile devices in detail.

Instead of (or in addition to) a keyboard and mouse, Tablet PCs provide a screen that doubles as an input device. With a special pen, called a *stylus*, you can actually write on the screen (see Figure 26-8). Just make sure you don't grab your fancy Cross ballpoint pen accidentally and start writing on the screen! Unlike some touch screens, most Tablet PC screens are not pressure sensitive—you have to use the stylus to write on the screen. Tablet PCs come in two main form factors: *convertibles*, which include a keyboard that you can fold out of the way, and *slates*, which do away with the keyboard entirely. The convertible Tablet PC in Figure 26-8, for example, looks and functions just like the typical clamshell laptop shown back in Figure 26-1. But here it's shown with the screen rotated 180 degrees and snapped flat so it functions as a slate. Pretty slick!

Early Tablet PCs ran Windows XP Tablet edition. Windows Vista and Windows 7 support tablet features in all editions. You'll recall from Chapter 20 the dedicated Pen and Input Devices applet in Windows Vista. Windows Vista and 7 have a specific Tablet PC Settings applet (see Figure 26-9) that enables you to configure the tablet to recognize handwriting, place menus conveniently for right- or left-handed users, and more.

Figure 26-8
A Tablet PC

Figure 26-9
Tablet PC Settings
applet

In applications that aren't "tablet-aware," the stylus acts just like a mouse, enabling you to select items, double-click, right-click, and so on. To input text with the stylus, you can either tap keys on a virtual keyboard (shown in Figure 26-10), write in the writing utility (shown in Figure 26-11), or use speech recognition software. With a little practice, most users find the computer's accuracy in recognizing their handwriting to be sufficient for most text input, although speedy touch-typists will probably still want to use a keyboard when typing longer documents.

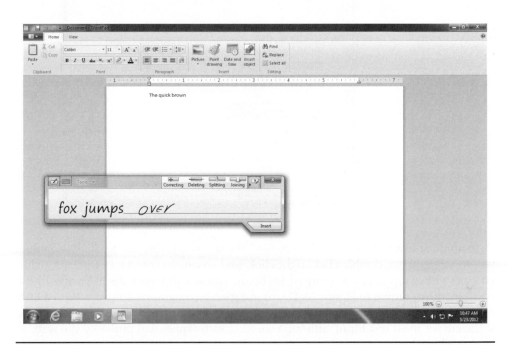

Figure 26-10 The virtual keyboard

Figure 26-11 The writing pad

Tablet PCs work well when you have limited space or have to walk around and use a laptop. Anyone who has ever tried to type with one hand while walking around the factory floor and holding the laptop with the other hand will immediately appreciate the beauty of a Tablet PC. In this scenario, Tablet PCs are most effective when combined with applications designed to be used with a stylus instead of a keyboard. An inventory control program, for example, might present drop-down lists and radio buttons to the user, making a stylus the perfect input tool. With the right custom application, Tablet PCs become indispensable tools.

Microsoft encourages software developers to take advantage of a feature they call *digital ink*, which allows applications to accept pen strokes as input without first converting the pen strokes into text or mouse-clicks. In Microsoft Journal, which comes with Tablet PCs, you can write on the screen just as though you were writing on a paper legal pad (see Figure 26-12). Many other applications, including Microsoft Office, allow you to add ink annotations. Imagine sitting on an airplane reviewing a Microsoft Word document and simply scribbling your comments on the screen (see Figure 26-13). No more printing out hard copy and breaking out the red pen for me! Imagine running a PowerPoint presentation and being able to annotate your presentation as you go.

Figure 26-12 Microsoft Journal preserves pen strokes as digital ink.

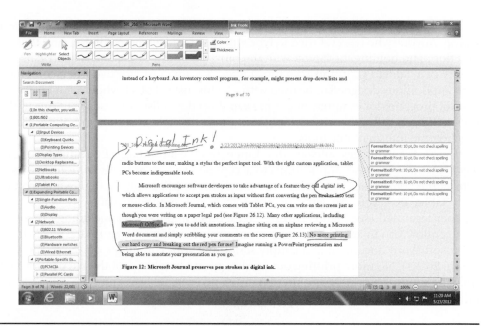

Figure 26-13 Microsoft Office supports digital ink.

Many useful third-party applications are designed specifically to take advantage of the Tablet PC form factor. In fields such as law and medicine, where Tablet PCs have been especially popular, the choices are endless. One handy free utility that anyone who spends time in front of an audience (teachers, salespeople, cult leaders, and so on) will appreciate is InkyBoard (www.cfcassidy.com/Inkyboard). InkyBoard provides a virtual dry-erase board, eliminating the need to find a real board when holding meetings. Ever wished you could have a record of everything that was written on the chalkboard in a class (or business meeting)? If the professor had used InkyBoard, creating and distributing a copy would be a snap.

Expanding Portable Computers

In the dark ages of mobile computing, you had to shell out top dollar for any device that would unplug, and what you purchased was what you got. Upgrade a laptop? Connect to external devices? You had few if any options, so you simply paid for a device that would be way behind the technology curve within a year and functionally obsolete within two.

Portable PCs today offer many ways to enhance their capabilities. Most feature external ports that enable you to add completely new functions to portables, such as attaching a scanner or mobile printer or both. You can take advantage of the latest wireless technology breakthrough simply by slipping a card into the appropriate slot on the laptop.

I'll first describe single-function ports, and then turn to networking options. Next, I'll cover card slots, and then finish with a discussion of general-purpose ports.

Single-Function Ports

All portable PCs come with one or more single-function ports. You'd have a hard time finding a portable computing device that doesn't have a speaker port, for example. Laptops invariably provide a video port such as a VGA or DVI connection for hooking up an external monitor.

Ports work the same way on portable PCs as they do on desktop models. You plug in a device to a particular port and, as long as Windows has the proper drivers, you will have a functioning device when you boot.

Audio

Portable PCs have a standard 3.5-mm audio out port and some have a similarly sized microphone in port (see Figure 26-14). You can plug in regular PC speakers or even a nice surround sound set to enable the laptop to play music just as well as a desktop computer can.

Figure 26-14
Standard audio ports

You control the sound (both out and in) through either the appropriate Control Panel applet in Windows or through some kind of switches on the laptop. The portable in Figure 26-15, for example, enables you to mute the speakers by pressing a special mute spot above the keyboard. Other portables use a combination of the FN key and another key to toggle mute on and off. You can also find many variations on how to control the volume coming out of the machine. Few portable PCs have a manual volume dial these days, instead relying on key combinations or special keys for control.

Figure 26-15
The mute spot on a laptop

Display

Most laptops support a second monitor via an analog VGA port or a digital port of some flavor, such as DVI, HDMI, Mini HDMI, Micro HDMI, or DisplayPort. With a second monitor attached, you can display Windows on only the laptop screen, on only the external monitor, or on both simultaneously. Not all portables can do all variations, but they're more common than not.

Most portables use the FN key plus another key on the keyboard to cycle through display options. Figure 26-16 shows a close-up of a typical keyboard with the Function key; note the other options you can access with the Function key, such as indicated on the F2 key. To engage the second monitor or to cycle through the modes, hold the Function key and press F2.

Figure 26-16

Laptop keyboard showing Function (FN) key that enables you to access additional key options, as on the F2 key

NOTE Although many laptops use the Function key method to cycle the monitor selections, that's not always the case. You might have to pop into the Display applet in the Control Panel to click a checkbox. Just be assured that if the laptop has a video output port, you can cycle through monitor choices!

You can control how the external monitor displays through the Display applet in the Control Panel. Open Display and click on *Change display settings* (see Figure 26-17). Under the Screen Resolution panel, click the drop-down arrow next to Multiple displays (see Figure 26-18). You'll see several options. *Extend these displays* makes your desktop encompass both the laptop and the external monitor. *Duplicate these displays* places the same thing on both displays. You'd use that for a presentation, for example, rather than for a work space. (The other two options shown in Figure 26-18 temporarily blank one or the other display.)

EXAM TIP The CompTIA A+ 802 exam objectives refer to multiple monitors as *dual displays*, though they can be in several modes.

Figure 26-17 Display applet

NOTE In Windows 7, the WINDOWS+P keyboard shortcut switches between multiple display modes.

Network

It's a rare item to find a portable computer without at least one network connection option. Today's laptops come with 802.11, Bluetooth, and wired Ethernet connections. Some still have modems for connecting to older-style telephone jacks. Generally they work exactly as you've seen in previous chapters, but you may stumble into a few issues that are unique to laptops.

802.11 Wireless

Most portables today have Wi-Fi built directly into the chipset for connecting the device to a wireless access point (WAP) and from there to a bigger network, such as the Internet. The 802.11b standard is common on older laptops; newer ones use 802.11g or 802.11n.

Figure 26-18 Multiple display options menu

Bluetooth

While not nearly as common as 802.11, plenty of laptops use Bluetooth as well. Bluetooth is really handy on a laptop because it gives you the ability to add wireless mice, keyboards, and headsets.

Hardware Switches

Laptops that come with 802.11 or Bluetooth have some form of on/off switch to toggle the antenna off or on so that you may use the laptop in areas where emissions aren't allowed (like a commercial aircraft). The switch may be hard wired, like the one shown in Figure 26-19, or it may be a toggle of the FN key plus another key on the keyboard. Also, if you're not using Wi-Fi or Bluetooth, turn them off to save electricity and lengthen the portable's battery life.

Wired Ethernet

Most laptops have an RJ-45 wired Ethernet connection like the one shown in Figure 26-20. These work exactly like any other Ethernet jack—they have link lights and connect via UTP cable.

Figure 26-19
Wireless switch

Figure 26-20
Ethernet port
on laptop

There are two issues with RJ-45s on laptops. First, they do not have an on/off switch like the 802.11 and Bluetooth connections. You can turn them off just like you would turn off the NIC on a desktop: disable the NIC in Device Manager or turn the NIC off in BIOS. The other issue is the relative weakness of the physical connection. If you ever plug a laptop into a wired network and Windows doesn't see a connection, check the RJ-45 port.

Portable-Specific Expansion Slots

The makers of portable computers have developed methods for you to add features to a portable via specialized connections known generically as *expansion slots*. Once a common feature on laptops, these specialized expansion slots are quickly fading away due to the dominance of USB. Yet you'll still find laptops with these slots (and they're covered on the CompTIA A+ exams), so let's take a look at expansion slots over the years.

PCMCIA

For many years, the *Personal Computer Memory Card International Association* (*PCMCIA*) established standards involving portable computers, especially when it came to expansion cards, which are generically called PC Cards. *PC Cards* are roughly credit card–sized devices that enhance and extend the functions of a portable PC. PC Cards are easy to use, inexpensive, and convenient. Figure 26-21 shows a typical PC Card.

Figure 26-21
PC Card

 EXAM TIP CompTIA uses the older term *PCMCIA cards* to describe PC Cards. Don't be shocked if you get that as an option on your exams! You'll hear many techs use the phrase as well.

Older portable PCs come with one or two PC Card slots, into which you insert a PC Card. Each card has at least one function, but many have two, three, or more! You can buy a PC Card that offers connections for removable media, for example, such as combination SD and CF card readers. You can also find PC Cards that enable you to plug into multiple types of networks. All PC Cards are hot-swappable, meaning you can plug them in without powering down the PC.

 EXAM TIP Many manufacturers use the term *hot-pluggable* rather than hot-swappable to describe the ability to plug in and replace PC Cards on the fly. Look for either term on the exams.

The PCMCIA established two versions of PC Cards, one using a parallel bus and the other using a serial bus. Each version, in turn, offers two technology variations as well as several physical varieties. This might sound complicated at first, but here's the map to sort it all out.

Parallel PC Cards

Parallel PC Cards come in two flavors, *16-bit* and *CardBus*, and each flavor comes in three physical sizes, called Type I, Type II, and Type III. The 16-bit PC Cards, as the name suggests, are 16-bit, 5-V cards that can have up to two distinct functions or devices, such as a modem/network card combination. CardBus PC Cards are 32-bit, 3.3-V cards that can have up to eight (!) functions on a single card. Regular PC Cards fit into and work in CardBus slots, but the reverse is not true. CardBus totally dominates the current PC Card landscape, but you might still run into older 16-bit PC Cards.

Type I, II, and III cards differ only in the thickness of the card (Type I being the thinnest, and Type III the thickest). All PC Cards share the same 68-pin interface, so any PC Card will work in any slot that accepts that card type. Type II cards are by far the most

common of PC Cards. Therefore, most older laptops have two Type II slots, one above the other, so the computer can accept two Type I or II cards or one Type III card (see Figure 26-22).

Figure 26-22
PC Card slots

Although PCMCIA doesn't require that certain sizes perform certain functions, most PC Cards follow their recommendations. Table 26-2 lists the sizes and typical uses of each type of PC Card.

Type	Length	Width	Thickness	Typical Use
Type I	85.6 mm	54.0 mm	3.3 mm	Flash memory
Type II	85.6 mm	54.0 mm	5.0 mm	I/O (modem, NIC, and so on)
Type III	85.6 mm	54.0 mm	10.5 mm	Hard drives

Table 26-2 PC Card Types and Their Typical Uses

ExpressCard

Slots for *ExpressCard*, the high-performance serial version of the PC Card, have replaced PC Card slots on laptop PCs over the last decade. ExpressCard comes in two widths: 34 mm and 54 mm, called *ExpressCard/34* and *ExpressCard/54*. Figure 26-23 shows both ExpressCard varieties. Both cards are 75 mm long and 5 mm thick, which makes them shorter than all previous PC Cards and the same thickness as a Type II PC Card.

Figure 26-23
34-mm and 54-mm
ExpressCards

ExpressCards connect to either the USB 2.0 bus or the PCI Express bus. These differ phenomenally in speed. The amazingly slow-in-comparison USB version has a maximum throughput of 480 Mbps. The PCIe version, in contrast, roars in at 2.5 Gbps in unidirectional communication.

Table 26-3 shows the throughput and variations for the parallel and serial PC Cards currently on the market.

Standard	Maximum Theoretical Throughput
PC Card using 16-bit bus	160 Mbps
CardBus PC Card using PCI bus	1056 Mbps
ExpressCard using USB 2.0 bus	480 Mbps
ExpressCard using PCIe bus	2.5 Gbps

Table 26-3 PC Card Speeds

PCMCIA announced ExpressCard 2.0 in 2009 with speeds up to 5 Gbps and support for SuperSpeed USB 3.0, and we expected to see devices roll out in 2010, but that's not what happened. PCMCIA has dissolved and shut its offices. The USB Implementer's Forum now manages all PC Card and ExpressCard standards, and there's not likely to be any further development.

NOTE You can find ExpressCards that supposedly support USB 3.0. While technically these cards have USB 3.0 ports, they connect to the PCIe bus and therefore aren't capable of true USB 3.0 speeds of up to 5 Gbps.

Storage Card Slots

Many portable computers offer one or more flash-memory card slots to enable you to add storage to the portable. These slots also enable the fast transfer of data from the card to the portable, and vice versa. They come in the standard varieties that you already know from Chapter 13, such as SD, CompactFlash, and xD.

General-Purpose Ports

Laptops rarely come with all of the hardware you want. Today's laptops usually include at least USB ports to give you the option to add more hardware. Some laptops still provide legacy general-purpose expansion ports (PS/2, RS-232 serial ports, and so on) for installing peripheral hardware, while other portables focus on more modern ports like eSATA and FireWire. If you're lucky, you will have a docking station or port replicator so you don't have to plug in all of your peripheral devices one at a time.

TIP Almost all handheld computing devices—such as iPod music players—connect to PCs through USB ports. Most come with a USB cable that has a standard connector on one end and a proprietary connector on the other. Don't lose the cable!

USB, FireWire, and eSATA

Universal serial bus (USB), FireWire (or more properly, IEEE 1394), and eSATA enable users to connect a device while the PC is running—you won't have to reboot the system to install a new peripheral. With USB, FireWire, and eSATA, just plug the device in and go! Because portable PCs don't have a desktop's multiple internal expansion capabilities, USB, FireWire, and eSATA are three of the more popular methods for attaching peripherals to laptops (see Figure 26-24).

Figure 26-24
Devices attached to USB on a portable PC

 EXAM TIP The small device resting in a stand in Figure 26-24 is called a *personal digital assistant (PDA)*, a precursor to modern smartphones and tablets such as the Apple iPhone and iPad. You could view pictures, take notes, check a calendar, listen to music, and more on these devices. Expect PDA as an answer choice in exam questions, but most likely as one of the wrong answers. PDAs are rarely used today.

Port Replicators

A *port replicator* plugs into a single port on the portable computer—often a USB port but sometimes a proprietary port—and offers uncommon and common PC ports, such as serial, parallel, USB, network, and PS/2. By plugging the port replicator into your notebook computer, you can instantly connect the computer to nonportable components such as a printer, scanner, monitor, or a full-sized keyboard. Port replicators are typically used at home or in the office with the nonportable equipment already connected. Figure 26-25 shows a Dell Inspiron laptop connected to a port replicator.

Figure 26-25
Port replicator for
a Dell portable
computer

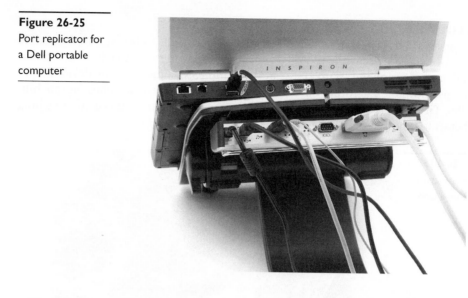

The computer can access any devices attached to the port replicator; you don't need to connect each individual device to the PC. As a side bonus, port replicators enable you to attach legacy devices, such as parallel printers, to a new laptop that only has modern multifunction ports such as USB and FireWire and not parallel or serial ports.

NOTE Although portable PCs most often connect to port replicators via USB ports, some manufacturers have proprietary connections for proprietary port replicators. As long as such a portable PC has a USB port, you can use either the proprietary hardware or the more flexible USB devices.

Docking Stations

Docking stations resemble port replicators in many ways, offering legacy and modern single- and multi-function ports (see Figure 26-26). The typical docking station uses a proprietary connection but has extra features built in, such as a DVD drive or PC Card slot for extra enhancements. You can find docking stations for many older small laptops. A docking station makes an excellent companion to such portables.

Figure 26-26
Docking station

Managing and Maintaining Portable Computers

Most portable PCs come from the factory solidly built and configured. Manufacturers know that few techs outside their factories know enough to work on them, so they don't cut corners. From a tech's standpoint, your most common work on managing and maintaining portables involves taking care of the batteries and extending the battery life through proper power management, keeping the machine clean, and avoiding excessive heat.

Everything you normally do to maintain a PC applies to portable PCs. You need to keep current on Windows patches and service packs and use stable, recent drivers. Run Check Disk with some frequency, and definitely defragment the hard drive. Disk Cleanup is a must if the laptop runs Windows. That said, let's look at issues specifically involving portables.

Batteries

Manufacturers have used three types of batteries for portable PCs: *Nickel-Cadmium (Ni-Cd)*, *Nickel-Metal Hydride (Ni-MH)*, and *Lithium-Ion (Li-Ion)*. Today, only Li-Ion is used because that battery chemistry provides the highest energy density for the weight and has few problems with external factors. Let's look at each battery type briefly.

Nickel-Cadmium

Ni-Cds were the first batteries commonly used in mobile PCs, which means the technology was full of little problems. Probably most irritating was a little thing called *battery memory*, or the tendency of a Ni-Cd battery to lose a significant amount of its rechargeability if it was charged repeatedly without being totally discharged. A battery that originally kept a laptop running for two hours would eventually only keep that same laptop going for 30 minutes or less. Figure 26-27 shows a typical Ni-Cd battery.

Figure 26-27
Ni-Cd battery

Nickel-Metal Hydride

Ni-MH batteries were the next generation of mobile PC batteries and are basically Ni-Cd batteries without most of the headaches. Ni-MH batteries are much less susceptible to memory problems, can tolerate overcharging better, can take more recharging, and can

last longer between rechargings. Like Ni-Cds, Ni-MH batteries are susceptible to heat, but at least they are considered less toxic to the environment. Figure 26-28 shows a typical Ni-MH battery.

Figure 26-28
Ni-MH battery

Lithium-Ion

The most common battery used today is Li-Ion. Li-Ion batteries are powerful, completely immune to memory problems, and last at least twice as long as comparable Ni-MH batteries on one charge. Sadly, they can't handle as many charges as Ni-MH types, but today's users are usually more than glad to give up total battery lifespan in return for longer periods between charges. Li-Ion batteries will explode if they are overcharged, so all Li-Ion batteries sold with PCs have built-in circuitry to prevent accidental overcharging. Lithium batteries can only be used on systems designed to use them. They can't be used as replacement batteries. Figure 26-29 shows a typical Li-Ion battery.

Figure 26-29
Li-Ion battery

NOTE *Lithium polymer (LiPO)* batteries are a variation of Li-Ion that places the heart of the battery—the electrolyte—into a solid polymer shape rather than an organic solvent. This enables the batteries to take on unusual forms beyond the simple cylinder or rectangle shapes. LiPO batteries haven't replaced Li-Ion in most portable PCs (with the Apple MacBook the obvious exception), but they are used heavily in smaller electronics such as tablets, smartphones, and portable media players.

The Care and Feeding of Batteries

In general, keep in mind the following basics. First, always store batteries in a cool place. Although a freezer is in concept an excellent storage place, the moisture, metal racks, and food make it a bad idea. Second, keep the battery charged, at least to 70–80 percent. Third, never drain a battery all the way down unless required to do so as part of a *battery calibration* (where you, in essence, reset the battery according to steps provided by the manufacturer). Rechargeable batteries have only a limited number of charge-discharge cycles before overall battery performance is reduced. Fourth, *never* handle a battery that has ruptured or broken; battery chemicals are very dangerous. Finally, always recycle old batteries.

TIP Got an old portable PC battery lying around? Well, you need to get rid of it, and there are some pretty nasty chemicals in that battery, so you can't just throw it in the trash. Sooner or later, you'll probably need to deal with such a battery. Here are a few tips for disposing of old batteries.

1. Do an online search to find the battery recycling center nearest to you.

2. Sometimes, you can take old laptop batteries to an auto parts store that disposes of old car batteries—I know it sounds odd, but it's true! See if you can find one in your area that will do this.

3. Many cities offer a hazardous materials disposal or recycling service. Check to see if and how your local government will help you dispose of your old batteries.

Power Management

Many different parts are included in the typical laptop, and each part uses power. The problem with early laptops was that every one of these parts used power continuously, whether or not the system needed that device at that time. For example, the hard drive continued to spin even when it was not being accessed, and the LCD panel continued to display even when the user walked away from the machine.

The optimal situation would be a system where the user could instruct the PC to shut down unused devices selectively, preferably by defining a maximum period of inactivity that, when reached, would trigger the PC to shut down the inactive device. Longer

periods of inactivity would eventually enable the entire system to shut itself down, leaving critical information loaded in RAM, ready to restart if a wake-up event (such as moving the mouse or pressing a key) told the system to restart. The system would have to be sensitive to potential hazards, such as shutting down in the middle of writing to a drive, and so on. Also, this feature could not add significantly to the cost of the PC. Clearly, a machine that could perform these functions would need specialized hardware and a specialized BIOS and operating system to operate properly. This process of cooperation among the hardware, the BIOS, and the OS to reduce power use is known generically as *power management*.

System Management Mode

Intel began the process of power management with a series of new features built into the 386SX CPU. These new features enabled the CPU to slow down or stop its clock without erasing the register information, as well as enabling power saving in peripherals. These features were collectively called *System Management Mode (SMM)*. All modern CPUs have SMM. Although a power-saving CPU was okay, power management was relegated to special "sleep" or "doze" buttons that would stop the CPU and all of the peripherals on the laptop. To take real advantage of SMM, the system needed a specialized BIOS and OS to go with the SMM CPU. To this end, Intel put forward the *Advanced Power Management (APM)* specification in 1992 and the *Advanced Configuration and Power Interface (ACPI)* standard in 1996.

Requirements for APM/ACPI

To function fully, APM and ACPI require a number of items. First, they require an SMM-capable CPU. As virtually all CPUs are SMM-capable, this is easy. Second, they need an APM-compliant BIOS that enables the CPU to shut off the peripherals when desired. The third requirement is devices that will accept being shut off. These devices are usually called Energy Star devices, which signals their compliance with the EPA's Energy Star standard. To be an Energy Star device, a peripheral must be able to shut down without actually turning off and show that it uses much less power than the non–Energy Star equivalent. Last, the system's OS must know how to request that a particular device be shut down, and the CPU's clock must be slowed down or stopped.

ACPI goes beyond the APM standard by supplying support for hot-swappable devices—always a huge problem with APM. This feature aside, it is a challenge to tell the difference between an APM system and an ACPI system at first glance.

 NOTE Don't limit your perception of APM, ACPI, and Energy Star just to laptops. Virtually all desktop systems and many appliances also use the power management functions.

APM/ACPI Levels

APM defined four power-usage operating levels for a system. These levels are intentionally fuzzy to give manufacturers considerable leeway in their use; the only real

difference among them is the amount of time each takes to return to normal usage. These levels are as follows:

- **Full On** Everything in the system is running at full power. There is no power management.

- **APM Enabled** CPU and RAM are running at full power. Power management is enabled. An unused device may or may not be shut down.

- **APM Standby** CPU is stopped. RAM still stores all programs. All peripherals are shut down, although configuration options are still stored. (In other words, to get back to APM Enabled, you won't have to reinitialize the devices.)

- **APM Suspend** Everything in the PC is shut down or at its lowest power-consumption setting. Many systems use a special type of Suspend called *hibernation*, where critical configuration information is written to the hard drive. Upon a wake-up event, the system is reinitialized, and the data is read from the drive to return the system to the APM Enabled mode. Clearly, the recovery time between Suspend and Enabled will be much longer than the time between Standby and Enabled.

ACPI, the successor to APM, handles all these levels plus a few more, such as "soft power on/off," that enables you to define the function of the power button. You should familiarize yourself with the following ACPI global (G) and sleeping (S) system power state specifications for both the CompTIA A+ exams and your own practical application:

- **G0 (S0)** Working state
- **G1** Sleeping state mode. Further subdivided into four *S* states:
 - **S1** CPU stops processing. Power to CPU and memory (RAM) is maintained.
 - **S2** CPU is powered down.
 - **S3** Sleep or Standby mode. Power to RAM still on.
 - **S4** Hibernation mode. Information in RAM is stored to nonvolatile memory or drive and powered off.
- **G2 (S5)** Soft power off mode. Certain devices used to wake a system—such as keyboard, LAN, USB, and other devices—remain on, while most other components are powered to a mechanical off state (G3).
- **G3** Mechanical off mode. The system and all components, with the exception of the real-time clock (RTC), are completely powered down.

Configuration of APM/ACPI

You configure APM/ACPI via CMOS settings or through Windows. Windows settings override CMOS settings. Although the APM/ACPI standards permit a great deal of flexibility, which can create some confusion among different implementations, certain settings apply generally to CMOS configuration. First is the ability to initialize power

management; this enables the system to enter the APM Enabled mode. Often CMOS then presents time frames for entering Standby and Suspend modes, as well as settings to determine which events take place in each of these modes.

Many CMOS versions present settings to determine wake-up events, such as directing the system to monitor a modem or a NIC (see Figure 26-30). You'll see this feature as *Wake on LAN*, or something similar. A true ACPI-compliant CMOS provides an ACPI setup option. Figure 26-31 shows a typical modern BIOS that provides this setting.

Figure 26-30 Setting a wake-up event in CMOS

Figure 26-31 CMOS with ACPI setup option

APM/ACPI settings can be found in the Control Panel applet Power Options. In Windows XP, the Power Options applet has several built-in *power schemes* such as Home/Office and Max Battery that put the system into Standby or Suspend after a certain interval (see Figure 26-32). You can also require the system to go into Standby after a set period of time or to turn off the monitor or hard drive after a time, thus creating your own custom power scheme. This is technically called adjusting the *sleep timers*.

Windows Vista and Windows 7 offer *power plans* that enable better control over power use by customizing a balanced, power saver, or high performance power plan (see Figure 26-33). You can customize a power saver plan for your laptop, for example, and configure it to turn off the display at a certain time interval while on battery or plugged in and configure it to put the computer to sleep as desired (see Figure 26-34).

Figure 26-32

The Windows XP
Power Options
applet's Power
Schemes tab

Power Options Properties

| Power Schemes | Advanced | Hibernate | UPS |

Select the power scheme with the most appropriate settings for this computer. Note that changing the settings below will modify the selected scheme.

Power schemes

Max Battery

Save As... Delete

Settings for Max Battery power scheme

Turn off monitor: After 15 mins

Turn off hard disks: Never

System standby: After 20 mins

System hibernates: After 45 mins

OK Cancel Apply

NOTE In Windows XP, you can also access your power options by right-clicking on the desktop, selecting Properties, and then clicking the Power button in the Monitor power section of the Screen Saver tab. In Windows Vista and 7, right-click the desktop, select Personalize, select Screen Saver, and then click on the *Change power settings* link.

Another feature, Hibernate mode, takes everything in active memory and stores it on the hard drive just before the system powers down. When the PC comes out of hibernation, Windows reloads all the files and applications into RAM. Figure 26-35 shows the Power Options Properties applet in Windows XP.

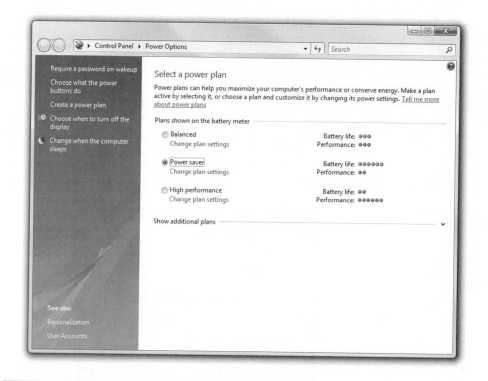

Figure 26-33 Windows Vista Balanced, Power saver, and High performance power plan options

Figure 26-34 Customizing a laptop power plan in Windows Vista

Figure 26-35
Windows XP
hibernation settings
in the Power
Options applet

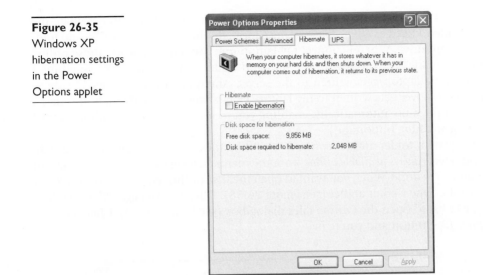

Manual Control over Power Use

Most portable PCs give you several manual options for reducing battery use in certain circumstances. We've already discussed using the on/off switch or keyboard combination for disabling the Wi-Fi antenna, for example, and shutting off Bluetooth. Laptops with backlit keyboards will have some way you can disable this feature when it's not needed, usually with a keyboard combination. You can also reduce the output of the LCD backlight using a combination of FN and another key to eke out a few more precious minutes of computing time before you have to shut down. Figure 26-36 shows a close-up of the FN-activated keys for adjusting screen brightness.

Figure 26-36
Keys for adjusting
screen brightness

One of the best ways to conserve battery use is to plan ahead for times when you'll be unplugged. When I travel, for example, and know that I'm going to need a certain set of files stored on my file server at the office, I put those files on my laptop before I leave, while it's still plugged into the AC. It's tempting to throw the files on a thumb drive so I don't have to break out my laptop at the office, right? Or to let Dropbox do my syncing for me when I get to a Wi-Fi hotspot, but both USB and Wi-Fi use electricity.

Better than that even, Windows Vista and Windows 7 enable me to designate the files and folders I need as *offline files*, storing a local, duplicate copy of the files and folders on my hard drive. When I connect my laptop into my office network, those offline files are automatically synced with the files and folders on the file server. Anything I changed on the laptop gets written to the server. Anything anyone changed in those folders on the server gets written to my laptop. (If changes were made on both sides, a sync conflict pops up automatically, enabling you to resolve problems without fear of overwriting anything important.)

To designate a folder and its contents as offline files, right-click on the folder you want and select *Always available offline* from the menu (see Figure 26-37). The sync will occur and you're done. When you want to open the files offline, go to the Control Panel and open the Sync Center applet (see Figure 26-38). Click the *Manage offline files* link in the Tasks list to open the Offline Files dialog box (see Figure 26-39). Click the *View your offline files* button and you're in.

Figure 26-37 Setting up offline files

Figure 26-38 Sync Center applet

Figure 26-39 Offline Files dialog box

Cleaning

Most portable PCs take substantially more abuse than a corresponding desktop model. Constant handling, travel, airport food on the run, and so on can radically shorten the life of a portable if you don't take action. One of the most important things you should do is clean the laptop regularly. Use an appropriate screen cleaner (not a glass cleaner!) to remove fingerprints and dust from the fragile LCD panel. (Refer to Chapter 21 for specifics.)

If you've had the laptop in a smoky or dusty environment where the air quality alone causes problems, try cleaning it with compressed air. Compressed air works great for blowing out the dust and crumbs from the keyboard and for keeping PC Card sockets clear. Don't use water on your keyboard! Even a minor amount of moisture inside the portable can toast a component.

Heat

To manage and maintain a healthy portable PC, you need to deal with issues of heat. Every portable has a stack of electronic components crammed into a very small space. Unlike their desktop brethren, portables don't have lots of freely moving air space that enables fans to cool everything down. Even with lots of low-power-consumption devices inside, portable PCs crank out a good deal of heat. Excessive heat can cause system lockups and hardware failures, so you should handle the issue wisely. Try this as a starter guide:

- Use power management, even if you're plugged into the AC outlet. This is especially important if you're working in a warm (more than 80 degrees Fahrenheit) room.

- Keep air space between the bottom of the laptop and the surface on which it rests. Putting a laptop on a soft surface, such as a pillow on your lap, creates a great heat-retention system—not a good thing! Always use a hard, flat surface.

- Don't use a keyboard protector for extended amounts of time.

- Listen to your fan, assuming the laptop has one. If it's often running very fast—you can tell by the high-pitched whirring sound—examine your power management settings and your environment, and change whatever is causing heat retention.

- Speaking of fans, be alert to a fan that suddenly goes silent. Fans do fail on laptops, causing overheating and failure. All laptop fans can be replaced easily.

Protecting the Machine

Although prices continue to drop for basic laptops, a fully loaded system is still pricey. To protect your investment, you'll want to adhere to certain best practices. You've already read tips in this chapter to deal with cleaning and heat, so let's look at the "portable" part of portable computers.

Tripping

Pay attention to where you run the power cord when you plug in a laptop. One of the primary causes of laptop destruction is people tripping over the power cord and knocking the laptop off of a desk. This is especially true if you plug in at a public place such as a café or airport. Remember, the life you save could be your portable PC's!

Storage

If you aren't going to use your laptop for a while, storing it safely will go a long way toward keeping it operable when you do power it up again. Investing in a quality case is worth the extra few dollars—preferably one with ample padding. Not only will this protect your system on a daily basis when transporting it from home to office, but it will keep dust and pet hair away as well. Lastly, protect from battery leakage by removing the battery if you'll be storing your device for an extended time.

Travel

If you're traveling with a laptop, take care to guard against theft. If possible, use a case that doesn't look like a computer case. A well-padded backpack makes a great travel bag for a laptop and appears less tempting to would-be thieves. Don't forget to pack any accessories you might need, like modular devices, spare batteries, and AC adapters. Make sure to remove any disks, such as optical or floppies, from their drives. Most importantly—back up any important data before you leave!

Make sure to have at least a little battery power available. Heightened security at airports means you might have to power on your system to prove it's really a computer and not a transport case for questionable materials. And never let your laptop out of your sight. If going through an x-ray machine, request a manual search. The x-ray won't harm your computer like a metal detector would, but if the laptop gets through the line at security before you do, someone else might walk away with it. If flying, stow your laptop under the seat in front of you where you can keep an eye on it.

If you travel to a foreign country, be very careful about the electricity. North America uses ~115-V power outlets, but most of the world uses ~230-V outlets. Many portable computers have *auto-switching power supplies*, meaning they detect the voltage at the outlet and adjust accordingly. For these portables, a simple plug converter will do the trick. Other portable computers, however, have *fixed-input power supplies*, which means they run only on ~115-V or on ~230-V power. For these portables, you need a full-blown electricity converting device, either a step-down or step-up *transformer*. You can find converters and transformers at electrical parts stores, such as Radio Shack in the United States.

Shipping

Much of the storage and travel advice can be applied to shipping. Remove batteries and optical discs from their drives. Pack the laptop well and disguise the container as best you can. Back up any data and verify the warranty coverage. Ship with a reputable

carrier and always request a tracking number and, if possible, delivery signature. It's also worth the extra couple of bucks to pay for the shipping insurance. And when the clerk asks what's in the box, it's safer to say "electronics" rather than "a new 20-inch laptop computer."

Security

The fact is, if someone really wants to steal your laptop, they'll find a way. There are, however, some things you can do to make yourself, and your equipment, less desirable targets. As you've already learned, disguise is a good idea. Although you don't need to camouflage your laptop or carry it in a brown grocery bag on a daily basis, an inconspicuous carrying case will draw less attention.

Another physical deterrent is a laptop lock. Similar to a steel bicycle cable, there is a loop on one end and a lock on the other. The idea is to loop the cable around a solid object, such as a bed frame, and secure the lock to the small security hole on the side of the laptop (see Figure 26-40). Again, if someone really wants to steal your computer, they'll find a way. They'll dismantle the bed frame if they're desperate. The best protection is to be vigilant and not let the computer out of your sight.

Figure 26-40
Cable lock

An alternative to physically securing a laptop with a lock is to use a software tracking system. Software makers, such as Computer Security Products, Inc., at www.computersecurity.com, offer tracking software that transmits a signal to a central office if the computer is stolen and connected to a phone line or the Internet. Even LoJack, the company famous for recovering stolen automobiles via its tracking devices, lends its name to a tracking product sold by Absolute Software (see Figure 26-41). The location of the stolen PC can be tracked, and sensitive files can even be deleted automatically with the aid of the stealth signal.

Figure 26-41
LoJack (photo
courtesy of
Absolute Software
Corporation)

Upgrading and Repairing Laptop Computers

A competent tech can upgrade and repair portable computers to a degree, though true laptop techs are specialists. Upgrading the basics usually means breaking out the trusty screwdriver and avoiding electrostatic discharge (ESD). *Repairing* portables successfully, on the other hand, requires research, patience, organization, special tools, and documentation. Plus you need a ridiculously steady hand. This section provides an overview of the upgrade and repair process.

Disassembly Process

Disassembling a portable PC is pretty easy. Putting it back together in working condition is the hard part! You need to follow a four-step process to succeed in disassembly/reassembly.

First, *document and label every cable and screw location*. Laptops don't use standard connectors or screws. Often you'll run into many tiny screws of varying threads. If you try to put a screw into the wrong hole, you could end up stripping the screw, stripping the hole, or getting the screw wedged into the wrong place.

Second, *organize any parts you extract from the laptop.* Seriously, put a big white piece of construction paper on your work surface, lay each extracted piece out in logical fashion, and clearly mark where each component connects and what it connects to as well.

Third, *refer to the manufacturer's documentation.* I can't stress this point enough. Unlike desktop PCs, portable PCs have no standardization of internal structure. Everything in the portable is designed according to the manufacturer's best engineering efforts. Two portables from the same manufacturer might have a similar layout inside, but it's far more likely that every model differs a lot.

Finally, you need to *use the appropriate hand tools.* A portable PC, especially on the inside, will have a remarkable variety of tiny screws that you can't remove/reinsert without tiny-headed Phillips or Torx drivers. You'll need tiny pry bars—metal and plastic—to open components. Figure 26-42 shows an entry-level toolkit for a laptop tech that you can order from iFixit.com (more on this site in a moment). Their professional version of the toolkit has 70 tools, plus there's an expansion kit! Like I said at the beginning of the chapter, portable techs are specialists.

Figure 26-42 Bare-minimum laptop repair tools

EXAM TIP Know the four-step disassembly process for the CompTIA A+ 220-802 exam:

1. Document and label cable and screw locations.
2. Organize parts.
3. Refer to the manufacturer's documentation.
4. Use appropriate hand tools.

Now that you have the official line on the disassembly process, let's get one thing clear: A lot of manufacturers don't provide documentation to just any tech, but only to authorized repair centers. So what do you do when faced with an unfamiliar laptop that a client brought in for repair?

You have essentially three options. First, you can find a dedicated laptop tech and refer your client to that person. If the problem is exceptionally complicated and the portable in question is mission critical, that's often the best option. If you want to tackle the problem or it looks like something you should be able to do, then you go to the sources: YouTube and iFixit.com.

Every portable computer has a specific make and model. Open up a Web browser and go to YouTube. Type in precisely what you want to do, such as "replace the keyboard on a Lenovo y530," and see what pops up (see Figure 26-43). You'll most likely be in shock and awe when you get the results back, especially if the laptop in question is a couple of years old. People all over the world have to deal with broken devices, so you're not alone.

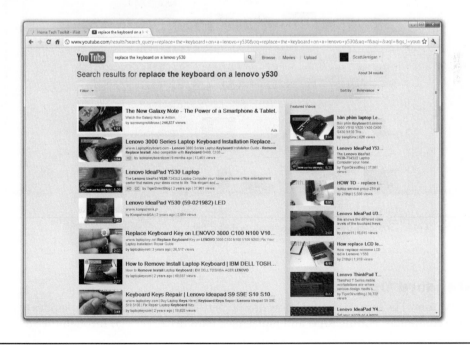

Figure 26-43 YouTube search result

Once you've found the appropriate video or something that's close enough to enable the repair attempt, watch it. If it's too difficult for your skill level or requires a set of expensive tools, then fall back to step one and go find that dedicated tech. Otherwise, figure out what tools and parts you need. Parts specific to a laptop (as in that Lenovo keyboard in the preceding example) will need to be purchased from the manufacturer. More generic parts, like hard drives, CPUs, and so on, can be purchased from Newegg (my favorite tech store) or some other online retailer.

For general tools, parts, and a lot of very detailed step-by-step instructions, I highly recommend iFixit.com. Billed as a "free repair manual you can edit," iFixit is built by techs like you who conquer a problem, document the steps, and post the details (see Figure 26-44). This means the next tech along who runs into the same problem doesn't have to reinvent the wheel. Just go to iFixit.com. The proceeds from parts and tools they sell, by the way, go toward supporting the site. It's not a for-profit enterprise.

Figure 26-44 Some of the Dell laptop repair walkthroughs at iFixit.com

Standard Upgrades

Every CompTIA A+ tech should know how to perform the two standard upgrades to portable computers: adding RAM and replacing a hard drive. Let's go through the steps.

 EXAM TIP One of the most striking contrasts between portable PCs and the tablets and smartphones you'll read about in Chapter 27 is in upgradability. You can and should upgrade portable PCs. Mobile devices, on the other hand, offer almost no upgradability at all.

RAM

Stock factory portable PCs almost always come with a minimal amount of RAM, so one of the first laptop upgrades you'll be called on to do is to add more RAM. Economy laptops running Windows 7 Home Premium routinely sit on store shelves and go home to consumers with as little as 1 GB of RAM, an amount guaranteed to limit the use and performance of the laptop. The OS alone will consume more than half of the RAM! Luckily, every decent laptop has upgradeable RAM slots. Ancient laptops use either 72-pin or 144-pin SO-DIMMs with SDRAM technology. DDR, DDR2, and DDR3 systems primarily use 200-pin SO-DIMMs (see Figure 26-45), although some laptops use micro-DIMMs.

Figure 26-45
200-pin SO-DIMM
stick (front and
back)

 TIP The amount of RAM needed to run a PC—portable or otherwise—smoothly and stably depends on both the type of applications that it will run and the needs of the OS. When making a recommendation to a client about upgrading a laptop's memory, you should ask the basic questions, such as what the client plans to do on the laptop. If the laptop will be used for e-mail, word processing, and Web surfing, a medium level of RAM, such as 1–2 GB, might be adequate. If the user travels, uses a high-end digital camera, and wants to use Photoshop to edit huge images, you'll need to augment the RAM accordingly. Then add the needs of the OS to give a good recommendation. Refer to Chapter 14 for specific OS RAM needs.

How to Add or Replace RAM Upgrading the RAM in a portable PC requires a couple of steps. First, you need to get the correct RAM. Many older portable PCs use proprietary RAM solutions, which means you need to order directly from Dell, HP, or Sony and pay exorbitant prices for the precious extra megabytes. Most manufacturers have taken pity on consumers in recent years and use standard SO-DIMMs or micro-DIMMs. Refer to the manufacturer's Web site or to the manual (if any) that came with the portable for the specific RAM needed.

Second, every portable PC offers a unique challenge to the tech who wants to upgrade the RAM, because there's no standard location for RAM placement in portables. More often than not, you need to unscrew or pop open a panel on the underside of the portable (see Figure 26-46). Then you press out on the restraining clips and the RAM stick pops up (see Figure 26-47). Gently remove the old stick of RAM and insert the new one by reversing the steps.

Figure 26-46
Removing a RAM panel

Figure 26-47
Releasing the RAM

Always remove all electrical power from the laptop before removing or inserting memory. Disconnect the AC cord from the wall outlet. Take out the battery! Failure to disconnect from power can result in a fried laptop.

Shared Memory Some laptops (and desktops) support *shared memory*. Shared memory reduces the cost of video cards by reducing the amount of memory on the video card itself. Instead of having 256 MB of RAM, the video card might have only 64 MB of RAM but be able to borrow 192 MB of RAM from the system. This equates to a 256 MB video card. The video card uses regular system RAM to make up for the loss.

The obvious benefit of shared memory is a less expensive video card (and a less expensive laptop!) with performance comparable to its mega-memory alternative. The downside is that your overall system performance will suffer because a portion of the system RAM is no longer available to programs. (The term *shared* is a bit misleading because the video card takes control of a portion of RAM. The video portion of system RAM is *not* shared back and forth between the video card processor and the CPU.) Shared memory technologies include TurboCache (developed by NVIDIA) and Hyper-Memory (developed by ATI).

 NOTE You cannot tell if a laptop is using shared memory in Windows. You have to go to CMOS to be sure.

Some systems give you control over the amount of shared memory, while others simply allow you to turn shared memory on or off. The settings are found in CMOS setup and only on systems that support shared memory. Shared memory is not reported to Windows, so don't panic if you have 1 GB of RAM in your laptop but Windows only sees 924 MB—the missing memory is used for video.

Adding more system RAM to a laptop with shared memory will improve laptop performance. Although it might appear to improve video performance, that doesn't tell the true story. It'll improve overall performance because the OS and CPU get more usable RAM. On some laptops, you can improve video performance as well, but that depends on the CMOS setup. If the shared memory is not set to maximum by default, increasing the overall memory and upping the portion reserved for video will improve video performance specifically.

HDD/SSD

You can replace a hard disk drive (HDD) or solid-state drive (SSD) in a portable PC fairly easily, especially if the laptop is only a few years old. SATA drives in the 2.5-inch drive format now rule in all laptops. Although much smaller than regular 3.5-inch hard drives, they use all the same features and configurations. These smaller hard drives have suffered, however, from diminished storage capacity as compared to their 3.5-inch brothers. Currently, large 2.5-inch hard drives hold up to 1 TB, while the 3.5-inch hard drives can hold more than 3 TB of data!

If you have a much older laptop, it might have a PATA drive, which means you need to pay more attention to cabling and jumpers. Some PATA drive manufacturers may require you to set the drive to use a cable-select setting as opposed to master or slave, so check with the laptop maker for any special issues. Otherwise, no difference exists between 2.5-inch drives and their larger 3.5-inch brethren (see Figure 26-48).

Figure 26-48
The 2.5-inch and 3.5-inch drives are mostly the same.

One of the best upgrades you can make on a laptop is to go from an HDD to an SSD. Obviously, you'll get a lot less storage capacity for the money, but the trade-offs can be worth it. First, the SSD will use a lot less electricity than an HDD, thus extending battery life. Second, any SSD is rip-roaringly faster than an HDD and performance across the board will be boosted.

The process of replacing a hard drive mirrors that of replacing RAM. You find the hard drive hatch—either along one edge or in a compartment on the underside of the computer—and release the screws (see Figure 26-49). Remove the old drive and then slide the new drive into its place (see Figure 26-50). Reattach the hatch or cover and boot the computer. Grab a Windows disc and prepare to reinstall.

Figure 26-49
Removing the drive compartment cover

Figure 26-50
Inserting a
replacement
drive

Hardware Replacement

Once you get beyond upgrading RAM and replacing a hard drive on a portable PC, you take the plunge into the laptop repair specialty. You can replace some components by lifting them out, detaching a ribbon cable, and then reversing the steps with the replacement part. Other parts require a full teardown of the laptop to the bare bones, which presents a much greater magnitude of difficulty. Because every portable PC differs from every other one, this section provides guidance, but not concrete steps, for replacement.

Components

Replaceable components require more work than the RAM or drive upgrades, but replacing them generally falls into the category of "doable." What I call *components* are the battery, keyboard, optical drive, internal speaker, and plastic parts.

Battery If a battery's performance falls below an acceptable level, you can replace it with a battery from the manufacturer or from an aftermarket vendor. Although this should be a simple swap replacement (and usually is), you might encounter a situation where the real problem wasn't the battery per se, but an inadequate or malfunctioning charging system. The new battery might not give you any better performance than the old one. Try it.

Keyboard Getting a keyboard off a laptop computer often requires little pry bars, but also look for screws, clips, and so on. Keyboards connect via a tiny, short, and very delicate cable, often held down by tape. Replacing one is tricky, but doable.

Mobile Experience

Mobile devices might seem, at first description, like PCs scaled down to fit in a backpack, purse, or pocket, but they bring a unique experience to users that differs substantially from the standard PC experience. Mobile devices have a default screen—like the desktop in Windows—called the *home screen* and have icons for applications (*apps*) for accomplishing specific tasks. But the first thing that will strike you when you handle one of these devices is that it's *not* the same thing as a small PC (see Figure 27-1). The most obvious difference is the interface, so we'll start there.

Figure 27-1 Small PC and tablet—cousins at best

Touch Interface

Mobile devices use a *touch interface*, meaning that to interact with them you touch the screen (see Figure 27-2). They don't come with a physical keyboard for typing or a mouse for clicking. (In fact, you can't add a mouse at all to most mobile devices.)

Different gestures with your fingers accomplish different tasks. To start a program, or app as they're called, you *tap* its icon, which means to poke it with your finger. If you've opened an app with multiple screens, you hold your finger on the screen and slide it across the screen, either right to left or top to bottom, depending on the type of application (see Figure 27-3). This is called a *swipe*.

Holding a finger on the home screen or on an open app screen in many devices brings up a context menu for accomplishing things like changing the background picture (the *wallpaper*), bookmarking a page, or editing (see Figure 27-4). Touching different parts of the screen when in an app can offer other options, such as closing the app or pushing the app to the background.

Figure 27-2
Mobile devices have
a touch interface.

Figure 27-3 Swiping to move to the next screen

Many mobile devices enable you to use multiple fingers to do tasks such as expand or shrink an image on the screen (see Figure 27-5). An open long document, such as a word processing document, for example, might give you two different responses when you scroll with one or two fingers. Using one finger might select text to edit, but two-fingered scrolling might move the document up or down. Different vendors call this feature different things, but the common term is *multitouch*.

Figure 27-4 Getting a context menu by touching and holding

Figure 27-5 Resizing and rotating an image using two fingers

This multitouch interface enables you to expand or contract some content on the screen. You can *pinch* an image, for example, between two fingers and make that picture bigger or smaller according to the way your fingers move.

Screen Technology Current *capacitive* touchscreens use electrical current in your body to determine movement of your fingers across the screen. They measure the difference between the electrical charge in your body and the static charge on the screen, which is quite cool when you think about it. Capacitive touchscreens require physical contact, so gloved fingers won't work. Older technologies used *resistive* touchscreens that responded to the pressure applied to the screen. Fingers worked, but best results came from using a special pointing stick called a *stylus* (see Figure 27-6).

Figure 27-6
Older mobile device with stylus

 EXAM TIP The resistive touchscreen devices required periodic *screen calibration*, which resets the touch screen for improved accuracy. Capacitive touchscreens don't require calibration.

Mobile devices use a variety of screen types. Most tablets use some type of LCD panel, just like portable PCs and desktop monitors. The less expensive ones use twisted nematic (TN); the better ones, like the Apple iPad, use an In-Plane Switching (IPS) panel for richer colors and better viewing angles.

Some smaller devices, like the better smartphones, use a related but different technology called *organic light-emitting diode (OLED)* screens where an organic compound provides the light for the screen. Applying an electric current causes the organic layer to glow in the precise spots desired. Displaying a checkerboard pattern of black and white, in other words, only lights up the white squares. OLEDs don't use backlights at all, which means they can display true black, they're lighter, and they use less electricity than LCDs of any sort. Screens larger than half a dozen inches, as of this writing, are too expensive to make for mainstream consumer devices.

EXAM TIP OLED screens use an organic compound exposed to electrical current for lighting; they don't have a traditional backlight.

Orientation Mobile devices feature rectangular screens, just like desktop displays, but all of them rotate easily. Plus, the orientation of the screen rotates right along with the display, so by default, up is always up. The underlying technology, called an *accelerometer*, enables you to switch easily from portrait view to landscape view. If you want to switch from reading a book to watching a movie, just turn the device on its side (see Figure 27-7). Figure 27-8 shows a wonderful use of the accelerometer in an iPhone, turning the device into an electronic level.

Figure 27-7
Switching
orientation

Figure 27-8
Hanging a picture
properly

Some devices feature a *gyroscope* that can detect the position of the tablet or phone in 3-D space. This enables more intuitive control over onscreen devices, such as a plane's joystick. Tilting the device forward, for example, would have the effect of pushing the plane's nose down; tilting backward "pulls back" on the stick, easing the plane's nose up. Few applications (and those primarily games) use the gyroscope as of this writing.

Mobile Operating Systems

Two operating systems power the vast majority of mobile devices. Apple *iOS* runs on all Apple devices, such as the iPhone smartphone and the iPad tablet. Google *Android* runs almost every non-Apple product. Microsoft has a very small presence in the mobile devices market, but you'll only find Windows Phone 7 on a few smartphones.

Apps

An *app* enables you to accomplish a specific task on a mobile device, such as check e-mail, surf the Web, play games, and so on. (Apps are the same thing as applications. For some reason, it's more hip to use the short term when discussing mobile devices.) Programmers write apps for specific mobile platforms and sometimes for specific devices. So an app written for a Windows Phone 7 phone, for example, won't work on an Apple iPhone, even though both are smartphones. This applies somewhat to apps written for a specific operating system as well. Apps written for an Apple iPhone can run on an Apple iPad, because both devices use Apple iOS for an operating system, but the same app optimized for the iPad will look and run better than a scaled-up iPhone app.

Different apps bring out different features of the mobile device. An electronic book reader, for example, shows an interface that appears like a book (see Figure 27-9). You swipe to change pages. A note-taking application, in contrast, will open a virtual keyboard that enables you to type as if you had a regular keyboard attached (see Figure 27-10). Finally, a racing game will turn the entire mobile device into a steering wheel, relying on the accelerometer to provide accurate turning (see Figure 27-11).

Figure 27-9

Reading an eBook

Figure 27-10

Typing on a virtual keyboard

Figure 27-11

Racing

Multimedia

Most mobile devices today come with one or two cameras for taking digital photos and movies and for video conferencing. Manufacturers initially offered low-resolution cameras and camcorders that produced poor-quality photos and grainy videos, but some current devices offer crystal-clear high-definition videos with flash photos and optical zoom.

Devices with two cameras, one pointed away and one pointed at the user, have some kind of button to switch when picture taking. The tablet in Figure 27-12, for example, enables the user to swap the focus of the picture-taking software by tapping the double-arrow button in the lower-right corner.

Figure 27-12
Switching from the
rear camera to the
front camera

Adding Apps

Mobile devices come from the manufacturer with a certain number of vital apps installed for accessing e-mail, surfing the Web, taking notes, making entries in a calendar, and so on. Almost all of them offer multimedia apps to enable you to listen to music, take pictures, watch YouTube videos, and view photos. You'll find instant messaging tools and, in the case of smartphones, telephone capabilities.

With no exceptions I've encountered, though, you'll want to add capabilities to the mobile device, and that means adding apps. Games are incredibly popular to add, with *Angry Birds* accounting for billions of dollars of lost worker productivity in the United States alone (see Figure 27-13). (And if you haven't played *Angry Birds*, I highly suggest downloading it right now!)

Figure 27-13
Angry Birds on an
ASUS tablet

NOTE The one big gotcha about Apple is that none of their mobile devices support Adobe Flash, making a surprising number of Web sites not available. You simply cannot add an app that makes Flash work on an Apple iPhone or iPad.

Even when the prebundled tools offer great functionality, often other software developers will take an idea and run with it to create something wholly unexpectedly cool. All the smartphones and nearly every tablet, for example, include some sort map tool that also includes *positioning software*. This software taps into the *Global Positioning System (GPS)* network of satellites maintained by the U.S. government to pinpoint your current location on a map (see Figure 27-14). This helps you find how to get from where you are to where you want to be.

Figure 27-14
GPS app showing current location (an excellent café in the Montrose neighborhood of Houston, Texas, in this example)

EXAM TIP The GPS aspect of mobile devices goes both ways. Because mobile devices tap into the Internet or cellular phone networks, the devices have identifying numbers such as a MAC address. The cell phone companies and government agencies can use the ID or MAC address to pinpoint where you are at any given time. This feature, called *geotracking*, clearly has a lot of room for abuse of power, though nothing major has happened as of this writing.

The Internet has turned the concept of map viewing into something much more powerful courtesy of tools like Google Earth. With Google Earth, you can zoom all over the world, seeing satellite images of cities, towns, and countryside. You can access embedded images of places (see Figure 27-15) and get information via Wikipedia. Adding Google Earth (or any other app) to a mobile device follows different patterns according to the operating system and manufacturer of a specific mobile device.

Figure 27-15 Image in Google Earth

NOTE Don't like the idea of Big Brother knowing where you are all the time? Turn off Location Services in iOS or GPS Services on your Android. Keep in mind that turning this off will keep all applications that need this information from working.

Apple and Closed Source

Apple makes the most popular mobile devices in the iPhone and the iPad (smartphone and tablet, respectively). Both devices use the iOS operating system. Unlike every other manufacturer, Apple tightly controls the user experience, insisting that all developers of apps for iOS follow the same guidelines.

Apple has created a *closed source* or *single source* system, meaning that if you want to get an app for your iPhone or iPad, you can only get it from the Apple App Store (see Figure 27-16). Apple must approve any app before it goes into the App Store, and Apple reserves the right to revoke permission on any app that fails to measure up.

Figure 27-16

App Store

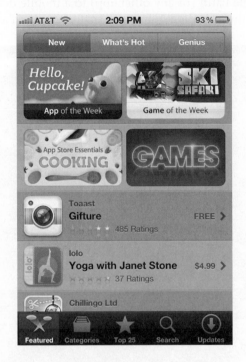

To add an app, select the App Store icon from the home screen. You can select from featured apps or view by category. You can check out the top 25 paid or free apps or simply search for what you want (see Figure 27-17).

The first time you try to purchase an app through the App Store, you'll be prompted to set up an account. You can use an account that you created previously through the Apple iTunes music and video store or create a new account using the Apple iCloud service. Creating a new iCloud account takes a few steps and a lot of typing in of passwords and such (see Figure 27-18), but eventually you'll get the account figured out. You'll need a valid credit card to set up the account.

Android Experience

Google Android powers a majority of smartphones and a solid percentage of tablets, but Android differs greatly from Apple iOS in that Google gives the OS away and developers create versions suited to their devices. That means in practice that when you have a smartphone or tablet that uses Google Android for an OS, you have to amend that description to include the manufacturer as well. A Samsung tablet, in other words, uses an OS that differs somewhat from the OS an ASUS tablet uses. HTC, for example, uses a custom interface for its Android devices called HTC Sense that changes the look and feel of Android.

Figure 27-17
Searching for
Google Earth

Figure 27-18
Creating an iCloud
account

EXAM TIP The CompTIA A+ 220-802 objectives mention "touch flow" as if it were a standard feature of mobile operating systems. In fact, HTC's Touch-FLO preceded HTC's Sense interface. TouchFLO is no longer used on HTC's Android phones.

When you want to get an app for an Android device, you have alternative sources for that app. Many vendors offer a store with apps developed or customized to work with their devices. These *vendor-specific* stores enable you to get apps that should work well with your Android smartphone or tablet.

You can also go to an *open source* market for apps developed "for Android" that probably will work with your device, but there's not a guarantee that they'll work on all Android devices. Google Play, for example, offers hundreds of thousands of apps. This Wild West approach to apps makes the Android experience vastly different from the iOS experience when it comes to smartphones and tablets.

NOTE Microsoft has a small but growing presence in the mobile devices market with Windows Phone 7 and Windows 8. Expect the market share to increase over the coming years. Microsoft embraces an app marketplace somewhere in between that of Apple and Google, with both Microsoft-created apps and those created by other developers available through the Windows Phone Marketplace and other venues.

Enhancing Hardware

A mobile device is a computer, just like your desktop PC or laptop, with the same basic components doing the same basic things. The construction centers around a primary circuit board, a *motherboard*, onto which every other component is attached. Each mobile device has a CPU and GPU, though not necessarily based on the same architecture as a portable PC. The Apple iPad uses an ARM processor, for example, rather than an Intel ×86 or ×64 processor. In contrast, the ASUS Transformer featured as the Android model in this chapter uses a processor called a Tegra from NVIDIA, billed as the first mobile super processor. It features two to four CPU cores with integrated GPU, Northbridge, Southbridge, and memory controller for awesome power and serious 3-D capabilities.

Mobile devices use storage, though usually not a traditional hard disk drive (HDD) with spinning platters. More commonly, mobile devices use a *solid state drive* (SSD) because SSDs use much less electricity than platter-based drives. Plus they're cooler in general, just like you.

Mobile devices vary from their larger brethren in two very significant areas of importance to techs. First, none of them offer any field-serviceable parts. If something breaks, you send the device back to the manufacturer. Second, you can't upgrade them at all. Even a laptop enables you to upgrade RAM or a hard drive, for example, but the mobile device you buy is exactly what you get. You want something better? Buy a new one.

 EXAM TIP Mobile devices have no field replaceable units (FRUs) and no upgradeability.

That said, every mobile device enables you to attach some kind of peripheral or external storage device. But every device offers different expansion capabilities, so it's hard to generalize about them.

The one exception to the rule that you can't generalize about mobile devices relates to sound. Every mobile device has a single 3.5-mm audio jack for plugging in earbuds or speakers (see Figure 27-19). This applies to smartphones and tablets from all vendors.

Figure 27-19
Earbuds plugged into a smartphone

Apple Expansion Options

Apple devices offer the least expansion capability of all the mobile devices, so even though they dominate the marketplace, there's not much to say about them. The iPhone and iPad use a single proprietary port that's used to recharge the device and to connect the few external devices available. Figure 27-20 shows the typical use for the port, a dongle that connects to a USB AC adapter for recharging.

Early iPhones and iPads had limited multimedia capabilities, but current devices enable you to mirror the screen to a multimedia device such as a projector. This enables seamless presentations, for example, through the excellent Apple Keynote program (see Figure 27-21). The multimedia connection requires another dongle adapter (see Figure 27-22).

Figure 27-20
Recharger dongle

Figure 27-21
Apple Keynote
on an iPad and a
projector

Android Expansion Options

Devices that use Google Android come with a variety of connections and expansion capabilities. Many offer microSD slots for adding storage in the form of the tiny flash memory cards (see Figure 27-23). Some offer bigger slots, and a few feature Micro USB or even full-sized USB ports.

Figure 27-22
Apple Digital AV
Adapter

Figure 27-23
MicroSD card
and slot

Many Android devices offer a proprietary socket that mimics the functions of Apple's dongle port, providing a way to recharge the tablet or smartphone and get data from a PC to the tablet and vice versa. Figure 27-24 shows a proprietary connector for power.

Figure 27-24
ASUS proprietary
power connector

Finally, many tablets sport a connector for attaching the device to an external monitor, such as a big screen or projector. (Smartphones don't generally have this connector.) Figure 27-25 shows a Micro-HDMI port and connector.

Figure 27-25
Micro-HDMI port
and connector

Bluetooth

The last way that mobile devices expand their physical capabilities is wirelessly, most often using the Bluetooth standard for adding a keyboard (all) or mouse (not with Apple products). In theory, you could attach all sorts of Bluetooth devices to the mobile device, but the reality seems limited to keyboards, headphones, and headsets. Figure 27-26 shows a diminutive Apple keyboard for the iPad and the iPad resting in a stand to make typing this chapter a little easier than using the virtual keyboard.

Figure 27-26
Keyboard associ-
ated with iPad

NOTE See the "Bluetooth" subsection of the "Configuration" section later in this chapter for the steps to set up a tablet with a Bluetooth keyboard.

Configuration

Mobile devices require some setup and configuration to function seamlessly in your online life. That means you need to set up network connectivity, add Bluetooth devices, configure e-mail account(s), and enable the devices to synchronize with a PC. Let's look at all four options.

Network Connectivity

Mobile devices connect to the outside world through the cellular networks or through various 802.11 Wi-Fi standards. You learned specifics about the standards in Chapter 23, so I won't rehash them here. This section looks at standard configuration issues from the perspective of a mobile device.

When you want to connect to a Wi-Fi network, you need to turn Wi-Fi on and then actively connect to a network. If the network is properly configured with WPA or WPA2 encryption, then you also need to have the logon information to access the network. The most common way to connect is through the Settings app (see Figure 27-27). (This applies to all iOS and Android devices.)

Figure 27-27
Selecting the
Settings icon

Settings enables you to do the vast majority of configuration necessary to a mobile device. To join a network, for example, tap the Wi-Fi (or Networks) option to see available networks (see Figure 27-28). Simply select the one you want to join and type in the passphrase or passcode. Give the mobile device a moment to get IP and DNS information from the DHCP server, and you're on the network.

Figure 27-28 Browsing available networks

After you connect to a network successfully, all mobile devices store that network access information automatically, creating a *profile* of that network based on the SSID (the name of the network). This works just like with any other device that connects to a Wi-Fi network. If the SSID of a network changes after you've connected to that network, your mobile device will fail to connect to the rechristened network. You need to delete the profile and reconnect. You do this through the Settings app by selecting the Wi-Fi network and selecting *Forget this network*.

EXAM TIP You can use the Settings app to turn Wi-Fi off or to go into Airplane Mode to stop the device from sending any signals out.

Data

Many mobile devices can use the cellular data services discussed in Chapter 24 to access the Internet. This way you can use your smartphone or tablet to get e-mail or browse the Web pretty much anywhere, even without a Wi-Fi hotspot.

By default, mobile devices that use cellular networks for Internet connectivity use *data roaming*, meaning they'll jump from cell tower to cell tower and from your provider to another provider without obvious notice. This is no big deal when you travel within your own country where competing providers have inexpensive roaming agreements.

Watch out for data roaming outside your country! If you travel outside of your country, your mobile device will also happily and seamlessly connect via some other available cell provider. This can lead to some shockingly huge bills from your cell phone company when you get back from that cruise or out-of-country trip. If you're going outside your cell provider's coverage area, get a plan that specifies that you're traveling. It'll still be more expensive than your regular plan, but not nearly as crazy as an accidental roaming charge.

If you don't need to connect when out of country, turn data roaming off. You'll find the feature in the Settings app, as you might expect. You can also turn off cellular data entirely or only turn off cellular services selectively if your device can do more than one type. (You would want to turn off cellular data, for example, if you don't have an unlimited data plan and are getting near your limits.)

Bluetooth

Pairing a Bluetooth device with a mobile device follows a similar, simple pattern through the Settings icon. You turn on Bluetooth on the smartphone or tablet, then power on the Bluetooth device. Return to the mobile device to select to pair with the Bluetooth device, and then enter the appropriate personal identification number (PIN) code. For a keyboard, for example, the smartphone or tablet will display a set of characters for you to type on the keyboard (see Figure 27-29). Once you type in the PIN code, the devices connect.

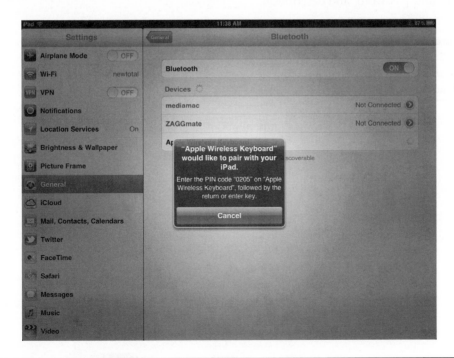

Figure 27-29 Prompting for PIN

EXAM TIP Not all Bluetooth pairings require a PIN code, but there's always some kind of pairing action to do on both devices to make a pairing. Note also that CompTIA uses the phrase *pin code* in lowercase to describe the pairing mechanism.

Always test the connectivity between a mobile device and a newly added Bluetooth accessory. If you've added a keyboard, for example, open up a note-taking app and start typing to make sure it works.

Most mobile devices have Bluetooth discovery disabled by default to conserve battery life. Actively seeking pairing uses electricity, as does completed pairing, so use Bluetooth when you need to use it and be prepared for the battery hit.

E-Mail

Setting up e-mail offers many levels of complexity with mobile devices, primarily because of the many different types of e-mail servers out there. The process is similar to that of setting up e-mail accounts that you learned about in Chapter 24. Apple devices go through the Settings app, then the Mail, Contacts, Calendars option (see Figure 27-30). Tap the Add Account option to bring up the default e-mail options (see Figure 27-31). If you want to connect to a Microsoft Exchange Server–based e-mail account, tap the appropriate option here and type in your e-mail address, domain, username, password, and description.

Figure 27-30
Mail, Contacts,
Calendars screen
on iPhone

.ıtll AT&T 📶	2:33 PM	90% 🔋

‹ Settings	**Mail, Contacts, Calen...**	

Work Email
Mail ›

Add Account... ›

Fetch New Data Off ›

Mail

Show 50 Recent Messages ›

Preview 2 Lines ›

Minimum Font Size Medium ›

Show To/Cc Label ⚪ OFF

Ask Before Deleting ON ⚪

Figure 27-31
Default e-mail
types on iPhone

If you want a more common POP3 or IMAP account set up, that's not one of Apple's default options, so you'd have to go through the Other option on the initial Add Account screen. Eventually you'll get prompted as you would expect to choose POP3 or IMAP and type in addresses for the sending and receiving servers.

Android-based tablets assume you'll have a Gmail account as your primary account, so that option is offered as a distinctive icon on the home screen (see Figure 27-32). You'll also have an Email icon for setting up Exchange, POP3, or IMAP accounts. You configure them the same way as you would a desktop e-mail application, including putting in the port setting and security type, such as SSL or TLS (see Figure 27-33).

Synchronization

Smartphones and tablets can *synchronize*, or *sync*, with local machines or over the Internet with cloud-based servers to keep files and data up-to-date. Older devices, such as BlackBerrys and Palm Pilots, had a specialized sync program that installed onto your PC that you could use to sync contacts, calendars, and so on. Today's devices either use a dedicated program or sync through the cloud.

Most tablets and many smartphones use a proprietary dongle for syncing through a USB port on the computer. This is the same dongle used to recharge the battery. Some devices can sync through Wi-Fi connections. Many smartphones use a micro USB to regular USB cable to connect to the PC.

Figure 27-32 Gmail account option

Figure 27-33 Setting up a secure IMAP account

iTunes and iCloud

Apple iPhones and iPads sync through Apple iTunes installed on a Mac or PC, a free program that you download from Apple. Everything, such as music, videos, contacts, pictures, and so on, can be stored locally. You can choose to back up all the apps on your iPhone or iPad to iTunes as well. This single source for backup makes it easy to recover from something catastrophic happening to your Apple device. If you replace an Apple device, for example, you can simply sync that new device and all your files, contact information, and apps copy to the new device.

EXAM TIP Apple iTunes will run on just about any Mac OS X machine. On Windows at the time of this writing, you need to be running Windows XP with Service Pack 2 or better or any later Windows OS.

The CompTIA A+ 802 competencies don't discuss hardware requirements. The only thing that's relevant to a tech is that hardware needs to scale up to play more complex media. You can play music with a 1-GHz CPU, for example, but need a 2.4-GHz CPU with two or more cores to play an HD video.

In late 2011, Apple introduced a cloud-based storage solution called iCloud. With iCloud, you can have all your iPhone or iPad data backed up and thus accessible from anywhere. This includes any media purchased through iTunes and calendars, contacts, reminders, and so forth.

Android and Gmail

Android-based mobile devices don't have a central desktop application like Apple devices. Rather, they sync over the Internet—but only some data. Contacts, calendars, and e-mail (through Gmail) are all that sync by default. For every other type of data or media, you treat the Android device like a fat thumb drive—you drag and drop files into the appropriate folder on the smartphone or tablet.

Sync In, Sync Out

One of the radical differences between an Apple device and an Android device is in the direction of syncing (or even copying, for that matter). With Apple, you can sync files—especially media files—to the iPhone or iPad. You cannot take that Apple device, connect it to another computer, and copy files *from* it to the PC. It's a one-way street.

Android devices, in contrast, happily share like a thumb drive. You can drag and drop from an Android smartphone or tablet to any PC.

Security

Mobile devices almost long to roam freely, so you need to take active steps to secure them against damage, loss, or theft. Let's look at all three issues.

Preventing Damage

Mobile devices cost a fair amount of money and thus aren't disposable media for most people. That means you need to take steps to prevent damage, both physical and software-based.

For physical damage, the first step you must take is to get a protective cover or sleeve for the mobile device. It doesn't help the HD camcorder in your new iPad if you get a scratch across the lens! You'll get a scratched, blurry movie even though the camcorder is capable of much, much more. Apple makes very nice covers for iPhones and iPads, plus you can get many third-party covers and sleeves (see Figure 27-34).

Figure 27-34
Putting an Apple
Smart cover on
an iPad

Depending on the amount of money you're willing to spend, you can get covers that help protect your screen from scratches, impacts, and small amounts of water. Like to scuba with your Android device? There are waterproof cases (as opposed to a cover) that enable you to check your Facebook account from 40 feet underwater. (These are specialty devices and not very typical.)

Do the obvious to protect your devices. Don't get them anywhere near liquids. Don't run your smartphone through the wash in your trousers. Don't even think about placing heavy objects on that ~$600 tablet! Use common sense.

Your options for software-based issues depend on your mobile platform. Android devices support a large number of antivirus applications, while iOS devices have no antivirus software. (Apple contends that such software is unnecessary on iOS.) You can also protect your mobile device with periodic *patching*, automatic updates and operating system patches from the device manufacturers.

 EXAM TIP There is no antivirus solution for iOS mobile devices.

Dealing with Loss

Losing a mobile device creates a series of issues that you need to address. First, protect your data from access by putting a good *passcode lock* on the device, which requires you to type in a series of letters, numbers, or motion patterns to unlock the mobile device each time you press the power button. Don't assume that you'll never set the phone down in the lavatory at an airport and forget about it or lose it to a thief. Most mobile devices enable you to set a passcode lock or screen lock from the Settings icon (see Figure 27-35). Do it right now! Some devices enable you to encrypt the contents of the SSD, so even if a "finder" dismantles the device to access the drive, he or she will not get your documents.

Figure 27-35
Screen lock option in Settings

Mobile devices also have a preset number of failed login attempt restrictions that, when exceeded, lock up the mobile device. This slows down someone trying to hack into a found mobile device while you use locator services or applications to try to recover it.

Both Apple and Google offer locator services for discovering the whereabouts of a misplaced mobile device. Google's service is okay, while Apple does a much better job with iCloud. Log in to your iCloud account and click the Find My iPhone button. (This works for both iPhones and iPads.) As soon as the device in question accesses the Internet (and thus receives an IP address and posts its MAC address), iCloud will pinpoint the location within a few yards (see Figure 27-36). Very slick!

Figure 27-36 Locating a device in iCloud

Recovering from Theft

If your mobile device gets stolen and contains sensitive information, then you have a couple of options for dealing with it. Certainly the locator services help, but if you have credit card information or other very damaging information on your mobile device, you need to act quickly.

First, make sure you have your data backed up. You should have everything synced to a local machine and, if possible, backed up to one of the remote backup applications—like iCloud—to put your data beyond the reach of even a disaster that takes out your house. With iCloud, go into Settings and select iCloud. Tap the Storage & Backup option and turn iCloud Backup from OFF (the default) to ON (see Figure 27-37). Note that this will stop automatic backups to your local machine when you sync with iTunes.

Second, you can remotely wipe your mobile device. Apple makes it supremely easy through iCloud. Log in, locate, and nuke your device (see Figure 27-38). You may never get the device back, but at least the bad guys won't have your data.

Figure 27-37
Turning on remote
backup

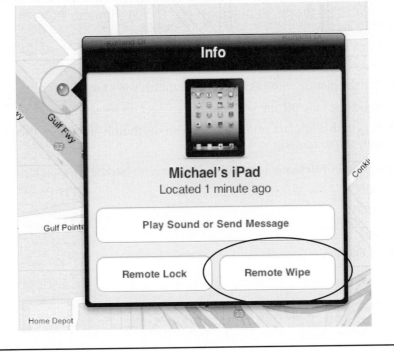

Figure 27-38 Remote wipe

Chapter Review

Questions

1. Placing your phone in a typical protective cover will *not* protect the phone from:

 A. Scratches

 B. Impact

 C. Small amounts of water

 D. Immersion in water

2. Which type of display responds to the difference in electrical potential between you and the screen?

 A. Capacitive

 B. LCD

 C. IPS

 D. Resistive

3. John has a high-resolution image on his iPad of his 2-year-old son and the family dog. The image initially displays smaller than the screen, so he wants to zoom in to get the details of his son's expression. How can he accomplish this task? (Select two.)

 A. Click the mouse in the middle of the picture to select it, then use the scroll wheel on the mouse to zoom in.

 B. Tap the picture with his index finger on his son's face.

 C. Right-click the picture with his index finger on his son's face.

 D. Touch his son's face on the screen with his thumb and finger, then pinch outward to scroll in.

4. Which mobile device screen technology uses no backlight?

 A. CCFL

 B. LCD

 C. LED

 D. OLED

5. What can a government use to determine your location at a specific time as long as you're using your mobile device?

 A. *Angry Birds*

 B. Geotracking

 C. Google Earth

 D. Gyroscope

6. What are the steps involved in pairing a Bluetooth keyboard with a tablet?

 A. Enable Bluetooth on the tablet; turn on the Bluetooth device; find the device with the tablet; enter a PIN code or other pairing sequence.

 B. Turn on the Bluetooth device; find the device with the tablet; enter a PIN code or other pairing sequence.

 C. Search for a Bluetooth device from the tablet; select **pair** from the options to enable the device.

 D. Enable Bluetooth on the tablet; turn on the Bluetooth device; find the device with the tablet; select **pair** from the options to enable the device.

7. A client calls, wanting to copy his music from his iPhone to his new PC. How can he accomplish this task?

 A. Connect the iPhone to the new PC. When it shows up as a new device, right-click it and select Properties. In the Properties dialog box, select Export media files.

 B. Connect the iPhone to the new PC. Double-click it and go to the Media folder. Drag and drop the desired music to the Music library on his new PC.

 C. Access the iPhone wirelessly from the PC. Drag and drop the desired music to the Music library on his new PC.

 D. He can't.

8. A client calls and is upset that he's misplaced his iPad. The mobile device has literally thousands of client records, including business addresses, e-mail addresses, phone numbers, and, in some cases, credit card information. What should he do first?

 A. There's nothing he can do.

 B. He should call his ISP and have them track his iPad.

 C. He should access his iCloud account and reset his iPad to erase all personal data.

 D. He should purchase another iPad and sync with his iTunes account. This automatically erases the information on the old tablet.

9. Name the primary feature that separates a smartphone from a tablet.

 A. iTunes

 B. OLED screen

 C. Capacitive touchscreen

 D. Capability to make telephone calls

10. What information do you need to connect an Android-based tablet to an IMAP account?

 A. POP3 server DNS name

 B. Username and password

 C. Username, password, sending and receiving server addresses

 D. Exchange server name, username, and password

Answers

1. **D.** A cover will not protect your phone from being immersed in water.

2. **A.** A capacitive touchscreen display responds to the difference in electrical potential between you and the screen.

3. **D.** John can pinch outward with his fingers to zoom in on the image.

4. **D.** OLED technology does not use a backlight.

5. **B.** Geotracking can locate you and your GPS-equipped mobile device.

6. **A.** To pair a Bluetooth keyboard with a tablet, enable Bluetooth on the tablet, turn on the Bluetooth device, find the Bluetooth device in the tablet's settings screen, then enter a PIN code or finalize the pairing.

7. **D.** You cannot copy music from an iPhone onto your PC.

8. **C.** To protect his data, the client should log in to his iCloud account and reset the iPad and erase all personal data.

9. **D.** A smartphone can make telephone calls, while a tablet cannot.

10. **C.** To connect an Android-based tablet to an IMAP account, you'll need a username and password and the sending and receiving server addresses.

Printers

In this chapter, you will learn how to
- Describe current printer technologies
- Explain the laser printing process
- Install a printer on a Windows PC
- Recognize and fix basic printer problems

Despite all of the talk about the "paperless office," printers continue to be a vital part of the typical office. In many cases, PCs are used exclusively for the purpose of producing paper documents. Many people simply prefer dealing with a hard copy. Programmers cater to this preference by using metaphors such as *page*, *workbook*, and *binder* in their applications. The CompTIA A+ certification strongly stresses the area of printing and expects a high degree of technical knowledge of the function, components, maintenance, and repair of all types of printers.

801

Printer Technologies

No other piece of your computer system is available in a wider range of styles, configurations, and feature sets than a printer, or at such a wide price variation. What a printer can and can't do is largely determined by the type of printer technology it uses—that is, how it gets the image onto the paper. Modern printers can be categorized into several broad types: impact, inkjet, dye-sublimation, thermal, laser, and solid ink.

Impact Printers

Printers that create an image on paper by physically striking an ink ribbon against the paper's surface are known as *impact printers*. Although *daisy-wheel* printers (essentially an electric typewriter attached to the PC instead of directly to a keyboard) have largely disappeared, their cousins, *dot-matrix printers*, still soldier on in many offices. Although dot-matrix printers don't deliver what most home users want—high quality and flexibility at a low cost—they're still widely found in businesses for two reasons: dot-matrix printers have a large installed base in businesses, and they can be used for multipart

forms because they actually strike the paper. Impact printers tend to be relatively slow and noisy, but when speed, flexibility, and print quality are not critical, they provide acceptable results. PCs that print multipart forms, such as *point of sale (POS)* machines, use special *impact paper* that can print receipts in duplicate, triplicate, or more. These POS machines represent the major market for new impact printers, although many older dot-matrix printers remain in use.

Dot-matrix printers use a grid, or matrix, of tiny pins, also known as *printwires*, to strike an inked printer ribbon and produce images on paper (see Figure 28-1). The case that holds the printwires is called a *printhead*. Using either 9 or 24 pins, dot-matrix printers treat each page as a picture broken up into a dot-based raster image. The 9-pin dot-matrix printers are generically called *draft quality*, while the 24-pin printers are known as *letter quality* or *near-letter quality (NLQ)*. The BIOS for the printer (either built into the printer or a printer driver) interprets the raster image in the same way a monitor does, "painting" the image as individual dots. Naturally, the more pins, the higher the resolution. Figure 28-2 illustrates the components common to dot-matrix printers. Many dot-matrix printers use continuous-feed paper with holes on its sides that are engaged by metal sprockets to pull the paper through—this is known as *tractor-feed paper* because the sprockets are reminiscent of the wheels on a tractor.

Figure 28-1
An Epson FX-880+ dot-matrix printer (photo courtesy of Epson America, Inc.)

Figure 28-2 Inside a dot-matrix printer

Inkjet Printers

Inkjet printers (also called *ink-dispersion printers*) like the one in Figure 28-3 are relatively simple devices. An inkjet printer uses a *printhead* connected to a *carriage* that contains the ink. A belt and motor move the carriage back and forth so the ink can cover the whole page. A *roller* grabs paper from a paper tray (usually under or inside the printer) or feeder (usually on the back of the printer) and advances it through the printer (see Figure 28-4).

Figure 28-3
Typical inkjet printer

Figure 28-4 Inside an inkjet printer

EXAM TIP Printers can also use *duplex assemblies*, which enable the printer to print automatically on both sides of the paper. Some printers include this feature built-in, while others require a piece of additional hardware that flips the paper for the printer.

The ink is ejected through tiny tubes. Most inkjet printers use heat to move the ink, while a few use a mechanical method. The heat-method printers use tiny resistors or electroconductive plates at the end of each tube that literally boil the ink; this creates a tiny air bubble that ejects a droplet of ink onto the paper, thus creating a portion of the image (see Figure 28-5).

Figure 28-5 Detail of the inkjet printhead

The ink is stored in special small containers called *ink cartridges*. Older inkjet printers had two cartridges: one for black ink and another for colored ink. The color cartridge had separate compartments for cyan (blue), magenta (red), and yellow ink, to print colors by using a method known as CMYK (you'll read more about CMYK later in this chapter). If your color cartridge ran out of one of the colors, you had to purchase a whole new color cartridge or deal with a messy refill kit.

Printer manufacturers began to separate the ink colors into three separate cartridges so that printers came with four cartridges: one for each color and a fourth for black (see Figure 28-6). This not only was more cost-effective for the user, but it also resulted

in higher quality printouts. Today you can find color inkjet printers with six, eight, or more color cartridges. In addition to the basic CMYK inks, the other cartridges provide for green, blue, gray, light cyan, dark cyan, and more. Typically, the more ink cartridges a printer uses, the higher the quality of the printed image—and the higher the cost of the printer.

Figure 28-6

Inkjet ink cartridges

The two key features of an inkjet printer are the *print resolution*—that is, the density of ink, which affects print quality—and the print speed. Resolution is measured in *dots per inch (dpi)*; higher numbers mean that the ink dots on the page are closer together, so your printed documents will look better. Resolution is most important when you're printing complex images such as full-color photos, or when you're printing for duplication and you care that your printouts look good. Print speed is measured in *pages per minute (ppm)*, and this specification is normally indicated right on the printer's box. Most printers have one (faster) speed for monochrome printing—that is, using only black ink—and another for full-color printing.

EXAM TIP Print resolution is measured in dots per inch (dpi) and print speed is measured in pages per minute (ppm).

Another feature of inkjet printers is that they can support a staggering array of print media. Using an inkjet printer, you can print on a variety of matte or glossy photo papers, iron-on transfers, and other specialty media; some printers can print directly onto specially coated optical discs, or even fabric. Imagine running a T-shirt through your printer with your own custom slogan (how about "I'm CompTIA A+ Certified!"). The inks have improved over the years, too, now delivering better quality and longevity than ever. Where older inks would smudge if the paper got wet or start to fade after a short time, modern inks are smudge proof and of archival quality—for example, some inks by Epson are projected to last up to 200 years.

Dye-Sublimation Printers

The term *sublimation* means to cause something to change from a solid form into a vapor and then back into a solid. This is exactly the process behind *dye-sublimation printing*, sometimes called *thermal dye transfer* printing. *Dye-sublimation printers* are used mainly for photo printing, high-end desktop publishing, medical and scientific imaging, and other applications for which fine detail and rich color are more important than cost and speed. Smaller, specialized printers called *snapshot* printers use dye-sublimation specifically for printing photos at a reduced cost compared to their full-sized counterparts.

The dye-sublimation printing technique is an example of the so-called CMYK (**c**yan, **m**agenta, **y**ellow, blac**k**) method of color printing. It uses a roll of heat-sensitive plastic film embedded with page-sized sections of cyan (blue), magenta (red), and yellow dye; many also have a section of black dye. A printhead containing thousands of heating elements, capable of precise temperature control, moves across the film, vaporizing the dyes and causing them to soak into specially coated paper underneath before cooling and reverting to a solid form. This process requires one pass per page for each color. Some printers also use a final finishing pass that applies a protective laminate coating to the page. Figure 28-7 shows how a dye-sublimation printer works.

Figure 28-7
The dye-sublimation printing process

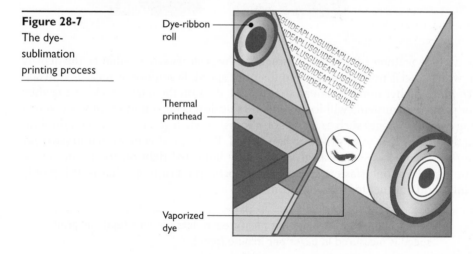

Dye-ribbon roll

Thermal printhead

Vaporized dye

Documents printed through the dye-sublimation process display *continuous-tone* images, meaning that the printed image is not constructed of pixel dots but a continuous blend of overlaid differing dye colors. This is in contrast to other print technologies' *dithered* images, which use closely packed, single-color dots to simulate blended colors. Dye-sublimation printers produce high-quality color output that rivals professional photo-lab processing.

Thermal Printers

Thermal printers use a heated printhead to create a high-quality image on special or plain paper. You'll see two kinds of thermal printers in use. The first is the *direct thermal* printer, and the other is the *thermal wax transfer* printer. Direct thermal printers use a heating element to burn dots into the surface of special heat-sensitive paper. If you remember the first generation of fax machines, you're already familiar with this type of printer. Many retail businesses still use it as a receipt printer, using large rolls of thermal paper housed in a feed assembly that automatically draws the paper past the heating element; some can even cut the paper off the roll for you.

Thermal wax printers work similarly to dye-sublimation printers, except that instead of using rolls of dye-embedded film, the film is coated with colored wax. The thermal printhead passes over the ribbon and melts the wax onto the paper. Thermal wax printers don't require special papers like dye-sublimation printers, so they're more flexible and somewhat cheaper to use, but their output isn't quite as good because they use color dithering.

Laser Printers

Using a process called *electro-photographic imaging, laser printers* produce high-quality and high-speed output of both text and graphics. Figure 28-8 shows a typical laser printer. Laser printers rely on the photoconductive properties of certain organic compounds. *Photoconductive* means that particles of these compounds, when exposed to light (that's the "photo" part), will *conduct* electricity. Laser printers usually use lasers as a light source because of their precision. Some lower-cost printers use LED arrays instead.

Figure 28-8
Typical laser printer

The first laser printers created only monochrome images. Today, you can also buy a color laser printer, although most laser printers produced today are monochrome. Although a color laser printer can produce complex full-color images such as photographs, they really shine for printing what's known as *spot color*—for example, eye-catching headings, lines, charts, or other graphical elements that dress up an otherwise plain printed presentation.

 CAUTION Some printers use consumables—such as ink—at a much faster rate than others, prompting the industry to rank printers in terms of their cost per page. Using an inexpensive printer (laser or inkjet) costs around 4 cents per page, while an expensive printer can cost more than 20 cents per page—a huge difference if you do any volume of printing. This hidden cost is particularly pernicious in the sub-$100 inkjet printers on the market. Their low prices often entice buyers, who then discover that the cost of consumables is outrageous—these days, a *single* set of color and black inkjet cartridges can cost as much as the printer itself, if not more!

Critical Components of the Laser Printer

The CompTIA A+ certification exams take a keen interest in the particulars of the laser printing process, so it pays to know your way around a laser printer (see Figure 28-9). Let's take a look at the many components of laser printers and their functions.

Figure 28-9 Components inside a laser printer

Toner Cartridge The *toner cartridge* in a laser printer is so named because of its most obvious activity: supplying the toner that creates the image on the page (see Figure 28-10). To reduce maintenance costs, however, many other laser printer parts, especially those that suffer the most wear and tear, have been incorporated into the toner cartridge. Although this makes replacement of individual parts nearly impossible, it greatly reduces the need for replacement; those parts that are most likely to break are replaced every time you replace the toner cartridge.

NOTE Color laser printers have four toner cartridges: black, cyan, magenta, and yellow.

Figure 28-10
Laser printer's
toner cartridge

Photosensitive Drum The *photosensitive drum* (also called the *imaging drum*) is an aluminum cylinder coated with particles of photosensitive compounds. The drum itself is grounded to the power supply, but the coating is not. When light hits these particles, whatever electrical charge they may have "drains" out through the grounded cylinder.

Erase Lamp The *erase lamp* exposes the entire surface of the photosensitive drum to light, making the photosensitive coating conductive. Any electrical charge present in the particles bleeds away into the grounded drum, leaving the surface particles electrically neutral.

Primary Corona/Charge Roller The *primary corona* wire (or *primary charge roller*, in newer laser printers), located close to the photosensitive drum, never touches the drum. When the primary corona or primary charge roller is charged with an extremely high voltage, an electric field (or corona) forms, enabling voltage to pass to the drum and charge the photosensitive particles on its surface. The *primary grid* regulates the transfer of voltage, ensuring that the surface of the drum receives a uniform negative voltage of between ~600 and ~1000 volts.

Laser The *laser* acts as the writing mechanism of the printer. Any particle on the drum struck by the laser becomes conductive and its charge is drained away into the grounded core of the drum. The entire surface of the drum has a uniform negative charge of between ~600 and ~1000 volts following its charging by the primary corona wire or charge roller. When particles are struck by the laser, they are discharged and left with a ~100-volt negative charge. Using the laser, we can "write" an image onto the drum. Note that the laser writes a positive image to the drum.

Toner The *toner* in a laser printer is a fine powder made up of plastic particles bonded to iron particles. The *toner cylinder* charges the toner with a negative charge of between ~200 and ~500 volts. Because that charge falls between the original uniform negative charge of the photosensitive drum (~600 to ~1000 volts) and the charge of the particles on the drum's surface hit by the laser (~100 volts), particles of toner are attracted to the areas of the photosensitive drum that have been hit by the laser (that is, areas that have a *relatively* positive charge with reference to the toner particles).

 EXAM TIP The toner used in laser printers is typically carbon particles mixed with a polyester resin.

Transfer Corona/Transfer Roller To transfer the image from the photosensitive drum to the paper, the paper must be given a charge that will attract the toner particles off of the drum and onto the paper. In older printers, the *transfer corona*, a thin wire, applied a positive charge to the paper, drawing the negatively charged toner particles to the paper. Newer printers accomplish the same feat using a *transfer roller* that draws the toner onto the paper. The paper, with its positive charge, is also attracted to the negatively charged drum. To prevent the paper from wrapping around the drum, a *static charge eliminator* removes the charge from the paper.

In most laser printers, the transfer corona/roller is outside the toner cartridge, especially in large, commercial-grade machines. The transfer corona/roller is prone to a build-up of dirt, toner, and debris through electrostatic attraction, and it must be cleaned. It is also quite fragile—usually finer than a human hair. Most printers with an exposed transfer corona/roller provide a special tool to clean it, but you can also—very delicately—use a cotton swab soaked in 90 percent denatured alcohol (don't use rubbing alcohol because it contains emollients). As always, never service any printer without first turning it off and unplugging it from its power source.

Fuser Assembly The *fuser assembly* is almost always separate from the toner cartridge. It is usually quite easy to locate, as it is close to the bottom of the toner cartridge and usually has two rollers to fuse the toner. Sometimes the fuser is somewhat enclosed and difficult to recognize because the rollers are hidden from view. To help you determine the location of the fuser, think about the data path of the paper and the fact that fusing is the final step of printing.

The toner is merely resting on top of the paper after the static charge eliminator has removed the paper's static charge. The toner must be permanently attached to the paper to make the image permanent. Two rollers, a pressure roller and a heated roller, are used to fuse the toner to the paper. The pressure roller presses against the bottom of the page, and the heated roller presses down on the top of the page, melting the toner into the paper. The heated roller has a nonstick coating such as Teflon to prevent the toner from sticking to the heated roller.

Power Supplies All laser printers have at least two separate power supplies. The first power supply is called the primary power supply or sometimes just the power supply. This power supply, which may actually be more than one power supply, provides power to the motors that move the paper, the system electronics, the laser, and the transfer corona/roller. The high-voltage power supply usually provides power only to the primary corona/charge roller. The extremely high voltage of the high-voltage power supply makes it one of the most dangerous devices in the world of PCs! Before opening a printer to insert a new toner cartridge, it is imperative that you *always turn off* a laser printer!

Turning Gears A laser printer has many mechanical functions. First, the paper must be picked up. Next, the photosensitive roller must be turned and the laser, or a mirror, must be moved from left to right. The toner must be evenly distributed, and the fuser assembly must squish the toner into the paper. Finally, the paper must be kicked out of the printer and the assembly must be cleaned to prepare for the next page.

All of these functions are served by complex gear systems. In most laser printers, these gear systems are packed together in discrete units generically called *gear packs* or *gearboxes*. Most laser printers have two or three gearboxes that you can remove relatively easily in the rare case when one of them fails. Most gearboxes also have their own motor or solenoid to move the gears.

System Board Every laser printer contains at least one electronic board. On this board is the main processor, the printer's ROM, and the RAM used to store the image before it is printed. Many printers divide these functions among two or three boards dispersed around the printer (also known as sub-logic boards, as seen in Figure 28-9). An older printer may also have an extra ROM chip and/or a special slot where you can install an extra ROM chip, usually for special functions such as PostScript.

On some printer models, you can upgrade the contents of these ROM chips (the *firmware*) by performing a process called *flashing* the ROM. Flashing is a lot like upgrading the system BIOS, which you learned about in Chapter 8. Upgrading the firmware can help fix bugs, add new features, or update the fonts in the printer.

Of particular importance is the printer's RAM. When the printer doesn't have enough RAM to store the image before it prints, you get a memory overflow problem. Also, some printers store other information in the RAM, including fonts or special commands. Adding RAM is usually a simple job—just snapping in a SIMM or DIMM stick or two—but getting the *right* RAM is important. Call or check the printer manufacturer's Web site to see what type of RAM you need. Although most printer companies will happily sell you their expensive RAM, most printers can use generic DRAM like the kind you use in a PC.

Ozone Filter The coronas inside laser printers generate ozone (O_3). Although not harmful to humans in small amounts, even tiny concentrations of ozone will cause damage to printer components. To counter this problem, most laser printers have a special ozone filter that needs to be vacuumed or replaced periodically.

Sensors and Switches Every laser printer has a large number of sensors and switches spread throughout the machine. The sensors are used to detect a broad range of conditions such as paper jams, empty paper trays, or low toner levels. Many of these sensors are really tiny switches that detect open doors and so on. Most of the time these sensors/switches work reliably, yet occasionally they become dirty or broken, sending a false signal to the printer. Simple inspection is usually sufficient to determine if a problem is real or just the result of a faulty sensor/switch.

Solid Ink

Solid ink printers use just what you'd expect—solid inks. The technology was originally developed by Tektronix, whose printer division was acquired by Xerox. Solid ink

printers use solid sticks of nontoxic "ink" that produce more vibrant color than other print methods. The solid ink is melted and absorbed into the paper fibers; it then solidifies, producing a continuous-tone output. Unlike dye-sublimation printers, all colors are applied to the media in a single pass, reducing the chances of misalignment. Solid ink sticks do not rely on containers like ink for inkjet printers and can be "topped off" midway through a print job by inserting additional color sticks without taking the printer offline.

These printers are fast, too! A full-color print job outputs the first page in about six seconds. Of course, all that speed and quality comes at a price. Xerox's base model starts at about twice the cost of a laser printer, with the expensive model selling for about six times the cost! Solid ink printers become a bit more affordable when you factor in the cost of consumables. A single stick of ink costs about as much as an inkjet cartridge, for example, but with a print capacity of 1000 pages, that completely beats the cost of inkjet cartridges over time.

Printer Languages

Now that you've learned about the different types of print devices and techniques, it's time to take a look at how they communicate with the PC. How do you tell a printer to make a letter *A* or to print a picture of your pet iguana? Printers are designed to accept predefined printer languages that handle both characters and graphics. Your software must use the proper language when communicating with your printer, so that your printer can output your documents onto a piece of paper. Following are the more common printer languages.

ASCII

You might think of the *American Standard Code for Information Interchange (ASCII)* language as nothing more than a standard set of characters, the basic alphabet in upper- and lowercase with a few strange symbols thrown in. ASCII actually contains a variety of control codes for transferring data, some of which can be used to control printers. For example, ASCII code 10 (or 0A in hex) means "Line Feed," and ASCII code 12 (0C) means "Form Feed." These commands have been standard since before the creation of IBM PCs, and all printers respond to them. Being highly standardized has advantages, but the control codes are extremely limited. Printing high-end graphics and a wide variety of fonts requires more advanced languages.

PostScript

Adobe Systems developed the *PostScript* page description language in the early 1980s as a device-independent printer language capable of high-resolution graphics and scalable fonts. PostScript interpreters are embedded in the printing device. Because PostScript is understood by printers at a hardware level, the majority of the image processing is done by the printer and not the PC's CPU, so PostScript printers print faster. Post-Script defines the page as a single raster image; this makes PostScript files extremely portable—they can be created on one machine or platform and reliably printed out on another machine or platform (including, for example, high-end typesetters).

Hewlett-Packard Printer Control Language (PCL)

Hewlett-Packard developed its *printer control language (PCL)* as a more advanced printer language to supersede simple ASCII codes. PCL features a set of printer commands greatly expanded from ASCII. Hewlett-Packard designed PCL with text-based output in mind; it does not support advanced graphical functions. The most recent version of PCL, PCL6, features scalable fonts and additional line drawing commands. Unlike PostScript, however, PCL is not a true page description language; it uses a series of commands to define the characters on the page. Those commands must be supported by each individual printer model, making PCL files less portable than PostScript files.

Windows GDI and XPS

Windows XP uses the *graphical device interface (GDI)* component of the operating system to handle print functions. Although you *can* use an external printer language such as PostScript, most users simply install printer drivers and let Windows do all the work. The GDI uses the CPU rather than the printer to process a print job and then sends the completed job to the printer. When you print a letter with a TrueType font in Windows, for example, the GDI processes the print job and then sends bitmapped images of each page to the printer. The printer sees a page of TrueType text, therefore, as a picture, not as text. As long as the printer has a capable enough raster image processor (explained later in this chapter) and plenty of RAM, you don't need to worry about the printer language in most situations. We'll revisit printing in Windows in more detail later in this chapter.

Windows Vista and Windows 7 support GDI printing, but they also include a printing subsystem called the *XML Paper Specification (XPS) print path*. XPS provides several improvements over GDI, including enhanced color management (which works with Windows Color System) and better print layout fidelity. The XPS print path requires a driver that supports XPS. Additionally, some printers natively support XPS, eliminating the requirement that the output be converted to a device-specific printer control language before printing.

Printer Connectivity

Most printers connect to one of two ports on the PC: a DB-25 parallel port or a USB port. The parallel connection is the classic way to plug in a printer, but most printers today use USB. You'll need to know how to support the more obscure parallel ports, cables, and connections as well as the plug-and-play USB connections.

Parallel Communication and Ports

The *parallel port* was included in the original IBM PC as a faster alternative to serial communication. The IBM engineers considered serial communication, limited to 1 bit at a time, to be too slow for the "high-speed" devices of the day (for example, dot-matrix printers). The standard parallel port has been kept around for backward compatibility despite several obvious weaknesses.

Parallel ports may be far faster than serial ports, but they are slow by modern standards. The maximum data transfer rate of a standard parallel port is still only approximately 150 kilobytes per second (KBps). Standard parallel communication on the PC

also relies heavily on software, eating up a considerable amount of CPU time that could be used better.

Parallel ports are hindered by their lack of true bidirectional capability. Although one-way communication was acceptable for simple line printers and dot-matrix printers, parallel communication also became popular for a wide range of external devices that required two-way communication. Although it is possible to get two-way communication out of a standard parallel port, the performance is not impressive.

 NOTE Many techs confuse the concept of duplex printing—a process that requires special printers capable of printing on both sides of a sheet of paper—with bidirectional printing. They are two different things!

IEEE 1284 Standard

In 1991, a group of printer manufacturers proposed to the *Institute of Electrical and Electronics Engineers* (*IEEE*) that a committee be formed to propose a standard for a backward-compatible, high-speed, bidirectional parallel port for the PC. The committee was the IEEE 1284 committee (hence the name of the standard).

The *IEEE 1284 standard* requires the following:

- Support for five distinct modes of operation: *compatibility mode, nibble mode, byte mode, EPP,* and *ECP*

- A standard method of negotiation for determining which modes are supported both by the host PC and by the peripheral device

- A standard physical interface (that is, the cables and connectors)

- A standard electrical interface (that is, termination, impedance, and so on)

Because only one set of data wires exists, all data transfer modes included in the IEEE 1284 standard are half-duplex: data is transferred in only one direction at a time.

 NOTE The five modes of operation for parallel printing specified in the IEEE 1284 standard (compatibility, nibble, byte, EPP, ECP) are inching closer to obsolescence as USB printers take over the market. If you find yourself needing to optimize the performance of a legacy parallel printer, you can look up these modes by name, using various Web search tools.

Parallel Connections, Cabling, and Electricity

Although no true standard exists, *standard parallel cable* usually refers to a printer cable with the previously mentioned male *DB-25 connector* on one end and a 36-pin *Centronics connector* on the other (see Figure 28-11). The shielding (or lack thereof) of the internal wiring and other electrical characteristics of a standard parallel printer cable

are largely undefined except by custom. In practice, these standard cables are acceptable for transferring data at 150 KBps, and for distances of less than 6 feet, but they would be dangerously unreliable for some transfer modes.

Figure 28-11
Standard parallel cable with 36-pin Centronics connector on one end and DB-25 connector on the other

For more reliability at distances up to 32 feet (10 meters), use proper IEEE 1284–compliant cabling. The transfer speed drops with the longer cables, but it does work, and sometimes the trade-off between speed and distance is worth it.

Installing a parallel cable is a snap. Just insert the DB-25 connector into the parallel port on the back of the PC and insert the Centronics connector into the printer's Centronics port and you're ready to go to press! If your PC didn't include a parallel port, you can always add one with a PCI or PCIe expansion card.

NOTE Some printers come with both USB and parallel connections, but this, like the parallel port in general, has become very rare. If you need a parallel printer for a system, be sure to confirm that the particular model you want will work with your system!

USB Printers

New printers now use USB connections that you can plug into any USB port on your computer. USB printers don't usually come with a USB cable, so you need to purchase one when you purchase a printer. (It's quite a disappointment to come home with your new printer only to find you can't connect it because it didn't come with a USB cable.) Most printers use the standard USB type A connector on one end and the smaller USB type B connector on the other end, although some use two type A connectors. Whichever configuration your USB printer has, just plug in the USB cable—it's that easy!

NOTE In almost all cases, you must install drivers before you plug a USB printer into your computer. You'll learn about installing printer drivers later in this chapter.

Network Printers

Connecting a printer to a network isn't just for offices anymore. More and more homes and home offices are enjoying the benefits of network printing. It used to be that to share a printer on a network—that is, to make it available to all network users—you would physically connect the printer to a single computer and then share the printer on the network. The downside to this was that the computer to which the printer was connected had to be left on for others to use the printer.

Today, the typical *network printer* comes with its own onboard network adapter that uses a standard RJ-45 Ethernet cable to connect the printer directly to the network by way of a router. Other printers include a built-in Wi-Fi adapter to enable wireless printing over the network. The printer can typically be assigned a static IP address, or it can acquire one dynamically from a DHCP server. (Don't know what a router, IP address, or DHCP server is? Take a look back at Chapters 5 and 22.) Once connected to the network, the printer acts independently of any single PC. Some of the more costly network printers come with a built-in Wi-Fi adapter to connect to the network wirelessly. Alternatively, some printers offer Bluetooth or infrared (IR) interfaces for networking.

 EXAM TIP The CompTIA A+ 220-801 exam objectives refer to a wireless print connection called "802.11x." This is not a new Wi-Fi standard. It's a generic term used to describe all Wi-Fi standards, including 802.11a, 802.11b, 802.11g, and 802.11n.

Even if a printer does not come with built-in Ethernet, Wi-Fi, or Bluetooth, you can purchase a standalone network device known as a *print server* to connect your printer to the network. These print servers, which can be Ethernet or Wi-Fi, enable one or several printers to attach via USB cable (or even parallel port, if you still have a printer that old). So take that ancient ImageWriter dot-matrix printer and network it—I dare you!

 EXAM TIP You'll find print servers outside standalone network devices. In fact, your Windows PC is capable of operating as a print server. Anytime you plug a printer into a PC and share the printer over the network, the sharing PC can be referred to as a print server. The CompTIA A+ exams, however, will most likely stick to standalone print server boxes, as opposed to Windows print servers.

Other Printers

Plenty of other connection types are available for printers. We've focused mainly on parallel, USB, and networked connections. Be aware that you may run into an old serial port printer or a SCSI printer. Although this is unlikely, know that it's a possibility.

The Laser Printing Process

The laser printing process can be broken down into seven steps, and the CompTIA A+ exams expect you to know them all. As a tech, you should be familiar with these phases, as this can help you troubleshoot printing problems. For example, if an odd line is printed down the middle of every page, you know there's a problem with the photosensitive drum or cleaning mechanism and the toner cartridge needs to be replaced.

The seven steps to the laser printing process may be performed in a different order, depending on the printer, but it usually goes like this:

1. Processing
2. Charging
3. Exposing
4. Developing
5. Transferring
6. Fusing
7. Cleaning

Processing

When you click the Print button in an application, several things happen. First, the CPU processes your request and sends a print job to an area of memory called the print spooler. The *print spooler* enables you to queue up multiple print jobs that the printer will handle sequentially. Next, Windows sends the first print job to the printer. That's your first potential bottleneck—if it's a big job, the OS has to dole out a piece at a time and you'll see the little printer icon in the notification area at the bottom right of your screen. Once the printer icon goes away, you know the print queue is empty—all jobs have gone to the printer.

Once the printer receives some or all of a print job, the hardware of the printer takes over and processes the image. That's your second potential bottleneck and has multiple components.

Raster Images

Impact printers transfer data to the printer one character or one line at a time, whereas laser printers transfer entire pages at a time to the printer. A laser printer generates a *raster image* (a pattern of dots) of the page, representing what the final product should look like. It uses a device (the laser) to "paint" a raster image on the photosensitive drum. Because a laser printer has to paint the entire surface of the photosensitive drum before it can begin to transfer the image to paper, it processes the image one page at a time.

A laser printer uses a chip called the *raster image processor (RIP)* to translate the raster image into commands to the laser. The RIP takes the digital information about fonts and graphics and converts it to a rasterized image made up of dots that can then be

printed. An inkjet printer also has a RIP, but it's part of the software driver instead of onboard hardware circuitry. The RIP needs memory (RAM) to store the data that it must process.

A laser printer must have enough memory to process an entire page. Some images that require high resolutions require more memory. Insufficient memory to process the image will usually be indicated by a memory overflow ("MEM OVERFLOW") error. If you get a memory overflow error, try reducing the resolution, printing smaller graphics, or turning off RET (see the following section for the last option). Of course, the best solution to a memory overflow error is simply to add more RAM to the laser printer.

Do not assume that every error with the word *memory* in it can be fixed simply by adding more RAM to the printer. Just as adding more RAM chips will not solve every conventional PC memory problem, adding more RAM will not solve every laser printer memory problem. The message "21 ERROR" on an HP LaserJet, for example, indicates that "the printer is unable to process very complex data fast enough for the print engine." This means that the data is simply too complex for the RIP to handle. Adding more memory would *not* solve this problem; it would only make your wallet lighter. The only answer in this case is to reduce the complexity of the page image (that is, fewer fonts, less formatting, reduced graphics resolution, and so on).

 TIP Inkjet printers use RIPs as well, but they're written into the device drivers instead of the onboard programming. You can also buy third-party RIPs that can improve the image quality of your printouts; for an example, see www.colorbytesoftware.com.

Resolution

Laser printers can print at different resolutions, just as monitors can display different resolutions. The maximum resolution that a laser printer can handle is determined by its physical characteristics. Laser printer resolution is expressed in dots per inch (dpi). Common resolutions are 600 × 600 dpi or 1200 × 1200 dpi. The first number, the horizontal resolution, is determined by how fine a focus can be achieved by the laser. The second number is determined by the smallest increment by which the drum can be turned. Higher resolutions produce higher-quality output, but keep in mind that higher resolutions also require more memory. In some instances, complex images can be printed only at lower resolutions because of their high memory demands. Even printing at 300 dpi, laser printers produce far better quality than dot-matrix printers because of *resolution enhancement technology (RET)*.

RET enables the printer to insert smaller dots among the characters, smoothing out the jagged curves that are typical of printers that do not use RET (see Figure 28-12). Using RET enables laser printers to output high-quality print jobs, but it also requires a portion of the printer's RAM. If you get a MEM OVERFLOW error, sometimes disabling RET will free up enough memory to complete the print job.

Figure 28-12
RET fills in gaps with smaller dots to smooth out jagged characters.

Charging

Now we turn to the physical side of the printing process. To make the drum receptive to new images, it must be charged (see Figure 28-13). Using the primary corona wire or primary charge roller, a uniform negative charge is applied to the entire surface of the drum (usually between ~600 and ~1000 volts).

Figure 28-13
Charging the drum with a uniform negative charge

Primary corona

Exposing

A laser is used to create a positive image on the surface of the drum. Every particle on the drum hit by the laser releases most of its negative charge into the drum.

Developing

Those particles with a lesser negative charge are positively charged relative to the toner particles and attracts them, creating a developed image (see Figure 28-14).

Figure 28-14 Writing the image and applying the toner

Primary corona

Imaging laser

Toner

Transferring

The printer must transfer the image from the drum onto the paper. The transfer corona or transfer roller gives the paper a positive charge; then the negatively charged toner particles leap from the drum to the paper. At this point, the particles are merely resting on the paper and must still be permanently fused to the paper.

Fusing

The particles have been attracted to the paper because of the paper's positive charge, but if the process stopped here, the toner particles would fall off the page as soon as you lift it. Because the toner particles are mostly composed of plastic, they can be melted to the page. Two rollers—a heated roller coated in a nonstick material and a pressure roller—melt the toner to the paper, permanently affixing it. Finally, a static charge eliminator removes the paper's positive charge (see Figure 28-15). Once the page is complete, the printer ejects the printed copy and the process begins again with the physical and electrical cleaning of the printer.

Cleaning

The printing process ends with the physical and electrical cleaning of the photosensitive drum (see Figure 28-16). Before printing another new page, the drum must be returned to a clean, fresh condition. All residual toner left over from printing the previous page must be removed, usually by scraping the surface of the drum with a rubber cleaning blade. If residual particles remain on the drum, they will appear as random black spots and streaks on the next page. The physical cleaning mechanism either deposits the residual toner in a debris cavity or recycles it by returning it to the toner supply in the toner cartridge. The physical cleaning must be done carefully. Damage to the drum will cause a permanent mark to be printed on every page.

Figure 28-15
Transferring the image to the paper and fusing the final image

Static eliminator

Fuser rollers

Transfer corona

Figure 28-16
Cleaning and erasing the drum

Erase lamp

Cleaning blade

The printer must also be electrically cleaned. One or more erase lamps bombard the surface of the drum with the appropriate wavelengths of light, causing the surface particles to discharge into the grounded drum. After the cleaning process, the drum should be completely free of toner and have a neutral charge.

Laser Printing in Color

Color laser printers follow the same general process as black and white laser printers, but color adds complexity. Color laser printers use four different colors of toner (cyan, magenta, yellow, and black) to create their printouts. Most models send each page through four different passes, adding one color at each pass to create the needed results, while others place all the colors onto a special *transfer belt* and then transfer them to the page in one pass. In some cases, the printer uses four separate toner cartridges and four lasers for the four toner colors, and in others the printer simply lays down one color after the other on the same drum, cleaning after each of four passes per page.

 CAUTION The heated roller produces enough heat to melt some types of plastic media, particularly overhead transparency materials. This could damage your laser printer (and void your warranty), so make sure you're printing on transparencies designed for laser printers!

Installing a Printer in Windows

You need to take a moment to understand how Windows handles printing, and then you'll see how to install, configure, and troubleshoot printers in these operating systems.

 EXAM TIP The CompTIA A+ exams test you on installing and troubleshooting printers, so read these sections carefully!

To Windows, a printer is not a physical device; it is a *program* that controls one or more physical printers. The *physical* printer is called a print device by Windows (although I continue to use the term "printer" for most purposes, just like almost every tech on the planet). Printer drivers and a spooler are still present, but in Windows, they are integrated into the printer itself (see Figure 28-17). This arrangement gives Windows amazing flexibility. For example, one printer can support multiple print devices, enabling a system to act as a print server. If one print device goes down, the printer automatically redirects the output to a working print device.

Figure 28-17
Printer driver and spooler in Windows

The general installation, configuration, and troubleshooting issues are basically identical in all modern versions of Windows. Here's a review of a typical Windows printer installation. I'll mention the trivial differences among Windows XP, Vista, and 7 as I go along.

Setting Up Printers

Setting up a printer is so easy that it's almost scary. Most printers are plug and play, so installing a printer is reduced to simply plugging it in and loading the driver if needed. With USB printers (and infrared printers, for that matter), Windows won't even wait for you to do anything—once you connect a printer (or point the IR beam at a compatible PC), Windows immediately detects and installs the printer. If the system does not detect the printer or if the printer is not plug and play, however, click Start | Printers and Faxes in Windows XP to open the Printers applet. In Windows Vista, you need to open the Control Panel and find the Printer menu item—it is either by itself or, in the categorized view, under Hardware. With Windows 7, go to Start | Devices and Printers. As you might guess, you install a new printer by clicking the Add a Printer icon/button (somehow Microsoft has managed to leave the name of this option unchanged through all Windows versions since 9x). This starts the Add Printer Wizard.

The Add Printer Wizard enables you to install a local printer or a network printer. This distinction is actually a little misleading. Windows divides printer installation into two scenarios: a printer connected directly to a PC (your local PC or another PC on a network), or a standalone printer directly connected to a switch or router. While you might think the local versus network installation options divide these scenarios nicely, they do not. Let's take a quick look at both local and network installations so you know when to use each.

Installing a Local Printer

At first glance, you might think the local printer installation option is used to install your standard USB printer, but don't forget that Windows will automatically detect and install USB printers (or any other plug-and-play printer). So what do you use it for? This option is most commonly used to install printers using a parallel connection or to install standalone network printers using an IP address. Using current versions of Windows and a modern printer, you shouldn't need to use the IP address to install a standalone network printer, but it can be a helpful alternative if Windows won't detect it any other way.

For parallel port printers, check the *Automatically detect and install my Plug and Play printer* option in Windows XP (see Figure 28-18). Windows won't automatically detect a new parallel device. When you check this box and click Next, Windows XP will run a search for any plug-and-play printers, including those connected via parallel cables. (Windows Vista and Windows 7 don't include this option; you'll need to configure parallel-connected printers manually by selecting a port and driver.)

If you need to install a standalone network printer using its IP address, uncheck the *Automatically detect and install my Plug and Play printer* option in Windows XP and click Next. In Windows Vista and Windows 7, click *Add a local printer*. In the *Create a new port* drop-down box, select Standard TCP/IP Port. Click Next. Type the IP address here.

Figure 28-18

Automatically detecting plug-and-play printers in Windows XP

NOTE Confusingly, you can also get to the IP address entry screen in Windows Vista and Windows 7 via the network installation option, but not directly. Only after the network option fails to automatically detect a networked printer can you enter the IP address manually by clicking *The printer that I want isn't listed* and selecting *Add a printer using a TCP/IP address or hostname.*

Whether you use a parallel port or a TCP/IP port, you'll need to manually select the proper driver (see Figure 28-19). Windows includes a lot of printer drivers, but you can also use the handy Have Disk option to use the disc that came with the printer. If you use the driver included on the disc, Windows will require administrator privileges to proceed; otherwise, you won't be able to finish the installation. The Windows Update button enables you to grab the latest printer drivers via the Internet.

Figure 28-19

Selecting drivers

 EXAM TIP You will be unable to install a printer using the drivers that came with a disc unless you have administrative privileges.

You'll be asked if the new local printer should be the default printer and whether or not you want to share it with other PCs on the network. And before you ask, yes, you can share a standalone network printer connected to your PC via a TCP/IP port using File and Printer Sharing, though the printer would be disabled for other users any time you turned off your PC. You'll be asked to print a test page to make sure everything works. Then you're done!

 CAUTION If you need to search for drivers online, make sure you download the driver designed for your operating system! If you have a 64-bit copy of Windows 7, the 32-bit Windows 7 drivers won't work.

Installing a Network Printer

Surprisingly, setting up network printers doesn't require much more effort than setting up local printers, unless you're using Windows XP—but isn't that always the case? When you try to install a network printer in Windows Vista or Windows 7, the Add Printer Wizard will scan for any available printers on your local network. More often than not, the printer you are looking for will pop up in a list (see Figure 28-20). When you select that printer and click Next, Windows will search for drivers. If you need to, you can pick from a list of available drivers or use the disc that came with the printer. Either way, you're already done.

![Add Printer dialog box titled "Select a printer" showing a list of printers with Printer Name and Address columns: HPMultiFax (HP Officejet Pro 8500 A909g) at http://[fe80::224:81ff:fe2b:922b%10]:3910/, Phaser 6180DN (Xerox) at 192.168.4.17, HP LaserJet 5 (Hewlett-Packard) at 192.168.4.15, Officejet Pro 8500 A909g (HP) at 192.168.4.18. Buttons for Search again, The printer that I want isn't listed, Next, and Cancel.]

Figure 28-20 List of available shared printers on a network

NOTE Remember printer sharing from Chapter 22? Here's the other side of the operation. Keep in mind that after you install a shared printer onto your PC, you can actually share that shared printer with others. Windows considers the shared printer *your* printer, so you can do what you want with it, including sharing it.

Windows XP doesn't include this automatic discovery feature, and if Windows Vista or Windows 7 fails to find your printer, you'll need to configure the network printer manually. Every version of Windows includes multiple methods of doing this. These methods change depending on whether you are connected to a domain or a workgroup.

If you are on a workgroup, you can browse for a printer on your network, connect to a specific printer (using its name or URL), or use a TCP/IP address or hostname (Windows Vista/7 only), as you can see in Figure 28-21. In a domain, most of those options remain the same, except that instead of browsing the workgroup, you can search and browse the domain using several search parameters, including printer features, printer location, and more. Once you've found your printer, you might be prompted for drivers. Provide them using the usual methods described earlier and then you are finished!

Figure 28-21 Options for finding network printers

NOTE If a computer is a member of a Windows 7 homegroup and printer sharing is enabled, all printers connected to the homegroup are shared with that computer automatically.

Remember that Windows doesn't always see your network's printers exactly how they are physically arranged. Imagine you have a network with three PCs. Andy's computer has a printer connected via USB, whereas Beth's computer and Carol's computer have no printers. There is, however, a second printer connected directly to their router via Ethernet. Beth has configured her PC to connect directly to the network printer using an IP address. Now that she's done that, she can actually share that printer with the rest of her network, even though it's not attached to her computer—Windows doesn't care where it is. The process for sharing a local printer and a network printer is identical because Windows considers both printers to be installed on your PC and under your control. So now Andy and Beth both share printers. When Carol goes looking for shared printers to use, the network printer attached to the router will look like Beth's printer, as if it were directly connected to Beth's machine.

> **NOTE** Depending upon how your network shares printers, you can end up seeing the same printer shared multiple ways. Everyone who has a shared printer installed can share the same printer again as their own printer. This can lead to some confusing printer usage, especially once people start turning off their computers and breaking the connections to the shared printer. Avoid this web of print sharing.

Figure 28-22 shows a typical Windows XP Printers and Faxes screen on a system with one printer installed. Note the small checkmark in the icon's corner; this shows that the device is the default printer. If you have multiple printers, you can change the default printer by right-clicking the printer's icon and selecting *Make Default Printer* in Windows XP or *Set as default printer* in Windows Vista/7.

Figure 28-22 Installed default printer in the Printers and Faxes applet

In addition to the regular driver installation outlined previously, some installations use printer emulation. *Printer emulation* simply means using a substitute printer driver for a printer, as opposed to using one made exclusively for that printer. You'll run into printer emulation in two circumstances. First, some new printers do not come with their own drivers. They instead emulate a well-known printer (such as an HP LaserJet 4) and run perfectly well on that printer driver. Second, you may see emulation in the "I don't have the right driver!" scenario. I keep about three different HP LaserJet and Epson inkjet printers installed on my PC because I know that with these printer drivers, I can print to almost any printer. Some printers may require you to set them into an *emulation mode* to handle a driver other than their native one.

 EXAM TIP In addition to the Devices and Printers applet, Windows 7 (excluding the Home Premium edition) also includes the Print Management console. This tool enables you to view and modify all the printers and drivers on your PC or connected to your network. You can also manage any Windows print servers connected to the network. Many of Print Management's advanced features go beyond the scope of the CompTIA A+ exams, but know that it centralizes (and in a few cases, enhances) the standard printer controls in Windows 7. You can find Print Management in Control Panel | Administrative Tools | Print Management.

Optimizing Print Performance

Although a quality printer is the first step toward quality output, your output relies on factors other than the printer itself. What you see on the screen may not match what comes out of the printer, so calibration is important. Using the wrong type of paper can result in less than acceptable printed documents. Configuring the printer driver and spool settings can also affect your print jobs.

Calibration

If you've ever tweaked that digital photograph so it looks perfect on your screen, only to discover that the final printout was darker than you had hoped, consider calibrating your monitor. *Calibration* matches the print output of your printer to the visual output on your monitor and governs that through software. All three parts need to be set up properly for you to print what you see consistently.

Computer monitors output in RGB—that is, they compose colors using red, green, and blue pixels, as discussed in Chapter 21—while printers mix their colors differently to arrive at their output. As mentioned earlier, the CMYK method composes colors from cyan (blue), magenta (red), yellow, and black.

 EXAM TIP The RGB color display model is used for displaying mixtures of red, green, and blue. The CMYK color printing model uses cyan, magenta, yellow, and black for producing colored printed images.

The upshot of all this is that the printer tries to output—by using CMYK (or another technique)—what you see on the screen using RGB. Because the two color modes do not create color the same way, you see color shifts and not-so-subtle differences between the onscreen image and the printed image. By calibrating your monitor, you can adjust the setting to match the output of your printer. You can do this manually through "eyeballing" it or automatically by using calibration hardware.

To calibrate your monitor manually, obtain a test image from the Web (try sites such as www.DigitalDog.net) and print it out. If you have a good eye, you can compare this printout to what you see on the screen and make the adjustments manually through your monitor's controls or display settings.

Another option is to calibrate your printer by using an International Color Consortium (ICC) color profile, a preference file that instructs your printer to print colors a certain way—for example, to match what is on your screen. Loading a different color profile results in a different color output. Color profiles are sometimes included on the installation media with a printer, but you can create or purchase custom profiles as well. The use of ICC profiles is not limited to printers; you can also use them to control the output of monitors, scanners, or even digital cameras. Windows Vista/7 include *Windows Color System* (*WCS*) to help build color profiles for use across devices. WCS is based on a new standard Microsoft calls *color infrastructure and translation engine* (*CITE*).

802

Troubleshooting Printers

As easy as printers are to set up, they are equally robust at running, assuming that you install the proper drivers and keep the printer well maintained. But printer errors do occasionally develop. Take a look at the most common print problems with Windows, as well as problems that crop up with specific printer types.

 NOTE Every printer is different. Read the documentation included with your printer to learn how you can perform the tasks listed in this section.

General Troubleshooting Issues

Printers of all stripes share some common problems, such as print jobs that don't go, strangely sized prints, and misalignment. Other issues include disposing of consumables, sharing multiple printers, and crashing on power-up. Let's take a look at these general troubleshooting issues, but start with a recap of the tools of the trade.

EXAM TIP Don't forget to check the obvious. Many printers include tiny displays that can clue you in to what's wrong. Most brands use a series of error codes that indicate the problem. Use the manual or the manufacturer's Web site to translate the error code into meaningful information.

Tools of the Trade

Before you jump in and start to work on a printer that's giving you fits, you'll need some tools. You can use the standard computer tech tools in your toolkit, plus a couple of printer-specific devices. Here are some that will come in handy:

- A multimeter for troubleshooting electrical problems such as faulty wall outlets
- Various cleaning solutions, such as denatured alcohol
- An extension magnet for grabbing loose screws in tight spaces and cleaning up iron-based toner
- An optical disc or USB thumb drive with test patterns for checking print quality
- Your trusty screwdriver—both a Phillips-head and flat-head, because if you bring just one kind, it's a sure bet that you'll need the other

Print Job Never Prints

If you click Print but nothing comes out of the printer, first check all the obvious things. Is the printer on? Is it connected? Is it online? Does it have paper?

If you can't connect to the printer, check all cables, ports, and power involved. If everything is plugged in and ready to go, check the appropriate printer applet for your version of Windows. If you don't see the printer you are looking for, you'll need to reinstall it using the Add Printer Wizard.

If you attempt to use a printer shared by another PC, but Windows pops up with an "Access Denied" error, you might not have permission to use the printer. Go to the host PC and check the Security tab of the Printer Properties dialog box. Make sure your user account is allowed to use the printer.

Assuming the printer is in good order, it's time to look at the spooler. You can see the spooler status either by double-clicking the printer's icon in the appropriate printer Control Panel applet or by double-clicking the tiny printer icon in the notification area if it's present. If you're having a problem, the printer icon will almost always be there. Figure 28-23 shows the print spooler open.

Document Name	Status	Owner	Pages	Size	Submitted	Port
F28-10.tif		michaels	1	2.73 MB	2:23:06 PM 4/20/2012	
Microsoft Word - 591_28w	Printing	michaels	1/67	88.2 KB/3.45 MB	2:22:20 PM 4/20/2012	laserjet4.totalhome

HP LaserJet 4 Plus — Printer / Document / View — 2 document(s) in queue

Figure 28-23 Print spooler

Print spoolers can easily overflow or become corrupt due to a lack of disk space, too many print jobs, or one of a thousand other factors. The status window shows all of the pending print jobs and enables you to delete, start, or pause jobs. I usually just delete the affected print job(s) and try again.

Print spoolers are handy. If the printer goes down, you can just leave the print jobs in the spooler until the printer comes back online. Some versions of Windows require you to select Resume Printing manually, but others automatically continue the print job(s). If you have a printer that isn't coming on anytime soon, you can simply delete the print job in the spooler window and try another printer.

If you have problems with the print spooler, you can get around them by changing your print spool settings. Go into the Printers and Faxes/Printers/Devices and Printers applet, right-click the icon of the printer in question, and choose Properties. In the resulting Properties dialog box (see Figure 28-24), choose the *Print directly to the printer* radio button and click OK; then try sending your print job again. Note that this window also offers you the choice of printing immediately—that is, starting to print pages as soon as the spooler has enough information to feed to the printer—or holding off on printing until the entire job is spooled.

If that isn't enough, try restarting the print spooler service. Open the Start menu and right-click on My Computer/Computer. Select Manage—you'll need administrator privileges to continue. In the column on the left, double-click on Services and Applications, and then click on Services. The Services console should appear in the center of the Computer Management window. Scroll down and find the service named Print Spooler. Right-click on the service and select Stop. After it has stopped, right-click on the service again and select Start. You should be able to print using the print spooler again.

Figure 28-24

Print spool settings

Another possible cause for a stalled print job is that the printer is simply waiting for the correct paper! Laser printers in particular have settings that tell them what size paper is in their standard paper tray or trays. If the application sending a print job specifies a different paper size—for example, it wants to print a standard No. 10 envelope, or perhaps a legal sheet, but the standard paper tray holds only 8.5 × 11 letter paper—the printer usually pauses and holds up the queue until someone switches out the tray or manually feeds the type of paper that this print job requires. You can usually override this pause, even without having the specified paper, by pressing the OK or GO button on the printer.

The printer's default paper tray and paper size options will differ greatly depending on the printer type and model. To find these settings, go into the printer's Properties dialog box from the Printers and Faxes/Printers/Devices and Printers applet, and then select the Device Settings tab. This list of settings includes Form To Tray Assignment, where you can specify which tray (in the case of a printer with multiple paper trays) holds which size paper.

Strange Sizes

A print job that comes out a strange size usually points to a user mistake in setting up the print job. All applications have a Print command and a Page Setup interface. The Page Setup interface enables you to define a number of print options, which vary from application to application. Figure 28-25 shows the Page Setup options for Microsoft Word. Make sure the page is set up properly before you blame the printer for a problem.

Figure 28-25
Page Setup options
for Microsoft Word

If you know the page is set up correctly, recheck the printer drivers. If necessary, uninstall and reinstall the printer drivers. If the problem persists, you may have a serious problem with the printer's print engine, but that comes up as a likely answer only when you continually get the same strangely sized printouts using a variety of applications.

Misaligned, Garbled, or Garbage Printouts

Misaligned or garbage printouts invariably point to a corrupted or incorrect driver. Make sure you're using the right driver (it's hard to mess this up, but not impossible) and then uninstall and reinstall the printer driver. If the problem persists, you may be asking the printer to do something it cannot do. For example, you may be printing to a PostScript printer with a PCL driver. Check the printer type to verify that you haven't installed the wrong type of driver for that printer!

Dealing with Consumables

All printers tend to generate a lot of trash in the form of *consumables*. Impact printers use paper and ribbons, inkjet printers use paper and ink cartridges, and laser printers use paper and toner cartridges. In today's environmentally sensitive world, many laws regulate the proper disposal of most printer components. Be sure to check with the local sanitation department or disposal services company before throwing away any component. Of course, you should never throw away toner cartridges—certain companies will *pay* for used cartridges!

When in doubt about what to do with a component, check with the manufacturer for a *material safety data sheet (MSDS)*. These standardized forms provide detailed information about not only the potential environmental hazards associated with different components but also proper disposal methods. For example, surf to www.hp.com/hpinfo/globalcitizenship/environment/productdata/index.html to find the latest MSDS for all Hewlett-Packard products. This isn't just a printer issue—you can find an MSDS for most PC components. When in doubt about how to get rid of any PC component, check with the manufacturer for an MSDS.

 EXAM TIP MSDSs contain important information regarding hazardous materials such as safe use procedures and emergency response instructions. An MSDS is typically posted anywhere a hazardous chemical is used.

Problems Sharing Multiple Printers

If you want to use multiple printers attached to the same parallel port, you have to use a switch box. Laser printers should never be used with mechanical switch boxes. Mechanical switch boxes create power surges that can damage your printer. If you must use a switch box, use a box that switches between printers electronically and has built-in surge protection.

Crashes on Power-up

Both laser printers and PCs require more power during their initial power-up (the POST on a PC and the warm-up on a laser printer) than once they are running. Hewlett-Packard recommends a *reverse power-up*. Turn on the laser printer first and allow it to finish its warm-up before turning on the PC. This avoids having two devices drawing their peak loads simultaneously.

Troubleshooting Impact Printers

Impact printers require regular maintenance but will run forever as long as you're diligent. Keep the platen (the roller or plate on which the pins impact) clean and the printhead clean with denatured alcohol. Be sure to lubricate gears and pulleys according to the manufacturer's specifications. Never lubricate the printhead, however, because the lubricant will smear and stain the paper. Don't forget to replace the ink ribbon every so often.

Bad-looking Text

White bars going through the text point to a dirty or damaged printhead. Try cleaning the printhead with a little denatured alcohol. If the problem persists, replace the printhead. Printheads for most printers are readily available from the manufacturer or from companies that rebuild them. If the characters look chopped off at the top or bottom, the printhead probably needs to be adjusted. Refer to the manufacturer's instructions for proper adjustment.

Bad-looking Page

If the page is covered with dots and small smudges—the "pepper look"—the platen is dirty. Clean the platen with denatured alcohol. If the image is faded, and you know the ribbon is good, try adjusting the printhead closer to the platen. If the image is okay on one side of the paper but fades as you move to the other, the platen is out of adjustment. Platens are generally difficult to adjust, so your best plan is to take it to the manufacturer's local warranty/repair center.

Troubleshooting Thermal Printers

Compared to other printer styles, thermal printers are simple to troubleshoot and maintain. With direct thermal printers, you only need to worry about three things: the heating element, the rollers, and the paper. With thermal wax printers, you also need to care for the wax ribbon.

To clean the heating element, turn off the thermal printer and open it according to the manufacturer's instructions. Use denatured alcohol and a lint-free cloth to wipe off the heating element. You might need to use a little pressure to get it completely clean. Clean the rollers with a cloth or compressed air. You want to keep them free of debris so they can properly grip the paper. Replacing the paper is as easy as sliding off the old roll and replacing it with a new one. Remember to feed the paper through the heating element, because otherwise you won't print anything. Replacing the ribbon is similar to

replacing the roll of paper; make sure to feed it past the heating element, or the printer won't work properly. Your printer's manufacturer should include any special instructions for installing a new ribbon.

Troubleshooting Inkjet Printers

Inkjet printers are reliable devices that require little maintenance as long as they are used within their design parameters (high-use machines will require more intensive maintenance). Because of the low price of these printers, manufacturers know that people don't want to spend a lot of money keeping them running. If you perform even the most basic maintenance tasks, they will soldier on for years without a whimper. Inkjets generally have built-in maintenance programs that you should run from time to time to keep your inkjet in good operating order.

Inkjet Printer Maintenance

Inkjet printers don't get nearly as dirty as laser printers, and most manufacturers do not recommend periodic cleaning. Unless your manufacturer explicitly tells you to do so, don't vacuum an inkjet. Inkjets generally do not have maintenance kits, but most inkjet printers come with extensive maintenance software (see Figure 28-26). Usually, the hardest part of using this software is finding it in the first place. Look for an option in Printing Preferences, a selection on the Start menu, or an icon on your desktop. Don't worry—it's there!

Figure 28-26
Inkjet printer maintenance screen

When you first set up an inkjet printer, it normally instructs you to perform a routine (sometimes confusingly referred to as *calibration*) to align the printheads properly, wherein you print out a page and select from sets of numbered lines. If this isn't done,

the print quality will show it, but the good news is that you can perform this procedure at any time. If a printer is moved or dropped or it's just been working away untended for a while, it's often worth running the alignment routine.

Inkjet Problems

Did I say that you never should clean an inkjet? Well, that may be true for the printer itself, but there is one part of your printer that will benefit from an occasional cleaning: the inkjet's printer head nozzles. The nozzles are the tiny pipes that squirt the ink onto the paper. A common problem with inkjet printers is the tendency for the ink inside the nozzles to dry out when not used even for a relatively short time, blocking any ink from exiting. If your printer is telling Windows that it's printing and feeding paper through, but either nothing is coming out (usually the case if you're just printing black text) or only certain colors are printing, the culprit is almost certainly dried ink clogging the nozzles.

NOTE All inkjet inks are water-based, and water works better than alcohol to clean them up.

Every inkjet printer has a different procedure for cleaning the printhead nozzles. On older inkjets, you usually have to press buttons on the printer to start a maintenance program. On more modern inkjets, you can access the head-cleaning maintenance program from Windows.

NOTE Cleaning the heads on an inkjet printer is sometimes necessary, but I don't recommend that you do it on a regular basis as preventive maintenance. The head-cleaning process uses up a lot of that very expensive inkjet ink—so do this only when a printing problem seems to indicate clogged or dirty printheads!

Another problem that sometimes arises is the dreaded multi-sheet paper grab. This is often not actually your printer's fault—humidity can cause sheets of paper to cling to each other—but sometimes the culprit is an overheated printer, so if you've been cranking out a lot of documents without stopping, try giving the printer a bit of a coffee break. Also, fan the sheets of the paper stack before inserting it into the paper tray.

Finally, check to see if excess ink overflow is a problem. In the area where the print-heads park, look for a small tank or tray that catches excess ink from the cleaning process. If the printer has one, check to see how full it is. If this tray overflows onto the main board or even the power supply, it will kill your printer. If you discover that the tray is about to overflow, you can remove excess ink by inserting a twisted paper towel into the tank to soak up some of the ink. It is advisable to wear latex or vinyl gloves while doing this. Clean up any spilled ink with a paper towel dampened with distilled water.

Troubleshooting Laser Printers

Quite a few problems can arise with laser printers, but before getting into those details, you need to review some recommended procedures for *avoiding* those problems.

 CAUTION Before you service a laser printer, always, *always* turn it off and unplug it! Don't expose yourself to the very dangerous high voltages found inside these machines.

Laser Printer Maintenance

Unlike PC maintenance, laser printer maintenance follows a fairly well established procedure. Of course, you'll need to replace the toner cartridge every so often, but keeping your laser printer healthy requires following these maintenance steps.

Keep It Clean Laser printers are quite robust as a rule. A good cleaning every time you replace the toner cartridge will help that printer last for many years. I know of many examples of original HP LaserJet I printers continuing to run perfectly after a dozen or more years of operation. The secret is that they were kept immaculately clean.

Your laser printer gets dirty in two ways: Excess toner, over time, will slowly coat the entire printer. Paper dust, sometimes called *paper dander*, tends to build up where the paper is bent around rollers or where pickup rollers grab paper. Unlike (black) toner, paper dust is easy to see and is usually a good indicator that a printer needs to be cleaned. Usually, a thorough cleaning using a can of compressed air to blow out the printer is the best cleaning you can do. It's best to do this outdoors, or you may end up looking like one of those chimney sweeps from *Mary Poppins*! If you must clean a printer indoors, use a special low-static vacuum designed especially for electronic components (see Figure 28-27).

EXAM TIP The CompTIA A+ 220-802 exam refers to a "toner vacuum," which is the same as a low-static vacuum.

Figure 28-27
Low-static vacuum

Every laser printer has its own unique cleaning method, but the cleaning instructions tend to skip one little area. Every laser printer has a number of rubber guide rollers through which the paper is run during the print process. These little rollers tend to pick up dirt and paper dust over time, making them slip and jam paper. They are easily cleaned with a small amount of 90 percent or better alcohol on a fibrous cleaning towel. The alcohol will remove the debris and any dead rubber. If the paper won't feed, you can give the rollers and separator pads a textured surface that will restore their feeding properties by rubbing them with a little alcohol on a nonmetallic scouring pad.

CAUTION The photosensitive drum, usually contained in the toner cartridge, can be wiped clean if it becomes dirty, but be very careful if you do so! If the drum becomes scratched, the scratch will appear on every page printed from that point on. The only repair in the event of a scratch is to replace the toner cartridge.

If you're ready to get specific, get the printer's service manual. They are a key source for information on how to keep a printer clean and running. Sadly, not all printer manufacturers provide these, but most do. While you're at it, see if the manufacturer has a Quick Reference Guide; these can be very handy for most printer problems!

Periodic Maintenance Although keeping the printer clean is critical to its health and well being, every laser printer has certain components that you need to replace periodically. Your ultimate source for determining the parts that need to be replaced (and when to replace them) is the printer manufacturer. Following the manufacturer's maintenance guidelines will help to ensure years of trouble-free, dependable printing from your laser printer.

Many manufacturers provide kits that contain components that you should replace on a regular schedule. These *maintenance kits* include sets of replacement parts, such as a fuser, as well as one or more rollers or pads. Typically, you need to reset the page counter after installing a maintenance kit so the printer can remind you to perform maintenance again after a certain number of pages have been printed.

Some ozone filters can be cleaned with a vacuum and some can only be replaced— follow the manufacturer's recommendation. You can clean the fuser assembly with 90 percent or better denatured alcohol. Check the heat roller (the Teflon-coated one with the light bulb inside) for pits and scratches. If you see surface damage on the rollers, replace the fuser unit.

Most printers will give you an error code when the fuser is damaged or overheating and needs to be replaced; others will produce the error code at a preset copy count as a preventive maintenance measure. Again, follow the manufacturer's recommendations.

NOTE Failure of the thermal fuse (used to keep the fuser from overheating) can necessitate replacing the fuser assembly. Some machines contain more than one thermal fuse. As always, follow the manufacturer's recommendations. Many manufacturers have kits that alert you with an alarm code to replace the fuser unit and key rollers and guides at predetermined page counts.

The transfer corona can be cleaned with a 90 percent denatured alcohol solution on a cotton swab. If the wire is broken, you can replace it; many just snap in or are held in by a couple of screws. Paper guides can also be cleaned with alcohol on a fibrous towel.

 CAUTION The fuser assembly operates at 200 to 300 degrees Fahrenheit, so always allow time for this component to cool down before you attempt to clean it.

Laser Printer Problems

Laser printers usually manifest problems by creating poor output. One of the most important tests you can do on any printer, not just a laser printer, is called a *diagnostic print page* or an *engine test page*. You do this by either holding down the On Line button as the printer is started or using the printer's maintenance software.

Blank Paper Blank sheets of paper usually mean the printer is out of toner. If the printer does have toner and nothing prints, print a diagnostic print page. If that is also blank, remove the toner cartridge and look at the imaging drum inside. If the image is still there, you know the transfer corona or the high-voltage power supply has failed. Check the printer's maintenance guide to see how to focus on the bad part and replace it.

Dirty or Smudged Printouts If the fusing mechanism in a laser printer gets dirty, it will leave a light dusting of toner all over the paper, particularly on the back of the page. When you see toner speckles on your printouts, you should get the printer cleaned.

If the printout looks smudged, the fuser isn't properly fusing the toner to the paper. Depending on the paper used, the fuser needs to reach a certain temperature to fuse the toner. If the toner won't fuse to the paper, try using a lighter-weight paper. You might also need to replace the fuser.

Ghosting Ghost images sometimes appear at regular intervals on the printed page. This happens when the imaging drum has not fully discharged and is picking up toner from a previous image or when a previous image has used up so much toner that either the supply of charged toner is insufficient or the toner has not been adequately charged. Sometimes it can also be caused by a worn-out cleaning blade that isn't removing the toner from the drum.

Light Ghosting versus Dark Ghosting A variety of problems can cause both light and dark ghosting, but the most common source of light ghosting is "developer starvation." If you ask a laser printer to print an extremely dark or complex image, it can use up so much toner that the toner cartridge will not be able to charge enough toner to print the next image. The proper solution is to use less toner. You can fix ghosting problems in the following ways:

- Lower the resolution of the page (print at 300 dpi instead of 600 dpi).
- Use a different pattern.
- Avoid 50 percent grayscale and "dot-on/dot-off patterns."
- Change the layout so that grayscale patterns do not follow black areas.
- Make dark patterns lighter and light patterns darker.
- Print in landscape orientation.
- Adjust print density and RET settings.
- Print a completely blank page immediately prior to the page with the ghosting image, as part of the same print job.

In addition to these possibilities, low temperature and low humidity can aggravate ghosting problems. Check your user's manual for environmental recommendations. Dark ghosting can sometimes be caused by a damaged drum. It may be fixed by replacing the toner cartridge. Light ghosting would *not* be solved in this way. Switching other components will not usually affect ghosting problems because they are a side effect of the entire printing process.

Vertical White Lines Vertical white lines usually happen when the toner is clogged, preventing the proper dispersion of toner on the drum. Try shaking the toner cartridge to dislodge the clog. If that doesn't work, replace the toner cartridge.

Blotchy Print Blotches are commonly a result of uneven dispersion of toner, especially if the toner is low. Shake the toner from side to side and then try to print. Also be sure that the printer is sitting level. Finally, make sure the paper is not wet in spots. If the blotches are in a regular order, check the fusing rollers and the photosensitive drum for any foreign objects.

Spotty Print If the spots appear at regular intervals, the drum may be damaged or some toner may be stuck to the fuser rollers. Try wiping off the fuser rollers. Check the drum for damage. If the drum is damaged, get a new toner cartridge.

Embossed Effect If your prints are getting an embossed effect (like putting a penny under a piece of paper and rubbing it with a lead pencil), there is almost certainly a foreign object on a roller. Use 90 percent denatured alcohol or regular water with a soft cloth to try to remove it. If the foreign object is on the photosensitive drum, you're going to have to use a new toner cartridge. An embossed effect can also be caused by the contrast control being set too high. The contrast control is actually a knob on the inside of the unit (sometimes accessible from the outside, on older models). Check your manual for the specific location.

Incomplete Characters You can sometimes correct incompletely printed characters on laser-printed transparencies by adjusting the print density. Be extremely careful to use only materials approved for use in laser printers.

Creased Pages Laser printers have up to four rollers. In addition to the heat and pressure rollers of the fuser assembly, other rollers move the paper from the source tray

to the output tray. These rollers crease the paper to avoid curling that would cause paper jams in the printer. If the creases are noticeable, try using a different paper type. Cotton bond paper is usually more susceptible to noticeable creasing than other bonds. You might also try sending the output to the face-up tray, which avoids one roller. There is no hardware solution to this problem; it is simply a side effect of the process.

Paper Jams Every printer jams now and then. If you get a jam, always refer first to the manufacturer's jam removal procedure. It is simply too easy to damage a printer by pulling on the jammed paper! If the printer reports a jam but there's no paper inside, you've almost certainly got a problem with one of the many jam sensors or paper feed sensors inside the printer, and you'll need to take it to a repair center.

Pulling Multiple Sheets If the printer grabs multiple sheets at a time, first try opening a new ream of paper and loading that in the printer. If that works, you have a humidity problem. If the new paper angle doesn't work, check the separation pad on the printer. The separation pad is a small piece of cork or rubber that separates the sheets as they are pulled from the paper feed tray. A worn separation pad looks shiny and, well, *worn!* Most separation pads are easy to replace. Check out www.printerworks. com to see if you can replace yours.

Warped, Overprinted, or Poorly Formed Characters Poorly formed characters can indicate either a problem with the paper (or other media) or a problem with the hardware.

Incorrect media cause a number of these types of problems. Avoid paper that is too rough or too smooth. Paper that is too rough interferes with the fusing of characters and their initial definition. If the paper is too smooth (like some coated papers, for example), it may feed improperly, causing distorted or overwritten characters. Even though you can purchase laser printer–specific paper, all laser printers print acceptably on standard photocopy paper. Try to keep the paper from becoming too wet. Don't open a ream of paper until it is time to load it into the printer. Always fan the paper before loading it into the printer, especially if the paper has been left out of the package for more than just a few days.

The durability of a well-maintained laser printer makes hardware a much rarer source of character printing problems, but you should be aware of the possibility. Fortunately, it is fairly easy to check the hardware. Most laser printers have a self-test function— often combined with a diagnostic printout but sometimes as a separate process. This self-test shows whether the laser printer can properly develop an image without actually having to send print commands from the PC. The self-test is quite handy to verify the question "Is it the printer or is it the computer?" Run the self-test to check for connectivity and configuration problems.

Possible solutions include replacing the toner cartridge, especially if you hear popping noises; checking the cabling; and replacing the data cable, especially if it has bends or crimps or if objects are resting on the cable. If you have a front menu panel, turn off advanced functions and high-speed settings to determine whether the advanced functions are either not working properly or not supported by your current software configuration (check your manuals for configuration information). If these solutions do not work, the problem may not be user serviceable. Contact an authorized service center.

Beyond A+

Multifunction Peripherals

It's a common theme in computing: why have two devices that do one thing each when you can have one device that does two things? In that spirit, manufacturers started gluing various peripherals together to create *multifunction peripherals*, or *MFPs* (see Figure 28-28). These devices can include printers, scanners, fax machines, photocopiers, and more. All of your standard connection options are available, including USB, parallel, Ethernet, Wi-Fi, and more.

Figure 28-28

All-in-one printer/scanner/fax machine/copier/coffee maker/iPod dock

One of the best parts of a multifunction device is that all of these functions are available using a single connection. On the other hand, because a multifunction device is much more complicated than a single-function device, you'll probably need to follow very specific instructions and use the manufacturer-supplied installation disc to get it all working. Many multifunction devices also include functions that don't require a PC at all, such as photocopying and faxing. You can even print files from a digital camera's memory card without plugging the MFP into a PC.

Chapter Review

Questions

1. What mechanism is used by most inkjet printers to push ink onto the paper?

 A. Electrostatic discharge

 B. Gravity

 C. Air pressure

 D. Electroconductive plates

2. With a laser printer, what creates the image on the photosensitive drum?

 A. Primary corona

 B. Laser imaging unit

 C. Transfer corona

 D. Toner

3. What is the proper order of the laser printing process?

 A. Process, clean, charge, expose, develop, transfer, and fuse

 B. Process, charge, expose, develop, transfer, fuse, and clean

 C. Clean, expose, develop, transfer, process, fuse, and charge

 D. Clean, charge, expose, process, develop, fuse, and transfer

4. On a dot-matrix printer, what physically strikes the ribbon to form an image?

 A. Electromagnets

 B. Printwires

 C. Character wheel

 D. Print hammers

5. Which of these items are considered to be dot-matrix printer consumables? (Select two.)

 A. Drive motor

 B. Paper

 C. Flywheel

 D. Ribbon

6. What part must be vacuumed or replaced periodically to prevent damage caused by the action of the corona?

 A. The rubber rollers

 B. The ozone filter

 C. The transfer filter

 D. The cleaning blade

7. Which of the following port types most commonly support printers? (Select two.)

 A. Parallel

 B. USB

 C. Infrared

 D. RS-232

8. A standalone printer prints a test page just fine, but it makes gobbledygook out of your term paper. What's probably wrong?

 A. Out of toner

 B. Fuser error

 C. Printer interface

 D. Faulty software configuration

9. What printing process uses heat-sensitive plastic files embedded with various color dyes?

 A. Dye-sublimation

 B. Inkjet

 C. Ink-dispersion

 D. Dye-dispersion

10. Which tool would help you determine why a print job didn't print?

 A. Printer driver

 B. Printer setup

 C. Print spooler

 D. System setup

Answers

1. **D.** Most inkjet printers use electroconductive plates to push the ink onto the paper.

2. **B.** The laser imaging unit creates an image on the photosensitive drum.

3. **B.** Process, charge, expose, develop, transfer, fuse, and clean is the proper process.

4. **B.** Printwires physically strike the ribbon in dot-matrix printers.

5. **B, D.** Both paper and ribbons are considered dot-matrix printer consumables.

6. **B.** The ozone filter should be periodically vacuumed or changed.

7. **A, B.** You'll find almost all printers hooked up to parallel or USB ports.

8. **D.** The application (software) that is trying to print is probably configured incorrectly.

9. **A.** Dye-sublimation printers use heat-sensitive plastic files embedded with various color dyes.

10. **C.** The print spooler can help you determine why a print job didn't print.

Securing Computers

In this chapter, you will learn how to

- Explain the threats to your computers and data
- Describe key security concepts and technologies
- Explain how to protect computers from network threats

Your PC is under siege. Through your PC, a malicious person can gain valuable information about you and your habits. He can steal your files. He can run programs that log your keystrokes and thus gain account names and passwords, credit card information, and more. He can run software that takes over much of your computer processing time and use it to send spam or steal from others. The threat is real and right now. Worse, he's doing one or more of these things to your clients as I write these words. You need to secure your computer and your users' computers from these attacks.

But what does *computer security* mean? Is it an antivirus program? Is it big, complex passwords? Sure, it's both of these things, but what about the fact that your laptop can be stolen easily or that improper ventilation can cause hard drives and other components to die?

To secure computers, you need both a sound strategy and proper tactics. From a strategic sense, you need to understand the threat from unauthorized access to local machines as well as the big threats posed when computers go onto networks. Part of the big picture means to know what policies, software, and hardware to put in place to stop those threats. From a tactical in-the-trenches sense, you need to master the details, to know how to implement and maintain the proper tools. Not only do you need to install antivirus programs in your users' computers, for example, but you also need to update those programs regularly to keep up with the constant barrage of new viruses.

 NOTE The majority of topics in this chapter apply exclusively to the 802 exam, but several 801 exam objectives fit well here too. I'll point out the 801 topics when they appear in the chapter.

801/802

Analyzing Threats

Threats to your data and PC come from two directions: accidents and malicious people. All sorts of things can go wrong with your computer, from users getting access to folders they shouldn't see to a virus striking and deleting folders. Files can be deleted, renamed, or simply lost. Hard drives can die, and optical discs get scratched and rendered unreadable. Accidents happen and even well-meaning people can make mistakes.

Unfortunately, a lot of people out there intend to do you harm. Add that intent together with a talent for computers, and you have a deadly combination. Let's look at the following issues:

- Unauthorized access
- Data destruction, accidental or deliberate
- Administrative access
- Catastrophic hardware failures
- Malware
- Environmental threats

Unauthorized Access

Unauthorized access occurs when a person accesses resources without permission. Resources in this case mean data, applications, and hardware. A user can alter or delete data; access sensitive information, such as financial data, personnel files, or e-mail messages; or use a computer for purposes the owner did not intend.

Not all unauthorized access is malicious—often this problem arises when users who are randomly poking around in a computer discover that they can access resources in a fashion the primary user did not intend. Unauthorized access becomes malicious when outsiders knowingly and intentionally take advantage of weaknesses in your security to gain information, use resources, or destroy data!

One of the ways to gain unauthorized access is through intrusion. You might imagine someone kicking in a door and hacking into a computer, but more often than not it's someone sitting at a home computer, trying various passwords over the Internet. Not quite as glamorous, but still....

Dumpster diving is the generic term for anytime a hacker goes through your refuse, looking for information. This is also a form of intrusion. The amount of sensitive information that makes it into any organization's trash bin boggles the mind! Years ago, I worked with an IT security guru who gave me and a few other IT people a tour of our office's trash. In one 20-minute tour of the personal wastebaskets of one office area, we had enough information to access the network easily, as well as to embarrass seriously more than a few people. When it comes to getting information, the trash is the place to look!

Shoulder surfing is another technique for gaining unauthorized access. Shoulder surfing is simply observing someone's screen or keyboard to get information, often passwords. As the name implies, it usually requires the bad guy looking over your shoulder to see what you are doing.

Social Engineering

Although you're more likely to lose data through accident, the acts of malicious users get the vast majority of headlines. Most of these attacks come under the heading of *social engineering*—the process of using or manipulating people inside the networking environment to gain access to that network from the outside—which covers the many ways humans can use other humans to gain unauthorized information. This unauthorized information may be a network login, a credit card number, company customer data—almost anything you might imagine that one person or organization may not want a person outside of that organization to access.

Social engineering attacks aren't hacking—at least in the classic sense of the word—although the goals are the same. Social engineering means people attacking an organization through the people in the organization or physically accessing the organization to get the information they need. Following are a few of the more classic types of social engineering attacks.

NOTE It's common for social engineering attacks to be used together, so if you discover one of them being used against your organization, it's a good idea to look for others.

Infiltration

Hackers can physically enter your building under the guise of someone who might have a legitimate reason for being there, such as cleaning personnel, repair technicians, or messengers. They then snoop around desks, looking for whatever they can find. They might talk with people inside the organization, gathering names, office numbers, department names—little things in and of themselves but powerful tools when combined later with other social engineering attacks.

Dressing the part of a legitimate user—with fake badge and everything—enables malicious people to gain access to locations and thus potentially your data. Following someone through the door, for example, as if you belong, is called *tailgating*. Tailgating is a common form of infiltration.

Telephone Scams

Telephone scams are probably the most common social engineering attack. In this case, the attacker makes a phone call to someone in the organization to gain information. The attacker attempts to come across as someone inside the organization and uses this to get the desired information. Probably the most famous of these scams is the "I forgot my user name and password" scam. In this gambit, the attacker first learns the

account name of a legitimate person in the organization, usually using the infiltration method. The attacker then calls someone in the organization, usually the help desk, in an attempt to gather information, in this case a password.

> **Hacker:** "Hi, this is John Anderson in accounting. I forgot my password. Can you reset it, please?"
>
> **Help Desk:** "Sure, what's your user name?"
>
> **Hacker:** "j_w_Anderson"
>
> **Help Desk:** "OK, I reset it to e34rd3."

Certainly telephone scams aren't limited to attempts to get network access. There are documented telephone scams against organizations aimed at getting cash, blackmail material, or other valuables.

Phishing

Phishing is the act of trying to get people to give their user names, passwords, or other security information by pretending to be someone else electronically. A classic example is when a bad guy sends you an e-mail that's supposed to be from your local credit card company asking you to send them your user name and password. Phishing is by far the most common form of social engineering done today.

Data Destruction

Often an extension of unauthorized access, data destruction means more than just intentionally or accidentally erasing or corrupting data. It's easy to imagine some evil hacker accessing your network and deleting all your important files, but authorized users may also access certain data and then use that data beyond what they are authorized to do. A good example is the person who legitimately accesses a Microsoft Access product database to modify the product descriptions, only to discover that she can change the prices of the products, too.

This type of threat is particularly dangerous when users are not clearly informed about the extent to which they are authorized to make changes. A fellow tech once told me about a user who managed to mangle an important database when someone gave him incorrect access. When confronted, the user said: "If I wasn't allowed to change it, the system wouldn't let me do it!" Many users believe that systems are configured in a paternalistic way that wouldn't allow them to do anything inappropriate. As a result, users often assume they're authorized to make any changes they believe are necessary when working on a piece of data they know they're authorized to access.

Administrative Access

Every operating system enables you to create user accounts and grant those accounts a certain level of access to files and folders in that computer. As an administrator, supervisor, or root user, you have full control over just about every aspect of the computer. Windows XP, in particular, makes it entirely too easy to give users administrative access to the computer, especially Windows XP Home, which has only two kinds of users:

administrators and limited users. Because you can't do much as a limited user, most home and small office systems simply use multiple administrator accounts. If you need to control access, you need to use non-Home versions of Windows.

System Crash/Hardware Failure

As with any technology, computers can and will fail—usually when you can least afford for it to happen. Hard drives crash, the power fails—it's all part of the joy of working in the computing business. You need to create redundancy in areas prone to failure (such as installing backup power in case of electrical failure) and perform those all-important data backups. Chapter 17 goes into detail about using backups and other issues involved in creating a stable and reliable system.

Physical Theft

A fellow network geek once challenged me to try to bring down his newly installed network. He had just installed a powerful and expensive firewall router and was convinced that I couldn't get to a test server he added to his network just for me to try to access. After a few attempts to hack in over the Internet, I saw that I wasn't going to get anywhere that way.

So I jumped in my car and drove to his office, having first outfitted myself in a techy-looking jumpsuit and an ancient ID badge I just happened to have in my sock drawer. I smiled sweetly at the receptionist and walked right by my friend's office (I noticed he was smugly monitoring incoming IP traffic by using some neato packet-sniffing program) to his new server.

I quickly pulled the wires out of the back of his precious server, picked it up, and walked out the door. The receptionist was too busy trying to figure out why her e-mail wasn't working to notice me as I whisked by her carrying the 65-pound server box. I stopped in the hall and called him from my cell phone.

> **Me (cheerily):** "Dude, I got all your data!"
>
> **Him (not cheerily):** "You rebooted my server! How did you do it?"
>
> **Me (smiling):** "I didn't reboot it—go over and look at it!"
>
> **Him (really mad now):** "YOU <EXPLETIVE> THIEF! YOU STOLE MY SERVER!"
>
> **Me (cordially):** "Why, yes. Yes, I did. Give me two days to hack your password in the comfort of my home, and I'll see everything! Bye!"

I immediately walked back in and handed him the test server. It was fun. The moral here is simple: Never forget that the best network software security measures can be rendered useless if you fail to protect your systems physically!

Malware

Networks are without a doubt the fastest and most efficient vehicles for transferring computer viruses among systems. News reports focus attention on the many malicious software attacks from the Internet, but a huge number of such attacks still come

from users who bring in programs on optical discs and USB drives. The "Network Security" section of this chapter describes the various methods of virus infection and other malware and what you need to do to prevent such attacks from damaging your networked systems.

Environmental Threats

Your computer is surrounded by a host of dangers all just waiting to wreak havoc: bad electricity from the power company, a host of chemicals that just by the nature of your business may or may not be near your computer, dust, heat, cold, wet…it's a jungle out there!

 EXAM TIP Expect questions on environmental threats on the 220-801 exam.

Power

We've covered power issues extensively back in Chapter 10. Don't ever fail to appreciate the importance of surge suppressors and uninterruptible power supplies (UPSs) to protect your electronics from surges, brownouts, and blackouts. Also remember that network devices need power protection as well. Figure 29-1 shows a typical UPS protecting a network rack.

Figure 29-1 UPS on rack

How's the Air in There?

Proper environmental controls help secure servers and workstations from the environmental impact of excessive heat, dust, and humidity. Such *environmental controls* include air conditioning, proper ventilation, air filtration, and monitors for temperature and humidity. A CompTIA A+ technician maintains an awareness of temperature, humidity level, and ventilation, so that he or she can tell very quickly when proper levels or settings are out of whack.

A PC works best in an environment where the air is clean, dry, and room temperature. CompTIA doesn't expect you to become an environmental engineer, but it does expect you to explain and deal with how dirty or humid or hot air can affect a computer. We've covered all of these topics to some extent throughout the book so let's just do a quick overview with security in mind.

Dirty Air Dust and debris aren't good for any electronic components. Your typical office air conditioning does a pretty good job of eliminating the worst offenders, but not all computers are in nice offices. No matter where the computers reside, you need to monitor your systems for dirt. The best way to do this is observation as part of your regular work. Dust and debris will show up all over the systems, but the best place to look are the fans. Fans will collect dust and dirt quickly (see Figure 29-2).

Figure 29-2
Dirty fan

All electronic components get dirty over time. To clean them, you need to use either compressed air or a nonstatic vacuum. So which one do you use? The rule is simple: If you don't mind dust blowing all over the place, use compressed air. If you don't want dust blowing all over the place, use a vacuum.

Equipment closets filled with racks of servers need proper airflow to keep things cool and to control dusty air. Make sure that the room is ventilated and air-conditioned (see Figure 29-3) and that the air filters are changed regularly.

If things are really bad, you can enclose a system in a dust shield. Dust shields come complete with their own filters to keep a computer clean and happy even in the worst of environments.

Temperature and Humidity Most computers are designed to operate at room temperature, which is somewhere in the area of 22°C (72°F) with the relative humidity in the 30–40 percent range. Colder and dryer is better for computers (but not for people), so the real challenge is when the temperature and the humidity go higher.

A modern office will usually have good air conditioning and heating, so your job as a tech is to make sure that things don't happen to prevent your air conditioning from doing its job. That means you're pretty much always on ventilation patrol. Watch for the following to make sure air is flowing:

- Make sure ducts are always clear of obstructions.
- Make sure ducts are adjusted (not too hot or too cold).
- Don't let equipment get too closed off from proper ventilation.

Figure 29-3
Air-conditioning
vent in a small
server closet

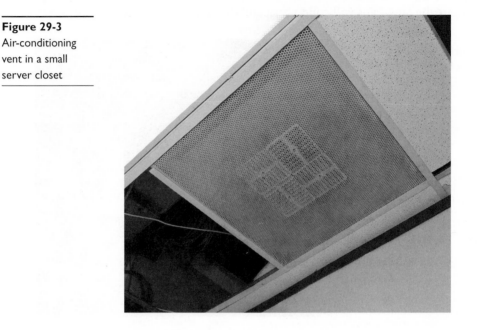

Toxic Materials

Every office is filled with chemicals, compositions that invariably get stored, spilled, or dumped. If something spills and it's not something you're familiar with, refer to the Material Safety Data Sheet (MSDS) for proper documentation for handling and disposal. Always comply with local government regulations when dealing with chemicals, including batteries and the metals on circuit boards.

TIP Most cities in the U.S. have one or more environmental services center that you can use to recycle electronic components. For your city, try a Google (or other search engine) search on the term "environmental services" and you'll almost certainly find a convenient place for e-waste disposal.

Security Concepts and Technologies

Once you've assessed the threats to your computers and networks, you need to take steps to protect those valuable resources. Depending on the complexity of your organization, this can be a small job encompassing some basic security concepts and procedures, or

it can be exceedingly complex. The security needs for a three-person desktop publishing firm, for example, would differ wildly from those of a defense contractor supplying top-secret toys to the Pentagon.

From a CompTIA A+ certified technician's perspective, you need to understand the big picture (that's the strategic side), knowing the concepts and available technologies for security. At the implementation level (that's the tactical side), you're expected to know where to find such things as security policies in Windows. A CompTIA Network+ or CompTIA Security+ tech will give you the specific options to implement. (The exception to this level of knowledge comes in dealing with malicious software such as viruses, but we'll tackle that subject as the last part of the chapter.) So let's look at three concept and technology areas: access control, data classification and compliance, and reporting.

Access Control

Access is the key. If you can control access to the data, programs, and other computing resources, you've secured your systems. *Access control* is composed of four interlinked areas that a good security-minded tech should think about: physical security, authentication, users and groups, and security policies. Much of this you know from previous chapters, but this section should help tie it all together as a security topic.

Secure Physical Area and Lock Down Systems

The first order of security is to block access to the physical hardware from people who shouldn't have access. This isn't rocket science. Lock the door to your workspace. Don't leave a PC unattended when logged in. In fact, don't ever leave a system logged in, even as a limited user. God help you if you walk away from a server still logged in as an administrator. You're tempting fate.

Employee ID badges are now so common that even relatively small organizations use them. Badges are a great way not only to control building access but also to store authentication tools such as radio frequency identification (RFID) or smart cards (see "Authentication" later in this chapter). Figure 29-4 shows a typical badge.

Figure 29-4
Typical employee badge/smart card

Be aware of the risk of shoulder surfing. One handy tool to prevent this is a privacy filter. A privacy filter is little more than a framed sheet or film that you apply to the front of your monitor. Privacy filters reduce the viewing angle, making it impossible to see the contents on the screen for anyone except those directly in front of the screen (see Figure 29-5).

Figure 29-5 Privacy filter

Security is more of an issue when users walk away from their computers, even for a moment. When you see a user's computer logged in and unattended, do the user and your company a huge favor and lock the computer. Just walk up and press WINDOWS LOGO KEY-L on the keyboard to lock the system. It works in all versions of Windows. Better yet, make a point to make users aware of this issue so they understand the risk and can take the precaution themselves. You should also instruct them how to password-protect their screensaver. When the password feature is enabled, a user won't be able to return to the desktop until they've entered the proper password. It's a little like locking the computer, and good for those who like using screensavers.

While you're looking at a user's monitor, examine around his or her desk. Is the user writing down passwords and putting them in plain sight? If so, tell the user to get rid of them! Teach users to create easy-to-remember passwords. Are critical, personal, or sensitive documents also lying about in plain sight? The user should put them in a closed, secure place. Documents no longer needed should be shredded immediately.

Authentication

Security requires properly implemented *authentication*, which means in essence how the computer determines who can or should access it and, once accessed, what that user can do. A computer can authenticate users through software or hardware, or a combination of both.

You can categorize ways to authenticate into three broad areas: knowledge factors, ownership factors, and inherent factors. A *knowledge factor* is something the user knows, like a password or personal identification number (PIN). An *ownership factor* is something the user has, like an ID card or security token. An *inherent factor* (also called a biometric) is something that is part of the user, like a fingerprint or retinal pattern.

NOTE A popular way to remember authentication factors is to think of them as something you know (passwords), something about you (biometric), and something you have (badge, key fob, or security token).

Multifactor authentication provides the best authentication, where a user must use two or more factors to prove his or her identity. Note that multifactor means more than one factor, not just more than one *thing*. Logging in with a user name and password is two things, for example, but because both fall into the category of what a user knows, it's not multifactor authentication.

Many organizations use *two-factor authentication*. An example is a key fob that generates a numeric key. A user authenticates by entering his or her user name and password (something you know) and is then prompted to enter the key (something you have).

EXAM TIP Remember the concept of *single sign-on* from Chapter 5? You can log on to any computer in a domain using one set of credentials. In addition to being a time-saver, this is also a great security feature that helps network administrators better control who can gain access to the network.

Software Authentication: Proper Passwords It's still rather shocking to me to power up a friend's computer and go straight to his or her desktop, or with my married-with-kids friends, to click one of the parents' user account icons and not be prompted for a password. This is just wrong! I'm always tempted to assign passwords right then and there—and not tell them the passwords, of course—so they'll see the error of their ways when they try to log on next. I don't do it but always try to explain gently the importance of good passwords.

You know about passwords from Chapter 16, so I won't belabor the point here. Suffice it to say that you must require that your users have proper passwords. Don't let them write passwords down or tape them to the underside of their mouse pads either!

It's not just access to Windows that you need to think about. There's always the temptation for people to do other mean things, such as changing CMOS settings, opening up the case, and even stealing hard drives. Any of these actions renders the computer inoperable to the casual user until a tech can undo the damage or replace components. All modern CMOS setup utilities come with a number of tools to protect your computer, such as drive lock, intrusion detection, and of course system access passwords such as the one shown in Figure 29-6. Refer to Chapter 8 to refresh yourself on what you can do at a BIOS level to protect your computer.

Figure 29-6
CMOS access
password request

Hardware Authentication Smart cards and biometric devices enable modern systems to authenticate users with more authority than mere passwords. *Smart cards* are credit card–sized cards with circuitry that can identify the bearer of the card. Smart cards are relatively common for such tasks as authenticating users for mass transit systems, for example, but are fairly uncommon in computers. Figure 29-7 shows a smart card and keyboard combination.

Figure 29-7
Keyboard-mounted
smart card reader
being used for a
commercial ap-
plication (photo
courtesy of Cherry
Corp.)

Security tokens are devices that store some unique information that the user carries on their person. They may be digital certificates, passwords, or biometric data. They may also store an RSA token. *RSA tokens* are random-number generators that are used with user names and passwords to ensure extra security. Most security tokens come in the form of key fobs, as shown in Figure 29-8.

Figure 29-8
RSA key fob (photo
courtesy of EMC
Corp.)

You can also get many types of security tokens as software. Anyone who plays *World of Warcraft* knows that there's an entire illegal industry known as "gold farmers" who like to hack accounts and steal all the hard-earned loot your character collects. It's a terrible feeling to log in to the game only to find your character cleaned out (see Figure 29-9).

Figure 29-9 I've been robbed! My fine armor is gone, my bags are empty, and my bank account only has a few copper pieces!

To counter this problem, Blizzard Entertainment, the folks who own *World of Warcraft*, provide free security tokens. Most folks think "hardware" in the form of key fobs when they hear the words "security tokens," but you can also download a security token as software—Blizzard offers an app for your smartphone, as shown in Figure 29-10.

Figure 29-10
Blizzard Entertainment security token for iPhone

People can guess or discover passwords, but it's a lot harder to forge someone's fingerprints. The keyboard in Figure 29-11 authenticates users on a local machine by using fingerprints. Other devices that will do the trick are key fobs and retinal scanners. Devices that require some sort of physical, flesh-and-blood authentication are called *biometric devices*.

Figure 29-11
Microsoft keyboard with fingerprint accessibility

 NOTE How's this for full disclosure? Microsoft does not claim that the keyboard in Figure 29-11 offers any security at all. In fact, the documentation specifically claims that the fingerprint reader is an accessibility tool, not a security device. Because it enables a person to log on to a local machine, though, I think it falls into the category of authentication devices.

Clever manufacturers have developed key fobs and smart cards that use RFID to transmit authentication information so users don't have to insert something into a computer or card reader. The Privaris plusID combines, for example, a biometric fingerprint fob with an RFID tag that makes security as easy as opening a garage door remotely! Figure 29-12 shows a plusID device.

Figure 29-12
plusID (photo courtesy of Privaris, Inc.)

For some reason, CompTIA lists *retinal scanners* as a form of biometric security. While retinal scanners do exist, I have been in hundreds of high-security facilities and have only seen one retinal scanner in operation in almost 30 years as a tech. CompTIA should remove this silly objective, but until they do, Figure 29-13 shows about the only image of a retinal scanner in operation you'll ever encounter.

Figure 29-13 Retinal scanner in *Half-Life 2*

NTFS, not FAT32!

The file system on a hard drive matters a lot when it comes to security. On a Windows machine with multiple users, you simply must use NTFS or you have no security at all. Not just primary drives but also any secondary drives in computers in your care should be formatted as NTFS, with the exception of removable drives such as the one you use to back up your system.

When you run into a multiple-drive system that has a second or third drive formatted as FAT32, you can use the *convert* command-line utility to go from FAT to NTFS. The syntax is pretty straightforward. To convert a D: drive from FAT or FAT32 to NTFS, for example, you'd type the following:

convert d: /fs:ntfs

You can substitute a mount name in place of the drive letter in case you have a mounted volume. The command has a few extra switches as well, so at the command prompt, type /? after the convert command to see all of your options.

Users and Groups

Windows uses user accounts and groups as the bedrock of access control. A user account is assigned to a group, such as Users, Power Users, or Administrators, and by association gets certain permissions on the computer. Using NTFS enables the highest level of control over data resources.

Assigning users to groups is a great first step in controlling a local machine, but this feature really shines once you go to a networked environment. Let's go there now.

User Account Management Through Groups

Access to user accounts should be restricted to the assigned individuals, and those who configure the permissions to those accounts must remember the Principle of Least Privilege discussed in Chapter 16: Accounts should have permission to access only the resources they need and no more. Tight control of user accounts is critical to preventing unauthorized access. Disabling unused accounts is an important part of this strategy, but good user account management goes far deeper than that.

Groups are a great way to achieve increased complexity without increasing the administrative burden on network administrators, because all operating systems combine permissions. When a user is a member of more than one group, which permissions does that user have with respect to any particular resource? In all operating systems, the permissions of the groups are *combined*, and the result is what you call the *effective permissions* the user has to access the resource. As an example, if Rita is a member of the Sales group, which has List Folder Contents permission to a folder, and she is also a member of the Managers group, which has Read and Execute permissions to the same folder, Rita will have both List Folder Contents *and* Read and Execute permissions to that folder.

Watch out for *default* user accounts and groups—they can become secret backdoors to your network! All network operating systems have a default Everyone group that can be used to sneak into shared resources easily. This Everyone group, as its name implies, literally includes anyone who connects to that resource. Windows gives full control to the Everyone group by default, for example, so make sure you know to lock this down! The other scary one is the Guest account. The Guest account is the only way to access a system without a user name and password. Unless you have a compelling reason to provide guest access, you should always make sure the Guest account is disabled.

All of the default groups—Everyone, Guest, Users—define broad groups of users. Never use them unless you intend to permit all of those folks access to a resource. If you use one of the default groups, remember to configure them with the proper permissions to prevent users from doing things you don't want them to do with a shared resource!

Security Policies

Although permissions control how users access shared resources, there are other functions you should control that are outside the scope of resources. For example, do you want users to be able to access a command prompt on their Windows system? Do you want users to be able to install software? Would you like to control what systems a user can log on to or at what time of day a user can log on? All network operating systems provide you with some capability to control these and literally hundreds of other security

parameters, under what Windows calls *policies*. I like to think of policies as permissions for activities, as opposed to true permissions, which control access to resources.

A policy is usually applied to a user account, a computer, or a group. Let's use the example of a network composed of Windows XP Professional systems with a Windows Server 2008 system. Every Windows XP system has its own local policies program, which enables policies to be placed on that system only. Figure 29-14 shows the tool you use to set local policies on an individual system, called *Local Security Policy*, being used to deny the user account Danar the capability to log on locally.

 NOTE When you open the Local Security Policy tool in Windows XP, note that the program is labeled "Local Security Settings," even though the icon is labeled "Local Security Policy." In Windows Vista and Windows 7, it is always called Local Security Policy.

Figure 29-14 Local Security Policy

Local policies work great for individual systems, but they can be a pain to configure if you want to apply the same settings to more than one PC on your network. If you want to apply policy settings *en masse*, you need to step up to Windows Active Directory domain-based *Group Policy*. By using Group Policy, you can exercise deity-like—Microsoft prefers to use the term *granular*—control over your network clients.

Want to set default wallpaper for every PC in your domain? Group Policy can do that. Want to make certain tools inaccessible to everyone except authorized users? Group Policy can do that, too. Want to control access to the Internet, redirect home folders, run scripts, deploy software, or just remind folks that unauthorized access to the network will get them nowhere fast? Group Policy is the answer. Figure 29-15 shows Group Policy; I'm about to change the default title on every instance of Internet Explorer on every computer in my domain!

Figure 29-15 Using Group Policy to make IE title say "provided by Mike!"

That's just one simple example of the settings you can configure by using Group Policy. You can apply literally hundreds of tweaks through Group Policy, from the great to the small, but don't worry too much about familiarizing yourself with each and every one. Group Policy settings are a big topic on most of the Microsoft certification tracks, but for the purposes of the CompTIA A+ exams, you simply have to be comfortable with the concept behind Group Policy.

Although I could never list every possible policy you can enable on a Windows system, here's a list of some commonly used ones:

- **Prevent Registry Edits** If you try to edit the Registry, you get a failure message.

- **Prevent Access to the Command Prompt** Keeps users from getting to the command prompt by turning off the Run command and the Command Prompt shortcut.

- **Log on Locally** Defines who may log on to the system locally.

- **Shut Down System** Defines who may shut down the system.

- **Minimum Password Length** Forces a minimum password length.

- **Account Lockout Threshold** Sets the maximum number of logon attempts a person can make before being locked out of the account.

- **Disable Windows Installer** Prevents users from installing software.
- **Printer Browsing** Enables users to browse for printers on the network, as opposed to using only assigned printers.

Although the CompTIA A+ exams don't expect you to know how to implement policies on any type of network, you are expected to understand that policies exist, especially on Windows networks, and that they can do amazing things to control what users can do on their systems. If you ever try to get to a command prompt on a Windows system only to discover the Run command is dimmed, blame it on a policy, not the computer!

Data Classification and Compliance

Larger organizations, such as government entities, benefit greatly from organizing their data according to its sensitivity—what's called *data classification*—and making certain that computer hardware and software stay as uniform as possible. In addition, many government and internal regulations apply fairly rigorously to the organizations.

Data classification systems vary by the organization, but a common scheme classifies documents as public, internal use only, highly confidential, top secret, and so on. Using a classification scheme enables employees such as techs to know very quickly what to do with documents, the drives containing documents, and more. Your strategy for recycling a computer system left from a migrated user, for example, will differ a lot if the data on the drive was classified as internal use only or top secret.

Compliance means, in a nutshell, that members of an organization or company must abide by or comply with all of the rules that apply to the organization or company. Statutes with funny names such as Sarbanes-Oxley impose certain behaviors or prohibitions on what people can and cannot do in the workplace.

From a technician's point of view, the most common compliance issue revolves around software, such as what sort of software users can be allowed to install on their computers or, conversely, why you have to tell a user that he can't install the latest application that may help him do the job more effectively because that software isn't on the approved list. This can lead to some uncomfortable confrontations, but it's part of a tech's job.

The concepts behind compliance in IT are not, as some might imagine at first blush, to stop you from being able to work effectively. Rather they're designed to stop users with not quite enough technical skill or knowledge from installing malicious programs or applications that will destabilize their systems. This keeps technical support calls down and enables techs to focus on more serious problems.

Reporting

As a final weapon in your security arsenal, you need to report any security issues so a network administrator or technician can take steps to make them go away. You can set up auditing within Windows so that the OS reports problems to you. *Event Viewer* enables you to read the logs created by auditing. You can then do your work and report those problems. Let's take a look.

Auditing

The Security section of Event Viewer doesn't show you anything by default. To unlock the full potential of Event Viewer, you need to set up auditing. *Auditing* in the security sense means to tell Windows to create an entry in the Security Log when certain events happen, such as when a user logs on—called *event auditing*—or tries to access a certain file or folder—called *object access auditing*. Figure 29-16 shows Event Viewer tracking logon and logoff events.

Figure 29-16 Event Viewer displaying security alerts

The CompTIA A+ certification exams don't test you on creating a brilliant auditing policy for your office—that's what network administrators do. You simply need to know what auditing does and how to turn it on or off so you can provide support for the network administrators in the field. To turn on auditing at a local level, go to Local Security Policy in Administrative Tools. Select Local Policies and then click Audit

Policy. Double-click one of the policy options and select one or both of the checkboxes in the Properties dialog box that opens. Figure 29-17 shows the Audit object access Properties dialog box.

Figure 29-17 Audit object access Properties dialog box, with Local Security Policy open in the background

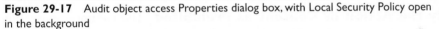 **NOTE** Event Viewer stores log files in %SystemRoot%\System32\Config.

Incidence Reporting

Once you've gathered data about a particular system or you've dealt with a computer or network problem, you need to complete the mission by telling your supervisor. This is called *incidence reporting*. Many companies have pre-made forms that you simply fill out and submit. Other places are less formal. Regardless, you need to do this!

Incidence reporting does a couple of things for you. First, it provides a record of work you've accomplished. Second, it provides a piece of information that, when combined with other information you might or might not know, reveals a pattern or bigger problem to someone higher up the chain. A seemingly innocuous security audit report, for example, might match other such events in numerous places in the building at the same time and thus show that conscious, coordinated action rather than a glitch was at work.

Evidence Handling

As a tech, you'll need to deal with people who use company computers in prohibited ways. In most cases, you're not paid to be the police and should not get involved. There are times, however, where something bad—really bad—takes place on one of the systems you support, and if you're the first tech person there, everyone is going to turn to you for action.

 EXAM TIP Look for evidence handling questions on the 220-801 exam.

A technician should ignore personal information in and around a person's computer. As mentioned back in Chapter 2, you should treat anything said to you and anything you see as a personal confidence, not to be repeated to customers, coworkers, or bosses. Here's Mike's Rule of Confidentiality: "Unless it's a felony or an imminent physical danger, you didn't see nothin'." This includes any confidential customer materials. Try not to look at anything that isn't directly related to your job. (Sometimes that's impossible, but limit your exposure.) If you're waiting on a printout at a printer and suddenly there's a bunch of printed pages coming out of the printer with employee payroll information, set it to the side and pretend you never saw it.

But what about the scary stuff? Obvious espionage? Pornography? People passing out personal information? Hacking? In these cases, you've just become the first line of defense and you need to act accordingly. Let's address the objectives as listed by CompTIA for the 220-801 exam.

Identify the Action or Content as Prohibited Use common sense, but keep in mind that most organizations have an Acceptable Use Policy that employees must sign. The Acceptable Use Policy defines what actions employees may or may not perform on company equipment. Remember that these polices aren't just for obvious issues such as using a computer for personal use. These policies cover computers, phones, printers, and even the network itself. This policy will define the handling of passwords, e-mail, and many other issues.

 NOTE The SANS Institute provides an excellent boilerplate Acceptable Use Policy on their Web site: www.sans.org/security-resources/policies/Acceptable_Use_Policy.pdf.

Report Through Proper Channels In most cases, you'll report any prohibited actions or content directly to your supervisor. There's also a chance your company will have a security officer or incident response leader who you'll contact instead. Do *not* speak to the person committing the infraction unless your supervisor approves that contact.

Data/Device Preservation You might end up in a situation serious enough that a computer or other device becomes evidence. In these cases, the location of the system and who has touched it may come into question, so you need to establish a *chain of custody*: a

documented history of who has been in possession of the system. You'll hopefully have a legal expert to guide you, but the following are fairly common rules:

1. Isolate the system. Shut down the system and store it in a place where no one else can access it.

2. Document when you took control of the system and the actions you took: shutting it down, unplugging it, moving it, and so on. Don't worry about too much detail, but you must track its location.

3. If another person takes control of the system, document the transfer of custody.

802

Network Security

Networks are under threat from the outside as well, so this section looks at issues involving Internet-borne attacks, firewalls, and wireless networking. This content is the security bread and butter for a CompTIA A+ technician, so you need to understand the concepts and procedures and be able to implement them properly.

Malicious Software

The beauty of the Internet is the ease of accessing resources just about anywhere on the globe, all from the comfort of your favorite chair. This connection, however, runs both ways, and people from all over the world can potentially access your computer from the comfort of their evil lairs. The Internet is awash with malicious software that is, even at this moment, trying to infect your systems.

The term *malware* defines any program or code (macro, script, and so on) that's designed to do something on a system or network that you don't want done. Malware comes in quite a variety of guises, such as grayware, spam, viruses, worms, macros, Trojan horses, and rootkits. Let's examine all these malware flavors and then explore how to deal with them.

Grayware

Programs that intrude unwanted into your computing experience but don't actually do any damage to your systems or data—what's called *grayware*—can make that computing experience less than perfect. On most systems, the Internet Web browser client is the most often used piece of software. Over the years, Web sites have come up with more and more ways to try to get you to see what they want you to see: their advertising. When the Web first got underway, we were forced to look at an occasional banner ad. In the past few years, Web site designers have become much more sophisticated, creating a number of intrusive and irritating ways to get you to part with your money in one form or another.

There are basically two irritating grayware types: pop-ups and spyware. *Pop-ups* are those surprise browser windows that appear automatically when you visit a Web site, proving themselves irritating and unwanted and nothing else. *Spyware*, meanwhile, defines a family of programs that run in the background on your PC, sending information about your browsing habits to the company that installed it on your system. Of the two, spyware is much less noticeable but far more nefarious.

NOTE The term *adware* generally refers to programs that support themselves using revenue from ads, like all those "free" Internet game sites. Every once in a while those ads can lead to spyware installing on a system, making many authors lump adware into the grayware category.

Pop-Ups Getting rid of pop-ups is actually rather tricky. You've probably noticed that most of these pop-up browser windows don't look like browser windows at all. They have no menu bar, button bar, or address window, yet they are separate browser windows. HTML coding permits Web site and advertising designers to remove the usual navigation aids from a browser window so all you're left with is the content. In fact, as I'll describe in a minute, some pop-up browser windows are deliberately designed to mimic similar pop-up alerts from the Windows OS. They might even have buttons similar to Windows' own exit buttons, but you might find that when you click them, you wind up with more pop-up windows instead! What to do?

The first thing you need to know when dealing with pop-ups is how to close them without actually having to risk clicking them. As I said, most pop-ups have removed all navigation aids, and many are also configured to appear on your monitor screen in a position that places the browser window's exit button—the little *X* button in the upper-right corner—outside of your visible screen area. Some even pop up behind the active browser window and wait there in the background. Most annoying! To remedy this, use alternate means to close the pop-up browser window. For instance, you can right-click the browser window's taskbar icon to generate a pop-up menu of your own. Select Close, and the window should go away. You can also press ALT-TAB to bring the browser window in question to the forefront and then press ALT-F4 to close it.

Most Web browsers have features to prevent pop-up ads in the first place, but I've found that these types of applications are sometimes *too* thorough. That is, they tend to prevent *all* new browser windows from opening, even those you want to view. Applications such as AdSubtract control a variety of Internet annoyances, including pop-up windows, cookies, and Java applets, and are more configurable—you can specify what you want to allow on any particular domain address—but the fully functional versions usually cost at least something, and that much control is too confusing for most novice-level users.

Spyware Some types of spyware go considerably beyond grayware's level of intrusion. They can use your computer's resources to run *distributed computing* applications, capture your keystrokes to steal passwords, reconfigure your dial-up settings to use a different phone number at a much higher connection charge, or even use your Internet

connection and e-mail address list to propagate itself to other computers in a virus-like fashion! Are you concerned yet?

Setting aside the legal and ethical issues—and there are many—you should at least appreciate that spyware can seriously impact your PC's performance and cause problems with your Internet connection. The threat is real, so what practical steps can you take to protect yourself? Let's look at how to prevent spyware installation and how to detect and remove any installed spyware.

How does this spyware get into your system in the first place? Obviously, sensible people don't download and install something that they know is going to compromise their computers. Makers of spyware know this, so they bundle their software with some other program or utility that purports to give you some benefit.

What kind of benefit? In 2005, Movieland (otherwise known as Movieland.com and Popcorn.net) released a "handy" movie download service. They didn't tell users, of course, that everyone who installed the software was "automatically enrolled" in a three-day trial. If you didn't cancel the "trial," a pop-up window filled your screen demanding you pay them for the service that you never signed up for. The best part, however, was that you couldn't uninstall the application completely. The uninstaller redirected users to a Web page demanding money again. (Movieland was shut down in 2007.) As you can see, spyware doesn't need to force its way into a PC. Instead, it saunters calmly through the front door.

Another popular spyware method is to use pop-up browser windows crudely disguised as Windows' own system warnings (see Figure 29-18). When clicked, these may trigger a flood of other browser windows, or may even start a file download.

Figure 29-18 A spyware pop-up browser window, disguised as a Windows alert

If Movieland was a problem back in 2005, what are the big spyware applications today? Unfortunately, I can't tell you—not because it's a secret, but because we don't know about them yet. Look at Figure 29-19: the dialog box asks the user if she trusts the Gator Corporation (a well-known spyware producer from several years ago). Because everyone eventually knew not to trust Gator, they would click No, and the company faded away several years ago. Gator, however, was incredibly well-known at the time. What about those small, unknown applications waiting in the dark corners of the Internet—the ones that just might have spyware hiding inside? How do you protect yourself from them?

Figure 29-19

Gator Corporation's acknowledgment warning

The lesson here is simple: *Don't install these programs*, at least not without researching the program first. Careful reading of the software's license agreement before you install a program is a good idea, but realistically, it does little to protect your PC. With that in mind, here are a couple of preventive measures you can take to keep parasitic software off of your system.

If you visit a Web site that prompts you to install a third-party application or plug-in that you've never heard of, *don't install it*. Well-known and reputable plug-ins, such as Adobe's Shockwave or Flash, are safe, but be suspicious of any others. Don't click *anywhere* inside of a pop-up browser window, even if it looks just like a Windows alert window or DOS command-line prompt—as I just mentioned, it's probably fake and the Close button is likely a hyperlink. Instead, use other means to close the window, such as pressing ALT-F4 or right-clicking the browser window's icon on the taskbar and selecting Close.

You can also install spyware detection and removal software on your system and run it regularly. Let's look at how to do that.

Some spyware makers are reputable enough to include a routine for uninstalling their software. Gator, for instance, made it fairly easy to get rid of their programs; you just used the Windows Add/Remove Programs or Programs and Features applet in the Control Panel. Others, however, aren't quite so cooperative. In fact, because spyware is

so—well, *sneaky*—it's entirely possible that your system already has some installed that you don't even know about. How do you discover it?

Windows comes with Windows Defender, a fine tool for catching most spyware, but it's not perfect. The better solution is to back up Windows Defender with a second spyware removal program. There are several on the market, but two that I highly recommend are Lavasoft's Ad-Aware (see Figure 29-20) and Safer Networking's Spybot Search & Destroy.

Figure 29-20 Lavasoft's Ad-Aware

Both of these applications work exactly as advertised. They detect and delete spyware of all sorts—hidden files and folders, cookies, Registry keys and values, you name it. Ad-Aware is free for personal use, while Spybot Search & Destroy is shareware (see Figure 29-21). Many times I've used both programs at the same time because one tends to catch what the other misses.

> **TIP** If you haven't done this already, do it now. Go to www.safer-networking .org and download the latest copy of Spybot Search & Destroy. Install it on your computer and run it. Did it find any spyware that slipped in past your defenses?

Spam

E-mail that comes into your Inbox from a source that's not a friend, family member, or colleague, and that you didn't ask for, can create huge problems for your computer and you. This unsolicited e-mail, called *spam*, accounts for a huge percentage of traffic

on the Internet. Spam comes in many flavors, from legitimate businesses trying to sell you products to scammers who just want to take your money. Hoaxes, pornography, and get-rich-quick schemes pour into the Inboxes of most e-mail users. They waste your time and can easily offend.

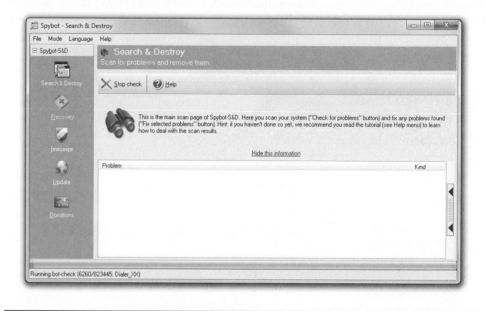

Figure 29-21 Spybot Search & Destroy

You can use several options to cope with the flood of spam. The first option is defense. Never post your e-mail address on the Internet. One study tested this theory and found that *over 97 percent* of the spam received during the study went to e-mail addresses they had posted on the public Internet.

Filters and filtering software can block spam at your mail server and at your computer. Google Mail has powerful blocking schemes, for example, that drop the average spam received by its subscribers by a large percentage, usually more than 90 percent. You can set most e-mail programs to block e-mail from specific people—good to use if someone is harassing you—or to specific people. You can block by subject line or keywords. Most people use a third-party antispam program instead of using the filters in their e-mail program.

A lot of spam contains malware or points to dangerous Web sites. Never click on any link or open an e-mail from someone you don't know! You might just save your computer.

Spam is also notorious for phishing scams. Phishing works by sending you an e-mail message that looks legitimate, like a bill or account information, hoping you will enter important personal information. If you receive an e-mail from Amazon.com, ebay. com, or some other site (like your bank), don't click on it! Like Admiral Ackbar said in *Star Wars*, "It's a trap!"

Virus

A *virus* is a program that has two jobs: to replicate and to activate. *Replication* means it makes copies of itself, often as code stored in boot sectors or as extra code added to the end of executable programs. *Activation* is when a virus does something like erase the boot sector of a drive. A virus only replicates to other drives, such as thumb drives or optical media. It does not replicate across networks. Plus, a virus needs human action to spread.

Worm

A *worm* functions similarly to a virus, though it replicates exclusively through networks. A worm, unlike a virus, doesn't have to wait for someone to use a removable drive to replicate. If the infected computer is on a network, a worm will immediately start sending copies of itself to any other computers on the network it can locate. Worms can exploit inherent flaws in program code like *buffer overflows*, where a buffer cannot hold all the data sent to it.

Macro

A *macro* is any type of virus that exploits application macros to replicate and activate. A *macro* is also programming within an application that enables you to control aspects of the application. Macros exist in any application that has a built-in macro language, such as Microsoft Excel, that users can program to handle repetitive tasks (among other things).

Trojan Horse

A *Trojan horse* is a piece of malware that looks or pretends to do one thing while, at the same time, doing something evil. A Trojan horse may be a game, like poker, or a free screensaver. The sky is the limit. The more "popular" Trojan horses turn an infected computer into a server and then open TCP or UDP ports so a remote user can control the infected computer. Trojan horses can be used to capture keystrokes, passwords, files, credit card information, and more. Trojan horses do not replicate.

Rootkit

For a virus or Trojan horse to succeed, it needs to come up with some method to hide itself. As awareness of malware has grown, anti-malware programs make it harder to find new locations on a computer to hide malware. A *rootkit* is a Trojan horse that takes advantage of very low-level operating system functions to hide itself from all but the most aggressive of anti-malware tools. Worse, a rootkit, by definition, gains privileged access to the computer. Rootkits can strike operating systems, hypervisors, and even firmware.

The most infamous rootkit appeared a few years ago as an antipiracy attempt by Sony on its music CDs. Unfortunately for the media giant, the rootkit software installed when you played a music CD and opened a backdoor that could be used for malicious intent.

Malware Signs and Symptoms

If your PC has been infected by malware, you'll bump into some strange things before you can even run an anti-malware scan. Like a medical condition, malware causes unusual symptoms that should stand out from your everyday computer use. You need to become a PC physician and understand what each of these symptoms means.

Malware's biggest strength is its flexibility: it can look like anything. In fact, a lot of malware attacks can feel like normal PC "wonkiness"—momentary slowdowns, random one-time crashes, and so on. Knowing when a weird application crash is actually a malware attack is half the battle.

A slow PC can mean you're running too many applications at once or you've been hit with malware. How do you tell the difference? In this case, it's the frequency. If it's happening a lot, even when all of your applications are closed, you've got a problem. This goes for frequent lockups, too. If Windows starts misbehaving (more than usual), run your anti-malware application right away.

Malware, however, doesn't always jump out at you with big system crashes. Some malware tries to rename system files, change file permissions, or hide files completely. Most of these issues are easily caught by a regular anti-malware scan, so as long as you remain vigilant, you'll be okay.

 EXAM TIP While it's not necessarily a malware attack, watch out for hijacked e-mail accounts, too, belonging either to you or to someone you know. Hackers can hit both e-mail clients and Webmail users. If you start receiving some fishy (or phishy) e-mail messages, change your Webmail user name and password or scan your PC for malware.

Some malware even fights back, defending itself from your many attempts to remove it. If your Windows Update feature stops working, preventing you from patching your PC, you've got malware. If other tools and utilities throw up an "Access Denied" road block, you've got malware. If you lose all Internet connectivity, either the malware is stopping you or removing the malware broke your connection. In this case, you might need to reconfigure your Internet connection: reinstall your NIC and its drivers, reboot your router, and so on.

Even your browser and anti-malware applications can turn against you. If you type in one Web address and end up at a different site than you anticipated, a malware infection might have overwritten your HOSTS file. The HOSTS file overrules any DNS settings and can redirect your browser to whatever site the malware adds to the file. Most browser redirections point you to phishing scams or Web sites full of free downloads (that are, of course, covered in malware). In fact, some free anti-malware applications are actually malware—what techs call a *rogue anti-malware* program. You can avoid these rogue applications by sticking to the recommended lists of anti-malware software found online.

Watch for security alerts in Windows, either from Windows' built-in security tools or from your third-party anti-malware program. Windows XP (SP2 and later) and Windows Vista include the Security Center, a Control Panel applet that monitors your software firewall, automatic updates, malware protection, and more. Windows 7 includes a similar

tool, but calls it the Action Center, which you learned about back in Chapter 19 (see Figure 29-22). You don't actually configure much using these applets; they just tell you whether or not you are protected. Both of these tools place an icon and pop up a notification in the notification area whenever Windows detects a problem. Windows XP and Vista use a red shield with a white × to notify you, while Windows 7 uses a white flag.

Figure 29-22 Windows 7 Action Center

Malware Prevention and Recovery

The only way to protect your PC permanently from getting malware is to disconnect it from the Internet and never permit any potentially infected software to touch your precious computer. Because neither scenario is likely these days, you need to use specialized anti-malware programs to help stave off the inevitable assaults. Even with the best anti-malware tools, there are times when malware still manages to strike your computer. When you discover infected systems, you need to know how to stop the spread of the malware to other computers, how to fix infected computers, and how to remediate (restore) the system as close to its original state as possible.

Dealing with Malware

You can deal with malware in several ways: anti-malware programs, training and awareness, patch management, and remediation.

At the very least, every computer should run an anti-malware program. If possible, add an appliance that runs anti-malware programs against incoming data from your

network. Also remember that an anti-malware program is only as good as its updates—keep everyone's definition file (explained a bit later) up to date with, literally, nightly updates! Users must be trained to look for suspicious ads, programs, and pop-ups, and understand that they must not click these things. The more you teach users about malware, the more aware they'll be of potential threats. Your organization should have policies and procedures in place so everyone knows what to do if they encounter malware. Finally, a good tech maintains proper incident response records to see if any pattern to attacks emerges. He or she can then adjust policies and procedures to mitigate these attacks.

EXAM TIP One of the most important malware mitigation procedures is to keep systems under your control patched and up to date through proper *patch management.* Microsoft does a very good job of putting out bug fixes and patches as soon as problems occur. If your systems aren't set up to update automatically, then perform manual updates regularly.

Anti-Malware Programs

An *anti-malware program* such as a classic *antivirus program* protects your PC in two ways. It can be both sword and shield, working in an active seek-and-destroy mode and in a passive sentry mode. When ordered to seek and destroy, the program scans the computer's boot sector and files for viruses and, if it finds any, presents you with the available options for removing or disabling them. Antivirus programs can also operate as *virus shields* that passively monitor a computer's activity, checking for viruses only when certain events occur, such as a program executing or a file being downloaded.

NOTE The term *antivirus* (and antispyware, or anti-anything) is becoming obsolete. Viruses are only a small component of the many types of malware. Many people continue to use the term as a synonym for anti-malware.

Antivirus programs use different techniques to combat different types of viruses. They detect boot sector viruses simply by comparing the drive's boot sector to a standard boot sector. This works because most boot sectors are basically the same. Some antivirus programs make a backup copy of the boot sector. If they detect a virus, the programs use that backup copy to replace the infected boot sector. Executable viruses are a little more difficult to find because they can be on any file in the drive. To detect executable viruses, the antivirus program uses a library of signatures. A *signature* is the code pattern of a known virus. The antivirus program compares an executable file to its library of signatures. There have been instances where a perfectly clean program coincidentally held a virus signature. Usually the antivirus program's creator provides a patch to prevent further alarms. Now that you understand the types of viruses and how antivirus programs try to protect against them, let's review a few terms that are often used when describing certain traits of viruses.

Polymorphic/Polymorphs A *polymorph virus* attempts to change its signature to prevent detection by antivirus programs, usually by continually scrambling a bit of useless code. Fortunately, the scrambling code itself can be identified and used as the signature—once the antivirus makers become aware of the virus. One technique used to combat unknown polymorphs is to have the antivirus program create a checksum on every file in the drive. A *checksum* in this context is a number generated by the software based on the contents of the file rather than the name, date, or size of that file. The algorithms for creating these checksums vary among different antivirus programs (they are also usually kept secret to help prevent virus makers from coming up with ways to beat them). Every time a program is run, the antivirus program calculates a new checksum and compares it with the earlier calculation. If the checksums are different, it is a sure sign of a virus.

Stealth The term "stealth" is more of a concept than an actual virus function. Most *stealth virus* programs are boot sector viruses that use various methods to hide from antivirus software. The AntiEXE stealth virus hooks on to a little-known but often-used software interrupt, for example, running only when that interrupt runs. Others make copies of innocent-looking files.

Recommended Anti-Malware Programs You can download many excellent anti-malware programs for free, either for extended trial periods or for indefinite use. Since you need these programs to keep your systems happy, download one or more anti-malware programs, such as the following:

- **Windows Defender** Windows Defender is a good antispyware program, but it won't protect you against any other form of malware. It's free with Windows, however, and better than nothing.

- **Microsoft Security Essentials** Recognizing the shortcomings of Windows Defender and no longer willing to count on users to download and install third-party programs, Microsoft offers a complete anti-malware solution called Microsoft Security Essentials. You can download this program for free from Microsoft (search for Microsoft Security Essentials). This program automatically shuts off Windows Defender when installed.

- **Malwarebytes Anti-Malware (www.malwarebytes.org)** Malwarebytes' Anti-Malware program rocks the house in terms of dealing with malicious software. They offer both a free version that scans your computer for malware and quarantines it and a PRO version that actively protects against any incoming malware. Anti-Malware is my first choice in dealing with malware on a client's computer.

- **Lavasoft Ad-Aware (www.lavasoft.com)** Ad-Aware is an excellent antispyware program. Ad-Aware will root out all sorts of files and programs that can cause your computer to run slowly (or worse).

- **Spybot Search & Destroy (www.safer-networking.org)** Spybot Search & Destroy from Safer Networking Ltd. is another superb antispyware program.

Many folks use both Ad-Aware and Spybot—though sometimes the two programs detect each other as spyware!

- **AVG Anti-Virus (http://free.avg.com)** AVG offers a free version of their antivirus software for noncommercial use. Updated regularly to add the latest virus signatures, the software will keep your system clean and bug free.

User Education

A powerful tool to prevent malware attacks and to reduce the impact of malware attacks when they happen is to educate your users. Teach users to be cautious of incoming e-mail they don't clearly recognize and to never click on an attachment or URL in an e-mail unless they are 100 percent certain of the source.

Explain to users the dangers of going to questionable Web sites and teach them how to react when they see questionable actions take place. Let's look at a few of the more evil ones. All Web browsers have built-in attack site warnings like the one shown in Figure 29-23.

Figure 29-23 Attack site warning

 NOTE Mozilla provides a sample Web site that displays the attack site sign—a great way to show users what it looks like: www.mozilla.org/firefox/its-an-attack.html.

Nobody wants their systems infected with malware. Users are motivated and happy when you give them the skills necessary to protect themselves. The bottom line is that educated and aware users will make your life a lot easier.

Malware Prevention Tips

The secret to preventing damage from a malicious software attack is to keep from getting malware on your system in the first place. As discussed earlier, for example, all good antivirus programs include a virus shield that scans e-mail, downloads, running programs, and so on automatically (see Figure 29-24).

Figure 29-24

A virus shield
in action

Use your antivirus shield. It is also a good idea to scan PCs daily for possible virus attacks. All antivirus programs include terminate-and-stay resident programs (TSRs) that run every time the PC is booted. Last but not least, know the source of any software before you load it. Although the chance of commercial, shrink-wrapped software having a virus is virtually nil (there have been a couple of well-publicized exceptions), that copy of *Call of Duty: Modern Warfare 3* you borrowed from a local hacker should definitely be inspected with care.

Keep your antivirus and anti-malware programs updated. New viruses and other malware appear daily, and your programs need to know about them. The list of virus signatures your antivirus program can recognize, for example, is called the *definition file*, and you must keep that definition file up to date so your antivirus software has the latest signatures. Fortunately, most antivirus programs update themselves automatically. Further, you should periodically update the core anti-malware software programming—called the *engine*—to employ the latest refinements the developers have included.

Boot CD Anti-Malware Tools

If you run anti-malware software and your computer still gets infected, especially after a reboot, you need a more serious anti-malware tool. Many anti-malware companies

provide bootable CDs or flash drives (or show you how to make one) that enable you to boot from a known-clean OS and run the same anti-malware software, but this time not corrupted by the malware on your system.

Malware Recovery Tips

When the inevitable happens and either your computer or one of your user's computers gets infected by malware such as a computer virus, you need to follow certain steps to stop the problem from spreading and get the computer back up safely into service. Try this five-step process.

1. Recognize
2. Quarantine
3. Search and destroy
4. Remediate
5. Educate

Recognize and Quarantine The first step is to identify and recognize that a potential malware outbreak has occurred. If you're monitoring network traffic and one computer starts spewing e-mail, that's a good sign. Or users might complain that a computer that was running snappily the day before seems very sluggish.

Many networks employ software such as the open source PacketFence that automatically monitors network traffic and can cut a machine off the network if that machine starts sending suspicious packets. You can also quarantine a computer manually, by disconnecting the network cable. Once you're sure the machine isn't capable of infecting others, you're ready to find the virus or other malware and get rid of it.

At this point, you should disable System Restore. If you make any changes going forward, you don't want the virus to be included in any saved restore points. To turn off System Restore in Windows XP, open the Start menu, right-click on My Computer, and select Properties. Switch to the System Restore tab and select Turn off System Restore. On the dialog box that pops up, confirm your selection by clicking Yes. To turn off System Restore in Windows Vista/7, open the Start menu, right-click on Computer, and select Properties. Click on the *System protection* link. In the Protection Settings section, select a drive and click on Configure. In the System Protection dialog box that opens, select *Turn off system protection*. Repeat the procedure for each hard drive on your Windows Vista/7 system.

Search and Destroy Once you've isolated the infected computer (or computers), you need to get to a safe boot environment and run anti-malware software. You can try Windows Safe Mode first, because it doesn't require anything but a reboot. If that doesn't work, or you suspect a boot sector virus, you need to turn to an external bootable source, such as a bootable CD or flash memory drive.

Get into the habit of keeping around a bootable anti-malware flash drive or optical media. If you suspect a virus or other malware, use the disc, even if your anti-malware program claims to have eliminated the problem. Turn off the PC and reboot it from the anti-malware disc. (You might have to change CMOS settings to boot to optical

media.) This will put you in a clean boot environment that you know is free from any boot sector viruses. If you only support fairly recent computers, most have an option to boot to a USB flash drive, so you can put a boot environment on a thumb drive for even faster start-up speeds.

You have several options for creating the bootable optical disc or flash drive. First, some antivirus software comes in a bootable version, such as the avast! Virus Cleaner Tool (see Figure 29-25).

Figure 29-25

avast! Virus Cleaner Tool

Second, you can download a copy of Linux that offers a live CD option such as Ubuntu. With a live CD, you boot to the CD and install a complete working copy of the operating system into RAM, never touching or accessing the hard drive, to give you full Internet-ready access to many online anti-malware sites. (You'll obviously need Internet access for those tools.) Kaspersky Labs provides a nice option at www.kaspersky.com.

Finally, you can download and burn a copy of the Ultimate Boot CD. It comes stocked with several antivirus and anti-malware programs, so you wouldn't need any other tool. Find it at www.ultimatebootcd.com. The only downside is that the anti-malware engines will quickly be out of date, as will their malware libraries.

EXAM TIP CompTIA considers the process of removing a virus part of the remediation step. Since you can't remediate a PC until after a virus is gone, I've laid out the steps as you see here.

Remediate Malware infections can do a lot of damage to a system, especially to sensitive files needed to load Windows, so you might need to remediate formerly infected systems after cleaning off the drive or drives. *Remediation* simply means that

you fix things the virus or other malware harmed. This can mean replacing corrupted Windows Registry files or even startup files.

If you can't start Windows after the malware scan is finished, you need to follow the steps outlined in Chapter 19 to boot to the Recovery Console in Windows XP, or boot from the Windows Preinstallation Environment into the Windows Recovery Environment in Windows Vista or Windows 7.

In the Windows XP Recovery Console, you'll have access to tools to repair the boot sector (or *boot blocks*, as CompTIA calls them) through the fixmbr and fixboot commands. You can run bootcfg to rebuild a corrupted boot.ini file.

With the Windows Vista/7 Recovery Environment, you have access to more repair tools, such as Startup Repair, System Restore, Windows Complete PC Restore (System Image Recovery in Windows 7), and the command prompt (see Figure 29-26). Run the appropriate option for the situation and you should have the machine properly remediated in a jiffy.

 EXAM TIP Remember to re-enable System Restore and create a new restore point once the system has been repaired.

Figure 29-26 System Recovery options in Windows Vista

Educate The best way to keep from having to deal with malware and grayware is education. It's your job as the IT person to talk to users, especially the ones whose systems you've just spent the last hour cleaning of nasties, about how to avoid these programs. Show them samples of dangerous e-mails they should not open, Web sites to avoid, and the types of programs they should not install and use on the network. Any user who understands the risks of questionable actions on their computers will usually do the right thing and stay away from malware.

Finally, have your users run antivirus and antispyware programs regularly. Schedule them while interfacing with the user so you know it will happen.

Firewalls

Firewalls are an essential tool in the fight against malicious programs on the Internet. *Firewalls* are devices or software that protect an internal network from unauthorized access to and from the Internet at large. Firewalls use a number of methods to protect networks, such as hiding IP addresses and blocking TCP/IP ports.

A typical network uses one of two types of firewalls: *hardware firewalls*, often built into routers, and *software firewalls* that run on your computers. Both types of firewall protect your computer and your network. You also run them at the same time. Let's look at both a typical SOHO router's firewall features and your computer's software firewall to see how they protect your network and your computers.

Hardware Firewall Settings

Most SOHO networks use a hardware firewall, often as a feature built into a router like the Linksys model you saw back in Chapter 24, shown in Figure 29-27. A hardware firewall hides and separates your internal LAN from outside connections like the Internet by using Network Address Translation (NAT), which you learned about back in Chapter 24. Routers, however, have a few other tricks up their sleeves. From the router's browser-based settings screen, you can configure a hardware firewall (see Figure 29-28). Let's walk through a few of the available settings.

Figure 29-27

Linksys router
as a firewall

A hardware firewall watches for and stops many common threats—all you have to do is turn it on (see Figure 29-29). Hardware firewalls use *Stateful Packet Inspection (SPI)* to inspect each incoming packet individually. SPI also blocks any incoming traffic that isn't in response to your outgoing traffic. You can even disable ports entirely, blocking all traffic in or out. But what if you want to allow outside users access to a Web server on the LAN? Because NAT hides the true IP address of that system, you'll need a way to allow incoming traffic past the router/firewall and a way to redirect that traffic to the right PC.

Figure 29-28 Default Web interface

Figure 29-29 SPI firewall settings

Port forwarding enables you to open a port in the firewall and direct incoming traffic on that port to a specific IP address on your LAN. In the case of the Web server referenced in the previous paragraph, you would open port 80 (for HTTP packets) and instruct the router to send all incoming traffic to the server machine. Figure 29-30 shows port forwarding configured to send all HTTP packets to an internal Web server.

Figure 29-30 Port forwarding

Port forwarding isn't the only way to open ports on a firewall. *Port triggering* enables you to open an incoming connection to one computer automatically based on a specific outgoing connection. The *trigger port* defines the outgoing connection, and the *destination port* defines the incoming connection. If you set the trigger port to 3434 and the destination port to 1234, for example, any outgoing traffic on port 3434 will trigger the router to open port 1234 and send any received data back to the PC with the original outgoing traffic. Figure 29-31 shows a router set up for port triggering of an Internet Relay Chat (IRC) server.

Figure 29-31 Port triggering

If you want to go beyond port forwarding and port triggering and open every port on a machine, you need a demilitarized zone (DMZ). A DMZ puts systems with the specified IP addresses outside the protection of the firewall, opening all ports and enabling all incoming traffic (see Figure 29-32). If you think this sounds incredibly dangerous, you are right! Any PC inside the DMZ will be completely exposed to outside attacks. Don't use it!

Software Firewalls

While a hardware firewall does a lot to protect you from outside intruders, you should also use a software firewall, such as the firewalls built into each version of Windows, called (appropriately) Windows Firewall. Windows Firewall handles the heavy lifting of port blocking, security logging, and more.

You can access Windows Firewall in Windows XP by opening the Windows Firewall applet in the Control Panel. The Windows XP's Windows Firewall applet (see Figure 29-33) looks a lot different from the one available in Windows 7 (see Figure 29-34), though their primary function remains the same. Configuring Windows Firewall involves turning it on or off, and choosing which programs and services can pass through the firewall, known as *exceptions*. If you wanted to play *Starcraft 2* (a PC game that requires an Internet connection), for example, it would need to be on the list of exceptions for your firewall—most programs you install add themselves to this list

automatically, otherwise Windows Firewall prompts you the first time you run it and asks if you want to add the program as an exception.

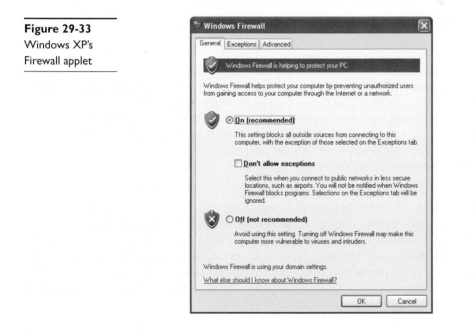

Figure 29-32 DMZ set up on a SOHO router

Figure 29-33
Windows XP's
Firewall applet

Figure 29-34 Windows 7 Firewall applet

EXAM TIP To turn Windows Firewall off (which I don't recommend doing), open the Windows Firewall applet. In Windows XP, click on the *Off (not recommended)* radio button. In Windows Vista, click on *Turn Windows Firewall on or off*, then select *Off (not recommended)*. In Windows 7, select *Turn Windows Firewall on or off*, then select *Turn off Windows Firewall (not recommended)* for each network type you use.

The Windows XP firewall's biggest shortcoming is that it fails to consider that a single PC, especially a portable, might connect to multiple networks. You don't necessarily want the same firewall settings used for both public and private networks. Microsoft needed to develop a way for you to separate trustworthy networks (like the one in your house or at the office) from non-trustworthy networks (like a public Wi-Fi Internet connection at the airport). To accomplish this, Microsoft included three network types in Windows Vista/7: Domain, Private, and Public.

- A *Domain* network is a Windows network controlled by a Windows domain controller. In this case, the domain controller itself tells your machine what it can and cannot share. You don't need to do anything when your computer joins a domain.

- A *Private* network enables you to share resources, discover other devices, and allow other devices to discover your computer safely.

- A *Public* network prevents your computer from sharing and disables all discovery protocols.

When your computer connects to a network for the first time, Windows Vista and 7 will prompt you to choose the network type: Home, Work, or Public location (see Figure 29-35).

Figure 29-35 Set Network Location in Vista

First, notice that Domain is not an option. There's a good reason for this: If your computer is on a domain, you won't see the dialog box in Figure 29-35. When your computer joins a domain, Windows automatically sets your network location to Domain (unless your domain controller chooses something different, which is unlikely).

So what exactly does Windows do when you select Home, Work, or Public location? Windows configures Windows Firewall to block or unblock discovery and sharing services. When running on a Private (Home or Work) network, Windows enables Network

Discovery and File and Printer Sharing as exceptions. When running on a Public network, Windows disables these exceptions.

EXAM TIP The Network Discovery setting dictates whether a computer can find other computers or devices on a network and vice versa. Even with Network Discovery activated, several firewall settings can overrule certain connections.

In Windows Vista, Microsoft cleverly used Windows Firewall and the network type to turn services on and off, but Microsoft made one mistake: the firewall configuration and network type remain the same for every connection. If your Windows machine never changes networks, you won't have a problem. But what about machines (mainly laptops) that hop from one network to another (see Figure 29-36)? In that case, you need different firewall settings for each network the system might encounter.

Figure 29-36 Many machines need more than one network setting.

In this regard, Windows 7 makes a big departure from Windows Vista. In Windows 7, the Set Network Location dialog box appears every time you connect to a new network. Windows 7 even includes three different firewall settings: one for Domains, one for Private networks (Home or Work), and one for Public networks.

Once you've picked a network type, you might want to customize the firewall settings further. If you click the Advanced Settings option in Windows Vista/7's Firewall applet, you'll discover a much deeper level of firewall configuration, one very different from the settings found in Windows XP (see Figure 29-37). In fact, it's an entirely different tool called Windows Firewall with Advanced Security.

Microsoft enhanced how Windows Vista/7 treat exceptions. In Windows XP, you can only choose a program and make it an exception, giving it permission to pass through the firewall. But programs both send and receive network data; Windows XP ignores the "inbound" and "outbound" aspect of firewalls. Windows Vista/7 takes the exceptions concept and expands it to include custom rules for both inbound and outbound data. Figure 29-38 shows the outbound rules for a typical Windows Vista/7 system.

Figure 29-37 Windows Firewall with Advanced Security

Figure 29-38 Outbound Rules list

A rule always includes at least the following:

- The name of the program
- Group: an organizational group that helps sort all the rules
- The associated profile (All, Domain, Public, Private)
- Enabled/disabled status
- Remote and local address
- Remote and local port number

You can add, remove, and customize any rule to your liking. It quickly gets complicated, so unless you need to set a lot of custom rules, stick to the standard Windows Firewall applet.

Authentication and Encryption

You know from previous chapters that the first step in securing data is authentication, through a user name and password. But when you throw in networking, you're suddenly not just a single user sitting in front of a computer and typing. You're accessing a remote resource and sending login information over the Internet. What's to stop someone from intercepting your user name and password?

Firewalls do a great job of controlling traffic coming into a network from the Internet and going out of a network to the Internet, but they do nothing to stop interceptor hackers who monitor traffic on the public Internet looking for vulnerabilities. Worse, once a packet is on the Internet itself, anyone with the right equipment can intercept and inspect it. Inspected packets are a cornucopia of passwords, account names, and other tidbits that hackers can use to intrude into your network. Because we can't stop hackers from inspecting these packets, we must turn to *encryption* to make them unreadable.

Network encryption occurs at many levels and is in no way limited to Internet-based activities. Not only are there many levels of network encryption, but each encryption level also provides multiple standards and options, making encryption one of the most complicated of all networking issues. You need to understand where encryption comes into play, what options are available, and what you can use to protect your network.

Network Authentication

Have you ever considered the process that takes place each time a person types in a user name and password to access a network, rather than just a local machine? What happens when this *network* authentication is requested? If you're thinking that when a user types in a user name and password, that information is sent to a server of some sort to be authenticated, you're right—but do you know how the user name and password get to the serving system? That's where encryption becomes important in authentication.

In a local network, authentication and encryption are usually handled by the OS. In today's increasingly interconnected and diverse networking environment, there is a motivation to enable different operating systems to authenticate any client system from any other OS. Modern operating systems such as Windows and Mac OS X use standard authentication encryptions such as MIT's *Kerberos*, enabling multiple brands of servers

to authenticate multiple brands of clients. These LAN authentication methods are usually transparent and work quite nicely, even in mixed networks.

Data Encryption

Encryption methods don't stop at the authentication level. There are a number of ways to encrypt network *data* as well. The choice of encryption method is dictated to a large degree by the method used by the communicating systems to connect. Many networks consist of multiple networks linked together by some sort of private connection, usually some kind of WAN connection such as DSL or T1. Microsoft's encryption method of choice for this type of network is called *IPSec* (derived from *IP security*). IPSec provides transparent encryption between the server and the client. IPSec also works in VPNs, but other encryption methods are more commonly used in those situations.

Application Encryption

When it comes to encryption, even TCP/IP applications can get into the swing of things. The most famous of all application encryptions is Netscape's *Secure Sockets Layer (SSL)* security protocol, which is used to create secure Web sites. Microsoft incorporates SSL into its more far-reaching *HTTPS* (HTTP over SSL) protocol. These protocols make it possible to create the secure Web sites people use to make purchases over the Internet. You can identify HTTPS Web sites by the *https://* (rather than http://) included in the URL (see Figure 29-39).

Figure 29-39 A secure Web site

To make a secure connection, your Web browser and the Web server must encrypt their data. That means there must be a way for both the Web server and your browser to encrypt and decrypt each other's data. To do this, the server sends a public key to your Web browser so the browser knows how to decrypt the incoming data. These public keys are sent in the form of a *digital certificate*. This certificate is signed by a trusted authority that guarantees that the public key you are about to get is actually from the Web server and not from some evil person trying to pretend to be the Web server. A number of companies issue digital certificates to Web sites, probably the most famous being VeriSign, Inc.

Your Web browser has a built-in list of trusted authorities. If a certificate comes in from a Web site that uses one of these highly respected companies, you won't see anything happen in your browser; you'll just go to the secure Web page, where a small lock will appear in the corner of your browser. Figure 29-40 shows the list of trusted authorities built into the Firefox Web browser.

Figure 29-40 Trusted authorities

If you receive a certificate from someone *not* listed in your browser, however, the browser will warn you and ask you if you wish to accept the certificate, as shown in Figure 29-41.

Figure 29-41 Incoming certificate

What you do here is up to you. Do you wish to trust this certificate? In most cases, you simply say yes, and this certificate is added to your SSL cache of certificates. An accepted certificate may become invalid, however, usually because of something boring; for instance, it may go out of date or the public key may change. This never happens with the "big name" certificates built into your browser—you'll see this more often when a certificate is used, for example, in-house on a company intranet and the administrator forgets to update the certificates. If a certificate goes bad, your browser issues a warning the next time you visit that site. To clear invalid certificates, you need to clear the SSL cache. The process varies in every browser, but in Internet Explorer, go to the Content tab under Internet Options and click the *Clear SSL state* button (see Figure 29-42).

Figure 29-42
Internet Options
Content tab in
Internet Explorer

Wireless Issues

Wireless networks add a whole level of additional security headaches for techs to face, as you know from Chapter 23. Some of the points to remember or to go back and look up are as follows:

- Set up wireless encryption, at least WEP but preferably WPA or the more secure WPA2, and configure clients to use it.
- Disable DHCP and require your wireless clients to use a static IP address.
- If you need to use DHCP, only allot enough DHCP addresses to meet the needs of your network, to avoid unused wireless connections.
- Change the WAP's SSID from default.
- Filter by MAC address to allow only known clients on the network.
- Change the default user name and password. Every hacker has memorized the default user names and passwords.
- Update the firmware as needed.
- If available, make sure the WAP's firewall settings are turned on.

Chapter Review

Questions

1. What is the process for using or manipulating people to gain access to network resources?

 A. Cracking

 B. Hacking

 C. Network engineering

 D. Social engineering

2. Which of the following might offer good hardware authentication?

 A. Strong passwords

 B. Encrypted passwords

 C. NTFS

 D. Smart cards

3. Which of the following tools would enable you to stop a user from logging on to a local machine but still enable him to log on to the domain?

 A. AD Policy Filter

 B. Group Policy Auditing

 C. Local Security Policy

 D. User Settings

4. Which hardware firewall feature enables incoming traffic on a specific port to reach an IP address on the LAN?

 A. Port forwarding

 B. NAT

 C. DMZ

 D. Multifactor authentication

5. Zander downloaded a game off the Internet and installed it, but as soon as he started to play, he got a Blue Screen of Death. Upon rebooting, he discovered that his My Documents folder had been erased. What happened?

 A. He installed spyware.

 B. He installed a Trojan horse.

 C. He broke the Group Policy.

 D. He broke the Local Security Policy.

6. Which of the following should Mary set up on her Wi-Fi router to make it the most secure?

 A. NTFS

 B. WEP

 C. WPA

 D. WPA2

7. What tool would you use to enable auditing on a local level?

 A. AD Policy

 B. Group Policy

 C. Local Security Policy

 D. User Settings

8. John dressed up in a fake security guard uniform that matched the uniforms of a company and then walked in with some legitimate employees in an attempt to gain access to company resources. What kind of attack is this?

 A. Administrative access

 B. Data destruction

 C. Spoofing

 D. Tailgating

9. The first day on the job, Jill received a spreadsheet that listed approved software for users and clear instructions not to allow any unapproved software. What kind of policy must she follow?

 A. Classification

 B. Compliance

 C. Group

 D. Security

10. Edna wants to put a policy in place at her company with regard to virus prevention or at least limitation. What policies would offer the best solution?

 A. Install antivirus software on every computer. Teach users how to run it.

 B. Install antivirus software on every computer. Set the software up to scan regularly.

 C. Install antivirus software on every computer. Set the software up to update the definitions and engine automatically. Set the software up to scan regularly.

 D. Install antivirus software on every computer. Set the software up to update the definitions and engine automatically. Set the software up to scan regularly. Educate the users about sites and downloads to avoid.

Answers

1. **D.** Social engineering is the process of using or manipulating people to gain access to network resources.

2. **D.** Smart cards are an example of hardware authentication devices.

3. **C.** You can use Local Security Policy to stop someone from logging on to a local machine.

4. **A.** To open a port on your hardware firewall and send incoming traffic to a specific PC, use port forwarding.

5. **B.** Zander clearly installed a Trojan horse, a virus masquerading as a game.

6. **D.** Mary should set up WPA2 on her Wi-Fi router.

7. **C.** You can enable local auditing through Local Security Policy.

8. **D.** John just practiced tailgating on the unsuspecting company.

9. **B.** Jill needs to enforce compliance to help keep the tech support calls at a minimum and the uptime for users at a maximum.

10. **D.** The best policy includes updating the software engine and definitions, scanning PCs regularly, and educating users.

Answers

1. D, S, and I....

2. Because such an example of both....

3. C. You can use it....

4. A. To attach a port on....

5. D....

6. A....

7. C. You should be an admin on the WCM....

8....

9....

10....

Virtualization

30

In this chapter, you will learn how to
- Describe the concepts of virtualization
- Explain why PC and network administrators have widely adopted virtualization
- Describe how virtualization manifests in modern networks

Virtualization takes your everyday notion of computing and turns it on its head. Left becomes right. Red becomes blue. Physical computers become virtual computers. It might sound complicated—properly configuring a real computer is hard enough—but once you see it in action, it makes perfect sense. In the simplest terms, *virtualization* is the process of using special software—a class of programs called *hypervisors* or *virtual machine managers*—to create a complete environment in which a guest operating system can function as though it were installed on its own computer. That guest environment is called a *virtual machine (VM)*. You learned about one very important virtual machine back in Chapter 19 called Windows XP Mode, which uses a program called Windows Virtual PC to run a virtual Windows XP operating system in Windows 7. Figure 30-1 shows another example: a system running Windows 7 using a program called VMware Workstation to host a virtual machine running Ubuntu Linux.

This chapter begins by explaining the ideas behind virtualization. The chapter then explores the motivating factors behind the widespread adoption of virtualization throughout the IT industry. The chapter concludes with an in-depth look at how modern networks implement virtualization. Some of the details presented here go beyond the CompTIA A+ 220-802 exam, but I include them to help you understand the scope and power of virtualization.

Historical/Conceptual

What Is Virtualization?

Ask 100 people what the term *virtual* means and you'll get a lot of different answers. Most people define *virtual* with words like "fake" or "pretend," but these terms only begin to describe it. Let's try to zero in on virtualization using a term that you've likely heard: *virtual reality*. For most of us, the idea of virtual reality starts with someone wearing headgear and gloves, as shown in Figure 30-2.

You also need to give the virtual machine a name (see Figure 30-11). By default, VMware Workstation uses a simple name. For this overview, accept the default name: Ubuntu. This dialog box also lets you decide where you want to store the files that comprise the virtual machine. Note that VMware uses a folder in the user's Documents folder called Virtual Machines.

Figure 30-11

Entering a VM name and location

New Virtual Machine Wizard

Name the Virtual Machine
What name would you like to use for this virtual machine?

Virtual machine name:

Ubuntu

Location:

C:\Users\mike\Documents\Virtual Machines\Ubuntu

Browse...

The default location can be changed at Edit > Preferences.

< Back Next > Cancel

TIP Use descriptive names for virtual machines. This will save you a lot of confusion when you have multiple VMs on a single hypervisor.

After you've gone through all the configuration screens, you can start using your virtual machine. You can start, stop, pause, add, or remove virtual hardware.

VMware is very convenient; it even configures the boot order in the virtual system setup to boot first from the installation media, making the Ubuntu installation automatic (see Figure 30-12).

After the virtual machine installs, you then treat the VM exactly as though it were a real machine. The only big difference is that VMware replaces CTRL-ALT-DELETE with CTRL-ALT-INSERT. Figure 30-13 shows VMware Workstation with the single VM installed but not running. A VM goes through a POST process just like any computer, as shown in Figure 30-14. If you wish, you can even access a complete virtual system setup utility by pressing the DELETE key just like on a real system.

Figure 30-12 Ubuntu installing into the new virtual machine

Figure 30-13 VMware Workstation with a single VM

Figure 30-14 POST in a virtual machine

Congratulations! You've just installed a *virtual desktop*. Virtual desktops were the first type of popular virtual machines seen in the PC world, championed by VMware and quickly copied by other virtualization programs.

There's a lot more to virtualization than just virtual desktops, however, but before I dive in too far, let's step back a moment and understand a very important question: Why do we virtualize?

Why Do We Virtualize?

Virtualization has taken the computing world by storm, but for those who have never seen virtualization, the big question has got to be: Why? Let's talk about the benefits of virtualization. While you read this section, keep in mind two important things:

- A single hypervisor on a single system will happily run as many virtual machines as its RAM, CPU, and drive space allow.

- A virtual machine that's shut down is little more than a file (or two) sitting on a hard drive.

While you're reading about the benefits of virtualization, don't forget about the costs. To run one or more virtual machines, you'll need a powerful machine—fast processor, loads of RAM (this is usually the limiting factor in how many virtual machines

you can run at the same time), and a good amount of hard drive space. If you want the virtual PC to connect to a network, your physical PC needs a NIC.

 EXAM TIP Virtualized operating systems use the same security features as real operating systems. For each virtual machine user account, you'll need to keep track of user names, passwords, permissions, and so on, just like on a normal PC.

Power Saving

Before virtualization, each installed OS needed to be on a unique physical system. With virtualization, you can place multiple virtual PCs on a single physical system, reducing electrical power use substantially. Rather than one machine running Windows Server 2008 (or Server 2008 R2) and acting as a file server and DNS server, and a second machine running Linux for a DHCP server, for example, the same computer can handle both operating systems simultaneously. Expand this electricity savings over an enterprise network or on a data server farm and the savings—both in terms of dollars spent and electricity used—are tremendous.

Hardware Consolidation

Similar to power saving, why buy a high-end server, complete with multiple processors, RAID arrays, redundant power supplies, and so on, and only run a single server? With virtualization, you can easily beef up the RAM and run a number of servers on a single box.

System Recovery

Possibly the most popular reason for virtualizing is to keep uptime percentage as high as possible. Let's say you have a Web server installed on a single system. If that system goes down—due to hacking, malware, or so on—you need to restore the system from a backup, which may or may not be easily at hand. With virtualization, you merely need to shut down the virtual machine and reload an alternative copy of it.

 CAUTION Rebooting virtual machines is easy, but keep an eye on your physical machine. If your PC goes down, it brings all your virtual machines down with it! Be sure to back up mission-critical virtual machines to an external hard drive— remember that a virtual machine is just a file on your hard drive. You can always install the backed-up virtual machines on another physical machine if necessary.

Think of virtual machines like you would a word processing document. Virtual machines don't have a "File | Save" equivalent, but they do have something called a *snapshot* that enables you to save an extra copy of the virtual machine as it is exactly at the moment the snapshot is taken. Figure 30-15 shows VMware Workstation saving a snapshot.

Figure 30-15 Saving a snapshot

System Duplication

Closely tied to system recovery, system duplication takes advantage of the fact that VMs are simply files, and like any file, they can be copied. Let's say you want to teach 20 students about Ubuntu Linux. Depending on the hypervisor you choose (VMware does this extremely well), you can simply install a hypervisor on 20 machines and copy a single virtual machine to all the computers. Equally, if you have a virtualized Web server and need to add another Web server (assuming your physical box has the hardware to support it), why not just make a copy of the server and fire it up as well?

Research

Here's a great example that happens in my own company. I sell my popular Total Tester test banks: practice questions for you to test your skills on a broad number of certification topics. As with any distributed program, I tend to get a few support calls. Running a problem through the same OS, even down to the service pack, helps me solve the problem. In the days before virtualization, I commonly had seven to ten PCs, using dual-boot, each keeping copies of a particular Windows version. Today, a single hypervisor enables me to support a huge number of Windows versions on a single machine (see Figure 30-16).

Figure 30-16

Lots of VMs used
for research

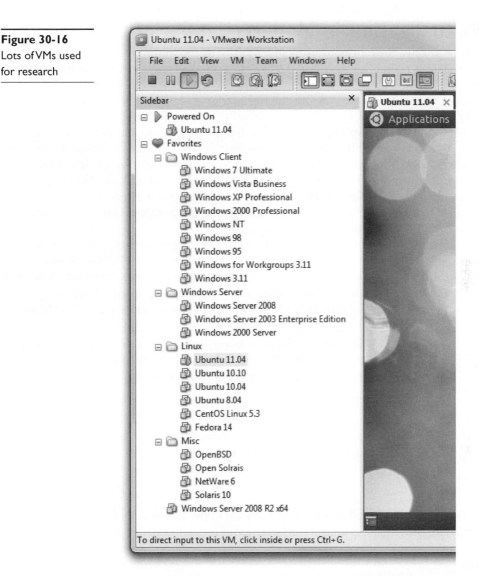

NOTE The system shown in Figure 30-16 could obviously never run all those
VMs at the same time.

Clearly there are a number of good reasons to virtualize some of the computers in a
network. Let's look at implementation now.

Virtualization in Modern Networks

You've already seen virtualization in action with the example shown using VMware Workstation earlier in this chapter. Many networks use a few virtual machines to augment and refine a traditional network closet. VMware Workstation is how I first performed virtualization on PCs, but the technology and power have grown dramatically over the past few years.

VMware Workstation requires an underlying operating system (such as Windows), so it functions essentially like a very powerful desktop application. What if you could remove the OS altogether and create a bare-metal implementation of virtualization?

VMware introduced ESX in 2001 to accomplish this goal. ESX is a hypervisor that's powerful enough to replace the host operating system on a physical box, turning the physical machine into a machine that does nothing but support virtual machines; no Windows, no Ubuntu—just ESX.

ESX by itself isn't much to look at; it's a tiny operating system/hypervisor that's usually installed on something other than a hard drive. Figure 30-17 shows how I loaded my copy of ESX: via a small USB thumb drive. Power up the server; the server loads ESX off the thumb drive; and in short order, a very rudimentary interface appears where I can input essential information, such as a master password and a static IP address.

NOTE For all you abbreviation lovers, I have some good news and some bad news about "ESX." Officially, it means nothing. Unofficially, it stands for "Elastic Sky," which is probably why it officially means nothing.

NOTE A free version of ESX is available. Called ESXi, it lacks a number of ESX's features but is still quite powerful.

Don't let ESX's small size fool you. It's small because it only has one job: to host virtual machines. ESX is an extremely powerful operating system/hypervisor.

NOTE Some writers will use the term *virtual machine manager* to describe virtual machine software that runs on top of a host operating system. They'll use the term *hypervisor* to describe only software that does not need a host operating system. Using this terminology, VMware Workstation is a virtual machine manager and ESX is a hypervisor. Other writers call both the hosted and bare-metal—or *native*—virtualization software products *hypervisors*, but make a distinction in other descriptive words (such as hosted or *native*).

Figure 30-17 USB drive on server system

Notice the built-in USB port shown in Figure 30-17. The popularity of hypervisors on dedicated servers makes these ports extremely common in a serious server box like the Dell system shown.

Powerful hypervisors like ESX are rarely administered directly at the box. Instead you use tools such as VMware's vSphere Client, so you can create, configure, and maintain virtual machines on the hypervisor server from the comfort of a client computer running this program. Once the VM is up and running, you can close the vSphere client, but the VM will continue to run happily on the server. For example, let's say you create a VM and install a Web server on that VM. As long as everything is running well on the Web server, you will find yourself using the vSphere client only to check on the Web server for occasional maintenance and administration.

So you now really have two different ways to virtualize: using virtual machine managers like VMware's Workstation to manage virtual desktops, and using powerful hypervisors like ESX to manage virtual servers. Granted, you could run a server like a Web browser in VMware Workstation, and you also could run a copy of Windows 7 Ultimate from an ESX system. Nothing is wrong with doing either of these.

Thus far, this chapter sounds like an advertisement for VMware. VMware really brought virtualization to the PC world and still holds a strong presence, but there are a number of alternatives to VMware products. Let's see what else is available.

Virtual Machine Managers

When it comes to the more basic virtual machine managers, you have a huge number of choices. The one you use is going to be determined by features and prices.

VMware Workstation

The granddaddy and front leader for virtualization, VMware Workstation, comes in both Windows and Linux versions. VMware Workstation runs virtually (pun!) on any operating system you'll ever need and is incredibly stable and proven. Too bad it's not free.

One of the more interesting features of VMware Workstation is VMTools. VMTools adds useful features such as copy/cut and paste between the virtual desktop and the real desktop.

Virtual PC

Microsoft has offered a few different virtual machine managers over the years, with the current mainstream product being Windows Virtual PC (see Figure 30-18). Windows Virtual PC is free, but has some serious limitations. First, it only works on Windows 7 Professional, Ultimate, and Enterprise. Second, it only officially supports Windows VMs, although a few intrepid souls have managed to get Linux working.

NOTE Remember Windows XP Mode from Chapter 19? It uses Virtual PC and a copy of Windows XP to create a virtual machine on your PC!

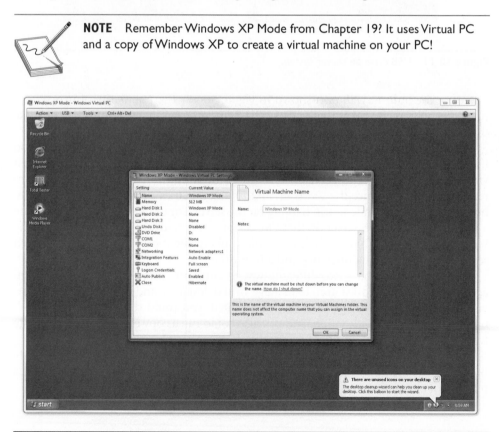

Figure 30-18 Windows Virtual PC

Parallels

Parallels is the most popular virtualization manager for Mac OS X (see Figure 30-19), although VMware Fusion is a close second. Parallels supports all popular operating systems, and even has a fair degree of 3-D graphics support; more so than even the mighty VMware. Parallels also offers Windows and Linux versions.

Figure 30-19 Parallels for Mac

KVM

Of course, the open source world has its players too. While picking a single product to represent the Linux/Unix world is hard, no one who knows virtualization would disagree that KVM from Red Hat is a dominant player. Unlike the other virtual machine managers discussed, KVM also supports a few non-x86 processors.

Don't think for a moment that this list is complete! There are lots of other virtual machine options for your desktop, especially if your host machine runs Linux. The most fun you'll have learning about virtualization is the playtime involved experimenting with the many options available.

Hypervisors

While you have lots of choices when it comes to virtual machine managers, your choices for real embedded hypervisors are limited to the two biggies: VMware's ESX and Microsoft's HyperV. There are others, such as Oracle's VM Server, but nothing has the market share of ESX or HyperV.

ESX

I've already discussed a few aspects of ESX, so instead I'll delve into the features that make ESX so popular. When it comes to real server virtualization, VMware truly leads the pack with a host of innovations (some of which are add-on products) that make ESX almost unstoppable. Here are a few examples:

- **Interface with large storage** ESX virtual machines easily integrate with network attached storage (NAS) and storage area networks (SANs) to handle massive data storage.

- **Transparent fault tolerance** ESX can monitor and automatically recover failed VMs with little or no input.

- **Transparent server transfer** You can move a *running* VM from one machine to another. How cool is that?

- **High virtual CPUs** Most hypervisors support a limited number of virtual CPUs, usually two at most. ESX can support up to 32 CPUs, depending on the vSphere product version you purchase to support it.

HyperV

Although HyperV can't stand toe-to-toe with ESX, it has a few aces up its sleeve that give it some intrigue. First, it's free. This is important in that ESX, with only a few extra add-ons, can cost thousands of dollars. Second, it comes as a stand-alone product or as part of Windows Server 2008 and even on some versions of Windows 7, making it easy for those who like to play to access it. Third, its simplicity makes it easier to learn for those new to using hypervisors. Watch HyperV. If Microsoft does one thing well, it's taking market share away from arguably better, more powerful competitors, while slowly making its product better.

Chapter Review

Questions

1. Upgrading which component of a host machine would most likely enable you to run more virtual machines simultaneously?

 A. CPU

 B. Hard drive

C. RAM

D. Windows

2. What is the difference between a virtual machine (VM) and an emulator?

 A. A VM converts commands to and from a host machine to an entirely different platform, whereas an emulator creates an environment based on the host machine and does no converting.

 B. An emulator converts commands to and from a host machine to an entirely different platform, whereas a VM creates an environment based on the host machine and does no converting.

 C. An emulator requires a host OS, whereas a VM runs on bare-metal servers without an OS.

 D. A VM requires a host OS whereas an emulator runs on bare-metal servers without an OS.

3. What do you make when you save a copy of a VM?

 A. Replacement

 B. Save

 C. Snapshot

 D. Zip

4. What do you need to install a legal copy of Windows 7 Professional into a virtual machine using VMware Workstation?

 A. A valid VM key

 B. A valid Windows 7 Professional installation media

 C. A valid ESX key

 D. A second NIC

5. What is one benefit of ESX over VMware Workstation?

 A. ESX costs less.

 B. ESX is easier to set up.

 C. ESX uses less electricity.

 D. You can move a running VM from one machine to another with ESX.

6. Which of the following is *not* a good reason for virtualization?

 A. Power saving

 B. Hardware consolidation

 C. System recovery

 D. Reduced hardware costs

7. With what does VMware Workstation replace CTRL-ALT-DELETE?

 A. A mouse click

 B. CTRL-ALT-INSERT

 C. CTRL-ALT-TAB

 D. CTRL-ALT-SHIFT

8. Powerful hypervisors like ESX are often booted from _____.

 A. Floppy diskettes

 B. USB thumb drives

 C. Firmware

 D. Windows

9. Which of the following virtualization programs works well with Mac OS X? (Select the best answer.)

 A. ESX

 B. KVM

 C. Parallels

 D. Virtual PC

10. When a virtual machine is not running, how is it stored?

 A. Firmware

 B. RAM drive

 C. Optical disc

 D. Files

Answers

1. **C.** Adding more RAM will enable you to run more simultaneous VMs. Upgrading a hard drive could help, but it's not the best answer here.

2. **B.** An emulator converts from one platform to another, whereas a virtual machine mirrors the host machine.

3. **C.** A copy or saved version of a VM is called a snapshot.

4. **B.** You need a copy of the Windows installation media to install Windows.

5. **D.** Among the many benefits of ESX over its little brother is the capability of moving a running VM from one machine to another.

6. **D.** Switching to virtual machines may or may not save money on hardware. A good virtual machine server can cost a lot more than a series of PCs, but operating costs are reduced.

7. **B.** VMware uses CTRL-ALT-INSERT for logon.

8. **B.** A good hypervisor can be tiny, loading from something as small as a USB thumb drive.

9. **C.** Parallels is the dominant virtualization program for Mac OS X.

10. **D.** VMs are just files, usually stored on a hard drive.

The Right PC for You

In this chapter, you will learn how to
- Research and build a standard thick client
- Customize a professional PC
- Build a specialized consumer PC

Now that you've learned all about PCs, you have the great joy of being able to build the PC of your desire, choose your favorite video card or motherboard, and assemble, from the ground up, the perfect system for you or your client. People will turn to you for advice, too: Which parts do I need? Where should I buy them? What do you think about this?

There's nothing wrong with buying a prebuilt system from a local brick-and-mortar or online store. If you want solid warranties, repair agreements, and so on, Dell or HP can help you out. But off-the-shelf computers aren't for everyone. Your needs or your client's needs might be too specific. In that case, it's time for you to do one of the most fun things a PC tech can do: the custom PC build!

For the first time in the history of the CompTIA A+ exams, CompTIA requires you to understand how to build certain types of PCs. This chapter will help you define these PC types, understand the issues involved in building these computers, and, at the same time, have a little fun.

Because this is a first for CompTIA, the creative team at Total Seminars took extra time to understand what CompTIA was trying to say. In general, we agree with the definitions of the custom configurations with the exception of the following two types. From the 220-801 exam objectives:

> 1.9 Evaluate and select appropriate components for a custom configuration, to meet customer specifications or needs.
>
> - Standard thick client
> - Desktop applications
> - Meets recommended requirements for running Windows
> - Thin client
> - Basic applications
> - Meets minimum requirements for running Windows

I'm not a fan of the term "client." It's outdated. What CompTIA calls a *thick client*, I'd call a *basic desktop*, and instead of a *thin client*, I'd call it a *single-purpose machine* (because that's all a thin client can handle). To CompTIA, the only real separation between a thick client and a thin client is meeting the "recommended" or "minimum" requirements for Windows, respectively. It's oversimplified. Even *that* might be okay, except Microsoft no longer provides minimum requirements for Windows 7. Oh well. We can only guess what CompTIA was thinking.

This chapter begins by explaining how to find the parts for a custom PC—you'll be doing a lot of reading, that's for sure. The rest of the chapter discusses the components you need for each custom build: thick clients, thin clients, virtualization and media workstations, home theater and server PCs, and (best of all) gaming PCs.

801

Building Your First PC

There's almost no better feeling than when you realize you know enough about PCs that you can say: "I think I'm comfortable building my own PC!" If you don't feel ready, let the information in this chapter be that extra push that takes you over the edge.

Building your first PC is both fun and scary. This is the first time you bring together everything you know about hardware. You'll make mistakes, and some brand-new piece of equipment you buy won't work the first time. You'll mount the CPU wrong and the system won't boot. That huge tower case with 23 fans will make too much noise and you'll hate it. But for all these mistakes, don't lose track of the fact that you're building your own PC. Your computer . . . your . . . precious (see Figure 31-1)!

Figure 31-1 Mike holding "Precious," his favorite self-built PC

Evaluating Parts

The most difficult (and most fun) part of buying a PC is picking which parts you want. Knowing which parts to buy for each type of PC is the cornerstone of this entire chapter. Let's take a moment to consider the processes and steps you can use to discover and evaluate the right parts for specific system types.

Read the Reviews

Every component has a review somewhere. Go to Google, type in the name and model number of a part, and add the word "review" at the end. There are two types of reviews: industry reviews written by professionals, and personal reviews written by people who purchased and use the part. Let the Google search I described show you how to the find the professional reviews. Newegg.com is one of my favorite places to read personal reviews.

Read the Fine Print

Learn everything you can about the part. Take some time to read the technical specifications. Check the return and warranty policy of the manufacturer and the retailer. Make sure you have some recourse if the part breaks or doesn't function as advertised.

Compare

Before you buy a part, see what folks say about the competitors' parts. Are there other parts that cost less, have better reviews, or use less power?

Put It in Your Hand

If you're lucky enough to live near a big retailer like Fry's Electronics or Micro Center, get in your car and go check out the part. Look for a display model. Look at the back of the box. See what extra parts are included. Talk to the salespeople about their experiences and the returns they've seen; ask about alternatives they like better.

Thick Client

CompTIA wants to call a general-purpose SOHO computer a *thick client*. Fine—let's have a laugh at the guy wearing the belt and suspenders, and then come up with some guidelines for building a thick client.

Thick clients are general-purpose machines. That means they don't have the fastest drives or the best video cards, but, by the same token, they don't use low-end parts, either. You need to create a platform that will support 90 percent of the folks wanting to use a computer in the home or office.

To begin researching parts for a thick client, look at the recommended hardware requirements for the operating system you intend to use. In this case, I want to install Windows 7 Ultimate 64-bit. I like Ultimate because it gives me the most flexibility, and the extra cost means nothing down the road if I later decide to join a Windows domain.

Here are the recommended system requirements for Windows 7 Ultimate 64-bit edition:

- 1 gigahertz (GHz) or faster 64-bit (x64) processor
- 2 GB RAM
- 20 GB available hard disk space
- DirectX 9 graphics device with WDDM 1.0 or higher driver

See Figure 31-2 for my opinion of the requirements.

Figure 31-2 Mike laughing uncontrollably

You can do a lot better. Here's my opinion of reasonable and modest hardware for a 64-bit thick client. These values aren't on the exam, but they should be.

- 2 GHz or faster 64-bit (x64) processor with at least two cores
- 4 GB RAM
- Blank 500-GB hard disk
- DirectX 11 video card

NOTE You should always go for a 64-bit edition of Windows when building a new PC—why limit yourself?

Size Matters

You can get into all kinds of mental confusion trying to decide how large of a case you want to use, but do yourself a favor and just get a mid-tower. Mid-towers have plenty of drive bays for future expansion without being so massive that they get in the way. A mid-tower will also support almost any motherboard you might choose to install. Take your time finding that perfect case. Unlike manufacturers of most other components, case manufacturers tend to keep making the same case model for many years (see Figure 31-3).

Figure 31-3
My Antec 900 mid-tower (because everything's bigger in Texas)

CPU and Motherboard

You begin the system build by deciding on the CPU/motherboard combination for your new system. I'm not going to tell you to buy an Intel or an AMD CPU. Do your own research and draw your own conclusions. I use plenty of both brands. Because this is a thick client and we don't need the most powerful CPU available, consider the following:

- Get a modern socket. You can get great deals on CPUs that use older sockets, but try to stick to whatever socket is current. This makes it possible to upgrade the CPU in the future.
- Avoid the low end *and* the high end. Both Intel and AMD make three levels of CPUs. Try to stick to the middle. Avoid the slowest and the fastest. Don't buy the CPU with the most cores or the fewest cores.

- When it comes to price, the sweet spot should be around $150 to $300. It's amazing, but CPU price points haven't changed much in over a decade. You can spend a lot more or a lot less, but either way is a waste of money or cheating yourself on power.

Now that you've got a CPU, it's time to find that magic motherboard. Your first big choice is the chipset. Take some time to learn about current chipsets that support the CPU of your choice and compare features. Consider the following:

- Total RAM support
- RAID support
- USB, including versions and number of ports
- Onboard video
- Onboard wireless

Once you narrow down your choice to a particular chipset, see which motherboards fit your plans:

- Just because a chipset supports certain features, don't assume the motherboard will as well. Double-check RAM limits, RAID support, USB ports and types, and so on.
- Check the manufacturer's reputation. Good names like ASUS and Intel are going to be better quality motherboards, but there are plenty of other good manufacturers, too.
- Read reviews of the motherboards you like. What are people saying about them?
- Think about how many expansion slots you need. Your motherboard should have at least one PCIe ×16 slot and a few smaller PCIe slots.
- Do you want to use integrated video? Many folks will think the onboard video is acceptable, and certainly well above Windows 7's Aero requirements. If not, you've always got that PCIe ×16 slot waiting for a new, dedicated video card.

Video

Regardless of whether you choose onboard or a dedicated video card, a thick client isn't going to push a graphics card very hard. Even lower-end cards include at least 1 GB of GDDR3 (or better) video RAM, solid processors, and plenty of extras like HDMI ports. You probably don't need to spend any more than about $150. If you spend more money than that, you're stretching into gaming PC territory.

 NOTE Go to www.tomshardware.com and check out their monthly "Best Graphics Cards for the Money" articles. They're the best source for what's the best graphics card available.

Be sure to check the reviews on a prospective video card and always be sure to do a Google search for a card's model number followed by "noise." Some videos cards are too loud—they'll drive you bonkers.

Monitors

Monitors are a personal choice, but remember that a good monitor will outlast several system builds, so don't be afraid to get a better monitor. A good-quality, widescreen, LED-backlit LCD monitor no smaller than 20 inches diagonally across will serve you well for a long time.

Storage

A thick client will do just fine with a single hard drive. Today's multiple-terabyte drives will store anything you might imagine and then some, and if you actually manage to fill a drive, your mid-tower will easily accept a second or even third drive.

Setting up a RAID array is probably not necessary. Of course, the system needs backup capability, but RAID might be overkill. At the same time, the low cost of drives and the ease of RAID installation makes at least RAID 1 a compelling option for your thick client.

Applications

The typical thick client is going to need a Web browser (or two) and some Microsoft Office–type applications. The recommended 4 GB of RAM won't have any difficulty supporting these types of applications or much more.

Workstation PCs

In modern times, people need computers to get work done. The type of computer you need is defined by the work you do and the way that your IT department decides to organize and network. For the most part, the thick client described earlier is the "go to" workstation PC, but CompTIA defines two other workstation types: the thin client and the virtualization workstation.

Thin Client

A *thin client* is a system designed to handle only very basic applications with an absolute minimum amount of hardware required by the operating system. Thin clients often serve as single-purpose systems, like point-of-sale machines (cash registers). Thin clients can be very small compared to a thick client, which makes them perfect when you want the PC tucked away. Figure 31-4 shows a typical thin client.

Figure 31-4
Thin client (photo courtesy of HP)

Thick client

Thin Client

Virtualization Workstations

Virtualization has taken the world of computing by storm over the past few years. As discussed in the previous chapter, virtualization is a powerful technology that enables you to run more than one operating system at the same time on a single computer. With virtualized servers, you can consolidate multiple, power-hungry machines into one box, saving floor space, electricity, and a lot of running around. With workstations, virtualization is most often used to run a second OS on top of the OS installed on the computer's hard drive.

For good performance on a virtualization workstation, install lots and lots of RAM. Each virtualization workstation needs enough memory to run the native operating system, the guest operating system, and any applications running in either OS, so RAM is the most important thing in virtualization. A powerful 64-bit CPU that supports hardware virtualization will also help virtual machines run smoothly. Many desktop computers can run virtual machines, but if you want the best possible performance, you want lots of RAM and a good CPU.

EXAM TIP You'll need lots of RAM and a fast CPU to get good performance out of a virtualization workstation.

Media Workstations

When George Lucas made the first *Star Wars* movie, he used camera tricks, miniature models, and stop-motion animation to create the illusion of massive spaceships and robots battling it out in a galaxy far, far away. Twenty years later, he filmed the *Star Wars*

prequels in front of massive green screens and used computer-generated imagery (CGI) to transform the bland sets into exotic planets and space stations. I won't get into an argument about which approach produced better movies, but the fact remains that the act of creating films has changed. It's not just films, either—computers have changed the way we create all types of media, including movies, television shows, photography, music, and more.

If you want to get involved in this creative revolution, you're going to need a mighty powerful computer. Workstations for creative professionals are customized for the type of media they create. We'll start by looking at graphics workstations (by which I mean workstations for editing still images and using computer-aided design/computer-aided manufacturing software), then move on to audio workstations and video workstations.

 NOTE *Computer-aided design (CAD)* and *computer-aided manufacturing (CAM)* software enable engineers to create and build components in an industrial setting.

Graphics Workstations

Professional photographers and graphic designers first and foremost need to have the clearest view possible of their images and image editing software. Whether you're editing photos in Adobe Photoshop or drafting mechanical components in SolidWorks, you need to make sure you can see what you're working on! Because of this, the primary need for a graphics workstation is a large, high-quality monitor. A $200 LCD panel from Best Buy won't help you here—you need to make sure that the colors you see on the screen are as accurate as possible. Expensive monitors will have higher contrast ratios for more vibrant images and they'll also give you more control over the image they output.

You learned in Chapters 21 and 25 that monitors and video cards use different techniques to display colors. For a workstation to display colors accurately on a monitor, you must properly calibrate the monitor. This is a simple process of using a small sensor, like the tool shown in Figure 31-5, on the screen to create a *profile* that enables the monitor to display more accurate colors. You can use a similar device with a printer to create a profile for it, too. That way, your printouts will match what you see on the monitor.

With a good enough monitor, almost any computer can be used as a graphics workstation, but ideally you'll want a fast, multicore 64-bit CPU and lots of RAM. If the processor is too slow or if the computer doesn't have enough RAM, it can take a long time to make changes to an image you're editing. A large hard drive is also a plus, since CAD files and photographs take up a lot of space. You'll also want to have an external drive to back up your work. If you're working with CAD/CAM software, you'll want a professional-level graphics card, such as an NVIDIA Quadro card (see Figure 31-6), though photo editing software won't see much of an advantage from such a card. Unlike typical graphics cards, these professional cards can cost thousands of dollars.

Figure 31-5
A monitor
calibrator

Figure 31-6
An NVIDIA
Quadro graphics
card (photo cour-
tesy of NVIDIA)

Graphic designers frequently make use of specialized input devices, too, such as digitizer tablets. These tablets enable designers to paint on their computers as if they were painting on a canvas, as shown in Figure 31-7.

Digital Audio Workstations

The requirements for audio workstations are very similar to those for graphics workstations—a fast, multicore CPU, gobs of RAM, a large monitor, and a big, high-speed hard drive. The difference is that you'll also need a high-quality audio interface.

An *audio interface* is a box that you hook up to your PC with inputs that enable you to connect professional microphones and instruments (see Figure 31-8). Functionally, an audio interface is just a really high-end sound card, though they usually connect to your computer via USB or FireWire rather than plug into the motherboard. Audio interfaces range in size from an interface you can fit in your hand, to one that will take up most of your desk. A more expensive interface includes more inputs and produces higher-quality sound, though you'll also need some expensive speakers to hear the difference.

Figure 31-7 Painting with a Wacom tablet

Figure 31-8
Audio interface
device (photo
courtesy of
PreSonus)

Just like with graphics workstations, audio workstations frequently make use of specialized input devices. These devices, referred to as *control surfaces*, mimic the look and feel of older, analog mixing consoles. They have a large number of programmable inputs that make controlling the software much faster and more accurate than with just a mouse and keyboard. These control surfaces range in size from small desktop units, all the way up to room-filling behemoths that are used in recording studios. Some of these boards also contain an audio interface.

Video Workstations

Video workstations combine the requirements of a graphics workstation and an audio workstation. Video editors often use two or more color-calibrated monitors so they can view the video stream they're working on with one monitor and see their video editor open on the other, making multiple monitors very useful. Video workstations require a very powerful CPU paired with as much RAM as possible, since video editing is a far more intensive process than graphics or audio editing. High-speed, high-capacity hard drives are also life-savers, since video files often take up multiple gigabytes of space. Many video workstations have multiple hard drives set up in a RAID for added storage capacity and read/write speed.

Video workstations, like CAD/CAM workstations, benefit enormously from a professional-level graphics card. This is almost as important as the fast CPU and piles of RAM, and you'll rarely see a video workstation without one.

Because video workstations are frequently used as audio workstations, too, you will often find video workstations with the same audio interfaces and control surfaces as you'd see on an audio workstation. There are also video interfaces that enable editors to connect to various cameras. Additionally, many video editors use custom keyboards that have special labels and controls for popular video editing software.

Specialized Consumer PCs

Once you move away from the office and into the house, your computing needs change. Home is for leisure, and the workplace is for, well, work! The three common types of home systems are home servers that store everything from your music collection to last year's income tax return, home theater PCs to play your music and your movies, and gaming PCs to play powerful, video-intensive games.

Building a Home Server PC

How many computing devices are in your house right now? If you're like me, the answer is "a lot." Between multiple smartphones, iPods, tablets, portables, and desktop computers, you might shock yourself with the count.

As more and more computing devices move into the home environment, there's a need for a centralized storage space, a *home server PC* to dish out files and folders on demand—a place for all your media to stream to multiple devices. This home server PC has very specialized needs that take it beyond the typical thick client.

A home server PC supplies three discrete functions: media streaming, file sharing, and print sharing. Media streaming often uses specialized software. Just like file and print sharing, though, it works fine through the default tools in Windows and Mac OS X. The home server PC has to have a very fast network connection and gobs of storage. Plus, that storage needs to be fault tolerant. Losing your video collection because of a hard drive crash would make for a very bad day.

Software

Any modern operating system enables you to share files and folders through standard sharing features. The same is true of sharing a printer. To turn that PC into a print server, open the Devices and Printers applet in the Control Panel, right-click on an installed printer, choose *Printer properties*, and then check the *Share this printer* checkbox on the Sharing tab (see Figure 31-9).

Figure 31-9

Sharing a printer

You can easily turn a Windows 7 PC into a media streaming server by selecting that option in the Control Panel. Open the Network and Sharing Center, select the *Change advanced sharing settings* link from the left Task menu, and then click the *Home or Work* option to get to the Advanced sharing settings screen (see Figure 31-10).

Halfway down the screen you'll find a link to *Choose media streaming options*. Click it. Figure 31-11 shows the Media streaming options screen. By default, Windows wants to share everything, though you can customize what's shared in case you have young children and don't want them to have access to inappropriate content.

Finally, both Windows Media Player and iTunes have a feature to share media files on a local network. Figure 31-12 shows iTunes sharing via the Bonjour protocol.

EXAM TIP Microsoft makes a perfectly fine server OS called Windows Home Server that you can use to set up a sweet home server machine. You probably won't find the OS on the CompTIA A+ exams, however.

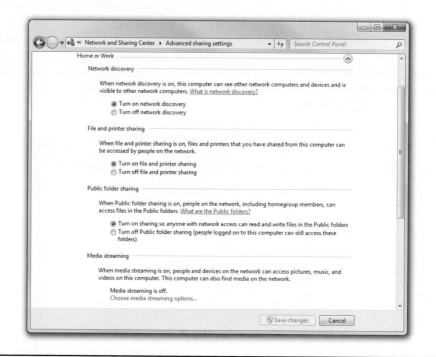

Figure 31-10 Advanced sharing settings

Figure 31-11 Media streaming options

Figure 31-12 Streaming with iTunes

Hardware

Hardware needs on a home server apply primarily to the network speed and hard drive capacity, at least according the CompTIA objectives. If you have a very active server, you should also pay attention to the amount of RAM it has and the speed of the CPU. Beefing both up above the standard thick client can help if you start getting some lag.

EXAM TIP You don't need to care at all about the video card in a server PC. Anything will do because you're not going to play anything directly on the server.

For the network, a wired Gigabit Ethernet NIC should be standard issue. Although it sounds cool to go wireless, you should limit the use of wireless to the single connection between the WAP and the client. The home server should connect via Ethernet to minimize any lag or dropped frames.

A file server's hard drives do the heavy and sustained lifting for the PC, so you should not stint on them. At a minimum, get two drives of identical size that have as much capacity as you can afford. No one *reduces* the amount of media in his or her collection over time, after all, especially if it's stored electronically. Plus, because you need fault tolerance on the data, you simply must use a RAID 1 configuration at a minimum (and thus the need to get two identical drives). If your budget can afford it and your motherboard supports it, get three identical drives and run in RAID 5.

Alternatives

Instead of building a custom home server box (the fun method), you can also purchase preconfigured devices that contain multiple hard drives and attach them to your network. Referred to as *network attached storage (NAS)*, these devices usually connect via Ethernet. Instead of connecting to the hard drive(s) on a server PC on the network, you connect to the NAS's hard drives. It plays the same role as a home server without all the fuss.

 EXAM TIP The CompTIA 801 objectives list "Ethernet" as a connection type for storage devices. While you won't find stand-alone external hard drives that support Ethernet connections, home servers and NAS devices can provide your PC with storage attached via Ethernet.

Setting Up a Home Theater PC

A home theater system enables you to play music and watch movies and television. If done well, the experience can rival that of watching a movie at a fine movie house. When coupled with a home theater PC, the home theater system enables the full computing experience as well.

An optimal home theater has five components:

- A monitor, television, or projector
- Surround sound speakers
- A stereo receiver
- A home theater PC
- Network connectivity (such as a cable box or Ethernet)

 NOTE You can certainly build a functional and very good home theater without the stereo receiver. My home theater doesn't use a stereo, for example, and isn't hooked up to a cable box either, yet it's great for watching movies and surfing the Internet.

This section looks at the specific components and issues involved with creating a home theater PC and connecting it to other components.

Output Killer Video

A home theater PC must provide support for large monitors at high resolution, a requirement that usually involves an HDMI connector on the video card (see Figure 31-13). The HDMI cable connects the home theater box to the stereo receiver, which then pushes the signal to the television. Figure 31-14 shows the basic home theater schematic.

Figure 31-13

HDMI output on
video card

Figure 31-14 Television, receiver, home theater PC

Both DVI and DisplayPort can support 1080p HDTV resolution, as you'll recall from Chapter 21. Many televisions today have a DVI port, so this is a viable solution, especially if you don't have a stereo receiver (see the following section).

Play It Loudly

A great home theater system simply must have surround sound and a thumping subwoofer, so the home theater PC needs a sound card or built-in sound processor that supports 5.1 or 7.1 stereo. For the best output, the sound card connects to the stereo receiver via S/PDIF, through either the optical connector or coaxial connector. The speakers then connect to the receiver. Figure 31-15 shows the schematic with speakers added.

Figure 31-15 PC, receiver, speakers

HDMI carries both the video signal and the surround sound audio signal, so if you plug it into the television directly from the PC, the rig will use the television's speakers by default. If you have the surround sound speakers plugged into the computer rather than a receiver, you need to go into the Sound applet in the Control Panel to select the playback device you prefer (see Figure 31-16).

Figure 31-16
Sound applet for choosing playback device

Look Cool in the Process

Home theater components look like traditional stacking stereo components, such as a receiver, equalizer, DVD player, and so on. It simply won't do to put a beige office computer case alongside your sleek, black-clad components (see Figure 31-17).

Figure 31-17
This is not right!

You can get a case for a PC that stacks nicely with other home theater components (see Figure 31-18). CompTIA calls this style of case an *HTPC*, although that's not an industry-standard form factor. I assume the letters stand for *home theater PC*.

Figure 31-18 HTPC case

Access the Media—Streaming and TV

The home theater PC needs access to content, usually through Gigabit Ethernet to get streaming media through the home server PC you created in the previous section of the chapter. The home theater could use Wi-Fi (802.11n or better), though wired is best, especially for HD content.

The home theater PC wouldn't normally have anything to do with a signal from the cable company or from a dedicated optical disc player, like a Blu-ray Disc box. Those signals go from the applicable box to the stereo receiver directly.

The only time the home theater PC should receive a television signal directly is through broadcast over the air. For this signal, the PC needs a television tuner, like you learned about in Chapter 25. You would use this to catch local news or sports programs.

Figure 31-19 shows the home theater schematic with all the media access methods included.

Figure 31-19 Final home theater

DLNA

Before we leave the hardware to look at software, I want to mention one topic that's outside the scope of the CompTIA A+ exams, but that you might run into in the field.

Digital Living Network Alliance (DLNA) certified devices connect to your home network, discover each other, and share media. In theory, DLNA devices should work with minimal setup or fuss, even if sourced from different manufacturers. If you share media files on a Windows PC, for example, a DLNA-equipped television, PlayStation 3, or other home theater device should be able to view those files. Look for the DLNA logo on devices as diverse as digital cameras, Blu-ray Disc players, network storage boxes, printers, and more.

Software Tools for Playback

Once you have the media center hardware set up properly, you need software to access streaming media. Microsoft includes Windows Media Center in some editions of Windows. If you don't have one of those editions (see Table 31-1), then you need to use a third-party tool, such as the excellent XBMC or Plex.

Windows XP	Windows Vista	Windows 7
Media Center	Home Premium	Home Premium
	Ultimate	Professional
		Ultimate

Table 31-1 Versions of Windows That Include Media Center

Windows Media Center enables you to stream content from a home server and watch content stored locally. You can even access some television shows broadcast over the Internet (see Figure 31-20). Most of the setup happens via wizards that run when you select an option. If you want to add content from networked computers, you'll need to add it to the appropriate library (in Windows 7) or connect to the shared folder(s) in Windows XP or Windows Vista.

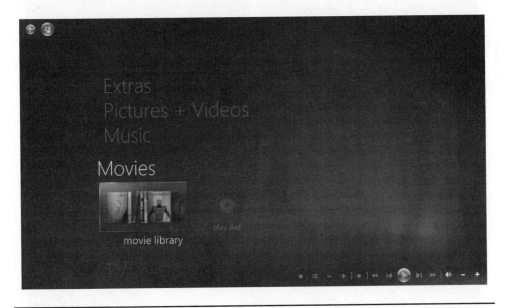

Figure 31-20 Windows Media Center

As cool as Windows Media Center is, you can find absolutely beautiful and functional third-party software for free, such as XBMC and Plex. XBMC in particular enables you to customize the look and feel of the interface, and many people have made awesome skins available too. Figure 31-21 shows the default skin for XBMC; Figure 31-22 shows the same content but displayed with a completely different skin. Plex is not

flashy, but it's totally functional. There are versions of XBMC and Plex available for Windows, Mac OS X, and Linux. You can download XBMC from xbmc.org. Get Plex at www.plexapp.com.

Figure 31-21 Default XBMC

Figure 31-22 XBMC sporting the Aeon skin

Gaming PC

And now for the grand finale, the PC you've been waiting for, the system you've always wanted to build. As an aspiring PC tech, you probably took your first apprehensive steps into the dark underbelly of PCs with a game: *Doom, Quake, Myst, The Sims, World of Warcraft* . . . you've played at least one of them. While casual gamers can get by with a standard desktop PC (like the thick client you read about earlier), those who take their gaming seriously want a powerful PC ready to pump out the latest graphics. A gamer goes through a game's graphics settings and sets everything to the max. And since games aren't all about how good they look, you'll also want a good sound card and headphones. (Okay—you also need a good game, but one thing at a time.)

First, I'm going to tell you about the optimal gaming PC—the best bang-for-your-buck gaming PC that will play every game out there without breaking your wallet. (It's cheaper than you think! You can get a lot for about $1000.) Then I'll show you how you can take PC gaming from a hobby to a lifestyle—your only lifestyle—with beyond-bleeding-edge components that you don't need but should buy anyway.

A Gaming PC That Won't Break Your Wallet

A gaming PC isn't that different from your run-of-the-mill thick client: all of the components are the same, but taken to the next level. The recommended Windows system requirements no longer cut it. Instead, you might turn your attention to the system requirements for your favorite PC game. Find a game that came out in the last year or two and see what it needs in a PC. You'll find that most games actually have pretty low system requirements.

A lot of modern PC games are *ports* or copies of console games (originally created for the for the Xbox 360 or PlayStation 3, for example). Because the consoles were launched so long ago—before Windows Vista!—their old hardware makes it easy for modern PCs to run ported games. Games designed specifically for PCs, however, can take advantage of every core and gigabyte you give them. Take a PC game's system requirements and bump them up a notch or two to keep your gaming PC future-proof. *Future-proofing* means building a PC in a way that keeps it relevant for a few years. You don't want your PC to be out of date a week after you build it. Going beyond the current requirements for a game will make it ready for new games that come out a year or two from now.

The Internals Most of the big improvements over a standard thick client will happen inside the case. Every game is coded differently—just like any other application—so each game will take advantage of your hardware to varying degrees. Some games, for example, are designed to use quad-core CPUs and others are not. If a game can only use one core, those three other cores in a quad-core CPU can't play along. But you want a quad-core CPU anyway. Why? Future-proofing and price. Why limit yourself now when more and more games can take advantage of multiple cores? And these days, the price is right. Find a quad-core Intel processor with a speed of 3 GHz or more. If you have a tighter budget, get the AMD equivalent.

NOTE Make sure you get a motherboard and CPU that are compatible with one another. I'll talk more about gaming motherboards later in this section.

For a budget-minded gaming PC, the processor is the first place you want to splurge a little bit. You don't need a special case or motherboard. You don't need more than 4 GB of RAM, and you only need enough hard drive space to store all your games. You don't need an extra monitor. Powering games revolves around two elements, so you'll spend the most money on these parts. I already told you about CPUs, so now let's talk about the biggest-ticket item, the graphics card.

A powerful graphics card (combined with a quality CPU) enables you to do two things: turn up the graphics quality and increase the performance (see Figure 31-23). The graphics-quality of the game depends as much on the graphics card as it does on the designers of the game. A good graphics card can't make an ugly game look pretty, but it can make a pretty game look gorgeous. At higher settings, all sorts of smoothing and filtering happens that would make weaker systems choke. At the same time, you also want to maximize performance. In games, we measure performance by the number of frames per second (FPS) displayed. Most games are designed to run at about 30 FPS, though the sky's the limit on the top end. If you're getting fewer than 20 FPS (everything will look very choppy and it will be difficult to play the game), you'll probably need to turn down the graphics settings in the game, and no one wants to do that!

Figure 31-23
An NVIDIA 680 graphics card (photo courtesy of NVIDIA)

So what should you look for in a graphics card? This can be a very "you get what you pay for" proposition, but NVIDIA and AMD—the two dominant graphics processing unit (GPU) manufacturers—have helpfully divided their products by number to show you at a glance how powerful they are. Yes, there are buses, cores, shaders, bandwidths, and so on, but it's all encapsulated into a (slightly random) number. The NVIDIA and AMD numbering systems, however, are entirely different, a little confusing, and sometimes loop back around to the beginning. I owned an NVIDIA GeForce4 MX 460 back in 2002. This is, of course, not the same as the NVIDIA GeForce GTX 460 released in 2010. And the NVIDIA GeForce GTX 460 is more powerful than an AMD Radeon 4850, even though AMD's number is bigger. Use each GPU manufacturer's Web site to learn

about the latest available graphics processors. When it comes time to buy, look for the third- or fourth-best card available in the latest generation's lineup. If the best card available is the "690," look for the "650" or "670" model. You can usually save hundreds of dollars and still get the best graphics and performance with modern games.

> **NOTE** Graphics card model numbers are organized by generations. As of 2012, NVIDIA cards were divided between the 500 and 600 generations, while AMD cards used the 6000 and 7000 series. Within each generation, a lower number means less power (and lower price), while a higher number means more power (and a higher price). The top NVIDIA card, for example, might be the 690 model, while the low-end model would use the 620 name. For the latest model information, check out the NVIDIA and AMD Web sites.

While the CPU and GPU will satisfy your eyes, don't forget about your ears. More and more games can take advantage of high-end sound cards that produce true surround sound rivaling blockbuster movies. Hear the squeal of your tires, the noise of your jet engine, and the fiery power of a wizard's spell in 5.1 surround sound! You'll need to spend a bit of money (almost as much as that graphics card you just found) to hear the difference, but if you're an audio geek, it's worth it. Look for sound cards that support extra channels (7.1), more bits (24-bit), and higher sample rates (192 KHz).

All of this power inside your case means it needs to handle a lot of extra heat. A more powerful CPU and GPU will put out more heat, and you'll need a cooling system that can handle it (see Figure 31-24). For a budget setup, you don't need to jump straight to liquid cooling (though it's always an option). Most cases have a few extra spots for fans that you can buy separately. Get some 120-mm fans and go to town. Your case cannot be too cool (and neither can you).

Figure 31-24
Powerful CPU fan
and heat sink

 EXAM TIP The key components of a great gaming PC include: a high-end processor, a powerful video card, a good sound card, and enough cooling (fans, heat sinks, liquid cooling) to keep all those parts from melting your machine.

The Externals For a budget gaming PC, there's not much to improve outside of your case. One monitor will work fine, but make sure it has a resolution of at least 1920 × 1080 and is 24 inches diagonally. That will enable you to easily watch 1080p HD video content and play console ports at or above their intended resolution. Likewise, a basic 2.1 or 5.1 speaker setup will work just fine with your nice sound card. Don't use cheap headphones, though. Invest in something nice (with a microphone, if you like to voice chat while gaming) that is comfortable and produces sounds that aren't tinny or hollow (see Figure 31-25).

Figure 31-25
Sennheiser HD 598

Many gamers like to buy fancy keyboards and mice, covered in extra buttons that can be customized to launch your wizard's fireball with a single click. Some keyboards even add little LCD screens that show you exactly how your keys have been customized and enable you to adjust your custom keyboard layout on the fly (see Figure 31-26). Keyboards and mice are very personal—get whatever best helps you game.

Figure 31-26 A nice keyboard with built-in LCD screen

 NOTE Like keyboards and mice, cases are a very personal choice. Some people like wild colors. Other people want lights and windows showing off their internal devices. Personally, I prefer a plain black case. No lights. No windows. No distractions.

A Gaming PC That Will Set Your Wallet on Fire

If money is no object, go buy a yacht, and on that yacht, set up your dream gaming PC. Here, no price is too high, no technology too frivolous, and no monitor too big. If it exists, you should have it, even if you'll never use it. Some of this will sound extreme, and that's the point. I'll point out the best places to spend too much money and transform your budget box into the ultimate gaming PC.

The Internals With the budget box, I told you why buying a quad-core processor was a good investment for future games that will take advantage of the technology. Now, quad-core isn't nearly enough. As of 2012, six-core processors like the Intel Core i7 Extreme Edition sit at the top of the CPU heap and will future-proof your PC for years to come. No game needs it, but at $1000, you can't afford not to get it.

If that wasn't extreme enough, get ready for your graphics card purchase, or should I say graphics *cards*? That's right: you'll need more than one high-end graphics card if you want the best of the best PC gaming experience. (And forget about not getting the very best card available—just look for the highest model number available and hand over your credit card.)

NVIDIA and AMD have both developed their own technology for linking multiple graphics cards. NVIDIA calls their technology *Scalable Link Interface (SLI)*, while AMD calls theirs *CrossFire*. Using a special cable (that looks sort of like a ribbon cable), the graphics cards can combine their power to increase graphical quality and performance (see Figure 31-27). With either technology, you can link up to four video cards together for more power than any current PC game could use. (But that's not the point.) Gamers will argue how effective these multicard setups really are—in fact, some games are so poorly optimized that they will run worse with multiple graphics cards. Read up on how each game you play works with multiple graphics cards and proceed accordingly.

 NOTE Installing multiple graphics cards requires a motherboard that can handle two or more PCIe cards, a power supply that produces enough wattage, a case it will all fit in, and a cooling system powerful enough to keep your PC from overheating (a liquid-cooling setup sounds nice right about now). Keep these things in mind when upgrading or building your PC.

While you're at it, you might as well get a bunch of extra RAM (16 GB sounds comfy). A solid-state drive (or two) will help load game levels into RAM that much faster. When you need a break from gaming, a Blu-ray Disc optical drive enables you to watch HD movies. Add to that a 7.1 sound card and Gigabit networking card for high-speed connections to other gamers, and you have the start of an unmatched gaming-performance machine.

Figure 31-27
An SLI cable

The Externals If you have multiple video cards, why not buy multiple monitors? You learned about multiple monitor setups when you read about audio/video workstations earlier in this chapter, and many games can take advantage of this feature. Picture, if you will, three monitors, side by side: the nose of your race car speeds down the track on the center monitor while the crowd whips by on the left and right monitors. With multiple monitors, your field of view doubles, triples, or more!

Instead of expanding your view left and right, you can also improve your display forward and backward with 3-D technology. More and more PC games are including support for 3-D displays. You'll need the slightly silly glasses to make it work, but for gaming, the effect is amazing. Lots of action games require a good sense of (virtual) depth perception to play. You can't hit the enemy warlock with your fireball if you can't aim it properly. With 3-D displays, distant enemies will *look and feel* distant. Everything becomes much more natural with 3-D technology. To use it, you'll need a display and video card that supports the technology.

NOTE For the ultimate graphics card/monitor combination, NVIDIA supports four graphics cards connected together via SLI, attached to three side-by-side 3-D monitors. I've never seen it in person, but I imagine it's as close as you can get to standing inside a video game world. (AMD CrossFireX also supports multiple video cards, but not connected to three monitors.)

For sound, why stop at puny PC speakers? Jump to big home theater surround sound speakers (see Figure 31-28). Get a gamepad, too (for the PC games that support it). While you're at it, buy a nice chair with good back support and padding. When you game for hours on end in a good chair, your neck, back, and bottom will thank you.

Figure 31-28
5.1 surround sound speakers (photo courtesy of Klipsch Group, Inc.)

That's it! Who knew it was so easy to spend $10,000 on a gaming PC? While most gamers will stick with something closer to the budget box, keep in mind that there is so much more power available—more than most games can handle. Whether you spend $100, $1000, or $10,000, don't forget to look for what *you* want out of your gaming PC. What games do you play? What do they require? What do you want? When you answer those questions, finding the parts you need becomes easy. Finding the right game, however, is an entirely different challenge.

NOTE If you skipped the other custom PC sections because this is the coolest kind of PC to build, don't forget to go back and read anything you missed. Who knows? You might decide to become a filmmaker instead of play games all day. (Yeah, right!)

Chapter Review

Questions

1. What is a thin client?

 A. A computer with a 32-bit-wide address bus

 B. A portable computer

 C. A system designed to handle only very basic applications with the minimum hardware required by the operating system

 D. A computer in a narrow, small form-factor case

2. What three functions does a home server PC provide? (Select three.)

 A. Media streaming

 B. File sharing

 C. Web hosting

 D. Print sharing

3. What's a good guide to use when deciding on hardware for a basic thick client?

 A. Buy whatever is on sale.

 B. Always start with the most expensive hardware.

 C. Check the recommended requirements for the OS you want to use.

 D. Check the MSDS for the OS you want to use.

4. How can you make sure that your printouts match the colors displayed on your monitor?

 A. Calibrate your GPU with a GPU calibrator.

 B. Calibrate your monitor and printer to use the same profile.

 C. Just buy an expensive monitor and printer; no setup is needed.

 D. Use RGB ink in your LaserJet printer.

5. How do you share a printer in Windows 7?

 A. Open Device Manager, right-click on the printer, select Properties, and select Share this printer.

 B. You have to install special drivers for your printer.

 C. Open the Devices and Printers applet in the Control Panel, right-click on the printer, select Printer properties, and then check the Share this printer checkbox on the Sharing tab.

 D. You have to have Windows Home Server in order to share printers.

6. What program that comes with some versions of Windows turns your PC into a home theater PC?

 A. XBMC

 B. Windows Media Center

 C. Plex

 D. Windows Home Theater

7. What term defines building your PC to run games that aren't out yet?

 A. Future-proofing

 B. Next-gen proofing

 C. Overbuilding

 D. Prebuilding

8. What does CompTIA call a PC case built for a home theater?

 A. Media center case

 B. XBMC

 C. HTPC

 D. Stereo case

9. Bob wants to build a new gaming computer, but he doesn't want to spend a ton of money. What parts should he spend the most money on? (Select two.)

 A. CPU

 B. Case

 C. Power supply

 D. Graphics card

10. What is the most important component for building a virtualization workstation?

 A. CPU

 B. Power supply

 C. RAM

 D. Large monitor

Answers

1. **C.** Thin clients rely on servers to perform anything beyond the most basic computing tasks.

2. **A, B, D.** Home servers share files, stream media, and share printers.

3. **C.** Knowing what hardware your OS requires is a good starting point for determining how powerful a PC you need to build.

4. **B.** Setting up identical color profiles on your printer and monitor will ensure accurate colors.

5. **C.** Printer sharing is done through the Devices and Printers applet.

6. **B.** Windows Media Center, included with some Windows editions, can turn a PC into an HTPC.

7. **A.** Future-proofing means building a PC that can play games that will come out in the near future.

8. **C.** HTPC cases blend your PC in with your home theater equipment.

9. **A, D.** A fast CPU and graphics card will get you the most bang for your buck when building a gaming PC.

10. **C.** Every virtual machine you run consumes a large share of RAM, so the more RAM you have, the more VMs you can run.

The Complete PC Tech

32

In this chapter, you will learn how to
- Describe how computers work
- Implement a troubleshooting methodology
- Describe a technician's toolkit

When a mission-critical computer goes down, regardless of the industry, people get upset. Workers can't work, so they feel guilty. Employers can't get product out on time, so they feel anxious. Supervisors blame employees for fouling things up, or at least the employees fear such blame, even if they did not break the machine.

Into this charged atmosphere comes the tech, ready to fix the computer and move on to the next challenge. Accomplishing this task, though, requires three things: First, a good tech must know the broken machine inside and out—how it's *supposed* to work when working properly. Second, the tech has to calm the workers and supervisors, and get answers to questions to gain relevant information about the problem. Third, the tech must troubleshoot the problem and fix the machine.

This chapter starts with an overview of how computers work and then describes a proven troubleshooting methodology to help you figure out the source of problems and point you to the fix quickly. The chapter wraps up by discussing the tools every tech should have.

802

How Computers Work

You've spent a lot of time going through this book, reading about technologies and components in great detail. Each chapter contained troubleshooting information and methodologies for the components explained in that chapter. In Chapter 6, for example, you learned all about CPUs, from how they work to how to install them. You also learned about issues specific to CPUs, including the potentially difficult task of adding or removing the fan and heat sink assembly that all CPUs require. In Chapters 11 and 12, you dove into hard drives in gory detail. With each chapter, you added more and more information about the pieces that make up the personal computer today.

In this chapter, I want you to distill that knowledge, to think about the computer as a coherent machine. Each of the computer's components works together with all the other components to enable people to produce some amazing things.

To master the art of troubleshooting as a PC tech, you need to approach a technical problem and answer one question: "What can be causing this problem?" Because every process involves multiple components, you must understand the interconnectedness of those components. If Jane can't get the printer to print her document, for example, what could the problem be? Connectivity? Drivers? Paper jam? Slow network connection? Frozen application? Solar flares? Let's look at the process.

Way back in Chapter 3, you learned about the four parts of the computing process: input, processing, output, and storage. Let's take a moment to review the computing process, this time to see how you can use it to help you fix computers.

When you run a program, your computer goes through three of the four stages of the *computing process*: input, processing, and output (see Figure 32-1). Input requires specific devices, such as the keyboard and mouse, which enable you to tell the computer to do something, such as open a program or type a word. The operating system (OS) provides an interface and tools so that the microprocessor and other chips can process your request. The image on the monitor or sound from the speakers effectively tells you that the computer has interpreted your command and spit out the result. The fourth stage, storage, comes into play when you want to save a document and when you first open programs and other files.

Figure 32-1
Input, processing, and output

Making this process work, though, requires the complex interaction of many components, including multiple pieces of hardware and layers of software. As a tech, you need to understand all the components and how they work together so that when something doesn't work right, you can track down the source and fix it. A look at a modern program reveals that even a seemingly simple action or change on the screen requires many things to happen within the computer.

Games such as *Second Life* (see Figure 32-2) are huge, taking up multiple gigabytes of space on an Internet server. They simply won't fit into the RAM in most computers, so developers have figured out ways to minimize RAM usage.

Figure 32-2 The *Second Life* virtual world

In *Second Life*, for example, you move through the online world in a series of more or less seamlessly connected areas. Crossing a bridge from one island to another triggers the game to quickly update the information you're about to see on the new island, so you won't be out of the action and the illusion of being in the game world remains intact. Here's what happens when you press the w key on your keyboard and your character steps across the invisible zone line.

NOTE *Second Life* is a massively multiplayer online role-playing game (MMORPG) that offers a unique twist on the genre. You can create just about anything you can imagine, as far as your time and talent can take you. *Second Life* has a functioning economy that spills out into the real world, meaning you can buy and sell things within the game and turn that into real U.S. dollars, although the more common scenario is to spend real money to get virtual possessions.

The keyboard controller reads the grid of your keyboard and, on discovering your input, sends the information to the CPU through the wires of the motherboard (see Figure 32-3). The CPU understands the keyboard controller because of a small program that was loaded into RAM from the ROM BIOS on the motherboard when the PC booted up.

Figure 32-3
Keyboard to CPU

The CPU and the application determine what should happen in the game, and on discovering that your character is about to cross the zone line, they trigger a whole series of actions. The application sends the signal to the OS that it needs a specific area loaded into RAM. The OS sends a signal to the CPU that it needs data stored on the hard drive plus information stored on the *Second Life* servers. The CPU then sends the commands to the hard drive controller for it to grab the proper stored data and send it to RAM, while at the same time sending a command to the NIC to download the updated information (see Figure 32-4).

The hard drive controller tells the hard drive to cough up the data—megabytes worth—and then sends that data through the motherboard to the memory controller, which puts it into RAM and communicates with the CPU when it's finished. The network card and network operating system communicate with the *Second Life* servers and download the necessary updated information. The CPU then uses the application and OS to process the new data, sending video data to the video card and sound data to the sound card, again through the wires on the motherboard (see Figure 32-5).

Figure 32-4 CPU to hard drive and NIC

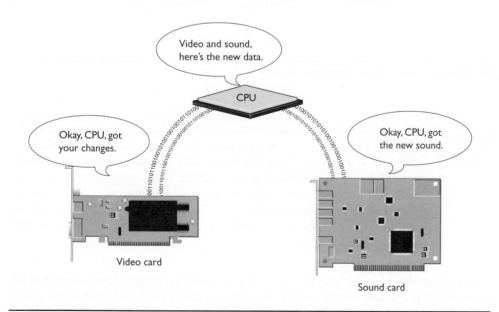

Figure 32-5 CPU to video card and sound card

The video card processor puts the incoming data into its RAM, processes the data, and then sends out commands to the monitor to update the screen. The sound card processor likewise processes the data and sends out commands to the speakers to play a new sound (see Figure 32-6).

Figure 32-6 Updating the screen and speakers

 TIP Modern Windows versions have raised the bar on video demands in a big way, so the video card in your users' systems can make a remarkable difference in their experience. Windows Vista/7 use the video card to produce many of the cool visual effects of the interface. This means that a low-end video card in an otherwise serviceable machine can cause Vista/7 to misbehave. Unless your client is gaming, there's no reason to drop $300+ on a video card, but assembling or recommending a system with yesterday's video is not necessarily a good thing!

For all of this to work, the PC has to have electricity, so the direct current (DC) provided by the power supply and the alternating current (AC) provided to the power supply must both be the proper voltage and amperage.

Finally, because *Second Life* is a network application, the OS has to send information through the NIC and onto the Internet to update everyone else's computer. That way, the other characters in the game world see you move forward a step (see Figure 32-7).

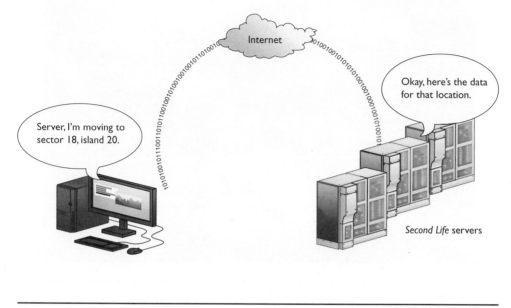

Figure 32-7 PC to *Second Life* servers

What do you see or hear with all these electrons zipping all over the place? Out of a seemingly blank vista (see Figure 32-8), a castle begins to appear, building itself piece by piece as your computer processes the new information and updates the video screen. You hear music begin to play from your speakers. Within a few seconds, with the data describing the new island fully downloaded and processed, the world on your monitor looks very different (see Figure 32-9). That's when all goes well. Many megabytes of data have flowed from your hard drive and across the Internet, been processed by multiple processors, and been sent to the monitor and the speakers.

To keep the action continuous and unbroken, *Second Life*, like many current online games, uses a process of continuous or *stream loading*: your computer constantly downloads updated information and data from the *Second Life* servers, so the world you see changes with every step you take. When done right, stream loading can do some amazing things. In the GameCube game *The Legend of Zelda: Wind Waker*, for example, the game anticipates where you will go next and loads that new area into RAM before you take the step. You can be in one area and use a telescope to zoom in on another fully developed area (see Figure 32-10), making the experience amazingly seamless, just like real life.

Figure 32-8 New area loading

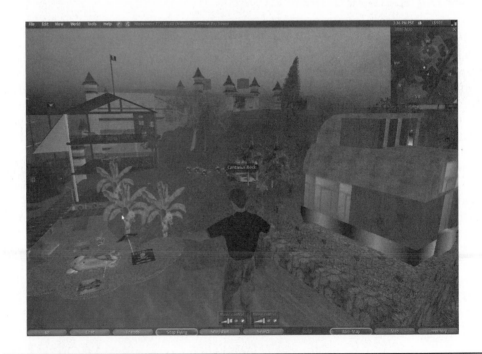

Figure 32-9 Castle completed

Figure 32-10
The Legend of Zelda: Wind Waker zoomed

Anytime a computer has a problem that's not immediately and clearly obvious (such as not powering up due to not having a power cord plugged in), you should use the computing process to help you zero in on the problem. But the computing process only defines the pieces and their interaction; good troubleshooting requires more than just rummaging around to find the problem. You need to combine the computing process with a troubleshooting theory to get the job done.

Troubleshooting Theory

Troubleshooting theory is nothing more than a set of mental steps you use along with the computing process to diagnose and fix a computer. Troubleshooting theory includes talking to users to determine how and when the problem took place, determining a cause, testing, verification, and documentation. Techs use a number of good troubleshooting theories. Luckily for those taking the CompTIA A+ 220-802 certification exam, CompTIA clearly defines their vision of troubleshooting theory:

 4.1 Given a scenario, explain the troubleshooting theory
- Identify the problem
 - Question the user and identify user changes to computer and perform backups before making changes
- Establish a theory of probable cause (question the obvious)
- Test the theory to determine cause
 - Once theory is confirmed, determine next steps to resolve problem
 - If theory is not confirmed, re-establish new theory or escalate
- Establish a plan of action to resolve the problem and implement the solution
- Verify full system functionality and if applicable implement preventative measures
- Document findings, actions and outcomes

Identify the Problem

There's a reason you're standing in front of a computer to repair it: something happened that the user of the computer has identified as "not good" and that's why you're here. First, you need to *identify the problem* by talking to the user. Get the user to show you what's not good. Is it an error code? Is something not accessible? Is a device not responding? Then ask the user that classic tech question (remember your communication skills here!): "Has anything recently changed on the computer that might have made this problem appear?" What you're really saying is: "Have you jacked with the computer? Did you install some evil program? Did you shove in a USB drive so hard you broke the connection?" Of course, you never say these things; simply ask nicely without accusing so the user can help you fix the problem (see Figure 32-11).

Figure 32-11
Tech asking nicely

In most troubleshooting situations, it's important to back up critical files before making changes to a system. To some extent, this is a matter of proper ongoing maintenance, but if some important bit of data disappears and you don't have a backup, you know who the user will blame, don't you?

 EXAM TIP The CompTIA A+ certification exams assume that all techs should back up systems *every time* before working on them, even though that's not how it works in the real world.

If you run into a partially functional system where you might have to reinstall the OS but can access the hard drive, you should definitely back up essential data, such as e-mail, browser favorites, important documents, and any data not stored on a regularly backed-up server. Because you can boot to a copy of Windows and go to the Recovery Console or System Recovery Options, you should never lose essential data, barring full-blown hard drive death.

NOTE Dead hard drives retain their data, so you can recover it—if you're willing to pay a lot of money. Having a good backup in place makes a lot more economic sense!

Establish a Theory of Probable Cause (Question the Obvious)

Now it's time to analyze the issue and come up with a theory as to what is wrong, a *theory of probable cause*. Personally, I prefer the word "guess" at this point because very few errors are so obvious that you'll know what to do. Fall back on your knowledge of the computing process to localize the issue based on the symptoms. Keep your guesses... err...theories...simple. One of the great problems for techs is their desire to overlook the obvious problems in their desire to dig into the system (see Figure 32-12).

Figure 32-12
Ford the Tech
misses the obvious.

Outside the Case

Take a moment to look for clues before you open up the case. Most importantly, use all your senses in the process.

What do you see? Is a connector mangled or a plastic part clearly damaged? Even if that connector or part works fine, the physical abuse could provide extra information. If the user can't connect to a network, check the cable. Was something rolled over it that could have broken the thin internal wires? Is that a jelly smear near the jammed optical drive door? (No pun intended, really!) A visual examination of the external computer is important.

When you put your hand on the system unit, does it feel hot? Can you feel or hear the vibrations of the fans? If not, that would be a clue to an overheating or overheated computer. Modern computers can run when overly hot, but generally run very sluggishly. If you run through basic malware fixes and a computer still runs poorly, think about excessive heat as a potential problem.

If you spend a moment listening to the PC, you might get some clues to problem sources. A properly running hard drive (as you'll recall from Chapter 12) doesn't make a lot of sound, just a regular hum from the spinning platters. If you hear clicking or grinding sounds from a drive, that's a very bad sign and a very important clue! Excessive thrashing or disk access can likewise lead to some potential problem areas, like insufficient RAM or a badly fragmented drive.

Finally, don't forget your nose. If you smell the unmistakable odor of ozone, you know that's the smell electronic components give off when they cook or are simply running much too hot.

Inside the Case

Use all your senses when you go inside the system unit as well. Do you see any physical damage? Check the motherboard capacitors if you have a dead PC. Properly working capacitors should be nice and (usually) blue; they definitely shouldn't look like partly melted batteries or be bulging at the seams. Fans should be spinning. The power supply shouldn't be blistering hot. You should be able to localize sounds better with the case off. And any smell of cooking components will definitely be stronger with the case off.

As you do your inspection, both outside and inside the case, don't jump to conclusions too quickly. When you see a problem that looks obvious, stop and give yourself an "Are you sure?" moment. Consider the possibility that a problem you've seen 50 times before might *not* be the problem this time. Of course, it probably *is* the same problem, but that quick rethink might save you trouble later.

Test the Theory to Determine Cause

Okay, so you've decided on a theory that makes sense. It's time to *test the theory* to see if it fixes the problem. The biggest challenge to fixing a computer is that the theory and the fix pretty much prove themselves at the same time. Let's go back to the situation where the power plug isn't plugged into the wall outlet. You observe that nothing happens when the PC power button is pressed. You check the back of the power supply and see that the power cable is plugged in. You then look at the wall outlet...not plugged in! So you quickly plug it in and *tada*! It works! You're a hero! In this simple case, your theory and your test are done in virtually the same move (see Figure 32-13).

Figure 32-13
Ford the Tech is
a hero!

Of course, most problems aren't that easy. In many cases, testing your theory does nothing more than verify that something is broken. Let's say you install an update for your video driver. You reboot, log on to Windows, and suddenly the screen freaks out. Ah, a bad video driver, right? To test, you reboot the computer and press F8 to get the boot options menu. You select VGA Mode (Windows XP) or Low Resolution Mode (Windows Vista/7) and reboot. Now the computer boots up just fine. You know what the problem is, but how do you fix it? Roll back the video driver? Reinstall an older driver? Try downloading another copy of the new driver and installing the video driver again? Any of these solutions may be the right one. Choose one and go for it (see Figure 32-14).

Uh oh, your first guess was wrong: the video is still messed up. No worries, just try another one of your theories. In most cases you'll just pick another theory and try again. But sometimes there's a point where the problem is bigger than you. It might be a problem on a server that you're not authorized to configure. It might be a problem with a user account, and techs in your company aren't allowed to change user accounts. It might be a problem with an in-house program and you don't have the skills to fix it. In these cases, you must *escalate* the problem.

Escalation is the process your company (or sometimes just you) goes through when you—the person assigned to repair a problem—are not able to get the job done. It's okay to escalate a problem because no one can fix every problem. All companies should have some form of escalation policy. It might mean calling your boss. It might mean filling out and sending some in-house form to another department. Escalation is sometimes

a more casual process. You might want to start researching the problem online; you might want to refer to in-house documentation to see if this problem has appeared in the past. (See "Document Findings, Actions, and Outcomes" later in this chapter.) You may want to call a coworker to come check it out (see Figure 32-15).

Figure 32-14
Ford the Tech takes a chance!

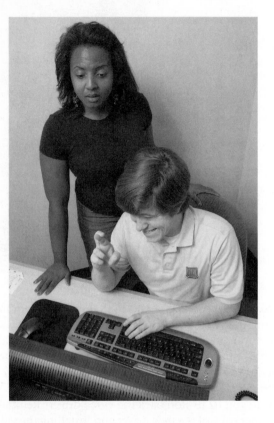

Figure 32-15
Ford the Tech asks for help from Scott.

Verify and Prevent

Fantastic! Through either your careful work or escalation, you've solved the problem, or so you think. Remember two items here. First, even though *you* think the problem is fixed, the user/customer might not think it's fixed. Second, try to do something to prevent the problem from happening again in the future, if possible.

Verify Full System Functionality

You need to *verify* full system functionality to make sure the user is happy. Let's say a user can't print. You determine that the printer spool is stalled due to a locked-up laser printer. You reset the printer and the jobs all start printing. Job done, right? Well, during your theory testing, you switched the default printer to another laser printer on the third floor. The user doesn't know how to set the default printer back to the one you just fixed.

The best way to verify full system functionality is to have the user do whatever she needs to do on the repaired system for a few minutes while you watch. Any minor errors (such as incorrect default printers) will quickly become apparent, and you might learn some interesting aspects of how the user does her job. Knowing what your users do is critical for good techs to help them do their jobs better (see Figure 32-16).

Figure 32-16
Ford the Tech
sticks around and
watches.

If Applicable, Implement Preventive Measures

A very smart tech once told me, "A truly good support tech's work goal should be to never have to get out of his chair." That's a pretty tall order, but it makes sense to me. Do whatever you can to prevent this problem from repeating. For some problems, there are obvious actions to take, such as making sure anti-malware is installed so a computer doesn't get infected again. Sometimes there's no action to take at all: nothing can prevent a hard drive that decides to die. But you can take one more critical action in almost

every case: education. Take advantage of the time with the user to informally train him about the problem. Show him the dangers of malware or tell him that sometimes hard drives just die. The more your users know, the less time you'll spend out of your chair.

Document Findings, Actions, and Outcomes

Based on his famous quote, "Those who cannot remember the past are condemned to repeat it," I think the philosopher George Santayana would have made a great PC technician. As a tech, the last step of every troubleshooting job should be to *document* your findings, actions, and results. This documentation might be highly formalized in some organizations, or it might just be a few notes you jot down for your own use, but you must document! What was the problem? What did you do to fix it? What worked? What didn't? The best guide to use for documentation is: "What would I have liked to have known about this problem before I walked up to it?" Good documentation is the strongest sign of a good PC tech (see Figure 32-17).

Figure 32-17
Ford documents a
successful fix.

Documenting problems helps you track the troubleshooting history of a machine over time, enabling you to make longer-term determinations about retiring it or changing out more parts. If you and fellow techs fix a specific problem with Mary's machine several times, for example, you might decide to swap out her whole system rather than fix it a fourth time.

Documenting helps fellow techs if they have to follow up on a task you didn't finish or troubleshoot a machine you've worked on previously. The reverse is also

true. If you get a call about Frank's computer, for example, and check the records to find other service calls on his computer, you might find that the fix for a particular problem is already documented. This is especially true for user-generated problems. Having documentation of what you did also means you don't have to rely on your memory when your coworker asks what you did to fix the weird problem with Jane's computer a year ago!

Documenting also comes into play when you or a user has an accident onsite. If your colleague Joe drops a monitor on his foot and breaks both the monitor and his foot, for example, you need to fill out an *incident report*, just as you would with any kind of accident: electrical, chemical, or physical. An *incident report* should detail what happened and where it happened. This helps your supervisors take the appropriate actions quickly and efficiently.

Tech Toolkit

Way back in Chapter 2, you learned the basic parts of a *tech toolkit*—a Phillips-head screwdriver and a few other useful tools, such as a Torx wrench and a pair of tweezers. Any good tech makes a point to carry around at least these tools (see Figure 32-18). Over time, you'll add more tools as your experience grows. But your toolkit won't stop at Phillips screwdrivers and Torx wrenches. You should include two other types of tools in your tech toolkit: utilities and field replaceable units (FRUs).

Figure 32-18
Typical technician
toolkit

Utilities

Windows comes with plenty of handy utilities, but there are times when you need to use stronger tools than these. The PC industry has thousands of third-party utilities that techs might use to diagnose and repair PCs. Sadly, there is no single selection of tools I can tell you to get: the tools one experienced tech uses differ from the tools I use based on experience, skills, and job functions. That doesn't mean you haven't been hearing my opinions! Throughout this book you've seen quite a few third-party utilities, and many of them are linked to on the media accompanying this book for you to use right away. Given that you already have my opinion on so many tools, let's instead talk about the types of third-party tools you'll find in most tech toolkits.

Many techs like to challenge me on the idea of carrying around tools. They say, "I know what I like; I'll just download them!" Well, sometimes you don't have Internet access and sometimes you need tools that are ready to go (see the next section). Granted, there are a number of tools that I would never carry on me. For example, device drivers change so often that keeping a copy on a thumb drive is a waste of time. The tools I'm listing here are the ones I promise you want with you, ready to go when you run into trouble.

Malware Cleaners

Ask any tech who works for Best Buy's Geek Squad, "What do you spend the most time doing on jobs?" and they will reply, "Cleaning malware." The first tech utilities you want in your toolkit are malware cleaners. To truly do it right, put your malware cleaners on a bootable optical disc because malware can sometimes attack a malware cleanup tool as you install. If you're not sure what to try first, grab a copy of the Ultimate Boot CD and try some of its fine cleanup tools.

Anti-Malware

After you clean the machine, make sure you have a copy of an anti-malware program that you can install so the user's machine doesn't get corrupted again. We talked about some of the popular freeware versions, but plenty of techs strongly prefer the pay versions and keep copies to sell to their customers.

Boot Tools

You need a tool that's better than the System Configuration utility at controlling what programs autostart on your Windows PC. OK, in this case, one tool stands out so strongly that you have to get it: Mark Russinovich's superb Autoruns. It's vastly superior to the built-in System Configuration utility and gives you incredible control of everything that's autostarting. Sure, there are others, but I love Autoruns. Get it at the Windows Sysinternals Web site, http://technet.microsoft.com/en-us/sysinternals.

Password Clearer

If you lose a Windows password, especially the Administrator password, and you can't log on to a system, you're in trouble. A number of tools let you reset any user's passwords. These programs don't let you *see* a password, only reset them, so if you have a user with encrypted folders, those won't be recoverable. None of these programs are easy to use, but when the alternative is not being able to log on, they will save you. Pretty much all of these programs run from bootable optical discs.

ZIP File Tool

Windows can read many compressed file formats (such as ZIP), but so many others are in use that it's often a good idea to have a third-party utility handy. I like 7-Zip (www .7-zip.org), but there are plenty of equally popular alternatives.

Backup

Odds are good that from time to time you'll need to do a backup for a system. I keep an external hard drive with a backup tool so I can go in fast and make backups of the most critical files.

Don't Forget Your Thumb Drives!

I guess I'm showing my age when I talk about putting all these tools on optical media. Sorry, I'm old. Almost all of these tools work equally well on USB thumb drives. I keep my tools on optical media because I still run into the occasional system that doesn't have CMOS settings for a bootable thumb drive.

Field Replaceable Units (FRUs)

Always carry several *field replaceable units (FRUs)*—a fancy way to say *spare parts*—when going to a job site or workstation. Having several known good components on hand enables you to swap out a potentially bad piece of hardware to see if that's the problem. Different technicians will have different FRUs. A printer specialist might carry a number of fusers, for example. Your employer will also have a big effect on what is an FRU and what is not. I generally carry a couple of RAM sticks (DDR, DDR2, and DDR3), a video card, a NIC, and a 300-watt power supply.

 EXAM TIP The CompTIA A+ exams expect you to know that FRUs are computer components such as cards, memory, hard drives, processors, or power supplies that can be easily replaced in the field.

Chapter 32 Review

Questions

1. Once you have assessed the problem with the user's machine, it is important to do what before making changes?

 A. Attach your grounding strap.

 B. Nothing; start fixing the problem immediately.

 C. Back up critical files.

 D. Get a signed release from the user.

2. While working at the help desk, you get a call from a distraught user who says she has a blank screen. What would be useful follow-up questions? (Select two.)

 A. Is the computer turned on?

 B. Is the monitor turned on?

 C. Did you reboot?

 D. What did you do?

3. Computers are complex machines, but many times the answer to a problem is what?

 A. Obscure

 B. Complex

 C. Obvious

 D. Very hard

4. What tool should be in every technician's toolkit?

 A. Pliers

 B. Hammer

 C. Flat-head screwdriver

 D. Phillips-head screwdriver

5. According to troubleshooting theory, what is the first thing you should do when you arrive to work on a computer?

 A. Identify the problem.

 B. Ask how the user broke the machine.

 C. Start working on the problem immediately.

 D. Back up critical data.

6. Once you have ascertained the computer's problem and backed up the critical data, what should you do?

 A. Establish a theory of probable cause.

 B. Start fixing the machine.

 C. Question users more to find out how they caused the problem.

 D. Document.

7. Once you have developed a theory of what has caused the problem, what should you do?

 A. Prepare the machine to be taken back to the workbench.

 B. Accuse the user of being an idiot for causing the problem.

 C. Test the theory to determine cause.

 D. Escalate the problem.

8. What should you do after successfully repairing a machine?

 A. Do nothing; your job is done.

 B. Admonish the user for causing so much work for the IT department.

 C. Document your findings.

 D. Lock it down so the user can't cause the same problem again.

9. You've just installed new printer drivers into Roland's computer for the big networked laser printer. What should you do to complete the assignment?

 A. Document that you installed new printer drivers.

 B. Tell Roland to print a test page.

 C. Print a test page and go to the printer to verify the results.

 D. Print a test page and go to the printer to verify the results. Document that you installed new printer drivers successfully.

10. What's an FRU?

 A. Foreign replacement unit—a cheaper part to replace an expensive American-made part

 B. Field replacement unit—a known good computer part to swap with a suspect part as part of the troubleshooting process

 C. Free repair unit—a gimmick used by some companies to provide free tech support for the first-time customer

 D. Short for FRU Linux, a Linux distribution

Answers

1. **C.** You should never lose data if you have an opportunity to back it up.

2. **A, B.** Go for the simple answer first. When faced with a blank screen, check to see if the computer and the monitor are on.

3. **C.** Don't overlook the obvious answer such as an unplugged power cord.

4. **D.** Every tech's toolkit should have a Phillips-head screwdriver, at the very least.

5. **A.** The first thing you should do is identify the problem.

6. **A.** You should establish a theory of probable cause once you have ascertained the problem and backed up data.

7. **C.** Once you think you know the cause, test your theory.

8. **C.** At the end of a repair you should always document your findings.

9. **D.** Always verify the results once you finish troubleshooting. Then document what you accomplished.

10. **B.** A field replacement unit is a known good computer part.

Mapping to the CompTIA A+ Objectives

222-801 Exam Objectives

Competency	Chapter(s)
1.0 PC Hardware	
1.1 Configure and apply BIOS settings.	
Install firmware upgrades – flash BIOS	8
BIOS component information	8
RAM	8
Hard drive	8
Optical drive	8
CPU	8
BIOS configurations	8
Boot sequence	8
Enabling and disabling devices	8
Date/time	8
Clock speeds	8
Virtualization support	8
BIOS security (passwords, drive encryption: TPM, lo-jack)	8
Use built-in diagnostics	8, 11
Monitoring	8
Temperature monitoring	8
Fan speeds	8
Intrusion detection/notification	8

Competency	Chapter(s)
Voltage	8
Clock	8
Bus speed	8
1.2 Differentiate between motherboard components, their purposes, and properties.	
Sizes	9
ATX	9
Micro-ATX	9
ITX	9
Expansion slots	9
PCI	9
PCI-X	9
PCIe	9
miniPCI	9
CNR	9
AGP 2x, 4x, 8x	9
RAM slots	7
CPU sockets	6
Chipsets	8
North Bridge	8, 9
South Bridge	8, 9
CMOS battery	8
Jumpers	9
Power connections and types	10
Fan connectors	9
Front panel connectors	9
USB	9
Audio	9
Power button	9
Power light	9
Drive activity lights	9
Reset button	9
Bus speeds	9
1.3 Compare and contrast RAM types and features.	
Types	7
DDR	7

Competency	Chapter(s)
DDR2	7
DDR3	7
SDRAM	7
SODIMM	7
RAMBUS	7
DIMM	7
Parity vs. non-parity	7
ECC vs. non-ECC	7
RAM configurations	7
Single channel vs. dual channel vs. triple channel	7
Single sided vs. double sided	7
RAM compatibility and speed	7
1.4 Install and configure expansion cards.	
Sound cards	25
Video cards	21
Network cards	22
Serial and parallel cards	20, 28
USB cards	20
Firewire cards	20
Storage cards	11
Modem cards	24
Wireless/cellular cards	23
TV tuner cards	25
Video capture cards	25
Riser cards	9
1.5 Install and configure storage devices and use appropriate media.	
Optical drives	13
CD-ROM	13
DVD-ROM	13
Blu-Ray	13
Combo drives and burners	13
CD-RW	13
DVD-RW	13
Dual Layer DVD-RW	13
BD-R	13

Competency	Chapter(s)
BD-RE	13
Connection types	
External	11
USB	11
Firewire	11
eSATA	11
Ethernet	31
Internal SATA, IDE and SCSI	11
IDE configuration and setup (Master, Slave, Cable Select)	11
SCSI IDs (0 – 15)	11
Hot swappable drives	11
Hard drives	11
Magnetic	11
5400 rpm	11
7200 rpm	11
10,000 rpm	11
15,000 rpm	11
Solid state/flash drives	11, 13
Compact flash	13
SD	13
Micro-SD	13
Mini-SD	13
xD	13
SSD	11
RAID types	11
0	11
1	11
5	11
10	11
Floppy drive	13
Tape drive	17
Media capacity	13
CD	13
CD-RW	13
DVD-RW	13

Competency	Chapter(s)
DVD	13
Blu-Ray	13
Tape	17
Floppy	13
DL DVD	13
1.6 Differentiate among various CPU types and features and select the appropriate cooling method.	
Socket types	6
Intel: LGA, 775, 1155, 1156, 1366	6
AMD: 940, AM2, AM2+, AM3, AM3+, FM1, F	6
Characteristics	6
Speeds	6
Cores	6
Cache size/type	6
Hyperthreading	6
Virtualization support	6, 8
Architecture (32-bit vs. 64-bit)	6
Integrated GPU	6
Cooling	6
Heat sink	6
Fans	6
Thermal paste	6
Liquid-based	6
1.7 Compare and contrast various connection interfaces and explain their purpose.	
Physical connections	
USB 1.1 vs. 2.0 vs. 3.0 speed and distance characteristics	20
Connector types: A, B, mini, micro	20
Firewire 400 vs. Firewire 800 speed and distance characteristics	20
SATA1 vs. SATA2 vs. SATA3, eSATA, IDE speeds	11
Other connector types	
Serial	20
Parallel	28
VGA	21
HDMI	21
DVI	21

Competency	Chapter(s)
Audio	25
RJ-45	5
RJ-11	5
Analog vs. digital transmission	21
VGA vs. HDMI	21
Speeds, distances and frequencies of wireless device connections	24
Bluetooth	23
IR	24
RF	24
1.8 Install an appropriate power supply based on a given scenario.	
Connector types and their voltages	10
SATA	10
Molex	10
4/8-pin 12v	10
PCIe 6/8-pin	10
20-pin	10
24-pin	10
Floppy	10
Specifications	10
Wattage	10
Size	10
Number of connectors	10
ATX	10
Micro-ATX	10
Dual voltage options	10
1.9 Evaluate and select appropriate components for a custom configuration, to meet customer specifications or needs.	
Graphic / CAD / CAM design workstation	31
Powerful processor	31
High-end video	31
Maximum RAM	31
Audio/Video editing workstation	31
Specialized audio and video card	31
Large fast hard drive	31
Dual monitors	31

Competency	Chapter(s)
Virtualization workstation	31
Maximum RAM and CPU cores	31
Gaming PC	31
Powerful processor	31
High-end video/specialized GPU	31
Better sound card	31
High-end cooling	31
Home Theater PC	31
Surround sound audio	31
HDMI output	31
HTPC compact form factor	31
TV tuner	31
Standard thick client	31
Desktop applications	31
Meets recommended requirements for running Windows	31
Thin client	31
Basic applications	31
Meets minimum requirements for running Windows	31
Home Server PC	31
Media streaming	31
File sharing	31
Print sharing	31
Gigabit NIC	31
RAID array	31
1.10 Given a scenario, evaluate types and features of display devices.	
Types	21
CRT	21
LCD	21
LED	21
Plasma	21
Projector	21
OLED	27
Refresh rates	21
Resolution	21
Native resolution	21

Competency	Chapter(s)
Brightness/lumens	21
Analog vs. digital	21
Privacy/antiglare filters	29
Multiple displays	21
1.11 Identify connector types and associated cables.	
Display connector types	21
DVI-D	21
DVI-I	21
DVI-A	21
Displayport	21
RCA	21
DB-15	21
BNC	21
miniHDMI	27
RJ-45	21
Din-6	21
Display cable types	21
HDMI	21
DVI	21
VGA	21
Component	21
Composite	21
S-video	21
RGB	21
Coaxial	21
Ethernet	21
Device connectors and various connector pin-outs	3, 5, 11, 20, 22, 25, 28
SATA	11
eSATA	11
PATA	11
IDE	11
EIDE	11
Floppy	13
USB	20
IEE1394	20

Competency	Chapter(s)
SCSI	11
PS/2	3
Parallel	28
Serial	20
Audio	25
RJ-45	5
Device cable types	5, 11, 13, 20, 28
SATA	11
eSATA	11
IDE	11
EIDE	11
Floppy	13
USB	20
IEE1394	20
SCSI	11
68pin vs. 50pin vs. 25pin	11
Parallel	28
Serial	20
Ethernet	5
Phone	5
1.12 Install and configure various peripheral devices.	
Input devices	20
Mouse	20
Keyboard	20
Touch screen	20
Scanner	20
Barcode reader	20
KVM	20
Microphone	25
Biometric devices	20
Game pads	20
Joysticks	20
Digitizer	20
Multimedia devices	20
Digital cameras	20
Microphone	25

Competency	Chapter(s)
DHCP	5
Subnet mask	5
Gateway	5
2.4 Explain common TCP and UDP ports, protocols, and their purpose.	
Ports	
21 – FTP	24
23 – TELNET	24
25 – SMTP	24
53 – DNS	24
80 – HTTP	24
110 – POP3	24
143 – IMAP	24
443 – HTTPS	24
3389 – RDP	24
Protocols	
DHCP	5, 22
DNS	5
LDAP	24
SNMP	24
SMB	24
SSH	24
SFTP	24
TCP vs. UDP	22
2.5 Compare and contrast wireless networking standards and encryption types.	
Standards	23
802.11 a/b/g/n	23
Speeds, distances and frequencies	23
Encryption types	23
WEP, WPA, WPA2, TKIP, AES	23
2.6 Install, configure, and deploy a SOHO wireless/wired router using appropriate settings.	
MAC filtering	23
Channels (1 – 11)	23
Port forwarding, port triggering	29
SSID broadcast (on/off)	23
Wireless encryption	23

Competency	Chapter(s)
Firewall	29
DHCP (on/off)	5, 22, 24
DMZ	29
NAT	24
WPS	23
Basic QoS	24
2.7 Compare and contrast Internet connection types and features.	
Cable	24
DSL	24
Dial-up	24
Fiber	24
Satellite	24
ISDN	24
Cellular (mobile hotspot)	24
Line of sight wireless internet service	24
WiMAX	24
2.8 Identify various types of networks.	
LAN	5
WAN	5
PAN	23
MAN	24
Topologies	5
Mesh	5
Ring	5
Bus	5
Star	5
Hybrid	5
2.9 Compare and contrast network devices and their functions and features.	
Hub	5
Switch	5
Router	5
Access point	23
Bridge	22
Modem	24
NAS	22, 31

Competency	Chapter(s)
Firewall	29
VoIP phones	24
Internet appliance	24
2.10 Given a scenario, use appropriate networking tools.	
Crimper	22
Multimeter	22
Toner probe	22
Cable tester	22
Loopback plug	22
Punchdown tool	22
3.0 Laptops	
3.1 Install and configure laptop hardware and components.	
Expansion options	26
Express card /34	26
Express card /54	26
PCMCIA	26
SODIMM	7
Flash	26
Hardware/device replacement	26
Keyboard	26
Hard Drive (2.5 vs. 3.5)	26
Memory	26
Optical drive	26
Wireless card	26
Mini-PCIe	26
Screen	26
DC jack	26
Battery	26
Touchpad	26
Plastics	26
Speaker	26
System board	26
CPU	26
3.2 Compare and contrast the components within the display of a laptop.	
Types	26

Competency	Chapter(s)
4.2 Given a scenario, install, and configure printers.	
Use appropriate printer drivers for a given operating system	28
Print device sharing	28
Wired	28
USB	28
Parallel	28
Serial	28
Ethernet	28
Wireless	28
Bluetooth	28
802.11x	28
Infrared (IR)	28
Printer hardware print server	28
Printer sharing	28
Sharing local/networked printer via Operating System settings	28
4.3 Given a scenario, perform printer maintenance.	
Laser	28
Replacing toner, applying maintenance kit, calibration, cleaning	28
Thermal	28
Replace paper, clean heating element, remove debris	28
Impact	28
Replace ribbon, replace print head, replace paper	28
5.0 Operational Procedures	
5.1 Given a scenario, use appropriate safety procedures.	
ESD straps	2
ESD mats	2
Self-grounding	2
Equipment grounding	2
Personal safety	2
Disconnect power before repairing PC	2
Remove jewelry	2
Lifting techniques	2, 21
Weight limitations	21
Electrical fire safety	10

Competency	Chapter(s)
CRT safety – proper disposal	2, 21
Cable management	2, 21
Compliance with local government regulations	2, 29
5.2 Explain environmental impacts and the purpose of environmental controls.	
MSDS documentation for handling and disposal	28-29
Temperature, humidity level awareness and proper ventilation	29
Power surges, brownouts, blackouts	10
Battery backup	10
Surge suppressor	10
Protection from airborne particles	29
Enclosures	29
Air filters	29
Dust and debris	29
Compressed air	29
Vacuums	29
Component handling and protection	2, 9
Antistatic bags	2
Compliance to local government regulations	29
5.3 Given a scenario, demonstrate proper communication and professionalism.	
Use proper language – avoid jargon, acronyms, slang when applicable	2
Maintain a positive attitude	2
Listen and do not interrupt the customer	2
Be culturally sensitive	2
Be on time (if late contact the customer)	2
Avoid distractions	2
Personal calls	2
Talking to co-workers while interacting with customers	2
Personal interruptions	2
Dealing with difficult customer or situation	2
Avoid arguing with customers and/or being defensive	2
Do not minimize customer's problems	2
Avoid being judgmental	2
Clarify customer statements (ask open ended questions to narrow the scope of the problem, restate the issue or question to verify understanding)	2

Competency	Chapter(s)
Set and meet expectations/timeline and communicate status with the customer	2
Offer different repair/replacement options if applicable	2
Provide proper documentation on the services provided	2
Follow up with customer/user at a later date to verify satisfaction	2
Deal appropriately with customers confidential materials	29
Located on a computer, desktop, printer, etc.	29
5.4 Explain the fundamentals of dealing with prohibited content/activity.	
First response	
Identify	29
Report through proper channels	29
Data/device preservation	29
Use of documentation/documentation changes	29
Chain of custody	29
Tracking of evidence/documenting process	29

222-801 Exam Objectives

Competency	Chapter
1.0 Operating Systems	
1.1 Compare and contrast the features and requirements of various Microsoft Operating Systems.	
Windows XP Home, Windows XP Professional, Windows XP Media Center, Windows XP 64-bit Professional	4
Windows Vista Home Basic, Windows Vista Home Premium, Windows Vista Business, Windows Vista Ultimate, Windows Vista Enterprise	4
Windows 7 Starter, Windows 7 Home Premium, Windows 7 Professional, Windows 7 Ultimate, Windows 7 Enterprise	4
Features:	
32-bit vs. 64-bit	4
Aero, gadgets, user account control, bit-locker, shadow copy, system restore, ready boost, sidebar, compatibility mode, XP mode, easy transfer, administrative tools, defender, Windows firewall, security center, event viewer, file structure and paths, category view vs. classic view	4, 7, 14, 16, 19, 29
Upgrade paths – differences between in place upgrades, compatibility tools, Windows upgrade OS advisor	14

Competency	Chapter
TRACERT	22
NETSTAT	24
IPCONFIG	22
NET	22
NSLOOKUP	22
NBTSTAT	22
OS	
KILL	15, 19
BOOTREC	19
SHUTDOWN	18
TLIST	15
MD	18
RD	18
CD	18
DEL	18
FDISK	12
FORMAT	18
COPY	18
XCOPY	18
ROBOCOPY	18
DISKPART	19
SFC	18
CHKDSK	18
[command name] /?	18
Recovery console	
Fixboot	19
Fixmbr	19
1.4 Given a scenario, use appropriate operating system features and tools.	
Administrative	
Computer management	4, 12
Device manager	4, 17
Users and groups	16
Local security policy	29
Performance monitor	15
Services	15
System configuration	17

Competency	Chapter
Task scheduler	17
Component services	15
Data sources	15
Print management	28
Windows memory diagnostics	19
Windows firewall	29
Advanced security	29
MSCONFIG	17
General	17
Boot	17
Services	17
Startup	17
Tools	17
Task Manager	15
Applications	15
Processes	15
Performance	15
Networking	15
Users	15
Disk management	12
Drive status	12
Mounting	12
Extending partitions	12
Splitting partitions	12
Assigning drive letters	12
Adding drives	12
Adding arrays	12
Other	
User Data Migration tool (UDMT)	4
User State Migration tool (USMT)	14
Run line utilities	
MSCONFIG	17
REGEDIT	15
CMD	4, 18
SERVICES.MSC	15
MMC	4

Competency	Chapter
MSTSC	24
NOTEPAD	18
EXPLORER	18
MSINFO32	17
DXDIAG	21
1.5 Given a scenario, use Control Panel utilities (the items are organized by "classic view/large icons" in Windows).	
Common to all Microsoft Operating Systems	
Internet options	24
Connections	24
Security	24
General	24
Privacy	24
Programs	24
Advanced	24
Display	21
Resolution	21
User accounts	16
Folder options	4, 16
Sharing	16
View hidden files	4
Hide extensions	4
Layout	4
System	(many)
Performance (virtual memory)	7
Hardware profiles	17
Remote settings	24
System protection	29
Security center	29
Windows firewall	29
Power options	26
Hibernate	26
Power plans	26
Sleep/suspend	26
Standby	26

Competency	Chapter
Unique to Windows XP	
Add/remove programs	17
Network connections	22
Printers and faxes	28
Automatic updates	17
Network setup wizard	24
Unique to Vista	
Tablet PC settings	26
Pen and input devices	20, 26
Offline files	4, 26
Problem ports and solutions	19
Printers	28
Unique to Windows 7	
HomeGroup	5
Action center	4, 19, 29
Remote applications and desktop applications	24
Troubleshooting	19
1.6 Setup and configure Windows networking on a client/desktop.	
HomeGroup, file/print sharing	5
WorkGroup vs. domain setup	5
Network shares/mapping drives	22
Establish networking connections	23, 24
VPN	24
Dialups	24
Wireless	23
Wired	22
WWAN (Cellular)	23, 24
Proxy settings	24
Remote desktop	24
Home vs. Work vs. Public network settings	29
Firewall settings	29
Exceptions	29
Configuration	29
Enabling/disabling Windows firewall	29

Competency	Chapter
User education	29
Principle of least privilege	16, 29
2.2 Compare and contrast common security threats.	
Social engineering	29
Malware	29
Rootkits	29
Phishing	29
Shoulder surfing	29
Spyware	29
Viruses	29
Worms	29
Trojans	29
2.3 Implement security best practices to secure a workstation.	
Setting strong passwords	16, 29
Requiring passwords	29
Restricting user permissions	29
Changing default user names	29
Disabling guest account	29
Screensaver required password	29
Disable autorun	19
2.4 Given a scenario, use the appropriate data destruction/disposal method.	
Low level format vs. standard format	14
Hard drive sanitation and sanitation methods	14
Overwrite	14
Drive wipe	14
Physical destruction	14
Shredder	14
Drill	14
Electromagnetic	14
Degaussing tool	14
2.5 Given a scenario, secure a SOHO wireless network.	
Change default user-names and passwords	23
Changing SSID	23
Setting encryption	23
Disabling SSID broadcast	23

Competency	Chapter
Remote wipes	27
Locator applications	27
Remote backup applications	27
Failed login attempts restrictions	27
Antivirus	27
Patching/OS updates	27
3.4 Compare and contrast hardware differences in regards to tablets and laptops.	
No field serviceable parts	27
Typically not upgradeable	27
Touch interface	27
Touch flow	27
Multitouch	27
Solid state drives	27
3.5 Execute and configure mobile device synchronization.	
Types of data to synchronize	27
Contacts	27
Programs	27
Email	27
Pictures	27
Music	27
Videos	27
Software requirements to install the application on the PC	27
Connection types to enable synchronization	27
4.0 Troubleshooting	
4.1 Given a scenario, explain the troubleshooting theory.	
Identify the problem	32
Question the user and identify user changes to computer and perform backups before making changes	32
Establish a theory of probable cause (question the obvious)	32
Test the theory to determine cause	32
Once theory is confirmed determine next steps to resolve problem	32
If theory is not confirmed re-establish new theory or escalate	32
Establish a plan of action to resolve the problem and implement the solution	32
Verify full system functionality and if applicable implement preventive measures	32
Document findings, actions and outcomes	32

Competency	Chapter
Tools	
Screwdriver	32
External enclosures	11
CHDKS	12
CHKDSK	12, 18
FORMAT	18
FDISK	12
File recovery software	19
4.4 Given a scenario, troubleshoot common video and display issues.	
Common symptoms	
VGA mode	21
No image on screen	21
Overheat shutdown	21
Dead pixels	21
Artifacts	21
Color patterns incorrect	21
Dim image	21
Flickering image	21
Distorted image	21
Discoloration (degaussing)	21
BSOD	21
4.5 Given a scenario, troubleshoot wired and wireless networks with appropriate tools.	
Common symptoms	
No connectivity	22, 24
APIPA address	22
Limited connectivity	24
Local connectivity	24
Intermittent connectivity	22
IP conflict	22
Slow transfer speeds	24
Low RF signal	23
Tools	
Cable tester	22
Loopback plug	22
Punch down tools	22

Competency	Chapter
Repair disks	19
Pre-installation environments	19
MSCONFIG	17
DEFRAG	17
REGSRV32	15
REGEDIT	15
Event viewer	19, 29
Safe mode	19
Command prompt	19
Emergency repair disk	17
Automated system recovery	17

4.7 Given a scenario, troubleshoot common security issues with appropriate tools and best practices.

Common symptoms	
Pop-ups	29
Browser redirection	29
Security alerts	29
Slow performance	29
Internet connectivity issues	29
PC locks up	29
Windows updates failures	29
Rogue antivirus	29
Spam	29
Renamed system files	29
Files disappearing	29
File permission changes	29
Hijacked email	29
Access denied	29

Tools	
Anti-virus software	29
Anti-malware software	29
Anti-spyware software	29
Recovery console	29
System restore	29
Pre-installation environments	19

Competency	Chapter
Faded prints	28
Ghost images	28
Toner not fused to the paper	28
Creased paper	28
Paper not feeding	28
Paper jam	28
No connectivity	28
Garbled characters on paper	28
Vertical lines on page	28
Backed up print queue	28
Low memory errors	28
Access denied	28
Printer will not print	28
Color prints in wrong print color	28
Unable to install printer	28
Error codes	28
Tools	
Maintenance kit	28
Toner vacuum	28
Compressed air	28
Printer spooler	28

About the CD-ROM

The disc included with this book comes with:

- An introduction to CompTIA A+ video from the author, Mike Meyers
- Digital copies of the CompTIA A+ 220-801 and 220-802 exam objectives
- Total Tester practice exam software with hundreds of practice exam questions
- A link to hours of Mike Meyers video training
- Links to a collection of Mike's current favorite tools and utilities for PC troubleshooting
- An electronic copy of the book in PDF format
- A Glossary of all the key terms in the book

The software can be installed on any Windows 98/NT/2000/XP/Vista/Windows 7 computer and must be installed to access the Total Tester practice exam software.

Playing the Mike Meyers Introduction Video

If your computer's optical drive is configured to auto-run, the menu will automatically start up upon inserting the disc. If the auto-run feature did not launch the disc, browse to the disc and double-click the Launch.exe icon.

From the opening screen you can launch the video message from Mike by clicking the Mike Meyers Introduction Video button. This launches the video file using your system's default video player.

Viewing the Glossary and the CompTIA Exam Objectives

To view the Glossary or the CompTIA A+ exam objectives, click the Objectives Maps and Glossary button from the main menu of the disc. On the next page, click the Glossary button, the CompTIA A+ (220-801) Objectives button, or the CompTIA A+ (220-802) Objectives button to open a PDF of the appropriate file. The objectives maps list the official exam objectives from CompTIA as of the date of publication. Please visit the CompTIA Web site for the most up-to-date exam objectives. A PDF-viewing program must be installed to view the Glossary or objectives lists. Adobe Acrobat Reader is available from www.acrobat.com.

System Requirements

The software requires Windows XP or higher, Internet Explorer 7 or higher or Firefox with Flash Player, and 30 MB of hard disk space for full installation.

Installing and Running Total Tester

From the main screen you may install the Total Tester by clicking the Software and Videos button, and then clicking the Total Tester A+ Practice Exams button. This will begin the installation process and place an icon on your desktop and in your Start menu. To run Total Tester, navigate to Start | (All) Programs | Total Seminars or double-click the icon on your desktop.

To uninstall the Total Tester software, go to Start | Settings | Control Panel | Add/ Remove Programs (XP) or Programs and Features (Vista / 7), and then select the A+ Total Tester program. Select Remove and Windows will completely uninstall the software.

Total Tester

Total Tester provides you with a simulation of the CompTIA A+ exams. You may select practice exams for CompTIA A+ Exam 801 or CompTIA A+ Exam 802. The exams can be taken in either Practice mode or Exam Simulation mode. Practice mode provides an assistance window with hints, references to the book, an explanation of the answer, and the option to check your answer as you take the test. Both Practice mode and Exam Simulation mode provide an overall grade and a grade broken down by certification objective. To take a test, launch the program, select a suite from the drop-down list at the top, and then click either Practice Exam or Exam Simulation. After making your selection, click Start Exam to begin.

Mike's Cool Tools

Mike loves freeware/open source PC tools! Most of the utilities mentioned in the text can be downloaded from the Internet using URLs provided on the disc on the Mike's Cool Tools page. You can access the menu by clicking on the Software and Videos button on the main page of the disc and then clicking the Access Mike's Cool Tools link.

Please read the Cool Tools page for a description of the utilities.

 CAUTION While all of the tools are "Mike Meyers Approved," there is no guarantee they will work for you. Read any and all documentation that comes with each utility before downloading and using that program.

Mike's Video Training

Your disc comes with a link to hours of free PC video training starring Mike Meyers. On the main page of the disc, click the Software and Videos link and then select Access

Mike Meyers Video Training. You'll have access to several training segments, with an option to purchase even more of Mike's instructional videos.

Electronic Book

The contents of this book are provided in PDF format on the CD. This file is viewable on your computer and many portable devices.

To view the file on your computer, Adobe's Acrobat Reader is required and has been included on the CD.

 NOTE For more information on Adobe Reader and to check for the most recent version of the software, visit Adobe's web site at www.adobe.com and search for the free Adobe Reader or look for Adobe Reader on the product page.

To view the electronic book on a portable device, copy the PDF file to your computer from the CD, and then copy the file to your portable device using a USB or other connection. Adobe offers a mobile version of Adobe Reader, the Adobe Reader mobile app, which currently supports iOS and Android. The Adobe web site also has a list of recommended applications.

Technical Support

For questions regarding the Total Tester software or operation of the CD, visit www .totalsem.com or e-mail support@totalsem.com.

For questions regarding the PDF book or video, e-mail techsolutions@mhedu.com or visit http://mhp.softwareassist.com.

For questions regarding book content, please e-mail customer.service@mheducation. com. For customers outside the United States, e-mail international_cs@mcgraw-hill.com.

INDEX

host bus adapter (HBA)
- AHCI (Advanced Host Controller Interface) and, 428–429
- for SATA drives, 427

hostname command, for viewing computer name, 806

hostnames, DNS, 1025–1026

hot keys, in Windows OSs, 116–117

hot- swappable
- FireWire devices, 52
- hardware RAID and, 442
- SATA drives, 427
- USB devices, 51

HTPC case, for home theatre PC, 1419

HTTP (Hypertext Transfer Protocol)
- as Internet application protocol, 1114
- as TCP/IP service, 1020

HTTPS (Hypertext Transfer Protocol Secure)
- application encryption, 1369
- as Internet application protocol, 1115

hubs
- in Ethernet networks, 167, 998
- USB, 886–887

humidity, environmental threats, 1327

hybrid hard drives (HHDs), 453

hybrid network topologies, 162

Hyper-Threading, 224, 240

Hypertext Transfer Protocol (HTTP)
- as Internet application protocol, 1114
- as TCP/IP service, 1020

Hypertext Transfer Protocol Secure (HTTPS)
- application encryption, 1369
- as Internet application protocol, 1115

HyperV, 1396

hypervisors
- ability to run multiple virtual machines, 1388
- ESX, 1392–1393
- managing virtual machines, 1380–1381
- naming virtual machines and, 1386
- options for, 1396
- overview of, 1377
- research and, 1390

I

I-cache, dual-core architectures and, 225

I/O Hub (IOH), Intel terminology for Northbridge, 331

IBSS (Independent Basic Service Set), 1061

ICANN (Internet Corporation for Assigned Names and Numbers), 176

ICC (International Color Consortium), 1305

ICH (Input/Output Controller Hub)
- on Intel chipset, 284
- Intel terminology for Southbridge, 331

iCloud
- backing up mobile devices to, 1272–1273
- creating account in, 1257
- locator service for Apple mobile devices, 1271–1272
- as storage solution, 1269

icons, configuring desktop look and feel, 965

ICS (Internet Connection Sharing), 1113–1114

IDE (integrated drive electronics). See also ATA (advanced technology attachment), 414

IE (Internet Explorer), configuring, 1117–1120

IEC-320 connector, for AC power, 370

IEEE (Institute of Electrical and Electronics Engineers)
- 802.11 standards. See 802.11
- 802.15 (Bluetooth) standard, 1070
- 1284 (parallel port) standard, 1290–1291
- 1394 standard. See FireWire (IEEE 1394)

IETF (Internet Engineering Task Force), 1029

image deployment, 574

image-editing software, 902

imaging drum. See photosensitive drum

IMAP (Internet Message Access Protocol)
- configuring e-mail, 1123

configuring e-mail on mobile devices, 1267–1268
- as Internet application protocol, 1114

IMC (integrated memory controller), in CPU technology, 225

impact paper, 1278

impact printers
- overview of, 1277–1278
- troubleshooting, 1310

in-place upgrade, 572

In-Plane Switching. See IPS (In-Plane Switching)

incident reports
- reporting security issues, 1341
- in troubleshooting, 1449

incremental backup, 761–763

Independent Basic Service Set (IBSS), 1061

industrial, scientific, and medical (ISM) radio bands, 1066

infiltration, as security threat, 1323

Information Technology (IT) workforce. See PC techs

infrared
- IrDA (Infrared Data Association) protocol, 1069
- motherboard support for, 329
- network printers and, 1292
- transceiver ports on portable computer devices, 1055–1056

Infrared Data Association (IrDA), 1069

infrastructure mode
- configuring wireless network in, 1072–1078
- overview of, 1061

inherent factors, in authentication, 1331

inheritance, NTFS permissions and, 693

ink cartridges, for inkjet printers, 1280–1281

ink, consumables used in printing, 1284

ink-dispersion printers. See inkjet printers

inkjet printers
- overview of, 1279–1281
- troubleshooting, 1311–1312

InkyBoard, 1202